Why does a 70% success rate sound better than a 30% failure rate? p. 283

How are we better off with imperfect memories? p. 194

Why might it be a good idea to sit in the same seat for an exam that you sat in during lecture? p. 177

Why shouldn't you study and watch TV at the same time? p. 135

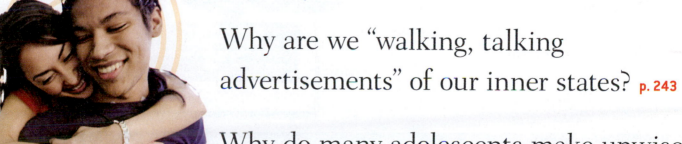

Why are we "walking, talking advertisements" of our inner states? p. 243

Why do many adolescents make unwise choices about sex? p. 332

WORTH PUBLISHERS

LEARNING*Curve*

Study Smarter with LearningCurve!

What is *LEARNINGCurve*?

LEARNINGCurve is a cutting-edge study tool designed to increase your understanding and memory of the core concepts in every chapter. Based on insights from the latest learning and memory research, the *LEARNINGCurve* system pairs multiple-choice and fill-in-the-blank questions with instantaneous feedback and a rich array of study tools including videos, animations, and lab simulations.

The *LEARNINGCurve* system is adaptive, so the quiz you take is customized to your level of understanding. The more questions you answer correctly, the more challenging the questions become. Best of all, the ebook of *Introducing Psychology*, Second Edition, is fully integrated, so you can easily review the text as you study and answer questions. *LEARNINGCurve* is a smart and fun way to master each chapter and prepare for your exam.

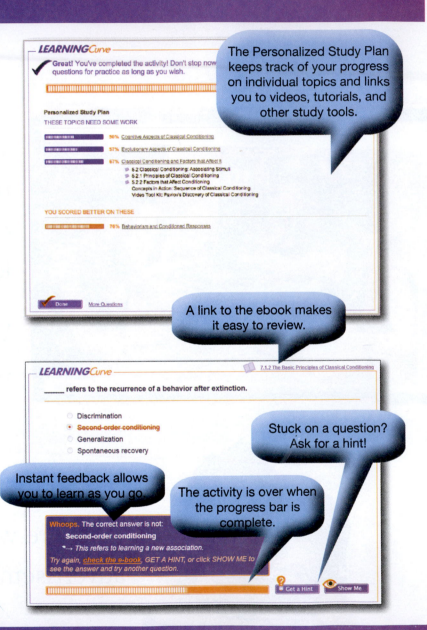

The Personalized Study Plan keeps track of your progress on individual topics and links you to videos, tutorials, and other study tools.

A link to the ebook makes it easy to review.

Stuck on a question? Ask for a hint!

Instant feedback allows you to learn as you go.

The activity is over when the progress bar is complete.

Introducing

Psychology

Jaume Plensa
SPIEGEL, 2010
Painted stainless steel
377 x 235 x 245 cm (each)

Site: Yorkshire Sculpture Park, UK
Artwork © Jaume Plensa

We love this cover, and not only because it has our names on it. In fact, our names kind of get in the way of an amazing sculpture by the Spanish artist, Jaume Plensa. Glance quickly at the sculpture and you see a human figure made of something like wire, tin, or cardboard. Look more closely and you see that the figure is actually made of symbols—some English letters, some Greek letters, and some letters that look suspiciously like Early Martian. What seems at first like an ordinary human figure is actually a story to be read, or better yet, a code to be broken. And what is the figure doing? Well, it looks like he's not doing much of anything at all—until you open the book, turn it over, and lay it flat so that you can see both the front and back covers at once. And then … aha! There are actually two of these coded figures, and they are deeply engaged in the act of decoding each other. To us, this artwork suggests that human beings are a mystery that human beings can solve, and we can think of no better maxim for the science of psychology.

SPECIAL UPDATE FOR DSM-5

Introducing Psychology

SECOND EDITION

DANIEL L. SCHACTER

HARVARD UNIVERSITY

DANIEL T. GILBERT

HARVARD UNIVERSITY

DANIEL M. WEGNER

HARVARD UNIVERSITY

WORTH PUBLISHERS

Senior Vice President, Editorial and Production: Catherine Woods
Publisher: Kevin Feyen
Acquisitions Editor: Daniel DeBonis
Assistant Editor: Nadina Persaud
Editorial Assistant: Agnes Baik
Marketing Manager: Lindsay Johnson
Marketing Assistant: Stephanie Ellis
Senior Developmental Editor: Valerie Raymond
Senior Media Editor: Christine Burak
Director of Development for Print and Digital Products: Tracey Kuehn
Associate Director of Market Research: Carlise Stembridge
Associate Managing Editor: Lisa Kinne
Photo Editor: Cecilia Varas
Art Director and Cover Designer: Babs Reingold
Text Designers: Lyndall Culbertson and Babs Reingold
Senior Designer and Chapter Opener Researcher: Lyndall Culbertson
Layout Designer: Paul Lacy
Project Editor: Jennifer Bossert
Illustrations: Matt Holt, Christy Krames, Don Stewart, and Todd Buck
Production Manager: Sarah Segal
Composition: MPS Ltd.
Printing and Binding: Quad/Graphics Versailles
Cover photographs: Front cover: Jaume Plensa, SPIEGEL, 2010, painted stainless steel,
377 × 235 × 425 cm (each), Site: Yorkshire Sculpture Park, UK. Artwork © Jaume Plensa;
Photo © Eric Murphy/Alamy.

Credits for art denoting the beginnings of chapters: pp. x and xxxvi: Con Ryan/Flickr/Getty
Images; pp. x and 30: kkgas/istockphoto; pp. xi and 56: © Adrianna Williams/Corbis; pp. xi and 90:
Hemera Technologies/© Getty Images; pp. xii and 130: Valentine Schmidt/Millennium Images/
Glasshouse Images; pp. xiii and 164: Kathryn Faulkner/Millennium Images/Glasshouse Images;
pp. xiii and 198: juanluisgx/Getty Images; pp. xiv and 234: Bigshots/Getty Images; pp. xiv and 266:
Peter Samuels/Getty Images; pp. xv and 306: Eva Serrabassa/iStockphoto; pp. xv and 344: Johner/
Glasshouse Images; pp. xvi and 374: © Corbis; pp. xvi and 404: Josefine Jonsson/Trigger Image/
Glasshouse Images; pp. xvii and 434: Will Crocker/Getty Images; pp. xvii and 464: FogStock/
Glasshouse

Library of Congress Control Number: 2012931180

ISBN-13: 978-1-4641-6350-0
ISBN-10: 1-4641-6350-2

©2015, 2011 by Worth Publishers

Printed in the United States of America

First printing

Worth Publishers
41 Madison Avenue
New York, NY 10010
www.worthpublishers.com

To our children and their children

Hannah Schacter

Emily Schacter

Arlo Gilbert

Shona Gilbert

Daylyn Gilbert

Sari Gilbert

Kelsey Wegner

Haley Wegner

About the Authors

Daniel Schacter is a professor of psychology at Harvard University. Dan received his BA degree from the University of North Carolina at Chapel Hill. He subsequently developed a keen interest in amnesic disorders associated with various kinds of brain damage. He continued his research and education at the University of Toronto, where he received his PhD in 1981. He taught on the faculty at Toronto for the next six years before joining the psychology department at the University of Arizona in 1987. In 1991, he joined the faculty at Harvard University. His research explores the relation between conscious and unconscious forms of memory, the nature of distortions and errors in remembering, and how people use memory to imagine future events. Many of Schacter's studies are summarized in his 1996 book, *Searching for Memory: The Brain, the Mind, and the Past*, and his 2001 book, *The Seven Sins of Memory: How the Mind Forgets and Remembers*, both winners of the American Psychological Association's William James Book Award. In 2009, Schacter received the Warren Medal from the Society of Experimental Psychologists for his research on true and false memories, and in 2012 received the Distinguished Scientific Contribution Award from the American Psychological Association.

Daniel Gilbert is a professor of psychology at Harvard University. After attending the Community College of Denver and completing his BA from the University of Colorado, Denver, he went on to earn his PhD from Princeton University. From 1985–1996, he taught at the University of Texas, Austin, and in 1996, he joined the faculty of Harvard University. He has received the American Psychological Association's Distinguished Scientific Award for an Early Career Contribution to Psychology, and has won teaching awards that include the Phi Beta Kappa Teaching Prize and the Harvard College Professorship Award. His research focuses on how, and how well, people think about their emotional reactions to future events. He is the author of the international bestseller *Stumbling on Happiness*, which won the Royal Society's General Prize for best popular science book of the year, and is the co-writer and host of the PBS television series, *This Emotional Life*.

Daniel Wegner is a professor of psychology at Harvard University. He received his BS in 1970 and PhD in 1974, both from Michigan State University. He began his teaching career at Trinity University in San Antonio, Texas before his appointments at the University of Virginia in 1990 and then Harvard University in 2000. His research focuses on thought suppression and mental control, transactive memory in relationships and groups, and the experience of conscious will. His work in thought suppression and consciousness served as the basis of two popular books, *White Bears and Other Unwanted Thoughts* and the *Illusion of Conscious Will*, which were both named *Choice* Outstanding Academic Books. In 2011, he received the William James Fellow Award from the Association for Psychological Science, the Distinguished Scientific Contribution Award from the American Psychological Association, and the Distinguished Scientist Award from the Society of Experimental Social Psychology.

Brief Contents

Contents

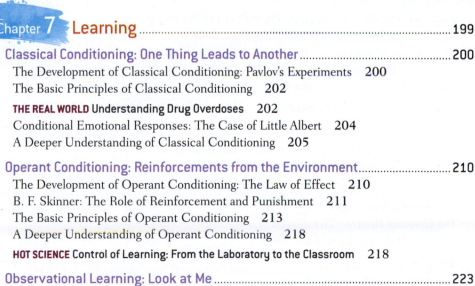

Preface

So why are you reading the preface? The book doesn't really get going for another 10 pages, so why are you here instead of there? Are you the kind of person who just can't stand the idea of missing something? Are you trying to justify the cost of the book by consuming every word? Did you just open to this page out of habit? Are you starting to think that might have been a major mistake?

For as long as we can remember, the three of us have been asking questions like these about ourselves, about our friends, and about anyone else who didn't run away fast enough. Our curiosity about why people think, feel, and act as they do drew each of us into our first psychology course, and though we remember being swept away by the lectures, we don't remember anything about the textbooks. That's probably because our textbooks were little more than colorful encyclopedias of facts, names, and dates. Little wonder that we sold our books back the moment we finished our final exams.

When we became psychology professors, we did the things that psychology professors often do: We taught classes, we conducted research, and we wore argyle socks long after they stopped being fashionable. We also wrote popular books that people really liked to read, and that made us wonder why no one had ever written an introductory psychology textbook that students really liked to read. After all, psychology is the most interesting subject in the known universe, so why shouldn't a psychology textbook be the most interesting thing in a student's backpack? We couldn't think of a reason, so we sat down and wrote the book that we wished we'd been given as students. *Psychology* was published in 2008 and the reaction was astounding. We'd never written a textbook before so we didn't know exactly what to expect, but never in our wildest dreams did we imagine that we would *win the Pulitzer Prize*!

Which was good, because we didn't. But we did get unsolicited letters and e-mails from students all over the country who wrote just to tell us how much they liked our book. They liked the content because, as we may have already mentioned, psychology is the most interesting subject in the known universe. But they also liked the fact that our textbook didn't *sound* like a textbook. It wasn't written in the stodgy voice of the announcer from one of those nature films we all saw in 7th-grade biology ("Behold the sea otter, nature's furry little scavenger"). Rather, it was written in *our* voices: the same voices we used to write books for ordinary people who didn't have highlighters in their hands and were allowed to throw the book away if they got bored. We made a conscious effort to tell the *story* of psychology—to integrate topics rather than just listing them, to illustrate ideas rather than just describing them. We recognized that because science is such a complicated and serious business, some teachers might think that a science textbook should be complicated and serious too. But we just didn't see it that way ourselves. Writing a textbook is the art of making complicated things seem simple and making serious things seem fun. The students who wrote to us seemed to agree.

Changes to the First Edition

The first edition of our book was a hit—so why have we replaced it with a second edition? Two reasons. First, we got tired of being asked about the guy on the cover of the first edition. He's gone now and we're only going to say this one more time: No, he isn't one of us, and yes, he probably was a little wired. The second and somewhat more important reason

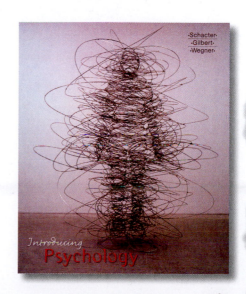

for bringing out a new edition is that things change. Science changes (psychologists know all sorts of things about the mind and the brain that they didn't know just a few years ago), the world changes (when we wrote the first edition, no one had heard of an iPad and LOLZ didn't mean anything to most people), and we change (our research and reading give us new perspectives on psychological issues, and our writing and teaching show us new ways to help students learn). With all of these changes happening around us and to us, we believed that our book should change as well. So what are some of the features you will see in this second brief edition?

Less *Still* Is More: A Focus on Core Topics

Every teacher knows that it is easier to prepare an hour-long talk than a 5-minute one. It is easy to carry on at great length about things you understand in great depth, but when asked to deliver a concise talk with a time restriction, you have to make hard decisions about what's important, how it can be conveyed with interest, and how the benefit to the audience can be maximized. These are the same challenges we faced in writing *Introducing Psychology*. We found that in a Brief Edition, you can't say all the same things but you can say them in the same way. For us, that meant retaining the aides, the touches of humor, and the broader story of psychology that is so important to understanding its influence. We have always believed that in presenting psychology to a new audience, the stories need to carry the facts, not vice versa. So, we have stayed true to the approach that so many found appealing in *Psychology*, asking our students to read, engage, think, and (we hope) enjoy their first encounter with psychology.

New Research

A textbook should give students a complete tour of the classics, of course, but it should also take them out dancing on the cutting edge. We want students to see that psychology is not a museum piece—not just a collection of past events but also of current events—and that this young and evolving science has a place for them if they want to claim it. So we've packed the second edition with information about what's happening in the field today—like right now, even as we type. Not only have we included more than 700 new citations, but we've featured some of the hottest new findings in the Hot Science boxes that you'll find in every chapter.

Chapter Number	Hot Science
2	Do Violent Movies Make Peaceful Streets ?
3	Mirror, Mirror, in my Brain
4	Expensive Taste
6	Sleep on It
7	Control of Learning: From the Laboratory to the Classroom
7	Even More Reason to Sleep
8	Fear Goggles
9	The Breast and the Brightest
10	Walk This Way
11	Personality on the Surface
12	The Color of Expectations
13	Autism and Childhood Disorders
13	Positive Psychology
14	Happy Pills? Antidepressants for Ordinary Sadness

A Focus on Culture

Although we're all middle-aged white guys named Dan, we realize that not everyone else is. That's why we pay special attention to cultural psychology, placing human behavior in the context of nations, ethnicities, religions, communities, and cultures. Culture influences just about everything we do—from how we perceive a line to how long we will stand in one—and this edition celebrates the rich diversity of human beings throughout, but especially in the Culture & Community boxes that you'll find in many of the chapters.

Chapter Number	Culture & Community
1	Do Illusions Affect Everyone the Same Way?
2	Best Place to Fall on Your Face
5	What Do Dreams Mean to Us around the World?
8	Is It What You Say or How You Say It?
9	Does Bilingualism Interfere with Cognitive Development?
12	Free Parking
13	Can People in Different Parts of the World Have Different Mental Disorders?
14	Is Psychology the Same around the World?
15	Can Being the Target of Discrimination Cause Stress and Illness?

Culture and Multicultural Experience

(Continued)

Organization

Our table of contents isn't like everyone else's. Well yes, it has titles and page numbers. But it also reflects our personal sense of how psychology is best taught in the 21st century (which is when we assume you will be taking your class). It is also a bit different than the table of contents in our first brief edition. For example, we've moved Social Psychology forward so that it can be closer to its cousin, Personality; we've moved Consciousness forward so that students will be better prepared to understand modern research on Memory and Learning; and we've clustered Psychological Disorders, Treatment of Psychological Disorders, and Stress and Health together to create a strong finish of clinically oriented material. The chapters seem happier in their new locations and we think you'll be happier too.

New Changing Minds Questions

What can 784 introductory psychology professors agree about? They can agree that students usually come into their first psychology class with a set of beliefs about the field and that most of those beliefs are wrong. With the help of the wonderful people at Worth Publishers (they made us say that), we conducted a survey of 784 introductory psychology teachers and asked them to name their students' most common misconceptions about psychology. We then created the Changing Minds questions you will see at the end of every chapter. These questions ask you to think about an everyday situation in which a common misconception might arise, and then to use the science you have just learned to overcome it. We hope these exercises will prepare you to apply what you learn—and maybe even change some minds about psychology (thereby justifying our corny title).

CHANGING MINDS

1. You catch a TV interview with a celebrity who describes his difficult childhood, living with a mother who suffered from major depression. "Sometimes my mother stayed in her bed for days, not even getting up to eat," he says. "At the time, the family hushed it up. My parents were immigrants, and they came from a culture where it was considered shameful to have mental problems. You are supposed to have enough strength of will to overcome your problems, without help from anyone else. So my mother never got treatment." How might the idea of a medical model of psychiatric disorders have helped the woman and her family in the decision whether to seek treatment?

Proven Pedagogy

Introductory psychology students have to learn many facts. This is made easier when the textbook supports learning by offering a proven pedagogy that helps students focus on the key points of each section and ask questions about the material they are reading.

The **cue questions** help you identify the most important concepts in every major section of the text.

Research shows that regular, short quizzes improve memory, so a **Summary Quiz** follows each major section to help you learn and remember key concepts.

A bulleted **Summary** at the end of each chapter also offers you the opportunity to test yourself and find out what you know (and more importantly, what you don't).

Critical Thinking Questions are included at the end of each chapter because you don't want to memorize words—you want to understand ideas. These questions get you thinking in a useful way about the things you've read.

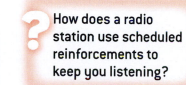

? How does a radio station use scheduled reinforcements to keep you listening?

SUMMARY QUIZ [12.3]

1. What is the process by which people come to understand others?
   a. dispositional attribution
   b. the accuracy motive
   c. social cognition
   d. cognitive dissonance

2. A common occupational stereotype is that lawyers are manipulative. Most people who subscribe to this stereotype
   a. believe that the stereotype applies to *all* lawyers.
   b. believe that the stereotype accurately applies to just a small percentage of lawyers.
   c. believe that lawyers are more likely than others to have this characteristic.
   d. would not be likely to misperceive lawyers when they actually meet.

3. The tendency to make a dispositional attribution even when a person's behavior was caused by the situation is referred to as
   a. comparison leveling.
   b. stereotyping.
   c. covariation.
   d. correspondence bias.

Emphasis on Practical Application and Debate

What would psychology be if it didn't have any application to the real world? (The answer is either philosophy or jazz, but we're not sure which.) The special-topic boxes are designed to bring psychology to life, and we've updated them for the second edition. The Real World boxes introduce practical applications of psychological science, and the Where Do You Stand? boxes ask you to weigh in on a current debate.

Chapter Number	The Real World
1	Improving Study Skills
1	Joining the Club
3	Brain Plasticity and Sensations in Phantom Limbs
4	Multitasking
5	Drugs and the Regulation of Consciousness
6	Dangerous Misattributions
7	Understanding Drug Overdoses
8	Jeet Jet?
9	Look Smart
10	When Mom's Away
11	Do Different Genders Lead to Different Personalities?
12	Making the Move
13	Suicide Risk and Prevention
14	Types of Psychotherapists
15	Why Sickness Feels Bad: Psychological Effects of Immune Response

Chapter Number	Where Do You Stand?
1	The Perils of Procrastination
2	The Morality of Immoral Experiments
3	Brain Death
4	Perception and Persuasion
5	Between NORML and MADD: What Is Acceptable Drug Use?
6	The Mystery of Childhood Amnesia
7	Learning for Rewards or for Its Own Sake?
8	Here Comes the Bribe
9	Making Kids Smart or Making Smart Kids?
10	A License to Rear
11	Personality Testing for Fun and Profit
12	The Model Employee
13	Genetic Tests for Risk of Psychological Disorders
14	Is Online Psychotherapy a Good Idea?
15	Should Smoking Appear on the Silver Screen?

Supplemental Resources and Media

Introducing Psychology, Second Edition, features a wide array of multimedia tools designed for the individual needs of students and teachers. For more information about any of the items below, visit Worth Publishers' online catalog at www.worthpublishers.com.

LaunchPad with LearningCurve Quizzing

A comprehensive web resource for teaching and learning psychology

LaunchPad combines Worth Publishers' awarding-winning media with an innovative platform for easy navigation. For students, it is the ultimate online study guide with rich interactive tutorials, videos, e-Book, and the new LearningCurve adaptive quizzing system. For instructors, LaunchPad is a full course space where class documents can be posted, quizzes are easily assigned and graded, and students' progress can be assessed and recorded. Whether you are looking for the most effective study tools or a robust platform for an online course, LaunchPad is a powerful way to enhance an introductory psychology class.

LaunchPad to Accompany *Introducing Psychology*, Second Edition, can be previewed and purchased at **www.worthpublishers.com/launchpad/schacterbrief2eDSM5e**.
   Introducing Psychology, Second Edition, and LaunchPad can be ordered together with ISBN-10: 1-4641-8517-4 / ISBN-13: 978-1-4641-8517-5

PsychPortal for *Introducing Psychology*, Second Edition, includes all the following resources:

> The **LearningCurve** quizzing system was designed based on the latest findings from learning and memory research. It combines adaptive question selection, immediate and valuable feedback, and a game-like interface to engage students in a learning experience that is unique to them. Each LearingCurve quiz is fully integrated with other resources in LaunchPad through the Personalized Study Plan, so students will be able to review with Worth's extensive library of videos, activities, and lab simulations. And state-of-the-art question analysis reports allow instructors to track the progress of their entire class.

> **An interactive e-Book** allows students to highlight, bookmark, and make their own notes, just as they would with a printed textbook. Digital enhancements include Google-style searching and in-text glossary definitions.

> **The Video Tool Kit for *Introductory Psychology*** includes engaging video modules that instructors can easily assign and customize for student assessment. Videos cover classic experiments, current news footage, and cutting-edge research, all of which are sure to spark discussion and encourage critical thinking.

> **PsychInvestigator: Laboratory Learning in *Introductory Psychology*** is a series of activities that model a virtual laboratory and are produced in association with Arthur Kohn, PhD, of Dark Blue Morning Productions. Students are introduced to core psychological concepts by a video host and then participate in activities that generate real data and lead to some startling conclusions! Like all activities in LaunchPad, PsychInvestigator activities can be assigned and automatically graded.

> The award-winning tutorials in Tom Ludwig's (Hope College) **PsychSim 5.0** and the new **Concepts in Action** provide an interactive, step-by-step introduction to key psychological concepts.

> **The Assignment Center** lets instructors easily construct and administer tests and quizzes from the book's Test Bank and course materials. Assignments can be automatically graded, and the results are recorded in a customizable Gradebook.

> **The *Scientific American* Newsfeed** delivers weekly articles, podcasts, and news briefs on the very latest developments in psychology from the first name in popular science journalism.

Additional Student Supplements

> **The Student Video Tool Kit for *Introductory Psychology*** is a DVD-based collection of more than 100 brief video clips (1–13 min) and activities from PsychPortal. It gives students a fresh way to experience both the classic experiments at the heart of psychological science and cutting-edge research conducted by the field's most influential investigators.

> The ***Introducing Psychology* Book Companion Web site** at **www.worthpublishers.com/schacterbrief2e** is the home of Worth Publishers' free study aids and supplemental content. The site includes online quizzes, interactive flashcards, and more.

> The **CourseSmart e-Book** offers the complete text of *Introducing Psychology*, Second Edition, in an easy-to-use, flexible format. Students can choose to view the CourseSmart e-Book online or download it to a personal computer or a portable media player, such as a smart phone or iPad. The CourseSmart e-Book for *Introducing Psychology*, Second Edition, can be previewed and purchased at **www.coursesmart.com**.

> The print **Study Guide** by Russell Frohardt and Alan Swinkels of St. Edward's University is a portable resource, ideal for students on the go who want to rehearse their mastery of concepts from the text with the following features:

> > "The Big Picture," a brief wrap-up of the chapter's main ideas and concepts

> > Chapter Objectives, which also appear in the Instructor's Resources and Test Bank

> > Chapter Overview, a fill-in-the-blank summary that is divided by major section

> > Three 10-question "Quick Quizzes"

> > "Hey, Guess What I Learned in Psychology Today," an essay question asking students to apply what they have learned

> > "Things to Ponder," a section that helps students extend and apply knowledge and think about where the material might be going

> > Web Links and Suggested Readings for further investigation

> > Answers section that includes in-depth explanations of complex topics

> ***Pursuing Human Strengths: A Positive Psychology Guide*** by Martin Bolt of Calvin College is a perfect way to introduce students to the amazing field of positive psychology as as their own personal strengths.

> ***The Critical Thinking Companion for Introductory Psychology*** by Jane S. Halonen of the University of West Florida and Cynthia Gray of Beloit College contains both a guide to critical thinking strategies as well as exercises in pattern recognition, practical problem solving, creative problem solving, scientific problem solving, psychological reasoning, and perspective taking.

> Worth Publishers is proud to offer several readers of articles taken from the pages of *Scientific American*. Drawing on award-winning science journalism, the ***Scientific American* Reader to Accompany *Psychology*, First Edition, by Daniel L. Schacter, Daniel T. Gilbert, and Daniel M. Wegner** features pioneering research across the fields of psychology. Selected by the authors themselves, this collection provides further insight into the fields of psychology through articles written for a popular audience.

> ***Psychology and the Real World: Essays Illustrating Fundamental Contributions to Society*** is a superb collection of essays by major researchers that describe their landmark studies. Published in association with the not-for-profit FABBS Foundation, this engaging reader includes Elizabeth Loftus's own reflections on her study of false memories, Eliot Aronson on his cooperative classroom study, and Daniel Wegner on his study of thought suppression. A portion of all proceeds is donated to FABBS to support societies of cognitive, psychological, behavioral, and brain sciences.

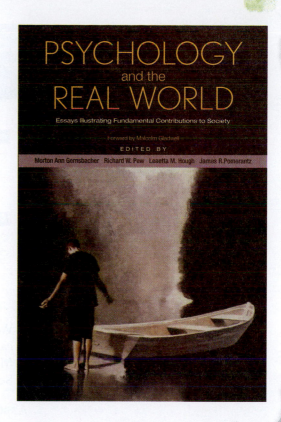

Take advantage of our most popular supplements!

Worth Publishers is pleased to offer cost-saving packages of *Introducing Psychology*, Second Edition, with our most popular supplements. Below is a list of some of the most popular combinations available for order through your local bookstore.

Introducing Psychology, 2nd Ed. & LaunchPad Access Card	ISBN-10: 1-4641-8517-4 / ISBN-13: 978-1-4641-8517-5
Introducing Psychology, 2nd Ed. & Study Guide	ISBN-10: 1-4641-8455-0 / ISBN-13: 978-1-4641-8455-0
Introducing Psychology, 2nd Ed. & iClicker	ISBN-10: 1-4641-8658-8 / ISBN-13: 978-1-4641-8658-5
Introducing Psychology, 2nd Ed. & *Scientific American* Reader	ISBN-10: 1-4641-8456-9 / ISBN-13: 978-1-4641-8456-7
Introducing Psychology, 2nd Ed. & *Psychology and the Real World*	ISBN-10: 1-4641-8457-7 / ISBN-13: 978-1-4641-8457-4

Faculty Support

> **New! Faculty Lounge** is an online forum provided by Worth Publishers where instructors can find and share favorite teaching ideas and materials, including videos, animations, images, PowerPoint slides, news stories, articles, Web links, and lecture activities. Sign up to browse the site or upload your favorite materials for teaching psychology at **www.worthpublishers.com/facultylounge**.

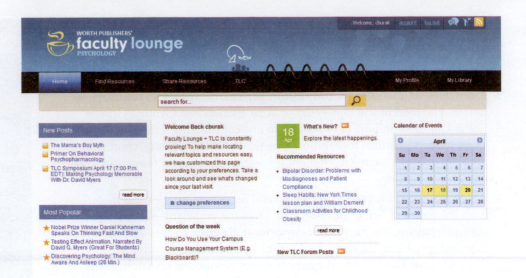

Course Management

> Worth Publishers supports multiple Course Management Systems with enhanced cartridges for upload into Blackboard, WebCT, Angel, Desire2Learn, Sakai, and Moodle. Cartridges are provided free upon adoption of *Introducing Psychology*, Second Edition, and can be downloaded at **www.macmillanhighered.com/lms**.

Assessment

> The **Printed Test Bank** by Chad Galuska of the College of Charleston features over 200 multiple-choice, true/false, and essay questions per chapter to test students' factual and conceptual knowledge and address the teaching outcomes set by the American Psychological Association.

> The **Computerized Test Bank** powered by Diploma includes all the test bank items for the easy creation of tests and quizzes. Created by Wimba, the Diploma software guides professors through the process of creating a test. It allows them to add, edit, or scramble an unlimited number of questions, format a test, drag-and-drop questions to create quizzes quickly and easily, and then print them for an exam. The computerized Test Bank will also allow you to export into a variety of formats compatible with many Internet-based testing products. For more information on Diploma, please visit Wimba's Web site: http://www.brownstone.net/publishers/products/dip6.asp.

> The **iClicker Classroom Response System** is a versatile polling system developed by educators for educators that makes class time more efficient and interactive. iClicker allows you to ask questions and instantly record your students' responses, take attendance, and gauge students' understanding and opinions. iClicker is available at a 10% discount when packaged with *Introducing Psychology*, Second Edition.

Presentation

> **New! Interactive Presentation Slides** are another great way to introduce Worth's *dynamic media* into the classroom without lots of advance preparation. Each presentation covers a major topic in psychology and integrates Worth's high-quality videos and animations for an engaging teaching and learning experience. These interactive presentations are complimentary to adopters of *Introducing Psychology*, Second Edition, and are a valuable resource for technology novices and experts alike.

> For teachers who want to promote interactive learning in the classroom, Worth Publishers is proud to offer **ActivePsych: Classroom Activities, Projects and Video Teaching Modules**. ActivePsych includes a robust collection of videos and

animations as well as two sets of activities created and class-tested by veteran introductory psychology teachers. The materials cover the entire introductory psychology curriculum with 32 flash-based demonstrations to promote discussion and critical thinking as well as 22 PowerPoint-based demonstrations designed to assess understanding that are compatible with the iClicker classroom response system.

> The **Instructor's Resources** by Jeffrey Henriques of The University of Wisconsin–Madison and Robin Freyberg of Stern College for Women, Yeshiva University, features a variety of materials that are valuable to new and veteran teachers alike. In addition to background on the chapter reading and suggestions for in-class lectures, the manual is rich with activities to engage students in different modes of learning. The Instructor's Resources can be downloaded from the Book Companion Web site at **www.worthpublishers.com/schacterbrief2e**.

A sample slide from the Worth Interactive Presentation Slides.

Video and DVD Resources

Worth Publisher's video collections—complimentary to adopters of *Introducing Psychology*, Second Edition—comprise over 300 unique video clips to enrich the classroom. These clips include clinical footage, interviews, animations, and news segments that vividly illustrate topics across the psychology curriculum.

> **New! Worth Introductory Psychology Videos**, produced in conjunction with **Scientific American** and **Nature**, is a breakthrough collection of NEW modular, tutorial videos on core psychology topics. This set includes animations, interviews with top scientists, and carefully selected archival footage, and is available on flash drive, DVD, or as part of the new Worth Video Anthology for Introductory Psychology.

> **New! The Worth Video Anthology for Introductory Psychology** is a complete collection, all in one place, of our video clips from the **Video Tool Kit**, the **Digital Media Archive**, the third edition of the **Scientific American Frontiers Teaching Modules**, as well as the new **Worth Introductory Psychology Videos** co-produced with **Scientific American** and **Nature**. Available on DVD or flash drive, the set is accompanied by its own Faculty Guide.

Acknowledgments

Despite what you might guess by looking at our photographs, we all found women who were willing to marry us. We thank Susan McGlynn, Marilynn Oliphant, and Toni Wegner for that particular miracle and also for their love and support during the years when we were busy writing this book.

Although ours are the names on the cover, writing a textbook is a team sport, and we were lucky to have an amazing group of professionals in our dugout. One in particular—Catherine E. Myers of *Rutgers University-Newark*—provided invaluable assistance in helping us to identify and communicate the essential parts of each chapter. We owe her a significant debt of thanks. We also greatly appreciate the contributions of Martin M. Antony, Mark Baldwin, Michelle A. Butler, Patricia Csank, Denise D. Cummins, Ian J. Deary, Howard Eichenbaum, Sam Gosling, Paul Harris, Shigehiro Oishi, Arthur S. Reber, Morgan T. Sammons, Dan Simons, Alan Swinkels, Richard M. Wenzlaff, and Steven Yantis.

We are grateful for the editorial, clerical, and research assistance we received from Clifford Robbins.

In addition, we would like to thank our core supplements authors. They provided insight into the role our book can play in the classroom and adeptly developed the materials to support it: Helen Just, Russ Frohardt, Alan Swinkels, Claire Etaugh, Chad Galuska, Jeff Henriques, and Robin Freyberg. We appreciate your tireless work in the classroom and the experience you brought to the book's supplements.

Over 1,000 students have class-tested chapters of *Introducing Psychology* in various stages of development. Not only are we encouraged by the overwhelmingly positive responses to *Introducing Psychology*, but we are also pleased to incorporate these students' insightful and constructive comments. In particular, we would like to thank the faculty who reviewed the manuscript in design, many of whom class-tested chapters with their introductory psychology students. They showed a level of engagement we have come to expect from our best colleagues and students:

Erica Altomare
University of Pittsburgh at Titusville

Stephanie Anderson
Central Community College

Jo Ann Armstrong
Patrick Henry Community College

Harold Arnold
Judson College

Cynthia Bane
Wartburg College

David Bauer
Viterbo University

Maida Berenblatt
Suffolk County Community College

Denise Berg
Santa Monica College

Cheryl Bluestone
Queensborough Community College

Cornelia Brentano
California State University

Richard Brewer
Southwest Baptist University

Wayne Briner
University of Nebraska at Kearney

Rita Butterfield
Sonoma State University

Thomas Capo
University of Maryland

Shawn Charlton
University of Central Arkansas

Veda Charlton
University of Central Arkansas

Arthur Cherdack
Los Angeles Valley College

Diana Ciesko
Valencia Community College

Shirley Clay
Northeast Texas Community College

Rick Collins
Eastern New Mexico University

Drew Curtis
Texas Woman's University

David Devonis
Graceland University

Adria DiBenedetto
Quinnipiac University

Dale Doty
Monroe Community College

Dewitt Drinkard
Danville Community College

Mirari Elcoro
Armstrong Atlantic State University

Michael Feiler
Merritt College

Claire Ford
Bridgewater State College

Carie Forden
Clarion University

Pamela Frazier-Anderson
Lincoln University

Danielle Gagne
Alfred University

Michael Gardner
Los Angeles Valley College

Marilyn Gibbons-Arhelger
Texas State University

Sandra Gibbs
Muskegon Community College

Arthur Gonchar
University of La Verne

Ray Gordon
Bristol Community College

Daniel Grangaard
Austin Community College

Gary Greenberg
University of Illinois at Chicago

Christina Grimes
Duke University

Marlene Groomes
Miami Dade College

Robert Guttentag
University of North Carolina at Greensboro

Shawn Haake
Iowa Central Community College

Charles Hallock
Pima County Community College

Scot Hamilton
University of West Georgia

Greg Harris
Polk State College

Christopher Hayashi
Southwestern College

Holly Haynes
Georgia Gwinnett College

Rebecca Helms McElroy
Wharton County Junior College

Ann Hennessey
Pierce College

Stacie Herzog
University of Wisconsin–Green Bay

James Higley
Brigham Young University

Elizabeth Hood
North Carolina Wesleyan College

David Iannaccone
Mount Wachusett Community College

Matthew Isaak
University of Louisiana

Lora Jacobi
Stephen F. Austin State University

Linda Jones
Blinn College

Diane Kobrynowicz
Austin Community College

Dana Kuehn
Florida State College at Jacksonville

Susan Lacke
Concordia University Wisconsin

Cindy Lahar
York County Community College

Lindette Lent
Arizona Western College

Christopher Long
Ouachita Baptist University

Karsten Look
Columbus State Community College

Sher'ri Madden Turner
Illinois Central College

Elizabeth Maloney
San Joaquin Delta College

John Marazita
Ohio Dominican University

Christopher Mayhorn
North Carolina State University

Dawn McBride
Illinois State University

Jason McCoy
Cape Fear Community College

Margaret McDevitt
McDaniel College

Marcia McKinley
Mount St. Mary's University

Barbara McMillan
Alabama Southern Community College

Glenn Meyer
Trinity University

Judith Luna Meyer
Beaufort County Community College

Daniel Miller
Wayne State College

Ronald Mossler
Los Angeles Valley College

Paulina Multhaupt
Macomb Community College

Tonya Nascimento
University of West Florida

Bryan Neighbors
Southwestern University

Jeffrey Nettle
University of New Haven

Caroline Olko
Nassau Community College

Tom Ollerman
Mesa Community College

Jennifer Ortiz Garza
Victoria College

Randall Osborne
Texas State University

Carol Pandey
Pierce College

Richard Pare
University of Maine at Bangor

David Payne
Wallace Community College

Jennifer Perry
Baldwin Wallace College

Kathleen Petrill
Ashland University

Linda Petroff
Central Community College

David Phillip
Santa Monica College

Kellie Pierson
Northern Kentucky University

James Previte
Victor Valley College

Frank Provenzano
Greenville Technical College

Michael Rodman
Middlesex Community College

Beverly Salzman
Housatonic Community College

Patricia Sawyer
Middlesex Community College

Nathan Saxon
Somerset Community College

Asani Seawell
Grinnell College

Leslie Sekerka
Menlo College

Brian Siers
Roosevelt University

Jerry Snead
*Coastal Carolina Community
College*

Jason Spiegelman
Community College of Beaver County

Susan Spooner
McLennan Community College

Jonathan Springer
Kean University

David Steitz
Nazareth College of Rochester

Krishna Stilianos
Oakland Community College

Dawn Strongin
California State University, Stanislaus

Eva Szeli
Arizona State University

Laura Talcott
Indiana University, South Bend

Kathleen Taylor
Sierra College

Melissa Terlecki
Cabrini College

Joan Thomas-Spiegel
Los Angeles Harbor College

Jeri Thompson
Hastings College

Michelle Tomaszycki
Wayne State University

Meral Topcu
Ferris State University

Sandra Trafalis
San Jose State University

Sarah Trost
Cardinal Stritch University

Ayme Turnbull
Adelpi University

Jyotsna Vaid
Texas A&M University

Linda Walsh
University of Northern Iowa

Mary Waterstreet
St. Ambrose University

Linda Weldon
*Community College of Baltimore
County*

Jan Wertz
Centre College

Melissa Weston
El Centro College

Peter Wooldridge
Durham Technical Community College

Nancy White
Coastal Carolina Community College

Jennifer Yates
Ohio Wesleyan University

Judith Wightman
Kirkwood Community College

Erin Young
Texas A&M University

Jeannetta Williams
St. Edward's University

Lee Zasloff
American River College

We learned a lot during the development of *Introducing Psychology* from focus group attendees, survey respondents, chapter reviewers, and class testers who read parts of our book, and we thank them for their time and insights, both of which were considerable. They include:

Maya Aloni
Middlesex Community College

Joelle Dayan
Dawson College

Steve Balsis
Texas A&M University

Peggy DeCooke
Purchase College

Arthur Beaman
University of Kentucky

Wendy Domjan
University of Texas, Austin

John Best
Eastern Illinois University

Evelyn Doody
College of Southern Nevada

Lyn T. Boulter
Catawaba College

Kimberley Duff
Cerritos College

Kate Byerwalter
Grand Rapids Community College

Anne Duran
California State University, Bakersfield

David Carroll
University of Wisconsin, Superior

Claire Etaugh
Bradley University

Elaine Cassel
Lord Fairfax Community College

Kimberly Fairchild
Manhattan College

Jenel Cavazos
Cameron University

Bryan D. Fantie
American University

Heather Chabot
New England College

Meredyth Fellows
West Chester University of Pennsylvania

Caroline Chochol
Dawson College

Sherecce Fields
Texas A&M University

Susan Cloninger
The Sage Colleges

Kevin Filter
Minnesota State University

Nathalie Cote
Belmont Abbey College

Krista Forrest
University of Nebraska

Catherine C. Crain
Cascadia Community College

Daniel Fox
Sam Houston State University

Christopher Cronin
Saint Leo University

Nelson Freedman
Queen's University

Robert DaPrato
Solano Community College

Elizabeth Freeman
Young Bentley University

Dale Fryxell
University of Hawaii, Manoa

Lisa Geraci
Texas A&M University

John Governale
Clark College

Erinn Green
University of Cincinnati

Andrew Guest
University of Portland

Rob Guttentag
University of North Carolina at Greensboro

David Haaga
American University

Gordon Hammerle
Adrian College

Moira Hanna
Greenville Technical College

Kathy Hipp
Daniel Webster College

Debra Hollister
Valencia Community College

Christine Homen
Bristol Community College

Suzy Horton
Mesa Community College

David Hothersall
The Ohio State University

Allen Huffcutt
Bradley University

Charles Huffman
James Madison University

Louise Jarrold
Dawson College

Annette Kujawski-Taylor
University of San Diego

Fred Leavitt
California State University, East Bay

Douglas Lenz
Metropolitan Community College of Omaha

Michael Levine
University of Illinois at Chicago

Nancey Lobb
Alvin Community College

Cynthia Lofaso
Central Virginia Community College

Anthony A. Lopez
Cerritos College

Christopher May
Carroll University

Ann McKay
Bristol Community College

Kyla McKay
Bristol Community College

Mitchell Metzger
Ashland University

Judith Meyer
Beaufort County Community College

Caroline Olko
Nassau Community College

Keith Pannell
El Paso Community College

Barb Philibert
Ashford University

Karyn Plumm
University of North Dakota

Julia Raehpour
Chippewa Valley Technical College

Bryan Raudenbush
Wheeling Jesuit University

Kimberly Renk
University of Central Florida

Tanya Renner
Kapiolani Community College

Vicki M. Ritts
St. Louis Community College

Ana Ruiz
Alvernia University

Stacy Seale
Eastern Kentucky University

Deirdre Slavik
Northwest Arkansas Community College

Helen Taylor
Bellevue College Washington

Melissa Terlecki
Cabrini College

Lawrence Venuk
North Valley Community College

Eleanor Webber
Johnson State College

Christopher Whelan
Community College of Southern Nevada

Paul Wellman
Texas A&M University

Jamie Workman
University of North Carolina at Greensboro

Thomas Westcott
University of West Florida

Frederic Wynn
County College of Morris

We are especially grateful to the extraordinary people of Worth Publishers: our senior publisher Catherine Woods and publisher Kevin Feyen, who provided guidance and encouragement at all stages of the project; our acquisitions editor, Dan DeBonis, who managed the project with intelligence, grace, and good humor; our development editors, Valerie Raymond and Mimi Melek; our director of development Tracey Kuehn, associate managing editor Lisa Kinne, project editor Jennifer Bossert, production manager Sarah Segal, and assistant editor Nadina Persaud, who through some remarkable alchemy turned a manuscript into a book; our art director Babs Reingold, designer Lyndall Culbertson, layout designer Paul Lacy, and photo editor Cecila Varas, who made the book an aesthetic delight; our senior media editor Christine Burak and editorial assistant Agnes Baik, who guided the development and creation of a superb supplements package; and our marketing manager Lindsay Johnson, associate director of market development Carlise Stembridge, and marketing assistant Stephanie Ellis who served as tireless public advocates for our vision. Thank you one and all. We look forward to working with you again.

Daniel L. Schacter   Daniel T. Gilbert   Daniel M. Wegner

Psychology: The Evolution of a Science

BACK IN 1860, ABRAHAM LINCOLN HAD JUST BEEN elected president of the United States, the Pony Express had just begun to deliver mail between Missouri and California, and a woman named Anne Kellogg had just given birth to a child who would grow up to invent the cornflake. But none of this mattered very much to William James, an 18-year-old man who had no idea what to do with his life. He loved to paint and draw but worried that he wasn't talented enough to become a serious artist. He had enjoyed studying biology in school but doubted that he could support a family on a naturalist's salary. So, like many young people faced with difficult decisions about their futures, William abandoned his dreams and chose to do something in which he had little interest but of which his family heartily approved. Alas, within a few months of arriving at Harvard Medical School, his initial lack of interest in medicine only blossomed. With a bit of encouragement from the faculty, he put his medical studies on hold to join a biological expedition to the Amazon. The adventure failed to focus his wandering mind (though he learned a great deal about leeches), and when he returned to medical school, both his physical and mental health began to deteriorate. It was clear to everyone that William James was not the sort of person who should be put in charge of a scalpel and a bag of drugs.

Dropping out of medical school, William decided to travel around Europe, where he met and talked with people developing a new science called *psychology* (from a combination of the Greek *psyche*, which means "soul," and *logos*, which means "to study"). As William learned more about psychology, he began to see that this new field was taking a modern, scientific approach to age-old questions about human nature—questions that had become painfully familiar to him during his personal search for meaning, but questions to which only poets and philosophers had ever before offered answers (Bjork, 1983; Simon, 1998). Excited about the new discipline, William returned to

MIKE HARRINGTON/GETTY IMAGES

▶ Over the years, many young people, like this happy pair, have turned to travel as they considered their next step in life. Thankfully, for the young William James, his travels led him to psychology.

1

NEW YORK TIMES CO./GETTY IMAGES

William James (1842–1910) was excited by the new field of psychology, which allowed him to apply a scientific approach to age-old questions about the nature of human beings.

America and quickly finished his medical degree. But he never practiced medicine. Rather, he became a professor at Harvard University and devoted the rest of his life to psychology. His landmark book—*The Principles of Psychology*—is still widely read and remains one of the most influential books ever written on the subject (James, 1890).

A lot has happened since then. Abraham Lincoln has become the face on a penny, the Pony Express has been replaced by e-mail and Twitter, and the Kellogg Company sells about $9 billion worth of cornflakes every year. If William James (1842–1910) were alive today, he would be amazed by all of these things. But he would probably be even more amazed by the intellectual advances that have taken place in the science that he helped create. Psychologists today are exploring perception, memory, creativity, consciousness, love, anxiety, addictions, and more. They use state-of-the-art technologies to examine what happens in the brain when people feel anger, recall a past experience, undergo hypnosis, or take an intelligence test. They examine the impact of culture on individuals, the origins and uses of language, the ways in which groups form and dissolve, and the similarities and differences between people from different backgrounds. Their research advances the frontiers of basic knowledge and has practical applications—from new treatments for depression and anxiety to new systems that allow organizations to function more effectively.

Psychology is *the scientific study of **mind** and **behavior.*** The **mind** refers to our *private inner experience,* the ever-flowing stream of consciousness that is made of perceptions, thoughts, memories, and feelings. **Behavior** refers to *observable actions of human beings and nonhuman animals,* the things that we do in the world, by ourselves or with others. As you will see in the chapters to come, psychology is an attempt to use scientific methods to address fundamental questions about mind and behavior that have puzzled people for millennia. Let's take a look at three key questions in psychology:

1. *What are the bases of perceptions, thoughts, memories, and feelings, or our subjective sense of self?*

    For thousands of years, philosophers tried to understand how the objective, physical world of the body was related to the subjective, psychological world of the mind. Today, psychologists know that all of our subjective experiences arise from the electrical and chemical activities of our brains. Modern psychologists and neuroscientists are using new technologies to explore this relationship in ways that would have seemed like science fiction only 20 years ago. For example, the technique known as *functional magnetic resonance imaging,* or fMRI, allows scientists to "scan" a brain and see which parts are active when a person reads a word, sees a face, learns a new skill, or remembers a personal experience. (You'll read more about this and related techniques in the upcoming chapters.) William James was interested in how people acquire complex skills such as the ability to play the violin, and he wondered how the brain enabled great musicians to produce virtuoso performances. What William James could only ponder, modern psychologists can observe.

    ? **What are the bases of perceptions, thoughts, memories, and feelings, or our subjective sense of self?**

2. *How does the mind usually allow us to function effectively in the world?*

    Scientists sometimes say that form follows function; that is, if we want to understand *how* something works (e.g., an engine or a thermometer), we need to know what it is working *for* (e.g., powering vehicles or measuring temperature). The function of the mind is to help us do what we have to do in order to prosper, such as acquiring food, shelter, and mates.

    For instance, perception allows us to recognize our families and avoid stumbling into oncoming traffic. Language allows us to organize our thoughts and commu-

psychology The scientific study of mind and behavior.

mind Our private inner experience of perceptions, thoughts, memories, and feelings.

behavior Observable actions of human beings and nonhuman animals.

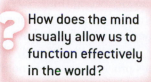

How does the mind usually allow us to function effectively in the world?

nicate them to others. Memory allows us to avoid solving the same problems over and over again every time we encounter them. Emotions allow us to react quickly to events that have "life or death" significance, and they enable us to form strong social bonds. The list goes on and on.

Given the adaptiveness of psychological processes, it is not surprising that people with deficiencies in those processes often have a pretty tough time. Consider the case of Elliot, a middle-aged husband and father with a good job, whose life was forever changed when surgeons discovered a tumor in the middle of his brain (Damasio, 1994). The surgeons were able to remove the tumor and save his life, but as time went on, Elliot seemed more likely than usual to make bad decisions. He couldn't prioritize tasks at work because he couldn't decide what to do first. Eventually he was fired, so he pursued a series of risky business ventures—and lost his life's savings. His wife divorced him, he married again, and his second wife divorced him too.

So what ruined Elliot's life? His intelligence was intact, and his ability to speak, to think, and to solve logical problems was every bit as sharp as it ever was. But Elliot was no longer able to experience emotions. For example, Elliot didn't experience any sorrow when his wives packed up and left him, and he didn't experience any regret or anger when his boss fired him. Most of us have wished from time to time that we could be as stoic and unflappable as that; after all, who needs anxiety, sorrow, and anger? The answer is that we all do. Emotions function as signals that tell us when we are putting ourselves in harm's way. If you felt no anxiety when you thought about taking an upcoming exam, borrowing your friend's car without permission, or cheating on your taxes, you would probably make a string of poor decisions that would leave you without a degree and possibly in jail. Elliot didn't have those feelings, and he paid a big price for it.

What good are emotions? Sometimes they just entertain us at the theater, but often they are adaptive and guide us to do what's good for us.

3. *Why does the mind occasionally function so ineffectively?*

The mind is an amazing machine that can do many things quickly. We can drive a car while talking to a passenger while recognizing the street address while remembering the name of the song that just came on the radio. But like all machines, the mind often trades accuracy for speed and versatility. This can produce occasional malfunctions in our otherwise-efficient mental processing. One of the most fascinating aspects of psychology is that we are *all* prone to a variety of errors and illusions.

Why does the mind occasionally function so ineffectively?

For example, consider a few examples from diaries of people who took part in a study concerning mental errors in everyday life (Reason & Mycielska, 1982, pp. 70–73):

> *I meant to get my car out, but as I passed the back porch on my way to the garage, I stopped to put on my boots and gardening jacket as if to work in the yard.*

> *I put some money into a machine to get a stamp. When the stamp appeared, I took it and said, "Thank you."*

> *On leaving the room to go to the kitchen, I turned the light off, although several people were there.*

If these lapses seem amusing, it is because they are. But they are also potentially important clues to human nature. For example, notice that the person who bought a stamp said "Thank you" to the machine, not "How do I find the

nativism The philosophical view that certain kinds of knowledge are innate or inborn.

philosophical empiricism The philosophical view that all knowledge is acquired through experience.

phrenology A now defunct theory that specific mental abilities and characteristics, ranging from memory to the capacity for happiness, are localized in specific regions of the brain.

subway?" In other words, the person did not just do *any* wrong thing; rather, he did something that would have been perfectly right in a real social interaction. As these examples suggest, people often operate on "autopilot," or behave automatically, relying on well-learned habits that they execute without really thinking. Understanding such lapses, errors, and mistakes provides a vantage point for understanding the normal operation of mental life and behavior.

Psychology is exciting because it addresses fundamental questions about human experience and behavior, and the three questions we've just considered are merely the tip of the iceberg. Think of this book as a guide to exploring the rest of the iceberg. But before we don our parkas and grab our pickaxes, we need to understand how the iceberg got here in the first place. To understand psychology in the 21st century, we need to become familiar with the psychology of the past.

Psychology's Roots: The Path to a Science of Mind

When the young William James interrupted his medical studies to travel in Europe during the late 1860s, he confronted a very different situation than a similarly curious student would confront today, largely because psychology did not yet exist as an independent field of study. As James cheekily wrote, "The first lecture in psychology that I ever heard was the first I ever gave." Of course, that doesn't mean no one had ever thought about human nature before. For 2,000 years, thinkers with scraggly beards and poor dental hygiene had pondered such questions, and, in fact, modern psychology acknowledges its deep roots in philosophy.

Psychology's Ancestors: The Great Philosophers

The desire to understand ourselves is not new. Greek thinkers such as Plato (428 BC–347 BC) and Aristotle (384 BC–322 BC) were among the first to struggle with fundamental questions about how the mind works (Robinson, 1995). Greek philosophers debated many of the questions that psychologists continue to debate today. For example, are cognitive abilities and knowledge inborn, or are they acquired only through experience? Plato argued in favor of **nativism,** which maintains that *certain kinds of knowledge are innate or inborn.* But his student Aristotle believed that the child's mind was a *tabula rasa* (a blank slate) on which experiences were written, and he argued for **philosophical empiricism,** which

? What fundamental question has puzzled philosophers ever since humans began thinking about behavior?

holds that *all knowledge is acquired through experience.* Although few modern psychologists believe that nativism or empiricism is entirely correct, the issue of just how much "nature" and "nurture" explain any given behavior is still a matter of controversy. In some ways, it is quite amazing that ancient philosophers were able to articulate so many of the important questions in psychology and offer so many excellent insights in their answers without any access to scientific evidence. Their ideas came from personal observations, intuition, and speculation. Although they were quite good at arguing with one another, they usually found it impossible to settle their disputes because their approach provided no means of testing their theories. As you will see in Chapter 2, the ability to test a theory is the cornerstone of the scientific approach and the basis for reaching conclusions in modern psychology.

How do young children learn about the world? Plato believed that certain kinds of knowledge are innate, whereas Aristotle believed that the mind is a blank slate on which experiences are written.

GEO MARTINEZ/FEATURE PICS

From the Brain to the Mind: The French Connection

We all know that the brain and the body are physical objects we can see and touch and that the subjective contents of our minds—our perceptions, thoughts, and feelings—are not. Inner experience is perfectly real, but where in the world is it? The French philosopher René Descartes (1596–1650) argued that body and mind are fundamentally different things—that the body is made of a material substance, whereas the mind (or soul) is made of an immaterial or spiritual substance. But if the mind and the body are different things made of different substances, then how do they interact? How does the mind tell the body to put its foot forward, and when the body steps on a rusty nail, why does the mind say, "Ouch"? This is the problem of *dualism,* or how mental activity can be reconciled and coordinated with physical behavior.

Descartes suggested that the mind influences the body through a tiny structure near the bottom of the brain known as the pineal gland. He was largely alone in this view, as other philosophers at the time either rejected his explanation or offered alternative ideas. For example, the British philosopher Thomas Hobbes (1588–1679) argued that the mind and body aren't different things at all; rather, the mind *is* what the brain *does.* From Hobbes's perspective, looking for a place in the brain where the mind meets the body is like looking for a place in a television where the picture meets the flat panel display.

The French physician Franz Joseph Gall (1758–1828) also thought that brains and minds were linked, but by size rather than by glands. After examining the brains of animals and of people who had died of disease, or as healthy adults, or as children, he observed that mental ability often increases with larger brain size and decreases with damage to the brain. These aspects of Gall's findings were generally accepted (and the part about brain damage still is today). But Gall went far beyond his evidence to develop a psychological theory known as **phrenology,** which held that *specific mental abilities and characteristics, ranging from memory to the capacity for happiness, are localized in specific regions of the brain* (**FIGURE 1.1**). The idea that different parts of the brain are specialized for specific psychological functions turned out to be right; as you'll learn later in the book, a part of the brain called the hippocampus is intimately involved in memory, just as a structure called the amygdala is intimately involved in fear. But Gall asserted that the size of bumps or indentations on the skull reflected the size of the brain regions beneath them and that by feeling those bumps, one could tell whether a person was friendly, cautious, assertive, idealistic, and so on. What Gall didn't realize was that bumps on the skull do not necessarily reveal anything about the shape of the brain underneath. Phrenology made for a nice parlor game and gave young people a good excuse for touching each other, but in the end it amounted to a series of strong claims based on weak evidence. Despite an initially large following, phrenology was quickly discredited (Fancher, 1979).

While Gall was busy playing bumpologist, other French scientists were beginning to link the brain and the mind in a more convincing manner. Biologists began to conduct experiments in which they surgically removed specific parts of the brain from dogs, birds, and other animals and found (not surprisingly!) that their actions and movements differed from those of animals with intact brains. Although no one conducted

? **How did work involving patients with brain damage help demonstrate the mind-brain connection?**

similar experiments on humans, clues were emerging on that front as well. For example, the surgeon Paul Broca (1824–80) worked with a patient who had suffered damage to a small part of the left side of the brain (now known as Broca's area). The patient was virtually unable to speak and could utter only the single syllable "tan." Yet the patient understood everything that was said to him and was able to communicate using gestures. Broca had the crucial insight that damage to a specific part of the brain impaired a specific mental

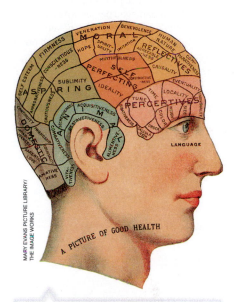

▲ Figure **1.1** **Phrenology** Franz Joseph Gall (1758–1828) developed a theory called phrenology, which suggested that psychological capacities (such as the capacity for friendship) and traits (such as cautiousness and mirth) were located in particular parts of the brain. The more of these capacities and traits a person had, the larger the corresponding bumps on the skull.

THE GRANGER COLLECTION

Surgeon Paul Broca (1824–80) worked with a brain-damaged person who could comprehend but not produce spoken language. Broca suggested that the mind is grounded in the material processes of the brain.

function, clearly demonstrating that the brain and mind are closely linked. This was important in the 19th century because at that time many people accepted Descartes' idea that the mind is separate from, but interacts with, the brain and the body. These studies demonstrated that the mind is grounded in a material substance; namely, the brain. Their work jump-started the scientific investigation of mental processes.

Structuralism: Applying Methods from Physiology to Psychology

In the middle of the 19th century, psychology benefited from the work of German scientists who were trained in the field of **physiology,** which is *the study of biological processes, especially in the human body.* Physiologists had developed methods that allowed them to measure such things as the speed of nerve impulses, and some of them had begun to use these methods to measure mental abilities. William James was drawn to the work of two such physiologists: Hermann von Helmholtz (1821–94) and Wilhelm Wundt (1832–1920). "It seems to me that perhaps the time has come for psychology to begin to be a science," wrote James in a letter written in 1867 during his visit to Berlin. "Helmholtz and a man called Wundt at Heidelberg are working at it."

Helmholtz, a brilliant experimenter with a background in both physiology and physics, had developed a method for measuring the speed of nerve impulses in a frog's leg, which he then adapted to the study of human beings. Helmholtz trained participants to respond when he applied a **stimulus**—*sensory input from the environment*—to different parts of the leg. He recorded his participants' **reaction time,** or *the amount of time taken to respond to a specific stimulus,* after applying the stimulus. Helmholtz found that people generally took longer to respond when their toe was stimulated than when their thigh was stimulated, and the difference between these reaction times allowed him to estimate how long it took a nerve impulse to travel to the brain. These results were astonishing to 19th-century scientists because at that time just about everyone thought that mental processes occurred instantaneously. Helmholtz showed that this wasn't true. In so doing, he also demonstrated that reaction time could be a useful way to study the mind and the brain.

Although Helmholtz's contributions were important, historians generally credit the official emergence of psychology to his research assistant, Wilhelm Wundt (Rieber, 1980). In 1867, Wundt taught what was probably the first university course in physiological psychology, a course that led to the publication of his book *Principles of Physiological Psychology* in 1874. In 1879, Wundt opened the first laboratory ever to be exclusively devoted to psychological studies, which marked the official birth of psychology as an independent field of study. The new lab was full of graduate students carrying out research on topics assigned by Wundt, and it soon attracted young scholars from all over the world who were eager to learn about the new science that Wundt had developed.

physiology The study of biological processes, especially in the human body.

stimulus Sensory input from the environment.

reaction time The amount of time taken to respond to a specific stimulus.

consciousness A person's subjective experience of the world and the mind.

structuralism The analysis of the basic elements that constitute the mind.

introspection The subjective observation of one's own experience.

functionalism The study of the purpose mental processes serve in enabling people to adapt to their environment.

Wundt believed that scientific psychology should focus on analyzing **consciousness,** *a person's subjective experience of the world and the mind.* Consciousness encompasses a broad range of subjective experiences.

? How did the work of chemists influence early psychology?

We may be conscious of sights, sounds, tastes, smells, bodily sensations, thoughts, or feelings. As Wundt tried to figure out a way to study consciousness scientifically, he noted that chemists try to understand the structure of matter by breaking down natural substances into basic elements. So he and his students adopted an approach called **structuralism,** *the analysis of the basic elements that constitute the mind.* This approach involved breaking consciousness down into elemental sensations and feelings. Some of Wundt's studies used the method of **introspection,** which involves *the subjective observation of one's own experience.* In a typical experiment, research partici-

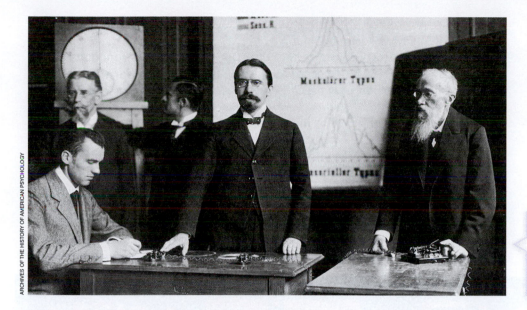

ARCHIVES OF THE HISTORY OF AMERICAN PSYCHOLOGY

Wilhelm Wundt (1832–1920), far right, founded the first laboratory devoted exclusively to psychology at the University of Leipzig in Germany.

pants were presented with a stimulus (usually a color or a sound) and asked to report their introspections, perhaps describing the brightness of the color or the loudness of the tone. By analyzing the relation between feelings and perceptual sensations, Wundt and his students hoped to uncover the basic structure of conscious experience.

The influence of the structuralist approach gradually faded, due mostly to the introspective method. Science requires replicable observations—we could never determine the structure of DNA or the life span of a dust mite if every scientist who looked through a microscope saw something different. Alas, however, even trained observers provided conflicting introspections about their conscious experiences ("I see a cloud that looks like a duck"—"No, I think that cloud looks like a horse"), thus making it difficult for different psychologists to agree on the basic elements of conscious experience. Indeed, some psychologists had doubts about whether it was even possible to identify such elements through introspection alone. One of the most prominent skeptics was someone you've already met—a young man with a bad attitude and a useless medical degree named William James.

James and the Functional Approach

By the time James returned from his European tour, he was still inspired by the idea of approaching psychological issues from a scientific perspective. He received a teaching appointment at Harvard (primarily because the president of the university was a neighbor and family friend), a position that enabled him to purchase laboratory equipment for classroom experiments. As a result, James taught the first course at an American university to draw on the new experimental psychology developed by Wundt and his German followers (Schultz & Schultz, 1987).

James agreed with Wundt on some points, including the importance of focusing on immediate experience and the usefulness of introspection as a technique (Bjork, 1983), but he disagreed with Wundt's claim that consciousness could be broken down into separate elements. James believed that trying to isolate and analyze a particular moment of consciousness (as the structuralists did) distorted the essential nature of consciousness. Consciousness, he argued, was more like a flowing stream than a bundle of separate elements. So James decided to approach psychology from a different perspective entirely, developing an approach known as **functionalism:** *the study of the purpose mental processes serve in enabling people to adapt to their environment.* In contrast to structuralism, which examined the structure of mental processes, functionalism set out to understand the functions those mental processes served. (See the Real World box for some strategies to enhance one of those functions—learning.)

James's thinking was inspired by the ideas in Charles Darwin's (1809–82) recently published book on biological evolution, *On the Origin of Species by Means of Natural Selection* (1859/1999). Darwin proposed the principle of **natural selection,** which states that *the features of an organism that help it survive and reproduce are more likely than other features to be passed on to subsequent generations.* From this perspective, James reasoned, mental abilities must have evolved because they were adaptive—that is, because they helped people solve problems and increased their chances of survival. Like other animals, people have always needed to avoid predators, locate food, build shelters, and attract mates. Applying Darwin's principle of natural selection, James (1890) reasoned that consciousness must serve an important biological function and that the task for psy-

? **How does functionalism relate to Darwin's theory of natural selection?**

THE REAL WORLD

Improving Study Skills

Psychologists have progressed a great deal in understanding how we remember and learn. We'll explore the science of memory and learning in Chapters 6 and 7, but here we focus on the practical implications of psychological research for your everyday life: how you can use psychology to improve your study skills.

One of the most important lessons from psychological research is that we acquire information most effectively when we think about its meaning and reflect on its significance. In fact, we don't even have to try to remember something if we think deeply enough about it; the act of reflection itself will virtually guarantee good memory. For example, suppose that you want to learn the basic ideas behind Skinner's approach to behaviorism. Pick a psychological issue that interests you, such as whether a mentally disturbed individual should be held responsible for

committing a crime. Given what you will read a little later in this chapter, what would Skinner's opinion on this issue have been? Do you agree? Why or why not? In attempting to answer such questions, you will need to review what you've learned about behaviorism and then relate it to other things you already know about. Such deep thinking about the basic principles of behaviorism will make it much easier to remember the information later.

Here are some other insights from psychology that can help you remember and learn the material in this textbook and prepare for your tests:

- Think about and review the information you have acquired in class on a regular basis. Don't wait until the last second to cram your review into one sitting; research shows that spacing out review leads to longer-lasting recall.

- Don't just re-read your class notes or this textbook; test yourself on the material as often as you can. Research shows that actively retrieving information you've acquired helps you to later remember that information more than does just reading it again.

- Take some of the load off your memory by developing effective note-taking and outlining skills. Students often scribble down vague and fragmentary notes during lectures, figuring that the notes will be good enough to jog memory later. But when the time comes to study, they've forgotten so much that their

▲ Anxious feelings about an upcoming exam may be unpleasant, but as you've probably experienced yourself, they can motivate much-needed study.

notes are no longer clear. Try to focus on making detailed notes about the main ideas, facts, and people mentioned in the lecture.

- Organize your notes into an outline that clearly highlights the major concepts. The act of organizing an outline will force you to reflect on the information in a way that promotes retention and will also provide you with a helpful study guide to promote self-testing and review.

To follow up on these suggestions and find much more detailed information on learning and study techniques, see the book *Improving Memory and Study Skills* by Hermann, Raybeck, and Gruneberg (2002)—or read on in this book.

"As I get older, I find I rely more and more on these sticky notes to remind me."

chologists was to understand what those functions are. Wundt and the other structuralists worked in laboratories, but James felt that such work was limited in its ability to tell us how consciousness functions in the natural environment. Wundt, in turn, felt that James did not focus enough on new findings from the laboratory that he and the structuralists had begun to produce. Commenting on *The Principles of Psychology*, Wundt conceded that James was a topflight writer but disapproved of his approach: "It is literature, it is beautiful, but it is not psychology" (quoted in Bjork, 1983, p. 12).

The rest of the world did not agree, and James's functionalist psychology quickly gained followers, especially in North America, where Darwin's ideas were influencing many thinkers. Psychology departments that embraced a functionalist approach started to spring up at many major American universities, and in a struggle for survival that would have made Darwin proud, functionalism became more influential than structuralism had ever been. By the time James died in 1910, functionalism was the dominant approach to psychology in North America.

natural selection Charles Darwin's theory that the features of an organism that help it survive and reproduce are more likely than other features to be passed on to subsequent generations.

hysteria A temporary loss of cognitive or motor functions, usually as a result of emotionally upsetting experiences.

SUMMARY QUIZ [1.1]

1. In the 1800s, French surgeon Paul Broca conducted research that demonstrated a connection between
   a. animals and humans.
   b. the mind and the brain.
   c. brain size and mental ability.
   d. skull indentations and psychological attributes.

2. What was the subject of the famous experiment conducted by Hermann von Helmholtz?
   a. reaction time
   b. childhood learning
   c. phrenology
   d. functions of specific brain areas

3. Wundt and his students sought to analyze the basic elements that constitute the mind, an approach called
   a. consciousness.
   b. introspection.
   c. structuralism.
   d. objectivity.

4. William James espoused _____, the study of the purpose mental processes serve in enabling people to adapt to their environment.
   a. empiricism
   b. nativism
   c. structuralism
   d. functionalism

The Development of Clinical Psychology

At about the same time that some psychologists were developing structuralism and functionalism in the laboratory, other psychologists working in the clinic were beginning to study patients with psychological disorders. They began to realize that one can often understand how something works by examining how it breaks, and their observations of mental disorders influenced the development of psychology.

The Path to Freud and Psychoanalytic Theory

French physician Jean-Martin Charcot (1825–93) interviewed patients who had developed a condition known then as **hysteria**, *a temporary loss of cognitive or motor functions, usually as a result of emotionally upsetting experiences*. Hysterical patients became blind, paralyzed, or lost their memories, even though there was no known physical cause of their problems. However, when the patients were put into a

In this photograph, Sigmund Freud (1856–1939) sits by the couch reserved for his psychoanalytic patients.

unconscious The part of the mind that operates outside of conscious awareness but influences conscious thoughts, feelings, and actions.

psychoanalytic theory Sigmund Freud's approach to understanding human behavior that emphasizes the importance of unconscious mental processes in shaping feelings, thoughts, and behaviors.

psychoanalysis A therapeutic approach that focuses on bringing unconscious material into conscious awareness to better understand psychological disorders.

humanistic psychology An approach to understanding human nature that emphasizes the positive potential of human beings.

> LASSIE!
> GET HELP!!

trancelike state through the use of hypnosis, their symptoms disappeared: Blind patients could see, paralyzed patients could walk, and forgetful patients could remember. After coming out of the hypnotic trance, however, the patients again showed their symptoms. They behaved like two different people in the waking versus hypnotic states.

These peculiar disorders were ignored by Wundt and other laboratory scientists, who did not consider them a proper subject for scientific psychology (Bjork, 1983). But William James believed it was important to capitalize on these mental disruptions as a way of understanding the normal operation of the mind (Taylor, 2001). During our ordinary conscious experience we are only aware of a single "me" or "self," but the aberrations described by Charcot and others suggested that the brain can create many conscious selves that are not aware of each other's existence (James, 1890, p. 400). These striking observations also fueled the imagination of a young physician from Vienna, Austria, who studied with Charcot in Paris. His name was Sigmund Freud (1856–1939).

After his visit to Charcot's clinic in Paris, Freud returned to Vienna, where he continued his work with hysteric patients. (The word *hysteria,* by the way, comes from the Latin word *hyster,* which means "womb." It was once thought that only women suffered from hysteria and that it was caused by a "wandering womb.") Freud began to make his own observations of hysterics and to develop theories to explain their strange behaviors and symptoms. He theorized that many of the patients' problems could be traced to the effects of painful childhood experiences that the person could not remember, and

? How was Freud influenced by work with hysterics?

he suggested that the powerful influence of these seemingly lost memories revealed the presence of an unconscious mind. According to Freud, the **unconscious** is *the part of the mind that operates outside of conscious awareness but influences conscious thoughts, feelings, and actions.* This idea led Freud to develop **psychoanalytic theory,** *an approach that emphasizes the importance of unconscious mental processes in shaping feelings, thoughts, and behaviors.* From a psychoanalytic perspective, it is important to uncover a person's early experiences and to illuminate the person's unconscious anxieties, conflicts, and desires. Psychoanalytic theory formed the basis for a therapy that Freud called **psychoanalysis,** which focuses on *bringing unconscious material into conscious awareness.* During psychoanalysis, patients recalled past experiences ("When I was a toddler, I was frightened by a masked man on a black horse") and related their dreams and fantasies ("Sometimes I close my eyes and imagine not having to pay for this session"). Psychoanalysts used Freud's theoretical approach to interpret what their patients said.

In the early 1900s, Freud and a growing number of followers formed a psychoanalytic movement. Carl Gustav Jung (1875–1961) and Alfred Adler (1870–1937) were prominent in the movement, but both were independent thinkers, and Freud apparently had little tolerance for individuals who challenged his ideas. Soon enough, Freud broke off his relationships with both men so that he could shape the psychoanalytic movement himself (Sulloway, 1992). Psychoanalytic theory became quite controversial (especially in America) because it suggested that understanding a person's thoughts, feelings, and behavior required a thorough exploration of the person's early sexual experiences and unconscious sexual desires. In those days these topics were considered far too racy for scientific discussion.

This famous psychology conference, held in 1909 at Clark University, brought together many notable figures, such as William James and Sigmund Freud. Both men are circled, with James on the left.

Most of Freud's followers, like Freud himself, were trained as physicians and did not conduct psychological experiments in the laboratory (though early in his career, Freud did do some nice laboratory work on the sexual organs of eels). By and large, psychoanalysts developed their ideas in isolation from the research-based approaches of Wundt, James, and others. An exception occurred in 1909, when William James and Sigmund Freud met for the first time, at a conference. Although James worked in an academic setting and Freud worked with clinical patients, both men believed that mental aberrations provide important clues into the nature of mind.

The Influence of Psychoanalysis and the Humanistic Response

Most historians consider Freud to be one of the most influential thinkers of the 20th century, and the psychoanalytic movement influenced everything from literature and history to politics and art. Within psychology, psychoanalysis had its greatest impact on clinical practice, but that influence has been considerably diminished over the past 40 years. This is partly because Freud's vision of human nature was a dark one, emphasizing limitations and problems rather than possibilities and potentials. He saw people as hostages to their forgotten childhood experiences and primitive sexual impulses, and the inherent pessimism of his perspective frustrated those psychologists who had a more optimistic view of human nature. Freud's ideas were also difficult to test, and a theory that can't be tested is of limited use in psychology or other sciences. Though Freud's emphasis on unconscious processes has had an enduring impact on psychology, psychologists began to have serious misgivings about many aspects of Freud's theory.

? Why are Freud's ideas less influential today?

In the years after World War II, psychologists such as Abraham Maslow (1908–70) and Carl Rogers (1902–87) pioneered a new movement called **humanistic psychology,** *an approach to understanding human nature that emphasizes the positive potential of human beings.* Humanistic psychologists focused on the highest aspirations that people had for themselves. Rather than viewing people as prisoners of events in their remote pasts, humanistic psychologists viewed them as free agents who have an inherent need to develop, grow, and attain their full potential. This movement reached its peak in

Carl Rogers (1902–87) (left) and Abraham Maslow (1908–70) (right) introduced a positive, humanistic psychology in response to what they viewed as the overly pessimistic view of psychoanalysis.

the 1960s when a generation of "flower children" found it easy to see psychological life as a kind of blossoming of the spirit. Humanistic therapists sought to help people realize their full potential; in fact, they called them "clients" rather than "patients." In this relationship, the therapist and the client (unlike the psychoanalyst and the patient) were on equal footing. The development of the humanistic perspective was one more reason why Freud's ideas eventually became less influential.

SUMMARY QUIZ [1.2]

1. To understand human behavior, French physician Jean-Martin Charcot studied people
   a. who appeared to be completely healthy.
   b. with psychological disorders.
   c. with damage in particular areas of the brain.
   d. who had suffered permanent loss of cognitive and motor function.

2. Building on the work of Charcot, Sigmund Freud developed
   a. psychoanalytic theory.
   b. the theory of hysteria.
   c. humanistic psychology.
   d. physiological psychology.

3. The psychological theory that emphasizes the positive potential of human beings is known as
   a. structuralism.
   b. psychoanalytic theory.
   c. humanistic psychology.
   d. functionalism.

The Search for Objective Measurement: Behaviorism Takes Center Stage

The schools of psychological thought that had developed by the early 20th century—structuralism, functionalism, and psychoanalysis—differed substantially from one another. But they shared an important similarity: Each tried to understand the inner workings of the mind by examining conscious perceptions, thoughts, memories, and feelings or by trying to elicit previously unconscious details, all of which were reported by participants in experiments or by patients in a clinical setting. In each case it proved difficult to establish with much certainty just what was going on in people's minds, due to the unreliable nature of the methodology. As the 20th century unfolded, a new approach developed as psychologists challenged the idea that psychology should focus on mental life. This new approach was called **behaviorism,** which advocated that psychologists should restrict themselves to *the scientific study of objectively observable behavior.* Behaviorism represented a dramatic departure from previous schools of thought.

? How did behaviorism help psychology advance as a science?

Watson and the Emergence of Behaviorism

John Broadus Watson (1878–1958) believed that private experience was too idiosyncratic and vague to be an object of scientific inquiry. Science required replicable, objective measurements of phenomena that were accessible to all observers, and the introspective methods used by structuralists and functionalists were far too subjective for that. So instead of describing conscious experiences, Watson proposed that psychologists focus entirely on the study of behavior—what people *do,* rather

behaviorism An approach that advocates that psychologists restrict themselves to the scientific study of objectively observable behavior.

response An action or physiological change elicited by a stimulus.

reinforcement The consequences of a behavior that determine whether it will be more likely that the behavior will occur again.

than what people *experience*—because behavior can be observed by anyone and can be measured objectively.

At the time, animal behavior specialists such as Margaret Floy Washburn (1871–1939) were arguing that nonhuman animals, much like human animals, have conscious mental experiences (Scarborough & Furumoto, 1987). Watson reacted to this claim with venom. Because we cannot ask pigeons about their private, inner experiences (well, we can *ask,* but they never tell us), Watson decided that the only way to understand how animals learn and adapt was to focus solely on their behavior, and he suggested that the study of human beings should proceed on the same basis.

In 1894, Margaret Floy Washburn (1871–1939) became the first woman to receive a PhD degree in psychology. Washburn went on to a highly distinguished career and contributed to the development of psychology as a profession.

Watson was influenced by the work of the Russian physiologist Ivan Pavlov (1849–1936), who carried out pioneering research on the physiology of digestion. In the course of this work, Pavlov noticed something interesting about the dogs he was studying (Fancher, 1979). Not only did the dogs salivate at the sight of food; they also salivated at the sight of the person who fed them. The feeders were not dressed in Alpo suits, so why should the mere sight of them trigger a basic digestive response in the dogs? To answer this question, Pavlov developed a procedure in which he sounded a tone every time he fed the dogs, and after a while he observed that the dogs would salivate when they heard the tone alone. In Pavlov's experiments, the sound of the tone was a stimulus—sensory input from the environment—that influenced the salivation of the dogs, which was a **response**—*an action or physiological change elicited by a stimulus.* Watson and other behaviorists made these two notions the building blocks of their theories, which is why behaviorism is sometimes called "stimulus-response," or "S-R," psychology.

Inspired by Watson's behaviorism, B. F. Skinner (1904–90) investigated the way an animal learns by interacting with its environment. Here, he demonstrates the "Skinner box," in which rats learn to press a lever to receive food.

B. F. Skinner and the Development of Behaviorism

Like William James, Burrhus Frederic Skinner (1904–90) was a young man who couldn't decide what to do with his life. He aspired to become a writer and wondered whether a novelist could portray a character without understanding why the character behaved as he or she did. When he came across Watson's books, he knew he had the answer. Skinner completed his PhD studies in psychology and began to develop a new kind of behaviorism. In Pavlov's experiments, the dogs had been passive participants that stood around, listened to tones, and drooled. Skinner recognized that in everyday life, animals don't just stand there—they do something! Animals *act* on their environments to find shelter, food, or mates. Skinner wondered if he could develop behaviorist principles that would explain how they *learned* to act in those situations.

Skinner built what he called a "conditioning chamber" but what the rest of the world would forever call a "Skinner box." The box had a lever and a food tray, and a hungry rat could get food delivered to the tray by pressing the lever. Skinner observed that when a rat was put in the box, it would wander around, sniffing and exploring, and would usually press the bar by accident, at which point a food pellet would drop into the tray. After that happened, the rate of bar pressing would increase dramatically and remain high until the rat was no longer hungry. Skinner saw evidence for what he called the principle of **reinforcement,** which states that *the consequences of a behavior determine whether it will be more or less likely to occur again.* The concept of reinforcement became the foundation for Skinner's new approach to behaviorism (see

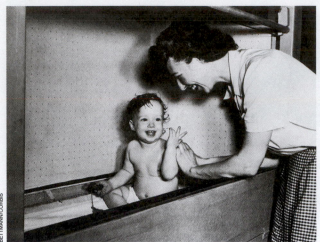

BETTMANN/CORBIS

Skinner's well-publicized questioning of such cherished notions as free will led to a rumor that he had raised his own daughter in a Skinner box. This urban legend, while untrue, likely originated from the climate-controlled, glass-encased crib that he invented to protect his daughter from the cold Minnesota winter. Skinner marketed the crib under various names, including the "Air-crib" and the "Heir Conditioner," but it failed to catch on with parents.

Chapter 7), which he formulated in a landmark book, *The Behavior of Organisms* (Skinner, 1938).

Skinner set out to use his ideas about reinforcement to help improve the quality of everyday life. He was visiting his daughter's fourth-grade class when he realized that he might be able to improve classroom instruction by breaking a complicated task into small bits and then using the principle of reinforcement to teach children each bit (Bjork, 1993). To learn how to solve a complicated math problem, for instance, students would first be asked an easy question about the simplest part of the problem. They would then be told whether the answer was right or wrong; if a correct response was made, they would move on to a more difficult question. Skinner thought that the satisfaction of knowing they were correct would be reinforcing and help students learn.

If fourth-graders and rats could be successfully trained, then why stop there? In the controversial books *Beyond Freedom and Dignity* (1971) and *Walden II* (1948/1986), Skinner laid out his vision of a utopian society in which behavior was controlled by the judicious application of the principle of reinforcement (Skinner, 1971). In those books he put forth the simple but stunning claim that our subjective sense of free will is an illusion and that when we think we are exercising free will, we are actually responding to present and past patterns of reinforcement. We do things in the present that have been rewarding in the past, and our sense of "choosing" to do them is nothing more than an illusion. Not surprisingly, that claim sparked an outcry from critics who believed that Skinner was giving away one of our most cherished attributes—free will—and calling for a repressive society that manipulated people for its own ends. In fact, Skinner did not want to turn society into a "dog obedience school" or strip people of their personal freedoms. Rather, he

? **Which of Skinner's claims provoked an outcry?**

argued that an understanding of the principles by which behavior is generated could be used to increase the social welfare, which is precisely what happens when a government launches advertisements to encourage citizens to drink milk or quit smoking. The result of all the controversy, however, was that Skinner's fame reached a level rarely attained by psychologists. A popular magazine that listed the 100 most important people who ever lived ranked Skinner just 39 points below Jesus Christ (Herrnstein, 1977).

SUMMARY QUIZ [1.3]

1. Behaviorism involves the study of
   a. observable actions and responses.
   b. the potential for human growth.
   c. unconscious influences and childhood experiences.
   d. human behavior and memory.

2. The experiments of Ivan Pavlov and John Watson centered on
   a. perception and behavior.   c. reward and punishment.
   b. stimulus and response.   d. conscious and unconscious behavior.

3. Who developed the concept of reinforcement?
   a. B. F. Skinner   c. John Watson
   b. Ivan Pavlov   d. Margaret Floy Washburn

The Return of the Mind: Psychology Expands

Watson, Skinner, and the behaviorists dominated psychology from the 1930s to the 1950s. The psychologist Ulric Neisser recalled the atmosphere when he was a student at Swarthmore in the early 1950s:

> Behaviorism was the basic framework for almost all of psychology at the time. It was what you had to learn. That was the age when it was supposed that no psychological phenomenon was real unless you could demonstrate it in a rat. (quoted in Baars, 1986, p. 275)

Behaviorism wouldn't dominate the field for much longer, however, and Neisser himself would play an important role in developing an alternative perspective.

"What about that! His brain still uses the old vacuum tubes."

The Emergence of Cognitive Psychology

Even at the height of behaviorist domination, there were a few revolutionaries whose research and writings were focused on mental processes. One such group of psychologists focused on the study of **illusions,** that is, *errors of perception, memory, or judgment in which subjective experience differs from objective reality.* For example, a German psychologist named Max Wertheimer (1880–1943) showed participants two lights that flashed quickly on a screen, one after the other. One light was flashed through a vertical slit, the other through a diagonal slit. When the time between two flashes was relatively long (one fifth of a second or more), an observer would see that it was just two lights flashing in alternation. But when Wertheimer reduced the time between flashes to around one twentieth of a second, observers saw a single flash of light moving back and forth (Fancher, 1979; Sarris, 1989).

Wertheimer reasoned that the perceived motion could not be explained in terms of the separate elements that cause the illusion (the two flashing lights) but instead that the moving flash of light is perceived as a *whole* rather than as the sum of its two parts. This unified whole, which in German is called *gestalt,* makes up the perceptual experience. Wertheimer's interpretation of the illusion led to the development of **Gestalt psychology,** *a psychological approach that emphasizes that we often perceive the whole rather than the sum of the parts.* In other words, the mind imposes organization on what it perceives, so people don't see what the experimenter actually shows them (two separate lights); instead they see the elements as a unified whole (one moving light).

? Why might people not see what an experimenter actually showed them?

Other cognitive psychologists gave people stories to remember and carefully observed the kinds of errors they made when they tried to recall them sometime later (Bartlett, 1932). The research participants often remembered what *should* have happened or what they *expected* to happen rather than what actually *did* happen. These and other errors led cognitive psychologists to suggest that memory is not a photographic reproduction of past experience and that our attempts to recall the past are powerfully influenced by our knowledge, beliefs, hopes, aspirations, and desires.

Meanwhile, the German psychologist Kurt Lewin (1890–1947) argued that one could best predict a person's behavior in the world by understanding the person's subjective experience of the world. A television soap opera is a meaningless series of unrelated physical movements unless one thinks about the characters' experiences—how Karen feels about Bruce, what Van was planning to say to Kathy about Emily, and whether Linda's sister, Nancy, will always hate their mother for meddling in her marriage. Lewin realized that it was not the stimulus, but rather the person's *construal* of the stimulus, that determined the person's subsequent behavior. A pinch on the cheek can be pleasant or unpleasant depending on who administers it, under what circumstances, and to which set of cheeks. Lewin used a special kind of mathematics

illusions Errors of perception, memory, or judgment in which subjective experience differs from objective reality.

gestalt psychology A psychological approach that emphasizes that we often perceive the whole rather than the sum of the parts.

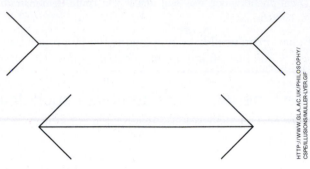

CULTURE & COMMUNITY

Do Illusions Affect Everyone the Same Way? Look at the two dark horizontal lines in the accompanying illustration. Which appears longer? If you're like most Americans, you'll find that the top line appears longer. But if you measure them with a ruler, you'll find that they're actually of equal length. This illusion occurs because the surrounding diagonal lines influence your perception of the horizontal lines. (You'll read more about this in Chapter 4.) But not everyone falls prey to this illusion. In a classic study, two groups of people classified culturally as European and non-European were asked to evaluate the length of the lines, called Müller-Lyer lines (Segall, Campbell, & Herskovits, 1963). Europeans came to the wrong conclusion that the lines are of different lengths considerably more often than did non-Europeans. The authors of the study inferred that people living in cities built of primarily rectangular shapes, as in European cities, see acute and obtuse angles drawn on paper as representative of 3-dimensional space. Because the non-Europeans in this study, primarily from rural hunting-and-gathering groups from southern Africa, did not make this mental leap, they were more likely to see the lines as they truly are: of the same length.

HTTP://WWW.GLA.AC.UK/PHILOSOPHY/CSPE/ILLUSIONS/MULLER-LYER.GIF

called *topology* to model the person's subjective experience; although his topological theories were not particularly influential, his attempts to model mental life and his insistence that psychologists study how people construe their worlds would have a lasting impact on psychology.

But, aside from a handful of pioneers such as these, psychologists happily ignored mental processes until the 1950s, when something important happened: the computer. The advent of computers had enormous practical impact, of course, but it also had an enormous conceptual impact on psychology. People and computers differ in important ways, but both seem to register, store, and retrieve information, leading psychologists to wonder whether the computer might be useful as a model for the human mind. Computers are information-processing systems, and the flow of information through their circuits is clearly no fairy tale. If psychologists could think of mental events—such as remembering, attending, thinking, believing, evaluating, feeling, and assessing—as the flow of information through the mind, then they might be able to study the mind scientifically after all. The emergence of the computer led to a reemergence of interest in mental processes all across the discipline of psychology, and it spawned a new approach called **cognitive psychology,** which is *the scientific study of mental processes, including perception, thought, memory, and reasoning.*

Technology and the Development of Cognitive Psychology

During World War II, the military had turned to psychologists to help understand how soldiers could best learn to use new technologies, such as radar. Radar operators had to pay close attention to their screens for long periods while trying to decide whether blips were friendly aircraft, enemy aircraft, or flocks of wild geese in need of a good chasing (Ashcraft, 1998; Lachman, Lachman, & Butterfield, 1979). How could radar operators be trained to make quicker and more accurate decisions? The answer to this question required that those who designed the equipment think about and talk about cognitive processes, such as perception, attention, identification, memory, and decision making.

cognitive psychology The scientific study of mental processes, including perception, thought, memory, and reasoning.

Meanwhile, by studying pilots, cognitive psychologists began to document what happens when people try to pay attention to several things at once. For instance, pilots can't attend to many different instruments at once and must actively move the focus of their attention from one to another (Best, 1992). In fact, the limited capacity to handle incoming information is a fundamental feature of human cognition, and this limit can explain many of the errors that pilots (and other people) make (Broadbent, 1958). There is a striking consistency in our capacity limitations across a variety of situations—we can pay attention to, and briefly hold in memory, about seven (give or take two) pieces of information (Miller, 1956). Cognitive psychologists began conducting experiments and devising theories to better understand the mind's limited capacity, a problem that behaviorists had ignored.

> **? What events prompted a new wave of cognitive studies?**

A computer is made of hardware (e.g., chips and disk drives today, magnetic tapes and vacuum tubes a half century ago) and software (stored on optical disks today and on punch cards a half century ago). If the brain is roughly analogous to the computer's hardware, then perhaps the mind was roughly analogous to a software program. This line of thinking led cognitive psychologists to begin writing computer programs to see what kinds of software could be made to mimic human speech and behavior (Newell, Shaw, & Simon, 1958). Meanwhile, the linguist Noam Chomsky (b. 1928) argued that just as a computer program contains a set of step-by-step rules for generating output, language relies on mental rules that allow people to understand and produce novel words and sentences. The ability of even a very young child to generate new sentences that he or she had never heard before flew in the face of the behaviorist claim that children learn to use language by reinforcement. Chomsky provided a clever, detailed, and thoroughly cognitive account of language that could explain many of the phenomena that the behaviorist account could not (Chomsky, 1959).

This 1950s computer was among the first generation of digital computers. Although different in many ways, computers and the human brain both process and store information, which led many psychologists at the time to think of the mind as a type of computer.

The Brain Meets the Mind: The Rise of Cognitive Neuroscience

Although cognitive psychologists studied the software of the mind, they had little to say about the hardware of the brain. And yet, as any computer scientist knows, the relationship between software and hardware is crucial: Each element needs the other to get the job done. Our mental activities often seem so natural and effortless—noticing the shape of an object, using words in speech or writing, recognizing a face as familiar—that we fail to appreciate the fact that they depend on intricate operations carried out by the brain. This dependence is revealed by dramatic cases in which damage to a particular part of the brain causes a person to lose a specific cognitive ability. Recall Broca's patient who, after damage to a limited area in the left side of the brain, could not produce words—even though he could understand them perfectly well. As you'll see later in the book, damage to other parts of the brain can also result in syndromes that are characterized by the loss of specific mental abilities (e.g., prosopagnosia, in which the person cannot recognize human faces) or by the emergence of bizarre behavior or beliefs (e.g., Capgras syndrome, in which the person believes that a close family member has been replaced by an imposter). These striking—sometimes startling—cases remind us that even the simplest cognitive processes depend on the brain.

Noam Chomsky's (b. 1928) theories of language signaled the end of behaviorism's dominance in psychology and helped spark the development of cognitive psychology.

Karl Lashley (1890–1958) conducted experiments he hoped would reveal a brain area that stores learned information. He removed different parts of animals' brains and observed the effects on the animals' behavior. Though he never found a specific area where learning is stored, his general approach had a major influence on behavioral neuroscience.

THE ARCHIVES OF THE HISTORY OF AMERICAN PSYCHOLOGY, THE UNIVERSITY OF AKRON

Karl Lashley (1890–1958), a psychologist who studied with John B. Watson, conducted a famous series of studies in which he trained rats to run mazes, surgically removed parts of their brains, and then measured how well they could run the maze again. Lashley hoped to find the precise spot in the brain where *learning* occurred. Alas, no one spot seemed to uniquely and reliably eliminate learning (Lashley, 1960). Rather, Lashley simply found that the more of a rat's brain he removed, the more poorly the rat ran the maze. He was frustrated by his inability to identify a specific site of learning, but his efforts inspired other scientists to take up the challenge. They developed a research area called *physiological psychology*. Today, this area has grown into **behavioral neuroscience,** which *links psychological processes to activities in the nervous system and other bodily processes*. To learn about the relationship between brain and behavior, behavioral neuroscientists observe animals' responses as the animals perform specially constructed tasks, such as running through a maze to obtain food rewards. The neuroscientists can record electrical or chemical responses in the brain as the task is being performed or later remove specific parts of the brain to see how performance is affected.

Of course, experimental brain surgery cannot ethically be performed on human beings; thus psychologists who want to study the human brain often have had to rely on nature's cruel and inexact experiments. Birth defects, accidents, and illnesses often cause damage to particular brain regions, and if this damage disrupts a particular ability, then psychologists deduce that the region is involved in producing the ability. For example, in Chapter 6 you'll learn about a patient whose memory was virtually wiped out by damage to a specific part of the brain, and you'll see how this tragedy provided scientists with remarkable clues about how memories are stored (Scoville & Milner, 1957). But in the late 1980s, technological breakthroughs led to the development of non-invasive "brain-scanning" techniques that made it possible for psychologists to watch what happens inside a human brain as a person performs a task such as reading, imagining, listening, or remembering (**FIGURE 1.2**). Brain scanning is an invaluable tool because it allows us to observe the brain in action and to see which parts are involved in which

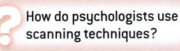

How do psychologists use scanning techniques?

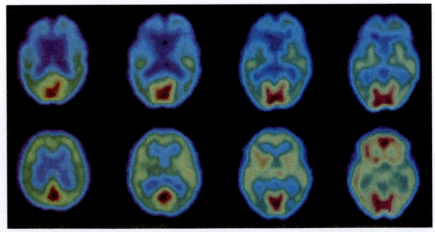

► FIGURE **1.2** **PET Scans of Living Human Brains** PET (positron emission tomography) scans are one of a variety of brain-imaging technologies that psychologists use to observe the living brain. The four brain images on the top each come from a person suffering from Alzheimer's disease; the four on the bottom each come from a healthy person of similar age. The red and green areas reflect higher levels of brain activity compared with the blue areas, which reflect lower levels of activity. In each image, the front of the brain is on the top and the back of the brain is on the bottom. As you can see, the person with Alzheimer's disease has less neural activity toward the front of the brain than does the healthy person.

ROGER RESSMEYER/CORBIS

operations (see Chapter 3). Psychologists can also use scanning techniques to observe healthy people performing various cognitive tasks in order to determine which brain areas are particularly active—and therefore probably intimately involved in—each kind of task (**FIGURE 1.3**). In fact, there's a name for this area of research. **Cognitive neuroscience** is the *field that attempts to understand the links between cognitive processes and brain activity* (Gazzaniga, 2000).

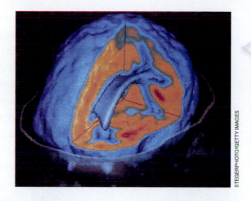

◄ FIGURE **1.3**   **More Ways to Scan a Brain** FMRI scanners produce more precise images than PET scanners do, allowing researchers to localize brain activity more accurately. FMRI scanners are also quicker at capturing images, allowing researchers to measure brain activity over briefer periods. Here, of the areas of the active brain during speech (yellow, red, and green areas), the areas in red were the most active.

The Adaptive Mind: The Emergence of Evolutionary Psychology

Psychology's renewed interest in mental processes and its growing interest in the brain were two developments that led psychologists away from behaviorism. A third development also pointed them in a different direction. Recall that one of behaviorism's key claims was that organisms are blank slates on which experience writes its lessons, and hence any one lesson should be as easily written as another. But in experiments conducted during the 1960s and 1970s, the psychologist John Garcia and his colleagues showed that rats can learn to associate nausea with the smell of food much more quickly than they can learn to associate nausea with a flashing light (Garcia, 1981). Why should this be? In the real world of forests, sewers, and garbage cans, nausea is usually caused by spoiled food, not by lightning, and although these particular rats had been born in a laboratory and had never left their cages, millions of years of evolution had "prepared" their brains to learn the natural association more quickly than the artificial one. In other words, it was not only the rat's learning history but the rat's *ancestors'* learning histories that determined the rat's ability to learn. Although that fact was at odds with the behaviorist doctrine, it was the credo for a new kind of psychology.

Evolutionary psychology *explains mind and behavior in terms of the adaptive value of abilities that are preserved over time by natural selection.* It has its roots in Charles Darwin's theory of natural selection, but it is only in the last few decades that evolutionary thinking has had an identifiable presence in psychology (Buss, 1999; Pinker, 1997; Tooby & Cosmides, 2000). Evolutionary psychologists think of the mind as a collection of specialized "modules" that are designed to solve the human problems our ancestors faced as they attempted to eat, mate, and reproduce over millions of years. According to evolutionary psychology, the brain is not an all-purpose computer that can do or learn one thing just as easily as it can do or learn another; rather, it is a computer that was built to do a few things well and everything else not at all. It is a computer that comes with a small suite of built-in applications that are designed to do the things that previous versions of that computer needed to have done.

? Why might so many of us have inherited "jealous genes"?

Consider, for example, how evolutionary psychology treats the emotion of jealousy. All of us who have been in romantic relationships have been jealous, if only because we noticed our partner noticing someone else. Jealousy can be a powerful, overwhelming emotion that we might wish to avoid, but according to evolutionary psychology, it exists today because it once served an adaptive function. If some of our hominid ancestors experienced jealousy and others did not, then the ones who experienced it might have been more likely to guard their mates and aggress against their rivals and thus may have been more likely to reproduce their "jealous genes" (Buss, 2000).

behavioral neuroscience An approach to psychology that links psychological processes to activities in the nervous system and other bodily processes.

cognitive neuroscience A field that attempts to understand the links between cognitive processes and brain activity.

evolutionary psychology A psychological approach that explains mind and behavior in terms of the adaptive value of abilities that are preserved over time by natural selection.

TIME LIFE PICTURES/GETTY IMAGES

Today's evolutionary psychologists embrace Charles Darwin's (1809–82) ideas, just as William James did more than a century ago. Darwin's theories of evolution, adaptation, and natural selection have provided insight into why brains and minds work the way they do.

Critics of the evolutionary approach point out that many current traits of people and other animals probably evolved to serve different functions than those they currently serve. For example, biologists believe that the feathers of birds probably evolved initially to perform such functions as regulating body temperature or capturing prey and only later served the entirely different function of flight. Likewise, people are reasonably adept at learning to drive a car, but nobody would argue that such an ability is the result of natural selection; the learning abilities that allow us to become skilled car drivers must have evolved for purposes other than driving cars.

Complications such as these have led critics to wonder how evolutionary hypotheses can ever be tested (Coyne, 2000; Sterelny & Griffiths, 1999). We don't have a record of our ancestors' thoughts, feelings, and actions, and fossils won't provide much information about the evolution of mind and behavior. Testing ideas about the evolutionary origins of psychological phenomena is indeed a challenging task, but not an impossible one (Buss et al., 1998; Pinker, 1997).

Start with the assumption that evolutionary adaptations should also increase reproductive success. So, if a specific trait or feature has been favored by natural selection, it should be possible to find some evidence of this in the numbers of offspring that are produced by the trait's bearers. Consider, for instance, the hypothesis that men tend to be tall because women prefer to mate with tall men. To investigate this hypothesis, researchers conducted a study in which they compared the numbers of offspring from short and tall men. They did their best to equate other factors that might affect the results, such as the level of education attained by short and tall men. Consistent with the evolutionary hypothesis, they found that tall men do indeed produce more offspring than short men (Pawlowski, Dunbar, & Lipowicz, 2000). This kind of study provides evidence that allows evolutionary psychologists to test their ideas. Not every evolutionary hypothesis can be tested, of course, but evolutionary psychologists are becoming increasingly inventive in their attempts.

SUMMARY QUIZ [1.4]

1. The study of mental processes such as perception and memory is called
   a. behavioral determinism.
   b. Gestalt psychology.
   c. social psychology.
   d. cognitive psychology.

2. The use of scanning techniques to observe the brain in action and to see which parts are involved in which operations helped the development of
   a. evolutionary psychology.
   b. cognitive neuroscience.
   c. cultural psychology.
   d. cognitive accounts of language formation.

3. Central to evolutionary psychology is the _____ function that minds and brains serve.
   a. emotional
   b. adaptive
   c. cultural
   d. physiological

Beyond the Individual: Social and Cultural Perspectives

Although psychologists often focus on the brain and the mind of the individual, they have not lost sight of the fact that human beings are fundamentally social animals who are part of a vast network of family, friends, teachers, and coworkers. Trying to understand people in the absence of that fact is a bit like trying to understand an ant or a bee without considering the function and influence of the colony or hive. People are the most important and most complex objects that we ever encounter; thus it is not surprising that our behavior is strongly influenced by their presence—or their absence. The two areas of psychology that most strongly emphasize these facts are social and cultural psychology.

social psychology A subfield of psychology that studies the causes and consequences of interpersonal behavior.

The Development of Social Psychology

Social psychology is *the study of the causes and consequences of interpersonal behavior*. Social psychology's development began in earnest in the 1930s and was driven by several historical events. The rise of Nazism led many of Germany's most talented scientists to immigrate to America; among them were psychologists such as Kurt Lewin, whom you met earlier. These psychologists had been strongly influenced by Gestalt psychology, which you'll recall held that "the whole is greater than the sum of its parts," and though the Gestaltists had been talking about the visual perception of objects, these psychologists felt that the phrase also captured a basic truth about the relationship between social groups and the individuals who constitute them. Phi-

"You're certainly a lot less fun since the operation."

? How did historical events influence the development of social psychology?

losophers had speculated about the nature of sociality for thousands of years, and political scientists, economists, anthropologists, and sociologists had been studying social life scientifically for some time. But these German refugees were the first to generate theories of social behavior that resembled the theories generated by natural scientists, and, more important, they were the first to conduct experiments to test their social theories.

Other historical events also shaped social psychology in its early years. For example, the Holocaust brought the problems of conformity and obedience into sharp

Social psychology studies how the thoughts, feelings, and behaviors of individuals can be influenced by the presence of others. Members of the Reverend Sun Myung Moon's Unification Church are often married to one another in ceremonies of 10,000 people or more; in some cases couples don't know each other before the wedding begins. Social movements such as this have the power to sway individuals.

cultural psychology The study of how cultures reflect and shape the psychological processes of their members.

focus, leading psychologists to examine the conditions under which people can influence one another to think and act in inhuman or irrational ways. The civil rights movement and the rising tensions between African Americans and White Americans led psychologists to study stereotyping, prejudice, and racism and to shock the world of psychology by suggesting that prejudice was the result of a perceptual error that was every bit as natural and unavoidable as an optical illusion (Allport, 1954). Social psychologists today study a wider variety of topics (from social memory to social relationships) and use a wider variety of techniques (from opinion polls to neuroimaging) than did their forebears, but this field of psychology remains dedicated to understanding the brain as a social organ, the mind as a social adaptation, and the individual as a social creature.

The Emergence of Cultural Psychology

North Americans and Western Europeans are sometimes surprised to realize that most of the people on the planet are members of neither culture. Although we're all more alike than we are different, there is nonetheless considerable diversity within the human species in social practices, customs, and ways of living. Culture refers to the values, traditions, and beliefs that are shared by a particular group of people. Although we usually think of culture in terms of nationality and ethnic groups, cultures can also be defined by age (youth culture), sexual orientation (gay culture), religion (Jewish culture), or occupation (academic culture). **Cultural psychology** is *the study of how cultures reflect and shape the psychological processes of their members* (Shweder & Sullivan, 1993). Cultural psychologists study a wide range of phenomena, ranging from visual perception to social interaction, as they seek to understand which of these phenomena are universal and which vary from place to place and time to time.

Perhaps surprisingly, one of the first psychologists to pay attention to the influence of culture was someone recognized today for pioneering the development of experimental psychology: Wilhelm Wundt. He believed that a complete psychological study would have to combine a laboratory approach with a broader cultural perspective (Wundt, 1908). But Wundt's ideas failed to spark much interest among other psychologists, who had their hands full trying to make sense of results from laboratory experiments and formulating general laws of human behavior. Outside of psychology,

The Skeen family from Texas (left), and the Namgay family from Shingkhey, Bhutan (right), display their respective family possessions in these two photos, both taken in 1993. Cultural psychology studies the similarities and differences in psychological processes that arise between people living in different cultures.

© PETER MENZEL PHOTOGRAPHY

anthropologists attempted to understand the workings of culture by traveling to far-flung regions of the world and carefully observing child-rearing patterns, rituals, religious ceremonies, and the like. Such studies revealed practices—some bizarre from a North American perspective—that served important functions in a culture, such as the painful ritual of violent body mutilation and bloodletting in mountain tribes of New Guinea, which initiates young boys into training to become warriors (Mead, 1935/1968; Read, 1965). Yet at the time, most anthropologists paid as little attention to psychology as psychologists did to anthropology.

Today, most psychologists agree that most psychological phenomena can be influenced by culture, some are completely determined by it, and others seem to be entirely unaffected. For example, the age of a person's earliest memory differs dramatically across cultures (MacDonald, Uesiliana, & Hayne, 2000), whereas judgments of facial attractiveness do not (Cunningham et al., 1995). As noted when we discussed evolutionary psychology, it seems likely that the most universal phenomena are those that are closely associated with the basic biology that all human beings share. Conversely, the least universal phenomena are those rooted in the varied socialization practices that different cultures evolve. Of course, the only way to determine whether a phenomenon is variable or constant across cultures is to design research to investigate these possibilities, and cultural psychologists do just that (Cole, 1996; Segall, Lonner, & Berry, 1998). We'll highlight the work of cultural psychologists at various points in the text in Culture & Community boxes like the one you read earlier in the chapter concerning cultural influences on the perception of a visual illusion.

? Why are psychological conclusions so often relative to the person, place, or culture described?

SUMMARY QUIZ [1.5]

1. Social psychology most differs from other psychological approaches in its emphasis on
   a. human interaction.
   c. the individual.
   b. behavioral processes.
   d. laboratory experimentation.

2. Cultural psychology emphasizes that
   a. all psychological processes are influenced to some extent by culture.
   b. psychological processes are the same across all human beings, regardless of culture.
   c. culture shapes some, but not all, psychological phenomena.
   d. insights gained from studying individuals from one culture will only rarely generalize to individuals from other cultures, who have different social identities and rituals.

The Profession of Psychology: Past and Present

You'll recall that when we last saw William James, he was wandering around Harvard University, expounding the virtues of the new science of psychology. In July 1892, James and six other psychologists came together for a meeting at Clark University. Although they were too few to make up a jury or even a respectable hockey team, these seven men decided that it was time to form an organization that represented psychology as a profession, and on that day the American Psychological Association (APA) was born. The seven psychologists could scarcely have imagined that today their little club would have more than 150,000 members. Although all of the original members were employed by universities or colleges, today academic psychologists make up only 20% of the membership, while nearly 70% of the members work in clinical and health-related settings. Because the APA is no longer as focused on academic psychology as it once was, the American Psychological Society (APS) was formed in 1988 by academic psychologists who wanted an organization that focused specifically on the needs of psychologists carrying out scientific research. The APS, renamed the Association for Psychological Science in 2006, grew quickly; today it comprises nearly 12,000 psychologists.

The Growing Role of Women and Minorities

In 1892, the APA had 31 members, all of whom were White and all of whom were male. Today, about half of all APA members are women, and the percentage of non-White members continues to grow. Surveys of recent PhD recipients reveal a picture of increasing diversification in the field. The proportion of students receiving PhDs in psychology who are female increased from only 15% in 1950 to 67% in 2004, and the

THE REAL WORLD

Joining the Club

Once upon a time, Western science was the hobby of wealthy European gentlemen. The pictures of the great figures in psychology's history you have seen in this chapter suggest that psychology likewise was once a narrow and exclusionary club. Fortunately, the face of this field has changed profoundly since its early days and continues to progress even now.

In fact, social changes have led to openness and diversity in psychology more swiftly and completely than in most other fields of study. In 2006, for example, while women were only poorly represented in engineering and the physical sciences, they received more than 71%

of new PhD degrees in psychology (Burrelli, 2008). Meanwhile, psychology PhDs to Hispanic, African American, and Native American students more than doubled from 1985 to 2005, and those to students of Asian and Pacific Islander heritage tripled (National Science Board, 2008). It is now the future, and in this future, psychology is the science of everyone.

Signs of the openness of psychology are all around. Just take a look at some of the students in undergraduate psychology clubs, *Psi Chi* (psychology's undergraduate and graduate student honorary society), or *Psi Beta* (the honorary society for community and junior college psychology students). Psychology students

now are far more often women than men (77%; Planty et al., 2008), and there is substantial representation of minority groups in psychology everywhere you look. Like its clubs and honorary societies, the study of psychology is open and welcoming to people of any age, sex, sexual orientation, race, different ability, color, religion, or national or ethnic origin. Please join us!

▼ Psychology students smiling for the camera include (right) Psi Chi from the University of Missouri and (left) Psi Chi of East Los Angeles College.

proportion who are minorities grew from a very small number to 15% during that same period. Clearly, psychology is increasingly reflecting the diversity of American society.

The current involvement of women and minorities in the APA, and psychology more generally, can be traced to early pioneers who blazed a trail that others followed. In 1905, Mary Calkins (1863–1930) became the first woman to serve as president of the APA. Calkins studied with William James at Harvard and later became a professor of psychology at Wellesley College. In her presidential address to the APA, Calkins described her theory of the

WELLESLEY COLLEGE ARCHIVES—MARGARET CLAPP LIBRARY

Mary Whiton Calkins (1863–1930), the first woman elected APA president, suffered from the sex discrimination that was common during her lifetime. Despite academic setbacks (such as Harvard University refusing to grant women an official PhD), Calkins went on to a distinguished career.

? How has the face of psychology changed as the field has evolved?

role of the "self" in psychological function. Arguing against Wundt's structuralist ideas that the mind can be dissected into components, Calkins claimed that the self is a single unit that cannot be broken down into individual parts. Calkins wrote four books and published over 100 articles during her illustrious career (Calkins, 1930; Scarborough & Furumoto, 1987; Stevens & Gardner, 1982). Today, women play leading roles in all areas of psychology. Some of the men who formed the APA might have been surprised by the prominence of women in the field today, but we suspect that William James, a strong supporter of Mary Calkins, would not be one of them.

The first member of a minority group to become president of the APA was Kenneth Clark (1914–2005), who was elected in 1970. Clark studied the self-image of African American children and argued that segregation of the races creates great psychological harm. Clark's conclusions had a large influence on public policy, and his research contributed to the Supreme Court's 1954 ruling (*Brown v. Board of Education*) to outlaw segregation in public schools (Guthrie, 2000). Clark's interest in psychology

ARCHIVES OF THE HISTORY OF AMERICAN PSYCHOLOGY

Francis Cecil Sumner (1895–1954) was the first African American to hold a PhD in psychology, receiving his from Clark University in 1920. Sumner conducted research on race relations, equality, and the psychology of religion.

WILLIAM E. SAURO/NEW YORK TIMES CO/GETTY IMAGES

Kenneth B. Clark (1914–2005) studied the developmental effects of prejudice, discrimination, and segregation on children. Clark's research was cited by the U.S. Supreme Court in its decision for the landmark *Brown v. Board of Education* case that ended school segregation.

was sparked as an undergraduate at Howard University when he took a course from Francis Cecil Sumner (1895–1954), who was the first African American to receive a PhD in psychology (from Clark University, in 1920). Sumner's main interest focused on the education of African American youth (Sawyer, 2000).

What Psychologists Do: Research Careers

So what should you do if you want to become a psychologist—and what should you fail to do if you desperately want to avoid this career? You can become "a psychologist" by a variety of routes, and the people who call themselves psychologists may hold a variety of different degrees. Students intending to pursue careers in psychology research typically finish college and enter graduate school to obtain a PhD (doctor of philosophy) degree in some particular area of psychology (e.g., social, cognitive, developmental). During graduate school, students generally gain exposure to the field by taking classes and learn to conduct research by collaborating with their professors. Although William James was able to master every area of psychology because the areas were so small during his lifetime, today a student can spend the better part of a decade mastering just one. After receiving a PhD, students can go on for more specialized research training by pursuing a postdoctoral fellowship under the supervision of an established researcher in their area or apply for a faculty position at a college or university or a research position in government or industry. Academic careers usually involve a combination of teaching and research, whereas careers in government or industry are typically dedicated to research alone.

But research is not the only career option for a psychologist. Most of the people who call themselves psychologists neither teach nor do research; rather, they assess or treat people with psychological problems. Most of these *clinical psychologists* work in private practice, often in partnerships with other psychologists or with psychiatrists (who have earned an MD, or medical degree, and are allowed to prescribe medication). Other clinical psychologists work in hospitals or medical schools, some have faculty positions at universities or colleges, and some combine private practice with an academic job. Many clinical psychologists focus on specific problems or disorders, such as depression or anxiety, whereas others focus on specific populations, such as children, ethnic minority groups, or elderly adults (**FIGURE 1.4**).

Just over 7% of APA members are *counseling psychologists,* who assist people in dealing with work or career issues and changes or help people deal with common crises such as divorce, the loss of a job, or the death of a loved one. Counseling psychologists may have a PhD or an MA (master's degree) in counseling psychology or an MSW (master of social work).

Psychologists are also quite active in educational settings. About 8% of APA members are *school psychologists,* who offer guidance to students, parents, and teachers. About 4% of APA members, known as *industrial/organizational psychologists,* focus on issues in the workplace. These psychologists typically work in business or industry and may be involved in assessing potential employees, finding ways to improve productivity, or helping staff and management develop effective planning strategies for coping with change or anticipated future developments.

Even this brief and incomplete survey of the APA membership provides a sense of the wide variety of contexts in which psychologists operate. You can think of psychol-

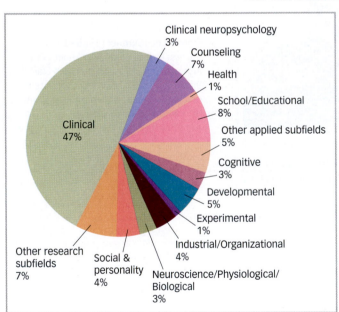

Clinical neuropsychology 3%
Counseling 7%
Health 1%
School/Educational 8%
Other applied subfields 5%
Cognitive 3%
Developmental 5%
Experimental 1%
Industrial/Organizational 4%
Neuroscience/Physiological/ Biological 3%
Social & personality 4%
Other research subfields 7%
Clinical 47%

▲ FIGURE **1.4** **The Major Subfields in Psychology** Psychologists are drawn to many different subfields in psychology. Here are the percentages of people receiving PhDs in various subfields. Clinical psychology makes up almost half of the doctorates awarded in psychology.

Source: 2004 Graduate Study in Psychology. Compiled by APA Research Office.

? In what ways does psychology contribute to society?

ogy as an international community of professionals devoted to advancing scientific knowledge; assisting people with psychological problems and disorders; and trying to enhance the quality of life in work, school, and other everyday settings.

SUMMARY QUIZ [1.6]

1. The largest organization of psychologists in the United States is the
   a. American Psychological Society.
   c. Association for Psychological Science.
   b. American Psychological Association.
   d. Psychonomic Society.

2. Mary Calkins
   a. studied with Wilhelm Wundt in the first psychology laboratory.
   b. did research on the self-image of African American children.
   c. was present at the first meeting of the APA.
   d. became the first woman president of the APA.

3. Kenneth Clark
   a. did research that influenced the Supreme Court decision to ban segregation in public schools.
   b. was one of the founders of the APA.
   c. was a student of William James.
   d. did research that focused on the education of African American youth.

Where Do You Stand?

The Perils of Procrastination

As you've read in this chapter, the human mind and behavior are fascinating in part because they are not error-free. The mind's mistakes interest us primarily as paths to achieving a better understanding of mental activity and behavior, but they also have practical consequences. Let's consider a malfunction that can have significant consequences in your own life: procrastination.

At one time or another, most of us have avoided carrying out a task or put it off to a later time. The task may be unpleasant, difficult, or just less entertaining than other things we could be doing at the moment. For college students, procrastination can affect a range of academic activities, such as writing a term paper or preparing for a test. Academic procrastination is not uncommon: Over 70% of college students report that they engage in some form of procrastination (Schouwenburg, 1995). Although it's fun to hang out with your friends tonight, it's not so much fun to worry for three days about your impending history exam or try to study at 4:00 a.m. on the day of the test. Studying now, or at least a little bit each day, robs procrastination of its power over you.

But some procrastinators defend the practice by claiming that they tend to work best under pressure or by noting that as long as a task gets done, it doesn't matter all that much if it is completed just before the deadline. Is there any merit to such claims, or are they just feeble excuses for counterproductive behavior?

A study of 60 undergraduate psychology college students provides some intriguing answers (Tice & Baumeister, 1997). At the beginning of the semester, the instructor announced a due date for the term paper and told students that if they could not meet the date, they would receive an extension to a later date. About a month later, students completed a scale that measures tendencies toward procrastination. At that same time, and then again during the last week of class, students recorded health symptoms they had experienced during the past week, the amount of stress they had experienced during that week, and the number of visits they had made to a health care center during the previous month.

Students who scored high on the procrastination scale tended to turn in their papers late. One month into the semester, these procrastinators reported less stress and fewer symptoms of physical illness than did nonprocrastinators. But at the end of the semester, the procrastinators reported *more* stress and *more* health symptoms than did the nonprocrastinators and also reported more visits to the health center. The procrastinators also received lower grades on their papers and on course exams.

So . . . when you put off a responsibility, is the reduced stress early on worth the price you pay as the deadline approaches? Where do you stand on procrastination?

Chapter Review

SUMMARY

Psychology's Roots: The Path to a Science of Mind

▶ Philosophers have pondered and debated ideas about human nature for millennia, but they have not provided empirical evidence to support their claims.

▶ Some of the earliest successful efforts to develop a *science* linking mind and behavior came from studies showing that damage to the brain can result in impairments to behavior and mental functions.

▶ Helmholtz furthered the science of the mind by developing methods for measuring reaction time. His student Wundt, credited with the founding of psychology as a scientific discipline, espoused structuralism—the idea that the mind could be studied by understanding its basic elements.

▶ William James emphasized the functions of consciousness and applied Darwin's theory of natural selection to the study of the mind.

The Development of Clinical Psychology

▶ Psychologists have often focused on patients with psychological disorders as a way of understanding human behavior.

▶ Freud developed psychoanalysis, which emphasized the importance of unconscious influences and childhood experiences in shaping thoughts, feelings, and behavior.

▶ Humanistic psychologists suggested that people are inherently disposed toward growth and can usually reach their full potential with a little help from their friends.

The Search for Objective Measurement: Behaviorism Takes Center Stage

▶ Behaviorism advocated the study of observable actions and responses and held that inner mental processes were private events that could not be studied scientifically.

▶ Pavlov and Watson studied the association between a stimulus and a response and emphasized the importance of the environment in shaping behavior.

▶ Skinner developed the concept of reinforcement, which states that that animals and humans repeat behaviors that generate pleasant results and avoid performing those that generate unpleasant results.

The Return of the Mind: Psychology Expands

▶ Cognitive psychologists study the inner workings of the mind and focus on inner mental processes such as perception, attention, memory, and reasoning.

▶ Cognitive neuroscience attempts to link the brain with the mind through studies of both brain-damaged and healthy people.

▶ Evolutionary psychology focuses on the adaptive function that minds and brains serve and seeks to understand the nature and origin of psychological processes in terms of natural selection.

Beyond the Individual: Social and Cultural Perspectives

▶ Social psychology recognizes that people exist as part of a network of other people and examines how individuals influence and interact with one another.

▶ Cultural psychology is concerned with the effects of the broader culture on individuals and with similarities and differences among people in different cultures.

The Profession of Psychology: Past and Present

▶ The American Psychological Association (APA) has grown dramatically since it was formed in 1892 and now includes over 150,000 members, working in clinical, academic, and applied settings.

▶ Through the efforts of pioneers such as Calkins, women have come to play an increasingly important role in the field and are now as well represented as men. Minority involvement in psychology took longer, but the pioneering efforts of Sumner, Clark, and others have led to increased participation of minorities in psychology.

▶ Psychologists prepare for research careers through graduate and postdoctoral training and work in a variety of applied settings, including schools, clinics, and industry.

KEY TERMS

psychology (p. 2)
mind (p. 2)
behavior (p. 2)
nativism (p. 4)
philosophical empiricism (p. 4)
phrenology (p. 5)
physiology (p. 6)
stimulus (p. 6)

reaction time (p. 6)
consciousness (p. 6)
structuralism (p. 6)
introspection (p. 6)
functionalism (p. 7)
natural selection (p. 8)
hysteria (p. 9)
unconscious (p. 10)

psychoanalytic theory (p. 10)
psychoanalysis (p. 10)
humanistic psychology (p. 11)
behaviorism (p. 12)
response (p. 13)
reinforcement (p. 13)
illusions (p. 15)
gestalt psychology (p. 15)

cognitive psychology (p. 16)
behavioral neuroscience (p. 18)
cognitive neuroscience (p. 19)
evolutionary psychology (p. 19)
social psychology (p. 21)
cultural psychology (p. 22)

CHANGING MINDS

1. One of your classmates says that she's only taking this class because it's required for her education major. "Psychology is all about understanding mental illness and treatment. I don't know why I have to learn this stuff when I'm going to be a teacher, not a psychologist." Why should your friend reconsider her opinion? What subfields of psychology are especially important for a teacher?

2. One of your friends confesses that he really enjoys his psychology courses, but he's decided not to declare a major in psychology. "You have to get a graduate degree to do anything with a psychology major," he says, "and I don't want to stay in school for the rest of my life. I want to get out there and work in the real world." Based on what you've read in this chapter about careers in psychology, what might you tell him?

3. On May 6, you spot a news item announcing that it's the birthday of Sigmund Freud, "the father of psychology." How accurate is it to call Freud the "father of psychology"? Having

read about psychology's subfields, do you think there are other people who are as important or more important than Freud?

4. One of your classmates has flipped ahead in the book, and he notices that there is going to be a lot of material—including an entire chapter—on the brain. "I don't see why we have to learn so much biology," he says. "I want to be a school counselor, not a brain surgeon. I don't need to understand the parts of the brain or chemical reactions in order to help people." How are the brain and the mind connected? In what specific ways might knowing about the brain help us to understand the mind?

5. Another classmate is very unsettled after reading about B. F. Skinner's claim that free will is an illusion. "Psychology always tries to treat human beings like lab rats whose behavior can be manipulated. I have free will, and I decide what I'm going to do next." What would you tell your friend? Does an understanding of the basic principles of psychology allow us to predict every detail of what individual humans will do?

CRITICAL THINKING QUESTIONS

1. William James thought Darwin's theory of natural selection might explain how mental abilities evolve, by conferring survival advantages on individuals who were better able to solve problems. How might a specific mental ability, such as the ability to recognize the facial expressions of others as signaling their emotional state, help an individual survive longer and produce more offspring?

2. Behaviorists explain behavior in terms of organisms learning to make particular responses that are paired with reinforcement (and to avoid responses that are paired with punishment). Evolutionary psychology focuses on how abilities are preserved over time if they contribute to an organism's ability to survive and reproduce. How might a proponent of each approach explain the fact that a rat placed in an unfamiliar environment will tend to stay in dark corners and avoid brightly lit open areas?

ANSWERS TO SUMMARY QUIZZES

Summary Quiz [1.1] 1. b; 2. a; 3. c; 4. d
Summary Quiz [1.2] 1. b; 2. a; 3. c
Summary Quiz [1.3] 1. a; 2. b; 3. a
Summary Quiz [1.4] 1. d; 2. b; 3. b
Summary Quiz [1.5] 1. a; 2. c
Summary Quiz [1.6] 1. b; 2. d; 3. a

Need more help? Additional resources are located at the book's free companion website at:
www.worthpublishers.com/schacterbrief2e

2

Methods in Psychology

LOUISE HAY IS ONE OF THE bestselling authors of all time (Oppenheimer, 2008). One of her books, *You Can Heal Your Life,* has sold over 35 million copies. Hay believes that everything that happens to us—including accidents and disease—is a result of the thoughts we choose to think. She claims that she cured herself of cancer by changing her thoughts, and she says that others can learn this trick by buying her books and attending her seminars. In a television interview, Hay explained why she's so sure that her technique works.

Interviewer: How do you know what you're saying is right?

Hay: Oh, my inner ding.

Interviewer: Ding?

Hay: My inner ding. It speaks to me. It feels right or it doesn't feel right. Happiness is choosing thoughts that make you feel good. It's really very simple.

Interviewer: But I hear you saying that even if there were no proof for what you believed, or even if there were scientific evidence against it, it wouldn't change.

Hay: Well, I don't believe in scientific evidence, I really don't. Science is fairly new. It hasn't been around that long. We think it's such a big deal, but it's, you know, it's just a way of looking at life.

Louise Hay says she doesn't believe in scientific evidence, but what could that mean? After all, if Hay's techniques really do cure cancer, then cancer victims who practice her technique ought to have a higher rate of remission than cancer victims who don't. That isn't some new or exotic way of "looking at life." That's just plain, old-fashioned common sense—exactly the kind of common sense that lies at the heart of science.

Science tells us that the only way to know for sure whether a claim is true is to go out and see for ourselves. But that sounds easier than it is. For example, how would you determine whether Louise Hay's claims are true? Would you go to one of her seminars and ask people in the audience whether or not they'd been healed? Would you examine the medical

► Louise Hay doesn't believe in scientific evidence and instead trusts her "inner ding."

MICHELE ASSELIN/CONTOUR BY GETTY IMAGES

empiricism The belief that accurate knowledge can be acquired through observation.

scientific method A set of principles about the appropriate relationship between ideas and evidence.

theory A hypothetical explanation of a natural phenomenon.

hypothesis A falsifiable prediction made by a theory.

empirical method A set of rules and techniques for observation.

records of people who had and hadn't bought her books? Would you invite people to sign up for a class that teaches her techniques and then wait to see how many got cancer? All of these tests sound reasonable, but the fact is that none of them would be particularly informative. There are a few good ways to test claims like this one and a whole lot of bad ways, and in this chapter you will learn to tell one from the other. Scientists have developed powerful tools for determining when an inner ding is right and when it is wrong. As the philosopher Bertrand Russell (1945, p. 527) wrote, "It is not *what* the man of science believes that distinguishes him, but *how* and *why* he believes it." And that goes for women of science too!

WE'LL START BY EXAMINING THE GENERAL PRINCIPLES THAT GUIDE scientific research and distinguish it from every other way of knowing. Next, we'll see that the methods of psychology are meant to answer two basic questions: *What* do people do, and *why* do they do it? Psychologists answer the first question by observing and measuring; they answer the second by looking for relationships between the things they measure. We'll see that scientific research allows us to draw certain kinds of conclusions but not others. Finally, we'll consider the unique ethical questions that confront scientists who study people and other animals.

The 17th-century astronomer Galileo Galilei was excommunicated and sentenced to prison for sticking to his own observations of the solar system rather than accepting the teachings of the church. In 1597 he wrote to his friend and fellow astronomer Johannes Kepler, "What would you say of the learned here, who, replete with the pertinacity of the asp, have steadfastly refused to cast a glance through the telescope? What shall we make of this? Shall we laugh, or shall we cry?" As it turned out, the answer was *cry*.

BETTMANN/CORBIS

Empiricism: How to Know Stuff

When ancient Greeks sprained their ankles, caught the flu, or accidentally set their beards on fire, they had to choose between two kinds of doctors: dogmatists (from *dogmatikos,* meaning "belief"), who thought that the best way to understand illness was to develop theories about the body's functions, and empiricists (from *empeirikos,* meaning "experience"), who thought that the best way to understand illness was to observe sick people. The rivalry between these two schools of medicine didn't last long because the people who went to see dogmatists tended to die a lot, which wasn't good for business. Today we use the word *dogmatism* to describe the tendency for people to cling to their assumptions and the word **empiricism** to describe *the belief that accurate knowledge can be acquired through observation.* The fact that we can answer questions about the natural world by examining it may seem obvious to you, but this fact has only recently gained wide acceptance. For most of human history, people trusted authority to answer important questions, and it is only in the last millennium (and especially in the past three centuries) that people began to trust their eyes and ears more than their elders.

Empiricism is the essential element of the **scientific method,** which is *a set of principles about the appropriate relationship between ideas and evidence*. In essence, the scientific method suggests that when we have an idea about the world—about how bats navigate, or where the moon came from, or why people can't forget traumatic events—we should gather empirical evidence relevant to that idea and then modify the idea to fit the evidence. Scientists usually refer to an idea of this kind as a **theory,** which is *a hypothetical explanation of a natural phenomenon.* We might theorize that bats navigate by making sounds and then listening for the echo, that the moon was formed when a small planet collided with the Earth, or that the brain responds to traumatic events by producing chemicals that facilitate

? What is the scientific method?

memory. Each of these theories is an explanation of how something in the natural world works.

Theories are ideas about how and why things work the way they do. So how do we decide if a theory is right? Most theories make predictions about what we should and should not be able to observe in the world. For example, if bats really do navigate by making sounds and then listening for echoes, then we should observe that deaf bats can't navigate. That "should statement" is technically known as a **hypothesis,** which is *a falsifiable prediction made by a theory.* The word *falsifiable* is a critical part of that definition. Some theories—such as "God created the universe"—do not specify what we should or should not observe if they are true, and thus no observations can falsify them. Because such theories do not give rise to hypotheses, they cannot be the sub-

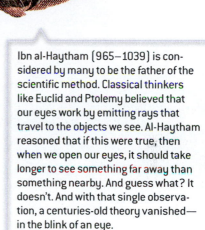

SCIENCE SOURCE

> **Why can't evidence ever prove a theory right?**

ject of scientific investigation. That doesn't mean they're wrong. It just means that we can't judge them by using the scientific method.

So what *can* we find out when we use the scientific method? Albert Einstein once lamented that "no amount of experimentation can ever prove me right, but a single experiment can prove me wrong." Why should that be? Well, just imagine what you could possibly learn about the navigation-by-sound theory if you observed a few bats. If you saw the deaf bats navigating every bit as well as the hearing bats, then the navigation-by-sound theory would instantly be proved wrong; but if you saw the deaf bats navigating more poorly than the hearing bats, your observation would be *consistent* with the navigation-by-sound theory but would not prove it. After all, even if you didn't see a deaf bat navigating perfectly today, it is still possible that someone else did or that you will see one tomorrow. When evidence is consistent with a theory, it increases our confidence in it, but it never makes us completely certain.

The scientific method suggests that the best way to learn the truth about the world is to develop theories, derive hypotheses from them, test those hypotheses by gathering evidence, and then use that evidence to modify the theories. Gathering evidence properly requires an **empirical method,** which is *a set of rules and techniques for observation.* Human behavior is relatively easy to observe, so you might expect psychology's empirical methods to be relatively simple. In fact, the empirical challenges facing psychologists are among the most daunting in all of modern science. Three things make people especially difficult to study:

> Ibn al-Haytham (965–1039) is considered by many to be the father of the scientific method. Classical thinkers like Euclid and Ptolemy believed that our eyes work by emitting rays that travel to the objects we see. Al-Haytham reasoned that if this were true, then when we open our eyes, it should take longer to see something far away than something nearby. And guess what? It doesn't. And with that single observation, a centuries-old theory vanished— in the blink of an eye.

> **What three things make people difficult to study?**

> *Complexity:* No galaxy, particle, molecule, or machine is as complicated as the human brain. Scientists can describe the birth of a star or the death of a cell in exquisite detail, but they can barely begin to say how the 500 million interconnected neurons that constitute the brain give rise to the thoughts, feelings, and actions that are psychology's core concerns.

> *Variability:* In almost all the ways that matter, one *E. coli* bacterium is pretty much like another. But people are as varied as their fingerprints. No two individuals ever do, say, think, or feel exactly the same thing under exactly the same circumstances, which means that when you've seen one, you've most definitely not seen them all.

> *Reactivity:* An atom of cesium-133 oscillates 9,192,631,770 times per second regardless of whether anyone is watching. But people often think, feel, and act one way when they are being observed and a different way when they are not. When people know they are being studied, they don't always behave as they otherwise would.

EDWARD KOREN/THE NEW YORKER COLLECTION/CARTOONBANK.COM

"Are you just pissing and moaning, or can you verify what you're saying with data?"

The fact that human beings are complex, variable, and reactive presents a major challenge to the scientific study of their behavior, but as you'll see, psychologists have developed two kinds of methods that are designed to meet these challenges head-on.

SUMMARY QUIZ [2.1]

1. The belief that accurate knowledge can be acquired through observation is
   - a. parsimony.
   - b. dogmatism.
   - c. empiricism.
   - d. scientific research.

2. Which of the following is the best definition of a hypothesis?
   - a. empirical evidence
   - b. a scientific investigation
   - c. a falsifiable prediction
   - d. a theoretical idea

3. The methods of psychological investigation take _____ into account because when people know they are being studied, they don't always behave as they otherwise would.
   - a. reactivity
   - b. complexity
   - c. variability
   - d. sophistication

Observation: Discovering What People Do

To *observe* means to use one's senses to learn about the properties of an event (e.g., a storm or a parade) or an object (e.g., an apple or a person). For example, when you observe a round, red apple, your brain is using the pattern of light that is falling on your eyes to draw an inference about the apple's identity, shape, and color. That kind of informal observation is fine for buying fruit but not for doing science. Why? First, casual observations are notoriously unstable. The same apple may appear red in the daylight and crimson at night or spherical to one person and elliptical to another. Second, casual observations can't tell us about all of the properties that might interest us. No matter how long and hard you look, you will never be able to discern an apple's crunchiness or pectin content simply by watching it. Luckily, scientists have devised measurement techniques that allow them to overcome these problems.

Measurement

The last time you said "Give me a second," you probably didn't know you were talking about atomic decay. Every unit of time has an **operational definition,** which is *a description of a property in concrete, measurable terms.* The operational definition of *a second* is "the duration of 9,192,631,770 cycles of microwave light absorbed or emitted by the hyperfine transition of cesium-133 atoms in their ground state undisturbed by external fields" (which takes roughly six seconds just to say). To actually count the cycles of light emitted as cesium-133 decays requires a **measure,** which is *a device that can detect the condition to which an operational definition refers.* A device known as a "cesium clock" can do just that, and when it counts 9,192,631,770 of them, a second has passed.

The steps we take to measure a physical property are the same steps we take to measure a psychological property. For example, if we wanted to measure a person's intelligence, or shyness, or happiness, we would have to start by developing an operational definition of that property—that is, by specifying some concrete, measurable event that indicates it. For example, we could define happiness as the frequency with which a person smiles, and we could then detect those smiles with an **electromyograph (EMG),** which is *a device that measures muscle contractions under the surface of a person's skin* (see **FIGURE 2.1**). Having an operational definition that specifies a

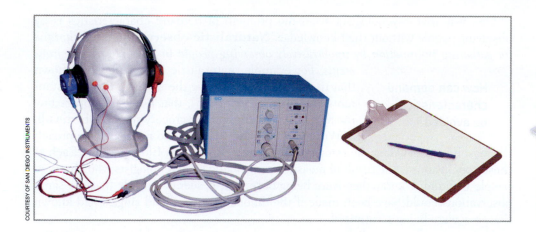

COURTESY OF SAN DIEGO INSTRUMENTS

◄ Figure **2.1 Psychological Measures**
Psychological measures may take a variety of forms. To measure happiness, we might use an electromyograph (EMG) to record electrical activity of the muscles in a person's face associated with smiling, or we might use a questionnaire that asks, "Are you happy?"

measurable event and a device that measures that event are the two keys to scientific measurement.

Of course, an EMG isn't the only possible way to measure a person's happiness. Instead, we could define happiness based on a person's answer to the question "How happy are you?" or we could define it based on the number of friends a person has. There are many ways to define and detect happiness, but some are clearly better than others. Good measures have three properties: validity, reliability, and power.

? What are three properties of a good measure?

1. **Validity** refers to *the extent to which a measurement and a property are conceptually related.* For example, frequency of smiling is a valid way to define happiness because people all over the world tend to smile more often when they feel happy. On the other hand, the number of friends a person has would not be a valid way to define happiness. Happy people do have more friends, but there are many other reasons why people might have lots of friends. Number of friends may be vaguely related to happiness, but the former really can't be taken as an indicator of the latter.

2. **Reliability** is *the tendency for a measure to produce the same measurement whenever it is used to measure the same thing.* For example, if a person's facial muscles produced precisely the same electrical activity on two different occasions, then an EMG should produce precisely the same readings on those two occasions. If it produced different readings—that is, if it detected differences that did not actually exist—it would be unreliable.

3. **Power** is *the ability of a measure to detect differences.* If a person's facial muscles produced different amounts of electrical activity on two occasions, then an EMG should detect those differences and produce two different readings. If it produced the same reading—that is, if it failed to detect a difference that actually existed—then it would be powerless.

Demand Characteristics

Once we have a valid, powerful, and reliable measure, then what do we do? The obvious answer is: Go measure something. But not so fast. While we are trying to measure how people behave, they may be trying to behave as they think we want them to or expect them to. **Demand characteristics** are *those aspects of an observational setting that cause people to behave as they think they should.* When someone you love asks, "Do these jeans make me look fat?" the right answer is always no. If you've ever been asked this question, then you have experienced demand. Demand characteristics make it hard to measure behavior as it normally unfolds.

operational definition A description of a property in concrete, measurable terms.

measure A device that can detect the condition to which an operational definition refers.

electromyograph (EMG) A device that measures muscle contractions under the surface of a person's skin.

validity The extent to which a measurement and a property are conceptually related.

reliability The tendency for a measure to produce the same measurement whenever it is used to measure the same thing.

power The ability of a measure to detect the concrete conditions specified in the operational definition.

demand characteristics Those aspects of an observational setting that cause people to behave as they think they should.

One way that psychologists avoid the problem of demand characteristics is by observing people without their knowledge. **Naturalistic observation** is *a technique for gathering information by unobtrusively observing people in their natural environ-*

> ❓ **How can demand characteristics be avoided?**

ments. For example, naturalistic observation has shown that the biggest groups leave the smallest tips in restaurants (Freeman et al., 1975), that hungry shoppers buy the most impulse items at the grocery store (Gilbert, Gill, & Wilson, 2002), and that men do not usually approach the most beautiful woman at a singles' bar (Glenwick, Jason, & Elman, 1978). Each of these conclusions is the result of measurements made by psychologists who observed people who didn't know they were being observed. It seems unlikely that the same observations could have been made if the diners, shoppers, and singles had known that they were being scrutinized.

Unfortunately, naturalistic observation isn't always a viable solution to the problem of demand characteristics. First, some of the things psychologists want to observe simply don't occur naturally. For example, if we wanted to know whether people who have undergone sensory deprivation perform poorly on motor tasks, we would have to hang around the shopping mall for a very long time before a few dozen blindfolded people with earplugs just happened to wander by and start typing. Second, some of the things that psychologists want to know can only be determined from direct interaction with a person—for example, by administering a survey, giving tests, conducting an interview, or hooking someone up to an EMG machine. If we wanted to know how often someone worried about dying, how accurately they could remember their high school graduation, or how quickly they could solve a logic puzzle, then simply watching them from the bushes won't do.

Luckily, there are other ways to avoid demand characteristics. For instance, people are less likely to be influenced by demand characteristics when they cannot be identified as the originators of their actions, and psychologists often take advantage of this fact by allowing people to respond privately (e.g., by having them complete questionnaires when they are alone) or anonymously (e.g., by not collecting personal information, such as the person's name or address). Another technique that psychologists often use to avoid demand characteristics is to measure behaviors that

CULTURE & COMMUNITY

Best Place to Fall on Your Face Robert Levine of California State University–Fresno sent his students to 23 large international cities for an observational study in the field. Their task was to observe helping behaviors in a naturalistic context. In one version of the experiment, students pretended to be either blind or injured while trying to cross a street; another student stood by to observe whether anyone would come to help.

The results showed that there was a wide range of response between cities. Rio de Janeiro, Brazil, came out on top as the most helpful city in the study with an overall helping score of 93%. Kuala Lumpur, Malaysia, came in last with a score of 40%, while New York City placed next to last with a score of 45%. On average, Latin American cities ranked as most helpful (Levine, Norenzayan, & Philbrick, 2001).

are not susceptible to demand. For instance, a person's behavior can't be influenced by demand characteristics if that behavior isn't under the person's voluntary control. You may not want a psychologist to know that you are feeling sexually aroused, but you can't prevent your pupils from dilating, which is what they do when you experience arousal.

A third way to avoid demand characteristics is to keep the people who are being observed from knowing the true purpose of

Why is it important for subjects to be "blind"?

the observation. When people are "blind" to the purpose of an observation, they can't behave the way they think they should behave because they don't *know* how they should behave. For instance, if you didn't know that a psychologist was studying the effects of music on mood, you wouldn't feel obligated to smile when music was played. This is why psychologists typically don't reveal the true purpose of an observation to the people who are being observed until the study is over.

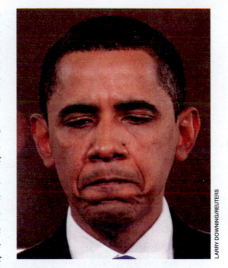

When people feel anxious, they tend to compress their lips involuntarily, as President Obama did during a difficult press conference in 2009. One way to avoid demand characteristics is to measure behaviors that people are unable or unlikely to control, such as facial expressions, blood pressure, reaction times, and so on.

LARRY DOWNING/REUTERS

Observer Bias

The people who are being observed aren't the only ones who can make measurement a bit tricky. When psychologists measure behavior, it is all too easy for them to see what they want to see or expect to see. This fact was demonstrated in a classic study in which students in a psychology class were asked to measure the speed with which a rat learned to run through a maze (Rosenthal & Fode, 1963). Some students were told that their rat had been specially bred to be "maze-dull" (i.e., slow to learn a maze) and others were told that their rat had been specially bred to be "maze-bright" (i.e., quick to learn a maze). Although all the rats were actually the of same breed, the students who *thought* they were measuring the speed of a maze-dull rat reported that their rats took longer to learn the maze than did the students who *thought* they were measuring the speed of a maze-bright rat. In other words, the measurements revealed precisely what the students expected them to reveal.

Why did this happen? First, *expectations can influence observations*. It is easy to make errors when measuring the speed of a rat, and expectations often determine the kinds of errors people make. Does putting one paw over the finish line count as "learning the maze"? If a rat runs a maze in 18.5 seconds, should that number be rounded up or rounded down before it is recorded in the log book? The answers to these questions may depend on whether one thinks the rat is bright or dull. The students who timed the rats probably tried to be honest, vigilant, and objective, but their expectations influenced their observations. Second, *expectations can influence reality*. Students who expected their rats to learn quickly may have unknowingly done things to help that learning along—for example, by muttering "Oh, no!" when the bright rat looked the wrong direction or by petting the dull rat less affectionately. (We'll discuss these phenomena more in Chapter 13.)

Why is it important for experimenters to be "blind"?

Observers' expectations, then, can have a powerful influence on both their observations and on the behavior of those whom they observe. Psychologists use many techniques to avoid these influences; one of the most common is the **double-blind** observation, which is *an observation whose true purpose is hidden from both the observer and the person being observed*. For example, if the students had not been told which rats were bright and

naturalistic observation A technique for gathering scientific information by unobtrusively observing people in their natural environments.

double-blind An observation whose true purpose is hidden from both the observer and the person being observed.

People's expectations can cause the phenomena they expect. In 1929, investors who expected the stock market to collapse sold their stocks and thereby caused the very crisis they feared. In this photo, panicked citizens stand outside the New York Stock Exchange the day after the crash, which the *New York Times* attributed to "mob psychology."

which were dull, then they wouldn't have *had* any expectations about their rats; thus their expectations couldn't have influenced their measurements. That's why it is common practice in psychology to keep the observers as blind as the participants. For example, measurements are often made by research assistants who do not know what is being studied or why—and who thus don't have any expectations about what the people being observed will or should do.

SUMMARY QUIZ [2.2]

1. When a measure produces the same measurement whenever it is used to measure the same thing, it is said to have
   a. validity.　　b. reliability.　　c. power.　　d. concreteness.

2. Aspects of an observational setting that cause people to behave as they think they should are called
   a. observer biases.　　　　　c. natural habitats.
   b. reactive conditions.　　　d. demand characteristics.

3. In a double-blind observation,
   a. the participants know what is being measured.
   b. people are observed in their natural environments.
   c. the purpose is hidden from both the observer and the person being observed.
   d. only objective, statistical measures are recorded.

variable A property whose value can vary across individuals or over time.

correlation Two variables are said to "be correlated" when variations in the value of one variable are synchronized with variations in the value of the other.

Explanation: Discovering Why People Do What They Do

Although scientific research always begins with the measurement of properties, its ultimate goal is typically the discovery of *causal relationships between properties*. For example, it is interesting to know that happy people are healthier than unhappy people, but what we *really* want to know is whether their happiness is the *cause* of their good health. It is interesting to know that attractive people earn more money, but what we *really* want to know is whether being attractive is a *cause* of higher income. These are the kinds of questions that even the most careful measurements cannot answer. By measuring we can learn *how much* happiness and health or attractiveness and wealth a particular group of people has, but we still cannot tell whether these things are related and, if so, whether one causes the other. As you are about to see, scientists have developed some clever ways of using their measurements to answer questions about causal relationships.

It doesn't hurt to be a redhead—or does it? In fact, studies show that redheads are more sensitive to pain than are brunettes or blondes. Does red hair cause pain sensitivity? Does pain sensitivity cause red hair? We'll give you the answer in a few pages.

Correlation

If you insult someone, he or she probably won't give you the time of day. If you have any doubt about this, you can demonstrate it by standing on a street corner, insulting a few people as they walk by ("Hello there, stupid ugly freak . . ."), not insulting others ("Hello there, Sir or Madam . . ."), and then asking everyone for the time of day (". . . could you please tell me what time it is?"). If you did this, the results of your investigation would probably look a lot like those shown in **TABLE 2.1**. Specifically, every person who was not insulted would give you the time of day, and every person who was insulted would refuse. Results such as these would probably convince you that being insulted *causes* people to refuse requests from the people who insulted them. But on what basis did you draw that conclusion? How did you manage to use measurement to learn not only about *how much* insulting and refusing had occurred, but also about the *relationship* between insulting and refusing?

How can we tell if two variables are correlated?

Measurements can tell us only about the properties of objects and events, but we can learn about the relationships between objects and events by comparing the *patterns of variation in a series of measurements*. When you performed your imaginary study of insults and requests, you did three things:

> First, you measured a pair of **variables,** which are *properties whose values can vary across individuals or over time*. You measured one variable whose value could vary from *not insulted* to *insulted,* and you measured a second variable whose value could vary from *refused* to *agreed*.

> Second, you did this again. And then again. And then again. That is, you made a *series* of measurements rather than making just one.

> Third and finally, you tried to discern a pattern in your series of measurements. If you look at Table 2.1, you will notice that whenever the value in the second column varies from *not insulted* to *insulted,* the value in the third column varies from *agreed* to *refused*. Thus, the patterns of variation in the two columns are synchronized or **correlated** (as in "co-related"). Two variables are said to "be correlated" when *variations in the value of one variable are synchronized with variations in the value of the other*. (See Appendix: Statistics for Psychology for more details.)

By looking for synchronized patterns of variation, we can use measurement to discover the relationships between variables. For example, you know that adults are

Table 2.1
Hypothetical Data of the Relationship Between Insults and Favors

Participant	Treatment	Response
1	Insulted	Refused
2	Insulted	Refused
3	Not insulted	Agreed
4	Not insulted	Agreed
5	Insulted	Refused
6	Insulted	Refused
7	Not insulted	Agreed
8	Not insulted	Agreed
9	Insulted	Refused
10	Insulted	Refused
11	Not insulted	Agreed
12	Not insulted	Agreed
13	Insulted	Refused
14	Insulted	Refused
15	Not insulted	Agreed
16	Not insulted	Agreed
17	Insulted	Refused
18	Insulted	Refused
19	Not insulted	Agreed
20	Not insulted	Agreed

When children line up by age, they also tend to line up by height. The pattern of variation in age (from youngest to oldest) is synchronized with the pattern of variation in height (from shortest to tallest).

PETER TURNLEY/CORBIS

generally taller than children, but this is just a shorthand way of saying that as the value of *age* varies from *young* to *old*, the value of *height* varies from *short* to *tall*. You know that people who eat a pound of spinach every day generally live longer than people who eat a pound of bacon every day, but this is just a shorthand way of saying that as the value of *daily food intake* varies from *spinach* to *bacon*, the value of *longevity* varies from *high* to *low*. As these statements suggest, correlations are the fundamental building blocks of knowledge.

Every correlation can be described in two equally reasonable ways. A positive correlation describes a relationship between two variables in "more-more"

> **? What's the difference between a positive and a negative correlation?**

or "less-less" terms. When we say that *more spinach* is associated with *more longevity* or that *less spinach* is associated with *less longevity*, we are describing a positive correlation. A negative correlation describes a relationship between two variables in "more-less" or "less-more" terms. When we say that *more bacon* is associated with *less longevity* or that *less bacon* is associated with *more longevity*, we are describing a negative correlation. How we choose to describe any particular correlation is usually just a matter of simplicity and convenience.

Causation

If you watched a cartoon in which a moving block collided with a stationary block, which then went careening off the screen, your brain would instantly make a very reasonable assumption, namely, that the moving block was the *cause* of the stationary block's motion (Heider & Simmel, 1944; Michotte, 1963). In fact, studies show that infants make such assumptions long before they have had a chance to learn anything about cartoons, blocks, collisions, or causality (Oakes & Cohen, 1990). For human beings, detecting causes and effects is as natural as sucking, sleeping, pooping, and howling, which is what led the philosopher Immanuel Kant (1781/1965) to suggest that people come into the world with cause-detectors built into their brains.

But those cause-detectors don't work perfectly. Sometimes we see causal relationships that don't actually exist: For centuries, people held superstitious beliefs such as "solar eclipses cause birth defects" or "human sacrifices bring rain," and, in fact, many still do. Just as we see causal relationships that don't exist, we sometimes fail to see causal relationships that do exist: It is only in the past century or so that surgeons have made it a practice to wash their hands before operating because before that, no one seemed to notice that dirty hands caused infections. Because our built-in cause-detectors are imperfect, we need a scientific method for discovering causal relationships. As you'll see, we've got one. But before learning about it, let's explore the problem it is meant to solve a bit more.

It isn't always easy to accurately detect causal relationships. For centuries, people sacrificed their enemies without realizing that doing so doesn't actually cause rain, and they smoked cigarettes without realizing that doing so actually does cause illness.

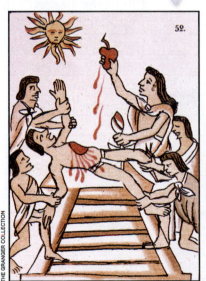

THE GRANGER COLLECTION

COLLECTION OF STANFORD UNIVERSITY/TOBACCO.STANFORD.EDU

The Third-Variable Problem

We observe correlations all the time—between automobiles and pollution, between bacon and heart attacks, between sex and pregnancy. **Natural correlations** are *the correlations we observe in the world around us*, and although such observations can tell us *whether* two variables have a relationship, they cannot tell us what *kind* of relationship these variables have. For example, many studies have found a positive correlation between the amount of violence to which a child is exposed through media such as television, movies, and video games (variable *X*) and the aggressiveness of the child's behavior (variable *Y*) (Anderson & Bushman, 2001; Anderson et al., 2003; Huesmann et al., 2003). The more media violence a child is exposed to, the more aggressive that child is likely to be. These variables clearly have a relationship—they are positively correlated—but why?

? Why can't we use natural correlations to infer causality?

One possibility is that exposure to media violence (*X*) causes aggressiveness (*Y*). For example, media violence may teach children that aggression is a reasonable way to vent anger and solve problems. A second possibility is that aggressiveness (*Y*) causes children to be exposed to media violence (*X*). For example, children who are naturally aggressive may be especially likely to seek opportunities to play violent video games or watch violent movies. A third possibility is that a *third variable* (*Z*) causes children to be aggressive (*Y*) and to be exposed to media violence (*X*), neither of which is causally related to the other. For example, lack of adult supervision (*Z*) may allow children to get away with bullying others and also to get away with watching television shows that adults would normally not allow. In other words, the relation between aggressiveness and exposure to media violence may be a case of **third-variable correlation,** which means that *two variables are correlated only because each is causally related to a third variable.* **FIGURE 2.2** shows three possible causes of any correlation.

? What is third-variable correlation?

How can we determine by simple observation which of these three possibilities best describes the relationship between exposure to media violence and aggressiveness? Take a deep breath. The answer is: *We can't.* When we observe a natural correlation, the possibility of third-variable correlation can never be dismissed. Don't take this claim on faith. Let's try to dismiss the possibility of third-variable correlation and you'll see why such efforts are always doomed to fail.

The most straightforward way to determine whether a third variable, such as lack of adult supervision (*Z*), causes exposure to media violence (*X*) and aggressive behavior (*Y*) is to eliminate differences in adult supervision (*Z*) among a group of children and see if the correlation between exposure (*X*) and aggressiveness (*Y*) is eliminated too. For instance, we could measure only children who are supervised by an adult exactly A% of the time, thus ensuring that every child who was exposed to media violence had exactly the same amount of adult supervision as every child who was not exposed. Alternatively, we could measure children who have different amounts of supervision but make sure that for every child we measure who is exposed to media violence and supervised B% of the time, we also observe a child who is not exposed to media violence and is supervised B% of the time, thus ensuring that children who are and are not exposed to media violence have the same amount of adult supervision on average. So if those who were exposed are on average more aggressive than those who were not exposed, we can be sure that lack of adult supervision was not the cause of this difference.

But even if we used these techniques to dismiss a *particular* third variable (such as lack of adult supervision), we would not be able to dismiss *all* third variables. For example, as soon as we finished making these observations, it might suddenly occur to us that emotional instability (*Z*) could cause children to gravitate toward violent television or video games (*X*) and to behave aggressively (*Y*). Emotional instability would be a new third variable, and we would have to design a new test to investigate

natural correlation A correlation observed in the world around us.

third-variable correlation The fact that two variables are correlated only because each is causally related to a third variable.

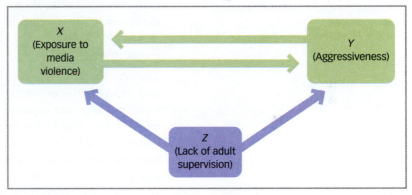

▼ Figure **2.2** **Causes of Correlation** If *X* (exposure to media violence) and *Y* (aggressiveness) are correlated, then there are at least three possible explanations: *X* causes *Y*, *Y* causes *X*, or *Z* (some other factor, such as lack of adult supervision) causes both *Y* and *X*, neither of which causes the other.

Some things just won't stay dead. Jason is one example. The third-variable problem is another.

©NEW LINE CINEMA/COURTESY EVERETT COLLECTION

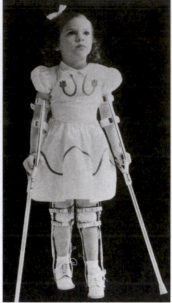

In 1949, Dr. Benjamin Sandler noticed a correlation between the incidence of polio and ice cream consumption; he concluded that sugar made children susceptible to the disease. Public health officials issued warnings. As it turned out, a third variable—warm weather—caused both an increase in disease (viruses become more active in the summer) and an increase in ice cream consumption.

whether it explains the correlation between exposure and aggression. Unfortunately, we could keep dreaming up new third variables all day long without ever breaking a sweat, and every time we dreamed one up, we would have to rush out and do a new test to determine whether *this* third variable was the cause of the correlation between exposure and aggressiveness.

Do you see the problem? Because there are an infinite number of third variables, there are an infinite number of reasons why X and Y might be correlated. And because we can't perform an infinite number of studies to rule out every possible third variable Z, we can never be absolutely sure that the correlation we observe between X and Y is evidence of a causal relationship between them. The **third-variable problem** refers to the fact that *a causal relationship between two variables cannot be inferred from the naturally occurring correlation between them because of the ever-present possibility of third-variable correlation.* In other words, if we care about causality, then naturally occurring correlations just won't tell us what we really want to know. But there is a technique that will!

Experimentation

The observational studies described above eliminated a single difference between two groups—the difference in adult supervision between groups of children who were and were not exposed to media violence. The problem is they eliminated only one difference and countless others remained. If we could just find a technique that eliminated *all* of these countless differences, then we *could* conclude that exposure and aggression are causally related. If exposed kids were more aggressive than unexposed kids, and if the two groups didn't differ in *any* way except for that exposure, then we could be sure that their level of exposure had caused their level of aggression.

In fact, scientists have a technique that does exactly that. It is called an **experiment,** which is *a technique for establishing the causal relationship between variables.* The most important thing to know about experiments is that you've been doing them all your life. Imagine that you are surfing the web on a laptop when all of a sudden you lose your wireless connection. You suspect that another device—say, your roommate's new cell phone—has somehow bumped you off the network. What would you do to test your suspicion? Observing a natural correlation wouldn't be much help. You could carefully note when you did and didn't have a connection and when your roommate did and didn't use his cell phone, but even if you observed a correlation between these two variables, you still couldn't conclude that the cell phone was *causing* your connection to fail. After all, if your roommate was afraid of loud noises and called his mommy for comfort whenever there was an electrical storm, and if that storm somehow zapped your wireless connection, then the storm (Z) would be the cause of both your roommate's cell phone usage (X) and your connectivity problem (Y).

So now could you test your suspicion? Rather than *observing* the correlation between cell phone usage and connectivity, you could try to *create* a correlation by making a call on your roommate's cell phone, hanging up, making another call, hanging up again, and observing changes in your laptop's connectivity as you did so. If you observed that

Experiments are the best way to establish causal relationships—and to win the Nobel Prize, as Dr. Elizabeth Blackburn did in 2009 for her discovery of how chromosomes protect themselves during cell division.

"connection off" occurred only in conjunction with "cell phone on," then you could conclude that your roommate's cell phone was the *cause* of your failed connection. The technique you used to solve the third-variable problem in this case was an experiment, and it included one of the hallmarks of experimentation—**manipulation,** which is *the creation of an artificial pattern of variation in a variable in order to determine its causal powers.*

Manipulation is a critical ingredient in an experiment. Up until now, we have approached science like polite dinner guests, taking what we were offered and making the best of it. Nature offered us children who differed in how much violence they were exposed to and who differed in how aggressively they behaved, and we dutifully measured the natural patterns of variation in these two variables and computed their correlations. In an experiment, rather than *measuring* exposure and *measuring* aggression and then computing the correlation between these two naturally occurring variables, we instead *manipulate* exposure in exactly the same way that you manipulated your roommate's cell phone. In essence, we need to systematically switch exposure on and off in a group of children and then watch to see whether aggression goes on and off too.

third-variable problem The fact that a causal relationship between two variables cannot be inferred from the naturally occurring correlation between them because of the ever-present possibility of third-variable correlation.

experiment A technique for establishing the causal relationship between variables.

manipulation The creation of an artificial pattern of variation in a variable in order to determine its causal powers.

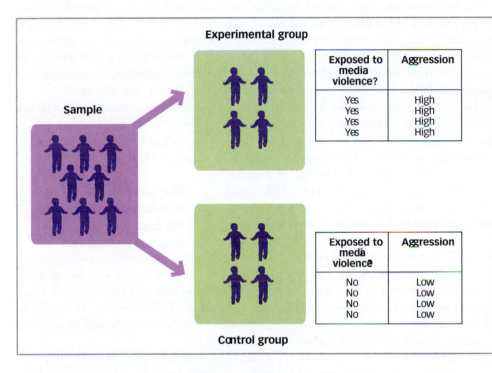

Experimental group

Sample

Exposed to media violence?	Aggression
Yes	High
Yes	High
Yes	High
Yes	High

Exposed to media violence?	Aggression
No	Low
No	Low
No	Low
No	Low

Control group

◄ Figure **2.3** **Manipulation** The independent variable is exposure to media violence and the dependent variable is aggression. Manipulation of the independent variable results in an experimental group and a control group. When we compare the behavior of participants in these two groups, we are actually computing the correlation between the independent variable and the dependent variable.

How do you determine whether eating 60 hotdogs will make you sick? You eat them one day, don't eat them the next day, and then see which day you barf. *That's* manipulation! BTW, world champion Joey Chestnut ate 60 hot dogs in 12 minutes by folding them up. *That's* manipulation too!

There are many ways to do this. For example, we might ask some children to participate in an experiment, then have half of them play violent video games for an hour and make sure the other half does not (see **FIGURE 2.3**). At the end of the study, we could measure the children's aggression and compare the measurements across the two groups. When we compared these measurements, we would essentially be computing the correlation between a variable that we manipulated (exposure) and a variable that we measured (aggression). Because we *manipulated* rather than *measured* exposure, we would never have to ask whether a third variable (such as lack of adult supervision) caused kids to experience different levels of exposure. After all, we already *know* what caused that. *We* did!

? **What are the three main steps in doing an experiment?**

Doing an experiment, then, involves three critical steps (and several technical terms):

independent variable The variable that is manipulated in an experiment.

experimental group The group of people who are treated in a particular way, as compared to the control group, in an experiment.

control group The group of people who are not treated in the particular way that the experimental group is treated in an experiment.

dependent variable The variable that is measured in a study.

self-selection A problem that occurs when anything about a person determines whether he or she will be included in the experimental or control group.

random assignment A procedure that uses a random event to assign people to the experimental or control group.

There is no evidence that Louise Hay's techniques can cure cancer. But even if cancer victims who bought her books *did* show a higher rate of remission than those who didn't, there would *still* be no evidence because buyers are self-selected and thus may differ from non-buyers in countless ways.

> First, we perform a manipulation. We call *the variable that is manipulated* the **independent variable** because it is under our control, and thus it is "independent" of what the participant says or does. When we manipulate an independent variable (such as exposure to media violence), we create at least two groups of participants: an **experimental group,** which is *the group of people who are treated in a particular way,* such as being exposed to media violence, and a **control group,** which is *the group of people who are not treated in this particular way.*

> Second, having manipulated one variable (exposure), we now measure the other variable (aggression). We call *the variable that is measured* the **dependent variable** because its value "depends" on what the person being measured says or does.

> Third and finally, we check to see whether our manipulation produced changes in the variable we measured.

Random Assignment

Imagine that we began our exposure and aggression experiment by finding a group of children and asking each child whether he or she would like to be in the experimental group or the control group. Imagine that half the children said that they'd like to play violent video games and the other half said they would rather not. Imagine that we let the children do what they wanted to do, measured aggression some time later, and found that the children who had played the violent video games were more aggressive than those who had not. Would this experiment allow us to conclude that playing violent video games causes aggression? Definitely not. But *why* not?

We went wrong when we let the children decide for themselves whether or not they would play violent video games. After all, children who ask to play such games are probably different in many ways from those who ask not to. They may be older, or stronger, or smarter. Or younger, or weaker, or dumber. Or less often supervised or more often supervised. The list of possible differences goes on and on. The whole point of doing the experiment was to divide children into two groups that differed *in only one way,* namely, in terms of their exposure to media violence. The moment we allowed the children to select their own groups, the two groups differed in countless ways, and any of those countless differences could have been a third variable that was responsible for any differences we observed in their measured aggression. **Self-selection** is *a problem that occurs when anything about a person determines whether he or she will be included in the experimental or control group.*

? **Why can't we allow people to select the condition of the experiment in which they will participate?**

If we want to be sure that there is one and only one difference between the children who are and are not exposed to media violence, then their inclusion in these groups must be *randomly determined.* One way to randomly determine assignment of children to groups is to flip a coin. For example, we could walk up to each child in our experiment, flip a coin, and, if the coin lands heads up, assign the child to play violent video games. If the coin lands heads down, then we assign the child to play no violent video games. **Random assignment** is *a procedure that uses a random event to assign people to the experimental or control group.*

What would happen if we assigned children to groups with a coin flip? As **FIGURE 2.4** shows, the first thing we would expect is that about half the children would be assigned to play violent video games and about half would not. Second—and *much more* important—we could expect the experimental group and the control group to have roughly equal numbers of supervised kids and unsupervised kids, roughly equal numbers of emotionally stable and unstable kids, roughly equal numbers of big kids and small kids, of active kids, fat kids, tall kids, funny kids, and kids with blue hair named Larry who can't stand to eat spinach. In other words, we could expect the two

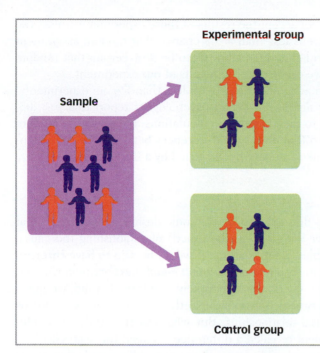

Experimental group

Exposed to media violence?	Adult supervision?	Aggression
Yes	Yes	High
Yes	No	High
Yes	Yes	High
Yes	No	High

Sample

Exposed to media violence	Adult supervision?	Aggression
No	Yes	Low
No	No	Low
No	Yes	Low
No	No	Low

Control group

◄ Figure 2.4 **Random Assignment** Children with adult supervision are shown in orange and those without adult supervision are shown in blue. The independent variable is exposure to media violence and the dependent variable is aggression. Random assignment ensures that participants in the experimental and the control groups are on average equal in terms of all possible third variables. In essence, it ensures that there is no correlation between a third variable and the dependent variable.

groups to have roughly equal numbers of kids who are anything-you-can-ever-name-and-everything-you-can't! Because the kids in the two groups will be the same *on average* in terms of height, weight, emotional stability, adult supervision, and every other variable in the known universe *except the one we manipulated*, we can be sure that the variable we manipulated (exposure) caused any changes in the variable we measured (aggression). Because exposure was the *only* difference between the two groups of children when we started the experiment, it *must* be the cause of any differences in aggression we observe at the end of the experiment.

? Why is random assignment so useful and important?

Significance

Random assignment is a powerful tool, but like a lot of tools, it doesn't work every time you use it. If we randomly assigned children to watch or not watch televised violence, we could expect the two groups to have roughly equal numbers of supervised and unsupervised kids, rich kids and poor kids, tall kids and short kids, and so on. The key word in that sentence is *roughly*. When you flip a coin 100 times, you can expect it to land heads up *roughly* 50 times. But every once in a while, 100 coin flips will produce 80 heads, or 90 heads, or even 100 heads, by sheer chance alone. This does not happen often, of course, but it does happen. Because random assignment is achieved by using a randomizing device such as a coin, every once in a long while the coin will assign more unsupervised, emotionally disturbed kids to play violent video games and more supervised, emotionally undisturbed kids to play none. When this happens, random assignment has failed—and when random assignment fails, the third-variable problem rises up out of its grave like a guy with a hockey mask and a grudge.

How can we tell when random assignment has failed? Unfortunately, we can't. But we can calculate the *odds* that random assignment has failed. It isn't important for you to know how to do this calculation, but it is important for you to understand how psychologists interpret its results. Psychologists perform a statistical calculation every time they

Here's the answer you've been waiting for. Redheads are especially sensitive to pain because a mutation in the MCR-1 gene causes both pain sensitivity and red hair.

internal validity The characteristic of an experiment that establishes the causal relationship between variables.

external validity A property of an experiment in which the variables have been operationally defined in a normal, typical, or realistic way.

ROBERT DALY/GETTY IMAGES

Do strawberries taste better when dipped in chocolate? If you dip the big juicy ones and don't dip the small dry ones, then you won't know if the chocolate is what made the difference. But if you randomly assign some to be dipped and others not to be dipped, and if the dipped ones taste better on average, then you will have demonstrated scientifically what every 6-year-old already knows.

Does piercing make a person more or less attractive? The answer, of course, depends entirely on how you operationally define *piercing*.

AP PHOTO/KEYSTONE, TI PRESS/SAMUEL GOLAY

do an experiment, and they do not accept the results of those experiments unless the calculation tells them that there is less than a 5% chance that random assignment failed. In other words, the calculation must allow us to be 95% certain that random assignment succeeded before we can accept the results of our experiment.

When the odds that random assignment failed are less than 5%, an experimental result is said to be *statistically significant*. When psychologists report that $p < .05$, they are saying that, according to their statistical calculations, the odds that random assignment failed are less than 5%, and thus the differences between the experimental and control groups were unlikely to have been caused by a third variable.

Drawing Conclusions

If we applied all the techniques discussed so far, we could design an experiment that had a very good chance (better than 95%, to be exact!) of establishing the causal relationship between two variables. That experiment would be said to have **internal validity,** which is *the characteristic of an experiment that establishes the causal relationship between variables.* When we say that an experiment is internally valid, we mean that everything *inside* the experiment is working exactly as it must in order for us to draw conclusions about causal relationships. But what exactly are those conclusions? If our imaginary experiment revealed a difference between the aggressiveness of children in the exposed and unexposed groups, then we could conclude that media violence *as we defined it* caused aggression *as we defined it* in the people *whom we studied.* Notice the phrases in italics. Each corresponds to an important restriction on the kinds of conclusions we can draw from an experiment, so let's consider each in turn.

Representative Variables

Whether an experiment shows that exposure to media violence causes aggression will depend in part on how these variables are defined. We are probably more likely to find that exposure causes aggression when we define exposure as "watching two hours of gory axe murders" rather than "watching 10 minutes of football" or when we define aggression as "interrupting another person" rather than "smacking someone with a tire iron." As you'll recall from our discussion of operational definitions, there are many ways to define the independent and dependent variables in an experiment, and how they are defined will have a huge impact on whether a manipulation of the former causes measurable changes in the latter. So what is the *right* way to define these variables?

One answer is that we should define them in an experiment as they are defined in the real world. **External validity** is *a property of an experiment in which variables have been operationally defined in a normal, typical, or realistic way.* It seems pretty clear that the kind of aggressive behavior that concerns teachers and parents lies somewhere between an interruption and an assault, and that the kind of media violence to which children are typically exposed lies somewhere between sports and torture. If the goal of an experiment is to determine whether the kinds of media violence to which children are typically exposed causes the kinds of aggression with which societies are typically concerned, then external validity is essential. When variables are defined in an experiment as they typically are in the real world, we say that the variables are *representative* of the real world.

STEWART FEREBEE/PHOTONICA/GETTY

External validity sounds like such a good idea that you may be surprised to learn that most psychology experiments are externally *in*valid—and that most psychologists don't mind. The reason for this is that psychologists are rarely trying to learn about the real world by creating tiny replicas of it in their laboratories. Rather, they are usually trying to learn about the real world by using experiments to test hypotheses and to gather evidence for or against those hypotheses, and externally invalid experiments can often do that splendidly (Mook, 1983).

? Why is external validity not always important?

Representative People

Our imaginary experiment on exposure to media violence and aggression would allow us to conclude that exposure as we defined it caused aggression as we defined it in the people *whom we studied*. That last phrase represents another important restriction on the kinds of conclusions we can draw from experiments.

Who are the people whom psychologists study? Psychologists rarely observe an entire **population,** which is *a complete collection of people*, such as the population of human beings (about 7 billion), the population of Californians (about 37 million), or the population of people with Down syndrome (about 1 million). Rather, they observe a **sample,** which is *a partial collection of people drawn from a population*. How big can a sample be? The size of a population is signified by the uppercase letter N, the size of a sample is signified by the lowercase letter n, and so $0 < n < N$.

? What is the difference between a population and a sample?

In some cases, $n = 1$. For example, sometimes a single individual is so remarkable that he or she deserves close study, and when psychologists study such people, they are using the **case method,** which is *a method of gathering scientific knowledge by studying a single individual*. We can learn a lot about memory by studying someone like Akira Haraguchi, who can recite the first 100,000 digits of pi, or about intelligence and creativity by studying someone like 14-year-old Jay Greenberg, whose musical compositions have been recorded by the Julliard String Quartet and the London Symphony Orchestra. Cases such as these are interesting in their own right, but they also provide important insights into how the rest of us work.

Of course, most of the psychological studies you will read about in the other chapters of this book included samples of ten, a hundred, a thousand, or a few thousand people. So how do psychologists decide which people to include in their samples? One way to select a sample from a population is by **random sampling,** which is

AP PHOTO/HO/COURTESY OF SONY BMG MASTERWORKS

Jay Greenberg was not a typical 14-year-old. According to the *New York Times,* the London Symphony Orchestra's recent recording of Greenberg's Symphony No. 5 reveals a "gift for drama and for lyricism, expressed in sophisticated colors and textures."

ULLSTEIN BILD/THE GRANGER COLLECTION

REUTERS/JIM YOUNG

Non-random sampling can lead to errors. In the presidential election of 1948, the *Chicago Tribune* mistakenly predicted that Thomas Dewey would beat Harry Truman. Why? Because polling was done by telephone, and Dewey Republicans were more likely to have telephones than were Truman Democrats. In the presidential election of 2004, exit polls mistakenly predicted that John Kerry would beat George Bush. Why? Because polling was done by soliciting voters as they left the polls, and Kerry supporters were more willing to stop and talk.

a technique for choosing participants that ensures that every member of a population has an equal chance of being included in the sample. When we randomly sample participants from a population, the sample is said to be *representative* of the population. This allows us to *generalize* from the sample to the population—that is, to conclude that what we observed in our sample would also have been observed if we had measured the entire population.

Random sampling sounds like such a good idea that you might be surprised to learn that most psychological studies involve non-random samples. Indeed, virtually every participant in every psychology experiment you will ever read about was a volunteer, and most were college students who were significantly younger, smarter, healthier, wealthier, and Whiter than the average Earthling. Why do psychologists sample non-randomly? Convenience. Even if there were an alphabetized list of all the world's human inhabitants from which we could randomly choose our research participants, how would we find the 72-year-old Bedouin woman whose family roams the desert so that we could measure the electrical activity in her brain while she watched cartoons? How would we convince the 3-week-old infant in New Delhi to complete a lengthy questionnaire about his political beliefs? As much as psychologists might *like* to randomly sample the population of the planet, the practical truth is that they are pretty much stuck studying the folks who volunteer for their studies.

? Why is the failure to sample randomly not always a problem?

HOT SCIENCE

Do Violent Movies Make Peaceful Streets?

In 2000, the American Medical Association and five other public health organizations issued a joint statement warning about the risks of exposure to media violence. They cited evidence from psychological experiments in which children and young adults who were exposed to violent movie clips showed a sharp increase in aggressive behavior immediately afterwards. They noted that "well over 1000 studies . . . point overwhelmingly to a causal connection between media violence and aggressive behavior."

Given the laboratory results, we might expect to see a correlation in the real world between the number of people who see violent movies in theaters and the number of violent crimes. When economists Gordon Dahl and Stefano Della Vigna (2009) analyzed crime statistics and box office statistics, they found just such a correlation—except that it was negative! In other words, on evenings when more people went to the theater to watch violent movies, there were *fewer* violent crimes. Why? The researchers suggested that violent movies are especially appealing to the people who are most likely to commit violent crimes. Because those people are busy watching movies for a few hours, violent crime drops. In other words, blood-and-bullet movies take criminals off the street by luring them to the theater!

Laboratory experiments clearly show that exposure to media violence *can* cause aggression. But as the movie theater data remind us, experiments are a tool for establishing the causal relationships between variables and are not meant to be miniature versions of the real world, where things are ever so much more complex.

UNIVERSAL STUDIOS/PHOTOFEST

◄ One thing we know about the people who went to see the movie *American Gangster* is that for 2 hours and 37 minutes they didn't shoot anybody.

So how can we learn *anything* from psychology experiments? Isn't the failure to randomly sample a fatal flaw? No, it's not, and there are three reasons why.

1. Sometimes the similarity of a sample and a population doesn't matter. Most people can't recite the first 100,000 digits of pi from memory, but Akira Haraguchi can—and when he did this in 2006, psychologists learned something important about the nature of human memory. An experimental result can be illuminating even when the sample isn't typical of the population.

2. When the ability to generalize an experimental result *is* important, psychologists perform new experiments that use the same procedures on different samples. For example, after measuring how some American children behaved after playing violent video games, we could replicate our experiment with Japanese children, or with teenagers, or with adults. If the results of our study were replicated in numerous non-random samples, we could be more confident (though never completely confident) that the results would generalize to the population at large.

3. Sometimes the similarity of the sample and the population is a reasonable assumption. For example, few of us would be willing to take an experimental medicine if a non-random sample of seven participants took it and died. Indeed, we would probably refuse the medicine even if the seven participants were mice. Although these non-randomly sampled participants were different from us in many ways (including tails and whiskers), most of us would be willing to generalize from their experience to ours because we know that even mice share enough of our basic biology to make it a good bet that what harms them can harm us too. By this same reasoning, if a psychology experiment demonstrated that some American children behaved violently after playing violent video games, we might ask whether there is a compelling reason to suspect that Ecuadorian college students or middle-aged Australians would behave any differently. If the answer is yes, then experiments would provide a way for us to investigate that possibility.

SUMMARY QUIZ [2.3]

1. When two variables are correlated, what keeps us from concluding that one is the cause and the other is the effect?
   a. the possibility of third-variable correlation
   b. the random assignment of control groups
   c. the existence of false positive correlation
   d. the impossibility of accurately measuring correlation strength

2. A researcher administers a questionnaire concerning attitudes toward global warming to people of both genders and of all ages who live all across the country. The dependent variable in the study is the _____ of the participants.
   a. age
   b. gender
   c. attitudes toward global warming
   d. geographic location

3. The characteristic of an experiment that allows conclusions about causal relationships to be drawn is called
   a. external validity.
   b. internal validity.
   c. random assignment.
   d. self-selection.

4. An experiment that operationally defines variables in a realistic way is said to be
   a. externally valid.
   b. controlled.
   c. operationally defined.
   d. statistically significant.

This mouse died after drinking the green stuff. Want to drink the green stuff? Why not? You're not a mouse, are you?

DAVID J. GREEN/ALAMY

The Ethics of Science: First, Do No Harm

Somewhere along the way, someone probably told you that it isn't nice to treat people like objects. And yet it may seem that psychologists do just that—creating situations that cause people to feel fearful or sad, to do things that are embarrassing or immoral, or to learn things about themselves and others that they might not really want to know. Don't be fooled by appearances. The fact is that psychologists go to great lengths to protect the well-being of their research participants, and they are bound by a code of ethics that is as detailed and demanding as the professional codes that bind physicians, lawyers, and accountants. That code requires that psychologists show respect for people, for animals, and for the truth. Let's examine each of these obligations in turn.

Respecting People

During World War II, Nazi doctors performed truly barbaric experiments on human subjects (see Where Do You Stand? at the end of the chapter). When the war ended, the international community developed the Nuremberg Code of 1947 and then the Declaration of Helsinki in 1964, which spelled out rules for the ethical treatment of human subjects. Unfortunately, not everyone obeyed them. For example, from 1932 until 1972, the U.S. Public Health Service conducted the infamous Tuskegee Experiment in which 399 African American men with syphilis were denied treatment so that researchers could observe the progression of the disease. As one journalist noted, the government "used human beings as laboratory animals in a long and inefficient study of how long it takes syphilis to kill someone" (Coontz, 2008).

In 1979, the U.S. Department of Health, Education and Welfare released what came to be known as the Belmont Report, which described three basic principles

? **What are three features of ethical research?**

that all research involving human subjects should follow. First, research should show *respect for persons* and their right to make decisions for and about themselves without undue influence or coercion. Second, research should be *beneficent*, which means that it should attempt to maximize benefits and reduce risks to the participants. Third, research should be *just*, which means that it should distribute benefits and risks equally to participants without prejudice toward particular individuals or groups.

The specific ethical code that psychologists follow incorporates these basic principles and expands them. (You can find the American Psychological Association's *Ethical Principles of Psychologists and Codes of Conduct* at http://www.apa.org/ethics/code/index.aspx.) Here are a few of the most important rules that govern the conduct of psychological research:

> *Informed consent*: Participants may not take part in a psychological study unless they have given **informed consent,** which is *a written agreement to participate in a study made by an adult who has been informed of all the risks that participation may entail*. This doesn't mean that the person must know everything about the study (e.g., the hypothesis), but it does mean that the person must know about anything that might potentially be harmful or painful. If people cannot give informed consent (e.g., because they are minors or are mentally incapable), then informed consent must be obtained from their legal guardians.

> *Freedom from coercion*: Psychologists may not coerce participation. Coercion means not only physical and psychological coercion but monetary coercion as well. It is unethical to offer people large amounts of money to persuade them to do something that they might otherwise decline to do.

informed consent A written agreement to participate in a study made by an adult who has been informed of all the risks that participation may entail.

debriefing A verbal description of the true nature and purpose of a study.

> *Protection from harm:* Psychologists must take every possible precaution to protect their research participants from physical or psychological harm. If there are two equally effective ways to study something, the psychologist must use the safer method.

> *Risk-benefit analysis:* Although participants may be asked to accept small risks, such as a minor shock or a small embarrassment, the psychologist must first demonstrate that these risks are outweighed by the social benefits of the new knowledge that might be gained from the study.

> *Deception:* Psychologists may use deception only when it is justified by the study's scientific, educational, or applied value and when alternative procedures are not feasible.

> *Debriefing:* If a participant is deceived in any way before or during a study, the psychologist must provide a **debriefing,** which is *a verbal description of the true nature and purpose of a study.*

> *Confidentiality:* Psychologists are obligated to keep private and personal information obtained during a study confidential.

© AMERICAN BROADCASTING COMPANIES, INC.

The man at this bar is upset. He just saw another man slip a drug into a woman's drink and he is alerting the bartender. What he doesn't know is that all the people at the bar are actors and that he is being filmed for the television show *What Would You Do?* Was it ethical for ABC to put this man in such a stressful situation without his consent? And how did men who didn't alert the bartender feel when they turned on their televisions months later and were confronted by their own shameful behavior?

These are just some of the rules that psychologists must follow. But how are those rules enforced? Almost all psychology studies are done by psychologists who work at institutions that have institutional review boards (IRBs) that are composed of instructors and researchers, university staff, and laypeople from the community (e.g., business leaders or members of the clergy). A psychologist may conduct a study only after the IRB has reviewed and approved it.

As you can imagine, the code of ethics and the procedure for approval are so strict that many studies simply cannot be performed anywhere, by anyone, at any time. For example, psychologists would love to know how growing up without exposure to language affects a person's subsequent ability to speak and think, but they cannot ethically manipulate that variable in an experiment. Because they can only study the natural correlations between language exposure and speaking ability, they may never be able to firmly establish the causal relationships between these variables. Indeed, there are many questions that psychologists will never be able to answer definitively because doing so would require unethical experiments that violate basic human rights.

Respecting Animals

Of course, not all research participants have human rights because not all research participants are human. Some are chimpanzees, rats, pigeons, or other nonhuman animals. The American Psychological Association's code specifically describes the special rights of these nonhuman participants; some of the more important ones are these:

? What steps must psychologists take to protect nonhuman subjects?

> All procedures involving animals must be supervised by psychologists who are trained in research methods and experienced in the care of laboratory animals as well as responsible for ensuring appropriate consideration of the animals' comfort, health, and humane treatment.

> Psychologists must make reasonable efforts to minimize the discomfort, infection, illness, and pain of animals.

> Psychologists may use a procedure that subjects an animal to pain, stress, or privation only when an alternative procedure is unavailable and when the procedure is justified by the scientific, educational, or applied value of the study.

> Psychologists must perform all surgical procedures under appropriate anesthesia and must minimize an animal's pain during and after surgery.

All good—but good enough? Some people don't think so. Some Americans consider it unethical to use nonhuman animals in research or believe that nonhuman animals should have the same fundamental rights as humans. On the other hand, a recent Gallup poll showed that about two thirds of Americans consider it morally acceptable to use nonhuman animals in research and would reject a governmental ban on such research (Kiefer, 2004; Moore, 2003). Indeed, most Americans see a sharp distinction between animal and human rights. Science is not in the business of resolving moral controversies, and every individual must draw his or her own conclusions about this issue. But it is worth noting that only a small percentage of psychological studies involve animals and that only a small percentage of those studies cause the animals any harm or pain. Psychologists mainly study people, and when they do study animals, they mainly study their behavior.

Some people consider it unethical to use animals for clothing or research. Others see an important distinction between these two purposes.

Respecting Truth

Institutional review boards ensure that data are collected ethically. But once the data are collected, who ensures that they are ethically analyzed and reported? Psychology, like all sciences, works on the honor system. You may find that a bit odd. After all, we don't use the honor system in stores ("Take the television set home and pay us next time you're in the neighborhood"), banks ("I don't need to look up your account; just tell me how much money you want to withdraw"), or courtrooms ("If you say you're innocent, well then, that's good enough for me"), so why would we expect it to work in science? Are scientists more honest than everyone else?

The honor system doesn't work because scientists are especially honest but because science is a community enterprise. When scientists claim to have discovered something important, other scientists don't just applaud; they start studying it too. When the physicist Jan Hendrik Schön announced in 2001 that he had produced a molecular-scale transistor, other physicists were deeply impressed—that is, until they tried to replicate his work and discovered that Schön had fabricated his data (Agin, 2007). Schön lost his job and had his doctoral degree revoked, but the important point is that such frauds can't last long because one scientist's conclusion is the next scientist's research question. This doesn't mean that all frauds are eventually uncovered, but it does mean that the important ones are.

? **What are psychologists expected to do when they report the results of their research?**

What exactly are psychologists obligated on their honor to do? At least three things. First, when they write reports of their studies and publish them in scientific journals, psychologists are obligated to report truthfully on what they did and what they found. They can't fabricate results (e.g., claiming to have performed studies that they never really performed) or "fudge" results (e.g., changing records of data that were actually collected), and they can't mislead by omission (e.g., by reporting only the results that confirm their hypothesis and saying nothing about the results that don't). Second, psychologists are obligated to share credit fairly by including as co-authors of their reports the other people who contributed to the work and by mentioning in their reports the other scientists who have done related work. And third, psychologists are obligated to share their data. The fact that anyone can check up on anyone else is part of why the honor system works as well as it does.

SUMMARY QUIZ [2.4]

1. A written agreement to participate in a study made by an adult who has been informed of all the risks that participation may entail is known as

   a. a memorandum of understanding. c. a signature of authorization.

   b. informed consent. d. debriefing.

2. Which of the following are true for participants in a psychology study?

   a. They do not have to be told about risks they may encounter by participating in the study if, by disclosing such risks, the experimenter feels that participants' behavior will be altered in such a way that any scientific results will be invalid.

   b. They may be paid for participation, as long as the amount of money is not so great that it might persuade them to do something they might not otherwise do.

   c. They must be mentally capable of providing informed consent.

   d. All of the above are true.

3. What are psychologists ethically required to do when reporting research results?

   a. to report findings truthfully c. to make data available for further research

   b. to share credit for research d. all of the above

REUTERS/LARRY DOWNING

Ethical reporting of research is not only an issue for scientists. Christie Todd Whitman was Administrator of the Environmental Protection Agency in 2003 when the agency wrote a scientific report and then removed references to studies showing that global warming is caused by human activity (Revkin & Seelye, 2003). Whitman denied that there was anything wrong with the way the report was written, but many scientists did not agree.

Where Do You Stand?

The Morality of Immoral Experiments

During World War II, Nazi doctors conducted barbaric medical studies on prisoners in concentration camps. They placed prisoners in decompression chambers and then dissected their living brains in order to determine how altitude affects pilots. They irradiated and chemically mutilated the reproductive organs of men and women in order to find inexpensive methods for the mass sterilization of "racially inferior" people. And in one of the most horrible experiments, prisoners were immersed in tanks of ice water so that the doctors could discover how long pilots would survive if they bailed out over the North Sea. The prisoners were frozen, thawed, and frozen again until they died. During these experiments, the doctors carefully recorded the prisoners' physiological responses.

These experiments were hideous. But the records of these experiments remain, and in some cases they provide valuable information that could never be obtained ethically. For example, because researchers cannot perform controlled studies that would expose volunteers to dangerously cold temperatures, there is still controversy among doctors about the best treatment for hypothermia. In 1988, Dr. Robert Pozos, a physiologist at the University of Minnesota Medical School, who had spent a lifetime studying hypothermia,

came across an unpublished report written in 1945 that described the results of the horrible freezing experiments performed on concentration camp prisoners, and it suggested that contrary to the conventional medical wisdom, rapid rewarming (rather than slow rewarming) might be the best way to treat hypothermia.

Should the Nazi medical studies have been published so that modern doctors might more effectively treat hypothermia? Many scientists and ethicists thought they should. "The victims' dignity was irrevocably lost in vats of freezing liquid forty years ago. Nothing can change that," argued bioethicist Arthur Caplan. Others disagreed. "I don't see how any credence can be given to the work of unethical investigators," wrote Dr. Arnold Relman, editor of the *New England Journal of Medicine*. "It goes to legitimizing the evil done," added Abraham Foxman, national director of the Anti-Defamation League (Siegel, 1988). The debate about this issue continues (Caplan, 1992). If we use data that were obtained unethically, are we rewarding those who collected it and legitimizing their actions? Or can we condemn such investigations but still learn from them? Where do you stand?

Chapter Review

Empiricism: How to Know Stuff

▶ Empiricism is the belief that the best way to understand the world is to observe it firsthand. It is only in the last few centuries that empiricism has come to prominence.

▶ Empiricism is at the heart of the scientific method, which suggests that our theories about the world give rise to falsifiable hypotheses and that we can thus make observations that test those hypotheses. The results of these tests can disprove our theories but cannot prove them.

▶ Observation doesn't just mean "looking." It requires a method. The methods of psychology are special because human beings are complex, variable, and reactive.

Observation: Discovering What People Do

▶ Measurement involves defining a property in terms of a concrete condition and then constructing a measure that can detect that condition.

▶ A good measure is valid (the concrete conditions it measures are conceptually related to the property of interest), reliable (it produces the same measurement whenever it is used to measure the same thing), and powerful (it can detect the concrete conditions when they actually exist).

▶ Demand characteristics are features of a setting that suggest to people that they should behave in a particular way. Psychologists try to reduce or eliminate demand characteristics by observing participants in their natural habitats or by hiding their expectations from the participants.

▶ Observer bias is the tendency for observers to see what they expect to see or cause others to behave as they expect them to behave. Psychologists try to eliminate observe bias by making double-blind observations.

Explanation: Discovering Why People Do What They Do

▶ To determine whether two variables are causally related, we must first determine whether they are related at all. This can be done by measuring each variable many times and then comparing the patterns of variation within each series of measurements. If the patterns covary, then the variables are correlated.

▶ Even when we observe a correlation between two variables, we can't conclude that they are causally related because there are an infinite number of third variables that might be causing them both. Experiments solve this third-variable problem by manipulating an independent variable, randomly assigning participants to the experimental and control groups that this manipulation creates, and measuring a dependent variable. These measurements are then compared across groups. If inferential statistics show that there was less than a 5% chance that random assignment failed, then differences in the measurements across groups are assumed to have been caused by the manipulation.

▶ An internally valid experiment establishes a causal relationship between variables as they were operationally defined and among the participants whom they included. When an experiment mimics the real world, it is externally valid. But most psychology experiments are not attempts to mimic the real world but rather to test hypotheses derived from theories.

The Ethics of Science: First, Do No Harm

▶ Institutional review boards ensure that the rights of human beings who participate in scientific research are based on the principles of respect for persons, beneficence, and justice.

▶ Psychologists are obligated to uphold these principles by getting informed consent from participants, not coercing participation, protecting participants from harm, weighing benefits against risks, avoiding deception, and keeping information confidential.

▶ Psychologists are obligated to respect the rights of animals and treat them humanely. Most people are in favor of using animals in scientific research.

▶ Psychologists are obligated to tell the truth about their studies, to share credit appropriately, and to grant others access to their data.

KEY TERMS

empiricism (p. 32)

scientific method (p. 32)

theory (p. 32)

hypothesis (p. 33)

empirical method (p. 33)

operational definition (p. 34)

measure (p. 34)

electromyograph (EMG) (p. 34)

validity (p. 35)

reliability (p. 35)

power (p. 35)

demand characteristics (p. 35)

naturalistic observation (p. 36)

double-blind (p. 37)

variable (p. 39)

correlation (p. 39)

natural correlation (p. 40)

third-variable correlation (p. 41)

third-variable problem (p. 42)

experiment (p. 42)

manipulation (p. 43)

independent variable (p. 44)

experimental group (p. 44)

control group (p. 44)

dependent variable (p. 44)

self-selection (p. 44)

random assignment (p. 44)

internal validity (p. 46)

external validity (p. 46)

population (p. 47)

sample (p. 47)

case method (p. 47)

random sampling (p. 47)

informed consent (p. 50)

debriefing (p. 51)

CHANGING MINDS

1. Back in Chapter 1, you read about B. F. Skinner, who studied the principle of reinforcement, which states that the consequences of a behavior determine whether it will be more or less likely to occur in the future. So, for example, a rat's rate of lever pressing will increase if it receives food reinforcement after each lever press. When you tell a classmate about this principle, she only shrugs. "That's obvious. Anyone who's ever owned a dog knows how to train animals. If you ask me, psychology is just common sense. You don't have to conduct scientific experiments to test things that everyone already knows are true." How would you explain the value of studying something that seems like "common sense"?

2. You're watching TV with a friend when a news program reports that a research study has found that people in Europe who work longer hours are less happy than those who work shorter hours, but in the United States it's the other way around: Americans who work longer hours are happier (Okulicz-Kozaryn, 2011). "That's an interesting experiment," he says. You point out that the news only said it was a research study, not an experiment. What would have to be true for it to be an experiment? Why aren't all research studies experiments?

3. After the first exam in a class, your professor says she's noticed a strong positive correlation between student seating and exam scores: "The students who scored the highest sit in the front four rows every class," she says. After class, a friend suggests you should both sit up front for the rest of the semester to improve your grades. Having read about correlation and causation, why should you be skeptical? What are some possible reasons that there could be a correlation between sitting up front and getting good grades? Could you design an experiment to test whether sitting up front actually causes good grades?

4. A classmate in your criminal justice class suggests that mental illness causes a majority of the violent crimes in the United States. As evidence, he mentions a highly publicized murder trial in which the convicted suspect was diagnosed with schizophrenia. What scientific evidence would he need to support this claim?

5. You ask a friend if he wants to go to the gym with you. "No," he says. "I never exercise." You tell him that regular exercise has all kinds of health benefits, including greatly reducing the risk of heart disease. "I don't believe that," he replies. "I had an uncle who got up at 6:00 a.m. every day of his life to go jogging, and he still died of a heart attack at age 53." What would you tell your friend? Does his uncle's case prove that exercise really doesn't protect against heart disease after all?

CRITICAL THINKING QUESTIONS

1. A good theory gives rise to testable hypotheses—predictions about what can and should happen. And yet, when we actually go out and test these hypotheses, the results can prove the theory wrong, but they can never prove it right. Why?

2. Demand characteristics are those aspects of a research setting that cause participants to behave as they think the researcher wants or expects them to behave. Suppose you wanted to know whether people are more likely to cheat when they feel sad than when they feel happy. People rarely cheat when they think someone is watching them, so how could you test this hypothesis in a way that minimized demand characteristics?

3. A newspaper article recently reported that couples who live together before marriage are less likely to stay married than are couples who don't live together before marriage. The article suggested that people who want to have long-lasting marriages should therefore avoid living together beforehand. Is that conclusion reasonable? How else could you explain this correlation?

ANSWERS TO SUMMARY QUIZZES

Summary Quiz [2.1] 1. c; 2. c; 3. a
Summary Quiz [2.2] 1. b; 2. d; 3. c
Summary Quiz [2.3] 1. a; 2. c; 3. b; 4. a
Summary Quiz [2.4] 1. b; 2. b; 3. d.

Need more help? Additional resources are located at the book's free companion website at:
www.worthpublishers.com/schacterbrief2e

3

Neuroscience and Behavior

IT WAS AN UNUSUAL NIGHT, even for the late shift in the hospital emergency room. First, 17-year-old David was brought in by some fellow members of his gang. They told the doctors that David had claimed he saw members of a rival gang sneaking up on him. At first David's friends listened to his warnings, but after repeated false alarms, they decided David had gone crazy. The doctors didn't find any problems with David's eyes. Instead, they discovered he was suffering from hallucinations—a side effect of abusing methamphetamine (McKetin et al., 2006). David's prolonged crystal meth habit had altered the normal functioning of some chemicals in his brain, distorting his perception of reality and "fooling" his brain into perceiving things that were not actually there.

Next, 75-year-old Betty arrived. She had fainted earlier in the day. After she was revived, Betty no longer recognized her husband, George, or their two sons. Her family brought her to the emergency room for examination. The doctor who examined Betty's eyes found her vision to be perfectly normal. A brain scan showed that Betty had suffered a stroke that damaged a small area on the right side of her brain. Doctors diagnosed Betty with a rare disorder called *prosopagnosia*, which is an inability to recognize familiar faces (Duchaine et al., 2006; Kleinschmidt & Cohen, 2006; Yin, 1970)—a result of the brain damage caused by her stroke.

David and Betty both complained of problems with their vision, but their symptoms were actually caused by disorders in the brain. Our ability to perceive the world around us depends not only on information we take in through our senses but, perhaps more important, on the interpretation of this information performed by the brain.

IN THIS CHAPTER, WE'LL CONSIDER HOW THE BRAIN WORKS, what happens when it doesn't, and how both states of affairs determine behavior. First, we'll introduce you to the basic unit of information processing in the brain, the neuron. The electrical and chemical activities of neurons are the starting point of all behavior, thought, and emotion. Next, we'll consider the anatomy of the central nervous system, focusing especially on the brain, its overall organization, and its evolutionary development. Finally, we'll discuss methods that allow us to study both damaged and healthy brains.

▶ Betty and David both complained of problems with their vision, but their symptoms were actually caused by disorders in the brain. Brain disorders, whether caused by taking drugs or suffering from a stroke, can produce bizarre and sometimes dangerous distortions of perception.

57

Neurons: The Origin of Behavior

An estimated 1 billion people watch the final game of World Cup soccer every four years. That's a whole lot of people, but it's still only a little over 14% of the estimated 7 billion people currently living on Earth. But a really, really big number is inside your skull right now: There are approximately *100 billion* cells in your brain that perform a variety of tasks to allow you to function as a human being. All of your thoughts, feelings, and behaviors spring from cells in the brain that take in information and produce some kind of output trillions of times a day. These cells are **neurons,** *cells in the nervous system that communicate with one another to perform information-processing tasks.*

Like cells in all organs of the body, neurons have a **cell body** (also called the *soma*), the largest component of the neuron that *coordinates the information-processing tasks and keeps the cell alive* (see **FIGURE 3.1**). Functions such as protein synthesis, energy production, and metabolism take place here. The cell body contains a *nucleus*; this structure houses chromosomes that contain your DNA, or the genetic blueprint of who you are. The cell body is surrounded by a porous cell membrane that allows molecules to flow into and out of the cell.

Unlike other cells in the body, neurons have two types of specialized extensions of the cell membrane that allow them to communicate: dendrites and axons. **Dendrites** *receive information from other neurons and relay it to the cell body*. The term *dendrite* comes from the Greek word for "tree"; indeed, most neurons have many dendrites that look like tree branches. The **axon** *transmits information to other neurons, muscles, or glands*. Each neuron has a single axon that sometimes can be very long, even stretching up to a meter from the base of the spinal cord down to the big toe.

In many neurons, the axon is covered by a **myelin sheath,** *an insulating layer of fatty material*. The myelin sheath is composed of **glial cells,** which are *support cells found in the nervous system*. Although there are 100 billion neurons busily processing information in your brain, there are 10 to 50 times that many glial cells serving a variety of functions. Some glial cells digest parts of dead neurons, others provide physical and nutritional support for neurons, and still others form myelin to help the axon transmit information more efficiently. Imagine for a minute the pipes coming from the water heater in the basement, leading upstairs to heat a house. When those pipes are wrapped in insulation, they usually perform their task more efficiently: The water inside stays hotter, the heater works more effectively, and so on. Myelin performs this same function for an axon: An axon insulated with myelin can more efficiently transmit signals to other neurons, organs, or muscles. In fact, with *demyelinating diseases*, such as multiple sclerosis, the myelin sheath deteriorates, slowing the transmission of information from one neuron to another (Schwartz & Westbrook, 2000). This leads to a variety of problems, including loss of feeling in the limbs, partial blindness, and difficulties in coordinated movement and cognition (Butler, Corboy, & Filley, 2009).

Although neurons look like they form a continuously connected lattice in the brain, the dendrites and axons of neurons do not actually touch each other. There's a small gap between the axon of one neuron and the dendrites or cell body of another. This gap is part of the **synapse:** *the junction or region between the axon of one neuron and the dendrites or cell body of another* (see **FIGURE 3.2**). Many of the 100 billion neurons in your brain have a few thousand synaptic junctions, so it should come as no shock that most adults have between 100 trillion and 500 trillion synapses. As you'll read shortly, the transmission of information across the synapse is fundamental to communication between neurons, a process that allows us to think, feel, and behave.

There are three major types of neurons, each performing a distinct function: sensory neurons, motor neurons, and interneurons. **Sensory neurons** *receive infor-*

neurons Cells in the nervous system that communicate with one another to perform information-processing tasks.

cell body The part of a neuron that coordinates information-processing tasks and keeps the cell alive.

dendrites The part of a neuron that receives information from other neurons and relays it to the cell body.

axon The part of a neuron that transmits information to other neurons, muscles, or glands.

myelin sheath An insulating layer of fatty material.

glial cells Support cells found in the nervous system.

synapse The junction or region between the axon of one neuron and the dendrites or cell body of another.

sensory neurons Neurons that receive information from the external world and convey this information to the brain via the spinal cord.

motor neurons Neurons that carry signals from the spinal cord to the muscles to produce movement.

interneurons Neurons that connect sensory neurons, motor neurons, or other interneurons.

mation from the external world and convey this information to the brain via the spinal cord. These neurons have specialized endings on their dendrites that receive signals for light, sound, touch, taste, and smell. **Motor neurons** *carry signals from the spinal cord to the muscles to produce movement.* These neurons often have long axons that can stretch to muscles at our extremities. However, most of the nervous system is composed of the third type of neuron, **interneurons,** which *connect sensory neurons, motor neurons, or other interneurons.* Some interneurons carry information from sensory neurons into the nervous system, others carry information from the nervous system to motor neurons, and still others perform a variety of information-processing functions within the nervous system.

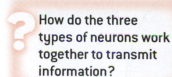

? How do the three types of neurons work together to transmit information?

▼ Figure **3.1** **Components of a Neuron**
A neuron is made up of three parts: a cell body that houses the chromosomes with the organism's DNA and maintains the health of the cell; dendrites that receive information from other neurons; and an axon that transmits information to other neurons, muscles, and glands.

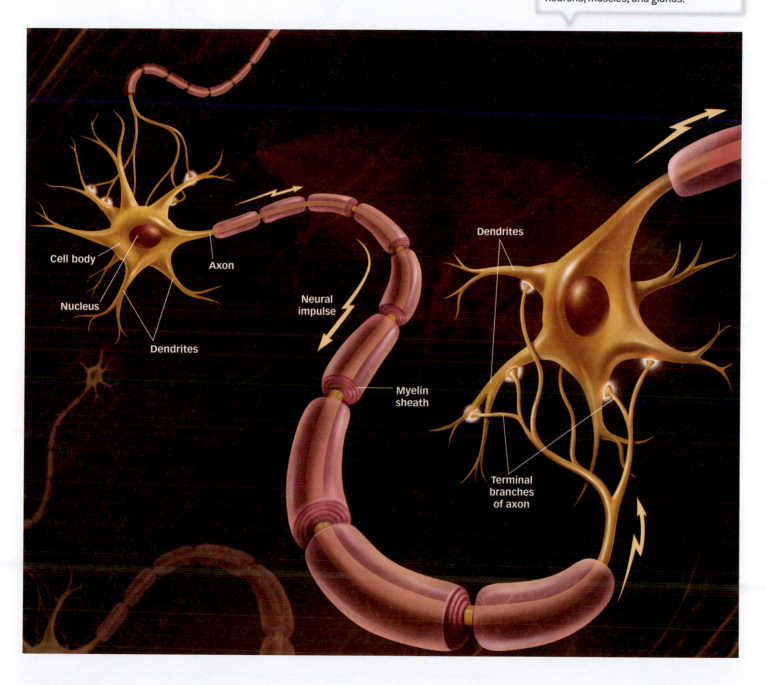

Cell body

Axon

Nucleus

Dendrites

Neural impulse

Myelin sheath

Dendrites

Terminal branches of axon

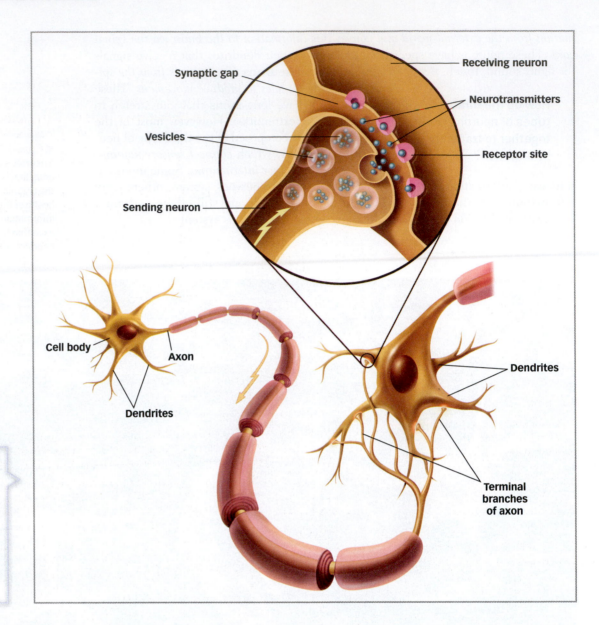

▶ Figure **3.2** **The Synapse**
The synapse is the junction between the dendrites of one neuron and the axon or cell body of another. Notice that neurons do not actually touch one another: There is a small space between them across which information is transmitted.

SUMMARY QUIZ [3.1]

1. Which of the following is *not* a function of a neuron?

   a. processing information

   b. communicating with other neurons

   c. processing nutrients

   d. sending messages to body organs and muscles

2. Signals from other neurons are received and relayed to the cell body by

   a. the nucleus.   b. dendrites.   c. axons.   d. glands.

3. Signals are transmitted from one neuron to another

   a. across a synapse.

   b. through a glial cell.

   c. by the myelin sheath.

   d. in the cell body.

4. Which type of neuron receives information from the external world and conveys this information to the brain via the spinal cord?

   a. sensory neuron   b. motor neuron   c. interneuron   d. axon

Information Processing in Neurons

Our thoughts, feelings, and actions depend on neural communication, but how does it happen? First, information has to travel inside the neuron—from the dendrite, to the cell body, to the axons. This information takes the form of an electrical signal that travels across the neuron. Then the signal has to be passed from one neuron, across the synapse, to another neuron. This information usually takes the form of chemical messengers. Let's look at both in more detail.

Electric Signaling: Conducting Information Within a Neuron

The neuron's cell membrane is porous, meaning that it has small holes ("pores") that allow small electrically charged molecules, called *ions,* to flow in and out of the cell. If you imagine using a strainer while you're preparing spaghetti, you'll get the idea. The mesh of the strainer cradles your dinner, but water can still seep in and out of it. Just as the flow of water out of a strainer enhances the quality of pasta, the flow of molecules across a cell membrane enhances the transmission of information in the nervous system.

The Resting Potential: The Origin of the Neuron's Electrical Properties

Neurons have a natural electric charge called the **resting potential,** which is *the difference in electric charge between the inside and outside of a neuron's cell membrane* (Kandel, 2000). The resting potential arises from the difference in concentrations of ions inside and outside the neuron's cell membrane (see **FIGURE 3.3a**). Ions can carry a positive (+) or a negative (−) charge. In the resting state, there are various positively and negatively charged ions on both sides of the membrane, but there is usually a higher concentration of positively charged potassium (K^+) ions inside the neuron's cell membrane than outside it. The concentration of K^+ inside and outside an axon

resting potential The difference in electric charge between the inside and outside of a neuron's cell membrane.

▼ Figure **3.3** **The Resting and Action Potentials** The resting and action potential neurons have a natural electric charge called a resting potential. Electric stimulation causes an action potential.

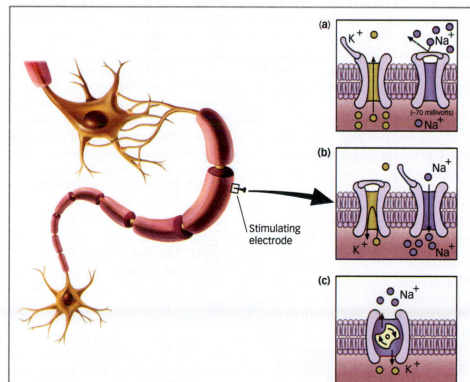

(a) The Resting Potential In the resting state, K^+ molecules flow freely across the cell membrane, but other molecules such as sodium (Na^+) are kept out, creating a difference in electric charge between the inside and outside of a neuron's cell membrane. The inside of the neuron has a charge of about −70 millivolts relative to the outside.

(b) The Action Potential Electric stimulation of the neuron shuts down the K^+ channels and opens the Na^+ channels, allowing Na^+ to rush in and increase the positive charge inside the axon relative to the outside, triggering the action potential.

(c) After the action potential, the imbalance in ions from the action potential is reversed by a chemical "pump" that moves Na^+ outside the cell and moves K^+ inside the cell. The neuron can now generate another action potential.

Stimulating electrode

action potential An electric signal that is conducted along a neruon's axon to a synapse.

refractory period The time following an action potential during which a new action potential cannot be initiated.

terminal buttons Knoblike structures that branch out from an axon.

neurotransmitters Chemicals that transmit information across the synapse to a receiving neuron's dendrites.

receptors Parts of the cell membrane that receive the neurotransmitter and initiate or prevent a new electric signal.

is controlled by channels in the axon membrane that allow molecules to flow in and out of the neuron. In the resting state, the channels that allow K⁺ molecules to flow freely across the cell membrane are open, while channels that allow the flow of larger negatively charged ions are generally closed. As K⁺ molecules flow out of the neuron through the open channels, this reduces the proportion of positively charged ions inside the neuron, leaving the inside of the neuron with a resting potential of about −70 millivolts relative to the outside. This degree of electric charge is roughly 1/200 of the charge of an AA battery (Stevens, 1971) and, just like in a battery, the resting potential creates the environment for a possible electrical impulse.

The Action Potential: Sending Signals Across the Neuron

The neuron maintains its resting potential most of the time. However, in the 1930s, biologists Alan Hodgkin and Andrew Huxley, while working with the giant squid axon, noticed that they could stimulate the axon with a brief electric shock, which resulted in the conduction of a large electric impulse down the length of the axon (Hausser, 2000; Hodgkin & Huxley, 1939). This electric impulse is called an **action potential,** which is *an electric signal that is conducted along the length of a neuron's axon to the synapse* (see **FIGURE 3.3***b*). The action potential occurs only when the electric shock reaches a certain level, or *threshold*. The action potential is *all or nothing*: Electric stimulation below the threshold fails to produce an action potential, whereas electric stimulation at or above the threshold always produces the action potential.

> **? Why is an action potential an all-or-nothing event?**

The action potential occurs when there is a change in the state of the axon's membrane channels. Remember, during the resting potential, only the K⁺ channels are open, leading to a net negative charge (−70 millivolts) inside the neuron relative to the outside. However, during an action potential, the K⁺ channels briefly shut down, and other channels that allow the flow of a *positively* charged ion, sodium (Na⁺), are opened. Na⁺ is typically much more concentrated outside the axon than inside. When the Na⁺ channels open, those positively charged ions flow inside, increasing the positive charge inside the axon relative to that outside. This flow of Na⁺ into the axon pushes the electric charge inside the neuron from negative (−70 millivolts) to positive (+40 millivolts).

The electrical current moves down the axon like a kind of chain reaction: As an action potential is generated at the beginning of the axon, it spreads a short distance, which generates an action potential at another nearby location, and so on, transmitting the charge down the length of the axon. The myelin sheath, which is made up of glial cells that coat and insulate the axon, facilitates the transmission of the action potential down the length of the axon. Myelin doesn't cover the entire axon; rather, it clumps around the axon with little break points between clumps, looking kind of like sausage links. These breakpoints are called the *nodes of Ranvier*, after French pathologist Louis-Antoine Ranvier, who discovered them (see **FIGURE 3.4**). When an electric current passes down the length of a myelinated axon, the charge seems to "jump" from node to node rather than having to traverse the entire axon (Poliak & Peles, 2003). This helps speed the flow of information down the axon.

After the action potential reaches its maximum, the membrane channels return to their original state, and K⁺ flows out until the axon returns to its resting potential (−70 millivolts). This leaves a lot of extra Na⁺ ions inside the axon and a lot of extra K⁺ ions outside the axon. During this period when the ions are imbalanced, the neuron cannot ini-

▼ Figure **3.4** **Myelin and Nodes of Ranvier** Myelin is formed by a type of glial cell, and it wraps around a neuron's axon to speed the transmission of the action potential along the length of the axon. Breaks in the myelin sheath are called the nodes of Ranvier. The electric impulse jumps from node to node, thereby speeding the conduction of information down the axon.

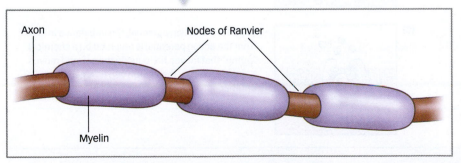

Axon

Nodes of Ranvier

Myelin

tiate another action potential, so it is said to be in a **refractory period,** *the time following an action potential during which a new action potential cannot be initiated.* The imbalance in ions is eventually reversed by an active chemical "pump" in the cell membrane that moves Na⁺ outside the axon and moves K⁺ inside the axon.

Chemical Signaling: Transmission Between Neurons

When the action potential reaches the end of an axon, you might think that it stops there. After all, the synaptic space between neurons means that the axon of one neuron and the neighboring neuron's dendrites do not actually touch one another. However, the electric charge of the action potential takes a form that can cross the relatively small synaptic gap by relying on a bit of chemistry.

? **How does a neuron communicate with another neuron?**

Axons usually end in **terminal buttons,** which are *knoblike structures that branch out from an axon.* A terminal button is filled with tiny *vesicles,* or "bags," that contain **neurotransmitters,** *chemicals that transmit information across the synapse to a receiving neuron's dendrites.* The dendrites of the receiving neuron contain **receptors,** *parts of the cell membrane that receive neurotransmitters and either initiate or prevent a new electric signal.*

The action potential travels down the length of the axon of the sending neuron, or *presynaptic neuron.* Once the action potential reaches the terminal buttons of the presynaptic neuron, it stimulates the release of neurotransmitters from vesicles into the synapse. These neurotransmitters float across the synapse and bind to receptor sites on a nearby dendrite of the receiving neuron, or *postsynaptic neuron.* A new electric potential is initiated in that neuron, which in turn may generate an action potential of its own. This process, called *synaptic transmission* (see **FIGURE 3.5**), allows neurons to communicate with one another.

What happens to the neurotransmitters left in the synapse after the chemical message is relayed to the postsynaptic neuron? Something must make neurotransmitters stop acting on neurons; otherwise, there'd be no end to the signals that they send. Neurotransmitters leave the synapse through three processes (Figure 3.5). First, neurotransmitters can be reabsorbed by the terminal buttons of the presynaptic neuron, a process called *reuptake.* Second, neurotransmitters can be broken down into their component molecules, a process called *deactivation.* Third, neurotransmitters can bind to receptor sites called *autoreceptors* on the presynaptic neuron. Autoreceptors detect how much of a neurotransmitter has been released into a synapse and signal the neuron to stop releasing the neurotransmitter when an excess is present.

▼ Figure **3.5** **Synaptic Transmission**
(1) The action potential travels down the axon and (2) stimulates the release of neurotransmitters from vesicles. (3) The neurotransmitters are released into the synapse, where they bind with receptor sites on a postsynaptic neuron. The neurotransmitters are cleared out of the synapse by (4) reuptake into the sending neuron, (5) being broken down in the synapse, or (6) binding to autoreceptors on the sending neuron.

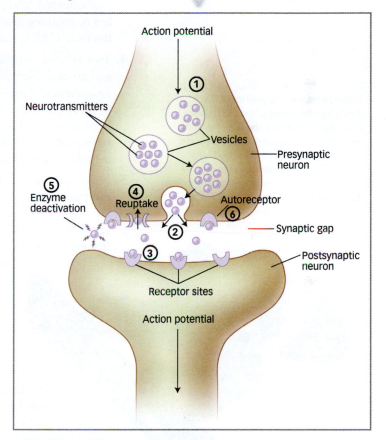

Types and Functions of Neurotransmitters

Now that you understand the basic process of how information moves from one neuron to another, let's refine things a bit. Today we know that some 60 chemicals play a role in transmitting information throughout the brain and body. How does a dendrite know which of the many neurotransmitters flooding into the synapse it should receive? Part of the answer is that neurotransmitters and receptor sites act like a lock-and-key system. Just as a particular key will only fit in a particular lock, so, too, will only some neurotransmitters bind to specific receptor sites on a dendrite. The molecular structure of the neurotransmitter must "fit" the molecular structure of the receptor site. Most neurotransmitters fit into a few major classes. We'll summarize those here, and you'll meet some of these neurotransmitters again, in later chapters.

1. *Acetylcholine* (ACh) is a neurotransmitter involved in a number of functions, including voluntary motor control. Acetylcholine is found in neurons of the brain and in the synapses where axons connect to muscles and body organs, such as the heart. Acetylcholine also contributes to the regulation of attention, learning, sleeping, dreaming, and memory (Gais & Born, 2004; Hasselmo, 2006; Wrenn et al., 2006). Alzheimer's disease, a medical condition involving severe memory impairments (Salmon & Bondi, 2009), is associated with the deterioration of ACh-producing neurons.

2. *Dopamine* is a neurotransmitter that regulates motor behavior, motivation, pleasure, and emotional arousal. Because of its association with the processing of motivation and pleasure, dopamine plays a role in drug addiction (Baler & Volkow, 2006). High levels of dopamine have been linked to schizophrenia (Winterer & Weinberger, 2004), while low levels have been linked to Parkinson's disease.

3. *Glutamate* is a major excitatory neurotransmitter in the brain, meaning that it enhances the transmission of information between neurons. *GABA* (gamma-aminobutyric acid), in contrast, is the primary inhibitory neurotransmitter in the brain, meaning that it tends to stop the firing of neurons. Too much glutamate, or too little GABA, can cause neurons to become overactive, causing seizures.

4. Two related neurotransmitters, *norepinephrine* and *serotonin*, influence mood and arousal. Norepinephrine is particularly involved in vigilance, or a heightened awareness of dangers in the environment (Ressler & Nemeroff, 1999). Serotonin is involved in the regulation of sleep and wakefulness, eating, and aggressive behavior (Dayan & Huys, 2009; Kroeze & Roth, 1998). Because both neurotransmitters affect mood and arousal, low levels of each have been implicated in mood disorders (Tamminga et al., 2002).

5. *Endorphins* are chemicals that act within the pain pathways and emotion centers of the brain to help dull the experience of pain and elevate moods (Keefe et al., 2001). The "runner's high" experienced by many athletes as they push their bodies to painful limits of endurance can be explained by the release of endorphins in the brain (Boecker et al., 2008).

> **?** How do neurotransmitters create the feeling of "runner's high"?

Each of these neurotransmitters affects thoughts, feelings, and behavior in different ways, so normal functioning involves a delicate balance of each. Even a slight imbalance—too much of one neurotransmitter or not enough of another—can dramatically affect behavior. People who smoke, drink alcohol, or take drugs, legal or not, are altering the balance of neurotransmitters in their brains. The drug LSD, for example, is structurally very similar to serotonin, so it binds very easily with serotonin receptors in the brain, producing similar effects on thoughts, feelings, or behavior. In the next section, we'll look at how some drugs are able to "trick" receptor sites in just this way.

How Drugs Mimic Neurotransmitters

Many drugs that affect the nervous system operate by increasing, interfering with, or mimicking the manufacture or function of neurotransmitters (Cooper, Bloom, & Roth, 2003; Sarter, 2006). **Agonists** are *drugs that increase the action of a neurotransmitter.* **Antagonists** are *drugs that block the function of a neurotransmitter.*

Shaun White won the gold medal in men's snowboarding at the Vancouver 2010 Olympics. When athletes like White engage in these kinds of extreme sports, they may experience subjective highs that result from the release of endorphins—chemical messengers acting in emotion and pain centers that elevate mood and dull the experience of pain.

REUTERS/MIKE BLAKE

Some drugs have a chemical structure so similar to a neurotransmitter that the drug is able to bind to receptors that are "keyed" to that neurotransmitter. If, by binding to a receptor, a drug mimics the neurotransmitter, it is an agonist; if it blocks the action of the neurotransmitter, it is an antagonist. For example, morphine is a drug that binds to endorphin receptors in the brain. The result is a calming and pleasurable effect, similar to that produced by the endorphins themselves. Thus, morphine is an agonist for the endorphins.

Other drugs alter a step in the production or release of the neurotransmitter. For example, a drug called L-dopa has been developed to treat Parkinson's disease, a

> **How does giving patients L-dopa alleviate symptoms of Parkinson's disease?**

movement disorder characterized by tremors and difficulty initiating movement and caused by the loss of neurons that use the neurotransmitter dopamine. Dopamine is created in neurons by a modification of a common molecule called L-dopa. Ingesting L-dopa will spur the surviving neurons to produce more dopamine. In other words, L-dopa acts as an agonist for dopamine. The use of L-dopa has been reasonably successful in the alleviation of Parkinson's disease symptoms (Muenter & Tyce, 1971; Schapira et al., 2009). However, the effectiveness of L-dopa typically decreases when used over a long period, so that many longtime users experience some symptoms of the disease. The actor Michael J. Fox, who was diagnosed with Parkinson's disease in 1991 and takes L-dopa, describes in his recent memoir the simple act of trying to brush his teeth:

> Grasping the toothpaste is nothing compared to the effort it takes to coordinate the two-handed task of wrangling the toothbrush and strangling out a line of paste onto the bristles. By now, my right hand has started up again, rotating at the wrist in a circular motion, perfect for what I'm about to do. My left hand guides my right hand up to my mouth, and once the back of the Oral-B touches the inside of my upper lip, I let go. It's like releasing the tension on a slingshot and compares favorably to the most powerful state-of-the-art electric toothbrush on the market. With no off switch, stopping means seizing my right wrist with my left hand, forcing it down to the sink basin, and shaking the brush loose as though disarming a knife-wielding attacker. (Fox, 2009, pp. 2–3)

Some unexpected evidence also highlights the central role of dopamine in regulating movement and motor performance. In 1982, six people ranging in age from 25 to 45 from the San Francisco Bay Area were admitted to emergency rooms with a bizarre set of symptoms: paralysis, drooling, and an inability to speak (Langston, 1995). A diagnosis of advanced Parkinson's disease was made, as these symptoms are consistent with the later stages of this degenerative disease. It was unusual for six fairly young people to come down with advanced Parkinson's at the same time in the same geographical area. In fact, none of the patients had Parkinson's, but they were all heroin addicts. These patients thought they were ingesting a synthetic form of heroin (called MPPP), but instead they had ingested a close derivative called MPTP, which unfortunately had the effects of destroying dopamine-producing neurons in an area of the brain crucial for motor performance. The patients experienced a remarkable recovery after they were given L-dopa. Just as L-dopa acts as an agonist by enhancing the production of dopamine, drugs such as MPTP act as antagonists by destroying dopamine-producing neurons.

For another example, think back to David in the opening vignette: His paranoid hallucinations were induced by his crystal meth habit. *Methamphetamine* affects pathways for dopamine, serotonin, and norepinephrine, making it difficult to interpret exactly how the drug works. But the combination of its agonist and antagonist effects alters the functions of neurotransmitters that help us perceive and interpret visual images. In David's case, it led to hallucinations that called his eyesight, and his sanity, into question. Other drugs—including prescription medications, street

Michael J. Fox vividly described his struggles with Parkinson's disease in his 2009 memoir. Fox's visibility has helped to increase awareness of the disease and perhaps also has resulted in greater efforts directed toward finding a cure.

agonists Drugs that increase the action of a neurotransmitter.

antagonists Drugs that block the function of a neurotransmitter.

drugs, and "legal" drugs such as caffeine, tobacco, and alcohol—also work by altering the actions of neurotransmitters. In later chapters, you'll read about more specific examples and the particular ways in which they alter brain function and influence behavior, emotions, and perceptions.

SUMMARY QUIZ [3.2]

1. The gap between the axon of one neuron and the dendrites of another is called the
   a. glial cell.   b. interneuron.   c. myelin sheath.   d. synapse.

2. An electric signal that is conducted along the length of a neuron's axon to the synapse is called
   a. a resting potential.   c. a node of Ranvier.
   b. an action potential.   d. an ion.

3. The chemicals that transmit information across the synapse to a receiving neuron's dendrites are called
   a. vesicles.   c. postsynaptic neurons.
   b. terminal buttons.   d. neurotransmitters.

The Organization of the Nervous System

We've seen how individual neurons communicate with each other. What's the bigger picture? Neurons work by forming circuits and pathways in the brain, which in turn influence circuits and pathways in other areas of the body. The **nervous system** *is an interacting network of neurons that conveys electrochemical information throughout the body.*

There are two major divisions of the nervous system: the central nervous system and the peripheral nervous system (see **FIGURE 3.6**). The **central nervous system (CNS)** *is composed of the brain and spinal cord.* It receives sensory information from the external world, processes and coordinates this information, and sends commands to the skeletal and muscular systems for action. The **peripheral nervous system (PNS)** *connects the central nervous system to the body's organs and muscles.* Let's look at each more closely.

The Peripheral Nervous System

The peripheral nervous system is composed of two major subdivisions, the somatic nervous system and the autonomic nervous system (see Figure 3.6). The **somatic nervous system** *is a set of nerves that conveys information into and out of the central nervous system.* Humans have conscious control over this system and use it to perceive, think, and coordinate their behaviors. For example, reaching for your morning cup of coffee involves the elegantly orchestrated activities of the somatic nervous system: Information from the receptors in your eyes travels to your brain, registering that a cup is on the table; signals from your brain travel to the muscles in your arm and hand; feedback from those muscles tells your brain that the cup has been grasped; and so on.

In contrast, the **autonomic nervous system (ANS)** *is a set of nerves that carries involuntary and automatic commands that control blood vessels, body organs, and glands.* As suggested by its name, this system works on its own to regulate bodily systems, largely outside of conscious control. The ANS has two major subdivisions, the sympathetic nervous system and the parasympathetic nervous system. Each exerts a dif-

nervous system An interacting network of neurons that conveys electrochemical information throughout the body.

central nervous system (CNS) The part of the nervous system that is composed of the brain and spinal cord.

peripheral nervous system (PNS) The part of the nervous system that connects the central nervous system to the body's organs and muscles.

somatic nervous system A set of nerves that conveys information into and out of the central nervous system.

autonomic nervous system (ANS) A set of nerves that carries involuntary and automatic commands that control blood vessels, body organs, and glands.

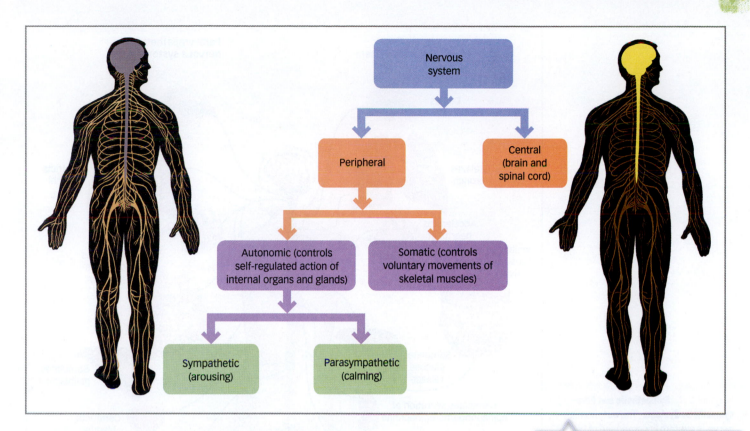

▲ Figure 3.6 **The Human Nervous System**
The nervous system is organized into the
peripheral and central nervous systems.
The peripheral nervous system is further
divided into the autonomic and somatic
nervous systems

ferent type of control on the body. The **sympathetic nervous system** is *a set of nerves that prepares the body for action in threatening situations*; the **parasympathetic nervous system** *helps the body return to a normal resting state* (see **FIGURE 3.7**). For example, imagine that you are walking alone late at night and frightened by footsteps behind you in a dark alley. Your sympathetic nervous system kicks into action at this point: It dilates your pupils to let in more light, increases your heart rate and respiration to pump more oxygen to muscles, diverts blood flow to your brain and muscles, and activates sweat glands to cool your body. To conserve energy, the sympathetic

What triggers the increase in your heart rate when you feel threatened?

nervous system inhibits salivation and bowel movements, suppresses the body's immune responses, and suppresses responses to pain and injury. The sum total of these fast, automatic responses is that they increase the likelihood that you can escape. Once you get away (or realize there is no threat), your body doesn't need to remain on red alert. Now the parasympathetic nervous system kicks in to reverse the effects of the sympathetic nervous system and return your body to its normal state. Thus, the parasympathetic nervous system constricts your pupils, slows your heart rate and respiration, diverts blood flow to your digestive system, and decreases activity in your sweat glands.

The Central Nervous System

Compared with the many divisions of the peripheral nervous system, the central nervous system may seem simple. After all, it has only two elements: the brain and the spinal cord. But those two elements are ultimately responsible for most of what we do as humans. The brain supports the most complex perceptual, motor, emotional, and cognitive functions of the nervous system. The spinal cord branches down from the brain to relay commands to the body.

sympathetic nervous system A set of nerves that prepares the body for action in threatening situations.

parasympathetic nervous system A set of nerves that helps the body return to a normal resting state.

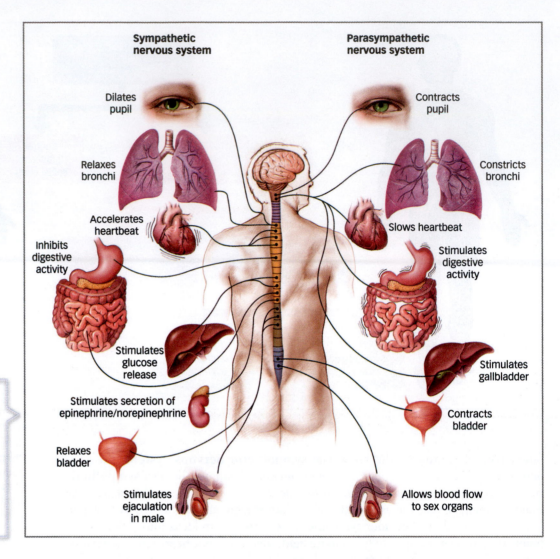

▶ Figure **3.7** **Sympathetic and Parasympathetic Systems** The autonomic nervous system is composed of two subsystems that complement each other. Activation of the sympathetic nervous system produces several aspects of arousal, whereas the parasympathetic nervous system returns the body to its normal resting state.

spinal reflexes Simple pathways in the nervous system that rapidly generate muscle contractions.

The spinal cord often seems like the brain's poor relation: The brain gets all the glory and the spinal cord just hangs around, carrying out the brain's orders. But for some very basic behaviors, the spinal cord doesn't need input from the brain at all. Connections between the sensory inputs and motor neurons in the spinal cord mediate **spinal reflexes,** *simple pathways in the nervous system that rapidly generate muscle contractions.* If you touch a hot stove, the sensory neurons that register pain send inputs directly into the spinal cord (see **FIGURE 3.8**). Through just a few synaptic connections within the spinal cord, interneurons relay these sensory inputs to motor neurons that connect to your arm muscles and direct you to quickly retract your hand.

? **What important functions does the spinal cord perform on its own?**

More elaborate tasks require the collaboration of the spinal cord and the brain. The peripheral nervous system communicates with the central nervous system through nerves that conduct sensory information into the brain, carry commands out of the brain, or both. The brain sends commands for voluntary movement through the spinal cord to motor neurons, whose axons project out to skeletal muscles and send the message to contract. Damage to the spinal cord severs the connection from the brain to the sensory and motor neurons that are essential to sensory perception and movement. The location of the spinal injury often determines the extent of the

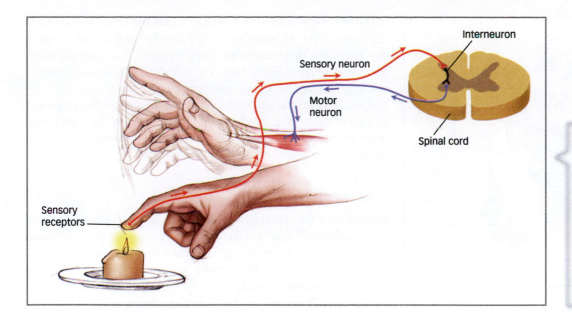

Interneuron

Sensory neuron

Motor neuron

Spinal cord

Sensory receptors

◀ Figure **3.8** **The Pain Withdrawal Reflex** Many actions of the central nervous system don't require the brain's input. For example, withdrawing from pain is a reflexive activity controlled by the spinal cord. Painful sensations (such as a pin jabbing your finger) travel directly to the spinal cord via sensory neurons, which then issue an immediate command to motor neurons to retract the hand.

abilities that are lost. Patients with damage at a particular level of the spinal cord lose sensations of touch and pain in body parts below the level of the injury as well as a loss of motor control of the muscles in the same areas. A spinal injury higher up the cord usually predicts a much poorer prognosis, such as quadriplegia (the loss of sensation and motor control over all limbs), breathing through a respirator, and lifelong immobility. On a brighter note, researchers are making progress in understanding the nature of spinal cord injuries and how to treat them by focusing on how the brain changes in response to injury (Blesch & Tuszynski, 2009; Dunlop, 2008), a process that is closely related to the concept of brain plasticity that we will examine later in this chapter (p. 76).

SUMMARY QUIZ [3.3]

1. The _____ automatically controls the organs of the body.
   a. autonomic nervous system   c. sympathetic nervous system
   b. parasympathetic nervous system d. somatic nervous system

2. When you feel threatened, your _____ nervous system prepares you to either fight or run away.
   a. central   b. somatic   c. sympathetic   d. parasympathetic

Structure of the Brain

Right now, your neurons and glial cells are busy humming away, giving you potentially brilliant ideas, consciousness, and feelings. But which neurons in which parts of the brain control which functions? To answer that question, neuroscientists first had to find a way of describing the brain. It can be helpful to talk about areas of the brain from "bottom to top," noting how the different regions are specialized for different kinds of tasks. In general, simpler functions are performed at the "lower levels" of the brain, whereas more complex functions are performed at successively "higher" levels (see **FIGURE 3.9**). Or, as you'll see shortly, the brain can also be approached in a "side-by-side" fashion: Although each side of the brain is roughly analogous, one half

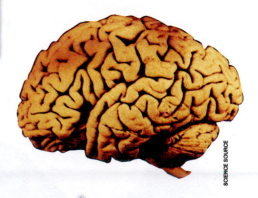

SCIENCE SOURCE

The human brain weighs only three pounds and isn't much to look at, but its accomplishments are staggering.

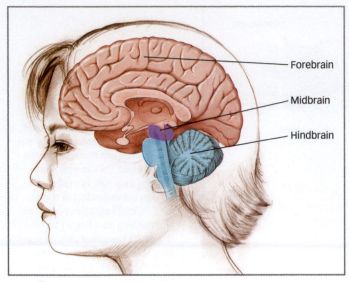

of the brain specializes in some tasks that the other half doesn't. Although these divisions make it easier to understand areas of the brain and their functions, keep in mind that none of these structures or areas in the brain can act alone: They are all part of one big, interacting, interdependent whole.

Let's look first at the divisions of the brain and the responsibilities of each part, moving from the bottom to the top. Using this view, we can divide the brain into three parts: the hindbrain, the midbrain, and the forebrain (see Figure 3.9).

The Hindbrain

If you follow the spinal cord from your tailbone to where it enters your skull, you'll find it difficult to determine where your spinal cord ends and your brain begins. That's because the spinal cord is continuous with the **hindbrain**, *an area of the brain that coordinates information coming into and out of the spinal cord*. The hindbrain, which looks like a stalk on which the rest of the brain sits, controls the most basic functions of life: respiration, alertness, and motor skills. There are three anatomical structures that make up the hindbrain: the medulla, the cerebellum, and the pons (see **FIGURE 3.10**).

The **medulla** is *an extension of the spinal cord into the skull that coordinates heart rate, circulation, and respiration.* Inside the medulla is a small cluster of neurons called the **reticular formation,** which *regulates sleep, wakefulness, and levels of arousal.* In one early experiment, researchers stimulated the reticular formation of a sleeping cat, causing the animal to awaken almost instantaneously and remain alert. Conversely, severing the connections between the reticular formation and the rest of the brain caused the animal to lapse into an irreversible coma (Moruzzi & Magoun, 1949). The reticular formation maintains the same delicate balance between alertness and unconsciousness in humans. In fact, many general anesthetics work by reducing activity in the reticular formation, rendering the patient unconscious.

▲ Figure **3.9** **The Major Divisions of the Brain** The brain can be organized into three parts, moving from the bottom to the top, from simpler functions to more complex ones: the hindbrain, the midbrain, and the forebrain.

▶ Figure **3.10** **The Hindbrain** The hindbrain coordinates information coming into and out of the spinal cord and controls the basic functions of life. It includes the medulla, the reticular formation, the cerebellum, and the pons.

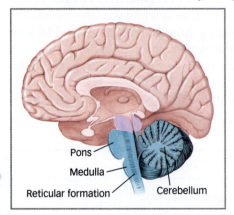

Olympic medalist Apolo Anton Ohno relies on his cerebellum to execute graceful, coordinated motions on the ice. The cerebellum, part of the hindbrain, helps direct the smooth action of a variety of motor behaviors.

Behind the medulla is the **cerebellum,** *a large structure of the hindbrain that controls fine motor skills. Cerebellum* is Latin for "little brain," and the structure does look like a small replica of the brain. The cerebellum orchestrates the proper sequence of movements when we ride a bike, play the piano, or maintain balance while walking and running. It contributes to the "fine tuning" of behavior, smoothing our actions to allow their graceful execution rather than initiating the actions (Smetacek, 2002). The initiation of behavior involves other areas of the brain; as you'll recall, different brain systems interact and are interdependent with one another.

? Which part of the brain helps to orchestrate movements that keep you steady on your bike?

The last major area of the hindbrain is the **pons,** *a structure that relays information from the cerebellum to the rest of the brain. Pons* means "bridge" in Latin. Although

AP PHOTO/KEVORK DJANSEZIAN

the detailed functions of the pons remain poorly understood, it essentially acts as a "relay station" or bridge between the cerebellum and other structures in the brain.

The Midbrain

Sitting on top of the hindbrain is the *midbrain,* which is relatively small in humans. As you can see in **FIGURE 3.11,** the midbrain contains two main structures: the *tectum* and the *tegmentum*. These structures help orient an organism in the environment and guide movement toward or away from stimuli. For example, when you're studying in a quiet room and you hear a *click* behind and to the right of you, your body will swivel and orient to the direction of the sound; this is your tectum in action. The midbrain may be relatively small, but it's important. In fact, you could survive if you had only a hindbrain and a midbrain. The structures in the hindbrain would take care of all the bodily functions necessary to sustain life, and the structures in the midbrain would orient you toward or away from pleasurable or threatening stimuli in the environment. But this wouldn't be much of a life. To understand where the abilities that make us fully human come from, we need to consider the last division of the brain.

hindbrain An area of the brain that coordinates information coming into and out of the spinal cord.

medulla An extension of the spinal cord into the skull that coordinates heart rate, circulation, and respiration.

reticular formation A brain structure that regulates sleep, wakefulness, and levels of arousal.

cerebellum A large structure of the hindbrain that controls fine motor skills.

pons A brain structure that relays information from the cerebellum to the rest of the brain.

subcortical structures Areas of the forebrain housed under the cerebral cortex near the very center of the brain.

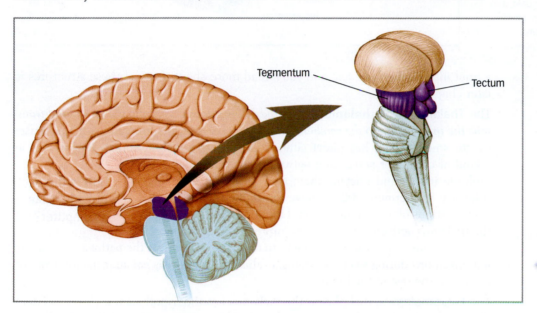

Tegmentum — Tectum

◂ Figure **3.11** **The Midbrain** The midbrain is important for orientation and movement. It includes structures such as the tectum and tegmentum.

The Forebrain

When you appreciate the beauty of a poem, detect the sarcasm in a friend's remark, plan to go skiing next winter, or notice the faint glimmer of sadness on a loved one's face, you are enlisting the forebrain. The *forebrain* is the highest level of the brain—literally and figuratively—and controls complex cognitive, emotional, sensory, and motor functions (see **FIGURE 3.12**). The forebrain itself is divided into two main sections: the cerebral cortex and the subcortical structures.

Subcortical Structures

The **subcortical structures** are *areas of the forebrain housed under the cerebral cortex near the very center of the brain.* The subcortical structures are nestled deep inside the brain, where they are quite protected. If you imagine sticking an index finger in each of your ears and pushing inward until they touch, that's about where you'd find the subcortical structures, including the thalamus, hypothalamus, pituitary gland, hippocampus, amygdala, and basal ganglia. Each of these subcortical structures plays an important role in relaying information throughout the brain, as well as performing specific tasks that allow us to think, feel, and behave as humans. Here, we'll give you

► Figure **3.12 The Forebrain** The forebrain is the highest level of the brain and is critical for complex cognitive, emotional, sensory, and motor functions. The forebrain is divided into two parts: the cerebral cortex and the underlying subcortical structures. These include the thalamus, hypothalamus, pituitary gland, hippocampus, amygdala, and basal ganglia. The corpus callosum (see page 74) connects the two hemispheres of the brain.

a brief introduction to each, and you'll read more about many of these structures in later chapters.

The Thalamus. The **thalamus** *relays and filters information from the senses and transmits the information to the cerebral cortex*. It receives inputs from all the major senses except smell, which has direct connections to the cerebral cortex. It also acts as a kind of computer server in a networked system, taking in multiple inputs and relaying them to a variety of locations (Guillery & Sherman, 2002). However, unlike the mechanical operations of a computer—"send input A to location B"— the thalamus actively filters sensory information, giving more weight to some inputs and less weight to others. It also closes the pathways of incoming sensations during sleep, providing a valuable function by *not* allowing information to pass to the rest of the brain.

How is the thalamus like a computer?

The Hypothalamus. Right below the thalamus lies the hypothalamus (*hypo-* is Greek for "under). The **hypothalamus** *regulates body temperature, hunger, thirst, and sexual behavior*. For example, lesions to some areas of the hypothalamus result in overeating, whereas lesions to other areas leave an animal with no desire at all for food (Berthoud & Morrison, 2008).

The Pituitary Gland. Below the hypothalamus lies the **pituitary gland,** *the "master gland" of the body's hormone-producing system, which releases hormones that direct the functions of many other glands in the body*. The hypothalamus sends hormonal signals to the pituitary gland, which in turn sends hormonal signals to other glands to control stress, digestive activities, and reproductive processes. For example, when we sense a threat, sensory neurons send signals to the hypothalamus, which stimulates the pituitary gland to release a specific hormone (called adrenocorticotropic hormone, or ACTH) that, in turn, stimulates the adrenal glands (above the kidneys) to activate the sympathetic nervous system (Selye & Fortier, 1950). As you read earlier in this chapter, the sympathetic nervous system prepares the body to either meet the threat head-on or flee from the situation.

The Hippocampus. The **hippocampus** (from the Latin for "sea horse," due to its shape) is *critical for creating new memories and integrating them into a network of knowledge so that they can be stored indefinitely in other parts of the cerebral cortex (see*

thalamus A subcortical structure that relays and filters information from the senses and transmits the information to the cerebral cortex.

hypothalamus A subcortical structure that regulates body temperature, hunger, thirst, and sexual behavior.

pituitary gland The "master gland" of the body's hormone-producing system, which releases hormones that direct the functions of many other glands in the body.

hippocampus A structure critical for creating new memories and integrating them into a network of knowledge so that they can be stored indefinitely in other parts of the cerebral cortex.

Figure 3.12). Patients with damage to the hippocampus can acquire new information and keep it in awareness for a few seconds, but as soon as they are distracted, they forget the information and the experience that produced it (Scoville & Milner, 1957; Squire, 2009). This kind of disruption is limited to everyday memory for facts and events that we can bring to consciousness; memory of learned habitual routines or emotional reactions remains intact (Squire, Knowlton, & Musen, 1993). As an example, people with damage to the hippocampus can remember how to drive and talk, but they cannot recall where they have recently driven or a conversation they have just had. You will read more about the hippocampus and its role in creating, storing, and combining memories in Chapter 6.

The Amygdala. Located at the tip of each horn of the hippocampus is the amygdala (named for the Latin word for "almond," also because of its shape). The **amygdala**

> ? **Why are you likely to remember details of a traumatic event?**

plays a central role in many emotional processes, particularly the formation of emotional memories (Aggleton, 1992). When we are in emotionally arousing situations, the amygdala stimulates the hippocampus to remember many details surrounding the situation (Kensinger & Schacter, 2005). For example, people who lived through the terrorist attacks of September 11, 2001, remember vivid details about where they were, what they were doing, and how they felt when they heard the news, even years later (Hirst et al., 2009). We'll have more to say about the amygdala's role in emotion and motivated behavior in Chapter 8. For now, keep in mind that a group of neurons the size of a lima bean buried deep in your brain help you to laugh, weep, or shriek in fright when the circumstances call for it.

The Basal Ganglia. Located near the thalamus and hypothalamus are the **basal ganglia,** *a set of subcortical structures that directs intentional movements.* The basal ganglia receive input from the cerebral cortex and send outputs to the motor centers in the brain stem (see Figure 3.12). One part of the basal ganglia, the *striatum,* is involved in the control of posture and movement. As we saw in the excerpt from Michael J. Fox's book, patients who suffer from Parkinson's disease typically show symptoms of uncontrollable shaking and sudden jerks of the limbs and are unable to initiate a sequence of movements to achieve a specific goal. This happens because the dopamine-producing neurons in the substantia nigra (found in the tegmentum of the midbrain) have become damaged (Dauer & Przedborski, 2003). The undersupply of dopamine then affects the striatum in the basal ganglia, which in turn leads to the visible behavioral symptoms of Parkinson's.

The Cerebral Cortex

Our tour of the brain has taken us from the very small (neurons) to the somewhat bigger (major divisions of the brain) to the very large: the cerebral cortex. The **cerebral cortex** is *the outermost layer of the brain, visible to the naked eye, and divided into two hemispheres.* The highest level of the brain, the cortex is responsible for the most complex aspects of perception, emotion, movement, and thought (Fuster, 2003). It sits over the rest of the brain, like a mushroom cap shielding the underside and stem, and it is the wrinkled surface you see when looking at the brain with the naked eye. The cerebral cortex occupies roughly the area of a newspaper page. Fitting that much cortex into a human skull is a tough task. But if you crumple a sheet of newspaper, you'll see that the same surface area now fits compactly into a much smaller space. The cortex, with its wrinkles and folds, holds a lot of brainpower in a relatively small package that fits comfortably inside the human skull.

amygdala A part of the limbic system that plays a central role in many emotional processes, particularly the formation of emotional memories.

basal ganglia A set of subcortical structures that directs intentional movements.

cerebral cortex The outermost layer of the brain, divided into two hemispheres.

> Crumpling a newspaper allows the same amount of surface area to fit into a much smaller space, just like the wrinkles and folds in the cortex allow a great deal of brain power to fit inside the human skull.

DONNA RANIERI

corpus callosum A thick band of nerve fibers that connects large areas of the cerebral cortex on each side of the brain and supports communication of information across the hemispheres.

occipital lobe A region of the cerebral cortex that processes visual information.

parietal lobe A region of the cerebral cortex whose functions include processing information about touch.

temporal lobe A region of the cerebral cortex responsible for hearing and language.

The functions of the cerebral cortex can be understood at three levels: the separation of the cortex into two hemispheres, the functions of each hemisphere, and the role of specific cortical areas.

1. **Organization Across Hemispheres.** The first level of organization divides the cortex into the left and right hemispheres. The two hemispheres are more or less symmetrical in their appearance and, to some extent, in their functions. However, each hemisphere controls the functions of the opposite side of the body. This is called *contralateral control*, meaning that your right cerebral hemisphere perceives stimuli from and controls movements on the left side of your body, whereas your left cerebral hemisphere perceives stimuli from and controls movement on the right side of your body (see **FIGURE 3.13**).

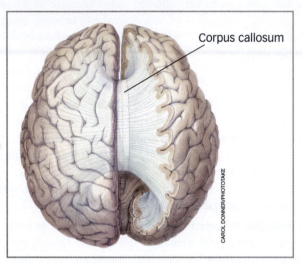

Corpus callosum

CAROL DONNER/PHOTOTAKE

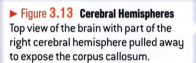

▶ Figure **3.13** **Cerebral Hemispheres** Top view of the brain with part of the right cerebral hemisphere pulled away to expose the corpus callosum.

The cerebral hemispheres are connected to each other by bundles of axons that make communication between parallel areas of the cortex in each half possible. The largest of these bundles is the **corpus callosum,** which *connects large areas of the cerebral cortex on each side of the brain and supports communication of information across the hemispheres*. This means that information received in the right hemisphere, for example, can pass across the corpus callosum and be registered, virtually instantaneously, in the left hemisphere.

2. **Organization Within Hemispheres.** The second level of organization in the cerebral cortex distinguishes the functions of the different regions within each hemisphere of the brain. Each hemisphere of the cerebral cortex is divided into four areas, or *lobes*: From back to front, these are the occipital lobe, the parietal lobe, the temporal lobe, and the frontal lobe, as shown in **FIGURE 3.14.** We'll examine the functions of these lobes in more detail later; for now, here's a brief overview of the main functions of each lobe.

The **occipital lobe,** located at the back of the cerebral cortex, *processes visual information*. Sensory receptors in the eyes send information to the thalamus, which in turn sends information to the primary areas of the occipital lobe, where simple features of the stimulus are extracted, such as the location and orientation of an object's edges (see p. 104 in Chapter 4 for more details). These features are then processed further in the occipital cortex, leading to comprehension of what's being seen. Damage to the primary visual areas of the occipital lobe can leave a person with partial or complete blindness. Information still enters the eyes, but without the ability to process and make sense of the information in the cerebral cortex, the information is as good as lost (Zeki, 2001).

▼ Figure **3.14** **Cerebral Cortex and Lobes** The four major lobes of the cerebral cortex are the occipital lobe, the parietal lobe, the temporal lobe, and the frontal lobe.

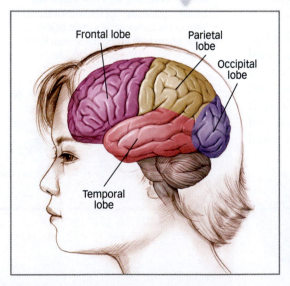

Frontal lobe

Parietal lobe

Occipital lobe

Temporal lobe

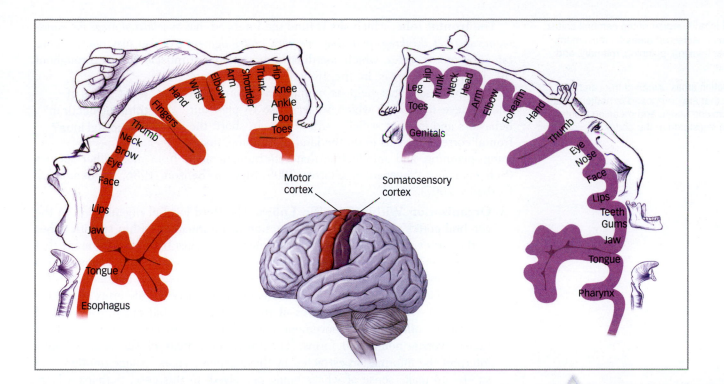

THE BRITISH MUSEUM, NATURAL HISTORY

▲ Figure **3.15** **Somatosensory and Motor Cortices** The motor cortex, a strip of brain tissue in the frontal lobe, represents and controls different skin and body areas on the contralateral side of the body. Directly behind the motor cortex, in the parietal lobe, lies the somatosensory cortex. Like the motor cortex, the somatosensory cortex represents skin areas of particular parts on the contralateral side of the body.

The homunculus is a rendering of the body in which each part is shown in proportion to how much of the somatosensory cortex is devoted to it.

The **parietal lobe,** located in front of the occipital lobe, carries out functions that include *processing information about touch.* The parietal lobe contains the *somatosensory cortex,* a strip of brain tissue running from the top of the brain down to the sides (see **FIGURE 3.15**). Within each hemisphere, the somatosensory cortex represents the skin areas on the contralateral surface of the body. Each part of the somatosensory cortex maps onto a particular part of the body. If a body area is more sensitive, a larger part of the somatosensory cortex is devoted to it. For example, the part of the somatosensory cortex that corresponds to the lips and tongue is larger than the area corresponding to the feet. The somatosensory cortex can be illustrated as a distorted figure, called a *homunculus* ("little man"), in which the body parts are rendered according to how much of the somatosensory cortex is devoted to them (Penfield & Rasmussen, 1950). Directly in front of the somatosensory cortex, in the frontal lobe, is a parallel strip of brain tissue called the *motor cortex.* As with the somatosensory cortex, different parts of the motor cortex correspond to different body parts. The motor cortex initiates voluntary movements and sends messages to the basal ganglia, cerebellum, and spinal cord. The motor and somatosensory cortices, then, are like sending and receiving areas of the cerebral cortex, taking in information and sending out commands.

The **temporal lobe,** located on the lower side of each hemisphere, is *responsible for hearing and language.* The *primary auditory cortex* in the temporal lobe is analogous to the somatosensory cortex in the parietal lobe and the primary visual areas of the occipital lobe—it receives sensory information from the ears based on the frequencies of sounds (Recanzone & Sutter, 2008). Secondary areas of the temporal lobe then process the information into meaningful units, such as speech and words. The temporal lobe also houses the visual association areas, which interpret the meaning of visual stimuli and help us recognize common objects in the environment (Martin, 2007).

frontal lobe A region of the cerebral cortex that has specialized areas for movement, abstract thinking, planning, memory, and judgment.

association areas Areas of the cerebral cortex that are composed of neurons that help provide sense and meaning to information registered in the cortex.

The **frontal lobe,** which sits behind the forehead, has *specialized areas for movement, abstract thinking, planning, memory, and judgment.* As you just read, it contains the motor cortex, which coordinates movements of muscle groups throughout the body. Other areas in the frontal lobe coordinate thought processes that help us manipulate information and retrieve memories, which we can use to plan our behaviors and interact socially with others. In short, the frontal cortex allows us to do the kind of thinking, imagining, planning, and anticipating that sets humans apart from most other species (Schoenemann, Sheenan, & Glotzer, 2005; Stuss & Benson, 1986; Suddendorf & Corballis, 2007).

> **?** What types of thinking occur in the frontal lobe?

3. **Organization Within Specific Lobes.** The third level of organization in the cerebral cortex involves the representation of information within specific lobes in the cortex. There is a hierarchy of processing stages from primary areas that handle fine details of information all the way up to **association areas,** which are *composed of neurons that help provide sense and meaning to information registered in the cortex.* For example, neurons in the primary visual cortex are highly specialized—some detect features of the environment that are in a horizontal orientation, others detect movement, and still others process information about human versus nonhuman forms. The association areas of the occipital lobe interpret the information extracted by these primary areas—shape, motion, and so on—to make sense of what's being perceived; in this case, perhaps a large cat leaping toward your face. Neurons in the association areas are usually less specialized and more flexible than neurons in the primary areas. As such, they can be shaped by learning and experience to do their job more effectively. This kind of shaping of neurons by environmental forces allows the brain flexibility, or "plasticity," our next topic.

Brain Plasticity

The cerebral cortex may seem like a fixed structure, one big sheet of neurons designed to help us make sense of our external world. Remarkably, though, sensory cortices are not fixed. They can adapt to changes in sensory inputs, a quality researchers call *plasticity* (i.e., "the ability to be molded"). As an example, if you lose your middle finger in an accident, the part of the somatosensory area that represents that finger

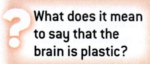

> **?** What does it mean to say that the brain is plastic?

is initially unresponsive (Kaas, 1991). After all, there's no longer any sensory input going from that location to that part of the brain. You might expect the "left middle finger neurons" of the somatosensory cortex to wither away. However, over time, that area in the somatosensory cortex becomes responsive to stimulation of the fingers *adjacent* to the missing finger. The brain is plastic: Functions that were assigned to certain areas of the brain may be capable of being reassigned to other areas of the brain to accommodate changing input from the environment (Feldman, 2009). This suggests that sensory inputs "compete" for representation in each cortical area. (See the Real World box for a striking illustration of "phantom limbs.")

Plasticity doesn't occur only to compensate for missing digits or limbs, however. An extraordinary amount of stimulation of one finger can result in that finger "taking over" the representation of the part of the cortex that usually represents other, adjacent fingers (Merzenich et al., 1990). For example, concert pianists have highly developed cortical areas for finger control: The continued input from the fingers commands a larger area of representation in the somatosensory cortices in the brain. Consistent with this observation, recent research indicates greater plasticity within the motor cortex of professional musicians compared with nonmusicians, perhaps

Brain Plasticity and Sensations in Phantom Limbs

Long after a limb is amputated, many patients continue to experience sensations where the missing limb would be, a phenomenon called *phantom limb syndrome.* Some even report feeling pain in their phantom limbs. Why does this happen? Some evidence suggests that phantom limb syndrome may arise in part because of plasticity in the brain.

Researchers stimulated the skin surface in various regions around the face, torso, and arms while monitoring brain activity in amputees and nonamputated volunteers (Ramachandran & Blakeslee, 1998; Ramachandran, Rodgers-Ramachandran, & Stewart, 1992). Brain-imaging techniques displayed the somatosensory cortical areas activated when the skin was stimulated. Stimulating areas of the face and upper arm activated an area in the somatosensory cortex that previously would have been activated by a now-missing hand. The face and arm were represented in the somatosensory cortex in an area adjacent to where the person's hand—

▶ **Mapping Sensations in Phantom Limbs** (a) Researchers lightly touch an amputee's face with a cotton swab, eliciting sensations in the "missing" hand. (b) Touching different parts of the cheek can even result in sensations in particular fingers or the thumb of the missing hand.

Cotton swab / Amputee / Thumb / Ball of thumb / Index finger / Pinkie finger

(a) (b)

▲ A mirror box creates the illusion that the phantom limb has been restored.

now amputated—would have been represented. Stimulating the face or arm produced phantom limb sensations in the amputees; they reported "feeling" a sensation in their missing limbs.

Brain plasticity can explain these results (Pascual-Leone et al., 2005). As you saw in Figure 3.15, the cortical representations for the face and the upper arm normally lie on either side of the representation for the hand. The somatosensory areas for the face and upper arm were larger in amputees and had taken over the part of the cortex normally representing the hand. Indeed, the new face and arm representations were now contiguous with each other, filling in the space occupied by the hand representation.

This idea has practical implications for dealing with the pain that can result from phantom limbs (Ramachandran & Altschuler, 2009). Researchers have used a "mirror box" to teach

patients a new mapping to increase voluntary control over their phantom limbs. For example, a patient would place his intact right hand and phantom left hand in the mirror box such that when looking at the mirror, he sees his right hand reflected on the left—where he has placed his phantom—creating the illusion the phantom has been restored. The phantom hand thus appears to respond to motor commands given by the patient, and with practice the patient can become better at "'moving'" the phantom in response to voluntary commands. As a result, when feeling the excruciating pain associated with a clenched phantom hand, the patient can now voluntarily unclench the hand and reduce the pain. This therapeutic approach based on brain plasticity has been applied successfully to a variety of patient populations (Ramachandran & Altschuler, 2009).

reflecting an increase in the number of motor synapses as a result of extended practice (Rosenkranz, Williamon, & Rothwell, 2007). Similar findings have been obtained with quilters (who may have highly developed areas for the thumb and forefinger, which are critical to their profession) and taxi drivers (who have overdeveloped brain areas in the hippocampus that are used during spatial navigation; Maguire, Woollett, & Spiers, 2006).

Plasticity is also related to a question you might not expect to find in a psychology text: How much exercise have you been getting lately? A large of number of studies in rats and other nonhuman animals indicate that physical exercise can increase the number of synapses and even promote the development of new neurons in the hippocampus (Hillman, Erickson, & Kramer, 2008; van Praag, 2009). Recent studies with people have begun to document the beneficial effects of cardiovascular exercise on aspects of brain function and cognitive performance (Colcombe et al., 2004, 2006). Though these effects tend to be seen most clearly in older adults (okay, so it's time for your textbook authors to get on a treadmill), benefits have also been documented throughout the life span (Hillman et al., 2008). It should be clear by now that the plasticity of the brain is not just an interesting theoretical idea; it has potentially important applications to everyday life.

MARK ANDERSEN/GETTY IMAGES

Everyday forms of exercise, such as running, can benefit not only your heart but also your brain.

SUMMARY QUIZ [3.4]

1. Which part of the hindbrain coordinates fine motor skills?

   a. the medulla   b. the cerebellum   c. the pons   d. the tegmentum

2. What part of the brain is involved in movement and orientation?

   a. the hindbrain   b. the midbrain   c. the forebrain   d. the reticular formation

3. The _____ regulates body temperature, hunger, thirst, and sexual behavior.

   a. cerebral cortex   b. pituitary gland   c. hypothalamus   d. hippocampus

4. What explains the apparent beneficial effects of cardiovascular exercise on aspects of brain function and cognitive performance?

   a. the different sizes of the somatosensory cortices

   b. the position of the cerebral cortex

   c. specialization of association areas

   d. neuron plasticity

The Evolution of Nervous Systems

As you've just read, far from being a single, elegant machine, the human brain is instead a system comprised of many distinct components that have been added at different times during the course of evolution. The human species has retained what worked best in earlier versions of the brain, then added bits and pieces to get us to our present state through evolution.

Evolutionary Development of the Central Nervous System

The central nervous system evolved from the very simple one found in simple animals to the elaborate nervous system in humans today. Even the simplest animals have sensory neurons and motor neurons for responding to the environment (Shepherd, 1988). For example, single-celled protozoa have molecules in their cell membrane that are sensitive to food in the water. These molecules trigger the movement of tiny threads called *cilia,* which help propel the protozoa toward the food source. The first neurons appeared in simple invertebrates, such as jellyfish; the sensory neurons in the jellyfish's tentacles can feel the touch of a potentially dangerous predator, which prompts the jellyfish to swim to safety. If you're a jellyfish, this simple neural system is sufficient to keep you alive. The first central nervous system worthy of the name, though, appeared in flatworms, which have a collection of neurons in the head—a simple kind of brain—that include sensory neurons for vision and taste and motor neurons that control feeding behavior.

During the course of evolution, a major split in the organization of the nervous system occurred between invertebrate animals (those without a spinal column) and vertebrate animals (those with a spinal column). In all vertebrates, the central nervous system is organized into a hierarchy, with lower levels executing simpler functions and higher levels performing more complex ones. As you saw earlier, in humans, reflexes are accomplished in the spinal cord. At the next level, the midbrain executes the more complex task of orienting toward an important stimulus in the environment. Finally, an even more complex task, such as imagining what your life will be like 20 years from now, is performed in the forebrain (Addis, Wong, & Schacter, 2007; Szpunar, Watson, & McDermott, 2007).

> **?** What is the difference in the organization of the nervous system between invertebrate and vertebrate animals?

The forebrain undergoes further evolutionary advances in vertebrates. In lower vertebrate species such as amphibians (frogs and newts), the forebrain consists only of small clusters of neurons at the end of the neural tube. In higher vertebrates, including reptiles, birds, and mammals, the forebrain is much larger, and it evolves in two different patterns. Reptiles and birds have almost no cerebral cortex. By contrast, mammals have a highly developed cerebral cortex, which develops multiple areas that serve a broad range of higher mental functions. This forebrain development has reached its peak—so far—in humans (**FIGURE 3.16**). This refinement of the forebrain allows for some remarkable, uniquely human abilities: self-awareness, sophisticated language use, social interaction, abstract reasoning, imagining, and empathy, among others.

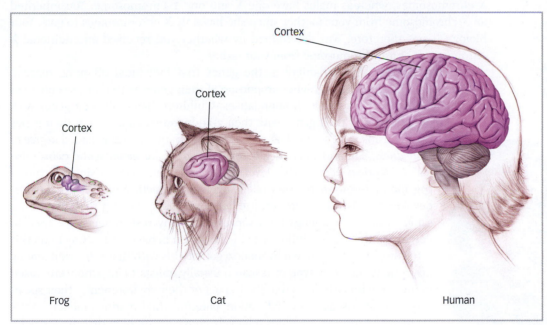

◀ Figure **3.16** **Development of the Forebrain** The human forebrain evolved to handle the increasingly complex demands of the environment.

Genes and the Environment

You may have heard the phrase "nature vs. nurture," which suggests that either genetics ("nature") or the environment ("nurture") plays a major role in producing particular behaviors, personality traits, psychological disorders, or pretty much any other thing that a human does. Do these twin influences grapple with each other for supremacy in directing a person's behavior? The emerging picture from current research is that both nature *and* nurture play a role in directing behavior, and the focus has shifted to examining the relative contributions of each influence rather than the absolute contributions of either influence alone. In short, it's the interaction of genes and environmental influences that determines what humans do (Gottesman & Hanson, 2005; Rutter & Silberg, 2002).

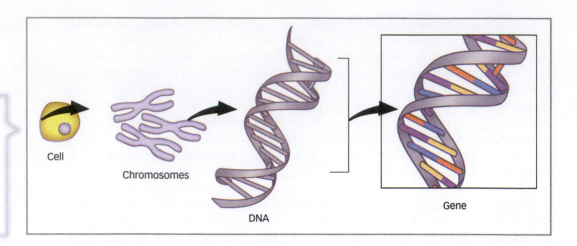

▶ Figure **3.17** **Genes, Chromosomes, and Their Recombination** The cell nucleus houses chromosomes, which are made up of double-helix strands of DNA. Every cell in our bodies has 23 pairs of chromosomes. Genes are segments on a strand of DNA with codes that make us who we are.

Cell

Chromosomes

DNA

Gene

Monozygotic twins (top) share 100% of their genes in common, while dizygotic twins (bottom) share 50% of their genes, the same as other siblings. Studies of monozygotic and dizygotic twins help researchers estimate the relative contributions of genes and environmental influences on behavior.

A **gene** is *the unit of hereditary transmission*. Genes are sections on a strand of DNA (deoxyribonucleic acid) and are organized into large threads called **chromosomes,** which are *strands of DNA wound around each other in a double-helix configuration* (see **FIGURE 3.17**). Chromosomes come in pairs, and humans have 23 pairs each. You inherit one member of each pair from your father and one from your mother. The chromosomes that determine sex are the X and Y chromosomes; females have two X chromosomes, whereas males have one X and one Y chromosome. You inherited an X chromosome from your mother since she has only X chromosomes to give. Your biological sex, therefore, was determined by whether you received an additional X chromosome or a Y chromosome from your father.

There is considerable variability in the genes that individual offspring receive. Nonetheless, children share a higher proportion of their genes with their parents than with more distant relatives or with nonrelatives. Children share half their genes with each parent, a quarter of their genes with their grandparents, an eighth of their genes with cousins, and so on. The probability of sharing genes is called *degree of relatedness*. The most genetically related people are *monozygotic twins* (also called *identical twins*), who develop from the splitting of a single fertilized egg and therefore share 100% of their genes. *Dizygotic twins (fraternal twins)* develop from two separate fertilized eggs and share 50% of their genes, the same as any two siblings born separately. Many researchers have tried to determine the relative influence of genetics on behavior. One way to do this is to compare a trait shown by monozygotic twins with that same trait among dizygotic twins. This type of research usually enlists twins who were raised in the same household so that the impact of their environment—their socioeconomic status, access to education, parental child-rearing practices, environmental stressors—remains relatively constant. Finding that monozygotic twins have a higher prevalence of a specific trait suggests a genetic influence (Boomsma, Busjahn, & Peltonen, 2002).

As an example, the likelihood that the dizygotic twin of a person who has schizophrenia (a mental disorder we'll discuss in greater detail in Chapter 13) will *also* develop schizophrenia is 27%. However, this statistic rises to 50% for monozygotic twins. That sounds scarily high—until you realize that 50% of the monozygotic twins of people with schizophrenia will *not* develop the disorder. That means that environmental influences must play an important role too. In short, genetics can contribute to the development, likelihood, or onset of a variety of traits. But a more complete picture of genetic influences on behavior must always take the environmental context into consideration. Genes express themselves within an environment, not in isolation.

SUMMARY QUIZ [3.5]

1. Compared with reptiles and birds, human have the most highly developed
   a. cerebral cortex.   b. cerebellum.   c. tectum.   d. thalamus.

2. The first true central nervous system appeared in
   a. flatworms.   b. jellyfish.   c. protozoa.   d. early primates.

3. Genes help determine the _____ that an individual will express specific characteristics.
   a. value   c. environmental possibilities
   b. likelihood   d. behavioral standards

gene The unit of hereditary transmission.

chromosomes Strands of DNA wound around each other in a double-helix configuration.

Investigating the Brain

So far, you've read a great deal about the nervous system: how it's organized, how it works, what its components are, and what those components do. But *how* do we know all of this? Anatomists can dissect a human brain and identify its structures, but they cannot determine which structures play a role in producing which behaviors by dissecting a nonliving brain.

Scientists use a variety of methods to understand how the brain affects behavior. Let's consider three of the main ones: testing people with brain damage and observing their deficits, studying electrical activity in the brain during behavior, and conducting brain scans while people perform various tasks.

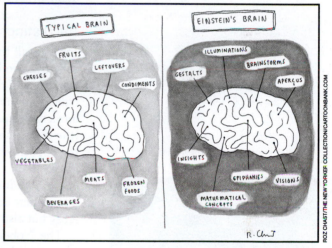

Learning About Brain Organization by Studying the Damaged Brain

Remember Betty, the 75-year-old woman at the beginning of this chapter admitted to the emergency room because she couldn't recognize her own husband? She had suffered a stroke caused by a blood clot that deprived her brain of oxygen and caused the death of neurons in the afflicted area. Betty's stroke affected part of the association area in her temporal lobe, where complex visual objects are identified. Betty's occipital lobe, the main area where visual processing takes place, was unaffected, so Betty could see her husband and two sons, but because of the damage to her temporal lobe, she could not recognize them.

> **?** How have brain disorders been central to our study of specific areas of the brain?

Much research in neuroscience correlates the loss of specific perceptual, motor, emotional, or cognitive functions with specific areas of brain damage (Andrewes, 2001; Kolb & Whishaw, 2003). By studying these instances, neuroscientists can theorize about the functions those brain areas normally perform. Studying people with brain damage highlights a theme illustrated many times in this book: To better understand the normal operation of a process, it is instructive to understand what happens when that process fails.

The Emotional Functions of the Frontal Lobes

As you've already seen, the human frontal lobes are a remarkable evolutionary achievement. However, psychology's first glimpse at some functions of the frontal lobes came

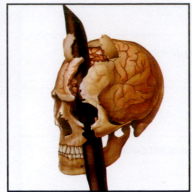

▲ Figure **3.18** **Phineas Gage** Phineas Gage's traumatic accident allowed researchers to investigate the functions of the frontal lobe and its connections with emotion centers in the subcortical structures. The likely path of the metal rod through Gage's skull is reconstructed here.

from a rather unremarkable fellow—so unremarkable, in fact, that a single event in his life defined his place in the annals of psychology's history (Macmillan, 2000). Phineas Gage was a muscular 25-year-old railroad worker. On September 13, 1848, in Cavendish, Vermont, he was packing an explosive charge into a crevice in a rock when the powder exploded, driving a 3-foot, 13-pound iron rod through his head at high speed (Harlow, 1848). As **FIGURE 3.18** shows, the rod entered through his lower left jaw and exited through the middle top of his head. Incredibly, Gage lived to tell the tale. But his personality underwent a significant change.

Before the accident, Gage had been mild mannered, quiet, conscientious, and a hard worker. After the accident, however, he became irritable, irresponsible, indecisive, and given to profanity. The sad decline of Gage's personality and emotional life nonetheless provided an unexpected benefit to psychology. His case study was the first to allow researchers to investigate the hypothesis that the frontal lobe is involved in emotion regulation, planning, and decision making. Furthermore, because the connections between the frontal lobe and the subcortical structures were affected, scientists were able to better understand how the amygdala, hippocampus, and related brain structures interacted with the cerebral cortex (Damasio, 2005).

The Distinct Roles of the Left and Right Hemispheres

You'll recall that the cerebral cortex is divided into two hemispheres, although typically the two hemispheres act as one integrated unit. Sometimes, though, disorders can threaten the ability of the brain to function, and the only way to stop them is with radical methods. This is sometimes the case with patients who suffer from severe, intractable epilepsy. Seizures that begin in one hemisphere cross the corpus callosum (the thick band of nerve fibers that allows the two hemispheres to communicate) to the opposite hemisphere and start a feedback loop that results in a kind of firestorm in the brain. To alleviate the severity of the seizures, surgeons can perform a *split-brain procedure* to sever the corpus callosum. As a result, a seizure that starts in one hemisphere cannot cross to the other side. This procedure helps patients with epilepsy but also produces some unusual, if not unpredictable, behaviors.

The Nobel laureate Roger Sperry (1913–94) designed several experiments that investigated the behaviors of human split-brain patients and in the process revealed a great deal about the independent functions of the left and right hemispheres (Sperry, 1964). Normally, any information that initially enters the left hemisphere is also registered in the right hemisphere and vice versa: The information comes in and travels across the corpus callosum, and both hemispheres understand what's going on. But in a split-brain patient, information entering one hemisphere stays there. In a series of experiments, Sperry and his colleagues had patients look at a spot in the center of a screen and then projected a stimulus on one side of the screen, isolating the stimulus to one hemisphere.

Roger Wolcott Sperry (1913–94) received the Nobel Prize in Physiology in 1981 for his pioneering work investigating the independent functions of the cerebral hemispheres.

The hemispheres themselves are specialized for different kinds of tasks. For example, language processing is largely a left-hemisphere activity. If an image was projected to a split-brain patient's left hemisphere and she was asked to verbally describe what it was, she'd have no problem: The left hemisphere has the information and it's the "speaking" hemisphere, so the patient should have no difficulty verbally describing what she saw. But this patient's right hemisphere has no clue what the object was because that information was received in the left hemisphere and was unable to travel to the right hemisphere! So even though the split-brain patient saw the object and could verbally describe it, she would be unable to use the right hemisphere to perform other tasks regarding that object, such as correctly selecting it from a group with her left hand (see **FIGURE 3.19**). Of course, information presented to the right hemisphere would produce complementary deficits. In this case, a patient might be presented with a familiar object in her left hand (such as a key), be able to demonstrate that she knew what it was (by twisting and turning the key in midair), yet be unable to verbally describe what she was holding. In this case, the information in the right hemisphere is unable to travel to the left hemisphere, which controls the production of speech.

These split-brain studies reveal that the two hemispheres perform different functions and can work together seamlessly as long as the corpus callosum is intact. Without a way to transmit information from one hemisphere to the other, information gets "stuck" in the hemisphere it initially entered and we become acutely aware of the different functions of each hemisphere. Of course, a split-brain patient can adapt to this by simply moving her eyes a little so that the same information independently enters both hemispheres. Split-brain studies have continued over the past few decades and continue to play an important role in shaping our understanding of how the brain works (Gazzaniga, 2006).

Listening to the Brain: Single Neurons and Global Activity

A second approach to studying the link between brain structures and behavior involves recording the pattern of electrical activity of neurons. An *electroencephalograph (EEG)* is a device used to record electrical activity in the brain. Typically electrodes are placed on the outside of the head, and even though the source of electrical activity in synapses and action potentials is far removed from these wires, the electric signals can be amplified several thousand times by the EEG. This provides a visual record of the underlying electrical activity, as shown in **FIGURE 3.20.** Using this technique, researchers can determine the amount of brain activity during different states of consciousness. For example, as you'll read in Chapter 5, the brain shows distinctive patterns of electrical activity when awake vs. asleep; in fact, there are even different brain-wave patterns associated with different stages of sleep. EEG recordings allow researchers to make these fundamental discoveries about the nature of sleep and wakefulness (Dement, 1978). The EEG can also be used to examine the brain's electrical activity when awake individuals engage in a variety of psychological functions, such as perceiving, learning, and remembering.

A different approach to recording electrical activity resulted in a more refined understanding of the brain's division of responsibilities, even at a cellular level. Nobel laureates David Hubel and Torsten Wiesel used a technique that inserted electrodes into the occipital lobes of anesthetized cats and observed the patterns of action potentials of individual neurons (Hubel, 1988). They discovered that neurons in the primary visual cortex are activated whenever a contrast between light and dark occurs in part of the visual field, such as a thick line of light against a dark background. They then found that each neuron responded vigorously only when presented with a contrasting edge at a particular orientation. Since then, many studies have shown that neurons in the primary visual cortex represent particular features of visual stimuli, such as contrast, shape, and color (Zeki, 1993).

These neurons in the visual cortex are known as *feature detectors* because they selectively respond to certain aspects of a visual image. For example, some neurons fire only when detecting a vertical line in the middle of the visual field, other neurons fire when a line at a 45-degree angle is perceived,

> **How does the EEG record electrical activity in the brain?**

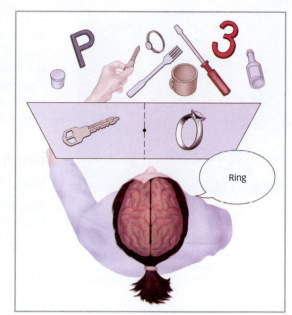

▲ Figure **3.19** **Split-Brain Experiment** When a split-brain patient is presented with the picture of a ring on the right and that of a key on the left side of a screen, she can verbalize *ring* but not *key* because the left hemisphere "sees" the ring and language is usually located in the left hemisphere. This patient would be able to choose a key with her left hand from a set of objects behind a screen. She would not, however, be able to pick out a ring with her left hand since what the left hemisphere "sees" is not communicated to the left side of her body.

▼ Figure **3.20** **EEG** The electroencephalograph (EEG) records electrical activity in the brain. Many states of consciousness, such as wakefulness and stages of sleep, are characterized by particular types of brain waves.

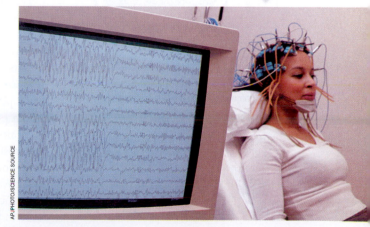

AP.IPHOTO/SCIENCE SOURCE

David Hubel (left, b. 1926) and Torsten Wiesel (right, b. 1924) received the Nobel Prize in Physiology in 1981 for their work on mapping the visual cortex.

and still others in response to wider lines, horizontal lines, lines in the periphery of the visual field, and so on (Livingstone & Hubel, 1988). The discovery of this specialized function for neurons was a huge leap forward in our understanding of how the visual cortex works. Feature detectors identify basic dimensions of a stimulus ("slanted line . . . other slanted line . . . horizontal line"); those dimensions are then combined during a later stage of visual processing to allow recognition and perception of a stimulus ("Oh, it's a letter *A*").

Brain Imaging: From Visualizing Structure to Watching the Brain in Action

The third major way that neuroscientists can peer into the workings of the human brain has only become possible in the past several decades. EEG readouts give an overall picture of a person's level of consciousness, and single-cell recordings shed light on the actions of particular clumps of neurons. The aspiration of neuroscience, however, has been to see the brain in operation while behavior is being enacted. This goal has been steadily achieved thanks to a wide range of *neuroimaging techniques* that use advanced technology to create images of the living, healthy brain (Posner & Raichle, 1994; Raichle & Mintun, 2006). *Structural brain imaging* provides information about the basic structure of the brain and allows clinicians or researchers to see abnormalities in brain structure. *Functional brain imaging*, in contrast, provides information about the activity of the brain when people perform various kinds of cognitive or motor tasks.

One structural neuroimaging technique is the *computerized axial tomography* (CT) *scan*. In a CT scan, a scanner rotates a device around a person's head and takes a series of x-ray photographs from different angles. Computer programs then combine these images to provide views from any angle. CT scans show different densities of tissue in the brain. For example, the higher-density skull looks white on a CT scan, the cortex shows up as gray, and the least dense fissures and ventricles in the brain look dark (see **FIGURE 3.21**). Another technique, *magnetic resonance imaging* (MRI), involves applying brief but powerful magnetic pulses to the head and recording how these pulses are absorbed throughout the brain. For very short periods, these magnetic pulses cause molecules in the brain tissue to twist slightly and then relax, which releases a small amount of energy. Differently charged molecules respond differently to the magnetic pulses, so the energy signals reveal brain structures with different molecular compositions. Magnetic resonance imaging produces pictures of soft tissue at a better resolution than a CT scan, as you can see in Figure 3.21. CT and MRI scans give psychologists a clearer picture of the structure of the brain and can help localize brain damage (as when someone suffers a stroke), but they reveal nothing about the functions of the brain.

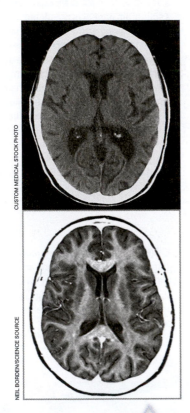

▲ Figure **3.21** **Structural-Imaging Techniques (CT and MRI)** CT (top) and MRI (bottom) scans are used to provide information about the structure of the brain and can help to spot tumors and other kinds of damage. Each scan shown here provides a snapshot of a single slice in the brain. Note that the MRI scan provides a clearer, higher-resolution image than the CT scan.

Two newer functional-brain-imaging techniques show researchers much more than just the structure of the brain by allowing us to actually watch the brain in action. These techniques rely on the fact that activated brain areas demand more energy for their neurons to work. This energy is supplied through increased blood flow to the activated areas. Functional-imaging techniques can detect such changes in blood flow. In *positron emission tomography* (PET), a harmless radioactive substance is injected into a person's bloodstream. Then the brain is scanned by radiation detectors as the person performs perceptual or cognitive tasks, such as reading or speaking. Areas of the brain that are activated during these tasks demand more energy and greater blood flow, resulting in a higher amount of radioactivity in that region. The radiation detectors record the level of radioactivity in each region, producing a computerized image of the activated areas (see **FIGURE 3.22**). In *functional magnetic resonance imaging* (fMRI), magnetic pulses cause the twisting of hemoglobin molecules. Hemoglobin is the molecule in the blood that carries oxygen to our tissues, including the brain. When active neurons demand more energy and blood flow, oxygenated hemoglobin concentrates in the active areas. fMRI detects the oxygenated hemoglobin and provides a picture of the level of activation in each brain area (see Figure 3.22). Both fMRI and PET allow

? **What does an fMRI track in an active brain?**

researchers to localize changes in the brain very accurately. However, fMRI has a couple of advantages over PET. First, fMRI does not require any exposure to a radioactive substance. Second, fMRI can localize changes in brain activity across briefer periods than PET, which makes it more useful for analyzing psychological processes that occur extremely quickly, such as reading a word or recognizing a face (see the Hot Science box.)

PET and fMRI provide remarkable insights into the types of information processing that take place in specific areas of the brain. For example, when people look at faces, fMRI reveals strong activity in a region located near the border of the temporal and occipital lobes called the *fusiform gyrus* (Kanwisher, McDermott, & Chun, 1997). When this structure is damaged, people experience problems with recognizing faces, as Betty did in the opening vignette. Further, when people perform a task that engages emotional processing, such as looking at sad pictures, researchers observe significant activation in the amygdala, which you learned earlier is linked with emotional arousal (Phelps, 2006). There is also increased activation in parts of the frontal lobe that are involved in emotional regulation—in fact, in the same areas that were most likely damaged in the case of Phineas Gage (Wang et al., 2005).

HOT SCIENCE

Mirror, Mirror, in My Brain

One of the most exciting recent advances in neuroscience is the discovery of mirror neurons, which are found in the frontal lobe (near the motor cortex) and in the parietal lobe (Rizzolatti & Craighero, 2004). As their name suggests, mirror neurons are activated when an animal performs a behavior, such as reaching for or manipulating an object, and also when another animal *observes* this animal performing the behavior. This kind of mirroring holds intriguing implications for understanding the brain's role in complex social behavior (Iacoboni, 2009).

A recent study on mirror neurons used fMRI to monitor the brains of humans as they watched each of three presentations (Iacoboni et al., 2005). Sometimes participants saw a hand making grasping motions but without a context. Sometimes they saw only the context, coffee cups or scrubbing sponges, but no hands making motions to go with them. Other times they saw hand motions in context, either grasping and moving a coffee cup to drink or cleaning dishes with a sponge.

The participants' mirror neurons responded more strongly when actions were embedded in a context. This suggests that the same set of

neurons involved in action recognition are also involved in understanding the intentions of others. Mirror neurons are active when watching someone perform a behavior, such as grasping in midair. But they are more highly activated when that behavior has some purpose or context, such as grasping a cup to take a drink. Recognizing another person's intentions means that the observer has inferred something about that person's goals, wants, or wishes ("Oh, she must be thirsty").

Why is this interesting? These results suggest a possible inborn neural basis for empathy. Grasping the intentions of another person—indeed, having your brain respond in kind as another person acts—allows us to understand other people's possible motivations and anticipate their future actions. In fact, these are the kinds of skills that people suffering from autism severely lack. Autism is a developmental disorder characterized by impoverished social interactions and communication skills (Frith, 2001). Recent evidence indicates that although children with autism can recognize the actions that another person is performing (e.g., grasping an object), they have difficulty understanding the intention behind the action (e.g.,

grasping an object in order to eat it) (Rizzolati, Fabbri-Destro, & Cattaneo, 2009). Research on mirror neurons may therefore offer one avenue for better understanding the origin and prognosis of this disorder (Iacoboni & Dapretto, 2006; Rizzolati et al., 2009).

▲ When one animal observes another engaging in a particular behavior, some of the same neurons become active in the observer as well as in the animal exhibiting the behavior. These mirror neurons seem to play an important role in social behavior.

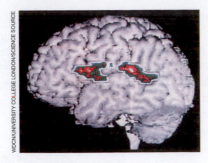

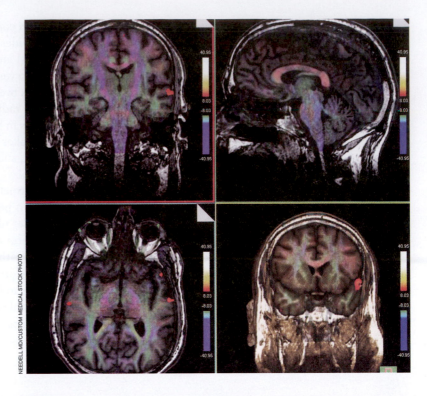

► Figure **3.22** **Functional-Imaging Techniques (PET and fMRI)**
PET and fMRI scans provide information about the functions of the brain by revealing which brain areas become more or less active in different conditions. The PET scan (directly above) shows areas in the left hemisphere (Broca's area, left; lower parietal-upper temporal area, right) that become active when people hold in mind a string of letters for a few seconds. The fMRI scans (all views to the right) indicate activity in the auditory cortex of a person listening to music.

As you may have noticed, then, the most modern brain-imaging techniques confirm what studies of brain damage from over 100 years ago suspected. It was pretty clear to the physician who examined Phineas Gage that the location of Gage's injuries played a major role in his drastic change in personality and emotionality. fMRI scans have since confirmed that the frontal lobe plays a central role in regulating emotion. It's always nice when independent methods—in these instances, very old case studies and very recent technology—arrive at the same conclusions. Although the human brain still holds many mysteries, researchers are developing increasingly sophisticated ways of unraveling them.

SUMMARY QUIZ [3.6]

1. Identifying the brain areas that are involved in specific types of motor, cognitive, or emotional processing is best achieved through
   a. recording patterns of electrical activity.
   b. observing psychological disorders.
   c. psychosurgery.
   d. brain imaging.

2. Split-brain studies have revealed that
   a. neurons in the primary visual cortex represent features of visual stimuli such as contrast, shape, and color.
   b. the two hemispheres perform different functions but can work together by means of the corpus callosum.
   c. when people perform a task that involves emotional processing, the amygdala is activated.
   d. brain locations for vision, touch, and hearing are separate.

3. Researchers can observe relationships between energy consumption in certain brain areas and specific cognitive and behavioral events using
   a. functional brain imaging.
   b. electroencephalography.
   c. inserting electrodes into individual cells.
   d. CT scans.

Where Do You Stand?

Brain Death

Andreas Vesalius (1514–64), a Belgian physician, is regarded as one of the founders of modern anatomy. According to one story, Vesalius conducted an autopsy in 1564 in front of a large crowd in Madrid, Spain. When the cadaver's chest was opened, the audience saw that the man's heart was still beating! The possibility that the patient was still alive created a scandal that forced Vesalius to leave Spain in disgrace.

We may never know whether this story is accurate. However, it raises a question that is still fiercely debated today. In Vesalius's time, if a patient didn't appear to be breathing, was generally unresponsive, or gave no strong evidence of a heartbeat, the person could safely be considered dead (despite the occasional misdiagnosis). Modern resuscitative techniques can keep the heart, lungs, and other organs functioning for days, months, or even years, so physicians have identified measures of brain function that allow them to decide more definitively when someone is dead.

Most medical professionals define brain death as the *irreversible loss of all functions of the brain*. Contrary to what you may think, brain death is not the same as being in a coma or being unresponsive to stimulation. Indeed, even a flat-line EEG does not indicate that all brain functions have stopped; the reticular formation in the hindbrain, which generates spontaneous respiration and heartbeat, may still be active.

Brain death came to the forefront of national attention during March 2005 in the case of Terri Schiavo, a woman who had been kept alive on a respirator for nearly 15 years in a Florida nursing home. Terri Schiavo's parents thought she had a substantial level of voluntary consciousness; they felt that she appeared to smile, cry, and turn toward the source of a voice. However, neurologists who specialize in these cases emphasized that these responses could be automatic reflexes supported by circuits in the thalamus and midbrain. These neurologists failed to see conclusive evidence of consciousness or voluntary behavior.

Terri's husband, Michael, asked the courts to remove the feeding tube that kept her alive, a decision a Florida court accepted. Nonetheless, Florida Governor Jeb Bush decreed in 2003 that doctors retain Terri's feeding tube and continue to provide medical care. Eventually, the court again ordered her feeding tube removed, resulting in her death.

The definition of brain death includes the term *irreversible*, suggesting that as long as *any* component of the brain can still function—with or without the aid of a machine—the person should be considered alive. But what qualifies as "life"? Is a simple consensus of qualified professionals—doctors, nurses, social workers—sufficient to decide whether someone is "still living" or at least "still living enough" to maintain whatever treatments may be in place? How should the wishes of family members be considered? For that matter, should the wishes of lawmakers and politicians play a role at all? Where do you stand?

Chapter Review

SUMMARY

Neurons: The Origin of Behavior

► Neurons process information received from the outside world, communicate with one another, and send messages to the body's muscles and organs.

► Neurons are composed of three major parts: the cell body, which contains the nucleus; the dendrites, which receive sensory signals; and the axon, which carries signals from the cell body to other neurons or to muscles and organs in the body.

► Neurons don't actually touch: They are separated by a small gap, which is part of the synapse across which signals are transmitted from one neuron to another.

► Neurons are differentiated according to the functions they perform. The three major types of neurons are sensory neurons, motor neurons, and interneurons.

Information Processing in Neurons

► Information is transmitted within a neuron by electrical signals, such as when the resting potential is changed by an electric impulse called an action potential, an all-or-nothing signal that moves down the axon.

► Communication between neurons takes place through chemical signals. The sending neuron releases neurotransmitters, which travel across the synapse to bind with receptors in the receiving neuron's dendrite.

▶ Neurotransmitters bind to specific receptor sites. Neurotransmitters leave the synapse through reuptake, through enzyme deactivation, and by binding to autoreceptors.

▶ Some of the major neurotransmitters are acetylcholine (ACh), dopamine, glutamate, GABA, norepinephrine, serotonin, and endorphins. Many (legal and illegal) drugs affect the brain by increasing or decreasing the action or influence of neurotransmitters.

The Organization of the Nervous System

▶ The nervous system is divided into the peripheral and the central nervous systems.

▶ The peripheral nervous system connects the central nervous system with the rest of the body. It is subdivided into the somatic nervous system, which conveys information into and out of the central nervous system and controls voluntary muscles, and the autonomic nervous system, which controls the body's blood flow, organs, and glands.

▶ The autonomic nervous system is further divided into the sympathetic nervous system, which prepares the body for action in threatening situations, and the parasympathetic nervous system, which returns the body to its normal state once the threat has passed.

▶ The central nervous system is composed of the spinal cord and the brain. The spinal cord can mediate some basic behaviors, such as spinal reflexes, without input from the brain.

Structure of the Brain

▶ The hindbrain generally coordinates information coming into and out of the spinal cord with structures such as the medulla, the reticular formation, the cerebellum, and the pons. These structures respectively coordinate breathing and heart rate, regulate sleep and arousal levels, coordinate fine motor skills, and communicate this information to the cortex.

▶ The midbrain, including the tectum and tegmentum, generally coordinates functions such as orientation to the environment and movement and arousal toward sensory stimuli.

▶ The forebrain generally coordinates higher-level functions, such as perceiving, feeling, and thinking. Subcortical structures, such as the thalamus, hypothalamus, hippocampus, amygdala, and basal ganglia, perform a variety of functions related to motivation and emotion. The cerebral cortex, composed of two hemispheres with four lobes each (occipital, parietal, temporal, and frontal), performs tasks that help make us fully human: thinking, planning, judging, perceiving, and behaving purposefully and voluntarily.

▶ Neurons in the brain can be shaped by experience and the environment, making the brain amazingly plastic.

The Evolution of Nervous Systems

▶ Nervous systems evolved from simple collections of sensory and motor neurons in simple animals, such as flatworms, to the elaborate centralized nervous systems found in mammals. The cerebral cortex is particularly highly developed in humans.

▶ The gene, or the unit of hereditary transmission, is built from strands of DNA in a double-helix formation that is organized into chromosomes.

▶ The study of genetics indicates that both genes and the environment work together to influence behavior.

Investigating the Brain

▶ One way to investigate brain function is by observing how specific perceptual, motor, intellectual, and emotional capacities are affected following damage to particular regions of the brain.

▶ Another technique is examining global electrical activity in the brain by using electroencephalography (EEG) or by recording the activity patterns of single neurons during specific perceptual or behavioral tasks.

▶ Functional-brain-imaging methods show areas of high energy consumption during specific types of perceptual, motor, cognitive, or emotional processing; brain areas with high energy consumption during those tasks are likely to be involved in performing those tasks.

KEY TERMS

neurons (p. 58)

cell body (p. 58)

dendrite (p. 58)

axon (p. 58)

myelin sheath (p. 58)

glial cells (p. 58)

synapse (p. 58)

sensory neurons (p. 58)

motor neurons (p. 59)

interneurons (p. 59)

resting potential (p. 61)

action potential (p. 62)

refractory period (p. 63)

terminal buttons (p. 63)

neurotransmitters (p. 63)

receptors (p. 63)

agonists (p. 64)

antagonists (p. 65)

nervous system (p. 66)

central nervous system (CNS) (p. 66)

peripheral nervous system (PNS) (p. 66)

somatic nervous system (p. 66)

autonomic nervous system (ANS) (p. 66)

sympathetic nervous system (p. 67)

parasympathetic nervous system (p. 67)

spinal reflexes (p. 68)

hindbrain (p. 70)

medulla (p. 70)

reticular formation (p. 70)

cerebellum (p. 70)

pons (p. 70)

subcortical structures (p. 71)

thalamus (p. 72)

hypothalamus (p. 72)

pituitary gland (p. 72)

hippocampus (p. 72)

amygdala (p. 73)

basal ganglia (p. 73)

cerebral cortex (p. 73)

corpus callosum (p. 74)

occipital lobe (p. 74)

parietal lobe (p. 75)

temporal lobe (p. 75)

frontal lobe (p. 76)

association areas (p. 76)

gene (p. 80)

chromosomes (p. 80)

CHANGING MINDS

1. While watching late-night TV, you come across an infomercial for all-natural BrainGro. "It's a well-known fact that most people use only 10% of their brain," the spokesman promises, "but with BrainGro you can increase that number from 10% to 99%!" Why should you be skeptical of the claim that we use only 10% of our brains? What would happen if a drug actually increased neuronal activity by tenfold?

2. Your friend has been feeling depressed and has gone to a psychiatrist for help. "He prescribed a medication that's supposed to increase serotonin in my brain. But my feelings depend on me, not on a bunch of chemicals in my head," she says. What examples could you give your friend to convince her that hormones and neurotransmitters really do influence our cognition, mood, and behavior?

3. A classmate has read the section in this chapter about the evolution of the central nervous system. "Evolution is just a theory," he says. "Not everyone believes in it. And even if it's true that we're all descended from monkeys, that doesn't have anything to do with the psychology of humans alive today." What is your friend misunderstanding about evolution? How would you explain to him the relevance of evolution to modern psychology?

4. A news program reports on a study (Hölzel et al., 2011) in which people who practiced meditation for about 30 minutes a day for 8 weeks showed changes in their brains, including increases in the size of the hippocampus and the amygdala. You tell a friend, who's skeptical. "The brain doesn't change like that. Basically, the brain you're born with is the brain you're stuck with for the rest of your life." Why is your friend's statement wrong? What are several specific ways in which the brain does change over time?

5. A friend announces that he's figured out why he's bad at math. "I read it in a book," he says. "Left-brained people are analytical and logical, but right-brained people are creative and artistic. I'm an art major, so I must be right-brained, and that's why I'm not good at math." Why is your friend's view too simplistic?

CRITICAL THINKING QUESTIONS

1. In this chapter you read about the various functions of different areas of the human cerebral cortex. Reptiles and birds have almost no cerebral cortex, while mammals such as rats and cats do have a cerebral cortex, but their frontal lobes are proportionately much smaller than the frontal lobes of humans and other primates.

   How might this explain the fact that only humans have developed complex language, computer technology, and calculus?

2. Different parts of the human cerebral cortex specialize in processing different types of information: The occipital lobe processes visual information, the parietal lobe processes information about touch, the temporal lobe is responsible for hearing and language, and the frontal lobe is involved in planning and judgment.

   Suppose a toddler is playing with the remote control and accidentally pushes the big red button, at which point her favorite cartoon disappears from the television screen. How would the different parts of her cortex encode information about this event so that she might learn not to make the same mistake twice?

3. In Chapter 2, you learned about the difference between correlation and causation; further, you learned that even if two events are correlated, this does not necessarily mean that one causes the other. In this chapter, you read about techniques such as fMRI and PET, which researchers can use to measure blood flow or activity in different regions while people perform particular tasks.

   Suppose a researcher designs an experiment in which participants view words on a screen and are asked to pronounce each word aloud while the researcher uses fMRI to examine brain activity. First, what areas of the brain would you expect to show activity on an fMRI scan as participants complete this task? Second, can the researcher now safely conclude that those brain areas are required for humans to pronounce words?

ANSWERS TO SUMMARY QUIZZES

Summary Quiz [3.1] 1. c; 2. b; 3. a; 4. a
Summary Quiz [3.2] 1. d; 2. b; 3. d
Summary Quiz [3.3] 1. a; 2. c
Summary Quiz [3.4] 1. b; 2. b; 3. c; 4. d
Summary Quiz [3.5] 1. a; 2. a; 3. b
Summary Quiz [3.6] 1. d; 2. b; 3. a

Need more help? Additional resources are located at the book's free companion website at:
www.worthpublishers.com/schacterbrief2e

4

Sensation and Perception

*N is sort of . . . rubbery . . . smooth, L is sort of the consistency of watery paint. . . .
Letters also have vague personalities, but not as strongly as numerals do.*
—Julieta

The letter A is blue, B is red, C is kind of a light gray, D is orange. . . .
—Karen

*I hear a note by one of the fellows in the band and it's one color. I hear the same note
played by someone else and it's a different color.*
—Jazz musician Duke Ellington (quoted in George, 1981, p. 226)

Basically, I taste words.
—Amelia

THESE COMMENTS ARE NOT FROM a recent meeting of the Slightly Odd
Society. They're the remarks of otherwise perfectly normal people describing experiences that—to them—are quite commonplace and genuine. These and many other people have at least one thing in common:
Their perceptual worlds seem to be quite different from most of ours.
These unusual perceptual events are varieties of *synesthesia*, the perceptual experience of one sense that is evoked by another sense [Hubbard & Ramachandran,
2003]. For some synesthetes, musical notes evoke the visual sensation of color.

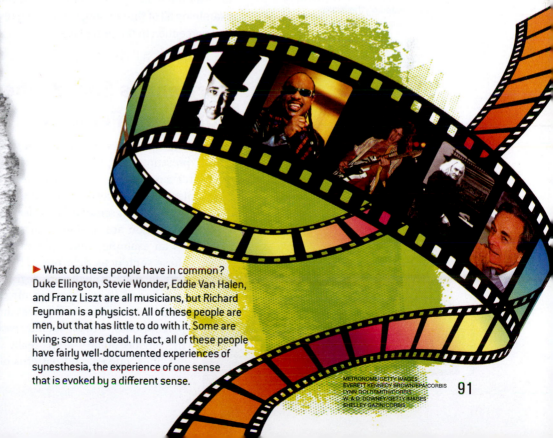

▶ What do these people have in common?
Duke Ellington, Stevie Wonder, Eddie Van Halen,
and Franz Liszt are all musicians, but Richard
Feynman is a physicist. All of these people are
men, but that has little to do with it. Some are
living; some are dead. In fact, all of these people
have fairly well-documented experiences of
synesthesia, the experience of one sense
that is evoked by a different sense.

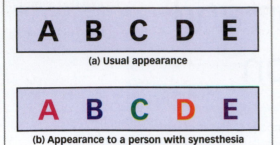

| A | B | C | D | E |

(a) Usual appearance

| A | B | C | D | E |

(b) Appearance to a person with synesthesia

▲ Figure **4.1** **Synesthesia** Most of us see letters printed in black as they appear in (a). Some people with synesthesia link their perceptions of letters with certain colors and perceive letters as printed in different colors, as shown in (b).

You can enjoy a tempting ice cream sundae even if you do not know that its sweet taste depends on a complex process of transduction, in which molecules dissolved in saliva are converted to neural signals processed by the brain.

Other people with synesthesia see printed letters (**FIGURE 4.1**) or numbers in specific, consistent colors (always seeing the digit 2 as pink and 3 as green, for example). Still others experience specific tastes when certain sounds are heard. For those of us who don't experience synesthesia, the prospect of tasting sounds or hearing colors may seem unbelievable or the product of some hallucinogenic experience. But some forms of synesthesia may be found in as many as one in every 100 people (Hubbard & Ramachandran, 2005).

Recent research has documented the psychological and neurobiological reality of synesthesia. For example, a synesthete who sees the digits 2 and 4 as pink and 3 as green will find it easier to pick out a 2 among a bunch of 3s than among a bunch of 4s, whereas a nonsynesthete will perform these two tasks equally well (Palmeri et al., 2002). Brain-imaging studies also show that in some synesthetes, areas of the brain involved in processing colors are more active when they hear words that evoke color than when they hear tones that don't evoke color; no such differences are seen among people in a control group (Mattingly, 2009; Nunn, Gregory, & Brammer, 2002).

So synesthesia is neither an isolated curiosity nor the result of faking. In fact, it may indicate that in some people, the brain is "wired" differently than in most, so that brain regions relating to different senses cross-activate one another (Ramachandran & Hubbard, 2003; Rouw & Scholte, 2007). Whatever the ultimate explanations, research on synesthesia can shed new light on how the brain is organized and how we sense and perceive the world.

IN THIS CHAPTER WE'LL EXPLORE KEY INSIGHTS into the nature of sensation and perception. We'll look at how physical energy in the world around us is encoded by our senses, sent to the brain, and enters conscious awareness. Vision is predominant among our senses; correspondingly, we'll devote a fair amount of space to understanding how the visual system works. Then we'll discuss how we perceive sound waves as words or music or noise, followed by an examination of the body senses, emphasizing touch, pain, and balance. We'll end with the chemical senses of smell and taste, which together allow you to savor the foods you eat. But before doing any of that, we will provide a foundation for examining all of the sensory systems by reviewing how psychologists measure sensation and perception in the first place.

Our Senses Encode the Information Our Brains Perceive

Sensation is *simple stimulation of a sense organ.* It is the basic registration of light, sound, pressure, odor, or taste as parts of your body interact with the physical world. After a sensation registers in your central nervous system, **perception** takes place at the level of your brain: It is *the organization, identification, and interpretation of a sensation in order to form a mental representation.* Sensation and perception are related—but separate—events. As an example, your eyes are coursing across these sentences right now. The sensory receptors in your eyeballs are registering different patterns of light reflecting off the page. Your brain is integrating and processing that light information into the meaningful perception of words, such as *meaningful*, *perception*, and *words*. Your eyes—the sensory organ—aren't really seeing words; they're simply encoding different lines, curves, and patterns of ink on a page. Your brain—the perceptual

? What role does the brain play in what we see and hear?

FOTOLARE/ISTOCKPHOTO

organ—is transforming those lines and curves into a coherent mental representation of words and concepts.

We all know that we have five senses: vision, hearing, touch, taste, and smell. Arguably, we possess several more senses besides these five. Touch, for example, encompasses distinct body senses, including sensitivity to pain and temperature, joint position and balance, and even the state of the gut. Despite the variety of our senses, they all depend on the process of **transduction,** which occurs *when many sensors in the body convert physical signals from the environment into encoded neural signals sent to the central nervous system.*

In vision, light reflected from surfaces provides the eyes with information about the shape, color, and position of objects. In audition, vibrations (from vocal cords or a guitar string, perhaps) cause changes in air pressure that move through space to a listener's ears. In touch, the pressure of a surface against the skin signals its shape, texture, and temperature. In taste and smell, molecules dispersed in the air or dissolved in saliva reveal the identity of substances that we may or may not want to eat. In each case, physical energy from the world is converted to neural energy inside the central nervous system (see **TABLE 4.1**).

sensation Simple stimulation of a sense organ.

perception The organization, identification, and interpretation of a sensation in order to form a mental representation.

transduction What takes place when many sensors in the body convert physical signals from the environment into encoded neural signals sent to the central nervous system.

Table 4.1

Transduction

The five senses convert physical energy from the world into neural energy, which is sent to the brain.

Sense	Sensory Input	Conversion into Neural Energy
Vision	Light reflected from surfaces, (for example from a leaf) provides the eyes with information about the shape, color, and positions of objects.	(See Figure 4.4 for a more detailed view.)
Audition (hearing)	Vibrations (from a guitar string, perhaps) cause changes in air pressure that move through space to the listener's ears.	(See Figure 4.23 for a more detailed view.)
Touch	Pressure of a surface against the skin signals its shape, texture, and temperature.	(See Figure 4.26 for a more detailed view.)
Taste and Smell	Molecules dispersed in the air or dissolved in saliva reveal the identity of substances that we may or may not want to eat.	(See Figures 4.27 and 4.29 for more detailed views.)

Psychophysics

It's intriguing to consider the possibility that our basic perceptions of sights or sounds might differ fundamentally from those of other people. After all, you can describe your experience to another person in words—*orange* and *beautiful*—but that person cannot know directly what you perceive when you look at a sunset. One reason we find synesthetes fascinating is because their perceptual experiences are so different from most of ours. But we won't get very far in understanding such differences by simply relying on casual self-reports. As you learned in Chapter 2, to understand a behavior, researchers must first *operationalize* it, and that involves finding a reliable way to measure it.

Any type of scientific investigation requires objective measurements. Measuring the physical energy of a stimulus, such as the wavelength of a light, is easy enough: You can probably buy the necessary instruments online to do that yourself. But how do you quantify a person's private, subjective *perception* of that light? It's one thing to know that a flashlight produces "100 candlepower" or gives off "8,000 lumens," but it's another matter entirely to measure a person's psychological experience of that light energy.

> **?** Why isn't it enough for a psychophysicist to measure only the strength of a stimulus?

In the mid-1800s, the German scientist and philosopher Gustav Fechner (1801–87) developed an approach to measuring sensation and perception called **psychophysics:** *methods that measure the strength of a stimulus and the observer's sensitivity to that stimulus* (Fechner, 1860/1966). In a typical psychophysics experiment, researchers ask people to make a simple judgment—whether or not they saw a flash of light, for example. The psychophysicist then relates the measured stimulus, such as the brightness of the light flash, to each observer's yes-or-no response.

Measuring Thresholds

Psychophysicists begin the measurement process with a single sensory signal to determine precisely how much physical energy is required to evoke a sensation in an observer. The simplest quantitative measurement in psychophysics is the **absolute threshold,** *the minimal intensity needed to just barely detect a stimulus.* A *threshold* is a boundary. The doorway that separates the inside from the outside of a house is a threshold, as is the boundary between two psychological states ("awareness" and "unawareness," for example). In finding the absolute threshold for sensation, the two states in question are *sensing* and *not sensing* some stimulus. **TABLE 4.2** lists the approximate sensory thresholds for each of the five senses.

To measure the absolute threshold for detecting a sound, for example, an observer sits in a soundproof room wearing headphones linked to a computer. The experimenter presents a pure tone (the sort of sound made by striking a tuning fork), using a computer to vary the loudness or the length of time each tone lasts and recording how often the observer reports hearing that tone under each condition. The outcome of such an experiment is graphed in **FIGURE 4.2**. Notice from the shape of the curve that the transition from *not hearing* to *hearing* is gradual rather than abrupt. Investigators typically define the absolute threshold as the loudness required for the listener to report hearing the tone on 50% of the trials.

If we repeat this experiment for many different tones, we can observe and record the thresholds for tones ranging from very low pitch to very high. It turns out that people tend to be most sensitive to the range of tones corresponding to human conversation. If the tone is low enough,

▼ Figure **4.2 Absolute Threshold** Absolute threshold is graphed here as the point where the increasing intensity of the stimulus enables an observer to detect it on 50% of the trials.

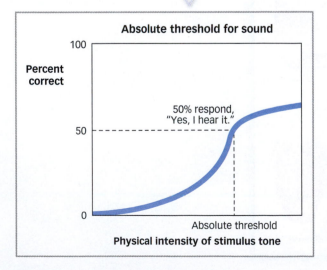

such as the lowest note on a pipe organ, most humans cannot hear it at all; we can only feel it. If the tone is high enough, we likewise cannot hear it, but dogs and many other animals can.

The absolute threshold is useful for assessing how sensitive we are to faint stimuli, but most everyday perception involves detecting differences among stimuli that are well above the absolute threshold. As a way of measuring this difference threshold, Fechner proposed the **just noticeable difference,** or **JND,** *the minimal change in a stimulus that can just barely be detected.* The JND is not a fixed quantity; rather, it is roughly proportional to the magnitude of the stimulus. This relationship was first noticed in 1834 by the German physiologist Ernst Weber; now called **Weber's law,** it states that *the just noticeable difference of a stimulus is a constant proportion despite variations in intensity.* As an example, the JND for weight is about 2% to 3%. If you picked up a one-ounce envelope, then a two-ounce envelope, you'd probably notice the difference between them. But if you picked up a twenty-pound package, then a twenty-pound, one-ounce package, you'd probably detect no difference. In fact, you'd probably need about a twenty-and-a-half-pound package to detect a JND. When calculating a difference threshold, it is the proportion between stimuli that is important; the measured size of the difference, whether in brightness, loudness, or weight, is irrelevant.

Signal Detection

Measuring absolute and difference thresholds requires a critical assumption: that a threshold exists! But much of what scientists know about biology suggests that such a discrete, all-or-nothing change in the brain is unlikely. Humans don't suddenly and rapidly switch between perceiving and not perceiving; in fact, the transition from *not sensing* to *sensing* is gradual. The very same physical stimulus, such as a dim light or a quiet tone, presented on several different occasions may be perceived by the same person on some occasions but not on others. Remember, an absolute threshold is operationalized as perceiving the stimulus 50% of the time . . . which means the other 50% of the time it might go undetected.

How accurate and complete are our perceptions of the world?

Our accurate perception of a sensory stimulus, then, can be somewhat haphazard. Whether in the psychophysics lab or out in the world, sensory signals face a lot of competition, or *noise,* which refers to all the other stimuli coming from the internal and external environment. Memories, moods, and motives intertwine with what you are seeing, hearing, and smelling at any given time. This internal "noise" competes with your ability to detect a stimulus with perfect, focused attention. Other sights, sounds, and smells in the world at large also compete for attention. As a consequence, you may not perceive everything that you sense, and you may even perceive things that you haven't sensed.

An approach to psychophysics called **signal detection theory** holds that *the response to a stimulus depends both on a person's sensitivity to the stimulus in the presence of noise and on a person's decision criterion.* That is, if a stimulus exceeds the criterion, it is detected; if it falls short of the criterion, it is not (Green & Swets, 1966; Macmillan & Creelman, 2005).

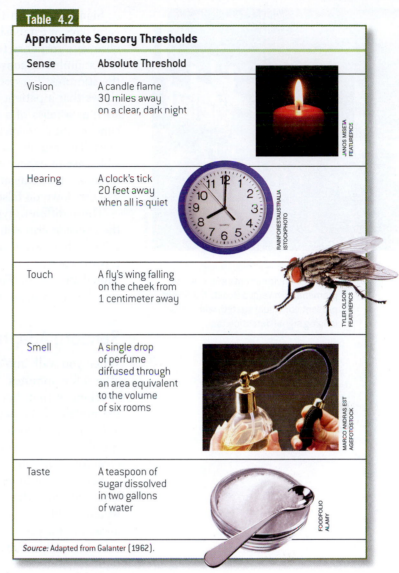

Table 4.2

Approximate Sensory Thresholds

Sense	Absolute Threshold
Vision	A candle flame 30 miles away on a clear, dark night
Hearing	A clock's tick 20 feet away when all is quiet
Touch	A fly's wing falling on the cheek from 1 centimeter away
Smell	A single drop of perfume diffused through an area equivalent to the volume of six rooms
Taste	A teaspoon of sugar dissolved in two gallons of water

Source: Adapted from Galanter (1962).

JANOS MISETA FEATUREPICS

RAINFORESTAUSTRALIA ISTOCKPHOTO

TYLER OLSON FEATUREPICS

MARCO ANDRAS EST AGEFOTOSTOCK

FOODFOLIO ALAMY

psychophysics Methods that measure the strength of a stimulus and the observer's sensitivity to that stimulus.

absolute threshold The minimal intensity needed to just barely detect a stimulus.

just noticeable difference (JND) The minimal change in a stimulus that can just barely be detected.

Weber's law The just noticeable difference of a stimulus is a constant proportion despite variations in intensity.

signal detection theory An observation that the response to a stimulus depends both on a person's sensitivity to the stimulus in the presence of noise and on a person's response criterion.

Cluttered environments such as this promenade in Venice Beach, California, present our visual system with a challenging signal detection task.

Signal detection theory is a more sophisticated approach than was used in the early days of establishing absolute thresholds because it explicitly takes into account observers' response tendencies, such as liberally saying "Yes" when there is any hint of a stimulus or conservatively reserving identifications only for obvious instances of the stimulus. For example, a radiologist may have to decide whether a mammogram shows that a patient has breast cancer. The radiologist knows that certain features, such as a mass of a particular size and shape, are associated with the presence of cancer. But noncancerous features can have a very similar appearance to cancerous ones. The radiologist may decide on a strictly liberal criterion and check every possible case of cancer with a biopsy. This decision strategy minimizes the possibility of missing a true cancer but leads to many false alarms. A strictly conservative criterion will cut down on false alarms but will miss some treatable cancers.

These different types of errors have to be weighed against one another in setting the decision criterion. Signal detection theory offers a practical way to choose among criteria that permit decision makers to take into account the consequences of hits, misses, false alarms, and correct rejections (McFall & Treat, 1999; Swets, Dawes, & Monahan, 2000). (For an example of a common everyday task that can interfere with signal detection, see the Real World box.)

Sensory Adaptation

When you walk into a bakery, the aroma of freshly baked bread overwhelms you, but after a few minutes, the smell fades. If you dive into cold water, the temperature is shocking at first, but after a few minutes, you get used to it. When you wake up in the middle of the night for a drink of water, the bathroom light blinds you, but after a few minutes, you no longer squint. These are all examples of **sensory adaptation,** the observation that *sensitivity to prolonged stimulation tends to decline over time as an organism adapts to current conditions.*

Sensory adaptation is a useful process for most organisms. Imagine what your sensory and perceptual world would be like without it. (If you had to constantly be aware of how your tongue feels while it is resting in your mouth, you'd be driven to distraction.) Our sensory systems respond more strongly to changes in stimulation than to constant stimulation. A stimulus that doesn't change usually doesn't require any action; your car probably emits a certain hum all the time that you've gotten used to. But a change in stimulation often signals a need for action. If your car starts making a different kind of noise, you're not only more likely to notice it, you're also more likely to do something about it.

? What conditions have you already adapted to today? Sounds? Smells?

sensory adaptation Sensitivity to prolonged stimulation tends to decline over time as an organism adapts to current conditions.

SUMMARY QUIZ [4.1]

1. Sensation involves _____ , while perception involves _____ .
   a. organization, coordination
   b. stimulation, interpretation
   c. identification, translation
   d. comprehension, information

2. What process converts physical signals from the environment into neural signals carried by sensory neurons into the central nervous system?
   a. representation
   c. propagation
   b. identification
   d. transduction

3. The smallest intensity needed to just barely detect a stimulus is called
   a. proportional magnitude.
   b. the absolute threshold.
   c. the just noticeable difference.
   d. Weber's law.

THE REAL WORLD

Multitasking

By one estimate, using a cell phone while driving makes having an accident four times more likely (McEvoy et al., 2005). In response to statistics such as this, state legislatures are passing laws that restrict, and sometimes ban, using mobile phones while driving. You might think that's a fine idea . . . for everyone else on the road. But surely *you* can manage to carry on a conversation while simultaneously driving in a safe and courteous manner. Right? In a word, *wrong*.

Talking on a cell phone while driving demands that you juggle two independent sources of sensory input—vision and audition—at the same time. This kind of *multitasking* creates problems when you need to react suddenly while driving. Researchers have tested experienced drivers in a highly realistic driving simulator, measuring their response times to brake lights and stop signs while they listened to the radio or carried on phone conversations (Strayer, Drews, & Johnston, 2003). These experienced drivers reacted significantly more slowly during phone conversations. Their slower braking response translated into an increased stopping distance that, depending on the driver's speed, could have resulted in a rear-end collision. Whether the phone was handheld or hands-free made little difference, and similar results have been obtained in field studies of actual driving (Horrey & Wickens, 2006). This suggests that

laws requiring drivers to use hands-free phones may have little effect on reducing accidents.

Why the poor driving? The tested drivers became so engaged in their phone conversations that their minds no longer seemed to be in the car. A phone conversation requires memory retrieval, deliberation, and planning what to say and often carries an emotional stake in the conversation topic. Tasks such as listening to the radio require far less attention. The situation is even worse when text messaging is involved: Compared with a no-texting control condition, when either sending or receiving a text message in the simulator, drivers spent dramatically less time looking at the road, had a much harder time staying in their lane, missed numerous lane changes, and had greater difficulty maintaining an appropriate distance behind the car ahead of them (Hosking, Young, & Regan, 2009).

Other researchers have measured brain activity using fMRI while people were shifting attention between visual and auditory information. The strength of visual and auditory brain activity was affected: When attention was directed to audition, activity in visual areas decreased compared with when attention was directed to vision (Shomstein & Yantis, 2004). It was as if the participants could adjust a mental "volume knob" to regulate the flow of incoming information according to which task they were attending to at the moment. Interestingly, people who report that they multi-

task frequently in everyday life have difficulty in laboratory tasks that require focusing attention in the face of distractions compared with individuals who do not multitask much in daily life (Ophir, Nass, & Wagner, 2009). So how well do you multitask in several thousand pounds of metal hurtling down the highway? Unless you have two heads with one brain each—one to talk and one to concentrate on driving—you would do well to keep your mind on the road, not on the phone.

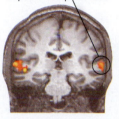

Superior temporal lobe   Fusiform gyrus

(a)   (b)

COURTESY OF SARAH SHOMSTEIN AND STEVEN YANTIS

▲ **Shifting Attention** Participants received fMRI scans as they performed tasks that required them to shift their attention between visual and auditory information. (a) When focusing on auditory information, a region in the superior (upper) temporal lobe involved in auditory processing showed increased activity (yellow/orange). (b) In striking contrast, a visual region, the fusiform gyrus, showed decreased activity when participants focused on auditory information (blue).

Vision I: How the Eyes and the Brain Convert Light Waves to Neural Signals

Humans have sensory receptors in their eyes that respond to wavelengths of light energy. When we look at people, places, and things, patterns of light and color give us information about where one surface stops and another begins. The array of light reflected from those surfaces preserves their shapes and enables us to form a mental representation of a scene (Rodieck, 1998). Understanding vision, then, starts with understanding light.

Sensing Light

Visible light is simply the portion of the electromagnetic spectrum that we can see, and it is an extremely small slice. You can think about light as waves of energy. Like ocean waves, light waves vary in height and in the distance between their peaks, or *wavelengths*, as **TABLE 4.3** shows. There are three properties of light waves, each of

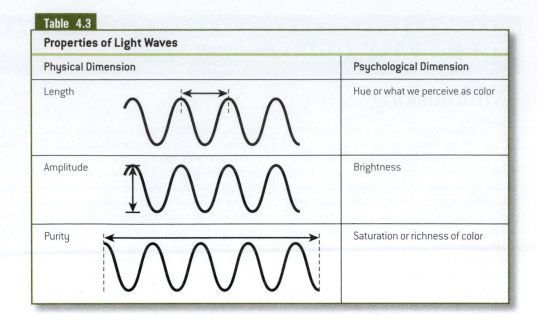

Table 4.3

Properties of Light Waves

Physical Dimension		Psychological Dimension
Length		Hue or what we perceive as color
Amplitude		Brightness
Purity		Saturation or richness of color

which has a physical dimension that produces a corresponding psychological dimension. The *length* of a light wave determines its hue, or what humans perceive as color. The intensity or *amplitude* of a light wave—how high the peaks are—determines what we perceive as the brightness of light. The *purity* is the number of distinct wavelengths that make up the light; it determines what humans perceive as saturation, or the richness of colors (see **FIGURE 4.3**). In other words, length, amplitude, and purity are intrinsic properties of the light waves themselves; what humans perceive from those properties are color, brightness, and saturation.

▶ Figure **4.3** **Electromagnetic Spectrum** The sliver of light waves visible to humans as a rainbow of colors from violet-blue to red is bounded on the short end by ultraviolet rays, which honeybees can see, and on the long end by infrared waves, which night-vision equipment reveals. Someone wearing night-vision goggles, for example, can detect another person's body heat in complete darkness.

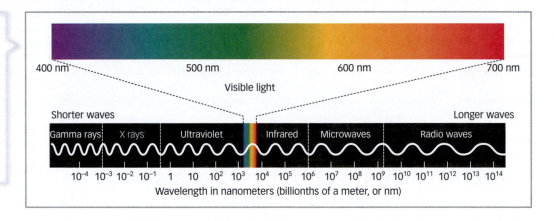

The Human Eye

Eyes have evolved as specialized organs to detect light. **FIGURE 4.4** shows the human eye in cross-section. Light that reaches the eyes passes first through a clear, smooth outer tissue, called the *cornea,* and then through the *pupil,* a hole in the colored part of the eye. This colored part is the *iris,* a translucent, doughnut-shaped muscle that controls the size of the pupil and hence the amount of light that can enter the eye.

Immediately behind the iris, muscles inside the eye control the shape of the *lens* to bend the light again and focus it onto the **retina,** *light-sensitive tissue lining the back of the eyeball.* The muscles change the shape of the lens to focus objects at different distances, making the lens flatter for objects that are far away or rounder for nearby

retina Light-sensitive tissue lining the back of the eyeball.

accommodation The process by which the eye maintains a clear image on the retina.

objects. This is called **accommodation,** *the process by which the eye maintains a clear image on the retina.* **FIGURE 4.5a** shows how accommodation works.

If your eyeballs are a little too long or a little too short, the lens will not focus images properly on the retina. If the eyeball is too long, images are focused in front of the retina, leading to near-sightedness (*myopia*), as shown in **FIGURE 4.5b**. If the eyeball is too short, images are focused behind the retina, and the result is far-sightedness (*hyperopia*), as shown in **FIGURE 4.5c**. Eyeglasses, contact lenses, and surgical procedures can correct either condition. For example, eyeglasses and contacts both provide an additional lens to help focus light more appropriately, and procedures such as LASIK physically reshape the eye's existing lens.

Light reflected from a surface enters the eyes via the transparent **cornea,** bending to pass through the **pupil** at the center of the colored **iris.**

Muscles to move eye

Behind the iris, the thickness and shape of the **lens** adjust to focus light on the **retina,** where the image appears upside down and backward. Vision is clearest at the **fovea.**

Light-sensitive receptor cells in the **retinal surface,** excited or inhibited by spots of light, influence the specialized neurons that signal the brain's visual centers through their bundled axons, which make up the **optic nerve.** The optic nerve creates the **blind spot.**

▲ Figure **4.4** **Anatomy of the Human Eye** Light reflected from a surface enters the eye via the transparent cornea, then through the pupil at the center of the colored iris. Behind the iris, the thickness and shape of the lens adjust to focus the light on the retina, where the image appears upside down and backward. Basically, this is how a camera lens works. Light-sensitive receptor cells in the retinal surface, excited or inhibited by spots of light, influence the specialized neurons that convey nerve impulses to the brain's visual centers through their axons, which make up the optic nerve.

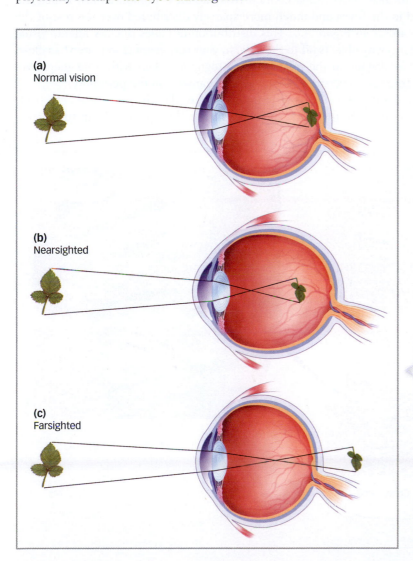

(a)
Normal vision

(b)
Nearsighted

(c)
Farsighted

◄ Figure **4.5** **Accommodation** Inside the eye, the lens changes shape to focus nearby or faraway objects on the retina. (a) People with normal vision focus the image on the retina at the back of the eye, both for near and far objects. (b) Nearsighted people see clearly what's nearby, but distant objects are blurry because light from them is focused in front of the retina, a condition called myopia. (c) Farsighted people have the opposite problem: Distant objects are clear, but those nearby are blurry because their point of focus falls beyond the surface of the retina, a condition called hyperopia.

cones Photoreceptors that detect color, operate under normal daylight conditions, and allow us to focus on fine detail.

rods Photoreceptors that become active under low-light conditions for night vision.

fovea An area of the retina where vision is the clearest and there are no rods at all.

blind spot A location in the visual field that produces no sensation on the retina because the corresponding area of the retina contains neither rods nor cones and therefore has no mechanism to sense light.

receptive field The region of the sensory surface that, when stimulated, causes a change in the firing rate of that neuron.

▼ Figure 4.6 **Close-up of the Retina** The surface of the retina is composed of photoreceptor cells, the rods and cones, beneath a layer of transparent neurons, the bipolar and retinal ganglion cells, connected in sequence. Viewed close up in this cross-sectional diagram is the area of greatest visual acuity, the fovea, where most color-sensitive cones are concentrated, allowing us to see fine detail as well as color. Rods, the predominant photoreceptors activated in low-light conditions, are distributed everywhere else on the retina.

Phototransduction in the Retina

How does a wavelength of light become a meaningful image? The retina is the interface between the world of light outside the body and the world of vision inside the central nervous system. Two types of *photoreceptor cells* in the retina contain light-sensitive pigments that transduce light into neural impulses. **Cones** *detect color, operate under normal daylight conditions, and allow us to focus on fine detail.* **Rods** *become active under low-light conditions for night vision* (see **FIGURE 4.6**).

Rods are much more sensitive to low light levels than cones, but this sensitivity comes at a cost: They provide no information about color because they sense only shades of gray. Think about this the next time you wake up in the middle of the night and make your way to the bathroom for a drink of water, and you'll notice that you see the room only in shades of gray. About 120 million rods are distributed more or less evenly around each retina except in the very center, the **fovea,** *an area of the retina where vision is the clearest and there are no rods at all.* The absence of rods in the fovea decreases the sharpness of vision in reduced light, but it can be overcome. For example, when amateur astronomers view dim stars through their telescopes at night, they know to look a little off to the side of the target so that the image will fall not on the rod-free fovea but on some other part of the retina that contains many highly sensitive rods.

> **?** What are the major differences between rods and cones?

In contrast to rods, each retina contains only about 6 million cones, which are densely packed in the fovea and much more sparsely distributed over the rest of the retina, as you can see in Figure 4.6. This distribution of cones directly affects visual acuity and explains why objects off to the side, in your *peripheral vision,* aren't so clear. The process is analogous to the quality of photographs taken with a six-megapixel digital camera (the fovea) versus a two-megapixel camera (in the periphery).

The retina is thick with cells. As seen in Figure 4.6, the photoreceptor cells (rods and cones) send signals to the oddly shaped *bipolar cells;* bipolar cells in turn trans-

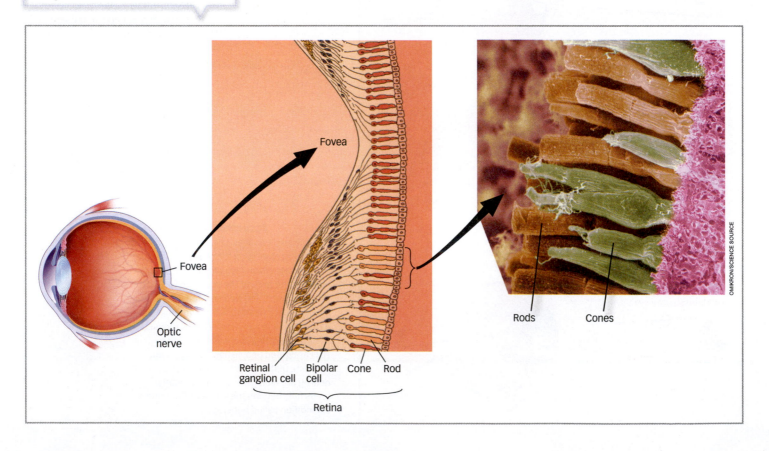

Fovea

Fovea

Optic nerve

Retinal ganglion cell   Bipolar cell   Cone   Rod

Retina

Rods   Cones

OMIKRON/SCIENCE SOURCE

The image on the left was taken at a higher resolution than the image on the right. The difference in quality is analogous to light falling on the fovea versus not.

mit signals to *retinal ganglion cells* (RGCs), which organize the signals and send them to the brain. The axons of RGCs form the *optic nerve*, which leaves the eye through a hole in the retina. Because it contains neither rods nor cones and therefore has no mechanism to sense light, this hole in the retina creates a **blind spot,** which is *a location in the visual field that produces no sensation on the retina.* Try the demonstration in **FIGURE 4.7** to find the blind spot in each of your own eyes.

Each RCG responds to input not from a single rod or cone but from an entire patch of adjacent photoreceptors in the retina (**FIGURE 4.8**). The RCG will thus respond to light falling anywhere within that small patch, which is called the cell's **receptive field,** *the region of the sensory surface that, when stimulated, causes a change in the firing rate of that neuron.* Although we'll focus on vision here, the general concept of receptive fields applies to all sensory systems. For example, the cells that connect to the touch centers of the brain have receptive fields, which are the part of the skin that, when stimulated, causes that cell's response to change in some way.

▲ Figure **4.7** **Blind Spot Demonstration** To find your blind spot, close your left eye and stare at the cross with your right eye. Hold the book 6 to 12 inches (15 to 30 centimeters) away from your eyes and move it slowly toward and away from you until the dot disappears. The dot is now in your blind spot and so is not visible. At this point the vertical lines may appear as one continuous line because the visual system fills in the area occupied by the missing dot. To test your left-eye blind spot, turn the book upside down and repeat with your right eye closed.

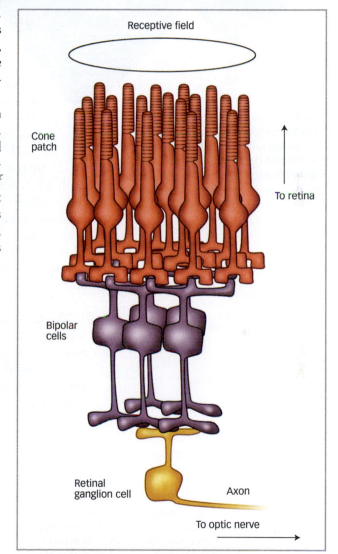

▲ Figure **4.8** **Receptive Field of a Retinal Ganglion Cell** The axon of a retinal ganglion cell, shown at the bottom of the figure, joins with all other RGC axons to form the optic nerve. Each RGC receives input from a cluster of five or six bipolar cells, which in turn receive input from a patch of photoreceptors connected to that bipolar cell. The RGC responds to a spot of light falling anywhere on that the patch, forming its receptive field.

Perceiving Color

Sir Isaac Newton pointed out around 1670 that color is not something "in" light. In fact, color is nothing but our perception of wavelengths (see Table 4.3) from the spectrum of visible light (see Figure 4.3). We perceive the shortest visible wavelengths as deep purple. As wavelengths increase, the color perceived changes gradually and continuously to blue, then green, yellow, orange, and, with the longest visible wavelengths, red. This rainbow of hues and accompanying wavelengths is called the *visible spectrum,* illustrated in **FIGURE 4.9**.

The full-color image on the left is what you'd see if your rods and cones were fully at work. The grayscale image on the right is what you'd see if only your rods were functioning.

You'll recall that rods are ideal for low-light vision but bad for distinguishing colors. Cones, by contrast, come in three types, each of which is especially sensitive to either red (long-wavelength), green (medium-wavelength), or blue (short-wavelength) light. Red, green, and blue are the primary colors of light; color perception results from different combinations of the three basic elements in the retina that respond to the wavelengths corresponding to the three primary colors of light. For example, lighting designers mix primary colors of light together, such as shining red and green spotlights on a surface to create a yellow light, as shown in **FIGURE 4.10a**. Notice that in the center of the figure, where the red, green, and blue lights overlap, the surface looks white. This demonstrates that a white surface really is reflecting all visible wavelengths of light.

By the way, as you may have discovered for yourself, slightly different rules apply when mixing paints: You can re-create any color found in nature by mixing only three colors—red, blue, and yellow—but stirring all of them together creates not white but a muddy approximation of black. This is because whereas spotlights *project* colors of light, painting a surface causes it to *absorb* colors of light. Red paint absorbs all the wavelengths *except* red, which is reflected back and can be detected by your eye, making the surface appear red. When you add additional colors of paint, more and more wavelengths are absorbed until—when you mix all the colors together—all the light is absorbed and none is reflected, creating the color black [**FIGURE 4.10b**].

The fact that three types of cones in the retina respond preferentially to different wavelengths (corresponding to blue, green, or red light) means that the pattern of responding across the three types of cones provides a unique code for each color. In fact, researchers can "read out" the wavelength of the light entering the eye by working backward from the relative firing rates of the three types of cones (Gegenfurtner & Kiper, 2003). A genetic disorder in which one of the cone types is missing—and, in some very rare cases, two or all three—causes a *color deficiency*. This trait is sex-linked, affecting men much more often than women.

▶ Figure **4.9** **Seeing in Color** We perceive a spectrum of color because objects selectively absorb some wavelengths of light and reflect others. Color perception corresponds to the summed activity of the three types of cones. Each type is most sensitive to a narrow range of wavelengths in the visible spectrum—short (bluish light), medium (greenish light), or long (reddish light). Rods, represented by the white curve, are most sensitive to the medium wavelengths of visible light but do not contribute to color perception.

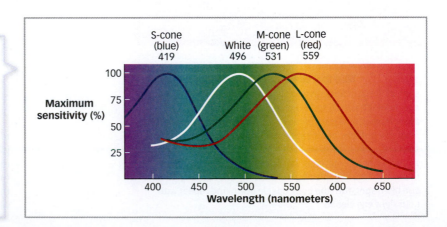

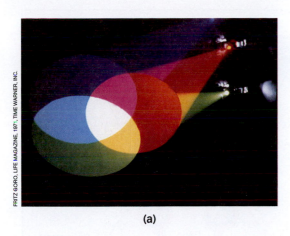
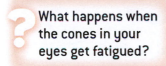
(a)

(b)

◀ Figure **4.10** **Color Mixing** The millions of shades of color that humans can perceive are products not only of a light's wavelength but also of the mixture of wavelengths a stimulus absorbs or reflects. (a) Colored spotlights work by causing the surface to reflect light of a particular wavelength, which stimulates the red, blue, or green photopigments in the cones. When all visible wavelengths are present, we see white. (b) Colored paints work by removing wavelengths, so that the painted surface absorbs all the wavelengths except those reflected by the paint. When all visible wavelengths are absorbed, we see black.

Color deficiency is often referred to as *color blindness,* but, in fact, people missing only one type of cone can still distinguish many colors, just not as many as someone who has the full complement of three cone types. Like synesthetes, people whose vision is color-deficient often do not realize that they experience color differently from others.

You can create a kind of temporary color deficiency by exploiting the idea of sensory adaptation. Just like the rest of your body, cones need an occasional break too.

? What happens when the cones in your eyes get fatigued?

Staring too long at one color fatigues the cones that respond to that color, producing a form of sensory adaptation that results in a *color afterimage.* To demonstrate this effect for yourself, follow these instructions for **FIGURE 4.11**:

> Stare at the small cross between the two color patches for about 1 minute. Try to keep your eyes as still as possible.

> After a minute, look at the lower cross. You should see a vivid color after effect that lasts for a minute or more. Pay particular attention to the colors in the afterimage.

Were you puzzled that the red patch produces a green afterimage and the green patch produces a red afterimage? When you view a color—say, green—the cones that respond most strongly to green become fatigued over time. Now, when you stare at a white or gray patch, which reflects all the colors equally, the green-sensitive cones respond only weakly compared with the still-fresh red-sensitive cones, which fire strongly. The result? You perceive the patch as tinted red.

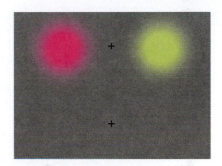

▲ Figure **4.11** **Color Afterimage Demonstration** Follow the accompanying instructions in the text, and sensory adaptation will do the rest. When the afterimage fades, you can get back to reading the chapter.

The Visual Brain

We have seen that a great deal of visual processing takes place within the retina itself. More complex aspects of vision, however, require more powerful processing, and that enlists the brain.

Half of the axons in the optic nerve that leave each eye come from retinal ganglion cells that code information in the right visual field, whereas the other half code information in the left visual field. These two nerve bundles link to the left and right hemispheres of the brain, respectively (see **FIGURE 4.12**). The optic nerve travels from each eye to the *thalamus,* and then to the back of the brain, to a location called **area V1,** the *part of the occipital lobe that contains the primary visual cortex.* Here the information is systematically mapped into a representation of the visual scene. There are about 30 to 50 brain areas specialized for vision, located mainly in the occipital lobe at the back of the brain and in the temporal lobes on the sides of the brain (Orban, Van Essen, & Vanduffel, 2004; Van Essen, Anderson, & Felleman, 1992).

area V1 The part of the occipital lobe that contains the primary visual cortex.

▶ Figure **4.12** **Visual Pathway from Eye Through Brain** Objects in the right visual field stimulate the left half of each retina, and objects in the left visual field stimulate the right half of each retina. The optic nerves, one exiting each eye, are formed by the axons of retinal ganglion cells emerging from the retina. Just before they enter the brain at the optic chiasm, about half the nerve fibers from each eye cross. The left half of each optic nerve, representing the right visual field, runs through the brain's left hemisphere via the thalamus, and the right half, representing the left visual field, travels this route through the right hemisphere. So information from the right visual field ends up in the left hemisphere and information from the left visual field ends up in the right hemisphere.

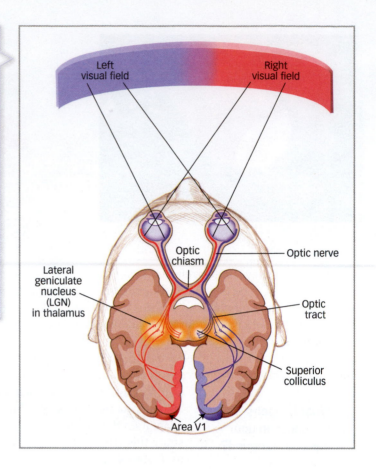

Neural Systems for Perceiving Shape

One of the most important functions of vision involves perceiving the shapes of objects; our day-to-day lives would be a mess if we couldn't reliably differentiate between a warm doughnut with glazed icing and a straight stalk of celery. Perceiving shape depends on the location and orientation of an object's edges. It is not surprising, then, that area V1 is specialized for encoding edge orientation.

As you read in Chapter 3, neurons in the visual cortex selectively respond to bars and edges in specific orientations in space (Hubel & Weisel, 1962, 1998). In effect, area V1 contains populations of neurons, each "tuned" to respond to edges oriented at each position in the visual field. This means that some neurons fire when an object in a vertical orientation is perceived, other neurons fire when an object in a horizontal orientation is perceived, still other neurons fire when objects in a diagonal orientation of 45 degrees are perceived, and so on (see **FIGURE 4.13**). The outcome of the coordinated response of all these feature detectors contributes to a sophisticated visual system that can detect where a doughnut ends and celery begins.

Pathways for What, Where, and How

From the occipital lobe, two functionally distinct pathways, or *visual streams*, project to visual areas in other parts of the brain (see **FIGURE 4.14**). One, the *ventral* ("below") *stream*, travels across the occipital lobe into the lower levels of the temporal lobes and includes brain areas that represent an object's shape and identity—in other words, what it is. The damage caused by Betty's stroke that you read about in Chapter 3 interrupted this "what pathway" (Tanaka, 1996). As a result, Betty could not recognize familiar faces even though she could still see them. The other pathway, the *dorsal* ("above")

? **What are the main jobs of the ventral and dorsal streams?**

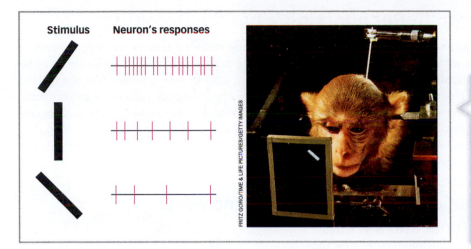

Stimulus   Neuron's responses

FRITZ GORO/TIME & LIFE PICTURES/GETTY IMAGES

◄ Figure **4.13** **Single-Neuron Feature Detectors** Area V1 contains neurons that respond to specific orientations of edges. Here a single neuron's responses are recorded (left) as the monkey views bars at different orientations (far left). This neuron fires continuously when the bar is pointing to the right at 45 degrees, less often when it is vertical, and not at all when it is pointing to the left at 45 degrees.

stream, travels up from the occipital lobe to the parietal lobes (including some of the middle and upper levels of the temporal lobes), connecting with brain areas that identify the location and motion of an object—in other words, where it is. Because the dorsal stream allows us to perceive spatial relations, researchers originally dubbed it the "where pathway" (Ungerleider & Mishkin, 1982). Neuroscientists later argued that because the dorsal stream is crucial for guiding movements, such as aiming, reaching, or tracking with the eyes, the "where pathway" should more appropriately be called the "how pathway" (Milner & Goodale, 1995).

Some of the most dramatic evidence for two distinct visual streams comes from studying the impairments that result from brain injury. A patient known as D. F. suffered permanent brain damage following exposure to toxic levels of carbon monoxide (Goodale et al., 1991). A large region of the lateral occipital cortex was destroyed, an area in the ventral stream that is very active when people recognize objects. D. F.'s ability to recognize objects by sight was greatly impaired, although her ability to recognize objects by touch was normal. This suggests that the *visual representation* of objects, not D. F.'s *memory* for objects, was damaged. Like Betty's inability to recognize familiar faces, D. F.'s brain damage belongs to a category called **visual-form agnosia,** *the inability to recognize objects by sight* (Goodale & Milner, 1992, 2004).

Frontal lobe

Parietal lobe

Dorsal stream

Occipital lobe

Area V1

Ventral stream

Temporal lobe

▲ Figure **4.14** **Visual Streaming** One interconnected visual system forms a pathway that courses from the occipital visual regions into the lower temporal lobe. This ventral pathway enables us to identify what we see. Another interconnected pathway travels from the occipital lobe through the upper regions of the temporal lobe into the parietal regions. This dorsal pathway allows us to locate objects, to track their movements, and to move in relation to them.

SUMMARY QUIZ [4.2]

1. Which is the correct sequence of eye parts that light passes through on the way to the brain?

   a. pupil, lens, cornea, retina

   b. cornea, pupil, lens, retina

   c. iris, lens, pupil, cornea

   d. lens, pupil, cornea, retina

2. Light striking the retina, causing a specific pattern of response in the three cone types, leads to our ability to see

   a. motion.   b. colors.   c. depth.   d. shadows.

3. In which part of the brain is the primary visual cortex, where encoded information is systematically mapped into a representation of the visual scene?

   a. the thalamus

   b. the lateral geniculate nucleus

   c. the fovea

   d. area V1

visual-form agnosia The inability to recognize objects by sight.

Vision II: Recognizing What We Perceive

Our journey into the visual system has already revealed how it accomplishes some pretty astonishing feats. But the system needs to do much more in order for us to be able to interact effectively with our visual worlds. Let's now consider how the system links together individual visual features into whole objects, allows us to recognize what those objects are, organizes objects into visual scenes, and detects motion and change in those scenes. Along the way we'll see that studying visual errors and illusions provides key insights into how these processes work, and we'll also revisit the intriguing world of synesthesia.

Attention: The "Glue" That Binds Individual Features into a Whole

As we've seen, specialized feature detectors in different parts of the visual system analyze each of the multiple features of a visible object—orientation, color, size, shape, and so forth. But how are different features combined into single, unified objects? What allows us to perceive that the man in the photo is wearing a red shirt and the woman is wearing a yellow shirt? Why don't we see free-floating patches of red and yellow? These questions refer to what researchers call the **binding problem** in perception, which concerns *how features are linked together so that we see unified objects in our visual world rather than free-floating or miscombined features* (Treisman, 1998, 2006).

Illusory Conjunctions: Perceptual Mistakes

In everyday life, we correctly combine features into unified objects so automatically and effortlessly that it may be difficult to appreciate that binding is ever a problem at all. However, researchers have discovered errors in binding that reveal important clues about how the process works. One such error is known as an **illusory conjunction,** *a perceptual mistake in which features from multiple objects are incorrectly combined.* In a pioneering study of illusory conjunctions, researchers briefly showed study participants visual displays in which black digits flanked colored letters, then instructed them first to report the black digits and second to describe the colored letters (Treisman & Schmidt, 1982). Participants frequently reported illusory conjunctions, claiming to have seen, for example, a blue A or a red X instead of the red A and the blue X that had actually been shown (see **FIGURE 4.15**). These illusory conjunctions were not just the result of guessing; they occurred more frequently than other kinds of errors, such as reporting a letter or color that was not present in the display.

Why do illusory conjunctions occur? Psychologist Anne Treisman and her colleagues have proposed a **feature integration theory** (Treisman, 1998, 2006; Treisman & Gelade, 1980; Treisman & Schmidt, 1982), which holds that *focused attention is not required to detect the individual features that comprise a stimulus, such as the color, shape, size, and location of letters, but is required to bind those individual features together.* From this perspective, attention provides the "glue" necessary to bind features together, and illusory conjunctions occur when it is difficult for participants to pay full attention to the features that need to be glued together. For example, in the experiments we just considered, participants were required to process the digits that flank the colored letters, thereby reducing attention to the letters and allowing illusory conjunctions to occur. When experimental conditions are changed so that participants can pay full attention to the colored letters, and they are able to correctly

We correctly combine features into unified objects, so, for example, we see that the man is wearing a red shirt and the woman is wearing a yellow shirt.

FUSE/PUNCHSTOCK

binding problem A phenomenon that concerns how features are linked together so that we see unified objects in our visual world rather than free-floating or miscombined features.

illusory conjunction A perceptual mistake where features from multiple objects are incorrectly combined.

feature integration theory The idea that focused attention is not required to detect the individual features that comprise a stimulus but is required to bind those individual features together.

? How does the study of illusory conjunctions help in understanding the role of attention in feature binding?

bind their features together, illusory conjunctions disappear (Treisman, 1998; Treisman & Schmidt, 1982).

The Role of the Parietal Lobe

The binding process makes use of feature information processed by structures within the ventral visual stream, the "what pathway" (Seymour et al., 2010; see Figure 4.14). But because binding involves linking together features that appear at a particular spatial location, it also depends critically on the parietal lobe in the dorsal stream, the "where pathway" (Robertson, 1999). For example, Treisman and others studied a patient, R. M., who had suffered strokes that destroyed both his left and right parietal lobes. Though many aspects of his visual function were intact, he had severe problems attending to spatially distinct objects. When presented with stimuli such as those in Figure 4.15, R. M. perceived an abnormally large number of illusory conjunctions, even when he was given as long as 10 seconds to look at the displays (Friedman-Hill, Robertson, & Treisman, 1995; Robertson, 2003).

These findings fit nicely with recent *transcranial magnetic stimulation* (TMS) studies. TMS is a benign technique that involves placing a powerful pulsed magnet over a person's scalp, which temporarily alters neuronal activity in the brain. Researchers have attempted to temporarily "turn off" the posterior

> **How have TMS studies increased our understanding of feature binding?**

parietal lobe while participants performed a feature-binding task involving colors and letters. Applying TMS during the task resulted in an increased number of illusory conjunctions but not in other kinds of perceptual errors (Braet & Humphreys, 2009). When TMS was applied to the occipital lobe, it had no effect on illusory conjunctions (Braet & Humphreys, 2009). These findings help to refine the original suggestion from feature integration theory that feature binding depends critically on attentional processes (Treisman, 1998).

Binding and Attention in Synesthesia

The findings and ideas we've just considered turn out to be highly relevant to synesthesia. Some synesthetes consistently perceive particular letters in a particular color (see Figure 4.1). Some researchers have characterized synesthesia as an instance of atypical feature binding. Normal binding of colors and letters, for example, is a response to actual features of the external stimulus, but in synesthesia, the color feature is not present in the external stimulus.

For example, fMRI studies of synesthetic individuals have revealed that the parietal lobe regions that are implicated in normal binding of color and shape become active during the experience of letter-color synesthesia (Weiss, Zilles, & Fink, 2005). Consistent with the idea that parietal activity is related to attentional processes needed for binding, other experiments have shown that synesthetic bindings, such as seeing a particular digit in a particular color, depend on attention (Mattingly, 2009; Robertson, 2003; Sagiv, Heer, & Robertson, 2006). For instance, when dots are quickly presented to a synesthetic individual together with digits (e.g., 7) that induce a synesthetic perception of green, the synesthete names the color of the dots more quickly when they are green than when they are orange—that is, when the dot color matches the color of the synesthetic perception. But when synesthetes are instructed to ignore the numbers, there is little difference in the amount of time taken to name the color of the green and orange dots, suggesting that attention is required to bind the synesthetic color to the digit (Robertson, 2003; Sagiv et al., 2006). Although our perceptual experiences differ substantially from those of synesthetes, they rely on the same basic mechanisms of feature binding.

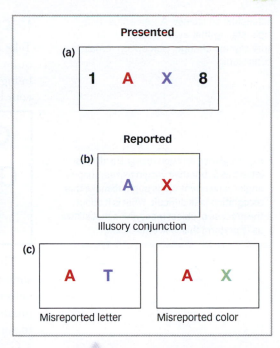

▲ Figure 4.15 **Illusory Conjunctions** Illusory conjunctions occur when features such as color and shape are combined incorrectly. (a) In one study, participants were shown a red A and blue X, flanked by black digits, and were instructed to report the digits first followed by the positions, colors, and names of any letters in the display. (b) They sometimes reported seeing a blue A and red X. (c) Other kinds of errors, such as a misreported letter (e.g., reporting "T" when no T was presented) or misreported color (reporting "green" when no green was presented), occured rarely, indicating that illusory conjunctions are not the result of guessing (based on Robertson, 2003).

perceptual constancy A perceptual principle stating that even as aspects of sensory signals change, perception remains consistent.

Recognizing Objects by Sight

Take a quick look at the letters in the accompanying illustration. Even though they're quite different from one another, you probably effortlessly recognized them as all being examples of the letter G. Now consider the same kind of demonstration using your best friend's face. Suppose one day your friend gets a dramatic new haircut—or

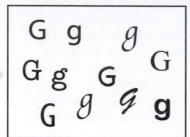

adds glasses, hair dye, or a nose ring. Even though your friend now looks strikingly different, you still recognize that person with ease. Just like the variability in Gs, you somehow are able to extract the underlying features of the face that allow you to accurately identify your friend. These examples illustrate the principle of **perceptual constancy:** *Even as aspects of sensory signals change, perception remains consistent.*

> A quick glance and you recognize all these letters as *G*, but their varying sizes, shapes, angles, and orientations ought to make this recognition task difficult. What is it about the process of object recognition that allows us to perform this task effortlessly?

This may seem trivial, but it's no small perceptual feat. If the visual system were somehow stumped each time a minor variation occurred in an object being perceived, the inefficiency of it all would be overwhelming. We'd have to effortfully process information just to perceive our friend as the same person from one meeting to another, not to mention laboring through the process of knowing when a G is really a G. In general, though, object recognition proceeds fairly smoothly, in large part because of the operation of the feature detectors we discussed earlier.

How do feature detectors help the visual system perform accurate perception of an object, such as your friend's face, in different circumstances? Some researchers argue for a *modular view*: that specialized brain areas, or modules, detect and represent faces or houses or even body parts. Using fMRI to examine visual processing in healthy young adults, researchers found a subregion in the temporal lobe that responds most strongly to faces compared with just about any other object category, while a nearby area responds most strongly to buildings and landscapes (Kanwisher, McDermott, & Chun, 1997). This view suggests we have not only feature detectors to aid in visual perception but also "face detectors," "building detectors," and possibly other types of neurons specialized for particular types of object perception (Downing et al., 2006; Kanwisher & Yovel, 2006).

Psychologists and researchers who argue for a more *distributed representation* of object categories challenge the modular view. Researchers have shown that although a subregion in the temporal lobes does respond more to faces than to any other category, parts of the brain outside this area may also be involved in face recognition. In this view, it is the pattern of activity across multiple brain regions that identifies any viewed object, including faces (Haxby et al., 2001). Each of these views explains some data better than the other one, and researchers are continuing to debate their relative merits.

> Our visual systems allows us to identify people as the same individual even when they change such features as their hairstyle, hair color, or jewelry. Despite the extreme changes between these actors in their natural state and as they appeared in the movie *Avatar*, can you tell that the same individuals are shown in each of the two photos?

Principles of Perceptual Organization

Before object recognition can even kick in, the visual system must perform another important task: grouping the image regions that belong together into a representation of an object. The idea that we tend to perceive a unified, whole object rather than a collection of separate parts is the foundation of Gestalt psychology, which you read about in Chapter 1. Gestalt principles characterize many aspects of human perception. Among the foremost are the Gestalt *perceptual grouping rules,* which govern how the features and regions of things fit together (Koffka, 1935). Here's a sampling:

> *Simplicity*: A basic rule in science is that the simplest explanation is usually the best. When confronted with two or more possible interpretations of an object's shape, the visual system tends to select the simplest or most likely interpretation (see **FIGURE 4.16a**).

> *Closure*: We tend to fill in missing elements of a visual scene, allowing us to perceive edges that are separated by gaps as belonging to complete objects (see **FIGURE 4.16b**).

> *Continuity*: Edges or contours that have the same orientation have what the Gestaltists called "good continuation," and we tend to group them together perceptually (see **FIGURE 4.16c**).

> *Similarity*: Regions that are similar in color, lightness, shape, or texture are perceived as belonging to the same object (see **FIGURE 4.16d**).

> *Proximity*: Objects that are close together tend to be grouped together (see **FIGURE 4.16e**).

> *Common fate*: Elements of a visual image that move together are perceived as parts of a single moving object (see **FIGURE 4.16f**).

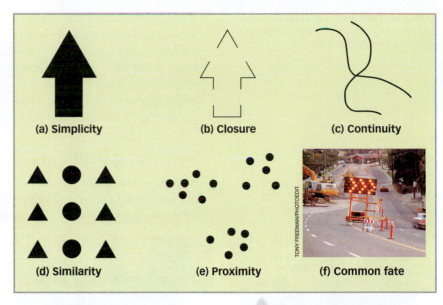

(a) Simplicity   (b) Closure   (c) Continuity
(d) Similarity   (e) Proximity   (f) Common fate

TONY FREEMAN/PHOTOEDIT

▲ Figure **4.16** **Perceptual Grouping Rules** Principles first identified by Gestalt psychologists demonstrate that the brain is predisposed to impose order on incoming sensations. One neural strategy for perception involves responding to patterns among stimuli and grouping like patterns together.

Separating Figure from Ground

Perceptual grouping is a powerful aid to our ability to recognize objects by sight. Grouping involves visually separating an object from its surroundings. In Gestalt terms, this means identifying a *figure* apart from the (back)*ground* in which it resides. For example, the words on this page are perceived as figural: They stand out from the ground of the sheet of paper on which they're printed. You certainly can perceive these elements differently, of course: The words *and* the paper are all part of a thing called "a page." Typically, though, our perceptual systems focus attention on some objects as distinct from their environments.

Size provides one clue to what's figure and what's ground: Smaller regions are likely to be figures, such as tiny letters on a big piece of paper. Another critical step toward object recognition is *edge assignment*. Given an edge, or boundary, between figure and ground, which region does that edge belong to? If the edge belongs to the figure, it helps define the object's shape, and the background continues behind the edge. Sometimes, though, it's not easy to tell which is which.

Edgar Rubin (1886–1951), a Danish psychologist, capitalized on this ambiguity in developing a famous illusion called the *Rubin vase* or, more generally, a *reversible figure-ground relationship*. You can view this "face-vase" illusion in **FIGURE 4.17** in two ways, either as a vase on a black background or as a pair of silhouettes facing each

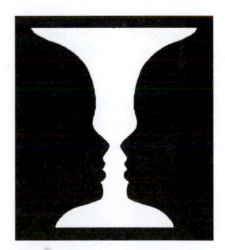

▲ Figure **4.17** **Ambiguous Edges** Here's how Rubin's classic reversible figure-ground illusion works: Fixate your eyes on the center of the image, and your perception will alternate between a vase and facing silhouettes, even as the sensory stimulation remains constant.

monocular depth cues Aspects of a scene that yield information about depth when viewed with only one eye.

other. Your visual system settles on one or the other interpretation and fluctuates between them every few seconds. This happens because the edge that would normally separate figure from ground is really part of neither: It equally defines the contours of the vase and the contours of the faces. Evidence from fMRIs shows, quite nicely, that when people are seeing the Rubin image as a face, there is greater activity in the face-selective region of the temporal lobe we discussed earlier than when they are seeing it as a vase (Hasson et al., 2001).

Perceiving Depth and Size

Objects in the world are arranged in three dimensions—length, width, and depth—but the retinal image contains only two dimensions, length and width. How does the brain process a flat, two-dimensional retinal image so that we perceive the depth of an object and how far away it is? The answer lies in a collection of *depth cues* that change as you move through space. Monocular and binocular depth cues all help visual perception (Howard, 2002).

THE PHOTO WORKS

▲ Figure **4.18** **Relative Size** When you view images of things you know well, such as the people in the left-hand photo, the object you perceive as smaller appears farther away. With a little image manipulation, you can see in the right-hand photo that the relative size difference projected on your retinas is far greater than you perceive. The image of the person in the blue vest is exactly the same size in both photos.

Monocular Depth Cues

Monocular depth cues are *aspects of a scene that yield information about depth when viewed with only one eye.* These cues rely on the relationship between distance and size. Even with one eye closed, the retinal image of an object you're focused on grows smaller as that object moves farther away and larger as it moves closer. Our brains routinely use these differences in retinal image size, or *relative size,* to perceive distance. Most adults, for example, fall within a familiar range of heights (perhaps five to seven feet tall), so retinal image size alone is usually a reliable cue to how far away they are. Our visual system automatically corrects for size differences and attributes them to differences in distance. **FIGURE 4.18** demonstrates how strong this effect is.

In addition to relative size, there are several more monocular depth cues, such as the following:

> *Linear perspective,* the phenomenon that parallel lines seem to converge as they recede into the distance (see **FIGURE 4.19a**)

> *Texture gradient,* the fact that the size of elements on a patterned surface, as well as the distance between them, appears to grow smaller as the surface recedes from the observer (see **FIGURE 4.19b**)

> *Interposition,* the fact that, when one object partly blocks another (see **FIGURE 4.19c**), you can infer that the block*ing* object is closer than the block*ed* object

> *Relative height in the image,* the fact that objects that are closer to you are lower in your visual field, while faraway objects are higher (see **FIGURE 4.19d**)

A famous illusion that makes use of a variety of monocular depth cues is the *Ames room,* which is trapezoidal in shape rather than square: Only two sides are parallel (see **FIGURE 4.20a**). A person standing in one corner of an Ames room is physically twice as far away from the viewer as a person standing in the other corner. But when viewed with one eye through the small peephole placed in one wall, the Ames room

(a)

(b)

(c)

(d)

◄ Figure **4.19** **Pictorial Depth Cues** Visual artists rely on a variety of monocular cues to make their work come to life. You can rely on cues such as (a) linear perspective, (b) texture gradient, (c) interposition, and (d) relative height in an image to infer distance, depth, and position, even if you're wearing an eye patch.

▼ Figure **4.20** **The Amazing Ames Room** (a) A diagram showing the actual proportions of the Ames room reveals its secrets. The sides of the room form a trapezoid with parallel sides but a back wall that's way off square. The uneven floor makes the room's height in the far back corner shorter than the other. Add misleading cues such as specially designed windows and flooring and position the room's occupants in each far corner and you're ready to lure an unsuspecting observer. (b) Looking into the Ames room through the viewing port with only one eye, the observer infers a normal size-distance relationship—that both people are the same distance away. But the different image sizes they project on the retina lead the viewer to conclude, based on the monocular cue of familiar size, that one person is very small and the other very large.

looks square because the shapes of the windows and the flooring tiles are carefully crafted to *look* square from the viewing port (Ittelson, 1952). The visual system perceives the far wall as perpendicular to the line of sight so that people standing at different positions along that wall appear to be at the same distance, and the viewer's judgments of their sizes are based directly on retinal image size. As a result, a person standing in the right corner appears to be much larger than a person standing in the left corner (see **FIGURE 4.20***b*).

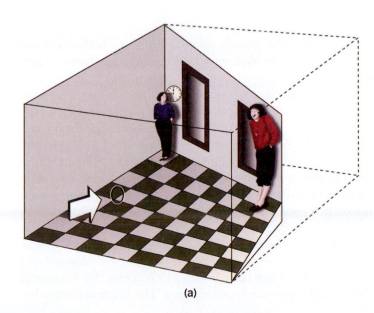

(a)

(b)

The View-Master has been a popular toy for decades. It is based on the principle of binocular disparity: Two images taken from slightly different angles produce a stereoscopic effect.

CORBIS/ALAMY

KODAK COLLECTION/SSPL/THE IMAGE WORKS

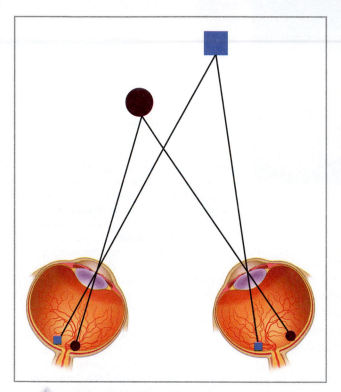

▲ Figure **4.21** **Binocular Disparity** We see the world in three dimensions because our eyes are a distance apart and the image of an object falls on the retinas of each eye at a slightly different place. In this two-object scene, the images of the square and the circle fall on different points of the retina in each eye. The disparity in the positions of the circle's retinal images provides a compelling cue to depth.

Binocular Depth Cues

We can also obtain depth information through **binocular disparity,** *the difference in the retinal images of the two eyes that provides information about depth.* Because our eyes are slightly separated, each registers a slightly different view of the world.

Your brain computes the disparity between the two retinal images to perceive how far away objects are, as shown in **FIGURE 4.21**. Viewed from above in the figure, the images of the more distant square and the closer circle each fall at different points on each retina. The View-Master toy and 3-D movies both make use of this phenomenon by showing slightly displaced images to each eye, creating the illusion of depth.

Perceiving Motion and Change

You should now have a good sense of how we see what and where objects are, a process made substantially easier when the objects stay in one place. But real life, of course, is full of moving targets; objects change position over time. Birds fly and horses gallop, rain and snow fall, trees bend in the wind. Understanding how we perceive motion and why we sometimes fail to perceive change can bring us closer to appreciating how visual perception works in everyday life.

Motion Perception

To sense motion, the visual system must encode information about both space and time. The simplest case to consider is an observer who does not move trying to perceive an object that does.

As an object moves across an observer's stationary visual field, it first stimulates one location on the retina, and then a little later it stimulates another location on the retina. Neural circuits in the brain can detect this change in position over time and respond to specific speeds and directions of motion (Emerson, Bergen, & Adelson, 1992). A region in the middle of the temporal lobe referred to as *MT* (part of the dorsal stream we discussed earlier) is specialized for the visual perception of motion (Born & Bradley, 2005; Newsome & Paré, 1988), and brain damage in this area leads to a deficit in normal motion perception (Zihl, von Cramon, & Mai, 1983).

Of course, in the real world, rarely are you a stationary observer. As you move around, your head and eyes move all the time, and motion perception is not simple. The motion-perception system must take into account the position and movement of your eyes, and ultimately of your head and body, in order to perceive the motions of objects correctly and allow you to approach or avoid them. The brain accomplishes this by monitoring your eye and head movements and "subtracting" them from the motion in the retinal image.

Motion perception, like color perception, is subject to sensory adaptation. A motion aftereffect called the *waterfall illusion* is analogous to color aftereffects. If you stare at the downward rush of a waterfall for several seconds, you'll experience an upward motion aftereffect when you then look at stationary objects near the waterfall such as trees or rocks. What's going on here?

Motion-sensitive neurons are connected to motion detector cells in the brain that encode motion in opposite directions. A sense of motion comes from the difference in the strength of these two opposing sensors. If one set of motion detector cells is fatigued through adaptation to motion in one direction, then the opposing sensor will take over. The net result is that motion is perceived in the opposite direction. Evidence from fMRIs indicates that when people experience the waterfall illusion while viewing a stationary stimulus, there is increased activity in region MT, which plays a key role in motion perception (Tootell et al., 1995).

> **?** **How can flashing lights on a casino sign give the impression of movement?**

The movement of objects in the world is not the only event that can evoke the perception of motion. The successively flashing lights of a Las Vegas casino sign can evoke a strong sense of motion. Recall, too, the Gestalt grouping rule of *common fate:* People perceive a series of flashing lights as a whole, moving object (see Figure 4.16f). This *perception of movement as a result of alternating signals appearing in rapid succession in different locations* is called **apparent motion.**

Video technology and animation depend on apparent motion. A sequence of still images sample the continuous motion in the original scene. In the case of motion pictures, the sampling rate is 24 frames per second (fps). A slower sampling rate would produce a much choppier sense of motion; a faster sampling rate would be a waste of resources because we would not perceive the motion as any smoother than it appears at 24 fps.

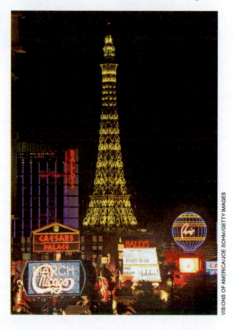

VISIONS OF AMERICA/JOE SOHM/GETTY IMAGES

> Want a powerful demonstration of apparent motion? Take a stroll down the Las Vegas strip.

Change Blindness and Inattentional Blindness

Motion involves a change in an object's position over time, but objects in the visual environment can change in ways that do not involve motion (Rensink, 2002). You might walk by the same clothing store window every day and notice when a new suit or dress is on display or register surprise when you see a friend's new haircut. Intuitively, we feel that we can easily detect changes to our visual environment. However, our comfortable intuitions have been challenged by experimental demonstrations of **change blindness,** which occurs *when people fail to detect changes to the visual details of a scene* (Rensink, 2002; Simons & Rensink, 2005). For example, Simons and Levin (1998) had an experimenter ask a person on a college campus for directions. While they were talking, two men walked between them holding a door that hid a second experimenter (see **FIGURE 4.22**). Behind the door, the two experimenters traded places, so that when the men carrying the door moved on, a different person was asking for directions than the one who had been there just a second or two earlier. Remarkably, only 7 of 15 participants reported noticing this change.

binocular disparity The difference in the retinal images of the two eyes that provides information about depth.

apparent motion The perception of movement as a result of alternating signals appearing in rapid succession in different locations.

change blindness A phenomenon that occurs when people fail to detect changes to the visual details of a scene.

(a)

(b)

(c)

(d)

FROM SIMONS & LEVIN (1998). FIGURE PROVIDED BY DANIEL SIMONS.

► Figure **4.22** **Change Blindness** The white-haired man was giving directions to one experimenter (a), who disappeared behind the moving door (b), only to be replaced by another experimenter (c). Like many other people, the man failed to detect a seemingly obvious change.

Although surprising, these findings once again illustrate the importance of focused attention for visual perception. We saw earlier that focused attention is critical for binding together the features of objects; experiments on change detection indicate that it is also necessary for detecting changes to objects and scenes (Rensink, 2002; Simons & Rensink, 2005). Change blindness is most likely to occur when people fail to focus attention on the changed object (even though the object is registered by the visual system) and is reduced for items that draw attention to themselves (Rensink, O'Regan, & Clark, 1997). Focused attention selects and binds together only some of the many visual features in the environment, and those bound features are the ones that comprise our conscious visual experience.

? How can a failure of focused attention explain change blindness?

The role of focused attention in conscious visual experience is also dramatically illustrated by the closely related phenomenon of **inattentional blindness,** which involves *a failure to perceive objects that are not the focus of attention.* In one study, researchers recruited a clown to ride a unicycle through a large square in the middle of the campus at Western Washington University (Hyman et al., 2010). The researchers then asked 151 students who had just walked through the square whether they saw the clown. Seventy-five percent of the students who were using cell phones failed to notice the clown, compared with less than 50% who were not using cell phones. Using cell phones draws on focused attention, resulting in increased inattentional blindness and emphasizing again that our conscious experience of the visual environment is restricted to those features or objects selected by focused attention. These findings have interesting implications for a world in which many of us are busy texting and talking on our cell phones while carrying on other kinds of everyday business.

College students who were using their cell phones while walking through campus failed to notice the unicycling clown more frequently than students who were not using their cell phones.

FROM IRA E. HYMAN, JR., ET AL., *APPLIED COGNITIVE PSYCHOLOGY* (2009), 24, 5, 597–607. © JOHN WILEY & SONS

SUMMARY QUIZ [4.3]

1. Our ability to visually combine details so that we perceive unified objects is explained by
   - a. feature integration theory.
   - b. illusory conjunction.
   - c. synesthesia.
   - d. ventral and dorsal streaming.

2. The idea that specialized brain areas represent particular classes of objects is
   - a. the modular view.
   - b. attentional processing.
   - c. distributed representation.
   - d. neuron response.

3. The principle of _____ holds that even as sensory signals change, perception remains consistent.
   - a. apparent motion
   - b. signal detection
   - c. perceptual constancy
   - d. closure

4. What kind of cues are relative size and linear perspective?
   - a. motion-based
   - b. binocular
   - c. monocular
   - d. template

Audition: More Than Meets the Ear

Vision is based on the spatial pattern of light waves on the retina. The sense of hearing, by contrast, is all about *sound waves*—changes in air pressure unfolding over time. Plenty of things produce sound waves: the collision of a tree hitting the forest floor, the impact of two hands clapping, the vibration of vocal cords during a stirring speech, the resonance of a bass guitar string during a thrash metal concert. Except for synesthetes who "hear colors," understanding most people's auditory experience requires understanding how we transform changes in air pressure into perceived sounds.

Sensing Sound

Striking a tuning fork produces a *pure tone,* a simple sound wave that first increases air pressure and then creates a relative vacuum. This cycle repeats hundreds or thousands of times per second as sound waves propagate outward in all directions from the source. Just as there are three dimensions of light waves corresponding to three dimensions of visual perception, so, too, there are three physical dimensions of a sound wave. Frequency, amplitude, and complexity determine what we hear as the pitch, loudness, and quality of a sound (see **TABLE 4.4**).

> The *frequency* of the sound wave, or its wavelength, depends on how often the peak in air pressure passes the ear or a microphone, measured in cycles per second, or hertz (abbreviated Hz). Changes in the physical frequency of a sound wave are perceived by humans as changes in **pitch,** *how high or low a sound is.*

> The *amplitude* of a sound wave refers to its height, relative to the threshold for human hearing (which is set at zero decibels, or dBs). Amplitude corresponds to **loudness,** or *a sound's intensity.* To give you an idea of amplitude and intensity, the rustling of leaves in a soft breeze is about 20 dB, normal conversation is measured at

"The ringing in your ears—I think I can help."

Table 4.4

Properties of Sound Waves

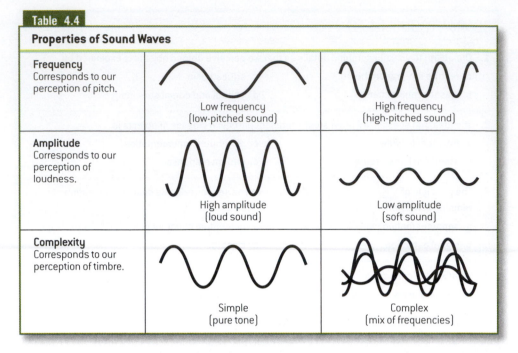

Frequency Corresponds to our perception of pitch.	Low frequency (low-pitched sound)	High frequency (high-pitched sound)
Amplitude Corresponds to our perception of loudness.	High amplitude (loud sound)	Low amplitude (soft sound)
Complexity Corresponds to our perception of timbre.	Simple (pure tone)	Complex (mix of frequencies)

JEWEL SAMAD/AFP/GETTY IMAGES

Foo Fighters star Dave Grohl has revealed that his deafness is causing problems in his marriage. "I'm virtually deaf . . . my wife asks me where we should go for dinner, and it sounds like the schoolteacher from the TV show *Charlie Brown*!"

about 40 dB, shouting produces 70 dB, a Slayer concert is about 130 dB, and the sound of the space shuttle taking off one mile away registers at 160 dB or more.

> Differences in the *complexity* of sound waves, or their mix of frequencies, correspond to **timbre,** *a listener's experience of sound quality or resonance.* Timbre (pronounced "TAM-ber") offers us information about the nature of sound. The same note played at the same loudness produces a perceptually different experience depending on whether it was played on a flute versus a trumpet, a phenomenon due entirely to timbre. Many "natural" sounds also illustrate the complexity of wavelengths, such as the sound of bees buzzing, the tonalities of speech, or the babbling of a brook. Unlike the purity of a tuning fork's hum, the drone of cicadas is a clamor of overlapping sound frequencies.

? Why does one note sound so different on a flute and a trumpet?

Of the three dimensions of sound waves, frequency provides most of the information we need to identify sounds. Amplitude and complexity contribute texture to our auditory perceptions, but it is frequency that allow us to identify the location of sounds, to understand speech, and to appreciate music—all skills that are valuable to our cultural survival. The focus in our discussion of hearing, then, is on how the auditory system encodes and represents sound-wave frequency (Kubovy, 1981).

The Human Ear

How does the auditory system convert sound waves into neural signals? The human ear is divided into three distinct parts, as shown in **FIGURE 4.23**: the *outer ear*, the *middle ear,* and the *inner ear.*

The outer ear consists of the visible part on the outside of the head (called the *pinna*); the auditory canal; and the eardrum, an airtight flap of skin that vibrates in response to sound waves gathered by the pinna and channeled into the canal. The middle ear, a tiny, air-filled chamber behind the eardrum, contains the three smallest bones in the body, called *ossicles*. Named for their appearance as hammer, anvil, and

timbre A listener's experience of sound quality or resonance.

cochlea A fluid-filled tube that is the organ of auditory transduction.

basilar membrane A structure in the inner ear that undulates when vibrations from the ossicles reach the cochlear fluid.

hair cells Specialized auditory receptor neurons embedded in the basilar membrane.

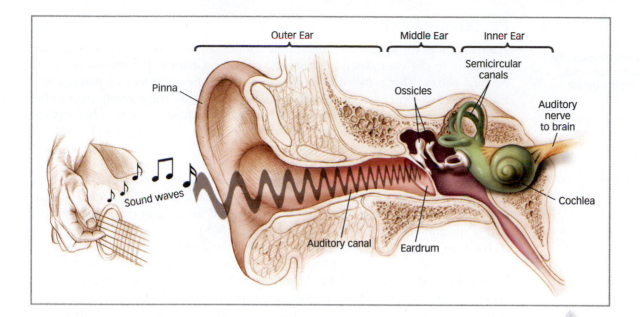

stirrup, the ossicles fit together into a lever that mechanically transmits and intensifies vibrations from the eardrum to the inner ear.

The inner ear contains the spiral-shaped **cochlea** (Latin for "snail"), *a fluid-filled tube that is the organ of auditory transduction.* The cochlea is divided along its length by the **basilar membrane,** *a structure in the inner ear that undulates when vibrations from the ossicles reach the cochlear fluid* (see **FIGURE 4.24**). Its wavelike movement stimulates thousands of tiny **hair cells,** *specialized auditory receptor neurons embedded in the basilar membrane.* The hair cells then release neurotransmitter molecules, initiating a neural signal in the auditory nerve that travels to the brain.

? How do hair cells in the ear enable us to hear?

▲ Figure **4.23** **Anatomy of the Human Ear** The pinna funnels sound waves into the auditory canal to vibrate the eardrum at a rate that corresponds to the sound's frequency. In the middle ear, the ossicles pick up the eardrum vibrations, amplify them, and pass them along by vibrating a membrane at the surface of the fluid-filled cochlea in the inner ear. Here fluid carries the wave energy to the auditory receptors that transduce it into electrochemical activity, exciting the neurons that form the auditory nerve, leading to the brain.

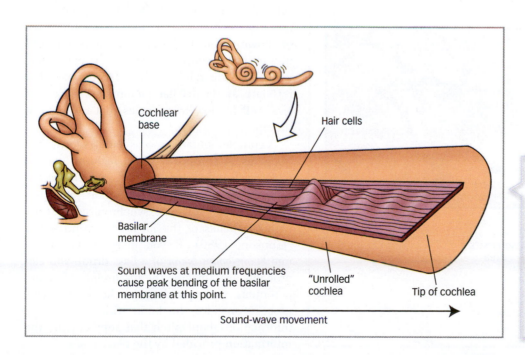

◄ Figure **4.24** **Auditory Transduction** Inside the cochlea, shown here as though it were uncoiling, the basilar membrane undulates in response to wave energy in the cochlear fluid. Waves of differing frequencies ripple varying locations along the membrane, from low frequencies at its tip to high frequencies at the base, and bend the embedded hair cell receptors at those locations. The hair-cell motion generates impulses in the auditory neurons, whose axons form the auditory nerve that emerges from the cochlea.

area A1 A portion of the temporal lobe that contains the primary auditory cortex.

place code The mechanism by which the cochlea encodes different frequencies at different locations along the basilar membrane.

temporal code The mechanism by which the cochlea registers low frequencies via the firing rate of action potentials entering the auditory nerve.

haptic perception The active exploration of the environment by touching and grasping objects with our hands.

▼ **Figure 4.25** **Primary Auditory Cortex** Area A1 is folded into the temporal lobe beneath the lateral fissure in each hemisphere. The left-hemisphere auditory areas govern speech in most people. (inset) The A1 cortex has a topographic organization, with lower frequencies mapping toward the front of the brain and higher frequencies toward the back, mirroring the organization of the basilar membrane along the cochlea (see Figure 4.24).

Perceiving Pitch

From the inner ear, action potentials in the auditory nerve travel to the thalamus and ultimately to the contralateral ("opposite side"; see Chapter 3) hemisphere of the cerebral cortex. This is called **area A1,** *a portion of the temporal lobe that contains the primary auditory cortex* (see **FIGURE 4.25**). For most of us, the auditory areas in the left hemisphere analyze sounds related to language and those in the right hemisphere specialize in rhythmic sounds and music. There is also evidence that the auditory cortex is composed of two distinct streams, roughly analogous to the dorsal and ventral streams of the visual system. Spatial ("where") auditory features, which allow you to locate the source of a sound in space, are handled by areas toward the back (caudal) part of the auditory cortex, whereas nonspatial ("what") features, such as temporal aspects of the acoustic signal, are handled by areas in the lower (ventral) part of the auditory cortex (Recanzone & Sutter, 2008).

Neurons in area A1 respond well to simple tones, and successive auditory areas in the brain process sounds of increasing complexity (Rauschecker & Scott, 2009; Schreiner, Read, & Sutter, 2000; Schreiner & Winer, 2007). Like area V1 in the visual cortex, area A1 has a topographic organization: Similar frequencies activate neurons in adjacent locations (see Figure 4.25, inset). A young adult with normal hearing ideally can detect sounds between about 20 and 20,000 Hz, although the ability to hear at the upper range decreases with age. But how is the frequency of a sound wave encoded in a neural signal?

Our ears have evolved two mechanisms to encode sound-wave frequency, one for high frequencies and one for low frequencies. The **place code,** used mainly for high frequencies, is active when *the cochlea encodes different frequencies at different locations along the basilar membrane.* Sounds of different frequencies cause waves that peak at different points on the basilar membrane (see Figure 4.24). When the frequency is low, the wide, floppy tip (*apex*) of the basilar membrane moves the most; when the frequency is high, the narrow, stiff end (*base*) of the membrane moves the most.

The movement of the basilar membrane causes hair cells to bend, initiating a neural signal in the auditory nerve. Axons fire the strongest in the hair

? How does the frequency of a sound wave relate to what we hear?

cells along the area of the basilar membrane that moves the most; in other words, the place of activation on the basilar membrane contributes to the perception of sound. The place code works best for relatively high frequencies that resonate at the basilar membrane's base and less well for low frequencies that resonate at the tip.

A complementary process handles lower frequencies. A **temporal code** *registers low frequencies via the firing rate of action potentials entering the auditory nerve.* Action potentials from the hair cells are synchronized in time with the peaks of the incoming sound waves (Johnson, 1980). If you imagine the rhythmic *boom-boom-boom* of a bass drum, you can probably also imagine the *fire-fire-fire* of action potentials corresponding to the beats. This process provides the brain with very precise information about pitch that supplements the information provided by the place code.

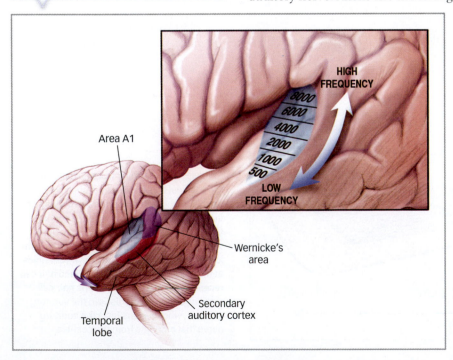

Area A1

HIGH
FREQUENCY

8000
6000
4000
2000
1000
500

LOW
FREQUENCY

Wernicke's area

Secondary auditory cortex

Temporal lobe

However, individual neurons can produce action potentials at a maximum rate of only about 1,000 spikes per second, so the temporal code does not work as well as the place code for high frequencies. Together, the place code and the temporal code work to cover the entire range of pitches that people can hear.

Localizing Sound Sources

Just as the differing positions of our eyes give us stereoscopic vision, the placement of our ears on opposite sides of the head gives us stereophonic hearing. The sound arriving at the ear closer to the sound source is louder than the sound in the farther ear, mainly because the listener's head partially blocks sound energy. This loudness difference decreases as the sound source moves from a position directly to one side (maximal difference) to straight ahead (no difference).

Another cue to a sound's location arises from timing: Sound waves arrive a little sooner at the near ear than at the far ear. The timing difference can be as brief as a few microseconds, but together with the intensity difference, it is sufficient to allow us to perceive the location of a sound. When the sound source is ambiguous, you may find yourself turning your head from side to side to localize it. By doing this, you are changing the relative intensity and timing of sound waves arriving in your ears and collecting better information about the likely source of the sound.

SUMMARY QUIZ [4.4]

1. What does the frequency of a sound wave determine?
   a. pitch   b. loudness   c. sound quality   d. timbre

2. The placement of our ears on opposite sides of the head is crucial to our ability to
   a. localize sound sources.   c. judge intensity.
   b. determine pitch.   d. recognize complexity.

3. The place code works best for encoding
   a. high intensities.   c. low frequencies.
   b. low intensities.   d. high frequencies.

The Body Senses: More Than Skin Deep

Vision and audition provide information about the world at a distance. By responding to light and sound energy in the environment, these "distance" senses allow us to identify and locate the objects and people around us. In comparison, the body senses, also called *somatosenses* (*soma*, from the Greek for "body"), are up close and personal. **Haptic perception** results from our *active exploration of the environment by touching and grasping objects with our hands*. We use sensory receptors in our muscles, tendons, and joints as well as a variety of receptors in our skin to get a feel for the world around us (see **FIGURE 4.26**).

Touch

Four types of receptors located under the skin's surface enable us to sense pressure, texture, pattern, or vibration against the skin (see Figure 4.26). The receptive fields of these specialized cells work together to provide a rich tactile (from Latin, "to touch") experience when you explore an object by feeling it or attempting to grasp it.

This rather unimposing geodesic dome sits on the floor of the Exploratorium, a science museum in San Francisco. The inside of the dome is pitch black; visitors must crawl, wiggle, slide, and otherwise navigate the unfamiliar terrain using only their sense of touch. How would you feel being in that environment for an hour or so?

© EXPLORATORIUM, www.exploratorium.edu

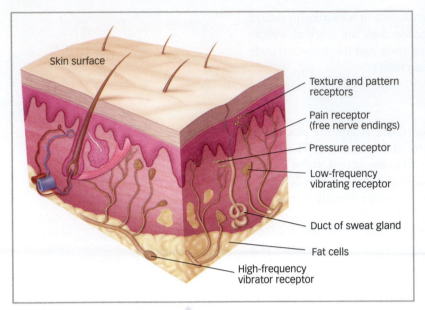

Skin surface

Texture and pattern receptors

Pain receptor (free nerve endings)

Pressure receptor

Low-frequency vibrating receptor

Duct of sweat gland

Fat cells

High-frequency vibrator receptor

▲ Figure **4.26** **Touch and Pain Receptors**
Touch receptors are specialized sensory neurons under the skin's surface that detect pressure, texture, temperature, or vibrations against the skin. Touch receptors respond to stimulation within their receptive fields, and their long axons enter the brain via the spinal or cranial nerves. Pain receptors are distributed around bones and within muscles and internal organs as well as under the skin surface. Some pain receptors transmit immediate, sharp pain sensations quickly and others signal slow, dull pain that lasts and lasts.

CKOU/CORBIS

Be warned for your next shopping trip: Touching the merchandise can lead you to value it more highly than just looking at it.

In addition, *thermoreceptors,* nerve fibers that sense cold and warmth, respond when your skin temperature changes. All these sensations blend seamlessly together in perception, of course, but detailed physiological studies have successfully isolated the parts of the touch system (Johnson, 2002).

Touch begins with the transduction of skin sensations into neural signals. Like cells in the retina of each eye, touch receptors have receptive fields that, when stimulated, cause that cell's response to change. The representation of touch in the brain follows a topographic scheme, much as vision and hearing do. Think back to the homunculus you read about in Chapter 3; you'll recall that different locations on the body project sensory signals to different locations in the somatosensory cortex in the parietal lobe.

There are three important principles regarding the neural representation of the body's surface:

1. The left half of the body is represented in the right half of the brain and vice versa. This is known as contralateral organization.

2. More of the brain is devoted to parts of the skin surface that have greater spatial resolution. For example, fingertips and lips, areas that are very good at discriminating fine spatial detail, have a relatively dense arrangement of touch receptors and a large topographical representation in the somatosensory cortex; comparatively, the lower back, hips, and calves have a relatively small representation (Penfield & Rasmussen, 1950).

   ? **Why might discriminating spatial detail be important for fingertips and lips?**

3. There is mounting evidence for a distinction between "what" and "where" pathways in touch analogous to similar distinctions we've already considered for vision and audition. The "what" system for touch provides information about the properties of surfaces and objects; the "where" system provides information about a location in external space that is being touched or a location on the body that is being stimulated (Lederman & Klatzky, 2009). FMRI evidence suggests that the "what" and "where" touch pathways involve areas in the lower and upper parts of the parietal lobe, respectively (Reed, Klatzky, & Halgren, 2005).

Touch information can have a powerful effect on our decisions and judgments. For example, recent research has shown that merely touching an object that we don't already own can increase our feeling of ownership and lead us to value the object more highly than when we view it but don't touch it (Peck & Shu, 2009); the longer we touch an object, the more highly we value it (Wolf, Arkes, & Muhanna, 2008). You might keep this "mere touch" effect in mind the next time you are in a store and considering buying an expensive item. Retailers are probably aware of this effect: During the 2003 holiday shopping season, the office of the Illinois state attorney general warned shoppers to be cautious in stores that encouraged them to touch the merchandise (Peck & Shu, 2009).

Pain

Although pain is arguably the least pleasant of sensations, this aspect of touch is among the most important for survival: Pain indicates damage or potential damage to the body. Without the ability to feel pain, we might ignore infections, broken bones, or serious burns. Children with congenital insensitivity to pain, a rare inherited disorder that specifically impairs pain perception, often mutilate themselves (biting into their tongues, for example, or gouging their skin while scratching) and are at increased risk of dying during childhood (Nagasako, Oaklander, & Dworkin, 2003).

Tissue damage is transduced by pain receptors, as shown in Figure 4.26. Fast-acting *A-delta fibers* transmit the initial sharp pain one might feel right away from a sudden injury, and slower *C fibers* transmit the longer-lasting, duller pain that persists after the initial injury. If you were running barefoot outside and stubbed your toe against a rock, you would first feel a sudden stinging pain transmitted by A-delta fibers that would die down quickly, only to be replaced by the throbbing but longer-lasting pain carried by C fibers. Both the A-delta and C fibers are impaired in cases of congenital insensitivity to pain, which is one reason why the disorder can be life threatening.

Neural signals for pain travel to two distinct areas in the brain and evoke two distinct psychological experiences (Treede et al., 1999). One pain pathway sends signals to the somatosensory cortex, identifying where the pain is occurring and what sort of pain it is (sharp, burning, dull). The second pain pathway sends signals to the motivational and emotional centers of the brain, such as the hypothalamus and amygdala, and to the frontal lobe. This is the aspect of pain that is unpleasant and motivates us to escape from or relieve the pain.

Pain typically feels as if it comes from the site of the tissue damage that caused it. If you burn your finger, you will perceive the pain as originating there. But we have pain receptors in many areas besides the skin—around bones and within muscles and internal organs as well. When pain originates internally, in a body organ, for example, we actually feel it on the surface of the body. This kind of **referred pain** occurs when *sensory information from internal and external areas converges on the same nerve cells in the spinal cord*. One common example is a heart attack: Victims often feel pain radiating from the left arm rather than from inside the chest.

Pain intensity cannot always be predicted solely from the extent of the injury that causes the pain (Keefe, Abernathy, & Campbell, 2005). For example, *turf toe* sounds like the mildest of ailments; it is pain at the base of the big toe as a result of bending or pushing off repeatedly, as a runner or football player might do during a sporting event. This small-sounding injury in a small area of the body can nonetheless sideline an athlete for a month with considerable pain. On the other hand, you've probably heard a story or two about someone treading bone-chilling water for hours on end, or dragging their shattered legs a mile down a country road to seek help after a tractor accident, or performing some other incredible feat despite searing pain and extensive tissue damage. Pain type and pain intensity show a less-than-perfect correlation, a fact that has researchers intrigued.

Some recent evidence indicates that subjective pain intensity may differ among ethnic groups. A study that examined responses to various kinds of experimentally induced pain, including heat pain and cold pain, found that compared with White young adults, African American young adults had a lower tolerance for several kinds of pain and rated the same pain stimuli as more intense and unpleasant (Campbell, Edward, & Fillingim, 2005).

One influential account of pain perception is known as **gate-control theory,** which holds that *signals arriving from pain receptors in the body can be stopped, or gated, by interneurons in the spinal cord via feedback from two directions* (Melzack & Wall, 1965). Pain can be gated by the skin receptors, for example, by rubbing the affected area. Rubbing your stubbed toe activates neurons that "close the gate" to stop pain signals from traveling to the brain. Pain can also be gated from the brain by modulating the activity of pain-transmission neurons. This neural feedback comes from a region in the midbrain called the *periaqueductal gray* (PAG). Under extreme conditions, such as high stress,

? Why does rubbing an injured area sometimes help alleviate pain?

referred pain Feeling of pain when sensory information from internal and external areas converges on the same nerve cells in the spinal cord.

gate-control theory A theory of pain perception based on the idea that signals arriving from pain receptors in the body can be stopped, or *gated*, by interneurons in the spinal cord via feedback from two directions.

The real-life subject of the movie *127 Hours,* Aron Ralston was hiking in a remote canyon in Utah when tragedy struck. A 1,000-pound boulder pinned him in a three-foot-wide space for 5 days, eventually leaving him no choice but to amputate his own arm with a pocketknife. He then applied a tourniquet, rappelled down the canyon, and hiked out to safety. These and similar stories illustrate that the extent of an injury is not perfectly correlated with the amount of pain felt.

MALCOM DALY

naturally occurring endorphins can activate the PAG to send inhibitory signals to neurons in the spinal cord that then suppress pain signals to the brain, thereby modulating the experience of pain. The PAG is also activated through the action of opiate drugs, such as morphine.

Body Position, Movement, and Balance

It may sound odd, but one aspect of sensation and perception is knowing where parts of your body are at any given moment. Your body needs some way to sense its position in physical space other than moving your eyes to constantly visually check the location of your limbs. Sensations related to position, movement, and balance depend on stimulation produced within our bodies. Receptors in the muscles, tendons, and joints signal the position of the body in space, whereas information about balance and head movement originates in the inner ear.

Maintaining balance depends primarily on the **vestibular system,** *the three fluid-filled semicircular canals and adjacent organs located next to the cochlea in each inner ear* (see Figure 4.23). The semicircular canals are arranged in three perpendicular orientations and studded with hair cells that detect movement of the fluid when the head moves or accelerates. This detected motion enables us to maintain our balance, or the position of our bodies relative to gravity. The movements of the hair cells encode these somatic sensations (Lackner & DiZio, 2005).

Vision also helps us keep our balance. If you see that you are swaying relative to a vertical orientation, such as the contours of a room, you move your legs and feet to keep from falling over. Psychologists have experimented with this visual aspect of balance by placing people in rooms that can be tilted forward and backward (Bertenthal, Rose, & Bai, 1997; Lee & Aronson, 1974). If the room tilts enough—particularly when small children are tested—people will topple over as they try to compensate for what their visual system is telling them. When a mismatch between the information provided by visual cues and vestibular feedback occurs, motion sickness can result. Remember this discrepancy the next time you try reading in the back seat of a moving car!

? Why is it so hard to stand on one foot with your eyes closed?

AP PHOTO/RICK RYCROFT

Hitting a ball with a bat or racket provides feedback as to where your arms and body are in space as well as to how the resistance of these objects affects your movement and balance. Successful athletes, such as Serena Williams, have particularly well-developed body senses.

SUMMARY QUIZ [4.5]

1. Which part of the body occupies the greatest area in the somatosensory cortex?
   a. calves   b. lips   c. lower back   d. hips

2. The location and type of pain we experience is indicated by signals sent to
   a. the amygdala.
   b. the spinal cord.
   c. pain receptors.
   d. the somatosensory cortex.

The Chemical Senses: Adding Flavor

Vision and audition sense energetic states of the world—light and sound waves—and touch is activated by physical changes in the body or on the body surface. The last set of senses we'll consider share a chemical basis to combine aspects of distance and proximity. The chemical senses of *olfaction* (smell) and *gustation* (taste) respond to the molecular structure of substances floating into the nasal cavity or dissolving in saliva. Smell and taste combine to produce the perceptual experience we call *flavor*.

Smell

Olfaction is the least understood sense and the only one directly connected to the forebrain, with pathways into the frontal lobe, amygdala, and other forebrain structures (the other senses connect first to the thalamus). This mapping indicates that smell has a close relationship with areas involved in emotional and social behavior. Smell seems to have evolved in animals as a signaling sense for the familiar—a friendly creature, an edible food, or a sexually receptive mate.

Countless substances release odors into the air, and some of their *odorant molecules* make their way into our noses, drifting in on the air we breathe. Situated along the top of the nasal cavity, shown in **FIGURE 4.27**, is a mucous membrane called the *olfactory epithelium,* which contains about 10 million **olfactory receptor neurons (ORNs),** *receptor cells that initiate the sense of smell.* Odorant molecules bind to sites on these specialized receptors, and if enough bindings occur, the ORNs send action potentials into the olfactory nerve (Dalton, 2003).

Each olfactory neuron has receptors that bind to some odorants but not to others, as if the receptor is a lock and the odorant is the key (see Figure 4.27). Humans possess about 350 different ORN types that permit us to discriminate among some 10,000 different odorants through the unique patterns of neural activity each odorant evokes. This setup is similar to our ability to see a vast range of colors based on only a small number of retinal cell types or to feel a range of skin sensations based on only a handful of touch receptor cell types.

? How many scents can humans smell?

Groups of ORNs send their axons from the olfactory epithelium into the **olfactory bulb,** *a brain structure located above the nasal cavity beneath the frontal lobes.* The axons of all ORNs of a particular type converge at a site called a *glomerulus* within the olfactory bulb; humans have about 350 glomeruli. Different odorant molecules produce varied patterns of activity (Rubin & Katz, 1999). A given odorant may strongly activate some glomeruli, moderately activate others, and have little effect on still others.

The olfactory bulb sends outputs to various centers in the brain, including the parts that are responsible for controlling basic drives, emotions, and memories. This explains why smells can have immediate effects on us, either strongly positive or strongly negative. If the slightest whiff of an apple pie baking brings back fond memories of childhood or the unexpected sniff of vomit mentally returns you to a particularly bad party you once attended, you've got the idea.

Our experience of smell is also determined by our previous experiences with an odor (Gottfried, 2008). Consistent with this idea, people rate the identical odor as more pleasant when it is paired with an appealing verbal label such as "cheddar cheese" rather than an unappealing one such as "body odor" (de Araujo et al., 2005; Herz

vestibular system The three fluid-filled semicircular canals and adjacent organs located next to the cochlea in each inner ear.

olfactory receptor neurons (ORNs) Receptor cells that initiate the sense of smell.

olfactory bulb A brain structure located above the nasal cavity beneath the frontal lobes.

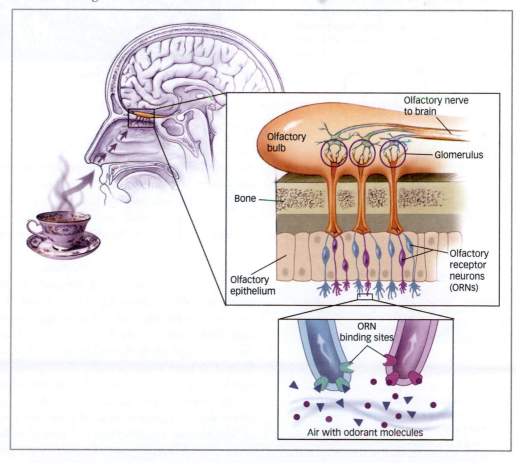

▼ Figure 4.27 **Anatomy of Smell** Along the roof of the nasal cavity, odorant molecules dissolve in the mucous membrane that forms the olfactory epithelium. Odorants may then bind to olfactory receptor neurons (ORNs) embedded in the epithelium. ORNs respond to a range of odors and, once activated, relay action potentials to their associated glomeruli in the olfactory bulb, located just beneath the frontal lobes. The glomeruli synapse on neurons whose axons form the olfactory nerve, which projects directly into the forebrain.

Olfactory nerve to brain

Olfactory bulb

Glomerulus

Bone

Olfactory receptor neurons (ORNs)

Olfactory epithelium

ORN binding sites

Air with odorant molecules

pheromones Biochemical odorants emitted by other members of its species that can affect an animal's behavior or physiology.

taste buds The organ of taste transduction.

& von Clef, 2001). FMRI evidence indicates that brain regions involved in coding the pleasantness of an experience, such as the orbiotofrontal cortex, respond more strongly to the identical odor when people think it is cheddar cheese than when they think it is a body odor (de Araujo et al., 2005; see the Hot Science box for a related finding concerning taste perception).

Smell may also play a role in social behavior. Humans and other animals can detect odors from **pheromones,** *biochemical odorants emitted by other members of its species that can affect the animal's behavior or physiology.* Parents can distinguish the smell of their own children from that of other people's children. An infant can identify the smell of its mother's breast from the smell of other mothers. Pheromones also play a role in reproductive behavior in insects and in several mammalian species, including mice, dogs, and primates (Brennan & Zufall, 2006), although research in humans has demonstrated no consistent tendency for people to prefer the odors of people of the opposite sex over other pleasant odors. However, odors related to testosterone (which is produced in men's sweat) activate the hypothalamus (a part of the brain that controls sexual behavior; see Chapter 3) in heterosexual women but not in heterosexual men. Strikingly, homosexual men responded in the same way as women did (Savic, Berglund, & Lindstrom, 2005; see **FIGURE 4.28**). Other common odors unrelated to sexual arousal were processed similarly by all three groups. These and related studies suggest that some human pheromones are related to sexual orientation.

▶ Figure **4.28** **Smell and Social Behavior** In a PET study, heterosexual women, homosexual men, and heterosexual men were scanned as they were presented with each of several odors. During the presentation of a testosterone-based odor (referred to in the figure as AND), there was significant activation in the hypothalamus for heterosexual women (left) and homosexual men (center) but not for heterosexual men (right) (Savic et al., 2005).

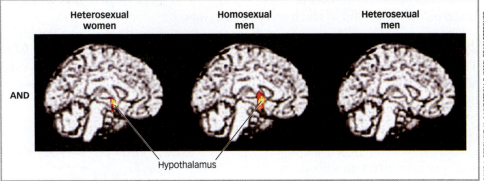

SAVIC, I, BERGLUND, H., & LINDSTROM, P. (2005). BRAIN RESPONSE TO PUTATIVE PHEROMONES IN HOMOSEXUAL MEN. PROCEEDINGS OF THE NATIONAL ACADEMY OF SCIENCES, USA, 102, 7356-7361.

Taste

One of the primary responsibilities of the chemical sense of taste is identifying things that are bad for you—as in "poisonous and lethal." Some aspects of taste perception are genetic, such as an aversion to extreme bitterness (which can indicate poison), and some are learned, such as an aversion to a particular food that once caused nausea. In either case, the direct contact between a tongue and possible foods allows us to anticipate whether something will be harmful or palatable.

Why is the sense of taste an evolutionary advantage?

The tongue is covered with thousands of small bumps, called *papillae*, which are easily visible to the naked eye. Within each papilla are hundreds of **taste buds,** *the organ of taste transduction* (see **FIGURE 4.29**). Most of our mouths contain between 5,000 and 10,000 taste buds fairly evenly distributed over the tongue, roof of the mouth, and upper throat (Bartoshuk & Beauchamp, 1994; Halpern, 2002). Each taste bud contains 50 to 100 taste receptor cells. Taste perception fades with age: On average, people lose half their taste receptors by the time they turn 20. This may help to explain why young children seem to be "fussy eaters," since their greater number of taste buds brings with it a greater range of taste sensations.

The human eye contains millions of rods and cones, the human nose contains some 350 different types of olfactory receptors, but the taste system contains just

Fussy eater or just too many taste buds? Our taste perception declines with age: We lose about half of our taste receptors by the time we're 20 years old. That can make childhood a time of either savory delight or a sensory overload of taste.

LESLIE BANKS/ISTOCKPHOTO.COM

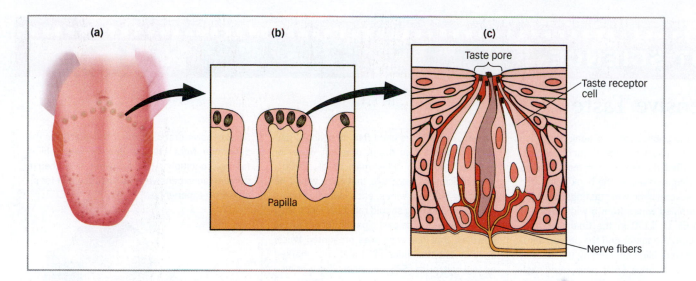

▲ Figure **4.29** **A Taste Bud** (a) Taste buds stud the bumps (papillae) on your tongue, shown here, as well as the back, sides, and roof of the mouth. (b) Each taste bud contains a range of receptor cells that respond to varying chemical components of foods called tastants. Tastant molecules dissolve in saliva and stimulate the taste receptor cells. (c) Each taste bud contacts the branch of a cranial nerve at its base.

five main types of taste receptors, corresponding to five primary taste sensations: salt, sour, bitter, sweet, and umami (savory). The first four are quite familiar, but *umami* may not be. In fact, perception researchers are still debating its existence. The umami receptor was discovered by Japanese scientists who attributed it to the tastes evoked by foods containing a high concentration of protein, such as meats and cheeses (Yamaguchi, 1998). If you're a meat eater and you savor the feel of a steak topped with butter or a cheeseburger as it sits in your mouth, you've got an idea of the umami sensation.

Of course, the variety of taste experiences greatly exceeds the five basic receptors discussed here. Any food molecules dissolved in saliva evoke specific, combined patterns of activity in the five taste receptor types. Although we often think of taste as the primary source for flavor, in fact, taste and smell collaborate to produce this complex perception. As any wine connoisseur will attest, the full experience of a wine's flavor cannot be appreciated without a finely trained sense of smell. Odorants from substances outside your mouth enter the nasal cavity via the nostrils, and odorants in the mouth enter through the back of the throat. This is why wine aficionados are taught to pull air in over wine held in the mouth: It allows the wine's odorant molecules to enter the nasal cavity through this "back door." (The taste of wine can also be influenced by cognitive factors, as illustrated in the Hot Science box.)

You can easily demonstrate the contribution of smell to flavor by tasting a few different foods while holding your nose, preventing the olfactory system from detecting their odors. If you have a head cold, you probably already know how this turns out. Your favorite spicy burrito or zesty pasta probably tastes as bland as can be.

Taste experiences also vary widely across individuals. About 50% of people report a mildly bitter taste in caffeine, saccharine, certain green vegetables, and other substances, while roughly 25% report no bitter taste. Members of the first group are called *tasters* and members of the second group are called *nontasters*. The remaining 25% of people are *supertasters*, who report that such substances, especially dark green vegetables, are extremely bitter, to the point of being inedible (Bartoshuk, 2000). Children start out as tasters or supertasters, which could help explain their early tendency toward fussiness in food preference. However, some children grow up to become nontasters. Because supertasters tend to avoid fruits and vegetables that contain tastes they experience as extremely bitter, they may be at increased health risk for

"We would like to be genetically modified to taste like Brussels sprouts."

HOT SCIENCE

Expensive Taste

In 2008, the publication of a book titled *The Wine Trials* (Goldstein & Herschkowitsch, 2008) ruffled the feathers of more than a few wine connoisseurs. The book described a study of several blind wine tastings, in which drinkers sampled wines from a wide range of prices ($1.65 to $150 in the Goldstein tastings), but both the taster and the person serving the wine were blind concerning the identity of the wine and its price. Each taster rated each wine on a scale from "bad" to "great." The study revealed a weak and slightly negative correlation between price and ratings, suggesting that, if anything, tasters liked the more expensive wines slightly *less* than the more inexpensive ones.

So why do people buy expensive wines, when cheaper ones taste just as good or better? Similar to olfaction (see p. 123), our experience of taste is partly determined by bottom-up influences, such as activity in our taste receptors, but it is also influenced by top-down factors, such as knowing what brand we are eating or drinking. For example, when people know that they are drinking either Pepsi or Coke, their subjective preferences and brain activity differ markedly from when they do not know which of the two beverages they are drinking (McClure et al., 2004).

To investigate the effects of price knowledge on the enjoyment of wine and associated brain activity, researchers used fMRI to scan 20 participants while they drank different wines or a control solution (Plassman et al., 2008). The participants were told that they would be sampling different wines, each identified by its price, and that they should rate how much they liked each wine. The participants did not know, however, that one wine was presented twice: once at its actual price ($5) and once marked up to a high price ($45); another wine was also presented once at its actual price ($90) and once at a lower price ($10). This design allowed the researchers to compare ratings and brain activity for the identical wine when participants thought it was expensive or cheap.

Participants reported liking both wines better when they were accompanied by a high price than by a low price. For the fMRI analysis, the researchers focused on the the medial orbitofrontal cortex (mOFC), a part of the frontal lobe that is involved in coding the pleasantness of an experience. There was greater mOFC activity for both wines when the tasters thought they were expensive than when the tasters thought the wines were cheap.

These results demonstrate that taste experience and associated neural activity can be influenced by top-down influences such as price knowledge. The results should provide some comfort to wine drinkers who are willing to pay for expensive brands. Even if they can't tell the difference from cheaper brands under blind tasting conditions, just knowing that they're drinking an expensive wine should make for an enjoyable experience.

▲ Taste and smell both contribute to what we perceive as flavor. This is why "smelling" the bouquet of a wine is an essential part of the wine-tasting ritual. The experience of wine tasting is also influenced by cognitive factors, such as knowledge of a wine's price.

diseases such as colon cancer. On the other hand, because they also tend to avoid fatty, creamy foods, they tend to be thinner and may have decreased risk of cardiovascular disease (Bartoshuk, 2000). There is evidence that genetic factors contribute to individual differences in taste perception (Kim et al., 2003), but much remains to be learned about the specific genes that are involved (Hayes et al., 2008; Reed, 2008).

SUMMARY QUIZ [4.6]

1. What best explains why smells can have immediate and powerful effects?
   a. the involvement in smell of brain centers for emotions and memories
   b. the vast number of olfactory receptor neurons we have
   c. our ability to detect odors from pheromones
   d. the fact that different odorant molecules produce varied patterns of activity

2. People lose about half their taste buds by the time they are
   a. 20.   b. 40.   c. 60.   d. 80.

Perception and Persuasion

We're used to seeing advertisements that feature exciting music and provocative or sexual images to sell products. The notion is that the sight and sound of exciting things will become associated with what might be an otherwise drab product. This form of advertising is known as *sensory branding* (Lindstrom, 2005).

Sensory branding is an intentional approach to marketing. That new-car smell you anticipate while you take a test drive? Actually, it's a manufactured fragrance sprayed into the car, carefully tested to evoke positive feelings among potential buyers. Bang and Olufsen, a Danish high-end stereo manufacturer, carefully designed its remote control units to have a certain distinctive "feel" in a user's hand. Singapore Airlines, which has consistently been rated "the world's best airline," has actually patented the smell of its airplane cabins (it's called Stefan Floridian Waters).

Another form of advertising that has grown dramatically in recent years is product placement: Companies pay to have their products appear prominently in movies and television shows. Do you notice when the star of a film drinks a can of a well-known beverage or drives a particular make of automobile in a car chase? Although viewers may not notice or even be aware of the product, advertisers believe that product placement benefits their bottom lines.

Video technology has advanced even to the point where products can be placed in movies after the fact. Princeton Video, using its L-VIS (live-video insertion) system, placed a Snackwell's cookie box on the kitchen counter of a *Bewitched* rerun from the 1960s, long before the Snackwell's brand existed (Wenner, 2004)! Currently, there's a wave of interest in developing product placement advertising for multiplayer online games, even to the extent that ads can be tailored to specific users based on their preferences and previous buying habits.

Is there any harm in marketing that bombards the senses or even sneaks through to perception undetected? Advertising is a business; like any business, it is fueled by innovation in search of profit. Perhaps these recent trends are simply the next clever step to get potential buyers to pay attention to a product message. On the other hand, is there a point when "enough is enough"? Do you want to live in a world where every sensory event is trademarked, patented, or test-marketed before reaching your perceptual system? Where do you stand?

Chapter Review

SUMMARY

Our Senses Encode the Information Our Brains Perceive

▶ Sensation is the simple stimulation of a sense organ. Perception organizes, identifies, and interprets sensation at the level of the brain.

▶ All our senses depend on the process of transduction, which converts physical signals from the environment into neural signals carried by sensory neurons into the central nervous system.

▶ Psychophysics is an approach to studying perception that measures the strength of a stimulus and an observer's sensitivity to that stimulus.

▶ The absolute threshold is the smallest intensity needed to detect a stimulus. The just noticeable difference (JND) is the smallest change in a stimulus that can be detected.

▶ Sensory adaptation occurs because sensitivity to lengthy stimulation tends to decline over time.

Vision I: How the Eyes and the Brain Convert Light Waves to Neural Signals

▶ Two types of photoreceptor cells in the retina—cones, which operate under normal daylight conditions and sense color, and rods, which are active under low-light conditions for night vision—transduce light into neural impulses.

▶ Light striking the retina causes a specific pattern of response in each of three cone types: short-wavelength (bluish) light, medium-wavelength (greenish) light, and long-wavelength (reddish) light. The overall pattern of response across the three cone types results in a unique code for each color.

▶ Information encoded by the retina travels to the brain along the optic nerve, which connects to the thalamus and then to the primary visual cortex, area V1, in the occipital lobe.

▶ Two functionally distinct pathways project from the occipital lobe to visual areas in other parts of the brain. The ventral stream projects to the areas of the temporal lobes that represent an object's shape and identity. The dorsal stream projects to areas of the parietal lobes that identify the location and motion of an object.

Vision II: Recognizing What We Perceive

▶ According to feature integration theory, attention provides the "glue" necessary to bind features together into the perception of a single object. The parietal lobe is important for attention and contributes to feature binding.

▶ Some regions in the occipital and temporal lobes respond selectively to specific object categories, supporting the modular view that specialized brain areas represent particular classes of objects.

▶ Gestalt principles of perceptual grouping, such as simplicity, closure, and continuity, govern how the features and regions of things fit together.

▶ Depth perception depends on monocular cues, such as familiar size and linear perspective, and binocular cues, such as retinal disparity.

▶ We experience a sense of motion through the differences in the strengths of output from motion-sensitive neurons. These processes can give rise to illusions such as apparent motion.

Audition: More Than Meets the Ear

▶ Sound waves have three physical dimensions: frequency; amplitude; and timbre, or differences in the complexity or mix of frequencies. Respectively, these determine our perception of pitch, loudness, and sound quality.

▶ Auditory perception begins in the ear, which consists of an outer ear that funnels sound waves toward the middle ear,

which in turn sends the vibrations to the inner ear, which contains the cochlea.

▶ Action potentials from the inner ear travel via the thalamus to the primary auditory cortex, area A1, in the temporal lobe.

▶ Auditory perception depends on both a place code and a temporal code, which together cover the full range of pitches that people can hear. Our ability to localize sound sources depends critically on the placement of our ears on opposite sides of the head.

The Body Senses: More Than Skin Deep

▶ Touch is represented in the brain according to a topographic scheme in which locations on the body project sensory signals to locations in the somatosensory cortex, a part of the parietal lobe.

▶ The experience of pain depends on signals that travel to the somatosensory cortex, which indicate the location and type of pain, and to the emotional centers of the brain, which result in unpleasant feelings.

▶ Balance and acceleration depend primarily on the vestibular system but are also influenced by vision.

The Chemical Senses: Adding Flavor

▶ Our experience of smell, or olfaction, is associated with odorant molecules binding to sites on specialized olfactory receptors, which converge at the glomerulus within the olfactory bulb. The olfactory bulb in turn sends signals to parts of the brain that control drives, emotions, and memories.

▶ Sensations of taste depend on taste buds, which are distributed across the tongue, roof of the mouth, and upper throat, and on taste receptors that correspond to the five primary taste sensations of salt, sour, bitter, sweet, and umami.

KEY TERMS

sensation (p. 92)
perception (p. 92)
transduction (p. 93)
psychophysics (p. 94)
absolute threshold (p. 94)
just noticeable difference (JND) (p. 95)
Weber's law (p. 95)
signal detection theory (p. 95)
sensory adaptation (p. 96)
retina (p. 98)
accommodation (p. 99)

cones (p. 100)
rods (p. 100)
fovea (p. 100)
blind spot (p. 101)
receptive field (p. 101)
area V1 (p. 103)
visual-form agnosia (p. 105)
binding problem (p. 106)
illusory conjunction (p. 106)
feature integration theory (p. 106)
perceptual constancy (p. 108)

monocular depth cues (p. 110)
binocular disparity (p. 112)
apparent motion (p. 113)
change blindness (p. 113)
inattentional blindness (p. 114)
pitch (p. 115)
loudness (p. 115)
timbre (p. 116)
cochlea (p. 117)
basilar membrane (p. 117)
hair cells (p. 117)
area A1 (p. 118)

place code (p. 118)
temporal code (p. 118)
haptic perception (p. 119)
referred pain (p. 121)
gate-control theory (p. 121)
vestibular system (p. 122)
olfactory receptor neurons (ORNs) (p. 123)
olfactory bulb (p. 123)
pheromones (p. 124)
taste buds (p. 124)

CHANGING MINDS

1. A friend of yours is taking a class in medical ethics. "We discussed a tough case today," she says. "It has to do with a patient who's been in a vegetative state for several years, and

the family has to decide whether to take him off life support. The doctors say he has no awareness of himself or his environment, and he is never expected to recover. But when light is shined in his eyes, his pupils contract. That shows he can sense light, so he has to have some ability to perceive his surroundings, doesn't he?" Without knowing any of the details of this particular case, how would you explain to your friend that a patient might be able to sense light but not perceive it? What other examples from the chapter could you use to illustrate the difference between sensation and perception?

2. In your philosophy class, the professor discusses the proposition that "perception is reality." From the point of view of philosophy, reality is the state of things that actually exists, whereas perception is how they appear to the observer. What does psychophysics have to say about this issue? What are three ways in which sensory transduction can alter perception, causing perceptions that may differ from absolute reality?

3. A friend comes across the story of an American soldier, Leroy Petry, who received the Medal of Honor for saving the lives of two of his men. The soldiers were in a firefight in Afghanistan when a live grenade landed at their feet; Petry picked up the grenade and tried to toss it away from the others, but it exploded, destroying his right hand. According to the news report, Petry didn't initially feel any pain; instead, he set about applying a tourniquet to his own arm while continuing to shout orders to his men as the firefight continued. "That's amazingly heroic," your friend says, "but that bit about not feeling the pain—that's crazy. He must just be so tough that he kept going despite the pain." What would you tell your friend? How can the perception of pain be altered?

CRITICAL THINKING QUESTIONS

1. Sensory adaptation refers to the fact that sensitivity to prolonged stimulation tends to decline over time. According to the theory of natural selection, inherited characteristics that provide a survival advantage tend to spread throughout the population across generations.

 Why might sensory adaptation have evolved? What survival benefits might it confer to a small animal trying to avoid predators? To a predator trying to hunt prey?

2. When visual light (light waves with particular length, amplitude, and purity) reaches the retina, it is transduced by rods and cones into visual signals, interpreted by the brain as color, brightness, and saturation.

 Many people (including about 5% of all males) inherit a common type of color blindness, in which the cones that

normally process green light are mildly deficient; these people have difficulty distinguishing red from green. Unfortunately, in the United States, traffic signals use red and green lights to indicate whether cars should stop or go through an intersection. Why do drivers with red-green color blindness not risk auto accidents every time they approach an intersection?

3. Color perception and motion perception both rely partially on opponent processing, which is why we fall prey to illusions such as color aftereffects and the waterfall illusion.

 How might the concept of aftereffects account for "sea legs," in which a person who has been on a small boat for a few hours has trouble walking on land because the ground seems to be rising and falling as if the person were still on the boat?

ANSWERS TO SUMMARY QUIZZES

Summary Quiz [4.1] 1. b; 2. d; 3. b
Summary Quiz [4.2] 1. b; 2. b; 3. d
Summary Quiz [4.3] 1. a; 2. a; 3. c; 4. c
Summary Quiz [4.4] 1. a; 2. a; 3. d
Summary Quiz [4.5] 1. b; 2. d
Summary Quiz [4.6] 1. a; 2. a

5

Consciousness

U NCONSCIOUSNESS IS SOMETHING YOU DON'T REALLY APPRECIATE until you need it. Belle Riskin needed it one day on an operating table, when she awoke just as doctors were pushing a breathing tube down her throat. She felt she was choking, but she couldn't see, breathe, scream, or move. Unable even to blink an eye, she couldn't signal to the surgeons that she was conscious. "I was terrified. . . . It was like being buried alive," she explained later. "I knew I was conscious, that something was going on during the surgery. I had just enough awareness to know I was being intubated" (Groves, 2004).

How could this happen? Anesthesia for surgery is supposed to leave the patient unconscious, "feeling no pain," and yet in about one in a thousand operations (Sandin et al., 2000), the patient regains consciousness at some point. The problem arises because muscle-relaxing drugs are used to keep the patient from moving involuntarily and making unhelpful contributions to the operation. Then, if the drugs that are given to induce unconsciousness fail to do the job, the patient with extremely relaxed muscles is unable to show or tell doctors that there is a problem.

Fortunately, new methods of monitoring wakefulness by measuring the electrical activity of the brain are being developed. One system uses sensors attached to the person's head and gives readings on a scale from 0 (no electrical activity signaling consciousness in the brain) to 100 (fully alert), providing a kind of "consciousness meter." Anesthesiologists using this index deliver anesthetics to keep the patient in the recommended range of 40 to 65 for general anesthesia during surgery. One of these devices in the operating room might have helped Belle Riskin settle into the unconsciousness she so dearly needed.

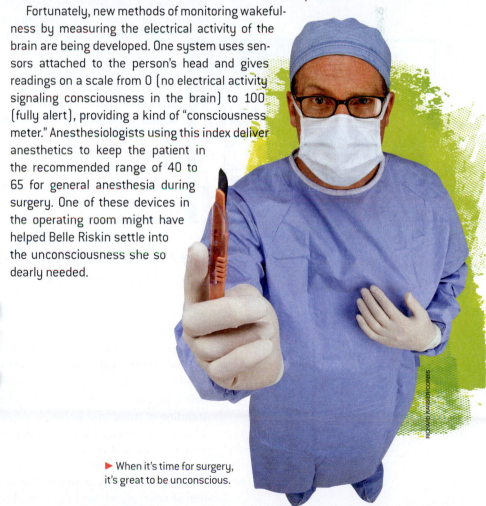

RICHARD RADSTONE/CORBIS

▶ When it's time for surgery,
it's great to be unconscious.

consciousness A person's subjective experience of the world and the mind.

phenomenology How things seem to the conscious person.

problem of other minds The fundamental difficulty we have in perceiving the consciousness of others.

mind/body problem The issue of how the mind is related to the brain and body.

MOST OF THE TIME, OF COURSE, CONSCIOUSNESS IS SOMETHING we cherish. How else could we experience a favorite work of art; the familiar strains of an oldie on the radio; the taste of a sweet, juicy peach; or the touch of a loved one's hand? **Consciousness** is *a person's subjective experience of the world and the mind.* Although you might think of consciousness as simply "being awake," the defining feature of consciousness is *experience,* which you have when you're not awake but experiencing a vivid dream. Conscious experience is essential to what it means to be human. The anesthesiologist's dilemma in trying to monitor Belle Riskin's consciousness is a stark reminder, though, that it is impossible for one person to experience another's consciousness. Your consciousness is utterly private, a world of personal experience that only you can know.

How can this private world be studied? We'll begin by examining consciousness directly, trying to understand what it is like and how it compares with the mind's *unconscious* processes. Then we'll examine its altered states: the departures from normal, everyday waking that occur during altered states such as sleep and dreams, intoxication with alcohol and other drugs, and hypnosis and meditation. Like the traveler who learns the meaning of *home* by roaming far away, we can learn the meaning of consciousness by exploring its exotic variations.

Conscious and Unconscious: The Mind's Eye, Open and Closed

What does it feel like to be you right now? It probably feels as though you are somewhere inside your head, looking out at the world through your eyes. You can feel your hands on this book, perhaps, and notice the position of your body or the sounds in the room when you orient yourself toward them. If you shut your eyes, you may be able to imagine things in your mind, even though all the while thoughts and feelings come and go, passing through your imagination. But where are "you," really? And how is it that this theater of consciousness gives you a view of some things in your world and your mind but not others? The theater in your mind doesn't have seating for more than one, making it difficult to share what's on our mental screen with our friends, a researcher, or even ourselves in precisely the same way a second time. We'll look first at the difficulty of studying consciousness directly, examine the nature of consciousness (what it is that can be seen in this mental theater), and then explore the unconscious mind (what is *not* visible to the mind's eye).

"We keep this section closed off."

The Mysteries of Consciousness

Other sciences, such as physics, chemistry, and biology, have the great luxury of studying *objects,* things that we all can see. Psychology studies objects, too, looking at people and their brains and behaviors, but it has the unique challenge of also trying to make sense of *subjects.* A physicist is not concerned with what it is like to be a neutron, but psychologists hope to understand what it is like to be a human, that is, grasping the subjective perspectives of the people that they study. Psychologists hope to include an understanding of **phenomenology,** *how things seem to the conscious person,* in their understanding of mind and behavior. After all, consciousness is an extraordinary human property that could well be unique to us. But including phenomenology in psychology brings up mysteries pondered by great thinkers almost since the beginning of thinking. Let's look at two of the more vexing mysteries of consciousness: the problem of other minds and the mind/body problem.

? What are the great mysteries of consciousness?

The Problem of Other Minds

One great mystery is called the **problem of other minds,** *the fundamental difficulty we have in perceiving the consciousness of others.* How do you know that anyone else is conscious? They tell you that they are conscious, of course, and are often willing to describe in depth how they feel, how they think, what they are experiencing, and how good or how bad it all is. But perhaps they are just *saying* these things. There is no clear way to distinguish a conscious person from someone who might do and say all the same things as a conscious person but who is *not* conscious.

Even the "consciousness meter" used by anesthesiologists falls short. It certainly doesn't give the anesthesiologist any special insight into what it is like to be the patient on the operating table; it only predicts whether patients will *say* they were conscious. We simply lack the ability to directly perceive the consciousness of others. In short, you are the only thing in the universe you will ever truly know what it is like to be.

The problem of other minds also means there is no way you can tell if another person's experience of anything is at all like yours. Although you know what the color red looks like to you, for instance, you cannot know whether it looks the same to other people. Maybe they're seeing what you see as blue and just *calling* it red in a consistent way. If their inner experience "looks" blue, but they say it looks hot and is the color of a tomato, you'll never be able to tell that their experience differs from yours. Of course, most people have come to trust one another in describing their inner lives, reaching the general assumption that other human minds are pretty much like their own. But they don't know this for a fact, and they can't know it directly.

How do people perceive other minds? Researchers conducting a large online survey asked people to compare the minds of 13 different targets, such as a baby, chimp, robot, man, and woman, on 18 different mental capacities, such as feeling pain, pleasure, hunger, and consciousness (see **FIGURE 5.1**) (Gray, Gray, & Wegner, 2007). Respondents who were judging the mental capacity to feel pain, for example, compared pairs of targets: Is a frog or a dog more able to feel pain? Is a 7-week-old fetus or a man in a persistent vegetative state more able to feel pain? Researchers examined all the comparisons on the different mental capacities, using a computational technique called factor analysis, and found two dimensions of mind perception. People judge minds according to the capacity for *experience* (such as the ability to feel pain, pleasure, hunger, consciousness, anger, or fear) and the capacity for *agency* (such as the ability for self-control, planning, memory, or thought). As shown in Figure 5.1, respondents rated some targets as having little experience or agency (the dead person), others as having experiences but little agency (the baby), and yet others as having both experience and agency (adult humans). Still others were perceived to have agency without experiences (the robot, God). The perception of minds, then, involves more than just whether something has a mind. People appreciate that minds both have experiences and act as agents that perform actions.

▼ Figure **5.1** **Dimensions of Mind Perception** When participants judged the mental capacities of 13 targets, two dimensions of mind perception were discovered (Gray et al., 2007). Participants perceived minds as varying in the capacity for experience (such as abilities to feel pain or pleasure) and in the capacity for agency (such as abilities to plan or exert self-control). They perceived normal adult humans (male, female, or "you," the respondent) to have minds on both dimensions, whereas other targets were perceived to have reduced experience or agency. The man in a persistent vegetative state ("PVS man"), for example, was judged to have only some experience and very little agency.

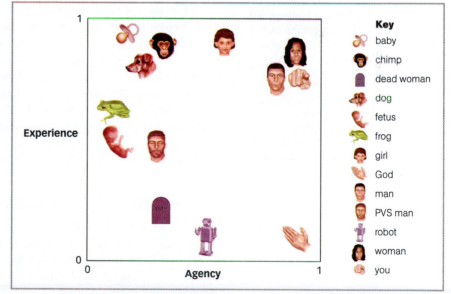

Key
baby
chimp
dead woman
dog
fetus
frog
girl
God
man
PVS man
robot
woman
you

The Mind/Body Problem

Another mystery of consciousness is the **mind/body problem,** *the issue of how the mind is related to the brain and body.* As you read in Chapter 1, René Descartes proposed that the human body is a machine made of physical matter but that the human mind or soul is a separate entity made of a "thinking substance." We now know that the mind and brain are connected everywhere to each other. In other words, "the mind is what the brain does" (Minsky, 1986, p. 287). But Descartes was right in pointing out the difficulty of reconciling the physical body with the mind. Most psychologists assume that mental events are intimately tied to brain events, such that every thought, perception, or feeling is associated with a particular pattern of activation of neurons in the brain (see Chapter 3). Thinking about a particular duck, for instance, occurs with a unique array of neural connections and activations. If the neurons repeat that pattern, then you must be thinking of the duck; conversely, if you think of the duck, the brain activity occurs in that pattern.

One telling set of studies, however, suggests that the brain's activities *precede* the activities of the conscious mind. The electrical activity in the brains of volunteers was measured using sensors placed on their scalps as they repeatedly decided when to move a hand (Libet, 1985). Participants were also asked to indicate exactly when they consciously chose to move by reporting the position of a dot moving rapidly around the face of a clock just at the point of the decision (**FIGURE 5.2a**). As a rule, the brain begins to show electrical activity around half a second before a voluntary action (535 milliseconds, to be exact). This makes sense since brain activity certainly seems to be necessary to get an action started.

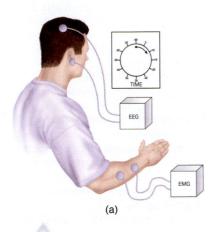

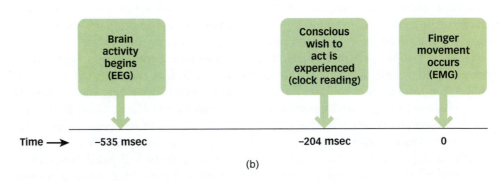

(a)

(b)

▲ Figure **5.2** **The Timing of Conscious Will** (a) In Benjamin Libet's experiments, the participant was asked to move fingers at will while simultaneously watching a dot move around the face of a clock to mark the moment at which the action was consciously willed. Meanwhile, EEG sensors timed the onset of brain activation and EMG sensors timed the muscle movement. (b) The experiment showed that brain activity (EEG) precedes the willed movement of the finger (EMG) but that the reported time of consciously willing the finger to move follows the brain activity.

But the experiment revealed that the brain also started to show electrical activity before the person's conscious decision to move. As shown in **FIGURE 5.2b**, these studies found that the brain becomes active more than 300 milliseconds before participants report that they are consciously trying to move. The feeling that you are consciously willing your actions, it seems, may be a result rather than a cause of your brain activity. Although your personal intuition is that you *think* of an action and *then* do it, these experiments suggest that your brain is getting started before *either* the thinking or the doing, preparing the way for both thought and action. Quite simply, it may appear to us that our minds are leading our brains and bodies, but the order of events may be the other way around (Haggard & Tsakiris, 2009; Wegner, 2002).

The Nature of Consciousness

How would you describe your own consciousness? Researchers have suggested that consciousness can be described based on its properties, its levels, and its contents. Each of these types of description is a different way of looking at the same problem, and each is useful in different contexts. Let's examine each of these points in turn.

Four Basic Properties

Researchers have described four basic properties of consciousness, based on people's reports of conscious experience:

1. Consciousness has *intentionality*, which is the quality of being directed toward an object. Consciousness is always *about* something. Despite all the lush detail you

NORTH CAROLINA MUSEUM OF ART/CORBIS

see in your mind's eye, the kaleidoscope of sights and sounds and feelings and thoughts, the object of your consciousness at any one moment is just a small part of all of this (see **FIGURE 5.3**).

2. Consciousness has *unity*, or resistance to division. One study had research participants divide their attention by reacting to two games superimposed on a television screen. The participants were easily able to follow one game at a time, but their error rate when attending to the two tasks was eight times greater than when attending to either task alone (Neisser & Becklen, 1975). Your attempts to study, in other words, could seriously interfere with a full appreciation of the TV show you're watching.

? Why shouldn't you study and watch TV at the same time?

3. Consciousness has *selectivity*, the capacity to include some objects but not others. How does consciousness decide what to filter in and what to tune out? The conscious system is most inclined to select information of special interest to the person. For example, in what has come to be known as the **cocktail party phenomenon,** *people tune in one message even while they filter out others nearby.* Perhaps you have noticed how abruptly your attention is diverted from whatever conversation you are having when someone else within earshot at the party mentions your name.

4. Consciousness has *transience*, or the tendency to change. Consciousness wiggles and fidgets like that toddler in the seat behind you on the airplane. The mind wanders not just sometimes, but incessantly, from one "right now" to the next "right now" and then on to the next (Wegner, 1997). William James, whom you met back in Chapter 1, famously described consciousness as a "stream" (James, 1890, Vol. 1, p. 239). The stream of consciousness partly reflects the limited capacity of the conscious mind. We humans can hold only so much information in mind, after all, so when more information is selected, some of what is currently there must disappear. As a result, our focus of attention keeps changing. The stream of consciousness flows so inevitably that it even changes our perspective when we view a constant object like a Necker Cube (see **FIGURE 5.4**).

Levels of Consciousness

Consciousness can also be understood as having levels, ranging from minimal consciousness to full consciousness to self-consciousness. These levels of consciousness would probably all register as "conscious" on that wakefulness meter for surgery patients you read about at the beginning of the chapter. The levels of consciousness are not a matter of degree of overall brain activity but instead involve different qualities of awareness of the world and of the self.

▲ Figure **5.3** **Bellotto's Dresden and Close-Up** The people on the bridge in the distance look very finely detailed in *View of Dresden with the Frauenkirche at Left,* by Bernardo Bellotto (1720–80) (left). However, when you examine the detail closely (right), you find that the people are made of brushstrokes merely *suggesting* people—an arm here, a torso there. Consciousness produces a similar impression of "filling in," as it seems to consist of extreme detail even in areas that are peripheral (Dennett, 1991).

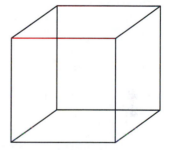

▲ Figure **5.4** **The Necker Cube** This cube has the property of reversible perspective in that you can bring one or the other of its two square faces to the front in your mind's eye. Although it may take awhile to reverse the figure at first, once people have learned to do it, they can reverse it regularly, about once every 3 seconds (Gomez et al., 1995). The stream of consciousness flows even when the target is a constant object.

cocktail party phenomenon A phenomenon in which people tune in one message even while they filter out others nearby.

1. **Minimal consciousness** is *consciousness that occurs when the mind inputs sensations and may output behavior* (Armstrong, 1980). This level of consciousness is a kind of sensory awareness and responsiveness, something that could even happen when someone pokes you during sleep and you turn over. Something seems to register in your mind but you may not think at all about having had the experience. It could be that animals or, for that matter, even plants can have this minimal level of consciousness. But because of the problem of other minds and the notorious reluctance of animals and plants to talk to us, we can't know for sure that they *experience* the things that make them respond.

2. Human consciousness is often more than minimal, of course, but what exactly gets added? Consider the glorious feeling of waking up on a spring morning as rays of sun stream across your pillow. It's not just that you are having this experience; being fully conscious means that you are also *aware* that you are having this experience. **Full consciousness** is *the level of awareness in which you know and are able to report your mental state.* Being fully conscious means that you are aware of having a mental state while you are experiencing the mental state itself. When you have a hurt leg and mindlessly rub it, for instance, your pain may be minimally conscious. After all, you seem to be experiencing pain because you have acted and are indeed rubbing your leg. It is only when you realize that it hurts, though, that the pain becomes fully conscious. Full consciousness involves not only thinking about things but also thinking about the fact that you are thinking about things (Jaynes, 1976).

   ? What is "full consciousness"?

3. **Self-consciousness** is *the level of consciousness in which the person's attention is drawn to the self as an object* (Morin, 2005). Most people report experiencing such self-consciousness when they are embarrassed, when they find themselves the focus of attention in a group, or when they look in a mirror. In fact, people go out of their way to avoid mirrors when they've done something they are ashamed of (Duval & Wicklund, 1972).

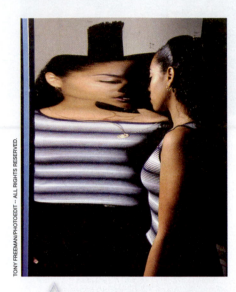

Self-consciousness is a curse and a blessing. Looking in a mirror can make people evaluate themselves on deeper attributes such as honesty as well as superficial ones such as looks.

Most animals don't appear to have such self-consciousness. The typical dog, cat, or bird seems mystified by a mirror, ignoring it or acting as though there is some other critter back there. However, chimpanzees sometimes behave in ways that suggest they recognize themselves in a mirror. To examine this, researchers painted an odorless red dye over the eyebrow of an anesthetized chimp and then watched when the awakened chimp was presented with a mirror (Gallup, 1977). If the chimp interpreted the mirror image as a representation of some other chimp with an unusual approach to cosmetics, we would expect it just to look at the mirror or perhaps to reach toward it. But the chimp reached toward its *own eye* as it looked into the mirror—not the mirror image—suggesting that it recognized the image as a reflection of itself. Other animals such as orangutans (Gallup, 1997), possibly dolphins (Reiss & Marino, 2001), and maybe even elephants (Plotnik, de Waal, & Reiss, 2006) and magpies (Prior, Schwartz, & Güntürkün, 2008) recognize their own mirror images. Dogs, cats, monkeys, and gorillas have been tested, too, but don't seem to know they are looking at themselves. Even humans don't have self-recognition right away. Infants don't recognize themselves in mirrors until they've reached about 18 months of age (Lewis & Brooks-Gunn, 1979). The experience of self-consciousness, as measured by self-recognition in mirrors, is limited to a few animals and to humans only after a certain stage of development.

Conscious Contents

What's on your mind? For that matter, what's on everybody's mind? One way to learn what is on people's minds is to ask them, and much research has called on people simply to *think aloud*. A more systematic approach is the *experience sampling tech-*

nique, in which people are asked to report their conscious experiences at particular times. Equipped with electronic beepers or called on cell phones, for example, participants are asked to record their current thoughts when asked at random times throughout the day (Csikszentmihalyi & Larson, 1987).

Experience sampling studies show that consciousness is dominated by the immediate environment: what is seen, felt, heard, tasted, and smelled. Beyond this orientation to the environment, consciousness turns to the person's *current concerns,* or what the person is thinking about repeatedly (Klinger, 1975). **TABLE 5.1** shows the results of a Minnesota study in which 175 college students were asked to report their current concerns (Goetzman, Hughes, & Klinger, 1994). The researchers sorted the concerns into the categories shown in the table. Keep in mind that these concerns are ones the students didn't mind reporting to psychologists; their private preoccupations may have been different and probably far more interesting.

The current concerns that populate consciousness can sometimes get the upper hand, transforming daydreams or everyday thoughts into rumination and worry. Thoughts that return again and again, or problem-solving attempts that never seem to succeed, can come to dominate consciousness. When this happens, people may exert **mental control,** *the attempt to change conscious states of mind.* For example, someone troubled by a recurring worry about the future ("What if I can't get a decent job when I graduate?") might choose to try not to think about this because it causes too much anxiety and uncertainty. Whenever this thought comes to mind, the person engages in **thought suppression,** *the conscious avoidance of a thought.* This may seem like a perfectly sensible strategy because it eliminates the worry and allows the person to move on to think about something else.

Or does it? The great Russian novelist Fyodor Dostoevsky (1821–1881) remarked on the difficulty of thought suppression: "Try to pose for yourself this task: not to think of a polar bear, and you will see that the cursed thing will come to mind every minute." Inspired by this observation, Daniel Wegner and his colleagues (1987) gave people this exact task in the laboratory. Participants were asked to try not to think about a white bear for 5 minutes while they recorded all their thoughts aloud into a

One concern on many students' minds is diet and exercise to keep in shape.

"Are you not thinking what I'm not thinking?"

TABLE 5.1

What's on Your Mind? College Students' Current Concerns

Current Concern Category	Example	Frequency of Students Who Mentioned the Concern
Family	Gain better relations with immediate family	40%
Roommate	Change attitude or behavior of roommate	29%
Household	Clean room	52%
Friends	Make new friends	42%
Dating	Desire to date a certain person	24%
Sexual intimacy	Abstaining from sex	16%
Health	Diet and exercise	85%
Employment	Get a summer job	33%
Education	Go to graduate school	43%
Social activities	Gain acceptance into a campus organization	34%
Religious	Attend church more	51%
Financial	Pay rent or bills	8%
Government	Change government policy	14%

minimal consciousness A low-level kind of sensory awareness and responsiveness that occurs when the mind inputs sensations and may output behavior.

full consciousness Consciousness in which you know and are able to report your mental state.

self-consciousness A distinct level of consciousness in which the person's attention is drawn to the self as an object.

mental control The attempt to change conscious states of mind.

thought suppression The conscious avoidance of a thought.

Go ahead—look away from the book for a minute and try not to think about a white bear.

LARRY WILLIAMS/CORBIS

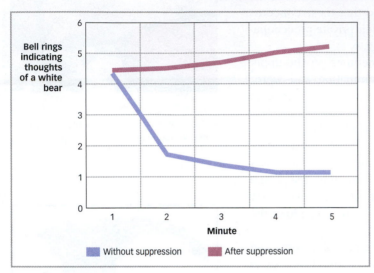

▲ Figure **5.5** **Rebound Effect** Research participants were first asked to try not to think about a white bear, and then they were asked to think about it and to ring a bell whenever it came to mind. Compared with those who were simply asked to think about a bear without prior suppression, those people who first suppressed the thought showed a rebound of increased thinking (Wegner et al., 1987).

rebound effect of thought suppression
The tendency of a thought to return to consciousness with greater frequency following suppression.

ironic processes of mental control Mental processes that can produce ironic errors because monitoring for errors can itself produce them.

dynamic unconscious An active system encompassing a lifetime of hidden memories, the person's deepest instincts and desires, and the person's inner struggle to control these forces.

repression A mental process that removes unacceptable thoughts and memories from consciousness.

tape recorder. In addition, they were asked to ring a bell if the thought of a white bear came to mind. On average, they mentioned the white bear or rang the bell (indicating the thought) more than once per minute. Thought suppression simply didn't work and instead produced a flurry of returns of the unwanted thought. What's more, when some research participants later were specifically asked to change tasks and deliberately *think* about a white bear, they became oddly preoccupied with it. A graph of their bell rings in **FIGURE 5.5** shows that these participants had the white bear come to mind far more often than did people who had only been asked to think about the bear from the outset, with no prior suppression. This **rebound effect of thought suppression,** *the tendency of a thought to return to consciousness with greater frequency following suppression,* suggests that attempts at mental control may be difficult indeed. The act of trying to suppress a thought may itself cause that thought to return to consciousness in a robust way.

As with thought suppression, other attempts to "steer" consciousness in any direction can result in mental states that are precisely the opposite of those desired. How ironic: Trying to consciously achieve one task may produce precisely the opposite outcome! These ironic effects seem most likely to occur when the person is distracted or under stress. People who are distracted while they are trying to get into a good mood, for example, tend to become sad (Wegner, Erber, & Zanakos, 1993), and those who are distracted while trying to relax actually become more anxious than those who are not trying to relax (Wegner, Broome, & Blumberg, 1997). Likewise, an attempt not to overshoot a golf putt, undertaken during distraction, often yields the unwanted overshot (Wegner, Ansfield, & Pilloff, 1998). The theory of **ironic processes of mental control** proposes that such *ironic errors occur because the mental process that monitors errors can itself produce them* (Wegner, 1994a, 2009). In the attempt not to think of a white bear, for instance, a small part of the mind is ironically *searching* for the white bear.

The ironic monitor is a process of the mind that works *outside* of consciousness, making us sensitive to all the things we do not want to think, feel, or do so that we can notice and consciously take steps to regain control if these things come back to mind. As this unconscious monitoring whirs along in the background, it unfortunately increases the person's sensitivity to the very thought that is unwanted. Ironic processes are mental functions that are needed for effective mental control—they help in the process of banishing a thought from consciousness—but they can sometimes yield the very failure they seem designed to overcome. Ironic effects of mental control arise from processes that work outside of consciousness, so they remind us that much of the mind's machinery may be hidden from our view, lying outside the fringes of our experience.

The Unconscious Mind

Many other mental processes are unconscious, too, in the sense that they occur without our experience of them. For example, think for a moment about the mental processes involved in simple addition. What happens in consciousness between hearing a problem ("What's 4 plus 5?") and thinking of the answer ("9")? Probably nothing—the answer just appears in the mind. Nothing conscious seems to bridge the gap; rather, the answer comes from the unconscious mind.

There are no conscious steps between hearing an easy problem ("What's 4 plus 5?") and thinking of the answer—unless you have to count on your fingers.

Freudian Unconscious

The true champion of the unconscious mind was Sigmund Freud. As you read in Chapter 1, Freud's psychoanalytic theory viewed conscious thought as the surface of a much deeper mind made up of unconscious processes. Far more than just a collection of hidden processes, Freud described a **dynamic unconscious**—*an active system encompassing a lifetime of hidden memories, the person's deepest instincts and desires, and the person's inner struggle to control these forces.* The dynamic unconscious might contain hidden sexual thoughts about one's parents, for example, or destructive urges aimed at a helpless infant—the kinds of thoughts people keep secret from others and may not even acknowledge to themselves. According to Freud's theory, the unconscious is a force to be held in check by **repression,** *a mental process that removes unacceptable thoughts and memories from consciousness and keeps them in the unconscious.* Without repression, a person might think, do, or say every unconscious impulse or animal urge, no matter how selfish or immoral. With repression, these desires are held in the recesses of the dynamic unconscious.

Freud looked for evidence of the unconscious mind in speech errors and lapses of consciousness, or what are commonly called "Freudian slips." Freud believed that

> **?** What do Freudian slips tell us about the unconscious mind?

errors are not random but instead have some surplus meaning that appear to have been created by an intelligent unconscious mind, even though the person consciously disavows this. For example, in the heat of his successful 2008 campaign for the presidency, Barack Obama slipped by referring to "my Muslim faith" in a televised interview. He is not Muslim and noted this immediately, but reporters seemed to agree with Freud, wondering what this slip might mean for the real loyalties of the African American candidate.

Did Obama's slip mean anything? Many of the meaningful errors Freud attributed to the dynamic unconscious are not predicted in advance and so seem to depend on clever after-the-fact interpretations. Such interpretations can be wrong. Suggesting a pattern to a series of random events is quite clever, but it's not the same as scientifically predicting and explaining when and why an event should occcur. Anyone can offer a reasonable, compelling explanation for an event after it has already happened, but the true work of science is to offer testable hypotheses that are evaluated based on reliable evidence. Freud's book *The Psychopathology of Everyday Life* (Freud, 1901/1938) suggests not so much that the dynamic unconscious produces errors but that Freud himself was a master at finding meaning in errors that might otherwise have seemed random. Obama's slip didn't mean that he was considering changing religions, after all, but rather that reporters were motivated for political reasons to interpret his gaffe as especially meaningful.

Barack Obama slipped in a televised interview with George Stephanopoulos, referring to "my Muslim faith." Obama is a member of the United Church of Christ.

A Modern View of the Cognitive Unconscious

Modern psychologists share Freud's interest in the impact of unconscious mental processes on consciousness and on behavior. However, rather than Freud's vision of the unconscious as a teeming menagerie of animal urges and repressed thoughts, the current study of the unconscious mind views it as the factory that builds the products of conscious thought and behavior (Kihlstrom, 1987; Wilson, 2002). The

Do people in a movie theater need any subliminal messages to get them to eat popcorn? Probably not. Would subliminal messages make them more likely to eat popcorn? Maybe, but not much.

Choosing a roommate can be like playing the lottery: You win some, you lose some, and then you lose some more.

cognitive unconscious includes *all the mental processes that are not experienced by a person but that give rise to the person's thoughts, choices, emotions, and behavior.*

One indication of the cognitive unconscious at work occurs when a person's thought or behavior is changed by exposure to information outside of consciousness. This happens in **subliminal perception,** when *thought or behavior is influenced by stimuli that a person cannot consciously report perceiving.* Worries about the potential of subliminal influence were first provoked in 1957, when a marketer claimed he had increased concession sales at a cinema by flashing the words "Eat Popcorn" and "Drink Coke" briefly on-screen during movies. It turns out his story was a hoax, and many attempts to increase sales using similar methods have failed. But the very idea of influencing behavior outside of consciousness created a wave of alarm about insidious "subliminal persuasion" that still concerns people (Epley, Savitsky, & Kachelski, 1999; Pratkanis, 1992).

Subliminal perception does occur, but the degree of influence it has on behavior is not very large (Dijksterhuis, Aarts, & Smith, 2005). One set of studies examined whether beverage choices could be influenced by brief visual exposures to thirst-related words while subjects were performing a computer task (Strahan, Spencer, & Zanna, 2002). Subliminal exposure did have an effect, but it was small and mainly limited to people who reported already feeling thirsty when the experiment started.

? What's an example of an idea that had an unconscious influence on you?

In some cases, however, the unconscious mind can make better decisions than the conscious mind. Participants in an experiment were asked to choose which of three hypothetical people with many different qualities they would prefer to have as a roommate (Dijksterhuis, 2004). One candidate was objectively better, with more positive qualities, and participants given 4 minutes to make a *conscious decision* tended to choose this one. A second group was asked for an *immediate decision* as soon as the information display was over, and a third group was encouraged to reach an *unconscious decision.* Like the conscious decision group, this group was allowed the same 4 minutes of time after the display ended to give their answer, but during this interval their conscious minds were occupied with solving a set of anagrams. As you can see in **FIGURE 5.6**, the unconscious decision group showed a stronger preference for the good roommate than did the immediate decision or conscious decision groups. Unconscious minds seemed *better able* than conscious minds to sort out the complex information and arrive at the best choice. You can sometimes end up more satisfied with decisions you make after just "going with your gut" than with the decisions you consciously agonize over.

▶ Figure **5.6** **Decisions** People making roommate decisions who had some time for unconscious deliberation chose better roommates than those who thought about the choice consciously or those who made snap decisions (Dijksterhuis, 2004).

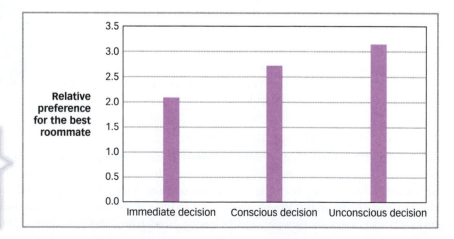

SUMMARY QUIZ [5.1]

1. Which of the following is *not* a basic property of consciousness?
   a. intentionality   b. disunity   c. selectivity   d. transience

2. Currently, unconscious processes are understood as
   a. a concentrated pattern of thought suppression.
   b. a hidden system of memories, instincts, and desires.
   c. a blank slate.
   d. unexperienced mental processes that give rise to thoughts and behavior.

3. The _____ unconscious is at work when subliminal and unconscious processes influence thought and behavior.
   a. minimal   b. repressive   c. dynamic   d. cognitive

Sleep and Dreaming: Good Night, Mind

What's it like to be asleep? Sometimes it's like nothing at all. Sleep can produce a state of unconsciousness in which the mind and brain apparently turn off the functions that create experience: The theater in your mind is closed. But this is an oversimplification because the theater actually seems to reopen during the night for special shows of bizarre cult films—in other words, dreams. Dream consciousness involves a transformation of experience that is so radical it is commonly considered an **altered state of consciousness**—*a form of experience that departs significantly from the normal subjective experience of the world and the mind*. Such altered states can be accompanied by changes in thinking, disturbances in the sense of time, feelings of the loss of control, changes in emotional expression, alterations in body image and sense of self, perceptual distortions, and changes in meaning or significance (Ludwig, 1966). The world of sleep and dreams, the two topics in this section, provides two unique perspectives on consciousness: a view of the mind without consciousness and a view of consciousness in an altered state.

? Why are dreams considered an altered state of consciousness?

Sleep

Consider a typical night. As you begin to fall asleep, the busy, task-oriented thoughts of the waking mind are replaced by wandering thoughts and images along with odd juxtapositions, some of them almost dreamlike. Eventually, your presence of mind goes away entirely. Time and experience stop, you are unconscious, and in fact there seems to be no "you" there to have experiences. But then come dreams, whole vistas of a vivid and surrealistic consciousness you just don't get during the day, a set of experiences that occur with the odd prerequisite that there is nothing "out there" you are actually experiencing. More patches of unconsciousness may occur, with more dreams here and there. And finally, the glimmerings of waking consciousness return again in a foggy and imprecise form as you enter postsleep consciousness and then awake, often with bad hair.

Sleep Cycle

The sequence of events that occurs during a night of sleep is part of one of the major rhythms of human life, the cycle of sleep and waking. This **circadian rhythm** is *a*

cognitive unconscious The mental processes that give rise to the person's thoughts, choices, emotions, and behavior even though they are not experienced by the person.

subliminal perception A thought or behavior that is influenced by stimuli that a person cannot consciously report perceiving.

altered states of consciousness Forms of experience that depart from the normal subjective experience of the world and the mind.

circadian rhythm A naturally occurring 24-hour cycle of sleeping and waking.

REM sleep A stage of sleep characterized by rapid eye movements and a high level of brain activity.

naturally occurring 24-hour cycle—from the Latin *circa,* "about," and *dies,* "day." Even people who are sequestered in underground buildings without clocks and are allowed to sleep when they want to tend to have a rest-activity cycle of about 25.1 hours (Aschoff, 1965). This slight deviation from 24 hours is not easily explained (Lavie, 2001), but it seems to underlie the tendency many people have to want to stay up a little later each night and wake up a little later each day. We're 25.1-hour people living in a 24-hour world.

The sleep cycle is far more than a simple on/off routine, however, as many bodily and psychological processes ebb and flow in this rhythm. EEG recordings reveal a regular pattern of changes in electrical activity in the brain accompanying the circadian cycle. During waking, these changes involve alternation between high-frequency activity (called *beta waves*) during alertness and lower-frequency activity (*alpha waves*) during relaxation. But the largest changes in EEG occur during sleep. These changes show a regular pattern over the course of the night that includes five sleep stages (see **FIGURE 5.7**). In the first stage of sleep, the EEG moves to frequency patterns even lower than alpha waves (*theta waves*). In the second stage of sleep, these patterns are interrupted by short bursts of activity called *sleep spindles* and *K complexes,* and the sleeper becomes somewhat more difficult to awaken. The deepest stages of sleep are 3 and 4, known as slow-wave sleep, in which the EEG patterns show activity called *delta waves.*

During the fifth sleep stage, **REM sleep,** *a stage of sleep characterized by rapid eye movements and a high level of brain activity,* EEG patterns become high-frequency

▶ Figure **5.7** **EEG Patterns During the Stages of Sleep** The waking brain shows high-frequency beta wave activity, which changes during drowsiness and relaxation to lower-frequency alpha waves. Stage 1 sleep shows lower-frequency theta waves, which are accompanied in stage 2 by irregular patterns called sleep spindles and K complexes. Stages 3 and 4 are marked by the lowest frequencies, delta waves. During REM sleep, EEG patterns return to higher-frequency sawtooth waves that resemble the beta waves of waking.

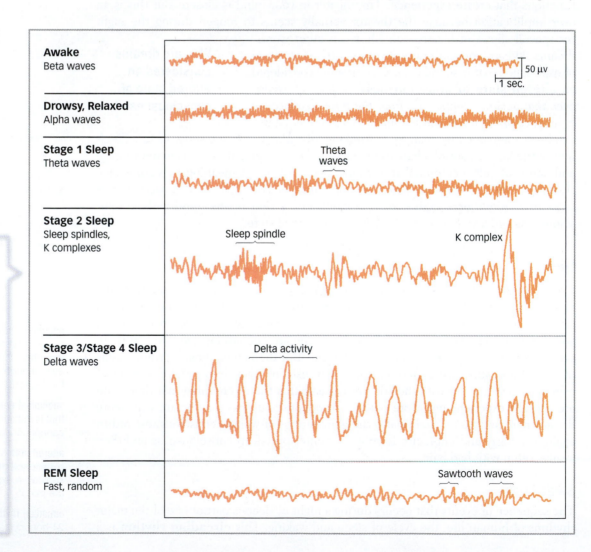

sawtooth waves, similar to beta waves, suggesting that the mind at this time is as active as it is during waking (see Figure 5.7). Sleepers wakened during REM periods report having dreams much more often than those wakened during non-REM periods (Aserinsky & Kleitman, 1953). During REM sleep, the pulse quickens, blood pressure rises, and there are telltale signs of sexual arousal. At the same time, measurements of muscle movements indicate that the sleeper is very still, except for a rapid side-to-side movement of the eyes. (Watch someone sleeping and you may be able to see the REMs through their closed eyelids. But be careful doing this with strangers down at the bus depot.)

Dreamers by Albert Joseph Moore (1882). Without measuring REM sleep, it's hard to know whether Moore's "Dreamers" are actually dreaming.

Although many people believe that they don't dream much (if at all), some 80% of people awakened during REM sleep report dreams. Some dreams are also reported in other sleep stages (non-REM sleep, also called *NREM sleep*) but not as many—and the dreams that occur at these times are described as less wild than REM dreams and more like normal thinking.

Putting EEG and REM data together produces a picture of how a typical night's sleep progresses through cycles of sleep stages (see **FIGURE 5.8**). In the first hour of the night, you fall all the way from waking to the fourth and deepest stage of sleep, the stage marked by delta waves. These slow waves indicate a general synchronization of neural firing, as though the brain is doing one thing at this time rather than many—the neuronal equivalent of "the wave" moving through the crowd at a stadium, as lots of individuals move together in synchrony. You then return to lighter sleep stages, eventually reaching REM and dreamland. Note that although REM sleep is lighter than that of lower stages, it is deep enough that you may be difficult to awaken. You then continue to cycle between REM and slow-wave sleep stages every 90 minutes or so throughout the night. Periods of REM last longer as the night goes on, and lighter sleep stages predominate between these periods, with the deeper slow-wave stages 3 and 4 disappearing halfway through the night. Although you're either unconscious or dream-conscious at the time, your brain and mind cycle through a remarkable array of different states each time you have a night's sleep.

? What are the stages in a typical night's sleep?

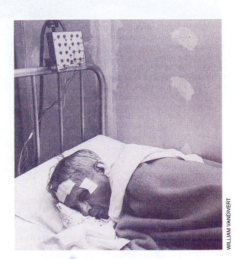

REM sleep discoverer Nathaniel Kleitman as a participant in his own sleep experiment with REM and EEG measurement electrodes in place.

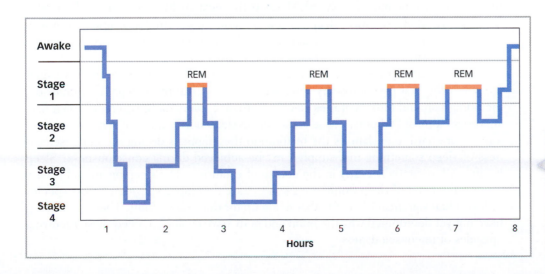

◄ Figure **5.8** **Stages of Sleep During the Night** Over the course of the typical night, sleep cycles into deeper stages early on and then more shallow stages later. REM periods become longer in later cycles, and the deeper slow-wave sleep of stages 3 and 4 disappears halfway through the night.

Sleep Needs and Deprivation

How much do people sleep? The answer depends on the age of the sleeper (Dement, 1999). Newborns will sleep 6 to 8 times in 24 hours, often totaling more than 16 hours. Their napping cycle eventually gets consolidated into "sleeping through the night," usually sometime between 9 and 18 months. The typical 6-year-old child might need 11 or 12 hours of sleep, and the progression to less sleep then continues into adulthood, when the average is about 7 to 7½ hours per night. With aging, people can get along with even a bit less sleep than that. Over a whole lifetime, we get about 1 hour of sleep for every 2 hours we are awake.

This is a lot of sleeping. Could we tolerate less? The world record for staying awake belongs to Randy Gardner, who at age 17 stayed up for 264 hours and 12 minutes in 1965 for a science project. When Randy finally did go to sleep, he slept only 14 hours and 40 minutes and awakened essentially recovered (Dement, 1978).

Feats like this one suggest that sleep might be expendable. This is the theory behind the classic "all-nighter" that you may have tried on the way to a rough exam. But it turns out that this theory is mistaken. When people learning a difficult perceptual task are kept up all night after they finished practicing the task, their learning of the task is wiped out (Stickgold et al., 2000). Sleep following learning appears to be essential for memory consolidation (see Hot Science: Sleep On It, p. 174 in Chapter 6). It is as though memories normally deteriorate unless sleep occurs to help keep them in place. Studying all night may help you cram for the exam, but it won't make the material stick—which pretty much defeats the whole point.

Sleep turns out to be a necessity rather than a luxury in other ways as well. At the extreme, sleep loss can be fatal. When rats are forced to break Randy Gardner's human waking record and stay awake even longer, they have trouble regulating their body temperature and lose weight although they eat much more than they normally do. Their bodily systems break down and they die, on average, in 21 days (Rechsthaffen et al., 1983). Shakespeare called sleep "nature's soft nurse," and it is clear that even for healthy young humans, a few hours of sleep deprivation each night can have a cumulative detrimental effect: reducing mental acuity and reaction time, increasing irritability and depression, and increasing the risk of accidents and injury (Coren, 1997).

REM sleep is also important psychologically, as memory problems and excessive aggression are observed in both humans and rats after only a few days of being wakened whenever REM activity starts (Ellman et al., 1991). Such REM deprivation causes a rebound of more REM sleep the next night (Brunner et al., 1990). Being deprived of slow-wave sleep (in stages 3 and 4), in turn, has primarily physical effects, with just a few nights of deprivation leaving people feeling tired, fatigued, and hypersensitive to muscle and bone pain (Lentz et al., 1999).

It's clearly dangerous to neglect the need for sleep. But why would we have such a need in the first place? Insects don't seem to sleep, but most "higher" animals do, including fish and birds. Giraffes sleep less than 2 hours daily, whereas brown bats snooze for almost 20 hours. These variations in sleep needs, and the very existence of a need, are hard to explain. Is the restoration that happens during the unconsciousness of sleep something that simply can't be achieved during consciousness? Sleep is, after all, potentially costly in the course of evolution. The sleeping animal is easy prey, so the habit of sleep would not seem to have developed so widely across species unless it had significant benefits that made up for this vulnerability. Theories of sleep have not yet determined why the brain and body have evolved to need these recurring episodes of unconsciousness.

Sleep deprivation can often be diagnosed without the help of any psychologists or brain-scanning equipment.

? What is the relationship between sleep and learning?

insomnia Difficulty in falling asleep or staying asleep.

sleep apnea A disorder in which the person stops breathing for brief periods while asleep.

somnambulism (sleepwalking) Occurs when the person arises and walks around while asleep.

narcolepsy A disorder in which sudden sleep attacks occur in the middle of waking activities.

Sleep Disorders

In answer to the question "Did you sleep well?," comedian Stephen Wright said, "No, I made a couple of mistakes." Sleeping well is something everyone would love to do, but for many people, sleep disorders are deeply troubling. Perhaps the most common sleep disorder is **insomnia,** *difficulty in falling asleep or staying asleep.* About 15% of adults complain of severe or frequent insomnia, and another 15% report having mild or occasional insomnia (Bootzin et al., 1993). Although people often overestimate the extent of their insomnia, the distress caused even by the perception of insomnia can be significant. There are many causes of insomnia, including anxiety associated with stressful life events, so insomnia may sometimes be a sign of other emotional difficulties. Although sedatives can be useful for brief sleep problems associated with emotional events, their long-term use is not effective. To begin with, most sleeping pills are addictive. People become dependent on the pills to sleep and may need to increase the dosage over time to achieve the same effect. Even in short-term use,

"I can't sleep. I think I'll get up and solve all my problems."

What are some problems caused by sleeping pills?

sedatives can interfere with the normal sleep cycle. Although they promote sleep, they reduce the proportion of time spent in REM and slow-wave sleep (Nishino, Mignot, & Dement, 1995), robbing people of dreams and their deepest sleep stages. As a result, the quality of sleep achieved with pills may not be as high as that without, and there may be side effects such as grogginess and irritability during the day. Finally, stopping the treatment suddenly can produce insomnia that is worse than before.

Sleep apnea is *a disorder in which the person stops breathing for brief periods while asleep.* A person with apnea usually snores, as apnea involves an involuntary obstruction of the breathing passage. When episodes of apnea occur for over 10 seconds at a time and recur many times during the night, they may cause many awakenings and sleep loss or insomnia. Apnea occurs most often in middle-aged overweight men (Partinen, 1994) and may go undiagnosed because it is not easy for the sleeper to notice. Bed partners may be the ones who finally get tired of the snoring and noisy gasping for air when the sleeper's breathing restarts, or the sleeper may eventually seek treatment because of excessive sleepiness during the day. Therapies involving weight loss, drugs, or external breathing aids may solve the problem.

Another sleep disorder is **somnambulism,** commonly called sleepwalking, which occurs when *a person arises and walks around while asleep.* Sleepwalking is more common in children, peaking around the age of 11 or 12, with as many as 25% of children experiencing at least one episode (Empson, 1984). Sleepwalking tends to happen early in the night, usually during slow-wave sleep, and sleepwalkers may awaken during their walk or return to bed without waking, in which case they will probably not remember the episode in the morning. The sleepwalker's eyes are usually open in a glassy stare, and walking with hands outstretched is uncommon except in cartoons. Sleepwalking is not usually linked to any additional problems and is only problematic in that sleepwalkers can hurt themselves. People who walk while they are sleeping do not tend to be very coordinated and can trip over furniture or fall down stairs. After all, they're sleeping. Contrary to popular belief, it is safe to wake sleepwalkers or lead them back to bed.

Is it safe to wake a sleepwalker?

Sleepwalkers in cartoons have their arms outstretched and eyes closed, but that's just for cartoons. A real-life sleepwalker usually walks normally with eyes open, sometimes with a glassy look.

There are other sleep disorders that are less common. **Narcolepsy** is *a disorder in which sudden sleep attacks occur in the middle of waking activities.* Narcolepsy involves the intrusion of a dreaming state of sleep into waking and is often accompanied by unrelenting excessive sleepiness and uncontrollable sleep attacks lasting

sleep paralysis The experience of waking up unable to move.

night terrors (or sleep terrors) Abrupt awakenings with panic and intense emotional arousal.

from 30 seconds to 30 minutes. This disorder appears to have a genetic basis, as it runs in families, and can be treated effectively with medication. **Sleep paralysis** is *the experience of waking up unable to move* and is sometimes associated with narcolepsy. This eerie experience usually lasts only a few moments and may occur with an experience of pressure on the chest (Hishakawa, 1976). **Night terrors** (or sleep terrors) are *abrupt awakenings with panic and intense emotional arousal.* These terrors, which occur mainly in boys ages 3 to 7, happen most often in NREM sleep early in the sleep cycle and do not usually have dream content the sleeper can report.

To sum up, there is a lot going on when we close our eyes for the night. Humans follow a pretty regular sleep cycle, going through five stages of NREM and REM sleep during the night. Disruptions to that cycle, caused by either sleep deprivation or sleep disorders, can produce consequences for waking consciousness. But something else happens during a night's sleep that affects our consciousness, both while asleep and when we wake up. It's dreaming, and we'll look at what psychologists know about dreams next.

Dreams

Pioneering sleep researcher William C. Dement (1959) said, "Dreaming permits each and every one of us to be quietly and safely insane every night of our lives." Indeed, dreams do seem to have a touch of insanity about them. Even more bizarre is the fact that we are the writers, producers, and directors of the crazy things we experience. Just what are these experiences, and how can they be explained?

Dream Consciousness

"Frank! Frank, honey, wake up! Your lamp—it's humongous!"

Dreams depart dramatically from reality. You may dream of being naked in public, of falling from a great height, of sleeping through an important appointment, of being chased, or even of flying (Holloway, 2001). These things don't happen much in reality unless you have a very bad life. The quality of consciousness in dreaming is also altered significantly from waking consciousness. There are five major characteristics of dream consciousness that distinguish it from the waking state (Hobson, 1988).

? What distinguishes dream consciousness from the waking state?

> We intensely feel *emotion,* whether it is bliss or terror or love or awe.

> Dream *thought* is illogical: The continuities of time, place, and person don't apply. You may find you are in one place and then another, for example, without any travel in between—or people may change identity from one dream scene to the next.

> *Sensation* is fully formed and meaningful; visual sensation is predominant, and you may also deeply experience sound, touch, and movement (although pain is very uncommon).

> Dreaming occurs with *uncritical acceptance,* as though the images and events were perfectly normal rather than bizarre.

> We have *difficulty remembering* the dream after it is over. People often remember dreams only if they are awakened during the dream and even then may lose recall for the dream within just a few minutes of waking. If waking memory were this bad, you'd be standing around half-naked in the street much of the time, having forgotten your destination, clothes, and lunch money.

Not all of our dreams are fantastic and surreal, however. We often dream about mundane topics that reflect prior waking experiences, or "day residue." Current conscious concerns pop up (Nikles et al., 1998), along with images from the recent past. The day residue does not usually include episodic memories, that is, complete daytime events replayed in the mind. Rather, dreams that reflect the day's experience tend to single out sensory experiences or objects from waking life. One study had research participants play the computer game Tetris and found that participants often reported dreaming about the Tetris geometrical figures falling down—even though they seldom reported dreams about being in the experiment or playing the game (Stickgold et al., 2001). The content of dreams takes snapshots from the day rather than retelling the stories of what you have done or seen. This means that dreams often come without clear plots or storylines, and so they may not make a lot of sense.

Some of the most memorable dreams are nightmares, and these frightening dreams can wake up the dreamer (Levin & Nielsen, 2009). One set of daily dream logs from college undergraduates suggested that the average student has about 24 nightmares per year (Wood & Bootzin, 1990), although some people may have them as often as every night. Children have more nightmares than adults, and people who have experienced traumatic events are inclined to have nightmares that relive those events. Following the 1989 earthquake in the San Francisco Bay Area, for example, college students who had experienced the quake reported more nightmares than those who had not and often reported that the dreams were about the quake (Wood et al., 1992).

The Nightmare by Henry Fuseli (1790). Fuseli depicts not only a mare in this painting but also an incubus—an imp perched on the dreamer's chest that is traditionally associated with especially horrifying nightmares.

Dream Theories

Dreams are puzzles that cry out to be solved. How could you *not* want to make sense out of these experiences? The search for dream meaning goes all the way back to biblical figures, who interpreted dreams and looked for prophecies in them. In the Old Testament, the prophet Daniel (a favorite of the three Daniels who authored this book) curried favor with King Nebuchadnezzar of Babylon by interpreting the king's dream. Unfortunately, the meaning of dreams is usually far from obvious.

In the first psychological theory of dreams, Freud (1900/1965) proposed that dreams are confusing and obscure because the dynamic unconscious creates them precisely *to be* confusing and obscure. According to Freud's theory, dreams represent wishes, and some of these wishes are so unacceptable, taboo, and anxiety producing that the mind can only express them in disguised form. For example, a dream about a tree burning down in the park across the street from where a friend once lived might represent a camouflaged wish for the death of the friend. In this case, wishing for the death of a friend is unacceptable, so it is disguised as a tree on fire. The problem with Freud's approach is that there are an infinite number of potential interpretations of any dream and finding the correct one is a matter of guesswork—and of convincing the dreamer that one interpretation is superior to the others.

Although dreams may not represent elaborately hidden wishes, there is evidence that they do feature the return of suppressed thoughts.

? What is the evidence that we dream about our suppressed thoughts?

Researchers asked volunteers to think of a personal acquaintance and then to spend 5 minutes before going to bed writing down whatever came to mind (Wegner, Wenzlaff, & Kozak, 2004). Some participants were asked to suppress thoughts of this person as they wrote, others were asked to focus on thoughts of the person, and yet others were asked just to write freely about anything. The next morning, participants wrote dream reports. Overall, all participants mentioned dreaming more about the person they had named than about other people. But they most often dreamed of the person they named if they were in the group that had been assigned to suppress thoughts of the person the night before. This finding suggests that Freud was

activation-synthesis model The theory that dreams are produced when the brain attempts to make sense of activations that occur randomly during sleep.

right to suspect that dreams harbor unwanted thoughts. Perhaps this is why actors dream of forgetting their lines, travelers dream of getting lost, and football players dream of fumbling the ball.

Another key theory of dreaming is the **activation-synthesis model** (Hobson & McCarley, 1977). This theory proposes that *dreams are produced when the mind attempts to make sense of random neural activity that occurs in the brain during sleep.* During waking consciousness, the mind is devoted to interpreting lots of information that arrives through the senses. You figure out that the odd noise you're hearing during class is your cell phone vibrating, for example, or you realize that the strange smell in the hall outside your room must be from burned popcorn. In the dream state, the mind doesn't have access to external sensations, but it keeps on doing what it usually does: interpreting information. Because that information now comes from neural activations that occur without the continuity provided by the perception of reality, the brain's interpretive mechanisms can run free. This might be why, for example, a person in a dream can sometimes change into someone else. There is no actual person being perceived to help the mind keep a stable view. In the mind's effort to perceive and give meaning to brain activation, the person you view in a dream about a grocery store might seem to be a clerk but then change into your favorite teacher when the dream scene moves to your school. The great interest people have in interpreting their dreams the next morning may be an extension of the interpretive activity they've been doing all night.

The Freudian theory and the activation-synthesis theory differ in the significance they place on the meaning of dreams. In Freud's theory, dreams begin with meaning, whereas in the activation-synthesis theory, dreams begin randomly—but meaning can be added as the mind lends interpretations in the process of dreaming. Dream research has not yet sorted out whether one of these theories or yet another might be the best account of the meaning of dreams.

CULTURE & COMMUNITY

What Do Dreams Mean to Us Around the World? A recent study (Morewedge & Norton, 2009) assessed how people from three different cultures evaluate their dreams. Participants were asked to rate different theories of dreaming on a scale of 1 (do not agree at all) to 7 (agree completely).

A significant majority of students from the United States, South Korea, and India agreed with the Freudian theory that dreams have meanings. Only small percentages believed the other options, that dreams provide a means to solve problems, promote learning, or are by-products of unrelated brain activity.

The accompanying figure illustrates the findings across all three cultural groups. It appears that in many parts of the world, people have an intuition that dreams contain something deep and relevant.

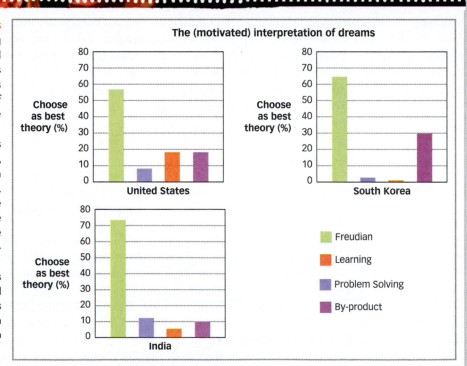

The (motivated) interpretation of dreams

Legend: Freudian, Learning, Problem Solving, By-product

The Dreaming Brain

What happens in the brain when we dream? Studies show that certain brain areas show changes in brain activation during REM sleep and that these changes correspond clearly with certain alterations of consciousness that occur in dreaming. **FIGURE 5.9** shows some of the patterns of activation and deactivation found in the dreaming brain (Schwartz & Maquet, 2002).

In dreams there are heights to look down from, dangerous people lurking, the occasional monster, some minor worries, and at least once in a while that major exam you've forgotten about until you walk into class. These themes suggest that the brain areas responsible for fear or emotion somehow work overtime in dreams, and it turns out that this is clearly visible in fMRI scans. The amygdala is involved in responses to threatening or stressful events, and indeed the amygdala is quite active during REM sleep.

The typical dream is also a visual wonderland, with visual events present in almost all dreams. However, there are fewer auditory sensations, even fewer tactile sensations, and almost no smells or tastes. This dream "picture show" doesn't involve actual perception, of course, just the imagination of visual events. It turns out that the areas of the brain responsible for visual perception are *not* activated during dreaming, whereas the visual association areas in the occipital lobe that are responsible for visual imagery *do* show activation (Braun et al., 1998). Your brain is smart enough to realize that it's not really seeing bizarre images but acts instead as though it's imagining bizarre images.

During REM sleep, the prefrontal cortex shows relatively less arousal than it usually does during waking consciousness. What does this mean for the dreamer? As a rule, the prefrontal areas are associated with planning and executing actions, and often dreams seem to be unplanned and rambling. Perhaps this is why dreams often don't have very sensible storylines—they've been scripted by an author whose ability to plan is inactive.

? Which areas are activated in the dreaming brain?

Another odd fact of dreaming is that while the eyes are moving rapidly, the body is otherwise very still. During REM sleep, the motor cortex is activated, but spinal neurons running through the brain stem inhibit the expression of this motor activation (Lai & Siegal, 1999). This turns out to be a useful property of brain activation in dreaming; otherwise, you might get up and act out every dream! People who are moving during sleep are probably not dreaming. The brain specifically inhibits movement during dreams, perhaps to keep us from hurting ourselves.

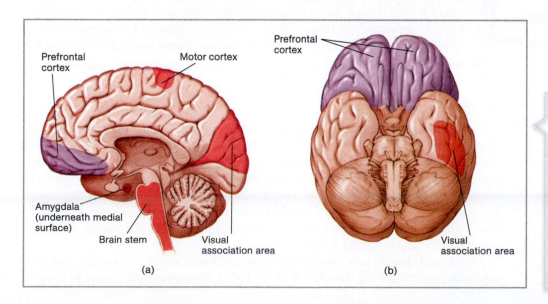

(a)   (b)

Prefrontal cortex — Motor cortex — Prefrontal cortex — Amygdala (underneath medial surface) — Brain stem — Visual association area — Visual association area

◀ Figure **5.9** **Brain Activation and Deactivation During REM Sleep** Brain areas shaded red are activated during REM sleep; those shaded blue are deactivated. (a) The medial view shows the activation of the amygdala, the visual association areas, the motor cortex, and the brain stem and the deactivation of the prefrontal cortex. (b) The ventral view shows the activation of other visual association areas and the deactivation of the prefrontal cortex (Schwartz & Maquet, 2002).

The seat of consciousness.

BRENT MADISON

Drugs and Consciousness: Artificial Inspiration

The author of the anti-utopian novel *Brave New World,* Aldous Huxley, once wrote of his experiences with the drug mescaline. His essay "The Doors of Perception" described the intense experience that accompanied his departure from normal consciousness. He described "a world where everything shone with the Inner Light, and was infinite in its significance. The legs, for example, of a chair—how miraculous their tubularity, how supernatural their polished smoothness! I spent several minutes—or was it several centuries?—not merely gazing at those bamboo legs, but actually *being* them" (Huxley, 1954).

Being the legs of a chair? This is better than being a seat cushion, but it sounds like an odd experience. Still, many people seek out such experiences, often through using drugs. **Psychoactive drugs** are *chemicals that influence consciousness or behavior by altering the brain's chemical message system.* You read about several such drugs in Chapter 3 when we explored the brain's system of neurotransmitters. And you will read about them in a different light when we turn to their role in the treatment of psychological disorders in Chapter 14. Whether these drugs are used for entertainment, for treatment, or for other reasons, they each exert their influence either by increasing the activity of a neurotransmitter (the agonists) or decreasing its activity (the antagonists). Like Huxley experiencing himself becoming the legs of a chair, people using drugs can have experiences unlike any they might find in normal waking consciousness or even in dreams. To understand these altered states, let's explore how people use and abuse drugs and examine the major categories of psychoactive drugs.

Drug Use and Abuse

Why do children sometimes spin around until they get dizzy and fall to the ground? There is something strangely attractive about states of consciousness that depart from the norm, and people throughout history have sought out these altered states by dancing, fasting, chanting, meditating, and ingesting a bizarre assortment of chemicals to intoxicate themselves (Tart, 1969). People pursue altered consciousness even when there are costs, from the nausea that accompanies dizziness to the life-wrecking obsession with a drug that can come with addiction. In this regard, the pursuit of altered consciousness can be a fatal attraction.

In one study researchers allowed rats to intravenously administer cocaine to themselves by pressing a lever (Bozarth & Wise, 1985). Rats given free access to cocaine increased their use over the course of the 30-day study. They not only continued to self-administer at a high rate but also occasionally binged to the point of giving themselves convulsions. They stopped grooming themselves and eating until they lost on average almost a third of their body weight. About 90% of the rats died by the end of the study. Studies of self-administration of drugs in laboratory animals show that animals will work to obtain not only cocaine but also alcohol, amphetamines, barbiturates, caffeine, opiates (such as morphine and heroin), nicotine, phencyclidine (PCP), MDMA (ecstasy), and THC (tetrahydrocannabinol, the active ingredient in marijuana). Rats are not tiny little humans, of course, so such research is not a firm basis for understanding human responses to cocaine. But these results do make it clear that these drugs are addictive and that the consequences of such addiction can be dire.

> **What is the allure of altered consciousness?**

People usually do not become addicted to a psychoactive drug the first time they use it. They may experiment a few times, then try again, and eventually find that their tendency to use the drug increases over time due to several factors, including **drug tolerance,** *the tendency for larger drug doses to be required over time to achieve the same effect.* Physicians who prescribe morphine to control pain in their patients are faced with tolerance problems because steadily greater amounts of the drug may be needed to dampen the same pain. With increased tolerance comes the danger of drug overdose; recreational users find they need to use more and more of a drug to produce the same high. But then, if a new batch of heroin or cocaine is more concentrated than usual, the "normal" amount the user takes to achieve the same high can be fatal.

Self-administration of addictive drugs can also be prompted by withdrawal symptoms, which result when drug use is abruptly discontinued. Some withdrawal symptoms signal *physical dependence,* when pain, convulsions, hallucinations, or other

> **What problems can arise in drug withdrawal?**

unpleasant symptoms accompany withdrawal. A common example is the "caffeine headache" some people complain of when they haven't had their daily jolt of java. Other withdrawal symptoms result from *psychological dependence,* a strong desire to return to the drug even when physical withdrawal symptoms are gone. For example, some ex-smokers report longing wistfully for an after-dinner smoke, even years after they've successfully quit the habit.

The psychological and social problems stemming from addiction are major. For many people, drug addiction becomes a way of life, and for some, it is a cause of death. But many people do overcome addictions. In one study, 64% of a sample of

psychoactive drug A chemical that influences consciousness or behavior by altering the brain's chemical message system.

drug tolerance The tendency for larger doses of a drug to be required over time to achieve the same effect.

> The antique coffee maker, a sight that warms the hearts of caffeine lovers around the world.

"At this point, we know it's addictive."

people who had a history of cigarette smoking had quit successfully, although many had to try again and again to achieve their success (Schachter, 1982). Another study of soldiers who became addicted to heroin in Vietnam found that 3 years after their return, only 12% remained addicted (Robins et al., 1980). Although addiction is dangerous, it may not be incurable.

It may not be accurate to view all recreational drug use under the umbrella of "addiction." Many people in the United States, for example, would not call the repeated use of caffeine an addiction, and some do not label the use of alcohol or tobacco in this way. In other times and places, however, each of these has been considered a terrifying addiction worthy of prohibition and public censure. In the early 17th century, for example, tobacco use was punishable by death in Germany, by castration in Russia, and by decapitation in China (Corti, 1931). Not a good time to be traveling around waving a cigar. By contrast, cocaine, heroin, marijuana, and amphetamines have each been popular and even recommended as medicines at several points throughout history (Inciardi, 2001). Societies react differently at different times, with some uses of drugs ignored, other uses encouraged, others simply taxed, and yet others subjected to intense prohibition (see the Real World box on p. 156). Rather than viewing *all* drug use as a problem, it is important to consider the costs and benefits of such use and to establish ways to help people choose behaviors that are informed by this knowledge (Parrott et al., 2004).

Types of Psychoactive Drugs

Four in five North Americans use caffeine in some form every day, but not all psychoactive drugs are this familiar. To learn how both the well-known and lesser-known drugs influence the mind, let's consider several broad categories of drugs: depressants, stimulants, narcotics, hallucinogens, and marijuana. **TABLE 5.2** summarizes what is known about the potential dangers of these different types of drugs.

TABLE 5.2

Dangers of Drugs

Drug	Dangers		
	Overdose (Can taking too much cause death or injury?)	Physical Dependence (Will stopping use make you sick?)	Psychological Dependence (Will you crave it when you stop using it?)
Depressants			
Alcohol	X	X	X
Benzodiazepines/Barbiturates	X	X	X
Toxic inhalants	X	X	X
Stimulants			
Amphetamines	X	X	X
MDMA (ecstasy)	X		?
Nicotine	X	X	X
Cocaine	X	X	X
Narcotics (opium, heroin, morphine, methadone, codeine)	X	X	X
Hallucinogens (LSD, mescaline, psilocybin, PCP, ketamine)	X		?
Marijuana			?

Depressants

Depressants are *substances that reduce the activity of the central nervous system.* Depressants have a sedative or calming effect, tend to induce sleep in high doses, and can arrest breathing in extremely high doses. Depressants can produce both physical and psychological dependence.

The most commonly used depressant is alcohol, the "king of the depressants," with its worldwide use beginning in prehistory, its easy availability in most cultures, and its widespread acceptance as a socially approved substance. Fifty-one percent of Americans over 12 years of age report having had a drink in the past month, and 23% have binged on alcohol (more than five drinks in succession) in that time. Young adults (ages 18 to 25) have even higher rates, with 62% reporting a drink in the previous month and 42% reporting a binge (*Health, United States*, 2008).

Alcohol's initial effects, euphoria and reduced anxiety, feel pretty positive. As it is consumed in greater quantities, drunkenness results, bringing slowed reactions, slurred speech, poor judgment, and other reductions in the effectiveness of thought and action. The exact way in which alcohol influences neural mechanisms is still not understood, but like other depressants, alcohol increases activity of the neurotransmitter GABA (De Witte, 1996). As you read in Chapter 3, GABA normally inhibits the transmission of neural impulses, so one effect of alcohol is as a disinhibitor—a chemical that lets transmissions occur that otherwise would be held in check. But there are many contradictions. Some people using alcohol become loud and aggressive, others become emotional and weepy, others become sullen, and still others turn giddy—and the same person can experience each of these effects in different circumstances. How can one drug do this? Two theories have been offered to account for these variable effects: *expectancy theory* and *alcohol myopia.*

> **?** Why do people experience being drunk differently?

Expectancy theory suggests that *alcohol effects are produced by people's expectations of how alcohol will influence them in particular situations* (Marlatt & Rohsenow, 1980). So, for instance, if you've watched friends or family drink at weddings and notice that this often produces hilarity and gregariousness, you could well experience these effects yourself should you drink alcohol on a similarly festive occasion. Seeing people getting drunk and fighting in bars, in turn, might lead to aggression after drinking. Evidence for the expectancy theory has been obtained in studies where some participants are given drinks containing alcohol and others are given a substitute liquid; some people in each group are led to believe they have alcohol and others are led to believe they do not. These experiments often show that the belief that one has had alcohol can influence behavior as strongly as the ingestion of alcohol itself (Goldman, Brown, & Christiansen, 1987).

Another approach to the varied effects of alcohol is the theory of **alcohol myopia,** which proposes that *alcohol hampers attention, leading people to respond in simple ways to complex situations* (Steele & Josephs, 1990). This theory recognizes that life is filled with complicated pushes and pulls, and our behavior is often a balancing act. Imagine that you are really attracted to someone who is dating your friend. Do you make your feelings known or focus on your friendship? The myopia theory holds that when you drink alcohol, your fine judgment is impaired. It becomes hard to appreciate the subtlety of these different options, and the inappropriate response is to veer full tilt one way or the other. So alcohol might lead you to make a wild pass at your friend's date or perhaps just cry in your beer over your timidity—depending on which way you happened to tilt in your myopic state.

Both the expectancy and myopia theories suggest that people using alcohol will often go to extremes (Cooper, 2006). In fact, it seems that drinking is a major contributing factor to social problems that result from extreme behavior. Drinking while

depressants Substances that reduce the activity of the central nervous system.

expectancy theory The idea that alcohol effects can be produced by people's expectations of how alcohol will influence them in particular situations.

alcohol myopia A condition that results when alcohol hampers attention, leading people to respond in simple ways to complex situations.

JEFF GREENBERG/THE IMAGE WORKS

People will often endure significant inconveniences to maintain their addictions.

driving is a main cause of auto accidents, for example, contributing to 32% of U.S. crash fatalities in 2006 (U.S. Department of Transportation, 2008). A survey of undergraduates revealed that alcohol contributes to as many as 90% of rapes and 95% of violent crimes on campus (Wechsler et al., 1994). Of the binge drinkers in the student sample, 41% reported that they had had unplanned sex due to drinking, and 22% said their drinking led to unprotected sex.

Compared with alcohol, other depressants are much less popular but still are widely used and abused. The *barbiturates*, such as Seconal or Nembutal, are prescribed as sleep aids and as anesthetics before surgery; the *benzodiazepines*, such as Valium and Xanax, are prescribed as antianxiety drugs. Physical dependence on these drugs is possible since withdrawal from long-term use can produce severe symptoms (including convulsions), and psychological dependence is common as well.

Finally, *toxic inhalants* are perhaps the most alarming substances in this category (Kurtzman, Otsuka, & Wahl, 2001). These drugs are easily accessible even to children in the vapors of glue, gasoline, or propane. Sniffing or "huffing" these vapors can promote temporary effects that resemble drunkenness, but overdoses are sometimes lethal, and continued use holds the potential for permanent brain damage (Fornazzari et al., 1983).

Stimulants

The **stimulants** are *substances that excite the central nervous system, heightening arousal and activity levels.* They include caffeine, amphetamines, nicotine, cocaine, modafinil, and ecstasy (MDMA), and sometimes they have a legitimate pharmaceutical purpose. For example, *amphetamines* (also called "speed") were originally prepared for use as diet drugs; however, some are widely abused, causing insomnia, aggression, and paranoia with long-term use. Stimulants increase the levels of dopamine and norepinephrine in the brain, thereby inducing higher levels of activity in the brain circuits that depend on these neurotransmitters. As a result, they increase alertness and energy in the user, often producing a euphoric sense of confidence and a kind of agitated motivation to get things done. Stimulants produce physical and psychological dependence, and their withdrawal symptoms involve depressive effects such as fatigue and negative emotions.

Ecstasy is an amphetamine derivative also known as MDMA, "X," or "e." Ecstasy is particularly known for making users feel empathic and close to those around them, but it has unpleasant side effects such as interfering with the regulation of body temperature, making users highly susceptible to heatstroke and exhaustion. Although ecstasy is not as likely as some other drugs to cause physical or psychological dependence, it nonetheless can lead to some dependence. What's more, the impurities sometimes found in "street" pills are also dangerous (Parrott, 2001). Ecstasy's potentially toxic effect on serotonin-activated neurons in the human brain is the subject of intense debate, and a good deal of research attention is being devoted to studying the effects of this drug on humans.

Cocaine is derived from leaves of the coca plant, which has been cultivated by indigenous peoples of the Andes for millennia and chewed as a medication. Yes, the urban legend is true: Coca-Cola contained cocaine until 1903 and still may use coca leaves (with cocaine removed) as a flavoring—although the company's not telling (Pepsi-Cola never contained cocaine and

Coca-Cola has been a popular product for more than a hundred years. In the early days, one of the fatigue-relieving ingredients was a small amount of cocaine.

DANNY LEHMAN/CORBIS

is probably made from something brown). Sigmund Freud tried cocaine and wrote effusively about it for a while. Cocaine (usually snorted) and crack cocaine (smoked) produce exhilaration and euphoria and are seriously addictive, both for humans and the rats you read about earlier in this chapter. Withdrawal takes the form of an unpleasant "crash," cravings are common, and antisocial effects like those generated by amphetamines—aggressiveness and paranoia—are frequent with long-term use. Although cocaine has enjoyed popularity as a "party drug," its extraordinary potential to create dependence should be taken very seriously.

Nicotine is something of a puzzle. This is a drug with almost nothing to recommend it to the newcomer. It usually involves inhaling smoke that doesn't smell that great, at least at first, and there's not much in the way of a "high" either—at best, some dizziness or a queasy feeling. So why do people do it? Tobacco use is motivated far more by the unpleasantness of quitting than by the pleasantness of using. The positive effects people report from smoking—relaxation and improved concentration, for example—come chiefly from relief from withdrawal symptoms (Baker, Brandon, & Chassin, 2004). The best approach to nicotine is never to get started.

Narcotics

Opium, which comes from poppy seeds, and its derivatives heroin, morphine, methadone, and codeine (as well as prescription drugs such as Demerol and OxyContin), are known as **narcotics** or **opiates,** *drugs derived from opium that are capable of relieving pain.* Narcotics induce a feeling of well-being and relaxation that is enjoyable but can also induce stupor and lethargy. The addictive properties of narcotics are powerful, and long-term use produces both tolerance and dependence. Because these drugs are often administered with hypodermic syringes, they also intro-

? Why are narcotics especially alluring?

duce the danger of diseases such as HIV when users share syringes. Unfortunately, these drugs are especially alluring because they are external mimics of the brain's own internal system of relaxation and well-being.

The brain produces endorphins or endogenous opioids, neurotransmitters that are closely related to opiates. As you learned in Chapter 3, endorphins play a role in how the brain copes internally with pain and stress. These substances reduce the experience of pain naturally. When you exercise for a while and start to feel your muscles burning, for example, you may also find that there comes a time when the pain eases—sometimes even *during* the exercise. Endorphins are secreted in the pituitary gland and other brain sites as a response to injury or exertion, creating a kind of natural remedy (like the so-called runner's high) that subsequently reduces pain and increases feelings of well-being. When people use narcotics, the brain's endorphin receptors are artificially flooded, however, reducing receptor effectiveness and possibly also depressing the production of endorphins. When external administration of narcotics stops, withdrawal symptoms are likely to occur.

Hallucinogens

The drugs that produce the most extreme alterations of consciousness are the **hallucinogens,** *drugs that alter sensation and perception, often causing hallucinations.* These include LSD (lysergic acid diethylamide), or acid; mescaline; psilocybin; PCP (phencyclidine); and ketamine (an animal anesthetic). Some of these drugs are derived from plants (mescaline from peyote cactus; psilocybin, or "shrooms," from mushrooms) and have been used by people since ancient times. For example, the ingestion of peyote plays a prominent role in some Native American religious practices. The other hallucinogens are largely synthetic.

These drugs produce profound changes in perception. Sensations may seem unusually intense, objects may seem to move or change, patterns or colors may appear, and these perceptions may be accompanied by exaggerated emotions ranging

stimulants Substances that excite the central nervous system, heightening arousal and activity levels.

narcotics or opiates Highly addictive drugs derived from opium that relieve pain.

hallucinogens Drugs that alter sensation and perception and often cause visual and auditory hallucinations.

Psychedelic art and music of the 1960s were inspired by some visual and auditory effects of drugs such as LSD.

MARTIN SHARP © PRIVATE COLLECTION/THE BRIDGEMAN ART LIBRARY

THE REAL WORLD

Drugs and the Regulation of Consciousness

Why does everyone have an opinion about drug use? Is consciousness something that governments should be able to legislate—or should people be free to choose their own conscious states (McWilliams, 1993)? After all, how can a "free society" justify regulating what people do inside their own heads?

Individuals and governments alike answer these questions by pointing to the costs of drug addiction, both to the addict and to the society that must "carry" unproductive people, pay for their welfare, and often even take care of their children. Drug users appear to be troublemakers and criminals. Widespread anger about the drug problem surfaced in the form of the "War on Drugs," a federal government program born in the Nixon years that focused on drug use as a criminal offense and attempted to stop drug use through the imprisonment of users.

Drug use did not stop with 40 years of the War on Drugs, though; instead, prisons filled with people arrested for drug use. From 1990 to 2007, the number of drug offenders in state and federal prisons increased from 179,070 to 348,736—a jump of 94% (Bureau of Justice Statistics, 2008)—not because of an increase in drug use but because of the rapidly increasing use of imprisonment for drug offenses. Many people who were being prevented from ruining their lives with drugs were instead having their lives ruined by prison. What can be done? The policy of the Obama administration is to focus on reducing the harm that drugs cause (Fields, 2009). This *harm reduction approach* originated in the Netherlands and England with tactics such as eliminating criminal penalties for some drug use or providing intravenous drug users with sterile syringes to help them avoid contracting HIV and other infections from shared needles (Des Jarlais et al., 2009). Harm reduction may even involve providing drugs for addicts to reduce the risks of poisoning and overdose they face when they get impure drugs of unknown strength from criminal suppliers.

Harm reduction seems to be working in the Netherlands. The Netherlands Ministry of Justice (1999) reported that the decriminalization of marijuana there in 1979 did not lead to increased use and that the use of other drugs remains at a level far below that of other European countries and the United States. A comparison of drug users in Amsterdam and San Francisco revealed that the city in which marijuana is criminalized—San Francisco—had higher rates of drug use for both marijuana and other drugs (Reinarman, Cohen, & Kaal, 2004). Separating the markets in which people buy marijuana and alcohol from those in which they get "hard" drugs such as heroin, cocaine, or methamphetamine may create a social barrier that reduces interest in the hard drugs.

Harm reduction strategies may not always find public support because they challenge the popular idea that the solution to drug and alcohol problems must always be prohibition: stopping use entirely. There may be solutions that

▲ In the Netherlands, marijuana use is not prosecuted. The drug is sold in "coffee shops" to those over 18.

find a middle ground between prohibition and deregulation as a way of reducing harm. Former president Jimmy Carter expressed it this way: "Penalties against drug use should not be more damaging to an individual than the use of the drug itself" (Carter, 1977).

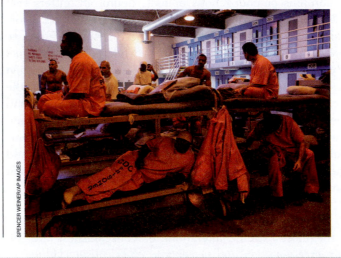

◀ There are many reasons that U.S. prisons are overcrowded—this country has the highest incarceration rate in the world. Treating drug abuse as a crime that requires imprisonment is one of the reasons.

from blissful transcendence to abject terror. These are the "I've-become-the-legs-of-a-chair!" drugs. But the effects of hallucinogens are dramatic and unpredictable, creating a psychological roller-coaster ride that some people find intriguing but others find deeply disturbing. Hallucinogens are the main class of drugs that animals *won't* work to self-administer, so it is not surprising that in humans these drugs are unlikely to be addictive. Hallucinogens do not induce significant tolerance or dependence, and overdose deaths are rare. Although hallucinogens still enjoy a marginal popularity with people interested in experimenting with their perceptions, they have been more a cultural trend than a dangerous attraction.

Marijuana

Marijuana is *derived from the leaves and buds of the hemp plant*. When smoked or eaten, either as is or in concentrated form as *hashish,* this drug produces an intoxication that is mildly hallucinogenic. Users describe the experience as euphoric, with heightened senses of sight and sound and the perception of a rush of ideas. Marijuana affects judgment and short-term memory and impairs motor skills and coordination—making driving a car or operating heavy equipment a poor choice during its use ("Where did I leave the darn bulldozer?"). The active ingredient in marijuana is known as THC, and researchers have found receptors in the brain that respond to THC (Stephens, 1999). These receptors normally respond to a naturally produced neurotransmitter called anandamide (Wiley, 1999), which is involved in the regulation of mood, memory, appetite, and pain perception and has been found temporarily to stimulate overeating in laboratory animals, much as marijuana does in humans (Williams & Kirkham, 1999). Some chemicals found in dark chocolate also mimic anandamide, although very weakly, perhaps accounting for the well-being some people claim they enjoy after a "dose" of chocolate.

? What are the risks of marijuana use?

The addiction potential of marijuana is not strong, as tolerance does not seem to develop, and physical withdrawal symptoms are minimal. Psychological dependence is possible, however, and some people do become chronic users. Marijuana use has been widespread throughout the world throughout recorded history, both as a medicine for pain and/or nausea and as a recreational drug, but its use remains controversial. Laws vary across the United States and Canada, with a number of states and provinces reducing penalties for the cultivation or possession of marijuana for medical use. The marijuana story is in flux, but right now the greatest danger of marijuana is that its use is illegal.

marijuana The leaves and buds of the hemp plant.

SUMMARY QUIZ [5.3]

1. Psychoactive drugs influence consciousness by altering the effects of
   a. agonists.   b. neurotransmitters.   c. amphetamines.   d. spinal neurons.

2. Tolerance to drugs involves
   a. larger doses being required over time to achieve the same effect.
   b. openness to new experiences.
   c. the initial attraction of drug use.
   d. the lessening of the painful symptoms that accompany withdrawal.

3. Drugs that heighten arousal and activity level by affecting the central nervous system are
   a. depressants.   b. stimulants.   c. narcotics.   d. hallucinogens.

4. Alcohol expectancy refers to
   a. alcohol's initial effects of euphoria and reduced anxiety.
   b. the widespread acceptance of alcohol as a socially approved substance.
   c. alcohol leading people to respond in simple ways to complex situations.
   d. people's beliefs about how alcohol will influence them in particular situations.

Hypnosis: Open to Suggestion

You may have never been hypnotized, but you have probably heard or read about it. When you think of hypnosis, you may envision people down on all fours acting like farm animals or perhaps "regressing" to early childhood and talking in childlike voices. Some of what you might think is true, but many of the common beliefs about hypnosis are false. **Hypnosis** is *an altered state of consciousness characterized by suggestibility and the feeling that one's actions are occurring involuntarily.*

Induction and Susceptibility

The essence of hypnosis is in leading people to expect that certain things will happen to them that are outside their conscious will (Wegner, 2002). To induce hypnosis, a hypnotist may ask a volunteer to sit quietly and focus on some item (such as a spot on the wall) and then suggest to the person what effects hypnosis will have (for example, "Your eyelids are slowly closing" or "Your arms are getting heavy"). Some of these suggestions seem to cause the actions—just thinking about their eyelids slowly closing, for instance, may make many people shut their eyes briefly or at least blink. In hypnosis, a series of behavior suggestions can induce in some people a state of mind that makes them susceptible to even very unusual suggestions, such as getting down on all fours and sniffing in the corner.

Not everyone is equally hypnotizable. Susceptibility varies greatly; while some hypnotic "virtuosos" are strongly influenced, most people are only moder-

? What makes someone easy to hypnotize?

ately influenced, and some people are entirely unaffected. One of the best indicators of a person's susceptibility is the person's own judgment. So if you think you might be hypnotizable, you may well be (Hilgard, 1965). People who have active, vivid imaginations, or who are easily absorbed in activities such as watching a movie, are also somewhat more prone to be good candidates for hypnosis (Sheehan, 1979; Tellegen & Atkinson, 1974).

Hypnotic Effects

From watching stage hypnotism, you might think that the major effect of hypnosis is making people do peculiar things. In fact, there have been some impressive demonstrations. At the 1849 festivities for Prince Albert of England's birthday, for example, a hypnotized guest was asked to ignore any loud noises and then didn't even flinch when a pistol was fired near his face. Other hypnotists claim that their volunteers can perform great feats not possible when the volunteers are fully conscious, such as becoming "stiff as a board" and lying unsupported with shoulders on one chair and feet on another. However, many people can perform these feats without hypnosis.

Hypnosis has also been touted as a cure for lost memory. The claim that hypnosis helps people to unearth memories that they are not able to retrieve in normal consciousness, however, seems to have surfaced because hypnotized people often make up memories to satisfy the hypnotist's suggestions. For example, Paul Ingram, a sheriff's deputy accused of sexual abuse by his daughters in the 1980s, was asked by interrogators in session after session to relax and imagine having committed the crimes. He emerged from these sessions having confessed to dozens of horrendous acts of "satanic ritual abuse." These confessions were called into question, however, when independent investigator Richard Ofshe used the same technique to ask Ingram about a crime that Ofshe had simply made

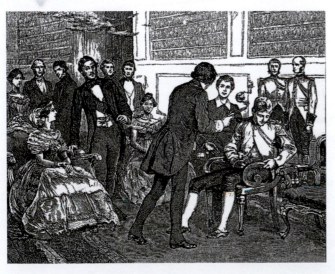

An 1849 demonstration of hypnosis at the festivities for Prince Albert's birthday. A pistol is discharged near the face of a young man in a trance, and he does not even flinch.

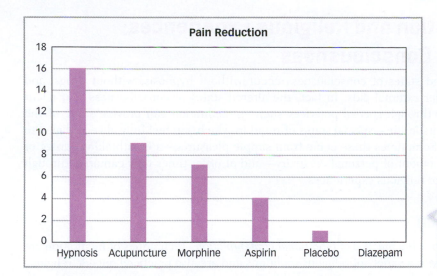

Pain Reduction

◄ Figure **5.10** **Hypnotic Analgesia**
The degree of pain reduction reported by people using different techniques for the treatment of laboratory-induced pain. Hypnosis wins. From Stern et al., 1977.

up out of thin air, something of which Ingram had never been accused. Ingram produced a three-page handwritten confession, complete with dialogue (Ofshe, 1992). Still, prosecutors in the case accepted Ingram's guilty plea, and he was only released in 2003 after a public outcry and years of work on his defense. After a person claims to remember something, even under hypnosis, it is difficult to convince others that the memory was false (Loftus & Ketchum, 1994).

Although all the preceding claims for hypnosis are somewhat debatable, one well-established effect is **hypnotic analgesia,** *the reduction of pain through hypnosis in people who are hypnotically susceptible.* For example, one study (see **FIGURE 5.10**) found that for pain induced in volunteers in the laboratory, hypnosis was more effective than morphine, diazepam (Valium), aspirin, acupuncture, or placebos (Stern et al., 1977). For people who are hypnotically susceptible, hypnosis can be used to control pain in surgeries and dental procedures, in some cases more effectively than any form of anesthesia (Druckman & Bjork, 1994; Kihlstrom, 1985). Evidence for pain control supports the idea that hypnosis is a different state of consciousness and not entirely a matter of skillful roleplaying on the part of highly motivated people.

? **Why do some argue that hypnosis is indeed a different state of consciousness?**

Stage hypnotists often perform an induction on a whole audience and then bring some of the more susceptible members onstage for further demonstrations.

SUMMARY QUIZ [5.4]

1. Hypnosis has been proven to have
   a. an effect on physical strength.
   b. a positive effect on memory retrieval.
   c. an analgesic effect.
   d. an age-regression effect.

2. Which of the following four individuals is *least* likely to be a good candidate for hypnosis?
   a. Jake, who spends lots of time watching movies
   b. Ava, who is convinced she is easily hypnotizable
   c. Evan, who has an active, vivid imagination
   d. Isabel, who loves to play sports

hypnosis An altered state of consciousness characterized by suggestibility and the feeling that one's actions are occurring involuntarily.

hypnotic analgesia The reduction of pain through hypnosis in people who are susceptible to hypnosis.

meditation The practice of intentional contemplation.

Meditation and Religious Experiences: Higher Consciousness

Some altered states of consciousness occur without hypnosis, without drugs, and without other external aids. In fact, the altered states of consciousness that occur naturally or through special practices such as meditation can provide some of the best moments in life—special states of mind in which you feel fully alive and glad to be human. Sometimes these come from simple pleasures—a breathtaking sunset or a magical moment of personal creativity—and at other times they can arise through meditative or religious experiences.

Meditation

Meditation is *the practice of intentional contemplation.* Techniques of meditation are associated with a variety of religious traditions and are also practiced outside religious contexts. Some forms of meditation call for attempts to clear the mind of thought, others involve focusing on a single thought (for example, thinking about a candle flame), and still others involve concentration on breathing or on a mantra, a repetitive sound such as *om.* At a minimum, the techniques have in common a period of quiet.

Meditation can confer physical and psychological benefits on its practitioners—but research has not yet determined how it might work.

PICTURE PRESS/PHOTONICA/GETTY

Why would someone meditate? The time spent meditating can be restful and revitalizing, and according to meditation enthusiasts, the repeated practice of meditation can enhance psychological well-being. The evidence for such long-term positive effects of meditation is controversial (Druckman & Bjork, 1994), but meditation does produce temporarily altered patterns of brain activation. Meditation influences EEG recordings of brain waves, usually producing patterns, known as *alpha waves,* that are associated with relaxation (Dillbeck & Orme-Johnson, 1987). A brain-scanning study of Buddhist practitioners during meditation found especially low levels of activation in the posterior superior parietal lobe (Newberg et al., 2001). This area is normally associated with judging physical space and orienting oneself in space—knowing angles, distances, and the physical landscape and distinguishing between the self and other objects in space. When this area is deactivated during meditation, its normal function of locating the self in space may subside to yield an experience of immersion and a loss of self.

? **What are some positive outcomes of meditation?**

Ecstatic Religious Experiences

In some religious traditions, people describe personal experiences of altered consciousness—feelings of ecstasy, rapture, conversion, or mystical union. Members of a religious group may "speak in tongues," or the celebrants may go into trances, report seeing visions, or feel as though they are possessed by spirits. These altered states may happen during prayer or worship or without any special religious activity. Over 40% of one sample of Americans reported having had a profound experience of this kind at least once in their lives (Greeley, 1975), and altered states of consciousness of one sort or another are associated with religious practices around the world (Bourguignon, 1968).

As with meditation, certain brain activation patterns are associated with ecstatic religious experiences. Some people who experience religious fervor show the same type of brain activation that occurs in some cases of epilepsy. Several prophets, saints, and founders of religions have been documented as having epilepsy—St. Joan of Arc, for example, had symptoms of epilepsy accompanying the religious visions that inspired her and her

? **What is the relationship between religious fervor and epilepsy?**

GAHAN WILSON/THE NEW YORKER COLLECTION/CARTOONBANK.COM

"Nothing happens next. This is it."

followers (Saver & Rabin, 1997). Similar symptoms occurred to St. Paul on the road to Damascus when he fell to the ground and suffered three days of blindness; the prophet Muhammad described falling episodes accompanied by religious visions; and Joseph Smith, who founded Mormonism, reported lapses of consciousness and speech arrest (Trimble, 2007). People asked to describe what it is like to have a seizure, in turn, sometimes report feeling what they call a religious "aura." One patient described his seizures as consisting of feelings of incredible contentment, detachment, and fulfillment, accompanied by the visualization of a bright light and soft music; sometimes he also saw a bearded man he assumed was Jesus Christ (Morgan, 1990). Surgery to remove a tumor in the patient's right anterior temporal lobe eliminated the seizures but also stopped his religious ecstasies. Cases such as this suggest the right anterior temporal lobe might be involved when people without epilepsy experience profound religious feelings. The special moments of connection that people feel with God or the universe may depend on the way in which brain activation promotes a religious state of consciousness.

The states of religious ecstasy and meditation are just two of the intriguing varieties of experience that consciousness makes available to us. Our consciousness ranges from the normal everyday awareness of walking, thinking, or gazing at a picture to an array of states that are far from normal or everyday—sleep, dreams, drug intoxication, hypnosis, and beyond. These states of mind stand as a reminder that the human mind is not just something that students of psychology can look at and study. The mind is something each of us looks *through* at the world and at ourselves.

Speaking in Tongues Part of worship in some churches involves being "filled with the Holy Spirit" and speaking in tongues. This usually means speaking in no recognizable language—although members of each congregation tend to have their own style and so sound alike.

SUMMARY QUIZ [5.5]

1. Meditation and religious ecstasy are altered states of consciousness that occur
   a. with the aid of drugs.
   b. through hypnosis.
   c. naturally or through special practices.
   d. as a result of dreamlike brain activity.

2. Meditation usually produces what kind of brain activity?
   a. delta waves   b. alpha waves   c. beta waves   d. theta waves

Where Do You Stand?

Between NORML and MADD: What Is Acceptable Drug Use?

Where is the line between drug use and abuse, between acceptable chemical alteration of consciousness and over-the-top, drug-crazed insanity? Some people think the line is drawn too strictly—organizations such as NORML (National Organization for the Reform of Marijuana Laws) lobby for the legalization of marijuana. Others think the line is too loose—MADD (Mothers Against Drunk Driving) asks bars and restaurants to end "happy hours" that promote alcohol consumption. At the extremes, some people advocate the legalization of cocaine and heroin (for instance, Jenny Tonge, member of the British Parliament), and others propose to fight caffeine addiction (for example, Rosemarie Ives, former mayor of Redmond, Washington).

Drug use is a controversial topic, and whenever it comes up, you may find yourself face-to-face with people who have very strong opinions. Talking with some people about drugs and alcohol may feel like talking with interrogators under a bright light down at the police station, and you may find yourself taking sides that do not reflect how you really feel. On the other hand, people you know who drink or use drugs may make you feel like a stick-in-the-mud if you don't always approve of what they're doing. Where do you stand? Should people be legally allowed to use psychoactive drugs and if yes, which ones? What about alcohol? Should there be restrictions on when or where these substances are used? For a legal drug, how old should a person be to use it?

Chapter Review

Conscious and Unconscious: The Mind's Eye, Open and Closed

▶ Consciousness is a mystery of psychology because other people's minds cannot be perceived directly and because the relationship between mind and body is perplexing.

▶ Consciousness has four basic properties: intentionality, unity, selectivity, and transience. It can also be understood in terms of levels: minimal consciousness, full consciousness, and self-consciousness.

▶ Conscious contents can include current concerns, daydreams, and unwanted thoughts.

▶ The cognitive unconscious is at work when subliminal perception and unconscious decision processes influence thought or behavior without the person's awareness.

Sleep and Dreaming: Good Night, Mind

▶ During a night's sleep, the brain passes in and out of five stages of sleep; most dreaming occurs in the REM sleep stage.

▶ Sleep needs decrease over the life span, but being deprived of sleep and dreams has psychological and physical costs.

▶ Sleep can be disrupted through disorders that include insomnia, sleep apnea, somnambulism, narcolepsy, sleep paralysis, and night terrors.

▶ fMRI studies of the dreaming brain reveal activations associated with visual activity, reductions of other sensations, increased sensitivity to emotions such as fear, lessened capacities for planning, and the prevention of movement.

Drugs and Consciousness: Artificial Inspiration

▶ Psychoactive drugs influence consciousness by altering the brain's chemical messaging system and intensifying or dulling the effects of neurotransmitters.

▶ Drug tolerance can result in overdose, and physical and psychological dependence can lead to addiction.

▶ Major types of psychoactive drugs include depressants, stimulants, narcotics, hallucinogens, and marijuana.

Hypnosis: Open to Suggestion

▶ Hypnosis is an altered state of consciousness characterized by suggestibility.

▶ Although many claims for hypnosis overstate its effects, hypnosis can create the experience that one's actions are occurring involuntarily and can even create analgesia in ways that suggest that hypnotic experiences are more than imagination.

Meditation and Religious Experiences: Higher Consciousness

▶ Meditation and religious ecstasy can be understood as altered states of consciousness.

▶ Meditation involves contemplation that may focus on a specific thought, sound, or action, or it may be an attempt to avoid any focus.

▶ Ecstatic religious experiences may have a basis in the same brain region—the right anterior temporal lobe—associated with some forms of epilepsy.

consciousness (p. 132)

phenomenology (p. 132)

problem of other minds (p. 133)

mind/body problem (p. 133)

cocktail party phenomenon (p. 135)

minimal consciousness (p. 136)

full consciousness (p. 136)

self-consciousness (p. 136)

mental control (p. 137)

thought suppression (p. 137)

rebound effect of thought suppression (p. 138)

ironic processes of mental control (p. 138)

dynamic unconscious (p. 139)

repression (p. 139)

cognitive unconscious (p. 140)

subliminal perception (p. 140)

altered state of consciousness (p. 141)

circadian rhythm (p. 141)

REM sleep (p. 142)

insomnia (p. 145)

sleep apnea (p. 145)

somnambulism (p. 145)

narcolepsy (p. 145)

sleep paralysis (p. 146)

night terrors (p. 146)

activation-synthesis model (p. 148)

psychoactive drugs (p. 150)

drug tolerance (p. 151)

depressants (p. 153)

expectancy theory (p. 153)

alcohol myopia (p. 153)

stimulants (p. 154)

narcotics or opiates (p. 155)

hallucinogens (p. 155)

marijuana (p. 157)

hypnosis (p. 158)

hypnotic analgesia (p. 159)

meditation (p. 160)

CHANGING MINDS

1. "I had a really weird dream last night," your friend tells you. "I dreamed that I was trying to fly like a bird, but I kept flying into clotheslines. I looked it up online, and dreams where you're struggling to fly mean that there is someone in your life who's standing in your way and preventing you from moving forward. I suppose that has to be my boyfriend, so maybe I'd better break up with him." Based on what you've read in this chapter, what would you tell your friend about the reliability of dream interpretation?

2. During an early-morning class, you notice your friend yawning, so you ask if he slept well the night before. "On weekdays, I'm in class all day, and I work the night shift," he says. "So I don't sleep much during the week. But I figure it's okay because I make up for it by sleeping in late on Saturday mornings." Is it realistic for your friend to assume that he can balance regular sleep deprivation with rebound sleep on the weekends?

3. You and a friend are watching the 2010 movie *Inception*, starring Leonardo DiCaprio as a corporate spy. DiCaprio's character is hired by a businessman named Mr. Saito to plant an idea in the unconscious mind of a competitor while he sleeps. According to the plan, when the competitor awakens, he'll be compelled to act on the idea, to the secret benefit of Saito's company. "It's a cool idea," your friend says, "but it's pure science fiction. There's no such thing as an unconscious mind and no way that unconscious ideas could influence the way you act when you're conscious." What would you tell your friend? What evidence do we have that the unconscious mind exists and can influence conscious behavior?

4. One of your friends has recently returned from a trip to India, and she tells you that in the city of Mumbai, the age limit for buying alcohol has recently been raised from 21 to 25. "Isn't that crazy?" she says. "People are considered old enough and responsible enough to vote at age 18, but even in the United States they don't allow you to drink alcohol until you're 21. They treat alcohol like it's some kind of drug." How would you explain to her that alcohol is, in fact, a drug? Why do some societies (including the United States) outlaw some drugs (e.g., cocaine, heroin), place age restrictions on others (e.g., alcohol, tobacco), and allow free use of others (such as caffeine, found in coffee, tea, and many sodas)?

CRITICAL THINKING QUESTIONS

1. Freud theorized that dreams represent unacceptable or anxiety-producing wishes that the mind can express only in disguised form. The activation-synthesis model of dreaming proposes that dreams are produced when the mind attempts to make sense of the random neural activity that occurs in the brain during sleep.

   Suppose a man is expecting a visit from his mother-in-law; the night before her arrival, he dreams that he comes home from work to find that his mother-in-law has driven a bus through the living room window of his house.

   How might Freud have interpreted such a dream? How might the activation-synthesis model interpret such a dream?

2. Alcohol has many effects that can differ from person to person and from situation to situation. Expectancy theory suggests that alcohol's effects are affected by people's expectations of how alcohol will influence them. The theory of alcohol myopia proposes that alcohol hampers attention, leading people to respond in simple ways to complex situations.

   Which one of these theories views a person's response to alcohol as being (at least partially) learned, through a process similar to observational learning?

3. Psychoactive drugs are chemicals that, when ingested, influence consciousness or behavior by altering the brain's chemical message system. Stimulant drugs can influence brain activity and often produce a sense of euphoria and well-being. Meditation is the practice of internal contemplation, and it can also temporarily influence brain activity and enhance the sense of well-being.

   Why do you think many cultures view psychoactive drugs as dangerous but meditation as healthful?

ANSWERS TO SUMMARY QUIZZES

Summary Quiz [5.1] 1. b; 2. d; 3. d
Summary Quiz [5.2] 1. a; 2. a; 3. c
Summary Quiz [5.3] 1. b; 2. a; 3. b; 4. d
Summary Quiz [5.4] 1. c; 2. d
Summary Quiz [5.5] 1. c; 2. b

Need more help? Additional resources are located at the book's free companion website at:
www.worthpublishers.com/schacterbrief2e

6

Memory

JILL PRICE WAS 12 years old when she began to suspect that she possessed an unusually good memory. Studying for a seventh-grade science final on May 30th, her mind drifted and she became aware that she could vividly recall everything she had been doing on May 30th of the previous year.

Remembering specifics of events that occurred a year ago may not seem so extraordinary—you can probably recall what you did on your last birthday or where you spent last Thanksgiving—but can you recall the details of what you did exactly 1 year ago today? Probably not—but Jill Price can.

As she grew older, Jill's memory flashes became even more frequent. Now in her mid-40s, Jill can recall clearly and in great detail what has happened to her *every single day since early 1980* (Price & Davis, 2008). This is not just Jill's subjective impression. Memory researchers tested Jill's memory over a period of a few years and came up with some shocking results (Parker, Cahill, & McGaugh, 2006). For example, they asked Jill to recall the dates of each Easter from 1980 to 2003, which is a pretty tough task considering that Easter can fall on any day between March 22nd and April 15th. Jill recalled the correct dates quickly and easily; nobody else the researchers tested came close. The researchers also asked Jill about the details of what she had been doing on various randomly chosen dates, and they checked Jill's recall against her personal diary. Again, Jill answered quickly and accurately: *July 1, 1986?*—"Tuesday. Went with [friend's name] to [restaurant name]." *October 3, 1987?*—"That was a Saturday. Hung out at the apartment all weekend, wearing a sling—hurt my elbow" (Parker et al., 2006, pp. 39–40).

Can you recall the day of the week and exactly what you were doing on, say, July 1, 2003, October 3, 2007, or April 27, 2009? One thing is certain: None of your textbook authors can.

Researchers still don't understand all the reasons why Jill Price can remember her past so much more fully than the rest of us, but Jill's memory is a gift we'd all love to have—right? Not necessarily. Here's what Jill has to say about her ability: "Most have called it a gift but I call it a burden. I run my entire life through my head every day and it drives me crazy!!!" (Parker et al., 2006, p. 35).

DAN TUFFS/GETTY IMAGES

▶ Jill Price can accurately remember just about everything that has happened to her during the past 30 years, as confirmed by her diary, but Jill's extraordinary memory is more of a curse than a blessing.

memory The ability to store and retrieve information over time.

encoding The process by which we transform what we perceive, think, or feel into an enduring memory.

storage The process of maintaining information in memory over time.

retrieval The process of bringing to mind information that has been previously encoded and stored.

elaborative encoding The process of actively relating new information to knowledge that is already in memory.

MEMORY *IS THE ABILITY TO STORE AND RETRIEVE INFORMATION OVER TIME.* Each of us has a unique identity that is intricately tied to the things we have thought, felt, done, and experienced. Memories are the residue of those events, the enduring changes that experience makes in our brains. If an experience passes without leaving a trace, it might just as well not have happened. But as Jill's story suggests, remembering all that has happened is not necessarily a good thing, either—a point we'll explore more fully later in the chapter.

The ease with which someone like Jill can remember her past shouldn't blind us from appreciating how complex the act of remembering really is. Because memory is so remarkably complex, it is also remarkably fragile (Schacter, 1996). We have all had the experience of forgetting something we desperately wanted to remember. Why does memory serve us so well in some situations and play such cruel tricks on us in others?

As you've seen in other chapters, the mind's mistakes provide key insights into its fundamental operation, and there is no better illustration of this than in the realm of memory. In this chapter, we will consider the three key functions of memory: **encoding**, *the process by which we transform what we perceive, think, or feel into an enduring memory;* **storage**, *the process of maintaining information in memory over time;* and **retrieval**, *the process of bringing to mind information that has been previously encoded and stored.* We'll then examine several different kinds of memory and focus on the ways in which errors, distortions, and imperfections can reveal the nature of memory itself.

Encoding: Transforming Perceptions into Memories

Bubbles P., a professional gambler with no formal education who spent most of his time shooting craps at local clubs or playing high-stakes poker, had no difficulty rattling off 20 numbers, in either forward or backward order, after just a single glance (Ceci, DeSimone, & Johnson, 1992). Most people can listen to a list of numbers and then repeat them from memory—as long as the list is no more than about seven items long (try it for yourself using **FIGURE 6.1**).

How did Bubbles accomplish his astounding feats of memory? For at least 2,000 years, people have thought of memory as a recording device that makes exact copies of information that comes in through our senses and then stores those copies for later use. This idea is simple and intuitive. It is also completely incorrect. Memories are made by combining information we *already* have in our brains with new information that comes in through our senses. Memories are *constructed*, not recorded, and encoding is the process by which we transform what we perceive, think, or feel into an enduring memory. Let's look at three types of encoding processes—elaborative encoding, visual imagery encoding, and organizational encoding—and then consider the possible survival value of encoding for our ancestors.

```
     2 8
    6 9 1
   0 4 7 3
  8 7 4 5 4
 9 0 2 4 8 1
5 7 4 2 2 9 6
6 4 7 1 9 3 0 4
3 5 6 7 1 8 4 8 5
1 0 2 8 8 3 4 7 2 9
4 7 2 0 8 2 7 4 2 6 4
7 3 1 0 9 3 4 3 5 1 3 8
```

▲ Figure **6.1** **Digit Memory Test** How many digits can you remember? Start on the first row and cover the rows below it with a piece of paper. Study the numbers in the row for 1 second and then cover that row back up again. After a couple of seconds, try to repeat the numbers. Then uncover the row to see if you were correct. If so, continue down to the next row, using the same instructions, until you can't recall all the numbers in a row. The number of digits in the last row you can remember correctly is your digit span. Bubbles P. could remember 20 random numbers, or about 5 rows deep. How did you do?

Elaborative Encoding

Memories are a combination of old and new information, so the nature of any particular memory depends as much on the old information already in our memories as it does on the new information coming in through our senses. In other words, how we remember something depends on how we think about it at the time. For example, as a professional gambler, Bubbles found numbers unusually meaningful, and so when he saw a string of digits, he tended to think about their meanings. He might have thought about how they related to his latest bet at the racetrack or to his winnings after a long night at the poker table. To memorize the string 22061823, Bubbles would think

? How do old memories influence new memories?

To test the two ideas, the researchers relied on a clever trick. Just after the letters disappeared from the screen, a tone sounded that cued the participants to report the letters in a particular row. A *high tone* cued participants to report the contents of the top row, a *medium* tone cued participants to report the contents of the middle row, and a *low* tone cued participants to report the contents of the bottom row. When asked to report only a single row, people recalled almost all of the letters in that row! Because the tone sounded *after* the letters disappeared from the screen, and participants couldn't know which of the three rows would be cued, the researchers concluded that people could have recalled the same number of letters from *any* of the rows had they been asked to. In fact, if the tone was substantially delayed, participants couldn't perform the task; the information had slipped away from their sensory memories. Like the afterimage of a flashlight, the 12 letters flashed on a screen are visual icons, a lingering trace stored in memory for a very short period.

Because we have more than one sense, we have more than one kind of sensory memory. **Iconic memory** is *a fast-decaying store of visual information*. A similar storage area serves as a temporary warehouse for sounds. **Echoic memory** is *a fast-decaying store of auditory information*. When you have difficulty understanding what someone has just said, you probably find yourself replaying the last few words— listening to them echo in your "mind's ear," so to speak. When you do that, you

> **?** How long is information held in iconic and echoic memory before it decays?

are accessing information that is being held in your echoic memory store. The hallmark of both the iconic and echoic memory stores is that they hold information for a very short time—usually a few seconds (Darwin, Turvey, & Crowder, 1972). These two sensory memory stores are a bit like doughnut shops: The products come in, they sit briefly on the shelf, and then they are discarded. If you want one, you have to grab it fast.

Short-Term Storage and Working Memory

A second kind of memory storage is **short-term memory,** which *holds nonsensory information for more than a few seconds but less than a minute*. For example, if someone tells you a telephone number, you can usually repeat it back with ease—but only for a few seconds. In one study, research participants were given consonant strings to remember, such as DBX and HLM. After seeing each string, participants were asked to count backward from 100 by 3s for varying amounts of time and were then asked to recall the strings (Peterson & Peterson, 1959). As shown in **FIGURE 6.6**, memory for the consonant strings declined rapidly, from approximately 80% after a 3-second delay to less than 20% after a 20-second delay. These results suggest that information can be held in the short-term memory store for about 15 to 20 seconds.

What if 15 to 20 seconds isn't enough time? What if we need the information for a while longer? We can use a trick that allows us to get around the natural limitations of our short-term memories. **Rehearsal** is *the process of keeping information in short-term memory by mentally repeating it*. If someone gives you a telephone number

> **?** Why is it helpful to repeat a phone number you want to remember?

and you don't have a pencil, you say it over and over to yourself until you find one. Each time you repeat the number, you are "reentering" it into short-term memory, giving it another 15 to 20 seconds of shelf life.

Short-term memory is limited in both how *long* it can hold information and how *much* information it can hold. Most people can keep approximately seven items in short-term memory, but if they

sensory memory A type of storage that holds sensory information for a few seconds or less.

iconic memory A fast-decaying store of visual information.

echoic memory A fast-decaying store of auditory information.

short-term memory A type of storage that holds nonsensory information for more than a few seconds but less than a minute.

rehearsal The process of keeping information in short-term memory by mentally repeating it.

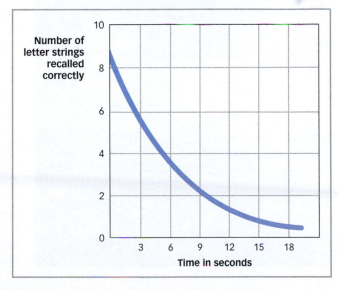

▼ Figure **6.6** **The Decline of Short-Term Memory** On a test for memory of three-letter strings, research participants were highly accurate when tested a few seconds after exposure to each string, but if the test was delayed another 15 seconds, people barely recalled the strings at all (Peterson & Peterson, 1959).

chunking Combining small pieces of information into larger clusters or chunks that are more easily held in short-term memory.

working memory Active maintenance of information in short-term storage.

long-term memory A type of storage that holds information for hours, days, weeks, or years.

anterograde amnesia The inability to transfer new information from the short-term store into the long-term store.

retrograde amnesia The inability to retrieve information that was acquired before a particular date, usually the date of an injury or operation.

put more new items in, then old ones begin to fall out (Miller, 1956). Those items can be numbers, letters, or even words or ideas. Therefore, one way to increase storage is to group several letters into a single meaningful item. **Chunking** involves *combining small pieces of information into larger clusters or chunks*. Waitresses who use organizational encoding (p. 168) to organize customer orders into groups are essentially chunking the information, giving themselves less to remember.

Short-term memory was originally conceived of as a kind of "place" where information is kept for a limited amount of time. A more dynamic model of a limited-capacity memory system has been developed and refined over the past few decades. **Working memory** refers to *active maintenance of information in short-term storage* (Baddeley & Hitch, 1974). It differs from the traditional view that short-term memory is simply a place to hold information and instead includes the operations and processes we use to work with information in short-term memory.

Working memory includes subsystems that store and manipulate visual images or verbal information, as well as a central executive that coordinates the subsystems (Baddeley, 2001). If you wanted to keep the arrangement of pieces on a chessboard in mind as you contemplated your next move, you'd be relying on working memory. Working memory includes the visual representation of the positions of the pieces, your mental manipulation of the possible moves, and your awareness of the flow of information into and out of memory, all stored for a limited amount of time. Brain-imaging studies indicate that the central executive component of working memory depends on regions within the frontal lobe that are important for controlling and manipulating information on a wide range of cognitive tasks (Baddeley, 2001).

Long-Term Storage

In contrast to the time-limited sensory memory and short-term memory stores, **long-term memory** *holds information for hours, days, weeks, or years*. In contrast to both sensory and short-term memory, long-term memory has no known capacity limits (see **FIGURE 6.7**). For example, most people can recall 10,000 to 15,000 words in their native language, tens of thousands of facts ("The capital of France is Paris" and "3 × 3 = 9"), and an untold number of personal experiences. Just think of all the song lyrics you can recite by heart, and you'll understand that you've got a lot of information tucked away in long-term memory!

Bruce Springsteen can count on his fans to know the words to almost all his songs.

KEVIN MAZUR/WIREIMAGE/GETTY IMAGES

The Role of the Hippocampus as Index

Where is long-term memory located in the brain? The clues to answering this question come from patients who are unable to store long-term memories. In 1953, a young man, known by the initials H. M., suffered from intractable epilepsy (Scoville & Milner, 1957). In a desperate attempt to stop the seizures, H. M.'s doctors removed parts of his temporal lobes, including the hippocampus and some surrounding regions (**FIGURE 6.8**). After the operation, H. M. could converse easily, use and understand language, and perform well on intelligence tests—but he could not remember anything that happened to him *after* the operation. H. M. could repeat a telephone number with no difficulty, suggesting that his short-term memory store was just fine (Corkin, 1984, 2002; Hilts, 1995; Squire, 2009). But after information left the short-term store, it was gone forever. For example, he would often forget that he had just eaten a meal or fail to recognize the hospital staff who helped him on a daily basis. H. M. now lacked the ability to hang on to the new memories he created. Studies of H. M. and others have shown that the hippocampal region of the brain is critical for putting new information

Maintenance rehearsal

Sensory input → Sensory memory → Attention → Short-term memory → Encoding / Retrieval → Long-term memory

Unattended information is lost.

Unrehearsed information is lost.

Some information may be lost over time.

◄ Figure **6.7** **The Flow of Information Through the Memory System** Information moves through several stages of memory as it gets encoded, stored, and made available for later retrieval

into the long-term store. When this region is damaged, patients suffer from a condition known as **anterograde amnesia,** which is *the inability to transfer new information from the short-term store into the long-term store.*

Some amnesic patients also suffer from **retrograde amnesia,** which is *the inability to retrieve information that was acquired before a particular date, usually the date of an injury or operation.* The fact that H. M. had much worse anterograde than retrograde amnesia suggests that the hippocampal region is not the site of long-term memory; indeed, research has shown that different aspects of a single memory—its sights, sounds, smells, emotional content—are stored in different places in the cortex (Damasio, 1989; Schacter, 1996; Squire & Kandel, 1999). Psychologists now believe that the hippocampal region acts as a kind of "index" that links together all of these otherwise separate bits and pieces so that we remember them as one memory (Schacter, 1996; Squire, 1992; Teyler & DiScenna, 1986). Over time, this index may become less necessary. You can think of the hippocampal-region index like a printed recipe. The first time you make a pie, you need the recipe to help you retrieve all the ingredients and then mix them together in the right amounts. As you bake more and more pies, though, you don't need to rely on the printed recipe anymore. Similarly, although the hippocampal-region index is critical when a new memory is first formed, it may become less important as the memory ages. Scientists are still debating the extent to which the hippocampal region helps us to remember details of our old memories (Bayley et al., 2005b; Kirwan et al., 2008; Moscovitch et al., 2006), but the notion of the hippocampus as an index explains why people like H. M. *cannot* make new memories and why they *can* remember old ones.

? How is using the hippocampal-region index like learning a recipe?

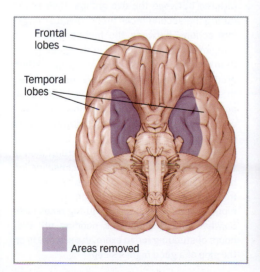

Frontal lobes

Temporal lobes

Areas removed

◄ Figure **6.8** **Patient H. M.** H. M. (right), whose real name was Henry Molaison, underwent surgery to stop his epileptic seizures; the surgery removed most of his hippocampus and adjacent structures of the medial temporal lobes (indicated by the shaded areas, left). As a result, he could not remember things that happened after the surgery. H. M. passed away in 2008, at the age of 82, after participating in countless memory experiments that made fundamental contributions to our understanding of memory and the brain.

consolidation The process by which memories become stable in the brain.

reconsolidation The process by which memories can become vulnerable to disruption when they are recalled, requiring them to become consolidated again.

Memory Consolidation

The idea that the hippocampus becomes less important over time for maintaining memories is related to the concept of **consolidation,** *a process by which memories become stable in the brain* (McGaugh, 2000). Shortly after encoding, memories exist in a fragile state in which they can be easily disrupted; once consolidation has occurred, they are more resistant to disruption. One type of consolidation operates over seconds or minutes. For example, when someone experiences a head injury in a car crash and later cannot recall what happened during the few seconds or minutes before the crash—but can recall other events normally—the head injury probably prevented consolidation of short-term memory into long-term memory. Another type of consolidation occurs over much longer periods—days, weeks, months, and years—and likely involves transfer of information from the hippocampus to more permanent storage sites in the cortex. The operation of this longer-term consolidation process is seen in the retrograde amnesia of patients like H. M. who can recall memories from childhood relatively normally but are impaired when recalling experiences that occurred just a few years prior to the time they became amnesic (Kirwan et al., 2008).

How does a memory become consolidated? The act of recalling a memory, thinking about it, and talking about it with others probably contributes to consolidation (Moscovitch et al., 2006). And as explained in the Hot Science box (below), mounting evidence indicates that sleep also plays an important role in memory consolidation.

Many researchers have long believed that a fully consolidated memory becomes a permanent fixture in the brain, more difficult to get rid of than a tenured professor. But even *seemingly consolidated memories can again become vulnerable to disruption*

HOT SCIENCE

Sleep on It

Thinking about pulling an all-nighter before your next big test? Here's reason to reconsider: We spend nearly one-third of our lives sleeping, and our minds don't simply shut off when we sleep (see Chapter 5). In fact, sleep may be as important to our memories as wakefulness.

Nearly a century ago, Jenkins and Dallenbach (1924) reported that recall of recently learned information is greater immediately after sleeping than after the same amount of time spent awake. They argued that being asleep passively protects us from encountering information that interferes with our ability to remember. As is explained later in the chapter (see p. 185), your ability to recall what happened yesterday can be impaired by new information that overwrites the earlier information. When you're asleep, you are not exposed to potentially interfering information, and so your memories may be protected compared

with an equivalent period of wakefulness. However, during the past few years, evidence has accumulated that sleep plays an active role in memory consolidation, doing more than simply protecting us from waking interference (Diekelmann, Wilhelm, & Born, 2009; Ellenbogen, Payne, & Stickgold, 2006).

In one study, participants studied a list of 90 word pairs in the evening, followed immediately by a test in which the first word of the pair was presented and they were instructed to recall the other word. Half the participants were then assigned to a sleep group that had two nights of normal sleep before receiving a second recall test. The other participants were assigned to a sleep-deprivation group that stayed up the first night and then had a recovery night's sleep before the second recall test.

The number of items recalled on the first test did not differ between the two groups, but participants in the sleep group recalled

more items on the second test than did participants in the sleep-deprivation group (Gais et al., 2007). Most important, brain activity differed between the two groups. fMRI scans during the second recall test showed stronger interactions between the hippocampus and a region in the frontal lobe in the sleep group than in the sleep-deprivation group. When brought back for a third test 6 months later, this frontal region again showed increased activity in the sleep group, but now the hippocampus was no longer engaged during correct recall.

What does it all mean? One interpretation is that sleep contributes to memory consolidation by increasing hippocampal interaction with the frontal lobe, aiding consolidation so that the hippocampus is less needed during recall later. So, when you find yourself nodding off after hours of studying for an exam, the science is on the side of a good night's sleep.

when they are recalled, thus requiring them to be consolidated again. This process is called **reconsolidation** (Nader & Hardt, 2009). Evidence for reconsolidation mainly comes from experiments with rats showing that when animals are cued to retrieve a new memory that was acquired a day earlier, giving the animal a drug (or an electrical shock) that prevents initial consolidation will cause forgetting (Nader, Shafe, & LeDoux, 2000; Sara, 2000). This finding is surprising because it was once thought that when memories are consolidated, drugs or shock that prevent initial consolidation no longer have any impact. To the contrary, it appears that each time they are retrieved, memories become vulnerable to disruption and have to be reconsolidated. Evidence of reconsolidation raises the intriguing possibility that it might be possible one day to eliminate painful memories by reminding individuals of traumatic experiences and injecting the right drug while the memory is held in mind (Brunet et al., 2008). While the possibility of selectively erasing painful memories makes for good entertainment in movies such as *Eternal Sunshine of the Spotless Mind*, research into reconsolidation is already beginning to turn such seemingly fanciful ideas into scientific reality.

The film *Eternal Sunshine of the Spotless Mind* builds on the premise that erasing some memories might be a good idea.

Memories, Neurons, and Synapses

We've already discussed parts of the brain that are related to memory storage, but exactly where in these regions are memories stored? Some of the answer comes from Erik Kandel's studies of the sea slug *Aplysia*, which has an extremely simple nervous system consisting of only 20,000 neurons (compared with roughly 100 billion in the human brain) (Kandel, 2006). When an experimenter stimulates *Aplysia*'s tail with a mild electric shock, the slug immediately withdraws its gill, and if the experimenter does it again a moment later, *Aplysia* withdraws its gill even more quickly. If the experimenter shocks *Aplysia* over and over, it develops an enduring "memory" that can last for days or even weeks. Research suggests that this long-term storage involves the growth of new connections between neurons (Abel et al., 1995; Kandel, 2006; Squire & Kandel, 1999). Specifically, when neurons communicate, the sending neuron releases neurotransmitters across the synapse, the small space between its own axon and the dendrites of the receiving neuron. The mere act of sending actually *changes* the synapse. Specifically, it strengthens the connection between the two neurons, making it easier for them to transmit to each other the next time. This is why researchers sometimes say, "Cells that fire together wire together" (Hebb, 1949).

The sea slug *Aplysia californica* is useful to researchers because it has an extremely simple nervous system that can be used to investigate the mechanisms of short- and long-term memory.

? Why are the spaces between neurons so important to memory?

If you're something more complex than a slug—say, a mammal or your roommate—a similar process of synaptic strengthening happens in the hippocampus, which we've seen is an area crucial for storing new long-term memories. In the early 1970s, researchers applied a brief electrical stimulus to a neural pathway in a rat's hippocampus (Bliss & Lømo,

Nobel Prize–winning neuroscientist Eric Kandel decided to take a risk and study the tiny sea slug *Aplysia* based in part on a lesson he had learned from his wife regarding their recent marriage, which encouraged him to trust his intuition: "Denise was confident that our marriage would work, so I took a leap of faith and went ahead. I learned from that experience that there are many situations in which one cannot decide on the basis of cold facts alone—because the facts are often insufficient. One ultimately has to trust one's unconscious, one's instincts, one's creative urge. I did this again in choosing *Aplysia*" (Kandel, 2006, p. 149).

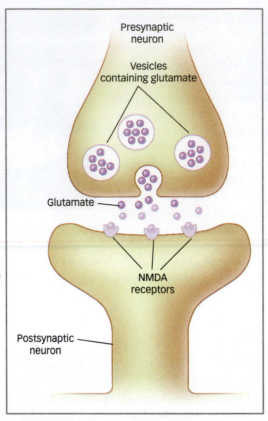

▶ Figure **6.9** **Long-Term Potentiation in the Hippocampus** The presynaptic neuron (top of figure) releases the neurotransmitter glutamate into the synapse. Glutamate then binds to the NMDA receptor sites on the postsynaptic neuron (bottom). At about the same time, excitation in the postsynaptic neuron takes place. The combined effect of these two processes initiates long-term potentiation and the formation of long-term memories.

1973). They found that the electrical current produced a stronger connection between synapses that lay along the pathway and that the strengthening lasted for hours or even weeks. They called this **long-term potentiation,** more commonly known as **LTP,** which is *a process whereby communication across the synapse between neurons strengthens the connection, making further communication easier.* Drugs that block LTP can turn rats into rodent versions of patient H.M.: The animals have great difficulty remembering where they've been recently and become easily lost in a maze (Bliss, 1999; Morris et al., 1986).

LTP in the hippocampus appears to depend on a neural receptor called NMDA (or, more formally, *N*-methyl-D-aspartate). The **NMDA receptor** *influences the flow of information between neurons by controlling the initiation of LTP in most hippocampal pathways* (Bliss, 1999; Li & Tsien, 2009). When a sending neuron releases glutamate (an excitatory transmitter), it may attach to an NMDA receptor on the receiving neuron, which may become active in turn. When this happens, LTP is initiated, which increases synaptic connections by allowing neurons that fire together to wire together (**FIGURE 6.9**). More work remains to be done in this area to conclusively show how LTP leads to the formation of long-term memories, but recent progress in understanding the workings of NMDA receptors may have important implications. For example, research on LTP and long-term memory formation may lead us to more effective treatments for Alzheimer's disease, a disorder that produces severe deficits in memory and other aspects of cognition in over 4 million older Americans (Li & Tsien, 2009).

SUMMARY QUIZ [6.2]

1. What kind of memory storage holds information for a second or two?

   a. retrograde memory

   b. working memory

   c. short-term memory

   d. sensory memory

2. The process by which memories become stable in the brain is called

   a. consolidation.

   b. long-term memory.

   c. iconic memory.

   d. hippocampal indexing.

3. Long-term potentiation occurs through

   a. the interruption of communication between neurons.

   b. the strengthening of synaptic connections.

   c. the reconsolidation of disrupted memories.

   d. sleep.

Retrieval: Bringing Memories to Mind

There is something fiendishly frustrating about piggy banks. You can put money in them, you can shake them around to assure yourself that the money is there, but you can't easily get the money out. If memories were like pennies in a piggy bank, stored but inaccessible, what would be the point of saving them in the first place? Retrieval is the process of bringing to mind information that has been previously encoded and stored, and it is perhaps the most important of all memory processes (Roediger, 2000; Schacter, 2001a).

Retrieval Cues: Reinstating the Past

One of the best ways to retrieve information from *inside* your head is to encounter information *outside* your head that is somehow connected to it. The information outside your head is called a **retrieval cue,** which is *external information that is associated with stored information and helps bring it to mind*. Retrieval cues can be incredibly effective. How many times have you said something like "I *know* who starred in *Pirates of the Caribbean,* but I just can't remember it," only to have a friend give you a hint ("Wasn't he in *Alice in Wonderland?*"), which instantly brings the answer to mind ("Johnny Depp!"). Such incidents suggest that information is sometimes *available* in memory even when it is momentarily *inaccessible* and that retrieval cues help us bring inaccessible information to mind.

Hints are one kind of retrieval cue, but they are not the only kind. The **encoding specificity principle** states that *a retrieval cue can serve as an effective reminder when it helps re-create the specific way in which information was initially encoded* (Tulving & Thomson, 1973). External contexts often make powerful retrieval cues (Hockley, 2008). For example, in one

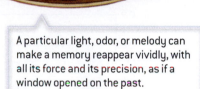

A particular light, odor, or melody can make a memory reappear vividly, with all its force and its precision, as if a window opened on the past.

study, divers learned some words on land and some other words underwater; they recalled the words best when they were tested in the same dry or wet environment in which they had initially learned them because the environment itself served as a retrieval cue (Godden

Why might it be a good idea to sit in the same seat for an exam that you sat in during lecture?

& Baddeley, 1975). Similarly, recovering alcoholics often experience a renewed urge to drink when visiting places in which they once drank because these places serve as retrieval cues. There may even be some wisdom to finding a seat in a classroom, sitting in it every day, and then sitting in it again when you take the test because the feel of the chair and the sights you see may help you remember the information you learned while you sat there.

Retrieval cues need not be external contexts—they can also be inner states. **State-dependent retrieval** is *the tendency for information to be better recalled when the person is in the same state during encoding and retrieval*. For example, retrieving information when you are in a sad or happy mood increases the likelihood that you will retrieve sad or happy episodes (Eich, 1995), which is part of the reason it is so hard to "look on the bright side" when you're feeling low. Being in a good mood affects patterns of electrical activity in parts of the brain responsible for semantic processing, suggesting that mood has a direct influence on semantic encoding (Kiefer et al., 2007). If the person's state at the time of retrieval matches the person's state at the time of encoding, the state itself serves as a retrieval cue—a bridge that connects the moment at which we experience something to the moment at which we remember it. Retrieval cues can even be thoughts themselves, as when one thought calls to mind another, related thought (Anderson et al., 1976).

The encoding specificity principle makes some unusual predictions. For example, you learned earlier that making semantic judgments about a word usually produces

long-term potentiation (LTP) A process whereby communication across the synapse between neurons strengthens the connection, making further communication easier.

NMDA receptor A receptor site on the hippocampus that influences the flow of information between neurons by controlling the initiation of long-term potentiation.

retrieval cue External information that helps bring stored information to mind.

encoding specificity principle The idea that a retrieval cue can serve as an effective reminder when it helps re-create the specific way in which information was initially encoded.

state-dependent retrieval The tendency for information to be better recalled when the person is in the same state during encoding and retrieval.

transfer-appropriate processing The idea that memory is likely to transfer from one situation to another when the encoding contexts of the situations match.

retrieval-induced forgetting A process whereby retrieving an item from long-term memory impairs subsequent recall of related items.

more durable memory for the word than does making rhyme judgments. So if you were asked to think of a word that rhymes with *brain* and your friend was asked to think about what *brain* means, we would expect your friend to remember the word better the next day if we simply asked you both "Hey, what was that word you saw yesterday?" However, if instead of asking that question, we asked you both "What was that word that rhymed with *train*?" we would expect you to remember it better than your friend did (Fisher & Craik, 1977). This is a fairly astounding finding. Semantic judgments almost always yield better memory than rhyme judgments. But in this case, the typical finding is turned upside down because the retrieval cue matched your encoding context better than it matched your friend's. The principle of **transfer-appropriate processing** states that *memory is likely to transfer from one situation to another when the encoding context of the situations match* (Morris, Bransford, & Franks, 1977; Roediger, Weldon, & Challis, 1989).

Consequences of Retrieval

Retrieval doesn't merely provide a readout of what is in memory; it also changes the state of the memory system in important ways. In this respect, human memory differs substantially from computer memory. Simply retrieving a file from my computer doesn't have any effect on the likelihood that the file will open again in the future. Not so with human memory.

Retrieval Can Improve Subsequent Memory

The simple act of retrieval can strengthen a retrieved memory, making it easier to remember that information at a later time (Bjork, 1975). In fact, the act of retrieving information from memory can strengthen the memory more than simply studying the information again. In one experiment, participants studied brief stories and then either studied them again or were given a test that required retrieving the stories (Roediger & Karpicke, 2006). Participants were then given a final recall test for the stories either 5 minutes, 2 days, or 1 week later. As shown in **FIGURE 6.10**, at the 5-minute delay, studying the stories twice resulted in slightly higher recall than studying and retrieving them. Critically, the opposite occurred at the 2-day and 1-week delays: Retrieval produced much higher levels of recall than did an extra study exposure.

These findings are especially important to college students, who are frequently preparing for exams: Students should spend more time testing themselves on the to-be-learned material rather than simply studying it over and over. You might think that this would be obvious to college students, but it's not. In one study of vocabulary learning, students made predictions about how well they would do with additional study or retrieval trials, and their predictions were totally unrelated to their actual performance (Karpicke & Roediger 2008)! We'll explore further some of the educational implications of these effects of retrieval on learning in Chapter 7.

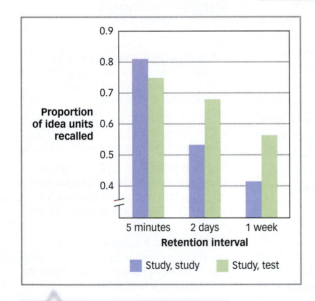

▲ Figure **6.10** **Memory Testing Benefits Long-Term Retention** With a 5-minute retention interval, the study-study condition results in slightly higher recall. But the results change dramatically with retention intervals of 2 days and 1 week: At these longer delays, the study-test condition yields much higher levels of recall than does the study-study condition (Roediger & Karpicke, 2006).

Retrieval Can Impair Subsequent Memory

As much as retrieval can help memory, that's not always the case. **Retrieval-induced forgetting** is *a process by which retrieving an item from long-term memory impairs subsequent recall of related items* (Anderson, 2003; Anderson, Bjork, & Bjork, 1994). It's as if our memory implements a kind of "survival of the fittest": When we try to recall some items but not others, the ones that are not recalled are weakened in memory. For example, when witnesses to a staged crime are questioned about some details of the crime scene, their ability to later recall related details that they were not asked about is impaired compared with witnesses who were not questioned at all initially

(MacLeod, 2002; Shaw, Bjork, & Handal, 1995). These findings suggest that initial interviews with eyewitnesses should be as complete as possible in order to avoid potential retrieval-induced forgetting of significant details that were not probed during the interview (MacLeod & Saunders, 2008).

Separating the Components of Retrieval

Before leaving the topic of retrieval, let's look at how the process actually works. There is reason to believe that *trying* to recall an incident and *successfully* recalling one are fundamentally different processes that occur in different parts of the brain (Moscovitch, 1994; Schacter, 1996). For example, regions in the left frontal lobe show heightened activity when people *try* to retrieve information that was presented to them earlier (Oztekin, Curtis, & McElree, 2009; Schacter et al., 1996a; Tulving et al., 1994). This activity may reflect the mental effort of struggling to dredge up the past event (Lepage et al., 2000). However, *successfully* remembering a past experience tends to be accompanied by activity in the hippocampal region (see FIGURE 6.11; Eldridge et al., 2000; Giovanello, Schnyer, & Verfaellie, 2004; Schacter et al., 1996a). Successful recall also activates parts of the brain that play a role in processing the sensory features of an experience. For instance, recall of previously heard sounds is accompanied by activity in the auditory cortex (the upper part of the temporal lobe), whereas recall of previously seen pictures is accompanied by activity in the visual cortex (in the occipital lobe) (Wheeler, Petersen, & Buckner, 2000). Although retrieval may seem like a single process, brain studies suggest that separately identifiable processes are at work.

> ? How is brain activity different when *trying* to recall vs. *successfully* recalling?

This sheds light on the phenomena we just discussed: retrieval-induced forgetting. Why might brains do such a thing? Recent fMRI evidence indicates that during memory retrieval, regions within the frontal lobe that are involved in retrieval effort play a role in suppressing competitors (Kuhl et al., 2007; Wimber et al., 2009). Once the competitor is suppressed, the frontal lobe no longer has to work as hard at controlling retrieval, ultimately making it easier to recall the target item (Kuhl et al., 2007). The odd phenomenon of retrieval-induced forgetting makes sense once we understand the specific roles played by particular brain regions in the retrieval process.

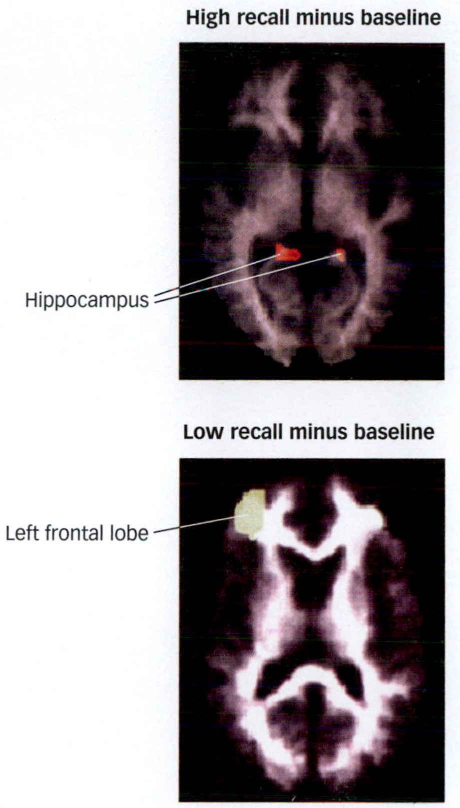

High recall minus baseline

Hippocampus

Low recall minus baseline

Left frontal lobe

▲ Figure **6.11** **PET Scans of Successful and Unsuccessful Recall** When people successfully remembered words they saw earlier in an experiment, achieving high levels of recall on a test, the hippocampus showed increased activity. When people tried but failed to recall words they had seen earlier, achieving low levels of recall on a test, the left frontal lobe showed increased activity (Schacter et al., 1996a).

SUMMARY QUIZ [6.3]

1. The increased likelihood of recalling a sad memory when you are in a sad mood is an illustration of
   a. the encoding specificity principle.
   c. transfer-appropriate processing.
   b. state-dependent retrieval.
   d. memory accessibility.

2. Which of the following statements regarding the consequences of memory retrieval is false?
   a. Retrieval-induced forgetting can affect eyewitness memory.
   b. The act of retrieval can strengthen a retrieved memory.
   c. Retrieval can impair subsequent memory.
   d. Retrieval boosts subsequent memory through the repetition of information.

3. Neuroimaging studies suggest that *trying* to remember activates the
   a. left frontal lobe.
   c. occipital lobe.
   b. hippocampal region.
   d. upper temporal lobe.

Multiple Forms of Memory: How the Past Returns

In 1977, the neurologist Oliver Sacks interviewed a young man named Greg who had a tumor in his brain that wiped out his ability to remember day-to-day events. One thing Greg could remember was his life during the 1960s, when his primary occupation seemed to be attending rock concerts by his favorite band, The Grateful Dead. Greg's memories of those concerts stuck with him over the following years, when he was living in a long-term-care hospital. In 1991, Dr. Sacks took Greg to a Dead concert at New York's Madison Square Garden, wondering whether such a momentous event might jolt his memory into action. "That was fantastic," Greg told Dr. Sacks as they left the concert. "I will always remember it. I had the time of my life." But when Dr. Sacks saw Greg the next morning and asked him whether he recalled the previous night's concert, Greg drew a blank: "No, I've never been to the Garden" (Sacks, 1995, pp. 76–77).

Although Greg was unable to form new memories, some of the new things that happened to him seemed to leave a mark. For example, Greg did not recall learning that his father had died, but he did seem sad and withdrawn for years after hearing the news. Similarly, H. M. could not make new memories after his surgery, but if he played a game in which he had to track a moving target, his performance gradually improved with each round (Milner, 1962). Greg could not consciously remember hearing about his father's death, and H. M. could not consciously remember playing the tracking game, but both showed clear signs of having been permanently changed by experiences that they so rapidly forgot. In other words, these patients *behaved* as though they were remembering things while claiming to remember nothing at all. This suggests that there must be several kinds of memory, some that are accessible to conscious recall and some that we cannot consciously access (Eichenbaum & Cohen, 2001; Schacter & Tulving, 1994; Schacter, Wagner, & Buckner, 2000; Squire & Kandel, 1999).

Explicit and Implicit Memory

The fact that people can be changed by past experiences without having any awareness of those experiences suggests that there must be at least two different classes of memory (**FIGURE 6.12**). **Explicit memory** occurs *when people consciously or intentionally retrieve past experiences.* Recalling last summer's vacation, incidents from a novel you just read, or facts you studied for a test all involve explicit memory. Indeed, anytime you start a sentence with, "I remember . . .," you are talking about an explicit memory. **Implicit memory** occurs when *past experiences influence later behavior and performance, even though people are not trying to recollect them and are not aware that they are remembering them* (Graf & Schacter, 1985; Schacter, 1987). Implicit memories are not consciously recalled, but their presence is "implied" by our actions.

One type of implicit memory, called **procedural memory,** refers to *the gradual acquisition of skills as a result of practice, or "knowing how" to do things.* H. M.'s improved performance on a tracking task that he didn't consciously remember doing is an example of procedural memory. So is the ability to ride a bike or tie your shoelaces or play guitar: You may know how to do these things, but you probably

? What type of memory is it when you just "know how" to do something?

can't describe how to do them. The fact that people who have amnesia can acquire new procedural memories suggests that the hippocampal structures that are usually damaged in these patients may be necessary for explicit memory, but not for implicit procedural memory. Rather, areas such as the motor cortex appear important for procedural memory (you'll read more about this in Chapter 7).

explicit memory The act of consciously or intentionally retrieving past experiences.

implicit memory The influence of past experiences on later behavior, even without an effort to remember them or an awareness of the recollection.

procedural memory The gradual acquisition of skills as a result of practice, or "knowing how" to do things.

priming An enhanced ability to think of a stimulus, such as a word or object, as a result of a recent exposure to the stimulus.

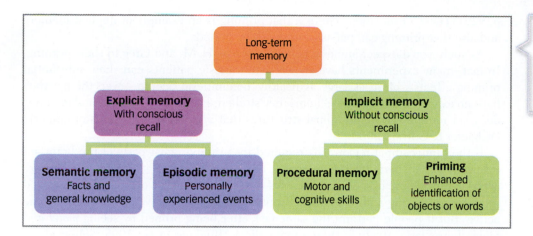

◄ Figure **6.12** **Multiple Forms of Memory**
Explicit and implicit memories are distinct from each other. Thus, a person with amnesia may lose explicit memory yet display implicit memory for material that she or he cannot consciously recall learning.

Not all implicit memories are procedural, or "how to," memories. For example, **priming** refers to *an enhanced ability to think of a stimulus, such as a word or object, as a result of a recent exposure to the stimulus* (Tulving & Schacter, 1990). In one experiment, college students were asked to study a long list of words, including items such as *avocado, mystery, climate, octopus,* and *assassin* (Tulving, Schacter, & Stark, 1982). Later, explicit memory was tested by showing participants some of these words along with new ones they hadn't seen and asking them which words were on the list. Implicit memory was tested by showing participants word fragments and asking them to come up with a word that fit the fragment. Try the test yourself:

```
ch____nk        o_t_p__        _og_y___        _l_m_te
```

You probably had difficulty coming up with the answers for the first and third fragments (*chipmunk, bogeyman*) but had little problem coming up with answers for the second and fourth (*octopus, climate*). Seeing *octopus* and *climate* on the original list made those words more accessible later, during the fill-in-the-blanks test. Similar priming effects are obtained from visual material, such as when participants first study drawings of objects and are later asked to identify the objects in fragmented drawings (D.B. Mitchell, 2006). Just as priming a pump makes water flow more easily, priming the memory system makes some information more accessible. In the fill-in-the-blanks experiment, people showed priming for studied words even when they failed to consciously remember that they had seen them earlier. This suggests that priming is an example of implicit, not explicit, memory.

How does priming make memory more efficient?

A truly stunning example of this point comes from a study by D. B. Mitchell (2006) in which participants first studied black-and-white line drawings depicting everyday objects. Later, the participants were shown fragmented versions of the drawings that are difficult to identify; some of them depicted objects that had been studied earlier in the experiment, whereas others depicted new objects that had not been studied. Mitchell found that participants correctly identified more fragmented drawings of studied than of new objects and identified more studied objects than did participants in a control group who had never seen the pictures—a clear demonstration of priming (see **FIGURE 6.13**). Here's the stunning part: The fragmented drawing test was given 17 years after presentation of the study list! By that time, participants had little or no explicit memory of having seen the drawings, and some had no recollection that they had ever participated in the experiment! "I'm sorry—I really don't remember this experiment at all," said one 36-year-old man who showed a strong priming effect. A 36-year-old female who showed even more priming stated simply, "Don't remember anything about it." (D.B. Mitchell, 2006,

▼ Figure **6.13** **Long-Term Priming of Visual Objects** Participants who viewed drawings of common objects, and 17 years later were given a test in which they tried to identify the objects from fragmented drawings (longitudinal group), showed a strong priming effect; by contrast, participants who had not seen the drawing 17 years earlier (control group) showed nonsignificant priming (D.B. Mitchell, 2006).

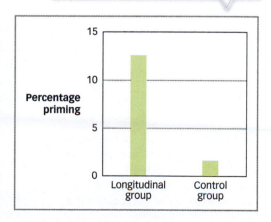

p. 929). These observations confirm that priming is an example of implicit memory and also that priming can persist over very long periods.

As such, you'd expect amnesic patients such as H. M. and Greg to show priming. In fact, many experiments have shown that amnesic patients can show substantial priming effects—often as large as healthy, nonamnesic people—even though they have no explicit memory for the items they studied. Priming, like procedural memory, does not require the hippocampal structures that are damaged in cases of amnesia (Schacter & Curran, 2000).

If the hippocampal region isn't required for priming, what parts of the brain are involved? When participants are shown the word stem *mot___* or *tab___* and are asked to provide the first word that comes to mind, parts of the occipital lobe involved in visual processing and parts of the frontal lobe involved in word retrieval become active. But if people perform the same task after being primed by seeing *motel* and *table*, there's less activity in these same regions (Buckner et al., 1995; Schott et al., 2005). Priming seems to make it easier for the parts of the cortex that are involved in perceiving a word or object to identify the item after a recent exposure to it (Schacter, Dobbins, & Schnyer, 2004; Wiggs & Martin, 1998). This suggests that the brain "saves" a bit of processing time after priming (see **FIGURE 6.14**).

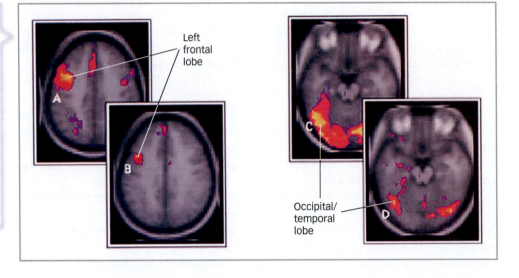

▶ Figure **6.14** **Primed and Unprimed Processing of Stimuli** Priming is associated with reduced levels of activation in the cortex on a number of different tasks. In each pair of fMRIs, the images on the upper left (A, C) show brain regions in the frontal lobe (A) and occipital/temporal lobe (C) that are active during an unprimed task (in this case, providing a word response to a visual word cue). The images on the lower right within each pair (B, D) show reduced activity in the same regions during the primed version of the same task.

From Schacter, D. L. & Buckner, R. L. (1998). Priming and the Brain. *Neuron, 20,* 185–195.

Semantic and Episodic Memory

Consider these two questions: (1) Why do Americans celebrate on July 4th? (2) What is the most spectacular Fourth of July celebration you've ever seen? Every American knows the answer to the first question (we celebrate the signing of the Declaration of Independence on July 4, 1776), but we all have our own answers to the second. Although both of these questions required you to search your long-term memory and explicitly retrieve information that was stored there, one required you to dredge up a fact that every American schoolchild knows and that is not part of your personal autobiography, and one required you to revisit a particular time and place—or episode—from your personal past. These memories are called *semantic* and *episodic* memories, respectively (Tulving, 1972, 1983, 1998). **Semantic memory** is *a network of associated facts and concepts that make up our general knowledge of the world,* whereas **episodic memory** is *the collection of past personal experiences that occurred at a particular time and place.*

Episodic memory is special because it is the only form of memory that allows us to engage in "mental time travel," projecting ourselves into the past and revisiting events that have happened to us. This ability allows us to connect our pasts and our

semantic memory A network of associated facts and concepts that make up our general knowledge of the world.

episodic memory The collection of past personal experiences that occurred at a particular time and place.

presents and to construct a cohesive story of our lives. People who have amnesia can usually travel back in time and revisit episodes that occurred before they became amnesic, but they are unable to revisit episodes that happened later. For example, Greg couldn't travel back to any time after 1969 because that's when he stopped being able to create new episodic memories. But can people with amnesia create new semantic memories?

What form of memory uses "mental time travel"?

Researchers have studied three young adults who suffered damage to the hippocampus during birth as a result of difficult deliveries that interrupted the oxygen supply to their brains (Brandt et al., 2009; Vargha-Khadem et al., 1997). Their parents noticed that the children could not recall what happened during a typical day, had to be constantly reminded of appointments, and often became lost and disoriented. In view of their hippocampal damage, you might also expect that each of the three would perform poorly in school. Remarkably, however, all three children learned to read, write, and spell; developed normal vocabularies; and acquired other kinds of semantic knowledge that allowed them to perform well in school. Based on this evidence, researchers have concluded that the hippocampus is not necessary for acquiring new *semantic* memories.

This contestant on the game show *Who Wants to Be a Millionaire?* is consulting her semantic memory in order to answer the question. The answer is B: Bulgaria.

Episodic Memory and Imagining the Future

We've already seen that episodic memory allows us to travel backward in time, but it turns out that episodic memory also plays a role in allowing to us to travel forward in time. An amnesic patient known by the initials K.C. provided an early clue. K.C. could not recollect any specific episodes from his past, and when asked to imagine a future episode—such as what he might do tomorrow—he reported a complete "blank" (Tulving, 1985). Consistent with this observation, most amnesic patients have difficulty imagining new experiences, such as sunbathing on a sandy beach (Hassabis et al., 2007). Something similar happens with aging. When asked either to recall episodes that actually occurred in their pasts or imagine new episodes that might occur in their futures, elderly adults provided fewer details about what happened, or what might happen, than did college students (Addis, Wong, & Schacter, 2008). Consistent with these findings, neuroimaging studies reveal that a network of brain regions known to be involved in episodic memory—including the hippocampus—shows similarly increased activity when people remember the past and imagine the future (Addis, Wong, & Schacter, 2007; Okuda et al., 2003; Szpunar, Watson, & McDermott, 2007; see **FIGURE 6.15**).

Taken together, these observations strongly suggest that we rely heavily on episodic memory to envision the future (Schacter, Addis, & Buckner, 2008). Episodic

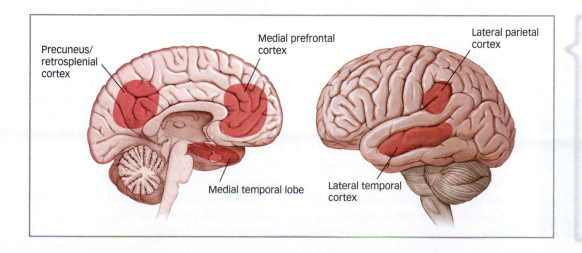

◀ Figure **6.15** **Remembering the Past and Imagining the Future Depend on a Common Network of Brain Regions** A common brain network is activated when people remember episodes that actually occurred in their personal pasts and when they imagine episodes that might occur in their personal futures. This network includes the hippocampus, a part of the medial temporal lobe long known to play an important role in episodic memory (Schacter, Addis, & Buckner, 2007).

transience Forgetting what occurs with the passage of time.

retroactive interference Situations in which information learned later impairs memory for information acquired earlier.

proactive interference Situations in which information learned earlier impairs memory for information acquired later.

memory is well suited to the task: It is a flexible system that allows us to recombine elements of past experience in new ways so that we can mentally "try out" different versions of what might happen (Schacter & Addis, 2007; Suddendorf & Corballis, 2007). For example, when you imagine having a difficult conversation with a friend that will take place in a couple of days, you can draw on past experiences to envisage different ways in which the conversation might unfold—and hopefully avoid saying things that, based on past experience, are likely to make the situation worse. As we'll discuss later, however, this flexibility of episodic memory might also be responsible for some kinds of memory errors.

SUMMARY QUIZ [6.4]

1. The act of consciously or intentionally retrieving past experiences is
   - a. priming.
   - b. procedural memory.
   - c. implicit memory.
   - d. explicit memory.

2. People who have amnesia are able to retain all of the following *except*
   - a. explicit memory.
   - b. implicit memory.
   - c. procedural memory.
   - d. priming.

3. Remembering a family reunion that you attended as a child illustrates
   - a. semantic memory.
   - b. procedural memory.
   - c. episodic memory.
   - d. perceptual priming.

Memory Failures: The Seven Sins of Memory

You probably haven't given much thought to breathing today, and the reason is that from the moment you woke up (not to mention while you were sleeping!), you've been doing it effortlessly and well. But the moment breathing fails, you are reminded of just how important it is. Memory is like that. Every time we see, think, notice, imagine, or wonder, we are drawing on our ability to use information stored in our brains, but it isn't until this ability fails that we become acutely aware of just how much we should treasure it. Like a lot of human behavior, we can better understand how a process works correctly by examining what happens when it works incorrectly. Such memory errors—the "seven sins" of memory—cast similar illumination on how memory normally operates and how often it operates well (Schacter, 1999, 2001b). We'll discuss each of the seven sins in detail below.

1. Transience

On March 6, 2007, I. Lewis "Scooter" Libby, former Chief of Staff to Vice President Dick Cheney, was convicted of perjury during an FBI investigation into whether members of the Bush administration had unlawfully disclosed the identity of a CIA agent to the media a few years earlier. According to Libby's defense team, any misstatements he might have made in response to FBI questioning were the result of faulty memory, not an intention to deceive. Libby's case resulted in a national debate about how much and what kind of forgetting is plausible for important events like those Libby claimed to have forgotten. Indeed, the case stimulated experimental research showing that people sometimes have mistaken intuitions about what factors influence forgetting of important events (Kassam et al., 2009).

I. Lewis "Scooter" Libby was convicted of perjury and obstructing justice, but he claimed that forgetting and related memory problems were responsible for any misstatements he made.

ALEX WONG/GETTY IMAGES

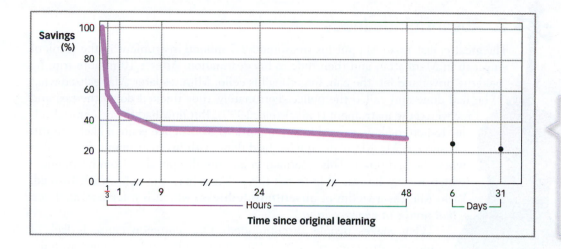

BETTMANN/CORBIS

◀ Figure **6.16** **The Curve of Forgetting** Hermann Ebbinghaus measured his retention at various delay intervals after he studied lists of nonsense syllables. Retention was measured in percent savings, that is, the percentage of time needed to relearn the list compared with the time needed to learn it initially.

Despite the controversy over forgetting in the Libby case, one thing is certain: Memories can and do degrade with time. The culprit here is **transience**—*forgetting what occurs with the passage of time.* Transience occurs during the storage phase of memory, after an experience has been encoded and before it is retrieved. You've already seen transience—rapid forgetting—in sensory storage and short-term storage. Transience also occurs in long-term storage, as was first illustrated in the late 1870s by Hermann Ebbinghaus, a German philosopher who measured his own memory for lists of nonsense syllables at different delays after studying them (Ebbinghaus, 1885/1964). Ebbinghaus charted his recall of nonsense syllables over time, creating the forgetting curve shown in **FIGURE 6.16**. Ebbinghaus noted a rapid drop-off in retention during the first few tests, followed by a slower rate of forgetting on later tests—a general pattern confirmed by many subsequent memory researchers (Wixted & Ebbesen, 1991). So, for example, when English

Hermann Ebbinghaus (1850–1909), a German philosopher and psychologist, conducted some of the first scientific studies of memory. Ebbinghaus trained himself to memorize lists of nonsense syllables, then kept track of how long he could retain the information. Ebbinghaus's research revealed a great deal about the nature of remembering and forgetting.

? How can memories interfere with one another?

speakers were tested for memory of Spanish vocabulary acquired during high school or college courses 1 to 50 years previously, there was a rapid drop-off in memory during the first 3 years after the students' last class, followed by tiny losses in later years (Bahrick, 1984, 2000). In all these studies, memories didn't fade at a constant rate as time passed; most forgetting happened soon after an event occurred, with increasingly less forgetting as more time passed.

Another way that memories can be distorted is by interference from other memories. For example, if you carry out the same activities at work each day, by the time Friday rolls around, it may be difficult to remember what you did on Monday because later activities blend in with earlier ones. This is an example of **retroactive interference,** which occurs when *later learning impairs memory for information acquired earlier* (Postman & Underwood, 1973). **Proactive interference,** in contrast, refers to situations in which *earlier learning impairs memory for information acquired later.* If you use the same parking lot each day at work or at school, you've probably gone out to find your car and then stood there confused by the memories of having parked it in a different spot on previous days.

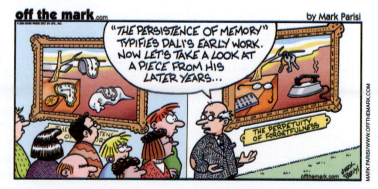

2. Absentmindedness

The great cellist Yo-Yo Ma put his treasured $2.5 million instrument in the trunk of a taxicab in Manhattan and then rode to his destination. After a 10-minute trip, he paid the driver and left the cab, forgetting his cello. Minutes later, Ma realized what he had done and called the police. Fortunately, they tracked down the taxi and recovered the instrument (Finkelstein, 1999). But how had the celebrated cellist forgotten about something so important? Transience is not a likely culprit. As soon as Mr. Ma realized what he'd done with his instrument, he recalled where he had put it. This information had not disappeared from his memory (which is why he was able to tell the police where the cello was). Instead, Yo-Yo Ma was a victim of **absentmindedness,** which is *a lapse in attention that results in memory failure.*

What makes people absentminded? One common cause is lack of attention. Attention plays a vital role in encoding information into long-term memory. Without proper attention, material is much less likely to be stored properly and recalled later. In one study, volunteers tried to learn a list of word pairs while researchers scanned their brains with positron emission tomography (PET) (Shallice et al., 1994). Some people simultaneously performed a task that took little attention (they moved a bar the same way over and over), whereas other people simultaneously performed a task that took a great deal of attention (they moved a bar over and over but in a novel, unpredictable way each time). This second group, whose attention was divided between the two tasks, showed worse list learning and also less activity in the lower left frontal lobe. As you saw earlier, greater activity in the lower left frontal region during encoding is associated with better memory. Dividing attention, then, prevents the lower left frontal lobe from playing its normal role in elaborative encoding, and the result is absentminded forgetting. More recent research using fMRI has shown that divided attention also leads to less hippocampal involvement in encoding (Kensinger, Clarke, & Corkin, 2003; Uncapher & Rugg, 2008). Given the importance of the hippocampus to episodic memory, this finding may help to explain why absentminded forgetting is sometimes so extreme, as when we forget where we put our keys or glasses only moments earlier.

How is memory affected for someone whose attention is divided?

Another common cause of absentmindedness is forgetting to carry out actions that we planned to do in the future. On any given day, you need to remember the times and places that your classes meet, which grocery items to pick up for dinner, and which page of this book you were on when you fell asleep. In other words, you have to remember to remember; this is called **prospective memory,** or *remembering to do things in the future* (Einstein & McDaniel, 1990, 2005).

3. Blocking

Have you ever tried to recall the name of a famous movie actor or a book you've read—and felt that the answer was "on the tip of your tongue," rolling around in your head *somewhere* but just out of reach it at the moment? This tip-of-the-tongue experience is a classic example of **blocking,** which is *a failure to retrieve information that is available in memory even though you are trying to produce it.* The sought-after information has been encoded and stored, and a cue is available that would ordinarily trigger recall of it. The information has not faded from memory, and you aren't forgetting to retrieve it. Rather, you are experiencing a full-blown retrieval failure, which makes

Yo-Yo Ma with his $2.5 million cello. The famous cellist lost it when he absentmindedly forgot that he'd placed the instrument in a taxicab's trunk minutes earlier.

Talking on a cell phone while driving is a common occurrence of divided attention in everyday life; texting is even worse. This can be dangerous, and an increasing number of states have banned the practice.

this memory breakdown especially frustrating. Researchers have described the tip-of-the-tongue state, in particular, as "a mild torment, something like [being] on the brink of a sneeze" (Brown & McNeill, 1966, p. 326).

Blocking occurs especially often for the names of people and places (Cohen, 1990; Semenza, 2009; Valentine, Brennen, & Brédart, 1996). Why? Because their links to related concepts and knowledge are weaker than those for common terms. That somebody's last name is Baker doesn't tell us much about the person, but saying that he *is* a baker does. To illus-

> **Why is Snow White's name easier to remember than Pinocchio's?**

trate this point, researchers showed people pictures of cartoon and comic strip characters, some with descriptive names that highlight key features of the character (e.g., Grumpy, Snow

White, Scrooge) and others with arbitrary names (e.g., Aladdin, Mary Poppins, Pinocchio) (Brédart & Valentine, 1998). Even though the two types of names were equally familiar to participants in the experiment, they blocked less often on the descriptive names than on the arbitrary names.

Although it's frustrating when it occurs, blocking is a relatively infrequent event for most of us. However, it occurs more often as we grow older, and it is a very common complaint among people in their 60s and 70s (Burke et al., 1991; Schwartz, 2002). Even more striking, some brain-damaged patients live in a nearly perpetual tip-of-the-tongue state (Semenza, 2009). One patient could recall the names of only 2 of 40 famous people when she saw their photographs, compared with 25 of 40 for healthy volunteers in the control group (Semenza & Zettin, 1989). Yet she could still recall correctly the occupations of 32 of these people—the same number as healthy people could recall. This case and similar ones have given researchers important clues about what parts of the brain are involved in retrieving proper names. Name blocking usually results from damage to parts of the left temporal lobe on the surface of the cortex, most often as a result of a stroke. In fact, studies that show strong activation of regions within the temporal lobe when people recall proper names support this idea (Damasio et al., 1996; Tempini et al., 1998).

4. Memory Misattribution

Shortly after the devastating 1995 bombing of the federal building in Oklahoma City, police set about searching for two suspects they called John Doe 1 and John Doe 2. John Doe 1 turned out to be Timothy McVeigh, who was quickly apprehended and later convicted of the crime and sentenced to death. John Doe 2, who had supposedly accompanied McVeigh when he rented a van 2 days before the bombing, was never

found. In fact, John Doe 2 had never existed; he was a product of the memory of Tom Kessinger, a mechanic who was present when McVeigh rented the van. The day after, two other men had also rented a van in Kessinger's presence. The first man, like McVeigh, was tall and fair. The second man was shorter and stockier, was dark-haired, wore a blue-and-white cap, and had a tattoo beneath his left sleeve—a match to the description of John Doe 2. Tom Kessinger had confused his recollections of men he had seen on separate days in the same place. He was a victim of **memory misattribution**—*assigning a recollection or an idea to the wrong source* (**FIGURE 6.17**).

Many people rely on memory aids such as calendars—and, more recently, personal digital assistants (PDAs)—to help them remember to perform a particular activity in the future.

absentmindedness A lapse in attention that results in memory failure.

prospective memory Remembering to do things in the future.

blocking A failure to retrieve information that is available in memory even though you are trying to produce it.

memory misattribution Assigning a recollection or an idea to the wrong source.

▼ Figure **6.17** **Memory Misattribution** In 1995, the Murrah Federal Building in Oklahoma City was bombed in an act of terrorism. The police sketch shows "John Doe 2," who was originally thought to have been culprit Timothy McVeigh's partner in the bombing. It was later determined that the witness had confused his memories of different men whom he had encountered on different days.

source memory Recall of when, where, and how information was acquired.

false recognition A feeling of familiarity about something that hasn't been encountered before.

Part of memory is knowing where our memories came from. This is known as **source memory**—*recall of when, where, and how information was acquired* (Johnson, Hashtroudi, & Lindsay, 1993; Mitchell & Johnson, 2009; Schacter, Harbluk, & McLachlan, 1984). People sometimes correctly recall a fact they learned earlier or accurately recognize a person or object they have seen before but misattribute the source of this knowledge—just as happened to Tom Kessinger (Davies, 1988). Such misattribution could be the cause of déjà vu experiences, where you suddenly feel that you have been in a situation before even though you can't recall any details. A present situation that is similar to a past experience may trigger a general sense of familiarity that is mistakenly attributed to having been in the exact situation previously (Brown, 2004; Reed, 1988).

> **?** What can explain a déjà vu experience?

Have you ever told someone a story or joke, only to have the person tell you—or eventually realize yourself—that you had already told him or her what you thought you were communicating for the first time? Although source memory errors are common in everyday life, we may be even more prone to mistakes in remembering whom we have told something before, a process called destination memory (Gopie & MacLeod, 2009ok). Recent experiments directly comparing source and destination memory revealed that participants made more errors when trying to remember whom they had told an interesting fact, compared with trying to remember who had told them an interesting fact. The effect seems to occur because when we are telling someone else a fact or a story, we are focused primarily on our own thoughts, resulting in a weak association between the fact and the person with whom we are communicating (Gopie & MacLeod, 2009).

Patients with damage to the frontal lobes are especially prone to memory misattribution errors (Schacter et al., 1984; Shimamura & Squire, 1987). This is probably because the frontal lobes play a significant role in effortful retrieval processes, which are required to dredge up the correct source of a memory. These patients sometimes produce bizarre misattributions. In 1991, a British photographer known as M. R. was overcome with feelings of familiarity about people he didn't know. He kept asking his wife whether each new passing stranger was "somebody"—a screen actor, television newsperson, or local celebrity. M. R.'s feelings were so intense that he often could not resist approaching strangers and asking whether they were indeed famous celebrities. Neurological exams revealed that M. R. suffered from multiple sclerosis, which had caused damage to his frontal lobes (Ward et al., 1999). Psychologists call the type of

Doonesbury

memory misattribution made by M. R. **false recognition,** which is *a feeling of famil-iarity about something that hasn't been encountered before.*

Other neurological patients exhibit a recently discovered type of memory misattri-bution called déjà vecu. Here, patients feel strongly—but mistakenly—that they have already lived through an experience and remember the details of what (supposedly) happened (Moulin et al., 2005). For example, when watching television, one patient was certain that he recalled seeing each show before, even when he watching an entirely new episode. When this patient went shopping, he constantly thought it was unnecessary to buy needed items because he remembered having done so already. Although the basis of this strange disorder is not well understood, it probably involves disruption to parts of the temporal lobe that normally generate a subjective feeling of remembering (Moulin et al., 2005).

We are all vulnerable to memory misattribution. Take the following test and there is a good chance that you will experience false recognition for yourself. First, study the two lists of words presented in **TABLE 6.1** by reading each word for about 1 second. When you are done, return to the paragraph you were reading for more instructions, but don't look back at the table!

Now, try to recognize which of the following words appeared on the list you just studied: *taste, bread, needle, king, sweet, thread.* If you think that *taste* and *thread* were on the lists you studied, you're right. And if you think that *bread* and *king* weren't on those lists, you're also right. But if you think that *needle* or *sweet* appeared on the lists, you're dead wrong.

Most people make exactly the same mistake, claiming with confidence that they saw *needle* and *sweet* on the list. This occurs because all the words in the lists are associated with *needle* or *sweet.* Seeing each word in the study list activates related words. Because *needle* and *sweet* are related to all of the words, they become more activated than other words—so highly activated that only minutes later, people swear that they actually studied the words (Deese, 1959; Gallo, 2006; Roediger & McDermott, 1995, 2000). In fact, brain-scanning studies using PET and fMRI show that many of the same brain regions are active during false recognition and true recognition, including the hippocampus (Cabeza et al., 2001; Schacter et al., 1996b; Slotnick & Schacter, 2004) (**FIGURE 6.18**).

Table 6.1	
False Recognition	
Sour	Thread
Candy	Pin
Sugar	Eye
Bitter	Sewing
Good	Sharp
Taste	Point
Tooth	Prick
Nice	Thimble
Honey	Haystack
Soda	Pain
Chocolate	Hurt
Heart	Injection
Cake	Syringe
Tart	Cloth
Pie	Knitting

▼ Figure **6.18 Hippocampal Activity During True and False Recognition** Many brain regions, including the hippocampus, show similar activation during true and false recognition. The figure shows results from an fMRI study of true and false recognition of visual shapes (Slotnick & Schacter, 2004). (a) A plot showing the activity level in the strength of the fMRI signal from the hippocampus over time. This shows that after a few seconds, there is comparable activation for true recognition of previously studied shapes (red line) and false recognition of similar shapes that were not presented (yellow line). Both true and false recognition show increased hippocampal activity compared with correctly classifying unrelated shapes as new (purple line). (b) A region of the left hippocampus that shows similar activation to true recognition and false recognition.

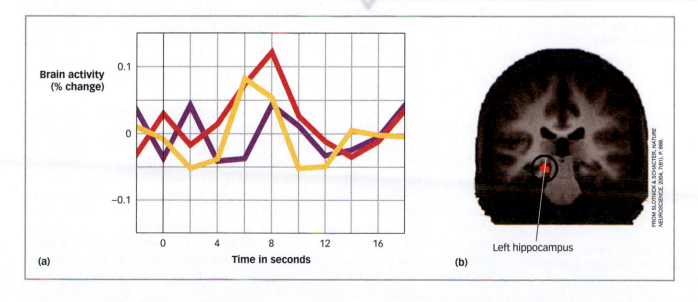

(a)

Brain activity (% change)

Time in seconds

(b)

Left hippocampus

FROM SLOTNICK & SCHACTER, *NATURE NEUROSCIENCE,* 2004, 7(6), P. 669.

It is possible to reduce or avoid false recognition by presenting distinctive information, such as a picture of *thread,* and encouraging participants to require specific recollections of seeing the picture before they say "yes" on a recognition test (Schacter, Israel, & Racine, 1999). Unfortunately, we do not always demand specific recollections before we say that we encountered a word in an experiment or—more important—make a positive identification of a suspect. When people experience a strong sense of familiarity about a person, object, or event but lack specific recollections, a potentially dangerous recipe for memory misattribution is in place. Understanding this point may be a key to reducing the dangerous consequences of misattribution in eyewitness testimony (see the Real World box).

5. Suggestibility

On October 4, 1992, an El Al cargo plane crashed into an apartment building in a southern suburb of Amsterdam, killing 39 residents and all four members of the airline crew. The disaster dominated news in the Netherlands for days as people viewed footage of the crash scene and read about the catastrophe. Ten months later, Dutch

ALBERT OVERBEEK/AP PHOTO

In 1992, an El Al cargo plane crashed into an apartment building in a suburb of Amsterdam. When Dutch psychologists asked students if they'd seen the television film of the plane crashing, most said they had. In fact, no such footage exists (Crombag et al., 1996).

psychologists asked a simple question of university students: "Did you see the television film of the moment the plane hit the apartment building?" Fifty-five percent answered "yes" (Crombag, Wagenaar, & Van Koppen, 1996). All of this might seem perfectly normal except for one key fact: There was no television film of the moment when the plane actually crashed. The researchers had asked a suggestive question that implied that television film of the crash had been shown. Respondents may have viewed television film of the post-crash scene, and they may have read, imagined, or talked about what might have happened when the plane hit the building, but they most definitely did not see it. The suggestive question led participants to misattribute information from these or other sources to a film that did not exist. **Suggestibility** is the *tendency to incorporate misleading information from external sources into personal recollections.*

If misleading details can be implanted in people's memories, is it also possible to suggest entire episodes that never occurred? The answer seems to be "yes" (Loftus, 1993, 2003). In one study, the research participant, a teenager named Chris, was asked by his older brother, Jim, to try to remember the time Chris had been lost in a shopping mall at age 5. He initially recalled nothing, but after several days, Chris produced a detailed recollection of the event. He recalled that he "felt so scared I would never see my family again" and remembered that a kindly old man wearing a flannel shirt found him crying (Loftus, 1993, p. 532). But according to Jim and other family members, Chris was never lost in a shopping mall. Of 24 participants in a larger study on implanted memories, approximately 25% falsely remembered being lost as a child in a shopping mall or in a similar public place (Loftus & Pickrell, 1995).

People develop false memories in response to suggestions for some of the same reasons memory misattribution occurs. We do not store all the details of our experiences in memory, making us vulnerable to accepting suggestions about what might have happened or should have happened. In addition, visual imagery plays an important role in constructing false memories (Goff & Roediger, 1998). Asking people to imagine an event like spilling punch all over the bride's parents at a wedding increases the likelihood that they will develop a false memory of it (Hyman & Pentland, 1996).

Suggestibility played an important role in a controversy that arose during the 1980s and 1990s concerning the accuracy of childhood memories that people recall during psychotherapy. One highly publicized example involved a woman named Diana Halbrooks (Schacter, 1996). After a few months in psychotherapy, she began

suggestibility The tendency to incorporate misleading information from external sources into personal recollections.

THE REAL WORLD

Dangerous Misattributions

On July 25, 1984, a 9-year-old girl was found dead in the woods near Baltimore after being brutally beaten and sexually assaulted. A witness identified 23-year-old Kirk Bloodsworth as the killer, based on a sketch police generated from five other witness accounts. Although Bloodsworth passionately maintained his innocence, a jury convicted him of first-degree murder and the judge sentenced him to death. In 1993, DNA testing revealed that Bloodsworth was not the source of incriminating semen stains in the victim's underwear. He was released from prison after serving 9 years, later received a full pardon, and returned to his quiet life as a crab fisherman (Chebium, 2000; Connors et al., 1997; Wells et al., 1998). The witness's memory misattribution cost Bloodsworth a decade of his life.

Bloodsworth is not alone. The first 40 cases in which DNA evidence led to the release of wrongfully imprisoned individuals revealed that 36 of the convictions—90%—were based partly or entirely on mistaken eyewitness identification (Wells et al., 1998). Fifty separate eyewitnesses were involved in these cases; they were all confident in their memories but seriously mistaken. These statistics are especially troubling because eyewitness testimony is frequently relied on in the courtroom: Each year more than 75,000 criminal trials are decided on the basis of eyewitness testimony (Ross et al., 1994, p. 918). Common lineup identification practices may often promote misattribution because people are encouraged to rely on general familiarity (Wells et al., 1998, 2000). In standard lineup procedures, witnesses are shown several suspects and attempt to identify the culprit. Under these conditions, witnesses tend to choose the person who, relative to the others in the lineup, looks most like the suspect. The problem is that even when the suspect is *not in* the lineup, witnesses still tend to choose the person who looks most like the suspect. There are ways to minimize this problem. For example, witnesses can be asked to make a "thumbs-up or thumbs-down" decision about each suspect immediately after

seeing each face instead of waiting until all suspects' faces have been displayed (Wells et al., 1998, 2000). This procedure encourages people to examine their memories more carefully and evaluate whether the pictured suspect matches the details of their recollections, sometimes (but not always) resulting in more accurate witness identification (Gronlund et al., 2009).

One encouraging development is that law-enforcement officials are listening to what psychologists have to say about the construction of lineups and other identification procedures that could promote inaccurate identification. There is still debate about what procedures work best in the real world (Mecklenburg, Bailey, & Larsen, 2008; Schacter, Dawes, et al., 2008; Turtle et al., 2008). But there is no debate that more controlled studies are needed to achieve the goal of minimizing eyewitness errors.

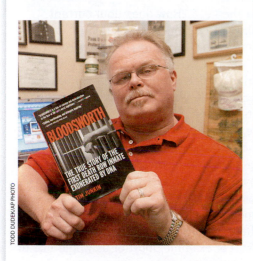

◄ Kirk Bloodsworth spent 9 years behind bars for a crime he didn't commit. He was released after DNA evidence led to the reversal of his conviction based on mistaken eyewitness testimony. Here he holds up the book that tells his story, by author and attorney Tim Junkin.

recalling disturbing incidents from her childhood—for example, that her mother had tried to kill her and that her father had abused her sexually. Although her parents denied that these events had ever occurred, her therapist encouraged her to believe in the reality of her memories. Eventually, Diana Halbrooks stopped therapy and came to realize that the "memories" she had recovered were inaccurate.

? Why can childhood memories be influenced by suggestion?

How could this happen? A number of the techniques used by psychotherapists to try to pull up forgotten childhood memories are clearly suggestive, such as encouraging clients to imagine incidents that might or might not have actually happened (Poole et al., 1995)—just the kind of techniques that can help create false memories in the lab (Garry et al., 1996; Hyman & Pentland, 1996; McConkey, Barnier, & Sheehan, 1998). In fact, some individuals who claim to have recovered memories of trauma also show unusually high rates of false memories on laboratory tests (Clancy et al., 2000, 2002). While some recovered memories—especially those that people remember on their own—are probably accurate (Gleaves et al., 2004), those recovered using techniques that are known to create false memories in the lab are suspect.

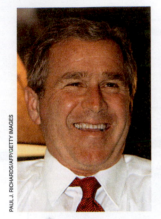 

How happy do you think you'd be if the candidate you supported won an election? Do you think you'd accurately remember your level of happiness if you recalled it several months later? Chances are good that bias in the memory process would alter your recollection of your previous happiness. Indeed, 4 months after they heard the outcome of the 2000 presidential election, Bush supporters overestimated how happy they were, while Gore supporters underestimated how happy they were.

6. Bias

In 2000, the outcome of a very close presidential race between George W. Bush and Al Gore was decided by the Supreme Court 5 weeks after the election had taken place.

The day after the election (when the result was still in doubt), supporters of Bush and Gore were asked to predict how happy they would be after the outcome of the election was determined (Wilson, Meyers, & Gilbert, 2003). These same respondents reported how happy they felt with the outcome on the day after Al Gore conceded. And 4 months later, the participants recalled how happy they had been right after the election was decided.

Bush supporters, whose candidate took office, were understandably happy on the day after the Supreme Court's decision. However, their retrospective accounts *over*estimated how happy they were at the time. Conversely, Gore supporters were not pleased with the outcome. But when polled 4 months after the election was decided, Gore supporters *under*estimated how happy they actually were at the time of the result. In both groups, recollections of happiness were at odds with existing reports of their actual happiness at the time (Wilson et al., 2003).

? How does your current outlook color your memory of a past event?

These results illustrate the problem of **bias**, which is *the distorting influences of present knowledge, beliefs, and feelings on recollection of previous experiences*. Sometimes what people remember from their pasts says less about what actually happened than about what they think, feel, or believe now. You already read that our current moods can bias our recall of past experiences, through the phenomenon of state-dependent retrieval. In addition to helping you recall actual sad memories, a sad mood can also bias your recollections of experiences that may not have been so sad. *Consistency bias* is the bias to reconstruct the past to fit the present.

Whereas consistency bias exaggerates the similarity between past and present, *change bias* is the tendency to exaggerate differences between what we feel or believe now and what we felt or believed in the past. For example, most of us would like to believe that our romantic attachments grow stronger over time. In one study, dating couples were asked, once a year for 4 years, to assess the present quality of their relationships and to recall how they felt in past years (Sprecher, 1999). Couples who stayed together for the 4 years recalled that the strength of their love had increased since they last reported on it. Yet their actual ratings at the time did not show any increases in love and attachment. Objectively, the couples did not love each other more today than yesterday. But they did from the subjective perspective of memory. Similarly, when college students tried to remember high school grades and their memories were checked against actual transcripts, they were highly accurate for grades of A (89% correct) and extremely inaccurate for grades of D (29% correct) (Bahrick, Hall, & Berger, 1996). People were remembering the past as they wanted it to be rather than the way it was.

The way each member of this happy couple recalls earlier feelings toward the other depends on how each currently views their relationship.

7. Persistence

The artist Melinda Stickney-Gibson awoke in her apartment to the smell of smoke. She jumped out of bed and saw black plumes rising through cracks in the floor. Raging flames had engulfed the entire building, and there was no chance to escape except by jumping from her third-floor window. Although she survived the fire and the fall, Melinda became overwhelmed by memories of the fire. When she sat down in front of a blank canvas to start a new painting, her memories of that awful night intruded. Her paintings, which were previously bright, colorful abstractions, became dark meditations that included only black, orange, and ochre—the colors of the fire (Schacter, 1996).

Melinda Stickney-Gibson's experiences illustrate memory's seventh and most deadly sin: **persistence,** or *the intrusive recollection of events that we wish we could forget.* Melinda's experience is far from unique: Persistence frequently occurs after disturbing or traumatic incidents. Although being able to quickly call up memories is usually considered a good thing, in the case of persistence, that ability mutates into an unwelcome burden.

Laboratory studies have revealed that emotional experiences tend to be better remembered than nonemotional ones. For instance, memory for unpleasant pictures, such as mutilated bodies, or pleasant ones, such as attractive men and women, is more accurate than for emotionally neutral pictures, such as household objects (Ochsner, 2000). Emotional arousal seems to focus our attention on the central features of an event. In one experiment, people who viewed an emotionally arousing sequence of slides involving a bloody car accident remembered more of the central themes and fewer peripheral details than people who viewed a sequence that was not emotionally arousing (Christianson & Loftus, 1987).

Intrusive memories are undesirable consequences of the fact that emotional experiences generally lead to more vivid and enduring recollections than nonemotional

? How does emotional trauma affect memory?

experiences do. One line of evidence comes from the study of **flashbulb memories,** which are *detailed recollections of when and where we heard about shocking events* (Brown & Kulick, 1977). For example, most Americans can recall exactly where they were and how they heard about the September 11, 2001 terrorist attacks on the World Trade Center and the Pentagon—almost as if a mental flashbulb had gone off automatically and recorded the event in long-lasting and vivid detail (Kvavilashvili et al., 2009). Several studies have shown that flashbulb memories are not always entirely accurate, but they are generally better remembered than mundane news events from the same time (Larsen, 1992; Neisser & Harsch, 1992). Enhanced retention of flashbulb memories is partly attributable to the emotional arousal elicited by events such as the September 11th terrorist attacks and partly attributable to the fact that we tend to talk and think a lot about these experiences. Recall that elaborative encoding enhances memory: When we talk about flashbulb experiences, we elaborate on them and thus further increase the memorability of those aspects of the experience that we discuss (Hirst et al., 2009).

Why do our brains succumb to persistence? A key player in the brain's response to emotional events is a small, almond-shaped structure called the amygdala, shown in **FIGURE 6.19**. The amygdala influences hormonal systems that kick into high gear when we experience an arousing event; these stress-related hormones, such as adrenaline and cortisol, mobilize the body in the face of threat—and they also enhance memory for the experience. Such amygdala activation during encoding of emotional events is one reason why people normally remember highly emotional events better than mundane ones (Cahill et al., 1996; Kensinger & Schacter, 2005,

bias The distorting influences of present knowledge, beliefs, and feelings on recollection of previous experiences.

persistence The intrusive recollection of events that we wish we could forget.

flashbulb memories Detailed recollections of when and where we heard about shocking events.

Some events are so emotionally charged, such as the Kennedy assassination and the terrorist attack on the World Trade Center, that we form unusually detailed memories of when and where we heard about them. These flashbulb memories generally persist much longer than memories for more ordinary events.

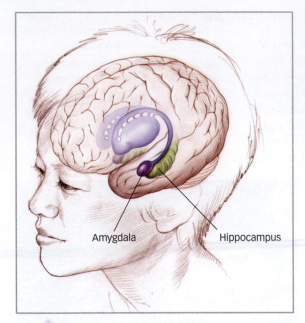

▲ Figure **6.19** **The Amygdala's Influence on Memory** The amygdala, located next to the hippocampus, responds strongly to emotional events. Patients with amygdala damage are unable to remember emotional events any better than nonemotional ones (Cahill & McGaugh, 1998).

2006). Patients with amygdala damage, however, do not remember emotional events any better than nonemotional ones—presumably because the emotional information does not receive this extra "kick" during encoding (Cahill & McGaugh, 1998).

In many cases, there are clear benefits to forming strong memories for highly emotional events, particularly those that are life-threatening. In the case of persistence, though, such memories may be too strong—strong enough to interfere with other aspects of daily life.

Are the Seven Sins Vices or Virtues?

You may have concluded that evolution burdened us with an extremely inefficient memory system that is so prone to error that it often jeopardizes our well-being. Not so. The seven sins are the price we pay for the many benefits that memory provides, the occasional result of the normally efficient operation of the human memory system (Schacter, 2001b).

Consider transience, for example. Wouldn't it be great to remember all the details of every incident in your life, no matter how much time had passed? Not necessarily. Do you remember the words of Jill Price, whom you met at the beginning of this chapter? Commenting on her own extraordinary memory, Jill complained that, "I run my entire life through my head every day and it drives me crazy!!!" (Parker et al., 2006, p. 35)

It is helpful and sometimes important to forget information that isn't current, like an old phone number. If we didn't gradually forget information over time, our minds would be cluttered with details we no longer need (Bjork & Bjork, 1988). Information that is used infrequently is less likely to be needed in the future than information that is used more frequently over the same period (Anderson & Schooler, 1991, 2000). Memory, in essence, makes a bet that when we haven't used information recently, we probably won't need it in the future. We win this bet more often than we lose it, making transience an adaptive property of memory. But we are acutely aware of the losses—the frustrations of forgetting—and are never aware of the wins. This is why people are often quick to complain about their memories: The drawbacks of forgetting are painfully evident, but the benefits of forgetting are hidden.

Similarly, absentmindedness and blocking can be frustrating, but they are side effects of our memory's usually successful attempt to sort through incoming information, preserving details that are worthy of attention and recall, and discarding those that are less worthy.

Memory misattribution and suggestibility both occur because we often fail to recall the details of exactly when and where we saw a face or learned a fact. Our memories carefully record such details only when we think they may be needed later, and most of the time we are better off for it. Further, we often use memories to anticipate possible future events. As discussed earlier, memory is flexible, allowing us to recombine elements of past experience in new ways so that we can mentally "try out" different versions of what might happen. But this very flexibility—a strength of memory—may sometimes produce misattribution errors in which elements of past experience are miscombined (Schacter & Addis, 2007). Bias skews our memories so that we depict ourselves in an overly favorable light—but it can produce the benefit of contributing to our overall sense of contentment. Holding positive illusions about ourselves can lead to greater psychological well-being (Taylor, 1989). Although persistence can cause us to be haunted by traumas that we'd be better off forgetting, overall, it is probably adaptive to remember threatening or traumatic events that could pose a threat to survival.

? How are we better off with imperfect memories?

Although each of the seven sins can cause trouble in our lives, they have an adaptive side as well. You can think of the seven sins as costs we pay for benefits that allow memory to work as well as it does most of the time.

SUMMARY QUIZ [6.5]

1. The rapid decline in memory, followed by more gradual forgetting, is reflected by

   a. chunking.
   c. absentmindedness.
   b. blocking.
   d. transience.

2. Eyewitness misidentification or false recognition is most likely a result of

   a. memory misattribution.
   c. bias.
   b. suggestibility.
   d. retroactive interference.

3. The fact that emotional arousal generally leads to enhanced memory is supported by

   a. egocentric bias.
   c. proactive interference.
   b. persistence.
   d. source memory.

Where Do You Stand?

The Mystery of Childhood Amnesia

You can easily recall many experiences from different times in your life, but there is one period from which you likely have few or no memories: the first few years of your life. This lack of memory for our early years is called *childhood amnesia* or *infantile amnesia*.

Try to recall your own earliest memory. As you mentally search for it, you may encounter a problem that has troubled researchers: How do you know the exact time when your recollection took place? Memory for dates is notoriously poor, so it is often difficult to determine precisely when your earliest memory occurred (Friedman, 1993). To address this problem, researchers asked people about memories for events that have clearly definable dates, such as the birth of a younger sibling, the death of a loved one, or a family move (Sheingold & Tenney, 1982; Usher & Neisser, 1993). In one study, researchers asked individuals between 4 and 20 years old to recall as much as they could about the birth of a younger sibling (Sheingold & Tenney, 1982). Participants who were at least 3 years old at the time of the birth remembered it in considerable detail, but participants who were younger than 3 years old remembered little or nothing. A more recent study found that individuals can recall events surrounding the birth of a sibling that occurred when they were about 2.4 years old; some people even showed evidence of recall from ages 2.0 to 2.4 years, although these memories were very sketchy (Eacott & Crawley, 1998).

It is difficult to draw firm conclusions from these kinds of studies because memories of early events may be based on family conversations that took place long after the events occurred. An adult or a child who remembers having ice cream in the hospital as a 3-year-old when his baby sister was born may be recalling what his parents told him after the event. Consistent with this idea, cross-cultural studies have turned up an interesting finding: Individuals from cultures that emphasize talking about the past, such as North American culture, tend to report earlier first memories than individuals from cultures that place less emphasis on talking about the past, such as Korean and other Asian cultures (MacDonald, Uesiliana, & Hayne, 2000; Mullen, 1994).

Recent research has examined whether the events that people say they remember from early childhood really are *personal recollections,* which involve conscious reexperiencing of some aspect of the event, or whether people *just know* about these events (perhaps from family photos and discussions), even though they don't truly possess personal recollections (Multhaup, Johnson, & Tetirick, 2005). Several experiments revealed that personal recollections tend to emerge later than memories based on "just knowing," with the transition from mostly "know" memories to mostly "recollect" memories occurring at 4.7 years of age.

Some events in your personal history are personal recollections. In other words, you actually remember the occurrence of the event. Other events from your past are ones that you know happened but are not personal recollections. In other words, you know the event occurred, but you cannot consciously recollect any aspect of what happened or of what you experienced at the time. Instead, your knowledge of the event is based on an external source of information, perhaps your parents and/or other family members, friends, pictures, photo albums, diaries, or family stories. Think about your own life and try to remember the following events: *You read your first book with chapters. You went to your first sleepover. You saw your first movie in a movie theater. You took your first swimming lesson.* Do you "recall" these events, or merely "know" that they happened? Where do you stand?

Chapter Review

Encoding: Transforming Perceptions into Memories

▶ Encoding is the process by which we transform sensory information into a lasting memory.

▶ Elaborative encoding, visual imagery encoding, and organizational encoding all increase memory, but they use different parts of the brain to accomplish that.

▶ Encoding information with respect to its survival value is a particularly effective method for increasing subsequent recall.

Storage: Maintaining Memories over Time

▶ There are several different types of memory storage: sensory memory, which holds information for a second or two; short-term or working memory, which retains information for about 15 to 20 seconds; and long-term memory, which stores information for anywhere from minutes to years or decades.

▶ The hippocampus and nearby structures play an important role in long-term memory storage and in memory consolidation, the process that makes memories increasingly resistant to disruption over time.

▶ Memory storage depends on changes in synapses, and long-term potentiation (LTP) increases synaptic connections.

Retrieval: Bringing Memories to Mind

▶ Successful retrieval of stored memories depends on whether retrieval cues are available to trigger recall. In addition to hints and prompts, moods and inner states can serve as retrieval cues.

▶ Retrieval improves subsequent memory of the retrieved information, but it can impair subsequent remembering of related information that is not retrieved.

▶ Retrieval can be separated into the effort we make while trying to remember what happened in the past, which activates the left frontal lobe, and the successful recovery of stored information, which activates the hippocampus and regions in the brain related to sensory aspects of an experience.

Multiple Forms of Memory: How the Past Returns

▶ Explicit memory is the act of consciously or intentionally retrieving past experiences, whereas implicit memory refers to the unconscious influence of past experiences on later behavior and performance.

▶ Two types of implicit memory are procedural memory, the acquisition of skills as a result of practice, and priming, a change in the ability to recognize or identify an object or a word as the result of past exposure to it.

▶ Two types of explicit memory are episodic memory, the collection of personal experiences from a particular time and place that allows us both to recollect the past and imagine the future, and semantic memory, a networked, general, impersonal knowledge of facts, associations, and concepts.

▶ People with amnesia have implicit memory, including procedural memory and priming, but they lack explicit memory.

Memory Failures: The Seven Sins of Memory

▶ Memory's mistakes can be classified into seven "sins"—the costs we pay for benefits that allow memory to work as well as it does most of the time.

▶ Some of these "sins" reflect inability to store or retrieve information we want: *Transience* is reflected by a rapid decline in memory followed by more gradual forgetting. *Absentmindedness* results from failures of attention, shallow encoding, and the influence of automatic behaviors. *Blocking* occurs when stored information is temporarily inaccessible, as when information is on the tip of the tongue. In contrast, *persistence* is the intrusive recollection of events we wish we could forget.

▶ Other "sins" reflect errors in memory content. *Memory misattribution* happens when we experience a sense of familiarity but don't recall, or mistakenly recall, the specifics of when and where an experience occurred. *Suggestibility* gives rise to implanted memories of small details or entire episodes. *Bias* reflects the influence of current knowledge, beliefs, and feelings on memory or past experiences.

Key Terms

memory (p. 166)
encoding (p. 166)
storage (p. 166)
retrieval (p. 166)
elaborative encoding (p. 167)
visual imagery encoding (p. 168)
organizational encoding (p. 169)
sensory memory (p. 170)
iconic memory (p. 171)

echoic memory (p. 171)
short-term memory (p. 171)
rehearsal (p. 171)
chunking (p. 172)
working memory (p. 172)
long-term memory (p. 172)
anterograde amnesia (p. 173)
retrograde amnesia (p. 173)
consolidation (p. 174)

reconsolidation (p. 174)
long-term potentiation (LTP) (p. 176)
NMDA receptor (p. 176)
retrieval cue (p. 177)
encoding specificity principle (p. 177)
state-dependent retrieval (p. 177)
transfer-appropriate processing (p. 178)

retrieval-induced forgetting (p. 178)
explicit memory (p. 180)
implicit memory (p. 180)
procedural memory (p. 180)
priming (p. 181)
semantic memory (p. 182)
episodic memory (p. 182)
transience (p. 185)

CHANGING MINDS

1. A friend of yours lost her father to cancer when she was a very young child. "I really wish I remembered him better," she says. "I know all the memories are locked in my head. I'm thinking of trying hypnotism to unlock some of those memories." You explain that we don't, in fact, have stored memories of everything that ever happened to us locked in our heads. What examples could you give of ways in which memories can be lost over time?

2. Another friend of yours has a very vivid memory of sitting with his parents in the living room on September 11, 2001, watching on live TV as the Twin Towers fell during the terrorist attacks. "I remember my mother was crying," he says, "and that scared me more than the pictures on the TV." Later, he goes home for a visit and discusses the events of 9/11 with his mother—and is stunned when she assures him that he was actually in school on the morning of the attacks and was only sent home at lunchtime, after the towers had fallen. "I don't understand," he tells you afterward. "I think she must be confused, because I have a perfect memory of that morning." Assuming your friend's mother is recalling events correctly, how would you explain to your friend the ways in which his "snapshot" memory could be wrong? What "memory sin" might be at fault?

3. You ask one of your psychology classmates if she wants to form a study group, to prepare for an upcoming exam. "No offense," she says, "but I can study the material best by just reading the chapter eight or nine times, and I can do that without a study group." What's wrong with your classmate's study plan? In what ways might the members of a study group help one another learn more effectively?

4. You and a friend go to a party on campus, where you meet a lot of new people. After the party, your friend says, "I liked a lot of the people we met, but I'll never remember all their names. Some people just have a good memory, and some don't, and there's nothing I can do about it." What advice could you give your friend to help him remember the names of people he meets at the next party?

5. A friend of yours who is taking a criminal justice class reads about a case in which the conviction of an accused murderer was later overturned, based on DNA evidence. "It's a travesty of justice," she says. "An eyewitness clearly identified the man by picking him out of a lineup and then identifying him again in court during the trial. No results from a chemistry lab should count more than eyewitness testimony." What is your friend failing to appreciate about eyewitness testimony? What sin of memory could lead an eyewitness to honestly believe she is identifying the correct man when she is actually making a false identification?

CRITICAL THINKING QUESTIONS

1. Elaborative encoding involves actively relating new information to facts you already know; visual imagery encoding involves storing new information by converting it into mental pictures.

   How might you use both kinds of encoding to help store a new fact, such as the date of a friend's birthday that falls on, say, November 1st?

2. Retrieval cues are "hints" that help bring stored information to mind. How does this explain the fact that most students prefer multiple-choice exams to fill-in-the-blank exams?

3. Transience, absentmindedness, and blocking, three of the seven "sins" of memory, involve ways in which memories can be temporarily or permanently lost.

   Suppose that, mentally consumed by planning for a psychology test the next day, you place your keys in an unusual spot and later forget where you put them. Is this more likely to reflect the "memory sin" of transience, absentmindedness, or blocking?

4. Misattribution, suggestibility, and bias are three memory "sins" involving memories that are not forgotten but are distorted.

   When researchers ask romantically involved couples to rate their relationships, and then ask again 2 months later, those couples whose relationships have since soured tend to recall their initial ratings as more negative than they really were. Is this more likely to reflect the "memory sin" of misattribution, suggestibility, or bias?

ANSWERS TO SUMMARY QUIZZES

Summary Quiz [6.1] 1. a; 2. c; 3. c.
Summary Quiz [6.2] 1. d; 2. a; 3. b
Summary Quiz [6.3] 1. b; 2. d; 3. a
Summary Quiz [6.4] 1. d; 2. a; 3. c
Summary Quiz [6.5] 1. d; 2. a; 3. b

Need more help? Additional resources are located at the book's free companion website at:
www.worthpublishers.com/schacterbrief2e

Learning

JENNIFER, A 45-YEAR-OLD CAREER MILITARY NURSE, lived quietly in a rural area of the United States with her spouse and two children before she served 19 months abroad during the Iraq war.

Jennifer served 4 months of her assignment in the Abu Ghraib prison hospital near Baghdad, where she witnessed many horrifying events. The prison was the target of relentless mortar fire, resulting in numerous deaths and serious casualties. Jennifer worked 12- to 14-hour shifts, trying to avoid incoming fire while tending to some of the most gruesomely wounded cases.

This repetitive trauma took a toll on Jennifer, and when she returned home, it became evident that she had not left her war experiences behind. The sight of blood or the smell of cooking meat made her sick to her stomach; the previously innocent sound of a helicopter approaching, which in Iraq signaled that new wounded bodies were about to arrive, now created in her heightened feelings of fear and anxiety. She regularly awoke from nightmares concerning her Iraq experiences. Jennifer was "forever changed" by her war experiences (Feczer & Bjorklund, 2009). And that is one reason why Jennifer's story is a compelling, though disturbing, introduction to the topic of learning.

Much of what happened to Jennifer after she returned home reflects the operation of a kind of learning based on association. Because sights, sounds, and smells in Iraq had become associated with negative emotions in a way that created an enduring bond, encountering similar sights, sounds, and smells at home elicited similarly intense negative feelings.

▼ During the 4 months that she served at the Abu Ghraib prison hospital near Baghdad during the Iraq war, Jennifer learned to associate the sound of an arriving helicopter with wounded bodies. That learned association had a long-lasting influence on her.

AP PHOTO/JOHN MOORE

learning The acquisition of new knowledge, skills, or responses from experience that result in a relatively permanent change in the state of the learner.

classical conditioning A phenomenon that occurs when a neutral stimulus produces a response after being paired with a stimulus that naturally produces a response.

unconditioned stimulus (US) Something that reliably produces a naturally occurring reaction in an organism.

unconditioned response (UR) A reflexive reaction that is reliably produced by an unconditioned stimulus.

conditioned stimulus (CS) A stimulus that is initially neutral and produces no reliable response in an organism.

conditioned response (CR) A reaction that resembles an unconditioned response but is produced by a conditioned stimulus.

Learning involves *the acquisition of new knowledge, skills, or responses from experience that result in a relatively permanent change in the state of the learner.* This definition emphasizes three key ideas: Learning is based on experience, learning produces changes in the organism, and these changes are relatively permanent.

Think about Jennifer's time in Iraq and you'll see all of these elements: Experiences such as the association between the sound of an approaching helicopter and the arrival of wounded bodies changed the way Jennifer responded to certain situations in a way that lasted for years.

In this chapter, we'll discuss the development and basic principles of two major approaches to learning: classical conditioning and operant conditioning. We'll then move on to see that some important kinds of learning occur simply by watching others and that such observational learning plays an important role in the cultural transmission of behavior. Finally, we'll discover that some kinds of learning can occur entirely outside of awareness.

Classical Conditioning: One Thing Leads to Another

You'll recall from Chapter 1 that American psychologist John B. Watson kick-started the behaviorist movement, arguing that psychologists should "never use the terms *consciousness, mental states, mind, content, introspectively verifiable, imagery,* and the like" (Watson, 1913, p. 166). Watson's firebrand stance was fueled in large part by the work of a Russian physiologist, Ivan Pavlov (1849–1936).

Pavlov studied the digestive processes of laboratory animals by surgically implanting test tubes into the cheeks of dogs to measure their salivary responses to different kinds of foods. Serendipitously, however, his explorations into spit and drool revealed the mechanics of one form of learning, which came to be called classical conditioning. **Classical conditioning** occurs *when a neutral stimulus produces a response after being paired with a stimulus that naturally produces a response.* Pavlov showed that dogs learned to salivate to neutral stimuli such as a bell or a tone after that stimulus had been associated with another stimulus that naturally evokes salivation, such as food.

The Development of Classical Conditioning: Pavlov's Experiments

Pavlov's basic experimental setup involved cradling dogs in a harness to administer the foods and to measure the salivary response, as shown in **FIGURE 7.1**. He noticed that dogs that had previously been in the experiment began to produce a kind of "anticipatory" salivary response as soon as they were put in the harness, before any food was presented. Pavlov and his colleagues regarded these responses as annoyances at first because they interfered with collecting naturally occurring salivary secretions. In reality, the dogs were exhibiting classical conditioning.

When the dogs were initially presented with a plate of food, they began to salivate. No surprise there. Pavlov called the presentation of food an **unconditioned stimulus (US),** or *something that reliably produces a naturally occurring reaction in an organism.* He called the dogs' salivation an **unconditioned response (UR),** or *a reflexive reaction that is reliably produced by an unconditioned stimulus.*

Pavlov soon discovered that he could make the dogs salivate to other stimuli, such as the sound of a buzzer or the flash of a light. Each of these stimuli was a **conditioned stimulus (CS),** or *a stimulus that is initially neutral and produces no*

"Perhaps, Dr. Pavlov, he could be taught to seal envelopes."

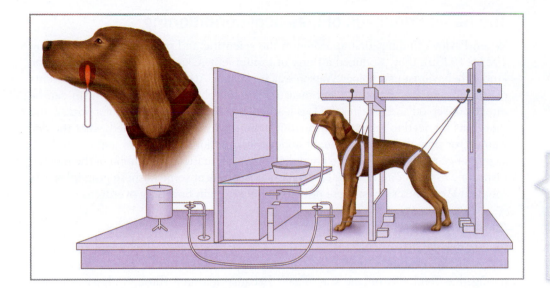

◄ Figure 7.1 **Pavlov's Apparatus for Studying Classical Conditioning** Pavlov presented auditory stimuli to the animals using a bell or a tuning fork. Visual stimuli could be presented on the screen. The inset shows a close-up of the tube inserted in the dog's salivary gland for collecting saliva.

reliable response in an organism (see **FIGURE 7.2**). When the conditioned stimulus, in this case the sound of a buzzer, is paired over time with the unconditioned stimulus, such as the sight of food, the animal will learn to associate food with the sound and eventually the CS is sufficient to produce a response, such as salivation. This response resembles the unconditioned response, but Pavlov called it the **conditioned response (CR),** or *a reaction that resembles an unconditioned response but is produced by a conditioned stimulus.*

Why do some dogs seem to know when it's dinnertime?

Consider your own dog (or cat). You probably think you have the only dog that can tell time because she always knows when dinner's coming and gets prepared, stopping short of pulling up a chair and tucking a napkin into her collar. It's as though she has one eye on the clock every day, waiting for the dinner hour. Sorry to burst your bubble, but your dog is no clockwatching wonder hound. Instead, the presentation of food (the US) has become associated with a complex CS—your getting up, moving into the kitchen, opening the cabinet, working the can opener—such that the CS alone signals to your dog that food is on the way and therefore initiates the CR of her getting ready to eat.

▼ Figure 7.2 **The Elements of Classical Conditioning** In classical conditioning, a previously neutral stimulus (such as the sound of a tuning fork) is paired with an unconditioned stimulus (such as the presentation of food). After several trials associating the two, the conditioned stimulus (the sound) alone can produce a conditioned response.

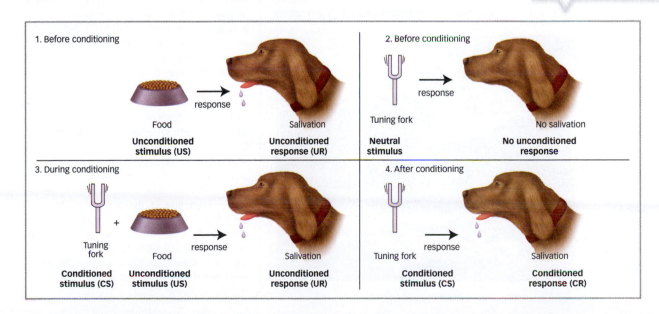

1. Before conditioning

Food → response → Salivation

Unconditioned stimulus (US) → **Unconditioned response (UR)**

2. Before conditioning

Tuning fork → response → No salivation

Neutral stimulus → **No unconditioned response**

3. During conditioning

Tuning fork + Food → response → Salivation

Conditioned stimulus (CS) **Unconditioned stimulus (US)** → **Unconditioned response (UR)**

4. After conditioning

Tuning fork → response → Salivation

Conditioned stimulus (CS) → **Conditioned response (CR)**

acquisition The phase of classical conditioning when the CS and the US are presented together.

second-order conditioning Conditioning in which the stimulus that functions as the US is actually the CS from an earlier procedure in which it acquired its ability to produce learning.

extinction The gradual elimination of a learned response that occurs when the US is no longer presented.

The Basic Principles of Classical Conditioning

When Pavlov's findings first appeared in the scientific and popular literature (Pavlov, 1923a, 1923b), they produced a flurry of excitement. Classical conditioning was the kind of behaviorist psychology Watson was proposing: An organism experiences events or stimuli that are observable and measurable, and changes in that organism can be directly observed and measured. Dogs learned to salivate to the sound of a buzzer, and there was no need to resort to explanations about why it had happened, what the dog wanted, or how the animal thought about the situation. Pavlov also appreciated the significance of his discovery and embarked on a systematic investigation of the mechanisms of classical conditioning. Let's take a closer look at some of these principles. (As the Real World box shows, these principles help explain how drug overdoses occur.)

Acquisition

Remember when you first got your dog? Chances are she didn't seem too smart, especially the way she stared at you vacantly as you went into the kitchen, not anticipating that food was on the way. That's because learning through classical condi-

THE REAL WORLD

Understanding Drug Overdoses

All too often, police are confronted with a perplexing problem: the sudden death of heroin addicts from a drug overdose. The victims are often experienced drug users, the dose taken is usually not larger than what they usually take, and the deaths tend to occur in unusual settings.

Classical conditioning provides some insight into how these deaths occur. First, when classical conditioning takes place, the CS is more than a simple bell or tone: It also includes the overall *context* within which the conditioning takes place. Indeed, Pavlov's dogs often began to salivate even as he approached the experi-

mental apparatus. Second, heroin causes many changes in the body, such as a slower breathing rate, so the body responds with compensatory reactions, such as speeding up breathing in order to maintain a state of balance.

These points help explain the seeming paradox of fatal heroin overdoses in experienced drug users (Siegel, 1984, 2005). When the drug is injected, the entire setting (the drug paraphernalia, the room, the lighting, the addict's usual companions) functions as the CS, and the addict's brain reacts to the heroin by secreting neurotransmitters that counteract its effects. Over time, this protective physiological response

becomes part of the CR, occurring in the presence of the CS but prior to the actual administration of the drug. These compensatory physiological reactions are also what make drug abusers take increasingly larger doses to achieve the same effect, producing *drug tolerance,* discussed in Chapter 5.

Based on these principles of classical conditioning, taking drugs in a new environment can be fatal for a longtime drug user. If an addict injects the usual dose in a setting that is sufficiently novel or where heroin has never been taken before, the CS is now altered, so the physiological compensatory CR that usually serves a protective function may not occur (Siegel et al., 2000). As a result, the addict's usual dose becomes an overdose and death often results.

Understanding these principles has led to treatments for drug addicts. For example, the brain's compensatory response to a drug, when elicited by the familiar contextual cues ordinarily associated with drug taking that constitute the CS, can be experienced by the addict as withdrawal symptoms. In *cue exposure therapies,* an addict is exposed to drug-related cues without being given the drug itself, eventually resulting in extinction of the association between the contextual cues and the compensatory CR. After such treatment, encountering familiar drug-related cues will no longer result in the CR, thereby making it easier for a recovering addict to remain abstinent (Siegel, 2005).

► Although opium dens and crack houses may be considered blight, it is often safer for addicts to use drugs there. The environment becomes part of the addict's CS, so, ironically, busting crack houses may contribute to more deaths from drug overdose when addicts are pushed to use drugs in new situations.

AP PHOTO/CHRIS GARDNER

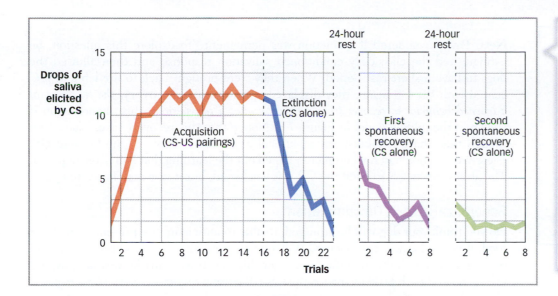

◀ Figure **7.3** **Acquisition, Extinction, and Spontaneous Recovery** In classical conditioning, the CS is originally neutral and produces no specific response. After several trials pairing the CS with the US, the CS alone comes to elicit the salivary response (the CR). Learning tends to take place fairly rapidly and then levels off as stable responding develops. In extinction, the CR diminishes quickly until it no longer occurs. A rest period, however, is typically followed by spontaneous recovery of the CR. In fact, a well-learned CR may show spontaneous recovery after more than one rest period even though there have been no additional learning trials.

tioning requires some period of association between the CS and US. This period is called **acquisition,** or *the phase of classical conditioning when the CS and the US are presented together.* During the initial phase of classical conditioning, typically there is a gradual increase in learning: It starts low, rises rapidly, and then slowly tapers off, as shown in the first panel of **FIGURE 7.3**. Pavlov's dogs gradually increased their amount of salivation over several trials of pairing a tone with the presentation of food; similarly, your dog eventually learned to associate your kitchen preparations with the subsequent appearance of food. After learning has been established, the CS by itself will reliably elicit the CR.

Second-Order Conditioning

After conditioning has been established, **second-order conditioning** can be demonstrated: *conditioning where the stimulus that functions as the US is actually the CS from an earlier procedure in which it acquired its ability to produce learning.* For example, in an early study Pavlov repeatedly paired a new CS, a black square, with the now-reliable tone. After a number of training trials, his dogs produced a salivary response to the black square even though the square itself had never been directly associated with the food. Second-order conditioning helps explain why some people desire money to the point that they hoard it and value it even more than the objects it purchases. Money is initially used to purchase objects that produce gratifying outcomes, such as an expensive car. Although money is not directly associated with the thrill of a drive in a new sports car, through second-order conditioning money can become linked with this type of desirable quality.

Extinction

After Pavlov and his colleagues had explored the process of acquisition extensively, they turned to the next logical question: What would happen if they continued to present the CS (tone) but stopped presenting the US (food)? Repeatedly presenting the CS without the US produces exactly the result you might imagine. As shown on the right side of the first panel in Figure 7.3, behavior declines abruptly ("extinguishes") and continues to drop until eventually the dog ceases to salivate to the sound of the tone. This process is called **extinction,** *the gradual elimination of a learned response that occurs when the US is no longer presented.*

? **How does conditioned behavior change when the unconditioned stimulus is removed?**

Some people desire money to the extent that they hoard it and value it more than the things it can buy. Multibillionaire Ingvar Kamprad, founder of the Swedish furniture company IKEA and ranked the fifth richest individual in the world by Forbes in 2009, drives an old Volvo, flies economy class, and dines at cheap restaurants. Such people may be showing the effects of second-order conditioning.

DENNIS THE MENACE

"I think Mom's using the can opener."

Spontaneous Recovery

Next, Pavlov wondered if extinction was permanent. To explore this question, he extinguished the classically conditioned salivation response and then allowed the dogs to have a short rest period. When they were brought back to the lab and presented with the CS again, they displayed **spontaneous recovery,** *the tendency of a learned behavior to recover from extinction after a rest period.* This phenomenon is shown in the middle panel in Figure 7.3. Notice that this recovery takes place even though there have not been any additional associations between the CS and US. Clearly, extinction had not completely wiped out the learning that had been acquired. The ability of the CS to elicit the CR was weakened, but it was not eliminated.

Generalization and Discrimination

Do you think your dog will be stumped, unable to anticipate the presentation of her food, if you get a new can opener? Will a whole new round of conditioning need to be established with this modified CS? Probably not. It wouldn't be very adaptive for an organism if each little change in the CS-US pairing required an extensive regimen of new learning. Rather, the phenomenon of **generalization** tends to take place, in which *the CR is observed even though the CS is slightly different from the original one used during acquisition.* This means that the conditioning "generalizes" to stimuli that are similar to the CS used during the original training. As you might expect, the more the new stimulus changes, the less conditioned responding is observed. If you replaced the original manual can opener with an electric can opener, your dog would probably show a much weaker conditioned response (Pearce, 1987; Rescorla, 2006).

> **?** How can a change in can opener affect a conditioned dog's response?

When an organism generalizes to a new stimulus, two things are happening. First, by responding to the new stimulus used during generalization testing, the organism demonstrates that it recognizes the similarity between the original CS and the new stimulus. Second, by displaying *diminished* responding to that new stimulus, it also tells us that it notices a difference between the two stimuli. In the second case, the organism shows **discrimination,** or *the capacity to distinguish between similar but distinct stimuli.*

Conceptually, generalization and discrimination are two sides of the same coin. The more organisms show one, the less they show the other, and training can modify the balance between the two.

Conditioned Emotional Responses: The Case of Little Albert

Watson and his followers thought that it was possible to develop general explanations of pretty much *any* behavior of *any* organism based on classical conditioning principles. As a step in that direction, Watson embarked on a controversial study with his research assistant Rosalie Rayner (Watson & Rayner, 1920). They enlisted the assistance of 9-month-old "Little Albert." Watson wanted to see if such a child could be classically conditioned to experience a strong emotional reaction—namely, fear.

Watson presented Little Albert with a variety of stimuli: a white rat, a dog, a rabbit, various masks, and a burning newspaper. Albert's reactions in most cases were curiosity or indifference; he showed no fear of any of the items. Watson also established that something *could* make Albert afraid. While Albert was watching Rayner, Watson unexpectedly struck a large steel bar with a hammer, producing a loud noise. Predictably, this caused Albert to cry, tremble, and be generally displeased.

spontaneous recovery The tendency of a learned behavior to recover from extinction after a rest period.

generalization A process in which the CR is observed even though the CS is slightly different from the original one used during acquisition.

discrimination The capacity to distinguish between similar but distinct stimuli.

Watson and Rayner then led Little Albert through the acquisition phase of classical conditioning. Albert was presented with a white rat. As soon as he reached out to touch it, the steel bar was struck. This pairing occurred again and again over several trials. Eventually, the sight of the rat alone caused Albert to recoil in terror, crying and clamoring to get away from it. In this situation, a US (the loud sound) was paired with a CS (the presence of the rat) such that the CS all by itself was sufficient to produce the CR (a fearful reaction). Little Albert also showed stimulus generalization. The sight of a white rabbit, a seal-fur coat, and a Santa Claus mask produced the same kinds of fear reactions in the infant.

Why did Albert fear the rat?

This study was controversial because of its cavalier treatment of a young child. Modern ethical guidelines that govern the treatment of research participants make sure that this kind of study could not be conducted today. So what was Watson's goal in all this? First, he wanted to show that a relatively complex reaction could be conditioned in humans using Pavlovian techniques. Second, he wanted to show that emotional responses such as fear and anxiety could be produced by classical conditioning and therefore need not be the product of deeper unconscious processes or early life experiences as Freud and his followers had argued (see Chapter 1). Instead, Watson proposed that fear reactions could be learned, just like any other behavior.

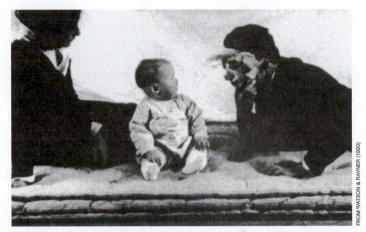

FROM WATSON & RAYNER (1920)

John Watson and Rosalie Rayner show Little Albert an unusual bunny mask. Why doesn't the mere presence of these experimenters serve as a conditioned stimulus in itself?

The kind of conditioned fear responses that were at work in Little Albert's case were also important in the chapter-opening case of Jennifer, who experienced fear and anxiety when hearing the previously innocent sound of an approaching helicopter as a result of her experiences in Iraq. Indeed, a therapy that has proven effective in dealing with such trauma-induced fears is based directly on principles of classical conditioning: Patients are repeatedly exposed to conditioned stimuli associated with their trauma in a safe setting in an attempt to extinguish the conditioned fear response (Bouton, 1988; Rothbaum & Schwartz, 2002). However, conditioned emotional responses are not limited to fear and anxiety responses. The warm and fuzzy feeling that envelops you when hearing a song on the radio that you used to listen to with a former boyfriend or girlfriend represents a type of conditioned emotional response.

A Deeper Understanding of Classical Conditioning

As a form of learning, classical conditioning could be reliably produced, it had a simple set of principles, and it had applications to real-life situations. In short, classical conditioning offered a good deal of utility for psychologists who sought to understand the mechanisms underlying learning, and it continues to do so today.

Like a lot of strong starters, though, classical conditioning has been subjected to deeper scrutiny in order to understand exactly how, when, and why it works. Let's examine three areas that give us a closer look at the mechanisms of classical conditioning: the cognitive, neural, and evolutionary elements.

The Cognitive Elements of Classical Conditioning

As we've seen, Pavlov's work was a behaviorist's dream come true. In this view, conditioning is something that *happens to* a dog, a rat, or a person, apart from what the organism thinks about the conditioning situation. However, although the dogs salivated

when their feeders approached (see Chapter 1), they did not salivate when Pavlov did so, and eventually someone was bound to ask: *Why not?* After all, Pavlov also delivered the food to the dogs, so why didn't he become a CS?

Maybe classical conditioning isn't such an unthinking, mechanical process as behaviorists originally had assumed (Rescorla, 1966, 1988). Somehow, Pavlov's dogs were sensitive to the fact that Pavlov was not a *reliable* indicator of the arrival of food. Pavlov was linked with the arrival of food, but he was also linked with other activities that had nothing to do with food, including checking on the apparatus, bringing the dogs from the kennel to the laboratory, and standing around and talking with his assistants. These observations suggest that perhaps cognitive components are involved in classical conditioning after all.

Robert Rescorla and Allan Wagner (1972) were the first to theorize that classical conditioning occurs only when an animal has learned to set up an *expectation*. The sound of a tone, because of its systematic pairing with food, set up this expectation for the laboratory dogs; Pavlov, because he had no reliable link with food, did not. In fact, in situations such as this, many responses are actually being conditioned. When the tone sounds, the dogs also wag their tails, make begging sounds, and look toward the food source (Jenkins et al., 1978). In short, what is really happening is something like the situation shown in **FIGURE 7.4**.

▼ Figure **7.4** **Expectation in Classical Conditioning** In the Rescorla-Wagner model of classical conditioning, a CS sets up an expectation. The expectation in turn leads to an array of behaviors associated with the presence of the CS.

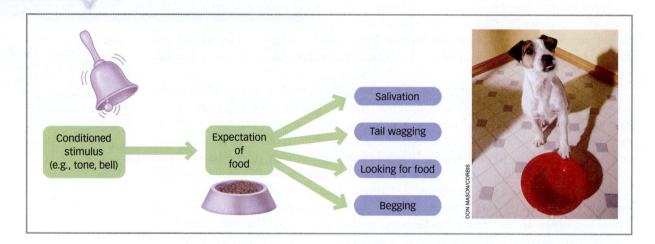

The *Rescorla-Wagner model* introduced a cognitive component that accounted for a variety of classical conditioning phenomena that were difficult to understand from a simple behaviorist point of view. For example, the model predicted that conditioning would be easier when the CS was an *unfamiliar* event than when it was familiar. The reason is that familiar events, being familiar, already have expectations associated with them, making new conditioning difficult. In short, classical conditioning might appear to be a primitive and unthinking process, but it is actually quite sophisticated and incorporates a significant cognitive element.

? **How does the role of expectation in conditioning challenge behaviorist ideas?**

The Role of Consciousness. One issue that arises from this cognitive view of classical conditioning concerns the role of consciousness. Is conscious awareness of the relationship between the CS and US necessary in order for conditioning to occur? Or can conditioning occur even without awareness of the CS-US relation? These questions have been addressed using two procedures for conditioning eyeblink responses that, on the surface, seem to be very similar to one another, yet have unexpectedly produced strikingly different results that initially puzzled researchers:

> In *delay conditioning*, the CS is a tone that is followed immediately by the US, such as a puff of air that elicits an eyeblink response. Importantly, the tone and air puff overlap in time—the tone remains on for a period, the air puff arrives later, and the tone and air puff end at the same time. After a few pairings of the tone and air puff, conditioning occurs and the tone alone elicits an eyeblink response (the CR).

> *Trace conditioning* uses the identical procedures, with one difference: In trace conditioning, there is a brief interval of time after the tone ends and before the air puff is delivered (see **FIGURE 7.5**).

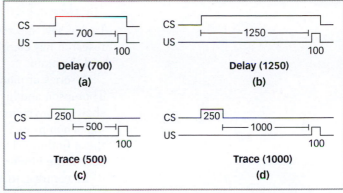

▲ Figure **7.5** **Delay and Trace Conditioning** Clark and Squire (1998) compared delay and trace conditioning. During delay conditioning, the CS (a tone) was presented for either 700 msec (a) or 1,250 msec (b), and then it remained on for 100 msec while the US (an air puff) was presented. During trace conditioning, the CS was presented for 250 msec (c and d) and was followed by a blank "trace" interval of either 500 msec (c) or 1000 msec (d) before presentation of the US for 100 msec. Trace conditioning depended on awareness of the relationship between the US and CS, whereas delay conditioning did not.

During the late 1990s, experiments revealed that amnesic patients—who, as you recall from Chapter 6, lack explicit memory of recent experiences—showed normal delay conditioning of eyeblink responses compared with nonamnesic control subjects. However, the amnesic patients failed to show trace conditioning (Clark & Squire, 1998; McGlinchey-Berroth et al., 1997). Intact delay conditioning in amnesic patients makes sense in light of findings indicating that amnesic patients often exhibit intact implicit memory (Chapter 6). Several researchers have suggested that classical conditioning draws on implicit but not explicit memory (Eichenbaum & Cohen, 2001; Squire & Kandel, 1999). But why would amnesic patients exhibit impaired trace conditioning?

In one study, healthy volunteers were given either delay or trace conditioning, followed by a true-false test with questions that probed their awareness of the contingency between the tone and the air puff, such as, "I believe the tone predicted when the air puff would come." Participants who scored significantly above chance on this test were classified as "aware"; those who did not score significantly above chance were classified as "unaware." Only aware participants showed trace conditioning, whereas both aware and unaware participants showed delay conditioning (Clark & Squire, 1998). These findings suggest a solution to the puzzle of why amnesic patients showed delay but not trace conditioning: Delay conditioning does not require awareness of the contingency between the tone and the air puff, whereas trace conditioning does.

Implications for Patients in a Vegetative State. In light of these findings, consider an intriguing question addressed in more recent work: Would patients in a vegetative state exhibit trace conditioning? As we discussed in Chapter 3, though such patients exhibit no overt signs of voluntary behavior or consciousness, fMRI studies have shown that some of them exhibit brain activity that may reflect conscious processing of spoken stimuli. Researchers examined trace conditioning in 22 patients in a vegetative state, using a standard trace conditioning procedure (Bekinschtein et al., 2009). Strikingly, the patients showed robust trace conditioning. In contrast, subjects who were rendered unconscious by the administration of anesthesia showed no trace conditioning.

Given evidence that trace conditioning depends on awareness of the contingency between the CS and the US, the researchers argued that trace conditioning in the vegetative state reflects some degree of conscious processing in these patients. Alternatively, the researchers acknowledged that they might have demonstrated a type of trace conditioning that occurs without conscious processing. Though more research needs to be done to sort out this issue, it is clear that comparing trace and delay conditioning can teach us a lot about the role of conscious awareness in learning.

The Neural Elements of Classical Conditioning

Pavlov saw his research as providing insights into how the brain works. Recent research has clarified some of what Pavlov hoped to understand about conditioning and the brain.

A series of pioneering experiments conducted across several decades by Richard Thompson and his colleagues, which focused on eyeblink conditioning in the rabbit, showed convincingly that the cerebellum is critical for both delay and trace conditioning (Thompson, 2005). Studies of patients with lesions to the cerebellum supported these findings (Daum et al., 1993). As you learned in Chapter 3, the cerebellum is part of the hindbrain and plays an important role in motor skills and learning.

In contrast to the cerebellum, the hippocampus is important for trace conditioning but not delay conditioning. Some of the supporting evidence for this point comes from Thompson's rabbit studies (Thompson, 2005) as well as the studies we just considered in which amnesic patients—who typically have damage to the hippocampus—exhibited intact delay conditioning along with impaired trace conditioning. Rounding out the picture, more recent neuroimaging findings in healthy young adults show greater hippocampal activation during trace than delay conditioning, together with similar amounts of activation in the cerebellum during the two types of conditioning (Cheng et al., 2008).

In addition to eyeblink conditioning, fear conditioning has been extensively studied. In Chapter 3, you saw that the amygdala plays an important role in the experience of emotion, including fear and anxiety. So

? What is the role of the amygdala in fear conditioning?

it should come as no surprise that the amygdala is also critical for emotional conditioning. Normally, rats trained to expect that a tone (CS) predicts an electric shock (US) come to produce an emotional CR such as *freezing,* where they crouch down and sit motionless. In addition, their autonomic nervous systems go to work: Heart rate and blood pressure increase, and various hormones associated with stress are released. The amygdala plays a role in producing all of these outcomes: If portions of the amygdala or its connections to other brain areas are damaged, the rat does not exhibit either the behavioral freezing response or the autonomic responses to the CS (LeDoux et al., 1988). Hence, the action of the amygdala is an essential element in fear conditioning, and its links with other areas of the brain are responsible for producing specific features of conditioning. The amygdala is involved in fear conditioning in people as well as rats and other animals (Phelps & LeDoux, 2005; Olsson & Phelps, 2007).

The Evolutionary Elements of Classical Conditioning

Evolutionary mechanisms also play an important role in classical conditioning. As you learned in Chapter 1, evolution and natural selection go hand in hand with adaptiveness: Behaviors that are adaptive allow an organism to survive and thrive in its environment.

Consider this example: A psychology professor was once on a job interview in Southern California, and his hosts took him to lunch at a Middle Eastern restaurant. Later, suffering from a case of bad hummus, he was up all night long—and developed a lifelong aversion to hummus.

On the face of it, this looks like a case of classical conditioning: The hummus was the CS, a bacterium or some other source of toxicity was the US, and the resulting nausea was the UR. The UR (nausea) became linked to the once-neutral CS (hummus) and became a CR (an aversion to hummus). However, there are several

Under certain conditions, people may develop food aversions. This serving of hummus looks inviting and probably tastes delicious, but at least one psychologist avoids it like the plague.

biological preparedness A propensity for learning particular kinds of associations over others.

peculiar aspects to this case. The psychologist's hosts also ate the hummus, yet none of them reported feeling ill. It's not clear, then, what the US was; it couldn't have been anything that was actually in the food. What's more, the time between eating the hummus and experiencing the distress was several hours; usually a UR follows a US fairly quickly. Most baffling, this aversion was cemented with a single acquisition trial. Usually it takes several pairings of a CS and US to establish learning.

These peculiarities are not so peculiar from an evolutionary perspective. Any species that forages or consumes a variety of foods needs to develop a mechanism by which it can learn to avoid any food that once made it ill. To have adaptive value, this mechanism should have several properties:

> There should be rapid learning that occurs in perhaps one or two trials. If learning takes more trials than this, the animal could die from eating a toxic substance.

> Toxic substances often don't cause illness immediately, so conditioning should be possible over very long intervals, perhaps up to several hours.

> The organism should develop the aversion to the smell or taste of the food rather than its ingestion. It's more adaptive to reject a potentially toxic substance based on smell alone than it is to ingest it.

> Learned aversions should occur more often with novel foods than familiar ones. It is not adaptive for an animal to develop an aversion to everything it has eaten on the particular day it got sick.

John Garcia and his colleagues illustrated the adaptiveness of classical conditioning in a series of studies with rats (Garcia & Koelling, 1966). They used a variety of CSs (visual, auditory, tactile, taste, and smell) and several different USs (injection of a toxic substance, radiation) that caused nausea and vomiting hours later. The researchers found weak or no conditioning when the CS was a visual, auditory, or tactile stimulus, but a strong food aversion developed with stimuli that have a distinct taste and smell.

? How has cancer patients' discomfort been eased by our understanding of food aversions?

This research had an interesting application. It led to the development of a technique for dealing with an unanticipated side effect of radiation and chemotherapy: Cancer patients who experience nausea from their treatments often develop aversions to foods they ate before the therapy. Broberg and Bernstein (1987) reasoned that, if the findings with rats generalized to humans, a simple technique should minimize the negative consequences of this effect. They gave their patients an unusual food (coconut- or root beer—flavored candy) at the end of the last meal before undergoing treatment. Sure enough, the conditioned food aversions that the patients developed were overwhelmingly for one of the unusual flavors and not for any of the other foods in the meal. Other than any root beer or coconut fanatics among the sample, patients were spared developing aversions to more common foods that they are more likely to eat.

Studies such as these suggest that evolution has provided each species with a kind of **biological preparedness,** *a propensity for learning particular kinds of associations over others,* so that some behaviors are relatively easy to condition in some species but not others. For example, the taste and smell stimuli that produce food aversions in rats do not work with most species of birds. Birds depend primarily on visual cues for finding food and are relatively insensitive to taste and smell. However, it is relatively easy to produce a food aversion in birds using an unfamiliar visual stimulus as the CS, such as a brightly colored food (Wilcoxon, Dragoin, & Kral, 1971). Indeed, most researchers agree that conditioning works best with stimuli that are biologically relevant to the organism (Domjan, 2005).

Rats can be difficult to poison because of learned taste aversions, which are an evolutionarily adaptive element of classical conditioning. Here a worker tries his best in the sewers of France.

BOYER/ROGER VIOLLET/GETTY IMAGES

operant conditioning A type of learning in which the consequences of an organism's behavior determine whether that behavior will be repeated in the future.

law of effect The principle that behaviors that are followed by a "satisfying state of affairs" tend to be repeated and those that produce an "unpleasant state of affairs" are less likely to be repeated.

operant behavior Behavior that an organism produces that has some impact on the environment.

reinforcer Any stimulus or event that functions to increase the likelihood of the behavior that led to it.

punisher Any stimulus or event that functions to decrease the likelihood of the behavior that led to it.

SUMMARY QUIZ [7.1]

1. In classical conditioning, a conditioned stimulus is paired with an unconditioned stimulus to produce
   a. a neutral stimulus.
   c. an unconditioned response.
   b. a conditioned response.
   d. another conditioned stimulus.

2. What occurs when a conditioned stimulus is no longer paired with an unconditioned stimulus?
   a. generalization
   c. extinction
   b. spontaneous recovery
   d. acquisition

3. What did Watson and Rayner seek to demonstrate about behaviorism through the Little Albert experiment?
   a. Conditioning involves a degree of cognition.
   b. Classical conditioning has an evolutionary component.
   c. Behaviorism alone cannot explain human behavior.
   d. Even sophisticated behaviors such as emotional reactions are subject to classical conditioning.

4. Which part of the brain is involved in the classical conditioning of fear?
   a. the amygdala
   c. the hippocampus
   b. the cerebellum
   d. the hypothalamus

Operant Conditioning: Reinforcements from the Environment

The study of classical conditioning is the study of behaviors that are *reactive*. Most animals don't voluntarily salivate or feel spasms of anxiety; rather, these animals exhibit these responses involuntarily during the conditioning process. But we also perform many voluntary behaviors. We engage in these voluntary behaviors in order to obtain rewards and avoid punishment; understanding them is essential to developing a complete picture of learning. **Operant conditioning** is *a type of learning in which the consequences of an organism's behavior determine whether it will be repeated in the future.* The study of operant conditioning is the exploration of behaviors that are *active*.

The Development of Operant Conditioning: The Law of Effect

The study of how active behavior affects the environment began at about the same time as the investigation of classical conditioning. In the 1890s, Edward Thorndike studied *instrumental behaviors,* that is, behavior that required an organism to *do* something—to solve a problem or otherwise manipulate elements of its environment (Thorndike, 1898). For example, Thorndike completed several experiments using a puzzle box, which was a wooden crate with a door that would open when a concealed lever was moved in the right way (see **FIGURE 7.6**). A hungry cat placed in a puzzle box would try various behaviors to get out—scratching at the door, meowing loudly, sniffing

What is the relationship between behavior and reward?

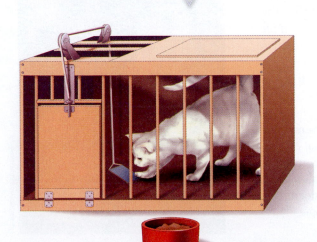

▼ Figure **7.6** **Thorndike's Puzzle Box** In Thorndike's original experiments, food was placed just outside the door of the puzzle box, where the cat could see it. If the cat triggered the appropriate lever, it would open the door and let the cat out.

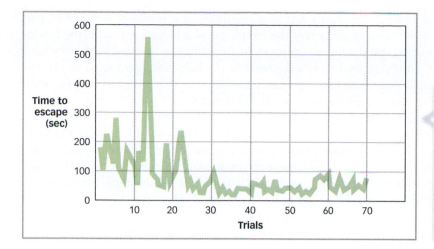

◂ Figure **7.7** **The Law of Effect** Thorndike's cats displayed trial-and-error behavior when trying to escape from the puzzle box. They made lots of irrelevant movements and actions until, over time, they discovered the solution. Once they figured out what behavior was instrumental in opening the latch, they stopped all other ineffective behaviors and escaped from the box faster and faster.

the inside of the box, putting its paw through the openings—but only one behavior opened the door and led to food: tripping the lever in just the right way. After this happened, Thorndike placed the cat back in the box for another round. Over time, the ineffective behaviors become less and less frequent, and the one instrumental behavior (going right for the latch) becomes more frequent (see **FIGURE 7.7**). From these observations, Thorndike developed the **law of effect,** which states that *behaviors that are followed by a "satisfying state of affairs" tend to be repeated and those that produce an "unpleasant state of affairs" are less likely to be repeated.*

Such learning is very different from classical conditioning. Remember that in classical conditioning experiments, the US occurred on every training trial no matter what the animal did. Pavlov delivered food to the dog whether it salivated or not. But in Thorndike's work, the behavior of the animal determined what happened next. If the behavior was "correct" (i.e., the latch was triggered), the animal was rewarded with food. Incorrect behaviors produced no results; the animal was stuck in the box until it performed the correct behavior. Although different from classical conditioning, Thorndike's work resonated with most behaviorists at the time: It was still observable, quantifiable, and free from explanations involving the mind (Galef, 1998).

B. F. Skinner: The Role of Reinforcement and Punishment

Several decades after Thorndike's work, B. F. Skinner (1904–90) coined the term **operant behavior** to refer to *behavior that an organism produces that has some impact on the environment.* In Skinner's system, all of these emitted behaviors "operated" on the environment in some manner, and the environment responded by providing events that either strengthened those behaviors (i.e., they *reinforced* them) or made them less likely to occur (i.e., they *punished* them) (Skinner, 1938, 1953). In order to study operant behavior scientifically, Skinner developed a variation on Thorndike's puzzle box. The *operant conditioning chamber,* or *Skinner box,* as it is commonly called, shown in **FIGURE 7.8**, allows a researcher to study the behavior of small organisms in a controlled environment.

Skinner's approach to the study of learning focused on *reinforcement* and *punishment.* These terms, which have commonsense connotations, have particular meaning in psychology in terms of their effect on behavior. A **reinforcer** is *any stimulus or event that functions to increase the likelihood of the behavior that led to it,* whereas a **punisher** is *any stimulus or event that functions to decrease the likelihood of the behavior that led to it.*

▾ Figure **7.8** **Skinner Box** In a typical Skinner box, or *operant conditioning chamber,* a rat, pigeon, or other suitably sized animal is placed in this environment and observed during learning trials that use operant conditioning principles.

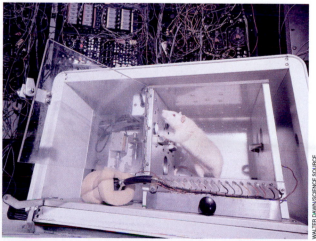

MICHELLE SELSENICK/FLICKR VISION

Negative reinforcement involves the removal of something unpleasant from the environment. When Daddy stops the car, he gets a reward: His little monster stops screaming. However, from the perspective of the child, this is positive reinforcement. The child's tantrum results in something positive added to the environment—stopping for a snack.

Whether a particular stimulus acts as a reinforcer or a punisher depends in part on whether it increases or decreases the likelihood of a behavior. Presenting food is usually reinforcing, producing an increase in the behavior that led to it; removing food is often punishing, leading to a decrease in the behavior. Turning on an electric shock is typically punishing (and decreases the behavior that led to it); turning it off is rewarding (and increases the behavior that led to it).

To keep these possibilities distinct, Skinner used the term *positive* for situations in which a stimulus was presented and *negative* for situations in which it was removed. Consequently, there is *positive reinforcement* (where a rewarding stimulus is presented) and *negative reinforcement* (where an unpleasant stimulus is removed), as well as *positive punishment* (where an unpleasant stimulus is administered) and *negative punishment* (where a rewarding stimulus is removed). Here the words *positive* and *negative* mean, respectively, something that is *added* or something that is *taken away*; they do not mean "good" or "bad" as they do in everyday speech. As you can see from **TABLE 7.1**, positive and negative reinforcement increase the likelihood of the behavior and positive and negative punishment decrease the likelihood of the behavior.

Table 7.1		
Reinforcement and Punishment		
	Increases the Likelihood of Behavior	**Decreases the Likelihood of Behavior**
Stimulus is presented	Positive reinforcement	Positive punishment
Stimulus is removed	Negative reinforcement	Negative punishment

These distinctions can be confusing at first; after all, "negative reinforcement" and "punishment" both sound like they should be "bad" and produce the same type of behavior. However, negative reinforcement, for example, involves something pleasant; it's the *removal* of something unpleasant, like a shock, and the absence of a shock is indeed pleasant.

Reinforcement is generally more effective than punishment in promoting learning. There are many reasons (Gershoff, 2002), but one reason is this: Punishment signals that an unacceptable behavior has occurred, but it doesn't specify what should be done instead. Spanking a young child for starting to run into a busy street certainly stops the behavior—which, in this case, is probably a good idea. But it doesn't promote any kind of learning about the *desired* behavior.

? Why is reinforcement more constructive than punishment in promoting desired behavior?

Reinforcers and punishers often gain their functions from basic biological mechanisms. Food, comfort, shelter, and warmth are examples of *primary reinforcers* because they help satisfy biological needs. However, the vast majority of reinforcers or punishers in our daily lives have little to do with biology: A handshake, verbal approval, an encouraging grin, a bronze trophy, or money all serve powerful reinforcing functions, yet none of them taste very good or help keep you warm at night. The point is, we learn to perform a lot of behaviors based on reinforcements that have little or nothing to do with biological satisfaction. These *secondary reinforcers* derive their effectiveness from their associations with primary reinforcers through classical conditioning. For example, money starts out as a neutral CS that, through its association with primary USs like acquiring food or shelter, takes on a conditioned emotional element. Flashing lights, originally a neutral CS, acquire powerful negative elements through association with a speeding ticket and a fine.

TOM CHENEY/THE NEW YORKER COLLECTION/CARTOONBANK.COM

"Oh, not bad. The light comes on, I press the bar, they write me a check. How about you?"

The Basic Principles of Operant Conditioning

After establishing how reinforcement and punishment produced learned behavior, Skinner and other scientists began to expand the parameters of operant conditioning. Let's look at some of these basic principles of operant conditioning.

Discrimination, Generalization, and the Importance of Context

We all take off our clothes at least once a day, but usually not in public. We scream at rock concerts but not in libraries. The underlying message is that learning takes place *in contexts*. As Skinner phrased it, most behavior is under *stimulus control,* meaning that a particular response only occurs when an appropriate discriminative stimulus is present. For example, in the presence of a *discriminative stimulus* (classmates drinking coffee together in Starbucks), a *response* (joking comments about a psychology professor's increasing waistline and receding hairline) produces a *reinforcer* (laughter among classmates). The same response in a different context—the professor's office—would most likely produce a very different outcome.

Stimulus control, perhaps not surprisingly, shows both discrimination and generalization effects similar to those we saw with classical conditioning. For example, in one study, the discriminative stimulus was either an Impressionist painting by Monet or a Cubist painting by Picasso (Watanabe, Sakamoto, & Wakita, 1995). Participants in the experiment were only reinforced if they responded when the appropriate painting was presented. After training, the participants discriminated appropriately; those trained with the Monet painting responded when other paintings by Monet were presented, but not when other Picasso paintings were shown. Picasso-trained participants showed the opposite behavior, responding to Picassos but not Monets. What's more, the research participants showed that they could generalize *across* painters as long as they were from the same artistic tradition. Those trained with Monet responded appropriately when shown other Impressionist paintings, and the Picasso-trained participants responded to other Cubist artwork, despite never having seen these paintings before. The results are especially striking because the participants were pigeons who were trained to key-peck to these various works of art. Stimulus control, and its ability to foster stimulus discrimination and stimulus generalization, is effective even if the stimulus has no meaning to the respondent.

B. F. Skinner with one of his many research participants.

In research on stimulus control, participants trained with Picasso paintings, such as the one on the left, responded to other paintings by Picasso or even to paintings by other Cubists. Participants trained with Monet paintings, such as the one on the right, responded to other paintings by Monet or by other French Impressionists. Interestingly, the participants in this study were pigeons.

Extinction

As in classical conditioning, operant behavior undergoes extinction when the reinforcements stop. Pigeons cease pecking at a key if food is no longer presented following the behavior. You wouldn't put more money into a vending machine if it failed to give you its promised candy bar or soda. On the surface, extinction of operant behavior looks like that of classical conditioning.

However, there is an important difference. In classical conditioning, the US occurs on every trial no matter what the organism does. In operant conditioning, the reinforcements occur only when the proper response has been made, and they don't always occur even then. Not every trip into the forest produces nuts for a squirrel, and researchers run many experiments that do not work out and never get published. Yet these behaviors don't weaken and gradually extinguish. Extinction is a bit more complicated in operant conditioning than in classical conditioning because it depends in part on how often reinforcement is received. In fact, this principle is an important cornerstone of operant conditioning that we'll examine next.

Schedules of Reinforcement

One day, Skinner was laboriously hand-rolling food pellets to reinforce the rats in his experiments. It occurred to him that perhaps he could save time and effort by not giving his rats a pellet for every bar press but instead delivering food on some intermittent schedule. The results of this hunch were dramatic. Not only did the rats continue bar pressing but they also shifted the rate and pattern of bar pressing depending on the timing and frequency of the presentation of the reinforcers (Skinner, 1979). Unlike classical conditioning, in which the sheer *number* of learning trials is important, in operant conditioning the *pattern* with which reinforcements appeared is crucial. Skinner explored dozens of what came to be known as *schedules of reinforcement* (Ferster & Skinner, 1957) (see **FIGURE 7.9**). We'll consider some of the most important here.

> Students cramming for an exam often show the same kind of behavior as pigeons being reinforced under a fixed interval schedule.

BRAND X PICTURES/JUPITERIMAGES

Interval Schedules. Under a **fixed interval (FI) schedule,** *reinforcers are presented at fixed times, provided that the appropriate response is made.* For example, on a 2-minute fixed interval schedule, a response will be reinforced, but only after 2 minutes have expired since the last reinforcement. Rats and pigeons in Skinner boxes produce predictable patterns of behavior under these schedules. They show little responding right after the presentation of reinforcement, but as the next time interval draws to a close, they show a burst of responding. Many undergraduates behave exactly like this. They do relatively little work until just before the upcoming exam, then engage in a burst of reading and studying.

Under a **variable interval (VI) schedule,** *a behavior is reinforced based on an average time that has expired since the last reinforcement.* For example, on a 2-minute variable interval schedule, responses will be reinforced every 2 minutes *on average.* Variable interval schedules typically produce steady, consistent respond-

> ▶ Figure **7.9 Reinforcement Schedules** Different schedules of reinforcement produce different rates of responding. These lines represent the amount of responding that occurs under each type of reinforcement. The black slash marks indicate when reinforcement was administered. Notice that ratio schedules tend to produce higher rates of responding than do interval schedules, as shown by the steeper lines for fixed ratio and variable ratio reinforcement.

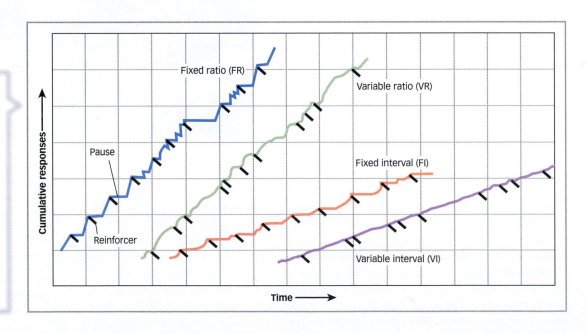

? How does a radio station use scheduled reinforcements to keep you listening?

ing because the time until the next reinforcement is less predictable. One example of a VI schedule might be radio promotional giveaways, such as tickets to rock concerts. The reinforcement—getting the tickets—might average out to once an hour across the span of the broadcasting day, but the presentation of the reinforcement is variable: It might come early in the 10:00 hour, later in the 11:00 hour, immediately into the 12:00 hour, and so on.

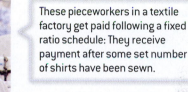

Radio station promotions and giveaways often follow a variable interval schedule of reinforcement.

Both fixed interval schedules and variable interval schedules tend to produce slow, methodical responding because the reinforcements follow a time progression that is independent of how many responses occur. It doesn't matter if a rat on a fixed interval schedule presses a bar 1 time during a 2-minute period or 100 times: The reinforcing food pellet won't drop out of the shoot until 2 minutes have elapsed, regardless of the number of responses.

Ratio Schedules. Under a **fixed ratio (FR) schedule,** *reinforcement is delivered after a specific number of responses have been made.* One schedule might present reinforcement after every fourth response, a different schedule might present reinforcement after every 20 responses; the special case of presenting reinforcement after *each* response is called *continuous reinforcement.* There are many examples of FR schedules in real life: Book clubs often give you a "freebie" after a set number of regular purchases, pieceworkers get paid after mak-

These pieceworkers in a textile factory get paid following a fixed ratio schedule: They receive payment after some set number of shirts have been sewn.

? How do ratio schedules work to keep you spending your money?

ing a fixed number of products, and some credit card companies return to their customers a percent of the amount charged. When a fixed ratio schedule is operating, it is possible, in principle, to know exactly when the next reinforcer is due. A laundry pieceworker on a 10-response fixed ratio schedule who has just washed and ironed the ninth shirt knows that payment is coming after the next shirt is done.

Under a **variable ratio (VR) schedule,** *the delivery of reinforcement is based on a particular average number of responses.* For example, slot machines in a modern casino pay off on variable ratio schedules that are determined by the random number generator that controls the play of the machines. A casino might advertise that they pay off on "every 100 pulls on average," which could be true. However, one player might hit a jackpot after 3 pulls on a slot machine, whereas another player might not hit until after 80 pulls. The ratio of responses to reinforcements is variable, which probably helps casinos stay in business.

Intermittent Reinforcement. Both variable and ratio schedules are examples of **intermittent reinforcement,** *when only some of the responses made are followed by reinforcement.* Intermittent reinforcement produces interesting behavior, particularly the **intermittent-reinforcement effect,** *the fact that operant behaviors that are maintained under intermittent-reinforcement schedules resist extinction better than those maintained under continuous reinforcement.* One way to think about

fixed interval (FI) schedule An operant conditioning principle in which reinforcements are presented at fixed times, provided that the appropriate response is made.

variable interval (VI) schedule An operant conditioning principle in which behavior is reinforced based on an average time that has expired since the last reinforcement.

fixed ratio (FR) schedule An operant conditioning principle in which reinforcement is delivered after a specific number of responses have been made.

variable ratio (VR) schedule An operant conditioning principle in which the delivery of reinforcement is based on a particular average number of responses.

intermittent reinforcement An operant conditioning principle in which only some of the responses made are followed by reinforcement.

intermittent-reinforcement effect The fact that operant behaviors that are maintained under intermittent-reinforcement schedules resist extinction better than those maintained under continuous reinforcement.

Slot machines in casinos pay out following a variable ratio schedule. This helps explain why some gamblers feel incredibly lucky, whereas others (like this chap) can't believe they can play a machine for so long without winning a thing.

this effect is to recognize that the more irregular and intermittent a schedule is, the more difficult it becomes for an organism to detect when it has actually been placed on a schedule that is intended to produce extinction. For example, if you've just put a dollar into a soda machine that, unbeknownst to you, is broken, no soda comes out. Because you're used to getting your sodas on a continuous-reinforcement schedule—one dollar produces one soda—this abrupt change in the environment is easily noticed and you are unlikely to put additional money into the machine: You'd quickly show extinction. However, if you've put your dollar into a slot machine that, unbeknownst to you, is broken, do you stop after one or two plays? Almost certainly not. If you're a regular slot player, you're used to going for many plays in a row without winning anything, so it's difficult to tell that anything is out of the ordinary. Under conditions of intermittent reinforcement, all organisms will show considerable resistance to extinction and continue for many trials before they stop responding.

Shaping Through Successive Approximations

Have you ever been to AquaLand and wondered how the dolphins learn to jump up in the air, twist around, splash back down, do a somersault, and then jump through a hoop, all in one smooth motion? Well, they don't. At least not all at once. Rather, elements of their behavior get shaped over time until the final product looks like one smooth motion.

Behavior rarely occurs in fixed frameworks where a stimulus is presented and then an organism has to engage in some activity or another. Most of our behaviors, then, are the result of **shaping,** or *learning that results from the reinforcement of successive steps to a final desired behavior.* The outcomes of one set of behaviors shape the next set of behaviors, whose outcomes shape the next set of behaviors, and so on.

? How can operant conditioning produce complex behaviors?

Skinner noted that if you put a rat in a Skinner box and wait for it to press the bar, you could end up waiting a very long time: Bar pressing just isn't very high in a rat's natural hierarchy of responses. However, it is relatively easy to "shape" bar pressing. Watch the rat closely: If it turns in the direction of the bar, deliver a food reward. This will reinforce turning toward the bar, making such a movement more likely. Now wait for the rat to take a step toward the bar before delivering food; this will reinforce moving toward the bar. After the rat walks closer to the bar, wait until it touches the bar before presenting the food. Notice that none of these behaviors is the final desired behavior—reliably pressing the bar. Rather, each behavior is a *successive approximation* to the final product, or a behavior that gets incrementally closer to the

B. F. Skinner shaping a dog named Agnes. In the span of 20 minutes, Skinner was able to use reinforcement of successive approximations to shape Agnes's behavior. The result was a pretty neat trick: to wander in, stand on hind legs, and jump.

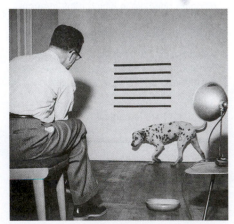

1 Minute

4 Minutes

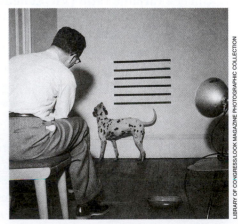

8 Minutes

overall desired behavior. In the dolphin example—and indeed, in many instances in which animals are trained to perform astoundingly complex behaviors—each smaller behavior is reinforced until the overall sequence of behavior is performed reliably.

shaping Learning that results from the reinforcement of successive steps to a final desired behavior.

Superstitious Behavior

Everything we've discussed so far suggests that one of the keys to establishing reliable operant behavior is the correlation between an organism's response and the occurrence of reinforcement. As you read in Chapter 2, however, just because two things are correlated (that is, they tend to occur together in time and space) doesn't imply that there is causality (that is, the presence of one reliably causes the other to occur).

Skinner (1948) designed an experiment that illustrates this distinction. He put several pigeons in Skinner boxes, set the food dispenser to deliver food every 15 seconds, and left the birds to their own devices. Later he returned and found the birds engaging in odd, idiosyncratic behaviors, such as pecking aimlessly in a corner or turning in circles. He referred to these behaviors as "superstitious" and offered a behaviorist's analysis of their occurrence: The pigeons were simply repeating behaviors that had been accidentally reinforced. A pigeon that just happened to have pecked randomly in the corner when the food showed up had connected the delivery of food to that behavior. Because this pecking behavior was "reinforced" by the delivery of food, the pigeon was likely to repeat it. Now pecking in the corner was more likely to occur, and it was more likely to be reinforced 15 seconds later when the food appeared again. Skinner's pigeons acted as though there was a causal relationship between their behaviors and the appearance of food when it was merely an accidental correlation.

? How would a behaviorist explain superstitions?

People believe in many different superstitions and engage in all kinds of superstitious behaviors. Many major league baseball players, for example, maintain a superstition of not stepping on the baselines when they enter or leave the field, as illustrated by former Baltimore Orioles pitcher Daniel Cabrera. Skinner thought superstitions resulted from the unintended reinforcement of inconsequential behavior.

Although some researchers questioned Skinner's characterization of these behaviors as "superstitious" (Staddon & Simmelhag, 1971), later studies have shown that people, like pigeons, behave as though there's a correlation between their responses and reward when in fact the connection is merely accidental (Bloom et al., 2007; Mellon, 2009; Ono, 1987; Wagner & Morris, 1987). For example, baseball players who hit several home runs on a day when they happened not to have showered are likely to continue that tradition, laboring under the belief that the accidental correlation between poor personal hygiene and a good day at bat is somehow causal. This "stench causes home runs" hypothesis is just one of many examples of human superstitions (Gilbert et al., 2000; Radford & Radford, 1949).

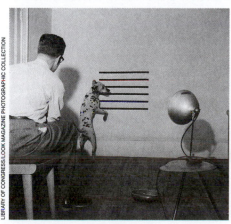

12 Minutes

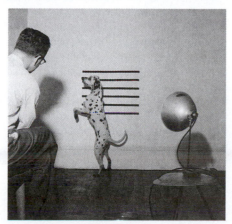

16 Minutes

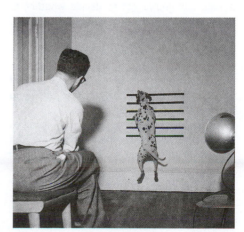

20 Minutes

A Deeper Understanding of Operant Conditioning

To behaviorists such as Watson and Skinner, an organism behaved in a certain way as a response to stimuli in the environment, not because there was any wanting, wishing, or willing by the animal in question. However, some research on operant conditioning digs deeper into the underlying mechanisms that produce the familiar outcomes of reinforcement. As we did earlier in the chapter with classical conditioning, let's examine three elements that expand our view of operant conditioning: the cognitive, neural, and evolutionary elements of operant conditioning.

The Cognitive Elements of Operant Conditioning

Edward Chace Tolman (1886–1959) was the strongest early advocate of a cognitive approach to operant learning. Tolman argued that there was more to learning than just knowing the circumstances in the environment (the properties of the stimulus) and being able to observe a particular outcome (the reinforced response). Instead, Tolman proposed that the conditioning experience produces knowledge or a belief that, in this particular situation, a specific reward will appear if a specific response is made. (For an example of one aspect of the reward [being ready for the test] given the response [decision to study], see the Hot Science box.) Tolman's ideas may remind you of the Rescorla-Wagner model of classical conditioning. In both Rescorla's and Tolman's theories, the stimulus does not directly evoke a response; rather, it establishes an internal cognitive state, which then produces the behavior.

Latent Learning and Cognitive Maps. In **latent learning,** *something is learned, but it is not manifested as a behavioral change until sometime in the future.* Latent learning can easily be established in rats and occurs without any obvious reinforcement, a finding that posed a direct challenge to the then-dominant behaviorist position that all learning required some form of reinforcement (Tolman & Honzik, 1930a).

BANCROFT LIBRARY/UNIVERSITY OF CALIFORNIA, BERKELEY

Edward Chace Tolman advocated a cognitive approach to operant learning and provided evidence that in maze-learning experiments, rats develop a mental picture of the maze, which he called a cognitive map.

HOT SCIENCE

Control of Learning: From the Laboratory to the Classroom

It's the night before the final exam in your introductory psychology course. You've put in a lot of work, but with just a little study time left you've got to decide whether to devote those precious remaining minutes to studying psychological disorders or social psychology. How do you choose? Recent research in cognitive psychology has shown that people's judgments about what they have learned play a critical role in guiding further study and learning (Metcalfe, 2009).

An important part of learning involves assessing how well we know something and how much more time we need to devote to studying it: what psychologists call "judgments of learning" (JOLs). But how accurate are JOLs?

To find out, researchers used an illusion that influences JOLs (Metcalfe & Finn, 2008). People are given lists of word pairs; some pairs are

studied three times, initially tested, and then studied one more time before the final test (3-1 condition); other pairs are studied once, initially tested, and then studied three more times before the final test (1-3 condition).

You should not be surprised to learn that on the initial test, people performed better on the 3-1 pairs (which they'd studied three times so far) than on the 1-3 pairs (which they'd studied only once). By the final test, people recalled the same number of 3-1 and 1-3 pairs, all of which had now been studied a total of four times. But before that final test, participants were asked for a JOL on each word pair. Strikingly, even though both 1-3 and 3-1 word pairs had been learned equally well, the participants' JOLs were higher for pairs in the 3-1 condition than the 1-3 condition. This illusion occurred because JOLs were influenced by the initial

test, on which participants recalled more 3-1 pairs than 1-3 pairs.

Similarly, after you read and re-read a chapter or article in preparation for a test, the material will likely feel quite familiar, and that feeling may convince you that you've learned the material well enough that you don't need to study it further. However, as in the study we just discussed, JOLs can be misleading. One way to avoid being fooled is to test yourself from time to time when studying for an exam under conditions similar to those that will occur during the exam. As we saw in Chapter 6, testing oneself improves later learning of the target material more than simply restudying it. You can use the results of those tests to help you decide which material requires further work. We can exert control over learning, but we also need to be aware of the possible pitfalls in attempting to exercise that control.

Tolman gave three groups of rats access to a complex maze every day for over 2 weeks. The control group never received any reinforcement for navigating the maze. They were simply allowed to run around until they reached the goal box at the end of the maze. In **FIGURE 7.10** you can see that over the 2 weeks of the study, this group (in green) got a little better at finding their way through the maze but not by much. A second group of rats received regular reinforcements; when they reached the goal box, they found a small food reward there. Not surprisingly, these rats showed clear learning, as can be seen in blue in Figure 7.10. A third group was treated exactly like the control group for the first 10 days and then rewarded for the last 7 days. This group's behavior (in orange) was quite striking. For the first 10 days, they behaved like the rats in the control group. However, during the final 7 days, they behaved a lot like the rats that had been reinforced every day. Clearly, the rats in this third group had learned a lot about the maze and the location of the goal

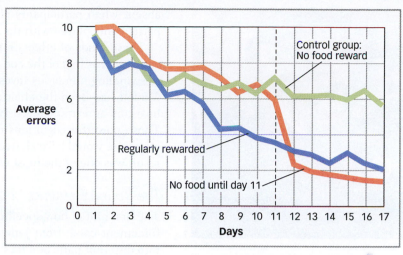

▲ Figure **7.10** **Latent Learning** Rats in a control group that never received any reinforcement (in green) improved at finding their way through the maze over 17 days but not by much. Rats that received regular reinforcements (in blue) showed fairly clear learning; their error rate decreased steadily over time. Rats in the latent learning group (in orange) were treated exactly like the control group rats for the first 10 days and then like the regularly rewarded group for the last 7 days. Their dramatic improvement on day 12 shows that these rats had learned a lot about the maze and the location of the goal box even though they had never received reinforcements. Notice also that on the last 7 days, these latent learners actually seem to make *fewer* errors than their regularly rewarded counterparts.

? What are cognitive maps and why are they a challenge to behaviorism?

box during those first 10 days even though they had not received any reinforcements for their behavior. In other words, they showed evidence of latent learning. These results suggested to Tolman that beyond simply learning "start here, end here," his rats had developed a sophisticated mental picture of the maze. Tolman called this a **cognitive map,** or *a mental representation of the physical features of the environment* (Tolman & Honzik, 1930b; Tolman, Ritchie, & Kalish, 1946). Later studies showed that, once a rat had learned to follow a particular pathway through the maze to obtain food, if that pathway was blocked, the rats immediately ran down an alternate pathway to the goal. The behaviorists would not have predicted this behavior because this alternate pathway had never been reinforced. Rather, it appeared that the rats had formed a sophisticated cognitive map of their environment and behaved in a way that suggested they were successfully following that map after the conditions had changed.

Learning to Trust: For Better or Worse. Cognitive factors also played a key role in an experiment examining learning and brain activity (using fMRI) in people who played a "trust" game with a fictional partner (Delgado, Frank, & Phelps, 2005). On each trial, a participant could either keep a $1 reward or transfer the reward to a partner, who would receive $3. The partner could then either keep the $3 or share half of it with the participant—so, when playing with a partner who was willing to share the reward, the participant would be better off transferring the money, but when playing with a partner who did not share, the participant would be better off keeping the reward in the first place. Participants in such experiments typically learn who is trustworthy on the basis of trial and error, and they give more money to partners who reinforce them by sharing.

In one study, participants were given detailed descriptions of their partners that portrayed the partners as either trustworthy, neutral, or suspect. Even though during the game itself the sharing behavior of the three types of partners did not differ—they each shared money 50% of the time—the participants' cognitions about their partners had powerful effects. Participants transferred more money to the "trustworthy" partner than to the others, essentially ignoring the trial-by-trial feedback that would ordinarily shape their playing behavior, and thus reduced the amount of reward they received. Highlighting the power of the cognitive effect, signals in a part of the brain that ordinarily distinguishes between positive and negative feedback were evident only when participants played with the "neutral" partner; these feedback signals were

latent learning A condition in which something is learned but it is not manifested as a behavioral change until sometime in the future.

cognitive map A mental representation of the physical features of the environment.

Bernard Madoff, shown here leaving a court hearing in March 2009, pleaded guilty to fraud after swindling billions of dollars from investors who trusted him.

AFP PHOTO/TIMOTHY A. CLARY/NEWSCOM

absent when participants played with the "trustworthy" partner and reduced when participants played with the "suspect" partner.

These kinds of effects might help us to understand otherwise perplexing real-life cases such as that of the con artist Bernard Madoff, who in March 2009 pleaded guilty to swindling numerous investors out of billions of dollars in a highly publicized case. Madoff had been the chairman of the NASDAQ stock exchange and seemed to his investors an extremely trustworthy figure with whom one could safely invest money. Those powerful cognitions might have caused investors to miss danger signals that otherwise would have alerted them to the true nature of Madoff's operation. If so, the result was one of the most expensive failures of learning in modern history.

The Neural Elements of Operant Conditioning

The first hint of how specific brain structures might contribute to the process of reinforcement came from James Olds and his associates, who inserted tiny electrodes into different parts of a rat's brain and allowed the animal to control electric stimulation of its own brain by pressing a bar. They discovered that some brain areas, particularly those in the limbic system (see Chapter 3), produced what appeared to be intensely positive experiences: The rats would press the bar repeatedly to stimulate these structures. The researchers observed that these rats would ignore food, water, and other life-sustaining necessities for hours on end simply to receive stimulation directly in the brain. They then called these parts of the brain "pleasure centers" (Olds, 1956) (see **FIGURE 7.11**).

In the years since these early studies, researchers have identified a number of structures and pathways in the brain that deliver rewards through stimulation (Wise, 1989, 2005). The neurons in the *medial forebrain bundle,* a pathway that meanders its way from the midbrain through the *hypothalamus* into the *nucleus accumbens,* are the most susceptible to stimulation that produces pleasure. This is not surprising as psychologists have identified this bundle of cells as crucial to behaviors that clearly involve pleasure, such as eating, drinking, and engaging in sexual activity. In addition, the neurons along this pathway, especially those in the nucleus accumbens itself, are all *dopaminergic;* that is, they secrete the neurotransmitter *dopamine.* Remember from Chapter 3 that higher levels of dopamine in the brain are usually associated with positive emotions. During recent years, several competing hypotheses about the precise role of dopamine have emerged, including the idea that dopamine is more closely linked with the expectation of reward than with reward itself (Fiorillo, Newsome, & Schultz, 2008; Schultz, 2006, 2007) and the theory that dopamine is more closely associated with wanting or even craving something rather than simply liking it (Berridge, 2007).

Whichever view turns out to be correct, researchers have found good support for a "reward center" in which dopamine plays a key role. First, as you've just seen, rats will work to stimulate this pathway at the expense of other basic needs (Olds & Fobes, 1981). However, if drugs that block the action of dopamine are administered to the rats, they cease stimulating the pleasure centers (Stellar, Kelley, & Corbett, 1983). Second, fMRI studies (see Chapter 3) show increased activity in the nucleus accumbens in heterosexual men looking at pictures of attractive women (Aharon et al., 2001) and in individuals who believe they are about to receive money (Cooper et al., 2009; Knutson et al., 2001). Finally, rats given primary reinforcers such as food or water show increased dopamine secretion in the nucleus accumbens—but only if the rats are hungry or thirsty (Damsma et al., 1992). This last finding is exactly what we might expect given our earlier

▼ Figure **7.11** **Pleasure Centers in the Brain** The nucleus accumbens, medial forebrain bundle, and hypothalamus are all major pleasure centers in the brain.

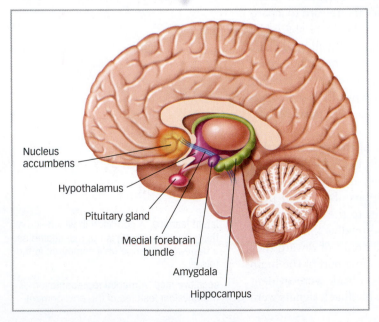

Nucleus accumbens

Hypothalamus

Pituitary gland

Medial forebrain bundle

Amygdala

Hippocampus

discussion of the complexities of reinforcement. After all, food tastes a lot better when we are hungry, and sexual activity is more pleasurable when we are aroused. These biological structures underlying rewards and reinforcements probably evolved to ensure that species engaged in activities that helped survival and reproduction.

The Evolutionary Elements of Operant Conditioning

As you'll recall, classical conditioning has an adaptive value that has been fine-tuned by evolution. Not surprisingly, we can also view operant conditioning from an evolutionary perspective. For example, researchers using simple T mazes like the one shown in **FIGURE 7.12** to study learning in rats discovered that if a rat found food in one arm of the maze on the first trial of the day, it typically ran down the *other* arm on the very next trial. A staunch behaviorist wouldn't expect the rats to behave this way. After all, the rats in these experiments were hungry and they had just been reinforced for turning in a particular direction. According to operant conditioning, this should *increase* the likelihood of turning in that same direction, not reduce it. With additional trials the rats eventually learned to go to the arm with the food, but they had to learn to overcome this initial tendency to go "the wrong way." How can we explain this?

What explains a rat's behavior in a T maze?

What was puzzling from a behaviorist perspective makes sense when viewed from an evolutionary perspective. Rats are foragers, and like all foraging species, they have evolved a highly adaptive strategy for survival. They move around in their environment looking for food. If they find it somewhere, they eat it (or store it) and then go look somewhere else for more. If they do not find food, they forage in another part of the environment. So, if the rat just found food in the *right* arm of a T maze, the obvious place to look next time is the *left* arm. The rat knows that there isn't any more food in the right arm because it just ate the food it found there! Indeed, foraging animals such as rats have well-developed spatial representations that allow them to search their environment efficiently. If given the opportunity to explore a complex environment like the multiarm maze shown in **FIGURE 7.13**, rats will systematically go from arm to arm collecting food, rarely returning to an arm they have previously visited (Olton & Samuelson, 1976).

Start

◀ Figure **7.12** **A Simple T Maze** When rats find food in the right arm of a typical T maze, on the next trial, they will often run to the *left* arm of the maze. This contradicts basic principles of operant conditioning: If the behavior of running to the right arm is reinforced, it should be more likely to occur again in the future. However, this behavior is perfectly consistent with a rat's evolutionary preparedness. Like most foraging animals, rats explore their environments in search of food and seldom return to where food has already been found. Quite sensibly, if food has already been found in the right arm of the T maze, the rat will search the left arm next to see if *more* food is there.

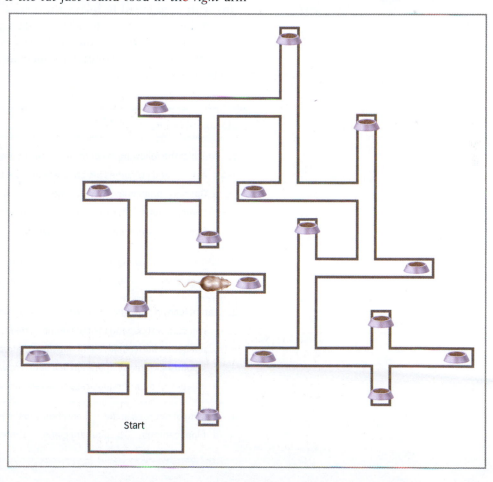

▶ Figure **7.13** **A Complex T Maze** Like many other foraging species, rats placed in a complex T maze such as this one show evidence of their evolutionary preparedness. These rats will systematically travel from arm to arm in search of food, never returning to arms they have already visited.

Start

JOHN WILKINSON ECOSCENE/CORBIS

MILLARD H. SHARP/SCIENCE SOURCE

The misbehavior of organisms: Pigs are biologically predisposed to root out their food just as raccoons are predisposed to wash their food. Trying to train them to behave differently can prove to be an exercise in futility.

Two of Skinner's former students, Keller Breland and Marian Breland, were among the first researchers to discover that it wasn't just rats in T mazes that presented a problem for behaviorists (Breland & Breland, 1961). The Brelands, who made a career of training animals for commercials and movies, often used pigs because pigs are surprisingly good at learning all sorts of tricks. However, they discovered that it was extremely difficult to teach a pig the simple task of dropping coins in a box. Instead of depositing the coins, the pigs persisted in rooting with them as if they were digging them up in soil, tossing them in the air with their snouts, and pushing them around. The Brelands tried to train raccoons at the same task, with different but equally dismal results. The raccoons spent their time rubbing the coins between their paws instead of dropping them in the box.

Having learned the association between the coins and food, the animals began to treat the coins as stand-ins for food. Pigs are biologically predisposed to root out their food, and raccoons have evolved to clean their food by rubbing it with their paws. That is exactly what each species of animal did with the coins.

The Brelands' work shows that each species, including humans, is biologically predisposed to learn some things more readily than others and to respond to stimuli in ways that are consistent with its evolutionary history (Gallistel, 2000). Such adaptive behaviors, however, evolved over extraordinarily long periods and in particular environmental contexts. If those circumstances change, some of the behavioral mechanisms that support learning can lead an organism astray. Raccoons that associated coins with food failed to follow the simple route to obtaining food by dropping the coins in the box; "nature" took over and they wasted time rubbing the coins together. The point is that although much of every organism's behavior results from predispositions sharpened by evolutionary mechanisms, these mechanisms can sometimes have ironic consequences.

SUMMARY QUIZ [7.2]

1. Which of the following is *not* an accurate statement concerning operant conditioning?
   a. Actions and outcomes are critical to operant conditioning.
   b. Operant conditioning involves the reinforcement of behavior.
   c. Complex behaviors cannot be accounted for by operant conditioning.
   d. Operant conditioning has associative mechanisms with roots in evolutionary behavior.

2. Which of the following mechanisms have *no* role in Skinner's approach to behavior?
   a. cognitive   b. neural   c. evolutionary   d. all of the above

3. Latent learning provides evidence for a cognitive element in operant conditioning because
   a. it occurs without any obvious reinforcement.
   b. it requires both positive and negative reinforcement.
   c. it points toward the operation of a neural reward center.
   d. it depends on a stimulus-response relationship.

4. Activity of neurons in the ___ contributes to the process of reinforcement.
   a. hippocampus   b. pituitary gland   c. medial forebrain bundle   d. parietal lobe

Observational Learning: Look at Me

Four-year-old Rodney and his 2-year-old sister Margie had always been told to keep away from the stove. Being a mischievous imp, however, Rodney decided one day to heat up a burner and place his hand over it until the singeing of his flesh led him to recoil, shrieking in pain. Rodney was more scared than hurt, really—and no one hearing this story doubts that he learned something important that day. But little Margie, who stood by watching these events unfold, *also* learned the same lesson. Rodney's story is a behaviorist's textbook example: The administration of punishment led to a learned change in his behavior. But how can we explain Margie's learning? She received neither punishment nor reinforcement—indeed, she didn't even have direct experience with the wicked appliance—yet it's arguable that she's just as likely to keep her hands away from stoves in the future as Rodney is.

? Why might a younger sibling appear to learn faster than a first-born?

observational learning A condition in which learning takes place by watching the actions of others.

Margie's is a case of **observational learning,** in which *learning takes place by watching the actions of others.* In all societies, appropriate social behavior is passed on from generation to generation, not only through deliberate training of the young but also through young people observing the patterns of behaviors of both their elders and one another (Flynn & Whiten, 2008). Tasks such as using chopsticks or learning to operate a TV's remote control are more easily acquired if we watch these activities being carried out before we try ourselves. And anyone who is about to undergo surgery is grateful for observational learning. Just the thought of a generation of surgeons acquiring their surgical techniques using the trial-and-error techniques studied by Thorndike or the shaping of successive approximations that captivated Skinner would make any of us very nervous.

Observational Learning in Humans

In a series of landmark studies, Albert Bandura and his colleagues investigated the parameters of observational learning (Bandura, Ross, & Ross, 1961). The researchers escorted individual preschoolers into a play area filled with toys that 4-year-olds typically like. An adult *model,* someone whose behavior might serve as a guide for others, then entered the room and sat in one corner, where there was a Bobo doll, which is a large inflatable plastic toy with a weighted bottom that allows it to bounce

? What did the Bobo doll experiment show about children and aggressive behavior?

back upright when knocked down. The adult played quietly for a bit but then started aggressing toward the Bobo doll, knocking it down, jumping on it, hitting it with a mallet, kicking it around the room, and yelling "Pow!" and "Kick him!" When the children who observed these actions were later allowed to play with a variety of toys, including a child-size Bobo doll, they were more than twice as likely to interact with it in an aggressive manner as a group of children who hadn't observed the aggressive model (**FIGURE 7.14**).

The children in these studies also showed that they were sensitive to the consequences of the actions they observed. When they saw the adult models being punished for behaving aggressively, the children showed considerably less aggression. When the children observed a model being rewarded and praised for aggressive behavior, they displayed an increase in aggression (Bandura, Ross, & Ross, 1963). The observational learning seen in Bandura's studies has implications for social learning and cultural transmission of behaviors, norms, and values (Bandura, 1977, 1994).

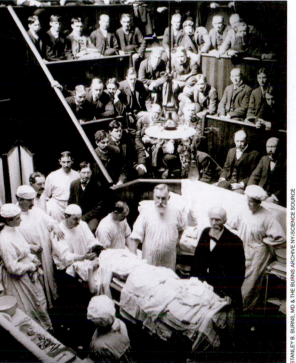

Observational learning plays an important role in surgical training, as illustrated by the medical students observing famed German surgeon Vincenz Czerny (beard and white gown) perform stomach surgery in 1901 at a San Francisco hospital.

© ALBERT BANDURA, DEPT. OF PSYCHOLOGY, STANFORD UNIVERSITY

▲ Figure **7.14 Beating Up Bobo** Children who were exposed to an adult model who behaved aggressively toward a Bobo doll were likely to behave aggressively themselves. This behavior occurred in the absence of any direct reinforcement. Observational learning was responsible for producing the children's behaviors.

Coaches rely on observational learning when they demonstrate techniques to athletes.

AP PHOTO/ROBERT F. BUKATY

Recent research with children has shown that observational learning is well suited to seeding behaviors that can spread widely across a culture through a process called a **diffusion chain,** where *individuals initially learn a behavior by observing another individual perform that behavior and then serve as a model from which other individuals learn the behavior* (Flynn, 2008; Flynn & Whiten, 2008). Experiments investigating the operation of diffusion chains in preschool-aged children have used a procedure in which a child (B) observes an adult model (A) performing a target act, such as using a novel tool to obtain a reward. Then, child B serves as a model for another child, C, who watches B perform the target act, followed by child D observing C perform the target act, and so forth. Initial studies of diffusion chains showed that behaviors such as novel tool use could be spread accurately across 10 or more children (Flynn & Whiten, 2008; Horner et al., 2006). These findings underscore the fact that observational learning is a potentially powerful means of influencing our culture.

Observational learning is important in many domains of everyday life. Sports provide a good example. Coaches rely on observational learning when they demonstrate critical techniques and skills to players, and athletes also have numerous opportunities to observe other athletes perform. But can merely observing a skill result in an improvement in performing that skill, without actually practicing it? A number of studies have shown that observing someone else perform a motor task, ranging from reaching for a target to pressing a sequence of keys, can produce robust learning in the observer—in fact, observational learning sometimes results in just as much learning as does practicing the task itself (Heyes & Foster, 2002; Mattar & Gribble, 2005; Vinter & Perruchet, 2002).

HOT SCIENCE

Even More Reasons to Sleep

Sleep has so much going for it, and yet here's something more. Observational learning can be enhanced by simply closing your eyes and going to sleep. We saw in Chapter 6 that sleep facilitates the consolidation of episodic memories, and other studies indicate that sleep can also facilitate consolidation of motor skills (Walker & Stickgold, 2006). To investigate effects on observational learning, researchers showed participants a video in which a hand performs a finger-tapping task (Van Der Werf et al., 2009). To prevent participants from subtly practicing the task while observing, the researchers required them to press two keys spaced apart on a keyboard using two of the fingers required for the tapping task.

Participants who saw the video in the evening and then went to sleep shortly after the observational learning period showed significant improvements when tested 12 or 24 hours later on the exact sequence they had observed compared with another sequence they had not observed. In contrast, participants who saw the video in the morning and then did not sleep within 12 hours of watching the video showed no such observational learning. The researchers conducted a follow-up experiment to rule out the possibility that the effects of sleep were due to watching the video in the evening instead of the morning: Participants who were tested immediately after observational learning without sleeping—either in the morning or in the evening—showed no benefit on performance. In this case, going to sleep soon after viewing the video was *necessary* in order to benefit from observational learning. If this effect generalizes to other instances of observational learning, coaches may want to consider hauling cots to practices in which they demonstrate techniques to their players.

Observational Learning in Animals

Humans aren't the only creatures capable of learning through observing. In one study, for example, pigeons watched other pigeons in a box get reinforced for either pecking at a feeder or stepping on a bar. When placed in the box later, the pigeons tended to use whatever technique they had observed other pigeons using earlier (Zentall, Sutton, & Sherburne, 1996).

One of the most important questions about observational learning in animals concerns whether monkeys and chimpanzees can learn to use tools by observing tool use in others, the way humans can. In one of the first controlled studies to examine this issue, chimpanzees observed a model (the experimenter) use a metal bar shaped like a T to pull items of food toward him (Tomasello et al., 1987). Compared with a group that did not observe any tool use, these chimpanzees showed more learning when later performing the task themselves. However, the researchers noted that the chimpanzees hardly ever used the tool in the exact same way that the model did. So, in a later experiment, they introduced a novel twist (Nagell, Olguin, & Tomasello, 1993). In one condition, a model used a rake in its normal position (with the teeth pointed to the ground) to capture a food reward, which was rather inefficient because the teeth were widely spaced and the food sometimes slipped between them. In a second condition, the model flipped over the rake so that the teeth were pointed up and the flat edge of the rake touched the ground—a more effective procedure for capturing the food. Both groups that observed tool use performed better when trying to obtain the food themselves than did a control group that did not observe a model use the tool. However, the chimpanzees who observed the more efficient procedure did not use it any more often than did those who observed the less efficient procedure; the two groups performed identically. By contrast, 2-year-old children exposed to the same conditions used the rake in the exact same way that each of the models did in the two observational learning conditions. The chimpanzees seemed only to be learning that the tool could be used to obtain food, whereas the children learned something specific about how to use the tool.

The chimpanzees in these studies had been raised by their mothers in the wild. In a related study, the researchers asked whether chimpanzees who had been raised

diffusion chain A phenomenon that occurs when individuals initially learn a behavior by observing another individual perform that behavior and then serve as a model from which other individuals learn the behavior.

in environments that also included human contact could learn to imitate the exact actions performed by a model (Tomasello, Savage-Rumbaugh, & Kruger, 1993). The answer was a resounding "yes": Chimpanzees raised in a more human-like environment showed more specific observational learning than did those who had been reared by their mothers, performing similarly to human children. This finding led Tomasello and colleagues (1993) to put forward what they termed the "enculturation hypothesis": Being raised in a human culture has a profound effect on the cognitive abilities of chimpanzees, especially their ability to understand the intentions of others when performing tasks such as using tools, which in turn increases their observational learning capacities. Others have criticized the hypothesis (Bering, 2004), noting that there is relatively little evidence in support of it beyond the results of this one study by Tomasello and colleagues (1993).

However, more recent research has found something similar in capuchin monkeys, which are known for their tool use in the wild, such as employing branches or stone hammers to crack open nuts (Boinski, Quatrone, & Swartz, 2000; Fragaszy et al., 2004) or using stones to dig up buried roots (Moura & Lee, 2004). Fredman and Whiten (2008) studied monkeys that had been reared either in the wild by their mothers or by human families in Israel as part of a project to train the monkeys to aid quadriplegics. A model demonstrated two ways of using a screwdriver to gain access to a food reward hidden in a box. Some monkeys observed the model poke through a hole in the center of the box, whereas others watched him pry open the lid at the rim of the box (see **FIGURE 7.15**). A control group did not observe any use of the tool. Both mother-reared and human-reared monkeys showed evidence of observational learning compared with the controls, but the human-reared monkeys carried out the exact action they had observed more often than the mother-reared monkeys.

While this evidence implies that there is a cultural influence on the cognitive processes that support observational learning, the researchers noted that the effects on observational learning could be attributed to any number of influences on the human-reared monkeys, including more experience with tools, more attention to a model's behavior, or, as originally suggested by Tomasello and colleagues (1993), increased sensitivity to the intentions of others. Thus, more work is needed to understand the exact nature of those processes (Bering, 2004; Tomasello & Call, 2004).

▲ Figure **7.15** **Observational Learning** Monkeys who had been reared by their mothers in the wild or by human families either watched a model poke a screwdriver through a hole in the center of a box to obtain a food reward (top) or pry open the lid (bottom). Both groups showed some evidence of observational learning, but the human-reared monkeys were more likely to carry out the exact action they watched.

Neural Elements of Observational Learning

Observational learning involves a neural component as well. As you read in Chapter 3, *mirror neurons* in the frontal and parietal lobes fire when an animal performs an action, such as when a monkey reaches for a food item (**FIGURE 7.16**). Mirror neurons also fire when an animal watches someone *else* perform the same specific task (Rizzolatti & Craighero, 2004). For example, monkeys' mirror neurons fired when they observed humans grasping for a piece of food, either to eat it or to place it in a container (Fogassi et al., 2005).

? What do mirror neurons do?

Mirror neurons occur in humans too. Studies of observational learning in healthy adults have shown that watching someone else perform a task engages some of the same brain regions that are activated when people actually perform the task themselves. Do you consider yourself a good dancer? Have you ever watched someone who is a good dancer—a friend or maybe a celebrity on *Dancing with the Stars*—in the hope of improving your own dance floor moves? In a recent fMRI study, participants performed two tasks for several days prior to scanning: practicing dance sequences to unfamiliar techno-dance songs and watching music videos containing other dance sequences accompanied by unfamiliar techno-dance songs (Cross et al., 2009). They were then scanned while viewing videos of sequences that they had previously danced or watched as well as videos of untrained sequences (i.e., sequences they had neither danced nor watched).

Analysis of the fMRI data revealed that in comparison with the unencountered sequences, viewing the previously danced or watched sequences recruited a largely similar brain network, including regions considered to be part of the mirror-neuron system. The results of a surprise dancing test given to participants after the conclusion of scanning showed that performance was better on sequences previously watched than on the untrained sequences, demonstrating significant observational learning, but was best of all on the previously danced sequences (Cross et al., 2009). So, while watching *Dancing with the Stars* might indeed improve your dancing skills, practicing on the dance floor should help even more.

Related evidence indicates that observational learning of some motor skills relies on the motor cortex, which is known to be critical for motor learning. For example, when participants watch another individual engage in a task that involves making a complex reaching movement, significant observational learning occurs (Mattar & Gribble, 2005). To examine whether the observational learning depends on the motor cortex, researchers applied transcranial magnetic stimulation, or TMS, to the motor cortex just after participants observed performance of the reaching movement (as you learned in Chapter 3, TMS results in a temporary disruption in the function of the brain region to which it is applied). Strikingly, applying TMS to the motor cortex greatly reduced the amount of observational learning, whereas applying TMS to a control region outside the motor cortex had no effect on observational learning (Brown, Wilson, & Gribble, 2009).

These findings indicate that some kinds of observational learning are grounded in brain regions that are essential for action. When one organism patterns its actions on another organism's behaviors, learning is speeded up and potentially dangerous errors—think of Margie, who won't burn her hand on the stove—are prevented.

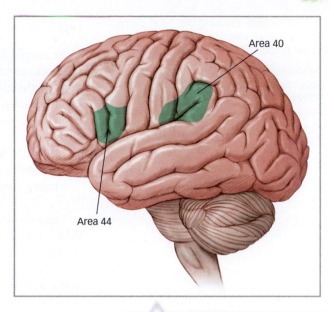

▲ Figure **7.16** **Mirror Neuron System** Regions in the frontal lobe (area 44) and parietal lobe (area 40) are thought to be part of the mirror-neuron system in humans.

Observing skilled dancers, such as Nicole Scherzinger and Derek Hough on *Dancing with the Stars,* engages many of the same brain regions as does actual dance practice and can produce significant learning.

SUMMARY QUIZ [7.3]

1. Which is true of observational learning?
   a. Although humans learn by observing others, nonhuman animals seem to lack this capability.
   b. If a child sees an adult engaging in a certain behavior, the child is more likely to imitate the behavior.
   c. Humans learn complex behaviors more readily by trial and error than by observation.
   d. Observational learning is limited to transmission of information between individuals of the same species.

2. Which of the following mechanisms does *not* help form the basis of observational learning?
   a. attention   b. perception   c. punishment   d. memory

3. Neural research indicates that observational learning is closely tied to brain areas that are involved in
   a. memory.   b. vision.   c. action.   d. emotion.

implicit learning Learning that takes place largely without awareness of the process or the products of information acquisition.

habituation A general process in which repeated or prolonged exposure to a stimulus results in a gradual reduction in response.

Implicit Learning: Under the Wires

Most people are attuned to linguistic, social, emotional, and sensorimotor events in the world around them—so much so that they gradually build up internal representations of those patterns that were acquired without explicit awareness. This process is often called **implicit learning,** or *learning that takes place largely independent of awareness of both the process and the products of information acquisition*. Because it occurs without awareness, implicit learning is knowledge that sneaks in "under the wires." As an example we've already seen, delay conditioning does not require awareness of the contingency between the CS and US, whereas trace conditioning does.

? How can you learn something without being aware of it?

Some forms of learning start out explicitly but become more implicit over time. When you first learned to drive a car, for example, you probably devoted a lot of attention to the many movements and sequences that need to be carried out simultaneously ("step lightly on the accelerator while you push the turn indicator and look in the rearview mirror while you turn the steering wheel"). That complex interplay of motions is now probably quite effortless and automatic for you. Explicit learning has become implicit over time. These distinctions in learning might remind you of similar distinctions in memory—and for good reason. In Chapter 6, you read about the differences between *implicit* and *explicit* memories. Do implicit and explicit learning mirror implicit and explicit memory?

? How are learning and memory linked?

It's not that simple, but it is true that learning and memory are inextricably linked. Learning produces memories, and, conversely, the existence of memories implies that knowledge was acquired, that experience was registered and recorded in the brain, or that learning has taken place.

Habituation: A Simple Case of Implicit Learning

One very basic form of implicit learning is known as **habituation,** *a general process in which repeated or prolonged exposure to a stimulus results in a gradual reduction in responding*. If you've ever lived under the flight path of your local airport, near railroad tracks, or by a busy highway, you've probably noticed the deafening noise when you first moved in. You probably also noticed that, after a while, the noise wasn't quite so deafening anymore and that eventually you ignored it. This welcome reduction in responding reflects the operation of habituation.

Habituation is considered a form of implicit learning in part because it occurs even in the simplest organisms that do not have the brain structures necessary for explicit learning, such as the hippocampus (Eichenbaum, 2008; Squire & Kandel, 1999). For example, in Chapter 6 you learned about the sea slug *Aplysia*. Even though *Aplysia* has no hippocampus, it exhibits habituation. In rats, which can exhibit both explicit and implicit learning, habituation is unaffected by lesions to the hippocampus, which impair explicit learning (Lee, Hunsaker, & Kesner, 2005).

? Why won't the noise from a highway near your home keep you awake at night?

Even in human beings, habituation can occur in the absence of explicit learning or memory. Consider a study in which two amnesic patients exhibited a form of implicit learning related to habituation in an experiment that explored how appetite changes as a function of experience (Higgs et al., 2008). Fifteen minutes after eating sandwiches to the point that they felt full, both amnesic patients and healthy control subjects indicated less desire for, and liking of, those sandwiches than they had prior to eating them. They also expressed less desire to eat the sandwiches than other foods that they had sampled lightly 15 minutes earlier. But the amnesic patients had

Living near a busy highway can be unpleasant. Most people who live near major highways become habituated to the sound of traffic.

MICHAEL KLINEC/ALAMY

no explicit memory that they had eaten any sandwiches 15 minutes earlier! Clearly, their reduction in liking and desire was based on implicit learning.

Habituation usually doesn't last very long. In most cases, a person will exhibit the original reaction if enough time has gone by. If you live near an airport and have habituated to the sounds of the jets, when you return home from a 2-week vacation, the roar of the jets will probably be just as loud as ever.

Cognitive Approaches to Implicit Learning

Most children, by the time they are 6 or 7 years old, are linguistically and socially fairly sophisticated. Yet most children have very little explicit awareness of what they have actually learned. As an example, although children are often given explicit rules of social conduct ("Don't chew with your mouth open"), they learn how to behave in a civilized way through experience. They're probably not aware of when or how they learned a particular course of action and may not even be able to state the general principle underlying their behavior. Yet most kids have learned not to eat with their feet, to listen when they are spoken to, and not to kick the dog.

In early laboratory studies investigating implicit learning, research participants were shown 15 or 20 letter strings and asked to memorize them. The letter strings, which at first glance look like nonsense syllables, were actually formed using a complex set of rules called an *artificial grammar* (see **FIGURE 7.17**). Participants were not told anything about the rules, but with experience, they gradually developed a vague, intuitive sense of the "correctness" of particular letter groupings and could get between 60% and 70% correct—but they were unable to provide much in the way of explicit awareness of the rules and regularities that they were using (Reber, 1967, 1996). The experience is like when you come across a sentence with a grammatical error—you are immediately aware that something is wrong. But unless you are a trained linguist, you'll probably find it difficult to articulate which rules of English grammar were violated.

Other studies of implicit learning have used a *serial reaction time* task (Nissen & Bullemer, 1987). Here research participants are presented with five small boxes on a computer screen. Each box lights up briefly, and when it does, the person is asked to press the button that is just underneath that box as quickly as possible. As with the artificial grammar task, the sequence of lights appears to be random, but in fact it follows a pattern. Research participants eventually get faster with practice as they learn to anticipate which box is most likely to light up next. But, if asked, they are generally unaware that there is a pattern to the lights.

Implicit learning is remarkably resistant to various disorders that are known to affect explicit learning. A group of patients suffering from various psychoses were so severely impaired that they could not solve simple problems that college students had little difficulty with. Yet these patients were able to solve an artificial grammar learning task about as well as college students (Abrams & Reber, 1988). Other studies have found that profoundly amnesic patients not only show normal implicit memories but also display virtually normal implicit learning of artificial grammar (Knowlton, Ramus, & Squire, 1992). In fact, these patients made accurate judgments about novel letter strings even though they had essentially no explicit memory of having been in the learning phase of the experiment! In contrast, several studies have shown that dyslexic children, who fail to acquire reading skills despite normal intelligence and good educational opportunities, exhibit deficits in implicit learning of artificial grammars (Pavlidou, Williams, & Kelly, 2009) and motor and spatial sequences on the serial reaction time task (Bennett et al., 2008; Orban, Lungu, & Doyon, 2008; Stoodley et al., 2008). These findings

▼ Figure **7.17** **Artificial Grammar and Implicit Learning** These are examples of letter strings formed by an artificial grammar. Research participants are exposed to the rules of the grammar and are later tested on new letter strings. Participants show reliable accuracy at distinguishing the valid, grammatical strings from the invalid, nongrammatical strings even though they usually can't explicitly state the rule they are following when making such judgments. Using an artificial grammar is one way of studying implicit learning (Reber, 1996).

Grammatical Strings	Nongrammatical Strings
VXJJ	VXTJJ
XXVT	XVTVVJ
VJTVXJ	VJTTVTV
VJTVTV	VJTXXVJ
XXXXVX	XXXVTJJ

Implicit learning, which is involved in acquiring and retaining the skills needed to ride a bicycle, tends to be less affected by age than explicit learning.

MICHAEL BLANN/GETTY IMAGES

suggest that problems with implicit learning play an important role in developmental dyslexia and need to be taken into account when developing remedial programs (Stoodley et al., 2008).

Implicit and Explicit Learning Use Distinct Neural Pathways

The fact that patients suffering amnesia show intact implicit learning strongly suggests that the brain structures that underlie implicit leaning are distinct from those that underlie explicit learning. As we learned in Chapter 6, amnesic patients are characterized by lesions to the hippocampus and nearby structures in the medial temporal lobe; accordingly, these regions are not necessary for implicit learning (Bayley, Frascino, & Squire, 2005a). What's more, it appears that distinct regions of the brain may be activated depending on how people approach a task.

For example, in one study, participants saw a series of dot patterns, each of which looked like an array of stars in the night sky (Reber et al., 2003). Actually, all the stimuli were constructed to conform to an underlying prototypical dot pattern. The dots, however, varied so much that it was virtually impossible for a viewer to guess that they all had this common structure. Before the experiment began, half of the participants were told about the existence of the prototype; in other words, they were given instructions that encouraged explicit processing. The others were given standard implicit-learning instructions: They were told nothing other than to attend to the dot patterns.

The participants were then scanned as they made decisions about new dot patterns, attempting to categorize them into those that conformed to the prototype and those that did not. Interestingly, both groups performed equally well on this task, correctly classifying about 65% of the new dot patterns. However, the brain scans revealed that the two groups were making these decisions using very different parts of their brains (see **FIGURE 7.18**). Participants who were given the explicit instructions showed *increased* brain activity in the prefrontal cortex, parietal cortex, hippocampus, and a variety of other areas known to be associated with the processing of explicit memories. Those given the implicit instructions showed *decreased* brain activation primarily in the occipital region, which is involved in visual processing. This finding suggests that participants recruited distinct brain structures in different ways depending on whether they were approaching the task using explicit or implicit learning.

Other studies have begun to pinpoint the brain regions that are involved in two of the most commonly used implicit-learning tasks: artificial grammar learning and sequence learning on the serial reaction time task. Several fMRI studies have shown that Broca's area—which, as you learned in Chapter 3, plays a key role in language production—is turned on during artificial grammar learning (Forkstam et al., 2006; Petersson, Forkstam, & Ingvar, 2004). Further, activating Broca's area by applying electrical stimulation to

? What technology shows that implicit and explicit learning are associated with separate structures of the brain?

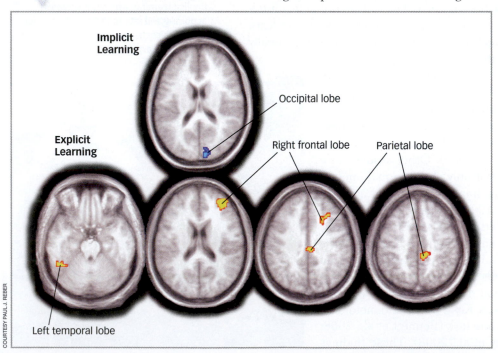

▼ Figure **7.18** **Implicit and Explicit Learning Activate Different Brain Areas** Research participants were scanned with fMRI while engaged in either implicit or explicit learning about the categorization of dot patterns. The occipital region (in blue) showed decreased brain activity after implicit learning. The areas in yellow, orange, and red showed increased brain activity during explicit learning, including the left temporal lobe (far left), right frontal lobe (second from left and second from right), and parietal lobe (second from right and far right) (Reber et al., 2003).

Implicit Learning

Explicit Learning

Occipital lobe

Right frontal lobe

Parietal lobe

Left temporal lobe

COURTESY PAUL J. REBER

the nearby scalp enhances implicit learning of artificial grammar, most likely by facilitating acquisition of grammatical rules (De Vries et al., 2010). In contrast, the motor cortex appears critical for sequence learning on the serial reaction time task. When the motor cortex was temporarily disabled by the application of a recently developed type of TMS that lasts for a long time, so that participants could perform the task without having TMS constantly applied while they were doing so, sequence learning was abolished (Wilkinson et al., 2010).

SUMMARY QUIZ [7.4]

1. What kind of learning takes place largely independent of awareness of both the process and the products of information acquisition?

   a. latent learning
   b. implicit learning
   c. observational learning
   d. conscious learning

2. The process in which repeated or prolonged exposure to a stimulus results in a gradual reduction in responding is called

   a. habituation.
   b. explicit learning.
   c. serial reaction time.
   d. delay conditioning.

3. Responding to implicit instructions results in decreased brain activation in which part of the brain?

   a. the hippocampus
   b. the parietal cortex
   c. the prefrontal cortex
   d. the occipital region

Where Do You Stand?

Learning for Rewards or for Its Own Sake?

The principles of operant conditioning have found their way into mainstream culture. The least psychology-savvy parent intuitively understands that rewarding a child's good behavior should make that behavior more likely to occur in the future; the "law of effect" may mean nothing to this parent, but the principle is readily appreciated nonetheless. And if reward shapes good behavior, then more reward must produce exemplary behavior, often in the form of good grades, high test scores, and overall clean living. So many parents shower children with gifts whenever a report card shows improvement. And it's not just the parents.

In fact, www.rewardsforgrades.com is a website that lists organizations that will give students external reinforcements for good grades, high test scores, perfect school attendance, and other behaviors that students are usually expected to produce just because they're students. Krispy Kreme offers a free doughnut for each A, Blockbuster gives free kids' movie rentals, Chick-fil-A rewards making the honor roll and achieving perfect attendance with free kids' meals, and Limited Too offers a $5 discount on merchandise if you present a report card "with passing grades" (which, in many school districts, might mean all Ds).

Before you get too excited by visions of a "grades for junk food" scam, you should know that there are often age limits on these offers. However, if you're a precocious fourth grader reading this textbook, feel free to cash in on the goods. Or if you happen to be enrolled at Wichita State University, you already might be familiar with the Cash for Grades initiative. The proposal is that an 8%-per-credit-hour increase to student fees would be used to then reward good student performance: $624 to a student with a 3.5 GPA at the end of a semester, $804 for straight As.

Where do you stand on this issue? Is this much ado about nothing or too much of a good thing? Some proponents of rewarding good academic performance argue that it mirrors the real world that, presumably, academic performance is preparing students to enter. After all, in most jobs, better performance is reinforced with better salaries, so why not model that in the school system? On the other hand, shouldn't the search for knowledge be reward enough? Is the subtle shift away from wanting to learn for its own sake to wanting to learn for a doughnut harmful in the long run?

Chapter Review

SUMMARY

Classical Conditioning: One Thing Leads to Another

► In classical conditioning, a neutral stimulus (the conditioned stimulus, or CS) is paired with a meaningful event or stimulus (the unconditioned stimulus, or US). Eventually the CS all by itself elicits a conditioned response (CR).

► Classical conditioning was embraced by behaviorists such as John B. Watson, who believed that no higher-level functions, such as thinking or awareness, needed to be invoked to understand behavior.

► Later researchers showed, however, that even simple species set up expectations and are sensitive to the degree to which the CS functions as a genuine predictor of the US, indicating that classical conditioning involves some degree of cognition.

► Different parts of the brain are involved in different types of classical conditioning: the cerebellum in delay conditioning, the hippocampus in trace conditioning, and the amygdala in fear conditioning.

► Each species is biologically predisposed to acquire particular CS-US associations based on its evolutionary history.

Operant Conditioning: Reinforcements from the Environment

► Operant conditioning is a process by which behaviors are reinforced and therefore become more likely to occur.

► Operant conditioning has clear cognitive components: Organisms behave as though they have expectations about the outcomes of their actions and adjust their actions accordingly.

Cognitive influences can sometimes override the trial-by-trial feedback that usually influences learning.

► Studies with both animals and people highlight the operation of a neural reward center that affects learning.

► The associative mechanisms that underlie operant conditioning have their roots in evolutionary biology.

Observational Learning: Look at Me

► Observational learning is an important process by which species gather information about the world around them, and it appears to be well suited for transmission of novel behaviors across individuals.

► Chimpanzees and monkeys can benefit from observational learning, especially those reared in settings that include humans.

► The mirror-neuron system becomes active during observational learning, and many of the same brain regions are active during observation and performance of a skill.

Implicit Learning: Under the Wires

► Implicit learning is a process that detects, learns, and stores patterns without the application of explicit awareness on the part of the learner.

► Simple behaviors such as habituation can reflect implicit learning, but complex behaviors, such as language use or socialization, can also be learned through an implicit process.

► Neuroimaging studies indicate that implicit and explicit learning recruit distinct brain structures, sometimes in different ways.

KEY TERMS

learning (p. 200)

classical conditioning (p. 200)

unconditioned stimulus (US) (p. 200)

unconditioned response (UR) (p. 200)

conditioned stimulus (CS) (p. 200)

conditioned response (CR) (p. 201)

acquisition (p. 203)

second-order conditioning (p. 203)

extinction (p. 203)

spontaneous recovery (p. 204)

generalization (p. 204)

discrimination (p. 204)

biological preparedness (p. 209)

operant conditioning (p. 210)

law of effect (p. 211)

operant behavior (p. 211)

reinforcer (p. 211)

punisher (p. 211)

fixed interval schedule (FI) (p. 214)

variable interval schedule (VI) (p. 214)

fixed ratio schedule (FR) (p. 215)

variable ratio schedule (VR) (p. 215)

intermittent reinforcement (p. 215)

intermittent-reinforcement effect (p. 215)

shaping (p. 216)

latent learning (p. 218)

cognitive map (p. 219)

observational learning (p. 223)

diffusion chain (p. 224)

implicit learning (p. 228)

habituation (p. 228)

CHANGING MINDS

1. A friend is taking a class in childhood education. "Back in the old days," she says, "teachers used physical punishment, but of course that's not allowed any more. Now a good teacher should only use reinforcement. When children behave, teachers should provide positive reinforcement, like praise. When children misbehave, teachers should provide negative reinforcement, like scolding or withholding privileges." What is your friend misunderstanding about reinforcement? Can you

give better examples of how negative reinforcement could be productively applied in an elementary school classroom?

2. A friend of your family is trying to train her daughter to make her bed every morning. You suggest she try positive reinforcement. A month later, the woman reports back to you. "It's not working very well," she says. "Every time she makes her bed, I put a gold star on the calendar, and at the end of the week, if there are seven gold stars, I give Vicky a reward—a piece of licorice. But so far, she's only earned the licorice twice." How could you explain why the desired behavior—bed making—might not increase as a result of this reinforcement procedure?

3. While studying for the exam, you ask your study partner to provide a definition of classical conditioning. "In classical conditioning," she says, "there's a stimulus, the CS, that predicts an upcoming event, the US. Usually, it's something bad, like an

electric shock, nausea, or a frightening loud noise. The learner makes a response, the CR, in order to prevent the US. Sometimes the US is good, like food for Pavlov's dogs, and then the learner makes the response in order to earn the US." What's wrong with this definition?

4. One of your classmates announces that he liked the last chapter, on memory, better than the current chapter, on learning. "I want to be a psychiatrist," he says, "so I mostly care about human learning. Conditioning might be a really powerful way to train animals to push levers or perform tricks. But it really doesn't have much relevance to how humans learn things." How similar is learning in humans and other animals? What real-world examples can you provide to show that conditioning does occur in humans?

CRITICAL THINKING QUESTIONS

1. Little Albert was exposed to the sight of a rat paired with a distressing loud noise; with repeated pairings of the rat and the noise, he began to show a CR to the rat—crying and trembling. Many people break into a cold sweat at the mere sound of a dentist's drill. How might this reaction be explained as a conditioned emotional response? [*Hint*: Assuming that human babies aren't born with a natural fear of drill sounds, then the cold sweat is a learned response (CR). What are the CS and US?]

2. In operant conditioning, a reinforcer is a stimulus or event that increases the likelihood of the behavior that led to it, and a punisher is a stimulus or event that decreases the likelihood of the behavior that led to it. Suppose you are the mayor of a suburban town and you want to institute some new policies to decrease the number of drivers who speed on residential streets. How might you use punishment to decrease the behavior you desire (speeding)? How might you use reinforcement to increase the behavior you desire (safe driving)? Based on the principles of operant conditioning you read about in this chapter, which approach do you think might be most fruitful?

3. In fixed ratio (FR) schedules, reinforcement is delivered after a specific number of responses have been made. In variable ratio (VR) schedules, reinforcement is delivered after an average number of responses. Both FR and VR schedules are examples of intermittent-reinforcement schedules, because only some responses are followed by reinforcement, and they are both more resistant to extinction than continuous-reinforcement schedules, in which a reinforcement is delivered after every response.

Imagine you own an insurance company and you want to encourage your salespeople to sell as much merchandise as possible. You decide to give them bonuses, based on the number of items sold. How might you set up a system of bonuses using an FR schedule? Using a VR schedule? Which system do you think would encourage your salespeople to work harder, in terms of making more sales?

4. Observational learning takes place when one individual watches and learns from the actions of others. By contrast, in classical conditioning, learning takes place when an individual directly experiences the consequences (US) associated with a stimulus or event (CS).

Monkeys can be classically conditioned to fear objects such as snakes or flowers if those objects are paired with an aversive US, such as an electric shock. Monkeys can also learn to fear snakes through observational learning if they see another monkey reacting with fear to the sight of a snake. But monkeys cannot be trained to fear flowers through observational learning—no matter how many times they watch another monkey who has been conditioned to fear the same flower. How does the principle of biological preparedness account for this finding?

5. In habituation, repeated or prolonged exposure to a stimulus that initially evoked a response results in a gradual reduction of that response.

How might psychologists use the concept of habituation to explain the fact that today's action movies tend to show much more graphic violence than movies of the 1980s, which in turn tended to show more graphic violence than movies of the 1950s?

ANSWERS TO SUMMARY QUIZZES

Summary Quiz [7.1] 1. b; 2. c; 3. d; 4. a
Summary Quiz [7.2] 1. c; 2. d; 3. a; 4. c
Summary Quiz [7.3] 1. b; 2. c; 3. c
Summary Quiz [7.4] 1. b; 2. a; 3. d

Need more help? Additional resources are located at the book's free companion website at:
www.worthpublishers.com/schacterbrief2e

8

Emotion and Motivation

LEONARDO IS 5 YEARS OLD AND CUTE AS a button. He can do many of the things that other 5-year-olds can do—solve puzzles, build towers of blocks, and play guessing games with grown-ups. But unlike other 5-year-olds, Leonardo has never been proud of his abilities, angry at his mother, or bored with his lessons. He has never laughed or cried. That's because Leonardo has a condition that makes him unable to experience emotions of any kind.

His mother has spent years teaching him how to make the facial expressions that indicate emotions such as surprise and sadness as well as how to detect those facial expressions in others. Leonardo now knows that he should smile when someone says something nice to him and that he should raise his eyebrow once in a while to show interest in what people are saying. Leonardo is a quick learner, and he's gotten so good at this that when strangers interact with him, they find it hard to believe that deep down inside he is feeling nothing at all.

So when Leonardo's mother smiles at him, he always smiles back. Yet she is keenly aware that Leonardo is merely making the faces he was taught to make and that he doesn't really love her.

▶ Leonardo is a typical 5-year-old in some ways, but not all.

ALEX CAO/JUPITER IMAGES

Leonardo and his "mom," MIT Professor Cynthia Breazeal.

"I never realized they had feelings."

But that's okay. Although Leonardo cannot return her affection, Dr. Cynthia Breazeal still considers him one of the greatest robots she's ever designed (Breazeal, 2009).

YES, LEONARDO IS A MACHINE. HE CAN SEE AND HEAR; he can remember and reason. But despite his adorable smile and knowing wink, he can't feel a thing, and that makes him infinitely different from us. Our ability to love and to hate, to be amused and annoyed, to feel elated and devastated is an essential element of our humanity, and a person who could not feel these things would seem a lot like a robot to the rest of us. But what exactly are these things we call emotions and why are they so essential? In this chapter we will explore these questions.

We'll start by discussing the nature of emotions and seeing how they relate to the states of our bodies and our brains. Next we'll see how people express their emotions and how they use those expressions to communicate with one another. Finally, we'll examine the essential role that emotions play in motivation—how they inform us and how they compel us do everything from making war to making love.

Emotional Experience: The Feeling Machine

Leonardo doesn't know what love feels likes and there's no way to teach him, because trying to describe the feeling of love to someone who has never experienced it is a bit like trying to describe the color green to someone who was born blind. We could tell Leonardo what causes the feeling ("It happens whenever I see Marilynn") and we

It is almost impossible not to feel something when you look at this photograph, and it is almost impossible to say exactly what you are feeling.

could tell him about its consequences ("I breathe hard and say goofy stuff"), but in the end these descriptions would miss the point because the essential feature of love—like the essential feature of all emotions—is the *experience*. It *feels* like something to love, and what it feels like is love's defining attribute.

What Is Emotion?

How can we study something whose defining attribute defies description? Although people can't always say what an emotional experience feels like, they can usually say how similar one experience is to another ("Love is more like happiness than like anger"). By asking people to rate the similarity of dozens of emotional experiences, psychologists have been able to use a technique known as *multidimensional scaling* to create a map of those experiences. The mathematics behind this technique is complex, but the logic is simple. If you drew up a list of the distances between half a dozen U.S. cities, handed the list to a friend, and challenged her to turn those distances into a map, your friend would have to draw a map of the United States (see **FIGURE 8.1**). Why? Because there is no other map that allows every city to appear at precisely the right distance from every other.

The same technique can be used to generate a map of the emotional landscape. If you listed the similarity of a large number of emotional experiences (assigning smaller "distances" to those that feel similar and larger "distances" to those that feel dissimilar) and then challenged a friend to incorporate them into a map,

? Why do psychologists use multidimensional scaling?

your friend would be forced to draw a map like the one shown in **FIGURE 8.2**. This is the unique map that allows every emotional experience to be precisely the right "distance" from every other. What good is this map? As it turns out, maps don't just show how close things are to one another: They also reveal the *dimensions* on which those things vary. For example, the map in **FIGURE 8.2** reveals that emotional experiences differ on two dimensions called *valence* (how positive or negative the experience is) and *arousal* (how active or

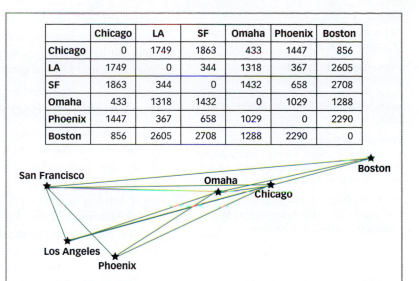

	Chicago	LA	SF	Omaha	Phoenix	Boston
Chicago	0	1749	1863	433	1447	856
LA	1749	0	344	1318	367	2605
SF	1863	344	0	1432	658	2708
Omaha	433	1318	1432	0	1029	1288
Phoenix	1447	367	658	1029	0	2290
Boston	856	2605	2708	1288	2290	0

▲ Figure **8.1** **From Distances to Maps** Knowing the distances between things—like cities, for example—allows us to draw a map that reveals the dimensions on which they vary.

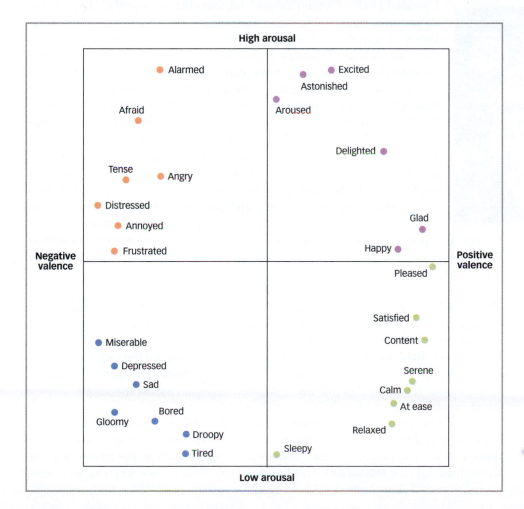

◀ Figure **8.2** **Two Dimensions of Emotion** Just as cities can be mapped by their longitude and latitude, emotions can be mapped by their arousal and valence.

emotion A positive or negative experience that is associated with a particular pattern of physiological activity.

James-Lange theory A theory which asserts that stimuli trigger activity in the autonomic nervous system, which in turn produces an emotional experience in the brain.

Cannon-Bard theory A theory which asserts that a stimulus simultaneously triggers activity in the autonomic nervous system and emotional experience in the brain.

two-factor theory A theory which asserts that emotions are inferences about the causes of physiological arousal.

passive the experience is). As such, **emotion** can be defined as *a positive or negative experience that is associated with a particular pattern of physiological activity.* As you are about to see, the first step in understanding emotion involves understanding how experience and physiological activity are related.

The Emotional Body

You probably think that if you walked into your kitchen right now and saw a bear nosing through the cupboards, you would feel fear, your heart would start to pound, and the muscles in your legs would prepare you for running. Presumably away. But in the late 19th century, William James suggested that the events that produce an emotion might actually happen in the opposite order: First you see the bear, then your heart starts pounding and your leg muscles contract, and *then* you experience fear, which is nothing more or less than your experience of your physiological response. Psychologist Carl Lange suggested something similar at about the same time; thus this idea is now known as the **James-Lange theory** of emotion, which asserts that *stimuli trigger activity in the autonomic nervous system, which in turn produces an emotional experience in the brain.* According to this theory, emotional experience is the consequence—not the cause—of our physiological reactions to objects and events in the world.

But James's former student, Walter Cannon, disagreed, and together with *his* student, Philip Bard, Cannon proposed an alternative to James's theory. The **Cannon-Bard theory** of emotion suggested that *a stimulus simultaneously triggers activity in the autonomic nervous system and emotional experience in the brain* (Bard, 1934; Cannon, 1927). Cannon favored his own theory over the James-Lange theory for several reasons. First, the autonomic nervous system reacts too slowly to account for the rapid onset of emotional experience. For example, a blush is an autonomic response to embarrassment that takes 15 to 30 seconds to occur, and yet one can feel embarrassed long before that, so how could the blush be the cause of the feeling? Second, people often have difficulty accurately detecting changes in their own autonomic activity, such as their heart rates. If people cannot detect increases in their heart rates, then how can they experience those increases as an emotion? Third, nonemotional stimuli—such as temperature—can cause the same pattern of autonomic activity that emotional stimuli do, so why don't people feel afraid when they get a fever? Finally, Cannon argued that there simply weren't enough unique patterns of autonomic activity to account for all the unique emotional experiences people have. If many different emotional experiences are associated with the same pattern of autonomic activity, then how could that pattern of activity be the sole determinant of the emotional experience?

These are all good questions, and about 30 years after Cannon asked them, psychologists Stanley Schachter and Jerome Singer supplied some answers (Schachter & Singer, 1962). James and Lange were right, they claimed, to equate emotion with the perception of one's bodily reactions. But Cannon and Bard were right, they claimed, to note that there are not nearly enough distinct bodily reactions to account for the wide variety of emotions that human beings can experience. Whereas James and Lange had suggested that different emotions are *different experiences* of *different patterns* of bodily activity, Schachter and Singer's **two-factor theory** of emotion claimed that *emotions are inferences about the causes of physiological arousal* (see **FIGURE 8.3**). So when you see a bear in your kitchen, your heart begins to pound. Your brain quickly scans the environment, looking for a reasonable

Did Princess Kate make Prince William blush by embarrassing him, or did she embarrass him by making him blush? The experience of embarrassment precedes blushing by up to 30 seconds, so it is unlikely that blushing is the cause of the emotional experience.

? How did the two-factor theory of emotion expand on earlier theories?

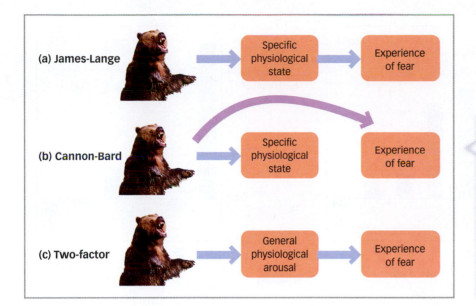

► Figure **8.3** **Classic Theories of Emotion** Classic theories make different claims about the origins of emotion. (a) The James-Lange theory suggests that stimuli trigger specific physiological states, which are then experienced as emotions. (b) The Cannon-Bard theory suggests that stimuli trigger both specific physiological states and emotional experiences independently. (c) The two-factor theory suggests that stimuli trigger general physiological arousal whose cause the brain interprets, and this interpretation leads to emotional experience.

explanation for all that pounding, and notices, of all things, a bear. Having noticed both a bear and a pounding heart, your brain then does what brains do so well: It puts two and two together, makes a logical inference, and interprets your arousal as fear. In other words, when you are physiologically aroused in the presence of something you think should scare you, you label that arousal as *fear*. But if you have precisely the same bodily response in the presence of something you think should delight you, then you label that arousal as *excitement*. According to Schachter and Singer, people have the same physiological reaction to all emotional stimuli, but they interpret that reaction differently on different occasions.

Schachter and Singer tested their theory by giving participants an injection of epinephrine, which causes increases in blood pressure, heart rate, blood flow to the brain, blood sugar levels, and respiration. Participants then interacted with another person who, unbeknownst to them, was a confederate of the experimenter and had been instructed to act in a particular way. Schachter and Singer predicted that those participants who experienced epinephrine-induced arousal, but who hadn't been informed of the injection's effects, would seek an explanation for their arousal—and that the confederate's behavior would supply it. In fact, that's what happened. When the confederate acted goofy, the participants concluded that they themselves were feeling *happy*; when the confederate acted nasty, they concluded that they themselves were feeling *angry*.

How has the two-factor model fared in the last half century? One of the model's claims has fared very well. Research has shown that when people are aroused—say, by having them ride an exercise bike in the laboratory—they subsequently find attractive people more attractive, annoying people more annoying, and funny cartoons funnier, as if they were interpreting their exercise-induced arousal as attraction, annoyance, or amusement (Byrne et al., 1975; Dutton & Aron, 1974; Zillmann, Katcher, & Milavsky, 1972). It appears that the two-factor model is right when it suggests that people make inferences about the causes of their arousal and that these inferences influence their emotional experience (Lindquist & Barrett, 2008).

However, research has not been so kind to the model's claim that all emotional experiences are merely different interpretations of the same bodily state. For example, researchers measured participants' physiological reactions as they experienced six different emotions and found that anger, fear, and sadness each produced a higher heart rate than disgust and that anger produced a larger increase in finger temperature than did fear (Ekman, Levenson, & Friesen, 1983) (see **FIGURE 8.4**).

Research shows that when people exercise, they sometimes misattribute their arousal to the attractiveness of those around them.

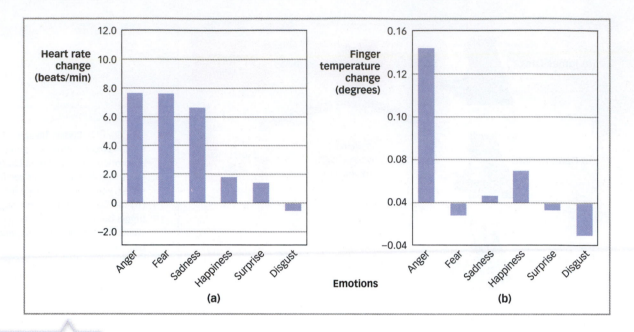

▲ Figure **8.4** **The Physiology of Emotion**
Contrary to the claims of the two-factor theory, different emotions do seem to have different underlying patterns of physiological arousal. (a) Anger, fear, and sadness all produce higher heart rates than happiness, surprise, and disgust. (b) Anger produces a much larger increase in finger temperature than any other emotion.

So James and Lange were right when they suggested that patterns of physiological response are not the same for all emotions. But Cannon and Bard were also right when they suggested that people are not perfectly sensitive to these patterns of response, which is why people must sometimes make inferences about what they are feeling. Our bodily activity and our mental activity are both the causes and the consequences of our emotional experience.

The Emotional Brain

The psychologist Heinrich Klüver and the physician Paul Bucy were studying the effects of hallucinogenic drugs in rhesus monkeys when they made an accidental discovery that Klüver would later call "the most striking behavior changes ever produced by a brain operation in animals" (Klüver, 1951, p. 151). After doing some brain surgery on a monkey named Aurora, they noticed that she would eat just about anything and have sex with just about anyone—as though she could no longer distinguish between good and bad food or good and bad mates. But the most striking thing about Aurora was that she did all this with an extraordinary lack of fear. She was eerily calm when being handled by experimenters or being confronted by snakes, both of which rhesus monkeys typically find alarming (Klüver & Bucy, 1937, 1939).

What explained this behavior? It turned out that during surgery, Klüver and Bucy had accidentally damaged a brain structure called the amygdala, which plays a special role in producing emotions such as fear. Before an animal can feel fear, its brain must first decide that there is something to be afraid of. This decision is called an **appraisal,** which is *an evaluation of the emotion-relevant aspects of a stimulus* (Arnold, 1960; Ellsworth & Scherer, 2003; Lazarus, 1984; Roseman, 1984; Roseman & Smith, 2001; Scherer, 1999, 2001). Many studies have shown that the amygdala is critical to making these appraisals. For example, some researchers performed an operation on monkeys so that information entering the monkey's left eye could be transmitted to the amygdala but infor-

The tourist and the tiger have something in common. Each has an amygdala that is trying to decide whether the other is a threat.

mation entering the monkey's right eye could not (Downer, 1961). When these monkeys were allowed to see a threatening stimulus with only their left eye, they responded with fear and alarm, but when they were allowed to see the threatening stimulus with only their right eye, they were calm and unruffled. These results suggest that if visual information doesn't reach the amygdala, then its emotional significance cannot be assessed. Research on human beings has reached a similar conclusion. For example, normal people have superior memory for emotionally evocative words such as *death* or *vomit,* but people whose amygdalae are damaged (LaBar & Phelps, 1998) or who take drugs that temporarily impair neurotransmission in the amygdala (van Stegeren et al., 1998) do not.

The amygdala is an extremely fast and sensitive "threat detector" that is activated even when potentially threatening stimuli (such as fearful faces) are shown at speeds so fast that people are unaware of having seen them (Whalen et al., 1998). Psychologist Joseph LeDoux (2000) mapped the route that information about a stimulus takes through the brain and found that it is transmitted simultaneously along two distinct routes: the "fast pathway," which goes from the thalamus directly to the amygdala, and the "slow pathway," which goes from the thalamus to the cortex and *then* to the amygdala (see **FIGURE 8.5**). This means that while the cortex is slowly using the information to conduct a full-scale investigation of the stimulus's identity and importance, the amygdala has already received the information directly from the thalamus and is making one very fast and very simple decision: "Is this a threat?" If the amygdala's answer to that question is "yes," it initiates the neural processes that ultimately produce the bodily reactions and conscious experience that we call fear.

The cortex takes much longer to process this information, but when it finally does, it sends a signal to the amygdala. That signal can tell the amygdala to maintain the state of fear ("We've now analyzed all the data up here, and sure enough, that thing is a bear—and bears bite!") or decrease it ("Relax, it's just some guy in a bear costume"). When experimental subjects are instructed to *experience* emotions such as happiness, sadness, fear, and anger, they show increased activity in the amygdala and decreased activity in the cortex (Damasio et al., 2000), but when they are asked to *inhibit* these emotions, they show increased cortical activity and decreased amygdala activity (Ochsner et al., 2002). In a sense, the amygdala presses the emotional gas pedal and the cortex then hits the brakes. That's why both adults with cortical damage and children (whose cortices are not well developed) have difficulty inhibiting their emotions (Stuss & Benson, 1986).

? How do the limbic system and cortex interact?

Studies of the brain confirm what psychologists have long suspected: Emotion is a primitive system that prepares us to react rapidly and on the basis of little information to things that are relevant to our survival and well-being. (See the Hot Science box.)

The Regulation of Emotion

We may not care whether we have cereal or eggs for breakfast, whether we play cricket or cards this afternoon, or whether we spend a few minutes thinking about hedgehogs, earwax, or the War of 1812. But we always care whether we are feeling happy or fearful, angry or relaxed, joyful or disgusted. Because we care so much about our emotional experiences, we work hard to have some and avoid others. **Emotion regulation** refers to *the cognitive and behavioral strategies people use to influence their own emotional experience.*

Nine out of 10 people report that they attempt to regulate their emotional experience at least once a day (Gross, 1998), and they describe more than a thousand

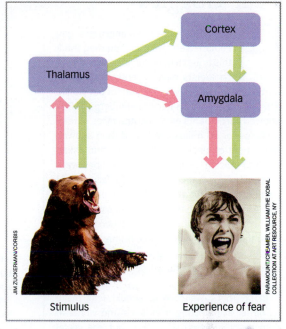

▲ Figure **8.5** **The Fast and Slow Pathways of Fear** According to Joseph LeDoux, information about a stimulus takes two routes simultaneously: the "fast pathway" (shown in pink), which goes from the thalamus directly to the amygdala, and the "slow pathway" (shown in green), which goes from the thalamus to the cortex and then to the amygdala. Because the amygdala receives information from the thalamus before it receives information from the cortex, people can be afraid of something before they know what it is.

appraisal An evaluation of the emotion-relevant aspects of a stimulus.

emotion regulation The use of cognitive and behavioral strategies to influence one's emotional experience.

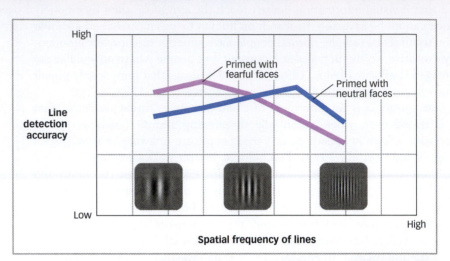

HOT SCIENCE

Fear Goggles

Have you ever been so angry that you couldn't see straight? You may think this is just a figure of speech, but psychologists have recently discovered that our emotions can actually affect our vision. Bruno Bocanegra and René Zeelenberg (2009) showed participants either neutral faces or fearful faces for 70 milliseconds and then showed them a set of black-and-white lines and asked them to quickly decide whether the lines were vertical or horizontal. Seeing fearful faces made participants better at detecting the orientation of the lines—but only when the lines were thick (or had "low spatial frequency"). When the lines were thin (or had "high spatial frequency"), the fearful faces had exactly the opposite effect: They made participants worse at detecting the orientation of the lines.

Okay. That's weird. Why should fear make us better at detecting thick lines and worse at detecting thin lines? As it turns out, the visual information that is critical to making the split-second decisions that ensure our survival—the decision to freeze, or run, or fight—typically has low spatial frequency. Information with high spatial frequency allows us to see fine detail, but you really don't need to be able to count a tiger's teeth when it's lunging at you. You just need to

▲ Low spatial frequency information (left) tells you that something big is coming, and high spatial frequency information (right) tells you exactly what it is.

see that something big is coming your way, and the dental exam can wait. Nature designed our brains so that the experience of fear momentarily enhances our ability to see what matters and

momentarily diminishes our tendency to be distracted by unimportant details.

Now if someone could just figure out how to keep the tigers from seeing *us*.

---

different strategies for doing so (Parkinson & Totterdell, 1999). Some of these are behavioral strategies (e.g., avoiding situations that trigger unwanted emotions, doing distracting activities, or taking drugs) and some are cognitive strategies (e.g., trying not to think about the cause of the unwanted emotion or recruiting memories that trigger the desired emotion).

Shooting heroin and singing in church would seem to have little in common, but both can be forms of emotion regulation. (We recommend singing.)

? How does reappraisal affect health?

Research suggests that one of the most effective strategies for emotion regulation is **reappraisal,** which involves *changing one's emotional experience by changing the meaning of the emotion-eliciting stimulus* (Ochsner et al., 2009ok).

For example, in one study, participants' brains were scanned as they saw photos that induced negative emotions, such as a photo of a woman crying during a funeral. Some participants were then asked to reappraise the picture, for example, by imagining that the woman in the photo was at a wedding rather than a funeral. The results showed that when participants initially saw the photo, their amygdalae became active. But as they reappraised the picture, several key areas of the cortex became active, and moments later, their amygdalae were deactivated (Ochsner et al., 2002). In other words, participants consciously and willfully turned down the activity of their own amygdalae simply by thinking about the photo in a different way.

The Roman emperor Marcus Aurelius wrote two millennia ago, "If you are distressed by anything external, the pain is not due to the thing itself, but to your estimate of it; and this you have the power to revoke at any moment." Is that true? As you will learn in Chapter 14, therapists often attempt to alleviate depression and distress by helping people find new ways to think about the events that happen to them. Indeed, reappraisal appears to be important for both mental and physical health (Davidson, Putnam, & Larson, 2000), and the inability to reappraise events lies at the heart of psychiatric disorders such as depression (Gross & Munoz, 1995). Nonetheless, the way we see the world is not entirely under our control, so while reappraisal can be a useful strategy for regulating emotions, it is not a panacea for all that ails us.

SUMMARY QUIZ [8.1]

1. Emotions can be described by their location on the two dimensions of
   a. motivation and scaling.
   b. arousal and valence.
   c. stimulus and reaction.
   d. pain and pleasure.

2. Which theorists claimed that that a stimulus simultaneously causes both an emotional experience and a physiological reaction?
   a. Cannon and Bard
   b. James and Lange
   c. Schacter and Singer
   d. Klüver and Bucy

3. Which brain structure is most directly involved in the rapid appraisal of whether a stimulus is good or bad?
   a. the cortex
   b. the hypothalamus
   c. the amygdala
   d. the thalamus

4. Through _____, we change an emotional experience by changing the meaning of the emotion-eliciting stimulus.
   a. deactivation
   b. appraisal
   c. valence
   d. reappraisal

Emotional Communication: Msgs w/o Wrds

Leonardo the robot may not be able to feel, but boy oh boy, can he smile. And wink. And nod. Indeed, one of the reasons why people who interact with him find it so hard to think of him as a machine is that Leonardo *expresses* emotions that he doesn't actually have. An **emotional expression** is *an observable sign of an emotional state,* and while robots have to be taught to exhibit them, human beings do it naturally.

Why are we "walking, talking advertisements" of our inner states?

Our emotional states influence just about everything we do: from the way we talk—intonation, inflection, loudness—to the way we walk, stand, or slump. But no part of the body is more exquisitely designed for communicating emotion than the face. Underneath every face lie 43 muscles that are capable of creating more than 10,000 unique configurations. Psychologists Paul Ekman and Wallace Friesen (1968) spent years cataloguing the muscle movements of which the human

reappraisal Changing one's emotional experience by changing the meaning of the emotion-eliciting stimulus.

emotional expression Any observable sign of an emotional state.

Leonardo's face is capable of expressing a wide range of emotions (Breazeal, 2003).

face is capable and isolated 46 unique movements. Research has shown that combinations of these muscle movements are reliably related to specific emotional states (Davidson et al., 1990). For example, when we feel happy, our *zygomatic major* (a muscle that pulls our lip corners up) and our *obicularis oculi* (a muscle that crinkles the outside edges of our eyes) produce a unique facial expression: smiling (Ekman & Friesen, 1982; Frank, Ekman, & Friesen, 1993; Steiner, 1986).

Communicative Expression

Why are our emotions written all over our faces? In 1872, Charles Darwin published a book titled *The Expression of the Emotions in Man and Animals,* in which he noted that human and nonhuman animals share certain facial and postural expressions, and

According to Charles Darwin, both human and nonhuman animals use facial expressions to communicate information about their internal states.

he suggested that these expressions were meant to communicate information about internal states. Darwin suggested that emotional expressions are a convenient way for one animal to let another animal know how it is feeling and hence how it is prepared to act. For example, if a dominant animal could bare its teeth and communicate the message, "I am angry at you," and if a subordinate animal could lower its head and communicate the message, "I am afraid of you," then the two could establish a pecking order without actually spilling any blood. In this sense, emotional expressions are a bit like the words of a nonverbal language.

The Universality of Expression

Of course, a language only works if everybody speaks the same one, and that fact led Darwin to develop the **universality hypothesis,** which suggests that *emotional expressions have the same meaning for everyone.* In other words, every human being naturally expresses happiness with a smile, and every human being naturally understands that a smile signifies happiness. Two lines of evidence suggest that Darwin was largely correct.

First, people are quite accurate at judging the emotional expressions of members of other cultures (Ekman & Friesen, 1971; Elfenbein & Ambady, 2002; Frank & Stennet,

universality hypothesis The hypothesis that emotional expressions have the same meaning for everyone.

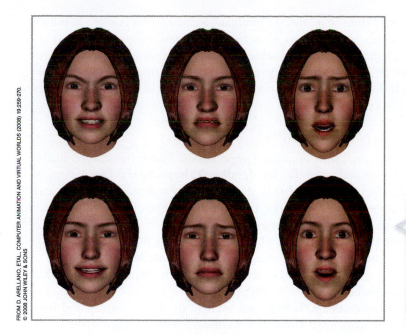

◀ Figure **8.6** **Six Basic Emotions** These computer-generated faces are displaying anger, disgust, fear, happiness, sadness, and surprise. The universality hypothesis suggests that no matter who you are or where you live, you will be able to identify the emotion in each face. Adapted from Arellano, Varona, & Perales, 2008.

2001; Haidt & Keltner, 1999). Not only do Chileans, Americans, and Japanese all recognize a smile as a sign of happiness and a frown as a sign of sadness, but so do members of preliterate cultures. In the 1950s, researchers took photographs of people expressing anger, disgust, fear, happiness, sadness, and surprise (see **FIGURE 8.6**) and showed them to members of the South Fore, a people who lived a Stone Age existence in the highlands of Papua New Guinea and had had little contact with the outside world. The researchers discovered that the Fore could recognize the emotional expressions of Americans about as accurately as Americans could, and vice versa. The one striking exception to this rule was that the Fore had trouble distinguishing expressions of surprise from expressions of fear, perhaps because for people who live in the wild, surprises are rarely pleasant.

The second line of evidence in favor of the universality hypothesis is that people who have never seen a human face make the same facial expressions as those who have. For instance, congenitally blind people

? **Why are some facial expressions universal?**

make all the facial expressions associated with the six emotions mentioned above (Galati, Scherer, & Ricci-Bitt, 1997; Matsumoto & Willingham, 2009). And 2-day-old infants (who have had virtually no exposure to human faces) react to sweet tastes with a smile and to bitter tastes with an expression of disgust (Steiner, 1973, 1979). In short, a good deal of evidence suggests that the facial displays of at least six emotions—*anger, disgust, fear, happiness, sadness,* and *surprise*—are universal. Recent evidence suggests that some other emotions, such as embarrassment, amusement, guilt, or shame, may have a universal pattern of facial expression as well (Keltner, 1995; Keltner & Buswell, 1996; Keltner & Haidt, 1999; Keltner & Harker, 1998).

Of course, just as a word (*bat*) can have more than one meaning ("wooden club" or "flying mammal"), so, too, can a facial expression. Is the man in the photo at the top of the next page feeling joy or sorrow? In fact, these two emotions often produce rather similar facial expressions—so how do we tell them apart? The answer is context. When someone says, "The centerfielder hit the ball with the bat," the sentence provides a context that

Why is Stevie Wonder smiling? Perhaps it's the 22 Grammy Awards he's won since 1974. Research shows that people who are born blind express emotion on their faces in the same ways that sighted people do.

Is this man feeling happy or sad? See p. 248.

tells us that *bat* means "club," not "flying mammal." Similarly, the context in which a facial expression occurs often tells us what that expression means (Aviezer et al., 2008; Meeren, van Heijnsbergen, & de Gelder, 2005). If you turn to p. 248 you will see the photo to the left in context, and you won't have any trouble knowing what the man is feeling. In fact, if you now return to the photo to the left, it will be very difficult for you *not* to see his expression.

The Cause and Effect of Expression

Emotional experiences can cause emotional expressions. But interestingly, it also works the other way around. The **facial feedback hypothesis** (Adelmann & Zajonc, 1989; Izard, 1971; Tomkins, 1981) suggests that *emotional expressions can cause the emotional experiences they signify.* For instance, people feel happier when they are asked to make the sound of a long *e* or to hold a pencil in their teeth (both of which cause contraction of the zygomatic major) than when they are asked to make the sound of a long *u* or to hold a pencil in their lips (Strack, Martin, & Stepper, 1988; Zajonc, 1989) (see **FIGURE 8.7**). Most researchers think that smiles and happiness become strongly associated through experience, with one generally bringing about the other. These expression-causes-emotion effects are not limited to the face.

? Why do emotional expressions cause emotional experience?

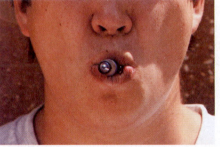

▲ Figure **8.7** **The Facial Feedback Hypothesis** Research shows that people who hold a pen with their teeth feel happier than those who hold a pen with their lips. These two postures cause contraction of the muscles associated with smiling and frowning, respectively.

For example, people who are asked to make a fist rate themselves as more assertive (Schubert & Koole, 2009) and people who are asked to extend their middle fingers rate others as more hostile (Chandler & Schwarz, 2009). (The odds seem pretty good that others would rate them as more hostile too).

The fact that emotional expressions can cause the emotional experiences they signify may help explain why people are generally so good at recognizing the emotional expressions of others. Many studies show that people unconsciously mimic other people's body postures and facial expressions (Chartrand & Bargh, 1999; Dimberg, 1982). When we see someone smile (or even when we read about someone smiling), our zygomatic major contracts ever so slightly (Foroni & Semin, 2009). The tendency to "ape" the facial expressions of our interaction partners is so natural that, yes, even apes do it (Davila Ross, Menzler, & Zimmermann, 2008).

What purpose does this mimicry serve? It appears that its main function is to help us figure out what others are feeling. Because of the expression-causes-emotion effect, when we mimic someone's facial expression, we also feel their emotions. On the other hand, people with amygdala damage, who have trouble experiencing fear and anger, are typically poor at recognizing the expressions of those emotions in others (Adolphs, Russell, & Tranel, 1999). And as you might expect, people who are naturally good at figuring out what others are feeling tend to be natural mimics (Sonnby-Borgstrom, Jonsson, & Svensson, 2003).

Deceptive Expressions

Given how important emotional expressions are, it's no wonder people have learned to use them to their advantage. Because you can control most of the muscles in your face, you don't have to display the emotion you are actually feeling. When your roommate makes a sarcastic remark about your haircut, you may make the facial expression for contempt (accompanied, perhaps, by a reinforcing hand gesture), but when your boss makes the same remark, you probably swallow hard and display a pained

facial feedback hypothesis The hypothesis that emotional expressions can cause the emotional experiences they signify.

display rules Norms for the control of emotional expression.

smile. Your expressions are moderated by your knowledge that it is permissible to show contempt for your peers but not for your superiors. **Display rules** are *norms for the control of emotional expression* (Ekman, 1972; Ekman & Friesen, 1968).

People in different cultures follow different display rules. For example, in one study, Japanese and American college students watched an unpleasant film of car accidents and amputations (Ekman, 1972; Friesen, 1972). When they didn't know that the experimenters were observing them, Japanese and American students made similar expressions of disgust, but when they realized that they were being observed, the Japanese students (but not the American students) masked their disgust with pleasant expressions. Many Asian societies have a cultural norm against displaying negative emotions in the presence of a respected person, and people in these societies may mask or neutralize their expressions.

> **How does emotional expression differ across cultures?**

Of course, our attempts to obey our culture's display rules don't always work. Darwin (1899/2007) noted that "those muscles of the face which are least obedient to the will, will sometimes alone betray a slight and passing emotion" (p. 64). Anyone who has ever watched the loser of a beauty pageant congratulate the winner knows that voices, bodies, and faces are "leaky" instruments that often betray a person's emotional state even when he or she is pretending to feel something else. For example, even when people smile bravely to mask their disappointment, their faces tend to express small bursts of disappointment that last just 1/5 to 1/25 of a second (Porter & ten Brinke, 2008). These "micro-expressions" happen so quickly that they are almost impossible to detect with the naked eye.

Other features are more readily observable (Ekman, 2003). For example, the facial muscle called the zygomatic major raises the corners of the mouth, and this happens when people smile spontaneously or when they force themselves to smile. But only a genuine, spontaneous smile engages the obicularis oculi, which crinkles the corners of the eyes (see **FIGURE 8.8**). Sincere expressions also tend to be symmetrical, to last for about 0.5 to 5 seconds, and tend to appear and disappear smoothly over a few seconds. So if you see someone giving an abrupt, lopsided smile that lasts for more than 5 seconds, it may be indicative of a display rule rather than of genuine happiness.

Our emotions don't just leak on our faces: They leak all over the place. Research has shown that many aspects of our verbal and nonverbal behavior are altered when we tell a lie (DePaulo et al., 2003). For example, liars speak more slowly, take longer to respond to questions, and respond in less detail than do those who are telling the truth. Liars are also less fluent, less engaging, more uncertain, more tense, and less pleasant than truth-tellers. Oddly enough, one of the telltale signs of a liar is that his or her performances tend to be just a bit too good. A liar's speech lacks the little imperfections that are typical of truthful speech, such as superfluous detail ("I noticed that the robber was wearing the same shoes that I saw on sale last week at Bloomingdale's and I found myself wondering what he paid for them"), spontaneous correction ("He was six feet tall . . . well, no, actually more like six-two"), and expressions of self-doubt ("I think he had blue eyes, but I'm really not sure").

Given the reliable differences between sincere and insincere expressions, you might think that people would be quite good at telling one from the other. In fact, studies show that human lie detection ability is pretty close to dreadful. Although trained professionals can learn to do it fairly well (Ekman & O'Sullivan, 1991; Ekman, O'Sullivan, & Frank, 1999), under most conditions ordinary people do barely better than chance (DePaulo, Stone, & Lassiter, 1985; Ekman, 1992; Zuckerman, DePaulo, & Rosenthal, 1981; Zuckerman & Driver,

▼ Figure **8.8** **Crinkle Eyes** Can you tell which of the two finalists in the 1986 Miss America pageant just won? Check out their eyes. Only one woman is showing the telltale "corner crinkle" that signifies genuine happiness. The winner is on the right, but don't feel too bad for the loser on the left. Her name is Halle Berry and she went on to have a pretty good acting career.

AP PHOTO/RAUL DEMOLINA

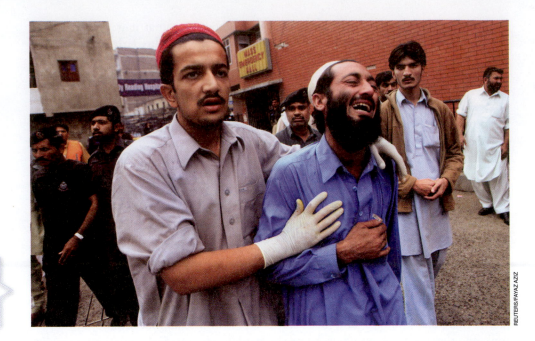

This Pakistani man is being led away from the scene of a Taliban suicide-bombing that killed his father.

1985). One reason for this is that people have a strong bias toward believing that others are sincere, which explains why people tend to mistake liars for truth-tellers more often than they mistake truth-tellers for liars (Gilbert, 1991).

When people can't do something well (e.g., adding numbers or picking up 10-ton rocks), they typically turn the job over to machines (see **FIGURE 8.9**). Can machines detect lies better than we can? The answer is "yes," but that's not saying much. The most widely used lie detection machine is the *polygraph,* which measures a variety of physiological responses that are associated with stress, which people often feel when they are

? **What is the problem with lie detection machines?**

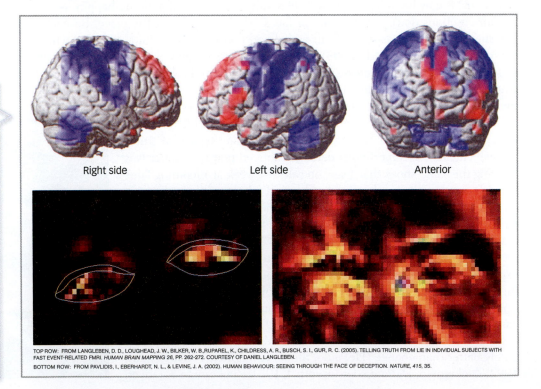

▶ Figure **8.9** **Lie Detection Machines** Some researchers hope to replace the polygraph with accurate machines that measure changes in blood flow in the brain and the face. As the top panel shows, some areas of the brain are more active when people tell lies than when they tell the truth (shown in red), and some are more active when people tell the truth than when they tell lies (shown in blue) (Langleben et al., 2005). The bottom panel shows images taken by a thermal camera that detects the heat caused by blood flow to different parts of the face. The images show a person's face before (left) and after (right) telling a lie (Pavlidis, Eberhardt, & Levine, 2002). Although neither of these new techniques is extremely accurate, that could soon change.

Right side   Left side   Anterior

CULTURE & COMMUNITY

Is It What You Say or How You Say It? We can learn a lot about people by paying attention both to what they say and to how they say it. But recent evidence (Ishii, Reyes, & Kitayama, 2003) suggests that some cultures place more of an emphasis on one of these than on the other.

Subjects heard a voice pronouncing pleasant or unpleasant words (such as *pretty* or *complaint*) in either a pleasant or an unpleasant tone of voice. On some trials, subjects were told to ignore the word and to classify the pleasantness of the voice; on other trials, subjects were told to ignore the voice and classify the pleasantness of the word.

Which of these kinds of information was more difficult to ignore? It depended on the subject's nationality. American subjects found it relatively easy to ignore the speaker's tone of voice but relatively difficult to ignore the pleasantness of the word being spoken. Japanese subjects, on the other hand, found it relatively easy to ignore the pleasantness of the word but relatively difficult to ignore the speaker's tone of voice.

It seems that, in America, what you say matters more than how you say it, but in Japan, just the opposite is true.

afraid of being caught in a lie. In fact, the machine is so widely used by governments and businesses that the National Research Council recently met to consider all the scientific evidence on its validity. After much study, it concluded that the polygraph can indeed detect lies at a rate that is significantly better than chance (National Research Council, 2003). However, it also concluded that "almost a century of research in scientific psychology and physiology provides little basis for the expectation that a polygraph test could have extremely high accuracy" (p. 212). In short, neither people nor machines are particularly good at lie detection, which is why lying remains such a popular sport.

SUMMARY QUIZ [8.2]

5. Which of the following does *not* provide any support for the universality hypothesis?
   a. Congenitally blind people make the facial expressions associated with the basic emotions.
   b. Infants only days old react to sweet tastes with smiles and to bitter tastes with expressions of disgust.
   c. Robots have been engineered to exhibit emotional expressions.
   d. Researchers have discovered that isolated people living a Stone Age existence with little contact with the outside world recognize the emotional expressions of people with contemporary lifestyles.

6. _____ is the idea that emotional expressions can cause emotional experiences.
   a. A display rule
   b. Expressional deception
   c. The universality hypothesis
   d. The facial feedback hypothesis

9. Which of the following statements is *not* accurate?
   a. Certain facial muscles are reliably engaged by sincere facial expressions.
   b. Even when people smile bravely to mask disappointment, their faces tend to express small bursts of disappointment.
   c. Studies show that human lie detection ability is extremely good.
   d. Polygraph machines detect lies at a rate better than chance, but their error rate is still quite high.

Motivation: Getting Moved

Leonardo the robot doesn't care about anything, doesn't value anything, doesn't desire anything. He can learn, but he cannot yearn. Because he doesn't have emotions, he isn't motivated in the same way that human beings are. **Motivation** refers to *the purpose for or psychological cause of an action,* and it is no coincidence that the words *emotion* and *motivation* share a common linguistic root that means "to move." Unlike robots, human beings act because their emotions move them, and emotions do this in two different ways: First, emotions provide people with *information* about the world, and second, emotions are the *objectives* toward which people strive. Let's examine each of these in turn.

The Function of Emotion

The first function of emotion is to provide us with information about the world. For example, people report having better lives when they are asked the question on a sunny day rather than a rainy day. Why? Because people feel happier on sunny days, and they use their happiness as information about the quality of their lives (Schwarz & Clore, 1983). People who are in good moods believe that they have a higher probability of winning a lottery than do people who are in bad moods. Why? Because people use their moods as information about the likelihood of succeeding at a task (Isen & Patrick, 1983). We all know that satisfying lives and bright futures make us feel good—so when we feel good, we conclude that our lives must be satisfying and our futures must be bright. Because the world influences our emotions, our emotions can provide information about the world (Schwarz, Mannheim, & Clore, 1988).

This information isn't just useful. It is critical. When neurologist Antonio Damasio was asked to examine a patient with an unusual form of brain damage, he asked the patient to choose between two dates for an appointment. It sounds like a simple decision, but for the next half hour, the patient enumerated reasons for and against each of the two possible dates, completely unable to decide in favor of one option or the other (Damasio, 1994). The problem wasn't any impairment of the patient's ability to think or reason. On the contrary, he could think and reason all too well. What he couldn't do was feel. The patient's injury had left him unable to experience emotion; thus when he entertained one option ("If I come next Tuesday, I'll have to cancel my lunch with Fred"), he didn't feel any better or any worse than when he entertained another ("If I come next Wednesday, I'll have to get up early to catch the bus"). And because he *felt* nothing when he thought about an option, he couldn't decide which was better. Studies show that when patients with this particular kind of brain damage are given the opportunity to gamble, they make a lot of reckless bets because they don't feel the twinge of anxiety that tells most of us that we're about to do something stupid. On the other hand, under certain conditions these patients make excellent investors, precisely because they are willing to take risks that others will not (Shiv et al., 2005).

The second function of emotion is to give us something to *do* with that information. People naturally prefer to experience positive rather than negative emotions; thus happiness, satisfaction, pleasure, and joy are often the goals, the ends, and the objectives toward which our behavior is aimed. The **hedonic principle** is *the claim that people are motivated to experience pleasure and avoid pain.* According to the hedonic principle, our emotional experience can be thought of as a gauge that ranges from bad to good, and our primary motivation—perhaps even our *sole* motivation—is to keep the needle on the gauge as close to *good* as possible. Even when we voluntarily do things that tilt the needle in the opposite direction, such as letting the

? Why do we need emotions to help us make decisions?

When we try to make a decision, we often ask how we "feel" about it. If we couldn't feel, then we wouldn't know which alternative to choose. Without emotions, Rihanna would just stand there until someone gave her a Grammy for Best Hot Pink Stiletto.

dentist drill our teeth or waking up early for a boring class, we are doing these things because we believe that they will nudge the needle toward *good* in the future and keep it there longer.

The Conceptualization of Motivation

The hedonic principle sets the stage for an understanding of motivation but leaves many questions unanswered. For example, if our primary motivation is to keep the needle on *good,* so to speak, then which things push the needle in that direction and which things push it away? And where do these things get the power to push our needle around, and exactly how do they do the pushing? The answers to such questions lie in two concepts that have played an unusually important role in the history of psychology: *instincts* and *drives*.

Instincts

When a newborn baby is given a drop of sugar water, it smiles, and when it is given a check for $10,000, it acts like it couldn't care less. By the time the baby goes to college, these responses pretty much reverse. It seems clear that nature endows us with certain motivations and that experience endows us with others. William James (1890) called the natural tendency to seek a particular goal an *instinct,* which he defined as "the faculty of acting in such a way as to produce certain ends, without foresight of the ends, and without previous education in the performance" (p. 383). According to James, nature hardwired penguins, parrots, puppies, and people to want certain things without training and to execute the behaviors that produce these things without thinking.

By 1930, the concept of instinct had fallen out of fashion. Not only did it fail to explain anything, but it also flew in the face of American psychology's hot new trend: behaviorism. Behaviorists rejected the concept of instinct on two grounds. First, they believed that behavior should be explained by the external stimuli that evoke it and not by the hypothetical internal states on which it depends. John Watson (1913) had written that "the time seems to have come when psychology must discard all reference to consciousness" (p. 163), and behaviorists saw instincts as just the sort of unnecessary "internal talk" that Watson forbade. Second, behaviorists wanted nothing to do with the notion of inherited behavior because they believed that all complex behavior was learned. Because instincts were inherited tendencies that resided inside the organism, behaviorists considered them doubly repugnant.

Drives

But within a few decades, some of Watson's younger followers began to realize that the strict prohibition against the mention of internal states made certain phenomena difficult to explain. For example, if all behavior is a response to an external stimulus, then why does a rat that is sitting still in its cage at 9:00 a.m. start wandering around and looking for food by noon? Nothing in the cage has changed, so why has the rat's behavior changed? What visible, measurable external stimulus is the wandering rat responding to? The obvious answer is that the rat is responding to something inside itself, which meant that Watson's young followers—the "new behaviorists" as they called themselves—were forced to look inside the rat to explain its wandering. How could they do that without talking about the "thoughts" and "feelings" that Watson had forbidden them to mention?

motivation The purpose for or psychological cause of an action.

hedonic principle The notion that all people are motivated to experience pleasure and avoid pain.

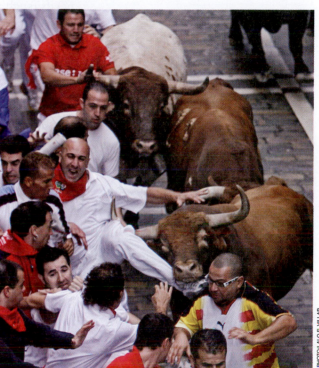

AP PHOTO/LALO R. VILLAR

All animals are born with instincts. In the annual "running of the bulls" in Pamplona, Spain, no one has to teach the bulls to chase the runners, and no one has to teach the runners to flee.

They began by noting that bodies are a bit like thermostats. When thermostats detect that the room is too cold, they send signals that initiate corrective actions such as turning on a furnace. Similarly, when bodies detect that they are underfed, they send signals that initiate corrective actions such as eating. To survive, an organism needs to maintain precise levels of nutrition, warmth, and so on, and when these levels depart from an optimal point, the organism receives a signal to take corrective action. That signal is called a **drive,** which is *an internal state caused by physiological needs.* According to this view, it isn't food per se that organisms find rewarding; it is the reduction of the drive for food. Hunger is a drive, a drive is an internal state, and when organisms eat, they are attempting to change their internal state.

Abraham Maslow (1954) attempted to organize the list of human drives—or, as he called them, *needs*—in a meaningful way (see **FIGURE 8.10**). He noted that some needs (such as the need to eat) must be satisfied before others (such as the need to have friends), and he built a hierarchy of needs that had the most immediate needs at the bottom and the most deferrable needs at the top. Maslow suggested that, as

? Why do some motivations take precedence over others?

a rule, people will not experience a need until all the needs below it are met. So when people are hungry or thirsty or exhausted, they will not seek intellectual fulfillment or moral clarity, which is to say that philosophy is a luxury of the well fed. Although many aspects of Maslow's theory have failed to win empirical support (e.g., a person on a hunger strike may value her principles more than her physical needs; see Wahba & Bridwell, 1976), the idea that some needs take precedence over others is clearly right. And although there are exceptions, the needs that typically take precedence are those related to our biology. Two of these biological needs—the need for food and the need for sex—are among the most powerful and well studied, so let's see how they work.

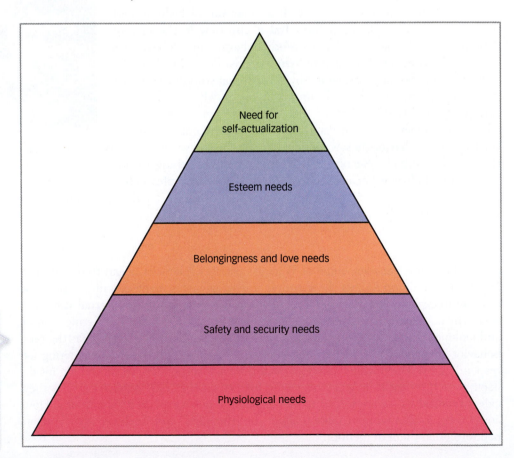

▶ Figure **8.10** **Maslow's Hierarchy of Needs** Human beings are motivated to satisfy a variety of needs. Psychologist Abraham Maslow thought these needs formed a hierarchy, with physiological needs forming a base and self-actualization needs forming a pinnacle. He suggested that people don't experience higher needs until the needs below them have been met.

Motivation for Food

Animals convert matter into energy by eating, and they are driven to do this by an internal state called hunger. But what is hunger and where does it come from? At every moment, your body is sending signals to your brain about its current energy state. If your body needs energy, it sends an *orexigenic* signal to tell your brain to switch hunger on, and if your body has sufficient energy, it sends an *anorexigenic* signal to tell your brain to switch hunger off (Gropp et al., 2005). No one knows precisely what these signals are or how they are sent and received, but research has identified a variety of candidates.

For example, *ghrelin,* a hormone that is produced in the stomach, appears to be a signal that tells the brain to switch hunger on (Inui, 2001; Nakazato et al., 2001). When people are injected with ghrelin, they become intensely hungry and eat about 30% more than usual (Wren et al., 2001). Interestingly, ghrelin also binds to neurons in the hippocampus and temporarily improves learning and memory (Diano et al., 2006) so that we become just a little bit better at locating food when our bodies need it most. *Leptin,* a chemical secreted by fat cells,

> **? What purpose does hunger serve?**

appears to be a signal that tells the brain to switch hunger off. It seems to do this by making food less rewarding (Farooqi et al., 2007). People who are born with a leptin deficiency have trouble controlling their appetites (Montague et al., 1997). For example, in 2002 medical researchers reported on the case of a 9-year-old girl who weighed 200 pounds, but after just a few leptin injections, she reduced her food intake by 84% and attained normal weight (Farooqi et al., 2002). Some researchers think the idea that chemicals turn hunger on and off is far too simple; they argue that there is no general state called hunger but rather that there are many different hungers, each of which is a response to a unique nutritional deficit and each of which is switched on by a unique chemical messenger (Rozin & Kalat, 1971). For example, rats that are deprived of protein will seek proteins while turning down fats and carbohydrates, suggesting that they are experiencing a specific "protein hunger," not a general hunger (Rozin, 1968).

Whether hunger is one signal or many, the primary receiver of these signals is the hypothalamus. Different parts of the hypothalamus receive different signals (see **FIGURE 8.11**). The *lateral hypothalamus* receives orexigenic signals and when it is destroyed, animals sitting in a cage full of food will starve themselves to death. The *ventromedial hypothalamus* receives anorexigenic signals and when it is destroyed, animals will gorge themselves to the point of illness and obesity (Miller, 1960; Steinbaum & Miller, 1965). These two structures were once thought to be the "hunger center" and "satiety center" of the brain, but recent research has shown that this view is far too simple (Woods et al., 1998). Hypothalamic structures play an important role in turning hunger on and off, but the precise way in which they execute these functions is complex and remains poorly understood (Stellar & Stellar, 1985).

Eating Disorders

Feelings of hunger tell us when to eat and when to stop. But for the 10 to 30 million Americans who have eating disorders, eating is a much more complicated affair (Hoek & van Hoeken, 2003). For instance, **bulimia nervosa** is *a disorder*

drive An internal state generated by departures from physiological optimality.

bulimia nervosa An eating disorder characterized by binge eating followed by purging.

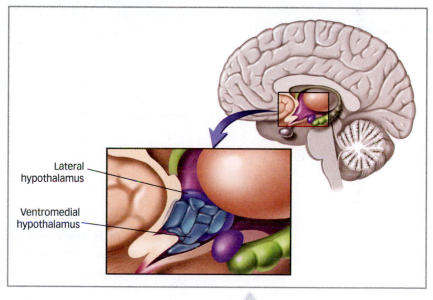

Lateral hypothalamus

Ventromedial hypothalamus

▲ Figure **8.11 Hunger, Satiety, and the Hypothalamus** The hypothalamus comprises many parts. In general, the lateral hypothalamus receives the signals that turn hunger on and the ventromedial hypothalamus receives the signals that turn hunger off.

Two fashion models look at Aya Barazani as she sits in her wheelchair. Aya suffers from anorexia. All three women are taking part in a photo shoot for a publicity campaign to convince modeling agencies not to feature malnourished women.

characterized by binge eating followed by purging. People with bulimia typically ingest large quantities of food in a relatively short period and then take laxatives or induce vomiting to purge the food from their bodies. These people are caught in a cycle: They eat to ease negative emotions such as sadness and anxiety, but then concern about weight gain leads them to experience negative emotions such as guilt and self-loathing, and these emotions then lead them to purge.

Anorexia nervosa is *a disorder characterized by an intense fear of being fat and severe restriction of food intake.* People with anorexia tend to have a distorted body image that leads them to believe they are fat when they are actually emaciated, and they tend to be high-achieving perfectionists who see their severe control of eating as a triumph of will over impulse. Contrary to what you might expect, people with anorexia have extremely *high* levels of ghrelin in their blood, which suggests that their bodies are trying desperately to switch hunger on but that hunger's call is being suppressed, ignored, or overridden (Ariyasu et al., 2001). Like most eating disorders, anorexia strikes more women than men, and 40% of newly identified cases of anorexia are among females who are 15 to 19 years old. Anorexia may have both cultural and biological causes. For example, women with anorexia typically believe that thinness equals beauty, and it isn't hard to understand why. The average American woman is 5'4″ tall and weighs 140 pounds, but the average American fashion model is 5'11″ tall and weighs 117 pounds. But anorexia is not just "vanity run amok" (Striegel-Moore & Bulik, 2007). Many researchers believe that there are as-yet-undiscovered biological and/or genetic components to the illness as well. For example, although anorexia primarily affects women, men have a sharply increased risk of becoming anorexic if they have a female twin who has the disorder (Procopio & Marriott, 2007), suggesting that anorexia may have something to do with prenatal exposure to female hormones.

? What causes anorexia?

Obesity

America's most pervasive eating-related problem is obesity. Obesity is defined as having a body mass index (or BMI) of 30 or greater. **TABLE 8.1** allows you to compute your body mass index, and the odds are that you won't like what you learn. Every year, obesity-related illnesses cost our nation about $147 billion (Finkelstein et al., 2009) and about 3 million lives (Allison et al., 1999). In addition to these physical risks, obese people tend to be viewed negatively by others, have lower self-esteem, and have a lower quality of life (Hebl & Heatherton, 1997; Kolotkin, Meter, & Williams, 2001). Obese women earn about 7% less than their nonobese counterparts (Lempert, 2007), and the stigma of obesity is so powerful that average-weight people are viewed negatively if they even have a relationship with someone who is obese (Hebl & Mannix, 2003). All of this is terribly unfair, of course. As one scientist noted, we need to declare "a war on obesity, not the obese" (Friedman, 2003).

We don't typically overbreathe, overdrink, or overmate—so why do we overeat? There are at least three reasons:

1. *Overeating can result from biochemical abnormalities.* For example, obese people are often leptin-resistant—that is, their brains do not respond to the chemical message that shuts hunger off—and even leptin injections don't help them

anorexia nervosa An eating disorder characterized by an intense fear of being fat and severe restriction of food intake.

Table 8.1

Body Mass Index Table

	Normal						Overweight					Obese					Extreme Obesity																			
BMI	19	20	21	22	23	24	25	26	27	28	29	30	31	32	33	34	35	36	37	38	39	40	41	42	43	44	45	46	47	48	49	50	51	52	53	54
Height (Inches)															Body Weight (pounds)																					
58	91	96	100	105	110	115	119	124	129	134	138	143	148	153	158	162	167	172	177	181	186	191	196	201	205	210	215	220	224	229	234	239	244	248	253	258
59	94	99	104	109	114	119	124	128	133	138	143	148	153	158	163	169	173	178	183	188	193	198	203	308	212	217	222	227	232	237	242	247	252	257	262	267
60	97	102	107	112	116	123	128	133	138	143	148	153	156	163	168	174	179	184	189	194	199	204	209	215	220	225	230	235	240	245	250	256	261	266	271	278
61	100	108	111	116	122	127	132	137	143	148	153	156	164	169	174	180	186	190	195	201	206	211	217	222	227	232	238	243	248	254	259	264	269	275	280	285
62	104	109	115	120	126	131	138	142	147	153	158	164	169	175	180	186	191	196	202	207	213	218	224	229	235	240	248	251	258	262	267	273	278	264	289	295
63	107	113	118	124	130	135	141	148	152	158	163	169	175	180	188	191	197	203	208	214	220	225	231	237	242	248	254	260	265	270	278	282	287	293	299	304
64	110	118	122	128	134	140	145	151	157	163	169	174	180	188	192	197	204	209	215	221	227	232	238	244	250	258	262	267	273	279	285	291	298	302	308	314
65	114	120	126	132	138	144	150	156	162	168	174	180	186	192	193	204	210	216	222	228	234	240	246	252	258	264	270	278	282	288	294	300	308	312	318	324
66	118	124	130	138	142	148	155	161	167	173	179	186	192	198	204	210	216	223	229	235	241	247	253	260	266	272	278	284	291	297	303	309	315	322	328	334
67	121	127	134	140	146	153	159	166	172	178	185	191	198	204	211	217	223	230	238	242	249	256	261	268	274	280	287	293	299	308	312	319	325	331	338	344
68	125	131	138	144	151	158	164	171	177	184	190	197	203	210	216	223	230	236	243	249	256	262	269	278	282	289	295	302	303	315	322	328	335	341	348	354
69	128	135	142	149	155	162	169	178	182	189	195	203	209	218	223	230	236	243	250	257	263	270	277	284	291	297	304	311	318	324	331	338	345	351	358	365
70	132	139	146	153	160	167	174	181	188	195	202	209	216	222	229	236	243	250	257	264	271	278	285	292	299	308	313	320	327	334	341	348	355	362	369	378
71	138	143	150	157	166	172	179	186	193	200	208	215	222	229	235	243	250	257	265	272	279	288	293	301	308	315	322	329	338	343	351	358	365	372	379	388
72	140	147	154	162	169	177	184	191	199	208	213	221	228	235	242	250	258	265	272	279	287	294	302	309	316	324	331	338	346	353	361	368	375	383	390	397
73	144	151	159	166	174	182	189	197	204	212	219	227	236	242	250	257	266	272	280	288	295	302	310	318	326	333	340	348	355	363	371	378	388	393	401	408
74	148	155	163	171	179	188	194	202	210	218	225	233	241	249	258	264	272	280	287	295	303	311	319	328	334	342	350	358	365	373	381	389	398	404	412	420
75	152	160	166	178	184	192	200	208	216	224	232	240	248	256	264	272	279	287	295	303	311	319	327	335	343	351	359	367	375	383	391	399	407	415	423	431
76	158	164	172	180	189	197	205	213	221	230	238	246	254	263	271	279	287	295	304	312	320	328	338	344	353	361	369	377	385	394	402	410	418	428	436	443

Source: Adapted from National Institutes of Health, 1998, *Clinical Guidelines on the Identification, Evaluation, and Treatment of Overweight and Obesity in Adults: The Evidence Report.*
This and other information about overweight and obesity can be found at www.nhlbi.nih.gov/guidelines/obesity/ob_home.htm.

(Friedman & Halaas, 1998; Heymsfield et al., 1999). For such people, the urge to eat is incredibly compelling, and they can't "just decide" to stop eating any more than you could just decide to stop breathing (Friedman, 2003).

2. *We often eat even when we aren't really hungry.* For example, we may eat to reduce negative emotions such as sadness or anxiety, we may eat out of habit ("I always have ice cream at night"), and we may eat out of social obligation ("Everyone else is ordering dessert") (Herman, Roth, & Polivy, 2003). Sometimes we eat simply because the clock tells us that we should (Schachter & Gross, 1968). (See the Real World box.)

3. *Nature designed us to overeat.* For most of our evolutionary history, the main food-related problem facing our ancestors was starvation. As a result, we developed a strong attraction to foods that provide large amounts of energy (calories) per bite—which is why most of us prefer hamburgers and milkshakes to celery and water. We also developed an ability to store excess food energy in the form of fat, which enabled us to eat more than we needed when food was plentiful and then live off our reserves when food was scarce. We are beautifully engineered for a world in which food is generally low-cal and scarce, but the problem is that we don't live in that world anymore. Instead, we live in a world in which the calorie-laden miracles of modern technology—from chocolate cupcakes to sausage pizzas—are inexpensive and readily available.

It is all too easy to overeat and become overweight or obese, and it is all too difficult to reverse course. The human body resists weight loss in two ways. First, when we gain weight, we experience an increase in both the size and the number of fat

Times have changed. People today are often astonished to see that ads once promised to help young women *gain* weight to become popular.

THE REAL WORLD

Jeet Jet?

Does the amount of food placed in front of people influence how much they eat?

Brian Wansink and colleagues (2005) sat research participants down in front of a large bowl of tomato soup and told them to eat as much as they wanted. In one condition of the study, a server came to the table and refilled the participant's bowl whenever it got down to about a quarter full. In another condition, unbeknownst to the participants, the bottom of the bowl was connected by a long tube to a large vat of soup, so whenever the participant ate from the bowl, it would slowly and almost imperceptibly refill itself.

What the researchers found was sobering. Participants who unknowingly ate from a "bottomless bowl" consumed a whopping 73% more soup than those who ate from normal bowls—

▲ Researcher Brian Wansink and his bottomless bowl of soup.

BOB FILA/CHICAGO TRIBUNE/NEWSCOM

and yet they didn't think they had consumed more and they didn't report feeling any more full.

It seems that we find it easier to keep track of what we are eating than how much, and this can cause us to overeat even when we are trying our best to do just the opposite. For instance, one study showed that diners at an Italian restaurant often chose to eat butter on their bread rather than dipping it in olive oil because they thought that doing so would reduce the number of calories per slice. And they were right. What they didn't realize, however, is that they would unconsciously compensate for this reduction in calories by eating 23% more bread during the meal (Wansink & Linder, 2003).

This and other research suggests that one of the best ways to reduce our waists is simply to count our bites.

---

cells in our bodies (usually in our abdomens if we are male and in our thighs and buttocks if we are female). But when we lose weight, we experience a decrease in the size of our fat cells but no decrease in their number. Once our bodies have added a fat cell, that cell is pretty much there to stay. It may become thinner when we diet, but it is unlikely to die. Second, our bodies respond to dieting by decreasing our **metabolism,** which is *the rate at which energy is used.* When our bodies sense that we are living through a famine (which is what they conclude when we refuse to feed them), they find more efficient ways to turn food into fat—a great trick for our ancestors but a real nuisance for us. The bottom line is that avoiding obesity is easier than overcoming it.

? **Why is dieting so difficult and ineffective?**

> One reason why obesity rates are rising is that "normal portions" keep getting larger. When researchers analyzed 52 depictions of "The Last Supper" that were painted between the years 1000 and 1800, they found that the average plate size increased by 66% (Wansink & Wansink, 2010).

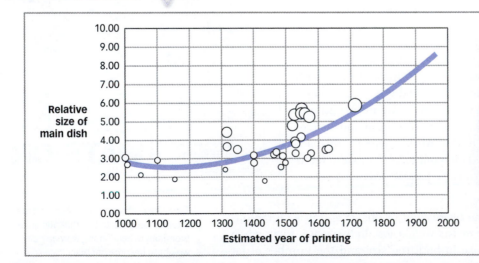

SCALA/ART RESOURCE, NY

Motivation for Sex

Food motivates us because it is essential to our survival. But sex is also essential to our survival—or at least to the survival of our DNA—and so evolution has ensured that a desire for sex is wired deep into the brain of almost every one of us.

A hormone called dihydroepiandosterone (DHEA) seems to be involved in the initial onset of sexual desire. Both males and females begin producing this slow-acting hormone at about the age of 6, which may explain why boys and girls both experience their initial sexual interest at about the age of 10. Two other hormones have more gender-specific effects. Both males and females produce testosterone and estrogen, but males produce more of the former and females produce more of the latter. As you will learn in Chapter 10, these two hormones are largely responsible for the physical and psychological changes that characterize puberty. But are they also responsible for the waxing and waning of sexual desire in adults?

The answer appears to be "yes"—as long as those adults are rats. Testosterone increases the sexual desire of male rats by acting on a particular area of the hypothalamus, and estrogen increases the sexual desire of female rats by acting on a different area of the hypothalamus. Lesions to these areas reduce sexual motivation in the respective genders, and when testosterone or estrogen is applied to these areas, sexual motivation increases.

The story for human beings is far more interesting. The females of most mammalian species—for example, dogs, cats, and rats—have little or no interest in sex except when their estrogen levels are high, which happens when they are ovulating (i.e., when they are "in estrus" or "in heat"). In other

Why don't female humans show clear signs of ovulation?

words, estrogen regulates both ovulation and sexual interest in these mammals. But female human beings can be interested in sex at any point in their monthly cycles. Although the level of estrogen in a woman's body changes dramatically over the course of her monthly menstrual cycle, studies suggest that her sexual desire changes little, if at all.

If estrogen is not the hormonal basis of women's sex drives, then what is? Two pieces of evidence suggests that the answer is testosterone—the same hormone that drives male sexuality. First, when women are given testosterone, their sex drives increase. Second, men naturally have more testosterone than women do, and they clearly have a stronger sex drive. Men are more likely than women to think about sex, have sexual fantasies, seek sex and sexual variety (whether positions or partners), masturbate, want sex at an early point in a relationship, and complain about low sex drive in their partners (Baumeister, Cantanese, & Vohs, 2001). All of this suggests that testosterone is the hormonal basis of the sex drive in both men and women.

While men and women may have different levels of sexual drive, their physiological responses during sex are fairly similar, and they also report similar reasons for having sex in the first place. Although sex is necessary for reproduction, the vast majority of sexual acts are not meant to produce babies. Research on college

metabolism The rate at which energy is used by the body.

"Come back, young man. He needs a booster shot."

The red coloration on the female gelada's chest (left) indicates that she is in estrus and amenable to sex. The sexual interest of a female human being (right) is not limited to a particular time in her monthly cycle.

Table 8.2

Reasons for Sex

Top Ten Reasons Why Men and Women Report Having Sex

	Women	Men
1	I was attracted to the person.	I was attracted to the person.
2	I wanted to experience the physical pleasure.	It feels good.
3	It feels good.	I wanted to experience the physical pleasure.
4	I wanted to show my affection to the person.	It's fun.
5	I wanted to express my love for the person.	I wanted to show my affection to the person.
6	I was sexually aroused and wanted the release.	I was sexually aroused and wanted the release.
7	I was "horny."	I was "horny."
8	It's fun.	I wanted to express my love for the person.
9	I realized I was in love.	I wanted to achieve an orgasm.
10	I was "in the heat of the moment."	I wanted to please my partner.

Source: Meston & Buss, 2007.

students (Meston & Buss, 2007) suggests that people have sex for four general reasons: because of *physical attraction* ("The person had beautiful eyes"), as a *means to an end* ("I wanted to be popular"), to increase *emotional connection* ("I wanted to communicate at a deeper level"), and to *alleviate insecurity* ("It was the only way my partner would spend time with me"). Although men are more likely than women to report having sex for purely physical reasons, **TABLE 8.2** shows that men and women don't differ dramatically in their most frequent responses. It is worth noting that not all sex is motivated by reasons like these: About half of college-age women and a quarter of college-age men report having unwanted sexual activity in a dating relationship (O'Sullivan & Allegeier, 1998). We will have much more to say about sexual attraction and relationships in Chapter 12.

Psychological Motivations

So is life nothing more than the pursuit of ice cream and orgasms? To be sure, eating and sex are fundamental motivations, but most of us care about a few other things as well. We may crave kisses of both the romantic and chocolate variety, but we also crave friendship and respect, security and certainty, wisdom and meaning. In addition to the biological motivations that we share with all mammals, we also have psychological motivations that make us unique.

For example, all animals strive to stay alive, but only human beings realize that this striving is ultimately in vain and that death is life's inevitable end. We and we alone know that every breath we take brings us just a little bit closer to our own demise. Some psychologists have suggested that this knowledge creates a sense of "existential terror" and that much of our behavior is merely an attempt to manage it. According to *terror management theory,* one of the ways that people cope with their existential terror is by developing a *cultural worldview*—a shared set of beliefs about what is good and right and true (Greenberg, Solomon, & Arndt, 2008; Solomon et al., 2004). These beliefs allow people to see themselves as more than mortal animals because they inhabit a world of meaning in which they can achieve symbolic immortality (e.g., by leaving a great legacy or having children) and perhaps even literal immortality (e.g., by being pious and earning a spot in the afterlife). According to this theory, our cultural worldview is a shield that buffers us against the anxiety that knowledge of our own mortality creates.

who arrived late to pick up their children, some of them instituted a financial penalty for tardiness. As **FIGURE 8.12** shows, the financial penalty caused an *increase* in late arrivals (Gneezy & Rustichini, 2000). Why? Because parents are intrinsically motivated to fetch their kids, and they generally do their best to be on time. But when the day-care centers imposed a fine for late arrival, the parents became extrinsically motivated to fetch their children—and because the fine wasn't particularly large, they decided to pay a small financial penalty in order to leave their children in day care for an extra hour. When threats and rewards change intrinsic motivation into extrinsic motivation, unexpected consequences can follow.

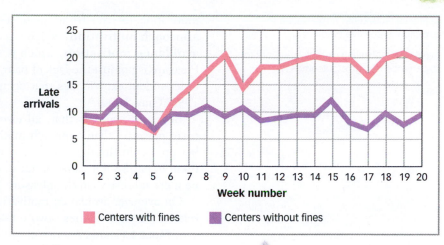

▲ Figure 8.12 **When Threats Backfire**
Threats can cause behaviors that were once intrinsically motivated to become extrinsically motivated. Day-care centers that instituted fines for late-arriving parents saw an increase in the number of parents who arrived late.

Conscious vs. Unconscious

When prizewinning artists or scientists are asked to explain their achievements, they typically say things like, "I wanted to liberate color from form" or "I wanted to cure diabetes." They almost never say, "I wanted to exceed my father's accomplishments, thereby proving to my mother that I was worthy of her love." People clearly have **conscious motivations,** which are *motivations of which people are aware,* but they also have **unconscious motivations,** which are *motivations of which people are not aware* (Aarts, Custers, & Marien, 2008; Bargh et al., 2001; Hassin, Bargh, & Zimerman, 2009).

Psychologists David McClelland and John Atkinson argued that people vary in their **need for achievement,** which is *the motivation to solve worthwhile problems* (McClelland et al., 1953). They argued that this basic motivation is unconscious. For example, when words such as *achievement* are presented on a computer screen so rapidly that people cannot consciously perceive them, those people will work especially hard to solve a puzzle (Bargh et al., 2001) and will feel especially unhappy if they fail (Chartrand & Kay, 2006).

What makes people conscious of their motivations?

What determines whether we are conscious of our motivations? Most actions have more than one motivation, and Robin Vallacher and Daniel Wegner have suggested that the ease or difficulty of performing the action determines which of these motivations we will be aware of (Vallacher & Wegner, 1985, 1987). When actions are easy (e.g., screwing in a lightbulb), we are aware of our most *general motivations* (e.g., to be helpful), but when actions are difficult (e.g., wrestling with a lightbulb that is stuck in its socket), we are aware of our more specific motivations (e.g., to get the threads aligned). For example, participants in an experiment drank coffee either from a normal mug or from a mug that had a heavy weight attached to the bottom, which made it difficult to manipulate. When asked what they were doing, those who were drinking from the normal mug explained that they were "satisfying needs," whereas those who were drinking from the weighted mug explained that they were "swallowing" (Wegner et al., 1984).

Michael Phelps is clearly high—in need for achievement, that is—which helped him win eight gold medals at the 2008 Olympics.

Approach vs. Avoidance

The author James Thurber (1956) wrote "All men should strive to learn before they die/what they are running from, and to, and why." The hedonic principle describes two conceptually distinct motivations: a motivation to "run to" pleasure and a

approach motivation A motivation to experience positive outcomes.

avoidance motivation A motivation not to experience negative outcomes.

motivation to "run from" pain. These motivations are what psychologists call an **approach motivation,** which is *a motivation to experience a positive outcome,* and an **avoidance motivation,** which is *a motivation not to experience a negative outcome.* Pleasure is not just the lack of pain, and pain is not just the lack of pleasure. They are independent experiences that occur in different parts of the brain (Davidson et al., 1990; Gray, 1990).

Research suggests that, all else being equal, avoidance motivations tend to be more powerful than approach motivations. Most people will turn down a chance to bet on a coin flip that would pay them $10 if it came up heads but would require them to pay $8 if it came up tails because they believe that the pain of losing $8 will be more intense than the pleasure of winning $10 (Kahneman & Tversky, 1979).

On average, avoidance motivation is stronger than approach motivation, but the relative strength of these two tendencies does differ somewhat from person to person. **TABLE 8.3** shows a series of questions that have been used to measure the relative strength of a person's approach and avoidance tendencies (Carver & White, 1994). Research shows that people who are described by the high-approach items are happier when rewarded than those who are not and that those who are described by the high-avoidance items are more anxious when threatened than those who are not

Table 8.3

BIS/BAS

To what extent do each of these items describe you? The items in red measure the strength of your avoidance tendency; the items in green measure the strength of your approach tendency.

- Even if something bad is about to happen to me, I rarely experience fear or nervousness. (LOW AVOIDANCE)
- I go out of my way to get things I want. (HIGH APPROACH)
- When I'm doing well at something, I love to keep at it. (HIGH APPROACH)
- I'm always willing to try something new if I think it will be fun. (HIGH APPROACH)
- When I get something I want, I feel excited and energized. (HIGH APPROACH)
- Criticism or scolding hurts me quite a bit. (HIGH AVOIDANCE)
- When I want something, I usually go all-out to get it. (HIGH APPROACH)
- I will often do things for no other reason than that they might be fun. (HIGH APPROACH)
- If I see a chance to get something I want, I move on it right away. (HIGH APPROACH)
- I feel pretty worried or upset when I think or know somebody is angry at me. (HIGH AVOIDANCE)
- When I see an opportunity for something I like, I get excited right away. (HIGH APPROACH)
- I often act on the spur of the moment. (HIGH APPROACH)
- If I think something unpleasant is going to happen, I usually get pretty "worked up." (HIGH AVOIDANCE)
- When good things happen to me, it affects me strongly. (HIGH APPROACH)
- I feel worried when I think I have done poorly at something important. (HIGH AVOIDANCE)
- I crave excitement and new sensations. (HIGH APPROACH)
- When I go after something, I use a "no holds barred" approach. (HIGH APPROACH)
- I have very few fears compared to my friends. (LOW AVOIDANCE)
- It would excite me to win a contest. (HIGH APPROACH)
- I worry about making mistakes. (HIGH AVOIDANCE)

Where Do You Stand?

Here Comes the Bribe

Americans prize their right to vote. They talk about it, they sing about it, and they die for it. They just don't use it very much.

The U.S. Census Bureau estimates that only about 60% of American citizens who are eligible to vote in a presidential election actually do so, and the numbers are significantly lower for "off-year" elections. Not all countries have this problem. Belgium, for instance, has a voter turnout rate close to 100% because, for the better part of a century, failing to vote in Belgium has been illegal. (If you failed to vote in Belgium, don't worry; this only applies to Belgians.) Belgians who fail to vote may be fined, and if they fail to vote several times in a row, they may be "legally disenfranchised," which makes it difficult for them to get a job. Although some people have suggested that America should join the long list of countries that have compulsory voting, Americans generally don't like the threat of punishment.

But they sure do love the possibility of reward—and that's what led Arizona ophthalmologist Mark Osterloh to propose the Arizona Voter Reward Act, which would have awarded $1 million to a randomly selected voter in every election. As soon as Osterloh announced his idea, principled people lined up against it. An editorial in Arizona's *Yuma Sun* newspaper stated: "A jackpot is not the right motivator for voting. . . . People should vote because they want to and because they think it is important. . . . Bribing people to vote is a superficial approach that will have no beneficial outcome to the process, except to make some people feel good that the turnout numbers are higher" (Editorial, 2006). Nonetheless, 185,902 of Osterloh's fellow Arizonans thought his idea had merit, and they signed their names to get his measure on the ballot.

In November 2006, Arizonans defeated the measure by a sound margin, but Osterloh wasn't dejected. "I believe somebody is eventually going to bring this back and get this approved somewhere around the world, and it's going to spread," he said days after the election. "If anybody has a better idea of how to get people to vote, let me know and I will support it" (quoted in Rotstein, 2006).

Should our government motivate people to vote with extrinsic rewards or punishments? We know where Arizonans stand on this issue. How about you?

(Carver, 2006). Just as some people seem to be more responsive to rewards than to punishments (and vice versa), some people tend to think about their behavior as attempts to get reward rather than to avoid punishment (and vice versa).

SUMMARY QUIZ [8.3]

1. The hedonic principle states that
   - a. emotions provide people with information.
   - b. people are motivated to experience pleasure and avoid pain.
   - c. people use their moods as information about the likelihood of succeeding at a task.
   - d. motivations are acquired solely through experience.

2. According to the early psychologists, an unlearned tendency to seek a particular goal is called
   - a. an instinct.
   - b. a drive.
   - c. a motivation.
   - d. a corrective action.

3. According to Maslow, which of the following needs is the most basic?
   - a. self-actualization
   - b. esteem
   - c. safety and security
   - d. belongingness and love

4. Which of the following is primarily a psychological motivation?
   - a. hunger
   - b. sexual interest
   - c. terror management
   - d. nutrition

5. Which of the following activities is most likely the result of extrinsic motivation?
   - a. completing a crossword puzzle
   - b. pursuing a career as a musician
   - c. having ice cream for dessert
   - d. flossing one's teeth

MICHAEL BROWN/GETTY IMAGES

People are motivated to avoid losses and achieve gains, but whether an outcome is seen as a loss or a gain often depends on how it is described. Smart retailers refer to price discrepancies such as this one as a "cash discount" rather than a "credit card surcharge."

Chapter Review

Emotional Experience: The Feeling Machine

▶ Emotional experiences are difficult to describe, but psychologists have identified their two underlying dimensions: arousal and valence.

▶ Several theories attempt to explain how emotional experience and physiological activity are related. The James-Lange theory suggests that a stimulus causes a physiological reaction, which leads to an emotional experience; the Cannon-Bard theory suggests that a stimulus causes both an emotional experience and a physiological reaction simultaneously; and Schachter and Singer's two-factor theory suggests that a stimulus causes undifferentiated physiological arousal about which people draw inferences. None of these theories is entirely right, but each has elements that are supported by research.

▶ Emotions are produced by the complex interaction of several brain structures. Information about a stimulus is sent simultaneously to the amygdala (which makes a quick appraisal of the stimulus's goodness or badness) and the cortex (which does a slower and more comprehensive analysis of the stimulus). In some instances, the amygdala will trigger an emotional experience that the cortex later inhibits.

▶ People care about their emotional experiences and use many strategies to regulate them. Reappraisal involves changing the way one thinks about an object or event; it is one of the most effective strategies for emotion regulation.

Emotional Communication: Msgs w/o Wrds

▶ The voice, the body, and the face all communicate information about a person's emotional state.

▶ Darwin suggested that these emotional expressions are the same for all people and are universally understood, and research suggests that this is generally true.

▶ Emotions cause expressions, but expressions can also cause emotions.

▶ Emotional mimicry allows people to experience and hence identify the emotions of others.

▶ Not all emotional expressions are sincere because people use display rules to help them decide which emotions to express.

▶ Different cultures have different display rules, but people enact those rules using the same techniques.

▶ There are reliable differences between sincere and insincere emotional expressions and between truthful and untruthful utterances, but people are generally poor at determining when an expression is sincere or an utterance is truthful. The polygraph can distinguish true from false utterances with better-than-chance accuracy, but its error rate is troublingly high.

Motivation: Getting Moved

▶ Emotions motivate us indirectly by providing information about the world, but they also motivate us directly.

▶ The hedonic principle suggests that people approach pleasure and avoid pain and that this basic motivation underlies all others.

▶ When the body experiences a deficit, we experience a drive to remedy it. Biological motivations, such as hunger and sexual interest, generally take precedence over psychological motivations, such as terror management.

▶ People have many motivations that can be classified in many ways, such as intrinsic vs. extrinsic motivations, general vs. specific motivations, and motivations for avoidance vs. approach.

emotion (p. 238)
James-Lange theory (p. 238)
Cannon-Bard theory (p. 238)
two-factor theory (p. 238)
appraisal (p. 240)
emotion regulation (p. 241)
reappraisal (p. 242)

emotional expression (p. 243
universality hypothesis (p. 244)
facial feedback hypothesis (p. 246)
display rules (p. 247)
motivation (p. 250)
hedonic principle (p. 250)

drive (p. 252)
bulimia nervosa (p. 253)
anorexia nervosa (p. 254)
metabolism (p. 256)
mortality-salience hypothesis (p. 259)
intrinsic motivation (p. 260)

extrinsic motivation (p. 260)
conscious motivation (p. 261)
unconscious motivation (p. 261)
need for achievement (p. 261)
approach motivation (p. 262)
avoidance motivation (p. 262)

CHANGING MINDS

1. A friend is nearing graduation and has received a couple of job offers. "I went on the first interview," she says, "and I really liked the company, but I know you shouldn't go with your first impressions on difficult decisions. You should be completely rational and not let your emotions get in the way." Are emotions always barriers to rational decision making? In what ways can emotions help guide our decisions?

2. While watching TV, you and a friend hear about a celebrity who punched a fan in a restaurant. "I just lost it," the celebrity said. "I saw what I was doing, but I just couldn't control myself." According to the TV report, the celebrity was sentenced to anger management classes. "I'm not excusing the violence," your friend says, "but I'm not sure anger management classes are any use either. You can't control your emotions; you just feel them." What example could you give your friend of ways in which we can attempt to control our emotions?

3. One of your friends has just been dumped by her boyfriend, and she's devastated. She's spent days in her room, crying and refusing to go out. You and your roommate decide to keep a close eye on her during this tough time. "Negative emotions are so destructive," your roommate says. "We'd all be better off without them." What would you tell your roommate? In what ways are negative emotions critical for our survival and success?

4. A friend is majoring in education. "We learned today about several cities, including New York and Chicago, that tried giving cash rewards to students who passed their classes or did well on achievement tests. That's bribing kids to get good grades, and as soon as you stop paying them, they'll stop studying." Your friend is assuming that extrinsic motivation undermines intrinsic motivation. In what ways is the picture more complicated?

5. One of your friends is a gym nut who spends all his free time working out and is very proud of his finely toned body. His roommate, though, is very overweight. "I keep telling him to diet and exercise," your friend says, "but he never loses any weight. If he just had a little more willpower, he could succeed." What would you tell your friend? When an individual has difficulty losing weight, what factors may contribute to this difficulty?

CRITICAL THINKING QUESTIONS

1. More than two millennia ago, the Roman emperor Marcus Aurelius wrote, "If you are distressed by anything external, the pain is not due to the thing itself, but to your estimate of it; and this you have the power to revoke at any moment." Does research support this claim? What about your personal experience? Have you ever had a painful emotion that you were able to revoke?

2. Although there is a rich variety of human languages across the globe, evidence suggests that facial displays of at least six primary emotions—anger, disgust, fear, happiness, sadness, and surprise—are universal. How can you explain this?

3. The hedonic principle is the notion that all people are motivated to experience pleasure and avoid pain. According to Aristotle, all other motivations rest on this one. If this is true, then how can you explain war?

ANSWERS TO SUMMARY QUIZZES

Summary Quiz [8.1] 1. b; 2. a; 3. c; 4. d
Summary Quiz [8.2] 1. c; 2. d; 3. c
Summary Quiz [8.3] 1. b; 2. a; 3. c; 4. c; 5. d

Need more help? Additional resources are located at the book's free companion website at:
www.worthpublishers.com/schacterbrief2e

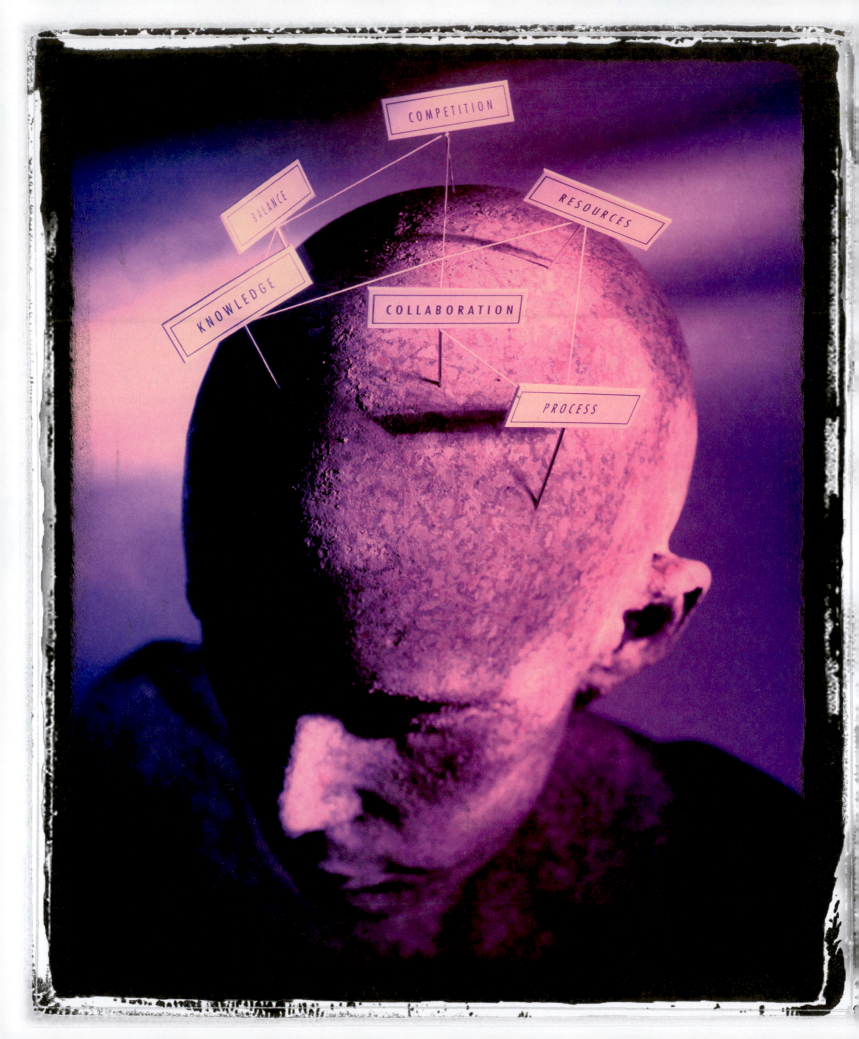

9

Language, Thought, and Intelligence

AN ENGLISH BOY NAMED CHRISTOPHER SHOWED AN AMAZING talent for languages. By the age of 6, he had learned French from his sister's schoolbooks; he acquired Greek from a textbook in only 3 months. His talent was so prodigious that grown-up Christopher could converse fluently in 16 languages. Presented with a made-up language, he figured out the complex rules easily, even though advanced language students found them virtually impossible to decipher (Smith & Tsimpli, 1995).

If you've concluded that Christopher is extremely smart, perhaps even a genius, you're wrong. His scores on standard intelligence tests are far below normal. He fails simple cognitive tests that 4-year-old children pass with ease, and he cannot even learn the rules for simple games like tic-tac-toe. Despite his dazzling talent, Christopher lives in a halfway house because he does not have the cognitive capacity to make decisions, reason, or solve problems in a way that would allow him to live independently.

▶ Christopher absorbed languages quickly from textbooks, yet he completely failed simple tests of other cognitive abilities.

ROMAN SIGAEV/STOCKPHOTO

267

CHRISTOPHER'S STRENGTHS AND WEAKNESSES offer compelling evidence that cognition is composed of distinct abilities. People who learn languages with lightning speed are not necessarily gifted at decision making or problem solving. People who excel at reasoning may have no special ability to master languages. In this chapter, you will learn about several key higher cognitive functions: acquiring and using language, forming concepts and categories, and making decisions: the components of intelligence itself. You'll also learn about where intelligence comes from, how it's measured, and whether it can be improved.

Honeybees communicate with each other about the location of food by doing a waggle dance that indicates the direction and distance of food from the hive.

Language and Communication: From Rules to Meaning

Most social species have systems of communication that allow them to transmit messages to one another. Honeybees communicate the location of food sources by means of a "waggle dance" that indicates both the direction and distance of the food source from the hive (Kirchner & Towne, 1994; Von Frisch, 1974). Vervet monkeys have three different warning calls that uniquely signal the presence of their main predators: a leopard, an eagle, and a snake (Cheney & Seyfarth, 1990). A leopard call provokes them to climb into a tree; an eagle call makes them look up into the sky. Each different warning call conveys a particular meaning and functions like a word in a simple language.

Language is *a system for communicating with others using signals that are combined according to rules of grammar and convey meaning.* **Grammar** is *a set of rules that specify how the units of language can be combined to produce meaningful messages.* The complex structure of human language distinguishes it from simpler signaling systems used by other species; it also allows us to express a wide range of ideas and concepts, including intangible concepts such as unicorn or democracy.

The Complex Structure of Human Language

Compared with other forms of communication, human language is a relatively recent evolutionary phenomenon, emerging as a spoken system no more than 1 to 3 million years ago and as a written system as little as 6,000 years ago. There are approximately 4,000 human languages, which linguists have grouped into about 50 language families (Nadasdy, 1995). Despite their differences, all of these languages share a basic structure involving a set of sounds and rules for combining those sounds to produce meanings.

? What do all languages have in common?

Basic Characteristics

The smallest units of sound that are recognizable as speech rather than as random noise are **phonemes**. These building blocks of spoken language differ in how they are produced. For example, when you say *ba*, your vocal cords start to vibrate as soon as you begin the sound, but when you say *pa*, there is a 60-millisecond lag between the time you start the *p* sound and the time your vocal cords start to vibrate.

Every language has **phonological rules** that *indicate how phonemes can be combined to produce speech sounds.* For example, the initial sound *ts* is acceptable in German but not in English. Typically, people learn these phonological rules without

language A system for communicating with others using signals that are combined according to rules of grammar and convey meaning.

grammar A set of rules that specify how the units of language can be combined to produce meaningful messages.

phoneme The smallest unit of sound that is recognizable as speech rather than as random noise.

phonological rules A set of rules that indicate how phonemes can be combined to produce speech sounds.

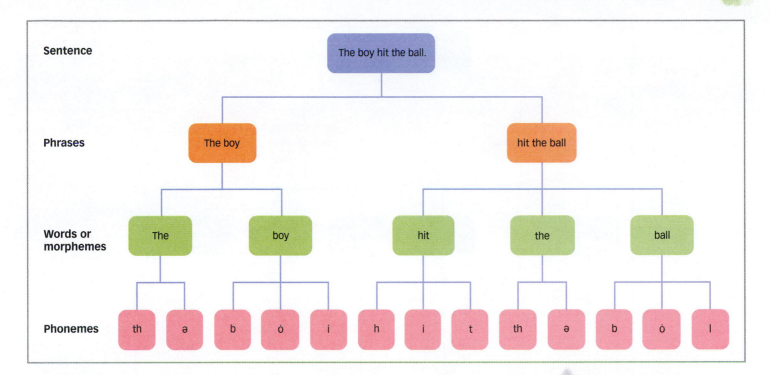

Sentence	The boy hit the ball.
Phrases	The boy / hit the ball
Words or morphemes	The / boy / hit / the / ball
Phonemes	th ə / b ȯ i / h i t / th ə / b ȯ l

▲ Figure **9.1** **Units of Language** A sentence—the largest unit of language—can be broken down into progressively smaller units: phrases, morphemes, and phonemes. In all languages, phonemes and morphemes form words, which can be combined into phrases and ultimately into sentences.

instruction, and if the rules are violated, the resulting speech sounds so odd that we describe it as speaking with an accent.

Phonemes are combined to make **morphemes**, *the smallest meaningful units of language* (see **FIGURE 9.1**). For example, your brain recognizes the *p* sound you make at the beginning of *pat* as a speech sound, but it carries no particular meaning. The morpheme *pat*, on the other hand, is recognized as an element of speech that carries meaning. **Morphological rules** indicate how morphemes can be combined to form words. Some morphemes are *content morphemes* that refer to things and events (e.g., "cat," "dog," "take"). Others are *function morphemes* that serve grammatical functions such as conjunctions, articles, and prepositions (e.g. "and," "the," "into"). About half the morphemes in human language are function morphemes, and it is the function morphemes that make human language complex enough to permit us to express abstract ideas.

Words can be combined and recombined to form an infinite number of new sentences, which are governed by **syntactical rules,** *rules that indicate how words can be combined to form phrases and sentences.* A simple syntactical rule in English is that every sentence must contain one or more nouns and one or more verbs (see **FIGURE 9.2**). So the utterance "dogs bark" is a full sentence but "the big gray dog over by the building" is not.

Meaning: Deep Structure vs. Surface Structure

Language usually conveys meaning quite well, but everyday experience shows us that misunderstandings can occur. These errors sometimes result from differences between the deep structure of sentences and their surface structure (Chomsky, 1957). **Deep structure** refers to *the meaning of a sentence*. **Surface structure** refers to *how a sentence is worded*. The sentences "The dog chased the cat" and "The cat was chased by the dog" mean the same thing (they have the same deep structure) even though on the surface their structures are different.

To generate a sentence, you begin with a deep structure (the meaning of the sentence) and create a surface structure (the particular words) to convey that meaning.

morphemes The smallest meaningful units of language.

morphological rules A set of rules that indicate how morphemes can be combined to form words.

syntactical rules A set of rules that indicate how words can be combined to form phrases and sentences.

deep structure The meaning of a sentence.

surface structure How a sentence is worded.

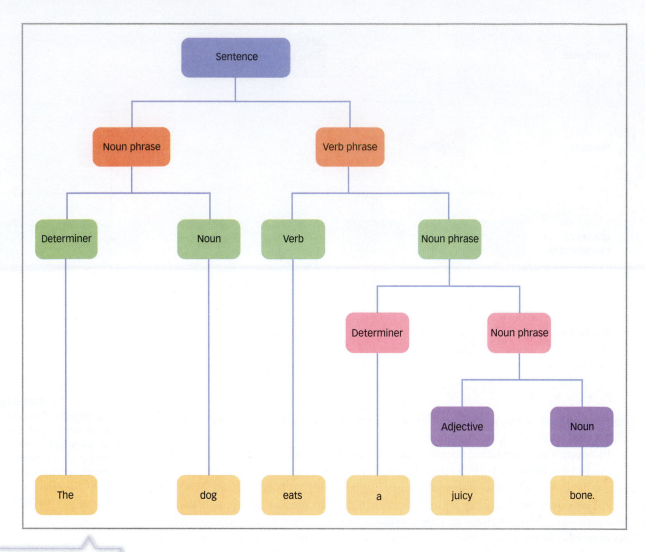

▲ Figure **9.2** **Syntactical Rules** Syntactical rules indicate how words can be combined to form sentences. Every sentence must contain one or more nouns, which may be combined with adjectives or articles to create a noun phrase. A sentence also must contain one or more verbs, which may be combined with noun phrases, adverbs, or articles to create a verb phrase.

When you comprehend a sentence, you do the reverse, processing the surface structure in order to extract the deep structure. After the deep structure is extracted, the surface structure is usually forgotten (Jarvella, 1970, 1971). In one study, researchers played tape-recorded stories to volunteers and then asked them to pick the sentences they had heard (Sachs, 1967). Participants frequently confused sentences they heard with sentences that had the same deep structure but a different surface structure. For example, if they heard the sentence "He struck John on the shoulder," they often mistakenly claimed they had heard "John was struck on the shoulder by him." In contrast, they rarely thought they has heard "John struck him on the shoulder" because this sentence has a different deep structure from the original sentence.

? **Is the meaning or wording of a sentence typically more memorable?**

Language Development

Language is a complex cognitive skill, yet we can carry on complex conversations with playmates and family before we begin school. Three characteristics of language development are worth bearing in mind. First, children learn language at an astonishingly rapid rate. The average 1-year-old has a vocabulary of 10 words, which expands to over 10,000 words in the next 4 years, requiring the child to learn, on average, about 6 or 7 new words *every day*. Second, children make few errors while learning to speak, and, as we'll see shortly, the errors they do make usually result from applying, but overgeneralizing, grammatical rules they've learned. Third, children's *passive mastery* of language (ability to understand) develops faster than their *active mastery* (ability to speak).

Distinguishing Speech Sounds

At birth, infants can distinguish all the sounds that occur in all human languages. Within the first 6 months of life, they lose this ability, and, like their parents, can distinguish only among the contrasting sounds in the language they hear being spoken around them.

> **?** **What language ability do babies have that adults do not?**

distinguish only among the contrasting sounds in the language they hear being spoken around them. For example, two distinct sounds in English are the *l* sound and the *r* sound, as in *lead* and *read*. These sounds are not distinguished in Japanese; instead, the *l* and *r* sounds fall within the same phoneme. Japanese adults cannot hear the difference between these two sounds, but American adults can distinguish between them easily—and so can Japanese infants.

In one study, researchers constructed a tape of a voice saying *"la-la-la"* or *"ra-ra-ra"* repeatedly (Eimas et al., 1971). They rigged a pacifier so that whenever an infant sucked on it, a tape player that broadcast the *"la-la"* tape was activated. When the *la-la* sound began playing in response to their sucking, the babies were delighted and kept sucking on the pacifier to keep the *la-la* sound playing. After a while, they began to lose interest, and sucking frequency declined to about half of its initial rate. At this point, the experimenters switched the tape so that the voice now said *"ra-ra-ra"* repeatedly. The Japanese infants began sucking again with vigor, indicating that they could hear the difference between the old, boring *la* sound and the new, interesting *ra* sound.

Although infants can distinguish speech sounds, they cannot produce them reliably, relying mostly on cooing, crying, laughing, and other vocalizations to communicate. Between the ages of about 4 and 6 months, they begin to babble speech sounds. Regardless of the language they hear spoken, all infants go through the same babbling sequence. For example, *d* and *t* appear in infant babbling before *m* and *n*. Even deaf babies babble sounds they've never heard, and they do so in the same order as hearing babies do (Ollers & Eilers, 1988). This is evidence that babies aren't simply imitating the sounds they hear and suggests that babbling is a natural part of the language development process.

In order for vocal babbling to continue, however, babies must be able to hear themselves. In fact, delayed babbling or the cessation of babbling merits testing for possible hearing difficulties. Babbling problems can lead to speech impairments, but they do not necessarily prevent language acquisition. Deaf infants whose parents

> In this videotaped test, the baby watches an animated toy animal while a single speech sound is repeated. After a few repetitions, the sound changes, and then the display changes, and then they both change again. If the baby switches her attention when the sound changes, she is anticipating the new display, which demonstrates that she can discriminate between the sounds.

fast mapping A phenomenon whereby children can map a word onto an underlying concept after only a single exposure.

telegraphic speech Speech that is devoid of function morphemes and consists mostly of content words.

Deaf infants who learn sign language from their parents start babbling with their hands around the same time that hearing infants babble vocally.

communicate using American Sign Language (ASL) begin to babble with their hands at the same age that hearing children begin to babble vocally—between 4 and 6 months (Petitto & Marentette, 1991). Their babbling consists of sign language syllables that are the fundamental components of ASL.

Language Milestones

At about 10 to 12 months of age, babies begin to utter (or sign) their first words. By 18 months, they can say about 50 words and can understand several times more than that. Toddlers generally learn nouns before verbs, and the nouns they learn first are names for everyday, concrete objects (e.g., chair, table, milk) (see **TABLE 9.1**). At about this time, their vocabularies undergo explosive growth. By the time the average child begins school, a vocabulary of 10,000 words is not unusual. By fifth grade, the average child knows the meanings of 40,000 words. By college, the average student's vocabulary is about 200,000 words. **Fast mapping**, in which *children map a word onto an underlying concept after only a single exposure*, enables them to learn at this rapid pace (Kan & Kohnert, 2008; Mervis & Bertrand, 1994). This astonishingly easy process contrasts dramatically with the effort required later to learn other concepts and skills, such as arithmetic or writing.

Around 24 months, children begin to form two-word sentences, such as "more milk" or "throw ball." Such sentences are referred to as **telegraphic speech** because they are *devoid of function morphemes and consist mostly of content words*. Yet despite the absence of function words, these two-word sentences tend to be grammatical; the words are ordered in a manner consistent with the syntactical rules of the language children are learning to speak. So, for example, toddlers will say "throw ball" rather than "ball throw" when they want you to throw the ball to them and "more milk" rather than "milk more" when they want you to give them more milk. With these seemingly primitive expressions, 2-year-olds show an appreciation of the syntactical rules of the language they are learning.

The Emergence of Grammatical Rules

If you listen to average 2- or 3-year-old children speaking, you may notice that they use the correct past-tense versions of common verbs, as in the expressions "I ran" and "You ate." By the age of 4 or 5, the same children will be using incorrect forms of

Table 9.1	
Language Milestones	
Average Age	**Language Milestones**
0–4 months	Can tell the difference between speech sounds (phonemes). Cooing, especially in response to speech.
4–6 months	Babbles consonants.
6–10 months	Understands some words and simple requests.
10–12 months	Begins to use single words.
12–18 months	Vocabulary of 30–50 words (simple nouns, adjectives, and action words).
18–24 months	Two-word phrases ordered according to syntactic rules. Vocabulary of 50–200 words. Understands rules.
24–36 months	Vocabulary of about 1,000 words. Production of phrases and incomplete sentences.
36–60 months	Vocabulary grows to more than 10,000 words; production of full sentences; mastery of grammatical morphemes (such as -ed for past tense) and function words (such as the, and, but). Can form questions and negations.

CHRISTINA KENNEDY/ALAMY

these verbs, saying such things as "I runned" or "You eated"—forms most children are unlikely to have ever heard (Prasada & Pinker, 1993). The reason is that very young children memorize the particular sounds (i.e., words) that express what they want to communicate. But as children acquire the grammatical rules of their language, they tend to overgeneralize. For example, if a child overgeneralizes the rule that the past tense is indicated by *-ed*, then *run* becomes *runned* or even *ranned* instead of *ran*.

> **?** **Why is it unlikely that children are using imitation to pick up language?**

These errors show that language acquisition is not simply a matter of imitating adult speech. Instead, children acquire grammatical rules by listening to the speech around them and using the rules to create verbal forms they've never heard. They manage this without explicit awareness of the grammatical rules they've learned. In fact, few children or adults can articulate the grammatical rules of their native language, yet the speech they produce obeys these rules.

By about 3 years of age, children begin to generate complete simple sentences that include function words (e.g., "Give me the ball" and "That belongs to me"). The sentences increase in complexity over the next 2 years. By 4 to 5 years of age, many aspects of the language acquisition process are complete. As children continue to mature, their language skills become more refined, with added appreciation of subtler communicative uses of language, such as humor, sarcasm, and irony.

Language Development and Cognitive Development

Language development typically unfolds in a sequence of steps. Nearly all infants begin with one-word utterances before moving on to telegraphic speech and then to simple sentences that include function morphemes. Despite what some proud parents claim, it's hard to find solid evidence of infants launching immediately into speaking in sentences. This orderly progression could result from general cognitive development that is unrelated to experience with a specific language (Shore, 1986; Wexler, 1999). For example, perhaps infants begin with one- and then two-word utterances because of initial limitations to their short-term memories; additional cognitive development might be necessary before they have the capacity to put together a simple sentence. By contrast, the orderly progression might depend on experience with a specific language, reflecting a child's emerging knowledge of that language (Bates & Goodman, 1997; Gillette et al., 1999). These two possibilities are difficult to tease apart, but recent research has begun to do so using a novel strategy: examining the acquisition of English by preschool-aged internationally adopted children who did not know any English prior to adoption (Snedeker, Geren, & Shafto, 2007).

> **?** **Why are studies of internationally adopted children especially useful?**

The researchers examined preschoolers ranging from 2½ to 5½ years old, 3 to 18 months after they were adopted from China (Snedeker et al., 2007). They did so by mailing materials to parents, who periodically recorded language samples in their homes and also completed questionnaires concerning specific features of language observed in their children. These data were compared to similar data obtained from monolingual infants. The main result was clear-cut: Language acquisition in preschool-aged internationally adopted children showed the same orderly progression of milestones that characterizes infants. These children began with one-word utterances before moving on to simple word combinations. Further, their vocabulary, just like that of infants, was initially dominated by nouns and they produced few function morphemes. While the internationally adopted children did add new words to their vocabularies more quickly than infants did, perhaps reflecting an influence of general cognitive development, the main message from this study is that some of the key milestones of language development depend on characteristics of language learning rather than general limitations of cognitive development.

Chinese preschoolers who are adopted by English-speaking parents progress through the same sequence of linguistic milestones as do infants born into English-speaking families, suggesting that these milestones reflect experience with English rather than general cognitive development.

MARVIN JOSEPH/WASHINGTON POST/GETTY IMAGES

nativist theory The view that language development is best explained as an innate, biological capacity.

genetic dysphasia A syndrome characterized by an inability to learn the grammatical structure of language despite having otherwise normal intelligence.

Theories of Language Development

We know a good deal about how language develops, but what underlies the process? The language acquisition process has been the subject of considerable controversy and (at times) angry exchanges among scientists coming from three different approaches: behaviorist, nativist, and interactionist.

Behaviorist Explanations

According to B. F. Skinner's behaviorist explanation of language learning, we learn to talk in the same way we learn any other skill: through reinforcement, shaping, extinction, and the other basic principles of operant conditioning that you learned about in Chapter 7 (Skinner, 1957). As infants mature, they begin to vocalize. Those vocalizations that are not reinforced gradually diminish, and those that are reinforced remain in the developing child's repertoire. So, for example, when an infant gurgles "prah," most parents are pretty indifferent. However, a sound that even remotely resembles "da-da" is likely to be reinforced with smiles, whoops, and cackles of "Goooood baaaaaby!" by doting parents. Maturing children also imitate the speech patterns they hear. Then parents or other adults shape those speech patterns by reinforcing those that are grammatical and ignoring or punishing those that are ungrammatical. "I no want milk" is likely to be squelched by parental clucks and titters, whereas "No milk for me, thanks" will probably be reinforced.

The behavioral explanation is attractive because it offers a simple account of language development, but it cannot account for many fundamental characteristics of language development (Chomsky, 1986; Pinker, 1994; Pinker & Bloom, 1990). First, parents don't spend much time teaching their children to speak grammatically. So, for example, when a child says "Nobody like me," his or her mother will respond with something like "Why do you think that?" rather than "Now listen carefully and repeat after me: Nobody *likes* me" (Brown & Hanlon, 1970. Second, children generate sentences that they've never heard before. This shows that children don't just imitate; they learn the rules for generating sentences. Third, as you read earlier, the errors children make when learning to speak tend to be overgeneralizations of grammatical rules. The behaviorist explanation would not predict these overgeneralizations if children were learning through trial and error or simply imitating what they hear.

Nativist Explanations

In a blistering reply to Skinner's behaviorist approach, linguist Noam Chomsky argued that language-learning capacities are built into the human brain and are separate from general intelligence. This **nativist theory** holds that *language development is best explained as an innate, biological capacity.* According to the nativist view, children learn the grammatical rules of human language with ease in part because they are "wired" to do so. The story of Christopher, whom you met earlier in the chapter, is consistent with the nativist view of language development—his genius for language acquisition, despite his low overall intelligence, indicates that language capacity can be distinct from other mental capacities. Other individuals show the opposite pattern: People with normal or nearly normal intelligence can find certain aspects of human language difficult or impossible to learn. This condition is known as **genetic dysphasia**, *a syndrome characterized by an inability to learn the grammatical structure of language despite having otherwise normal intelligence.* For example, one child with the disorder, asked to describe what she did over the weekend, wrote "On Saturday I watch TV." Notice that the idea this child is trying to communicate is intelligent; only the grammar is wrong. Her teacher corrected the sentence to "On Saturday, I watched TV," drawing attention to the *-ed* rule for describing past events. The following week, the child was asked to write another account of what she did over

"Got idea. Talk better. Combine words. Make sentences."

the weekend. She wrote "On Saturday I wash myself and I watched TV and I went to bed." Notice that although she had memorized the past-tense forms *watched* and *went*, she could not generalize the rule to form the past tense of another word (*washed*).

Also consistent with the nativist view is evidence that language can be acquired only during a restricted period of development. This was dramatically illustrated by the tragic case of Genie (Curtiss, 1977). At the age of 20 months, Genie was tied to a chair by her parents and kept in virtual isolation. Her father forbade Genie's mother and brother to speak to her, and he himself only growled and barked at her. She remained in this brutal state until she was rescued at the age of 13. Genie's life improved substantially, and she received years of language instruction. But it was too late. Her language skills remained extremely primitive. She developed a basic vocabulary and could communicate her ideas, but she could not grasp the grammatical rules of English.

MICHAEL NEWMAN/PHOTOEDIT

Immigrants who learn English as a second language are more proficient if they start to learn English before puberty rather than after.

Less dramatic evidence for a restricted period for language learning comes from studies of language acquisition in immigrants. In one study, the proficiency with which immigrants spoke English depended not on how long they'd lived in the United States, but on their age at immigration, with those who arrived as children being more proficient than those who arrived after puberty (Johnson & Newport, 1989). More recent work using fMRI shows that acquiring a second language early in childhood (between 1 and 5 years of age) results in very different representation of that language in the brain than does acquiring that language much later (after 9 years of age; Bloch et al., 2009).

Interactionist Explanations

Nativist theories are often criticized because they do not explain *how* language develops; they merely explain *why*. The interactionist approach holds that, although infants are born with an innate ability to acquire language, social interaction also plays a crucial role in language. Interactionists point out that parents tailor their verbal interactions with children in ways that simplify the language acquisition process: They speak slowly, enunciate clearly, and use simpler sentences than they do when speaking with adults (Bruner, 1983; Farrar, 1990).

? How does the interactionist theory of language acquisition differ from behaviorist and nativist theories?

A group of deaf children in Nicaragua created their own sign language, complete with grammatical rules, without receiving formal instruction. The language has evolved and matured over the past 25 years.

Further evidence of the interaction of biology and experience comes from a fascinating study of deaf children's creation of a new language (Senghas, Kita, & Ozyurek, 2004). Prior to about 1980, deaf children in Nicaragua stayed at home and usually had little contact with other deaf individuals. In 1981, some deaf children began to attend a new school. At first, the school did not teach a formal sign language, and none of the children had learned to sign at home, but the children gradually began to communicate using hand signals that they invented. Initially, the gestures were simple, but over the past three decades, the Nicaraguan sign language has developed considerably; it now contains many of the same features as more mature languages, including signs to describe separate components of complex concepts. These acts of creation nicely illustrate the interplay of nativism (the predisposition to use language) and experience (growing up in an insulated deaf culture).

SUSAN MEISELAS/MAGNUM

Language Development and the Brain

In early infancy, language processing is distributed across many areas of the brain. But as the brain matures, language processing becomes more and more concentrated in two areas: Broca's area and Wernicke's area. *Broca's area* is located in the left frontal cortex; it is involved in the production of the sequential patterns in vocal and sign languages (see **FIGURE 9.3**). *Wernicke's area*, located in the left temporal cortex, is involved in language comprehension (whether spoken or signed).

Together, Broca's area and Wernicke's area are sometimes referred to as the language centers of the brain; damaging them results in a serious condition called **aphasia**, defined as *difficulty in producing or comprehending language*. As you saw in Chapter 1, patients with damage to Broca's area understand language relatively well, although they have increasing difficulty as grammatical structures get more complex. But their real struggle is with speech production; typically, they speak in short, staccato phrases: "Ah, Monday, uh, Casey park. Two, uh, friends, and, uh, 30 minutes." On the other hand, patients with damage to Wernicke's area can produce grammatical speech, but it tends to be meaningless: "Feel very well. In other words, I used to be able to work cigarettes. I don't know how. Things I couldn't hear from are here."

As important as Broca's and Wernicke's areas are for language, they are not the entire story (for additional insight into brain and language in relation to bilingualism, see the Culture & Community box). The right cerebral hemisphere also contributes

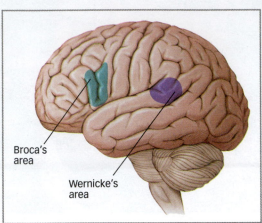

▲ Figure **9.3** **Broca's and Wernicke's Areas** Neuroscientists study people with brain damage in order to better understand how the brain normally operates. When Broca's area is damaged, patients have a hard time producing sentences. When Wernicke's area is damaged, patients can produce sentences, but they tend to be meaningless.

CULTURE & COMMUNITY

Does Bilingualism Interfere with Cognitive Development?

Question: What do you call someone who speaks more than one language?
Answer: A polyglot.
Question: What do you call someone who speaks only one language?
Answer: An American.

Nearly half of the world's population grows up speaking more than one language (Bialystok & Hakuta, 1994; Hakuta, 1986, 1999). Despite this, bilingualism is the source of considerable controversy in the United States. The concern is that communicating with children in more than one language might hinder the proper acquisition and retrieval of crucial conceptual knowledge as well as slow the development of language skills. Is there any evidence for these assumptions?

The available evidence indicates that bilingual and monolingual children do not differ significantly in the course and rate of language development (Nicoladis & Genesee, 1997). In fact, middle-class participants who are fluent in two languages score higher than monolingual participants on several measures of cognitive functioning (Bialystok, 1999, 2009; Campbell & Sais, 1995). On the other hand, bilinguals tend to have a smaller vocabulary in each language than their monolingual peers (Portocarrero, Burright, & Donovick, 2007); they also process language more slowly than monolinguals and can sometimes take longer to formulate sentences (Bialystock, 2009; Taylor & Lambert, 1990).

Recent research on the brains of bilingual individuals indicates that when first learning a new language, there is much greater activity in the frontal lobe for reading second-language than first-language words, probably reflecting great cognitive effort to read the newly learned words (Stein et al., 2009). However, these differences are reduced after just a few months of experience with the second language, suggesting that the first and second languages come to depend increasingly on a shared brain network as second-language proficiency increases (Stein et al., 2009). Further, learning a second language produces lasting changes in a part of the left parietal lobe that is involved in language (Mechelli et al., 2004). The gray matter in this region is denser in bilinguals than in monolinguals, and the increased density is most pronounced in those individuals who are most proficient in using their second language. Thus, learning a second language seems to increase the ability of the left parietal lobe to handle linguistic demands.

to language processing (Jung-Beeman, 2005). Neuroimaging studies show that the right hemisphere is activated during language tasks; patients with damage to the right hemisphere sometimes have problems with language comprehension, while children with damage to the left hemisphere can sometimes recover many of their language abilities. These findings demonstrate that all language processing is not limited to the left hemisphere.

aphasia Difficulty in producing or comprehending language.

concept A mental representation that groups or categorizes shared features of related objects, events, or other stimuli.

SUMMARY QUIZ [9.1]

1. The combining of words to form phrases and sentences is governed by
   a. phonological rules.
   b. morphological rules.
   c. structural rules.
   d. syntactical rules.

2. Which of the following statements about language development is *not* accurate?
   a. Language acquisition is largely a matter of children imitating adult speech.
   b. Deep structure refers to the meaning of a sentence, while surface structure refers to how it is constructed.
   c. By the time the average child begins school, a vocabulary of 10,000 words is not unusual.
   d. Children's passive mastery of language develops faster than their active mastery.

3. Language development as an innate, biological capacity is explained by
   a. fast mapping.
   b. behaviorism.
   c. nativist theory.
   d. interactionist explanations.

4. Damage to the brain region called Broca's area results in
   a. failure to comprehend language.
   b. difficulty in producing grammatical speech.
   c. the reintroduction of infant babbling.
   d. difficulties in writing.

Concepts and Categories: How We Think

In October 2000, a 69-year old man known by the initials J.B. went for a neurological assessment because he was having difficulty understanding the meaning of words, even though he still performed well on many other perceptual and cognitive tasks. In 2002, as his problems worsened, he began participating in a research project concerned with the role of language in naming, recognizing, and classifying colors (Haslam et al., 2007). As the researchers observed J.B. over the next 15 months, they documented that his color language deteriorated dramatically; he had great difficulty naming colors and could not even match objects with their typical colors (e.g., strawberry and red, banana and yellow). Yet even as his language deteriorated, J.B. could still classify colors normally, sorting color patches into groups of green, yellow, red, and blue in exactly the same manner that healthy participants did. J.B. retained an intact concept of colors despite the decline of his language ability—a finding that suggests that we need to look at factors in addition to language in order to understand concepts (Haslam et al., 2007).

A **concept** is a *mental representation that groups or categorizes shared features of related objects, events, or other stimuli.* A concept is an abstract representation, description, or definition that serves to designate a class or category of things. The brain organizes our concepts

"Attention, everyone! I'd like to introduce the newest member of our family."

family resemblance theory The theory that members of a category have features that appear to be characteristic of category members but may not be possessed by every member.

prototype The "best" or "most typical member" of a category.

exemplar theory A theory of categorization that argues that we make category judgments by comparing a new instance with stored memories for other instances of the category.

about the world, classifying them into categories based on shared similarities. Our category for "dog" may be something like "small, four-footed animal with fur that wags its tail and barks." Our category for "bird" may be something like "small, winged, beaked creature that flies." We form these categories in large part by noticing similarities among objects and events that we experience in everyday life. For example, your concept of a chair might include such features as sturdiness, relative flatness, an object that you can sit on. That set of attributes defines a category of objects in the world—desk chairs, recliner chairs, flat rocks, bar stools, and so on—that can all be described in that way. Concepts are fundamental to our ability to think and make sense of the world.

? Why are concepts useful to us?

Psychological Theories of Concepts and Categories

What is your definition of *dog*? Can you come up with a rule of "dogship" that includes all dogs and excludes all nondogs? Most people can't, but they still use the term *dog* intelligently, easily classifying objects as dogs or nondogs. Three theories seek to explain how people perform these acts of categorization.

Family Resemblance Theory

Eleanor Rosch developed a theory of concepts based on **family resemblance**—that is, *features that appear to be characteristic of category members but may not be possessed by every member* (Rosch, 1973, 1975; Rosch & Mervis, 1975; Wittgenstein, 1953/1999). For example, you and your brother may have your mother's eyes, but you and your sister may have your father's high cheekbones. There is a strong family resemblance among you, your parents, and your siblings despite the fact that there is no necessarily defining feature that you all have in common. Similarly, many members of the "bird" category have feathers and wings, so these are the characteristic features. Anything that has these features is likely to be classified as a bird because of this "family resemblance" to other members of the "bird" category (see **FIGURE 9.4**).

Prototype Theory

Building on the idea of family resemblance, Rosch also proposed that categories are organized around a **prototype**, which is *the "best" or "most typical member" of the category*. A prototype possesses most (or all) of the most characteristic features of the category. For North Americans, the prototype of the "bird" category would be something like a wren: a small animal with feathers and wings that flies through the air, lays eggs, and migrates (see **FIGURE 9.5**). People make category judgments by comparing new instances to the category's prototype. According to prototype theory, if your prototypical bird is a wren, then a canary would be considered a better example of a bird than would an ostrich because a canary has more features in common with a wren than an ostrich does.

Exemplar Theory

In contrast to prototype theory, **exemplar theory** holds that *we make category judgments by comparing a new instance with stored memories for other instances of the category* (Medin & Schaffer, 1978). Imagine that you're out walking in the woods, and from the corner of your eye you spot a four-legged animal that might be a wolf but that reminds you of your cousin's German shepherd. You figure it must be a dog and continue to enjoy your walk rather than fleeing in a panic. You probably categorized this new ani-

▼ Figure **9.4** **Family Resemblance Theory** The family resemblance here is unmistakable, even though no two Smith brothers share all the family features. The prototype is brother 9. He has it all: brown hair, large ears, large nose, mustache, and glasses.

Properties	Generic bird	Wren	Blue heron	Golden eagle	Domestic goose	Penguin
Flies regularly	✔	✔	✔	✔		
Sings	✔	✔	✔			
Lays eggs	✔	✔	✔	✔	✔	✔
Is small	✔	✔				
Nests in trees	✔	✔				

◀ Figure **9.5 Critical Features of a Category** We tend to think of a generic bird as possessing a number of critical features, but not every bird possesses all of those features. In North America, a wren is a "better example" of a bird than a penguin or an ostrich.

mal as a dog because it bore a striking resemblance to other dogs you've encountered; in other words, it was a good example (or an exemplar) of the category "dog." Exemplar theory does a better job than prototype theory in accounting for certain aspects of categorization, especially in that we recall not only what a prototypical dog looks like but also what specific dogs look like. **FIGURE 9.6** illustrates the difference between prototype theory and exemplar theory.

Exemplars

Prototype

Exemplar Theory

Prototype Theory

New stimulus

◀ Figure **9.6 Prototype Theory and Exemplar Theory** According to prototype theory, we classify new objects by comparing them with the prototype (or most typical) member of a category. According to exemplar theory, we classify new objects by comparing them with all category members.

category-specific deficit A neurological syndrome that is characterized by an inability to recognize objects that belong to a particular category although the ability to recognize objects outside the category is undisturbed.

rational choice theory The classical view that we make decisions by determining how likely something is to happen, judging the value of the outcome, and then multiplying the two.

Concepts, Categories, and the Brain

Studies that have attempted to link concepts and categories to the brain have helped to make sense of the theories we just considered. For example, researchers using neuroimaging techniques have concluded that we use both prototypes and exemplars when forming concepts and categories. The visual cortex is involved in forming prototypes, whereas the prefrontal cortex and basal ganglia are involved in learning exemplars (Ashby & Ell, 2001; Ashby & O'Brien, 2005). This evidence suggests that exemplar-based learning involves analysis and decision making (prefrontal cortex), whereas prototype formation is a more holistic process involving image processing (visual cortex).

Some of the most striking evidence linking concepts and categories with the brain comes from patients with brain damage. One such patient could not recognize a variety of human-made objects or retrieve any information about them—but his knowledge of living things and foods was perfectly normal (Warrington & McCarthy, 1983). Other patients exhibited the reverse pattern: They could recognize information about human-made objects, but their ability to recognize information about living things and foods was severely impaired (Warrington & Shallice, 1984). Such unusual cases became the basis for a syndrome called **category-specific deficit**, *an inability to recognize objects that belong to a particular category although the ability to recognize objects outside the category is undisturbed.*

> **?** How is an exemplar different from a prototype?

The type of category-specific deficit suffered depends on where the brain is damaged. Deficits usually result when an individual suffers damage to areas in the left hemisphere of the cerebral cortex (Martin & Caramazza, 2003). Damage to the front part of the left temporal lobe results in difficulty identifying humans, damage to the lower left temporal lobe results in difficulty identifying animals, and damage to the region where the temporal lobe meets the occipital and parietal lobes impairs the ability to retrieve names of tools (Damasio et al., 1996). Similarly, when healthy people undertake the same task, imaging studies have demonstrated that the same regions of the brain are more active during naming of tools than animals and vice versa, as shown in **FIGURE 9.7** (Martin, 2007; Martin & Chao, 2001).

How do particular brain regions develop category preferences for objects such as tools or animals? In one fMRI study, blind and sighted individuals each heard a series of words, including some words that referred to animals and others that referred to tools. Category-preferential regions showed highly similar patterns of activity in the blind and sighted individuals. These results provide compelling evidence that category-specific organization of visual regions does not depend on an individual's visual experience. The simplest explanation may be that some brain regions are "prewired" to respond more strongly to some categories than others (Mahon et al., 2009).

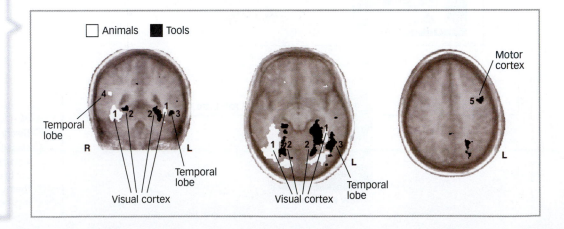

▶ Figure **9.7 Brain Areas Involved in Category-Specific Processing** Participants were asked to silently name pictures of animals and tools while they were scanned with fMRI. The fMRIs revealed greater activity in the areas in white when participants named animals, and areas in black showed greater activity when participants named tools. Specific regions indicated by numbers include areas within the visual cortex (1, 2), parts of the temporal lobe (3, 4), and the motor cortex (5). Note that the images are left/right reversed.

SUMMARY QUIZ [9.2]

1. The "most typical" member of a category is a(n)
   a. prototype.   b. exemplar.   c. concept.   d. definition.

2. Which theory of how we form concepts is based on our judgment of features that appear to be characteristic of category members but may not be possessed by every member?
   a. prototype theory   c. exemplar theory
   b. family resemblance theory   d. heuristic theory

3. The inability to recognize objects that belong to a particular category even though the ability to recognize objects outside the category is undisturbed is called
   a. category-preferential organization.   c. a category-specific deficit.
   b. a cognitive-visual deficit.   d. aphasia.

Decision Making: Rational and Otherwise

We use categories and concepts to guide the hundreds of decisions and judgments we make during the course of an average day. Some decisions are easy—what to wear, what to eat for breakfast, and whether to walk, ride a bicycle, or drive to class—and some are more difficult—which car to buy, which apartment to rent, who to hang out with on Friday night, and even which job to take after graduation. Some decisions are made based on sound judgments. Others are not.

The Rational Ideal

Economists contend that if we are rational and are free to make our own decisions, we will behave as predicted by **rational choice theory**: *We make decisions by determining how likely something is to happen, judging the value of the outcome, and then multiplying the two* (Edwards, 1955). This means that our judgments will vary depending on the value we assign to the possible outcomes. Suppose, for example, you were asked to choose between a 10% chance of gaining $500 and a 20% chance of gaining $2,000. The rational person would choose the second alternative because the expected payoff is $400 ($2,000 × 20%), whereas the first offers an expected gain of only $50 ($500 × 10%). Selecting the option with the highest expected value seems very straightforward. But how well does this theory describe decision making in our everyday lives? In many cases, the answer is "not very well."

The Irrational Reality

Is the ability to classify new events and objects into categories always a useful skill? Alas, no. The same principles that allow cognition to occur easily and accurately can pop up to bedevil our decision making. Here are five examples:

BILL GREENBLATT/NEWSMAKERS/GETTY IMAGES

People don't always make rational choices. When a lottery jackpot is larger than usual, more people will buy lottery tickets, thinking that they might well "win big." However, more people buying lottery tickets reduces the likelihood probability of any one person's winning the lottery. Ironically, people have a better chance at winning a lottery with a relatively small jackpot.

1. Judging Frequencies and Probabilities

Consider the following list of words:

block table block pen telephone block disk glass table block telephone block watch table candy

frequency format hypothesis The proposal that our minds evolved to notice how frequently things occur, not how likely they are to occur.

availability bias The tendency to mistakenly judge items that are more readily available in memory as having occurred more frequently.

conjunction fallacy An error that occurs when people think that two events are more likely to occur together than either individual event.

You probably noticed that the words *block* and *table* occurred more frequently than the other words did. In fact, studies have shown that people are quite good at estimating *frequency*, or the number of times something will happen. In contrast, we perform poorly on tasks that require us to think in terms of *probabilities*, or the likelihood that something will happen.

> **?** Why do we process information about frequency with comparative ease?

In one experiment, 100 physicians were asked to predict the incidence of breast cancer among women whose mammograms showed possible evidence of breast cancer. The physicians were told to take into consideration the rarity of breast cancer (1% of the population at the time the study was done) and radiologists' record in diagnosing the condition (correctly recognized only 79% of the time and falsely diagnosed almost 10% of the time). Of the 100 physicians, 95 estimated the probability of cancer to be about 75%! The correct answer was 8% (Eddy, 1982). Dramatically different results were obtained when the study was repeated using frequency information instead of probability information. Stating the problem as "10 out of every 1,000 women actually have breast cancer" instead of "1% of women actually have breast cancer" led 46% of the physicians to derive the right answer (Hoffrage & Gigerenzer, 1998).

The **frequency format hypothesis** suggests that *our minds evolved to notice how frequently things occur, not how likely they are to occur* (Gigerenzer, 1996; Gigerenzer & Hoffrage, 1995). Thus, we interpret, process, and manipulate information about frequency with comparative ease because that's the way quantitative information usually occurs in natural circumstances. Presenting statistical information in frequency format rather than probability format capitalizes on our evolutionary strengths (Gigerenzer & Hoffrage, 1995; Hertwig & Gigerenzer, 1999). Therefore, the frequency format hypothesis provides an explanation for why physicians do so much better at predicting the incidence of breast cancer when the relevant information is presented as frequencies rather than probabilities.

Jennifer Aniston	Robert Kingston
Judy Smith	Gilbert Chapman
Frank Carson	Gwyneth Paltrow
Elizabeth Taylor	Martin Mitchell
Daniel Hunt	Thomas Hughes
Henry Vaughan	Michael Drayton
Agatha Christie	Julia Roberts
Arthur Hutchinson	Hillary Clinton
Jennifer Lopez	Jack Lindsay
Allan Nevins	Richard Gilder
Jane Austen	George Nathan
Joseph Litton	Britney Spears

▲ Figure 9.8 **Availability Bias** Looking at this list of names, estimate the number of women's and men's names.

2. Availability Bias

Take a look at the list of names in **FIGURE 9.8**. Now look away from the book and estimate the number of male names and female names in the figure. Did you notice that some of the women on the list are famous and none of the men are? Was your estimate off because you thought the list contained more women's than men's names (Tversky & Kahneman, 1973, 1974)? People typically fall prey to **availability bias**, in which *items that are more readily available in memory are judged as having occurred more frequently*.

The availability bias affects our estimates because memory strength and frequency of occurrence are directly related. Frequently occurring items are remembered more easily than infrequently occurring ones, so you naturally conclude that items for which you have better memory must also have been more frequent. Unfortunately, better memory in this case was due not to greater frequency but to greater familiarity.

3. The Conjunction Fallacy

Consider the following description:

> Linda is 31 years old, single, outspoken, and very bright. In college, she majored in philosophy. As a student, she was deeply concerned with issues of discrimination and social justice and also participated in antinuclear demonstrations.
> Which state of affairs is more probable?
>
> **a.** Linda is a bank teller.
> **b.** Linda is a bank teller and is active in the feminist movement.

In one study, 89% of participants rated option b as more probable than option a (Tversky & Kahneman, 1983). This is called the **conjunction fallacy** because *people think that two events are more likely to occur together than either individual event.* In reality, the probability of two or more events occurring simultaneously (in conjunction) is always less than the probability of each event occurring alone, as you can see in **FIGURE 9.9**.

4. Representativeness Heuristic

Think about the following situation:

> A panel of interviewers wrote descriptions of 100 people, including 70 engineers and 30 lawyers. You will be shown a random selection of these descriptions. Read each and then decide if it is more likely that the person is an engineer or a lawyer.
>
> 1. Jack enjoys reading books on social and political issues. During the interview, he displayed particular skill at argument.
> 2. Tom is a loner who enjoys working on mathematical puzzles during his spare time. During the interview, his speech remained fairly abstract and his emotions were well controlled.
> 3. Harry is a bright man and an avid racquetball player. During the interview, he asked many insightful questions and was very well spoken.

Research participants were shown a series of descriptions like these and asked after each one to judge the likelihood that the person described was a lawyer or an engineer (Kahneman & Tversky, 1973). Remember, of the descriptions, 70 were of engineers and 30 were of lawyers. If participants took this proportion into consideration, their judgments should have reflected the fact that there were more than twice as many engineers as lawyers. But researchers found that people instead based their judgments solely on how closely the description matched their concepts of lawyers and engineers. So the majority of participants thought Jack was more likely to be a lawyer and Tom more likely to be an engineer. Harry's description doesn't sound like a lawyer's or an engineer's, so most people said he was equally likely to hold either occupation. But the pool contains more than twice as many engineers as lawyers, so it is far more likely that he is an engineer. People seem to ignore information about the probability of an event, instead basing their judgments on similarities to categories. Researchers call this the **representativeness heuristic**—*making a probability judgment by comparing an object or event to a prototype of the object or event* (Kahneman & Tversky, 1973).

5. Framing Effects

If people are told that a particular drug has a 70% effectiveness rate, they're usually pretty impressed. Tell them instead that 30% of the time the drug does no good and they typically perceive it as risky and potentially harmful. Notice that the information is the same either way. The way the information is presented, however, leads to substantially different conclusions (Tversky & Kahneman, 1981). This is called the **framing effect**, which occurs *when people give different answers to the same problem depending on how the problem is phrased (or framed).*

Why does a 70% success rate sound better than a 30% failure rate?

One of the most striking framing effects is the **sunk-cost fallacy**, which occurs when *people make decisions about a current situation based on what they have previously invested in the situation.* Imagine waiting in line for 3 hours, paying $100 for a ticket to the Warped Tour to see your favorite bands, and waking on the day of the outdoor concert to find that it's bitterly cold and rainy. If you go, you'll feel miserable. But you go anyway, reasoning that the $100 you paid for the ticket and the time you spent in line will have been wasted if you stay home.

Notice that you have two choices: (1) Stay comfortably at home. (2) Endure many uncomfortable hours in the rain. The $100 is gone in either case; it's a sunk cost. But

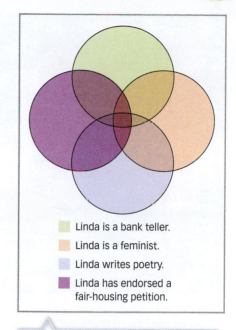

▲ Figure **9.9** **The Conjunction Fallacy** People often think that with each additional bit of information, the probability that all the facts are simultaneously true of a person increases. In fact, the probability decreases dramatically. Notice how the intersection of all these possibilities is much smaller than the area of any one possibility alone.

Linda is a bank teller.
Linda is a feminist.
Linda writes poetry.
Linda has endorsed a fair-housing petition.

representativeness heuristic A mental shortcut that involves making a probability judgment by comparing an object or event to a prototype of the object or event.

framing effects Phenomena that occur when people give different answers to the same problem depending on how the problem is phrased (or framed).

sunk-cost fallacy A framing effect in which people make decisions about a current situation based on what they have previously invested in the situation.

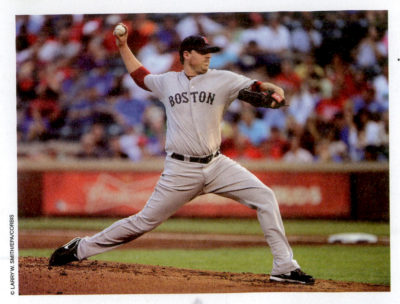

© LARRY W. SMITH/EPA/CORBIS

Worth the cost? Sports teams sometimes try to justify their investment in an expensive player who is underperforming, an example of a sunk-cost effect. John Lackey is a highly paid major league baseball pitcher, but his performance has not recently lived up to his salary.

because you invested time and money, you feel obligated to follow through, even though it's something you no longer want to do.

Even the National Basketball Association (NBA) is guilty of a sunk-cost fallacy. The most expensive players are given more time on court and are kept on the team longer than cheaper players, even if the costly players are not performing up to par (Staw & Hoang, 1995). Coaches act to justify their team's investment in an expensive player rather than recognize the loss. Framing effects can be costly!

Another kind of framing effect occurs when information is presented in terms of losses instead of in terms of savings. For example, imagine you're renting a new apartment, and as part of a promotion you're given a choice between a $300 rebate on your first month's rent or spinning a wheel that offers an 80% chance of getting a $400 rebate. Which would you choose? If you're like most people, you'll choose the sure $300 over the risky $400.

But suppose the lease offers you a choice of paying a penalty for damaging the apartment of either $300 or spinning a wheel that has an 80% of a $400 fine. Now which would you choose? Most people will choose to gamble by spinning the wheel, taking a chance of avoiding the fine altogether, even though the odds are they'll wind up paying more than the sure $300.

Prospect theory argues that *people choose to take risks when evaluating potential losses and avoid risks when evaluating potential gains* (Tversky & Kahneman, 1992). This asymmetry in risk preferences shows that we are willing to take on risk if we think it will ward off a loss, but we're risk-averse if we expect to lose some benefits.

Decision Making and the Brain

A patient identified as "Elliot" (whom you met briefly in Chapter 1) was a successful businessman, husband, and father prior to developing a brain tumor. After surgery, his intellectual abilities seemed intact, but he was unable to differentiate between important and unimportant activities. He lost his job and got involved in several risky financial ventures that bankrupted him. He had no difficulty discussing what had happened, but his descriptions were so detached and dispassionate that it seemed as though his abstract intellectual functions had become dissociated from his social and emotional abilities.

Research confirms that this interpretation of Elliot's downfall is right on track. In one study, researchers looked at how healthy volunteers differed from people with prefrontal lobe damage on a gambling task that involves risky decision making (Bechara et al., 1994, 1997). Participants were allowed to choose cards one-at-a-time from any of four decks; each card specified an amount of play money won or lost. Unbeknownst to the subjects, two of the decks had mostly cards with large payoffs and large losses (the "risky" decks). The other two decks had mostly cards with small payoffs and small losses (the "safe" decks). Early on, most healthy participants choose from each set of decks equally, but they gradually shifted to choosing primarily from the safe decks, where potential payoffs were smaller—but so were potential losses. In contrast, patients with prefrontal damage continued to select equally from the risky and safe decks, leading most to eventually go bankrupt in the game. This performance mirrors Elliot's real-life problems. The healthy participants also showed skin conductance response (SCR) that jumped dramatically when they were thinking about choosing a card from a risky deck—an anticipatory emotional response

prospect theory The proposal that people choose to take risks when evaluating potential losses and avoid risks when evaluating potential gains.

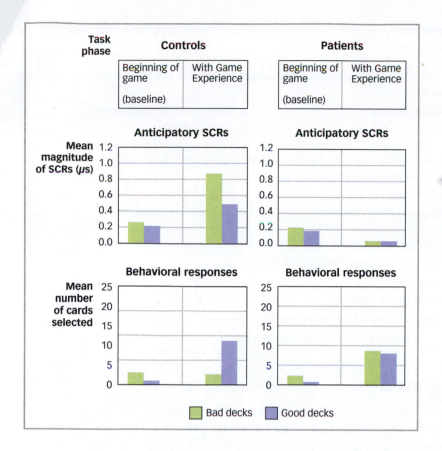

◄ Figure **9.10** **The Neuroscience of Risky Decision Making**
In a study of risky decision making, researchers compared healthy controls' choices with those made by people with damage to the prefrontal cortex. Participants played a game in which they selected a card from one of four decks. Two of the decks were made up of riskier cards, that is, cards that provided large payoffs or large losses. The other two contained "safer" cards—those with much smaller payoffs and losses. At the beginning of the game, both groups chose cards from the two sets of decks with equal frequency. Over the course of the game, the healthy controls avoided the bad decks and showed large emotional responses (SCRs, or skin conductance responses) when they even considered choosing a card from a "risky" deck. Patients with prefrontal brain damage, on the other hand, continued to choose cards from the two sets of decks with equal frequency and showed no evidence of emotional learning. These participants eventually went bankrupt.
After Bechara et al. (1997)

(Bechara et al., 1997). The patients with prefrontal damage didn't show these anticipatory responses when they were thinking about selecting a card from a risky deck. Apparently their emotional reactions did not guide their thinking, and so they continued to make risky decisions, as shown in **FIGURE 9.10**.

Further studies of these patients suggest that their risky decision making grows out of insensitivity to the future consequences of their behavior (Naqvi, Shiv, & Bechara, 2006). Unable to think beyond immediate consequences, they could not shift their choices in response to a rising rate of losses or a declining rate of rewards (Bechara, Tranel, & Damasio, 2000). Interestingly, substance-dependent individuals, such as alcoholics and cocaine addicts, act the same way. Most perform as poorly on the gambling task as do patients with prefrontal damage (Bechara et al., 2001). More recent work has extended these impairments on the gambling task across cultures to Chinese adolescents with binge-drinking problems (C. A. Johnson et al., 2008).

? **What is the relationship of the prefrontal cortex to risky behavior?**

Neuroimaging studies of healthy individuals have provided evidence that fits well with the patient studies: When performing the gambling task, an area in the prefrontal cortex is activated when participants need to make risky decisions as compared with safe decisions (Fukui et al., 2005; Lawrence et al., 2009). Indeed, the activated region is in the part of the prefrontal cortex that is typically damaged in patients who perform poorly on the gambling task, and greater activation in this region is correlated with better task performance in healthy individuals (Fukui et al., 2005; Lawrence et al., 2009). Taken together, the neuroimaging and lesion studies show that aspects of risky decision making depend critically on the contributions of the prefrontal cortex.

SUMMARY QUIZ [9.3]

1. People give different answers to the same problem depending on how the problem is phrased because of
   a. the availability bias.
   b. the conjunction fallacy.
   c. the representativeness heuristic.
   d. framing effects.

2. The view that people choose to take on risk when evaluating potential losses and avoid risks when evaluating potential gains describes
   a. expected utility.
   b. the frequency format hypothesis.
   c. prospect theory.
   d. the sunk-cost fallacy.

3. People with damage to the prefrontal cortex are prone to
   a. heightened anticipatory emotional reactions.
   b. risky decision making.
   c. skin conductance response.
   d. extreme sensitivity to behavioral consequences.

Intelligence

Remember Christopher, the boy who could learn languages but not tic-tac-toe? Would you call him intelligent? It seems odd to say that someone is intelligent when he can't master a simple game, but it seems equally odd to say that someone is unintelligent when he can master 16 languages. In a world of Albert Einsteins and Homer Simpsons, we'd have no trouble distinguishing the geniuses from the dullards. But ours is a world of people like Christopher and people like us—people who are sometimes brilliant, typically competent, and occasionally dimmer than broccoli. Psychologists generally define **intelligence** as the *ability to direct one's thinking, adapt to one's circumstances, and learn from one's experiences* (Gottfredson, 1997). As you are about to see, psychologists have learned a lot over the last hundred years about this prized and elusive quality.

The Intelligence Quotient

Few things are more dangerous than a man with a mission. In the 1920s, psychologist Henry Goddard administered intelligence tests to arriving immigrants at Ellis Island and concluded that the overwhelming majority of Jews, Hungarians, Italians, and Russians were "feebleminded." Goddard also used his tests to identify feebleminded American families and suggested that the government should segregate them in isolated colonies and "take away from these people the power of procreation" (Goddard, 1913, p 107). The United States subsequently passed laws restricting the immigration of people from Southern and Eastern Europe, and 27 states passed laws requiring the sterilization of "mental defectives."

> **?** Why were intelligence tests originally developed?

From Goddard's day to our own, intelligence tests have been used to rationalize prejudice and discrimination against people of different races, religions, and nationalities. This is especially ironic because such tests were developed for the most noble of purposes: to help underprivileged children succeed in school. At the end of the 19th century, France instituted a sweeping set of education reforms that made a primary school education available to children of every social class, and suddenly

intelligence The ability to direct one's thinking, adapt to one's circumstances, and learn from one's experiences.

ratio IQ A statistic obtained by dividing a person's mental age by the person's physical age and then multiplying the quotient by 100 (see *deviation IQ*).

When immigrants arrived at Ellis Island in the 1920s, they were given intelligence tests, which supposedly revealed whether they were "feebleminded."

French classrooms were filled with a diverse mix of children who differed dramatically in their readiness to learn. The French government called on psychologist Alfred Binet and physician Theodore Simon to develop a test that would allow educators to develop remedial programs for those children who lagged behind their peers. "Before these children could be educated," Binet (1909) wrote, "they had to be selected. How could this be done?"

Binet and Simon set out to develop an objective test that would provide an unbiased measure of a child's ability. They began, sensibly enough, by looking for tasks that the best students in a class could perform and that the worst students could not—in other words, tasks that could distinguish the best and worst students and thus predict

? How do the two kinds of intelligence quotients differ?

a future child's success in school. The tasks they tried included solving logic problems, remembering words, copying pictures, making rhymes, and answering questions such as "When anyone has offended you and asks you to excuse him, what ought you to do?" Binet and Simon settled on 30 of these tasks and assembled them into a test that they claimed could measure a child's "natural intelligence," meaning the child's *aptitude* for learning independent of the child's prior educational *achievement*. They suggested that teachers could use their test to estimate a child's "mental level" simply by computing the average test score of children in different age groups and then finding the age group whose average test score was most like that of the child's. For example, a child who was 10 years old but whose score was about the same as the score of the average 8-year-old was considered to have the mental level of an 8-year-old and thus to need remedial education.

This simple idea became the basis for the most common measure of intelligence: the intelligence quotient, or **ratio IQ,** which is *a statistic*

Alfred Binet (left, 1857–1911) and Theodore Simon (right, 1872–1961) developed the first intelligence test to identify children who needed remedial education.

▶ FIGURE **9.11** **The Normal Curve of Intelligence** Deviation IQ scores produce a normal curve. This chart shows the percentage of people who score in each interval of IQ.

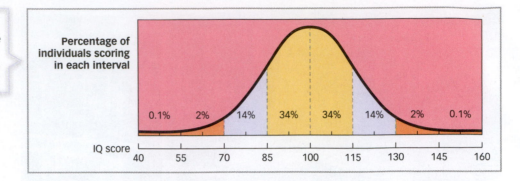

Percentage of individuals scoring in each interval

0.1% 2% 14% 34% 34% 14% 2% 0.1%

IQ score
40   55   70   85   100   115   130   145   160

The magazine columnist Marilyn vos Savant is said to have the world's highest measured IQ. The relatively stupid guy standing next to her is her husband, Dr. Robert Jarvik, who invented the artificial heart.

Caller I.Q.

YOUR HUSBAND 112

deviation IQ A statistic obtained by dividing a person's test score by the average test score of people in the same age group and then multiplying the quotient by 100 (see *ratio IQ*).

obtained by dividing a person's mental age by the person's physical age and then multiplying the quotient by 100. Thus, a 10-year-old child whose test score was about the same as the average 10-year-old child's test score would have a ratio IQ of 100 because (10/10) × 100 = 100. But a 10-year-old child whose test score was about the same as the average 8-year-old child's test score would have a ratio IQ of 80 because (8/10) × 100 = 80. This formula doesn't work so well for adults (after all, there's nothing wrong with a 60-year-old who has the mental level of someone much younger). Instead, adult intelligence is usually measured using the **deviation IQ,** which is *a statistic obtained by dividing a person's test score by the average test score of people in the same age group and then multiplying the quotient by 100.* According to this formula, a person who scored the same as the average person his or her age would have a deviation IQ of 100. Modern researchers typically compute the ratio IQ for children and the deviation IQ for adults. **FIGURE 9.11** shows the percentage of people who typically score at each level of IQ on a standard intelligence test.

The Logic of Intelligence Testing

Binet and Simon's test did a good job of predicting a child's performance in school, and intelligence is one of the factors that contribute to that performance. But surely there are others. Affability, motivation, intact hearing, doting parents—all of these seem likely to influence a child's scholastic performance. Binet and Simon's test identified students who were likely to perform poorly in school, but was it a test of intelligence?

As you learned in Chapter 2, measurement always requires that we generate an operational definition of the property we wish to measure. To design an intelligence test, we begin with the assumption that a *property* called intelligence leads people to experience a wide variety of *consequences* such as getting good grades in school, earning a large income, finding the best route to the gym, or inventing a greaseless burrito. Because it would be highly impractical to actually measure these consequences, we instead devise an easily administered set of tasks (e.g., a geometric puzzle) and questions (e.g., "*Butterfly* is to *caterpillar* as *woman* is to _____") whose successful completion is correlated with those consequences. We could call this "an intelligence test" as long as we understand that what we mean by that phrase is "a measurement of a person's performance on tasks that are correlated with the consequences that intelligence produces." In other words, intelligence tests do not "measure" intelligence in the same way that thermometers measure temperature. Rather, they measure the ability to answer questions and perform tasks that are highly correlated with the ability to get good grades, solve real-world problems, and so on.

Finding such questions and tasks isn't easy, and since Binet and Simon's day, psychologists have worked hard to construct intelligence tests that can predict the consequences of intelligence. Today the most widely used intelligence tests are the *Stanford-Binet* (a test that is based on Binet and Simon's original test but that has been modified and updated many times) and the *WAIS* (the Wechsler Adult Intelligence Scale). Both tests require respondents to answer a variety of questions and solve a variety of problems. For example, the WAIS's 13 subtests involve seeing similarities and differences, working out and applying rules, articulating the meaning of words, recalling general knowledge, explaining practical actions in everyday life, working with numbers, and so forth.

A person's score on a standard intelligence test is a good predictor of that person's academic performance and the number of years of education that person will receive, which is in part why these scores also predict a person's occupational status and income (Nyborg & Jensen, 2001) (see the Real World box). Intelligence test scores predict a wide variety of other important consequences—from how likely people are to commit crimes to how long people are likely to live (Deary et al., 2008; Der, Batty, & Deary, 2009; Gottfredson & Deary, 2004; Leon et al., 2009; Richards et al., 2009; Rushton & Templer, 2009; Whalley & Deary, 2001) (see **FIGURE 9.12**). All in all, intelligence tests scores are excellent predictors of a remarkable range of important consequences. IQ clearly matters.

> **?** What important consequences do intelligence scores predict?

At a singles event in Chicago, Mary Kravenas quickly raises her hand and answers "yes" to the question: "Is your IQ greater than your eyeglass prescription?" Does that question count as a test of intelligence?

Is Intelligence One Ability or Many?

During the 1990s, Michael Jordan won the National Basketball Association's Most Valuable Player award five times, led the Chicago Bulls to six league championships, and had the highest regular season scoring average in the history of the game. ESPN named him the greatest athlete of the century. So when Jordan quit professional basketball in 1993 to join professional baseball, he was as surprised as anyone to find that he . . . well, sucked. One of his teammates lamented that Jordan "couldn't hit a curveball with an ironing board," and a major league manager called him "a disgrace

Intelligence is highly correlated with income. Ken Jennings has won more money on television game shows than any other human being—a whopping $3,623,414.

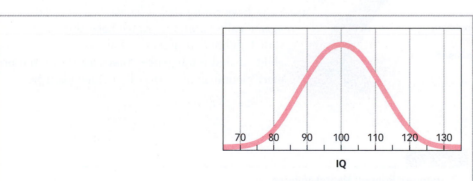

Percentage of people at each IQ level who experience these outcomes

Unemployed more than 1 month out of year (men)	12	10	7	7	2
Divorced in 5 years	21	22	23	15	9
Lives in poverty	30	16	6	3	2
Ever incarcerated (men)	7	7	3	1	0
Chronic welfare recipient (mothers)	31	17	8	2	0
High school dropout	55	35	6	.4	0

◀ FIGURE **9.12** **Life Outcomes and Intelligence** People with lower intelligence test scores typically have poorer life outcomes. This chart shows the percentage of people at different levels of IQ who experience the negative life outcomes listed in the leftmost column.

to the game" (quoted in Wulf, 1994). Michael Jordan's brilliance on the basketball court and his mediocrity on the baseball field proved beyond all doubt that these two sports require different abilities that are not necessarily possessed by the same individual. But if the two sports require different abilities, then what does it mean to say that someone is the greatest athlete of the century? Is *athleticism* just a meaningless abstraction? The science of intelligence has grappled with a similar question for more than a hundred years. As we have seen, intelligence scores predict important outcomes, from academic success to longevity. But is that because they measure a real property of the human mind, or is intelligence just a meaningless abstraction?

To investigate this question, Charles Spearman—a student of Wilhelm Wundt, whom you met in Chapter 1—measured how well school-aged children could discriminate small differences in color, auditory pitch, and weight, and he then correlated these scores with the children's grades in different academic subjects as well as with their teachers' estimates of their intellectual ability. He found that most of these measures were indeed positively correlated: Children who scored high on one measure—for example, distinguishing the musical note C# from D—tended to score high on the other measures—for example, solving algebraic equations. On the other hand, the correlation wasn't perfect: The child who had the highest score on one measure didn't necessarily have the highest score on *every* measure. Spearman combined these two facts into a **two-factor theory of intelligence,** which suggested that *every task requires a combination of a general ability* (g) *and skills that are specific to the task* (s).

As sensible as Spearman's conclusions were, not everyone agreed with them. Louis Thurstone (1938) noticed that while scores on most tests were indeed positively correlated, scores on verbal tests were more highly correlated with each other than they were with scores on perceptual tests. Thurstone took this "clustering of correlations" to mean that there was actually no such thing as g and that there were instead a few stable and independent mental abilities such as perceptual ability, verbal ability, and numerical ability, which he called the *primary mental abilities.* In essence, Thurstone argued that just as we have games called *baseball* and *basketball* but no game called *athletics,* so we have abilities such as verbal ability and perceptual ability but no general ability called intelligence. **TABLE 9.2** shows the primary mental abilities that Thurstone identified.

Michael Jordan was an extraordinary basketball player and a mediocre baseball player. So was he or wasn't he a great athlete?

PATRICK MURPHY-RACEY/SPORTS ILLUSTRATED/GETTY IMAGES

two-factor theory of intelligence Spearman's theory suggesting that every task requires a combination of a general ability (which he called *g*) and skills that are specific to the task (which he called *s*).

Table 9.2

Thurstone's Primary Mental Abilities

Primary Mental Ability	Description
Word fluency	Ability to solve anagrams and to find rhymes, etc.
Verbal comprehension	Ability to understand words and sentences
Number	Ability to make mental and other numerical computations
Space	Ability to visualize a complex shape in various orientations
Memory	Ability to recall verbal material, learn pairs of unrelated words, etc.
Perceptual speed	Ability to detect visual details quickly
Reasoning	Ability to induce a general rule from a few instances

THE REAL WORLD

Look Smart

Your interview is in 30 minutes. You've checked your hair twice, eaten your weight in breath mints, combed your résumé for typos, and rehearsed your answers to all the standard questions. Now you have to dazzle them with your intelligence whether you've got it or not. Because intelligence is one of the most valued of all human traits, we are often in the business of trying to make others think we're smart regardless of whether that's true. So we make clever jokes and drop the names of some of the longer books we've read in the hope that prospective employers, prospective dates, prospective customers, and prospective in-laws will be appropriately impressed.

But are we doing the right things, and, if so, are we getting the credit we deserve? Research shows that ordinary people are, in fact, reasonably good judges of other people's intelligence (Borkenau & Liebler, 1995). For example, observers can look at a pair of photographs and reliably determine which of the two people in them is smarter (Zebrowitz et al., 2002). When observers watch 1-minute videotapes of different people engaged in social interactions, they can accurately estimate which person has the highest IQ—even if they see the videos without sound (Murphy, Hall, & Colvin, 2003).

People base their judgments of intelligence on a wide range of cues, from physical features (being tall and attractive) to dress (being well groomed and wearing glasses) to behavior (walking and talking quickly). And yet none of

these cues is actually a reliable indicator of a person's intelligence. The reason why people are such good judges of intelligence is that in addition to all these useless cues, they also take into account one very useful cue: eye gaze. As it turns out, intelligent people hold the gaze of their conversation partners both when they are speaking and when they are listening, and observers know this, which is what enables them to accurately estimate a person's intelligence despite their mythical beliefs about the informational value of spectacles and neckties (Murphy et al., 2003). All of this is especially true when the observers are women (who tend to be better judges of intelligence) and the people being observed are men (whose intelligence tends to be easier to judge).

The bottom line? Breath mints are fine and a little gel on the cowlick certainly can't hurt, but when you get to the interview, don't forget to stare.

◄ Wahad Mehood is interviewing for a job as a petroleum engineer with EPC Global. Studies show that when a job candidate holds an interviewer's gaze, the interviewer is more likely to consider the candidate to be intelligent. And the interviewer is right!

The debate among Spearman, Thurstone, and other mathematical giants raged for half a century as psychologists hotly debated the existence of *g*. But in the 1980s, new mathematical techniques brought the debate to a quiet close by revealing that Spearman and Thurstone had each been right in his own way. Specifically, the correlations between scores on different mental ability tests are best described by a three-level hierarchy (see **FIGURE 9.13**) with a *general factor* (like Spearman's *g*) at the top, *specific factors* (like Spearman's *s*) at the bottom, and a set of factors called *group factors* (like Thurstone's *primary mental abilities*) in the middle (Gustafsson, 1984). A reanalysis of massive amounts of data collected over 60 years has shown that almost every study done over the past half century results in a three-level hierarchy of this kind (Carroll, 1993). This hierarchy suggests that people have a very general ability called intelligence, which is made up of a small set of middle-level

How was the debate between Spearman and Thurstone resolved?

Dr. Olufunmilayo Olopade received a so-called genius award from the MacArthur Foundation for her work in molecular genetics. Spearman's two-factor theory of intelligence suggests that because she's a brilliant scientist, we should expect her to be a competent (though not necessarily brilliant) musician.

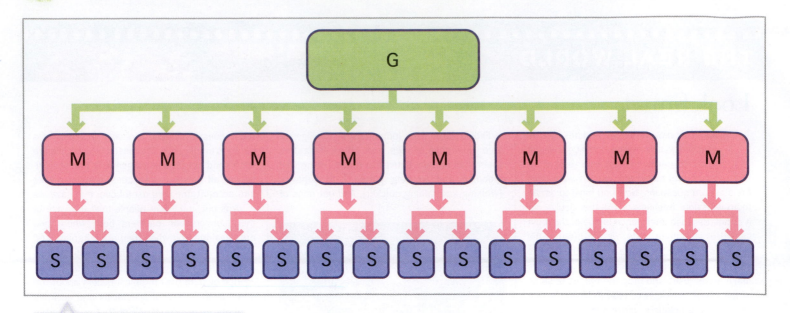

▲ FIGURE **9.13** **A Three-Level Hierarchy** Most intelligence test data are best described by a three-level hierarchy with general intelligence (*g*) at the top, specific abilities (*s*) at the bottom, and a small number of middle-level abilities (*m*) (sometimes called group factors) in the middle.

▼ FIGURE **9.14** **Raven's Progressive Matrices Test** This item from Raven's Progressive Matrices Test measures nonverbal reasoning abilities and is unlikely to be culturally biased.

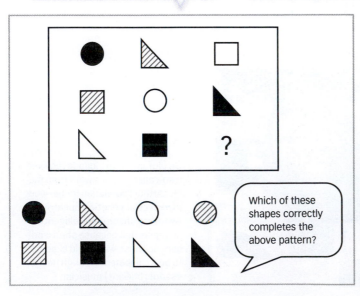

abilities, which are made up of a large set of specific abilities that are unique to particular tasks. Although this resolution to a hundred years of disagreement is not particularly exciting, it appears to have the compensatory benefit of being true.

So what are these middle-level abilities, exactly? Based on intelligence test scores from nearly 500 studies conducted over half a century, psychologist John Carroll suggested that there are eight middle-level abilities: *memory and learning, visual perception, auditory perception, retrieval ability, cognitive speediness, processing speed, crystallized intelligence,* and *fluid intelligence* (Carroll, 1993). Although most of the abilities on this list are self-explanatory, the last two are not. **Fluid intelligence** is *the ability to see abstract relationships and draw logical inferences,* and **crystallized intelligence** is *the ability to retain and use knowledge that was acquired through experience* (Horn & Cattell, 1966). If we think of the brain as an information-processing device, then crystallized intelligence refers to the "information" part and fluid intelligence refers to the "processing" part (Salthouse, 2000). Whereas crystallized intelligence is generally assessed by tests of vocabulary, factual information, and so on, fluid intelligence is generally assessed by tests that pose novel, abstract problems that must be solved under time pressure, such as Raven's Progressive Matrices Test, shown in **FIGURE 9.14**.

Other psychologists have come to different conclusions about the nature of middle-level abilities. For example, psychologist Robert Sternberg believes that there are three kinds of intelligence, which he calls *analytic intelligence, creative intelligence,* and *practical intelligence.* Analytic intelligence is the ability to identify and define problems and to find strategies for solving them; creative intelligence is the ability to generate solutions that other people do not; practical intelligence is the ability to apply and implement these solutions in everyday settings. Some studies suggest that these different kinds of intelligence are independent. For example, workers at milk-processing plants develop complex strategies for efficiently combining partially filled cases of milk, and not only do they outperform highly educated white-collar workers, but their performance is also unrelated to their scores on intelligence tests, suggesting that practical and analytic intelligence are not the same thing (Scribner, 1984). Sternberg has argued

"I don't have to be smart, because someday I'll just hire lots of smart people to work for me."

fluid intelligence The ability to see abstract relationships and draw logical inferences.

crystallized intelligence The ability to retain and use knowledge that was acquired through experience.

prodigy A person of normal intelligence who has an extraordinary ability.

savant A person of low intelligence who has an extraordinary ability.

that tests of practical intelligence are better than tests of analytic intelligence at predicting a person's job performance, though such claims have been criticized (Brody, 2003; Gottfredson, 2003).

Yet another psychologist, Howard Gardner, also believes that standard intelligence tests fail to measure some important human abilities. His observations of ordinary people, people with brain damage, **prodigies** (*people of normal intelligence who have an extraordinary ability*), and **savants** (*people of low intelligence who have an extraordinary ability*) have led him to conclude that there are eight distinct kinds of intelligence: *linguistic, logical-mathematical, spatial, musical, bodily-kinesthetic, interpersonal, intrapersonal,* and *naturalistic.* Moreover, he argues that standard intelligence tests measure only the first three of these abilities because they are the abilities most valued by Western culture but that other cultures may conceive of intelligence differently. For instance, the Confucian tradition emphasizes the ability to behave properly, the Taoist tradition emphasizes humility and self-knowledge, and the Buddhist tradition emphasizes determination and mental effort (Yang & Sternberg, 1997). Westerners regard people as intelligent when they speak quickly and often, but Africans regard people as intelligent when they are deliberate and quiet (Irvine, 1978). Unlike Western societies, many African and Asian societies conceive of intelligence as including social responsibility and cooperativeness (Azuma & Kashiwagi, 1987; Serpell, 1974; White & Kirkpatrick, 1985), and the word for *intelligence* in Zimbabwe, *ngware,* means "to be wise in social relationships." Definitions of intelligence may even differ within a culture: Californians of Latino ancestry are more likely to equate

Unlike Americans, Africans describe people as intelligent when they are deliberate and quiet. "Thought is hallowed in the lean oil of solitude," wrote Nigerian poet Wole Soyinka, who won the Nobel Prize in Literature in 1986.

emotional intelligence The ability to reason about emotions and to use emotions to enhance reasoning.

intelligence with social competence, while Californians of Asian ancestry are more likely to equate it with cognitive skill (Okagaki & Sternberg, 1993). Some researchers take all this to mean that different cultures have radically different conceptualizations of intelligence, but others argue that every culture values the ability to solve important problems and that what really distinguishes cultures is the *kinds* of problems that are considered to be important.

> **?** How does the concept of intelligence differ across cultures?

One of the most important kinds of problems in any culture are emotional problems. How do you tell a friend that she talks too much without hurting her feelings? How do you cheer yourself up after failing a test? How do you know whether you are feeling anxious or angry? Psychologists John Mayer and Peter Salovey define **emotional intelligence** as *the ability to reason about emotions and to use emotions to enhance reasoning* (Mayer, Roberts, & Barsade, 2008; Salovey & Grewal, 2005). Emotionally intelligent people know what kinds of emotions a particular event will trigger; they can identify, describe, and manage their emotions; they know how to use their emotions to improve their decisions; and they can identify other people's emotions from facial expressions and tones of voice. Furthermore, they do all this quite easily, which is why emotionally intelligent people show *less* neural activity when solving emotional problems than emotionally unintelligent people do (Jausovec & Jausovec, 2005; Jausovec, Jausovec, & Gerlic, 2001).

All of these skills turn out to be quite important, especially when it comes to social relationships. Emotionally intelligent children have better social skills and more friends (Eisenberg et al., 2000; Mestre et al., 2006; Schultz, Izard, & Bear, 2004); emotionally intelligent students are judged to be more competent in their interactions (Brackett et al., 2006); emotionally intelligent adults have better romantic relationships (Brackett, Warner, & Bosco, 2005) and better workplace relationships (Elfenbein et al., 2007; Lopes et al., 2006). Given all this, it isn't surprising that emotionally intelligent people tend to be happier (Brackett & Mayer, 2003; Brackett et al., 2006) and more satisfied with their lives (Ciarrochi, Chan, & Caputi, 2000; Mayer, Caruso, & Salovey, 1999).

The data-based and theory-based approaches identify many of the core competencies that constitute intelligence. It isn't entirely clear how many of these there are or what they should be called, but it *is* clear that some people have a lot more of them than others. So what makes smart people so smart? We'll tackle that question next.

Two items from a test of emotional intelligence. Item 1 (left) measures the accuracy with which a person can read emotional expressions and Item 2 (right) measures the ability to predict emotional responses to external events. The correct answer to both questions is A.

From Mayer et al. (2008)

1.	

COURTESY OF DANIEL GILBERT

Emotion	Select one:
a. Happy	○
b. Angry	○
c. Fearful	○
d. Sad	○

2.

Tom felt worried when he thought about all the work he needed to do. He believed he could handle it—if only he had the time. When his supervisor brought him an additional project, he felt _____. (Select the best choice.)

Emotion	Select one:
a. Frustrated and anxious	○
b. Content and calm	○
c. Ashamed and accepting	○
d. Sad and guilty	○

SUMMARY QUIZ [9.4]

1. Which of the following abilities is *not* an accepted feature of intelligence?

   a. the ability to direct one's thinking

   b. the ability to adapt to one's circumstances

   c. the ability to care for oneself

   d. the ability to learn from one's experiences

2. Intelligence tests

   a. were first developed to help children who lagged behind their peers.

   b. were developed to measure aptitude rather than educational achievement.

   c. have been used for detestable ends.

   d. are described by all of the above.

3. Intelligence tests have been shown to be predictors of

   a. academic performance.

   b. health.

   c. attitudes.

   d. all of the above.

4. People who score well on one test of mental ability usually score well on others, suggesting that

   a. tests of mental ability are perfectly correlated.

   b. intelligence cannot be measured meaningfully.

   c. there is a general ability called intelligence.

   d. intelligence is genetic.

5. Most scientists now believe that intelligence is best described

   a. as a set of group factors.

   b. by a two-factor framework.

   c. as a single, general ability.

   d. by a three-level hierarchy.

Where Does Intelligence Come From?

The notion that intelligence is "in the blood" has been with us for a long time. For example, in *The Republic,* the philosopher Plato suggested that some people are born to rule, others to be soldiers, and others to be tradesmen. But it wasn't until late in the 19th century that this suggestion became the subject of scientific inquiry. Sir Francis Galton was a half cousin of Charles Darwin, and his contributions to science ranged from meteorology to fingerprinting. Late in life, Galton (1869) became interested in the origins of intelligence. He did careful genealogical studies of eminent families and collected measurements from over 12,000 people that ranged from head size to the ability to discriminate tones. As the title of his book *Hereditary Genius* suggests, he concluded that intelligence was inherited. Was he right?

Genetic Influences on Intelligence

The fact that intelligence appears to "run in families" isn't very good evidence of genetic influence. After all, brothers and sisters share genes, but they share many other things as

©BETTMANN/CORBIS

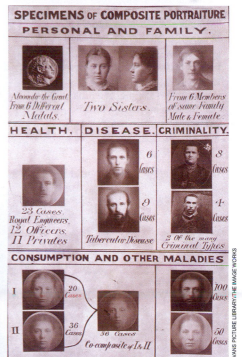

Sir Francis Galton (1822-1911) studied the physical and psychological traits that appeared to run in families. In his book *Hereditary Genius,* he concluded that intelligence was largely inherited.

MARY EVANS PICTURE LIBRARY/THE IMAGE WORKS

Small genetic differences can make a big difference. A single gene on chromosome 15 determines whether a dog will be too small for your pocket or too large for your garage.

well. They typically grow up in the same house, go to the same schools, read many of the same books, and have many of the same friends. Members of a family may have similar levels of intelligence because they share genes, environments, or both. To separate the influence of genes and environments, we need to examine the intelligence test scores of people who share genes but not environments (e.g., biological siblings who are separated at birth and raised by different families), people who share environments but not genes (e.g., adopted siblings who are raised together), and people who share both (e.g., biological siblings who are raised together).

? Why are the intelligence test scores of relatives so similar?

There are several kinds of siblings with different degrees of genetic relatedness. When siblings have the same biological parents but different birthdays, they share on average 50% of their genes. **Fraternal twins** (also called *dizygotic twins*) are *twins who develop from two different eggs that were fertilized by two different sperm*; although they happen to have the same birthday, they are merely siblings who shared a womb and they, too, share on average 50% of their genes. **Identical twins** (also called *monozygotic twins*) are *twins who develop from the splitting of a single egg that was fertilized by a single sperm*; unlike other siblings, they are genetic copies of each other, sharing 100% of their genes.

These different degrees of genetic relatedness allow psychologists to assess the influence that genes have on intelligence. Studies show that the intelligence test scores of identical twins are strongly correlated when the twins are raised in the same household, but they are also strongly correlated when they are raised in different households—for example, when they are separated at birth and adopted by different families. In fact, identical twins who are raised apart have more similar intelligence scores than do fraternal twins who are raised together.

What this means is that people who share all their genes have similar intelligence test scores regardless of whether they share their environments. Indeed, the correlation between the intelligence test scores of identical twins who have never met is about the same as the correlation between the intelligence test scores of a single person who has taken the test twice! By comparison, the intelligence test scores of unrelated people raised in the same household—for example, two siblings, one or both of whom were adopted—are correlated only modestly (Bouchard & McGue, 2003). These patterns suggest that genes play an important role in determining intelligence. This shouldn't surprise us. Intelligence is in part a function of how well a brain works, and given that brains are designed by genes, it would be quite remarkable if genes *didn't* play a role in determining a person's intelligence.

So why don't two identical twins with the same genes score exactly the same on intelligence tests? Even identical twins who live in the same household will have *some* but not *all* of their experiences in common. The **shared environment** refers to *those environmental factors that are experienced by all relevant members of a household*. For example, siblings raised in the same household have about the same level of affluence, the same number and types of books, the same diet, and so on. The **nonshared environment** refers to *those environmental factors that are not experienced by all relevant members of a household*. Siblings raised in the same household may have very different friends and teachers and may contract different illnesses. This may be why the correlation between the IQ scores of siblings decreases as the age difference between them increases (Sundet, Eriksen, & Tambs, 2008). As psychologist Eric Turkheimer (2000, p. 162) notes, "The appropriate conclusion [to draw from twin studies] is not so much that the family environment does not matter for development, but rather that the part of the family environment that is shared by siblings does not matter. What does matter is the individual environments of children, their peers, and the aspects of their parenting that they do not share."

Tamara Rabi and Adrian Scott were 20 years old when they met in a McDonald's parking lot in New York. "I'm just standing there looking at her," Adriana recalled. "It was a shock. I saw me" (Gootman, 2003). The two soon discovered that they were twins who had been separated at birth and adopted by different families.

Environmental Influences on Intelligence

Americans believe that every individual should have an equal chance to succeed in life, and one of the reasons why we bristle when we hear about genetic influences on intelligence is that we mistakenly believe that this means that our genes are our destinies—that "genetic" is a synonym for "unchangeable" (Pinker, 2003). In fact, traits that are strongly influenced by genes may also be strongly influenced by the environment. Height is a heritable trait, which is why tall parents tend to have tall children; yet the average height of Korean boys has increased by more than seven inches in the last 50 years simply because of changes in nutrition (Nisbett, 2009). Genes may explain why two people who have the same diet differ in height—that is, why Chang-sun is taller than Kwan-ho—but they do not dictate how tall either of these boys will actually grow up to be.

> **? In what ways is intelligence like height?**

Is intelligence like height? It depends on whether we are talking about relative or absolute intelligence. *Relative intelligence* is generally stable over time. For example, when people are given intelligence tests many years apart, the same people who got the best (or worst) scores when the test was administered the first time tend to get the best (or worst) scores when it is administered the second time. Indeed, studies show that those who are most intelligent at age 11 are likely to be most intelligent at age 80 (Deary, 2000; Deary et al., 2004, 2008).

On the other hand, as **FIGURE 9.15** shows, an individual's *absolute intelligence* can change considerably over time (Owens, 1966; Schaie, 1996, 2005; Schwartzman, Gold, & Andres, 1987). Studies show that intelligence tends to increase between adolescence and middle age and to decline in old age (Kaufman, 2001; Salthouse, 1996a, 2000; Schaie, 2005), which may be due to a general slowing of the brain's processing speed (Salthouse, 1996b; Zimprich & Martin, 2002). Absolute intelligence also tends to *increase* across generations. The *Flynn Effect* refers to the accidental discovery by the philosopher James Flynn that the average intelligence test score has been rising by about .3% every year, which is to say that the average person today scores about 15 IQ points higher than the average person did just 50 years ago (Dickens & Flynn, 2001; Flynn, 1984, 1987). Some researchers have suggested that these improvements are the result of better nutrition (Lynn, 2009) or better parenting and schooling (Neisser, 1998), and some have suggested that they are a result of the fact that the least intelligent people in each generation are being left out of the mating game (Mingroni, 2007). Others (including Flynn himself) believe that industrial and technological revolutions have changed the nature of daily living such

fraternal twins (also called dizygotic twins) Twins who develop from two different eggs that were fertilized by two different sperm (see *identical twins*).

identical twins (also called monozygotic twins) Twins who develop from the splitting of a single egg that was fertilized by a single sperm (see *fraternal twins*).

shared environment Those environmental factors that are experienced by all relevant members of a household (see *nonshared environment*).

nonshared environment Those environmental factors that are not experienced by all relevant members of a household (see *shared environment*).

AP PHOTO/BINSAR BAKKARA

105-year-old Khatijah (front row, second from right) sits with five generations of her family. The Flynn Effect suggests that intelligence is increasing across generations.

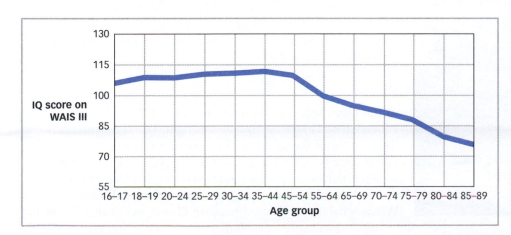

IQ score on WAIS III

Age group

◀ FIGURE **9.15**
Absolute Intelligence Changes over Time
Data from Kaufman (2001).

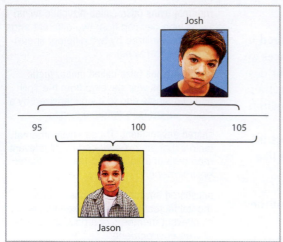

Josh

95   100   105

Jason

▲ FIGURE **9.16** **Genes and Environment**
Genes may establish the range in which
a person's intelligence *may* fall, but
environment determines the point in that
range at which the person's intelligence
will fall. Even though Jason's genes give
him a better chance to be smart than do
Josh's, differences in their diets could
easily cause Josh to have a higher IQ
than Jason.

Although their school was burned by
attackers in 2006, the students at the
Girls High School of Mondrawet in Afghanistan continue to attend. Studies show
that education increases intelligence.

that people now spend more and more time solving precisely the kinds of
abstract problems that intelligence tests include—and as we all know, practice makes perfect (Flynn, 2009; Neisser, 1998). In other words, these scientists argue, people today score better than their grandparents did because
modern life is becoming more like an IQ test!

All of these studies of change over the life span and across generations clearly show that intelligence is not "a fixed quantity that cannot be
increased." Genes may determine the *range* in which a person's IQ is *likely*
to fall, but environments determine the exact *point* in that range at which
the person's IQ actually *will* fall (see **FIGURE 9.16**). Intelligence can and does
change—so what kinds of things can and do change it?

Economics

Perhaps money can't buy love, but it sure can buy intelligence. One of the
best predictors of a person's intelligence is the material wealth of the family in which he or she was raised—what scientists call *socioeconomic status,* or SES.
Studies suggest that being raised in a high-SES family rather than a low-SES family
is worth between 12 and 18 IQ points (Nisbett, 2009; van IJzendoorn, Juffer, & Klein
Poelhuis, 2005).

Exactly how does SES influence intelligence?
One way is by influencing the structure of the
brain itself. Low-SES children have poorer nutri-
tion and medical care, they experience greater daily stress, and they are more likely to
be exposed to environmental toxins such as air pollution and lead—all of which can
impair brain development (Chen, Cohen, & Miller, 2010; Evans, 2004; Hackman
& Farah, 2008). Low-SES children are also less likely to be breast-fed, and breast-
feeding is known to enhance IQ by about 6 points (Anderson, Johnstone, & Remley,
1999; Kramer et al., 2008) (see the Hot Science box).

SES also has cultural effects. For example, research shows that children who grow
up in more intellectually stimulating environments tend to be more intelligent. High-
SES parents are more likely to read to their children and to connect what they are
reading to the outside world ("Billy has a rubber ducky. Who do you know who has a
rubber ducky?") (Heath, 1983; Lareau, 2003). When high-SES parents talk to their
children, they tend to ask stimulating questions ("Do you think a ducky likes to eat
grass?"), whereas low-SES parents tend to give instructions ("Please put your ducky
away") (Hart & Risley, 1995). By the age of 3, the average high-SES child has heard
30 million different words, while the average low-SES child has heard only 10 million; as a result, the high-SES child knows 50% more words than his or her low-
SES counterpart. These differences in the intellectual richness of
the home environment may explain why children from low-SES
families show a decrease in intelligence during the summer, when
school is not in session, whereas children from high-SES families
do not (Burkham et al., 2004; Cooper et al., 1996). Clearly, poverty
is the enemy of intelligence.

? Why are wealthier people
more intelligent?

Education

Alfred Binet believed that if poverty was intelligence's enemy, then
education was its friend. And he was right. The correlation between
the amount of formal education a person receives and his or her
intelligence is quite strong (Ceci, 1991; Neisser et al., 1996). One
reason is that smart people tend to stay in school, but the other reason is that school makes people smarter (Ceci & Williams, 1997).
When schooling is delayed because of war, political strife, or the

ANDY NELSON/CHRISTIAN SCIENCE MONITOR VIA GETTY IMAGES

HOT SCIENCE

The Breast and the Brightest

Scientists have been studying the effects of numerous intelligence-enhancing drugs. Although the jury is still out on most of them, one has now been conclusively shown to increase both academic performance and measured intelligence—and to have a variety of other health benefits to boot. What's the name of this mystery molecule? Mother's milk.

Researchers have known for some time that babies who are breast-fed grow up to have higher IQs than do babies who are formula-fed (Anderson et al., 1999). The problem is that almost all of the studies showing this effect are observational—that is, they show that children whose mothers *elected* to breast-feed end up being more intelligent than children whose mothers *elected* not to. As you learned in Chapter 2, this is a methodological problem called *self-selection,* and it has kept researchers from knowing whether breast-feeding is actually the *cause* of increased intelligence.

But recently, a clever study seems to have settled the matter (Kramer et al., 2008). First, the researchers located several maternity hospitals. Next, they randomly selected half of these hospitals and paid them a visit. During their visits they spoke with new mothers and promoted breast-feeding. The visits worked:

◀ These women are among the 3,738 Filipino mothers who came together in 2006 to set a world's record for simultaneous breast-feeding. A new study shows that breast-feeding leads to increased intelligence. For the babies, that is.

PHOTO/BULLIT MARQUEZ

Mothers in the visited hospitals were seven times more likely than mothers in the unvisited hospitals to exclusively breast-feed their babies. Finally, the researchers sat back and waited for the babies to grow.

Six years later, the researchers measured the intelligence of nearly 14,000 children who had been born in either a visited or an unvisited hospital. They found that children who had

been born in a visited hospital had significantly higher IQs than those who had been born in an unvisited hospital. What's more, the teachers of those children (who didn't know that they'd been breast-fed) gave them higher marks in a variety of subjects.

The jury is in: You can make kids smart with milk from the start. However, scientists still don't know the cause of bad rhymes.

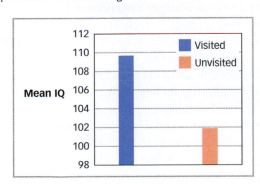

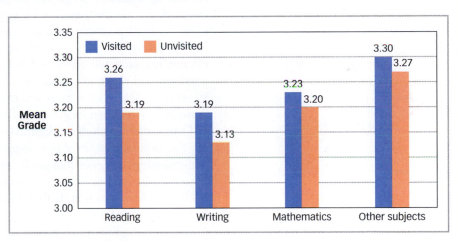

simple lack of qualified teachers, children show a measurable decline in intelligence (Nisbett, 2009). Indeed, children born in the first 9 months of a calendar year typically start school an entire year earlier than those born in the last 3 months of the same year, and sure enough, people with late birthdays tend to have lower intelligence test scores than people with early birthdays (Baltes & Reinert, 1969).

Does this mean that anyone can become a genius just by showing up for class? Unfortunately not. Although education reliably increases intelligence, its impact is small, and some studies suggest that it tends to enhance test-taking ability more than general cognitive ability and that its effects vanish within a few years (Perkins & Grotzer, 1997). In other words, education seems to produce increases in intelligence that are smaller, narrower, and shorter-lived than we would like. That might mean that education can't change intelligence all that much, or it might mean that education is potentially very powerful but that modern schools aren't very good at providing it. Research leans toward the latter conclusion. Although most experiments in education—from magnet schools and charter schools to voucher systems and Head Start programs—have failed to produce substantial intellectual gains for students, a few have been quite successful (Nisbett, 2009), which shows that education *can* increase intelligence substantially even if it usually doesn't. No one knows just how big the impact of an optimal education could be, but it seems clear that our current educational system is less than optimal.

Improving Intelligence

How else might we boost the national IQ? *Cognitive enhancers* are drugs that produce improvements in the psychological processes that underlie intelligent behavior. For example, stimulants such as Ritalin (methylphenidate) and Adderall (mixed amphetamine salts) can enhance cognitive performance (Elliott et al., 1997; Halliday et al., 1994; McKetin et al., 1999), which is why there has been an increase in their use by healthy students over the past few years. These drugs improve people's ability to focus attention, manipulate information in working memory, and flexibly control responses (Sahakian & Morein-Zamir, 2007). Cognitive performance can also be enhanced by a new class of drugs called ampakines (Ingvar et al., 1997). Modafinil is one such drug, and it has been shown to improve short-term memory and planning abilities in healthy, young volunteers (Turner et al., 2003).

How might your children enhance their intelligence?

Although everyone worries about the abuse of these drugs, the distinction between enhancing cognition by taking drugs and enhancing it by other means is not crystal clear. As one distinguished group of scientists recently concluded, "Drugs may seem distinctive among enhancements in that they bring about their effects by altering brain function, but in reality so does any intervention that enhances cognition. Recent research has identified beneficial neural changes engendered by exercise, nutrition and sleep, as well as instruction and reading" (Greely et al., 2008, p. 703). In other words, if both drugs and exercise enhance cognition by altering the way the brain functions, then what's the difference between them?

Other scientists believe cognitive enhancement will soon be achieved not by altering the brain's chemistry in college but by altering its basic structure at birth. By manipulating the genes that guide hippocampal development, scientists have created a strain of "smart mice" that have extraordinary memory and learning abilities, leading the researchers to conclude that "genetic enhancement of mental and cognitive attributes such as intelligence and memory in mammals is feasible" (Tang et al., 1999, p. 64). Although no one has yet developed a safe and powerful "smart pill" or "smart gene therapy," many experts believe that this will happen in the next few years (Farah et al., 2004; Rose, 2002; Turner & Sahakian, 2006). Clearly, we are about to enter a brave new world.

Are Some Groups More Intelligent Than Others?

In the early 1900s, Stanford professor Lewis Terman improved on Binet and Simon's work and produced the intelligence test now known as the Stanford-Binet. Among the things his test revealed was that Whites performed much better than non-Whites. "Are the inferior races really inferior, or are they merely unfortunate in their lack of opportunity to learn?" he asked, and then answered unequivocally: "Their dullness seems to be racial, or at least inherent in the family stocks from which they come." He went on to suggest that "children of this group should be segregated into separate classes . . . [because] they cannot master abstractions but they can often be made into efficient workers" (Terman, 1916, pp. 91–92).

A century later, these sentences make us cringe. But you may be surprised to learn that virtually all scientists agree that intelligence *is* influenced by genes and that some groups *do* perform better than others on intelligence tests.

Let's be clear about one thing: Between-group differences in intelligence are not inherently troubling. No one is troubled by the possibility that Nobel laureates are on average more intelligent than shoe salesmen, and that includes the shoe salesmen. But most of us are extremely troubled by the possibility that people of one gender, race, or nationality may be more intelligent than people of another because intelligence is a valuable commodity and it just doesn't seem fair for a few groups to corner the market by accidents of birth or geography.

But fair or not, the fact is that some groups routinely outscore others on intelligence tests. Whites routinely outscore Latinos, who routinely outscore Blacks (Neisser et al., 1996; Rushton, 1995). Women routinely outscore men on tests that require rapid access to and use of semantic information, production and comprehension of complex prose, fine motor skills, and perceptual speed of verbal intelligence; men routinely outscore women on tests that require transformations in visual or spatial memory, certain motor skills, spatiotemporal responding, and fluid reasoning in abstract mathematical and scientific domains (Halpern, 1997; Halpern et al., 2007). Indeed, group differences in performance on intelligence tests "are among the most thoroughly documented findings in psychology" (Suzuki & Valencia, 1997, p. 1104). But do group differences in intelligence test *scores* reflect group differences in *actual intelligence?*

No test is perfect. Might the imperfections of intelligence tests give one group an advantage over another? There is little doubt that the earliest intelligence tests did exactly that by asking questions whose answers were more likely to be known by members of one group (usually White Europeans) than by members of another.

How might intelligence testing disadvantage one group more than another?

When Binet and Simon asked students "When anyone has offended you and asks you to excuse him, what ought you to do?" they were looking for answers such as "Accept the apology graciously"; the answer "Demand three goats" would have been counted as wrong. But intelligence tests have come a long way in a century, and one would have to look hard to find questions on a modern intelligence test that have the same blatant cultural bias that Binet and Simon's test did (Suzuki & Valencia, 1997). Moreover, group differences emerge even on those portions of intelligence tests that measure nonverbal skills, such as Raven's Progressive Matrices Test (see Figure 9.14). It would be difficult to argue that the large differences betweens the average scores of different groups is due entirely—or even largely—to a cultural bias in IQ tests.

Of course, even when test *questions* are unbiased, testing *situations* may not be. For example, studies show that African American students perform more poorly on tests if they are asked to report their race at the top of the answer sheet because doing so causes them to feel anxious about confirming racial stereotypes (Steele & Aronson, 1995) and anxiety naturally interferes with test performance (Reeve, Heggestad, & Lievens, 2009). European American students do not show the same effect when asked to report their race. Similarly, when women read an essay suggesting that mathematical ability is strongly influenced by genes, they perform more poorly on subsequent

Research suggests that men tend to outperform women in abstract mathematical and scientific domains and women tend to outperform men on production and comprehension of complex prose. Sonya Kovalevsky (1850–91), who was regarded as one of the greatest mathematicians of her time, wrote: "It seems to me that the poet must see what others do not see, must look deeper than others look. And the mathematician must do the same thing. As for myself, all my life I have been unable to decide for which I had the greater inclination, mathematics or literature."

"I don't know anything about the bell curve, but I say heredity is everything."

These high school juniors in South Carolina are taking the SAT. When people are anxious about the possibility of confirming a racial or gender stereotype, their test performance can suffer.

AP PHOTO/MARY ANN CHASTAIN

math tests (Dar-Nimrod & Heine, 2006). Findings such as these remind us that the situation in which intelligence tests are administered can affect members of different groups differently and may cause group differences in performance that do not reflect group differences in actual intelligence.

There is broad agreement among scientists that environment also plays a major role. For example, in comparison to European American children, African American children have lower birth weights, poorer diets, higher rates of chronic illness, and poorer medical care; they also attend worse schools and are three times more likely to live in single-parent households (Acevedo-Garcia et al., 2007; National Center for Health Statistics, 2004). Given the vast differences between the SES of European Americans and African Americans, it isn't very surprising that African Americans score on average 10 points lower on IQ tests than do European Americans. Do genes play any role in this difference? So far, scientists have not found a single fact that requires such a conclusion. Although scientists have discovered some genes that are weakly associated with intelligence (Burdick et al., 2006), they have not found these genes to be more prevalent in one group than in another. Until that happens, psychologists are unlikely to embrace genetic explanations of between-group differences in intelligence. Indeed, some experts, like psychologist Richard Nisbett, believe the debate is all but over: "Genes account for none of the difference in IQ between blacks and whites; measurable environmental factors plausibly account for all of it" (Nisbett, 2009, p. 118).

SUMMARY QUIZ [9.5]

1. Intelligence is influenced by
   a. genes alone.
   b. genes and environment.
   c. environment alone.
   d. neither genes nor environment.

2. Relative intelligence _____ over time; absolute intelligence _____ over time.
   a. changes; is generally stable
   b. is generally stable; changes
   c. is generally stable; is generally stable
   d. changes; changes

3. A person's socioeconomic status has a(n) _____ effect on intelligence.
   a. powerful   b. negligible   c. unsubstantiated   d. unknown

Making Kids Smart or Making Smart Kids?

Once upon a time, babies were a surprise. Until the day they were born, no one knew if Mom would deliver a girl, a boy, or perhaps one of each. Advances in medicine such as amniocentesis and ultrasound technology have allowed parents to look inside the womb and learn about the gender and health of their fetuses long before they meet them. Now parents can do more than just look. For example, IVF (in vitro fertilization) involves creating dozens of human embryos in the laboratory, determining which have genetic abnormalities, and then implanting only the normal embryos in a woman's womb. Gene therapy involves replacing the faulty sections of an embryo's DNA with healthy sections. These and other techniques may be used to reduce a couple's chances of having a child with a devastating illness such as Tay-Sachs, early-onset Alzheimer's, sickle-cell disease, hemophilia, or muscular dystrophy. But in the not-too-distant future they may also enable a couple to increase the odds that their baby will have the traits they value—such as intelligence.

If scientists do find genes or gene complexes that are directly related to intelligence, IVF and gene therapy will provide methods of increasing a couple's chances of having an intelligent—and perhaps even an extraordinarily intelligent—child. Those who oppose the selection or manipulation of embryos fear that there is no bright line that separates repairing or selecting genes that cause disease and repairing or de-selecting genes that cause normal intelligence. This could ultimately lead to a lot of interesting people never being born. As Shannon Brownlee (2002) of the New America Foundation noted, "Today, Tom Sawyer and Huck Finn would have been diagnosed with attention-deficit disorder and medicated. Tomorrow, they might not be allowed out of the petri dish."

People on the other side of this debate wonder what the fuss is about. After all, people can already select their offspring for high IQ by mating with the smartest partners they can find. And once their babies are born, most parents will work hard to enhance their children's intelligence by giving them everything from carrots to cello lessons. Science writer Ron Bailey predicts that "parents will someday screen embryos for desirable traits such as tougher immune systems, stronger bodies, and smarter brains. What horrors do such designer babies face? Longer, healthier, smarter, and perhaps even happier lives? It is hard to see any ethical problem with that" (Bailey, 2002).

Should parents be allowed to use genetic screening or gene therapy to increase the intelligence of their children? Where do you stand?

Chapter Review

SUMMARY

Language and Communication: From Rules to Meaning

► Human language is characterized by a complex organization— from phonemes to morphemes to phrases and finally to sentences.

► Grammatical rules are acquired early in development, even without being taught explicitly. Instead, children appear to be biologically predisposed to process language in ways that allow them to extract these grammatical rules from the language they hear.

► Our abilities to produce and comprehend language depend on distinct regions of the brain, with Broca's area critical for language production and Wernicke's area critical for comprehension.

Concepts and Categories: How We Think

► We organize knowledge about objects, events, or other stimuli by creating concepts.

► Family resemblance theory states that items in the same category share certain, although not necessarily all, features; prototype theory states that we use the most "typical" member of a category to assess new items; exemplar theory states that we compare new items with stored memories of other members of the category.

► Neuroimaging studies have shown that prototypes and exemplars are processed in different parts of the brain; they suggest that certain brain areas may be "prewired" to respond strongly to distinct categories, such as living things and human-made things.

Decision-Making: Rational and Otherwise

► Human decision making often departs from a completely rational process, and the mistakes that accompany this departure tell us a lot about how the human mind works.

- We can make irrational decisions when we fail to estimate probabilities accurately or when we fall prey to the availability bias, the conjunction fallacy, the representative heuristic, or framing effects.

- Some of our decision-making errors can be explained by prospect theory, the idea that people are more likely to take on risk when evaluating potential losses than potential gain, and the frequency format hypothesis, the idea that we evolved to notice how frequently things occur, not how likely they are to occur.

- The prefrontal cortex plays an important role in decision making, and patients with prefrontal damage make more risky decisions than do healthy controls.

Intelligence

- *Intelligence* is a mental ability that enables people to direct their thinking, adapt to their circumstances, and learn from their experiences.

- Intelligence tests produce a score known as an *intelligence quotient* or IQ. *Ratio IQ* is the ratio of a person's mental to physical age; *deviation IQ* is the deviation of a person's test score from the average score of his or her peers.

- Intelligence test scores predict a person's academic performance, job performance, health, wealth, and attitudes.

- People who score well on one test of mental ability *usually* score well on others, which suggests that there is a property called g (general intelligence), but they don't *always* score well on others, which suggests that there are also properties called s (specific abilities). Research reveals that between g and s are several *middle-level abilities*.

Where Does Intelligence Come From?

- Both genes and environments influence intelligence.

- Relative intelligence is generally stable over time, but absolute intelligence changes.

- SES has a powerful influence on intelligence, and education has a moderate influence.

- Human intelligence can be temporarily increased by cognitive enhancers such as Ritalin and Adderall, and nonhuman intelligence has been permanently increased by genetic manipulation.

- Some groups outscore others on intelligence tests because (a) testing situations impair the performance of some groups more than others and (b) some groups live in less healthful and stimulating environments, but there is no compelling evidence to suggest that between-group differences in intelligence are due to genetic differences.

KEY TERMS

language (p. 268)
grammar (p. 268)
phoneme (p. 268)
phonological rules (p. 268)
morphemes (p. 269)
morphological rules (p. 269)
syntactical rules (p. 269)
deep structure (p. 269)
surface structure (p. 269)
fast mapping (p. 272)
telegraphic speech (p. 272)

nativist theory (p. 274)
genetic dysphasia (p. 274)
aphasia (p. 276)
concept (p. 277)
family resemblance theory (p. 278)
prototype (p. 278)
exemplar theory (p. 278)
category-specific deficit (p. 280)
rational choice theory (p. 281)
frequency format hypothesis (p. 282)

availability bias (p. 282)
conjunction fallacy (p. 282)
representativeness heuristic (p. 283)
framing effects (p. 283)
sunk-cost fallacy (p. 283)
prospect theory (p. 284)
intelligence (p. 286)
ratio IQ (p. 287)
deviation IQ (p. 288)
two-factor theory of intelligence (p. 290)

fluid intelligence (p. 292)
crystallized intelligence (p. 292)
prodigy (p. 293)
savant (p. 293)
emotional intelligence (p. 294)
fraternal twins (p. 296)
identical twins (p. 296)
shared environment (p. 296)
nonshared environment (p. 296)

CHANGING MINDS

1. In September, 2011, *Wired* magazine ran an article discussing the "fourth down decisions" of NFL coaches. On the fourth down, a team can either take a big risk by trying to run or pass for a first down, or they can take a smaller risk by kicking the ball. Statistical analyses show that the riskier play is usually the better one but that coaches choose the safer play over 90% of the time. Reading this article, one of your friends is incredulous. "Coaches aren't stupid, and they want to win," he says. "Why would they always make the wrong decision?" Your

friend is assuming that humans are rational decision makers. In what ways is your friend wrong? What might be causing the irrational decision making by football coaches?

2. In biology class, the topic turns to genetics. The professor describes the "Doogie" mouse, named after a 1990s TV show starring Neil Patrick Harris as a child genius named Doogie Howser. Doogie mice have a genetic manipulation that makes them smarter than genetically normal mice. Your classmate turns to you. "I knew it," she says. "There's a 'smart gene' after

all; some people have it and some people don't, and that's why some people are intelligent and some people aren't." What would you tell her about the role genetics plays in intelligence? What other factors, besides genes, play an important role in determining an individual's intelligence?

3. One of your friends tells you about his sister. "We're very competitive," he says. "But she's smarter. We both took IQ tests when we were kids, and she scored 104 but I only scored 102." What would you tell your friend about the relationship between IQ scores and intelligence? What do IQ scores really measure?

4. A speaker visiting your university notes that there are still gender differences in academia; for example, in math departments across the country, women make up only about 26% of assistant professors and 10% of full professors. One of your classmates notes that the statistic isn't surprising: "Girls don't do as well as boys at math," he says. "So it's not surprising that fewer girls choose math-related careers." Based on what you've read in the text about group differences in intelligence, why might women perform more poorly then men on tests of math or science—even if the groups actually have similar ability?

5. One of your cousins has a young son, and she's very proud of the boy's accomplishments. "He's very smart," she says. "I know this because he has a great memory: He gets 100% on all his vocabulary tests." What kind of skills do vocabulary tests measure? While these skills are important for intelligence, what other abilities contribute to an individual's overall intelligence?

CRITICAL THINKING QUESTIONS

1. To create a sentence, you have to change the deep structure of an idea into the surface structure of a sentence. The person receiving the message translates the surface structure of the sentence back into the deep structure of the idea.

With surface structure so important to communication, why are we able to communicate effectively when we quickly forget the surface structure of sentences? Why might this forgetfulness of the surface structure be an evolutionary benefit?

2. According to rational choice theory, people evaluate all options when making a decision and choose the alternative with the greatest benefit to them. However, psychological research shows us that this is not always the case. Indeed, we are often forced to make decisions without all the information present.

In these conditions, we are often fooled into making a different decision than we normally would because of how the options are presented to us.

Think back to a recent election. How might some political candidates use the conjunction fallacy, framing effects, or prospect theory to influence voters' evaluations of their opponents or their opponents' views?

3. Intelligence tests have been used to rationalize prejudice and discrimination, and their results can be influenced by features of the testing situation. On the other hand, they are excellent predictors of success in life. Given this, do you support or oppose giving intelligence tests to children in school?

ANSWERS TO SUMMARY QUIZZES

Summary Quiz [9.1] 1. d; 2. a; 3. c; 4. b
Summary Quiz [9.2] 1. a; 2. b; 3. c
Summary Quiz [9.3] 1. d; 2. c; 3. b
Summary Quiz [9.4] 1. c; 2. d; 3. d; 4. c; 5. d
Summary Quiz [9.5] 1. b; 2. b; 3. a

Need more help? Additional resources are located at the book's free companion website at:
www.worthpublishers.com/schacterbrief2e

10

Development

HIS MOTHER CALLED HIM ADI AND SHOWERED him with affection, but his father was not so kind. As his sister later recalled, "Adi challenged my father to extreme harshness and got his sound thrashing every day." Although his father wanted him to become a civil servant, Adi's true love was art, and his mother quietly encouraged that gentler interest. Adi was just 18 years old when his mother was diagnosed with terminal cancer, and he was heartbroken when she died. Even her physician remarked that "in all my career, I have never seen anyone so prostrate with grief."

But Adi had little time for grieving. As he wrote, "Poverty and hard reality compelled me to make a quick decision. I was faced with the problem of somehow making my own living." Adi resolved to make his living as an artist. He moved to the city and applied to art school, but he was flatly rejected. Motherless and penniless, Adi wandered the city streets for 5 long years, sleeping on park benches, living in homeless shelters, and eating in soup kitchens, while trying desperately to sell his sketches and watercolors. Ten years later, Adi had achieved the fame he so desired, but not as an artist. Because while the artist's mother called him Adi, the rest of us know him as Adolf Hitler.

▶ One of Adi's paintings, *Village Scene,* sold at auction in 2006 for almost $20,000.

AP PHOTO/BARRY GOMER

MAKSYM BONDARCHUK/SHUTTERSTOCK.COM

307

WHY IS IT SO DIFFICULT TO IMAGINE THE GREATEST mass murderer of the 20th century as a gentle child who loved to draw, as a compassionate adolescent who cared for his ailing mother, or as a dedicated young adult who suffered cold and hunger for the sake of beauty? After all, none of us began as the people we are now. From birth to infancy, from childhood to adolescence, from young adulthood to old age, one of the most obvious facts about human beings is that we change over time. Their development includes both dramatic transformations and striking consistencies in the way we look, think, feel, and act. **Developmental psychology** is *the study of continuity and change across the life span.*

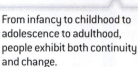
From infancy to childhood to adolescence to adulthood, people exhibit both continuity and change.

We'll start where it all starts by examining the 9-month period between conception and birth, and we'll see how prenatal events set the stage for everything to come. Next, we'll examine childhood, during which children must learn how to think about the world and their relationship to it, to understand and bond with others, to tell the difference between right and wrong. We'll examine the relatively modern invention called adolescence, the stage at which children become both independent actors and sexual creatures. Finally, we'll examine adulthood, the stage at which people typically leave their parents, find mates, have children, and grow old—with some surprising results.

Prenatality: A Womb with a View

You probably calculate your age by counting your birthdays, but the fact is that when you were born, you were already 9 months old. The *prenatal stage* of development ends with birth, but it begins when about 200 million sperm begin a hazardous journey from a woman's vagina, through her uterus, and on to her fallopian tubes. Many of these sperm have defects that prevent them from swimming vigorously enough to make progress, and others get stuck in the spermatazoidal equivalent of a traffic jam. Of those that manage to make their way through the uterus, many take a wrong turn and end up in the fallopian tube that does not contain an egg. A mere 200 or so of the original 200 million sperm manage to get close enough to an egg to release digestive enzymes that erode the egg's protective outer layer. As soon as one of these sperm manages to penetrate the coating, the egg quickly releases a chemical that seals the coating and keeps all the remaining sperm from entering. After triumphing

developmental psychology The study of continuity and change across the life span.

zygote A fertilized egg that contains chromosomes from both a sperm and an egg.

germinal stage The 2-week period of prenatal development that begins at conception.

embryonic stage The period of prenatal development that lasts from the second week until about the eighth week.

fetal stage The period of prenatal development that lasts from the ninth week until birth.

over massive odds, the one successful sperm sheds its tail and fertilizes the egg. In about 12 hours, the nuclei of the sperm and the egg merge, and the prenatal development of a unique human being begins.

Prenatal Development

A **zygote** is *a fertilized egg that contains chromosomes from both a sperm and an egg.* From the first moment of its existence, a zygote has one thing in common with the person it will ultimately become: gender. Each human sperm cell and each human egg cell contain 23 *chromosomes* that contain *genes,* which provide the blueprint for all biological development. One of these chromosomes (the 23rd) can come in two variations: X or Y. Some sperm carry an X chromosome, others carry a Y chromosome. If the egg is fertilized by a sperm that carries a Y chromosome, then the zygote is male; if the egg is fertilized by a sperm that carries an X chromosome, the zygote is female.

The 2-week period that begins at conception is known as the **germinal stage.** During this stage the one-celled zygote begins to divide—into two cells that divide into four, which then divide into eight, and so on. By the time of birth, the zygote has divided into trillions of cells, each of which contains exactly one set of 23 chromosomes from the sperm and one set of 23 chromosomes from the egg. During the germinal stage, the zygote migrates back down the fallopian tube and implants itself in the wall of the uterus. This is a difficult journey, and about half of all zygotes do not complete it, either because they are defective or because they implant themselves in an inhospitable part of the uterus. Male zygotes are especially unlikely to complete this journey, but no one understands why (though some people suspect it's because male zygotes are especially unwilling to stop and ask for directions).

? **What are the three prenatal stages?**

When the zygote implants itself on the uterine wall, a new stage of development begins. The **embryonic stage** is *a period that lasts from the second week until about the eighth week* (see **FIGURE 10.1**). During this stage, the zygote continues to divide and its cells begin to differentiate. The zygote at this stage is known as an *embryo,* and although it is just an inch long, it already has a beating heart and other body parts, such as arms and legs. Male embryos begin to produce a hormone called testosterone, which masculinizes their reproductive organs. Without testosterone, the embryo continues developing as a female.

The **fetal stage** is *a period that lasts from the ninth week until birth.* The embryo at this stage is known as a *fetus,* and it has a skeleton and muscles that make it capable of movement. During the fetal stage, the size of the fetus increases rapidly. It

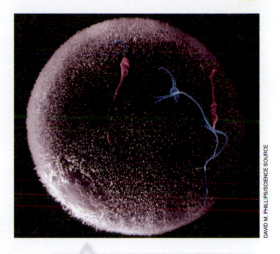

This electron micrograph shows a false-color image of several human sperm, one of which is fertilizing an egg.

▼ Figure **10.1** **Prenatal Development** Human beings undergo amazing changes in the 9 months of prenatal development. These images show an embryo at 30 days, an embryo at 8 to 9 weeks, and a fetus at 5 months.

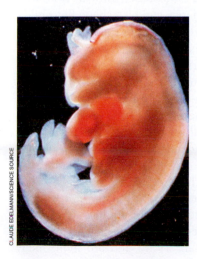
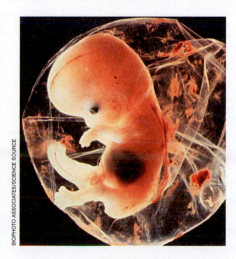
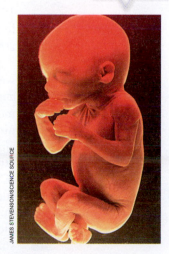

myelination The formation of a fatty sheath around the axons of a neuron.

teratogens Agents that damage the process of development, such as drugs and viruses.

fetal alcohol syndrome A developmental disorder that stems from heavy alcohol use by the mother during pregnancy.

infancy The stage of development that begins at birth and lasts between 18 and 24 months.

develops a layer of insulating fat beneath its skin, and its digestive and respiratory systems mature. The cells that ultimately become the brain divide and begin to generate axons and dendrites (which permit communication with other brain cells). They also begin to undergo a process (described in Chapter 3) known as **myelination,** which is *the formation of a fatty sheath around the axons of a neuron.* Just as plastic sheathing insulates a wire, myelin insulates a brain cell and prevents the leakage of neural signals that travel along the axon. This process starts during the fetal stage but doesn't end for years; the myelination of the cortex, for example, continues into adulthood.

Although the brain undergoes rapid and complex growth during the fetal period, at birth it is nowhere near its adult size. Whereas a newborn chimpanzee's brain is nearly 60% of its adult size, a newborn human's brain is only 25% of its adult size, which is to say that 75% of the brain's development occurs outside the womb. Why are human beings born with such underdeveloped brains when other primates are not? There

? Why are human beings born with underdeveloped brains?

are at least two reasons. First, the human brain has nearly tripled in size in just 2 million years of evolution, and bigger brains require bigger heads to house them. If a newborn's head were closer to its adult size, the baby could not pass through its mother's birth canal. Second, one of our species' greatest talents is its ability to adapt to a wide range of novel environments that differ in terms of climate, social structure, and so on. Rather than arriving in the world with a fully developed brain that may or may not meet the requirements of its environment, human beings arrive with brains that do much of their developing *within* the very environments in which they will function. The fact that our underdeveloped brains are specifically shaped by the unique social and physical environment into which we are born allows us to be exceptionally adaptable.

Prenatal Environment

The womb is an environment that influences development in a multitude of ways (Coe & Lubach, 2008; Wadhwa, Sandman, & Garite, 2001). For example, the *placenta* is the organ that physically links the bloodstreams of the mother and the developing embryo or fetus and permits the exchange of materials. As such, the foods a woman eats during pregnancy can affect her fetus. The children of mothers who received insufficient nutrition during pregnancy tend to have both physical problems (Stein et al., 1975) and psychological problems, most notably an increased risk of schizophrenia and antisocial personality disorder (Neugebauer, Hoek, & Susser, 1999; Susser, Brown, & Matte, 1999). The foods a woman eats during pregnancy can also shape her child's food preferences: Infants tend to like the foods and spices that their mothers ate while they were in utero (Mennella, Johnson, & Beauchamp, 1995).

? How does the uterine environment affect the unborn child?

In fact, almost anything a woman eats, drinks, inhales, injects, or otherwise comes into contact with can pass through the placenta. *Agents that damage the process of development* are called **teratogens,** which literally means "monster makers." The most common teratogen is alcohol. **Fetal alcohol syndrome** (FAS) *is a developmental disorder that stems from heavy alcohol use by the mother during pregnancy;* children with FAS have a variety of distinctive facial features, brain abnormalities, and cognitive deficits (Carmichael Olson et al., 1997; Streissguth et al., 1999). Some studies suggest that light drinking does not harm the fetus, but at present there is no medical consensus about what constitutes a "safe" amount (Warren & Hewitt, 2009). Tobacco is another common teratogen. Babies whose mothers smoke have lower birth weights (Horta et al., 1997) and are more likely

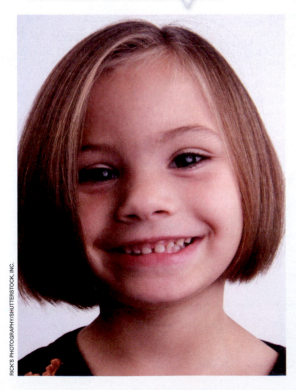

This child has some of the telltale facial features associated with FAS: short eye openings, a flat midface, a flat ridge under the nose, a thin upper lip, and an underdeveloped jaw.

to have perceptual and attentional problems in childhood (Fried & Watkinson, 2000). Even secondhand smoke can lead to reduced birth weight and deficits in attention and learning (Makin, Fried, & Watkinson, 1991; Windham, Eaton, & Hopkins, 1999). Other teratogens include environmental poisons such as lead in the water, paint dust in the air, and mercury in fish.

The prenatal environment is rich with chemicals, but it is also rich with information. Unlike an automobile, which operates only after it has been fully assembled, the human brain is operating even as it is being built, and research shows that the developing fetus can sense stimulation and learn from it. For example, the fetus can hear its mother's heartbeat, the gastrointestinal sounds associated with her digestion, and her voice. Newborns suck a nipple more vigorously when they hear the sound of their mother's voice than when they hear the voice of a female stranger (Querleu et al., 1984), suggesting that they are more familiar with the former than the latter. Newborns whose mothers read aloud from *The Cat in the Hat* during their pregnancies reacted as though the story was familiar (DeCasper & Spence, 1986). Clearly, the fetus is listening.

SUMMARY QUIZ [10.1]

1. The sequence of prenatal development is
   - a. fetus, embryo, zygote.
   - b. zygote, embryo, fetus.
   - c. embryo, zygote, fetus.
   - d. zygote, fetus, embryo.

2. Learning begins
   - a. in the womb.
   - b. at birth.
   - c. in the newborn stage.
   - d. in infancy.

3. Which is true of vulnerability to tetrogens?
   - a. Heavy alcohol use during the early stages of pregnancy will probably not damage the fetus because critical brain systems have not yet developed.
   - b. Exposure of the mother to environmental poisons such as lead in the drinking water can interfere with the development of the fetus.
   - c. The babies of women who smoke while pregnant may have impaired development, but exposure to secondhand smoke is okay.
   - d. All of the above are true.

Infancy and Childhood: Becoming a Person

Newborns may appear to be capable of little more than squalling and squirming, but in the last decade, researchers have discovered that they are actually quite sophisticated. **Infancy** is *the stage of development that begins at birth and lasts between 18 and 24 months,* and as you will see, much more happens during this stage than meets the untrained eye.

Perceptual and Motor Development

New parents like to stand around the crib and make goofy faces at the baby because they think the baby will be amused. In fact, newborns have a rather limited range of vision. How do we know what newborns are seeing? In one study, newborns were shown a circle with diagonal stripes over and over again. The babies stared a lot at first, and then less and less on each subsequent presentation. Recall from Chapter 7

Infants mimic the facial expressions of adults. And vice versa.

Some children develop motor skills earlier than others.

that *habituation* is the tendency for organisms to respond less intensely to a stimulus as the frequency of exposure to that stimulus increases, and babies habituate just like the rest of us do. But when the researchers rotated the circle 90 degrees, the newborns once again stared intently, indicating that they had noticed the change in the circle's orientation (Slater, Morison, & Somers, 1988).

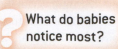

What do babies notice most?

Newborns are even more attentive to social stimuli. For example, in one study, researchers stood close to some newborns while sticking out their tongues and stood close to other newborns while pursing their lips. Newborns in the first group stuck out their own tongues more often than those in the second group did, and newborns in the second group pursed their lips more often than those in the first group did (Meltzoff & Moore, 1977). Indeed, newborns have been shown to mimic facial expressions in their very first *hour* of life (Reissland, 1988).

Although infants can use their eyes right away, they must spend considerably more time learning how to use most of their other parts. **Motor development** is *the emergence of the ability to execute physical actions* such as reaching, grasping, crawling, and walking. Infants are born with a small set of **reflexes,** which are *specific patterns of motor response that are triggered by specific patterns of sensory stimulation.* For example, the *rooting reflex* is the tendency for infants to move their mouths toward any object that touches their cheek, and the *sucking reflex* is the tendency to suck any object that enters their mouths. These two reflexes allow newborns to find their mother's nipple and begin feeding—a behavior so vitally important that nature took no chances and hardwired it into every one of us. Interestingly, these and other reflexes that are present at birth seem to disappear in the first few months as children learn to execute more sophisticated motor behavior.

The development of these more sophisticated behaviors tends to obey two general rules. The first is the **cephalocaudal rule** (or the "top-to-bottom" rule), which describes *the tendency for motor skills to emerge in sequence from the head to the feet.*

In what order do infants learn to use parts of their bodies?

Infants tend to gain control over their heads first, their arms and trunks next, and their legs last. A young baby who is placed on her stomach may lift her head and may even lift her chest by using her arms for support, but she typically has little control over her legs. The second rule is the **proximodistal rule** (or the "inside-to-outside" rule), which describes *the tendency for motor skills to emerge in sequence from the center to the periphery.* Babies learn to control their trunks before their elbows and knees, and they learn to control their elbows and knees before their hands and feet (see **FIGURE 10.2**). Motor skills generally emerge in an orderly sequence but not on a strict timetable. Rather, the timing of these skills is influenced by many factors, such as the baby's incentive for reaching, body weight, muscular development, and general level of activity. For example, in one study, babies who had visually stimulating mobiles hanging above their cribs began reaching for objects 6 weeks earlier than babies who did not (White & Held, 1966).

Cognitive Development

What are the three essential tasks of cognitive development?

Infants can see and move. But can they think? In the first half of the 20th century, a Swiss biologist named Jean Piaget noticed that when confronted with difficult problems—Does the big glass have more liquid in it than the small glass? Can Billy see what you see?—children of the same age made precisely the same mistakes. And as they aged, they stopped making these mistakes. This led Piaget to suspect that children move through discrete stages of **cognitive development,** which is *the emergence of the ability to think and understand.* Between infancy and adulthood,

motor development The emergence of the ability to execute physical action.

reflexes Specific patterns of motor response that are triggered by specific patterns of sensory stimulation.

cephalocaudal rule The "top-to-bottom" rule that describes the tendency for motor skills to emerge in sequence from the head to the feet.

proximodistal rule The "inside-to-outside" rule that describes the tendency for motor skills to emerge in sequence from the center to the periphery.

cognitive development The emergence of the ability to think and understand.

sensorimotor stage A stage of development that begins at birth and lasts through infancy in which infants acquire information about the world by sensing it and moving around within it.

schemas Theories about or models of the way the world works.

assimilation The process by which infants apply their schemas in novel situations.

accommodation The process by which infants revise their schemas in light of new information.

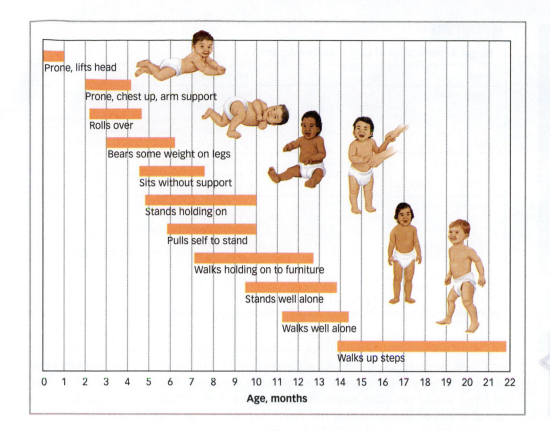
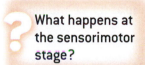

Prone, lifts head
Prone, chest up, arm support
Rolls over
Bears some weight on legs
Sits without support
Stands holding on
Pulls self to stand
Walks holding on to furniture
Stands well alone
Walks well alone
Walks up steps

0 1 2 3 4 5 6 7 8 9 10 11 12 13 14 15 16 17 18 19 20 21 22
Age, months

◄ **Figure 10.2 Motor Development** Infants learn to control their bodies from head to feet and from center to periphery. These skills emerge in a strict sequence.

children must come to understand (1) how the physical world works, (2) how their minds represent it, and (3) how other minds represent it. These are the three essential tasks of cognitive development, so let's see how children master them.

Discovering the World

Piaget suggested that cognitive development occurs in four stages: the *sensorimotor* stage, the *preoperational* stage, the *concrete operational* stage, and the *formal operational* stage (Piaget, 1954) (see **TABLE 10.1**). The **sensorimotor stage** is *a stage of development that begins at birth and lasts through infancy.*

? What happens at the sensorimotor stage?

As the word *sensorimotor* suggests, infants at this stage use their ability to *sense* and their ability to *move* to acquire information about the world in which they live. By actively exploring their environments with their eyes, mouths, and fingers, infants begin to construct **schemas,** which are *theories about or models of the way the world works.*

As every scientist knows, the key advantage of having a theory is that one can use it to predict and control what will happen in novel situations. If an infant learns that tugging at a stuffed animal causes the toy to come closer, then that observation is incorporated into the infant's theory about how physical objects behave, and the infant can later use that theory when he or she wants a different object to come closer, such as a rattle or a ball. Piaget called this process **assimilation,** which occurs when *infants apply their schemas in novel situations.* Of course, if the infant tugs the tail of the family cat, the cat is likely to sprint in the opposite direction. Infants' theories about the world ("Things come closer if I pull them") are occasionally disconfirmed; thus infants must occasionally adjust their schemas in light of their new experiences ("Aha! *Inanimate* things come closer when I pull them"). Piaget called this process **accommodation,** which occurs when *infants revise their schemas in light of new information.*

During the sensorimotor stage, infants explore with their hands and mouths, learning important lessons about the physical world, such as "If you whack Jell-O hard enough, you can actually wear it as a mask."

MICHAEL HAGEDORN/CORBIS

FARRELL GREHAN/CORBIS

Jean Piaget (1896–1980) was the father of modern developmental psychology as well as the last man to look good in a beret.

Table 10.1

Piaget's Four Stages of Cognitive Development

Stage	Age	Characteristics
Sensorimotor	Infancy (Birth–2 years old)	• Experience the world through movement and senses • Develop schemas; learn to revise them through assimilation and accommodation • Begin to understand object permanence
Preoperational	Early childhood (2–6 years old)	• Acquire motor skills • Learn about "physical" (concrete) objects • Egocentric thinking
Concrete operational	Middle childhood (6–11 years old)	• Learn how actions, or "operations," can influence objects • Understand conservation of physical properties • Develop mental representations of objects and a theory of mind
Formal operational	Late childhood through adulthood (11+ years old)	• Learn and reason about abstract concepts

Piaget also suggested that infants do not have—and hence must acquire—some very basic understandings about the physical world. For example, when you put a pair of socks in a drawer, you know that the socks exist even after you close the drawer, and you would be quite surprised if you opened the drawer a moment later and found it empty. But according to Piaget, this would not surprise an infant because infants do not have a theory of **object permanence,** which is *the idea that objects continue to exist even when they are not visible.* Piaget noted that in the first few months of life, infants act as though objects stop existing the moment they are out of sight. For instance, he observed that a 2-month-old infant will track a moving object with her eyes, but once the object leaves her visual field, she will not search for it.

? When do children acquire a theory of object permanence?

Was Piaget right? Recent research suggests that when infants are tested in other ways, they demonstrate a sense of object permanence much earlier than Piaget realized (Shinskey & Munakata, 2005). For instance, in one study, babies were shown a miniature drawbridge that flipped up and down (see **FIGURE 10.3**). Once the babies

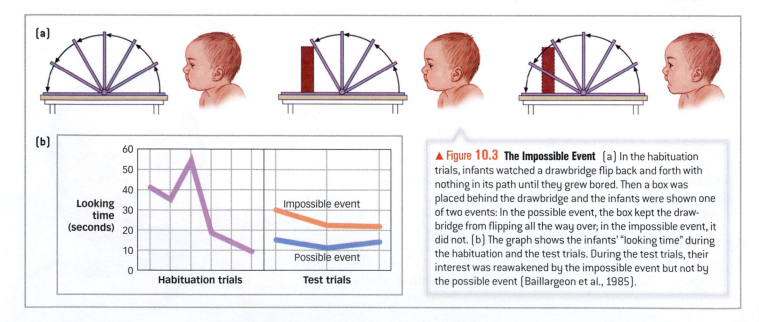

▲ Figure **10.3** **The Impossible Event** (a) In the habituation trials, infants watched a drawbridge flip back and forth with nothing in its path until they grew bored. Then a box was placed behind the drawbridge and the infants were shown one of two events: In the possible event, the box kept the drawbridge from flipping all the way over; in the impossible event, it did not. (b) The graph shows the infants' "looking time" during the habituation and the test trials. During the test trials, their interest was reawakened by the impossible event but not by the possible event (Baillargeon et al., 1985).

got used to this, they watched as a box was placed behind the drawbridge—in its path but out of their sight. Some infants then saw a *possible* event: The drawbridge began to flip and then suddenly stopped, as if impeded by the box that the infants could not see. Other infants saw an *impossible* event: The drawbridge began to flip and then continued, as if unimpeded by the box. What did infants do? Four-month-old infants stared longer at the impossible event than at the possible event, suggesting that they were puzzled by it (Baillargeon, Spelke, & Wasserman, 1985). The only thing that could have made it puzzling, of course, was the existence of an unseen box (Fantz, 1964). Studies such as these suggest that infants have some understanding of object permanence by the time they are just 4 months old. Although infants seem to have a better understanding of the physical world than Piaget suspected, it is still true that, as Piaget (1927/1977) wrote: "The child's first year of life is unfortunately still an abyss of mysteries for the psychologist. If only we could know what is going on in a baby's mind while observing him in action, we could certainly understand everything there is to psychology."

Discovering the Mind

The long period following infancy is called **childhood,** which is *the stage of development that begins at about 18 to 24 months and lasts until adolescence, which begins between ages 11 and 14.* According to Piaget, childhood consists of two stages. The first is a **preoperational stage,** which is *the stage of development that begins at about age 2 and ends at about age 6,* during which the child

learns about physical, or "concrete," objects. The second is the **concrete operational stage,** which is *the stage of development that begins at about age 6 and ends at about age 11,* during which the child learns how various actions or "operations" can affect or transform those objects.

? **What distinguishes the preoperational and concrete operational stages?**

The difference between these stages is illustrated by an experiment in which Piaget showed children a row of cups and asked them to place an egg in each. Preoperational children were able to do this, and afterward they readily agreed that there were just as many eggs as there were cups. Then Piaget removed the eggs and spread them out in a long line that extended beyond the row of cups. Preoperational children incorrectly claimed that there were now more eggs than cups, pointing out that the row of eggs was longer than the row of cups and hence there must be more of them. Concrete operational children, on the other hand, correctly reported that the number of eggs did not change when they were spread out in a longer line. They understood that *quantity* is a property of a set of concrete objects that does not change when an operation such as *spreading out* alters the set's appearance (Piaget, 1954). Piaget called the child's insight **conservation,** which is *the notion that the quantitative properties of an object are invariant despite changes in the object's appearance.*

The main reason why preoperational children do not fully grasp the notion of conservation is that they do not fully grasp the fact that they have *minds* and that these minds contain *mental representations* of the world. As adults, we all distinguish between appearances and realities. We realize that things aren't always as they seem—that a wagon can *be* red but *look* gray at dusk, a highway can *be*

object permanence The idea that objects continue to exist even when they are not visible.

childhood The stage of development that begins at about 18 to 24 months and lasts until adolescence.

preoperational stage The stage of development that begins at about age 2 and ends at about age 6, during which children have a preliminary understanding of the physical world.

concrete operational stage The stage of development that begins at about age 6 and ends at about age 11, during which children learn how various actions, or "operations," can affect or transform "concrete" objects.

conservation The notion that the quantitative properties of an object are invariant despite changes in the object's appearance.

When preoperational children are shown two equal-size glasses filled with equal amounts of liquid, they correctly say that neither glass "has more." But when the contents of one glass are poured into a taller, thinner glass, they incorrectly say that the taller glass now "has more." Concrete operational children don't make this mistake because they recognize that operations such as pouring change the appearance of the liquid but not its actual volume.

formal operational stage The stage of development that begins around the age of 11 and lasts through adulthood, during which children can solve nonphysical problems.

egocentrism The failure to understand that the world appears differently to different observers.

theory of mind The idea that human behavior is guided by mental representations.

dry but *look* wet in the heat. We make a distinction between the way things *are* and the way we *see* them. But preoperational children don't make this distinction so easily. When something *looks* gray or wet, they tend to assume it *is* gray or wet.

As children develop into the concrete operational stage, they begin to realize that the way the world *appears* is not necessarily the way the world really *is*. For instance, concrete operational children can understand that when a ball of clay is rolled, stretched, or flattened, it is still the same amount of clay despite the fact that it looks larger in one form than in another. Once children can make a distinction between objects and their mental representations of objects, between an object's properties and an object's appearance, they can begin to understand that some operations change what an object *looks* like without changing what the object *is* like.

? What is the essential feature of the formal operational stage?

Children at the concrete operational stage can solve a variety of physical problems. But it isn't until they move on to the **formal operational stage,** which is *the stage of development that begins around the age of 11 and lasts through adulthood,* that they can solve nonphysical problems with similar ease. Childhood ends when formal operations begin and people are able to reason systematically about abstract concepts such as *liberty* and *love* and about events that will happen, that might have happened, and that never happened. The ability to generate, consider, reason about, or otherwise operate on abstract objects is the hallmark of formal operations.

Discovering Other Minds

As children develop, they discover their own minds, but they also discover the minds of others. Because preoperational children don't fully grasp the fact that they have minds that mentally represent objects, they also don't fully grasp the fact that other people have minds that may mentally represent the same objects in different ways. Hence, they generally expect others to see the world as they do. **Egocentrism** is *the failure to understand that the world appears differently to different observers.* When 3-year-old children are asked what a person on the opposite side of a table is seeing, they typically claim that the other person sees what

? What does the false belief test show?

they see. They also have trouble understanding that others may not know what they know. In one study using the *false belief test,* children saw a puppet named Maxi deposit some chocolate in a cupboard and then leave the room. A second puppet

Because children are egocentric, they think that others see what they see. When small children are told to hide, they sometimes cover their eyes. Because they cannot see themselves, they think that others can't see them either.

COURTESY OF DANIEL GILBERT

arrived a moment later, found the chocolate, and moved it to a different cupboard. The children were then asked where Maxi would look for the chocolate when he returned—in the first cupboard where he had initially put it or in the second cupboard where the children knew it was currently. Most 5-year-olds realized that Maxi would search the first cupboard because, after all, Maxi had not seen the chocolate being moved. But 3-year-olds typically claimed that Maxi would look in the second cupboard because, after all, that's where *the children* knew the chocolate really was (Wimmer & Perner, 1983). Children all over the world begin to pass the *false belief test* somewhere between the ages of 4 and 6 (Callaghan et al., 2005), and no one yet understands why children in some cultures pass it earlier than children in others (Liu et al., 2008).

Children also take quite a long time to understand that other people may have emotional reactions unlike their own. When 5-year-olds hear a story in which Little Red Riding Hood knocks on her grandmother's door, unaware that a wolf is inside waiting to devour her, they realize that Little Red Riding Hood does not know what they know; nonetheless, they expect Little Red Riding Hood to feel what they feel, namely, afraid (Bradmetz & Schneider, 2004; DeRosnay et al., 2004; Harris et al., 1989). It is only at about 6 years of age that children come to understand that because they and others have different knowledge, they and others may also experience different emotions in the same situation.

Once children understand that different people can have different perceptions, beliefs, and emotional responses, they are said to have acquired a **theory of mind,** which is *the idea that human behavior is guided by mental representations.* The age at which children acquire a theory of mind appears to be influenced by a variety of factors, such as the number of siblings the child has, the frequency with which the child engages in pretend play, whether the child has an imaginary companion, and the socioeconomic status of the child's family. But of all the factors researchers have studied, language seems to be the most important (Astington & Baird, 2005). Children's language skills are an excellent predictor of how well they perform on false belief tests (Happé, 1995). Language—especially language about thoughts and feelings—is an important tool for helping children make sense of their own and others' minds (Harris, de Rosnay, & Pons, 2005).

Two groups of children lag far behind their peers in acquiring a theory of mind. *Autism* is a relatively rare disorder that affects approximately 1 in 2,500 children (Frith, 2003). Some psychologists have suggested that autistic children fail to acquire a theory of mind. Although children with autism are typically normal—and sometimes far *better* than normal—on most intellectual dimensions (Dawson et al., 2007), they have difficulty understanding the inner life of other people. Specifically, they do not seem to understand that other people can have false beliefs (Baron-Cohen, Leslie, & Frith, 1985; Senju et al., 2009), belief-based emotions (Baron-Cohen, 1991), or self-conscious emotions such as embarrassment and shame (Heerey, Keltner, & Capps, 2003). The second group of children who lag behind their peers in acquiring a theory of mind are deaf children whose parents do not know sign language. These children are slow to learn to communicate because they do not have ready access to any form of conventional language, and this restriction seems to slow the development of their understanding of other minds. Like children with autism, they display difficulties in understanding false beliefs even at 5 or 6 years of age (DeVilliers, 2005; Peterson & Siegal, 1999). Just as learning a spoken language seems to help hearing children

"You're five. How could you possibly understand the problems of a five-and-a-half-year-old?"

Daniel Tammet has autism. He cannot drive a car or tell left from right. But he recently broke a European record by spending 5 hours, 9 minutes, and 24 seconds reciting the first 22,514 digits of pi from memory. "I just wanted to show people that disability needn't get in the way," he said (quoted in Johnson, 2005). Although only 10% of people with autism have extraordinary abilities such as this, they are 10 times more likely than other people to have such abilities. No one knows why.

acquire a theory of mind, so does learning a sign language help deaf children do the same (Pyers & Senghas, 2009).

Cognitive development—from the sensorimotor stage to formal operations—is a complex journey, and Piaget's ideas about it were nothing less than groundbreaking. Although many of these ideas have held up quite well, psychologists have discovered two important ways in which his claims must be qualified. First, Piaget thought that children graduate from one stage to another in the

? What did Piaget get wrong?

same way that they graduate from kindergarten to first grade: A child is in kindergarten *or* first grade, he is never in both, and there is a particular moment of transition to which everyone can point. Modern psychologists see development as a more continuous and less step-like progression than Piaget believed. Children who are transitioning between stages may perform more mature behaviors one day and less mature behaviors the next. Cognitive development is more like the change of seasons than it is like graduation. Second, children acquire many of the abilities that Piaget described much *earlier* than he realized. Every year, it seems, research lowers the age at which babies can demonstrate their ability to perform sophisticated cognitive tasks.

GEORGE VILLIERS, DUKE OF BUCKINGHAM AND HIS BROTHER, LORD FRANCIS VILLIERS, 1635, AFTER VAN DYCK, ROBSON, THOMAS (1798-1871) / © WARRINGTON MUSEUM AND ART GALLERY, CHESHIRE, UK /THE BRIDGEMAN ART LIBRARY

As this 1635 painting by Van Dyke shows, children have typically been portrayed as little adults, with adult features, proportions, gestures, and dress. But modern research shows that children and adults think about the world in fundamentally different ways.

Discovering Our Cultures

Piaget saw the child as a lone scientist who made observations, developed theories, and then revised those theories in light of new observations. Yet most scientists don't start from scratch. Rather, they receive training from more experienced scientists. According to Russian psychologist Lev Vygotsky, children do much the same thing. Vygotsky believed that cognitive development was largely the result of the child's interaction with members of his or her own culture rather than his or her interaction with concrete objects (Vygotsky, 1978).

? How does culture affect cognitive development?

For example, in English, the numbers beyond 20 are named by a decade (twenty) that is followed by a digit (one), and their names follow a logical pattern (twenty-one, twenty-two, twenty-three, etc.). In Chinese, the numbers from 11 to 19 are similarly constructed (ten-one, ten-two, ten-three . . .). But in English, the names of the numbers between 11 and 19 either reverse the order of the decade and the digit (sixteen, seventeen) or are entirely arbitrary (eleven, twelve). The difference in the regularity of these two systems makes a big difference to the children who must learn them. It is obvious to a Chinese child that 12—which is called "ten-two"—can be decomposed into 10 and 2, but it is not so obvious to an American child, who calls the number "twelve" (see **FIGURE 10.4**). In one study, children from many countries were asked to hand an experimenter a certain number of bricks. Some of the bricks were single, and some were glued together in strips of 10. When Asian children were asked to hand the experimenter 26 bricks, they tended to hand over two strips of 10 plus six singles. Non-Asian children tended to use the clumsier strategy of counting out 26 single bricks (Miura et al., 1994). Results such as these suggest that the regularity of the counting system that children inherit can promote or discourage their discovery of the fact that two-digit numbers can be decomposed (Gordon, 2004; Imbo & LeFevre, 2009).

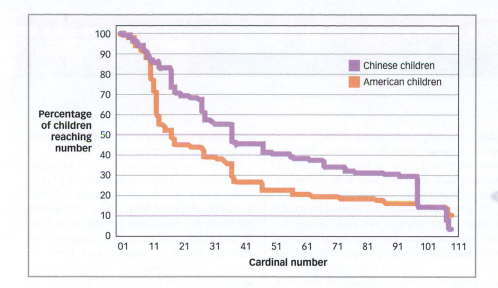

◄ Figure **10.4** **Twelve or Two-Teen?** As this graph shows, the percentage of American children who can count through the cardinal numbers drops off suddenly when they hit the number 10, whereas the percentage of Chinese children shows a more gradual decline (Miller, Smith, & Zhu, 1995).

Children's ability to learn skills, such as counting, from others depends on three fundamental skills that they acquire early on (Meltzoff et al., 2009; Striano & Reid, 2006).

1. *Joint attention*: the ability to focus on what another person is focused on. If an adult turns her head to the left, both young infants (3 months) and older infants (9 months) will look to the left; but if the adult first closes her eyes and then looks to the left, the young infant will look to the left but the older infant will not (Brooks & Meltzoff, 2002). This suggests that older infants are not following the adult's head movements, but rather, they are following her gaze—trying to see what they think she is seeing (see **FIGURE 10.5**).

2. *Social referencing*: the ability to use another person's reactions as information. An infant who approaches a new toy will often stop and look back at his or her mother, examining her face for cues about whether mom thinks the toy is or isn't dangerous (Kim, Walden, & Knieps, 2010; Walden & Ogan, 1988). (See the Hot Science box.)

3. *Imitation*: the ability to do what another person does (or meant to do). Infants are natural mimics and will do what they see adults do (Jones, 2007). But very early on, infants learn to mimic adults' intentions rather than their actions. When an 18-month-old infant sees an adult's hand slip as the adult tries to pull the lid off a jar, the infant won't copy the slip. Rather, the infant will perform the *intended* action by removing the lid (Meltzoff, 1995).

Joint attention, social referencing, and imitation are the three basic skills that allow infants to learn more sophisticated skills from other members of their species.

▼ Figure **10.5** **Joint Attention** Joint attention allows children to learn from others. When a 12-month-old infant interacts with an adult (a) who then looks at an object (b), the infant will typically look at the same object (c)—but only when the adult's eyes are open (Meltzoff et al., 2009).

(a)

(b)

(c)

MELTZOFF ET AL. 2009

HOT SCIENCE

Walk This Way

Parents often complain that their children won't take their advice. But recent research shows that even 18-month-old infants know when to listen to their parents—and when to ignore them.

Researchers (Tamis-LeMonda et al., 2008) built a slope whose steepness could be adjusted (as shown in the accompanying photo), put infants at the top and moms at the bottom, and then watched to see whether the infants would attempt to walk down the plane and toward their mothers. Sometimes the slope was clearly flat and safe, sometimes it was clearly steep and risky, and sometimes it was somewhere between these two extremes. Mothers were instructed either to encourage their infants to walk down the plane or to discourage them from doing so.

So what did the babies do? Did they trust their mothers or did they trust their eyes? As you can see in the accompanying figure, when the slope was clearly safe or clearly risky, infants ignored their mothers. They typically trotted down the flat plane even when mom advised against it and refused to try the risky plane even when mom said it was okay. But when the plane was somewhere between safe and risky, the infants tended to follow mom's advice.

These data show that infants use social information in a very sophisticated way. When their senses provide unambiguous information about the world, they ignore what people tell them. But when their senses leave them unsure about what to do, they readily accept parental advice. It appears that from the moment children start to walk, they know when to listen to their parents and when to shake their heads, roll their eyes, and do what they darn well please.

COURTESY OF KAREN ADOLPH

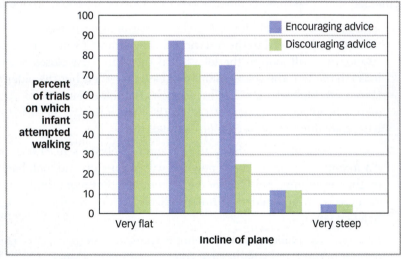

Social Development

During World War II, psychologists studied infants who were living in orphanages while awaiting adoption. Although these children were warm, safe, and well fed, many were physically and developmentally retarded (Spitz, 1949). Shortly thereafter, psychologist Harry Harlow (1958; Harlow & Harlow, 1965) discovered that baby rhesus monkeys that were warm, safe, and well fed but were allowed no social contact for the first 6 months of their lives developed a variety of pathologies. The socially isolated monkeys turned out to be incapable of communicating with or learning from others of their kind, and when the females matured and became mothers, they ignored, rejected, and sometimes even attacked their own babies. Harlow also discovered that when socially isolated monkeys were put in a cage with two "artificial mothers"—one that was made of wire and dispensed food and one that was made of cloth and dispensed no food—they spent most of their time clinging to the soft cloth mother despite the fact that the wire mother was the source of their nourishment. Clearly, infants of both species require something more from their caregivers than mere sustenance. But what?

Becoming Attached

When Konrad Lorenz was a child, he wanted to be a goose. "On realizing that this was impossible," he explained in his Nobel Prize acceptance speech, "I got a one-day-old duckling and found, to my intense joy, that it transferred its following response to my person." Every farmer knows that a baby goose will normally follow its mother everywhere she goes, but Lorenz discovered that a newly hatched gosling will faithfully follow the first moving object to which it is exposed—even if that object is a human being or a tennis ball. Lorenz theorized that the first moving object a hatchling saw was somehow *imprinted* on its bird brain as "the thing I must always stay near" (Lorenz, 1952).

Harlow's monkeys preferred the comfort and warmth of a soft cloth mother (right) to the wire mother (left) even when the wire mother was associated with food.

Psychiatrist John Bowlby was fascinated by this work, and he sought to understand how human infants form attachments to their caregivers (Bowlby, 1969, 1973, 1980). Bowlby began by noting that from the moment they are born, goslings waddle after their mothers and monkeys cling to their mothers' furry chests because the newborns of both species must stay close to their caregivers to survive. Human babies, he suggested, have a similar need, but they are much less physically developed and cannot waddle or cling. Because they cannot stay close to their caregivers, human babies do things that cause their caregivers to stay close to them. When a baby cries, gurgles, coos, makes eye contact, or smiles, most adults reflexively move toward the baby, and Bowlby claimed that this is *why* the baby emits these "come hither" signals.

? What is attachment?

Bowlby claimed that babies begin their lives by sending these signals to anyone within range to receive them, but during their first 6 months, they begin to target their signals to the *primary caregiver*—the person who responds most often and most promptly. This person quickly becomes the emotional center of the infant's universe. Infants feel secure in the primary caregiver's presence and will happily crawl around, exploring their environments with their eyes, ears, fingers, and mouths. But if their primary caregiver gets too far away, infants begin to feel insecure, and like the imprinted gosling, they take action to decrease the distance between themselves and their primary caregiver, perhaps by crawling toward their caregiver or by crying until

Like goslings, human babies need to stay close to their mothers to survive. Unlike goslings, though, human babies know how to get their mothers to come to them rather than the other way around.

Children are naturally social creatures who readily develop relationships with caregivers and peers. A recent study shows that toddlers who spend time with a responsive robot will begin to treat it like a classmate instead of like a toy (Tanaka, Cicourel, & Movellan, 2007).

their caregiver moves toward them. Human infants, Bowlby suggested, are predisposed to form an **attachment**—that is, *an emotional bond*—with a primary caregiver. Later work by psychologist Mary Ainsworth suggested that most infants show one of four basic styles of attachment (Ainsworth et al., 1978):

1. *Secure attachment*: If the caregiver leaves, then returns, infants who had been distressed by her absence go to her and are calmed by her proximity, while those who had not been distressed acknowledge her return with a glance or greeting.

2. *Avoidant attachment*: These infants are generally not distressed when their caregiver leaves the room, and they generally do not acknowledge her when she returns.

3. *Ambivalent attachment*: These infants are almost always distressed when their caregiver leaves the room, but when she returns they rebuff her attempt to calm them, arching their backs and squirming to get away.

4. *Disorganized attachment*: These infants show no consistent pattern of responses when their caregiver leaves or returns.

Most American infants (about 60%) display secure attachment styles, with about 20% showing avoidant attachment and about 15% showing ambivalent attachment; very few American infants (< 5%) display disorganized attachment. Secure attachment is likewise the most common style all over the world (van IJzendoorn & Kroonenberg, 1988), but other attachment styles vary across cultures. For example, German children (whose parents tend to foster independence) are more likely to have avoidant than ambivalent attachment styles, whereas Japanese children (whose mothers typically stay home and do not leave them in the care of others) are more likely to have ambivalent than avoidant attachment styles (Takahashi, 1986).

Working Models

The capacity for attachment may be innate, but the quality of that attachment is influenced by the child, the primary caregiver, and their interaction. Infants seem to keep track of the responsiveness of their primary caregiver and use this information to create an **internal working model of relationships,** which is *a set of beliefs about the self, the primary caregiver, and the relationship between them* (Bretherton & Munholland, 1999). Infants with different attachment styles appear to have different working models of relationships. Specifically, infants with a secure attachment style act as though they are certain that their primary caregiver will respond when they feel insecure, infants with an avoidant attachment style act as though they are certain that their primary caregiver will not respond, and infants with an ambivalent attachment style act as though they are uncertain about whether their primary caregiver will respond or not. Infants with a disorganized attachment style seem to be confused about their caregivers, which has led some psychologists to speculate that this style primarily characterizes children who have been abused (Carolson, 1998; Cicchetti & Toth, 1998).

Attachment is an interaction between two people; thus both of them—the primary caregiver and the child—play a role in determining the nature of the child's working model. On the one hand, different children are born with different **temperaments,** or *characteristic patterns of emotional reactivity* (Thomas & Chess, 1977). Very young children vary in their tendency toward fearfulness, irritability, activity, positive affect, and other emotional traits (Rothbart & Bates, 1998). These differences in temperament seem to emerge from stable differences in biology. For example, 10% to 15% of infants have highly reactive limbic systems that produce an "inhibited" temperament. These infants thrash and cry when shown a new toy or a new person; they grow into children who tend to avoid novel people, objects, and situations; and they ultimately become quiet, cautious, and sometimes shy adults (Schwartz et al., 2003). These studies sug-

attachment The emotional bond that forms between newborns and their primary caregivers.

internal working model of relationships A set of beliefs about the self, the primary caregiver, and the relationship between them.

temperaments Characteristic patterns of emotional reactivity.

gest that from the earliest moments of life, some infants are prone to feel insecure when their primary caregiver leaves a room and to be inconsolable when she returns.

At the same time, a caregiver's behavior also has an important influence on the infant's working model and attachment style. In particular, securely attached infants tend to have parents who also have secure working models of attachment (van IJzendoorn, 1995). Mothers of securely attached infants tend to be especially sensitive to signs of their child's emotional state, especially good at detecting their infant's "request" for

> **How do caregivers influence an infant's attachment style?**

reassurance, and especially responsive to that request (Ainsworth et al., 1978; De Wolff & van IJzendoorn, 1997). (See the Real World box.) Mothers of infants with an ambivalent attachment style tend to respond inconsistently, only sometimes attending to their infants when they show signs of distress. Mothers of infants with an avoidant attachment style are typically indifferent to their child's need for reassurance and may even reject their attempts at physical closeness (Isabelle, 1993). While these data are merely correlational, there is reason to suspect that the mothers' behavior does indeed help *cause* the infants' attachment style. For example, when mothers of irritable or difficult children are trained to be more sensitive to their babies' emotional signals, and to be more responsive to those signals, their children are more likely to develop a secure attachment style than the children whose mothers do not receive the training (van den Boon, 1994, 1995).

THE REAL WORLD

When Mom's Away

In 1947, about 30% of married American women worked outside the home. Sixty years later, that figure had doubled (Blau & Kahn, 2007). So what are all those working mothers doing with their children? The vast majority of working mothers entrust their children's care to someone else for some part of the day (see the accompanying figure). Some mothers worry that spending so much time away from their kids will impair the attachment process. Indeed, when asked what advice he had for working mothers, John Bowlby—the father of attachment theory—remarked, "I would remind them, if you want a job done properly, do it yourself" (Steele, 2008).

Was Bowlby right? To find out, the National Institute for Child Health and Human Development conducted a massive, long-term study of the effects of non-maternal day care on approximately 1,300 children living in a wide variety of settings in North America. The children were tracked from birth to age 15. The results surprised everyone: Non-maternal day care, it seems, has little effect on the quality of the attachment that children establish with their mothers (Friedman & Boyle, 2008). Although the attachment styles of infants and toddlers are strongly influenced by their mother's sensitivity and responsiveness, they are generally not influenced by the quality, amount, age of entry, stability, or type of day care they receive. As the scientific coordinator of the study explained, "We're finding again and again that child care is not the source of worry that existed when we started the study" (Shapiro, 2005).

But the results were not all good news. Although non-maternal day care had no large, direct effects on children's attachments, there was evidence of a subtle interaction. Infants who had insensitive and unresponsive mothers *and* who were left in poor-quality day care for more than 10 hours a week were especially likely to be insecurely attached. The bottom line? Most day care is just fine for most children. But if a child gets a double whammy—bad day care combined with a mother who is unresponsive and insensitive—the attachment process may well be impaired.

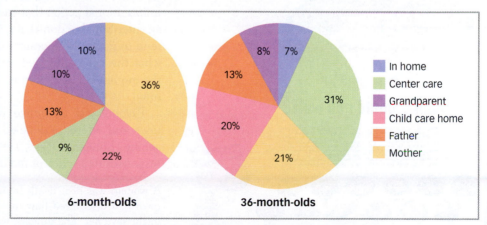

▲ **Time in Child Care** Who is watching the baby? Although "Mom" is a popular answer, children are watched more often by others than by mothers.

preconventional stage A stage of moral development in which the morality of an action is primarily determined by its consequences for the actor.

conventional stage A stage of moral development in which the morality of an action is primarily determined by the extent to which it conforms to social rules.

postconventional stage A stage of moral development in which the morality of an action is determined by a set of general principles that reflect core values.

Moral Development

From the moment of birth, human beings can make one distinction quickly and well, and that's the distinction between pleasure and pain. But as they mature, they begin to notice that their pleasures ("Throwing food is fun") are often someone else's pains ("Throwing food makes Mom mad"). This is a problem. Human beings need one another to survive and thrive, and when people make others feel bad, then others tend to avoid them, exclude them, or retaliate against them. We are social animals, and it is in our own selfish interests to learn how to balance our needs and the needs of others. We do this by developing a new distinction—the distinction between right and wrong. "Bad behavior" usually involves the gratification of our own desires at the expense of someone else's, and most moral systems are a set of recommendations for balancing different people's competing needs (cf. Haidt, 2008; Turiel, 2006).

Knowing What's Right

How do children think about right and wrong? Piaget spent time playing marbles with children and quizzing them about how they came to know the rules of the game and what they thought should happen to children who broke them. By listening carefully to what children said, Piaget noticed that their moral thinking changed systematically over time in three important ways (Piaget, 1932/1965).

First, Piaget noticed that children's moral thinking tends to shift *from realism to relativism*. Very young children regard moral rules as real, inviolable truths about the world. For the young child, right and wrong are like day and night—they exist in the world and do not depend on what people think or say. As they mature, children begin to realize that some moral rules (e.g., wives should obey their husbands) are inventions, not discoveries, and that groups of people can therefore agree to adopt them, change them, or abandon them entirely. Second, children's moral thinking tends to shift *from prescriptions to principles*. Young children think of moral rules as guidelines for specific actions in specific situations ("Children should take turns playing marbles"). As they mature, children come to see that rules are expressions of more general principles, such as fairness and equity, which means that specific rules can be abandoned or modified when they fail to uphold the general principle ("If a child missed his turn, then it would be fair to give him two turns"). Third and finally, children's moral thinking tends to shift from *outcomes* to *intentions*. For the young child, an unintentional action that causes great harm seems "more wrong" than an intentional action that causes slight harm because young children tend to judge the morality of an action by its outcome rather than by what the actor intended. As they mature, children begin to see that the morality of an action is critically dependent on the actor's state of mind.

Psychologist Lawrence Kohlberg picked up on Piaget's observations and offered a detailed theory of the development of moral reasoning (Kohlberg, 1963, 1986). Kohlberg based his theory on people's responses to a series of moral dilemmas such as this one:

A woman was near death from a special kind of cancer. The druggist in town had discovered how to make a new drug that the doctors thought might save her. The druggist was charging $2,000 for a small dose of the drug, even though it only cost him $200 to make. The sick woman's husband, Heinz, only had $1,000. He told the druggist that his wife was dying

> **?** According to Piaget, what three shifts characterize moral development?

> How do children learn to decide what is right and what is wrong?

"Well...could you wait?"

Well, *could* you? With that beautiful, mouth-melting Velvet-Crumb Cake just sitting there asking to be eaten . . . could you wait till dessert time? Golly, maybe you can't even wait to make this old-timey tasting cake. And the surprise is that you do it with Bisquick. Betty Crocker put her directions for Velvet-Crumb Cake

right on the Bisquick package . . . along with some real good ways to fancy it up. (Fancy enough to make a lovely gift for your best neighbor. A whole dozen heartwarming gift ideas are down there at the bottom of the page. Make your list.) It's a beautiful fact, minus, for feeding a family, you can't beat Bisquick!

For feeding a family you can't beat **Bisquick**

COURTESY OF JON WILLIAMSON.COM

and asked him to sell the drug cheaper. But the druggist said: "No, I discovered the drug and I'm going to make money from it." So Heinz got desperate and broke into the druggist's store to steal the drug for his wife. Should Heinz have done that?

Kohlberg proposed three stages of moral development:

1. The **preconventional stage** is *a stage of moral development in which the morality of an action is primarily determined by its consequences for the actor.* Immoral actions are those for which one is punished, and the appropriate resolution to any moral dilemma is to choose the behavior with the least likelihood of punishment. For example, children at this stage often base their moral judgment of Heinz on the relative costs of one decision ("It would be bad if he got blamed for his wife's death") versus another ("It would be bad if he went to jail for stealing"). Kohlberg believed that most children are at the preconventional stage.

? What are Kohlberg's three stages of moral development?

2. The **conventional stage** is *a stage of moral development in which the morality of an action is primarily determined by the extent to which it conforms to social rules.* Individuals at this stage believe that everyone should uphold the generally accepted norms of their cultures, obey the laws of society, and fulfill their civic duties and familial obligations. They believe that Heinz must weigh the dishonor he will bring upon himself and his family by stealing (i.e., breaking a law) against the guilt he will feel if he allows his wife to die (i.e., failing to fulfill a duty). Kohlberg believed that children move to this stage around adolescence.

3. The **postconventional stage** is *a stage of moral development in which the morality of an action is determined by a set of general principles that reflect core values,* such as the right to life, liberty, and the pursuit of happiness. When a behavior violates these principles, it is immoral, and if a law requires that these principles to be violated, then it should be disobeyed. For a person who has reached the postconventional stage, a woman's life is always more important than a shopkeeper's profits, so stealing the drug is not only a moral behavior, it is a moral obligation. Kohlberg believed that some (but not all) individuals reach this stage of moral development in adulthood.

Research supports Kohlberg's general claim that moral reasoning shifts from an emphasis on punishment to an emphasis on social rules and finally to an emphasis on ethical principles (Walker, 1988). But research also suggests that these stages are not quite as discrete as Kohlberg thought. For instance, a person may use preconventional, conventional, and postconventional thinking in different circumstances, which suggests that people do not "reach a stage" so much as they "acquire a skill" that they may or may not use on particular occasions.

During World War II, Albanian Muslims shielded their Jewish neighbors from the Nazis because of a moral code they called *besa*, which means "oath of faith." "There was no government conspiracy; no underground railroad; no organized resistance of any kind. Only individual Albanians, acting alone, to save the lives of people whose lives were in immediate danger," wrote Norman Gershman, who photographed Muslims such as Baba Haxhi Dede Reshatbardhi (pictured) who saved so many Jewish lives.

Feeling What's Right

Research on moral reasoning portrays children as little jurists who use rational analysis—sometimes simple and sometimes sophisticated—to distinguish between right and wrong. But moral dilemmas don't just make us think. They also make us *feel*. Consider the following scenario:

You are standing on a bridge. Below you can see a runaway trolley hurtling down the track toward five people who will be killed if it remains on its present course. You can save these people by flipping a lever that will switch the trolley onto a different track, where it will kill just one person instead of five. Is it morally permissible to divert the trolley and prevent five deaths at the cost of one?

Now consider a slightly different version of this problem:

You and a large man are standing on a bridge. Below you can see a runaway trolley hurtling down the track toward five people who will be killed if it remains on its present course. You can save these people by pushing the large man onto the track, where his body will be caught up in the trolley's wheels and stop it before it kills the five people. Is it morally permissible to push the large man and prevent five deaths at the cost of one?

These scenarios are illustrated in **FIGURE 10.6**. If you are like most people, you believe that it is morally permissible to sacrifice one person for the sake of five in the first case but not in the second. And if you are like most people, you can't say why. Indeed, you probably didn't reach this conclusion by moral reasoning at all. Rather, you had a negative emotional reaction to the mere thought of pushing another human being into the path of an oncoming trolley, and that reaction was sufficient to convince you that pushing him would be wrong. You may have come up with a few good arguments to support this position, but those arguments probably followed rather than preceded your conclusion (Greene et al., 2001).

The way people respond to cases such as these has convinced some psychologists that moral judgments are the consequences—not the causes—of emotional reactions (Haidt, 2001). According to this *moral intuitionist* perspective, we have evolved to react emotionally to a small family of events that are particularly relevant to reproduction and survival, and we have developed the distinction between right and wrong as a way of labeling and explaining these emotional reactions (Hamlin, Wynn, & Bloom, 2007).

? Do moral judgments come before or after emotional reactions?

According to the moral intuitionist perspective, the reason most people consider it permissible to stop a trolley by pulling a switch but not by pushing someone onto the tracks is that people have negative emotional reactions to other people's physical pain (Greene et al., 2001). This aversion to others' suffering begins early in childhood (Warneken & Tomasello, 2009). When adults in one study pretended to hit their thumbs with a hammer, even very young children seemed alarmed and attempted to comfort them (Zahn-Waxler et al., 1992). These efforts are occasionally clumsy or inappropriate—for example, a toddler may offer a distressed adult a teddy bear—but they suggest that children are moved by other people's pain. Indeed, even very young children distinguish between actions that are wrong because they violate a social rule and actions that are wrong because they cause suffering. When asked whether it would be okay to leave toys on the floor in a school that allowed such behavior, young children tend to say it would. But when asked whether it would be okay to hit another child in a school that allowed such behavior, young children tend to say it would not (Smetana, 1981; Smetana & Braeges, 1990). Indeed, young children say that hitting is wrong even if an adult instructs someone to do it (Laupa & Turiel, 1986).

Children clearly think about transgressions that cause others to be observably distressed (e.g., hitting) differently from transgressions that do not (e.g., eating with one's fingers). Why might that be? One possibility is that observing distress automatically triggers an empathic reaction in the brain of the observer. Recent research has shown that some of the brain regions that are activated when people

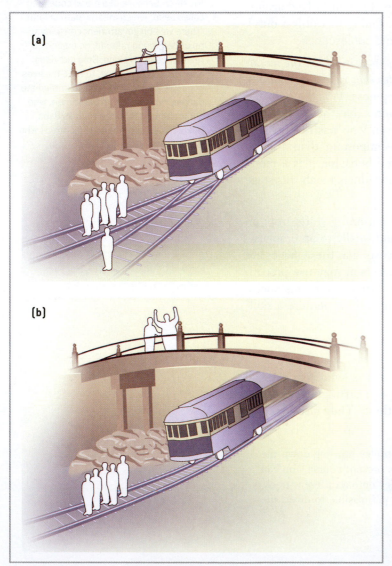

▼ Figure **10.6** **The Trolley Problem** Why does it seem permissible to trade one life for five lives by pulling a switch but not by pushing a man from a bridge? Research suggests that the scenario shown in (b) elicits a more negative emotional response than does the scenario shown in (a), and this emotional response may be the basis for our moral intuitions.

(a)

(b)

experience an unpleasant emotion are also activated when people see someone else experience that emotion (Carr et al., 2003). (See the discussion of mirror neurons in Chapter 3.) In one study, women received a shock or watched their romantic partners receive a shock on different parts of their bodies. The regions of the women's brains that processed information about the location of the shock were activated only when the women experienced the shock themselves, but the regions that processed emotional information were activated whether the women received the shock or observed it (Singer et al., 2004). Similarly, the emotion-relevant brain regions that are activated when a person smells a foul odor are also activated when the person sees someone else smelling the foul odor (Wicker et al., 2003). Studies such as these suggest that our brains respond to other people's *expressions* of distress by creating within us the *experience* of distress, and this mechanism may have evolved because it allows us to know instantly what others are feeling. The fact that we can actually *feel* another person's distress may explain why even a small child who is incapable of sophisticated moral reasoning still considers it wrong to inflict distress on others.

> **?** **What are the two kinds of transgressions between which children clearly distinguish?**

© CREASOURCE/CORBIS

Most people are upset by the suffering of others, and research suggests that even young children have this response, which may be the basis of their emerging morality.

SUMMARY QUIZ [10.2]

1. Piaget believed that infants construct _____, which are theories about the way the world works.
   a. assimilations
   b. accommodations
   c. schemas
   d. habituations

2. Once children understand that human behavior is guided by mental representations, they are said to have acquired
   a. joint attention.
   b. a theory of mind.
   c. formal operational ability.
   d. egocentrism.

3. When infants in a new situation examine their mother's face for cues about what to do, they are demonstrating an ability known as
   a. joint attention.
   b. social referencing.
   c. imitation.
   d. all of the above

4. The capacity for attachment may be innate, but the quality of attachment is influenced by
   a. the child's temperament.
   b. the primary caregiver's ability to read the child's emotional state.
   c. the interaction between the child and the primary caregiver.
   d. all of the above

5. According to Kohlberg, each stage in the development of moral reasoning is characterized by a specific focus. What is the correct sequence of these stages?
   a. focus on consequences, focus on ethical principles, focus on social rules
   b. focus on ethical principles, focus on social rules, focus on consequences
   c. focus on consequences, focus on social rules, focus on ethical principles
   d. focus on social rules, focus on consequences, focus on ethical principles

adolescence The period of development that begins with the onset of sexual maturity (about 11 to 14 years of age) and lasts until the beginning of adulthood (about 18 to 21 years of age).

puberty The bodily changes associated with sexual maturity.

primary sex characteristics Bodily structures that are directly involved in reproduction.

secondary sex characteristics Bodily structures that change dramatically with sexual maturity but that are not directly involved in reproduction.

Adolescence: Minding the Gap

Between childhood and adulthood is an extended developmental stage that may not qualify for a "hood" of its own but that is clearly distinct from the stages that come before and after. **Adolescence** is *the period of development that begins with the onset of sexual maturity (about 11 to 14 years of age) and lasts until the beginning of adulthood (about 18 to 21 years of age).* Unlike the transition from embryo to fetus or from infant to child, this transition is both sudden and clearly marked. In just 3 or 4 years, the average adolescent gains about 40 pounds and grows about 10 inches. Girls' growth rates begin to accelerate around the age of 10, and they reach their full heights at around 15½ years. Boys experience an equivalent growth spurt about 2 years later and reach their full heights at around 17½ years.

The growth spurt signals the onset of **puberty,** which refers to *the bodily changes associated with sexual maturity.* These changes involve **primary sex characteristics,** which are *bodily structures that are directly involved in reproduction,* for example, the onset of menstruation in girls and the enlargement of the testes, scrotum, and penis and the emergence of the capacity for ejaculation in boys. They also involve **secondary sex characteristics,** which are *bodily structures that change dramatically with sexual maturity but that are not directly involved in reproduction,* for example, the enlargement of the breasts and the widening of the hips in girls and the appearance of facial hair, pubic hair, underarm hair, and the lowering of the voice in both genders. This pattern of changes is caused by increased production of sex-specific hormones: estrogen in girls and testosterone in boys.

? How does the brain change at puberty?

Just as the body changes during adolescence, so, too, does the brain. Between the ages of 6 and 13, the connections between the temporal lobe (the brain region specialized for language) and the parietal lobe (the brain region specialized for understanding spatial relations) multiply rapidly and then stop—just about the time that the critical period for learning a language ends (see **FIGURE 10.7**). There is also

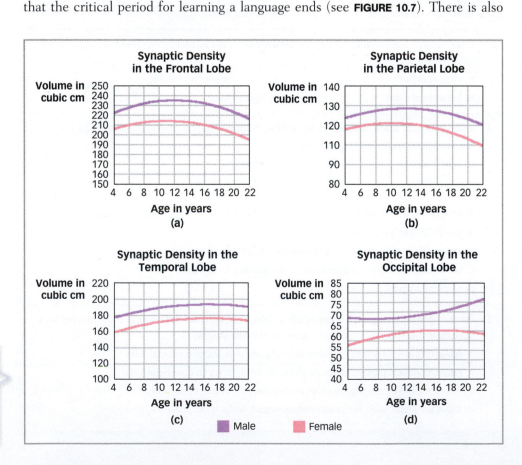

▶ Figure **10.7** **Your Brain on Puberty** The development of neurons peaks in the frontal and parietal lobes at about age 12 (a, b), and in the temporal lobe at about age 16 (c), and continues to increase in the occipital lobe through age 20 (d).

Adolescents are often described as gawky because different parts of their faces and bodies mature at different rates. But as musician Justin Timberlake can attest, the gawkiness generally clears up.

a massive wave of proliferation of new synapses in the prefrontal cortex just before puberty, followed by a period of synaptic pruning during adolescence, as those connections that are not frequently used are eliminated (Giedd et al., 1999). Clearly, the adolescent brain is a work in progress.

The Protraction of Adolescence

Although the onset of puberty is largely determined by a genetic program (no one reaches puberty at 2 or 72), there is considerable variation across individuals (e.g., people tend to reach puberty at about the same age as their same-sex parent did)

How has the onset of puberty changed over the last century?

and across cultures (e.g., African American girls tend to reach puberty before European American girls do; see **FIGURE 10.8**). There is also considerable variation across generations (Malina, Bouchard, & Beunen, 1988). For example, in the United States, the age of

first menstruation was between age 16 and 17 in the 19th century but was approximately age 13 in 1960. Puberty is accelerated by body fat (Kim & Smith, 1998), and the decrease in the age of the onset of puberty is due at least in part to improved diet and health (Ellis & Garber, 2000). But some scientists worry that physical maturity in

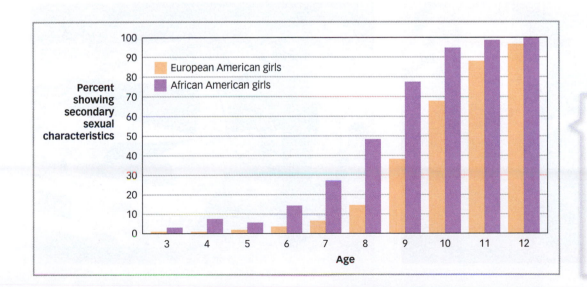

◄ Figure **10.8** **Secondary Sexual Characteristics** The graph shows the percentage of girls in each age group who show breast and/or pubic hair development. These characteristics appear earlier in African American than European American girls. There is no evidence that African American boys mature earlier than European American boys (Herman-Giddens et al., 1997).

women is being hastened by exposure to endocrine-disrupting chemicals that mimic estrogen in the body.

The increasingly early onset of puberty has important psychological consequences. Just two centuries ago, the gap between childhood and adulthood was relatively brief because people became physically adult at roughly the same time that they were ready to accept adult roles in society, and these roles did not normally require them to have extensive schooling. But in modern societies, people typically spend 3 to 10 years in school after they reach puberty. Thus, while the age at which people become physically adult has decreased, the age at which they are prepared or allowed to take on adult responsibilities has increased, and so the period between childhood and adulthood has become *protracted*.

Adolescence is often characterized as a time of internal turmoil and external recklessness, and some psychologists have speculated that the protraction of adolescence is in part to blame for its bad reputation (Moffitt, 1993). According to these theorists, adolescents are adults who have temporarily been denied a place in adult society. As such, they feel especially compelled to do things to demonstrate their adulthood, such as smoking, drinking, using drugs, having sex, and committing crimes. As one researcher noted, "Isolated from adults and wrongly treated like children, it is no wonder that some teens behave, by adult standards, recklessly or irresponsibly" (Epstein, 2007).

But the storm and stress of adolescence is by no means inevitable (Steinberg & Morris, 2001). Teenagers in many cultures show few signs of adolescent turmoil and seem more intent on learning to become adults than on rebelling against them (Epstein, 2007b). Indeed, research suggests that even in American society, the "moody adolescent" who is a victim of "raging hormones" is largely a myth. Adolescents are no moodier than children (Buchanan, Eccles, & Becker, 1992), and fluctu-

? Are adolescent problems inevitable?

About 60% of preindustrial societies don't even have a word for adolescence (Schlegel & Barry, 1991). When a Krobo female menstruates for the first time, older women take her into seclusion for 2 weeks and teach her about sex, birth control, and marriage. Afterward, a public ceremony called the *durbar* is held, and the young female who that morning was regarded as a child is thereafter regarded as an adult.

BOB BURCH / INDEX STOCK

These students at the University of Missouri (left) may be experimenting with reckless behavior, but they are unlikely to become reckless adults. Of course, the Vermont State Trooper (right) who is inspecting the car in which four teens died after a night of drinking would probably remind us that this only applies to those who live.

AP PHOTO/L.G. PATTERSON

AP PHOTO/ALDEN PELLETT, FILE

ations in their hormone levels have only a tiny impact on their moods (Brooks-Gunn, Graber, & Paikoff, 1994). Adolescents do tend to experiment with misbehavior, but most adolescents who try drugs or break the law end up becoming sober, law-abiding adults (Steinberg, 1999). In short, adolescence is not a terribly troubled time for most people, and adolescents typically "age out" of the troubles they get themselves into (Sampson & Laub, 1995).

Sexuality

Adolescence is not an easy time for anyone, but it is especially difficult for some. Boys who reach puberty later than their peers often find this period especially stressful because immature boys may be less athletic and may feel less "manly" than their peers (Petersen, 1985). Among girls, it is those who reach puberty earlier than their peers who are most likely to experience negative consequences (Caspi & Moffitt, 1991; Mendle, Turkheimer, & Emery, 2007) (see **FIGURE 10.9**). Early-maturing girls don't have as much time as their peers do to develop the skills necessary to cope with adolescence (Petersen & Grockett, 1985), and they also tend to receive attention from older males, who may lead them into a variety of unhealthy activities (Ge, Conger, & Elder, 1996). Some research suggests that the *timing* of puberty has a greater influence on emotional and behavioral problems than does the occurrence of puberty itself (Buchanan et al., 1992).

For some adolescents, puberty is additionally complicated by the fact that they are attracted to members of the same sex. In a recent survey (Pew Research Center for People & the Press, 2009b), about half of all Americans said that homosexuality is morally wrong—and America is more accepting of homosexuality than are many other nations (see **FIGURE 10.10**). For example, 98% of Nigerians and Kenyans believe that "homosexuality can never be morally justified" (Pew Research Center for People & the Press, 2006), and Uganda recently considered instituting the death penalty as punishment for homosexual behavior. Given so much social disapproval, it is little wonder that between 2% and 10% of adults classify themselves as homosexual but only .5% of young teenagers are willing to do the same (Garofalo et al., 1999).

? **Is sexual orientation a matter of nature or nurture?**

What determines whether a person is sexually oriented toward the same or the opposite sex? Psychologists used to believe that a person's sexual orientation depended primarily on his or her upbringing, suggesting, for example, that boys who grow up with a domineering mother and a submissive father are less likely to identify with their father and are thereby more likely to become homosexual. But the fact is that scientific research has failed to identify *any* aspect of parenting that has a significant impact on sexual orientation (Bell, Weinberg, & Hammersmith, 1981). Indeed, children raised by homosexual couples and heterosexual couples are equally likely to become heterosexual adults (Patterson, 1995). There is also little support for the idea that a person's early sexual encounters have a lasting impact on his or her sexual orientation (Bohan, 1996).

On the other hand, there is mounting evidence that genes and biology play an important role in determining sexual orientation. The identical twin of a gay man (with

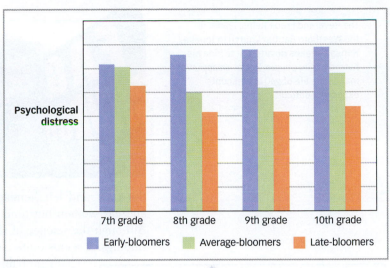

▲ Figure **10.9** **Early Puberty** Early puberty is a source of psychological distress for women (Ge et al., 1996).

▼ Figure **10.10** **Attitudes Toward Homosexuality** It isn't surprising that homosexual adolescents are reluctant to reveal their sexual orientations. A 2009 public opinion survey shows that about half of all Americans disapprove of homosexuality, though this attitude varies significantly by race, age, and level of education (Pew Research Center for People & the Press, 2009b).

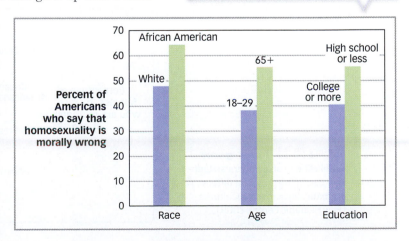

The Reverend Fred Phelps, leader of the Westboro Baptist Church in Topeka, Kansas, makes no attempt to hide his hatred of gay people. Social disapproval makes the life of gay adolescents especially difficult.

whom he shares 100% of his genes) has a 50% chance of being gay, whereas the fraternal twin or nontwin brother of a gay man (with whom he shares 50% of his genes) has only a 15% chance (Bailey & Pillard, 1991; Gladue, 1994). A similar pattern has emerged in studies of women (Bailey et al., 1993). Some studies have found that the brains of gay people look like the brains of straight people of the opposite gender (Savic & Lindstrom, 2008). For example, the right and left hemispheres tend to be of different sizes among straight men and gay women but tend to be of equal sizes among straight women and gay men. Although the science of sexual orientation is still young and fraught with conflicting findings, it seems quite clear that sexual orientation is *not* simply a matter of choice. That's probably why the so-called conversion therapies that attempt to change people's sexual orientations have proved so ineffective (American Psychological Association, 2009).

Sexual orientation may not be a choice, but sexual behavior is—and American teenagers typically choose it. More than 65% of American women report having had sexual intercourse by age 18 and 90% by age 21 (Hogan, Sun, & Cornwell, 2000). Unfortunately, teenagers' interest in sex often surpasses their knowledge about it. The United States has the highest rate of teen pregnancy in the developed world and the highest abortion rate in the Western world, not because American teens have more sex than others but because they are less knowledgeable about it.

Despite what some people believe, evidence suggests that sex education lowers the likelihood that teenagers will get pregnant or catch a sexually transmitted disease (Satcher, 2001) and increases the likelihood that they will use birth control (Mueller, Gavin, & Kulkarni, 2008). Viewed this way, abortion, AIDS, and other sexually transmitted diseases are unfortunate consequences of sexual ignorance. Teenage pregnancy is another (see **FIGURE 10.11**). Teenage mothers fare more poorly than teenage women without children on almost every measure of academic and economic achievement, and their children fare more poorly on most measures of educational success and emotional well-being than do the children of older mothers (Olausson et al., 2001).

? Why do many adolescents make unwise choices about sex?

▶ Figure **10.11** **Teen Pregnancy** The likelihood of an American teenager becoming pregnant differs dramatically across subcultures (Pew Hispanic Center, 2009).

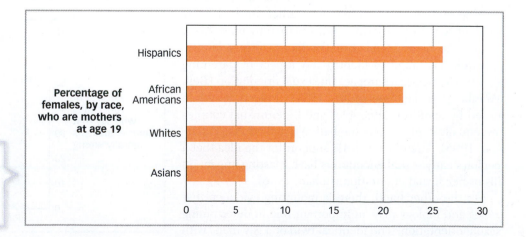

Percentage of females, by race, who are mothers at age 19

Parents and Peers

Children's views of themselves and their worlds are tightly tied to the views of their parents, but puberty creates a new set of needs that begins to snip away at these bonds by orienting adolescents toward peers rather than parents. Whereas children define themselves almost entirely in terms of their relationships with parents and siblings, adolescence marks a shift in emphasis from family relations to peer relations. Two things can make this shift difficult. First, children cannot choose their parents, but adolescents can choose their peers. As such, adolescents have the power to shape themselves by joining groups that will lead them to develop new values, attitudes, beliefs, and perspectives. In a sense, adolescents have the opportunity to invent the adults they will soon become, and the responsibility this opportunity entails can be overwhelming. Second, as adolescents strive for greater autonomy, their parents naturally rebel. For instance, parents and adolescents tend to disagree about the age at which certain adult behaviors, such as staying out late or having sex, become permissible (Holmbeck & O'Donnell, 1991). Because adolescents and parents often have different ideas about who should control the adolescent's behavior, their relationships may become more conflictive and less close and their interactions briefer and less frequent (Larson & Richards, 1991).

? How do family and peer relationships change during adolescence?

But these conflicts and tensions are not as dramatic, pervasive, and inevitable as many seem to believe (Chung, Flook, & Fuligni, 2009). For example, adolescents tend to have aspirations and values that are quite similar to those of their parents (Elder & Conger, 2000), and familial bickering tends to be about much smaller issues, such as dress and language, which explains why teenagers argue more with their mothers (who are typically in charge of such issues) than with their fathers (Caspi et al., 1993). Furthermore, in cultures that emphasize the importance of duty and obligation, parents and adolescents may show few if any signs of tension and conflict (Greenfield et al., 2003).

As adolescents pull away from their parents, they move toward their peers. Studies show that across a wide variety of cultures, historical epochs, and even species, peer relations evolve in a similar way (Dunphy, 1963; Weisfeld, 1999). Young adolescents initially form groups, or "cliques" (Brown, Mory, & Kinney, 1994), with others of their gender. Next, male cliques and female cliques begin to meet in public places, such as town squares or shopping malls, and to interact—but only in groups and only in public. After a few years, the older members of these single-sex cliques "peel off" and form smaller, mixed-sex cliques, which may assemble in private as well as in public but usually assemble as a group. Finally, couples (typically a male and a female) "peel off" from the small, mixed-sex clique and begin romantic relationships.

Studies show that throughout adolescence, people spend increasing amounts of time with opposite-sex peers while maintaining the amount of time they spend with same-sex peers (Richards et al., 1998), and they accomplish this by spending less time with their parents (Larson & Richards, 1991). Although peers exert considerable influence on the adolescent's beliefs and behaviors—both for better and for worse—this influence generally occurs because adolescents

"So I blame you for everything—whose fault is that?"

Adolescents form same-sex cliques that meet opposite-sex cliques in public places. Eventually, these people will form mixed-sex cliques, pair off into romantic relationships, get married, and have children who will take their places at the mall.

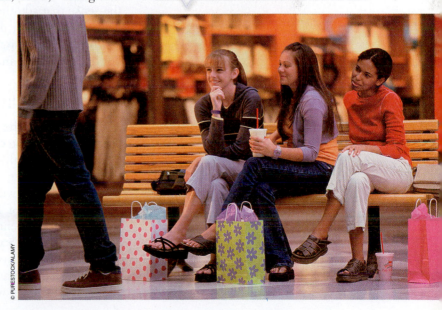

respect, admire, and like their peers, not because their peers pressure them (Susman et al., 1994). In fact, as they age, adolescents show an increasing tendency to resist peer pressure (Steinberg & Monahan, 2007). Acceptance by peers is of tremendous importance to adolescents, and those who are rejected by their peers tend to be withdrawn, lonely, and depressed (Pope & Bierman, 1999). Fortunately for those of us who were seventh-grade nerds, individuals who are unpopular in early adolescence can become popular in later adolescence as their peers become less rigid and more tolerant (Kinney, 1993).

SUMMARY QUIZ [10.3]

1. Evidence indicates that American adolescents are
   a. moodier than children.
   b. victims of raging hormones.
   c. likely to develop drinking problems.
   d. living in a protracted gap between childhood and adulthood.

2. Scientific evidence suggests that _____ play a key role in determining a person's sexual orientation.
   a. personal choices
   b. parenting styles
   c. sibling relationships
   d. genes and biology

3. Adolescents place the greatest emphasis on relationships with
   a. peers.
   b. parents.
   c. siblings.
   d. nonparental authority figures.

Adulthood: Going Happily Downhill

It takes fewer than 7,000 days for a single-celled zygote to become a registered voter. The speed of our physical development is initially quite rapid and then slows in **adulthood,** which is *the stage of development that begins around age 18 to 21 and ends at death.* Because physical change slows from a gallop to a crawl, we sometimes have the sense that adulthood is a destination to which development delivers us and that, once we've arrived, our journey is complete. But that's not true. Although they are less noticeable, many physical, cognitive, and emotional changes take place between our first legal beer and our last legal breath (see **FIGURE 10.12**).

Changing Abilities

The early 20s are the peak years for health, stamina, vigor, and prowess, and because our psychology is so closely tied to our biology, these are also the years during which most of our cognitive abilities are at their sharpest. At this very moment you see farther, hear better, remember more, and weigh less than you ever will again. Enjoy it. Somewhere between the ages of 26 and 30, you will begin the slow and steady decline that does not end until you do. A mere 10 or 15 years after puberty, your body will begin to deteriorate in almost every way: Your muscles will be replaced by fat, your skin will become less elastic, your hair will thin and your bones will weaken, your sensory abilities will become less acute, and your

? **What physical and psychological changes are associated with adulthood?**

adulthood The stage of development that begins around age 18 to 21 and ends at death.

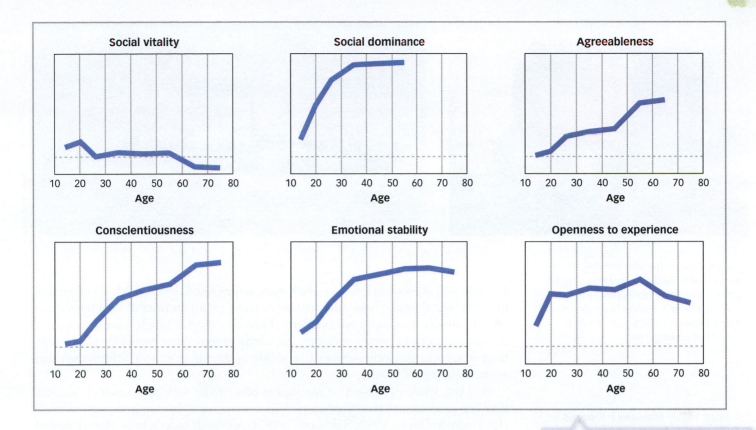

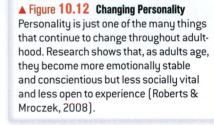

▲ Figure **10.12** **Changing Personality**
Personality is just one of the many things that continue to change throughout adulthood. Research shows that, as adults age, they become more emotionally stable and conscientious but less socially vital and less open to experience (Roberts & Mroczek, 2008).

brain cells will die at an accelerated rate. Eventually, if you are a woman, your ovaries will stop producing eggs and you will become infertile. Eventually, if you are a man, your erections will be fewer and farther between. Indeed, other than being more resistant to colds and less sensitive to pain, older bodies just don't work as well as younger ones do.

As these physical changes accumulate, they will begin to have measurable psychological consequences (Salthouse, 2006) (see **FIGURE 10.13**). For instance, as your brain ages, your prefrontal cortex will deteriorate more quickly than will the other areas of your brain (Raz, 2000); thus you will experience the most noticeable cognitive decline on tasks that require effort, initiative, or strategy. Everyone knows that memory gets worse with age, but not all kinds of memory worsen at the same rate.

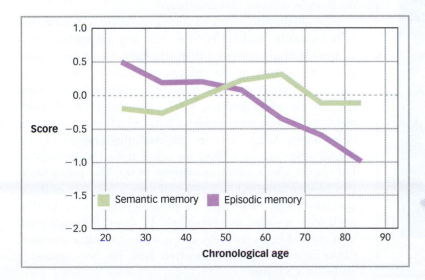

◄ Figure **10.13** **Cognitive Decline** Knowledge lasts a lifetime, but the ability to use it does not. After the age of 20, people show dramatic declines on most measures of cognitive performance even though their level of knowledge remains stable (Salthouse, 2006).

AP PHOTO/NOAH BERGER

AP PHOTO/STEVEN DAY

One week before his 58th birthday, US Airways pilot Chesley Sullenberger made a perfect emergency landing on the Hudson River and saved the lives of everyone on board. None of the passengers wishes they'd had a younger pilot.

▼ Figure **10.14** **Bilaterality in Older and Younger Brains** Across a variety of tasks, older adult brains show bilateral activation and younger adult brains show unilateral activation. One possible explanation for this is that older brains compensate for the declining abilities of one neural structure by calling on other neural structures for help (Cabeza, 2002).

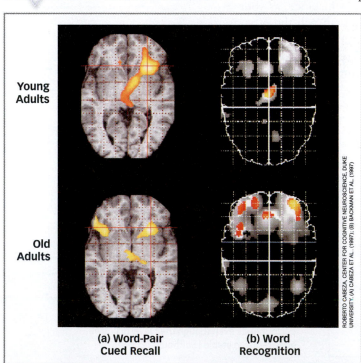

Young Adults

Old Adults

(a) **Word-Pair Cued Recall**

(b) **Word Recognition**

ROBERTO CABEZA, CENTER FOR COGNITIVE NEUROSCIENCE, DUKE UNIVERSITY. (A) CABEZA ET AL. (1997); (B) BÄCKMAN ET AL. (1997)

For example, older adults show a much more pronounced decline on tests of working memory (the ability to hold information "in mind") than on tests of long-term memory (the ability to retrieve information). They also show a much more pronounced decline on tests of episodic memory (the ability to remember particular past events) than on tests of semantic memory (the ability to remember general information such as the meanings of words).

And yet, while the cognitive machinery gets rustier with age, research suggests that the operators of that machinery often compensate by using it more skillfully (Bäckman & Dixon, 1992; Salthouse, 1987). Although older chess players *remember* chess positions more poorly than younger players do, they *play* as well as younger players because they search the board more efficiently (Charness, 1981). Although older typists *react* more slowly than younger typists do, they *type* as quickly and accurately as younger typists because they are better at anticipating the next word (Salthouse, 1984). Older airline pilots are considerably worse than younger pilots when it comes to keeping a list of words in short-term memory, but this age difference disappears when those words are the "heading commands" that pilots receive from the control tower every day (Morrow et al., 1994). This pattern of errors suggests that older adults are somehow compensating for age-related declines in memory and attention.

? Why how do adults compensate for their declining abilities?

How do they do it? When young adults try to keep verbal information in working memory, the left prefrontal cortex is more strongly activated than the right, and when young adults try to keep spatial information in working memory, the right prefrontal cortex is more strongly activated than the left (Smith & Jonides, 1997). But this *bilateral asymmetry* is not seen among older adults, which may mean that older brains compensate for the declining abilities of one neural structure by calling on other neural structures to help out (Cabeza, 2002; see **FIGURE 10.14**). The young brain can be characterized as a group of specialists, but as these specialists age, they begin to work together on tasks that each once handled independently. In short, the machinery of body and brain do break down with age, but a seasoned driver in an old jalopy can often hold his own against a rookie in a hot rod.

Changing Goals

One reason why Grandpa can't find his car keys is that his prefrontal cortex doesn't function like it used to. But another reason is that the location of car keys just isn't the sort of thing that grandpas spend their precious time memorizing. According to *socioemotional selectivity theory* (Carstensen & Turk-Charles, 1994), younger adults

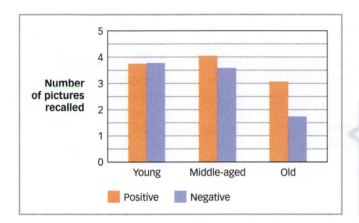

? How do informational goals change in adulthood?

are generally oriented toward the acquisition of information that will be useful to them in the future (e.g., reading news), whereas older adults are generally oriented toward information that brings emotional satisfaction in the present (e.g., reading novels). Because young people have such long futures, they *invest* their time attending to, thinking about, and remembering potentially *useful information* that may serve them well in the many days to come. But older people have shorter futures, so they *spend* their time attending to, thinking about, and remembering *positive information* that serves them well in the moment (see **FIGURE 10.15**).

◀ Figure **10.15** **Memory for Pictures**
Memory in general declines with age, but the ability to remember negative information—such as unpleasant pictures—declines much more quickly than the ability to remember positive information (Carstensen et al., 2000).

Older people perform much more poorly than younger people when they are asked to remember a series of unpleasant faces but perform only slightly more poorly when they are asked to remember a series of pleasant ones (Mather & Carstensen, 2003). Whereas younger adults show activation of the amygdala when they see both pleasant and unpleasant pictures, older adults show greater activation when they see pleasant pictures than when they see unpleasant ones (Mather et al., 2004). Apparently, older adults just don't attend to information that doesn't make them happy. What's more, older people seem better able than younger people to sustain their positive emotional experiences and to curtail their negative ones (Lawton et al., 1992; Mather & Carstensen, 2005).

These cognitive and emotional changes influence the activities in which older people engage. Because a shortened future orients people toward emotionally satisfying rather than intellectually profitable information, older adults become more selective about their interaction partners, choosing to spend time with family and a few close friends rather than with a large circle of acquaintances. One study that followed a group of people from the 1930s to the 1990s found that their rate of interaction with acquaintances declined from early to middle adulthood but their rate of interaction with spouses, parents, and siblings remained stable or increased (Carstensen, 1992).

As people age, they prefer to spend time with family and a few close friends rather than with large circles of acquaintances.

COURTESY OF DANIEL GILBERT

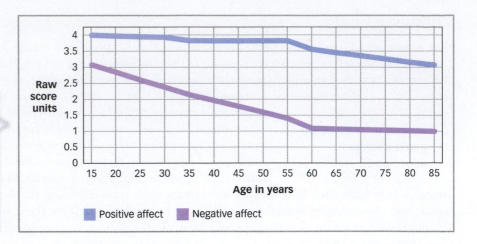

▶ Figure **10.16** **Happiness and Age** Despite what our youth-oriented culture would have you believe, people's overall happiness generally increases with age. As this graph shows, people experience a small decrease in positive affect beginning around age 55, but this is more than compensated for by the large decrease in negative affect that begins around the age of 15 and continues through middle age (Charles, Reynolds, & Gatz, 2001).

Together, these cognitive, emotional, and behavioral changes tend to make later adulthood one of the most satisfying periods of a human life (see **FIGURE 10.16**). In a recent survey, 38% of people over 65 described themselves as very happy, but only 28% of 18- to 29-year-olds said the same (Pew Research Center for the People & the Press, 1997). One reason why Western culture is so obsessed with youth is that young adults vastly overestimate the problems of aging (Pew Research Center for People & the Press, 2009a) (see **FIGURE 10.17**). Research suggests that aging doesn't have to be bad at all and that it is one of the best ways to increase one's share of happiness.

? Is late adulthood a happy or unhappy time for most people?

Changing Roles

The psychological separation from parents that begins in adolescence usually becomes a physical separation in adulthood. In virtually all human societies, young adults leave home, get married, and have children of their own. The average college-age American is likely to get married at around the age of 27, have approximately 1.8 children, and consider both partner and children to be sources of great joy.

But do marriage and children really make us happy? Research has consistently shown that married people live longer, have more frequent sex (and enjoy that sex

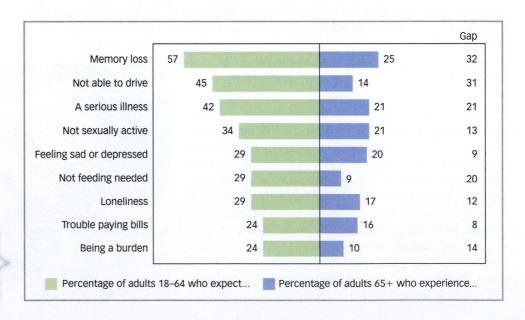

▶ Figure **10.17** **Not So Bad** Research shows that young adults overestimate the problems of old age (Pew Research Center for People & the Press, 2009a).

In 2008, Min Bahadur Sherchan, 76, became the oldest person to scale Mount Everest. Data suggest that for many people the last decades of life are the most satisfying.

AP PHOTO/BINOD JOSH

more), and earn several times as much money as unmarried people do (Waite, 1995). Given these differences, it is no surprise that married people consistently report being happier than unmarried people—whether those unmarried people are single, widowed, divorced, or cohabiting (Johnson & Wu, 2002). That's why many researchers consider marriage one of the best investments individuals can make in their own happiness. But other researchers suggest that married people may be happier because happy people may be more likely to get married and that marriage may be the consequence—not the cause—of happiness (Lucas et al., 2003). The general consensus among scientists seems to be that both of these positions have merit: Even before marriage, people who end up married tend to be happier than those who never marry, but marriage does seem to confer further benefits.

? What does research say about marriage, children, and happiness?

Children are another story. In general, research suggests that children decrease rather than increase their parents' happiness (DiTella, MacCulloch, & Oswald, 2003). For example, parents typically report lower marital satisfaction than do nonparents— and the more children they have, the less satisfaction they report (Twenge, Campbell, & Foster, 2003). Studies suggest that marital satisfaction starts out high, plummets at about the time that the children are in diapers, begins to recover, plummets again when the children are in adolescence, and returns to its premarital levels only when children leave home (see **FIGURE 10.18**). Women with young children are especially likely to experience role conflicts ("How am I supposed to manage being a full-time lawyer and a full-time mother?") and restrictions of freedom ("I never get to play tennis anymore"). One study found that American women were less happy when taking care of their children than when eating, exercising, shopping, napping, or watching television—and only slightly happier than when they were doing housework (Kahneman et al., 2004). *Thinking* about children is a delight, but *raising* children is hard work. Perhaps that's why when women in a national survey were asked to name a mother's most important quality, mothers of grown children were most likely to name

Does marriage make people happy, or do happy people tend to get married?

COURTESY OF DANIEL GILBERT

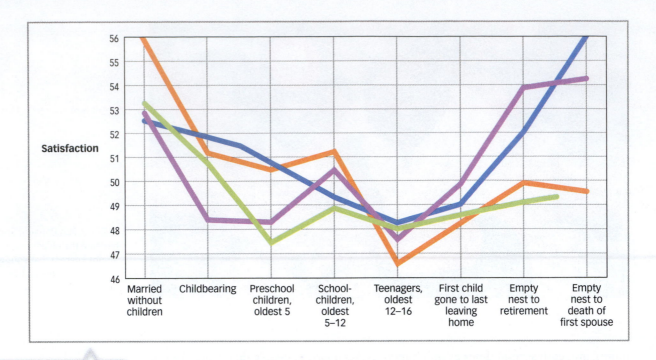

Satisfaction

| | Married without children | Childbearing | Preschool children, oldest 5 | School-children, oldest 5–12 | Teenagers, oldest 12–16 | First child gone to last leaving home | Empty nest to retirement | Empty nest to death of first spouse |

► Figure **10.18** **Marital Satisfaction over the Life Span** This graph shows the results of four independent studies of marital satisfaction among men and women. All four studies suggest that marital satisfaction is highest before children are born and after they leave home (Walker, 1977).

"love," whereas mothers of young children were most likely to name "patience" (Pew Research Center for People & the Press, 1997).

Does all of this mean that people would be happier if they didn't have children? Not necessarily. Because researchers cannot randomly assign people to be parents or nonparents, studies of the effects of parenthood are necessarily correlational. People who want children and have children may be somewhat less happy than people who neither want them nor have them, but it is possible that people who want children would be even less happy if they didn't have them. What seems clear is that raising children is a challenging job that most people find to be meaningful and rewarding—especially when it's over.

SUMMARY QUIZ [10.4]

1. The peak years for health, stamina, vigor, and prowess are
   a. childhood.
   b. the early teens.
   c. the early 20s.
   d. the early 30s.

2. Data suggest that, for most people, the last decades of life are
   a. characterized by an increase in negative emotions.
   b. spent attending to the most useful information.
   c. extremely satisfying.
   e. a time during which they begin to interact with a much wider circle of people.

3. Which is true of marital satisfaction over the life span?
   a. It increases steadily.
   b. It decreases steadily.
   c. It is remarkably stable.
   d. It shows peaks and valleys, corresponding to the presence and ages of children.

A License to Rear

Common law states that "when practice of a profession or calling requires special knowledge or skill and intimately affects public health, morals, order or safety, or general welfare, legislature may prescribe reasonable qualifications for persons desiring to pursue such professions or calling and require them to demonstrate possession of such qualifications by examination." Most of us would probably agree that this is reasonable and that people who want to operate automobiles, use firearms, pilot airplanes, or perform surgeries should be required to demonstrate their proficiency and obtain a license. After all, if people were allowed to practice law or build bridges without first demonstrating their knowledge and skill, the public welfare would be gravely compromised.

So why not apply this logic to parenting? Why not outlaw reproduction by citizens who can't qualify for a parenting license? This suggestion may sound outrageous, but it has actually become the subject of serious debate among ethicists who are trying to decide how best to balance the interests of parents against the damage that bad parenting does to children and society (Tittle, 2004; Warnock, 2003). The arguments *against* parental licensing are obvious: People have a fundamental right to reproduce; people have different definitions of "good parenting"; a licensing system would invite abuse by governments that want to limit the reproduction of citizens who have the wrong genes, the wrong skin color, or the wrong political beliefs. Americans are naturally suspicious of governmental intrusion into private affairs, and what could be more private than the decision to have a child?

But the arguments in favor of licensing are also quite compelling. Consider just a few:

- Bad flossing is a private affair. Bad parenting is not. Every one of us pays the price when parents abuse, neglect, or fail to educate their children. Bad parents impose significant social and economic burdens on the rest of society—not to mention on their own children. Society has a clear interest in *preventing* (not just punishing) abusive and negligent parenting.

- Licensing is not meant to stop people from having children—it is meant to make bad parents into good ones. Driver's education turns bad drivers into good drivers, but most people wouldn't sign up for such training if they didn't have to in order to qualify for a driver's license. Licensing would motivate people to learn the things that every parent should know.

- If we demand that people meet certain standards before they are allowed to *adopt* children, then why should we not demand that they meet the same standards before being allowed to *bear* children? Are our biological children worth less than our adopted ones?

Anyone who has read George Orwell's *1984* or Aldous Huxley's *Brave New World* will find the notion of parental licensing more than a little frightening. And yet the arguments in its favor are not absurd. Bad parenting is a real problem. Is parental licensing the right solution, or is it a cure that's worse than the illness? Where do you stand?

Chapter Review

SUMMARY

Prenatality: A Womb with a View

▶ Developmental psychology studies continuity and change across the life span.

▶ The prenatal stage of development begins when a sperm fertilizes an egg, producing a zygote. The zygote, which contains chromosomes from both the egg and the sperm, develops into an embryo at 2 weeks and then into a fetus at 8 weeks.

▶ The environment has important physical and psychological influences on the fetus. In addition to the food a pregnant woman eats, teratogens, or agents that impair fetal development, can affect the fetus. Common teratogens are tobacco and alcohol.

▶ The fetus can hear sounds and become familiar with those it hears often, such as its mother's voice.

Infancy and Childhood: Becoming a Person

▶ Infants have a limited range of vision, but they can see and remember objects. They learn to control their bodies from the top down and from the center out.

▶ Infants slowly develop theories about how the world works. Piaget believed that these theories developed through four stages, in which children learn basic facts about the world.

▶ Cognitive development also comes about through social interactions in which children are given tools for understanding that have been developed over millennia by members of their cultures.

▶ At a very early age, human beings develop strong emotional ties to their primary caregivers. The quality of these ties is determined both by the caregiver's behavior and the child's temperament.

▶ Children's reasoning about right and wrong is initially based on an action's consequences, but as they mature, children begin to consider the actor's intentions as well as the extent to which the action obeys abstract moral principles.

Adolescence: Minding the Gap

▶ Adolescence is a stage of development that begins with a growth spurt and with puberty, the onset of sexual maturity of the human body.

▶ Adolescents are somewhat more prone to do things that are risky or illegal, but they rarely inflict serious or enduring harm on themselves or others.

▶ During adolescence, sexual interest intensifies, and in some cultures, sexual activity begins. Although most people are attracted to members of the opposite sex, some are not, and research suggests that biology plays a key role in determining a person's sexual orientation.

▶ As adolescents seek to develop their adult identities, they seek increasing autonomy from their parents and become more peer-oriented, forming single-sex cliques, followed by mixed-sex cliques, and finally pairing off as couples.

Adulthood: Going Happily Downhill

▶ Gradual physical decline begins early in adulthood.

▶ Older adults show declines in working memory, episodic memory, and retrieval tasks, but they often develop strategies to compensate.

▶ Older people are more oriented toward emotionally satisfying information, which influences their basic cognitive performance, the size and structure of their social networks, and their general happiness.

▶ People who get married are typically happier, but children and the responsibilities that parenthood entails present a significant challenge.

KEY TERMS

developmental psychology (p. 308)
zygote (p. 309)
germinal stage (p. 309)
embryonic stage (p. 309)
fetal stage (p. 309)
myelination (p. 310)
teratogens (p. 310)
fetal alcohol syndrome (p. 310)
infancy (p. 311)
motor development (p. 312)

reflexes (p. 312)
cephalocaudal rule (p. 312)
proximodistal rule (p. 312)
cognitive development (p. 312)
sensorimotor stage (p. 313)
schemas (p. 313)
assimilation (p. 313)
accommodation (p. 313)
object permanence (p. 314)
childhood (p. 315)
preoperational stage (p. 315)

concrete operational stage (p. 315)
conservation (p. 315)
formal operational stage (p. 316)
egocentrism (p. 316)
theory of mind (p. 317)
attachment (p. 322)
internal working model of relationships (p. 322)
temperaments (p. 322)

preconventional stage (p. 325)
conventional stage (p. 325)
postconventional stage (p. 325)
adolescence (p. 328)
puberty (p. 328)
primary sex characteristics (p. 328)
secondary sex characteristics (p. 328)
adulthood (p. 334)

CHANGING MINDS

1. One of your friends is recently married, and the couple is now planning to have children. You tease your friend that, once she's pregnant, she'll have to stop drinking on the weekends. She scoffs at the idea. "They make it sound like, if a pregnant woman drinks alcohol, she's murdering her baby. The human race got along just fine for thousands of years before anybody decided pregnant women shouldn't drink." What is your friend failing to understand about the effects of alcohol on prenatal development? What other teratogens might you tell her about?

2. The same friend is out with you, buying groceries, when you spot a crying child in a stroller. The mother picks up the child

and cuddles it until it stops crying. "Now, that's bad parenting," your friend says. "If you pick up and cuddle a child every time it cries, you're reinforcing the behavior, and the result will be one spoiled child." Do you agree with your friend? What do studies of attachment tell us about the effects of picking up and holding children when they cry?

3. You and your roommate are watching a movie in which a young man tells his parents that he's gay; the parents react badly and decide that they should send him to a "camp" where he can learn to change his sexual orientation. Your roommate turns to you: "Do you know anything about this? Can you really change

someone from gay to straight, just by sending them to camp?" Based on what you've read in this text, what would you tell your friend about the factors determining sexual preference?

4. One of your cousins has just turned 30 and, to his horror, has just discovered a gray hair. "This is terrible," he says. "I sup-

pose the next thing is I'll start losing my eyesight and my hearing, and after that I'll begin forgetting where I put the keys or how to program a cell phone. Aging is just one slow, terrible decline." What could you tell your cousin to cheer him up? Does everything in life get worse with aging?

CRITICAL THINKING QUESTIONS

1. Young children don't realize that other people can see the world differently than they do. That statement describes most little kids, but it also describes most adults from time to time. What are some examples of adult egocentrism, and why doesn't it ever completely go away?

2. Some parents believe that teaching adolescents about birth control and then expecting them to abstain is like giving them the keys to a car and then expecting them not to drive. Other

parents believe that adolescents make their own decisions about sex and that it is better for those decisions to be made on the basis of knowledge rather than ignorance. How would you design a study to help settle this argument?

3. Data suggest that later adulthood is an especially rewarding time of life for most people. So why do so many of us think that being young is better than being old? Is this just a matter of ignorance, or does our society actively perpetrate this myth?

ANSWERS TO SUMMARY QUIZZES

Summary Quiz [10.1] 1. b; 2. a; 3. b
Summary Quiz [10.2] 1. c; 2. b; 3. b; 4. d; 5. c
Summary Quiz [10.3] 1. d; 2. d; 3. a
Summary Quiz [10.4] 1. c; 2. c; 3. d

Need more help? Additional resources are located at the book's free companion website at
www.worthpublishers.com/schacterbrief2e

Personality

GROWING UP, STEFANI JOANNE ANGELINA GERMANOTTA seemed to have personality. As a child, she was said to have shown up at the occasional family gathering naked. As the pop star now known as Lady Gaga, she continues the tradition of being different. Her first albums, titled *The Fame* and *The Fame Monster*, hinted she might have issues. And look at her website: THE WHOLE THING IS IN CAPS, A STYLE WE ALL KNOW IS LIKE SCREAMING. It seems almost natural, then, that she would wear a meat dress to the Video Music Awards. But it's not all show. She supports humanitarian and personal causes, including equality for people who are gay, bisexual, lesbian, or transgendered (as in her song "Born This Way"). Even the meat dress was for a cause—turned into jerky and preserved at the Rock and Roll Hall of Fame. Lady Gaga is one of a kind. She has personality in an important sense—she has qualities that make her psychologically different from other people.

▶ Singer Lady Gaga in her meat dress at the MTV Video Music Awards, September 2010.

PRESS ASSOCIATION VIA AP IMAGES

345

THE FORCES THAT CREATE ANY ONE PERSONALITY ARE ALWAYS something of a mystery. Your personality is different from anyone else's and expresses itself pretty consistently across settings—at home, in the classroom, and elsewhere. But how and why do people differ psychologically? By studying many unique individuals, psychologists seek to gather enough information to scientifically answer these, the central questions of personality psychology.

Personality *is an individual's characteristic style of behaving, thinking, and feeling.* Whether Lady Gaga's quirks are real or merely concocted for publicity, they are certainly hers and show her distinct personality. In this chapter, we will explore personality, first by looking at what it is and how it is measured and then by focusing on each of four main approaches to understanding personality—trait-biological, psychodynamic, humanistic-existential, and social cognitive. (Psychologists have personalities, too, so their different approaches, even to the topic of personality, shouldn't be that surprising.) At the end of the chapter, we will discuss the psychology of self to see how our views of what we are like can shape and define our personality.

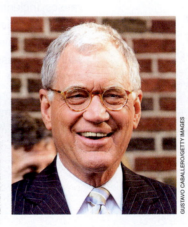

How would you describe each of these personalities?

Personality: What It Is and How It Is Measured

If someone said "You have no personality," how would you feel? Like a cookie-cutter person, a boring, grayish lump who should go out and get a personality as soon as possible? As a rule, people don't usually strive for a personality—one seems to develop naturally as we travel through life. As psychologists have tried to understand the process of personality development, they have pondered questions of description (How do people differ?), explanation (Why do people differ?), and the more quantitative question of measurement (How can personality be assessed?).

Describing and Explaining Personality

Most personality psychologists focus on specific, psychologically meaningful individual differences—characteristics such as honesty or anxiousness or moodiness. Still, personality is often in the eye of the beholder. When one person describes another as "a conceited jerk," for example, you may wonder whether you have just learned more about the describer or the person being described. Interestingly, studies that ask acquaintances to describe one another find a high degree of similarity among any one individual's descriptions of many different people ("Jason thinks that Bob is considerate, Renata is kind, and Gina is nice to others"). In contrast, resemblance is quite low when many people describe one person ("Bob thinks Jason is smart, Renata

? What does it mean to say that personality is in the eye of the beholder?

thinks he is competitive, and Gina thinks he has a good sense of humor") (Dornbusch et al., 1965).

What leads Lady Gaga to all her entertaining extremes? In general, explanations of personality differences are concerned with (1) *prior events* that can shape an individual's personality or (2) *anticipated events* that might motivate the person to reveal particular personality characteristics. In a biological prior event, Stefani Germanotta received genes from her parents that may have led her to develop into the sort of person who loves putting on a display (not to mention putting on raw meat) and stirring up controversy. Researchers interested in events that happen prior to our behavior delve into our subconscious and into our circumstances and interpersonal surroundings as well as studying our biology and brains.

The consideration of *anticipated events* emphasizes the person's own perspective and often seems intimate and personal in its reflection of the person's inner life—hopes, fears, and aspirations. Of course, our understanding of how the baby named Stefani Germanotta grew into the adult Lady Gaga—or the life of any woman or man—also depends on insights into the interaction between the past and future: We need to know how her history may have shaped her motivations. Personality psychologists study questions of how our personalities are determined by the forces in our minds and in our personal history of heredity and environment and by the choices we make and the goals we seek.

"Do you mind if I say something helpful about your personality?"

Measuring Personality

Of all the things psychologists have set out to measure, personality must be one of the toughest. How do you capture the uniqueness of a person—like a moonbeam in a jar? The general personality measures can be classified broadly into personality inventories and projective techniques.

Personality Inventories

To learn about an individual's personality, you could follow the person around and, clipboard in hand, record every single thing the person does, says, thinks, and feels—including how long this goes on before the person calls the police. Some observations might involve your own impressions ("Day 5: seems to be getting irritable"); others would involve objectively observable events that anyone could verify ("Day 7: grabbed my pencil and broke it in half, then bit my hand").

Psychologists have figured out ways to obtain objective data on personality without driving their subjects to distraction. The most popular technique is the **self-report**—*a series of answers to a questionnaire that asks people to indicate the extent to which sets of statements or adjectives accurately describe their own behavior or mental state.* Scales based on the content of self-reports have been devised to assess a whole range of personality characteristics, all the way from general tendencies such as overall happiness (Lyubomirsky, 2008; Lyubomirsky & Lepper, 1999) to specific ones such as responding rapidly to insults (Swann & Rentfrow, 2001) or complaining about poor service (Lerman, 2006).

For example, the **Minnesota Multiphasic Personality Inventory (MMPI-2)**, *a well-researched, clinical questionnaire used to assess personality and psychological problems,* consists of more than 500 descriptive statements—for example, "I often feel like breaking things," "I think the world is a dangerous place," and "I'm good at socializing"—to which the respondent answers "true," "false," or "cannot say." Researchers then combine the answers to get a score on 10 main subscales, each describing some aspect of personality. The MMPI-2 measures tendencies toward clinical problems—for example, depression, hypochondria, anxiety, paranoia, and unconventional ideas or bizarre thoughts and beliefs—as well as some general personality characteristics, such as degree of masculine and feminine gender role

personality An individual's characteristic style of behaving, thinking, and feeling.

self-report A series of answers to a questionnaire that asks people to indicate the extent to which sets of statements or adjectives accurately describe their own behavior or mental state.

Minnesota Multiphasic Personality Inventory (MMPI) A well-researched, clinical questionnaire used to assess personality and psychological problems.

identification, sociability versus social inhibition, and impulsivity. The MMPI-2 also includes *validity scales* that assess a person's attitudes toward test taking and any tendency to try to distort the results by faking answers.

Personality inventories such as the MMPI-2 are easy to administer: Just give someone a pencil and away they go. The person's scores can be calculated by computer and compared with the average ratings of thousands of other test takers. Because no interpretation of the responses is needed, biases are minimized. Of course, an accurate reading of personality will occur only if people provide honest responses—especially about characteristics that might be unflattering—and if they don't always agree or always disagree, a phenomenon known as *response style*. The validity scales cannot eliminate these problems altogether, but they can detect them well enough to make personality inventories a generally effective means of testing, classifying, and researching many personality characteristics.

> **?** What are some limitations of personality inventories?

Projective Techniques

The second major class of tools for evaluating personality, the **projective techniques,** consist of *a standard series of ambiguous stimuli designed to elicit unique responses that reveal inner aspects of an individual's personality.* The developers of projective tests assumed that people would project personality factors that are out of awareness—wishes, concerns, impulses, and ways of seeing the world—onto ambiguous stimuli and would not censor these responses. If you and a friend were looking at the sky one day and she became upset because one cloud looked to her like a monster, her response might reveal more about her inner life than her answer to a direct question about her fears.

Probably the best-known projective technique is the **Rorschach Inkblot Test,** *a projective personality test in which individual interpretations of the meaning of a set of unstructured inkblots are analyzed to identify a respondent's inner feelings and interpret his or her personality structure.* An example inkblot is shown in **FIGURE 11.1.** Responses are scored according to complicated systems (derived in part from research with patients) that classify what people see (Exner, 1993; Rapaport, 1946). For example, most people who look at Figure 11.1 report seeing birds or people, so someone who is unable to see obvious items when he or she responds to a blot may be having difficulty perceiving the world as others do.

The **Thematic Apperception Test (TAT)** is *a projective personality test in which respondents reveal underlying motives, concerns, and the way they see the social world through the stories they make up about ambiguous pictures of people.* To get a sense of the test, look at **FIGURE 11.2.** Who are those people, and what are they doing and thinking? Different people tell very different stories about this image, as they do about the standard images in the TAT set. In creating the stories, the test taker is thought to identify with the main characters and to project his or her view of others and the world onto the other details in the drawing. Here is one young woman's response to the sample card shown in Figure 11.2—one that seems to reveal her own personal situation and a conflict between her wish for independence and fear that this is wrong and is punishable by a tragic loss: "The old lady in

▼ Figure **11.1** **Sample Rorschach Inkblot** Test takers are shown a card such as this sample and asked, "What might this be?" Their responses are assumed to reflect unconscious aspects of their personality.
Behn-Rorschach Test, Verlag Hans Huber, Bern, Switzerland, 1941.

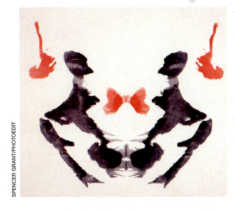

SPENCER GRANT/PHOTOEDIT

▶ Figure **11.2** **Sample TAT Card** Test takers are shown cards with ambiguous scenes, such as this sample, and are asked to tell a story about what is happening in the picture. The main themes of the story, the thoughts and feelings of the characters, and how the story develops and resolves are considered useful indices of unconscious aspects of an individual's personality (Murray, 1943).

SPENCER GRANT/PHOTOEDIT—ALL RIGHTS RESERVED

the background seems angry and thinks the younger one is making a big mistake. Maybe they're related. . . . Everything the young woman does is wrong in her mother's eyes. The daughter just wants to get away and live her own life but is too guilty to leave her mother's side, thinking it will hurt her. In the end, hmm? The girl does leave and the mother dies."

Projective tests remain controversial in psychology. Critics argue that tests such as the Rorschach and the TAT are open to the subjective interpretation and theoretic biases of the examiner. Although a TAT story like the above may *seem* revealing, the examiner must always add an interpretation (Was this about the client's actual mother, about her own conflicted desires for independence, or about trying to be funny or creative or oddball?), and that interpretation could well be the scorer's *own* projection into the mind of the test taker. Thus, despite the rich picture of a personality and the insights into an individual's motives that these tests offer, projective tests should be understood primarily as a way in which a psychologist can get to know someone personally and intuitively (McClelland et al., 1953). When measured by rigorous scientific criteria, projective tests such as the TAT and the Rorschach have not been found to be reliable or valid in predicting behavior (Lilienfeld, Lynn, & Lohr, 2003).

> **?** Why might a projective test like the TAT be less than reliable?

New personality measurement methods are moving beyond both personality inventories and projective tests (Robins, Fraley, & Krueger, 2007). High-tech methods such as wireless communication, real-time computer analysis, and automated behavior identification open the door to personality measurements that are leaps beyond "following the person around with a clipboard"—and can lead to surprising findings. The stereotype that women are more talkative than men, for example, was challenged by findings when 396 college students in the United States and Mexico each spent several days wearing an "EAR"—an electronically activated recorder—that captured random snippets of their talk (Mehl et al., 2009). The result? Women and men were *equally* talkative, each averaging about 16,000 words per day. The advanced measurement of how people differ (and how they do not) is a key step in understanding personality.

projective techniques A standard series of ambiguous stimuli designed to elicit unique responses that reveal inner aspects of an individual's personality.

Rorschach Inkblot Test A projective personality test in which individual interpretations of the meaning of a set of unstructured inkblots are analyzed to identify a respondent's inner feelings and interpret his or her personality structure.

Thematic Apperception Test (TAT) A projective personality test in which respondents reveal underlying motives, concerns, and the way they see the social world through the stories they make up about ambiguous pictures of people.

The electronically activated recorder sampled conversations of hundreds of participants and found that women and men are equally talkative (Mehl et al., 2009).

SUMMARY QUIZ [11.1]

1. From a psychological perspective, personality refers to
   a. a person's characteristic style of behaving, thinking, and feeling.
   b. physiological predispositions that manifest themselves psychologically.
   c. past events that have shaped a person's current behavior.
   d. choices people make in response to cultural norms.

2. Which of the following is *not* a drawback of self-report measures such as the MMPI-2?
   a. People may respond in ways that put themselves in flattering light.
   b. Some people tend to always agree or always disagree with the statements on the test.
   c. Interpretation is subject to the biases of the researcher.
   d. People are unaware of some of their personality characteristics and thus cannot answer accurately.

3. Projective techniques to assess personality involve
   a. personal inventories.   c. responses to ambiguous stimuli.
   b. self-reporting.   d. actuarial methodology.

The Trait Approach: Identifying Patterns of Behavior

Imagine writing a story about the people you know. To capture their special qualities, you might describe their traits: Lulu is *friendly, aggressive,* and *domineering;* Seth is *flaky, humorous,* and *superficial.* With a dictionary and a free afternoon, you might even be able to describe Gino as *perspicacious, flagitious,* and *callipygian.* The trait approach to personality uses such trait terms to characterize differences among individuals. In attempting to create manageable and meaningful sets of descriptors, trait theorists face two significant challenges: narrowing down the almost infinite set of adjectives and answering the more basic question of why people have particular traits—whether they arise from biological or hereditary foundations.

Traits as Behavioral Dispositions and Motives

Gordon Allport (1937), one of the first trait theorists, believed people could be described in terms of traits just as an object could be described in terms of its properties. He saw a **trait** as *a relatively stable disposition to behave in a particular and consistent way.* For example, a person who keeps his books organized alphabetically in bookshelves, hangs his clothing neatly in the closet, keeps a clear agenda in a daily planner, and lists birthdays of friends and family in his calendar can be said to have the trait of *orderliness.* This trait consistently manifests itself in a variety of settings.

The "orderliness" trait describes a person but doesn't explain his or her behavior. *Why* does the person behave in this way? Allport saw traits as preexisting dispositions, causes of behavior that reliably trigger the behavior. The person's orderliness, for example, is an inner property of the person that will cause the person to straighten things up and be tidy in a wide array of situations. Other personality theorists, such as Henry Murray (the originator of the TAT), sug-

> **?** How might traits explain behavior?

gested instead that traits reflect motives. Just as a hunger motive might explain someone's many trips to the snack bar, a need for orderliness might explain the neat closet and organized calendar (Murray & Kluckhohn, 1953). As a rule, researchers examining traits as causes have used personality inventories to measure them, whereas those examining traits as motives have more often used projective tests.

The Search for Core Traits

Picking a single trait such as orderliness and studying it in depth doesn't get us very far in the search for the core of human character—for the basic set of traits that define how humans differ from one another. How have researchers tried to discover such core traits?

Classification Using Language

The study of core traits began with an exploration of how personality is represented in the store of wisdom we call language. Generation after generation, people have described people with words, so early psychologists proposed that core traits could be discerned by finding the main themes in all the adjectives used to describe personality. In one such analysis, a painstaking count of relevant words in a dictionary of English resulted in a list of more than 18,000 potential traits (Allport & Odbert, 1936)! Attempts to narrow down the list to a more manageable set depend on the idea that traits might be related in a hierarchical pattern, with more general or abstract traits, such as neuroticism, at higher levels than more specific or concrete traits, such as

trait A relatively stable disposition to behave in a particular and consistent way.

Big Five The traits of the five-factor model: conscientiousness, agreeableness, neuroticism, openness to experience, and extraversion.

quickness to anger. The highest-level traits are sometimes called dimensions or *factors* of personality.

But how many factors are there? Different researchers have proposed different answers. Cattell (1950) proposed a 16-factor theory of personality—way down from 18,000, but still a lot—whereas others have proposed theories with far fewer basic dimensions (John, Naumann, & Soto, 2008). Hans Eysenck (1967) simplified things nicely with a model of personality with only two

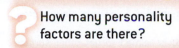

How many personality factors are there?

major traits (although he later expanded that to three). Eysenck identified one dimension that distinguished people who are sociable and active (extraverts) from those who are more introspective and quiet (introverts). He also identified a second dimension ranging from the tendency to be very neurotic or emotionally unstable to the tendency to be more emotionally stable. He believed that many behavioral tendencies could be understood in terms of their relation to these core traits.

The Big Five Dimensions of Personality

Today many personality researchers agree that personality is best captured by 5 factors rather than by 2, 3, 16, or 18,000 (John & Srivastava, 1999; McCrae & Costa, 1999). The **Big Five,** as they are affectionately called, are *the traits of the five-factor model of personality: conscientiousness, agreeableness, neuroticism, openness to experience, and extraversion* (see **TABLE 11.1**). (Remember them by the initials CANOE.) The five-factor model, which overlaps with the pioneering work of Cattell and Eysenck, is now widely preferred for several reasons. First, modern mathematical analysis techniques con-

What are the strengths of the five-factor model?

firm that this set of five factors strikes the right balance between accounting for as much variation in personality as possible while avoiding overlapping traits. Second, in a large number of studies using different kinds of data—people's descriptions of their own personalities, other people's descriptions of their personalities, interviewer checklists, and behavioral observation—the same five factors have emerged. Third, and perhaps most important, the basic five-factor structure seems to show up across a wide range of participants, including children, adults in other cultures, and even among those who speak other languages, suggesting that the Big Five may be universal (John & Srivastava, 1999).

The Big Five can also be used to predict patterns of behavior (see the Hot Science box). People identified as high in extraversion, for example, tend to choose to spend time with lots of other people and are more likely than introverts to look people in the eye. People high in conscientiousness generally perform well at work and tend to live longer. People low on conscientiousness and low in agreeableness are more likely than average to be juvenile delinquents (John & Srivastava, 1999).

Research on the Big Five has shown that people's personalities tend to remain stable through their lifetime, scores at one time in life correlating strongly with scores at later dates, even later decades (Caspi, Roberts, & Shiner, 2005). William James offered the opinion that "... in most of us, by the age of thirty, the character has set like plaster, and will never soften again" (James, 1890, p. 121), but this turns out to be too strong a view. Some variability is typical in childhood, and though there is less in adolescence, some personality change can even occur in adulthood for some people (Srivistava et al., 2003).

Table 11.1		
The Big Five Factor Model		
Conscientiousness	organized.................disorganized careful...........................careless self-disciplined.............weak-willed	
Agreeableness	softhearted....................ruthless trusting.......................suspicious helpful...................uncooperative	
Neuroticism	worried...........................calm insecure........................secure self-pitying...............self-satisfied	
Openness to experience	imaginative..............down-to-earth variety...........................routine independent.................conforming	
Extraversion	social...........................retiring fun loving........................sober affectionate..................reserved	

Source: McCrae & Costa, 1990, 1999.

HOT SCIENCE

Personality on the Surface

When you judge someone as friend or foe, interesting or boring, how do you do it? It's nice to think that your impressions of personality are based on something deep. You wouldn't judge personality based on something as shallow as someone's looks, would you? Or what about the appearance of a person's room? The music he prefers? His web page? It turns out that some accurate personality judgments can be made from exactly such superficial cues.

People in one study were asked to make personality judgments of the occupants of business offices and dormitory rooms (Gosling et al., 2002). The occupants were not present, and photos and identifying information were hidden, leaving only the rooms' contents and arrangement to go on. Even so, observers rating occupants on the Big Five trait dimensions were very accurate in judging openness to experience, conscientiousness, and extraver-

sion. How could they do this? They reported using specific cues: Occupants high in openness had distinctive, unconventional rooms; those high in conscientiousness had spaces that were well organized and uncluttered; those high in extraversion had rooms that were warm, decorated, and inviting. Agreeableness and neuroticism, on the other hand, were not linked to specific room features. Not every personality trait reveals itself in your stuff.

Are music preferences also surface indicators of your personality? One study examining the music picks of some 3,000 students in Texas found that people who like their music upbeat and conventional (pop, country) tend to be extraverted, agreeable, and conscientious (Rentfrow & Gosling, 2003). Those who prefer more reflective and complex music (jazz, classical) or more intense and rebellious music (rock, alternative) are high in openness to experience. You may not think you're reveal-

ing your personality by playing your stereo, but you are.

Personality is related to yet other surface characteristics. Extraverts smile more than others and appear more stylish and healthy (Naumann et al., 2009), while people high in openness to experience are more likely to have tattoos and other body modifications (Nathanson, Paulhus, & Williams, 2006). Findings like these suggest that people can manipulate their surface identities to try to make desired impressions on others—and that surface signs of personality might therefore be false or misleading. However, a study of Facebook pages—which are clearly surface expressions of personality intended for others to see—found that the personalities people project online are highly related to their real personalities (Back et al., 2010). The signs of personality that appear on the surface may be more than skin deep.

▲ A closet isn't just a place for clothes. In some cases, it's a personality test.

Traits as Biological Building Blocks

Can we explain *why* a person has a stable set of personality traits? Many trait theorists have argued that immutable brain and biological processes produce the remarkable stability of traits over the life span. Brain damage certainly can produce personality change, as the classic case of Phineas Gage so vividly demonstrates (see Chapter 3). You may recall that after the blasting accident that blew a steel rod through his frontal lobes, Gage showed a dramatic loss of social appropriateness and conscientiousness (Damasio, 1994). In fact, when someone experiences a profound change in personality, testing often reveals the presence of such brain pathologies as Alzheimer's disease, stroke, or brain tumor (Feinberg, 2001). The administration of antidepressant medication and other pharmaceutical treatments that change brain chemistry can also trigger personality changes, making people, for example, somewhat more extraverted and less neurotic (Bagby et al., 1999; Knutson et al., 1998).

Genes, Traits, and Personality

Some of the most compelling evidence for the importance of biological factors in personality comes from the domain of behavioral genetics. Simply put, the more genes you have in common with someone, the more similar your personalities are likely to be. In one review of studies involving more than 24,000 twin pairs, for example, identical twins, who share the same genes, proved markedly more similar to each other in personality than did fraternal twins, who share on average only half their genes

? What do studies of twins tell us about personality?

(Loehlin, 1992). And although environment and life experiences also help shape personality, identical twins reared apart in adoptive families end up at least as similar in personality as those who grew up together (McGue & Bouchard, 1998; Tellegen et al., 1988).

It's unlikely that a specific gene controls neuroticism or extraversion or any other personality factor. Rather, more genes interacting may produce a specific physiological characteristic such as a tendency for extraversion. This biological factor may then shape the person's behavior, leading him to be more likely to chat with strangers at a party than someone whose genes produce a tendency for introversion.

From an evolutionary perspective, differences in personality reflect alternative adaptations that species—human and nonhuman—have evolved to deal with the challenges of survival and reproduction. For example, if you were to hang around a bar for an evening or two, you would soon see that humans have evolved more than one way to attract and keep a mate. People who are extraverted would probably show off to attract attention, whereas you'd be likely to see people high in agreeableness displaying affection and nurturance (Buss, 1996). Both approaches might work well to attract mates and reproduce successfully—depending on the environment. Through this process of natural selection, those characteristics that have proved successful in our evolutionary struggle for survival have been passed on to future generations (see the Real World Box).

Traits in the Brain

But what neurophysiological mechanisms influence the development of personality traits? Much of the thinking on this topic has focused on the extraversion/introversion dimension. In his personality model, Eysenck (1967) speculated that extraversion and introversion might arise from individual differences in alertness. Extraverts may need to seek out social interaction, parties, and even mayhem in the attempt to achieve full mental stimulation, whereas introverts may avoid these situations because they are so sensitive that such stimulation is unpleasant.

Behavioral and physiological research generally supports Eysenck's view. When introverts and extraverts are presented with a range of intense stimuli, introverts respond more strongly, including salivating more when a drop of lemon juice is placed on their tongues and reacting more negatively to electric shocks or loud

THE REAL WORLD

Do Different Genders Lead to Different Personalities?

Do you think there is a typical "female" personality or a typical "male" personality? Researchers have found some reliable differences between men and women with respect to their self-reported traits, attitudes, and behaviors (Feingold, 1994). Some of these findings conform to North American stereotypes of "masculine" and "feminine." For example, researchers have found women to be more verbally expressive, more sensitive to nonverbal cues, and more nurturing than are men. Men are more physically aggressive than women, but women engage in more social relationship aggression (e.g., ignoring someone) than do men (Eagly & Steffen, 1986). On the Big Five, women tend to be higher on agreeableness and neuroticism than men, but the genders do not differ in openness to experience. On a variety of other personality characteristics, including helpfulness and sexual desire, men and women on average show no reliable differences. Overall, men and women seem to be far more similar in personality than they are different (Hyde, 2005).

An evolutionary biological perspective on gender differences in personality holds that men and women have evolved different personality characteristics in part because their reproductive success depends on different behaviors. For instance, aggressiveness in men may have an adaptive value in intimidating sexual rivals; women who are agreeable and nurturing may have evolved to protect and ensure the survival of their offspring (Campbell, 1999) as well as

GIFT OF JEAN AND FRANCIS MARSHALL/UNIVERSITY OF CALIFORNIA,
BERKELEY ART MUSEUM/PACIFIC FILM ARCHIVE

to secure a reliable mate and provider (Buss, 1989). In contrast, a social cognitive perspective known as *social role theory* holds that personality differences between men and women result from cultural standards and expectations that assign them socially permissible jobs, activities, and family positions (Eagly & Wood, 1999). Because of their physical size and their freedom from childbearing, men historically took roles of greater power—roles that in postindustrial society don't necessarily require physical strength. These differences then snowball, with

◀ Cultures differ in their appreciation of male and female characteristics, but the Hindu deity Ardhanarishvara represents the value of combining both parts of human nature. Male on one side and female on the other, this god is symbolic of the dual nature of the sacred. The only real problem with such side-by-side androgyny comes in finding clothes to fit.

men generally taking roles that require assertiveness and aggression (e.g., executive, school principal, surgeon) and women pursuing roles that emphasize greater supportiveness and nurturance (e.g., nurse, day-care worker, teacher).

Regardless of the source of gender differences in personality, the degree to which people identify personally with masculine and feminine stereotypes may tell us about important personality differences between individuals. Researcher Sandra Bem (1974) suggested that psychologically *androgynous* people—those who adopt the "best of both worlds," identifying both with positive feminine traits (such as kindness) and positive masculine traits (such as assertiveness)—might be better adjusted than are people who identify strongly with only one sex role. Androgyny has benefits (Lefkowitz & Zeldow, 2006), but it is particularly beneficial for women—perhaps because many of the traits stereotypically associated with masculinity (such as assertiveness and achievement) are related to psychological health (Cook, 1985).

---

noises (Bartol & Costello, 1976; Stelmack, 1990). This reactivity has an impact on the ability to concentrate: Extraverts tend to perform well at tasks that are done in a noisy, arousing context, such as bartending or teaching, whereas introverts are better at tasks that require concentration in tranquil contexts, such as the work of a librarian or nighttime security guard (Geen, 1984; Lieberman & Rosenthal, 2001; Matthews & Gilliland, 1999).

? What neurological differences explain why extraverts pursue more stimulation than introverts?

Refining Eysenck's ideas about arousability, Jeffrey Gray (1970) proposed that the dimensions of extraversion/introversion and neuroticism reflect two basic brain systems. The *behavioral activation system* (*BAS*), essentially a "go" system, activates approach behavior in response to the anticipation of reward. The extravert has a highly reactive BAS and will actively engage the environment, seeking social reinforcement and on the "go." The *behavioral inhibition system* (*BIS*), a "stop" system, inhibits behavior in response to stimuli signaling punishment. The emotionally unstable person, in turn, has a highly reactive BIS and will focus on negative outcomes and be on the lookout for "stop" signs. Studies of brain electrical activity (electroencephalograms—EEGs) and functional brain imaging (fMRI) suggest that individual differences in activation and inhibition arise through the operation of distinct brain systems underlying these tendencies (DeYoung & Gray, 2009).

psychodynamic approach An approach that regards personality as formed by needs, strivings, and desires, largely operating outside of awareness-motives that can also produce emotional disorders.

id The part of the mind containing the drives present at birth; it is the source of our bodily needs, wants, desires, and impulses, particularly our sexual and aggressive drives.

SUMMARY QUIZ [11.2]

1. A relatively stable disposition to behave in a particular and consistent way is a
   a. motive.   b. goal.   c. trait.   d. reflex.

2. Which of the following is *not* one of the Big Five personality factors?
   a. conscientiousness   c. neuroticism
   b. agreeableness   d. orderliness

3. Compelling evidence for the importance of biological factors in personality is best seen in studies of
   a. parenting styles.   c. brain damage.
   b. identical twins reared apart.   d. responses on the MMPI-2.

The Psychodynamic Approach: Forces That Lie Beneath Awareness

Rather than trying to understand personality in terms of broad theories for describing individual differences, Freud looked for personality in the details—the meanings and insights revealed by careful analysis of the tiniest blemishes in a person's thoughts and behavior. Working with patients who came to him with disorders that did not seem to have any physical basis, he began by interpreting the origins of their everyday mistakes and memory lapses—errors that have come to be called "Freudian slips."

The theories of Freud and his followers (discussed in Chapter 14) are referred to as the **psychodynamic approach.** According to this approach, *personality is formed by needs, strivings, and desires largely operating outside of awareness—motives that can produce emotional disorders.* The real engines of personality, in this view, are forces of which we are largely unaware.

Sigmund Freud was the first psychology theorist to be honored with his own bobble-head doll. Let's hope he's not the last.

The Structure of the Mind: Id, Ego, and Superego

To explain the emotional difficulties that beset his patients, Freud proposed that the mind consists of three independent, interacting, and often conflicting systems: the id, the ego, and the superego.

The most basic system, the **id,** is *the part of the mind containing the drives present at birth; it is the source of our bodily needs, wants, desires, and impulses, particularly our sexual and aggressive drives.* The id motivates the tendency to seek immediate gratification of any impulse. If governed by the id alone, you would never be able to tolerate the buildup of hunger while waiting to be served at a restaurant but would simply grab food from tables nearby.

The timeless illustration of the "bad side" and "good side" fighting for the person's mind resembles what Freud described as the inner struggle between the id and superego for control of the ego.

All that the id can do is wish. The **ego** is *the component of personality, developed through contact with the external world, that enables us to deal with life's practical demands.* The ego is a regulating mechanism that enables the individual to delay gratifying immediate needs and function effectively in the real world. The ego helps you resist the impulse to snatch others' food—and also find the restaurant and pay the check.

The final system of the mind is the **superego,** *the mental system that reflects the internalization of cultural rules, mainly learned as parents exercise their authority.* The superego acts as a kind of conscience, punishing us when it finds we are doing or thinking something wrong (by producing guilt or other painful feelings) and rewarding us (with feelings of pride or self-congratulation) for living up to ideal standards.

According to Freud, the relative strength of the interactions among the three systems of mind—that is, which system is usually dominant—determines an individual's basic personality structure. The id force of personal needs, the superego force of social pressures to quell those needs, and the ego force of reality's demands together create constant controversy, almost like a puppet theater or a bad play.

> **?** How is personality shaped by the interaction of the id, ego, and superego?

Dealing with Inner Conflict

According to Freud, the dynamics among the id, ego, and superego are largely governed by *anxiety,* an unpleasant feeling that arises when unwanted thoughts or feelings occur—such as when the id seeks a gratification that the ego thinks will lead to real-world dangers or the superego sees as eliciting punishment. When the ego receives an "alert signal" in the form of anxiety, it launches into a defensive position in an attempt to ward off the anxiety. According to Freud, it first tries *repression,* which, as you read in Chapter 5, is a mental process that removes painful experiences and unacceptable impulses from the conscious mind. Repression is sometimes referred to as "motivated forgetting." Indeed, functional imaging studies suggest that the repression of memories may involve decreased activation of the hippocampus—a region (as discussed in Chapter 6) that is central to memory (Anderson et al., 2004) (see **FIGURE 11.3**).

Repression may not be adequate to keep unacceptable drives from entering consciousness. When such material begins to surface, the ego can employ other means of self-deception, called **defense mechanisms,** which are *unconscious coping mechanisms that reduce the anxiety generated by threats from unacceptable impulses.* Anna Freud (1936), Freud's daughter and a psychodynamic theorist, identified a number of defense mechanisms and detailed how they operate. Let's look at a few of the most common.

> ▶ **Rationalization** is *a defense mechanism that involves supplying a reasonable-sounding explanation for unacceptable feelings and behavior to conceal (mostly from oneself) one's underlying motives or feelings.* For example, someone who drops a

▶ Figure **11.3** **Decreased Hippocampal Activity during Memory Suppression** FMRI scans of people intentionally trying to forget a list of words reveal reduced activation (shown in blue) in the left and right hippocampal areas. (From Anderson et al., 2004.)

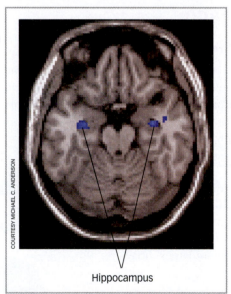

Hippocampus

ego The component of personality, developed through contact with the external world, that enables us to deal with life's practical demands.

superego The mental system that reflects the internalization of cultural rules, mainly learned as parents exercise their authority.

defense mechanisms Unconscious coping mechanisms that reduce the anxiety generated by threats from unacceptable impulses.

rationalization A defense mechanism that involves supplying a reasonable-sounding explanation for unacceptable feelings and behavior to conceal (mostly from oneself) one's underlying motives or feelings.

class after having failed an exam might tell herself that she is quitting because poor ventilation in the classroom made it impossible to concentrate.

> **Reaction formation** is *a defense mechanism that involves unconsciously replacing threatening inner wishes and fantasies with an exaggerated version of their opposite.* Examples include being excessively nice to someone you dislike or being cold and indifferent toward someone to whom you are strongly attracted.

> **Projection** is *a defense mechanism that involves attributing one's own threatening feelings, motives, or impulses to another person or group.* For example, people who think that they themselves are overly rigid or dishonest may have a tendency to judge other people as having the same qualities (Newman, Baumeister, & Duff, 1995).

> **Regression** is *a defense mechanism in which the ego deals with internal conflict and perceived threat by reverting to an immature behavior or earlier stage of development,* a time when things felt safer and more secure. Examples of regression include an adult's return to teddy bear cuddling or watching cartoons in response to something distressing.

> **Displacement** is *a defense mechanism that involves shifting unacceptable wishes or drives to a neutral or less threatening alternative.* Displacement should be familiar to you if you've ever slammed a door, thrown a textbook across a room, or yelled at your roommate or your cat when you were really angry at your boss.

> **Identification** is *a defense mechanism that helps deal with feelings of threat and anxiety by enabling us unconsciously to take on the characteristics of another person who seems more powerful or better able to cope.* A child whose parent bullies or severely punishes her may later take on the characteristics of that parent and begin bullying others.

> **Sublimation** is *a defense mechanism that involves channeling unacceptable sexual or aggressive drives into socially acceptable and culturally enhancing activities.* Football, rugby, and other contact sports, for example, may be construed as culturally sanctioned and valued activities that channel our aggressive drives.

Through reaction formation, a person defends against underlying feelings, such as covering hostility with an exaggerated display of affection. Maybe there's more to this sibling squeeze than love?

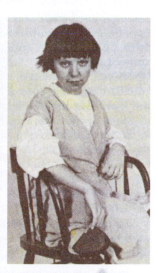

A photo of regression? The young woman shown in the photograph on the left grew up under harsh circumstances: family strife, instability, and substance abuse, among other horrors. At age 17, she discovered a photograph of herself taken when she was 5 years old (middle), after which she adopted the look and mannerisms of a 5-year-old child. The image on the right shows the same woman after regression. (Masserman, 1961.)

reaction formation A defense mechanism that involves unconsciously replacing threatening inner wishes and fantasies with an exaggerated version of their opposite.

projection A defense mechanism that involves attributing one's own threatening feelings, motives, or impulses to another person or group.

regression A defense mechanism in which the ego deals with internal conflict and perceived threat by reverting to an immature behavior or earlier stage of development.

displacement A defense mechanism that involves shifting unacceptable wishes or drives to a neutral or less threatening alternative.

identification A defense mechanism that reduces feelings of threat and anxiety by enabling us unconsciously to take on the characteristics of another person who seems more powerful or better able to cope.

sublimation A defense mechanism that involves channeling unacceptable sexual or aggressive drives into socially acceptable and culturally enhancing activities.

psychosexual stages Distinct early life stages through which personality is formed as children experience sexual pleasures from specific body areas and caregivers redirect or interfere with those pleasures.

oral stage The first psychosexual stage, in which experience centers on the pleasures and frustrations associated with the mouth, sucking, and being fed.

anal stage The second psychosexual stage, which is dominated by the pleasures and frustrations associated with the anus, retention and expulsion of feces and urine, and toilet training.

phallic stage The third psychosexual stage, during which experience is dominated by the pleasure, conflict, and frustration associated with the phallic-genital region as well as coping with powerful incestuous feelings of love, hate, jealousy, and conflict.

Defense mechanisms are useful (Cramer, 2008). They help us overcome anxiety and engage effectively with the outside world. The ego's capacity to use defense mechanisms in a healthy and flexible fashion may depend on the nature of early experiences with caregivers, the defense mechanisms they used, and possibly some biological and temperamental factors as well (McWilliams, 1994). Our characteristic style of defense becomes our signature in dealing with the world—and an essential aspect of our personality.

 **How can our defense mechanisms be useful?**

Psychosexual Stages and the Development of Personality

Freud believed that a person's basic personality is formed before 6 years of age during a series of five sensitive periods, or life stages, when experiences influence all that will follow. Freud called these periods **psychosexual stages,** defined as *distinct early life stages through which personality is formed as children experience sexual pleasures from specific body areas and caregivers redirect or interfere with those pleasures.* Each stage represents a battleground between the child's id impulses and the adult external world. Problems and conflicts encountered at any psychosexual stage, Freud believed, will influence personality in adulthood.

1. In the first year and a half of life, Freud believed the infant is in the **oral stage,** *during which experience centers on the pleasures and frustrations associated with the mouth, sucking, and being fed.* Infants who are deprived of pleasurable feeding or indulgently overfed may develop an oral personality; that is, their lives will center on issues related to fullness and emptiness and what they can "take in" from others and the environment. Personality traits associated with the oral stage include depression, lack of trust, envy, and demandingness.

2. Between 2 and 3 years of age, the child moves on to the **anal stage,** *during which experience is dominated by the pleasures and frustrations associated with the anus, retention and expulsion of feces and urine, and toilet training.* From the toddler's perspective, the soiling of one's diapers is a wonderful convenience that can feel pretty good. But sooner or later caregivers begin to disagree, and their opinions are voiced more strongly as the child gets older. Individuals who have had difficulty negotiating this conflict may develop a rigid personality and remain preoccupied with issues of control of others and of themselves and their emotions. They may be preoccupied with their possessions, money, issues of submission and rebellion, and concerns about cleanliness versus messiness.

3. Between the ages of 3 and 5 years, the child is in the **phallic stage,** *during which experience is dominated by the pleasure, conflict, and frustration associated with the phallic-genital region as well as coping with powerful incestuous feelings of love, hate, jealousy, and conflict.* According to Freud, boys in the phallic stage experience the **Oedipus conflict,** *a developmental experience in which a child's conflicting feelings toward the opposite-sex parent are (usually) resolved by identifying with the same-sex parent.* (In Greek myth, Oedipus was a young man who, unknowingly, killed his father and ended up marrying his mother.) Freud thought that, around age 4 or 5, boys grow jealous of Mommy's relationship with Daddy and experience jealousy. Males who are unable to resolve the Oedipus conflict and who get stuck in the phallic stage tend to be unusually preoccupied with issues of seduction, jealousy, competition, power, and authority. Females stuck in this phase, Freud thought, would display seductiveness, flirtatiousness, and jealousy.

4. A more relaxed period in which children are no longer struggling with the power of their sexual and aggressive drives occurs between the ages of 5 and 13, as children experience the **latency stage,** *during which the primary focus is on the further development of intellectual, creative, interpersonal, and athletic skills.*

One of the id's desires is to make a fine mess—a desire that is often frustrated early in life, perhaps during the anal stage. Famous painter Jackson Pollack found a way to make extraordinarily fine messes—behavior that at some level all of us envy.

SMITHSONIAN INSTITUTION, GIFT OF THE ESTATE OF HANS NAMUTH

5. At puberty and thereafter, the fifth and final stage of personality development occurs. This, the **genital stage,** is *the time for the coming together of the mature adult personality with a capacity to love, work, and relate to others in a mutually satisfying and reciprocal manner.* The degree to which the individual is encumbered by unresolved conflicts at the earlier stages will affect whether he or she will be able to achieve healthy adult sexuality and a well-adjusted adult personality.

What should we make of all this? On the one hand, psychoanalytic theory picks up on themes that seem to ring true in many cases—you may very well know people who seem to be "oral" or "anal," for example, or who have issues about sexuality that seem to have had a great influence on their personalities. On the other hand, critics argue that psychodynamic explanations tend to focus on after-the-fact interpretation rather than testable prediction. The psychosexual stage theory offers a compelling set of story plots for interpreting lives once they have unfolded but has not generated the kinds of clear-cut predictions that inspire research.

? Why do critics say Freud's psychosexual stages are more interpretation than explanation?

THE GRANGER COLLECTION, NEW YORK

Oedipus Rex, **Classical Greek Play by Sophocles**
According to the psychodynamic approach, at 4 or 5 years of age children are in the throes of the Oedipus conflict. At this time, children experience intense feelings of love, hate, jealousy, and anxiety related to their longings toward their parents and the wish for an exclusive love relationship with their fathers or mothers.

SUMMARY QUIZ [11.3]

1. Which of Freud's systems of the mind would impel you to, if hungry, start grabbing food off people's plates upon entering a restaurant?

   a. the id   b. the superego   c. the ego   d. the volvo

2. After performing poorly on an exam, you drop a class, saying that you and the professor are just a poor match. According to Freud, what defense mechanism are you employing?

   a. regression   b. rationalization   c. projection   d. reaction formation

3. According to Freud, a person who is preoccupied with his or her possessions, money, issues of submission and rebellion, and concerns about cleanliness versus messiness is stuck at which psychosexual stage?

   a. the oral stage   b. the anal stage   c. the latency stage   d. the genital stage

The Humanistic-Existential Approach: Personality as Choice

In the 1950s and 1960s, psychologists began to try to understand personality from a quite different viewpoint. Humanistic and existential theorists turned attention to how humans make *healthy choices* that create their personalities. *Humanistic psychologists* emphasized a positive, optimistic view of human nature that highlights people's inherent goodness and their potential for personal growth. *Existentialist psychologists* focused on the individual as a responsible agent who is free to create and live his or her life while negotiating the issue of meaning and the reality of death. The *humanistic-existential approach* integrates these insights with a focus on how a personality can become optimal.

Human Needs and Self-Actualization

Humanists see the **self-actualizing tendency,** *the human motive to realize our inner potential,* as a major factor in personality. The pursuit of knowledge, the expression of one's creativity, the quest for spiritual enlightenment, and the desire to give to society

Oedipus conflict A developmental experience in which a child's conflicting feelings toward the opposite-sex parent are (usually) resolved by identifying with the same-sex parent.

latency stage The fourth psychosexual stage, during which the primary focus is on the further development of intellectual, creative, interpersonal, and athletic skills.

genital stage The final psychosexual stage, a time for the coming together of the mature adult personality with a capacity to love, work, and relate to others in a mutually satisfying and reciprocal manner.

self-actualizing tendency The human motive to realize our inner potential.

Being All You Can Be The area called "Garbage City" outside Cairo is becoming known as one of the "green" places on Earth. Recycling and repurposing salvages almost 80% of waste here. To self-actualize, you don't have to start with much.

are all examples of self-actualization. As you saw in Chapter 8, the noted humanistic theorist Abraham Maslow (1970) proposed a *hierarchy of needs,* a model in which basic physiological and safety needs must be satisfied before a person can afford to focus on higher-level psychological needs, culminating in *self-actualization*—the need to be good, to be fully alive, and to find meaning in life.

? What does it mean to be self-actualized?

Humanist psychologists explain individual personality differences as arising from the various ways that the environment facilitates—or blocks—attempts to satisfy psychological needs. Like a wilting plant deprived of water, sunshine, and nutrients, an individual growing up in an arid social environment can fail to develop his or her unique potential. For example, someone with the inherent potential to be a great scientist, artist, parent, or teacher might never realize these talents if his or her energies and resources are instead directed toward meeting basic needs of security, belongingness, and the like. Research indicates that when people shape their lives around goals that do not match their true nature and capabilities, they are less likely to be happy than those whose lives and goals do match (Ryan & Deci, 2000).

It feels great to be doing exactly what you are capable of doing. Mihaly Csikszentmihalyi (1990) found that engagement in tasks that exactly match one's abilities creates a mental state of energized focus that he called *flow*. Tasks that are below our abilities cause boredom, those that are too challenging cause anxiety, and those that are "just right" lead to the experience of flow. If you know how to play the piano, for example, and are playing a Chopin prelude that you know well enough that it just matches your abilities, you are likely to experience this optimal state. People report being happier at these times than at any other times. Humanists believe that such peak experiences, or states of flow, reflect the realization of one's human potential and represent the height of personality development.

Personality as Existence

Existentialists agree with humanists about many of the features of personality but focus on challenges to the human condition that are more profound than the lack of a nurturing environment. For existentialists, specific aspects of the human condition, such as awareness of our own existence and the ability to make choices about how to behave, have a double-edged quality: They bring an extraordinary richness and dignity to human life, but they also force us to confront realities that are difficult to face, such as the prospect of our own death. The **existential approach** *regards personality as governed by an individual's ongoing choices and decisions in the context of the realities of life and death.*

According to the existential perspective, the difficulties we face in finding meaning in life and in accepting the responsibility of making free choices provoke a type of anxiety existentialists call *angst* (the anxiety of fully being). The human ability to consider limitless numbers of goals and actions is exhilarating, but it can also open the door to profound questions such as "Why am I here?" and "What is the meaning of my life?"

? What is angst, and how is it created?

Thinking about the meaning of existence also can evoke an awareness of the inevitability of death. What, then, should we do with each moment? What is the purpose of living if life as we know it will end one day, perhaps even today? Alternatively, does

existential approach A school of thought that regards personality as governed by an individual's ongoing choices and decisions in the context of the realities of life and death.

social cognitive approach An approach that views personality in terms of how the person thinks about the situations encountered in daily life and behaves in response to them.

life have more meaning given that it is so temporary? Existential theorists do not suggest that people consider these profound existential issues on a day-to-day and moment-to-moment basis. Rather than ruminate about death and meaning, people typically pursue superficial answers that help them deal with the angst and dread they experience, and the defenses they construct form the basis of their personalities (Binswanger, 1958; May, 1983). Such defenses might include the pursuit of superficial relationships, a focus on obtaining consumer goods, or addictive behaviors that numb the mind to existential realities.

Unfortunately, security-providing defense mechanisms can be self-defeating and stifle the potential for personal growth. For existentialists, being fully human means confronting existential realities rather than denying them or embracing comforting illusions. This requires the courage to accept the inherent anxiety and the dread of nonbeing that is part of being alive. Such courage may be bolstered by developing supportive relationships with others who can supply unconditional positive regard. There's something about being loved that helps take away the angst.

SUMMARY QUIZ [11.4]

1. Humanists see personality as directed toward the goal of
   a. existentialism.
   b. self-actualization.
   c. healthy adult sexuality.
   d. sublimation.

2. According to the existential perspective, the difficulties we face in finding meaning in life and in accepting the responsibility for making free choices provoke a type of anxiety called
   a. angst.
   b. flow.
   c. the self-actualizing tendency.
   d. mortality salience.

The Social Cognitive Approach: Personalities in Situations

What is it like to be a person? The social cognitive approach to personality explores what it is like to be a person who tries to understand what to do in life's many encounters with people, events, and situations. The **social cognitive approach** *views personality in terms of how the person thinks about the situations encountered in daily life and behaves in response to them.* Bringing together insights from social psychology, cognitive psychology, and learning theory, this approach emphasizes how the person experiences and construes situations (Bandura, 1986; Mischel & Shoda, 1999; Ross & Nisbett, 1991; Wegner & Gilbert, 2000).

The idea that situations cause behavior became clear in basic studies of learning. B. F. Skinner, the strict behaviorist and observer of rats and pigeons (see Chapter 7), would hold that differences in behavior patterns reflect differences in how the behaviors have been rewarded in past situations.

Researchers in social cognition agree that the situation and learning history are key determinants of behavior, but they go much further than Skinner would have in looking inside the psychological "black box" of the mind to examine the thoughts and feelings that come between the situation and the person's response

The Situation Mike "The Situation" Sorrentino is on the *Jersey Shore* reality TV show. Sometimes personalities think they're situations.

MICHAEL GERMANA/ZUMAPRESS/NEWSCOM

to it. Because human "situations" and "reinforcements" are radically open to interpretation, social cognitive psychologists focus on how people *perceive* their environments. People think about their goals, the consequences of their behavior, and how they might achieve certain things in different situations (Lewin, 1951). The social cognitive approach looks at how personality and situation interact to cause behavior, how personality contributes to the way people construct situations in their own minds, and how people's goals and expectancies influence their responses to situations.

? How do researchers in social cognition agree with behaviorists and how do they disagree?

Consistency of Personality Across Situations

Although social cognitive psychologists attribute behavior both to the individual's personality and to his or her situation, situation can often trump personality. For example, a person would have to be pretty strange to act exactly the same way at a memorial service and at a toga party. In their belief that the strong push and pull of situations can influence almost everyone, social cognitive psychologists are somewhat at odds with the basic assumptions of classic personality psychology—that is, that personality characteristics (such as traits, needs, unconscious drives) cause people to behave in the same way across situations and over time. At the core of the social cognitive approach is a natural puzzle, the **person-situation controversy,** which focuses on *the question of whether behavior is caused more by personality or by situational factors.*

This controversy began in earnest when Walter Mischel (1968) argued that measured personality traits often do a poor job of predicting individuals' behavior. Mischel reviewed decades of research that compared scores on standard personality tests with actual behavior, looking at evidence from studies asking questions such as "Does a person with a high score on a test of introversion actually spend more time alone than someone with a low score?" Mischel's disturbing conclusion: The average correlation between trait and behavior is only about .30. This is certainly better than zero (i.e., chance) but not very good when you remember that a perfect prediction is represented by a correlation of 1.0.

Mischel also noted that knowing how a person will behave in one situation is not particularly helpful in predicting the person's behavior in another situation. For example, in classic studies Hartshorne and May (1928) assessed children's honesty by examining their willingness to cheat on a test and found that such dishonesty was not consistent from one situation to another. The assessment of a child's trait of honesty in a cheating situation was of almost no use in predicting whether the child would act honestly in a different situation—such as when given the opportunity to steal money. Mischel proposed that measured traits do not predict behaviors very well because behaviors are determined more by situational factors than personality theorists were willing to acknowledge.

Is a student who cheats on a test more likely than others to steal candy or lie to her grandmother? Social cognitive research indicates that behavior in one situation does not necessarily predict behavior in a different situation.

Is there no personality, then? Do we all just do what situations require? It turns out that information about both personality and situation are necessary to predict behavior (Fleeson, 2004; Mischel, 2004). Some situations are particularly powerful, leading most everyone to behave similarly regardless of personality (Cooper &

Withey, 2009). At a funeral, after all, most everyone looks somber, and at an earthquake, most everyone shakes. But in situations that are weaker, personality can come forward to influence behavior (Funder, 2001). Among the children in Hartshorne and May's studies, cheating versus not cheating on a test was actually a fairly good predictor of cheating on a test later—as long as the situation was similar (Hartshorne & May, 1928). Personality consistency, then, appears to be a matter of when and where a certain kind of behavior tends to be shown. Social cognitive theorists believe these patterns of personality consistency in response to situations arise from the ways different people construe situations and from the ways different people pursue goals within situations.

Personal Constructs

How can we understand differences in the way situations are interpreted? George Kelly (1955) long ago realized that differences in perspective could be used to understand the *perceiver's* personality. He suggested that people view the social world from differing perspectives and that these different views arise through the application of **personal constructs,** *dimensions people use in making sense of their experiences.* Consider, for example, different individuals' personal constructs of a clown: One person may see him as a source of fun, another as a tragic figure, and yet another as so frightening that the circus is off-limits.

Why doesn't everyone love clowns?

Here's how Kelly assessed personal constructs about social relationships: He'd ask people to (1) list the people in their life, (2) consider three of the people and state a way in which two of them were similar to each other and different from the third, and (3) repeat this for other triads of people to produce a list of the dimensions used to classify friends and family. One respondent might focus on the degree to which people (self included) are lazy or hardworking, for example; someone else might attend to the degree to which people are sociable or unfriendly.

Kelly proposed that different personal constructs are the key to personality differences and lead to disparate behaviors. Taking a long break from work for a leisurely lunch might seem lazy to you. To your friend, the break might seem an ideal opportunity for catching up with friends, so he will wonder why you always choose to eat at your desk. Social cognitive theory explains different responses to situations with the idea that people see things in different ways.

Are two of these people taller and one shorter? Are two bareheaded while one wears a hood? Or are two the daughters and one the mom? George Kelly held that the personal constructs we use to distinguish among people in our lives are basic elements of our own personalities.

Personal Goals and Expectancies

Social cognitive theories also recognize that a person's unique perspective on situations is reflected in his or her personal goals, which are often conscious. In fact, people can usually tell you their goals, whether they are to "find a date for this weekend," "get a good grade in psych," "establish a fulfilling career," or just "get this darn bag of chips open." These goals often reflect the tasks that are appropriate to the person's situation (Cantor, 1990; Klinger, 1977; Little, 1983; Vallacher & Wegner, 1985). For instance, common goals for adolescents include being popular, achieving greater independence from parents and family, and getting into their first-choice college. Common goals for adults include developing a meaningful career, finding a mate, securing financial stability, and starting a family.

People translate goals into behavior in part through **outcome expectancies,** *a person's assumptions about the likely consequences of a future behavior.* Just as a

person-situation controversy The question of whether behavior is caused more by personality or by situational factors.

personal constructs Dimensions people use in making sense of their experiences.

outcome expectancies A person's assumptions about the likely consequences of a future behavior.

Table 11.2

Rotter's Locus-of-Control Scale

For each pair of items, choose the option that most closely reflects your personal belief. Then turn the book upside down to see if you have more of an internal or external locus of control.

1. a. Many of the unhappy things in people's lives are partly due to bad luck.
   b. People's misfortunes result from the mistakes they make.

2. a. I have often found that what is going to happen will happen.
   b. Trusting to fate has never turned out as well for me as making a decision to take a definite course of action.

3. a. Becoming a success is a matter of hard work; luck has little or nothing to do with it.
   b. Getting a good job depends mainly on being in the right place at the right time.

4. a. When I make plans, I am almost certain that I can make them work.
   b. It is not always wise to plan too far ahead because many things turn out to be a matter of good or bad fortune anyhow.

Source: Rotter, 1966.

Answer: A more internal locus of control would be reflected in choosing options 1b, 2b, 3a, and 4a.

Some days you feel like a puppet on a string. If you have an external locus of control, you may feel that way most days.

laboratory rat learns that pressing a bar releases a food pellet, we learn that "if I am friendly toward people, they will be friendly in return" or "if I ask people to pull my finger, they will withdraw from me." So we learn to perform behaviors that we expect will have the outcome of moving us closer to our goals. Outcome expectancies are learned through direct experience, both bitter and sweet, and through merely observing other people's actions and their consequences. Outcome expectancies combine with a person's goals to produce the person's characteristic style of behavior. We do not all want the same things from life, clearly, and our personalities largely reflect the goals we pursue and the expectancies we have about the best ways to pursue them.

People also differ in their expectancy of achieving goals. Some people seem to feel that they are fully in control of what happens to them in life, whereas others feel that the world doles out rewards and punishments to them irrespective of their actions. A person's **locus of control** is the *tendency to perceive the control of rewards as internal to the self or external in the environment* (Rotter, 1966). Locus of control can be measured using questionnaires such as the one shown in **TABLE 11.2**. People whose answers suggest that they believe they control their own destiny are said to have an *internal* locus of control, whereas those who believe that outcomes are random, determined by luck, or controlled by other people are described as having an *external* locus of control. These beliefs translate into individual differences in emotion and behavior. For example, people with an internal locus of control tend to be less anxious, achieve more, and cope better with stress than do people with an external orientation (Lefcourt, 1982). To get a sense of your standing on this trait dimension, choose one of the options for each of the sample items from the locus-of-control scale in Table 11.2.

? What is the advantage of an internal locus of control?

SUMMARY QUIZ [11.5]

1. Which of the following is *not* an emphasis of the social cognitive approach?
   a. how personality and situation interact to cause behavior
   b. how personality contributes to the way people construct situations in their own minds
   c. how people's goals and expectancies influence their responses to situations
   d. how people confront realities rather than embrace comforting illusions

2. According to social cognitive theorists, _____ are the dimensions people use in making sense of their experiences.
   a. personal constructs
   b. outcome expectancies
   c. loci of control
   d. personal goals

3. Tyler has been getting poor evaluations at work. He attributes this to having a mean boss who always assigns him the hardest tasks. This suggests that Tyler has
   a. an external locus of control
   b. an internal locus of control
   c. high performance anxiety
   d. poorly developed personal constructs

The Self: Personality in the Mirror

Imagine that you wake up tomorrow morning, drag yourself into the bathroom, look into the mirror, and don't recognize the face looking back at you. This was the plight of a woman, married for 30 years and the mother of two grown children, who one day began to respond to her mirror image as if it were a different person (Feinberg, 2001). She talked to and challenged the person in the mirror. When there was no response, she tried to attack it as if it were an intruder. Her husband, shaken by this bizarre behavior, brought her to a neurologist, who was gradually able to convince her that the image in the mirror was in fact herself.

Most of us are pretty familiar with the face that looks back at us from every mirror. We developed the ability to recognize ourselves in mirrors by 18 months of age (as discussed in Chapter 5), and self-recognition in mirrors signals our amazing capacity for reflexive thinking, for directing attention to our own thoughts, feelings, and actions. This ability enables us to construct ideas about our own personality: what we think about ourselves—our *self-concept*—and on how we feel about ourselves—our *self-esteem*. Self-concept and self-esteem are critically important facets of personality, not only because they reveal how we see our own personalities but also because they also guide how we think others will see us.

locus of control A person's tendency to perceive the control of rewards as internal to the self or external in the environment.

Self-Concept

If asked to describe yourself, you might mention your physical characteristics (male or female, tall or short, dark-skinned or light-skinned), your activities (listening to hip-hop, alternative rock, jazz, or classical music), your personality traits (extraverted or introverted, agreeable or independent), or your social roles (student, son or daughter, member of a hiking club, manager of a noodle factory). These features make

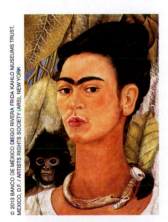

What do these self-portraits of Frida Kahlo, Vincent Van Gogh Salvador Dalí, Wanda Wulz, and Jean-Michel Basquiat reveal about each artist's self-concept?

up the **self-concept,** *a person's explicit knowledge of his or her own behaviors, traits, and other personal characteristics.* A person's self-concept develops from social experiences and has a profound effect on a person's behavior throughout life.

Self-Concept Organization

Our knowledge of ourselves seems to be organized in two ways—as narratives about episodes in our lives and in terms of traits (as would be suggested by the distinction between episodic and semantic memory discussed in Chapter 6).

The aspect of the self-concept that is a *self-narrative*—a story that we tell about ourselves—can be brief or very lengthy. Your life story could start with your birth and upbringing, describe a series of defining moments, and end where you are today. Self-narrative organizes the highlights (and low blows) of your life into a story in which you are the leading character and binds them together into your self-concept (McAdams, 1993; McLean, 2008).

? **What is your life story as you see it—your self-narrative?**

Self-concept is also organized in terms of personality traits. Just as you can judge an object on its attributes ("Is this apple green?"), you are able to judge yourself on any number of traits—whether you are considerate or smart or lazy or active or, for that matter, green. Each person finds certain unique personality traits particularly important for conceptualizing the self (Markus, 1977). One person might define herself as independent, for example, whereas another might not care much about her level of independence but instead emphasize her sense of style.

How do our behavior self-narratives and trait self-concepts compare? These two methods of self-conceptualization don't always match up. You may think of yourself as an honest person, for example, but also recall that time you nabbed a handful of change from your parents' dresser and conveniently forgot to replace it. The traits

? **Why don't traits always reflect knowledge of behavior?**

we use to describe ourselves are generalizations, and not every episode in our life stories may fit. In fact, research suggests that the stores of knowledge about our behaviors and traits are not very well integrated (Kihlstrom, Beer, & Klein, 2002). In people who develop amnesia, for example, memory for behaviors can be lost even though the trait self-concept remains stable (Klein, 2004). People can have a pretty strong sense of who they are even though they may not remember a single example of when they acted that way.

HIDEO KURIHARA/ALAMY

A key element in personality involves the stories, myths, and fairy tales we tell ourselves about our lives. Are you living the story of the prince or princess in a castle—or are you the troll in the woods?

Causes and Effects of Self-Concept

How do self-concepts arise, and how do they affect us? Although we can gain self-knowledge in private moments of insight, we more often arrive at our self-concepts through interacting with others. Young children in particular receive plenty of feedback from their parents, teachers, siblings, and friends about their characteristics, and this helps them to form an idea of who they are. Even adults would find it difficult to hold a view of the self as "kind" or "smart" if no one else ever shared this impression. The sense of self, then, is largely developed and maintained in relationships with others.

Over the course of a lifetime, however, we become less and less impressed with what others have to say about us. Social theorist George Herbert Mead (1934) observed that all the things people have said about us accumulate after a while into what we see as a kind of consensus held by the "generalized other." We typically adopt this general view of ourselves that is as stable as our concept of anything at all and hold on to it stubbornly. Just as we might argue vehemently with someone who tried to tell us that a refrigerator is a pair of underpants or that up is actually down and to the left, we are likely to defend our self-concept against anyone whose view of us departs from our own.

? How does self-concept influence behavior?

Because it is so stable, a major effect of the self-concept is to promote consistency in behavior across situations (Lecky, 1945). As existential theorists emphasize, people derive a comforting sense of familiarity and stability from knowing who they are. We tend to engage in what William Swann (1983, 2010) has called **self-verification,** *the tendency to seek evidence to confirm the self-concept,* and we find it disconcerting if someone sees us quite differently from the way we see ourselves. In one study, Swann (1983) gave people who considered themselves submissive feedback that they seemed very dominant and forceful. Rather than accepting this discrepant information, they went out of their way to act in an extremely submissive manner. Our tendency to project into the world our concept of the self contributes to personality coherence.

"I don't want to be defined by who I am."

Self-Esteem

When you think about yourself, do you feel good and worthy? Do you like yourself, or do you feel bad and have negative, self-critical thoughts? **Self-esteem** is *the extent to which an individual likes, values, and accepts the self.* Researchers who study self-esteem typically ask participants to fill out a self-esteem questionnaire, such as one shown in **TABLE 11.3** (Rosenberg, 1965). People who strongly agree with the positive statements about themselves and strongly disagree with the negative statements are considered to have high self-esteem. In general, compared with people with low self-esteem, those with high self-esteem tend to live happier and healthier lives, cope better with stress, and be more likely to persist at difficult tasks.

Table 11.3				
Rosenberg Self-Esteem Scale				
Consider each statement and circle SA for strongly agree, A for agree, D for disagree, and SD for strongly disagree.				
1. On the whole, I am satisfied with myself.	SA	A	D	SD
2. At times, I think I am no good at all.	SA	A	D	SD
3. I feel that I have a number of good qualities.	SA	A	D	SD
4. I am able to do things as well as most other people.	SA	A	D	SD
5. I feel I do not have much to be proud of.	SA	A	D	SD
6. I certainly feel useless at times.	SA	A	D	SD
7. I feel that I'm a person of worth, at least on an equal plane with others.	SA	A	D	SD
8. I wish I could have more respect for myself.	SA	A	D	SD
9. All in all, I am inclined to feel that I am a failure.	SA	A	D	SD
10. I take a positive attitude toward myself.	SA	A	D	SD

Source: Rosenberg, 1965.

Scoring: For items 1, 3, 4, 7, and 10, SA = 3, A = 2, D = 1, SD = 0; for items 2, 5, 6, 8, and 9, the scoring is reversed, with SA = 0, A = 1, D = 2, SD = 3. The higher the total score, the higher one's self-esteem.

self-concept A person's explicit knowledge of his or her own behaviors, traits, and other personal characteristics.

self-verification The tendency to seek evidence to confirm the self-concept.

self-esteem The extent to which an individual likes, values, and accepts the self.

SHAUN BOTTERILL/GETTY IMAGES

Silver medalist Duje Draganja of Croatia, gold medalist Gary Hall Jr. of the United States, and bronze medalist Roland Schoeman of South Africa show off their medals following their 50-meter swimming final. Notice the expression on Draganja's face compared with those of the gold and bronze medalists.

Sources of Self-Esteem

An important factor in self-esteem is whom people choose for comparison. For example, James (1890) noted that an accomplished athlete who is the second best in the world should feel pretty proud, but this athlete might not if the standard of comparison involves being best in the world. In fact, athletes in the 1992 Olympics who had won silver medals looked less happy during the medal ceremony than those who had won bronze (Medvec, Madey, & Gilovich, 1995). If the actual self is seen as falling short of the ideal self—the person they would like to be—people tend to feel sad or dejected; when they become aware that the actual self is inconsistent with the self they have a duty to be, they are likely to feel anxious or agitated (Higgins, 1987).

? How do comparisons with others affect self-esteem?

Fleeting thoughts of authorities can influence self-esteem. Catholic girls subliminally shown photos of Pope John Paul II experienced reduced self-esteem.

SEAN GALLUP/GETTY IMAGES

Unconscious perspectives we take on feedback we get about ourselves can also affect our sense of self-worth. In one study, researchers examined the self-esteem of young, Catholic, female participants who had read an article from *Cosmopolitan* that described a woman's sexual dream (in PG-13 language) and who had either seen a photo of a disapproving-looking pope or a photo of an unfamiliar disapproving person. The photos were shown subliminally—that is, in such brief flashes that the women could not consciously recognize whom they had seen. In self-ratings made afterward, the women in the disapproving-pope group showed a marked reduction in self-esteem compared with the other women: They rated themselves as less competent, more anxious, and less moral. In the words of the researchers, self-esteem can be influenced when an important authority figure is "watching you from the back of your mind" (Baldwin, Carrell, & Lopez, 1989, p. 435).

Self-esteem is also affected by what kinds of domain we consider most important in our self-concept. One person's self-worth might be entirely contingent on, for example, how well she does in school, whereas another's self-worth might be based on his physical attractiveness (Crocker & Wolfe, 2001; Pelham, 1985). The first person's self-esteem might receive a big boost when she gets an A on an exam but much less of a boost when she's complimented on her new hairstyle—and this effect might be exactly reversed in the second person.

The Desire for Self-Esteem

What's so great about self-esteem? Why do people want to see themselves in a positive light? Three key theories on the benefits of self-esteem focus on status, belonging, and security.

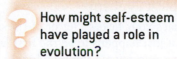

? **How might self-esteem have played a role in evolution?**

self-serving bias People's tendency to take credit for their successes but downplay responsibility for their failures.

narcissism A trait that reflects a grandiose view of the self combined with a tendency to seek admiration from and exploit others.

1. **Social Status.** People with high self-esteem seem to carry themselves in a way that is similar to high-status animals of other social species. Dominant male gorillas, for example, appear confident and comfortable, not anxious or withdrawn. Perhaps high self-esteem in humans reflects high social status or suggests that the person is worthy of respect, and this perception triggers natural affective responses (Barkow, 1980; Maslow, 1937).

2. **Belongingness.** Evolutionary theory holds that early humans who managed to survive to pass on their genes were those able to maintain good relations with others rather than being cast out to fend for themselves. Clearly, belonging to groups is adaptive, as is knowing whether you are accepted. Thus, self-esteem could reflect how much a person feels included by others at any given moment (Leary & Baumeister, 2000). According to evolutionary theory, then, we seek higher self-esteem because we have evolved to seek out belongingness in our families, work groups, and culture, and higher self-esteem indicates that we are being accepted.

3. **Security.** Existentialist approaches suggest that the source of distress underlying negative self-esteem is ultimately the fear of death (Solomon, Greenberg, & Pyszczynski, 1991). In this view, humans find it terrifying to contemplate their own mortality, so they try to defend against this awareness by immersing themselves in activities (such as earning money or dressing up to appear attractive) that their culture defines as meaningful and valuable. The desire for self-esteem is a need to find value in ourselves as a way of escaping the anxiety associated with recognizing our mortality. The higher our self-esteem, the less anxious we feel with the knowledge that someday we will no longer exist.

Whatever the reason that low self-esteem feels so bad and high self-esteem feels so good, people are generally motivated to see themselves positively. In fact, we often process information in a biased manner in order to feel good about ourselves. Research on the **self-serving bias** shows that *people tend to take credit for their successes but downplay responsibility for their failures.* You may have noticed this tendency in yourself, particularly in terms of the attributions you make about exams when you get a good grade ("I studied really intensely, and I'm good at that subject") or a bad grade ("The test was ridiculously tricky and the professor is a nimnutz"). The self-serving bias may be adaptive, however. People who do not engage in this self-serving bias to boost their self-esteem tend to be more at risk for depression, anxiety, and related health problems (Taylor & Brown, 1988).

"I got into the stupidest thing with my reflection this morning."

On the other hand, a few people take positive self-esteem to the extreme—a trait called **narcissism,** *a grandiose view of the self combined with a tendency to seek admiration from and exploit others.* At its extreme, narcissism is considered a personality disorder. (Personality disorders are discussed further in Chapter 13). Research has documented disadvantages of an overinflated view of self, most of which arise from the need to defend that grandiose view at all costs. For example, when highly narcissistic adolescents were given reason to be ashamed of their performance on a task, their aggressiveness increased—in the form of willingness to deliver loud blasts of noise to punish their opponent in a laboratory game (Thomaes et al., 2008).

Implicit Egotism

What's your favorite letter of the alphabet? About 30% of people answer by picking what just happens to be the first letter of their first name. Could this choice indicate that some people think so highly of themselves that they base judgments of seemingly unrelated topics on how much it reminds them of themselves?

This *name-letter effect* was discovered some years ago (Nuttin, 1985), but only recently have researchers gone on to discover how broad the egotistic bias in preferences can be. When researchers examined the rolls of people moving into several southern states, for example, they found people named George were more likely than those with other names to move to Georgia (Pelham, Mirenberg, & Jones, 2002). The same was true for Florences (Florida), Kenneths (Kentucky), and Louises (Louisiana). You can guess where the Virginias tended to relocate. Although the biases are small (if your name is Wally, you don't *have* to move to Walla Walla), they are consistent across many tests of the hypothesis. These biases have been called expressions of *implicit egotism* because people are not typically aware that they are influenced by the wonderful sound of their own names (Pelham, Carvallo, & Jones, 2005).

? Do people choose homes and occupations based in part on their own names?

At some level, of course, a bit of egotism is probably good for us. It's sad to meet someone who hates her own name or whose snap judgment of self is "I'm worthless." Yet in another sense, implicit egotism is a curiously subtle error—a tendency to make biased judgments of what we will do and where we will go in life just because we happen to have a certain name. Yes, the bias is only a small one. But your authors wonder: Could we have found better people to work with had we not fallen prey to this bias in our choice of colleagues?

The self is the part of personality that the person knows and can report about. Some of the personality measures we have seen in this chapter—such as person-

If you were trying to light up a room with a letter, would your first choice also be your initial?

MAXSTOCK/ALAMY IMAGES

ality inventories based on self-reports—are really no different from measures of self-concept. Both depend on the person's perceptions and memories of the self's behavior and traits. But personality runs deeper than this as well. The unconscious forces identified in psychodynamic approaches provide themes for behavior, and sources of mental disorder, that are not accessible for self-report. The humanistic and existential approaches remind us of the profound concerns we humans face and the difficulties we may have in understanding all the forces that shape our self-views. Finally, in emphasizing how personality shapes our perceptions of social life, the social cognitive approach brings the self back to center stage. The self, after all, is the hub of each person's social world.

SUMMARY QUIZ [11.6]

1. What we think about ourselves is referred to as our _____, and how we feel about ourselves is referred to as our _____.
   a. self-narrative; self-verification
   b. self-concept; self-esteem
   c. self-concept; self-verification
   d. self-esteem; self-concept

2. On what do the key theories on the benefits of self-esteem focus?
   a. status   b. belonging   c. security   d. all of the above

3. When people take credit for their successes but downplay responsibility for their failures, they are exhibiting
   a. narcissism.
   b. implicit egoism.
   c. the self-serving bias.
   d. the name-letter effect.

Where Do You Stand?

Personality Testing for Fun and Profit

Many people enjoy taking personality tests. In fact, dozens of websites, magazine articles, and popular books offer personality tests as well as handy summaries of test scores. Google *personality test* and you'll see. Unfortunately, many personality tests are no more than a collection of questions someone has put together to offer entertainment to test takers. These tests yield a sense of self-insight that is no more valid than what you might get from the random "wisdom" of a fortune cookie or your daily horoscope.

The personality tests discussed in this chapter are more valid, of course: They have been developed and refined to offer reliable predictions of a person's tendencies. Still, the validity of many personality tests, particularly the projective tests, remains controversial, and critics question whether personality tests should be used for serious purposes.

Would one or more personality tests help you decide what career path to follow after college? Research findings have demonstrated correlations between personality dimensions and certain work-related indicators. In research on the Big Five, for example, people who are high in extraversion have been found to do well in sales and management positions, while people high in agreeableness and low in neuroticism do well in jobs that require working in groups (John & Srivastava, 1999).

In fact, business, government, and the military often use personality tests in hiring. Although such tests have been criticized for their flimsy theoretical and research foundations (Paul, 2004), businesses have not abandoned them. The possibility also exists that such tests might someday be used to predict whether criminals behind bars have been rehabilitated or might return to crime if released. If tests could be developed that would predict whether a person would be likely to commit a violent crime or become a terrorist or a sexual predator, do you think such tests should be used to make decisions about people's lives?

Think of all you have learned about the different approaches to personality, the strengths and weaknesses of different kinds of tests, the person-situation controversy, and the fact that personality measures do correlate significantly (although not perfectly) with a person's behaviors. Are existing personality tests useful for making decisions about people now? If such tests were perfected, should they be used in the future? Where do you stand?

Chapter Review

Personality: What It Is and How It Is Measured

▶ In psychology, personality refers to a person's characteristic style of behaving, thinking, and feeling.

▶ Personality psychologists attempt to find the best ways to describe personality, to explain how personalities come about, and to measure personality.

▶ Two general classes of personality tests are personality inventories, such as the MMPI-2, and projective techniques, such as the Rorschach Inkblot Test and the TAT.

The Trait Approach: Identifying Patterns of Behavior

▶ The trait approach tries to identify personality dimensions that can be used to characterize an individual's behavior. Researchers have attempted to boil down the potentially huge array of things people do, think, and feel into some core personality dimensions.

▶ Many personality psychologists currently focus on the Big Five personality factors: conscientiousness, agreeableness, neuroticism, openness to experience, and extraversion.

▶ To address the question of why traits arise, trait theorists often adopt a biological perspective, seeing personality largely as the result of genetic influences on brain mechanisms.

The Psychodynamic Approach: Forces That Lie Beneath Awareness

▶ Freud believed that the personality results from forces that are largely unconscious, shaped by the interplay among id, ego, and superego.

▶ Defense mechanisms are methods the mind may use to reduce anxiety generated from unacceptable impulses.

▶ Freud also believed that the developing person passes through a series of psychosexual stages and that individuals who fail to progress beyond one of the stages have corresponding personality traits.

The Humanistic-Existential Approach: Personality as Choice

▶ Humanists see personality as directed by an inherent striving toward self-actualization and development of our unique human potentials.

▶ Existentialists focus on angst and the defensive response people often have to questions about the meaning of life and the inevitability of death.

The Social Cognitive: Personalities in Situations

▶ The social cognitive approach focuses on personality as arising from individuals' behavior in situations.

▶ According to social cognitive personality theorists, the same person may behave differently in different situations but should behave consistently in similar situations.

▶ People translate their goals into behavior through outcome expectancies, their assumptions about the likely consequences of future behaviors.

The Self: Personality in the Mirror

▶ The self-concept is a person's knowledge of self, including both specific self-narratives and more abstract personality traits.

▶ People's self-concept develops through social feedback, and people often act to try to confirm these views through a process of self-verification.

▶ Self-esteem is a person's evaluation of self; it is derived from being accepted by others as well as by how we evaluate ourselves in comparison to others. Theories proposed to explain why we seek positive self-esteem suggest that we do so to achieve perceptions of status, or belonging, or of being symbolically protected against mortality.

▶ People strive for positive self-views through self-serving biases and implicit egotism.

personality (p. 346)

self-report (p. 347)

Minnesota Multiphasic Personality Inventory (MMPI-2) (p. 347)

projective techniques (p. 348)

Rorschach Inkblot Test (p. 348)

Thematic Apperception Test (TAT) (p. 348)

trait (p. 350)

Big Five (p. 351)

psychodynamic approach (p. 355)

id (p. 355)

ego (p. 356)

superego (p. 356)

defense mechanisms (p. 356)

rationalization (p. 356)

reaction formation (p. 357)

projection (p. 357)

regression (p. 357)

displacement (p. 357)

identification (p. 357)

sublimation (p. 357)

psychosexual stages (p. 358)

oral stage (p. 358)

anal stage (p. 358)

phallic stage (p. 358)

Oedipus conflict (p. 358)

latency stage (p. 358)

genital stage (p. 359)

self-actualizing tendency (p. 359)

existential approach (p. 360)

social cognitive approach (p. 361)

person-situation controversy (p. 362)

personal constructs (p. 363)

outcome expectancies (p. 363)

locus of control (p. 364)

self-concept (p. 366)

self-verification (p. 367)

self-esteem (p. 367)

self-serving bias (p. 369)

narcissism (p. 369)

CHANGING MINDS

1. A presidential candidate makes a Freudian slip on live TV, calling his mother "petty"; he corrects himself quickly and says he meant to say "pretty." The next day the video has gone viral, and the morning talk shows discuss the possibility that the candidate has an unresolved Oedipus conflict; if so, he's stuck in the phallic stage and is likely a relatively unstable person preoccupied with issues of seduction, power, and authority (which may be why he wants to be president). Your roommate knows you're taking a psychology class and asks for your opinion: "Can we really tell that a person is sexually repressed, and maybe in love with his own mother, just because he stumbled over a single word?" How would you reply? How widely are Freud's ideas about personality accepted by modern psychologists?

2. While reading a magazine, you come across an article on the nature-nurture controversy in personality. The article describes several adoption studies in which adopted children (who share no genes with each other but grow up in the same household) are no more like each other than complete strangers. This suggests that the influence of family environment—and of parental behavior—on personality is very weak. You show the article to a friend, who has trouble believing the results. "I always thought parents who don't show affection produce kids

who have trouble forming lasting relationships." How would you explain to your friend the relationship among nature, nurture, and personality?

3. One of your friends has found an online site that offers personality testing. He takes the test and reports that the results prove he's an "intuitive" rather than a "sensing" personality, someone who likes to look at the big picture rather than focusing on tangible here-and-now experiences. "This explains a lot," he says, "like why I have trouble remembering details like other people's birthdays and why it's hard for me to finish projects before the deadline." Aside from warning your friend about the dangers of self-diagnosis via Internet quizzes, what would you tell him about the relationship between personality types and behavior? How well do scores on personality tests predict a person's actual behavior?

4. You are watching a TV program that claims several international terrorist organizations specifically try to recruit adolescents, believing that early indoctrination into a belief or culture can be particularly effective in shaping lifelong attitudes and, indeed, in determining an individual's whole personality. Is this belief accurate? How stable is personality across the life span?

CRITICAL THINKING QUESTIONS

1. Research on men who report *homophobia*—the dread of gay men and lesbians—revealed an interesting result (Adams, Wright, & Lohr, 1996). Homophobic participants—heterosexual men who agreed with statements such as "I would feel nervous being with a group of homosexuals"—and a comparison group of nonhomophobic men were shown videos of sexual activity, including heterosexual, gay male, and lesbian segments. Each man's sexual arousal was then assessed by means of a device that measures penile swelling. Curiously, the homophobic men showed greater arousal to the male homosexual images than did the men in the control group. The psychoanalytic interpretation seems clear: Men troubled by their own homosexual arousal

form opposite reactions to this unacceptable feeling, turning their unwanted attraction into "dread." Do these results imply that homophobia is a defense mechanism? If so, which one?

2. The text says that "there's something about being loved that helps take away the angst." According to a humanist or existentialist, what are some specific ways love could take away angst?

3. The text discusses how behavior self-narratives and trait self-concepts don't always match up. Think about your own self-narrative and self-concept. Are there areas that don't match up? How might you explain that?

4. Is it possible for someone to have too much self-esteem?

ANSWERS TO SUMMARY QUIZZES

Summary Quiz [11.1] 1. a; 2. c; 3. c
Summary Quiz [11.2] 1. c; 2. d; 3. b
Summary Quiz [11.3] 1. a; 2. b; 3. b
Summary Quiz [11.4] 1. b; 2. a
Summary Quiz [11.5] 1. d; 2. a; 3. a
Summary Quiz [11.6] 1. b; 2. d; 3. c

Need more help? Additional resources are located at the book's free companion website at www.worthpublishers.com/schacterbrief2e

12

Social Psychology

TERRY, ROBERT, AND JOHN have one thing in common: They've all been tortured. Terry was a journalist when he was kidnapped by guerrillas, Robert was a boxer when he was sent to prison, and John was a soldier when he was captured by the enemy. All three endured a variety of tortures, and all agree about which one was the worst.

> "I'm beginning to lose my mind, to lose control completely," wrote the journalist. "I wish I could die."

> "It was a nightmare," wrote the prisoner. "I saw men so desperate that they ripped prison doors apart, starved and mutilated themselves."

> "It's an awful thing," wrote the solider. "It crushes your spirit and weakens your resistance more effectively than any other form of mistreatment."

The technique these three men are describing has nothing to do with electric shock or water-boarding. It does not require wax, rope, or razor blades. It is a remarkably simple technique that has been used for thousands of years to break the body and destroy the mind. It is called solitary confinement. Between them, Terry Anderson, Robert King, and John McCain spent a total of 38 years alone in a cell.

When we think of torture, we usually think of techniques designed to cause pain by depriving people of something they desperately need, such as oxygen, water, food, or sleep. But the need for social interaction is every bit as vital. Studies of prisoners show that extensive periods of physical isolation can induce symptoms typical of psychosis (Grassian, 2006), and ordinary people who are socially isolated are more prone to depression, illness, and premature death. In fact, feeling isolated is as bad for your health as being obese or smoking (Cacioppo & Patrick, 2008; House, Landis, & Umberson, 1988).

▼ **Terry Anderson** (left), **Robert King** (middle), and **John McCain** (right) each spent years in isolation and described it as the worst form of torture.

WHAT KIND OF ANIMAL GETS SICK OR GOES CRAZY when left alone? Our kind. Human beings are the most social species on the planet and everything about us—from the structure of our brains to the structure of our societies—is influenced by that fact. **Social psychology** is *the study of the causes and consequences of sociality.* We'll start our tour of social psychology by examining *social behavior*—how people interact with one another—and we'll see how social behavior solves a problem that every living creature faces. Next we'll examine *social influence*—how people change one another—and we'll see that people have three basic motivations that make them susceptible to influence. Finally, we'll examine *social cognition*—how people understand one another—and we'll see how people use information about another person's affiliations and actions to make judgments. And to make mistakes!

Social Behavior: Interacting with People

Centipedes aren't social. Neither are snails or brown bears. In fact, most animals are loners who prefer solitude to company. So why don't we?

All animals must survive and reproduce, and being social is one strategy for accomplishing these two important goals. When it comes to finding food or fending off enemies, herds and packs and flocks can often do what individuals can't, and that's why over millions of years many different species have found it useful to become social. But of the thousands and thousands of social species on our planet, only four types of animal have become *ultrasocial,* which means that they form societies in which large numbers of individuals divide labor and cooperate for mutual benefit. Those four are the hymenoptera (i.e., ants, bees, and wasps), the termites, the naked mole rats, and us (Haidt, 2006). Of these four, we are the only one whose societies consist of genetically *un*related individuals, and some scientists believe that the primary reason why we evolved such big brains is to deal with the complexities that these large-scale societies introduce (Dunbar & Shultz, 2007; Smith et al., 2010).

Being the most social of the ultrasocial animals has allowed our species to outsurvive and outreproduce everyone else. If 10,000 years ago you had rounded up all the mammals on Earth and placed them on a gigantic bathroom scale, human beings would have accounted for about .01% of the total weight. Today we would account for 98%. We are world champions of survival and reproduction because we are so deeply social, and as you are about to see, much of our social behavior revolves around these two basic goals.

Survival: The Struggle for Resources

Every living creature faces the same problem: survival. To survive, animals need resources such as food, water, and shelter. These resources are always scarce because if they were plentiful, then the animal population would increase until they weren't. Human beings deal with the problem of scarce resources by hurting one another and by helping one another. *Hurting* and *helping* are antonyms and you might expect them to have little in common, but as you will see, these very different behaviors are merely two solutions to one problem (Hawley, 2002).

Aggression

The simplest way to solve the problem of scarce resources is to take the resources and kick the beans out of anyone who tries to stop you. **Aggression** is *behavior whose purpose is to harm another* (Anderson & Bushman, 2002; Bushman & Huesmann, 2010); it is a strategy used by just about every animal on the planet. Aggression is not something that animals do for its own sake but, rather, as a way of getting the resources they

social psychology The study of the causes and consequences of sociality.

aggression Behavior whose purpose is to harm another.

frustration-aggression hypothesis A principle stating that animals aggress only when their goals are thwarted.

want. This idea is captured by the **frustration-aggression hypothesis,** which suggests that *animals aggress when and only when their goals are frustrated* (Dollard et al., 1939). The chimp wants the banana (goal) but the pelican is about to take it (frustration), so the chimp threatens the pelican with its fist (aggression). The robber wants the money (goal) but the teller has it all locked up (frustration), so the robber threatens the teller with a gun (aggression).

The frustration-aggression hypothesis may be right, but some psychologists believe it is incomplete. They argue that the real cause of aggressive behavior is negative affect, and that the inability to reach a goal is just one of many things that brings about negative affect (Berkowitz, 1990). In fact, animals do aggress when they feel bad. Laboratory rats that are given painful electric shocks will attack anything in their cage, including other animals, stuffed dolls, or even tennis balls (Kruk et al., 2004). People who are asked to put their hands in ice water, or to smell an unpleasant odor, or to sit in a very hot room are more likely to aggress against others (Anderson, 1989; Anderson, Bushman, & Groom, 1997). The idea that aggression is a response to negative affect may even explain why so many acts of aggression—from violent crime to athletic brawls—are more likely to occur on hot days when people are feeling irritated and uncomfortable (see **FIGURE 12.1**).

Of course, not everyone aggresses every time they feel bad. So who does—and why? Both biology and culture play a role in determining if and when people will aggress.

Biology and Aggression. The single best predictor of aggression is gender (Wrangham & Peterson, 1997). Crimes such as assault, battery, and murder are almost exclusively perpetrated by men—and especially by young men (Strueber, Lueck, & Roth, 2006). Although most societies encourage males to be more aggressive than females, male aggressiveness is not merely the product of socialization. Many studies show that aggression is strongly correlated with the presence of testosterone, which is typically higher in men than in women (see Chapter 10), in younger men than in older men, and in violent criminals than in nonviolent criminals (Dabbs et al., 1995).

Testosterone doesn't just "turn aggression on" (Eisenegger et al., 2010); rather, it seems to promote aggression by making people feel concerned with their status,

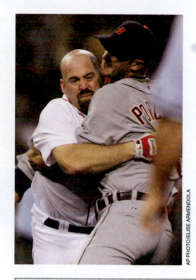

◀ Figure **12.1** **Hot and Bothered** In this 2009 baseball game, Boston Red Sox slugger Kevin Youkilis is about to tackle Detroit Tigers pitcher Rick Porcello after being hit by a pitch. Professional pitchers have awfully good aim, so when they hit batters with the baseball, it's safe to assume that it wasn't an accident. This figure shows the average number of batters who were hit by pitches per game during the 1986–1988 major-league seasons. As you can see, the temperature on the field was highly correlated with the likelihood of being beaned.

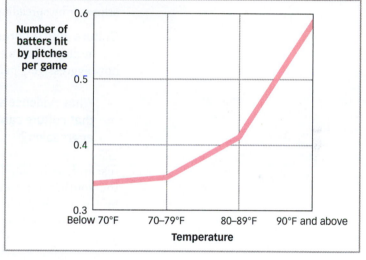

? Why are men more physically aggressive than women?

powerful, and confident in their ability to prevail. Indeed, three quarters of all murders can be classified as "status competitions" or "contests to save face" (Daly & Wilson, 1988). Contrary to popular wisdom, it isn't men with *low* self-esteem but men with unrealistically *high* self-esteem who are most prone to aggression because such men are especially likely to perceive others' actions as a challenge to their inflated sense of their own status (Baumeister, Smart, & Boden, 1996).

Although women can be just as aggressive as men, their aggression tends to be more focused on attaining or protecting a resource than on attaining or protecting their status. Women are *much* less likely than men to aggress without provocation or to aggress in ways that cause physical injury, but they are only *slightly* less likely than men to aggress when provoked or to aggress in ways that cause psychological injury (Bettencourt & Miller, 1996; Eagly & Steffen, 1986). Indeed, women may even be

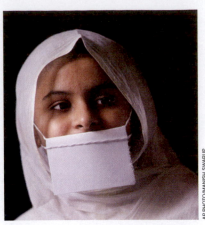

Culture has a strong influence on violence. In Iraq, where murder is a part of everyday life, young boys stage a mock execution. In India, a teenager who is a member of the Jain religion wears a mask at all times so that she will not harm insects or microbes by inhaling them.

more likely than men to aggress by causing social harm—for example, by ostracizing others or by spreading malicious rumors about them (Crick & Grotpeter, 1995).

Culture and Aggression. Although aggression is clearly part of our evolutionary heritage, it isn't inevitable. Cultures play an important role in determining how aggressively people behave. For example, violent crime in the United States is much more prevalent in the South, where men are taught to react aggressively when they feel their status has been challenged (Brown, Osterman, & Barnes, 2009; Nisbett & Cohen, 1996). In one set of experiments, researchers insulted volunteers from northern and southern states and found that the southerners were more likely to feel that their status had been diminished by the insult (Cohen et al., 1996). The southerners also experienced a greater increase in testosterone than did the northerners, and they were physically more assertive when a 6'3", 250-pound man got in their way as they left the experimental room. As **FIGURE 12.2** shows, aggression varies quite a bit with geography, which suggests that culture determines how and when our biological predisposition toward aggression is expressed.

? What evidence suggests that culture can influence aggression?

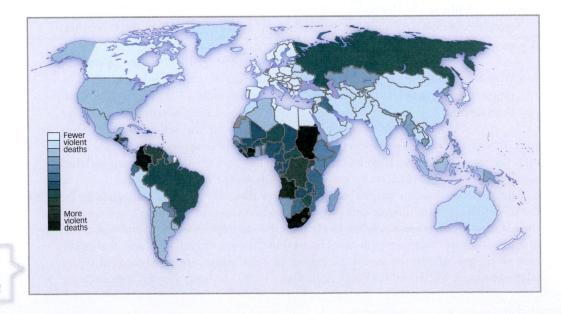

Fewer violent deaths

More violent deaths

▶ Figure **12.2 The Geography of Violence** When it comes to violence, culture matters a lot!

Cooperation

Aggression is one way to solve the problem of scarce resources, but when individuals work together they can each get more resources than either could get alone. **Cooperation** is *behavior by two or more individuals that leads to mutual benefit* (Deutsch, 1949; Pruitt, 1998), and it is one of our species' greatest achievements—right up there with language, fire, and opposable thumbs (Axelrod, 1984; Axelrod & Hamilton, 1981; Nowak, 2006). Every roadway and supermarket, every iPod and cell phone, every ballet and surgery is the result of cooperation, and it is difficult to think of an important human achievement that could have occurred without it.

Risk and Trust. If the benefit of cooperation is so clear, then why don't we cooperate all the time? The answer is that cooperation is *risky*, and a simple game called *the prisoner's dilemma* illustrates why. Imagine that you and a friend have been arrested for

What makes cooperation risky?

a crime. You are now being interrogated separately. The detectives tell you that if you and your friend both confess, you'll each get 10 years in prison, and if you both refuse to confess, you'll each get 1 year in prison. However, if one of you confesses and the other doesn't, then the one who confesses will go free and the one who doesn't confess will be put away for 30 years. What should you do? If you study **FIGURE 12.3**, you'll see that you and your friend would both be wise to cooperate with each other, in which case you will both get a light sentence. But look what happens if you trust your friend and then he double-crosses you: He gets to go home while you spend the next three decades making license plates!

The prisoner's dilemma is more than a game. It mirrors the risks and benefits of cooperation in everyday life. For example, if everyone pays taxes, then the tax rate stays low and everyone enjoys the benefits of sturdy bridges and first-rate museums. If no one pays taxes, then the bridges fall down and the museums shut their doors. There is clearly a *moderate* benefit to everyone if everyone pays taxes, but there is a *huge* benefit to the few noncooperators who don't pay taxes while everyone else does because they get to use the bridges and enjoy the museums for free. This dilemma makes it difficult for people to decide whether to pay taxes and risk being chumps or to cheat and risk having the bridges collapse and the museums shut down. If you are like most people, you would be perfectly willing to cooperate in this sort of dilemma but you worry that others won't do the same. It's no wonder that when people are asked what single trait they most want those around them to have, the answer is *trustworthiness* (Cottrell, Neuberg, & Li, 2007).

Groups and Favoritism. Cooperation requires that we take a risk by benefiting those who have not yet benefited us and then *trusting* them to do the same. But other than Mom, whom can we really trust?

A **group** is *a collection of people who have something in common that distinguishes them from others.* Every one of us is a member of many groups—from families and teams to religions and nations. **Prejudice** is *a positive or negative evaluation of another person based on that person's group membership,* and **discrimination** is *a positive or negative behavior toward another person based on that person's group membership* (Dovidio & Gaertner, 2010). One of the defining characteristics of groups is that their members are

How do groups lessen the risks of cooperation?

positively prejudiced toward other members and tend to discriminate in their favor. It doesn't take much to create this kind of favoritism (Efferson, Lalive, & Fehr, 2008). In one set of studies, participants were shown abstract paintings by two artists and were then divided into two groups based on their preference for one artist or the other (Tajfel, 1970; Tajfel et al., 1971). When participants were subsequently asked

cooperation Behavior by two or more individuals that leads to mutual benefit.

group A collection of people who have something in common that distinguishes them from others.

prejudice A positive or negative evaluation of another person based on that person's group membership.

discrimination Positive or negative behavior toward another person based on that person's group membership.

	COOPERATION (B does not confess)	NONCOOPERATION (B confesses)
COOPERATION (A does not confess)	A gets 1 year B gets 1 year	A gets 30 years B gets 0 years
NONCOOPERATION (A confesses)	A gets 0 years B gets 30 years	A gets 10 years B gets 10 years

▲ Figure **12.3** **The Prisoner's Dilemma Game** The prisoner's dilemma game illustrates the benefits and costs of cooperation. Players A and B receive benefits whose size depends on whether they independently decide to cooperate. Mutual cooperation leads to a relatively moderate benefit to both players, but if only one player cooperates, then the cooperator gets no benefit and the noncooperator gets a large benefit.

Kevin Hart owns the Gator Motel in Fargo, Georgia, which he runs on an honor system: Guests arrive, stay as long as they like, and leave their payment on the dresser. If just a few people cheated, it would not affect the room rates, but if too many cheated, then prices would have to rise. How would you decide whether to pay or to cheat? Before answering this question, please notice the large dog.

to allocate money to other participants, they consistently allocated more money to those in their group (Brewer, 1979). It appears that simply knowing that "I'm one of *us* and not one of *them*" is sufficient to produce favoritism. Because group members favor other group members, cooperation within the group is less risky.

But if groups have benefits, they also have costs. People in groups sometimes do terrible things that none of their members would do alone (Yzerbyt & Demoulin, 2010). Lynching, rioting, gang-raping—why do we behave so badly when we assemble in groups? One reason is **deindividuation,** which occurs *when immersion in a group causes people to become less concerned with their personal values.* We may want to grab the Rolex from the jeweler's window or plant a kiss on the attractive stranger in the library, but we don't do these things because they conflict with our personal values. Being assembled in groups draws our attention to others and *away* from ourselves. As a result, we are less likely to consider our own personal values and instead to adopt the group's values (Postmes & Spears, 1998). A second reason why we behave badly in groups is **diffusion of responsibility,** which occurs when *individuals feel diminished responsibility for their actions because they are surrounded by others who are acting the same way.* When we're all alone, we know it is up to us to do the right thing; but when we see lots of other people around us, we may feel that it is somebody else's job (Darley & Latané, 1968). If you and one other student were taking an exam and you saw the other student cheating, you'd probably feel more responsible for reporting the incident than if you were taking that test in a room full of students (see **FIGURE 12.4**).

If groups encourage bad behavior, then might we be better off without them? Probably not. One of the best predictors of a person's general well-being is the quality and extent of his or her social relationships and group memberships (Myers & Diener, 1995). People who are excluded from groups are typically anxious, lonely, depressed, and at increased risk for illness and premature death (Cacioppo & Patrick, 2008; Cohen, 1988; Leary, 1990). Indeed, being excluded from a group activates areas of the brain that are normally activated by physical pain (Eisenberger, Lieberman, & Williams, 2003). Groups may cause us to misbehave, but they seem to be key to our happiness and well-being.

Altruism

Cooperation is a way to solve the problem of scarce resources. But is this the only reason we cooperate with others? Aren't we ever just . . . well, *nice*? **Altruism** is *behavior that benefits another without benefiting oneself,* and for a very long time scientists and philosophers have debated whether people are ever truly altruistic.

▶ Figure **12.4** **Mob Size and Level of Atrocity** Groups are capable of horrible things. These two men were rescued by police just as residents of their town prepared to lynch them for stealing a car. Because larger groups provide more opportunity for deindividuation and diffusion of responsibility, their atrocities become more horrible as the ratio of mob members to victims becomes larger (Leader, Mullen, & Abrams, 2007).

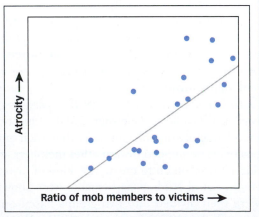

Altruism appears to be common among animals—but appearances can be deceiving. For example, birds and squirrels give "alarm calls" when they see a predator, which puts them at increased risk of being eaten but allows their fellow birds and squirrels to escape. Ants and bees spend their lives caring for the offspring of the queen rather than bearing offspring of their own. But these behaviors are not really altruistic because the animals being helped are related to the animals doing the helping. Any animal that promotes the survival of its relatives is actually promoting the survival of its own genes (Hamilton, 1964). **Kin selection** is *the process by which evolution selects for individuals who cooperate with their relatives,* which means that cooperating with relatives is not really altruistic. Even cooperating with nonrelatives isn't necessarily proof of altruism. Male baboons will risk injury to help an unrelated male baboon win a fight, and monkeys will spend time grooming unrelated monkeys when they could be doing something else. Is that altruism? Not necessarily. Careful studies of primates reveal that the individuals who perform such favors tend to receive favors in return. **Reciprocal altruism** is *behavior that benefits another with the expectation that those benefits will be returned in the future,* and despite the second word in this term, it isn't really very altruistic at all (Trivers, 1971). Indeed, reciprocal altruism is merely cooperation extended over long periods.

Ground squirrels put themselves in danger when they warn others about predators, but those they warn share their genes, so the behavior is not truly altruistic. In contrast, Christine Karg-Palreiro donated her kidney anonymously to someone she'd never even met. "If I had a spare, I'd do it again," she said.

The behavior of nonhuman animals provides little if any evidence of genuine altruism. But what about us? Are we any different? Like other animals, we tend to help our kin more than strangers (Burnstein, Crandall, & Kitayama, 1994; Komter, 2010) and we tend to expect those we help to help us in return (Burger et al., 2009). But unlike other animals, we do sometimes provide benefits to complete strangers who have no chance of repaying us (Batson, 2002; Warneken & Tomasello, 2009). We make anonymous donations to charity, tip waiters in restaurants to which we will never return, and hold the door for people who share precisely none of our genes. As the World Trade Center burned on the morning of September 11, 2001, civilians in sailboats headed *toward* the destruction rather than away from it, initiating the largest waterborne evacuation in the history of the United States. As one observer remarked, "If you're out on the water in a pleasure craft and you see those buildings on fire, in a strictly rational sense you should head to New Jersey. Instead, people went into potential danger and rescued strangers" (Dreifus, 2003). Human beings can be heroes, and some studies even suggest that altruism is more common than we realize (Miller & Ratner, 1998).

? Are human beings really altruistic?

Reproduction: The Quest for Immortality

All animals have two goals: to survive and to reproduce. Social behavior facilitates the first of these goals, but it is an essential requirement for the second. Because we are a sexual species, we can't reproduce without getting very, very social. There are many steps on the road to reproduction, but the first one invariably involves finding someone of the opposite gender who wants to travel that road with us. How do we do that?

Selectivity

With the exception of a few well-known celebrities, people don't seem to mate randomly. Rather, they *select* their sexual partners, and women tend to be more selective than men (Feingold, 1992a; Fiore et al., 2010). In one study, an attractive person (who was working for the experimenters) approached an opposite-sex stranger on a college

deindividuation A phenomenon that occurs when immersion in a group causes people to become less aware of their individual values.

diffusion of responsibility The tendency for individuals to feel diminished responsibility for their actions when they are surrounded by others who are acting the same way.

altruism Behavior that benefits another without benefiting oneself.

kin selection The process by which evolution selects for individuals who cooperate their relatives.

reciprocal altruism Behavior that benefits another with the expectation that those benefits will be returned in the future.

campus and asked one of two questions: "Would you go out tonight?" or "Would you go to bed with me?" About half of the men and women who were approached agreed to go out with the attractive person; but while *none* of the women agreed to go to bed with the person, *three quarters* of the men did (Clark & Hatfield, 1989).

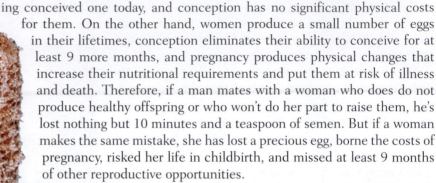

? **Why are women choosier than men?**

Why are women the choosier gender? One reason is that sex is potentially more costly for women than for men (Buss & Schmitt, 1993; Trivers, 1972). Men produce billions of sperm in their lifetimes, their ability to conceive a child tomorrow is not inhibited by having conceived one today, and conception has no significant physical costs for them. On the other hand, women produce a small number of eggs in their lifetimes, conception eliminates their ability to conceive for at least 9 more months, and pregnancy produces physical changes that increase their nutritional requirements and put them at risk of illness and death. Therefore, if a man mates with a woman who does do not produce healthy offspring or who won't do her part to raise them, he's lost nothing but 10 minutes and a teaspoon of semen. But if a woman makes the same mistake, she has lost a precious egg, borne the costs of pregnancy, risked her life in childbirth, and missed at least 9 months of other reproductive opportunities.

Basic biology may push women to be choosier then men, but culture can push just as hard. When cultures glorify promiscuous men as *playboys* and disparage promiscuous women as *sluts,* women may be more selective than men simply because the reputational costs of sex are much higher; but when cultures lower the costs of sex for women by providing access to effective birth control, by promoting the financial independence of women, or by adopting communal styles of child-rearing, women become less selective (Eagly & Wood, 1999; Kasser & Sharma, 1999). And when sex becomes expensive for men—for example, when they are choosing a long-term mate for a monogamous relationship rather than a short-term mate for a weekend—they turn out to be every bit as selective as women (Kenrick et al., 1990). Indeed, small changes in the courtship ritual can actually cause men to become *choosier* than women (see the Real World box). The point is that biology makes sex a riskier proposition for women than for men, but cultures can exaggerate, equalize, or even reverse those risks. The higher the risk, the more selective people tend to be.

DR. PAUL ZAHL/ SCIENCE SOURCE

CREATAS IMAGES PICTUREQUEST

If men could become pregnant, how might their behavior change? Among sea horses, it is the male that carries the young; not coincidentally, males are more selective than are females.

Attraction

For most of us, there are a very small number of people with whom we are willing to have sex, an even smaller number of people with whom we are willing to have children, and a staggeringly large number of people with whom we are unwilling to have either. So when we meet someone new, how do we decide which of these categories that person belongs in? Many things go into choosing a date, a lover, or a partner for life, but perhaps none is more important than the simple feeling we call *attraction* (Berscheid & Reiss, 1998). Research suggests that this feeling is caused by situational, physical, and psychological factors.

1. Situational Factors. One of the best predictors of any kind of interpersonal relationship is the physical proximity of the people involved (Nahemow & Lawton, 1975). For example, in one study, students who had been randomly assigned to university housing were asked to name their three closest friends, and nearly half named their next-door neighbor (Festinger, Schachter, & Back, 1950ok). We tend to think that we select our romantic partners on the basis of their personalities, appearances, and so

THE REAL WORLD

Making the Move

When it comes to selecting romantic partners, women tend to be choosier than men, and most scientists think that has a lot to do with differences in their reproductive biology. But it might also have something to do with the nature of the courtship dance itself.

When it comes to approaching a potential romantic partner, the person with the most interest should be most inclined to "make the first move." Of course, in most cultures, men are *expected* to make the first move. Could it be that making the first move *causes* men to think they have more interest than women do?

To find out, researchers created two kinds of speed-dating events (Finkel & Eastwick, 2009). In the "traditional event," the women stayed in their seats and the men moved around the room, stopping to spend a few minutes chatting with each woman. In the "nontraditional event," the men stayed in their seats and the women moved around the room. When the event was over, the researchers asked each man and woman privately whether they wanted to exchange phone numbers with any of the potential partners they'd met.

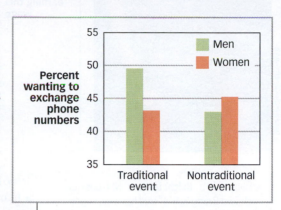

The results were striking (see the accompanying figure). When men made the move (as they traditionally do), women were the choosier gender. That is, men wanted to get a lot more phone numbers than women wanted to give. But when women made the move, men were the choosier gender, and women asked for more numbers than men were willing to hand over. Apparently, approaching someone makes us eager and being approached makes us cautious. One reason why women are so often the choosier gender may simply be that, in most cultures, men are expected to make the first move.

GREG GILBERT/THE SEATTLE TIMES/MCT/NEWSCOM

on—and we do—but we get to select only from the pool of people whom we have met. Before you ever start auditioning and ruling out potential mates, geography has already ruled out 99.999% of the world's population for you. Proximity not only provides the opportunity for attraction but also provides the motivation: People work especially hard to like those with whom they expect to have interaction (Darley & Berscheid, 1967). When you are assigned a roommate in college, you know that day-to-day existence will be a whole lot easier if you like that person than if you don't, so you go out of your way to notice the person's good qualities and ignore the bad ones.

? Why does proximity influence attraction?

2. **Physical Factors.** You already know that appearance influences attraction, but research suggests that this influence may be stronger than you think. In one study, researchers arranged a dance for first-year university students and randomly assigned each student to an opposite-sex partner. Midway through the dance, the students confidentially reported how much they liked their partner, how attractive they thought their partner was, and how much they would like to see their partner again. The researchers measured many of the students' attributes—from their attitudes to their personalities—and they found that the partner's physical appearance was the *only* attribute that influenced the students' feelings of attraction (Walster et al.,

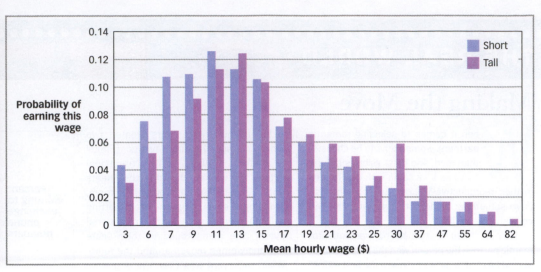

▲ Figure **12.5** **Height Matters** NFL quarterback Tom Brady is 6′4″ and his wife, supermodel Gisele Bündchen, is 5′10″. Research shows that tall people earn $789 more per inch per year. The graph shows the average hourly wage of adult White men in the United States classified by height (Mankiw & Weinzierl, 2010).

1966). Field studies have revealed the same thing. For instance, one study found that a man's height and a woman's weight were among the best predictors of how many responses a personal ad received (Lynn & Shurgot, 1984); another study found that physical attractiveness was the *only* factor that predicted the online dating choices of both women and men (Green, Buchanan, & Heuer, 1984).

Appearance is important in just about every context (Etcoff, 1999; Langlois et al., 2000). Beautiful people have more friends, more dates, more sex, and more fun than the rest of us do (Curran & Lippold, 1975), and they even earn about 10% more money over the courses of their lives (Hamermesh & Biddle, 1994; see **FIGURE 12.5**). We tend to think that beautiful people also have superior personal qualities (Dion, Berscheid, & Walster, 1972; Eagly et al., 1991), and in some cases they do. For instance, because beautiful people have more friends and more opportunities for social interaction, they tend to have better social skills than less beautiful people (Feingold, 1992b). Appearance is so powerful that it even influences how mothers treat their own children: Mothers are more affectionate and playful when their children are attractive than unattractive (Langlois et al., 1995). It is interesting to note that although men and women seem to be equally influenced by the appearance of their potential partners, men are more likely than women to acknowledge this fact (Feingold, 1990).

So yes, it pays to be beautiful. But what exactly constitutes beauty? There is no doubt that standards of beauty can vary across time and culture. In the United States, for example, most women want to be slender, but in Mauritania, young girls are forced to drink up to 5 gallons of high-fat milk every day so that they will someday be obese

Standards of beauty differ across cultures. Mauritanian women long to be obese (left), and Ghanian men are grateful to be short (right).

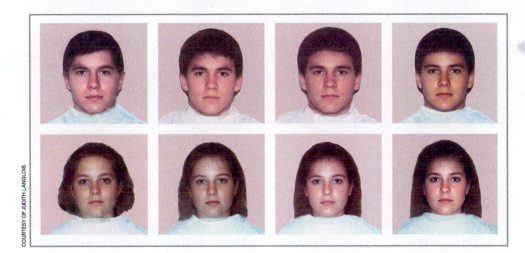

◄ **Figure 12.6** **The Attractive Norm** When photos of human faces are "morphed" to create a composite, people tend to judge the composite as more attractive than its components because the composites are closer to the human average. The faces shown are (from left to right) composites of 4, 8, 16, and 22 faces, and most people think the faces on the right are more attractive than the faces on the left.

Langlois & Roggman (1990).

enough to attract a husband. As one Mauritanian woman noted, "Men want women to be fat, and so they are fat. Women want men to be skinny, and so they are skinny" (LaFraniere, 2007). In the United States, most men want to be tall, but in Ghana, most men are short and consider height a curse. "To be a tall person can be quite embarrassing," said one particularly tall Ghanaian man. "When you are standing in a crowd, the short people start to jeer at you," said another (quoted in French, 1997).

On the other hand, some standards of beauty are common across many cultures; for example, human faces are generally considered more attractive when they are bilaterally symmetrical—that is, when the left half is a mirror image of the right (Perrett et al., 1999) and when their features approximate the average of the human population (Langlois & Roggman, 1990; Langlois, Roggman, & Musselman, 1994; see **FIGURE 12.6**). In fact, both symmetry and averageness are signs of good genetic health (Jones et al., 2001; Thornhill & Gangestad, 1993), so nature may have designed us to be attracted to faces with these features because the people wearing them are potentially good, healthy mates. Of course, attraction is one thing, and action is another. Studies show that while everyone may desire the most beautiful person in the room, most people tend to approach, date, and marry someone who is about as attractive as they are (Berscheid et al., 1971; Lee et al., 2008).

? What kind of information does physical appearance convey?

3. Psychological Factors. If attraction is all about big biceps and high cheekbones, then why don't we just skip the small talk and pick our mates from photographs? Because for human beings, attraction is about much more than that. Physical appearance may determine who draws our attention and quickens our pulse, but once people begin interacting, they quickly move beyond appearances (Cramer, Schaefer, & Reid, 1996; Regan, 1998). People's *inner* qualities—their personalities, points of view, attitudes, beliefs, values, ambitions, and abilities—play an important role in determining their sustained interest in each other, and there isn't much mystery about the kinds of inner qualities that most people find attractive. For example, intelligence, sense of humor, sensitivity, and ambition seem to be high on just about everybody's list (Daniel et al., 1985).

But just how much wit and wisdom do we want our mate to have? Research suggests that we are most attracted to people who are generally similar to us (Byrne, Ervin, & Lamberth, 1970; Byrne & Nelson, 1965; Hatfield & Rapson, 1992; Neimeyer & Mitchell, 1988). We marry people with similar levels of education, religious backgrounds, ethnicities, socioeconomic statuses, and personalities (Botwin, Buss, & Shackelford, 1997; Buss, 1985; Caspi & Herbener, 1990). Why is similarity

Similarity is a very strong source of attraction.

? Why is similarity such a powerful determinant of attraction?

so attractive? First, it's easy to interact with people who are similar to us because we can instantly agree on a wide range of issues, such as what to eat, where to live, how to raise children, and how to spend our money. Second, when someone shares our attitudes and beliefs, we feel a bit more confident that those attitudes and beliefs are correct (Byrne & Clore, 1970). Third, if we like people who share our attitudes and beliefs, then we can reasonably expect them to like us for the same reason—and *being* liked is a powerful source of attraction (Aronson & Worchel, 1966; Backman & Secord, 1959; Condon & Crano, 1988). Although we tend to like people who like us, it is worth noting that we *especially* like people who like us and who *don't* like anyone else (Eastwick et al., 2007).

Relationships

Selecting and attracting a mate is a prerequisite for reproduction. But the real work consists of bearing and raising the kids! For human beings, that work is ordinarily done in the context of committed, long-term, romantic relationships such as a marriage (Clark & Lemay, 2010). Only a few animals have relationships of this kind, so why are we among them?

One answer is that we're born half baked. Human beings have large heads to house their large brains; thus a fully developed human infant could not pass through its mother's birth canal. As such, human infants are *born before they are fully developed* and thus need a great deal of care—often more than one parent can provide. If human infants were more like tadpoles—ready at birth to swim, find food, and escape predators—then their parents might not need to form and maintain relationships. But human infants are remarkably helpless creatures that require years of intense care before they can fend for themselves, so human adults do almost all of their reproducing in the context of committed, long-term relationships. (By the way, some baby birds also require more food than one adult caretaker can provide, and the adults of those species also tend to form long-term relationships.)

In most cultures, committed, long-term relationships are signified by marriage, and ours is no exception. The probability of marrying by age 40 is currently 81% for American men and 86% for American women (Goodwin, McGill, & Chandra, 2009). And most of those who marry will say they married for love. The fact that people marry for love seems so obvious that you may be surprised to learn that, throughout history, marriage has traditionally served a variety of economic (and decidedly unromantic) functions, ranging from cementing agreements between clans to paying back debts—and in many cultures, that's precisely how it is still regarded. Ancient Greeks and Romans married, but they considered love a form of madness (Heine, 2010). Twelfth-century Europeans married but thought of love as a game to be played by knights and ladies of the court (who happened to be married, but not to the knights). Indeed, it wasn't until the 17th century that Westerners began seriously considering the possibility that love might actually be a *reason* to get married.

Are people more like cattle or robins? In most ways, we are more like any mammal than we are like any bird, but songbirds and people do share one thing that cattle don't: Their young are helpless at birth and thus require significant parental care. Interestingly, adult robins and adult human beings (but not adult cattle) have enduring relationships. And sing.

JUPITER IMAGES

CRAIG LOVELL/CORBIS

LIGHTSCAPES PHOTOGRAPHY, INC./CORBIS

But is it? People who get married usually think they will stay married, and a whole lot of them are wrong. For every two couples who got married in 2008, one couple got divorced (Tejada-Vera & Sutton, 2009). Although there are many reasons for divorce (Gottman, 1994; Karney & Bradbury, 1995), one is that couples don't always have a clear understanding of what love is. Indeed, a language that uses the same word to describe the deepest forms of intimacy ("I love Emily") and the most shallow forms of satisfaction ("I love ketchup") is bound to confuse the people who speak it (Reis & Aron, 2008). Psychologists try to sidestep this confusion by distinguishing between two basic kinds of love—**passionate love**, which is *an experience involving feelings of euphoria, intimacy, and intense sexual attraction*, and **companionate love**, which is *an experience involving affection, trust, and concern for a partner's well-being* (Acevedo & Aron, 2009; Hatfield, 1988; Rubin, 1973; Sternberg, 1986). The ideal romantic relationship gives rise to both types of love, but the speeds, trajectories, and durations of the two experiences are markedly different (**FIGURE 12.7**).

Passionate love is what brings people together; it has a rapid onset, reaches its peak quickly, and begins to diminish within just a few months (Aron et al., 2005). Companionate love is what keeps people together; it takes some time to get started, grows slowly, and need never stop growing (Gonzaga et al., 2001). In other words, the love we feel early in a relationship is not the same love we feel later. When people marry for passionate love, they may not choose a partner with whom they can easily develop companionate love, and if they don't understand how quickly passionate love cools, they may blame their partners when it does. In many cultures, parents try to keep children from making these mistakes by choosing their marriage partners for them. Some studies suggest that these "arranged marriages" yield greater satisfaction over the long term than do "love matches" (Yelsma & Athappilly, 1988), but other studies suggest the opposite (Xiaohe & Whyte, 1990). If there *are* any benefits to arranged marriage, they may derive from the fact that parents are less likely to pick partners on the basis of passionate love and more likely to pick partners who have a high potential for companionate love (Haidt, 2006).

Although feelings of love, happiness, and satisfaction may lead us to marriage, the lack of those feelings doesn't seem to lead us to divorce. Marital satisfaction is only weakly correlated with marital stability (Karney & Bradbury, 1995), suggesting that relationships break up or remain intact for reasons other than the satisfaction of those involved (Drigotas & Rusbult, 1992; Rusbult & Van Lange, 2003). Relationships offer benefits, such as love, sex, and financial security, but they also exact costs, such as increased responsibility, increased conflict, and loss of freedom. **Social exchange** is *the hypothesis that people remain in relationships only as long as they perceive a favorable ratio of costs to benefits* (Homans, 1961; Thibaut & Kelley, 1959). A relationship that provides an acceptable level of benefits at a reasonable cost will probably be maintained, and one that doesn't won't. Research suggests that this hypothesis is generally true, with three important caveats:

? How do people weigh the costs and benefits of their relationships?

1. People compare their cost-benefit ratios with those they believe they deserve or could attain in another relationship (Rusbult et al., 1991; Thibaut & Kelley, 1959). For example, a cost-benefit ratio that is acceptable to two people who are stranded on a desert island might not be acceptable to the same two people if they were living in a large city where each had access to other potential partners.

2. People may want their cost-benefit ratios to be high, but they also want them to be about the same as their partner's (Bolton & Ockenfels, 2000; Messick &

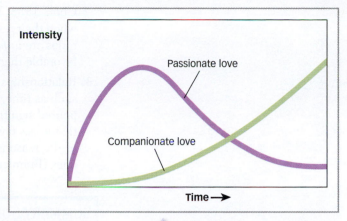

▲ Figure **12.7** **Passionate and Companionate Love** Companionate and passionate love have different time courses and trajectories. Passionate love begins to cool within just a few months, but companionate love can grow slowly but steadily over years.

passionate love An experience involving feelings of euphoria, intimacy, and intense sexual attraction.

companionate love An experience involving affection, trust, and concern for a partner's well-being.

social exchange The hypothesis that people remain in relationships only as long as they perceive a favorable ratio of costs to benefits.

Cook, 1983; Walster, Walster, & Berscheid, 1978). Spouses are more distressed when their respective cost-benefit ratios are *different* than when their cost-benefit ratios are *unfavorable*—and this is true even when their cost-benefit ratio is *more* favorable than their partner's (Schafer & Keith, 1980).

3. Relationships can be thought of as investments into which people pour resources such as time, money, and affection, and research suggests that after people have poured significant resources into their relationships, they are more willing to settle for less favorable cost-benefit ratios (Kelley, 1983; Rusbult, 1983). This is one of the reasons why people are much more likely to end new marriages than old ones (Bramlett & Mosher, 2002; Cherlin, 1992).

SUMMARY QUIZ [12.1]

1. Why are acts of aggression—from violent crimes to athletic brawls—more likely to occur on hot days when people are feeling irritated and uncomfortable?
   a. frustration
   b. negative affect
   c. resource scarcity
   d. biology and culture interaction

2. The prisoner's dilemma game illustrates
   a. the hypothesis-confirming bias.
   b. the diffusion of responsibility.
   c. group polarization.
   d. the benefits and costs of cooperation.

3. Which of the following *best* describes reciprocal altruism?
   a. people becoming less concerned with personal values through immersion in a group
   b. anxiety, loneliness, and depression being caused by exclusion from a group
   c. cooperation extended over long periods
   d. the evolutionary process by which individuals cooperate with their relatives

4. Which of the following is *not* an explanation for greater selectivity by women in choosing a mate?
   a. Sex is potentially more costly for women than for men.
   b. Communal styles of child-rearing argue for increased selectivity.
   c. The reputational costs of sex are historically much higher for women than for men.
   d. Pregnancy increases women's nutritional requirements and puts them at risk of illness and death.

5. The hypothesis that people remain in relationships only as long as they perceive a favorable ratio of costs to benefits is referred to as
   a. companionate love.
   b. the exposure effect.
   c. social exchange.
   d. equity.

Social Influence: Controlling People

Those of us who grew up watching cartoons on Saturday mornings have usually thought a bit about which of the standard superpowers we'd most like to have. Superstrength and superspeed have obvious benefits, invisibility could be interesting as well as lucrative, and there's a lot to be said for flying. But when it comes right down to it, the ability to control other people would surely be most useful. After all, who needs to lift a tractor or catch a bad guy if they can get someone else to do it for them? The things we want from life—gourmet food, interesting jobs, big houses, fancy cars—can be given to us by others, and the things we want most—loving families, loyal friends, admiring children, appreciative employers—cannot be had in any other way.

social influence The ability to control another person's behavior.

Social influence is *the ability to control another person's behavior* (Cialdini & Trost, 1998). But how does it work? If you want people to give you their time, money, allegiance, or affection, you'd be wise to consider first what it is *they* want. People have three basic motivations that make them susceptible to social influence (Bargh, Gollwitzer, & Oettingen, 2010). People are motivated to experience pleasure and to avoid experiencing pain (the *hedonic motive*), they are motivated to be accepted and to avoid being rejected (the *approval motive*), and they are motivated to believe what is right and to avoid believing what is wrong (the *accuracy motive*). As you will see, most social influence attempts appeal to one or more of these motives.

The Hedonic Motive: Pleasure Is Better Than Pain

If there is an animal that prefers pain to pleasure, it must be very good at hiding because scientists have never seen it. Pleasure-seeking is the most basic of all motives, and social influence often involves creating situations in which others can achieve more pleasure by doing what we want them to do than by doing something else. Parents, teachers, governments, and businesses often try to influence our behavior by offering rewards and threatening punishments (see **FIGURE 12.8**). There's nothing mysterious about how these influence attempts work, and they are often quite effective. When the Republic of Singapore warned its citizens that anyone caught chewing gum in public would face a year in prison and a $5,500 fine, the rest of the world seemed either outraged or amused. When all the criticism and chuckling subsided, though, it was hard to ignore the fact that the incidence of felonious gum-chewing in Singapore had fallen to an all-time low.

? How effective are rewards and punishments?

You'll recall from Chapter 6 that even a sea slug will repeat behaviors that are followed by rewards and avoid behaviors that are followed by punishments. Although the same is generally true of human beings, there are some instances in which rewards and punishments can backfire. For example, children in one study were allowed to play with colored markers and then some were given a "Good Player Award." When the children were given markers the next day, those who had received an award were less likely to play with them than were those who had not received an award (Lepper, Greene, & Nisbett, 1973). Why? Because children who had received an award the first day came to think of drawing as something one did to receive rewards, and if no one was going to give them an award, then why should they do it (Deci, Koestner, & Ryan, 1999)? Similarly, reward and punishment can backfire simply because people

According to *Time*, the world's most influential person in 2010 was Mir-Hossein Mousavi, the leader of a political movement that opposes the government of Iran.

▼ Figure **12.8 The Cost of Speeding** The penalty for speeding in Massachusetts used to be a modest fine. In 2006, the legislature changed the law so that drivers under 18 who are caught speeding now lose their licenses for 90 days—and to get them back they have to pay $500, attend 8 hours of training classes, and retake the state's driving exam. Guess what? Deaths among drivers under 18 fell by 38% in just 3 years. In other words, more than 8,000 young lives were saved by appealing to the hedonic motive

[http://www.boston.com/news/local/massachusetts/articles/2010/04/18/steep_drop_in_teen_driver_fatalities/].

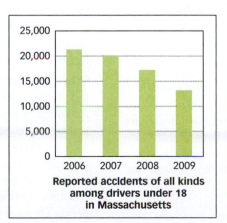

Reported accidents of all kinds among drivers under 18 in Massachusetts

CULTURE & COMMUNITY

Free Parking People don't like to be manipulated, and they get upset when someone threatens their freedom to do as they wish. Is this a uniquely Western reaction? To find out, psychologists asked college students for one of two favors and then measured how irritated the students felt (Jonas et al., 2009). In one case, they asked students if they would give up their right to park on campus for a week ("Would you mind if I used your parking card so I can participate in a research project in this building?"). In the other case, they asked students if they would give up *everyone's* right to park on campus for a week ("Would you mind if we closed the entire parking lot for a tennis tournament?"). How did students react to these requests?

It depended on their culture. As the accompanying figure shows, European American students were more irritated by a request that limited their freedom than by a request that limited everyone's freedom ("If nobody can park, that's inconvenient. But if everybody except *me* can park, that's unfair!"). But Latino students and Asian American students had precisely the opposite reactions ("The needs of the requestor outweigh the needs of one student, but they don't outweigh the needs of all students"). It appears that people do indeed value freedom—but not necessarily their own.

FUSE/JUPITERIMAGES

don't like to feel manipulated. Researchers placed signs in two restrooms on a college campus—one reading "Please don't write on these walls" and another reading "Do not write on these walls under any circumstances." Two weeks later, the walls in the second restroom had more graffiti than the walls in the first restroom did, presumably because students didn't appreciate the threatening tone of the second sign and wrote on the walls just to prove to themselves that they could (Pennebaker & Sanders, 1976).

The Approval Motive: Acceptance Is Better Than Rejection

Other people stand between us and starvation, predation, loneliness, and all the other things that make getting shipwrecked such a bad idea. We depend on others for safety, sustenance, and solidarity, and thus we are powerfully motivated to have others like us, accept us, and approve of us (Baumeister & Leary, 1995; Leary, 2010). Like any motive, this one leaves us vulnerable to social influence.

Normative Influence

When getting on an elevator, you are supposed to face forward, and you shouldn't talk to the person next to you unless you are the only two people on the elevator. Although no one ever taught you this rule, you probably picked it up somewhere along the way. The unwritten rules that govern social behavior are called **norms,** which are *customary standards for behavior that are widely shared by members of a culture* (Miller & Prentice, 1996). **Normative influence** occurs when *another person's behavior provides information about what is appropriate* (see **FIGURE 12.9**). For example, every human culture has a **norm of reciprocity,** which is *the unwritten rule*

? How are we influenced by other people's behavior?

---

norm A customary standard for behavior that is widely shared by members of a culture.

normative influence A phenomenon that occurs when another person's behavior provides information about what is appropriate.

norm of reciprocity The unwritten rule that people should benefit those who have benefited them.

door-in-the-face technique A strategy that uses reciprocating concessions to influence behavior.

conformity The tendency to do what others do simply because others are doing it.

that *people should benefit those who have benefited them* (Gouldner, 1960). When a friend buys you lunch, you return the favor; if you don't, your friend gets miffed. Indeed, the norm of reciprocity is so strong that waiters and waitresses get bigger tips when they give customers a piece of candy along with the bill because customers feel obligated to do "a little extra" for those who have done "a little extra" for them (Strohmetz et al., 2002).

The norm of reciprocity always involves swapping, but the swapping doesn't always involve favors. The **door-in-the-face technique** is *a strategy that uses reciprocating concessions to influence behavior.* Here's how it works: You ask someone for something more valuable than you really want, you wait for that person to refuse (to "slam the door in your face"), and then you ask the person for what you really want. In one study, researchers asked college students to volunteer to supervise adolescents who were going on a field trip, and only 17% of the students agreed. But when the researchers first asked students to commit to spending 2 hours per week for 2 years working at a youth detention center (to which every one of the students said "no") and *then* asked them if they'd be willing to supervise the field trip, 50% of the students agreed (Cialdini et al., 1975). Why? The norm of reciprocity. The researchers began by asking for a large favor, which the student refused. Then the researchers made a concession by asking for a smaller favor. Because the researchers made a concession, the norm of reciprocity demanded that the student make one too—and half of them did!

On average, your risk of becoming obese increases by ...

... 57% if someone you consider a friend becomes obese.

... 171% if a very close friend becomes obese.

... 100% if you are a man and your male friend becomes obese.

... 38% if you are a woman and your female friend becomes obese.

... 37% if your spouse becomes obese.

... 40% if one of your siblings becomes obese.

... 67% if you are a woman and your sister becomes obese.

... 44% if you are a man and your brother becomes obese.

©FRANCIS DEAN/DEAN PICTURES/THE IMAGE WORKS

▲ Figure **12.9** **The Perils of Connection** Other people's behavior defines what's "normal," which is one of the reasons why obesity "spreads" through social networks (Christakis & Fowler, 2007).

Source: Analysis of 12,067 participants in the Framingham Heart Study from 1971 to 2003 James Abundis/Globe Staff

Conformity

People can influence us by invoking familiar norms. But if you've ever found yourself sneaking a peek at the diner next to you, hoping to discover whether the little fork is supposed to be used for the shrimp or the salad, then you know that other people

? Why do we do what we see other people doing?

can also influence us by defining *new* norms in ambiguous, confusing, or novel situations. **Conformity** is *the tendency to do what others do simply because others are doing it.*

In a classic study, participants sat in a room with seven other people who appeared to be ordinary participants but who were actually actors (Asch, 1951, 1956). An experimenter explained that the participants would be shown cards with three printed lines and that their job was simply to say which of the three lines matched a "standard line" that was printed on another card (**FIGURE 12.10**). The experimenter held up a card and then asked each person to answer in turn. The real participant was among the last to be called on. Everything was normal on the first two trials, but on the third trial, something odd happened: The actors all began giving the same wrong answer! What did the real participants do? Seventy-five percent of them conformed and announced the wrong answer on at least one trial. Subsequent research has shown that these participants didn't actually misperceive the length of the lines but were instead succumbing to normative influence (Asch, 1955; Nemeth & Chiles, 1988). Giving the wrong answer was apparently the right thing to do, and so participants did it.

▼ Figure **12.10** **Asch's Conformity Study** If you were asked which of the lines on the right—A, B, or C—matches the standard line on the left, what would you say? Research on conformity suggests that your answer would depend, in part, on how other people in the room answered the same question.

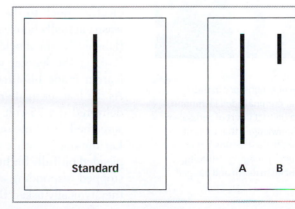

Standard

A B C

The perplexed research participant (center), flanked by confederates (who are "in" on the experiment), is on the verge of conformity in one of Solomon Asch's line-judging experiments.

▲ Figure **12.11** **Normative Influence at Work**

The behavior of others can tell us what is proper, appropriate, expected, and accepted—in other words, it can define a norm—and once a norm is defined, we feel obliged to honor it. When the Sacramento Municipal Utility District randomly selected 35,000 customers and sent them electric bills showing how their energy consumption compared with that of their neighbors (see **FIGURE 12.11**), consumption fell by 2% (Kaufman, 2009). Clearly, normative influence can be a force for good.

Obedience

In most situations there are a few people whom we all recognize as having special authority both to define the norms and to enforce them. The usher at a movie theater may be an underpaid high school student who isn't allowed to drink, drive, vote, or stay up past 10:00 p.m. on a school night, but in the context of the theater, the usher is the authority. So when the usher asks you to take your feet off the seat in front of you, you obey. **Obedience** is *the tendency to do what powerful people tell us to do.*

Why do we obey powerful people? Well, yes, sometimes they have guns. But while powerful people are often capable of rewarding and punishing us, research shows that much of their influence is *normative* (Tyler, 1990). Psychologist Stanley Milgram (1963) demonstrated this in one of psychology's most infamous experiments. The participants in this experiment met a middle-aged man who was introduced as another participant but who was actually a trained actor. An experimenter in a lab coat explained that the participant would play the role of *teacher* and the actor would play the role of *learner*. The teacher and learner would sit in different rooms, the teacher would read words to the learner over a microphone, and the learner would then repeat the words back to the teacher. If the learner made a mistake, the teacher would press a button that delivered an electric shock to the learner (**FIGURE 12.12**). The shock-generating machine (which wasn't actually hooked up, of course) offered 30 levels of shock, ranging from 15 volts (labeled "slight shock") to 450 volts (labeled "Danger: severe shock").

? Why do we do what others tell us?

After the learner was strapped into his chair, the experiment began. When the learner made his first mistake, the participant dutifully delivered a 15-volt shock. As the learner made more mistakes, he received more shocks. When the participant delivered the 75-volt shock, the learner cried out in pain. At 150 volts, the learner screamed, "Get me out of here. I told you I have heart trouble . . . I refuse to go on. Let me out!" With every shock, the learner's screams become more agonized as he pleaded pitifully for his freedom. Then, after receiving the 330-volt shock, the learner stopped responding altogether. Participants were naturally upset by all of this, and they typically asked the experimenter to stop the experiment. But the experimenter

Is this the face of a monster? In this photo, Nazi war criminal Adolf Eichmann sits before the District Court of Jerusalem. Eichmann acknowledged that he sent millions of Jews to their deaths but argued that he was merely obeying authority. He was sentenced to death and hanged in 1962.

◄ Figure **12.12** **Milgram's Obedience Studies** The learner (left) being hooked up to the shock generator (right) that was used in Stanley Milgram's obedience studies.

simply replied, "You have no choice; you must go on." The experimenter never threatened the participant with punishment of any kind. Rather, he just stood there with his clipboard in hand and calmly instructed the participant to continue. What did the participants do? Eighty percent of the participants continued to shock the learner even after he screamed, complained, pleaded, and then fell silent. And 62% went all the way, delivering the highest possible voltage. Although Milgram's study was conducted half a century ago, a recent replication revealed about the same rate of obedience (Burger, 2009).

Would normal people electrocute a stranger just because some guy in a lab coat told them to? The answer, it seems, is "yes"—as long as *normal* means being sensitive to social norms. The participants in this experiment knew that hurting others is *often* wrong but not *always* wrong: Doctors give painful injections, and teachers give painful exams. There are many situations in which it is permissible—and even desirable—to cause someone to suffer in the service of a higher goal. The experimenter's calm demeanor and persistent instruction suggested that he, not the participant, knew what was appropriate in this particular situation, so the participant did as ordered.

The Accuracy Motive: Right Is Better Than Wrong

When you are hungry, you open the refrigerator and grab an apple because you know that apples (1) taste good and (2) are in the refrigerator. This action, like most actions, relies on both an **attitude,** which is *an enduring positive or negative evaluation of an object or event,* and a **belief,** which is *an enduring piece of knowledge about an object or event.* In a sense, our attitudes tell us what we should do ("Eat an apple") and our beliefs tell us how to do it ("Start by opening the fridge"). If our attitudes or beliefs are inaccurate—that is, if we can't tell good from bad or right from wrong—then our actions are likely to be fruitless. Because we rely so much on our attitudes and beliefs, it isn't surprising that we are motivated to have the right ones. And that motivation leaves us vulnerable to social influence.

Informational Influence

If everyone in the shopping mall suddenly ran screaming for the exit, you'd probably join them—not because you were afraid that they would otherwise disapprove of you, but because their behavior would suggest to you that there was something worth running from. **Informational influence** occurs when *another person's behavior provides information about what is good or right.* You can observe the power of informational influence yourself just by standing in the middle of the sidewalk, tilting back your head, and staring at the top of a tall building. Research shows that within just a few minutes, other people will stop and stare too (Milgram, Bickman, & Berkowitz,

> **How do informational and normative influence differ?**

obedience The tendency to do what powerful people tell us to do.

attitude An enduring positive or negative evaluation of an object or event.

belief An enduring piece of knowledge about an object or event.

informational influence A phenomenon that occurs when a person's behavior provides information about what is good or right.

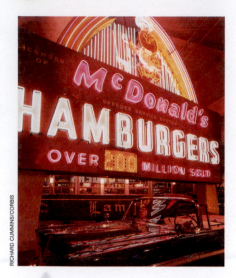

Is McDonald's trying to keep track of sales from the parking lot? Probably not. Rather, it wants you to know that other people are buying its hamburgers, which suggests that they are worth buying, which suggests that you just might want to stop and have one yourself right about now.

1969). Why? They will assume that if you are looking, then there must be something worth looking at.

You are the constant target of informational influence. Advertisements that refer to soft drinks as "popular" or books as "best sellers" are reminding you that other people are buying these particular sodas and novels, which suggests that they know something you don't and that you'd be wise to follow their example. Situation comedies provide "laugh tracks" because the producers know that when you hear other people laughing, you will mindlessly assume that something must be funny (Nosanchuk & Lightstone, 1974). In short, the world is full of objects and events that we know little about, and we can often cure our ignorance by paying attention to the way in which others are acting toward them. Alas, the very thing that makes us open to information leaves us open to manipulation as well.

Persuasion

When the next presidential election rolls around, two things will happen. First, the candidates will say that they intend to win your vote by making arguments that focus on the issues. Second, the candidates will then avoid arguments, ignore issues, and attempt to win your vote with a variety of cheap tricks. What the candidates promise to do and what they actually do reflect two basic forms of **persuasion,** which occurs when *a person's attitudes or beliefs are influenced by a communication from another person* (Albarracín & Vargas, 2010; Petty & Wegener, 1998). The

? When is it more effective to appeal to reason or to emotion?

candidates will promise to engage in **systematic persuasion,** which refers to *the process by which attitudes or beliefs are changed by appeals to reason,* but they will spend most of their time and money engaged in **heuristic persuasion,** which refers to *the process by which attitudes or beliefs are changed by appeals to habit or emotion* (Chaiken, 1980; Petty & Cacioppo, 1986). (*Heuristics* are simple shortcuts or "rules of thumb.") Which form of persuasion will be more effective depends on whether the person is willing and able to weigh evidence and analyze arguments.

For example, in one study, university students heard a speech that contained either strong or weak arguments in favor of instituting comprehensive exams at their school (Petty, Cacioppo, & Goldman, 1981). Some students were told that the speaker was a Princeton University professor, and others were told that the speaker was a high school student—a bit of information that could be used as a shortcut to decide whether to believe the speech. Some students were told that their university was considering implementing these exams right away, motivating them to analyze the evidence; other students were told that their university was considering implementing these exams in 10 years, which gave them less motivation to analyze the evidence (because they'd presumably be long gone by the time the exams were given). When students were motivated to analyze the evidence, they were systematically persuaded—that is, their attitudes and beliefs were influenced by the strength of the arguments but not by the status of the speaker. But when students were not motivated to analyze the evidence, they were heuristically persuaded—that is, their attitudes and beliefs were influenced by the status of the speaker but not by the strength of the arguments.

Because cars are relatively expensive, people are motivated to process information about them and are therefore persuaded by facts. Because shoes are relatively inexpensive, people are not motivated to process information about them and are therefore persuaded by celebrity endorsements.

To crash with a Volvo is extremely safe.

If you're sitting in a Saab.

Saab 9-5. Sweden's safest car. In real life.

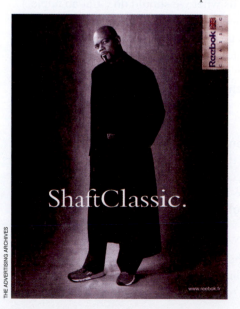

ShaftClassic.

www.reebok.fr

Consistency

If a friend told you that rabbits had just staged a coup in Antarctica and were halting all carrot exports, you probably wouldn't Google it to see if it was true. You'd know right away that your friend was joking because the statement is logically inconsistent with other things that you know are true—for example, that Antarctica does not export carrots. People evaluate the accuracy of new beliefs by assessing their *consistency* with old beliefs, and although this is not a foolproof method for determining whether something is true, it provides a pretty good approximation. We are motivated to be accurate, and because consistency is a rough measure of accuracy, we are motivated to be consistent as well (Cialdini, Trost, & Newsom, 1995).

Why do we care about being consistent?

That motivation leaves us vulnerable to social influence. For example, the **foot-in-the-door** technique is *a technique that involves a small request followed by a larger request* (Burger, 1999). In one study (Freedman & Fraser, 1966), experimenters went to a neighborhood and knocked on doors to see if they could convince homeowners to agree to have a big ugly "Drive Carefully" sign installed in their front yards. One group of homeowners was simply asked to install the sign, and only 17% said yes. A second group of homeowners was first asked to sign a petition urging the state legislature to promote safe driving (which almost all agreed to do) and was *then* asked to install the ugly sign. And 55% said yes! Why would homeowners be more likely to grant two requests than one?

Just imagine how the homeowners in the second group felt. They had already signed a petition stating that they thought safe driving was important, and yet they knew they didn't want to install an ugly sign in their front yards. As they wrestled with this inconsistency, they probably began to experience a feeling called **cognitive dissonance,** which is *an unpleasant state that arises when a person recognizes the inconsistency of his or her actions, attitudes, or beliefs* (Festinger, 1957). When people experience cognitive dissonance, they naturally try to alleviate it, and one way to alleviate cognitive dissonance is to change one's actions, attitudes, or beliefs in order to restore consistency among them (Aronson, 1969; Cooper & Fazio, 1984). For the homeowners, changing their minds and allowing the sign to be installed in their yards did precisely that.

We are motivated to be consistent, but there are inevitably times when we just can't—for example, when we tell a friend that her new hairstyle is "daring" when it actually resembles a wet skunk after an unfortunate encounter with a snowblower. Why don't we experience cognitive dissonance under such circumstances and come

persuasion A phenomenon that occurs when a person's attitudes or beliefs are influenced by a communication from another person.

systematic persuasion The process by which attitudes or beliefs are changed by appeals to reason.

heuristic persuasion The process by which attitudes or beliefs are changed by appeals to habit or emotion.

foot-in-the-door technique A technique that involves a small request followed by a larger request.

cognitive dissonance An unpleasant state that arises when a person recognizes the inconsistency of his or her actions, attitudes, or beliefs.

DILBERT

to believe our own lies? Because while telling a friend that her hairstyle is daring is inconsistent with the belief that her hairstyle is hideous, it is perfectly consistent with the belief that one should be nice to one's friends. When small inconsistencies are *justified* by large consistencies, cognitive dissonance is reduced.

SUMMARY QUIZ [12.2]

1. The _____ motive describes how people are motivated to experience pleasure and to avoid experiencing pain.
   a. emotional   b. accuracy   c. approval   d. hedonic

2. The tendency to do what authorities tell us to do simply because they do so is known as
   a. persuasion.   b. obedience.   c. conformity.   d. the self-fulfilling prophecy.

3. Andrea and Jeff had to wait in line for over an hour to get into an exclusive restaurant. Despite being served a mediocre meal, they glowingly praised the restaurant to their friends. This behavior was probably a result of
   a. conformity.   c. perceptual confirmation.
   b. the norm of reciprocity.   d. cognitive dissonance.

Social Cognition: Understanding People

Of the millions of objects you might encounter, other human beings are the most important. **Social cognition** is *the process by which people come to understand others,* and you do it all day long. Whether you know it or not, your brain is constantly making inferences about others people's thoughts and feelings, beliefs and desires, abilities and aspirations, intentions, needs, and characters. It bases these inferences on two kinds of information: the categories to which people belong and the things they do and say.

Stereotyping: Drawing Inferences From Categories

You'll recall from Chapter 9 that categorization is the process by which people identify a stimulus as a member of a class of related stimuli. Once we have identified a novel stimulus as a member of a category ("That's a textbook"), we can then use our knowledge of the category to make educated guesses about the properties of the novel stimulus ("It's probably expensive") and act accordingly ("I think I'll download it illegally").

Why are stereotypes useful?

What we do with textbooks we also do with people. No, not the illegal downloading part. The educated guessing part. **Stereotyping** is *the process by which we draw inferences about others based on knowledge of the categories to which they belong.* The moment we categorize a person as an adult, a male, a baseball player, and a Russian, we can use our knowledge of those categories to make some educated guesses about him—for example, that he shaves his face but not his legs, that he understands the infield fly rule, and that he knows more about vodka than we do. When we offer children candy instead of cigarettes or ask gas station attendants for directions instead of dating advice, we are making inferences about people whom we have never met before based solely on their category membership. As these examples suggest, stereotyping is a very useful process (Allport, 1954). Yet ever since the word was coined in 1936, it has had a distasteful connotation. Why? Because stereotyping is a useful process that can often produce harmful results, and it does so because stereotypes tend to have four properties: They are inaccurate, overused, self-perpetuating, and automatic.

social cognition The processes by which people come to understand others.

stereotyping The process by which people draw inferences about others based on their knowledge of the categories to which others belong.

1. Stereotypes Can Be Inaccurate

The inferences we draw about individuals are only as accurate as our stereotypes about the categories to which they belong. Although there was no evidence to indicate that Jews were especially materialistic or that African Americans were especially lazy, American college students held such beliefs for most of the last century (Gilbert, 1951; Karlins, Coffman, & Walters, 1969; Katz & Braly, 1933). They weren't born holding these beliefs, so how did they acquire them? There are only two ways to acquire a belief about anything: to see for yourself or to take somebody else's word for it. In fact, most of what we know about the members of human categories is hearsay—stuff we picked up from friends and uncles, from novels and newspapers, from jokes and movies and late-night television. Many of the people who believe stereotypes about Jews or African Americans have never actually met someone who is Jewish or African American, and their beliefs are a result of listening too closely to what others told them. In the process of inheriting the wisdom of our culture, it is inevitable that we also will inherit its ignorance too.

2. Stereotypes Can Be Overused

Because all thumbtacks are pretty much alike, our beliefs about thumbtacks ("small, cheap, painful when chewed") are quite useful, and we will rarely be mistaken if we generalize from one thumbtack to another. Human categories, however, are so variable that our stereotypes may offer only the vaguest of clues about the individuals who populate those categories. You probably believe that men have greater upper body strength than women do, and this belief is right *on average*. But the upper body strength of individuals *within* each of these categories is so varied that you cannot easily predict how much weight a particular person can lift simply by knowing that person's gender. The inherent variability of human categories makes stereotypes much less useful than they might otherwise be.

Alas, we don't always recognize this because the mere act of categorizing a stimulus tends to warp our perceptions of that category's variability.

? How does categorization warp perception?

For instance, we all identify colors as members of categories such as *blue* or *green*, and this leads us to overestimate the similarity of colors that share a category label and to underestimate the similarity of colors that do not. That's why we see discrete *bands* of color when we look at rainbows, which are actually a smooth continuum of colors (see **FIGURE 12.13** and the Hot Science box). That's also why we tend to underestimate the distance between cities that are in the same country, such as Memphis and Pierre, and overestimate the distance between cities that are in different countries, such as Memphis and Toronto (Burris & Branscombe, 2005). What's true of

Stereotypes can be inaccurate. Shlomo Koenig does not fit most people's stereotype of a police officer or a rabbi, but he is both.

▼ Figure **12.13** **Perceiving Categories** Categorization can influence how we see colors and how we estimate distances.

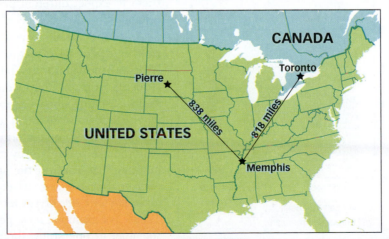

HOT SCIENCE

The Color of Expectations

Psychologists often say that people see what they expect to see, and research shows that this is true in the most literal sense (Hansen et al., 2006). Subjects were shown pictures of different-colored objects on a computer display and were asked to adjust the color on the display until the object appeared gray. When the object was a yellow blob, subjects did this quite well; but when the object was a yellow banana, they went

beyond gray and made it slightly blue (see the accompanying figure). Why? Because even after the banana had objectively become gray, subjects continued to see it as slightly yellow because they expected a banana to be yellow; thus they kept adjusting the knob toward blue. Psychologists have long known that expectations can color our perceptions of people, but apparently they can color our perceptions of color as well.

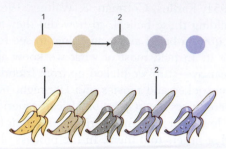

▲ When trying to make a yellow object look gray, subjects adjusted from 1 to 2.

colors and distances is true of people as well. The mere act of categorizing people as Blacks or Whites, Jews or Gentiles, artists or accountants, can cause us to underestimate the variability within those categories ("All artists are wacky") and to overestimate the variability between them ("Artists are much wackier than accountants"). When we underestimate the variability of a human category, we overestimate how useful our stereotypes can be.

3. Stereotypes Can Be Self-Perpetuating

When we meet a man who likes ballet more than football or a senior citizen who likes hip-hop more than easy-listening, why don't we recognize that our stereotypes are inaccurate? Stereotypes are a bit like viruses: Once they take up residence inside us, they perpetuate themselves and resist even our most concerted efforts to eradicate them. Stereotypes are self-perpetuating for three reasons. First, *we have a tendency to see what we expect to see*. In one study, participants listening to a radio broadcast of a basketball game were asked to

? **In what way is a stereotype like a virus?**

evaluate the performance of one of the players. Those participants who had previously been led to believe that the player was African American thought he had exhibited more athletic ability than those who had been led to believe that he was White (Stone, Perry, & Darley, 1997). Participants' stereotypes led them to expect different performances from athletes of different racial origins—and they perceived just what they expected.

A second reason why stereotypes are self-perpetuating is that *we can cause what we expect to see*. In one study (Steele & Aronson, 1995), African American and White students were given a test, and half the students in each group were asked to list their race at the top of the exam. Students who were not asked to list their race performed well; but when students were asked to list their races, African American students became anxious and performed poorly (**FIGURE 12.14**). Stereotypes perpetuate themselves in part by causing the stereotyped individual to behave in ways that confirm the stereotype. Finally, stereotypes can be self-perpetuating because, *when faced with evidence to the contrary, we tend to modify our stereotypes rather than abandon them* (Weber & Crocker, 1983). For example, most people believe that public relations agents are sociable; in one study, though, when participants learned about a PR

▼ Figure 12.14 **Stereotype Threat** When asked to indicate their race before starting a test, African American students perform more poorly than their SAT scores suggest they should.

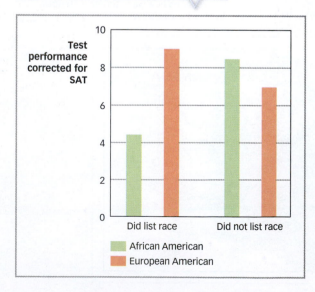

Test performance corrected for SAT

- African American
- European American

agent who was extremely unsociable, they tended to consider him as an "exception to the rule" and thereby preserve their stereotypes about PR agents in general (Kunda & Oleson, 1997).

4. Stereotyping Can Be Automatic

If stereotypes are inaccurate and self-perpetuating, then why don't we just stop using them? The answer is that stereotyping happens *unconsciously* (which means that we don't always know we are doing it) and *automatically* (which means that we often cannot avoid doing it them even when we try) (Banaji & Heiphetz, 2010; Greenwald, McGhee, & Schwartz, 1998; Greenwald & Nosek, 2001).

? Can we decide not to stereotype?

For example, in one study, photos of Black or White men holding guns or cameras were flashed on a computer screen for less than 1 second each. Participants earned money by pressing a button labeled "shoot" whenever the man on the screen was holding a gun but lost money if they shot a man holding a camera. The participants made some mistakes, of course, but the kinds of mistakes they made were quite disturbing: Participants were more likely to shoot a man holding a camera when he was Black and less likely to shoot a man holding a gun when he was White (Correll et al., 2002). Although the photos appeared on the screen so quickly that participants did not have enough time to consciously consult their stereotypes, those stereotypes worked unconsciously, causing them to mistake a camera for a gun when it was in the hands of a Black man and a gun for a camera when it was in the hands of a White man. Interestingly, Black participants were just as likely to make this pattern of errors as White participants.

Although stereotyping is unconscious and automatic, it is not inevitable (Blair, 2002; Kawakami et al., 2000; Milne & Grafman, 2001; Rudman, Ashmore, & Gary, 2001). For instance, police officers who receive special training before participating in the "camera or gun" experiment described earlier do not show the same biases that ordinary people do (Correll et al., 2007). Like ordinary people, they take a few milliseconds longer to decide not to shoot a Black man than a White man, indicating that stereotypes influenced their thinking. But unlike ordinary people, they don't actually *shoot* Black men more often than White men, indicating that they have learned how to keep their stereotypes from influencing their behavior.

In 2007, Reuters news photographer Namir Noor-Eldeen was shot to death in Iraq by American soldiers in a helicopter who mistook his camera for a weapon. Would they have made the same mistake if Noor-Eldeen had been blonde or female?

Attribution: Drawing Inferences From Actions

In 1963, Dr. Martin Luther King Jr. gave a speech in which he described his vision for America: "I have a dream that my four children will one day live in a nation where they will not be judged by the color of their skin but by the content of their character." Research on stereotyping demonstrates that Dr. King's concerns were well justified. We do indeed judge others by the color of their skin—as well as by their gender, nationality, religion, age, and occupation—and in so doing, we sometimes make tragic errors. But are we any better at judging people by the content of their character? If we could "turn off" our stereotypes and treat each person as an individual, would we judge these individuals accurately?

Not necessarily. Treating a person as an individual means judging that person by his or her own words and deeds. This is more difficult than it sounds because the relationship between what a person *is* and what a person *says or does* is not always straightforward. An honest person may lie to save a friend from embarrassment, and a dishonest person may tell the truth to bolster her credibility. Happy people have

"For God's sake, think! Why is he being so nice to you?"

some rotten days, polite people can be rude in traffic, and people who despise us can be flattering when they need a favor. In short, people's behavior sometimes tells us about the kind of people they are, but sometimes it simply tells us about the kind of situation they happen to be in.

To understand people, we need to know not only what they did but also why they did it. Is the batter who hit the home run a talented slugger, or was the wind blowing in just the right direction? Is the politician who gave the pro-life speech really opposed to abortion, or was she just trying to win the conservative vote? When we answer questions such as these, we are making **attributions,** which are *inferences about the causes of people's behaviors* (Epley & Waytz, 2010; Gilbert, 1998). We make *situational attributions* when we decide that a person's behavior was caused by some temporary aspect of the situation in which it happened ("He was lucky that the wind carried the ball into the stands"), and we make *dispositional attributions* when we decide that a person's behavior was caused by his or her relatively enduring tendency to think, feel, or act in a particular way ("He's got a great eye and a powerful swing").

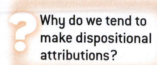

? Why do we tend to make dispositional attributions?

As sensible as this seems, research suggests that people don't always make attributions correctly. The **correspondence bias** is *the tendency to make a dispositional attribution even when a person's behavior was caused by the situation* (Gilbert & Malone, 1995; Jones & Harris, 1967; Ross, 1977). This bias is so common that it is sometimes called the *fundamental attribution error.* For example, volunteers in one experiment played a trivia game in which one participant acted as the "quizmaster" and made up a list of unusual questions, another participant acted as the "contestant" and tried to answer those questions, and a third participant acted as the "observer" and simply watched the game. The quizmasters tended to ask tricky questions based on their own idiosyncratic knowledge, and contestants were generally unable to answer them. After watching the game, the observers were asked to decide how knowledgeable the quizmaster and the contestant were. Although the quizmasters had asked good questions and the contestants had given bad answers, it should have been clear to the observers that all this asking and answering was a product of the roles they had been assigned to play and that the contestant would have asked equally good questions and the quizmaster would have given equally bad answers had their roles been reversed. And yet observers tended to rate the quizmaster as more knowledgeable than the contestant (Ross, Amabile, & Steinmetz, 1977) and were more likely to choose the quizmaster as their own partner in an upcoming game (Quattrone, 1982). Even when we know that a successful athlete had a home field advantage or that a successful entrepreneur had family connections, we tend to attribute their success to talent and tenacity.

Although the correspondence bias is quite robust, it is more likely to occur under some circumstances than others (Choi, Nisbett, & Norenzayan, 1999; D'Agostino & Fincher-Kiefer, 1992; Fein, Hilton, & Miller, 1990). For example, we are more prone to correspondence bias when judging other people's behavior than when judging our own. The **actor-observer effect** is *the tendency to make situational attributions for our own behaviors while making dispositional attributions for the identical behavior of others* (Jones & Nisbett, 1972). When college students are asked to explain why they and their friends chose their majors, they tend to explain their own choices in terms of situations ("I chose economics because my parents told me I have to support myself as soon as I'm done with

When passing a homeless man on the street, do you tend to make situational attributions ("He's probably just down on his luck.") or dispositional attributions ("He's probably too lazy to get a job.")?

college") and their friends' choices in terms of dispositions ("Norma chose economics because she's materialistic") (Nisbett et al., 1973). The actor-observer effect occurs because people typically have more information about the situations that caused their own behavior than about the situations that caused other people's behavior. We can remember getting the please-major-in-something-practical lecture from our parents, but we weren't at Norma's house to see her get the same lecture. As observers, we are naturally focused on another person's behavior, but as actors, we are focused on the situations in which our behavior occurs. Indeed, when people are shown videotapes of their conversations that allow them to see themselves from their partner's point of view, they tend to make dispositional attributions for their own behavior and situational attributions for their partner's (Storms, 1973ok; Taylor & Fiske, 1975).

attribution An inference about the cause of a person's behavior.

correspondence bias The tendency to make a dispositional attribution even when a person's behavior was caused by the situation.

actor-observer effect The tendency to make situational attributions for our own behaviors while making dispositional attributions for the identical behavior of others.

SUMMARY QUIZ [12.3]

1. What is the process by which people come to understand others?
   a. dispositional attribution
   b. the accuracy motive
   c. social cognition
   d. cognitive dissonance

2. A common occupational stereotype is that lawyers are manipulative. Most people who subscribe to this stereotype
   a. believe that the stereotype applies to *all* lawyers.
   b. believe that the stereotype accurately applies to just a small percentage of lawyers.
   c. believe that lawyers are more likely than others to have this characteristic.
   d. would not be likely to misperceive lawyers when they actually meet.

3. The tendency to make a dispositional attribution even when a person's behavior was caused by the situation is referred to as
   a. comparison leveling.
   b. stereotyping.
   c. covariation.
   d. correspondence bias.

Where Do You Stand?

The Model Employee

When Elizabeth Nill walks into an Abercrombie & Fitch store, she is usually offered a job. "Every time this happens my little sister says 'Not again'" (quoted in Greenhouse, 2003). Is it her years of retail experience or her keen eye for fashion? Nope. Elizabeth is tall, slender, young, and gorgeous—and according to a former assistant store manager, it is the company's policy to recruit such people to the sales force. "We were supposed to approach someone in the mall who we think will look attractive in our store. If that person said, 'I never worked in retailing before,' we said: 'Who cares? We'll hire you.' But if someone came in who had lots of retail experience and not a pretty face, we were told not to hire them at all."

Recruiting people on the basis of their looks seems more than a little unfair (Rhode, 2010). After all, not everyone is blessed with flawless skin and shiny hair. Retailers can't discriminate against people on the basis of race or religion, so why should they be allowed to discriminate on the basis of physical attractiveness? Retailers respond by noting that they didn't invent human nature and that customers simply prefer to shop at stores staffed by attractive people. As one shopper admitted, "If you see an attractive person working in the store wearing Abercrombie clothes, it makes you want to wear it too." Most people think that businesses have the right to hire the person for the job, and if a salesperson's job is to sell clothing, then attractive people may do the job best.

Should businesses be required to disregard a person's physical attractiveness when making hiring decisions, or do they have a right to give customers what they want? Where do you stand?

Chapter Review

Social Behavior: Interacting with People

► Survival and reproduction require scarce resources, and aggression and cooperation are two ways to get them.

► Aggression often results from negative affect. The likelihood that people will aggress when they feel negative affect is determined both by biological factors (such as testosterone level) and cultural factors.

► Cooperation is beneficial but risky, and one strategy for reducing its risks is to form groups whose members are biased in favor of one another. Unfortunately, groups often show prejudice and discrimination toward those who are not members, and they may even take extreme actions that no individual member would take alone.

► Human beings can behave altruistically, though behaviors that appear to be altruistic sometimes have hidden benefits for the person who does them.

► Attraction is determined by situational factors (such as proximity), physical factors (such as symmetry), and psychological factors (such as similarity).

► Human reproduction usually occurs within the context of a long-term relationship. People weigh the costs and benefits of their relationships and tend to dissolve them when they think they can or should do better, when they and their partners

have very different cost-benefit ratios, or when they have little invested in the relationship.

Social Influence: Controlling People

► People are motivated to experience pleasure and avoid pain (the hedonic motive) and thus can be influenced by rewards and punishments, though these can sometimes backfire.

► People are motivated to attain the approval of others (the approval motive) and thus can be influenced by social norms, such as the norm of reciprocity.

► People are motivated to know what is true (the accuracy motive) and thus can be influenced by other people's behaviors and communications. This motivation also causes them to seek consistency among their attitudes, beliefs, and actions.

Social Cognition: Understanding People

► People make inferences about others based on the categories to which the others people belong (stereotyping). This method can lead them to misjudge others because stereotypes can be inaccurate, overused, self-perpetuating, unconscious, and automatic.

► People make inferences about others based on their behaviors. This method can lead them to misjudge others because people tend to attribute actions to dispositions even when they should attribute them to situations.

KEY TERMS

social psychology (p. 376)
aggression (p. 376)
frustration-aggression hypothesis (p. 377)
cooperation (p. 379)
group (p. 379)
prejudice (p. 379)
discrimination (p. 379)
deindividuation (p. 380)

diffusion of responsibility (p. 380)
altruism (p. 380)
kin selection (p. 381)
reciprocal altruism (p. 381)
passionate love (p. 387)
companionate love (p. 387)
social exchange (p. 387)
social influence (p. 389)
norms (p. 390)

normative influence (p. 390)
norm of reciprocity (p. 390)
door-in-the-face technique (p. 391)
conformity (p. 391)
obedience (p. 392)
attitude (p. 393)
belief (p. 393)
informational influence (p. 393)
persuasion (p. 394)

systematic persuasion (p. 394)
heuristic persuasion (p. 394)
foot-in-the-door technique (p. 395)
cognitive dissonance (p. 395)
social cognition (p. 396)
stereotyping (p. 396)
attribution (p. 400)
correspondence bias (p. 400)
actor-observer effect (p. 400)

CHANGING MINDS

1. One of the senators from your state is supporting a bill that would impose heavy fines on aggressive drivers who cut off others in traffic, run red lights, and generally engage in dangerous driving. You're discussing this idea with one of your classmates, who thinks it's a good idea. "We read in the chapter that people can become less aggressive. If we punish aggression, then by the rules of conditioning, the frequency of the punished behaviors should decline." Your classmate has a point, but how might the planned laws backfire? What other policies might be suggested, based on the principles of social psychology, to promote safe driving?

2. One of your friends is outgoing and funny as well as a star athlete on the women's basketball team. She has started to date a man who is introverted and prefers playing computer games to attending parties. When you tease her about the contrast in personalities, she replies, "Well, opposites attract." Is your friend correct? Why or why not?

3. In late 2011, a federal judge ruled that the New York City Fire Department had long pursued discriminatory hiring practices, resulting in systematic exclusion of minorities from the force – which at the time included almost 97% Whites although the city's population is about 25% Black. Your roommate reads about the case and scoffs. "People are always so quick to claim racism. And of course there are still a few racist people out there. But the fact is, ever since the 1960s, we've had equal rights in this country, and racism on a large scale just doesn't exist in the United States." What would you tell your friend about racism in the United States? What explanations could you give for why discrimination has been such a difficult problem to eradicate from human culture?

4. One of your friends has a very . . . unique fashion sense, always wearing clothes that are just a little bit different from what everyone else is wearing—from his neon orange track shoes to his battered fedora. Most of the time, you appreciate your friend for his quirky personality. One day, he tells you that he chooses his clothes carefully to make a fashion statement. "Most people follow the crowd," he announces. "I don't. I'm an individual, and I make my own choices, without influence from anyone else." Despite your friend's assertion, he's subject to social influence just like all other human beings. What

examples might you provide your friend to show how a college student is subject to the hedonic motive, the approval motive, and the accuracy motive?

5. A classmate is shaken after learning about the Milgram (1963) study, in which participants were willing to obey orders to administer painful electric shocks to another human, even after he begged them to stop. Worse, the Burger (2009) study shows that it wasn't just humans "back then" who were capable of this behavior—modern participants showed virtually identical obedience rates to those in the Milgram study. "It's horrible to think that people are capable of such violence in the name of following orders," she says. "I know that you or I wouldn't behave like that, but it's really scary that so many other people would." Can we each really be sure that we would not, in fact, obey orders in a replication of the Milgram experiment? What type of social influence produces a tendency to obey people in authority even if their orders seem wrong or incorrect?

6. When your family gathers for Thanksgiving, your cousin Mary brings her new fiancé; it's the first time he's met the whole family, and his behavior is a little strained: He talks too much, laughs too loudly, and generally gets under everyone's skin. Later, when you're alone with your mother, she rolls her eyes. "It's hard to imagine Mary wanting to spend the rest of her life married to someone whose personality is as annoying as that." You decide to be more generous because you think your mother might have fallen prey to the correspondence bias. How could you explain the behavior of Mary's fiancé using situational attribution rather than dispositional attribution? Does this excuse the behavior?

CRITICAL THINKING QUESTIONS

1. Both culture and biology can make people more or less likely to respond to negative affect by aggressing. If the president of the United States asked you to come up with three ways to reduce aggression in America, what would you suggest?

2. If you could take a pill that made you completely immune to social influence, would you do it? Would you want others to do it? What would be the benefits and what would be the costs?

3. Stereotypes are natural, essential, and harmful. Even though we can't eliminate them, we might be able to eliminate some of their most harmful effects. How could that be accomplished?

ANSWERS TO SUMMARY QUIZZES

Summary Quiz [12.1] 1. b; 2. d; 3. c; 4. b; 5. c
Summary Quiz [12.2] 1. d; 2. b; 3. d
Summary Quiz [12.3] 1. c; 2. c; 3. d

Need more help? Additional resources are located at the book's free companion website at
www.worthpublishers.com/schacterbrief2e

Psychological Disorders

VIRGINIA WOOLF LEFT HER WALKING STICK on the bank of the river, put a large stone in the pocket of her coat, and made her way into the water. Her body was found 3 weeks later. She had written to her husband: "Dearest, I feel certain I am going mad again. . . . And I shan't recover this time. I begin to hear voices, and I can't concentrate. So I am doing what seems the best thing to do" (quoted in Dally, 1999, p. 182). Thus life ended for the prolific novelist and essayist, a victim of lifelong "breakdowns," with swings in mood between wretched depression and manic excitement.

The madness afflicting Woolf is now known as bipolar disorder. At one extreme were her episodes of depression—sullen, despondent, she was sometimes bedridden for months by her illness. These periods alternated with mania, when, as her husband recounted, "She talked almost without stopping for 2 or 3 days, paying no attention to anyone in the room or anything said to her" (quoted in Dally, 1999, p. 240). She refused to eat, wrote pages of nonsense, and launched tirades of abuse at her husband and her companions. Between these phases, Woolf somehow managed a brilliant literary life, producing nine novels, a play, five volumes of essays, and more than 14 volumes of diaries and letters. In a letter to a friend, she remarked, "As an experience, madness is terrific . . . and not to be sniffed at, and in its lava I still find most of the things I write about" (quoted in Dally, 1999, p. 240). The price that Woolf paid for her genius, of course, was a dear one. Disorders of the mind can create immense pain.

▶ English novelist and critic Virginia Woolf (1882–1941), 1937. Her lifelong affliction with bipolar disorder ended in suicide, but the manic phases of her illness helped to fuel her prolific writing.

THE PRINT COLLECTOR/ALAMY

SYMPTOMS REFLECTING ABNORMALITIES OF THE MIND, CALLED *psychological,* or *mental, disorders,* are hard to define and explain. Psychiatrists and psychologists agree that a psychological disorder is not, say, extreme anxiety before a chemistry test or deep sadness at the break-up of a relationship. To qualify as a mental disorder, thoughts, feelings, and emotions must be persistent, harmful to the person experiencing them, and uncontrollable. About half of Americans will develop some type of mental disorder during the course of their lives (Kessler et al., 2005)—at a substantial cost in health, productivity, and happiness. Data compiled by the Global Burden of Disease study reveal that, after cardiovascular disease, mental disorders are the second-greatest contributor to a loss of years of healthy life (Rodgers et al., 2004). Problems of the head are nearly as great a plague on humanity as problems of the heart.

Psychologists who study mental disorders seek to uncover ways to understand, treat, and prevent such human misery. The study of psychological disorders can be unsettling because you may well see yourself mirrored in the various conditions. Like medical stu-

dents who come to worry about their own symptoms with each new disease they examine, students of abnormal psychology can catch their own version of "medical students' disease," noticing personal oddities as they read about the peculiarities of others (Woods, Natterson, & Silverman, 1966). Is your late-night frenzy to finish an assignment a kind of mania? Is your fear of snakes a phobia? Does forgetting where you left your keys qualify you for diagnosis with a dissociative disorder? Please relax. You may not always avoid self-diagnosis, but you're not alone. Studying mental disorders heightens everyone's sensitivity to his or her own eccentricities. In fact, you would be "abnormal" if studying mental disorders *didn't* make you reflect on yourself.

In this chapter, we first consider the question: What is abnormal? Virginia Woolf's bouts of depression and mania and her eventual suicide certainly seem abnormal, but at times, she was fine. The enormously complicated human mind can produce behaviors, thoughts, and emotions that change radically from moment to moment. How do psychologists decide that a particular mind is disordered? We will examine the key factors that must be weighed in making such a decision. We will then focus on several major forms of mental disorder, including anxiety disorders, mood disorders, dissociative disorders, schizophrenia, and personality disorders. As we view each of these problems, we will look at how they can influence the person's thoughts and behaviors and at what is known about their prevalence and their causes.

Identifying Psychological Disorders: What Is Abnormal?

medical model The conceptualization of psychological abnormalities as diseases that, like physical diseases, have biological causes, defined symptoms, and possible cures.

DSM-5 *(Diagnostic and Statistical Manual of Mental Disorders [Fifth Edition].)* A classification system that describes the features used to diagnose each recognized mental disorder and indicates how the disorder can be distinguished from other, similar problems.

The idea of a *psychological disorder* is a relatively recent invention, historically speaking. People who act strangely or report bizarre thoughts or emotions have been known since ancient times, but their difficulties were often interpreted as possession by animal spirits or demons, as enchantment by a witch or shaman, or as God's punishment for wrongdoing. In many societies, including our own, people with psychological disorders have been feared and ridiculed, and they have often been treated as criminals—punished, imprisoned, or put to death for their "crime" of deviating from the normal.

Over the past 200 years, these ways of looking at psychological abnormalities have largely been replaced in industrialized areas of the world by a **medical model,** *the conceptualization of psychological disorders as diseases that, like physical diseases, have* *biological causes, defined symptoms, and possible cures.* Treating abnormal behavior in the way we treat illness suggests that a first step is to determine the nature of the problem through *diagnosis.* In diagnosis, clinicians seek to determine the nature of the patient's mental disease by assessing *symptoms*—behaviors, thoughts, and emotions suggestive of an underlying abnormal *syndrome,* a coherent cluster of symptoms usually due to a single cause. So, for example, just as a fever, sniffles, and cough are symptoms of a cold, Virginia Woolf's extreme moods, alternating between despondency and wild enthusiasm, can be seen as symptoms of her bipolar disorder.

> **?** **What's the first step in helping someone with a psychological disorder?**

As useful as the medical model can be, it should nonetheless be viewed with some skepticism. Every action or thought suggestive of abnormality cannot be traced to an underlying disease (American Psychiatric Association, 2000; Keisler, 1999; Persons, 1986). And, as you will discover in Chapter 14, some of the most successful treatments for abnormal behavior or thought focus on simply eliminating the behavior or thought; no effort is made to treat the root "syndrome." Nevertheless, the medical model is still a vast improvement over older alternatives—such as viewing psychological disorders as the work of witchcraft or as punishment for sin. Viewing psychological disorders as medical problems reminds us that people who are suffering deserve care and treatment, not condemnation.

Classification of Disorders

To facilitate diagnosis, psychologists have generally adopted an approach developed by psychiatrists—physicians concerned with treatment of mental disorders—who use a system for classifying mental disorders. In 1952, in recognition of the need to have a consensual diagnostic system for therapists and researchers, the first version of the *Diagnostic and Statistical Manual of Mental Disorders (DSM)* was published. This provided a common language for talking about disorders, but the diagnostic criteria were still often vague and based on tenuous theoretical assumptions.

The current version of this manual is the *Diagnostic and Statistical Manual of Mental Disorders (Fifth Edition),* or *DSM-5* (American Psychiatric Association, 2013), with a new version which was published in 2013. The **DSM-5** is *a classification system that describes the features used to diagnose each recognized mental disorder and indicates how the disorder can be distinguished from other, similar problems.* Each disorder is named and classified as though it were a distinct illness. The major mental disorders distinguished in the *DSM-5* are shown in **TABLE 13.1.**

Social disorder isn't mental disorder. Violence erupted in Athens in March 2010 as protesters were outraged by government cutbacks made in response to huge budget deficits. Rioting might seem disordered on the surface, but the *DSM-5* definition of mental disorders rules out political dissidence and social deviance.

ARIS MESSINIS/AFP/GETTY IMAGES

A major misconception is the idea that a mental disorder can be defined entirely in terms of deviation from the average, the typical, or "healthy." Yes, people who have mental disorders may behave, think, or experience emotions in unusual ways, but simple departure from the norm can't be the whole picture, or we'd rapidly be diagnosing mental disorders in anyone whose ideas deviate from those around them. And unfortunately, diagnosing people with mental disorders when they do things you don't like is not all that uncommon. Physicians before the Civil War diagnosed escaped slaves with "drapetomania" (Szasz, 1987), and it was only in 1974 that homosexuality was dropped from the list of psychological disorders

> **?** **Why is it difficult to make reliable diagnoses?**

Table 13.1

Main *DSM-5* Categories of Mental Disorders

1. Neurodevelopmental Disorders: These are conditions the begin early in development and cause significant impairments in functioning, such as Intellectual Disability (formerly called "Mental Retardation"), Autism Spectrum Disorder, and Attention-Deficit/Hyperactivity Disorder.

2. Schizophrenia Spectrum and Other Psychotic Disorders: This is a group of disorders characterized by major disturbances in perception, thought, language, emotion, and behavior.

3. Bipolar and Related Disorders: These disorders include major fluctuations in mood — from mania to depression — and also can include psychotic experiences, which is why they are placed between the psychotic and depressive disorders in DSM-5.

4. Depressive Disorders: These are conditions characterized by extreme and persistent periods of depressed mood.

5. Anxiety Disorders: These are disorders characterized by excessive fear and anxiety that are extreme enough to impair a person's functioning, such as panic disorder, generalized anxiety disorder, and specific phobia.

6. Obsessive-Compulsive and Related Disorders: These are conditions characterized by the presence of obsessive thinking followed by compulsive behavior in response to that thinking.

7. Trauma- and Stressor-Related Disorders: These are disorders that develop in response to a traumatic event, such as Post-Traumatic Stress Disorder.

8. Dissociative Disorders: These are conditions characterized by disruptions or discontinuity in consciousness, memory, or identity, such as Dissociative Identity Disorder (formerly called "Multiple Personality Disorder").

9. Somatic Symptom and Related Disorders: These are conditions in which a person experiences bodily symptoms (e.g., pain, fatigue) associated with significant distress or impairment,

10. Feeding and Eating Disorders: These are problems with eating that impair health or functioning, such as Anorexia Nervosa and Bulimia Nervosa.

11. Elimination Disorders: These involve inappropriate elimination of urine or feces (e.g., bed-wetting).

12. Sleep-Wake Disorders: These are problems with the sleep-wake cycle, such as Insomnia, Narcolepsy, and Sleep Apnea.

13. Sexual Dysfunctions: These are problems related to unsatisfactory sexual activity, such as Erectile Disorder and Premature Ejaculation.

14. Gender Dysphoria: This is a single disorder characterized by incongruence between a person's experienced/ expressed gender and assigned gender.

15. Disruptive, Impulse-Control, and Conduct Disorders: These are conditions involving problems controlling emotions and behaviors, such as Conduct Disorder, Intermittent Explosive Disorder, and Kleptomania.

16. Substance-Related and Addictive Disorders: This collection of disorders involves persistent use of substances or some other behavior (e.g., gambling) despite the fact that it leads to significant problems.

17. Neurocognitive Disorders: These are disorders of thinking caused by conditions such as Alzheimer's Disease or Traumatic Brain Injury.

18. Personality Disorders: These are enduring patterns of thinking, feeling, and behaving that lead to significant life problems.

19. Paraphilic Disorders: These are conditions characterized by inappropriate sexual activity, such as Pedophilic Disorder.

20. Other Mental Disorders: This is a residual category for conditions that do not fit into one of the above categories but are associated with significant distress or impairment, such as an unspecified mental disorder due to a medical condition.

21. Medication-Induced Movement Disorders and Other Adverse Effects of Medication: These are problems with physical movement (e.g., tremors, rigidity) that are caused by medication.

22. Other Conditions that May be the Focus of Clinical Attention: These include problems related to abuse, neglect, relationship, and other issues.

Source: From the *DSM-5* (American Psychiatric Association, 2013).

(Kutchins & Kirk, 1997). The definition of psychological disorder shouldn't be a popularity contest.

The *DSM-5* definition takes these concerns into account by focusing on three key elements that must be present for a cluster of symptoms to qualify as a potential mental disorder:

> A disorder is manifested in symptoms that involve *disturbances in behavior, thoughts, or emotions.*

> The symptoms are associated with significant *personal distress or impairment.*

> The symptoms stem from an *internal dysfunction* (biological, psychological, or both).

So, on the one hand, if someone experiences mild sadness and distress after a break-up, this would not be indicative of a mental disorder because this is a normal, expected response that does not originate from internal dysfunction. On the other hand, a prolonged period of unremitting sadness that interferes with a person's ability to perform the activities of everyday life might indeed indicate depression, which is an example of a mood disorder.

As these examples suggest, determining the degree to which a person has a psychological disorder is always difficult. Psychological disorder exists along a continuum from normal to abnormal without a bright line of separation. There is increasing recognition among researchers and clinicians that many disorders are dimensional, rather than categorical, and that psychological disorder occurs when a person is at the extreme end of a given dimension (e.g., extremely emotional, extremely impulsive).

Even so, the path to reliable diagnosis remains thorny. Many diagnostic categories in the *DSM-5* depend on interpretation-based criteria rather than on observable behavior, and diagnosis continues to focus on patient self-reports (which are susceptible to censorship and distortion). Diagnostic difficulty is further increased when a person suffers from more than one disorder (see **FIGURE 13.1**). *The co-occurrence of two or more disorders in a single individual* is referred to as **comorbidity** and is relatively common in patients seen within the *DSM* diagnostic system (Kessler et al., 1994). Comorbidity raises a host of confusing possibilities: A person could be depressed because a phobia makes social situations impossible, or the person could be phobic about showing a despairing mood in public, or the disorders could be unrelated but co-occurring. Diagnosticians try hard to solve the problem of comorbidity because understanding the underlying basis for a person's disorder may suggest methods of treatment.

"First off, you're not a nut. You're a legume."

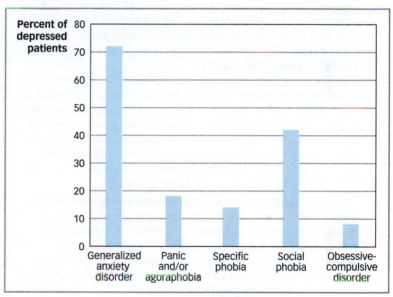

▲ FIGURE **13.1** **Comorbidity of Depression and Anxiety Disorders** The comorbidity of depression and anxiety disorders is substantial. Of 102 patients whose primary diagnosis was depression (major depressive disorder or dysthymia), large percentages also had a secondary diagnosis of one or more anxiety disorders.
(Brown et al., 2001.)

Causation of Disorders

The medical model of psychological disorders suggests that knowing a person's diagnosis is useful because any given category of mental illness is likely to have a distinctive cause. In other words, just as different viruses, or bacteria, or types of trauma, or genetic abnormalities cause different physical illnesses, so a specifiable pattern of causes (or *etiology*) may exist for different psychological disorders. The medical model also suggests that each category of psychological disorder is likely to have a common *prognosis*, a typical course over time and a susceptibility to treatment and cure. Unfortunately, this basic medical model is usually an oversimplification; it is

comorbidity The co-occurrence of two or more disorders in a single individual.

diathesis-stress model A model suggesting that a person may be predisposed for a mental disorder that remains unexpressed until triggered by stress.

rarely useful to focus on a *single cause* that is *internal* to the person and that suggests a *single cure*.

An integrated perspective that incorporates biological, psychological, and environmental factors offers the most comprehensive and useful framework for understanding most psychological disorders. On the biological side, the focus is on genetic influences, biochemical imbalances, and structural abnormalities of the brain. The psychological perspective focuses on maladaptive learning and coping, cognitive biases, dysfunctional attitudes, and interpersonal problems. Environmental factors include poor socialization, stressful life circumstances, and cultural and social inequities. The complexity of causation suggests that different individuals can experience a similar psychological disorder (e.g., depression) for different reasons. A person might fall into depression as a result of biological causes (e.g., genetics, hormones), psychological causes (e.g., faulty beliefs, hopelessness, poor strategies for coping with loss), environmental causes (e.g., stress or loneliness), or, more likely, some combination of these factors. And, of course, multiple causes mean there may not be single cures.

? **Why does assessment require looking at a number of factors?**

The observation that most disorders have both internal (biological and psychological) *and* external (environmental) causes has given rise to a theory known as the **diathesis-stress model,** which suggests that *a person may be predisposed for a psychological disorder that remains unexpressed until triggered by stress.* The diathesis is the internal predisposition, which could be genetic, and the stress is the external trigger. For example, most people were able to cope with their strong emotional reactions to the terrorist attacks of September 11, 2001. However, for some who had a predisposition to negative emotions or were already contending with major life stressors, the horror of the events may have overwhelmed their ability to cope, thereby precipitating a psychological disorder. Although diatheses can be inherited, it's important to remember that heritability is not destiny. A person who inherits a diathesis may never encounter the precipitating stress, whereas someone with little genetic propensity to a disorder may come to suffer from it given the right pattern of stress.

Searching for the biological causes of psychological disorders tends to invite a particular error in explanation—the *intervention-causation fallacy*. This fallacy involves the assumption that if a treatment is to be effective, it must address the cause of the problem. To get a sense of the error in this logic, imagine that you've spent many sleepless nights worrying about a loved one who was recently hospitalized with a serious illness. You discover that taking a sleeping medicine before bed helps you sleep. On the basis of your favorable response, should we conclude that your insomnia was caused by a deficiency of sleeping pills—that a part of your brain needed the chemicals in the pills? Of course not. Your anxiety and sleeplessness were due to your loved one's illness, not to the absence of

CULTURE & COMMUNITY

How Are Mental Disorders Experienced Differently in Different Parts of the World? Many of the disorders described in *DSM-5*, such as schizophrenia, look very similar all around the world. However, other disorders are experienced differently in different cultures. For instance, stress typically leads to depression or anxiety in Western cultures, but is more likely to be manifested in physical symptoms, such as fatigue or weakness, in Eastern cultures (Kleinman, 1986, 1988).

To aid researchers and clinicians in understanding how cultural factors can influence the experience, understanding, and expression of mental illness, the *DSM-5* suggests the use of the Cultural Formulation Interview, a series of 16 questions that inquire about how the patient understands their current clinical problem and what ideas they have about how to best treat it. In addition, the *DSM-5* includes a description of various cultural concepts of distress, or ways in which distress can be differentially experienced, understood, and expressed in different cultures. Here's a sample:

- *Ataque de nervios.* "Attack of nerves" (translation from Spanish) is principally reported among Latinos and is characterized by symptoms of intense anxiety or anger; attacks of crying, trembling, and heat in the chest; and uncontrollable screaming and shouting. Related conditions are Indisposition in Haiti, blacking out in the Southern US, and falling out in the West Indies. Ataque de nervios is closest to the DSM-5 concepts of Panic Disorder and Intermittent Explosive Disorder.

- *Kufungisisa.* "Thinking too much" (translation from Shona) is primarily reported among the Shona of Zimbabwe and is characterized by persistent worry and rumination about upsetting thoughts. The symptoms of Kufungisisa include depression, irritability, excessive worry and anxiety, and panic attacks. "Thinking too much" has been described in other cultures in Africa, Latin America, the Carribean, East Asia, and in Native Americans. The closest concepts in *DSM-5* are Major Depressive Disorder and Generalized Anxiety Disorder.

- *Taijin kyofusho.* "Interpersonal fear disorder" (translation from Japanese) is characterized by anxiety and avoidance of interpersonal situations for fear that one is inadequate or offensive to others (e.g., due to body odor, inappropriate eye contact, or excessive blushing). Taijin kyofusho is reported most often in Japan, but also has been documented in the US, Australia and New Zealand. A related condition is Taein kong po, reported in Korea. The closest concepts in *DSM-5* are Social Anxiety Disorder and Body Dysmorphic Disorder.

a pill. Be cautious about drawing inferences about causality based on responsiveness to treatment: The cure does not necessarily point to the cause.

Dangers of Labeling

An important complication in the diagnosis and classification of psychological disorders is the effect of labeling. Psychiatric labels can have negative consequences, since many of these labels carry the baggage of negative stereotypes and stigma, such as the idea that mental disorder is a sign of personal weakness or the idea that psychiatric patients are dangerous. The stigma associated with mental disorders may explain why nearly 70% of people with diagnosable psychological disorders do not seek treatment (Kessler et al., 1996; Regier et al., 1993; Sussman, Robins, & Earls, 1987).

Unfortunately, educating people about mental disorders does not dispel the stigma borne by those with these diseases (Phelan et al., 1997). In fact, expectations created by psychiatric labels can sometimes even compromise the judgment of mental health professionals (Garb, 1998; Langer & Abelson, 1974; Temerlin & Trousdale, 1969). In a classic demonstration of this phenomenon, researchers reported to different mental hospitals complaining of "hearing voices"—a symptom sometimes found in people with schizophrenia. Each was admitted to a hospital, and each promptly reported that the symptom had ceased. Even so, hospital staff were reluctant to identify these "patients" as normal: It took an average of 19 days for these "patients" to secure their release, and even then they were released with the diagnosis of "schizophrenia in remission" (Rosenhan, 1973). Apparently, once hospital staff had labeled these "patients" as having a psychological disease, the label stuck.

Labeling may even affect how the labeled person views him- or herself; persons given such a label may come to view themselves not just as mentally disordered, but as hopeless or worthless. Such a view may cause these persons to develop an attitude of defeat and, as a result, to fail to work toward their own recovery. As one small step toward counteracting such consequences, clinicians have adopted the important practice of applying labels to the disorder, not to the person with the disorder. For example, a patient might be described as "a person with schizophrenia," not as "a schizophrenic." You'll notice that we follow this model in the text.

SUMMARY QUIZ [13.1]

1. The conception of psychological disorders as diseases that have symptoms and possible cures is referred to as
   a. the medical model.
   b. physiognomy.
   c. the root syndrome framework.
   d. a diagnostic system.

2. The *DSM-5* is best described as a
   a. medical model.
   b. classification system.
   c. set of theoretical assumptions.
   d. collection of psychological definitions.

3. Comorbidity of disorders refers to
   a. symptoms stemming from internal dysfunction.
   b. the relative risk of death arising from a disorder.
   c. the co-occurrence of two or more disorders in a single individual.
   d. the existence of disorders on a continuum from normal to abnormal.

anxiety disorders Mental disorders in which anxiety is the predominant feature.

generalized anxiety disorder (GAD) A disorder characterized by chronic excessive worry accompanied by three or more of the following symptoms: restlessness, fatigue, concentration problems, irritability, muscle tension, and sleep disturbance.

phobic disorders Disorders characterized by marked, persistent, and excessive fear and avoidance of specific objects, activities, or situations.

specific phobia A disorder that involves an irrational fear of a particular object or situation that markedly interferes with an individual's ability to function.

social phobia A disorder that involves an irrational fear of being publicly humiliated or embarrassed.

Anxiety and Obsessive-Compulsive Disorders: When Fears Take Over

"Okay, time for a pop quiz that will be half your grade for this class!" If your instructor had actually said that, you would probably have experienced a wave of anxiety and dread. Your reaction would not be a sign that you have a mental disorder. In fact, situation-related anxiety is normal and can be adaptive—in this case, perhaps

? When is anxiety harmful, and when is it helpful?

by reminding you to keep up with your textbook assignments so you are prepared for pop quizzes. When anxiety arises that is out of proportion to real threats and challenges, however, it is maladaptive: It can take hold of people's lives, stealing their peace of mind and undermining their ability to function normally. Pathological anxiety is expressed as an **anxiety disorder,** *the class of mental disorder in which anxiety is the predominant feature.* Among the anxiety disorders recognized in the *DSM-5* are *generalized anxiety disorder, phobic disorders, panic disorder,* and *obsessive-compulsive disorder.*

Generalized Anxiety Disorder

Terry, a 31-year-old man, began to experience debilitating anxiety during his first year as an internal medicine resident. The 36-hour on-call periods were grueling, and he became concerned that he and other interns were making too many errors and oversights. He worried incessantly for a year and finally resigned his position. However, he continued to be plagued with anxiety about making mistakes—self-doubt that extended to his personal relationships. When he eventually sought treatment, he described himself as "worthless" and unable to control his debilitating anxiety, and he complained of headaches and constant fatigue (Vitkus, 1996).

Terry's symptoms are typical of **generalized anxiety disorder (GAD)**—called *generalized* because the unrelenting worries are not focused on any particular threat. In people suffering from GAD, *chronic excessive worry is accompanied by three or more of the following symptoms: restlessness, fatigue, concentration problems, irritability, muscle tension, and sleep disturbance.* The uncontrollable worrying produces a sense of loss of control that can so erode self-confidence that simple decisions seem fraught with dire consequences. For example, Terry needed to buy a new suit for a special occasion but began shaking and sweating when he approached a clothing store because he was afraid of choosing the "wrong" suit. He became so anxious that he could not even enter the store.

About 5% of North Americans are estimated to suffer from GAD at some time in their lives (Kessler et al., 1994). GAD occurs more frequently in lower socioeconomic groups than in middle- and upper-income groups (Blazer et al., 1991) and is approximately twice as common in women as in men (Eaton et al., 1994). Research suggests that both biological and psychological factors contribute to the risk of GAD. Family studies indicate a mild to modest level

? What factors contribute to GAD?

of heritability (Norrholm & Ressler, 2009). Although identical twin studies of GAD are rare, some evidence suggests that compared with fraternal twins, identical twins have modestly higher *concordance rates* (the percentage of pairs that share the characteristic) (Hettema, Neale, & Kendler, 2001). Moreover, teasing out environmental versus personality influences on concordance rates is quite difficult.

Some patients with GAD respond to certain prescription drugs that appear to stimulate the neurotransmitter *gamma-aminobutyric acid (GABA)*, which suggests that neurotransmitter imbalances may play a role in the disorder. However, other drugs that do not directly affect GABA levels (e.g., antidepressants such as Prozac) can also be helpful in the treatment of GAD (Gobert et al., 1999; Michelson et al., 1999; Roy-Byrne & Cowley, 1998). To complicate matters, these different prescription drugs do not help all patients and, in some cases, can produce serious side effects and dependency. Psychological explanations focus on anxiety-provoking situations in explaining high levels of GAD. The condition is especially prevalent among people who have low incomes, are living in large cities, or are trapped in environments rendered unpredictable by political and economic strife. The relatively high rates of GAD among women may also be related to stress because women are more likely than men to live in poverty, experience discrimination, or be subjected to sexual or physical abuse (Koss, 1990; Strickland, 1991). Research shows that unpredictable traumatic experiences in childhood increase the risk of developing GAD, and this evidence also supports the idea that stressful experiences play a role (Torgensen, 1986). Moreover, major life changes (new job, new baby, personal loss, physical illness, etc.) often immediately precede the development of GAD (Blazer, Hughes, & George, 1987). Still, many people who might be expected to develop GAD don't, supporting the diathesis-stress notion that personal vulnerability must also be a key factor in this disorder.

Potential anxiety victims? Generalized anxiety disorder is more common for women and children living below the poverty line than for others.

Phobic Disorders

Mary, a 47-year-old mother of three, sought treatment for *claustrophobia*—an intense fear of enclosed spaces. She traced her fear to childhood, when her older siblings would scare her by locking her in closets and confining her under blankets. She wanted to find a job but could not because of a terror of elevators and other confined places that, she felt, shackled her to her home (Carson, Butcher, & Mineka, 2000). Many people feel anxious in enclosed spaces, but Mary's fears were abnormal and dysfunctional because they were wildly disproportional to any actual risk and because they imposed unwanted restrictions on her life. Mary's condition is a **phobic disorder,** a *marked, persistent, and excessive fear and avoidance of specific objects, activities, or situations.* An individual with a phobic disorder recognizes that the fear is irrational but cannot prevent it from interfering with everyday functioning.

A **specific phobia** is *an irrational fear of a particular object or situation that markedly interferes with an individual's ability to function.* Specific phobias recognized by the *DSM* include fear of animals (e.g., dogs, snakes, spiders), natural environments (e.g., heights, darkness), situations (e.g., bridges, enclosed places), blood or injury, and illness or death. Approximately 11% of people in the United States will develop a specific phobia during their lives and—for unknown reasons—the risk seems to be increasing in younger generations (Magee et al., 1996). With few exceptions (e.g., fear of heights), specific phobias are much more common among women than among men, with a ratio of about 4 to 1 (Kessler et al., 1994; Kessler et al., 1996).

Social phobia involves *an irrational fear of being publicly humiliated or embarrassed.* Social phobia can be restricted to situations such as public speaking or

No fear of heights here. Construction workers eat their lunches atop a steel beam 800 feet above ground during the 1932 construction of the RCA Building (now the GE Building) in Rockefeller Center in Manhattan.

preparedness theory The idea that people are instinctively predisposed toward certain fears.

panic disorder A disorder characterized by the sudden occurrence of multiple psychological and physiological symptoms that contribute to a feeling of stark terror.

agoraphobia An extreme fear of venturing into public places.

generalized to a variety of social situations that involve being observed or interacting with unfamiliar people. Individuals with social phobia try to avoid situations in which unfamiliar people might evaluate them, and they experience intense anxiety and distress when public exposure is unavoidable. Social phobia can develop in childhood, but it typically emerges between early adolescence and the age of 25 (Schneier et al., 1992). About 11% of men and 15% of women qualify for diagnosis of social phobia at some time in their lives (Kessler et al., 1994). Even higher rates are found among people who are undereducated, have low incomes, or both (Magee et al., 1996).

Why are phobias so common? The high rates of both specific and social phobias suggest a predisposition to be fearful of certain objects and situations. Indeed, most of the situations and objects of people's phobias could pose a real threat—for example, falling from a high place or being attacked by a vicious dog or poisonous snake or spider. Social situations have their own dangers. A roomful of strangers may not attack or bite, but they could form impressions that affect your prospects for friends, jobs, or marriage. And of course, in some very rare cases, they could attack or bite.

? Why might we be predisposed to certain phobias?

Observations such as these are the basis for the **preparedness theory** of phobias, which maintains that *people are instinctively predisposed toward certain fears* (Seligman, 1971). The preparedness theory is supported by research showing that both humans and monkeys can quickly be conditioned to have a fear response for stimuli such as snakes and spiders but not for neutral stimuli such as flowers or toy rabbits (Cook & Mineka, 1989; Öhman, Dimberg, & Ost, 1985). Similarly, research on facial expressions has shown that people are more easily conditioned to fear angry facial expressions than other types of expressions (Öhman, 1996; Öhman et al., 1985; Woody & Nosen, 2008). Phobias are particularly likely to form for objects that evolution has predisposed us to avoid. This idea is also supported by studies of the heritability of phobias. Family studies of specific phobias indicate greater concordance rates for identical than for fraternal twins (Kendler, Myers, & Prescott, 2002; Kendler et al., 1992; O'Laughlin & Malle, 2002). Other studies have found that more than 30% of first-degree relatives (parents, siblings, or children) of patients with specific phobias also have a phobia (Fryer et al., 1990).

Neurobiological factors may also play a role. Abnormalities in the neurotransmitters serotonin and dopamine are more common in individuals who report phobias than among people who don't (Stein, 1998). In addition, individuals with phobias sometimes show abnormally high levels of activity in the amygdala, an area of the brain linked with the development of emotional associations (discussed in Chapter 8 and in Hirschfeld et al., 1992; Stein, Chavira, & Jang, 2001).

This evidence does not rule out the influence of environments and upbringing on the development of phobic overreactions. As learning theorist John Watson (1924) demonstrated many years ago, phobias can be classically conditioned (see our Chapter 7 discussion of Little Albert and the white rat). Similarly, the discomfort of a dog bite could create a conditioned association between dogs and pain, resulting in an irrational fear of all dogs. The idea that phobias are learned from emotional experiences with feared objects, however, is not a complete explanation for the occurrence of phobias. Most studies find that people with phobias are no more likely than people without phobias to recall personal experiences with the feared object that could have

The preparedness theory explains why most merry-go-rounds carry children on beautiful horses. This mom might have some trouble getting her daughter to ride on a big spider or snake.

COURTESY OF DANIEL WEGNER

provided the basis for classical conditioning (Craske, 1999; McNally & Steketee, 1985). Moreover, many people are bitten by dogs, but few develop phobias. Despite its shortcomings, however, the idea that this is a matter of learning provides a useful model for therapy (see Chapter 14).

Panic Disorder

Mindy, a 25-year-old art director, had been having panic attacks with increasing frequency, often two or three times a day, when she finally sought help at a clinic. The attacks began with a sudden wave of "horrible fear" that seemed to come out of nowhere, often accompanied by trembling, nausea, and a tightening of the chest. The attacks began when she was in high school and had continued intermittently ever since (Spitzer et al., 1994).

Mindy's condition, called **panic disorder,** is characterized by *the sudden occurrence of multiple psychological and physiological symptoms that contribute to a feeling of stark terror.* The acute symptoms of a panic attack typically last only a few minutes and include shortness of breath, heart palpitations, sweating, dizziness, feelings of detachment or unreality, and a fear that one is going crazy or about to die. Not surprisingly, panic attacks often send people rushing to emergency departments or their physicians' offices for what they believe is either an acute cardiac, respiratory, or neurological episode (Hirschfeld, 1996).

A common complication of panic disorder is **agoraphobia,** *a specific phobia involving a fear of venturing into public places.* Many individuals with agoraphobia are not frightened of public places themselves; instead, they are afraid of having a panic attack in a public place or around strangers who might view them with disdain or fail to help them. In severe cases, people who have panic disorder with agoraphobia are unable to leave home, sometimes for years on end.

? What is it about public places that many agoraphobics fear?

Approximately 22% of the U.S. population reports having had at least one panic attack (Kessler et al., 2006), typically during a period of intense stress (Telch, Lucas, & Nelson, 1989). An occasional episode is not sufficient for a diagnosis of panic disorder—the individual also has to experience significant dread and anxiety about having another attack. When this criterion is applied, approximately 3.5% of people will have diagnosable panic disorder sometime in their lives, and of those, about 43% will also develop agoraphobia (Kessler et al., 1994). Panic disorder is twice as prevalent among women as men (Weissman et al., 1997). Family studies suggest a modest hereditary component to panic disorder. If one identical twin has the disorder, the likelihood of the other twin having it is about 30% (Crowe, 1990; Kendler et al., 1995; Torgensen, 1983).

People who experience panic attacks may be hypersensitive to physiological signs of anxiety, which they interpret as having disastrous consequences for their well-being. Supporting this cognitive explanation is research showing that people who are high in anxiety sensitivity (i.e., they believe that bodily arousal and other symptoms of anxiety can have dire consequences) have an elevated risk for experiencing panic attacks (Li & Zinbarg, 2007). Thus, panic attacks may be traceable to the fear of fear itself.

In panic disorder with agoraphobia, the fear of having a panic attack in public may prevent the person from going outside.

obsessive-compulsive disorder (OCD)
A disorder in which repetitive, intrusive thoughts (obsessions) and ritualistic behaviors (compulsions) designed to fend off those thoughts interfere significantly with an individual's functioning.

mood disorders Mental disorders that have mood disturbance as their predominant feature.

major depressive disorder A disorder characterized by a severely depressed mood that lasts 2 weeks or more and is accompanied by feelings of worthlessness and lack of pleasure, lethargy, and sleep and appetite disturbances.

seasonal affective disorder (SAD) Depression that involves recurrent depressive episodes in a seasonal pattern.

> Have you ever counted the tiles in the ceiling just out of boredom in a class? What if you were obsessed with counting tiles and came upon the Nasr ol Molk mosque in Shiraz, Iran? There goes the weekend.

VLADIMIR MELNIK/SHUTTERSTOCK

Obsessive-Compulsive Disorder

Karen, a 34-year-old with four children, sought treatment after several months of experiencing intrusive, repetitive thoughts in which she imagined that one of her children was having a serious accident. In addition, an extensive series of protective counting rituals hampered her daily routine. For example, when grocery shopping, Karen had the feeling that if she selected the first item on a shelf, something terrible would happen to her oldest child. If she selected the second item, some unknown disaster would befall her second child, and so on for the four children. Karen's preoccupation with numbers extended to other activities. For example, if she drank one cup of coffee, she felt compelled to drink four more to protect her children from harm. She acknowledged that her counting rituals were irrational, but she found that she became extremely anxious when she tried to stop (Oltmanns, Neale, & Davison, 1991).

Karen's symptoms are typical of **obsessive-compulsive disorder (OCD),** in which *repetitive, intrusive thoughts (obsessions) and ritualistic behaviors (compulsions) designed to fend off those thoughts interfere significantly with an individual's functioning.* Anxiety plays a role in this disorder because the obsessive thoughts typically produce anxiety, and the compulsive behaviors are performed to reduce it. It is not uncommon for people to have occasional intrusive thoughts that prompt ritualistic behavior (e.g., double- or triple-checking to be sure the garage door is closed or the oven is off), but the obsessions and compulsions of OCD are intense, frequent, and experienced as irrational and excessive. Attempts to cope with the obsessive thoughts by trying to suppress or ignore them are of little or no benefit. In fact (as discussed in Chapter 5), thought suppression can backfire, increasing the frequency and intensity of the obsessive thoughts (Wegner, 1989; Wenzlaff & Wegner, 2000).

? How effective is willful effort at curing OCD?

Approximately 1.3% of people will develop OCD sometime in their lives, with somewhat lower rates in Asian cultures (Somers et al., 2006). Women tend to be more susceptible than men, but the difference is not large (Karno & Golding, 1991). Although compulsive behavior is always excessive, it can vary considerably in intensity and frequency. For example, fear of contamination may lead to 15 minutes of hand washing in some individuals, while others may need to spend hours with disinfectants and extremely hot water, scrubbing their hands until they bleed.

Family studies indicate a moderate genetic heritability for OCD: Identical twins show a higher concordance than do fraternal twins. Relatives of individuals with OCD may not have the disorder themselves, but they are at greater risk for other types of anxiety disorders than are members of the general public (Billet, Richter, & Kennedy, 1998). Researchers have not determined the biological mechanisms that may contribute to OCD (Friedlander & Desrocher, 2006), but one hypothesis implicates heightened neural activity in the caudate nucleus of the brain, a portion of the basal ganglia (discussed in Chapter 3) known to be involved in the initiation of intentional actions (Rappoport, 1990). Drugs that increase the activity of the neurotransmitter serotonin in the brain can inhibit the activity of the caudate nucleus and relieve some of the symptoms of obsessive-compulsive disorder (Hansen et al., 2002). However, this finding does not indicate that overactivity of the caudate nucleus is the cause of OCD. It could also be an effect of the disorder: Patients with OCD often respond favorably to psychotherapy and show a corresponding reduction in activity in the caudate nucleus (Baxter et al., 1992).

Depressive and Bipolar Disorders: At the Mercy of Emotions

You're probably in a mood right now. Maybe you're happy that it's almost time to get a snack or saddened by something you heard on the radio—or you may feel good or bad without having a clue why. Moods are relatively long-lasting, nonspecific emotional states—and *nonspecific* means we often may have no idea what has caused a mood. Changing moods lend variety to our experiences, like different-colored lights shining on the stage as we play out our lives. However, for people like Virginia Woolf and others with mood disorders, moods can become so intense that they are pulled or pushed into life-threatening actions. **Mood disorders**—*mental disorders that have mood disturbance as their predominant feature*—take two main forms: depression and bipolar disorder.

Depressive Disorders

R.A., a 58-year-old man, had difficulties falling asleep and staying asleep that left him chronically fatigued. Over the past 6 months, he'd stopped exercising and gained 12 pounds and had lost interest in socializing. Nothing he normally enjoyed, including sexual activity, could give him pleasure anymore; he had trouble concentrating and was forgetful, irritable, impatient, and frustrated (Lustman, Caudle, & Clouse, 2002). R.A.'s sense of hopelessness and weariness and his lack of normal pleasures goes far beyond normal sadness; it is also different from the normal responses of sorrow and grief that accompany a tragic situation such as the death of a loved one (Bowlby, 1980). Instead, depressive mood disorders are dysfunctional, chronic, and fall outside the range of socially or culturally expected responses.

Major depressive disorder, also known as unipolar depression, is characterized by *a severely depressed mood that lasts 2 or more weeks and is accompanied by feelings of worthlessness and lack of pleasure, lethargy, and sleep and appetite disturbances.* Great sadness or despair is not always present, although intrusive thoughts of failure or ending one's life are not uncommon (see the Real World box). Some people experience *recurrent depressive episodes in a seasonal pattern,* commonly known as **seasonal affective disorder (SAD).** In most cases, the episodes begin in fall or winter and remit in spring, a pattern that is due to reduced levels of light during the colder seasons (Westrin & Lam, 2007). Recurrent summer depressive episodes are not unknown. A winter-related pattern of depression appears to be more prevalent in higher latitudes.

A time for seasonal affective disorder. When the sun goes away, sadness can play.

ARCTIC IMAGES/ALAMY

helplessness theory The idea that individuals who are prone to depression automatically attribute negative experiences to causes that are internal (i.e., their own fault), stable (i.e., unlikely to change), and global (i.e., widespread).

On average, major depression lasts about 12 weeks (Eaton et al., 2008). However, without treatment, approximately 80% of individuals will experience at least one recurrence of the disorder (Judd, 1997; Mueller et al., 1999). Genetic factors appear to play a role in vulnerability to depression; a relatively large study of twins found that the concordance rates for severe major depression were quite high, with a rate of

THE REAL WORLD

Suicide Risk and Prevention

Overall, suicide is the eleventh leading cause of death in the United States and the third most common form of death among high school and college students (King, 1997). Approximately 50% of those who kill themselves do so during a depressive episode (Isacsson & Rich, 1997). In the United States, women attempt suicide about two to three times more often than men. However, because men typically use more lethal methods than do women (such as guns versus pills), men are three to four times more likely to actually kill themselves than are women (Canetto & Lester, 1995). The tragic effects of suicide extend beyond the loss of life, compounding the grief of families and loved ones who must contend with feelings of abandonment, guilt, shame, and futility.

Researchers have identified a variety of motives for suicide, including a profound sense of alienation, intolerable psychological or physical suffering or both, hopelessness, an escape from feelings of worthlessness, and a desperate cry for help (Durkheim, 1951; Joiner, 2006).

How can you tell if someone is at risk for suicide? Unfortunately, definitive prediction is impossible, but a variety of warning signs can

suggest an increased risk (Substance Abuse and Mental Health Services Administration, 2005). Any one sign is a cause for concern, and the risk is especially serious when several occur together. Some signs:

- Talk about suicide. About 90% of people who are suicidal discuss their intentions. Although most people who threaten suicide do not actually attempt it, they are at greater risk than those who do not talk about it.

- An upturn in mood following a prolonged depressive episode. Surprisingly, suicide risk increases at this point. A sudden lifting of mood may reflect relief at the prospect that suicide will end the emotional suffering.

- A failed love interest, romantic breakup, or loss of a loved one through separation or death.

- A severe, stressful event that is especially shameful or humiliating.

- A family history of suicide, especially of a parent.

- Unusual reckless or risky behavior, seemingly carried out without thinking.

- An unexplained decline in school or workplace performance.

- Withdrawal from friends, family, and regular activities.

- Expressing feelings of being trapped, as though there's "no way out."

- "Cleaning house" by giving away prized possessions.

- Increased alcohol or drug use. Substance abuse is associated with approximately 25% to 50% of suicides and is especially associated with adolescent suicides (Conwell et al., 1996; Woods et al., 1997).

Although discussing suicide with someone possibly at risk might seem to increase actual risk, a caring listener can help put issues in better perspective and reduce feelings of isolation. Anyone who is potentially suicidal should be encouraged to seek professional help. Colleges and universities have student counseling centers, and most cities have suicide prevention centers with 24-hour hotlines and walk-in emergency counseling. The U.S. National Suicide Prevention Lifeline is 1-800-273-TALK.

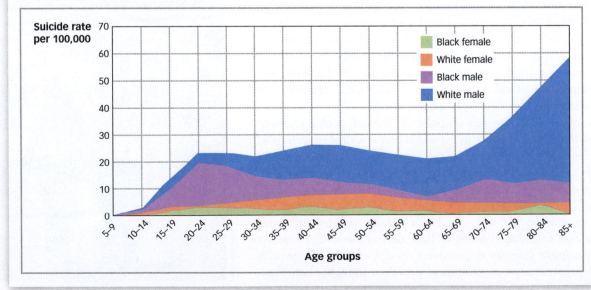

◀ Suicide rates in the United States reveal that men are more likely to commit suicide than women at all ages, that men's likelihood of suicide grows in early adulthood, and that White men remain most suicide-prone throughout life—with a spike in the later years.

[From National Institute of Mental Health, 2003.]

59% for identical twins and 30% for fraternal twins (Bertelsen, Harvald, & Hauge, 1977). Women are diagnosed with depression at a rate twice that of men (Grigoriadis & Robinson, 2007). It is possible that the higher rate of depression in women reflects greater willingness by women to face their depression and seek out help, leading to higher rates of diagnosis. Sex differences in hormones are another possibility: Estrogen, androgen, and progesterone influence depression; some women experience *postpartum depression* (depression following childbirth) due to changing hormone balances.

Other neurotransmitters, norepinephrine and serotonin, have also been implicated in depression because drugs such as Prozac and Zoloft that increase levels of these neurotransmitters sometimes reduce depression (see Chapter 14). However, this cannot be the whole story. For example, some studies have found *increases* in norepinephrine activity among depressed patients (Thase & Howland, 1995). Moreover, even though the antidepressant medications change neurochemical transmission in less than a day, they typically take at least 2 weeks to relieve depressive symptoms. A biochemical model of depression has yet to be developed that accounts for all the evidence.

Depression may involve diminished activity in the left prefrontal cortex and increased activity in the right prefrontal cortex (see **FIGURE 13.2**)—areas of the brain involved in the processing of emotions (Davidson, 2004; Davidson et al., 2002). These abnormal activity patterns may be effects of the mood disturbance, or they may cause people to be more susceptible to depression. The role of distinct brain regions in vulnerability to depression is still not well understood (Koenigs et al., 2008).

Turning to psychological factors, researchers have proposed a theory of depression that emphasizes the role of people's negative inferences about the causes of their experiences (Abramson, Seligman, & Teasdale, 1978). **Helplessness**

Actress Brooke Shields experienced severe postpartum depression and wrote a book about it.

? **What is helplessness theory?**

theory maintains that *individuals who are prone to depression automatically attribute negative experiences to causes that are internal (i.e., their own fault), stable (i.e., unlikely to change), and global (i.e., widespread).* For example, a student at risk for depression might view a bad grade on a math test as a sign of low intelligence (internal) that will never change (stable) and that will lead to failure in all his or her future endeavors (global). In contrast, a student without this tendency might have the opposite response, attributing the grade to something external (poor teaching), unstable (a missed study session), and/or specific (boring subject).

Individuals at risk for depression may normally struggle to suppress negative thoughts that threaten their emotional well-being. Thought suppression is an effortful process that can be disrupted when cognitive resources are depleted (see Chapter 5). Not surprisingly, then, when cognitive demands arise (time pressures, distraction, stress, and so forth), individuals who are at risk for depression often display heightened levels of negative thinking (Wenzlaff & Bates, 1998; Wenzlaff & Eisenberg, 2001). They may worry about failures, think that people are avoiding them, or wonder whether anything is worthwhile. This breakdown in mental control may explain why stressful life events such as a prolonged illness or the loss of a loved one often precede a descent into depression (Monroe & Reid, 2009). Ironically, thought suppression itself may intensify depressive thoughts and ultimately contribute to relapse (Beevers & Meyer, 2008; Wenzlaff, 2005).

▼ FIGURE **13.2** **Brain and Depression** Reduced activation in the left dorsolateral prefrontal cortex (blue) and increased activation in the right dorsolateral prefrontal cortex (red) have been found to be linked with depression in several studies.

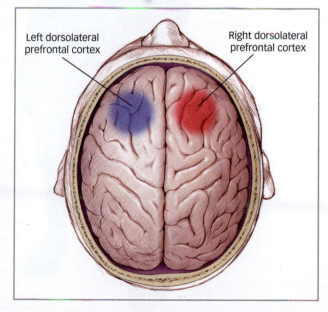

Left dorsolateral prefrontal cortex

Right dorsolateral prefrontal cortex

"Those? Oh, just a few souvenirs from my bipolar-disorder days."

Bipolar Disorder

Julie, a 20-year-old college sophomore, had gone 5 days without sleep and was extremely active and expressing bizarre thoughts and ideas. She proclaimed to friends that she did not menstruate because she was "of a third sex, a gender above the two human sexes," that she had switched souls with the senior senator from her state, and that she could save the world from nuclear destruction (Vitkus, 1999).

In addition to her manic episodes, Julie—like Woolf—had a history of depression. The diagnostic label for this constellation of symptoms is **bipolar disorder,** *an unstable emotional condition characterized by cycles of abnormal, persistent high mood (mania) and low mood (depression).* The depressive phase of bipolar disorder is often clinically indistinguishable from major depression (Johnson et al., 2009). In the manic phase, mood can be elevated, expansive, or irritable. Other prominent symptoms include grandiosity, decreased need for sleep, talkativeness, racing thoughts, distractibility, and reckless behavior (such as compulsive gambling, sexual indiscretions, and unrestrained spending sprees).

The lifetime risk for bipolar disorder is about 1.3% for both men and women (Wittchen, Knauper, & Kessler, 1994). Unfortunately, bipolar disorder tends to be persistent. In one study, 24% of patients had relapsed within 6 months of recovery from an episode, and 77% had at least one new episode within 4 years of recovery (Coryell et al., 1995).

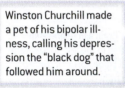

Winston Churchill made a pet of his bipolar illness, calling his depression the "black dog" that followed him around.

Among the various mental disorders, bipolar disorder has the highest rate of heritability, with concordance from 40% to 70% for identical twins and 10% for fraternal twins (Craddock & Jones, 1999). Occasional families are found in which a single gene gives rise to the disorder, but most often the disorder is *polygenic,* arising from the interaction of multiple genes, and these have been difficult to identify (Goodwin & Ghaemi, 1998; Plomin et al., 1997). Biochemical imbalances may be involved in bipolar disorder, but specific neurotransmitters have not been identified.

? **How does stress relate to manic-depressive episodes?**

Psychological factors also play a role. Stressful life experiences often precede manic and depressive episodes (S. L. Johnson et al., 2008). One study found that severely stressed patients took an average of three times longer to recover from an episode than did patients not affected by stress (Johnson & Miller, 1997). Personality characteristics such as neuroticism and conscientiousness have also been found to predict increases in bipolar symptoms over time (Lozano & Johnson, 2001). Finally, patients living with family members who are hostile toward or critical of the patient are more likely to relapse than patients with supportive families (Miklowitz et al., 1988).

A significant minority of people with bipolar disorder are highly creative, artistic, or otherwise outstanding in some way. Before the mania becomes too pronounced, the energy, grandiosity, and ambition that it supplies may help people achieve great things. In addition to Virginia Woolf, notable individuals thought to have had the disorder include Abraham Lincoln, Ernest Hemingway, Winston Churchill, and Theodore Roosevelt.

SUMMARY QUIZ [13.3]

1. Major depression is characterized by a severely depressed mood that lasts at least
   a. 2 weeks. b. 1 week. c. 1 month. d. 6 months.

2. Extreme mood swings between _____ characterize bipolar disorder.
   a. depression and mania
   b. stress and lethargy
   c. anxiety and arousal
   d. obsessions and compulsions

3. Which of the following is true regarding mood disorders?
   a. People with mood disorders show abnormally high levels of norepinephrine and serotonin.
   b. People who attribute their failures to external and unstable causes are more prone to depression.
   c. People with major depression often show increased activity in the left frontal cortex and diminished activity in the right prefrontal cortex.
   d. Close relatives of individuals with mood disorders have a heightened risk for developing mood disorders themselves, indicating that heredity plays a role.

bipolar disorder An unstable emotional condition characterized by cycles of abnormal, persistent high mood (mania) and low mood (depression).

dissociative disorder A condition in which normal cognitive processes are severely disjointed and fragmented, creating significant disruptions in memory, awareness, or personality that can vary in length from a matter of minutes to many years.

dissociative identity disorder (DID) The presence within an individual of two or more distinct identities that at different times take control of the individual's behavior.

Dissociative Disorders: Going to Pieces

Mary, a 35-year-old social worker being treated with hypnosis for chronic pain in her forearm, mentioned to her doctor that she often found her car low on fuel in the morning despite her having filled it with gas the day before. Overnight the odometer would gain 50 to 100 miles, even though she had no memory of driving the car. During one hypnotic session, Mary suddenly blurted out in a strange voice, "It's about time you knew about me." In the new voice, she identified herself as "Marian" and described the drives that she took at night, which were retreats to the nearby hills to "work out problems." Mary knew nothing of "Marian" and her nighttime adventures. Marian was as abrupt and hostile as Mary was compliant and caring. In the course of therapy, six other personalities emerged (including one who claimed to be a 6-year-old child) (Spitzer et al., 1994).

Mary suffers from a type of **dissociative disorder,** *a condition in which normal cognitive processes are severely disjointed and fragmented, creating significant disruptions in memory, awareness, or personality that can vary in length from a matter of minutes to many years.* To some extent, a bit of dissociation, or "splitting," of cognitive processes is normal. For example, we can engage in more than one activity or mental process while maintaining only dim awareness of the perceptions and decisions that guide other behaviors (such as talking while driving a car). Our ordinary continuity of memory and awareness of our personal identity contrasts with Mary's profound cognitive fragmentation and blindness to her own mental processes and states.

Joanne Woodward played Eve White, a woman with dissociative identity disorder, in the 1957 film *The Three Faces of Eve*. This film and others dramatized the disorder and, by increasing public awareness, stimulated more frequent diagnosis of this problem. It is not clear, though, whether the increased awareness led to greater accuracy in finding cases of the disorder that were already present or if it shaped how people behaved (and what therapists tried to find) and so *created* more cases of the disorder.

Dissociative Identity Disorder

Dissociative identity disorder (DID) is characterized by *the presence within an individual of two or more distinct identities that at different times take control of the individual's behavior.* The number of alternate personalities (or "alters") can range considerably, with some cases numbering more

A moment ago she was the nicest girl in town...
A moment from now she will be anybody's pick-up!

The Three Faces of Eve
CinemaScope
JOANNE WOODWARD · DAVID WAYNE · LEE J. COBB · NUNNALLY JOHNSON

dissociative amnesia The sudden loss of memory for significant personal information.

dissociative fugue The sudden loss of memory for one's personal history, accompanied by an abrupt departure from home and the assumption of a new identity.

schizophrenia A disorder characterized by the profound disruption of basic psychological processes; a distorted perception of reality; altered or blunted emotion; and disturbances in thought, motivation, and behavior.

delusion A patently false belief system, often bizarre and grandiose, that is maintained in spite of its irrationality.

than one hundred. Sometimes alters assume different vocal patterns, dialects, ages, morals, and even gender identities. No longer called "multiple personality disorder" because the term implies that more than one person is in "residence," the disorder is now conceptualized as involving multiple patterns of thought and behavior, each of which is associated with a different identity.

Recent estimates are that between .5% and 1% of the general population suffers from the disorder, with a female-to-male prevalence of about 9 to 1 (Maldonado & Butler, 1998). Most patients are diagnosed when they are in their 20s or 30s, although the actual age of onset is probably during childhood (Maldonado & Butler, 1998; Putnam et al., 1986).

Many patients with DID report a history of severe childhood abuse and trauma (Coons, 1994; Putnam et al., 1986), and such evidence supports an explanation rooted in psychodynamic theory. From this viewpoint, the helpless child, confronted with intolerable abuse and trauma, responds with the primitive psychological defense of splitting or dissociating to escape the pain and horror. But the theory linking trauma and dissociation has some problems. For example, the evidence of abuse in DID patients is seldom corroborated by anyone other than the patient (Piper & Merskey, 2004).

What accounts for the variation in DID diagnoses?

Critics of the psychodynamic explanation of DID have raised the possibility that individuals who exhibit both trauma and DID may be responding to their therapists' expectations that the two are linked (Humphreys & Dennett, 1989; Kluft, 1991; Lalonde et al., 2001). Research suggests that at least some cases represent patients who are vulnerable to suggestive procedures such as hypnosis and who are cajoled or coaxed by well-meaning therapists into reporting evidence of alternate personalities (Acocella, 1999). What we know for sure is that DID is poorly understood and that deep questions exist about what it is, how it arises, and how it can be treated.

Dissociative Amnesia

"Burt," a 42-year-old short-order cook in a small town, got into a heated altercation with another man in a diner. When the police took "Burt" to the hospital, they discovered that he had no identification documents and was clueless about his past. Police matched his description to that of Gene Saunders, a resident of a city 200 miles away who had disappeared a month earlier. When Gene's wife came to identify him, he denied knowing her and his real identity. Before he disappeared, Gene had been experiencing considerable difficulties at home and at work and had become withdrawn and irritable. Two days before he left, he had a violent argument with his 18-year-old son, who accused him of being a failure (Spitzer et al., 1994).

A related condition, **dissociative amnesia,** is *the sudden loss of memory for significant personal information.* The memory loss is typically for a traumatic specific event or period but can involve extended periods (months or years) of a person's life (Kihlstrom, 2005). Dissociative amnesia may be temporary: People have lost significant personal memories and then recovered them later (Brenneis, 2000; Schooler, Bendiksen, & Ambadar, 1997).

Burt's case is an example of **dissociative fugue,** a subtype of dissociative amnesia involving *the sudden loss of memory for one's personal history, accompanied by an abrupt departure from home and the assumption of a new identity.* The fugue state is usually associated with stressful life circumstances and can be brief or lengthy.

To be classified as dissociative amnesia or dissociative fugue, the patient's memory loss cannot result from normal forgetting or brain injury, drugs, or another mental disorder (such

How do dissociative fugue and dissociative amnesia differ from other kinds of memory impairments?

Call me "Al." A man identified only by the name "Al" gave a news conference in Denver in 2006 in hopes that someone might be able to tell him more about himself. A victim of a dissociative fugue state, he had no memory of his identity or his life. His fiancée recognized him on TV and confirmed his identity as Jeffrey Alan Ingram, an unemployed machinist from Olympia, Washington.

AP PHOTO/THE DENVER POST, KARL GEHRING

as post-traumatic stress disorder, covered in Chapter 15). Both dissociative amnesia and dissociative fugue usually emerge in adulthood and rarely occur after the age of 50 (Sackeim & Devanand, 1991). Dissociative fugue states usually end rather abruptly, and victims typically recover their memories and personal identities. Dissociative amnesia may also be temporary: People have lost significant personal memories and then recovered them later (Brenneis, 2000; Schooler et al., 1997).

SUMMARY QUIZ [13.4]

1. A dissociative disorder is characterized by significant disruptions in which of the following?
   a. memory
   b. awareness
   c. personality
   d. all of the above

2. Which of the following is an accurate statement regarding dissociative identity disorder?
   a. The disorder is also called "multiple personality disorder."
   b. The "host" individual is aware of the alternate personalities.
   c. Some researchers believe the disorder is created in therapy.
   d. Recent estimates are that approximately 5% of the population suffers from the disorder.

3. Pat was involved in a severe auto accident and is unable to recall the event. Pat is displaying
   a. dissociative amnesia.
   b. dissociative fugue.
   c. dissociative identity disorder.
   d. multiple personality disorder.

Schizophrenia: Losing the Grasp on Reality

Margaret, a 39-year-old mother, believed that God was punishing her for marrying a man she did not love and bringing two children into the world. As her punishment, God had made her and her children immortal so that they would have to suffer in their unhappy home life forever. She saw evidence for this belief in everyday events, reading arcane meanings into the way items were lying in the kitchen sink and the programs playing on television (Oltmanns et al., 1991).

Symptoms and Types of Schizophrenia

Margaret was suffering from **schizophrenia**, a disorder characterized by *the profound disruption of basic psychological processes; a distorted perception of reality; altered or blunted emotion; and disturbances in thought, motivation, and behavior.* Symptoms can include *delusion, hallucination, disorganized speech, grossly disorganized behavior* or *catatonic behavior,* and *negative symptoms.* The various symptoms of schizophrenia do not all occur in every case. Let's consider each symptom in detail.

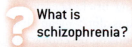
What is schizophrenia?

> **Delusion** is *a patently false belief system, often bizarre and grandiose, that is maintained in spite of its irrationality.* For example, an individual with schizophrenia may believe that he or she is Jesus Christ, Napoleon, Joan of Arc, or some other famous person. Such delusions of identity have helped foster the misconception that schizophrenia involves multiple personalities. Unlike dissociative identity disorder, however, adopted identities in schizophrenia do not alternate, exhibit amnesia for one another, or otherwise "split." Delusions of persecution are also common. The patient's belief that the CIA, demons, extraterrestrials, or other malevolent forces are conspiring to harm the patient

"I want to see other hallucinations."

Patients with schizophrenia are sometimes able to express their experiences in drawings.

or control his or her mind may represent an attempt to make sense of the tormenting delusions (Roberts, 1991). People with schizophrenia have little or no insight into their disordered perceptual and thought processes (Karow et al., 2007). Without understanding that they have lost control of their own minds, they may develop unusual beliefs and theories that attribute control to external agents.

> **Hallucination** is *a false perceptual experience that has a compelling sense of being real despite the absence of external stimulation.* These experiences can include hearing, seeing, or smelling things that are not there. Among people with schizophrenia, some 65% report hearing voices repeatedly (Frith & Fletcher, 1995). The voices typically command, scold, or offer snide comments. One patient reported a voice saying, "He's getting up now. He's going to wash. It's about time." (Frith & Fletcher, 1995).

> **Disorganized speech** is *a severe disruption of verbal communication in which ideas shift rapidly and incoherently from one to another unrelated topic.* For example, asked by her doctor, "Can you tell me the name of this place?" one patient with schizophrenia responded, "I have not been a drinker for 16 years. I am taking a mental rest after a 'carter' assignment of 'quill.' You know, a 'penwrap.' I had contracts with Warner Brothers Studios and Eugene broke phonograph records but Mike protested." (quoted in Carson et al., 2000, p. 474).

> **Grossly disorganized behavior** is *behavior that is inappropriate for the situation or ineffective in attaining goals, often with specific motor disturbances.* A patient might exhibit constant childlike silliness, improper sexual behavior (such as masturbating in public), disheveled appearance, or loud shouting or swearing.

> **Negative symptoms** include *emotional and social withdrawal; apathy; poverty of speech; and other indications of the absence or insufficiency of normal behavior, motivation, and emotion.* These symptoms refer to things missing in people with schizophrenia, in contrast to the positive symptoms (such as hallucinations) that appear more in people with schizophrenia than in other people.

Schizophrenia occurs in about 1% of the population (Jablensky, 1997) and is slightly more common in men than in women (McGrath et al., 2008). The first episode typically occurs in late adolescence or early adulthood (Gottesman, 1991). Despite its relatively low frequency, schizophrenia is the primary diagnosis for nearly 40% of all admissions to state and county mental hospitals; it is the second most frequent diagnosis for inpatient psychiatric admission at other institutions (Rosenstein, Milazzo-Sayre, & Manderscheid, 1990). The disproportionate rate of hospitalization for schizophrenia is a testament to the devastation it causes in people's lives.

Some of the symptoms found in schizophrenia appear in people without the disorder. For example, 71% of college students report hearing brief, occasional hallucinated voices (Posey & Losch, 1983). These observations don't mean that schizophrenia is widespread—they remind us instead that diagnosing psychological disorders must take into account the complexity of the mind and the glimmerings of madness in us all.

hallucination A false perceptual experience that has a compelling sense of being real despite the absence of external stimulation.

disorganized speech A severe disruption of verbal communication in which ideas shift rapidly and incoherently from one to another unrelated topic.

grossly disorganized behavior Behavior that is inappropriate for the situation or ineffective in attaining goals, often with specific motor disturbances.

negative symptoms Emotional and social withdrawal, apathy, poverty of speech, and other indications of the absence or insufficiency of normal behavior, motivation, and emotion.

Biological Factors

What is the role of genetics in schizophrenia?

As shown in **FIGURE 13.3**, the closer a person's genetic relatedness to a person with schizophrenia, the greater the likelihood of developing the disorder (Gottesman, 1991). Almost every study finds the average concordance rates higher for identical twins (48%) than for fraternal twins (17%), which strongly suggests a genetic component for the disorder (Torrey et al., 1994).

HOT SCIENCE

Austism Spectrum Disorder and Childhood Disorders

Are psychological disorders in children just junior versions of the adult disorders? Or are childhood disorders unique? There are many parallels between childhood and adult mental problems—anxiety disorders and mood disorders, for example, appear with similar symptoms no matter when they occur in the life span. But there are also *early-onset disorders* recognized in the *DSM* as problems in children: intellectual disability, learning disorders, communication disorders, motor skill disorders, eating and elimination disorders, conduct disorders, attention-deficit/hyperactivity disorder, and Autism Spectrum Disorder (ASD). Some of these problems resolve as the person develops, but others do not.

One childhood disorder is the focus of new research attention because it has become increasingly prevalent in recent years (Fombonne, 2009). *Autism Spectrum Disorder* involves abnormal or impaired development of communication and a markedly restricted repertoire of activities or interests. Signs of autism can arise in early infancy. Most infants respond to facial expressions in the first few months, sometimes even rewarding a smile with a smile in return—

▲ It's a good sign when a baby smiles for you. Even better if the baby can fly. COURTESY OF DANIEL WEGNER

whereas a baby with profound autism may not do this even at 6 months of age. Some children who become autistic progress normally for the first years, only to develop the disorder at age 2 or 3 or even later.

Whenever it emerges, autism can be profoundly debilitating. The disorder often involves an inability to interact socially, with little eye contact or social responsiveness, and it can lead to restricted, repetitive behaviors and even recurring self-harm. Autism is not always severe, with various degrees of disorder along a spectrum that includes milder forms such as Asperger's syndrome (Goldstein, Naglieri, & Ozonoff, 2008). Sometimes the disorder can even bring unique talents. People with autism may show remarkable abilities—for example, the ability to perceive or remember details or to master symbol systems such as mathematics or music (Happé & Vital, 2009). These gifts come with the cost, however, of poor social perception—a limited ability to perceive others' minds and desires.

So what happens to people with autism when they are no longer children? Some develop ways to cope and even channel their unique talents, such as renowned behavioral scientist and author Temple Grandin, who is a university professor and the central character in an HBO movie based on her life. But people diagnosed with autism as children have highly variable trajectories, with some achieving normal or better-than-normal functioning and others remaining the victims of profound disorder. Autism is a childhood disorder that in adulthood can turn out many ways.

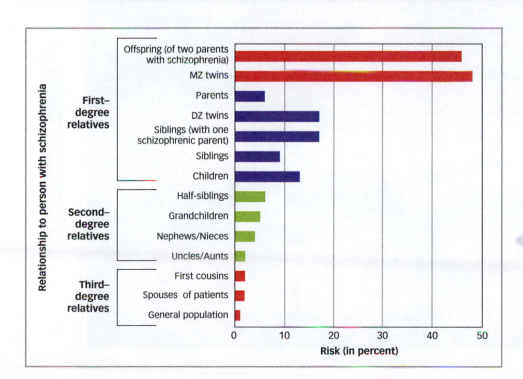

▶ FIGURE **13.3** **Average Risk of Developing Schizophrenia** The risk of schizophrenia among biological relatives is greater for those with greater degrees of relatedness. An identical (MZ) twin of a twin with schizophrenia has a 48% risk of developing schizophrenia, for example, and offspring of two parents with schizophrenia have a 46% risk of developing the disorder.

(Adapted from Gottesman, 1991.)

However, other biological factors play a role too. The **dopamine hypothesis** is *the idea that schizophrenia involves an excess of dopamine activity.* Many drugs that can alleviate schizophrenic symptoms work by reducing dopamine transmission in certain brain tracts, and amphetamines, which increase dopamine levels, often aggravate the symptoms of schizophrenia (Iverson, 2006). However, many individuals with schizophrenia do not respond favorably to dopamine-blocking drugs, and those who do seldom show a complete remission of symptoms. Moreover, the drugs block dopamine receptors very rapidly, yet individuals with schizophrenia typically do not show a beneficial response for weeks. Finally, research has implicated other neurotransmitters in schizophrenia, suggesting that the disorder may involve a complex interaction among a host of different biochemicals (Risman et al., 2008; Sawa & Snyder, 2002). In sum, the precise role of neurotransmitters in schizophrenia has yet to be determined.

Finally, neuroimaging studies provide evidence of a variety of brain abnormalities in schizophrenia. Some of the most well documented changes include a progressive tissue loss beginning in the parietal lobe and eventually encompassing much of the brain (Thompson et al., 2001) (see **FIGURE 13.4**). All adolescents lose some gray matter over time in a kind of normal "pruning" of the brain, but in the case of those developing schizophrenia, the loss was dramatic enough to seem pathological. A variety of specific brain changes found in other studies suggest a clear relationship between biological changes in the brain and the progression of schizophrenia (Shenton et al., 2001).

▼ FIGURE **13.4** **Brain Tissue Loss in Adolescent Schizophrenia** MRI scan composites reveal brain tissue loss in adolescents diagnosed with schizophrenia. Normal brains (top) show minimal loss due to "pruning." Early deficit scans (middle) reveal loss in the parietal areas. Patients at this stage may experience symptoms such as hallucinations or bizarre thoughts. Scans 5 years later (bottom) reveal extensive tissue loss over much of the cortex. Patients at this stage are likely to suffer from delusions, disorganized speech and behavior, and negative symptoms such as social withdrawal. (From Thompson et al., 2001)

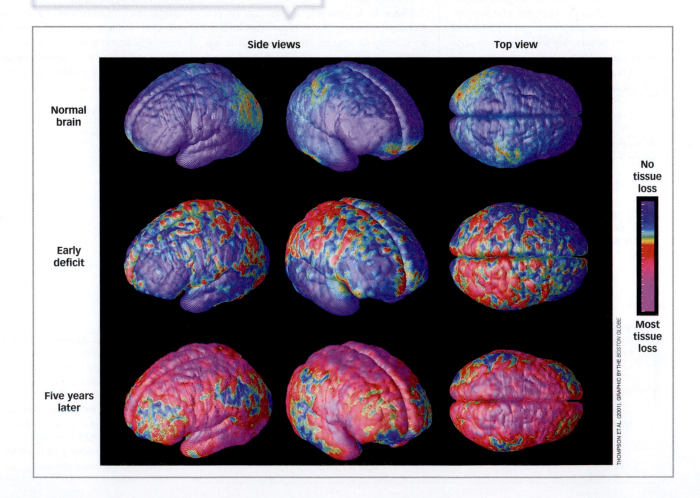

THOMPSON ET AL. (2001). GRAPHIC BY THE BOSTON GLOBE.

Psychological Factors

With all these potential biological contributors to schizophrenia, you might think there would be few psychological or social causes of the disorder. However, several studies do suggest that the family environment plays a role in the development of and recovery from the condition. One large-scale study compared the risk of schizophrenia in children adopted into healthy families and those adopted into severely disturbed families (Tienari et al., 2004). (Disturbed families were defined as those with extreme conflict, lack of communication, or chaotic relationships.) Among children whose biological mothers had schizophrenia, the disturbed environment increased the likelihood of developing schizophrenia—an outcome that was not found among children who were also reared in disturbed families but whose biological mothers did *not* have schizophrenia. This finding provides support for the diathesis-stress model described earlier.

dopamine hypothesis The idea that schizophrenia involves an excess of dopamine activity.

personality disorders Disorders characterized by deeply ingrained, inflexible patterns of thinking, feeling, relating to others, or controlling impulses that cause distress or impaired functioning.

SUMMARY QUIZ [13.5]

1. Schizophrenia is characterized by which of the following?
   a. hallucinations
   b. disorganized thoughts and behavior
   c. emotional and social withdrawal
   d. all of the above

2. Schizophrenia affects approximately _____ % of the population and accounts for approximately _____ % of admissions to state and county mental hospitals.
   a. 5; 20
   b. 5; 5
   c. 1; 1
   d. 1; 40

3. Keith believes that he is an alien who was born on a different planet and that the CIA is monitoring all his thoughts by means of a wireless transmitter they have implanted inside his head. Keith is experiencing
   a. hallucinations.
   b. disorganized speech.
   c. delusions.
   d. grossly disorganized behavior.

Personality Disorders: Going to Extremes

Think for a minute about high school acquaintances whose personalities made them stand out—not necessarily in a good way. Was there a space ball, for example, a person who didn't seem to make sense, wore strange outfits, sometimes wouldn't respond in conversation—or would respond by bringing up weird things like astrology or mind reading? Or perhaps a drama queen, whose theatrics and exaggerated emotions turned everything into a big deal? And don't forget the neat freak, who had the perfectly organized locker, precisely arranged hair, and a sweater with zero lint balls. One way to describe such people is to say they simply have *personalities,* the unique patterns of traits we explored in Chapter 11. But sometimes personality traits can become so rigid and confining that they blend over into mental disorders. **Personality disorders** are *disorders characterized by deeply ingrained, inflexible patterns of thinking, feeling, relating to others, or controlling impulses that cause distress or impaired functioning.* Let's look at the types of personality disorders and then take a closer look at one that sometimes lands people in jail—*antisocial personality disorder.*

Types of Personality Disorders

The *DSM-5* lists 10 personality disorders (see **TABLE 13.2**). They fall into three clusters—*odwd/eccentric, dramatic/erratic,* and *anxious/inhibited.* The high school space

Ever browse a copy of *Architectural Digest* and wonder who would live in one of those perfect homes? A person with obsessive-compulsive personality disorder might fit right in. This personality disorder (characterized by excessive perfectionism) should not be mistaken, by the way, for obsessive-compulsive disorder—the anxiety disorder in which the person suffers from repeated unwanted thoughts or actions.

Table 13.2

Clusters of Personality Disorders

Cluster	Personality Disorder	Characteristics
A. Odd/Eccentric	Schizotypal	Peculiar or eccentric manners of speaking or dressing. Strange beliefs. "Magical thinking" such as belief in ESP or telepathy. Difficulty forming relationships. May react oddly in conversation, not respond, or talk to self. Speech elaborate or difficult to follow. (Possibly a mild form of schizophrenia.)
	Paranoid	Distrust in others, suspicion that people have sinister motives. Apt to challenge the loyalties of friends and read hostile intentions into others' actions. Prone to anger and aggressive outbursts but otherwise emotionally cold. Often jealous, guarded, secretive, overly serious.
	Schizoid	Extreme introversion and withdrawal from relationships. Prefers to be alone, little interest in others. Humorless, distant, often absorbed with own thoughts and feelings, a daydreamer. Fearful of closeness, with poor social skills; often seen as a "loner."
B. Dramatic/Erratic	Antisocial	Impoverished moral sense or "conscience." History of deception, crime, legal problems, impulsive and aggressive or violent behavior. Little emotional empathy or remorse for hurting others. Manipulative, careless, callous. At high risk for substance abuse and alcoholism.
	Borderline	Unstable moods and intense, stormy personal relationships. Frequent mood changes and anger, unpredictable impulses. Self-mutilation or suicidal threats or gestures to get attention or manipulate others. Self-image fluctuation and a tendency to see others as "all good" or "all bad."
	Histrionic	Constant attention seeking. Grandiose language, provocative dress, exaggerated illnesses, all to gain attention. Believes that everyone loves them. Emotional, lively, overly dramatic, enthusiastic, and excessively flirtatious. Shallow and labile true emotions. "Onstage."
	Narcissistic	Inflated sense of self-importance, absorbed by fantasies of self and success. Exaggerates own achievement, assumes others will recognize they are superior. Good first impressions but poor longer-term relationships. Exploitative of others.
C. Anxious/Inhibited	Avoidant	Socially anxious and uncomfortable unless they are confident of being liked. In contrast with schizoid person, yearns for social contact. Fears criticism and worries about being embarrassed in front of others. Avoids social situations due to fear of rejection.
	Dependent	Submissive, dependent, requiring excessive approval, reassurance, and advice. Clings to people and fears losing them. Lacking self-confidence. Uncomfortable when alone. May be devastated by end of close relationship or suicidal if breakup is threatened.
	Obsessive-compulsive	Conscientious, orderly, perfectionist. Excessive need to do everything "right." Inflexibly high standards and caution can interfere with their productivity. Fear of errors can make them strict and controlling. Poor expression of emotions. (*Not* the same as obsessive-compulsive disorder.)

Source: From *DSM-5* (American Psychiatric Association, 2013).

ball, for example, could have *schizotypal personality disorder* (odd/eccentric cluster); the drama queen could have *histrionic personality disorder* (dramatic/erratic cluster); the neat freak could have *obsessive-compulsive personality disorder* (anxious/inhibited cluster). Don't rush to judgment, however. Most of those kids are probably quite healthy and fall far short of qualifying for a diagnosis—after all, high school can be a rocky time for everyone. Still, the array of personality disorders suggests that there are multiple ways an individual's gift of a unique personality could become a burden.

Personality disorders are the most controversial classifications in the *DSM-5* for several reasons. First, critics question whether having a problem personality is really a disorder. Given that 14.8% of the U.S. population has a personality disorder that fits a *DSM* description (Grant et al., 2004), perhaps it might be better just to admit that a lot of people are difficult and leave it at that. Another question is whether personality problems correspond to "disorders" or might be better understood as extreme values on trait dimensions such as the Big Five discussed in Chapter 11 (Trull & Durrett, 2005). Finally, definitions of many personality problems share characteristics with the major disorders and may be mild versions of these conditions. Overall, for example, roughly half of people with an anxiety or mood disorder have a comorbid personality disorder (Van Velzen & Emmelkamp, 1996). Research is ongoing on these various questions (Oldham, Skodol, & Bender, 2005).

Many people with personality disorders won't admit to them, and this adds a further diagnostic complication. Personality measurement depends largely on self-reports—a pointless undertaking

? **Why is self-reporting a problem in diagnosing personality disorders?**

when self-insight is the exception rather than the rule. To solve this problem, some researchers have turned to *peer nomination* measures, reports by others who know the person. Research on peer nominations in college sororities and fraternities and in groups of military recruits reveals that groups arrive at remarkably homogeneous assessments of their personality-disordered members (Oltmanns & Turkheimer, 2006). Peer nominations using basic reports of the behavior of people in a group can predict which members will have further problems—such as dropping out of college or being discharged early from the military (Fiedler, Oltmanns, & Turkheimer, 2004).

The common feature of personality disorders is a failure to take other people's perspectives, particularly on the self. People with personality disorders often blame others, society, or the universe for their difficulties, distorting their perceptions of the world in a way that makes the personality disorder seem perfectly normal—at least to them. In many of the personality disorders, this blindness perpetuates the disorder and so hurts the person who suffers from it: People with personality disorders are often unhappy or depressed. Antisocial personality disorder, however, is particularly likely to go beyond harm to self and to exact a cost on anyone who knows the person—because the individual with antisocial personality disorder also lacks insight into what it means to hurt others.

TECH. SGT. DENISE A. RAYDER

Military recruits going through basic training develop knowledge of one another's personalities. Their judgments of one another at the end of training—peer nominations—produce valid predictions of who will later receive early discharge from the military.

Antisocial Personality Disorder

Henri Désiré Landru began using the personal columns to attract a woman "interested in matrimony," and he succeeded in seducing 10 of them. He bilked them of their savings, poisoned them, and cremated them in his stove, also disposing of a boy and two dogs along the way. He recorded his murders in a notebook and maintained a marriage and a mistress all the while. The gruesome actions of serial killers such as Landru leave us frightened and wondering; however, bullies, compulsive liars, and even drivers who regularly speed through a school zone share the same shocking blindness to human pain. **Antisocial personality disorder (APD)** is defined as *a pervasive pattern of disregard for and violation of the rights of others that begins in childhood or early adolescence and continues into adulthood.*

Adults with an antisocial personality diagnosis typically have a history of problems as children and adolescents, such as aggression, destruction of property, lying, stealing, and cruelty to animals. As adults, diagnostic signs include illegal behavior, deception, impulsivity, physical aggression, recklessness, irresponsibility, and a lack of remorse for wrongdoing. About 3.6% of the general population has antisocial personality disorder, and the

? **What are some of the factors that contribute to APD?**

rate of occurrence in men is three times the rate in women (Grant et al., 2004). The terms *sociopath* and *psychopath* describe people with APD who are especially cold-hearted, manipulative, and ruthless—yet may be glib and charming (Cleckley, 1976; Hare, 1998). Many people with APD commit crimes, and many are caught because of the frequency and flagrancy of their infractions. Among 22,790 prisoners in one study, 47% of the men and 21% of the women were diagnosed with antisocial personality disorder (Fazel & Danesh, 2002). Statistics such as these support the notion of a "criminal personality."

antisocial personality disorder (APD) A pervasive pattern of disregard for and violation of the rights of others that begins in childhood or early adolescence and continues into adulthood.

Both the early onset of conduct problems and the lack of success in treatment suggest that career criminality has an internal cause (Lykken, 1995). Evidence of brain abnormalities in people with APD is also accumulating (Blair, Peschardt, & Mitchell, 2005). For example, criminal psychopaths who are shown negative emotional words such as *hate* or *corpse* exhibit less activity in the amygdala and hippocampus than do noncriminals (Kiehl et al., 2001). These two brain areas are involved in the process of fear conditioning (Patrick, Cuthbert, & Lang, 1994), so their relative inactivity in such studies suggests that psychopaths are less sensitive to fear than are other people. Violent psychopaths can target their aggression toward the self as well as others, often behaving in reckless ways that lead to violent ends. It might seem peaceful

HOT SCIENCE

Positive Psychology

You are now familiar with some of the most difficult challenges we face—profound, painful mental problems that can cause great unhappiness. However, psychologists' interests go beyond the negative aspects of life. Most recently, a flourishing movement known as *positive psychology* emphasizes an approach that seeks to understand what makes our lives pleasant, good, and meaningful.

The positive psychology movement has been particularly effective in stimulating research on happiness (Snyder & Lopez, 2009). Each of us claims to be something of an expert on what will make us happy (Chocolate, please! Or maybe world peace? No, no, a speedboat . . .), but it is often surprising just how mistaken we can be about what will bring us the joy we desire (Gilbert, 2006). Research supplies some happy facts:

- Money can buy happiness, but only a little. Wealthy people are only the tiniest bit happier than the average person (Diener, Horwitz, & Emmons, 1985).

- Friends make you happy. People report that the main source of their happiness is relationships—with their friends, spouses, and children (*Time* poll, 2005). As the old saying goes, people on their deathbed never say, "I should have spent more time at work."

- Married people are happier than singles, especially right after getting married and then again when their children are grown (Coombs, 1991). Their greater happiness, however, may be because they were happier to begin with (Lucas et al., 2003).

- Happiness is born, not made. Twin studies reveal that as much as 50% of variability in happiness is due to genetic factors (Lykken & Tellegen, 1996). Ideally, try to be born happy.

- People regularly overestimate the degree to which positive events (such as winning the lottery) will make them happy. They fail to appreciate their own tendency to adjust psychologically to emotional experiences and "get over it," no matter what "it" is (Gilbert & Wilson, 2009).

- Although happiness decreases gradually until about age 50, it then rises steadily for about the next 25 years (Stone et al., 2010).

- Happiness comes from goodness. Doing good deeds or seeing them done can lead to feelings of elevation and happiness (Haidt, 2006).

More happy facts are surfacing every day, as many researchers have joined the movement toward positive psychology (Gable & Haidt, 2005). This movement provides a balance to the common focus of the field on the negative side, the psychological disorders. Knowing about these disorders does aid in understanding how the mind works. But, like the good physician who brings to a patient's bedside both an analytical appreciation of the patient's disorder and a warm smile to help the patient through the rough times, the field of psychology must temper the bitter with the sweet. Psychological science can be most effective when it unites the problem-solving approach of studying disorders with the ideals and optimism of studying wellness.

Virtue	Definition	Specific Strengths
Wisdom and knowledge	Cognitive strengths that entail the acquisition and use of knowledge	Creativity, open-mindedness, curiosity, love of learning, perspective
Courage	Emotional strengths that involve the exercise of will to accomplish goals in the face of opposition, external or internal	Authenticity, bravery, persistence, zest
Humanity	Interpersonal strengths that involve tending and befriending others	Kindness, love, social intelligence
Justice	Civic strengths that underlie healthy community life	Fairness, leadership, teamwork
Temperance	Strengths that protect against excess	Forgiveness, modesty, prudence, self-regulation
Transcendence	Strengths that forge connections to the larger universe and provide meaning	Appreciation of beauty and excellence, gratitude, hope, humor, religiousness

Source: From Peterson and Seligman (2004), *Character Strengths and Virtues.*

to go through life "without fear," but perhaps fear is useful in keeping people from the extremes of antisocial behavior.

The psychological disorders we have examined in this chapter represent a tragic loss of human potential. The contentment, peace, and love that people could be enjoying are crowded out by pain and suffering when the mind goes awry to create disorders (see the Hot Science box). A scientific approach to mental disorders that views them through a medical model is beginning to sort out their symptoms and causes. As we will see in the next chapter, this approach already offers treatments for some disorders that are remarkably effective and for other disorders offers hope that pain and suffering can be alleviated in the future.

Henri Désiré Landru (1869–1922) was a serial killer who met widows through ads he placed in newspapers' lonely hearts columns. After obtaining enough information to embezzle money from them, he murdered 10 women and the son of one of the women. He was executed for serial murder in 1922.

SUMMARY QUIZ [13.6]

1. Which of the following is a feature common to all personality disorders?
   a. failure to take other people's perspectives
   b. excessive fear of rejection
   c. unstable moods
   d. overly dramatic attempts at attention seeking

2. Which of the following is *not* one of the identified personality disorder clusters?
   a. odd/eccentric
   b. dramatic/erratic
   c. anxious/inhibited
   d. impulsive/aggressive

3. Jim was diagnosed as having antisocial personality disorder based on the fact that he
   a. is emotionally distant, suspicious of others, and has an intense fear of rejection.
   b. avoids social interaction, has very poor social skills, and is often seen as a "loner."
   c. is very peculiar in his speech and dress and has difficulty forming relationships.
   d. is manipulative, impulsive, and shows little emotional empathy.

Where Do You Stand?

Genetic Tests for Risk of Psychological Disorders

Today, you don't have to worry about it. Genetic testing for psychological disorders is not advanced enough that you could learn if you're genetically prone toward a disorder. But in the not-too-distant future, you may be able to find out if your genes show an elevated risk for a problem—merely by providing a saliva specimen. Genetic patterns underlying certain forms of bipolar mood disorder, for example, may be clear enough that genetic testing for risk of the disorder is possible (Couzin, 2008; Joo et al., 2009).

A genetic diagnosis could be very helpful. If your life is miserable and you're overwhelmed with problems, it might be nice to put a label on what's wrong, even if that diagnosis is not good news. In the case of bipolar disorder, years may elapse between the onset of symptoms and a diagnosis, and

the end of the uncertainty that comes with knowing the problem may bring a kind of relief. Having a name for the disorder doesn't guarantee effective treatment, of course, but it is a key first step.

But what if you have a genetic tendency toward the disorder but don't have any symptoms? Then would you want to know about your genes? For that matter, you might have a genetic tendency that will never be expressed— suspicious saliva with no actual disorder. Suspecting that you might become bipolar could create problems all by itself. Every little symptom could be meaningful. Was I being manic just now? Was I acting depressed? Any mood shift might be an alarm bell, and worrying about your genes could be a constant source of stress. So would you want to know your genetic risk for a psychological disorder, or would you rather not? Where do you stand?

Chapter Review

Identifying Psychological Disorders: What Is Abnormal?

▶ The study of psychological disorders follows a medical model in which symptoms are understood to indicate an underlying disorder.

▶ The *DSM-5* is a classification system that defines a psychological disorder as occurring when the person experiences disturbances of thought, emotion, or behavior that produce distress or impairment and that arise from internal sources.

▶ Many psychological disorders arise from multiple causes or as a result of the interaction of diathesis (internal predisposition) and stress. It is a common error to assume that an intervention that cures a disorder reflects the cause of the disorder.

Anxiety and Obsessive-Compulsive Disorders Disorders: When Fears Take Over

▶ People with anxiety disorders have irrational worries and fears that undermine their ability to function normally.

▶ Generalized anxiety disorder (GAD) involves a chronic state of anxiety, whereas phobic disorders involve anxiety tied to a specific object or situation.

▶ People who suffer from panic disorder experience a sudden and intense attack of anxiety that is terrifying and can lead them to become agoraphobic and housebound for fear of public humiliation.

▶ People with obsessive-compulsive disorder experience recurring, anxiety-provoking thoughts that compel them to engage in ritualistic, irrational behavior.

Depressive and Bipolar Disorders Disorders: At the Mercy of Emotions

▶ Mood disorders are mental disorders in which a disturbance in mood is the predominant feature.

▶ Major depression (or unipolar depression) is characterized by a severely depressed mood; symptoms include excessive self-criticism, guilt, difficulty concentrating, suicidal thoughts, sleep and appetite disturbances, and lethargy.

▶ Bipolar disorder is an unstable emotional condition involving extreme mood swings of depression and mania, periods of abnormally and persistently elevated, expansive, or irritable mood.

Dissociative Disorders: Going to Pieces

▶ Dissociative disorders involve severely disjointed and fragmented cognitive processes reflected in significant disruptions in memory, awareness, or personality.

▶ People with dissociative identity disorder (DID) shift between two or more identities that are distinctive from each other in terms of personal memories, behavioral characteristics, and attitudes.

▶ Dissociative amnesia involves significant memory loss that is too extensive to be the result of normal forgetting and cannot be attributed to brain injury, drugs, or another mental disorder.

Schizophrenia: Losing the Grasp on Reality

▶ Schizophrenia is a severe psychological disorder involving hallucinations, disorganized thoughts and behavior, and emotional and social withdrawal. It affects only 1% of the population, but it accounts for a disproportionate share of psychiatric hospitalizations.

▶ Drugs that reduce the availability of dopamine sometimes reduce the symptoms of schizophrenia, suggesting that the disorder involves an excess of dopamine activity, but recent research suggests that schizophrenia may involve a complex interaction among a variety of neurotransmitters.

▶ Risks for developing schizophrenia include genetic factors, biochemical factors (perhaps a complex interaction among many neurotransmitters), brain abnormalities, and a stressful home environment.

Personality Disorders: Going to Extremes

▶ Personality disorders are deeply ingrained, inflexible patterns of thinking, feeling, relating to others, or controlling impulses that cause distress or impaired functioning.

▶ Classification of personality disorders is controversial because they may be no more than extreme examples of normal personality, may represent personality dimensions rather than types of disorder, and are often comorbid with other disorders.

▶ Antisocial personality disorder is associated with a lack of moral emotions and behavior; people with antisocial personality disorder can be manipulative, dangerous, and reckless, often hurting others and sometimes hurting themselves

KEY TERMS

medical model (p. 406)

DSM-5 (p. 407)

comorbidity (p. 409)

diathesis-stress model (p. 410)

anxiety disorders (p. 412)

generalized anxiety disorder (GAD) (p. 412)

phobic disorders (p. 413)

specific phobia (p. 413)

social phobia (p. 413)

preparedness theory (p. 414)

panic disorder (p. 415)

agoraphobia (p. 415)

obsessive-compulsive disorder (OCD) (p. 416)

mood disorders (p. 417)

major depressive disorder (p. 417)

seasonal affective disorder (SAD) (p. 417)

helplessness theory (p. 419)

bipolar disorder (p. 420)

dissociative disorder (p. 421)

dissociative identity disorder (DID) (p. 421)

dissociative fugue (p. 422)

dissociative amnesia (p. 422)

schizophrenia (p. 423)

delusion (p. 423)

hallucination (p. 424)

disorganized speech (p. 424)

grossly disorganized behavior
 (p. 424)

negative symptoms (p. 424)

dopamine hypothesis (p. 426)

personality disorders (p. 427)

antisocial personality disorder
 (APD) (p. 429)

CHANGING MINDS

1. You catch a TV interview with a celebrity who describes his difficult childhood, living with a mother who suffered from major depression. "Sometimes my mother stayed in her bed for days, not even getting up to eat," he says. "At the time, the family hushed it up. My parents were immigrants, and they came from a culture where it was considered shameful to have mental problems. You are supposed to have enough strength of will to overcome your problems, without help from anyone else. So my mother never got treatment." How might the idea of a medical model of psychiatric disorders have helped the woman and her family in the decision whether to seek treatment?

2. You're studying for your upcoming psychology exam when your roommate breezes in, saying: "I was just at the gym and I ran into Sue. She's totally schizo: nice one minute, mean the next." You can't resist the opportunity to set the record straight. What psychiatric disorder is your roommate attributing to Sue? How is this different from schizophrenia?

3. A friend of yours has a family member who is experiencing severe mental problems, including delusions and loss of motivation. "We went to one psychiatrist," she says, "and got a diagnosis of schizophrenia. We went for a second opinion, and the other doctor said it was probably bipolar disorder. They're both good doctors, and they're both using the same *DSM*—how can they come up with different diagnoses?" How would you reply to her?

4. After reading the chapter, one of your classmates turns to you with a sigh of relief. "I finally figured it out. I have a deadbeat brother who always gets himself into trouble and then blames other people for his problems. Even when he gets a ticket for speeding, he never thinks it's his fault—the police were picking on him, or his passengers were urging him to go too fast. I always thought he was just a loser—but now I realize he has a personality disorder!" Do you agree with your classmate's diagnosis of his brother? How would you caution your classmate about the dangers of self-diagnosis or diagnosis of friends and family?

CRITICAL THINKING QUESTIONS

1. Psychological disorders can be caused by biological, psychological, and environmental factors. The diathesis-stress model suggests that a person may be predisposed for a psychological disorder that remains unexpressed until triggered by stress. Suppose that two identical twins (with the same genetic profile) grow up in the same household (sharing the same parents, the same basic diet, the same access to television, etc.). As a teenager, one twin but not the other develops a mental disorder such as schizophrenia. How could this be?

2. Phobias are anxiety disorders that involve excessive and persistent fear of a specific object, activity, or situation. Some phobias may be learned through classical conditioning, in which a conditioned stimulus (CS) that is paired with an anxiety-evoking stimulus (US) itself comes to elicit a fear response (CR). Suppose your friend has a phobia of dogs that is so

intense that he is afraid to go outside in case one of his neighbors' dogs barks at him. Using the principles of classical conditioning you learned in Chapter 7, how might you help him overcome his fear?

3. Major depression (also known as unipolar depression) is characterized by a severely depressed mood, accompanied by feelings of worthlessness and lack of pleasure and by sleep and appetite disturbances. To be characterized as major depression, the episode must last at least 2 weeks, but on average episodes last about 6 months.

 Both seasonal affective disorder (SAD) and bipolar disorder involve shorter, but cyclically recurring, depressive episodes. If you have a friend who experiences recurring periods of severe depression, how would you determine whether she is suffering from SAD or bipolar disorder?

ANSWERS TO SUMMARY QUIZZES

Summary Quiz [13.1] 1. a; 2. b; 3. c

Summary Quiz [13.2] 1. d; 2. d; 3. b

Summary Quiz [13.3] 1. a; 2. a; 3. d

Summary Quiz [13.4] 1. d; 2. c; 3. a

Summary Quiz [13.5] 1. d; 2. d; 3. c

Summary Quiz [13.6] 1. a; 2. d; 3. d

Need more help? Additional resources are located at the book's free companion website at:
www.worthpublishers.com/schacterbrief2e

Treatment of Psychological Disorders

THE PLANE WAS STILL AT THE GATE, but Lisa was buckled in her seat with her hands tightly squeezing the armrests, her knuckles white. She glanced out the window, swallowed hard, and then stole a look at the people across the aisle. They seemed calm, but she didn't feel calm at all. Her heart was pounding, and then she noticed that the plane was starting to move. She was deathly afraid of flying, but she hoped that this flight might be easier. After all, she wasn't really in a plane. Instead, she was seated in a psychologist's office, wearing virtual reality goggles that projected the sights and sounds of the flight all around her. She was in therapy.

Psychological therapy takes many forms. In this case, Lisa's fear was being treated with a relatively new technique called *virtual reality therapy*. The therapist sat nearby during the virtual flight and encouraged Lisa to progress at her own pace through the stages of air travel that made her anxious—sitting on a plane with the engines off, sitting on a plane with the engines on, taxiing on the runway, a smooth takeoff and a smooth flight, a smooth landing, a close pass similar to a missed landing, a rough landing, a turbulent flight, and a rough takeoff. Lisa came back for six sessions over several weeks, and at the end of her virtual travels she reported feeling no anxiety about any of these virtual events. With the therapist's encouragement, she soon took the step of flying in a real plane (Rothbaum et al., 1996). For many people who might otherwise have debilitating fears or phobias, virtual reality therapy offers a treatment option that can be remarkably effective (Powers & Emmelkamp, 2008).

ROZA/DREAMSTIME.COM

THIERRY BERROD/MONA LISA PRODUCTION/SCIENCE PHOTO LIBRARY/SCIENCE SOURCE

Virtual reality therapy offers new possibilities for treating people with psychological disorders, especially phobias. Clients can practice engaging in "virtual experiences" before tackling the real-life experiences they fear. The top photo shows a therapist conducting a virtual flight; the bottom photo shows the client's virtual "view" out the "plane" window.

THERE ARE A NUMBER OF WAYS TO TREAT MOST psychological disorders, with the goal of changing a person's thoughts, behaviors, emotions, or coping skills. Treatments requiring a person to wear wraparound video goggles are not yet commonplace, but the variety and ingenuity of goggle-free treatment techniques are remarkable. In this chapter, we will explore the most common approaches to psychological treatment. We will examine why people need to seek psychological help in the first place, look at how psychotherapy for individuals is built on the major theories of the causes and cures of disorders—including psychoanalytic, behavioral, cognitive, and humanistic/existential theories—and explore how psychotherapy can be conducted for people in groups as well. We'll also look into medical and biological approaches to treatment that focus on understanding the brain's role in disorders. Finally, we'll discuss whether treatment works as well as how we know that treatment works.

Treatment: Getting Help to Those Who Need It

Estimates suggest that almost one in five people suffer from some type of mental disorder (Narrow et al., 2002). The personal costs of these disorders involve anguish to the sufferers as well as interference in their ability to carry on the activities of daily life, affecting family life, the ability to work, maintenance of friendships, and more. For example, people with anxiety disorders report levels of impairment in their daily lives that are comparable with or higher than those of people with chronic medical illnesses, such as multiple sclerosis or end-stage renal disease (Antony et al., 1998b). There are financial costs too. One study found that the annual cost of anxiety disorders alone in the United States was $42.3 billion, or $1,542 per sufferer, including costs of treatment, diminished productivity, and absenteeism in the workplace (Greenberg et al., 1999). If we add in similar figures for schizophrenia, mood disorders, substance abuse, and all the other psychological problems, the overall costs are astronomical. In addition to the personal benefits of treatment, then, society also stands to benefit from the effective treatment of psychological disorders.

Why People Cannot or Will Not Seek Treatment

A physical symptom such as a toothache would send most people to the dentist—a trip that usually results in a successful treatment. The clear source of pain and the obvious solution make for a quick and effective response. In contrast, the path from a mental disorder to a successful treatment is often far less clear. Despite the high prevalence of psychological problems in the general population, most people who suffer from such problems do not receive help. One survey of more than 1,600 adults diagnosed with depression or an anxiety disorder found that only 30% received appropriate treatment for the problem—despite the fact that 83% had seen a health care provider in the previous year (Young et al., 2001). People may fail to get treatment because of three major problems:

? What are the obstacles to help/treatment for the mentally ill?

1. *People may not realize that their disorder needs to be treated.* Mental illness is often not taken nearly as seriously as physical illness, perhaps because the origin of mental illness is "hidden" and usually cannot be diagnosed by a blood test or x-ray.

2. *There may be barriers to treatment, such as beliefs and circumstances that keep people from getting help.* Individuals may believe that they should be able to handle

things themselves. In some cases, families discourage their loved ones from seeking help because the public acknowledgment of a psychological disorder may be seen as an embarrassment to the family. In other cases, there may be financial obstacles to getting treatment, such as lack of medical insurance that covers treatment for mental health disorders. Cultural and gender factors may also affect who seeks treatment and who does not. For example, among college students, men may be less likely than women to seek psychological services (Komiya, Good, & Sherrod, 2000).

3. *Even people who acknowledge they have a problem may not know where to look for services.* Like finding a good lawyer or plumber, finding the right psychologist can be more difficult than simply flipping through the yellow pages or searching online. This confusion is understandable given the plethora of different types of treatments available (see the Real World box).

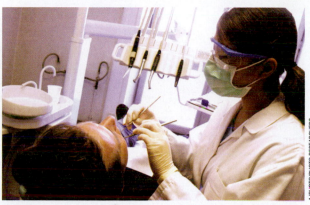

When your tooth hurts, you go to a dentist. But how do you know when to see a psychologist?

THE REAL WORLD

Types of Psychotherapists

Therapists have widely varying backgrounds and training, and this affects the kinds of services they offer. There are several major "flavors":

- *Psychologists:* A psychologist who practices psychotherapy holds a doctorate with specialization in clinical psychology (a PhD or PsyD). The psychologist will have extensive training in therapy, the assessment of psychological disorders, and research. The psychologist will sometimes have a specialty, such as working with adolescents or helping people overcome sleep disorders. Psychologists must be licensed by the state.

- *Psychiatrists:* A psychiatrist is a medical doctor who has completed an MD with specialized training in assessing and treating mental disorders. Psychiatrists can prescribe medications, and some also practice psychotherapy. General practice physicians can also prescribe medications for mental disorders, but they do not typically receive much training in the diagnosis or treatment of mental disorders and do not practice psychotherapy.

- *Social workers:* Social workers have a master's degree in social work and have training in working with people in dire life situations such as poverty, homelessness, or family conflict. Clinical or psychiatric social workers also receive training to help people in these situations who have mental disorders.

- *Counselors:* In some states, a counselor must have a master's degree and extensive training in therapy; other states require minimal training or relevant education. Counselors who work in schools usually have a master's degree and specific training in counseling in educational settings.

Some people offer therapy under made-up terms that sound professional—"mind/body healing therapist" or "marital adjustment adviser." Often these terms are simply invented to mislead clients and avoid licensing boards. To be safe, it

▲ Which one? Finding the right psychotherapist can seem like finding the best watermelon: You won't really know until you've had a taste. Shoppers sometimes thump melons on the theory that the sweetest ones sound different, but no one quite knows how a good one will sound. In the case of psychotherapists, fortunately, no thumping is required. You can find out about their qualifications in advance and even talk to several to see which one seems right.

is important to shop wisely for a therapist whose training and credentials inspire confidence. People you know—your general practice physician, a school counselor, or a trusted friend or family member—might be able to recommend a good therapist. Or you can visit the Internet site of an organization, such as the American Psychological Association, that offers referrals to licensed mental health care providers.

Before you agree to see a therapist for treatment, you should ask questions to evaluate whether the therapist is a good match for your problem:

- What type of therapy do you practice?
- What types of problems do you usually treat?
- For how long do you usually see people in therapy?
- Will our work involve "talking" therapy, medications, or both?
- How effective is this type of therapy for the type of problem I'm having?
- What are your fees for therapy, and will health insurance cover them?

Armed with these answers, you can make an informed decision about the type of service you need. The therapist's personality is also critically important. You should seek out someone who is willing to answer questions and who shows general respect and empathy for you. A therapist is someone you are entrusting with your mental health, and you should enter into such a relationship only when you and the therapist have good rapport.

Even when people seek and find help, they sometimes do not receive the most effective treatments. For example, although cognitive and behavioral therapies yield the best results for treating anxiety disorders, most people do not receive these treatments. In one study, most individuals seeking help in a clinic specializing in anxiety disorders reported having previously received treatments other than cognitive or behavioral therapy for their anxiety problems even though there is little evidence for the effectiveness of these other approaches for anxiety disorders. Only about one third of people reported previously receiving the treatment approaches most strongly supported by prior research (Rowa et al., 2000). Clearly, before choosing or prescribing a therapy, we need to know what kinds of treatments are available and understand which treatments are best for particular disorders.

Approaches to Treatment

Treatments can be divided broadly into two kinds: psychotherapy, in which a person interacts with a psychotherapist, and medical or biological treatments, in which the mental disorder is treated with drugs or surgery. In some cases, both psychotherapy *and* biological treatments are used. Lisa's fear of flying, for example, might be treated not only with the virtual reality therapy you read about (a form of psychotherapy) in preparation for the real flight but also with antianxiety medications in the hours before the actual takeoff. As you'll see later in the chapter, often the most effective treatments combine both psychotherapy and medications.

Early mental health workers used water dowsing, or "hydrotherapy," for psychological disorders. Here a patient at the Pennsylvania Hospital for the Insane gets a cold "douche bath" (Haskell, 1869). Such treatments were given in the forlorn hope that something might work, but often they were simply torture—not unlike the waterboarding used in CIA interrogations during the George W. Bush administration.

COURTESY UNIVERSITY OF MICHIGAN'S ©MAKING OF AMERICA/HTTP://MCAMOA.UMICH.EDU

CULTURE & COMMUNITY

Is Psychotherapy the Same Around the World? Not at all. Some psychotherapies are indigenous to particular cultures. For example, two well-known therapies influenced by Buddhism originated in Japan: Morita therapy and Naikan therapy (Sato, 2001).

Morita therapy instructs patients that feelings cannot be changed and are to be accepted. Actions can be taken to achieve goals, in spite of feelings, and these actions may in turn increase positive feelings. In Naikan, patients are asked to think about what they can do for others. They examine instances of care and benevolence they received from another person, recollect memories of what they returned to that person, and recall any trouble or worries they have given to that person. The goal of Naikan therapy is to have patients realize their indebtedness to their significant others, their mothers in particular.

psychotherapy An interaction between a therapist and someone suffering from a psychological problem, with the goal of providing support or relief from the problem.

eclectic psychotherapy Treatment that draws on techniques from different forms of therapy, depending on the client and the problem.

psychodynamic psychotherapies A general approach to treatment that explores childhood events and encourages individuals to develop insight into their psychological problems.

Psychological Therapies: Healing the Mind Through Interaction

Psychological therapy, or **psychotherapy,** is *an interaction between a therapist and someone suffering from a psychological problem, with the goal of providing support or relief from the problem.* Currently more than 400 different systems of psychotherapy exist. A survey of 1,000 psychotherapists asked them to describe their main theoretical orientation (Norcross, Hedges, & Castle, 2002; see **FIGURE 14.1**). More than one third reported using **eclectic psychotherapy,** *a form of psychotherapy that involves drawing on techniques from different forms of therapy, depending on the client and the problem.* This allows the therapists to apply an appropriate theoretical perspective that is suited to the problem at hand rather than adhering to a single theoretical perspective for all clients and all types of problems. Nevertheless, as Figure 14.1 shows, the majority of psychotherapists use a single approach, such as psychodynamic therapy, behavioral and cognitive therapies, humanistic and existential therapies, or group therapy. We'll examine each of those four major branches of psychotherapy in turn.

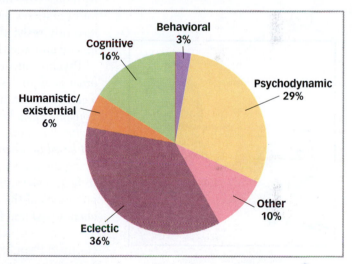

▲ Figure **14.1** **Approaches to Psychotherapy in the 21st Century** This chart shows the percentage of psychologists (from among 1,000 members of the American Psychological Association's Division of Psychotherapy) who have various primary psychotherapy orientations (adapted from Norcross et al., 2002).

Psychodynamic Therapy

Psychodynamic psychotherapy has its roots in Freud's psychoanalytically oriented theory of personality (see Chapter 11). **Psychodynamic psychotherapies** *explore childhood events and encourage individuals to use this understanding to develop insight into their psychological problems.* There are a number of different psychodynamic therapies that can vary substantially, but they all share the belief that the path to overcoming psychological problems is to develop insight into the unconscious memories, impulses, wishes, and conflicts that are assumed to underlie these problems.

? What is the commonly held belief behind all psychodynamic therapies?

Psychoanalysis

As you saw in Chapter 11, *psychoanalysis* assumes that humans are born with aggressive and sexual urges that are repressed during childhood development through the use of defense mechanisms. Psychoanalysts encourage their clients to bring these repressed conflicts into consciousness so that the clients can understand them and reduce their unwanted influences.

Traditional psychoanalysis takes place over an average of 3 to 6 years, with four or five sessions per week (Ursano & Silberman, 2003). During a session, the client reclines on a couch, facing away from the analyst, and is asked to express whatever thoughts and feelings come to mind. Occasionally, the analyst may comment on some of the information presented by the client, but the analyst does not express his or her values and judgments. The stereotypic image you might have of psychological therapy—a person lying on a couch talking to a person sitting in a chair—springs from this approach.

The goal of psychoanalysis is for the client to understand the unconscious in a process Freud called *developing insight*. Some key techniques that psychoanalysts use to help the client develop insight include free association, in which the client reports every thought that enters the mind and the therapist looks for recurring themes, and dream analysis, in which the therapist looks for dream elements that symbolize unconscious conflicts or wishes. Psychoanalysts also assess the client's **resistance,** or *reluctance to cooperate with treatment for fear of confronting unpleasant unconscious material*. For example, the therapist might suggest that the client's problem with obsessive health worries could be traced to a childhood rivalry with her mother for her father's love and attention. The client could find the suggestion insulting and fervently resist the interpretation, which might signal to the therapist that this is indeed an issue the client could be directed to confront in order to develop insight.

Psychoanalytic techniques may be used over the course of an intensive and lengthy process of analysis. During this process, the client and psychoanalyst often develop a close relationship. Freud believed that the development and resolution of this relationship was a key process of psychoanalysis. **Transference** occurs *when the analyst begins to assume a major significance in the client's life and the client reacts to the analyst based on unconscious childhood fantasies*. Successful psychoanalysis involves analyzing the transference so that the client understands this reaction and why it occurs. In fact, insight, the ultimate goal of psychoanalysis, may be enhanced because interpretations of the client's interaction with the therapist also have implications for the client's past and future relationships (Andersen & Berk, 1998).

"Not so fast, Mr. Hodges."

VICTORIA ROBERTS/THE NEW YORKER COLLECTION/CARTOONBANK.COM

Beyond Psychoanalysis

Although Freud's insights and techniques are fundamental, modern psychodynamic theory reflects the contributions of many who followed. Carl Jung (1875–1961) and Alfred Adler (1870–1937) agreed with Freud that insight was a key therapeutic goal but disagreed that insight usually involves unconscious conflicts about sex and aggression (Arlow, 2000). Instead, Jung emphasized what he called the *collective unconscious,* the culturally determined symbols and myths that are shared among all people that, he argued, could serve as a basis for interpretation beyond sex or aggression. Adler believed that emotional conflicts are the result of perceptions of inferiority and that psychotherapy should help people overcome problems resulting from inferior social status, sex roles, and discrimination.

Other analysts to break with Freud were Melanie Klein (1882–1960), who believed that primitive fantasies of loss and persecution (e.g., worrying about a parent

? In what common ways do other psychodynamic theories differ from Freudian analysis?

dying or about being bullied) were important factors underlying mental illness, and Karen Horney (1885–1952), who disagreed with Freud about inherent differences in the psychology of men and women and traced such differences to society and culture rather than biology. All of these approaches to psychotherapy stress that the individual is part of a larger society and that conflicts can reflect the individual's role in that society.

Modern psychodynamic psychotherapies differ from classical psychoanalysis in many ways. For starters, the therapist and client typically sit face-to-face. In addition, therapy is less intensive, with meetings often occurring only once a week and therapy lasting months rather than years. In contrast to classical psychoanalysis, modern psychodynamic therapists are more likely to see relief from symptoms as a reasonable goal for therapy (in addition to the goal of facilitating insight), and they are more likely to offer support or advice in addition to interpretation (Henry et al., 1994). Therapists are also now less likely to interpret a client's statements as a sign of unconscious sexual or aggressive impulses. However, other concepts, such as transference and fostering insight into unconscious processes, remain features of most psychodynamic therapies. Psychodynamic psychotherapy has had an enormous impact on how emotional problems are treated, influencing most subsequent schools of therapy in some form. Freud's couch has cast a long shadow.

Sigmund Freud with his mother, Amalia.

Psychodynamic therapists Carl Jung (1875–1961), Alfred Adler (1870–1937), Melanie Klein (1882–1960), and Karen Horney (1885–1952).

Behavioral and Cognitive Therapies

Unlike psychodynamic psychotherapy, which emphasizes early developmental processes as the source of psychological dysfunction, behavioral and cognitive treatments emphasize the current factors that contribute to the problem—maladaptive behaviors and dysfunctional thoughts.

Behavior Therapy

The idea of focusing treatment on the client's behavior rather than the client's unconscious was inspired by behaviorism. As you read in Chapter 1, behaviorists rejected theories that were based on "invisible" mental properties that were difficult to test and impossible to observe directly. Behaviorists found psychoanalytic ideas particularly hard to test: How do you know whether a person has an unconscious conflict? Behavioral principles, in contrast, focused solely on behaviors that could be observed (e.g., avoidance of a feared object, such as refusing to get on an airplane). **Behavior therapy** *assumes that disordered behavior is learned and that symptom relief is achieved through changing overt maladaptive behaviors into more*

? What primary problem did behaviorists have with psychoanalytic ideas?

resistance A reluctance to cooperate with treatment for fear of confronting unpleasant unconscious material.

transference An event that occurs in psychoanalysis when the analyst begins to assume a major significance in the client's life and the client reacts to the analyst based on unconscious childhood fantasies.

behavior therapy A type of therapy that assumes that disordered behavior is learned and that symptom relief is achieved through changing overt maladaptive behaviors into more constructive behaviors.

token economy A form of behavior therapy in which clients are given "tokens" for desired behaviors, which they can later trade for rewards.

exposure therapy An approach to treatment that involves confronting an emotion-arousing stimulus directly and repeatedly, ultimately leading to a decrease in the emotional response.

cognitive therapy A form of psychotherapy that involves helping a client identify and correct any distorted thinking about self, others, or the world.

cognitive restructuring A therapeutic approach that teaches clients to question the automatic beliefs, assumptions, and predictions that often lead to negative emotions and to replace negative thinking with more realistic and positive beliefs.

mindfulness meditation A form of cognitive therapy that teaches an individual to be fully present in each moment; to be aware of his or her thoughts, feelings, and sensations; and to detect symptoms before they become a problem.

cognitive behavioral therapy (CBT) A blend of cognitive and behavioral therapeutic strategies.

constructive behaviors. A variety of behavior therapy techniques have been developed for many disorders, based on the learning principles you encountered in Chapter 7. Here are three examples of behavior therapy techniques in action:

Eliminating Unwanted Behaviors. How would you change a 3-year-old boy's habit of throwing tantrums at the grocery store? A behavior therapist might investigate what happens after the tantrum: Did the child get candy to "shut him up"? Did the mortified parent provide a lot of attention, begging the child to be quiet? The study of operant conditioning shows that behavior can be predicted by its *consequences* (the reinforcing or punishing events that follow). Adjusting these might help change the behavior. Making the consequences less reinforcing (no candy) and more punishing (a period of time-out in the car while the parent watches from nearby rather than providing a rush of attention) could eliminate the problem behavior.

Promoting Desired Behaviors. A behavior therapy technique sometimes used in psychiatric hospitals is the **token economy,** which involves *giving clients "tokens" for desired behaviors, which they can later trade for rewards.* Tokens for behaviors such as cleaning their rooms, getting exercise, or helping other patients signal positive reinforcement because they can be exchanged for rewards such as time away from the hospital, television privileges, and special foods. Token economies have proven to be effective while the system of rewards is in place, but the learned behaviors are not usually maintained when the reinforcements are discontinued (Glynn, 1990).

Reducing Unwanted Emotional Responses. One of the most powerful ways to reduce fear is by gradual *exposure* to the feared object or situation (Wolpe, 1958). **Exposure therapy** involves *confronting an emotion-arousing stimulus directly and repeatedly, ultimately leading to a decrease in the emotional response.* This technique depends on the processes of habituation and response extinction that were originally discovered in the study of classical conditioning (see Chapter 7). Behavioral therapists use an exposure hierarchy to expose the client gradually to the feared object or situation. Easier situations are practiced first; as fear decreases, the client progresses to more difficult or frightening situations (see **TABLE 14.1**).

Table 14.1

Exposure Hierarchy for Social Phobia	
Item	**Fear (0–100)**
1. Have a party and invite everyone from work	99
2. Go to a holiday party for 1 hour without drinking	90
3. Invite Cindy to have dinner and see a movie	85
4. Go for a job interview	80
5. Ask boss for a day off work	65
6. Ask questions in a meeting at work	65
7. Eat lunch with coworkers	60
8. Talk to a stranger on the bus	50
9. Talk to cousin on the telephone for 10 minutes	40
10. Ask for directions at the gas station	35

An exposure therapy client with obsessive-compulsive disorder who fears contamination in public restrooms might be given "homework" to visit three such restrooms in a week, turn the water in the sink on and off, and then *not* wash up.

MAJOR PIX/ALAMY IMAGES

Cognitive Therapy

Whereas behavior therapy focuses on an individual's behavior, **cognitive therapy** focuses on *helping a client identify and correct any distorted thinking about self, others, or the world* (e.g., Beck & Weishaar, 2000). For example, behaviorists might explain a phobia as the outcome of a classical conditioning experience. For example, a dog bite could lead to the development of a dog phobia through the simple association of the dog with the experience of pain. Cognitive theorists might instead emphasize the *meaning* of the event. In the case of a dog bite, cognitive theorists might focus on a person's new or strengthened belief that dogs are dangerous to explain the fear.

MAJOR PIX/ALAMY IMAGES

Cognitive therapist Aaron Beck's direct and rational approach to psychotherapy helps people change maladaptive thinking patterns. Beck's approach to psychotherapy helps people change maladaptive thinking patterns in a direct and rational approach.

Cognitive therapies use a technique called **cognitive restructuring,** which *involves teaching clients to question the automatic beliefs, assumptions, and predictions that often lead to negative emotions and to replace negative thinking with more realistic and positive beliefs.* Specifically, clients are taught to examine the evidence for and

? How might a client restructure a negative self-image into a positive one?

against a particular belief or to be more accepting of outcomes that may be undesirable yet still manageable. For example, a depressed client may believe that she is stupid and will never pass her college courses—all on the basis of one poor grade. In this situation, the therapist would work with the client to examine the validity of this belief. The therapist would consider relevant evidence such as grades on previous exams, performance on other coursework, and examples of intelligence outside school. **TABLE 14.2** shows a variety of potentially irrational ideas—beliefs and convictions that could be true or could be false and that serve to unleash unwanted emotions such as anger, depression, or anxiety. Any of these irrational beliefs might bedevil a person with serious emotional problems if left unchallenged and so are potential targets for cognitive restructuring.

Some forms of cognitive therapy include techniques for coping with unwanted thoughts and feelings, techniques that resemble meditation (see Chapter 5). One such technique, called **mindfulness meditation,** *teaches an individual to be fully present in each moment; to be aware of his or her thoughts, feelings, and sensations; and to detect symptoms before they become a problem.* Researchers have found mindfulness meditation to be helpful for preventing relapse in depression. In one study, people recovering from depression were about half as likely to relapse during a 60-week assessment period if they received mindfulness meditation—based cognitive therapy than if they received treatment as usual (Teasdale, Segal, & Williams, 2000).

Table 14.2

Common Irrational Beliefs and the Emotional Responses They Can Cause

Belief	Emotional Response
I have to get this done immediately. I must be perfect. Something terrible will happen.	Anxiety, stress
Everyone is watching me. I won't be able to make friends. People know something is wrong with me.	Embarrassment, social anxiety
I'm a loser and will always be a loser. Nobody will ever love me.	Sadness, depression
She did that to me on purpose. He is evil and should be punished. Things ought to be different.	Anger, irritability

Cognitive Behavioral Therapy

Historically, cognitive and behavioral therapies were considered distinct systems of therapy. Today, most therapists working with anxiety and depression use *a blend of cognitive and behavioral therapeutic strategies,* often referred to as **cognitive behavioral therapy (CBT).** In contrast to traditional behavior therapy and cognitive therapy,

There's nothing funny about depression.

ADRI BERGER/GETTY IMAGES

CBT is "problem focused," meaning that it is undertaken for specific problems (e.g., reducing the frequency of panic attacks or allowing the client to return to work after a bout of depression), and "action oriented," meaning that the therapist tries to assist the client in selecting specific strategies to help address those problems. The client is expected to *do* things, such as practice relaxation

? Why do most therapists use a blend of cognitive and behavioral strategies?

exercises or use a diary to monitor relevant symptoms (e.g., the severity of depressed mood or panic attack symptoms). This is in contrast to psychodynamic or other therapies where goals may not be explicitly discussed or agreed on and the client's only necessary action is to attend the therapy session.

Cognitive behavioral therapies have been found to be effective for a number of disorders (Butler et al., 2006), including unipolar depression, generalized anxiety disorder, panic disorder, social phobia, post-traumatic stress disorder, and childhood depressive and anxiety disorders.

Humanistic and Existential Therapies

Humanistic and existential therapies emerged in part as a reaction to the negative views that psychodynamic psychotherapies hold about human nature. Humanistic and existential therapies share the assumption that psychological problems stem

? How does a humanistic view of human nature differ from a psychodynamic view?

from feelings of alienation and loneliness and that these feelings can be traced to failure to reach one's potential (in the humanistic approach) or failure to find meaning in life (in the existential approach). Although interest in these approaches peaked in the 1960s and 1970s, some therapists continue to use them today. Two well-known types are person-centered therapy (a humanistic approach) and Gestalt therapy (an existential approach).

Person-Centered Therapy

Person-centered therapy (also known as client-centered therapy) *assumes that all individuals have a tendency toward growth and that this growth can be facilitated by acceptance and genuine reactions from the therapist.* In person-centered therapy, the therapist tends not to provide advice or suggestions about what the client should be doing. Instead, the therapist paraphrases the client's words, mirroring the client's thoughts and sentiments (e.g., "I think I hear you saying . . ."). Person-centered therapists believe that, with adequate support, the client will recognize the right things to do.

Person-centered therapists should demonstrate three basic qualities. The first is *congruence,* or being open and honest in the therapeutic relationship and communicating the same message at all levels. For example, the same message must be communicated in the therapist's words, facial expression, and body language. Saying "I think your concerns are valid" while smirking would simply not do. The second quality, *empathy,* refers to the continuous process of trying to understand the client by getting inside his or her way of thinking, feeling, and understanding the world, which enables the therapist to better appreciate the client's apprehensions, worries, or fears. The third quality is *unconditional positive regard,* meaning the therapist must provide a nonjudgmental, warm, and accepting environment in which the client can feel safe when expressing his or her thoughts and feelings.

person-centered therapy An approach to therapy that assumes all individuals have a tendency toward growth and that this growth can be facilitated by acceptance and genuine reactions from the therapist.

gestalt therapy An existentialist approach to treatment with the goal of helping the client to become aware of his or her thoughts, behaviors, experiences, and feelings and to "own" or take responsibility for them.

Gestalt Therapy

Gestalt therapy *has the goal of helping the client to become aware of his or her thoughts, behaviors, experiences, and feelings and to "own" or take responsibility for them.* Gestalt therapists are encouraged to be enthusiastic and warm toward their clients, an approach they share with person-centered therapists. To help facilitate the client's awareness, Gestalt therapists also reflect their impressions of the client back to the client.

Gestalt therapy emphasizes the experiences and behaviors that are occurring at that particular moment in the therapy session. For example, if a client is talking about something stressful that occurred during the previous week, the therapist might ask, "How do you feel as you describe what happened to you?" This technique is known as focusing. Clients are also encouraged to put their feelings into action. One way to do this is the empty chair technique, in which the client imagines that another person (e.g., a spouse, a parent, a coworker) is in an empty chair, sitting directly across from the client. The client then moves from chair to chair, alternating between role-playing what he or she would say to the other person and how he or she imagines the other person would respond. Gestalt techniques are now often used in both counseling and "life coaching," which is used to help people prepare for new job or family situations (Grant, 2008).

As part of Gestalt therapy, clients may be encouraged to imagine that another person is sitting across from them in a chair. The client then moves from chair to chair, role-playing what he or she would say to the imagined person and what that person would answer.

Groups in Therapy

It is natural to think of psychopathology as an illness that affects only the individual. Yet each person lives in a world of other people, and interactions with others may intensify and even create disorders. A depressed person may be lonely after moving away from friends and loved ones, or an anxious person could be worried about pressures from parents. These ideas suggest that people might be able to recover from disorders in the same way they got into them—not just as an individual effort but through social processes.

What to do when your marriage is in a rut? One option is to enter couples therapy. Another option is to go out on a screwball comedy "date night" and fall into a wacky mistaken-identity misadventure with several unsavory characters on the way to rediscovering the magic in your marriage. Your choice.

Couples and Family Therapy

When a couple is "having problems," neither individual may be suffering from any psychopathology. Rather, it may be the relationship itself that is disordered. In *couples therapy,* a married, cohabiting, or dating couple is seen together in therapy to work on problems usually arising within the relationship. For example, a couple might seek help because they are unhappy with their relationship. In this scenario, both members of the couple are expected to attend therapy sessions and the problem is seen as arising from their interaction rather than from the problems of one half of the couple. Treatment strategies would target changes in *both* parties, focusing on ways to break their repetitive dysfunctional pattern (Watzlawick, Beavin, & Jackson, 1967).

There are cases when therapy with even larger groups is warranted. An individual may be having a problem—say, an adolescent is abusing alcohol—but the source of the problem is the individual's relationships with family members; perhaps the mother is herself an alcoholic who subtly encourages the adolescent to drink and the father travels and neglects the family. In this case, it could be useful for the therapist to work with the whole group at once in *family therapy*—psychotherapy

Families enter therapy for many reasons, sometimes to help particular members and other times because there are problems in one or more of the relationships in the family.

involving members of a family. As in couples therapy, the problems and solutions are seen as arising from the *interaction* of individuals in the family, rather than simply from any one family member.

Group Therapy

Taking these ideas one step further, if individuals (or families) can benefit from talking with a psychotherapist, perhaps they can also benefit from talking with other clients. This is **group therapy,** *a technique in which multiple participants (who often do not know one another at the outset) work on their individual problems in a group atmosphere.* The therapist in group therapy serves more

? **What are the advantages of a group therapy approach?**

as a discussion leader than as a personal therapist, conducting the sessions both by talking with individuals and by encouraging them to talk with one another.

Why do people choose group therapy? One advantage is that groups provide a context in which clients can practice relating to others. People in group therapy have a "built-in" set of peers whom they have to talk to and get along with on a regular basis. This can be especially helpful for clients who are otherwise socially isolated. Second, attending a group with others who have similar problems shows clients that they are not alone in their suffering. Third, group members model appropriate behaviors for one another and share their insights about how to deal with their problems. Fourth, group therapy is often just as effective as individual therapy (e.g., Jonsson & Hougaard, 2008), so, on average, whoever is paying for group therapy gets a bargain.

Self-Help and Support Groups

An important offshoot of group therapy is the concept of *self-help groups* and *support groups,* which are discussion or Internet chat groups that are often run by peers who have themselves struggled with the same issues. The most famous self-help and support groups are Alcoholics Anonymous (AA), Gamblers Anonymous, and Al-Anon

Self-help groups are a cost-effective, time-effective, and treatment-effective solution for dealing with some types of psychological problems.

(a program for the family and friends of those with alcohol problems). Other self-help groups offer support to people with mood disorders, eating disorders, substance abuse problems, and self-harming disorders—in fact, self-help and support groups exist for just about every psychological disorder.

In addition to being cost-effective, self-help and support groups allow people to realize that they are not the only ones with a particular problem and give them the opportunity to offer guidance and support to one another based on personal experiences of success.

? What are the pros and cons of self-help support groups?

group therapy Therapy in which multiple participants (who often do not know one another at the outset) work on their individual problems in a group atmosphere.

In some cases, though, self-help and support groups can do more harm than good. Some members may be disruptive or aggressive or encourage one another to engage in behaviors that are countertherapeutic (e.g., avoiding feared situations or using alcohol to cope). People with moderate problems may be exposed to others with severe problems and may become oversensitized to symptoms they might otherwise have not found disturbing. Because self-help and support groups are usually not led by trained therapists, mechanisms to evaluate these groups or to ensure their quality are rarely in place.

Today, AA has more than 2 million members in the United States, with 185,000 group meetings that occur around the world (Mack, Franklin, & Frances, 2003). Members are encouraged to follow "12 steps" to reach the goal of lifelong abstinence from all drinking; the steps include believing in a higher power, practicing prayer and meditation, and making amends for harm to others. A few studies examining the effectiveness of AA have been conducted, and it appears that individuals who participate tend to overcome problem drinking with greater success than those who do not participate in AA (Fiorentine, 1999; Morgenstern et al., 1997). However, several tenets of the AA philosophy are not supported by the research. We know that the general AA program is useful, but questions about which parts of this program are most helpful have yet to be studied.

Considered together, the many social approaches to psychotherapy reveal how important interpersonal relationships are for each of us. It may not always be clear how psychotherapy works, whether one approach is better than another, or what particular theory should be used to understand how problems have developed. What is clear, however, is that social interactions between people—both in individual therapy and in all the different forms of therapy in groups—can be useful in treating psychological disorders.

SUMMARY QUIZ [14.2]

1. The different psychodynamic therapies all share an emphasis on
   a. the influence of the collective unconscious.
   b. the importance of taking responsibility for psychological problems.
   c. combining behavioral and cognitive approaches.
   d. developing insight into the unconscious sources of psychological disorders.

2. Which type of therapy would likely work best for someone with an irrational fear of heights?
   a. psychodynamic   c. behavioral
   b. cognitive   d. humanistic

3. Self-help groups are an important offshoot of
   a. cognitive behavioral therapy.   c. person-centered therapy.
   b. support groups.   d. group therapy.

antipsychotic drugs Medications that are used to treat schizophrenia and related psychotic disorders.

psychopharmacology The study of drug effects on psychological states and symptoms.

antianxiety medications Drugs that help reduce a person's experience of fear or anxiety.

antidepressants A class of drugs that help lift people's mood.

Medical and Biological Treatments: Healing the Mind Through the Brain

Ever since someone discovered that a whack to the head can affect the mind, people have suspected that direct brain interventions might hold the key to a cure for psychological disorders. Archaeological evidence, for example, indicates that the occasional human thousands of years ago was "treated" for some malady by the prac-

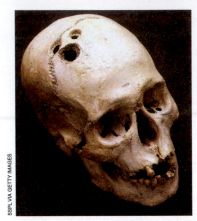

tice of trepanning—drilling a hole in the skull, perhaps in the belief that this would release evil spirits that were affecting the mind (Alt et al., 1997). Surgery for psychological disorders is a last resort nowadays, and treatments that focus on the brain usually involve interventions that are less dramatic. The use of drugs to influence the brain was also discovered in prehistory (alcohol, for example, has been around for a long time). Since then, drug treatments have grown in variety and effectiveness to become what is now the most common medical approach in treating psychological disorders.

This is a trepanned skull from the Bronze Age (about 2200–2000 BCE). The bones show signs of healing, indicating the patient lived afterward. Don't try this at home.

Antipsychotic Medications

Antipsychotic drugs *treat schizophrenia and related psychotic disorders*. The first antipsychotic drug, back in the 1950s, was chlorpromazine (brand name Thorazine), which was originally developed as a sedative. Other related medications, such as thioridazine (Mellaril) and haloperidol (Haldol), followed. Before the introduction of antipsychotic drugs, people with schizophrenia often exhibited bizarre symptoms and were sometimes so disruptive and difficult to manage that the only way to protect them (and other people) was to keep them in asylums. In the period following the introduction of these drugs, the number of people in psychiatric hospitals decreased by more than two thirds. Antipsychotic drugs made possible the deinstitutionalization of hundreds of thousands of people and gave a major boost to the field of **psychopharmacology,** *the study of drug effects on psychological states and symptoms*.

Antipsychotic medications are believed to block dopamine receptors. As you read in Chapter 13, the effectiveness of schizophrenia medications led to the "dopamine hypothesis," suggesting that schizophrenia may be caused by excess dopamine in the brain. Research has indeed found that dopamine overactivity in some areas of the brain is related to positive symptoms of schizophrenia, such as hallucinations and delusions (Marangell et al., 2003). Unfortunately, the negative symptoms of schizophrenia, such as emotional numbing and social withdrawal, may be related to dopamine *under*activity in other areas of the brain. This may help explain why antipsychotic medications do not relieve negative symptoms well.

After the introduction of antipsychotic medications, there was little change in the available treatments for schizophrenia for more than a quarter of a century. However, in the 1990s, a new class of antipsychotic drugs was introduced. These newer drugs, which include clozapine (Clozaril), risperidone (Risperidal), and olanzepine (Zyprexa), have

? What are the advantages of the newer, atypical antipsychotic medications?

"The drug has, however, proved more effective than traditional psychoanalysis."

become known *as atypical antipsychotics* (the older drugs are now often referred to as *conventional* or *typical* antipsychotics). Unlike the older antipsychotic medications, these newer drugs appear to block both dopamine and serotonin receptors. Serotonin has been implicated in some mood disorders, which may explain why atypical antipsychotics can provide relief for both positive and negative symptoms (Bradford, Stroup, & Lieberman, 2002).

Like most medications, antipsychotic drugs have side effects. These can include motor disturbances such as involuntary movements of the face, mouth, and extremities. In fact, patients often need to take another medication to treat the unwanted side effects of the conventional antipsychotic drugs. Side effects of the newer medications tend to be different and sometimes milder than those of the older antipsychotics. For that reason, the atypical antipsychotics are now usually the front-line treatments for schizophrenia (Marangell et al., 2003).

Antianxiety Medications

Antianxiety medications are *drugs that help reduce a person's experience of fear or anxiety.* The most commonly used antianxiety medications are the benzodiazepines, a type of tranquilizer that works by facilitating the action of the neurotransmitter gamma-aminobutyric acid (GABA). As you read in Chapter 3, GABA inhibits certain neurons in the brain, producing a calming effect for the person. Commonly prescribed benzodiazepines include diazepam (Valium), lorazepam (Ativan), and alprazolam (Xanax). The benzodiazepines typically take effect in a matter of minutes and are effective for reducing symptoms of anxiety disorders (Roy-Byrne & Cowley, 2002).

? **What are some reasons for caution when prescribing antianxiety medications?**

Nonetheless, these days doctors are relatively cautious when prescribing benzodiazepines. One concern is that these drugs can be highly addictive. Another consideration when prescribing benzodiazepines is their side effects. The most common side effect is drowsiness, although benzodiazepines can also have negative effects on coordination and memory. And benzodiazapines combined with alcohol can depress respiration, potentially causing accidental death.

Antidepressants and Mood Stabilizers

Antidepressants are *a class of drugs that help lift people's moods.* Two classes of antidepressants were introduced in the 1950s, the *monoamine oxidase inhibitors (MAOIs)* and the *tricyclic antidepressants.* MAOIs prevent the enzyme monoamine oxidase from breaking down neurotransmitters such as norepinephrine, serotonin, and dopamine (**FIGURE 14.2**). However, despite their effectiveness, MAOIs are seldom prescribed anymore due to side effects such as dizziness and loss of sexual interest, as well as potentially dangerous interactions with other common medications. The tricyclic antidepressants block the reuptake of norepinephrine and serotonin, thereby increasing the amount of neurotransmitter in the synaptic space between neurons. Tricyclic antidepressants are still sometimes used, but they also have serious side effects, including dry mouth, constipation, difficulty urinating, blurred vision, and racing heart (Marangell et al., 2003).

Today, the most commonly used antidepressants include the *selective serotonin reuptake inhibitors,* or SSRIs, which include drugs such as fluoxetine (Prozac), citalopram (Celexa), and paroxetine (Paxil). The SSRIs work by blocking the reuptake of serotonin in the brain, which makes more serotonin available in the

People with schizophrenia are two to three times more likely to smoke tobacco than the average person (Kelly & McCreadie, 2000). Several explanations are being tested for this, including the possibility that people with schizophrenia seek out nicotine to reduce their symptoms. If this is true, their "self-medication" may point the way toward new drug treatments for the disorder that might be more helpful and less harmful than smoking.

"Your therapy will be a combination of drugs and clowns."

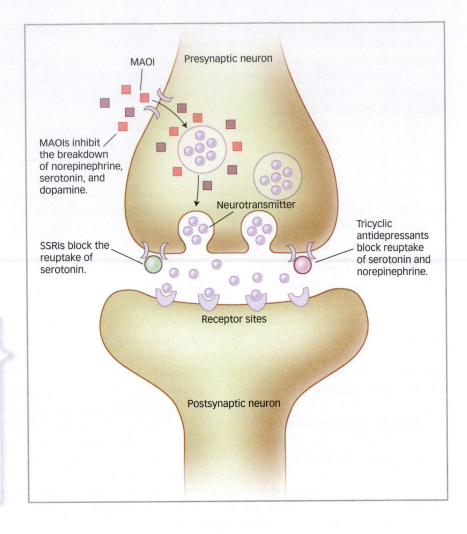

▶ Figure **14.2** **Antidepressant Drug Actions**
Antidepressant drugs, such as MAOIs, SSRIs, and tricyclic antidepressants, act on neurotransmitters such as serotonin, dopamine, and norepinephrine by inhibiting their breakdown and blocking reuptake. These actions make more of the neurotransmitter available for release and leave more of the neurotransmitter in the synaptic gap to activate the receptor sites on the postsynaptic neuron. These drugs relieve depression and often alleviate anxiety and other disorders.

synaptic space between neurons. The greater availability of serotonin in the synapse gives the neuron a better chance of "recognizing" and using this neurotransmitter in sending the desired signal. The SSRIs were developed based on hypotheses that low levels of serotonin are a causal factor in depression (see Chapter 13). Supporting this hypothesis, SSRIs are effective for depression as well as for a wide range of other problems. SSRIs are called "selective" because, unlike the tricyclic antidepressants, which work on the serotonin and norepinephrine systems, SSRIs work more specifically on the serotonin system.

? **What are the most common antidepressants used today? How do they work?**

Finally, antidepressants such as Effexor (venlafaxine) and Wellbutrin (bupropion) offer other alternatives. Effexor is an example of a serotonin and norepinephrine reuptake inhibitor (SNRI); whereas SSRIs act only on serotonin, SNRIs act on both serotonin and norepinephrine. Wellbutrin, in contrast, is a norepinephrine and dopamine reuptake inhibitor. These and other newly developed antidepressants appear to have fewer (or at least different) side effects than the tricyclic antidepressants and MAOIs.

Most antidepressants can take up to 1 month before they start to have an effect on mood. Besides relieving symptoms of depression, almost all of the antidepressants effectively treat anxiety disorders, and many of them can resolve other problems, such as eating disorders. In fact, several companies that manufacture SSRIs have marketed their drugs as treatments for anxiety disorders rather than for their antidepressant effects. Although antidepressants can be effective in treating major

HOT SCIENCE

Happy Pills? Antidepressants for Ordinary Sadness

Imagine a world in which no one ever needs to be sad because sadness can be erased with a drug. This was the dystopian vision of novelist Aldous Huxley's *Brave New World* (1932), where people of the future use *soma,* a happiness drug. After the pills were taken, "Eyes shone, cheeks were flushed, the inner light of universal benevolence broke out on every face in happy, friendly smiles." In Huxley's fictional world, soma for everyone didn't turn out so well because of unexpected side effects— the loss of anger, passion, and ambition. Could antidepressants have a similar downside in our world?

Antidepressant drugs indeed come with side effects. In the case of the tricyclics and MAOIs, these can be unpleasant and dangerous enough that people risk them only to escape debilitating depression. The SSRIs, however, have milder side effects, at least at first, and so seem attractive for those who are not seriously depressed and are simply hoping to feel happier. Books like *Listening to Prozac* (Kramer, 1993) suggest that these drugs can fine-tune happiness and increase the quality of life for anyone. People taking Prozac do report increased extraversion and decreased neuroticism, improve-

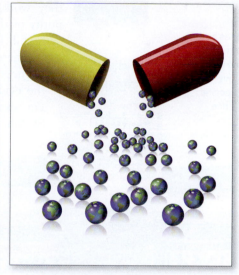

▲ In our world, just as in Huxley's *Brave New World*, there is no perfect pill for happiness. Antidepressant drugs come with side effects.

ETEIMAGING/SHUTTERSTOCK

ments in personality that most anyone would desire (Tang et al., 2009). Commentators are increasingly wondering if ordinary sadness should be treated as a psychological disorder (Horwitz & Wakefield, 2007). Should we be popping antidepressants like vitamins?

The answer is clearly "no." It turns out that antidepressants have not just one catch but several. The main problem is that SSRIs increase happiness only for people who are clinically depressed; for people who are suffering only from ordinary sadness, SSRIs are no better than placebo treatments (Fournier et al., 2010). People who are not seriously depressed, but who claim to have found new happiness with SSRI treatment, may well be responding to the improvement in hopefulness for a cure that accompanies any nonspecific treatment.

And unfortunately, side effects of SSRIs are very real (Masand & Gupta, 2002). Common initial complaints include nausea, dry mouth, and headache, which can be followed by later problems of weight gain and loss of sexual interest or ability. Interactions of SSRIs with other drugs can be serious and must be monitored, and unpleasant symptoms following discontinuation of treatment can be severe. Risking these side effects in return for nothing more than a placebo seems a steep price. No wonder SSRIs are called antidepressants rather than happy pills—they're only really useful if you are depressed.

depression (see the Hot Science box), they are not recommended for treating bipolar disorder, which is characterized by depressive and manic episodes (see Chapter 13), because they might actually trigger a manic episode. Instead, bipolar disorder is commonly treated with *mood stabilizers,* which are medications used to suppress swings between mania and depression.

Herbal and Natural Products

In a survey of more than 2,000 Americans, 7% of those suffering from anxiety disorders and 9% of those suffering from severe depression reported using alternative

? Why are herbal remedies used? Are they actually effective?

"medications" such as herbal medicines, megavitamins, homeopathic remedies, or naturopathic remedies to treat these problems (Kessler et al., 2001). Major reasons people use these products are that they are easily available over the counter, can be less expensive, and are perceived as "natural" alternatives to "drugs." Are herbal and natural products effective in treating mental health problems, or are they just so much "snake oil"?

The answer to this question isn't simple. Herbal products are not considered medications by regulatory agencies (e.g., the U.S. Food and Drug Administration) and are exempt from rigorous research to establish their safety and effectiveness. Instead, herbal products are classified as nutritional supplements and regulated in the same way as are foods. There is little scientific information about herbal products, including possible interactions with other medications, possible tolerance and withdrawal symptoms, side effects, appropriate dosages, how they work, or even *whether* they work—and the purity of these products often varies from brand to brand (Jordan, Cunningham, & Marles, 2010).

Many of the "natural" remedies and treatments available at health food and supplement stores come with little or no evidence of effectiveness and no claims for any specific benefit on the label, but the price tag is usually quite clear.

There is some research support for the effectiveness of some herbal and natural products, but the evidence is not overwhelming (Lake, 2009). For example, some studies have shown that St. John's wort (a wort, it turns out, is an herb) has an advantage over a placebo condition in relieving depression (e.g., Lecrubier et al., 2002), but others show no advantage (e.g., Hypericum Depression Trial Study Group, 2002). Although herbal medications and treatments are worthy of continued research, these products should be closely monitored and used judiciously until more is known about their safety and effectiveness. After all, a drug with no documented main effects could still have very serious side effects.

Combining Medication and Psychotherapy

Psychologists looking for effective ways to treat psychological disorders get pretty excited about the progress of drug therapy. At the same time, as we have seen, drugs can be blunt instruments as treatment devices, producing general changes in mood or relieving unpleasant symptoms—but leaving specific problems untreated. How can we bring medication and psychotherapy together to produce comprehensive treatments?

Many studies have compared psychological treatments, medication, and combinations of these approaches for addressing psychological disorders. For example, in the cases of schizophrenia and bipolar disorder, researchers have found that medication is a necessary part of treatment, and studies have tended to examine whether adding psychotherapeutic treatments, such as social skills training or cognitive behavioral treatment, can be helpful. But in the case of anxiety disorders, medication and psychotherapy may be about equally effective. One study compared cognitive behavioral therapy, imipramine (a tricyclic antidepressant), and the combination of these treatments (CBT plus imipramine) with a placebo (administration of an inert medication) for the treatment of panic disorder (Barlow et al., 2000). After 12 weeks of treatment, either CBT alone or imipramine alone was found to be superior to a placebo. The CBT-plus-imipramine condition was also better than placebo but was not significantly better than either CBT or imipramine alone. In other

"These medicines all taste pretty good—let's approve them."

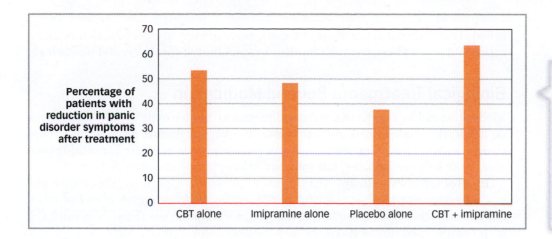

◄ Figure **14.3** **The Effectiveness of Medication and Psychotherapy for Panic Disorder** One study of CBT and medication (imipramine) for panic disorder found that the effects of CBT, medication, and combined treatment (CBT and medication) were not significantly different over the short term, though all three were superior to the placebo condition (Barlow et al., 2000).

words, either treatment was better than nothing, but the combination of treatments was not significantly more effective than one or the other (see **FIGURE 14.3**).

Given that both therapy and medications are effective, one question is whether they work through similar mechanisms. A study of people with social phobia examined patterns of cerebral blood flow following treatment using either citalopram (an SSRI) or CBT (Furmark et al., 2002). Patients in both groups were alerted to the possibility that they would soon have to speak in public. In both groups, those who responded to treatment showed similar reductions in activation in the amygdala, hippocampus, and neighboring cortical areas during this challenge (see **FIGURE 14.4**). As you'll recall from Chapter 6, the amygdala and hippocampus play significant roles in memory for emotional information. These findings suggest that both therapy and medication affect the brain in regions associated with a reaction to threat.

? Do therapy and medications work through similar mechanisms?

One complication in combining medication and psychotherapy is that these treatments are often provided by different people. Psychiatrists are trained in the administration of medication in medical school (and they may also provide psychotherapy), whereas psychologists provide psychotherapy but cannot prescribe medication. This means that the coordination of treatment often requires cooperation between psychologists and psychiatrists.

The question of whether psychologists should be licensed to prescribe medications has been a source of debate (Fox et al., 2009). Opponents argue that psychologists do not have the medical training to understand how medications interact with other drugs. On the other hand, proponents of prescription privileges argue that patient

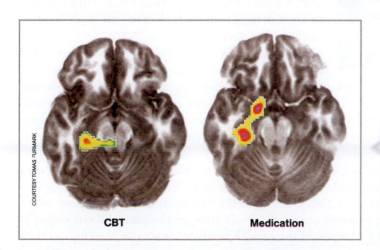

CBT   Medication

◄ Figure **14.4** **The Effects of Medication and Therapy in the Brain** PET scans of patients with social phobia showed similar reductions in activations of the amygdala/hippocampus region after they had received treatment with CBT (shown on the left) and citalopram, an SSRI (shown on the right) (from Furmark et al., 2002).

safety would not be compromised as long as rigorous training procedures were established. This issue remains a focus of debate, so, at present, the coordination of medication and psychotherapy usually involves a team effort of psychiatry and psychology.

Biological Treatments Beyond Medication

Medication can be an effective biological treatment, but for some people medications do not work or side effects are intolerable. If a patient doesn't respond to psychotherapy either, what other options exist to provide symptom relief? Some additional avenues of help are available, but some are risky or poorly understood.

Electoconvulsive theapy (ECT), more commonly known as "shock therapy," is *a treatment that involves inducing a mild seizure by delivering an electrical shock to the brain.* The shock is applied to the person's scalp for less than a second. ECT is primarily used to treat severe depression, although it may also be useful for treating mania (Mukherjee, Sackeim, & Schnur, 1994). Patients are pretreated with muscle relaxants and are under general anesthetic, so they are not conscious of the procedure. The main side effect of ECT is impaired short-term memory, which usually improves over the first month or two after the end of treatment. In addition, patients undergoing this procedure sometimes report headaches and muscle aches afterward (Marangell et al., 2003). Despite these side effects, the treatment can be effective: ECT is more effective than simulated ECT, placebo, and antidepressant drugs such as tricyclics and MAOIs (Pagnin et al., 2008).

? **Where do people turn if medication and therapy are unsuccessful?**

Transcranial magnetic stimulation (TMS) is *a treatment that involves placing a powerful magnet over a person's scalp, which alters neuronal activity in the brain* (George, Lisanby, & Sackeim, 1999). Unlike ECT, TMS is noninvasive and side effects are minimal; they include mild headache and a small risk of seizure, but TMS has no impact on memory or concentration. TMS may be particularly useful in treating depression that is unresponsive to medication (Avery et al., 2009). In fact, a study comparing TMS to ECT found that both procedures were effective, with no significant differences between them (Janicak et al., 2002). Other studies have found that TMS can also be used to treat auditory hallucinations in schizophrenia (Aleman, Sommer, & Kahn, 2007).

Phototherapy, which *involves repeated exposure to bright light,* may be helpful to people who have a seasonal pattern to their depression. This could include people suffering from seasonal affective disorder (SAD; see Chapter 13), which often occurs in the winter months due to the lack of light. Typically, the patient is exposed to bright light in the mornings, using a lamp designed for this purpose. Treatments lasting 2 hours each day for a week seem to be effective, at least in the short term (Terman et al., 1989).

Psychosurgery, *the surgical destruction of specific brain areas,* is a very rarely used procedure for treating certain psychological disorders. Psychosurgery has a controversial history, beginning in the 1930s with the invention of the lobotomy, which involved inserting an instrument into the brain through the patient's eye socket or through holes drilled in the side of the head. The objective was to sever connections

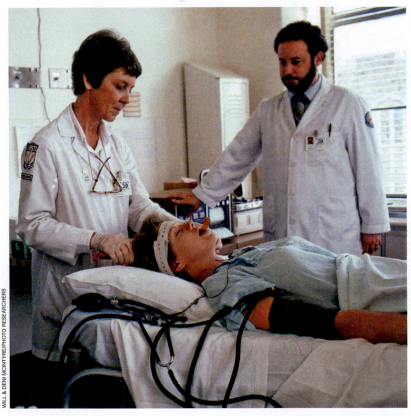

Electroconvulsive therapy (ECT) can be an effective treatment for severe depression. To reduce the side effects, it is administered under general anesthesia.

WILL & DENI MCINTYRE/PHOTO RESEARCHERS

between the frontal lobes and inner brain structures such as the thalamus, known to be involved in emotion, and thereby reduce violence or agitation. Although some lobotomies produced highly successful results, significant side effects such as extreme lethargy or childlike impulsivity detracted from these benefits. Today, psychosurgeries are far more precise in targeting particular brain areas to lesion, and they produce far better results. For example, patients suffering from obsessive-compulsive disorder (OCD) who fail to respond to treatment (including several trials of medications and cognitive behavioral treatment) may benefit from specific surgical procedures that destroy parts of the cingulate gyrus and corpus callosum (see Chapter 3) or that disrupt the pathway between the caudate nucleus and putamen. Long-term follow-up studies suggest that more than one quarter of patients with OCD who do not respond to standard treatments report significant benefit following psychosurgery, with relatively few side effects (Baer et al., 1995; Cumming et al., 1995; Hay et al., 1993). However, due to the intrusive nature of psychosurgery and a lack of controlled studies, these procedures are currently reserved for the most severe cases.

Not all psychosurgery works by destroying brain tissue. In *deep brain stimulation,* a treatment pioneered only recently, a small, battery-powered device is implanted in the brain. This technique has been successful for OCD treatment (Abelson et al., 2009) and can provide benefits for people with a variety of neurologic conditions. The tremor that accompanies Parkinson's disease has proven to be treatable in this way (Perlmutter & Mink, 2006), as have some cases of severe depression that are otherwise untreatable (Mayberg et al., 2005). The early view of psychosurgery as a treatment of last resort is being replaced by a cautious hope that certain direct interventions in the brain can have beneficial effects.

Rosemary Kennedy, sister of President John F. Kennedy, was intellectually challenged from childhood and had violent tantrums and rages that began in her early 20s. Her family agreed to her treatment with a lobotomy at St. Elizabeth's Hospital in Washington, D.C., in 1942, but it went very wrong. She became permanently paralyzed on one side, incontinent, and unable to speak coherently; she spent the rest of her life in institutions.

SUMMARY QUIZ [14.3]

1. Antipsychotic drugs were developed to treat
   a. depression.
   b. schizophrenia.
   c. anxiety.
   d. mood disorders.

2. Which of the following statements is *not* accurate regarding antidepressants?
   a. Current antidepressants act on combinations of different neurotransmitter systems.
   b. Antidepressants have had significantly positive results in the treatment of bipolar disorder.
   c. Antidepressants are also prescribed to treat anxiety.
   d. Most antidepressants can take up to a month before they start to have an effect on mood.

3. What do electroconvulsive therapy, transcranial magnetic stimulation, and phototherapy all have in common?
   a. They incorporate herbal remedies in their treatment regimens.
   b. They may result in the surgical destruction of certain brain areas.
   c. They are considered biological treatments beyond medication.
   d. They are typically used in conjunction with psychotherapy.

electroconvulsive therapy (ECT) A treatment that involves inducing a mild seizure by delivering an electrical shock to the brain.

transcranial magnetic stimulation (TMS) A treatment that involves placing a powerful pulsed magnet over a person's scalp, which alters neuronal activity in the brain.

phototherapy A treatment for seasonal depression that involves repeated exposure to bright light.

psychosurgery Surgical destruction of specific brain areas.

Treatment Effectiveness: For Better or for Worse

Think back to our fearful flyer Lisa at the beginning of the chapter. What if, instead of virtual reality therapy, Lisa had been assigned by her therapist to a drug treatment or to psychosurgery? For that matter, what if her therapy was to walk around for a week wearing a large false nose? Could these alternatives have been just as effective for treating her phobia? Throughout this chapter, we have explored various psychological and biomedical treatments that may help people with psychological disorders. But do these treatments actually work, and, if so, which ones work better than the others?

As you learned in Chapter 2, pinning down a specific cause for an effect can be a difficult detective exercise. The detection is made even more difficult because people may approach treatment evaluation very unscientifically, often by simply noticing an improvement (or no improvement) and reaching a conclusion based on that sole observation. Treatment evaluation can be susceptible to illusions that can only be overcome by scientific evaluation of the effectiveness of treatments.

Treatment Illusions

Imagine you're sick and the doctor says, "Take a pill." You follow the doctor's orders, and you get better. To what do you attribute your improvement? If you're like most people, you reach the conclusion that the pill cured you. How could this be an illusion? There are at least three ways: Maybe you would have gotten better anyway; maybe the pill wasn't the active ingredient in your cure; or maybe, after you're better, you mistakenly remember having been more ill than you really were. These possibilities point to three potential illusions of treatment—illusions produced by natural improvement, by nonspecific treatment effects, and by reconstructive memory. Let's look more closely at each.

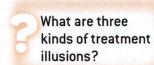

What are three kinds of treatment illusions?

1. *Natural improvement* is the tendency of symptoms to return to their mean, or average, level. People typically turn to therapy or medication when their symptoms are at their worst. When this is the case, the client's symptoms will often improve regardless of whether there was any treatment at all; when you're at rock bottom, there's nowhere to go but up. In most cases, for example, depression that becomes severe enough to make a person a candidate for treatment will tend to lift in several months. A person who enters therapy for depression may develop an illusion that the therapy works because the therapy coincides with the typical course of the illness and the person's natural return to health.

2. Another treatment illusion could be produced by *nonspecific treatment effects* that are not related to the specific mechanisms by which treatment is supposed to work. For example, simply knowing that you are getting a treatment can be a nonspecific treatment effect. These instances include the positive influences that can be produced by a **placebo,** *an inert substance or procedure that has been applied with the expectation that a healing response will be produced.* Research shows that a large percentage of individuals with anxiety, depression, and other emotional problems experience significant improvement after a placebo treatment. For example, in one study adolescents with obsessive-compulsive disorder were treated with Prozac (an SSRI) or a placebo (Geller et al., 2001). Participants receiving medication showed a dramatic decrease in symptoms over the course of the 13-week study—and so did those taking a placebo (**FIGURE 14.5**). The difference between the Prozac and placebo groups only became significant in the seventh week of treatment. In fact, some psychologists estimate that up to 75% of

placebo An inert substance or procedure that has been applied with the expectation that a healing response will be produced.

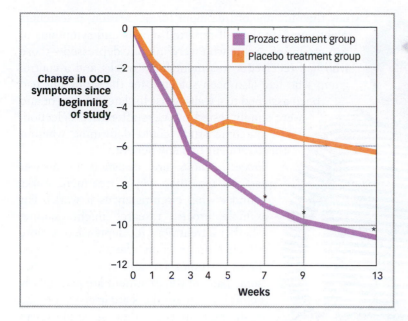

P. C. VEY/THE NEW YORKER COLLECTION/CARTOONBANK.COM

◄ Figure **14.5** **The Placebo Effect** Two groups of patients were given pills to treat OCD. The first group was given Prozac, an antidepressant, and the second group was given an inert sugar pill, a placebo. Interestingly, both groups showed significant improvement in their OCD symptoms until week 7, when the benefits of taking the placebo leveled off. As shown by the asterisks (*), Prozac reduced symptoms significantly more than did placebo pills by weeks 7, 9, and 13 (Geller et al., 2001).

the effects shown by antidepressant medications are due to the placebo effect (Kirsch & Sapirstein, 1998).

3. A third treatment illusion can come about when the client's motivation to get well causes errors in *reconstructive memory* for the original symptoms. You might think that you've improved because of a treatment when in fact you're simply misremembering—mistakenly believing that your symptoms before treatment were worse than they actually were. A client who forms a strong expectation of success in therapy might conclude later that even a useless treatment had worked wonders—by recalling past symptoms and troubles as worse than they were and thereby making the treatment seem effective.

A person who enters treatment is often anxious to get well and so may be especially likely to succumb to errors and illusions in assessing the effectiveness of the treatment. Treatments can look as if they worked when illusions lead us to ignore natural improvement, to overlook nonspecific treatment effects (e.g., the placebo effect), and to reconstruct our pretreatment history as worse than it was. Such treatment illusions can be overcome by using scientific methods to evaluate treatments rather than trusting only our potentially faulty personal skills of observation.

"If this doesn't help you don't worry, it's a placebo."

Treatment Studies

How can treatment be evaluated in a way that allows us to choose treatments that work and not waste time with procedures that may be useless or even harmful? Treatment studies depend generally on the research design concepts covered in Chapter 2, but they also depend on some ideas that are unique to the evaluation of psychological treatments.

There are two main types of treatment studies: outcome studies and process studies. *Outcome studies* are designed to evaluate *whether* a particular treatment works, often in relation to some other treatment or a control condition. For example, to

Many psychological disorders don't play favorites with one gender or the other, but anxiety and depression are more common for women than for men.

COLLEEN CAHILL/AGEFOTOSTOCK

study the outcome of treatment for depression, researchers might compare the self-reported moods and symptoms of two groups of people who were initially depressed—those who had received a treatment for 6 weeks and a control group who had also been selected for the study but had been assigned to a waiting list for later treatment and were simply tested 6 weeks after their selection. The outcome study could determine whether this treatment had any benefit.

Process studies are designed to answer questions regarding *why* a treatment works or under what circumstances it works. For example, process research might examine whether a treatment for depression is more effective for certain clients than others. Process studies can also examine whether some parts of the treatment are particularly helpful, whereas others are irrelevant to the treatment's success. Process studies can refine therapies and target their influence to make them more effective.

Both outcome and process studies can be plagued by treatment illusions, so scientists usually design their research to overcome them. For example, the treatment illusions caused by natural improvement and reconstructive memory happen when people compare their symptoms before treatment with their symptoms after treatment. To avoid this, a treatment (or experimental) group and a control group need to be randomly selected from the same population of patients before the study and then compared at the end of treatment. That way, natural improvement or motivated reconstructive memory can't cause illusions of effective treatment.

But what should happen to the control group during the treatment? If they simply stay home waiting until they can get treatment later (a wait-list control group), they won't receive the nonspecific effects of the treatment that the treatment group enjoys (such as visiting the comforting therapist or taking a medication). So, ideally, a treatment should be assessed in a *double-blind experiment*—a study in which both the patient and the researcher/therapist are uninformed about which treatment the patient is receiving (see Chapter 2). In the case of drug studies, this isn't hard to arrange because active drugs and placebos can be made to look alike to both the

? Why is a double-blind experiment so important in assessing treatment effectiveness?

patients and the researchers during the study. Keeping both patients and researchers "in the dark" is much harder in the study of psychotherapy; in fact, it may even be impossible. Both the patient and the therapist can easily notice the differences in treatments such as psychoanalysis and behavior therapy, for example, so there's no way to keep the beliefs and expectations of both patient and therapist out of the picture in evaluating the effectiveness of psychotherapy.

DILBERT

Which Treatments Work?

The distinguished psychologist Hans Eysenck (1916-97) reviewed the relatively few studies of psychotherapy effectiveness available in 1957 and raised a furor among therapists by concluding that psychotherapy—particularly psychoanalysis—not only was ineffective but also seemed to *impede* recovery (Eysenck, 1957). Much larger numbers of studies have been examined statistically since then, and they support a more optimistic conclusion: The typical psychotherapy client is better off than three quarters of untreated individuals (Seligman, 1995; Smith, Glass, & Miller, 1980). Although critiques of psychotherapy continue to point out weaknesses in how patients are tested, diagnosed, and treated (Baker, McFall, & Shoham, 2009; Dawes, 1994), strong evidence generally supports the effectiveness of many treatments (Nathan & Gorman, 2007), including psychodynamic therapy (Shedler, 2010). The key question then becomes: Which treatments are effective for which problems (Hunsley & Di Giulio, 2002)?

? **What are the current controversies surrounding evaluation of the effectiveness of psychotherapy?**

Some psychologists have argued that most psychotherapies work about equally well. In this view, it is the nonspecific factors shared by all forms of psychotherapy, such as contact with and empathy from a professional, that contribute to change (Luborsky et al., 2002; Luborsky & Singer, 1975). In contrast, others have argued that there are important differences among therapies and that certain treatments are more effective for treating particular types of problems (Beutler, 2002; Hunsley & Di Giulio, 2002). In 1995, the American Psychological Association (APA) published one of the first attempts to define criteria for determining whether a particular type of psychotherapy is effective for a particular problem (Task Force on Promotion and Dissemination of Psychological Procedures, 1995). The official criteria for empirically validated treatments defined two levels of empirical support: *well-established treatments*, those with a high level of support, and *probably efficacious treatments*, those with preliminary support. After these criteria were established, a list of empirically supported treatments was published by the APA (Chambless et al., 1998; Woody & Sanderson, 1998). **TABLES 14.3** and **14.4** show examples of each kind of treatment.

Even trickier than the question of establishing whether a treatment works is whether a psychotherapy or medication might actually do damage. The dangers of drug treatment should be clear to anyone who has read a magazine ad for a drug—and studied the fine print with its list of side effects, potential drug interactions, and complications. Many drugs used for psychological treatment may be addictive, creating long-term dependency with serious withdrawal symptoms. The strongest

Table 14.3

Some Well-Established Psychological Treatments

Type of Treatment	Patient's Problem
Cognitive behavioral therapy	Panic disorder with and without agoraphobia
Cognitive therapy	Depression
Cognitive therapy	Bulimia
Interpersonal therapy	Depression
Behavior therapy (exposure and response prevention)	Obsessive-compulsive disorder
Behavior therapy	Childhood enuresis (bed wetting)
Behavior therapy	Marital difficulties

Table 14.4

Some Probably Efficacious Psychological Treatments

Type of Treatment	Patient's Problem
Behavior therapy	Cocaine abuse
Brief psychodynamic therapy	Opiate dependence
Cognitive behavioral therapy	Opiate dependence
Brief psychodynamic therapy	Depression
Interpersonal therapy	Bulimia
Behavior therapy	Offensive sexual behavior

critics of drug treatment claim that drugs do no more than trade one unwanted symptom for another—trading depression for lack of sexual interest, anxiety for intoxication, or agitation for lethargy and dulled emotion (see, e.g., Breggin, 2000).

The dangers of psychotherapy are more subtle, but one is clear enough that there is actually a name for it: **Iatrogenic illness** is *a disorder or symptom that occurs as a result of a medical or psychotherapeutic treatment itself* (e.g., Boisvert & Faust, 2002). Such an illness might arise, for example, when a psychotherapist becomes convinced that a client has a disorder that in fact the client does not

How might psychotherapy cause harm?

have. As a result, the therapist works to help the client accept that diagnosis and participate in psychotherapy to treat that disorder. Being treated for a disorder can, under certain conditions, make a person show signs of that very disorder—and so an iatrogenic illness is born.

There are cases of patients who have been influenced through hypnosis and repeated suggestions in therapy to believe that they have dissociative identity disorder (even coming to express multiple personalities) or to believe that they were subjected to traumatic events as a child and "recover" memories of such events when investigation reveals no evidence for these problems prior to therapy (Acocella, 1999; McNally, 2003; Ofshe & Watters, 1994). Needless to say, a therapy that leads patients to develop such bizarre beliefs is doing more harm than good.

To regulate the potentially powerful influence of therapies, psychologists hold themselves to a set of ethical standards for the treatment of people with mental disorders (American Psychological Association, 2002). Adherence to these standards is required for membership in the American Psychological Association, and state licensing boards also monitor adherence to ethical principles in therapy. These ethical standards include (1) striving to benefit clients and taking care to do no harm; (2) establishing relationships of trust with clients; (3) promoting accuracy, honesty, and truthfulness; (4) seeking fairness in treatment and taking precautions to avoid biases; and (5) respecting the dignity and worth of all people. When people suffering from mental disorders come to psychologists for help, adhering to these guidelines is the least that psychologists can do. Ideally, in the hope of relieving this suffering, they can do much more.

iatrogenic illness A disorder or symptom that occurs as a result of a medical or psychotherapeutic treatment.

SUMMARY QUIZ [14.4]

1. Which treatment illusion occurs when a client or therapist attributes the client's improvement to a feature of treatment even though that feature wasn't really the active element that caused improvement?
   a. nonspecific treatment effects
   b. natural improvement
   c. error in reconstructive memory
   d. regression to the mean

2. Current studies indicate that the typical psychotherapy client is better off than _____ of untreated individuals.
   a. one half
   b. the same number
   c. one fourth
   d. three fourths

3. Dr. Carolyn Johnson is studying whether Drug X is more effective in treating anxiety in women than in men. Her research is an example of a(n)
   a. double-blind experiment.
   b. placebo control.
   c. outcome study.
   d. process study.

Where Do You Stand?

Is Online Psychotherapy a Good Idea?

If you're on the Internet and have an hour and a credit card, you can get psychotherapy right now. Online psychotherapy, or e-therapy, is offered by dozens of web services—therapy by e-mail, live chat, message posting, interactive blogging, and more. Yes, you can be old fashioned and get therapy by phone—but better yet, switch on your laptop camera for a Skype videoconference with a therapist, or create an avatar for yourself and get therapy in the Second Life virtual world.

An avatar might be a bit much, but some of this sounds like a great idea. E-therapy is as convenient as the nearest online computer, and there's something enticing about therapy you get at your own pace and in your own space. In addition, e-therapy can be less expensive than standard therapy and offers greater anonymity. For those who live far from a therapist, e-therapy may be the only way to get the help you want.

So what's the downside? There are several. In fact, the rapid growth of e-therapy has led to rapid growth in debate about its ethics and effectiveness (Abbott, Klein, & Ciechomski, 2008; Childress, 2000; Humphreys, Winzelberg, & Klaw, 2000). It's not easy to judge the trustworthiness of a website selling hubcaps, after all, let alone one offering psychological services that could change your life. You should be careful to learn the therapist's credentials and find out what the thera-

pist is likely to do, just as you would offline (see the Real World box on types of psychotherapists, p. 437). When you find the right therapist, e-therapy can be effective (e.g., Germain et al., 2009)—but you should be aware that it has some shortcomings.

Electronic communication means both you and the therapist must bridge the gap from reading on-screen messages to understanding a real, live human. With e-therapy (unless you're on video), you lose the nonverbal communication that usually helps you understand a person's meaning and genuineness—tone of voice, gestures, facial expressions, and those hard-to-describe nuances that really let people know each other. E-therapy can also be awkward as client and therapist take turns without immediate feedback, and it can be hard for a therapist to recognize and intervene in crisis situations (Rochlen, Zack, & Speyer, 2004). On top of all this, there is also the *online disinhibition effect* (Suler, 2004): People online seem to self-disclose more deeply and act on impulse more frequently than they would in person. For a therapist trying to discern a client's true feelings and offer help, such online "flaming" can tangle communication.

So is psychotherapy online a good way to get people convenient help? Or is it a poor substitute for real therapy that may cause miscommunication and undermine psychological health? Where do you stand?

Chapter Review

Treatment: Getting Help to Those Who Need It

▶ Because mental illness is often misunderstood, it too often goes untreated, affecting an individual's ability to function and also causing social and financial burdens.

▶ Many people who suffer from mental illness do not get the help they need; they may be unaware that they have a problem, they may face obstacles to getting treatment, or they simply may not know where to turn.

▶ Treatments include psychotherapy, which focuses on the mind, and medical and biological methods, which focus on the brain and body.

Psychological Therapies: Healing the Mind Through Interaction

▶ Psychodynamic therapies, including psychoanalysis, emphasize helping clients gain insight into their unconscious conflicts.

▶ Behavior therapy applies learning principles to specific behavior problems; cognitive therapy aims at challenging irrational thoughts. Cognitive behavioral therapy (CBT) merges these approaches.

▶ Humanistic approaches (e.g., person-centered therapy) and existential approaches (e.g., Gestalt therapy) focus on helping people to develop a sense of personal worth.

▶ Group therapies target couples, families, or groups of clients brought together for the purpose of therapy.

Medical and Biological Treatments: Healing the Mind Through the Brain

▶ Medications have been developed to treat many psychological disorders, including antipsychotic medications (schizophrenia and psychotic disorders), antianxiety medications (anxiety disorders), and antidepressants (depression and related disorders).

▶ Medications are often combined with psychotherapy.

▶ Other biomedical treatments include electroconvulsive therapy (ECT), transcranial magnetic stimulation (TMS), and psychosurgery—this last used in extreme cases, when other methods of treatment have been exhausted.

Treatment Effectiveness: For Better or for Worse

▶ Observing improvement during treatment does not necessarily mean that the treatment was effective; it might instead reflect natural improvement, nonspecific treatment effects (e.g., the placebo effect), or reconstructive memory processes.

▶ Treatment studies focus on both treatment outcomes and processes, using scientific research methods such as double-blind techniques and placebo controls.

▶ Treatments for psychological disorders are generally more effective than no treatment at all, but some are more effective than others for certain disorders, and both medication and psychotherapy have dangers that ethical practitioners must consider carefully.

psychotherapy (p. 439)

eclectic psychotherapy (p. 439)

psychodynamic psychotherapies (p. 439)

resistance (p. 440)

transference (p. 440)

behavior therapy (p. 441)

token economy (p. 442)

exposure therapy (p. 442)

cognitive therapy (p. 443)

cognitive restructuring (p. 443)

mindfulness meditation (p. 443)

cognitive behavioral therapy (CBT) (p. 443)

person-centered therapy (p. 444)

Gestalt therapy (p. 445)

group therapy (p. 446)

antipsychotic drugs (p. 448)

psychopharmacology (p. 448)

antianxiety medications (p. 449)

antidepressants (p. 449)

electroconvulsive therapy (ECT) (p. 454)

transcranial magnetic stimulation (TMS) (p. 454)

phototherapy (p. 454)

psychosurgery (p. 454)

placebo (p. 456)

iatrogenic illness (p. 460)

1. One of your friends recently lost a close family member in a tragic car accident, and he's devastated. He's not been attending classes, and when you check up on him, you learn that he's not sleeping well or eating regularly. You want to help him but feel a little out of your depth, so you suggest he visit the campus counseling center and talk to a therapist. "Only crazy people go to therapy," he says. What could you tell your friend to dispel his assumption?

2. While you're talking to your bereaved friend, his roommate comes in. The roommate agrees with your suggestion about therapy but takes it further. "I'll give you the name of my therapist. He helped me quit smoking—he'll be able to cure your depression in no time." Why is it dangerous to assume that a good therapist can cure anyone and anything?

3. Back in Chapter 2, you read about Louise Hay, whose best-selling book *You Can Heal Your Life* promotes a kind of psychotherapy: teaching readers how to change their thoughts and thereby improve not only their inner lives but also their physical health. The chapter quotes Hay as saying that scientific evidence is unnecessary to validate her claims. Is there a scientific basis for the major types of psychotherapy described in this chapter? How is scientific experimentation used to assess their effectiveness?

4. In June 2009, pop icon Michael Jackson died after receiving a fatal dose of the anesthetic propofol, which is sometimes used off-label as an antianxiety drug; autopsy confirmed that his body contained a cocktail of prescription drugs, including the benzodiazepines lorazepam and diazepam. (Jackson's cardiologist, Dr. Conrad Murray, was later convicted of involuntary manslaughter for administering the fatal dose.) Other celebrities whose deaths have been attributed to medications commonly prescribed for anxiety and depression include Heath Ledger in 2008 and Anna Nicole Smith in 2007. "These drugs are dangerous," your roommate notes. "People who have psychological problems should seek out talk therapy for their problems and stay away from the medications, even if they're prescribed by a responsible doctor." You agree that medications can be dangerous if misused, but how would you justify the use of drug treatment for serious mental disorders?

CRITICAL THINKING QUESTIONS

1. Psychodynamic psychotherapies focus on exploring childhood events to understand current psychological problems. In contrast, behavioral therapy assumes that disordered behavior is learned and that symptom relief is achieved through changing behaviors, sometimes through conditioning principles, while cognitive therapies use cognitive restructuring to teach clients to replace negative thinking with more realistic and positive beliefs.

Suppose a young man comes to visit a therapist, reporting that he's been extremely depressed since the death of his mother, who raised him single-handedly after his father died; it's been over a year since her death, but the man is still experiencing extreme sadness and hopelessness as well as loss of appetite and trouble sleeping.

How might a psychologist who follows each of the above systems begin therapy?

2. Some antidepressant medications, called benzodiazepines, work by facilitating the action of the neurotransmitter GABA, which inhibits certain types of neurons in the brain.

Back in Chapter 5, you read about a widely used, legally available psychoactive drug that also increases GABA. What was it? How are the effects of this drug similar to those of the benzodiazepines?

3. Treatment illusions occur when an individual's improvement is mistakenly attributed to a treatment for a mental disorder.

Suppose you experience a severe panic attack every time you walk into your organic chemistry class; the symptoms are so bad that you can't concentrate on the lesson, and you're sure you'll fail the class. You visit a psychiatrist, who prescribes an antianxiety medication. The next time you attend the class, you feel much calmer and more confident. Possibly the medication is causing chemical changes in your brain that are resulting in a reduction of anxiety. But name three other ways in which treatment illusions could be responsible for your reduction in symptoms.

ANSWERS TO SUMMARY QUIZZES

Summary Quiz [14.1] 1. b; 2. d; 3. c
Summary Quiz [14.2] 1. d; 2. c; 3. d
Summary Quiz [14.3] 1. b; 2. b; 3. c
Summary Quiz [14.4] 1. a; 2. d; 3. d

Need more help? Additional resources are located at the book's free companion website at
www.worthpublishers.com/schacterbrief2e

15

Stress and Health

THE 53-YEAR-OLD PATIENT WAS SEMICOMATOSE WITH severe bronchial asthma when he was admitted to a hospital on July 13, 1960. Mr. X (fortunately, not his real name) was treated and discharged symptom-free after a few days and went directly to his mother's home—where, in a matter of hours, he was wheezing so badly that he arrived back at the hospital in near-terminal condition. After two more severe attacks at his mother's house, a psychotherapist recommended that he not visit his mother again. A month later, Mr. X phoned his mother. He was found an hour later blue and gasping for breath and was pronounced dead shortly thereafter.

How did Mr. X die? The autopsy report cited heart damage from lack of oxygen as the cause of death, but interviews with his family and doctors revealed a more complicated story (Mathis, 1964). His first asthma attack had occurred shortly after he received a profitable offer for the family business and told his mother he wanted to sell. His mother was upset, but he decided to take the offer. In an angry confrontation, his mother said, "Do this and something dire will happen to you." Two days later he had his first incident of mild wheezing. During his many hospitalizations, Mr. X recognized that his troubles might be due to fear of his mother's curse. On the day of his death, he told his mother that he thought he was getting better. She replied by repeating her warning of "dire results."

▶ Imagine that someone ordered an authentic voodoo doll from New Orleans, named it after you, and started sticking it with pins in your presence. Even if you didn't believe in curses at all, might this be stressful?

ISTOCKPHOTO

stressors Specific events or chronic pressures that place demands on a person or threaten the person's well-being.

stress The physical and psychological response to internal or external stressors.

health psychology The subfield of psychology concerned with ways psychological factors influence the causes and treatment of physical illness and the maintenance of health.

chronic stressor A source of stress that occurs continuously or repeatedly.

CAN A PERSON LITERALLY BE FRIGHTENED TO DEATH? Perhaps. Clearly there is a profound connection between mind and body. Just as physical trauma can reduce blood pressure, cause a rapid and shallow pulse, and deprive the body's vital organs of oxygen, great fear can evoke physiological reactions that eventually result in death (Cannon, 1942). Although such deaths are rare and their causes are always open to interpretation, the case of Mr. X shows how harm to the mind may provoke illness of the body.

Now, on an average day, you probably don't get a death curse from your mom. But modern life has its **stressors**, *specific events or chronic pressures that place demands on a person or threaten the person's well-being.* Although such stressors rarely result in sudden death, they do have both immediate and cumulative effects that can influence health.

In this chapter, we'll look at what psychologists and physicians have learned about the kinds of life events that produce **stress**, *the physical and psychological response to internal or external stressors,* typical responses to such stressors, and ways to manage stress. Stress has such a profound influence on health that we consider stress and health together in this chapter. And because sickness and health are not merely features of the physical body, we then consider the more general topic of **health psychology**, *the subfield of psychology concerned with ways psychological factors influence the causes and treatment of physical illness and the maintenance of health.* You will see how perceptions of illness can affect its course and how health-promoting behaviors can improve the quality of people's lives.

Sources of Stress: What Gets to You

Stressors can be natural catastrophes, such as a hurricane or earthquake. But for most of us, stressors are personal events that affect the comfortable pattern of our lives and little annoyances that bug us day after day. Let's look at the life events that can cause stress, chronic sources of stress, and the relationship between lack of perceived control and the impact of stressors.

Stressful Events

People often seem to get sick after major life events (Holmes & Rahe, 1967). In fact, simply assigning points to a person's life changes and adding them up provides a significant indicator of the person's future illness (Miller, 1996). A person who gets divorced and loses a job and has a friend die all in a year, for example, is more likely to get sick than one who escapes the year with only a divorce.

A checklist adapted for the life events of college students (and sporting the snappy acronym CUSS, for College Undergraduate Stress Scale) is shown in **TABLE 15.1**. To assess your stressful events, check off any events that have happened to you in the past year and sum your point total. In a large sample of students in an introductory psychology class, the average was 1,247 points, ranging from 182 to 2,571 (Renner & Mackin, 1998).

Looking at the list, you may wonder why positive events such as getting married are included. Compared with negative events, positive events produce less psychological distress and fewer physical symptoms (McFarlane et al., 1980), and the happiness can sometimes even

? Where are you on the stress scale?

Students under stress. When you signed up for college, did they mention walking to early morning exams in the cold? Probably not.

AP PHOTO/THE GRAND RAPIDS PRESS, REX LARSEN

Table 15.1

College Undergraduate Stress Scale

Event	Stress Rating	Event	Stress Rating
Being raped	100	Lack of sleep	69
Finding out that you are HIV positive	100	Change in housing situation (hassles, moves)	69
Being accused of rape	98	Competing or performing in public	69
Death of a close friend	97	Getting in a physical fight	66
Death of a close family member	96	Difficulties with a roommate	66
Contracting a sexually transmitted disease (other than AIDS)	94	Job changes (applying, new job, work hassles)	65
Concerns about being pregnant	91	Declaring a major or concerns about future plans	65
Finals week	90	A class you hate	62
Concerns about your partner being pregnant	90	Drinking or use of drugs	61
Oversleeping for an exam	89	Confrontations with professors	60
Flunking a class	89	Starting a new semester	58
Having a boyfriend or girlfriend cheat on you	85	Going on a first date	57
Ending a steady dating relationship	85	Registration	55
Serious illness in a close friend or family member	85	Maintaining a steady dating relationship	55
Financial difficulties	84	Commuting to campus or work or both	54
Writing a major term paper	83	Peer pressures	53
Being caught cheating on a test	83	Being away from home for the first time	53
Drunk driving	82	Getting sick	52
Sense of overload in school or work	82	Concerns about your appearance	52
Two exams in one day	80	Getting straight A's	51
Cheating on your boyfriend or girlfriend	77	A difficult class that you love	48
Getting married	76	Making new friends; getting along with friends	47
Negative consequences of drinking or drug use	75	Fraternity or sorority rush	47
Depression or crisis in your best friend	73	Falling asleep in class	40
Difficulties with parents	73	Attending an athletic event	20
Talking in front of class	72		

Source: Renner & Mackin (1998). *Note:* To compute your personal life change score, sum the stress ratings for all events that have happened to you in the last year.

counteract the effects of negative events (Fredrickson, 2000). However, positive events often require readjustment and preparedness that many people find extremely stressful (e.g., Brown & McGill, 1989), so these events are included in computing life-change scores.

Chronic Stressors

Life would be simpler if an occasional stressful event such as a wedding or a lost job was the only pressure we faced. At least each event would be limited in scope, with a beginning, a middle, and, ideally, an end. Unfortunately, though, life brings with it continued exposure to **chronic stressors,** *sources of stress that occur continuously or*

"I can't find that much hair in a drain and not see stress issues."

repeatedly. Strained relationships, long lines at the supermarket, nagging relatives, overwork, money troubles—small stressors that might be easy to ignore if they happened only occasionally can accumulate to produce distress and illness. People who report having a lot of daily hassles also report more psychological symptoms (Kanner et al., 1981) and physical symptoms (Delongis et al., 1982), and these effects often have a greater and longer-lasting impact than major life events.

Many chronic stressors are linked to particular environments. For example, features of city life—noise, traffic, crowding, pollution, and even the threat of violence—provide particularly insistent sources of chronic stress. In one study, children who attended schools under the flight path of an airport had higher blood pressure and gave up more easily when working on difficult problems compared with children of similar race, economic background, and ethnicity who attended nearby schools away from the noise (Cohen et al., 1980). Rural areas have their own chronic stressors, of course, especially isolation and lack of access to amenities such as health care. The realization that chronic stressors are linked to environments has spawned the subfield *environmental psychology,* the scientific study of environmental effects on behavior and health.

? What are some examples of environmental factors that cause chronic stress?

Perceived Control Over Stressful Events

Paradoxically, events are most stressful when there is *nothing to do*—no way to deal with the challenge. In classic studies of *perceived control,* participants were asked to solve puzzles in a room filled with noise as loud as that in classrooms under the airport flight path mentioned above (Glass & Singer, 1972). The bursts of noise hurt people's performance on the tasks. However, this dramatic decline in performance was prevented among participants who were told during the noise period that they could stop the noise just by pushing a button. They didn't actually take this option, but access to

CULTURE & COMMUNITY

Can Being the Target of Discrimination Cause Stress and Illness? It is difficult to be a stranger in a strange land. It's even worse if the people in this land discriminate against you. In a study by Suarez-Morales and Lopez (2009), preadolescents in Miami-Dade County, Florida, who had immigrated from Cuba and other Hispanic cultures were asked to report whether they had experienced discrimination in the United States (agreeing, e.g., that "Because of the group I am in, I don't get the grades I deserve"). Those who reported discrimination also reported higher levels of worrying, anxiety, and bodily symptoms of stress.

You might wonder whether the discrimination caused the stress symptoms or whether there is some other causal connection. For example, maybe people who complain about problems in one area tend to complain about other problems as well. Studies looking at which comes first—suffering discrimination or experiencing health problems—show that discrimination is indeed the culprit (Pascoe & Richman, 2009). Being a stranger in a strange land can make you sick.

MEDIACOLOR/ALAMY

When the flight attendant announces that "we have a full cabin on this flight," conditions can be stressful not so much because of the crowding but because one has no obvious control over the crowding. Taking control—for example, by keeping busy or wearing headphones to decrease contact with others or even by talking with people and getting to know them—may help decrease the stress.

the "panic button" shielded them from the detrimental effects of the noise. Similarly, the stressful effects of crowding appear to stem from the feeling that you aren't in control—that you can't get away from the crowded conditions (Sherrod, 1974).

SUMMARY QUIZ [15.1]

1. If you live in a dense urban area with considerable traffic, noise, and pollution, to what kinds of stressors are you likely exposed?
   a. cultural stressors
   b. intermittent stressors
   c. chronic stressors
   d. positive stressors

2. In an experiment, two groups are subject to distractions while attempting to complete a task. Group A is told they can quiet the distractions by pushing a button. This information is withheld from group B. Why will group A's performance at the task likely be better than group B's?
   a. Group B is working in a different environment.
   b. Group A has perceived control over a source of performance-impeding stress.
   c. Group B is less distracted than group A.
   d. The distractions affecting group B are now chronic.

3. According to the College Undergraduate Stress Scale, which of the following events is most stressful?
   a. concerns about your appearance
   b. lack of sleep
   c. getting sick
   d. confrontation with professors

Stress Reactions: All Shook Up

An accident at the Three Mile Island nuclear plant near Harrisburg, Pennsylvania, on March 28, 1979, created a near meltdown in the reactor and released radioactivity into the surrounding area. Local residents fled. Most eventually returned when the danger had subsided, but a year and a half later, local residents showed physical signs of stress: They had relatively high levels of stress-related hormones, and they had fewer white blood cells available to fight infection (Fleming et al., 1985;

A near-meltdown occurred at the Three Mile Island nuclear plant near Harrisburg, Pennsylvania, on March 28, 1979. Residents of the area showed both physical and psychological stress responses—just from knowing they were in danger.

JOHN S. ZEEDICK/GETTY IMAGES

Schaeffer et al., 1985). The residents also suffered psychological effects, including higher levels of anxiety, depression, and alienation compared with people elsewhere. Because the radiation released was not sufficient to account for any of these effects, they were attributed to the aftermath of stress. Stress can produce changes in every system of the body and mind, stimulating both physical and psychological reactions. Let's consider each in turn.

Physical Reactions

The **fight-or-flight response** is *an emotional and physiological reaction to an emergency that increases readiness for action.* The mind asks, "Should I stay and battle this somehow, or should I run like mad?" And the body prepares to react. If you're a cat at this time, your hair stands on end. If you're a human, your hair stands on end, too, but not as visibly.

Brain activation in response to threat occurs in the hypothalamus, which initiates a cascade of bodily responses that include stimulation of the pituitary gland, which in turn causes stimulation of the adrenal glands. This pathway, shown in **FIGURE 15.1**, is sometimes called the *HPA axis* (for *h*ypothalamus, *pi*tuitary, *a*drenal). The adrenal glands release hormones, including the *catecholamines* (epinephrine and norepinephrine), which increase sympathetic nervous system activation (and therefore increase heart rate, blood pressure, and respiration rate) and decrease parasympathetic activation (see Chapter 3). The increased respiration and blood pressure make more oxygen available to the muscles to energize attack or to initiate escape. The adrenal glands also release *cortisol,* a hormone that increases the concentration of glucose in the blood to make fuel available to the muscles. Everything is prepared for a full-tilt response to the threat.

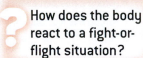

? **How does the body react to a fight-or-flight situation?**

▼ Figure **15.1 HPA Axis** Just a few seconds after a fearful stimulus is perceived, the hypothalamus activates the pituitary gland, which in turn activates the adrenal glands to release catecholamines and cortisol, which energize the fight-or-flight response.

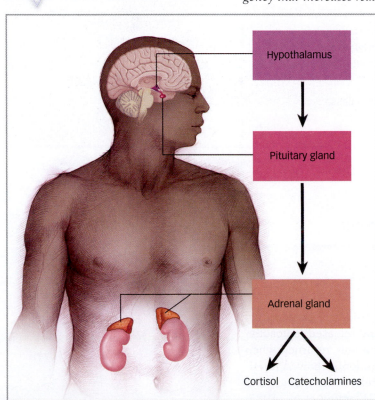

Hypothalamus

Pituitary gland

Adrenal gland

Cortisol   Catecholamines

General Adaptation Syndrome

What might have happened to Three Mile Island's neighbors if the sirens had wailed again and again for days or weeks at a time? Canadian physician Hans Selye subjected rats to heat, cold, infection, trauma, hemorrhage, and other prolonged stressors; he made few friends among the rats but found physiological responses that included an enlarged adrenal cortex, shrinking of the lymph glands, and ulceration of the stomach. Noting that many different kinds of stressors caused similar patterns of physiological change, he called the reaction the **general adaptation syndrome (GAS),** *a three-stage physiological stress response that appears regardless of the stressor that is encountered.* The first phase of the GAS is the *alarm* phase, in which the body displays the fight-or-flight response, rapidly mobilizing its resources to respond

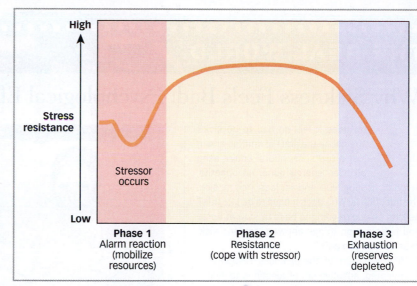

? **What are the three phases of GAS?**

to the threat (see **FIGURE 15.2**). Energy is required, so the body calls on its stored fat and muscle. Next, in the *resistance* phase, the body adapts to its high state of arousal as it tries to cope with the stressor. It shuts down unnecessary processes, such as digestion, growth, and sex drive. If the resistance phase goes on long enough, the third phase, *exhaustion,* sets in, which can include susceptibility to infection, tumor growth, aging, irreversible organ damage, or death.

▲ Figure **15.2** **Selye's Three Phases of Stress Response** In Selye's theory, resistance to stress builds over time but then can only last so long before exhaustion sets in.

Stress Effects on the Immune Response

The **immune system** is *a complex response system that protects the body from bacteria, viruses, and other foreign substances.* The immune system is remarkably responsive to psychological influences. Stressors can cause hormones known as glucocorticoids to flood the brain, wearing down the immune system and making it less able to fight invaders (Webster Marketon & Glaser, 2008). For example, in one study, medical student volunteers agreed to receive small wounds to the roof of the mouth. Researchers observed that these wounds healed more slowly during exam periods than during summer vacation (Marucha, Kiecolt-Glaser, & Favagehi, 1998).

? **How does stress affect the immune system?**

The effect of stress on immune response may help to explain why social status is related to health. The stress of living life at the bottom levels of society may increase risk of infections by weakening the immune system. People who perceive themselves as low in social status are more prone to suffer from respiratory infections, for example, than those who do not bear this social burden—and the same holds true for low-status male monkeys (Cohen, 1999).

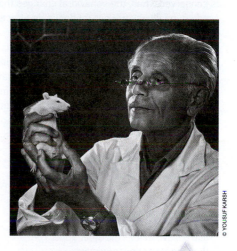

Hans Selye with rat. Given all the stress Selye put rats under, this one looks surprisingly calm.

Stress and Cardiovascular Health

The heart and circulatory system are also sensitive to stress. Chronic stress is a major contributor to coronary heart disease (Krantz & McCeney, 2002) because prolonged stress-activated arousal of the sympathetic nervous system raises blood pressure and gradually damages the blood vessels. In one study, men who exhibited elevated blood pressure in response to stress and who reported that their work environment was especially stressful showed progressive atherosclerosis during the 4-year study (Everson et al., 1997).

? **How does chronic stress increase the chance of a heart attack?**

fight-or-flight response An emotional and physiological reaction to an emergency that increases readiness for action.

general adaptation syndrome (GAS) A three-stage physiological response that appears regardless of the stressor that is encountered.

immune system A complex response system that protects the body from bacteria, viruses, and other foreign substances.

THE REAL WORLD

Why Sickness Feels Bad: Psychological Effects of Immune Response

Why does it feel so bad to be sick? You notice the start of sniffles and in just a few short hours, you're achy all over, energy gone, no appetite, feverish, feeling dull and listless. You're sick. The question is: Why does it have to be like this? As long as you're going to have to stay at home and miss out on things anyway, couldn't sickness be less of a pain?

Misery is part of the *sickness response,* a coordinated, adaptive set of reactions to illness organized by the brain (Hart, 1988; Watkins & Maier, 2005). Feeling sick keeps you home, where you'll spread germs to fewer people. More important, the sickness response makes you withdraw from activity and lie still, conserving the energy for fighting illness that you'd normally expend on other behavior. Appetite loss is similarly helpful: The energy spent on digestion is conserved. Thus, the behavioral changes that accompany illness are not random side effects; they help the body fight disease.

How does the brain know it should do this? The immune response to an infection begins with the activation of white blood cells that "eat" microbes and also release *cytokines,* proteins that circulate through the body and communicate among the other white blood cells—and also communicate the sickness response to the

SICK GIRL BY CHRISTIAN KROHG/NASJONALGALLERIET, OSLO, NORWAY/THE BRIDGEMAN ART LIBRARY

▲ Sickness not only feels bad; it also shows. The pain of being ill has an emotional wallop like mild depression.

brain (Maier & Watkins, 1998). Administration of cytokines to an animal can artificially create the sickness response, and administration of drugs that oppose the action of cytokines can block the sickness response even during an ongoing infection. Cytokines do not enter the brain, but they activate the vagus nerve that runs from the intestines, stomach, and chest to the brain and induce the "I am infected" message (Goehler et al., 2000).

Interestingly, the sickness response can be prompted merely by the introduction of stress. The stressful presence of a predator's odor, for instance, can produce the sickness response of lethargy in an animal—along with symptoms of infection such as fever and increased white blood cell count (Maier & Watkins, 2000). In humans, the connection among the sickness response, immune reaction, and stress is illustrated in depression, a condition in which all the sickness machinery runs at full speed. So in addition to fatigue and malaise, depressed people show signs characteristic of infection, including high levels of cytokines circulating in the blood (Maes, 1995). Just as illness can make you feel a bit depressed, severe depression seems to recruit the brain's sickness response and make you feel ill (Watkins & Maier, 2005).

Road rage starts to make sense when you believe that all the other drivers on the road are trying to kill you.

ROY MORSCH/AGE FOTOSTOCK

In the 1950s, cardiologists interviewed and tested 3,000 healthy middle-age men and then tracked their subsequent cardiovascular health (Friedman & Rosenman, 1974). Some of the men displayed a **Type A behavior pattern,** characterized by *a tendency toward easily aroused hostility, impatience, a sense of time urgency, and competitive achievement strivings.* Other men displayed a less driven behavior pattern (sometimes called *Type B*). The Type A men were identified by their answers to questions in the interview (agreeing that they walk and talk fast, work late, set goals for themselves, work hard to win, and easily get frustrated and angry at others) and also by the pushy and impatient way in which they answered the questions. In the decade that followed, men who had been classified as Type A were twice as likely to have heart attacks compared with the Type B men. A later study of stress and anger found that medical students who responded to stress with anger and hostility were three times more likely to develop premature heart disease and six times more likely to have an early heart attack than were students who did not respond with anger (Chang et al., 2002). Stress affects the cardiovascular system to some degree in everyone but is particularly harmful in people who respond to stressful events with hostility (see also **FIGURE 15.3**).

Psychological Reactions

The body's response to stress is intertwined with responses of the mind. Perhaps the first thing the mind does is try to sort things out—to interpret whether an event is threatening and, if it is, whether something can be done about it.

Stress Interpretation

The interpretation of a stimulus as stressful or not is called *primary appraisal* (Lazarus & Folkman, 1984). Primary appraisal allows you to realize that a small dark spot on your shirt is a stressor

> **?** **What is the difference between a threat and a challenge?**

("Spider!") or that a 70-mile-per-hour drop from a great height in a small car full of screaming people may not be ("Roller coaster!").

The next step in interpretation is *secondary appraisal*—determining whether the stressor is something you can handle—that is, whether you have control over the event (Lazarus & Folkman, 1984). Interestingly, the body responds differently depending on whether the stressor is perceived as a *threat* (a stressor you believe you might *not* be able to overcome) or a *challenge* (a stressor you feel fairly confident you can control) (Blascovich & Tomaka, 1996). The same midterm exam could be a challenge if you are well prepared and a threat if you had neglected to study. Although both threats and challenge raise heart rate, threats also cause constriction of the blood vessels, which can lead to high blood pressure.

Stress Disorders

Psychological reactions to stress can lead to stress disorders. For example, a person who lives through a terrifying and uncontrollable experience may develop **post-traumatic stress disorder (PTSD),** a disorder characterized by *chronic physiological arousal, recurrent unwanted thoughts or images of the trauma, and avoidance of things that call the traumatic event to mind.* For example, many soldiers returning from combat have PTSD symptoms, including flashbacks of battle, exaggerated anxiety and startle reactions, and even medical conditions that do not arise from physical damage (e.g., paralysis or chronic fatigue). Such symptoms are normal, appropriate responses to horrifying events; for most people, the symptoms subside with time. In PTSD, the symptoms can last much longer. For example, the Centers for Disease Control (1988) found that even 20 years after the Vietnam War, 15% of veterans who had seen combat continued to report lingering symptoms. This long-term psychological response is now recognized not only among the victims, witnesses, and perpetrators of war but also among ordinary people

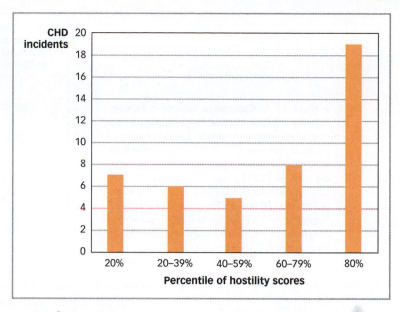

▲ Figure **15.3** **Hostility and Coronary Heart Disease** Of 2,280 men studied over the course of 3 years, 45 suffered coronary heart disease (CHD) incidents, such as heart attack. Many more of these incidents occurred in the group who had initially scored above the 80th percentile in hostility (Niaura et al., 2002).

The traumatic events of war leave many debilitated by PTSD. But because PTSD is an invisible wound that is difficult to diagnose with certainty, the Pentagon has decided that psychological casualties of war are not eligible for the Purple Heart—the hallowed medal given to those wounded or killed by enemy action (Alvarez & Eckholm, 2009).

Type A behavior pattern The tendency toward easily aroused hostility, impatience, a sense of time urgency, and competitive achievement strivings.

post-traumatic stress disorder (PTSD) A disorder characterized by chronic physiological arousal, recurrent unwanted thoughts or images of the trauma, and avoidance of things that call the traumatic event to mind.

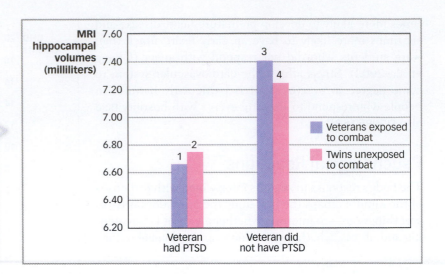

▶ Figure **15.4** **Hippocampal Volumes of Vietnam Veterans and Their Identical Twins** Average hippocampal volumes were smaller both in combat-exposed veterans with PTSD (group 1) and their twins who had not been exposed to combat and did not have PTSD (group 2), in comparison with veterans without PTSD (group 3) and their unexposed twins (group 4). This pattern of findings suggests that an inherited smaller hippocampus may make some people sensitive to conditions that cause PTSD (Gilbertson et al., 2002).

who are traumatized by terrible events. At some time over the course of their lives, about 8% of Americans are estimated to suffer from PTSD (Kessler et al., 1995).

Not everyone who is exposed to a traumatic event develops PTSD, suggesting that people differ in their degree of sensitivity to trauma. Some studies report that the hippocampus is smaller in volume among individuals with PTSD than those without PTSD (Stein et al., 1997). This raises an important question: Does the reduced hippocampal volume reflect a preexisting condition that makes the brain sensitive to stress, or does the traumatic stress itself somehow kill nerve cells? One study suggests that although a group of combat veterans with PTSD showed reduced hippocampal volume, so do the identical (monozygotic) twins of those men (see **FIGURE 15.4**)—even though those twins had never had any combat exposure or developed PTSD (Gilbertson et al., 2002). This suggests that the veterans' reduced hippocampal volumes weren't caused by the combat exposure; instead, both these veterans and their twin brothers might have had a smaller hippocampus to begin with, a preexisting condition that made them susceptible to developing PTSD when they were later exposed to trauma.

? What structure in the brain might be an indicator for susceptibility to PTSD?

Burnout

Did you ever take a class from an instructor who had lost interest in the job? Maybe the teacher looked distant and blank, almost robotic, giving predictable and humdrum lessons each day—as if it didn't matter whether anyone was listening. Now imagine *being* this instructor. You decided to teach because you wanted to shape young minds. You worked hard, and for a while things were great. But one day, you look up to see a roomful of miserable students who are bored and don't care about anything you have to say. They text-message while you talk and start putting papers away long before the end of class. You're happy at work only when you're not in class. When people feel this way, especially about their careers, they are suffering from **burnout,** *a state of physical, emotional, and mental exhaustion created by long-term involvement in an emotionally demanding situation and accompanied by lowered performance and motivation.*

Burnout is a particular problem in the helping professions (Freudenberger, 1974; Pines & Aronson, 1988). Teachers, nurses, clergy, doctors, dentists, psychologists, social workers, police officers,

Is there anything worse than taking a horribly boring class? How about being the teacher of that class?

CHRIS RYAN/GETTY IMAGES

and others who repeatedly encounter emotional turmoil on the job may only be able to work productively for a limited time before succumbing to overwhelming exhaustion, a deep cynicism about and detachment from the job, and a sense of ineffectiveness and lack of accomplishment (Maslach, 2003).

Why is burnout a problem especially in the helping professions?

What causes burnout? One theory suggests that the culprit is using your job to give meaning to your life (Pines, 1993). If you define yourself only by your career and gauge your self-worth by success at work, you risk having nothing left when work fails. For example, a teacher in danger of burnout might do well to invest time in family, hobbies, or other self-expressions. Others argue that some emotionally stressful jobs lead to burnout no matter how they are approached and that active efforts to overcome the stress before burnout occurs are important. The stress management techniques discussed in the next section may be lifesavers for people in such jobs.

burnout A state of physical, emotional, and mental exhaustion created by long-term involvement in an emotionally demanding situation and accompanied by lowered performance and motivation.

SUMMARY QUIZ [15.2]

1. According to the general adaptation syndrome, during the _____ phase, the body adapts to its high state of arousal as it tries to cope with a stressor.
   a. exhaustion   b. alarm   c. resistance   d. energy

2. Which of the following statements is most accurate regarding the physiological response to stress?
   a. Type A behavior patterns have psychological but not physiological ramifications.
   b. The link between work-related stress and coronary heart disease is unfounded.
   c. Stressors can cause hormones to flood the brain, strengthening the immune system.
   d. The immune system is remarkably responsive to psychological influences.

3. Which of the following is *not* an accurate statement regarding the psychological reaction to stress?
   a. Stress disorders do not have a psychological basis.
   b. The body's response to stress is intertwined with responses of the mind.
   c. Stress levels depend on the psychological interpretation of a stimulus.
   d. Emotionally stressful jobs can lead to psychological disorders.

Stress Management: Dealing With It

Most college students (92%) say they occasionally feel overwhelmed by the tasks they face, and more than one third say they have dropped courses or received low grades in response to severe stress (Deuenwald, 2003). No doubt you are among the lucky 8% who are entirely cool and report no stress. But just in case you're not, you may appreciate our exploration of stress management techniques. These techniques resemble some of the forms of cognitive behavior therapy we explored in Chapter 14, but they are strategies people often exercise on their own, without the help of a therapist.

Mind Management

Stressful events are magnified in the mind. If you fear public speaking, for example, just the thought of an upcoming presentation to a group can create anxiety. And if you do break down during a presentation—going blank, for example, or blurting out

repressive coping Avoiding situations or thoughts that are reminders of a stressor and maintaining an artificially positive viewpoint.

rational coping Facing a stressor and working to overcome it.

reframing Finding a new or creative way to think about a stressor that reduces its threat.

relaxation therapy A technique for reducing tension by consciously relaxing muscles of the body.

something embarrassing—intrusive memories of this stressful event could echo in your mind afterward. A significant part of stress management, then, is control of the mind. Let's look at three specific strategies.

1. Repressive Coping

Controlling your thoughts isn't easy, but some people do seem to be able to banish unpleasant thoughts from mind. **Repressive coping** is *characterized by avoiding situations or thoughts that are reminders of a stressor and maintaining an artificially positive viewpoint.* Everyone has *some* problems, of course, but repressors are good at deliberately ignoring them (Barnier, Levin, & Maher, 2004). So, for example, when repressors suffer a heart attack, they are less likely than other people to report intrusive thoughts of their heart problems in the days and weeks that follow (Ginzburg, Solomon, & Bleich, 2002).

Like Mr. X, who was persuaded to avoid his mother's home as a way of keeping her frightening threats out of mind, people often rearrange their lives in order to avoid stressful situations. Many victims of rape, for example, not only avoid the place where the rape occurred but may move away from their home or neighborhood (Ellis, 1983). It may make sense to try to avoid stressful thoughts and situations if you're the kind of person who is good at putting unpleasant thoughts and emotions out of mind (Coifman et al., 2007). For some people, however, the avoidance of unpleasant thoughts and situations is so difficult it can turn into a grim preoccupation (Parker & McNally, 2008; Wegner & Zanakos, 1994). For those who can't avoid negative emotions effectively, it may be better to come to grips with them. This is the basic idea of rational coping.

? When is it useful to avoid stressful thoughts and when is avoidance a problem?

2. Rational Coping

Rational coping involves *facing the stressor and working to overcome it.* This strategy is the opposite of repressive coping and may seem to be the most unpleasant and unnerving thing you could do when faced with stress. It requires approaching rather than avoiding a stressor in order to lessen its longer-term negative impact (Hayes, Strosahl, & Wilson, 1999). Rational coping is a three-step process. The first step is *acceptance,* coming to realize that the stressor exists and cannot be wished away.

How do you cope rationally with an earthquake? This survivor of the devastating January 2010 Haitian earthquake looks for belongings in the wreckage.

The second step is *exposure,* attending to the stressor, thinking about it, and even seeking it out. Psychotherapy may be useful during the exposure step by helping victims confront and think about what happened. Sometimes reliving the traumatic event in memory or even returning to the scene of the trauma can help. In one study, rape survivors were instructed to seek out objectively safe situations that caused them anxiety or that they had avoided. This sounds like bitter medicine indeed, but it is remarkably effective, producing significant reductions in anxiety and PTSD symptoms (Foa et al., 1999).

? What are the three steps in rational coping?

The third element of rational coping involves *understanding,* working to find the meaning of the stressful events. A trauma victim may wonder again and again, "Why me?" or "How did it happen?" or "Why?" Survivors of incest frequently voice the desire to make sense of their trauma (Silver, Boon, & Stones, 1983)—a process that is difficult, even impossible, during bouts of suppression and avoidance.

3. Reframing

Changing the way you think is another way to cope with stressful thoughts. **Reframing** involves *finding a new or creative way to think about a stressor that reduces its threat.* If you experience anxiety at the thought of public speaking, for example, you might reframe by shifting from thinking of an audience as evaluating you to thinking of yourself as evaluating them, and this might make speech-giving easier.

Reframing apparently can take place spontaneously if people are given the opportunity to spend time thinking and writing about stressful events. For example, the physical health of a group of col-

? How has writing about stressful events been shown to be helpful?

lege students improved after they spent a few hours writing about their deepest thoughts and feelings: Compared with students who had written about something else, they were less likely in subsequent months to visit the student health center; they also used less aspirin and got better grades (Pennebaker & Chung, 2007). In fact, engaging in such expressive writing was found to improve immune function (Pennebaker, Kiecolt-Glaser, & Glaser, 1988), while suppressing emotional topics weakened it (Petrie, Booth, & Pennebaker, 1998). The positive effect of self-disclosing writing may reflect its usefulness in reframing trauma and reducing stress.

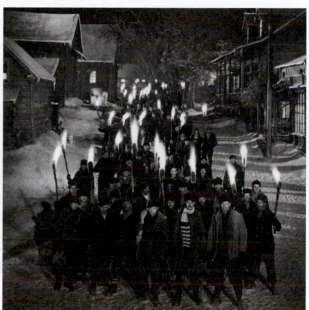

COURTESY EVERETT COLLECTION

Stressed about giving a speech? One way to reframe is to appreciate that at least your audience probably doesn't look like this.

Body Management

Stress can express itself as tension in your neck muscles, back pain, a knot in your stomach, sweaty hands, or the harried face you glimpse in the mirror. Because stress so often manifests itself through bodily symptoms, body management can reduce stress. Here are three techniques.

1. Relaxation

Imagine for a moment that you are scratching your chin. Don't actually do it; just think about it and notice that your body participates by moving ever so slightly, tensing and relaxing in the sequence of the imagined action. Our bodies respond to all the things we think about doing every day. These thoughts create muscle tension even when we think we're doing nothing at all.

Relaxation therapy is *a technique for reducing tension by consciously relaxing muscles of the body.* A person in relaxation therapy may be asked to relax specific muscle groups one at a time or to imagine warmth flowing through the body or to think

relaxation response A condition of reduced muscle tension, cortical activity, heart rate, breathing rate, and blood pressure.

biofeedback The use of an external monitoring device to obtain information about a bodily function and possibly gain control over that function.

social support The aid gained through interacting with others.

about a relaxing situation. Meditation, hypnosis, yoga, and prayer have some elements in common with relaxation therapy (see Chapter 5). These activities all draw on a **relaxation response,** *a condition of reduced muscle tension, cortical activity, heart rate, breathing rate, and blood pressure* (Benson, 1990). Basically, as soon as you get in a comfortable position, quiet down, and focus on something repetitive or soothing that holds your attention, you relax.

> **?** **What do meditation, hypnosis, yoga, and prayer have in common?**

Relaxing on a regular basis can reduce symptoms of stress (Carlson & Hoyle, 1993) and even reduce blood levels of cortisol, the biochemical marker of the stress response (McKinney et al., 1997). For example, in patients who are suffering from tension headache, relaxation reduces the tension that causes the headache; in people with cancer, relaxation makes it easier to cope with stressful treatments; in people with stress-related cardiovascular problems, relaxation can reduce the high blood pressure that puts the heart at risk (Mandle et al., 1996).

2. Biofeedback

Wouldn't it be nice if, instead of having to learn to relax, you could just flip a switch and relax as fast as possible? **Biofeedback,** *the use of an external monitoring device to obtain information about a bodily function and possibly gain control over that function,* was developed with this goal of high-tech relaxation in mind. You might not be aware right now of whether your fingers are warm or cold, for example, but with an electronic thermometer displayed before you, the ability to sense your temperature might allow you (with a bit of practice) to make your hands warmer or cooler at will (e.g., Roberts & McGrady, 1996).

> **?** **How does biofeedback work?**

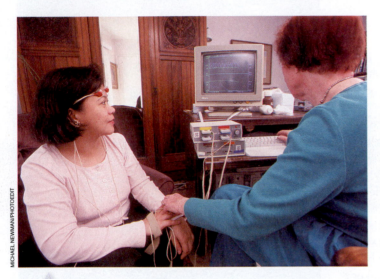

MICHAEL NEWMAN/PHOTOEDIT

Biofeedback gives people access to visual or audio feedback showing levels of psychophysiological functions such as heart rate, breathing, brain electrical activity, or skin temperature that they would otherwise be unable to sense directly.

Biofeedback can even help people control physiological functions they are not otherwise aware of. For example, you probably have no idea right now what brain-wave patterns you are producing. But people can change their brain waves from alert beta patterns to relaxed alpha patterns and back again when they are permitted to monitor their own brains using the electroencephalograph (also called the EEG and discussed in Chapter 3). Often, however, the use of biofeedback to produce relaxation in the brain turns out to be a bit of technological overkill and may not be much more effective than simply having the person stretch out in a hammock and hum a happy tune. People who find that they cannot relax successfully through relaxation therapy, however, may find biofeedback a useful alternative.

3. Aerobic Exercise

Studies indicate that *aerobic exercise* (exercise that increases heart rate and oxygen intake for a sustained period) is associated with psychological well-being (Hassmen, Koivula, & Uutela, 2000). In one study, mildly depressed college women were randomly placed in a 10-week program of aerobic exercise (1 hour, twice each week), a program of relaxation, or no treatment. The exercise group became less depressed over the course of the program, improving more than the relaxation group and the control group (McCann & Holmes, 1984). Subsequent studies have found that as little as 10 minutes of exercise at a time can yield a positive mood boost (Hanson, Stevens, & Coast, 2001).

The reasons for this positive effect are unclear. Researchers have suggested that the effect results from increases in the body's production of neurotransmitters such as serotonin, which can have a positive effect on mood (as discussed in Chapter 3), or from increases in the production of endorphins— the endogenous opioids discussed in Chapters 3 and 5 (Jacobs, 1994). Perhaps the simplest thing you can do to improve your happiness and health, then, is to regularly participate in an aerobic activity. Pick something you find fun: Sign up for a dance class, get into a regular basketball game, or start paddling a canoe—just not all at once.

? What are the benefits of exercise?

Situation Management

After you have tried to manage stress by managing your mind and managing your body, what's left to manage? Look around and you'll notice a whole world out there. Situation management involves changing your life situation as a way of reducing the impact of stress on your mind and body.

1. Social Support

The wisdom of the National Safety Council's first rule—"Always swim with a buddy"—is obvious when you're in water over your head, but people often don't realize that the same principle applies whenever danger threatens. Other people can offer help in times of stress. **Social support** is *aid gained through interacting with others.* Good ongoing relationships with friends and family as well as participation in social activities and religious groups can be as healthy for you as exercising and avoiding smoking (House, Landis, & Umberson, 1988; Umberson et al., 2006). Lonely people are more likely than others to be stressed and depressed (Baumeister & Leary, 1995), and they can be more susceptible to illness because of lower-than-normal levels of immune functioning (Kiecolt-Glaser et al., 1984).

Many first-year college students experience something of a crisis of social support. No matter how outgoing and popular they were in high school, newcomers typically find the task of developing satisfying new social relationships quite daunting. Not surprisingly, research shows that students reporting the greatest feelings of isolation also show reduced immune responses to flu vaccinations (Pressman et al., 2005). Time spent getting to know people in new social situations can be an investment in your own health.

The value of social support in protecting against stress may be very different for women and men: Whereas women seek support under stress, men do not. In fact, the fight-or-flight response to stress may be largely a male reaction, according to research by Shelley Taylor (2002). Taylor suggests that the female response to stress is to *tend-and-befriend* by taking care of people and bringing them together. Like males, human females respond to stressors with sympathetic nervous system arousal and the release of epinephrine and norepinephrine; but unlike males, they also release *oxytocin,* a hormone secreted by the pituitary gland in pregnant and nursing mothers. In the presence of estrogen, oxytocin triggers social responses—a tendency to seek out social contacts, nurture others, and create and maintain cooperative groups.

? Why is the hormone oxytocin a health advantage for women?

After a hard day at work, a man may come home frustrated and worried about his job and end up drinking a beer and fuming alone. A woman under the same type of stress may instead play with her kids or talk to friends on the phone. The tend-and-befriend response to stress may help to explain why women are healthier and have a longer life span than do men. The typical male response amplifies the unhealthy effects of stress, whereas the female response takes a lesser toll on her mind and body—and provides social support for the people around her as well.

AP PHOTO/MATT DUNHAM

Exercise is helpful for the reduction of stress, unless, like John Stibbard, your exercise involves carrying the Olympic torch on a wobbly suspension bridge over a 70-meter gorge.

2. Humor

Wouldn't it be nice to laugh at your troubles and move on? Most of us recognize that humor can diffuse unpleasant situations and reduce stress. Is laughter truly the best medicine? Should we close down the hospitals and send in the clowns?

In fact, humor can reduce sensitivity to pain and distress. In one study, participants were more tolerant of the pain of an overinflated blood pressure cuff during a laughter-inducing comedy audiotape than during a neutral tape or instructed relaxation (Cogan et al., 1987).

Humor can also reduce the time needed to calm down after a stressful event. For example, men viewing a highly stressful film about three industrial accidents were asked to narrate the film aloud either by describing the events seriously or by making their commentary as funny as possible. Although men in both groups reported feeling tense while watching the film and showed increased levels of sympathetic nervous arousal (increased heart rate, decreased skin temperature), those looking for humor in the experience bounced back to normal arousal levels more quickly than did those in the serious-story group (Newman & Stone, 1996).

? How does humor mitigate stress?

"I don't think it's anything serious."

PERCIVAL/CARTOONSTOCK.COM

SUMMARY QUIZ [15.3]

1. Engaging in aerobic exercise is a way of managing stress by managing the
   - a. mind.
   - b. body.
   - c. situation.
   - d. intake of air.

2. Finding a new or creative way to think about a stressor that reduces its threat is called
   - a. stress inoculation.
   - b. repressive coping.
   - c. reframing.
   - d. rational coping.

3. According to the research of Shelley Taylor, a woman is *least* likely to respond to stress by doing which of the following?
   - a. taking a long drive by herself
   - b. playing with her child
   - c. talking to a friend on the phone
   - d. visiting an elderly relative

The Psychology of Illness: When It's in Your Head

One of the mind's main influences on the body's health and illness is the mind's sensitivity to bodily symptoms. No doubt Mr. X, discussed at the beginning of this chapter, had his attention radically reoriented toward his body by his mother's repeated warning that something bad would happen. This sensitivity may have then amplified his fear of dying and so aggravated his asthma. Noticing what is wrong with the body can be helpful when it motivates a search for treatment, but sensitivity can also lead to further problems when it snowballs into a preoccupation with illness that itself can cause harm.

Recognizing Illness and Seeking Treatment

You probably weren't thinking about your breathing a minute ago, but now that you're reading this sentence, you notice it. Sometimes we are very attentive to our bodies. At other times, the body seems to be on "automatic," running along unnoticed until specific symptoms announce themselves or are pointed out by an annoying textbook writer.

psychosomatic illness An illness produced by an interaction between mind and body.

somatoform disorder A psychological disorder in which the patient displays physical symptoms not fully explained by a general medical condition.

hypochondriasis A psychological disorder in which a person is preoccupied with minor symptoms and develops an exaggerated belief that the symptoms signify a life-threatening illness.

People differ substantially in the degree to which they attend to and report bodily symptoms. People who report many physical symptoms tend to be negative in other ways as well—describing themselves as anxious, depressed, and under stress (Watson & Pennebaker, 1989). Do people with many complaints about symptoms truly have a lot of problems or are they just high-volume complainers? Volunteers underwent several applications of a thermal stimulus (of 110° to 120°F) to the leg, and, as you might expect, some of the participants found it more painful than did others. fMRI brain scans during the painful events revealed that the anterior cingulate cortex, somatosensory cortex, and prefrontal cortex (areas known to respond to painful body stimulation) were particularly active in those participants who reported higher levels of pain experience. Because other brain areas sensitive to pain, such as the thalamus, were not particularly active (see **FIGURE 15.5**), the researchers concluded that more reporting of pain is suggestive of greater activation of only some of the brain areas linked with pain (Coghill, McHaffie, & Yen, 2003).

What is the relationship between pain and activity in the brain?

In contrast to complainers are those who underreport symptoms and pain or ignore or deny the possibility that they are sick. Insensitivity to symptoms comes with costs: It can delay the search for treatment, sometimes with serious repercussions. When it comes to your own health, protecting your mind from distress through the denial of illness can put your body in great danger.

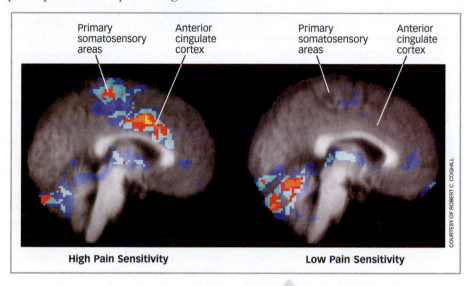

High Pain Sensitivity **Low Pain Sensitivity**

▲ Figure **15.5** **The Brain in Pain** fMRI scans of brain activation in high- (left) and low-pain-sensitive (right) individuals during painful stimulation. The anterior cingulate cortex and primary somatosensory areas show greater activation in high-pain-sensitive individuals. Levels of activation are highest in yellow and red, then light blue and dark blue (Coghill et al., 2003).

Somatoform Disorders

The flip side of denial is excessive sensitivity to illness, and it turns out that sensitivity also has its perils. Indeed, hypersensitivity to symptoms or to the possibility of illness underlies a variety of psychological problems and can also undermine physical health. Psychologists studying **psychosomatic illness,** *an interaction between mind and body that can produce illness,* explore ways in which mind (*psyche*) can influence body (*soma*) and vice versa. The study of mind-body interactions focuses on psychological disorders called **somatoform disorders,** in which *the patient displays physical symptoms not fully explained by a general medical condition.* These are psychological disorders like those discussed in Chapter 14, but their association with symptoms in the body makes them relevant to this chapter's concern with health.

How can hypersensitivity to symptoms undermine health?

The most well-known somatoform disorder is **hypochondriasis,** *a psychological disorder in which a person is preoccupied with minor symptoms and develops an exaggerated belief that the symptoms signify a life-threatening illness.* You may know people who constantly worry about their health, and these poor souls can mentally turn every cough into tuberculosis and every headache into a brain tumor. For a hypochondriac, the tendency to catastrophize symptoms by imagining their worst possible interpretation can become a chronic source of anxiety.

Somatoform disorders fascinated Sigmund Freud and other physicians early in the history of psychology because they demonstrated that the mind could produce physical illnesses without any physiological cause. Current theories focus on the idea that such symptoms occur as a result of breakdowns in the psychological processes underlying voluntary movement and attention (Hallett et al., 2005).

"There are many questions, of course, that won't be answered till the autopsy."

On Being a Patient

Getting sick is more than a change in physical state; it can involve a transformation of identity. This change can be particularly profound with a serious illness: A kind of cloud settles over you, a feeling that you are now different, and this transformation can influence everything you feel and do in this new world of illness. You even take on a new role in life: a **sick role**—*a socially recognized set of rights and obligations linked with illness* (Parsons, 1975). The sick person is absolved of responsibility for many everyday obligations and enjoys exemption from normal activities. For example, in addition to skipping school and homework and staying on the couch all day, a sick child can watch TV and avoid eating anything unpleasant at dinner. In return for these exemptions, the sick role also incurs obligations. The properly "sick" individual cannot appear to enjoy the illness and must also take care to pursue treatment to end this "undesirable" condition. You may recall times when you have felt the conflict between sickness and health as though it were a moral decision: Should you drag yourself out of bed and try to make it to the chemistry exam or just slump back under the covers and wallow in your "pain"?

Some people feign medical or psychological symptoms to achieve something they want, a behavior called *malingering*. Because many symptoms of illness cannot be faked—even facial expressions of pain are difficult to simulate (Williams, 2002)—malingering is possible only with a restricted number of illnesses. Faking illness is suspected when the secondary gains of illness—such as the ability to rest, to be freed from performing unpleasant tasks, or to be helped by others—outweigh the costs. Such gains can be very subtle, as when a child stays in bed because of the comfort provided by an otherwise distant parent, or they can be obvious, as when insurance benefits turn out to be a cash award for Best Actor. Some behaviors that could lead to illness may not be under the patient's control; for example, self-starvation may be part of an uncontrollable eating disorder (see Chapter 8). For this reason, malingering can be difficult to diagnose and treat (Feldman, 2004).

? What benefits might come from being ill?

Patient-Practitioner Interaction

Medical care usually occurs through a strange interaction. On one side is a patient, often miserable, who expects to be questioned and examined and possibly prodded, pained, or given bad news. On the other side is a health care provider, who hopes to obtain useful information from the patient, help in some way, cope with the emotional part of the interaction, and achieve all of this as efficiently as possible because more patients are waiting. To offer successful treatment, the physician must simultaneously understand the patient's physical state and psychological state. Physicians often err on the side of failing to acknowledge patients' emotions, focusing instead on technical issues of the case (Suchman et al., 1997). This is particularly unfortunate because a substantial percentage of patients who seek medical care do so for treatment of psychological and emotional problems (Taylor, 1986). The best physician treats the patient's mind as well as the patient's body.

Another important part of the medical care interaction is motivating the patient to follow the prescribed regimen of care (Cohen, 1979). When researchers check

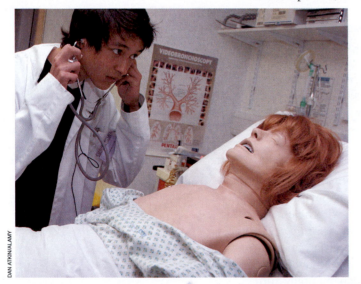

Doctor and patient have two modes of interaction, the technical and the interpersonal. Medical training with robot patients may help doctors learn the technical side of health care, but it is likely to do little to improve the interpersonal side.

compliance by counting the pills remaining in a patient's bottle after a prescription has been under way, they find that patients often do an astonishingly poor job of following doctors' orders. Compliance deteriorates when the treatment must be *frequent,* such as dispensing eyedrops for glaucoma every few hours, or *inconvenient* or *painful,* such as drawing blood or administering injections in managing diabetes. Finally, compliance decreases *as the number of treatments increases.* This is a worrisome

> **Why is it important that a physician be empathic?**

problem especially for older patients, who may have difficulty remembering when to take which pill. Failures in medical care may stem from the failure of health care providers to recognize the psychological challenges that are involved in self-care. Helping people to follow doctors' orders involves psychology, not medicine, and is an essential part of promoting health.

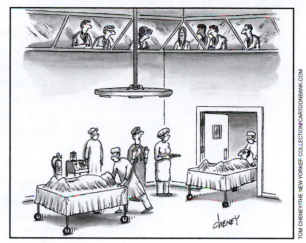

"Next, an example of the very same procedure when done correctly"

SUMMARY QUIZ [15.4]

1. A person who is preoccupied with minor symptoms and believes they signify a life-threatening illness is likely to be diagnosed with
   a. post-traumatic stress disorder.
   b. repressive coping.
   c. hypochondriasis.
   d. somatization disorder.

2. Enjoying an illness is a violation of
   a. malingering.
   b. somatoform disorder.
   c. the sick role.
   d. the Type B pattern of behavior.

3. Which of the following describes a successful health care provider?
   a. displays empathy
   b. pays attention to both the physical and psychological state of the patient
   c. uses psychology to promote patient compliance
   d. all of the above

The Psychology of Health: Feeling Good

Two kinds of psychological factors influence personal health: health-relevant personality traits and health behavior. Personality can influence health through relatively enduring traits that make some people particularly susceptible to health problems or stress while sparing or protecting others. The Type A behavior pattern is an example. Because personality is not typically something we choose ("I'd like a bit of that sense of humor and extraversion over there, please, but hold the whininess"), this source of health can be outside personal control. In contrast, engaging in positive health behaviors is something anyone can do, at least in principle.

Personality and Health

Different health problems seem to plague different social groups. For example, men are more susceptible to heart disease than are women, and African Americans are more susceptible to asthma than are Asian or European Americans. Beyond these general social categories, personality turns out to be a factor in wellness, with individual differences in optimism and hardiness important influences.

sick role A socially recognized set of rights and obligations linked with illness.

Optimism

An optimist who believes that "in uncertain times, I usually expect the best" is likely to be healthier than a pessimist who believes that "if something can go wrong for me, it will." In a study of 309 patients who had undergone coronary artery bypass surgery, for example, patients with higher levels of overall optimism (not merely optimism about the particular surgery) were less likely than other patients after their surgery to need rehospitalization for complications such as infection, heart attacks, or further surgery (Scheier et al., 1999).

Such findings are encouraging for optimists (what wouldn't be?), but studies like this one showing that optimism directly improves physical health are relatively rare (Segerstrom, 2005). Rather than improving physical health directly, optimism seems to aid in the maintenance of *psychological* health in the face of physical health problems. When sick, optimists are more likely than pessimists to maintain positive emotions, avoid negative emotions such as anxiety and depression, stick to medical regimens their caregivers have prescribed, and keep up their relationships with others. Among women who have surgery for breast cancer, for example, optimists are less likely to experience distress and fatigue after treatment than are pessimists, largely because they keep up social contacts and recreational activities during their treatment (Carver, Lehman, & Antoni, 2003).

> **?** Who's healthier, the optimist or the pessimist? Why?

The benefits of optimism raise an important question: If the traits of optimism and pessimism are stable over time—even resistant to change—can pessimists ever hope to gain any of the advantages of optimism (Heatherton & Weinberger, 1994)? Research has shown that even die-hard pessimists can be trained to become significantly more optimistic and that this training can improve their psychosocial health outcomes. For example, pessimistic breast cancer patients who received 10 weeks of training in stress management techniques became more optimistic and were less likely than those who received only relaxation exercises to suffer distress and fatigue during their cancer treatments (Antoni et al., 2001).

Hardiness

Some people seem to be thick-skinned, somehow able to take stress or abuse that could be devastating to others. Suzanne Kobasa (1979) studied a group of stress-resistant business executives. These individuals reported high levels of stressful life events but had histories of relatively few illnesses compared with a similar group, who succumbed to stress by getting sick. The stress-resistant group (Kobasa called them *hardy*) shared several traits, all conveniently beginning with the letter C. They showed a sense of *commitment,* an ability to become involved in life's tasks and encounters rather than just dabbling. They exhibited a belief in *control,* the expectation that their actions and words would have a causal influence on their lives and environment. And they were willing to accept *challenge,* undertaking change and accepting opportunities for growth.

Sometimes hardiness tips over the edge into foolhardiness. Members of the Coney Island Polar Bear Club take that plunge every Sunday of winter.

Can anyone develop hardiness? In one study, participants attended 10 weekly "hardiness-training" sessions, in which they were encouraged to examine their stressors, develop action plans for dealing with them, explore their bodily reactions to stress, and find ways to compensate for unchangeable situations without falling into self-pity. Compared with control groups (who engaged in relaxation and meditation training or in group discussions about stress), the hardiness-training group reported greater reductions in their perceived personal stress as well as fewer symptoms of illness (Maddi, Kahn, & Maddi, 1998). Hardiness training can have similar positive effects in college students, for some even boosting their GPAs (Maddi et al., 2009).

JAY DICKMAN/NATIONAL GEOGRAPHIC STOCK

Health-Promoting Behaviors and Self-Regulation

Even without changing our personalities at all, we can do certain things to be healthy. The importance of healthy eating, safe sex, and giving up smoking are common knowledge. But we don't seem to be acting on the basis of this knowledge. At the turn of the 21st century, 67% of Americans over 20 are overweight or obese (National Center for Health Statistics, 2008). The prevalence of unsafe sex is difficult to estimate, but 15 million people contract one or more sexually transmitted diseases (STDs) each year (Weinstock, Berman, & Cates, 2004)—and another million live with human immunodeficiency virus/acquired immune deficiency syndrome (HIV/AIDS), which is usually contracted through unprotected sex with an infected partner (Centers for Disease Control and Prevention, 2006). And despite endless warnings, 21% of Americans still smoke cigarettes (Pleis, Lucas, & Ward, 2009). What's going on?

Self-Regulation

Doing what is good for you is not necessarily easy. Engaging in health-promoting behaviors involves **self-regulation,** *the exercise of voluntary control over the self to bring the self into line with preferred standards.* When you decide on a salad rather than a cheeseburger, for instance, you control your impulse and behave in a way that will help make you the kind of person you would prefer to be—a healthy one. Self-regulation often involves putting off immediate gratification for longer-term gains (see Chapter 5).

One theory suggests that self-control is a kind of strength that can be fatigued (Baumeister, Heatherton, & Tice, 1995; Baumeister, Vohs, & Tice, 2007). In other words, trying to exercise control in one area may exhaust self-control, leaving behavior in other areas unregulated. To test this theory, researchers seated hungry volunteers near a batch of fresh, hot chocolate chip cookies. They asked some participants to leave the cookies alone but to help themselves to a healthy snack of radishes, whereas

> **? Why is it difficult to achieve and maintain self-control?**

others were allowed to indulge. When later challenged with an impossibly difficult figure-tracing task, the self-control group was more likely than the self-indulgent group to abandon the difficult task—behavior interpreted as evidence that they had depleted their pool of self-control (Baumeister et al., 1998). The take-home message from this experiment is that to control behavior successfully, we need to choose our battles, exercising self-control mainly on the personal weaknesses that are most harmful to health.

Sometimes, though, self-regulation is less a matter of brute force than of strategy. Martial artists claim that anyone can easily overcome a large attacker with the use of the right moves, and overcoming our own unhealthy impulses may also be a matter of finesse. Let's look carefully at healthy approaches to some key challenges for self-regulation—eating, safe sex, and smoking—to learn what "smart moves" can aid us in our struggles.

Eating Wisely

In many Western cultures, the weight of the average citizen is increasing alarmingly. One explanation is based on our evolutionary history: In order to ensure their survival, our ancestors found it useful to eat well in times of plenty to store calories for leaner times. In postindustrial societies in the 21st century, however, there are no leaner times, and people can't burn all of the calories they consume (Pinel, Assanand, & Lehman, 2000). But why, then, are people in France leaner on average than Americans even though their foods are high in fat? One reason has to do with average portion, which is far smaller in France than in the United States. Activity level in France is also greater.

Short of moving to France, what can you do? Studies indicate that dieting doesn't always work because the process of conscious self-regulation can be easily undermined by stress, leading people who are trying to control themselves to lose control by

self-regulation The exercise of voluntary control over the self to bring the self into line with preferred standards.

> Nobody ever said self-control was easy. Probably the only reason you're able to keep yourself from eating this cookie is that it's just a picture of a cookie. Really. Don't eat it.

JEAN SANDLER/FEATUREPICS

overindulging in the very behavior they had been trying to overcome. This may remind you of a general principle discussed in Chapter 5: Trying hard not to do something can often directly produce the unwanted behavior (Wegner, 1994a, 1994b). Rather than dieting, then, heading toward normal weight should involve a new emphasis on exercise and nutrition (Prochaska & Sallis, 2004). In emphasizing what is good to eat, the person can freely think about food rather than trying to suppress thoughts about it. Self-regulation is more effective when it focuses on what to do rather than on what not to do (Molden, Lee, & Higgins, 2009; Wegner & Wenzlaff, 1996).

? Why is exercise a more effective weight-loss choice than dieting?

Avoiding Sexual Risks

People put themselves at risk when they have unprotected vaginal, oral, or anal intercourse with many sexual partners or with partners who themselves have many sexual partners, exhibit symptoms of STDs, are HIV-positive, or are intravenous drug users. Sexually active adolescents and adults are usually aware of such risks, not to mention the risk of unwanted pregnancy, and yet many behave in risky ways nonetheless.

Why doesn't awareness translate into avoidance? Risk-takers harbor an *illusion of unique invulnerability,* a systematic bias toward believing that they are less likely to fall victim to the problem than are others (Perloff & Fetzer, 1986). For example, a study of sexually active female college students found that respondents judged their own likelihood of getting pregnant in the next year as under 10% but estimated the average for other females at the university to be 27% (Burger & Burns, 1988).

Risky sex is often the impulsive result of last-minute decisions. When thought is further blurred by alcohol or recreational drugs, people often fail to use the latex condoms that can reduce their exposure to the risks of pregnancy, HIV, and many other STDs. One approach to reducing sexual risk-taking, then, is simply finding ways to help people plan ahead. Sex education programs offer adolescents just such a chance by encouraging them at a time when they have not had much sexual experience to think about what they might do when they will need to make decisions. Although sex education is sometimes criticized as increasing adolescents' awareness of and interest in sex, the research evidence is clear: Sex education reduces the likelihood that adolescents will engage in unprotected sexual activity and benefits their health (American Psychological Association, 2005). The same holds true for adults.

? Why does planning ahead reduce sexual risk-taking?

Not Smoking

One in two smokers dies prematurely from smoking-related diseases such as lung cancer, heart disease, emphysema, and cancer of the mouth and throat. Although the overall rate of smoking in the United States is declining, new smokers abound, and many can't seem to stop. College students are puffing away along with everyone else, with 20% of college students currently smoking (Thompson et al., 2007). In the face of all the devastating health consequences, why don't people quit?

Nicotine, the active ingredient in cigarettes, is addictive, so smoking is difficult to stop once the habit is established (discussed in Chapter 5). As in other forms of self-regulation, the resolve to quit smoking is fragile and seems to break down under stress. In the months following 9/11, for example, cigarette sales jumped 13% in Massachusetts (Phillips, 2002). And for some time after quitting, ex-smokers remain sensitive to cues in the environment: Eating or drinking, a bad mood, anxiety, or just seeing someone else smoking is enough to make them

want a cigarette (Shiffman et al., 1996). The good news is that the urge decreases and people become less likely to relapse the longer they've been away from nicotine.

Psychological programs and techniques to help people kick the habit include nicotine replacement systems such as gum and skin patches, counseling programs, and hypnosis—but these programs are not always successful. Trying again and again in different ways is apparently the best approach (Schachter, 1982). After all, to quit smoking forever, you only need to quit one more time than you start up. But like the self-regulation of eating and sexuality, the self-regulation of smoking can require effort and thought. The ancient Greeks blamed self-control problems on *akrasia,* or "weakness of will." Modern psychology focuses less on blaming a person's character for poor self-regulation and points instead toward the difficulty of the task. Keeping healthy by behaving in healthy ways is one of the great challenges of life.

? **To quit smoking forever, how many times do you need to quit?**

SUMMARY QUIZ [15.5]

1. When sick, optimists are more likely than pessimists to
   a. maintain positive emotions.
   b. become depressed.
   c. ignore their caregiver's advice.
   d. avoid contact with others.

2. Which of the following is *not* a trait associated with hardiness?
   a. a sense of commitment
   b. an aversion to criticism
   c. a belief in control
   d. a willingness to accept challenge

3. Stress _____ the self-regulation of behaviors such as eating and smoking.
   a. strengthens
   b. has no effect on
   c. disrupts
   d. normalizes

Where Do You Stand?

Should Smoking Appear on the Silver Screen?

When Sigourney Weaver's character smoked on-screen in the film *Avatar,* public health watchdogs complained. A spokesman for the Center for Tobacco Control Research and Education at the University of California, San Francisco, suggested that the smoking in the movie created millions of dollars in free advertising for tobacco companies. *Avatar* director James Cameron defended the movie, claiming that Weaver's character was rude and obnoxious—not likely to be an inspirational role model to teenagers (Cieply, 2010). But the question remains: Does smoking in movies cause adolescents to take up the habit?

This is a difficult question for research. How could you in good conscience do an experiment in which adolescents are randomly assigned to watch movies featuring smoking? Even if just one adolescent in the exposed group takes up smoking as a result, that seems like too many. Researchers have resorted, then, to tracking the movies that teenagers freely choose to watch in real life to see whether there is any association between exposure to smoking in movies and the tendency to take up smoking. There is, and the association is strong across many studies (Charlesworth & Glantz, 2005).

As we've noted before, such an association does not establish causation. But studies of adolescent smoking reveal interesting details that help to fill out the causal theory. For example, adolescents whose favorite stars smoke on-screen are more inclined to be smokers than are adolescents whose favorite stars don't smoke. Those whose favorite star smoked in several films (for example, Leonardo DiCaprio, Sharon Stone, or John Travolta) were three times more likely themselves to smoke than those whose favorite star did not smoke on-screen (Tickle et al., 2001). There are clear hints, then, that smoking in movies may cause nonsmokers to take it up—but without experimental research, we can't know this for certain. The question then becomes: Should smoking be shown on-screen? Where do you stand?

Chapter Review

Sources of Stress: What Gets to You

▶ Stressors are events and threats that place specific demands on a person or threaten well-being.

▶ Sources of stress include major life events (even the happy ones), catastrophic events, and chronic hassles—some of which can be traced to an environment.

▶ Events are most stressful when we perceive that there is no way to control them or deal with the challenge.

Stress Reactions: All Shook Up

▶ The body responds to stress with an initial fight-or-flight reaction, which activates the hypothalamus-pituitary-adrenal (HPA) axis and prepares the body to face the threat or run away from it.

▶ Chronic stress can overtax the body, causing susceptibility to infection, aging, tumors and organ damage, and death.

▶ The psychological response to stress can, if prolonged, lead to anxiety disorders such as PTSD or to burnout.

Stress Management: Dealing With It

▶ The management of stress involves strategies for influencing the mind, the body, and the situation.

▶ Mind management strategies include repressing stressful thoughts (or avoiding the situations that produce them), rationally coping with the stressor, and reframing.

▶ Body management strategies involve attempting to reduce stress symptoms through relaxation, biofeedback, and aerobic exercise.

▶ Situation management strategies can involve seeking out social support or attempting to find humor in stressful events.

The Psychology of Illness: When It's in Your Head

▶ The psychology of illness concerns how sensitivity to the body leads people to recognize illness and seek treatment.

▶ Somatoform disorders, such as hypochondriasis, can stem from too much sensitivity.

▶ The sick role is a set of rights and obligations linked with illness; some people fake illness in order to accrue those rights.

▶ Successful health care providers interact with their patients to understand both the physical state and the psychological state.

The Psychology of Health: Feeling Good

▶ The personality traits of optimism and hardiness are associated with reduced risk for illnesses, perhaps because people with these traits can fend off stress.

▶ The self-regulation of behaviors such as eating, engaging in sex, and smoking is difficult for many people because self-regulation is easily disrupted by stress.

stressors (p. 466)

stress (p. 466)

health psychology (p. 466)

chronic stressor (p. 467)

fight-or-flight response (p. 471)

general adaptation syndrome (GAS) (p. 471)

immune system (p. 471)

Type A behavior pattern (p. 472)

post-traumatic stress disorder (PTSD) (p. 473)

burnout (p. 474)

repressive coping (p. 476)

rational coping (p. 476)

reframing (p. 477)

relaxation therapy (p. 477)

relaxation response (p. 478)

biofeedback (p. 478)

social support (p. 479)

psychosomatic illness (p. 481)

somatoform disorder (p. 481)

hypochondriasis (p. 481)

sick role (p. 482)

self-regulation (p. 485)

1. In 2002, researchers compared severe acne in college students during a relatively stress-free period and during a highly stressful exam period. After adjusting for other variables such as changes in sleep or diet, the researchers concluded that increased acne severity was strongly correlated with increased levels of stress. Learning about the study, your roommate is surprised. "Acne is a skin disease," your roommate says. "I don't see how it could have anything to do with your mental state." How would you weigh in on the role of stress in medical diseases? What other examples could you give of ways in which stress can affect health?

2. One of your friends has just gotten news that his sister has been diagnosed with bipolar disorder. He begins researching treatments online and comes across a website promoting a

stress reduction treatment that, the author claims, can prevent or reverse many disorders—without requiring drugs, surgery, or anything but "positive thinking." What would you tell your friend? Are most psychological disorders caused primarily by too much stress?

3. A friend of yours, who is taking a heavy courseload, confides that he's feeling overwhelmed. "I can't take the stress," he says. "Sometimes I daydream of living on an island somewhere, where I can just lie in the sun and have no stress at all." What would you tell your friend about stress? Is all stress bad? What would a life with no stress really be like?

4. One of your classmates spent the summer interning in a neurologist's office. "One of the most fascinating things," she says, "was the patients with psychosomatic illness. Some had seizures or partial paralysis of an arm, and there were no neurological causes—so it was all psychosomatic. The neurologist tried to refer these patients to psychiatrists, but a lot of the patients thought he was accusing them of faking their symptoms and were very insulted." What would you tell your friend about psychosomatic illness? Could a disease that's "all in the head" really produce symptoms such as seizures or partial paralysis, or are these patients definitely faking their symptoms?

CRITICAL THINKING QUESTIONS

1. Review the events in the stress scale (Table 15.1 on p. 467), and evaluate which of them are something a person has control over and which are not. How does the potential for control of an event relate to the stress rating?

2. Have you ever experienced burnout? If so, what coping techniques worked for you? What techniques could be used to help people in helping professions—such as teachers, doctors, or nurses—prevent burnout from stress?

3. Have you ever ridden on public transportation sitting next to a person with a hacking cough? We are bombarded by advertisements for medicines designed to suppress symptoms of illness so we can keep going. Is staying home with a cold socially acceptable or considered malingering? How does this jibe with the concept of the sick role, a socially recognized set of rights and obligations linked with illness?

4. People in France are leaner on average than Americans, even though their foods are high in fat. At a McDonald's in France, eating a meal takes an average of 22 minutes, whereas in the United States, eating the average fast-food meal takes less than 15 minutes (Rozin, Bauer, & Cantanese, 2003). How could the length of the average meal influence an individual's body weight?

ANSWERS TO SUMMARY QUIZZES

Summary Quiz [15.1] 1. c; 2. b; 3. b
Summary Quiz [15.2]: 1. c; 2. d; 3. a
Summary Quiz [15.3]: 1. b; 2. c; 3. a
Summary Quiz [15.4]: 1. c; 2. c; 3. d
Summary Quiz [15.5]: 1. a; 2. b; 3. c

APPENDIX

Essentials of Statistics for Psychological Science

Graphic Representations

In Chapter 2, you learned how to operationally define a property; how to design a valid, reliable, and powerful measure of that property; and how to use that measure while avoiding demand characteristics and observer bias. So where does that leave you? With a big page filled with numbers, and if you are like most people, a big page filled with numbers just doesn't seem very informative. Psychologists feel the same way, and that's why they have techniques for making sense of big pages full of numbers. One technique involves making graphic representations.

The most common kind of graphic representation is the **frequency distribution,** which is *a graphic representation of measurements arranged by the number of times each measurement was made.* **FIGURE A.1** shows a pair of frequency distributions that represent the hypothetical performances of a group of men and women who took a test of fine motor skill (i.e., the ability to manipulate things with their hands). Every possible test score is shown on the horizontal axis. The number of times (or the *frequency* with which) each score was observed is shown on the vertical axis. Although a frequency distribution can have any shape, a common shape is the *bell curve,* which is technically known as the *Gaussian distribution* or the **normal distribution,** which is *a mathematically defined frequency distribution in which most measurements are concentrated around the middle.* The normal distribution is symmetrical (i.e., the left half is a mirror image of the right half), has a peak in the middle, and trails off at both ends.

The picture in Figure A.1 reveals in a single optical gulp what a page full of numbers never can. For instance, the shape of the distributions instantly tells you that most people have moderate motor skills and that only a few have exceptionally good or exceptionally bad motor skills. You can also see that the distribution of men's scores is displaced a bit to the left of the distribution of women's scores, which instantly tells you that women tend to have somewhat better motor skills than men. Finally, you can see that the two distributions have a great deal of overlap, which tells you that although women tend to have better motor skills than men, there are still plenty of men who have better motor skills than plenty of women.

Descriptive Statistics

A frequency distribution depicts every measurement and thus provides a complete picture of those measurements. But sometimes we want a brief summary statement instead. In psychology, brief summary statements that capture the essential information from a frequency distribution are called *descriptive statistics.* There are two important kinds of descriptive statistics: those that describe the *central tendency* of a frequency distribution and those that describe the *variability* in a frequency distribution.

frequency distributions A graphic representation of measurements arranged by the number of times each measurement was made.

normal distribution A mathematically defined frequency distribution in which most measurements are concentrated around the middle.

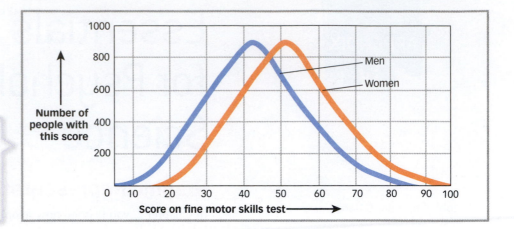

▶ Figure **A.1** **Frequency Distributions** This graph shows how a hypothetical group of men and women scored on a test of motor skill. Test scores are listed along the horizontal axis, and the frequency with which each score was obtained is represented along the vertical axis.

Descriptions of Central Tendency

Descriptions of central tendency are summary statements about the value of the measurements that tend to lie near the center of the frequency distribution. A common description of central tendency is the **mean** (*the average value of all the measurements*). When you hear a descriptive statistic such as "the average American college student sleeps 8.3 hours per day," you are hearing about the mean of a frequency distribution. Other descriptive statistics are the **mode** (*the value of the most frequently observed measurement*) and the **median** (*the value that is "in the middle"– i.e., greater than or equal to half the measurements and less than or equal to half the measurements*). **FIGURE A.2** shows how each of these descriptive statistics is calculated.

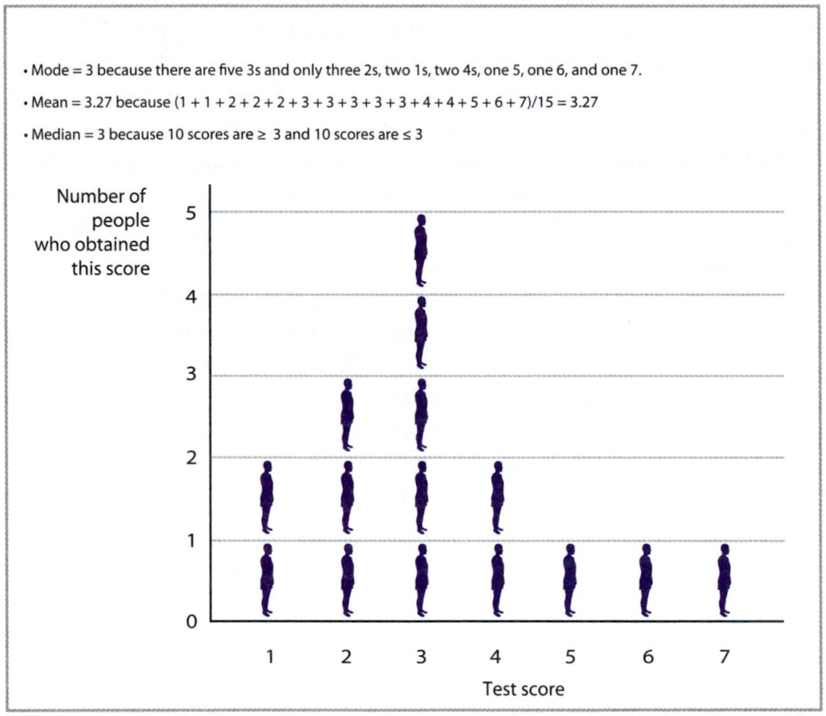

The normal distribution, the mean, median, and mode all have the same value, but when the distribution is not normal, these three descriptive statistics can differ. For example, imagine that you measured the net worth of 40 college professors and Bill Gates. The frequency distribution of your measurements would not be normal, but *positively skewed*. As you can see in **FIGURE A.3**, the mode and the median of a positively skewed distribution are much lower than the mean because the mean is more strongly influenced by the value of a single extreme measurement (which, in case you've been sleeping for the last few years, would be the net worth of Bill Gates). When distributions become skewed, the mean gets dragged off toward the tail, the mode stays home at the hump, and the median goes to live between the two. When distributions are skewed, a single measure of central tendency can paint a misleading picture of the measurements. For example, the average net worth of the people you measured is probably about a billion dollars, but that statement makes the college professors sound a whole lot richer than they are. You could provide a much better description of the net worth of the people you measured if you also mentioned that the median net worth is $300,000 and that the modal net worth is $288,000. Indeed, you should always be suspicious when you hear some new fact about "the average person" but don't hear anything about the shape of the frequency distribution.

• Mode = 3 because there are five 3s and only three 2s, two 1s, two 4s, one 5, one 6, and one 7.

• Mean = 3.27 because (1 + 1 + 2 + 2 + 2 + 3 + 3 + 3 + 3 + 3 + 4 + 4 + 5 + 6 + 7)/15 = 3.27

• Median = 3 because 10 scores are ≥ 3 and 10 scores are ≤ 3

▲ Figure **A.2** **Some Descriptive Statistics** This frequency distribution shows the scores of 15 individuals on a 7-point test. Descriptive statistics include measures of central tendency (such as the mean, median, and mode) and measures of variability (such as the range and the standard deviation).

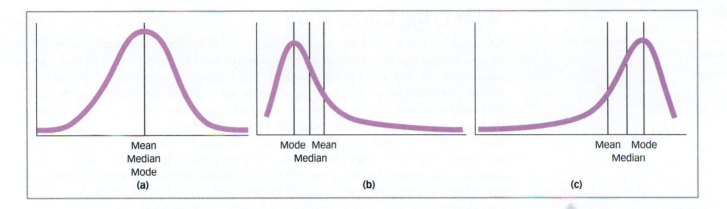

(a)   (b)   (c)

▲ Figure **A.3** **Skewed Distributions**
When a frequency distribution is normal
(a), the mean, median, and mode are
all the same, but when it is positively
skewed (b) or negatively skewed (c),
these three measures of central tendency
are quite different.

Descriptions of Variability

Whereas descriptions of central tendency are statements about the location of the measurements in a frequency distribution, descriptions of variability are statements about the extent to which the measurements differ from each other. The simplest description of variability is the **range,** which is *the value of the largest measurement in a frequency distribution minus the value of the smallest measurement.* The range is easy to compute, but like the mean it can be dramatically affected by a single measurement. If you said that the net worth of the people you had measured ranged from $40,000 to $40,000,000,000, a listener might get the impression that these people were all remarkably different from each other when, in fact, they were all quite similar save for one rich guy from Seattle.

Other descriptions of variability aren't quite as susceptible to this problem. For example, the **standard deviation** is *a statistic that describes the average difference between the measurements in a frequency distribution and the mean of that distribution.* In other words, on average, how far are the measurements from the center of the distribution? As **FIGURE A.4** shows, two frequency distributions can have the same mean but very different ranges and standard deviations. For example, studies show that men and women have the same mean IQ but that men have a larger range and standard deviation, which is to say that a man is more likely than a woman to be much more or much less intelligent than the average person of his or her own gender.

mean The average value of all the measurements.

mode The value of the most frequently observed measurement.

median The value that is "in the middle"– i.e., greater than or equal to half the measurements and less than or equal to half the measurements.

range The value of the largest measurement in a frequency distribution minus the value of the smallest measurement.

standard deviation A statistic that describes the average distance between the measurements in a frequency distribution and the mean of that distribution.

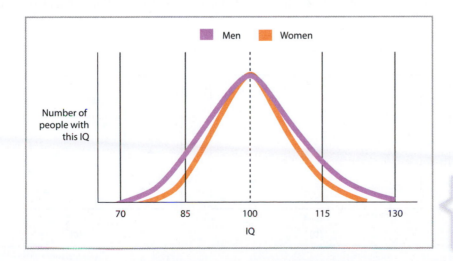

Number of people with this IQ

70   85   100   115   130

IQ

◄ Figure **A.4** **IQ of Men and Women**
Men and women have the same average IQ, but men are more variable than women.

correlation coefficient A measure of the direction and strength of a correlation, symbolized by the letter *r* (as in "relationship").

Measuring Correlation

In Chapter 2 you learned about correlation, using a hypothetical example (Table 2.1) in which there was a correlation between whether or not you insulted a passerby and whether or not that same passerby would then respond to your request for the time of day. The variables in this made-up example are perfectly correlated: that is, each and every time *not insulted* changes to *insulted*, *agreed* also changes to *refused*, and there are no exceptions to this rule. But perfect correlations are so rare in everyday life that we had to make up a hypothetical study just to show you one. There really *is* a correlation between age and height, and if we predict that a child will be shorter than an adult we will be right more often than we are wrong. But we *will* be wrong in some instances because there are *some* tall kids and *some* short adults. So how much confidence should we have in predictions based on correlations?

Statisticians have developed a way to estimate just how accurate a particular prediction is likely to be by measuring the *strength* of the correlation on which it is based. The **correlation coefficient** is *a measure of the direction and strength of a correlation,* and it is symbolized by the letter *r* (as in "relationship").

> ▶ If every time the value of one variable increases the value of the second variable also increases, then the relationship between the variables is called a *perfect positive correlation* and $r = 1$. For example, if every increase in age of 1 year was associated with an increase in height of .3 inches, then age and height would be *perfectly positively correlated* **(FIGURE A.5a)**.

> ▶ If every time the value of one variable increases by a fixed amount the value of the second variable *decreases* by a fixed amount, then the relationship between the variables is called a *perfect negative correlation* and $r = -1$. For example, if every increase in age of 1 year was associated with a decrease in height of .3 inches, then age and height would be *perfectly negatively correlated* **(FIGURE A.5b)**.

> ▶ If every time the value of one variable increases by a fixed amount the value of the second variable does not increase or decrease systematically, then the two variables are said to be *uncorrelated* and $r = 0$. For example, if increases in age of 1 year were sometimes associated with increases in height, sometimes associated with decreases in height, and sometimes associated with no change in height, then age and height would be uncorrelated **(FIGURE A.5c)**.

In the real world, perfect positive and negative correlations are rare; more commonly, two variables are correlated to varying degrees—but there are some exceptions to the rule (the tall kids and the short adults). We note this by giving *r* intermediate values between 0 and 1 (for positive correlations) or between 0 and −1 (for negative correlations). In each case, the farther *r* is from 0, the stronger the correlation

▼ **Figure A.5 Three Kinds of Correlations** This figure illustrates pairs of variables that have (a) a perfect positive correlation $(r = +1)$, (b) a perfect negative correlation $(r = -1)$, and (c) no correlation $(r = 0)$.

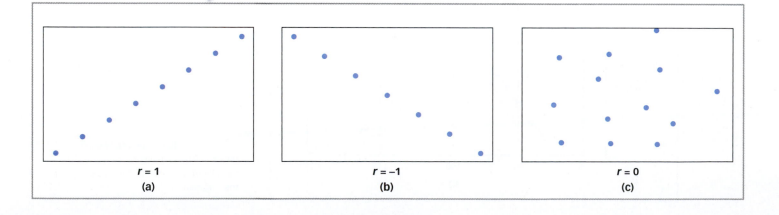

| $r = 1$ | $r = -1$ | $r = 0$ |
| (a) | (b) | (c) |

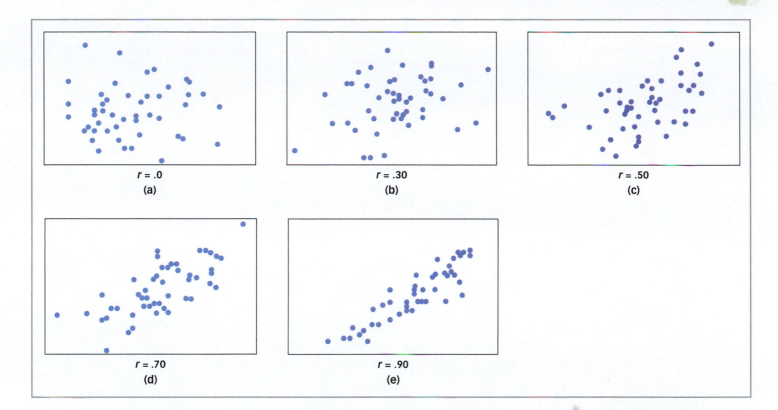

$r = .0$
(a)

$r = .30$
(b)

$r = .50$
(c)

$r = .70$
(d)

$r = .90$
(e)

between the variables. **FIGURE A.6** shows cases in which two variables are positively correlated but have different numbers of exceptions and therefore different values of r. Two variables can have a perfect correlation ($r = 1$), a strong correlation (for example, $r = .90$), a moderate correlation (for example, $r = .70$), or a weak correlation (for example, $r = .30$). The correlation coefficient, then, is a measure of both the *direction* and *strength* of the relationship between two variables. The sign of r (plus or minus) tells us the direction of the relationship and the absolute value of r (between 0 and 1) tells us about the number of exceptions to the rule.

▲ Figure A.6 **Correlations of Different Strengths** These graphs represent different degrees of correlation between two variables. When there are few exceptions to the rule $X = Y$, then the correlation is strong and r is closer to 1. When there are many exceptions to this rule, the correlation is weak and r is closer to 0.

Glossary

absentmindedness A lapse in attention that results in memory failure. (p. 186)

absolute threshold The minimal intensity needed to just barely detect a stimulus. (p. 94)

accommodation The process by which infants revise their schemas in light of new information. (p. 313)

accommodation The process by which the eye maintains a clear image on the retina. (p. 99)

acquisition The phase of classical conditioning when the CS and the US are presented together. (p. 203)

action potential An electric signal that is conducted along a neruon's axon to a synapse. (p. 62)

activation-synthesis model The theory that dreams are produced when the brain attempts to make sense of activations that occur randomly during sleep. (p. 148)

actor-observer effect The tendency to make situational attributions for our own behaviors while making dispositional attributions for the identical behavior of others. (p. 400)

adolescence The period of development that begins with the onset of sexual maturity (about 11 to 14 years of age) and lasts until the beginning of adulthood (about 18 to 21 years of age). (p. 328)

adulthood The stage of development that begins around age 18 to 21 and ends at death. (p. 334)

aggression Behavior whose purpose is to harm another. (p. 376)

agonists Drugs that increase the action of a neurotransmitter. (p. 64)

agoraphobia An extreme fear of venturing into public placces. (p. 415)

alcohol myopia A condition that results when alcohol hampers attention, leading people to respond in simple ways to complex situations. (p. 153)

altered states of consciousness Forms of experience that depart from the normal subjective experience of the world and the mind. (p. 141)

altruism Behavior that benefits another without benefiting oneself. (p. 380)

amygdala A part of the limbic system that plays a central role in many emotional processes, particularly the formation of emotional memories. (p. 73)

anal stage The second psychosexual stage, which is dominated by the pleasures and frustrations associated with the anus, retention and expulsion of feces and urine, and toilet training. (p. 358)

anorexia nervosa An eating disorder characterized by an intense fear of being fat and severe restriction of food intake. (p. 254)

antagonists Drugs that block the function of a neurotransmitter. (p. 65)

anterograde amnesia The inability to transfer new information from the short-term store into the long-term store. (p. 173)

antianxiety medications Drugs that help reduce a person's experience of fear or anxiety. (p. 449)

antidepressants A class of drugs that help lift people's mood. (p. 449)

antipsychotic drugs Medications that are used to treat schizophrenia and related psychotic disorders. (p. 448)

antisocial personality disorder (APD) A pervasive pattern of disregard for and violation of the rights of others that begins in childhood or early adolescence and continues into adulthood. (p. 429)

anxiety disorders Mental disorders in which anxiety is the predominant feature. (p. 412)

aphasia Difficulty in producing or comprehending language. (p. 276)

apparent motion The perception of movement as a result of alternating signals appearing in rapid succession in different locations. (p. 113)

appraisal An evaluation of the emotion-relevant aspects of a stimulus. (p. 240)

approach motivation A motivation to experience positive outcomes. (p. 262)

area A1 A portion of the temporal lobe that contains the primary auditory cortex. (p. 118)

area V1 The part of the occipital lobe that contains the primary visual cortex. (p. 103)

assimilation The process by which infants apply their schemas in novel situations. (p. 313)

association areas Areas of the cerebral cortex that are composed of neurons that help provide sense and meaning to information registered in the cortex. (p. 76)

attachment The emotional bond that forms between newborns and their primary caregivers. (p. 322)

attitude An enduring positive or negative evaluation of an object or event. (p. 393)

attribution An inference about the cause of a person's behavior. (p. 400)

autonomic nervous system (ANS) A set of nerves that carries involuntary and automatic commands that control blood vessels, body organs, and glands. (p. 66)

availability bias The tendency to mistakenly judge items that are more readily available in memory as having occurred more frequently. (p. 282)

avoidance motivation A motivation not to experience negative outcomes. (p. 262)

axon The part of a neuron that transmits information to other neurons, muscles, or glands. (p. 58)

basal ganglia A set of subcortical structures that directs intentional movements. (p. 73)

basilar membrane A structure in the inner ear that undulates when vibrations from the ossicles reach the cochlear fluid. (p. 117)

behavior Observable actions of human beings and nonhuman animals. (p. 2)

behavior therapy A type of therapy that assumes that disordered behavior is learned and that symptom relief is achieved through changing overt maladaptive behaviors into more constructive behaviors. (p. 441)

behavioral neuroscience An approach to psychology that links psychological processes to activities in the nervous system and other bodily processes. (p. 18)

behaviorism An approach that advocates that psychologists restrict themselves to the scientific study of objectively observable behavior. (p. 12)

belief An enduring piece of knowledge about an object or event. (p. 393)

bias The distorting influences of present knowledge, beliefs, and feelings on recollection of previous experiences. (p. 192)

Big Five The traits of the five-factor model: conscientiousness, agreeableness, neuroticism, openness to experience, and extraversion. (p. 351)

binding problem A phenomenon that concerns how features are linked together so that we see unified objects in our visual world rather than free-floating or miscombined features. (p. 106)

binocular disparity The difference in the retinal images of the two eyes that provides information about depth. (p. 112)

biofeedback The use of an external monitoring device to obtain information about a bodily function and possibly gain control over that function. (p. 478)

biological preparedness A propensity for learning particular kinds of associations over others. (p. 209)

bipolar disorder An unstable emotional condition characterized by cycles of abnormal, persistent high mood (mania) and low mood (depression). (p. 420)

blind spot A location in the visual field that produces no sensation on the retina because the corresponding area of the retina contains neither rods nor cones and therefore has no mechanism to sense light. (p. 101)

blocking A failure to retrieve information that is available in memory even though you are trying to produce it. (p. 196)

bulimia nervosa An eating disorder characterized by binge eating followed by purging. (p. 253)

burnout A state of physical, emotional, and mental exhaustion created by long-term involvement in an emotionally demanding situation and accompanied by lowered performance and motivation. (p. 474)

cannon-bard theory A theory which asserts that a stimulus simultaneously triggers activity in the autonomic nervous system and emotional experience in the brain. (p. 238)

case method A method of gathering scientific knowledge by studying a single individual. (p. 47)

category-specific deficit A neurological syndrome that is characterized by an inability to recognize objects that belong to a particular category although the ability to recognize objects outside the category is undisturbed. (p. 280)

cell body The part of a neuron that coordinates information-processing tasks and keeps the cell alive. (p. 58)

central nervous system (CNS) The part of the nervous system that is composed of the brain and spinal cord. (p. 66)

cephalocaudal rule The "top-to-bottom" rule that describes the tendency for motor skills to emerge in sequence from the head to the feet. (p. 312)

cerebellum A large structure of the hindbrain that controls fine motor skills. (p. 70)

cerebral cortex The outermost layer of the brain, divided into two hemispheres. (p. 73)

change blindness A phenomenon that occurs when people fail to detect changes to the visual details of a scene. (p. 113)

childhood The stage of development that begins at about 18 to 24 months and lasts until adolescence. (p. 315)

chromosomes Strands of DNA wound around each other in a double-helix configuration. (p. 80)

chronic stressor A source of stress that occurs continuously or repeatedly. (p. 467)

chunking Combining small pieces of information into larger clusters or chunks that are more easily held in short-term memory. (p. 172)

circadian rhythm A naturally occurring 24-hour cycle of sleeping and waking. (p. 141)

classical conditioning A phenomenon that occurs when a neutral stimulus produces a response after being paired with a stimulus that naturally produces a response. (p. 200)

cochlea A fluid-filled tube that is the organ of auditory transduction. (p. 117)

cocktail party phenomenon A phenomenon in which people tune in one message even while they filter out others nearby. (p. 135)

cognitive behavioral therapy (CBT) A blend of cognitive and behavioral therapeutic strategies. (p. 443)

cognitive development The emergence of the ability to think and understand. (p. 312)

cognitive dissonance An unpleasant state that arises when a person recognizes the inconsistency of his or her actions, attitudes, or beliefs. (p. 395)

cognitive map A mental representation of the physical features of the environment. (p. 219)

cognitive neuroscience A field that attempts to understand the links between cognitive processes and brain activity. (p. 19)

cognitive psychology The scientific study of mental processes, including perception, thought, memory, and reasoning. (p. 16)

cognitive restructuring A therapeutic approach that teaches clients to question the automatic beliefs, assumptions, and predictions that often lead to negative emotions and to replace negative thinking with more realistic and positive beliefs. (p. 443)

cognitive therapy A form of psychotherapy that involves helping a client identify and correct any distorted thinking about self, others, or the world. (p. 443)

cognitive unconscious The mental processes that give rise to the person's thoughts, choices, emotions, and behavior even though they are not experienced by the person. (p. 140)

comorbidity The co-occurrence of two or more disorders in a single individual. (p. 409)

companionate love An experience involving affection, trust, and concern for a partner's well-being. (p. 387)

concept A mental representation that groups or categorizes shared features of related objects, events, or other stimuli. (p. 227)

concrete operational stage The stage of development that begins at about age 6 and ends at about age 11, during which children learn how various actions, or "operations," can affect or transform "concrete" objects. (p. 315)

conditioned response (CR) A reaction that resembles an unconditioned response but is produced by a conditioned stimulus. (p. 201)

conditioned stimulus (CS) A stimulus that is initially neutral and produces no reliable response in an organism. (p. 200)

cones Photoreceptors that detect color, operate under normal daylight conditions, and allow us to focus on fine detail. (p. 100)

conformity The tendency to do what others do simply because others are doing it. (p. 391)

conjunction fallacy An error that occurs when people think that two events are more likely to occur together than either individual event. (p. 282)

conscious motivation A motivation of which one is aware. (p. 261)

consciousness A person's subjective experience of the world and the mind. (p. 6)

conservation The notion that the quantitative properties of an object are invariant despite changes in the object's appearance. (p. 315)

consolidation The process by which memories become stable in the brain. (p. 174)

control group The group of people who are not treated in the particular way that the experimental group is treated in an experiment. (p. 44)

conventional stage A stage of moral development in which the morality of an action is primarily determined by the extent to which it conforms to social rules. (p. 325)

cooperation Behavior by two or more individuals that leads to mutual benefit. (p. 379)

corpus callosum A thick band of nerve fibers that connects large areas of the cerebral cortex on each side of the brain and supports communication of information across the hemispheres. (p. 74)

correlation Two variables are said to "be correlated" when variations in the value of one variable are synchronized with variations in the value of the other. (p. 39)

correlation coefficient A measure of the direction and strength of a correlation, symbolized by the letter *r* (as in "relationship"). (p. A-4)

correspondence bias The tendency to make a dispositional attribution even when a person's behavior was caused by the situation. (p. 400)

crystallized intelligence The ability to retain and use knowledge that was acquired through experience. (p. 292)

cultural psychology The study of how cultures reflect and shape the psychological processes of their members. (p. 22)

debriefing A verbal description of the true nature and purpose of a study. (p. 51)

deep structure The meaning of a sentence. (p. 269)

defense mechanisms Unconscious coping mechanisms that reduce the anxiety generated by threats from unacceptable impulses. (p. 356)

deindividuation A phenomenon that occurs when immersion in a group causes people to become less aware of their individual values. (p. 380)

delusion A patently false belief system, often bizarre and grandiose, that is maintained in spite of its irrationality. (p. 423)

demand characteristics Those aspects of an observational setting that cause people to behave as they think they should. (p. 35)

dendrite The part of a neuron that receives information from other neurons and relays it to the cell body. (p. 58)

dependent variable The variable that is measured in a study. (p. 44)

depressants Substances that reduce the activity of the central nervous system. (p. 153)

developmental psychology The study of continuity and change across the life span. (p. 308)

deviation IQ A statistic obtained by dividing a person's test score by the average test score of people in the same age group

and then multiplying the quotient by 100 (see *ratio IQ*). (p. 288)

diathesis-stress model A model suggesting that a person may be predisposed for a mental disorder that remains unexpressed until triggered by stress. (p. 410)

diffusion chain A phenomenon that occurs when *individuals initially learn a behavior by observing another individual perform that behavior and then serve as a model from which other individuals learn the behavior.* (p. 224)

diffusion of responsibility The tendency for individuals to feel diminished responsibility for their actions when they are surrounded by others who are acting the same way. (p. 380)

discrimination Positive or negative behavior toward another person based on that person's group membership. (p. 204)

discrimination The capacity to distinguish between similar but distinct stimuli. (p. 379)

disorganized speech A severe disruption of verbal communication in which ideas shift rapidly and incoherently from one to another unrelated topic. (p. 424)

displacement A defense mechanism that involves shifting unacceptable wishes or drives to a neutral or less threatening alternative. (p. 357)

display rules Norms for the control of emotional expression. (p. 247)

dissociative amnesia The sudden loss of memory for significant personal information. (p. 422)

dissociative disorder A condition in which normal cognitive processes are severely disjointed and fragmented, creating significant disruptions in memory, awareness, or personality that can vary in length from a matter of minutes to many years. (p. 421)

dissociative fugue The sudden loss of memory for one's personal history, accompanied by an abrupt departure from home and the assumption of a new identity. (p. 422)

dissociative identity disorder (DID) The presence within an individual of two or more distinct identities that at different times take control of the individual's behavior. (p. 421)

door-in-the-face technique A strategy that uses reciprocating concessions to influence behavior. (p. 391)

dopamine hypothesis The idea that schizophrenia involves an excess of dopamine activity. (p. 426)

double-blind An observation whose true purpose is hidden from both the observer and the person being observed. (p. 37)

drive An internal state generated by departures from physiological optimality. (p. 252)

drug tolerance The tendency for larger doses of a drug to be required over time to achieve the same effect. (p. 151)

DSM-5 (*Diagnostic and Statistical Manual of Mental Disorders [Fifth Edition].*) A classification system that describes the features used to diagnose each recognized mental disorder and indicates how the disorder can be distinguished from other, similar problems. (p. 407)

dynamic unconscious An active system encompassing a lifetime of hidden memories, the person's deepest instincts and desires, and the person's inner struggle to control these forces. (p. 139)

echoic memory A fast-decaying store of auditory information. (p. 171)

eclectic psychotherapy Treatment that draws on techniques from different forms of therapy, depending on the client and the problem. (p. 439)

ego The component of personality, developed through contact with the external world, that enables us to deal with life's practical demands. (p. 356)

egocentrism The failure to understand that the world appears differently to different observers. (p. 316)

elaborative encoding The process of actively relating new information to knowledge that is already in memory. (p. 167)

electroconvulsive therapy (ECT) A treatment that involves inducing a mild seizure by delivering an electrical shock to the brain. (p. 454)

electromyograph (EMG) A device that measures muscle contractions under the surface of a person's skin. (p. 34)

embryonic stage The period of prenatal development that lasts from the second week until about the eighth week. (p. 309)

emotion A positive or negative experience that is associated with a particular pattern of physiological activity. (p. 238)

emotion regulation The use of cognitive and behavioral strategies to influence one's emotional experience. (p. 241)

emotional expression Any observable sign of an emotional state. (p. 243)

emotional intelligence The ability to reason about emotions and to use emotions to enhance reasoning. (p. 294)

empirical method A set of rules and techniques for observation. (p. 33)

empiricism The belief that accurate knowledge can be acquired through observation. (p. 32)

encoding The process by which we transform what we perceive, think, or feel into an enduring memory. (p. 166)

encoding specificity principle The idea that a retrieval cue can serve as an effective reminder when it helps re-create the specific way in which information was initially encoded. (p. 177)

episodic memory The collection of past personal experiences that occurred at a particular time and place. (p. 182)

evolutionary psychology A psychological approach that explains mind and behavior in terms of the adaptive value of abilities that are preserved over time by natural selection. (p. 19)

exemplar theory A theory of categorization that argues that we make category judgments by comparing a new instance with stored memories for other instances of the category. (p. 278)

existential approach A school of thought that regards personality as governed by an individual's ongoing choices and decisions in the context of the realities of life and death. (p. 360)

expectancy theory The idea that alcohol effects can be produced by people's expectations of how alcohol will influence them in particular situations. (p. 153)

experiment A technique for establishing the causal relationship between variables. (p. 42)

experimental group The group of people who are treated in a particular way, as compared to the control group, in an experiment. (p. 44)

explicit memory The act of consciously or intentionally retrieving past experiences. (p. 180)

exposure therapy An approach to treatment that involves confronting an emotion-arousing stimulus directly and repeatedly, ultimately leading to a decrease in the emotional response. (p. 442)

external validity A property of an experiment in which the variables have been operationally defined in a normal, typical, or realistic way. (p. 46)

extinction The gradual elimination of a learned response that occurs when the US is no longer presented. (p. 203)

extrinsic motivation A motivation to take actions that are not themselves rewarding but that lead to reward. (p. 260)

facial feedback hypothesis The hypothesis that emotional expressions can cause the emotional experiences they signify. (p. 246)

false recognition A feeling of familiarity about something that hasn't been encountered before. (p. 189)

family resemblance theory The theory that members of a category have features that appear to be characteristic of category members but may not be possessed by every member. (p. 278)

fast mapping A phenomenon whereby children can map a word onto an underlying concept after only a single exposure. (p. 272)

feature integration theory The idea that focused attention is not required to detect the individual features that comprise a stimulus but is required to bind those individual features together. (p. 106)

fetal alcohol syndrome A developmental disorder that stems from heavy alcohol use by the mother during pregnancy. (p. 310)

fetal stage The period of prenatal development that lasts from the ninth week until birth. (p. 309)

fight-or-flight response An emotional and physiological reaction to an emergency that increases readiness for action. (p. 471)

fixed interval (FI) schedule An operant conditioning principle in which reinforcements are presented at fixed time periods, provided that the appropriate response is made. (p. 214)

fixed ratio (FR) schedule An operant conditioning principle in which reinforcement is delivered after a specific number of responses have been made. (p. 215)

flashbulb memories Detailed recollections of when and where we heard about shocking events. (p. 193)

fluid intelligence The ability to see abstract relationships and draw logical inferences. (p. 292)

foot-in-the-door technique A technique that involves a small request followed by a larger request. (p. 395)

formal operational stage The stage of development that begins around the age of 11 and lasts through adulthood, during which children can solve nonphysical problems. (p. 316)

fovea An area of the retina where vision is the clearest and there are no rods at all. (p. 100)

framing effects Phenomena that occur when people give different answers to the same problem depending on how the problem is phrased (or framed). (p. 283)

fraternal twins (also called **dizygotic twins**) Twins who develop from two different eggs that were fertilized by two different sperm (see *identical twins*). (p. 296)

frequency distributions A graphic representation of measurements arranged by the number of times each measurement was made. (p. A-1)

frequency format hypothesis The proposal that our minds evolved to notice how frequently things occur, not how likely they are to occur. (p. 282)

frontal lobe A region of the cerebral cortex that has specialized areas for movement,

abstract thinking, planning, memory, and judgment. (p. 76)

frustration-aggression hypothesis A principle stating that animals aggress only when their goals are thwarted. (p. 377)

full consciousness Consciousness in which you know and are able to report your mental state. (p. 136)

functionalism The study of the purpose mental processes serve in enabling people to adapt to their environment. (p. 7)

gate-control theory A theory of pain perception based on the idea that signals arriving from pain receptors in the body can be stopped, or *gated*, by interneurons in the spinal cord via feedback from two directions. (p. 121)

gene The unit of hereditary transmission. (p. 80)

general adaptation syndrome (GAS) A three-stage physiological response that appears regardless of the stressor that is encountered. (p. 471)

generalization A process in which the CR is observed even though the CS is slightly different from the original one used during acquisition. (p. 204)

generalized anxiety disorder (GAD) A disorder characterized by chronic excessive worry accompanied by three or more of the following symptoms: restlessness, fatigue, concentration problems, irritability, muscle tension, and sleep disturbance. (p. 412)

genetic dysphasia A syndrome characterized by an inability to learn the grammatical structure of language despite having otherwise normal intelligence. (p. 274)

genital stage The final psychosexual stage, a time for the coming together of the mature adult personality with a capacity to love, work, and relate to others in a mutually satisfying and reciprocal manner. (p. 359)

germinal stage The 2-week period of prenatal development that begins at conception. (p. 359)

Gestalt psychology A psychological approach that emphasizes that we often perceive the whole rather than the sum of the parts. (p. 15)

Gestalt therapy An existentialist approach to treatment with the goal of helping the client to become aware of his or her thoughts, behaviors, experiences, and feelings and to "own" or take responsibility for them. (p. 445)

glial cells Support cells found in the nervous system. (p. 58)

grammar A set of rules that specify how the units of language can be combined to produce meaningful messages. (p. 268)

grossly disorganized behavior Behavior that is inappropriate for the situation or ineffective in attaining goals, often with specific motor disturbances. (p. 424)

group A collection of people who have something in common that distinguishes them from others. (p. 379)

group therapy Therapy in which multiple participants (who often do not know one another at the outset) work on their individual problems in a group atmosphere. (p. 446)

habituation A general process in which repeated or prolonged exposure to a stimulus results in a gradual reduction in response. (p. 228)

hair cells Specialized auditory receptor neurons embedded in the basilar membrane. (p. 117)

hallucination A false perceptual experience that has a compelling sense of being real despite the absence of external stimulation. (p. 424)

hallucinogens Drugs that alter sensation and perception and often cause visual and auditory hallucinations. (p. 155)

haptic perception The active exploration of the environment by touching and grasping objects with our hands. (p. 119)

health psychology The subfield of psychology concerned with ways psychological factors influence the causes and treatment of physical illness and the maintenance of health. (p. 466)

hedonic principle The notion that all people are motivated to experience pleasure and avoid pain. (p. 250)

helplessness theory The idea that individuals who are prone to depression automatically attribute negative experiences to causes that are internal (i.e., their own fault), stable (i.e., unlikely to change), and global (i.e., widespread). (p. 419)

heuristic persuasion The process by which attitudes or beliefs are changed by appeals to habit or emotion. (p. 394)

hindbrain An area of the brain that coordinates information coming into and out of the spinal cord. (p. 70)

hippocampus A structure critical for creating new memories and integrating them into a network of knowledge so that they can be stored indefinitely in other parts of the cerebral cortex. (p. 72)

humanistic psychology An approach to understanding human nature that emphasizes the positive potential of human beings. (p. 11)

hypnosis An altered state of consciousness characterized by suggestibility and the feeling that one's actions are occurring involuntarily. (p. 158)

hypnotic analgesia The reduction of pain through hypnosis in people who are susceptible to hypnosis. (p. 159)

hypochondriasis A psychological disorder in which a person is preoccupied with minor symptoms and develops an exaggerated belief that the symptoms signify a life-threatening illness. (p. 481)

hypothalamus A subcortical structure that regulates body temperature, hunger, thirst, and sexual behavior. (p. 72)

hypothesis A falsifiable prediction made by a theory. (p. 33)

hysteria A temporary loss of cognitive or motor functions, usually as a result of emotionally upsetting experiences. (p. 9)

iatrogenic illness A disorder or symptom that occurs as a result of a medical or psychotherapeutic treatment. (p. 460)

iconic memory A fast-decaying store of visual information. (p. 171)

id The part of the mind containing the drives present at birth; it is the source of our bodily needs, wants, desires, and impulses, particularly our sexual and aggressive drives. (p. 355)

identical twins (also called **monozygotic twins**) Twins who develop from the splitting of a single egg that was fertilized by a single sperm (see *fraternal twins*). (p. 296)

identification A defense mechanism that reduces feelings of threat and anxiety by enabling us unconsciously to take on the characteristics of another person who seems more powerful or better able to cope. (p. 357)

illusions Errors of perception, memory, or judgment in which subjective experience differs from objective reality. (p. 15)

illusory conjunction A perceptual mistake where features from multiple objects are incorrectly combined. (p. 106)

immune system A complex response system that protects the body from bacteria, viruses, and other foreign substances. (p. 471)

implicit learning Learning that takes place largely without awareness of the process or the products of information acquisition. (p. 228)

implicit memory The influence of past experiences on later behavior, even without an effort to remember them or an awareness of the recollection. (p. 180)

inattentional blindness A failure to perceive objects that are not the focus of attention. (p. 114)

independent variable The variable that is manipulated in an experiment. (p. 44)

infancy The stage of development that begins at birth and lasts between 18 and 24 months. (p. 311)

informational influence A phenomenon that occurs when a person's behavior provides information about what is good or right. (p. 393)

informed consent A written agreement to participate in a study made by an adult who has been informed of all the risks that participation may entail. (p. 50)

insomnia Difficulty in falling asleep or staying asleep. (p. 145)

intelligence The ability to direct one's thinking, adapt to one's circumstances, and learn from one's experiences. (p. 286)

intermittent reinforcement An operant conditioning principle in which only some of the responses made are followed by reinforcement. (p. 215)

intermittent-reinforcement effect The fact that operant behaviors that are maintained under intermittent-reinforcement schedules resist extinction better than those maintained under continuous reinforcement. (p. 215)

internal validity The characteristic of an experiment that establishes the causal relationship between variables. (p. 46)

internal working model of relationships A set of beliefs about the self, the primary caregiver, and the relationship between them. (p. 322)

interneurons Neurons that connect sensory neurons, motor neurons, or other interneurons. (p. 59)

intrinsic motivation A motivation to take actions that are themselves rewarding. (p. 260)

introspection The subjective observation of one's own experience. (p. 6)

ironic processes of mental control Mental processes that can produce ironic errors because monitoring for errors can itself produce them. (p. 138)

James-Lange theory A theory which asserts that stimuli trigger activity in the autonomic nervous system, which in turn produces an emotional experience in the brain. (p. 238)

just noticeable difference (JND) The minimal change in a stimulus that can just barely be detected. (p. 95)

kin selection The process by which evolution selects for individuals who cooperate their relatives. (p. 381)

language A system for communicating with others using signals that are combined according to rules of grammar and convey meaning. (p. 268)

latency stage The fourth psychosexual stage, during which the primary focus is on the further development of intellectual, creative, interpersonal, and athletic skills. (p. 358)

latent learning A condition in which something is learned but it is not manifested as a behavioral change until sometime in the future. (p. 218)

law of effect The principle that behaviors that are followed by a "satisfying state of affairs" tend to be repeated and those that produce an "unpleasant state of affairs" are less likely to be repeated. (p. 211)

learning The acquisition of new knowledge, skills, or responses from experience that result in a relatively permanent change in the state of the learner. (p. 200)

locus of control A person's tendency to perceive the control of rewards as internal to the self or external in the environment. (p. 364)

long-term memory A type of storage that holds information for hours, days, weeks, or years. (p. 172)

long-term potentiation (LTP) A process whereby communication across the synapse between neurons strengthens the connection, making further communication easier. (p. 176)

loudness A sound's intensity. (p. 115)

major depressive disorder A disorder characterized by a severely depressed mood that lasts 2 weeks or more and is accompanied by feelings of worthlessness and lack of pleasure, lethargy, and sleep and appetite disturbances. (p. 417)

manipulation The creation of an artificial pattern of variation in a variable in order to determine its causal powers. (p. 43)

marijuana The leaves and buds of the hemp plant. (p. 157)

mean The average value of all the measurements. (p. A-2)

measure A device that can detect the condition to which an operational definition refers. (p. 34)

median The value that is "in the middle"– i.e., greater than or equal to half the measurements and less than or equal to half the measurements. (p. A-2)

medical model The conceptualization of psychological abnormalities as diseases that, like physical diseases, have biological causes, defined symptoms, and possible cures. (p. 406)

meditation The practice of intentional contemplation. (p. 160)

medulla An extension of the spinal cord into the skull that coordinates heart rate, circulation, and respiration. (p. 70)

memory The ability to store and retrieve information over time. (p. 166)

memory misattribution Assigning a recollection or an idea to the wrong source. (p. 187)

mental control The attempt to change conscious states of mind. (p. 137)

metabolism The rate at which energy is used by the body. (p. 256)

mind Our private inner experience of perceptions, thoughts, memories, and feelings. (p. 2)

mind/body problem The issue of how the mind is related to the brain and body. (p. 133)

mindfulness meditation A form of cognitive therapy that teaches an individual to be fully present in each moment; to be aware of his or her thoughts, feelings, and sensations; and to detect symptoms before they become a problem. (p. 443)

minimal consciousness A low-level kind of sensory awareness and responsiveness that occurs when the mind inputs sensations and may output behavior. (p. 136)

Minnesota Multiphasic Personality Inventory (MMPI) A well-researched, clinical questionnaire used to assess personality and psychological problems. (p. 347)

mode The value of the most frequently observed measurement. (p. A-2)

monocular depth cues Aspects of a scene that yield information about depth when viewed with only one eye. (p. 110)

mood disorders Mental disorders that have mood disturbance as their predominant feature. (p. 417)

morphemes The smallest meaningful units of language. (p. 269)

morphological rules A set of rules that indicate how morphemes can be combined to form words. (p. 269)

mortality-salience hypothesis The prediction that people who are reminded of their own mortality will work to reinforce their cultural worldviews. (p. 259)

motivation The purpose for or psychological cause of an action. (p. 250)

motor development The emergence of the ability to execute physical action. (p. 312)

motor neurons Neurons that carry signals from the spinal cord to the muscles to produce movement. (p. 59)

myelin sheath An insulating layer of fatty material. (p. 58)

myelination The formation of a fatty sheath around the axons of a neuron. (p. 310)

narcissism A trait that reflects a grandiose view of the self combined with a tendency to seek admiration from and exploit others. (p. 369)

narcolepsy A disorder in which sudden sleep attacks occur in the middle of waking activities. (p. 145)

narcotics or opiates Highly addictive drugs derived from opium that relieve pain. (p. 155)

nativism The philosophical view that certain kinds of knowledge are innate or inborn. (p. 4)

nativist theory The view that language development is best explained as an innate, biological capacity. (p. 274)

natural correlation A correlation observed in the world around us. (p. 40)

natural selection Charles Darwin's theory that the features of an organism that help it survive and reproduce are more likely than other features to be passed on to subsequent generations. (p. 8)

naturalistic observation A technique for gathering scientific information by unobtrusively observing people in their natural environments. (p. 36)

need for achievement The motivation to solve worthwhile problems. (p. 261)

negative symptoms Emotional and social withdrawal, apathy, poverty of speech, and other indications of the absence or insufficiency of normal behavior, motivation, and emotion. (p. 424)

nervous system An interacting network of neurons that conveys electrochemical information throughout the body. (p. 66)

neurons Cells in the nervous system that communicate with one another to perform information-processing tasks. (p. 58)

neurotransmitters Chemicals that transmit information across the synapse to a receiving neuron's dendrites. (p. 63)

night terrors (or sleep terrors) Abrupt awakenings with panic and intense emotional arousal. (p. 146)

NMDA receptor A receptor site on the hippocampus that influences the flow of information between neurons by controlling the initiation of long-term potentiation. (p. 176)

nonshared environment Those environmental factors that are not experienced by all relevant members of a household (see *shared environment*). (p. 296)

norm A customary standard for behavior that is widely shared by members of a culture. (p. 390)

norm of reciprocity The unwritten rule that people should benefit those who have benefited them. (p. 390)

normal distribution A mathematically defined frequency distribution in which most measurements are concentrated around the middle. (p. A-1)

normative influence A phenomenon that occurs when another person's behavior provides information about what is appropriate. (p. 390)

obedience The tendency to do what powerful people tell us to do. (p. 392)

object permanence The idea that objects continue to exist even when they are not visible. (p. 314)

observational learning A condition in which learning takes place by watching the actions of others. (p. 223)

obsessive-compulsive disorder (OCD) A disorder in which repetitive, intrusive thoughts (obsessions) and ritualistic behaviors (compulsions) designed to fend off those thoughts interfere significantly with an individual's functioning. (p. 416)

occipital lobe A region of the cerebral cortex that processes visual information. (p. 74)

Oedipus conflict A developmental experience in which a child's conflicting feelings toward the opposite-sex parent are (usually) resolved by identifying with the same-sex parent. (p. 358)

olfactory bulb A brain structure located above the nasal cavity beneath the frontal lobes. (p. 123)

olfactory receptor neurons (ORNs) Receptor cells that initiate the sense of smell. (p. 123)

operant behavior Behavior that an organism produces that has some impact on the environment. (p. 211)

operant conditioning A type of learning in which the consequences of an organism's behavior determine whether that behavior will be repeated in the future. (p. 210)

operational definition A description of a property in concrete, measurable terms. (p. 34)

oral stage The first psychosexual stage, in which experience centers on the pleasures and frustrations associated with the mouth, sucking, and being fed. (p. 358)

organizational encoding The process of categorizing information according to the relationships among a series of items. (p. 169)

outcome expectancies A person's assumptions about the likely consequences of a future behavior. (p. 169)

panic disorder A disorder characterized by the sudden occurrence of multiple psychological and physiological symptoms that contribute to a feeling of stark terror. (p. 415)

parasympathetic nervous system A set of nerves that helps the body return to a normal resting state. (p. 67)

parietal lobe A region of the cerebral cortex whose functions include processing information about touch. (p. 75)

passionate love An experience involving feelings of euphoria, intimacy, and intense sexual attraction. (p. 387)

perception The organization, identification, and interpretation of a sensation in order to form a mental representation. (p. 92)

perceptual constancy A perceptual principle stating that even as aspects of sensory signals change, perception remains consistent. (p. 108)

peripheral nervous system (PNS) The part of the nervous system that connects the central nervous system to the body's organs and muscles. (p. 66)

persistence The intrusive recollection of events that we wish we could forget. (p. 193)

person-centered therapy An approach to therapy that assumes all individuals have a tendency toward growth and that this growth can be facilitated by acceptance and genuine reactions from the therapist. (p. 444)

person-situation controversy The question of whether behavior is caused more by personality or by situational factors. (p. 362)

personal constructs Dimensions people use in making sense of their experiences. (p. 363)

personality An individual's characteristic style of behaving, thinking, and feeling. (p. 346)

personality disorders Disorders characterized by deeply ingrained, inflexible patterns of thinking, feeling, relating to others, or controlling impulses that cause distress or impaired functioning. (p. 427)

persuasion A phenomenon that occurs when a person's attitudes or beliefs are influenced by a communication from another person. (p. 394)

phallic stage The third psychosexual stage, during which experience is dominated by the pleasure, conflict, and frustration associated with the phallic-genital region as well as coping with powerful incestuous feelings of love, hate, jealousy, and conflict. (p. 358)

phenomenology How things seem to the conscious person. (p. 132)

pheromones Biochemical odorants emitted by other members of its species that can affect an animal's behavior or physiology. (p. 124)

philosophical empiricism The philosophical view that all knowledge is acquired through experience. (p. 4)

phobic disorders Disorders characterized by marked, persistent, and excessive fear and avoidance of specific objects, activities, or situations. (p. 413)

phoneme The smallest unit of sound that is recognizable as speech rather than as random noise. (p. 268)

phonological rules A set of rules that indicate how phonemes can be combined to produce speech sounds. (p. 268)

phototherapy A treatment for seasonal depression that involves repeated exposure to bright light. (p. 454)

phrenology A now defunct theory that specific mental abilities and characteristics, ranging from memory to the capacity for happiness, are localized in specific regions of the brain. (p. 5)

physiology The study of biological processes, especially in the human body. (p. 6)

pitch How high or low a sound is. (p. 115)

pituitary gland The "master gland" of the body's hormone-producing system, which releases hormones that direct the functions of many other glands in the body. (p. 72)

place code The mechanism by which the cochlea encodes different frequencies at different locations along the basilar membrane. (p. 118)

placebo An inert substance or procedure that has been applied with the expectation that a healing response will be produced. (p. 456)

pons A brain structure that relays information from the cerebellum to the rest of the brain. (p. 70)

population The complete collection of participants who might possibly be measured. (p. 47)

postconventional stage A stage of moral development in which the morality of an action is determined by a set of general principles that reflect core values. (p. 325)

post-traumatic stress disorder (PTSD) A disorder characterized by chronic physiological arousal, recurrent unwanted thoughts or images of the trauma, and avoidance of things that call the traumatic event to mind. (p. 473)

power The ability of a measure to detect the concrete conditions specified in the operational definition. (p. 35)

preconventional stage A stage of moral development in which the morality of an action is primarily determined by its consequences for the actor. (p. 325)

prejudice A positive or negative evaluation of another person based on that person's group membership. (p. 379)

preoperational stage The stage of development that begins at about age 2 and ends at about age 6, during which children have a preliminary understanding of the physical world. (p. 315)

preparedness theory The idea that people are instinctively predisposed toward certain fears. (p. 414)

primary sex characteristics Bodily structures that are directly involved in reproduction. (p. 328)

priming An enhanced ability to think of a stimulus, such as a word or object, as a result of a recent exposure to the stimulus. (p. 181)

proactive interference Situations in which information learned earlier impairs memory for information acquired later. (p. 185)

problem of other minds The fundamental difficulty we have in perceiving the consciousness of others. (p. 133)

procedural memory The gradual acquisition of skills as a result of practice, or "knowing how" to do things. (p. 180)

prodigy A person of normal intelligence who has an extraordinary ability. (p. 293)

projection A defense mechanism that involves attributing one's own threatening feelings, motives, or impulses to another person or group. (p. 357)

projective techniques A standard series of ambiguous stimuli designed to elicit unique responses that reveal inner aspects of an individual's personality. (p. 348)

prospect theory The proposal that people choose to take risks when evaluating potential losses and avoid risks when evaluating potential gains. (p. 284)

prospective memory Remembering to do things in the future. (p. 186)

prototype The "best" or "most typical member" of a category. (p. 278)

proximodistal rule The "inside-to-outside" rule that describes the tendency for motor skills to emerge in sequence from the center to the periphery. (p. 312)

psychoactive drug A chemical that influences consciousness or behavior by altering the brain's chemical message system. (p. 150)

psychoanalysis A therapeutic approach that focuses on bringing unconscious material into conscious awareness to better understand psychological disorders. (p. 10)

psychoanalytic theory Sigmund Freud's approach to understanding human behavior that emphasizes the importance of unconscious mental processes in shaping feelings, thoughts, and behaviors. (p. 10)

psychodynamic approach An approach that regards personality as formed by needs, strivings, and desires, largely operating outside of awareness—motives that can also produce emotional disorders. (p. 355)

psychodynamic psychotherapies A general approach to treatment that explores childhood events and encourages individuals to develop insight into their psychological problems. (p. 439)

psychology The scientific study of mind and behavior. (p. 2)

psychopharmacology The study of drug effects on psychological states and symptoms. (p. 448)

psychophysics Methods that measure the strength of a stimulus and the observer's sensitivity to that stimulus. (p. 94)

psychosexual stages Distinct early life stages through which personality is formed as children experience sexual pleasures from specific body areas and caregivers redirect or interfere with those pleasures. (p. 358)

psychosomatic illness An illness produced by an interaction between mind and body. (p. 481)

psychosurgery Surgical destruction of specific brain areas. (p. 454)

psychotherapy An interaction between a therapist and someone suffering from a psychological problem, with the goal of providing support or relief from the problem. (p. 439)

puberty The bodily changes associated with sexual maturity. (p. 328)

punisher Any stimulus or event that functions to decrease the likelihood of the behavior that led to it. (p. 211)

random assignment A procedure that uses a random event to assign people to the experimental or control group. (p. 44)

random sampling A technique for choosing participants that ensures that every member of a population has an equal chance of being included in the sample. (p. 47)

range The value of the largest measurement in a frequency distribution minus the value of the smallest measurement. (p. A-3)

ratio IQ A statistic obtained by dividing a person's mental age by the person's physical age and then multiplying the quotient by 100 (see *deviation IQ*). (p. 287)

rational choice theory The classical view that we make decisions by determining how likely something is to happen, judging the value of the outcome, and then multiplying the two. (p. 281)

rational coping Facing a stressor and working to overcome it. (p. 476)

rationalization A defense mechanism that involves supplying a reasonable-sounding explanation for unacceptable feelings and behavior to conceal (mostly from oneself) one's underlying motives or feelings. (p. 356)

reaction formation A defense mechanism that involves unconsciously replacing threatening inner wishes and fantasies with an exaggerated version of their opposite. (p. 357)

reaction time The amount of time taken to respond to a specific stimulus. (p. 6)

reappraisal Changing one's emotional experience by changing the meaning of the emotion-eliciting stimulus. (p. 242)

rebound effect of thought suppression The tendency of a thought to return to consciousness with greater frequency following suppression. (p. 138)

receptive field The region of the sensory surface that, when stimulated, causes a change in the firing rate of that neuron. (p. 101)

receptors Parts of the cell membrane that receive the neurotransmitter and initiate or prevent a new electric signal. (p. 63)

reciprocal altruism Behavior that benefits another with the expectation that those benefits will be returned in the future. (p. 381)

reconsolidation The process by which memories can become vulnerable to disruption when they are recalled, requiring them to become consolidated again. (p. 174)

referred pain Feeling of pain when sensory information from internal and external areas converges on the same nerve cells in the spinal cord. (p. 121)

reflexes Specific patterns of motor response that are triggered by specific patterns of sensory stimulation. (p. 312)

refractory period The time following an action potential during which a new action potential cannot be initiated. (p. 63)

reframing Finding a new or creative way to think about a stressor that reduces its threat. (p. 477)

regression A defense mechanism in which the ego deals with internal conflict and perceived threat by reverting to an immature behavior or earlier stage of development. (p. 357)

rehearsal The process of keeping information in short-term memory by mentally repeating it. (p. 171)

reinforcement The consequences of a behavior that determine whether it will be more likely that the behavior will occur again. (p. 13)

reinforcer Any stimulus or event that functions to increase the likelihood of the behavior that led to it. (p. 211)

relaxation response A condition of reduced muscle tension, cortical activity, heart rate, breathing rate, and blood pressure. (p. 478)

relaxation therapy A technique for reducing tension by consciously relaxing muscles of the body. (p. 477)

reliability The tendency for a measure to produce the same measurement whenever it is used to measure the same thing. (p. 35)

REM sleep A stage of sleep characterized by rapid eye movements and a high level of brain activity. (p. 142)

representativeness heuristic A mental shortcut that involves making a probability judgment by comparing an object or event to a prototype of the object or event. (p. 283)

repression A mental process that removes unacceptable thoughts and memories from consciousness. (p. 139)

repressive coping Avoiding situations or thoughts that are reminders of a stressor and maintaining an artificially positive viewpoint. (p. 476)

resistance A reluctance to cooperate with treatment for fear of confronting unpleasant unconscious material. (p. 440)

response An action or physiological change elicited by a stimulus. (p. 13)

resting potential The difference in electric charge between the inside and outside of a neuron's cell membrane. (p. 61)

reticular formation A brain structure that regulates sleep, wakefulness, and levels of arousal. (p. 70)

retina Light-sensitive tissue lining the back of the eyeball. (p. 98)

retrieval The process of bringing to mind information that has been previously encoded and stored. (p. 166)

retrieval cue External information that helps bring stored information to mind. (p. 177)

retrieval-induced forgetting A process whereby retrieving an item from long-term memory impairs subsequent recall of related items. (p. 178)

retroactive interference Situations in which information learned later impairs memory for information acquired earlier. (p. 185)

retrograde amnesia The inability to retrieve information that was acquired before a particular date, usually the date of an injury or operation. (p. 173)

rods Photoreceptors that become active under low-light conditions for night vision. (p. 100)

Rorschach Inkblot Test A projective personality test in which individual interpretations of the meaning of a set of unstructured inkblots are analyzed to identify a respondent's inner feelings and interpret his or her personality structure. (p. 348)

sample The partial collection of people drawn from a population. (p. 47)

savant A person of low intelligence who has an extraordinary ability. (p. 293)

schemas Theories about or models of the way the world works. (p. 313)

schizophrenia A disorder characterized by the profound disruption of basic psychological processes; a distorted perception of reality; altered or blunted emotion; and disturbances in thought, motivation, and behavior. (p. 423)

scientific method A set of principles about the appropriate relationship between ideas and evidence. (p. 32)

seasonal affective disorder (SAD) Depression that involves recurrent depressive episodes in a seasonal pattern. (p. 417)

second-order conditioning Conditioning in which the stimulus that functions as the US is actually the CS from an earlier procedure in which it acquired its ability to produce learning. (p. 203)

secondary sex characteristics Bodily structures that change dramatically with sexual maturity but that are not directly involved in reproduction. (p. 328)

self-actualizing tendency The human motive to realize our inner potential. (p. 359)

self-concept A person's explicit knowledge of his or her own behaviors, traits, and other personal characteristics. (p. 366)

self-consciousness A distinct level of consciousness in which the person's attention is drawn to the self as an object. (p. 136)

self-esteem The extent to which an individual likes, values, and accepts the self. (p. 367)

self-regulation The exercise of voluntary control over the self to bring the self into line with preferred standards. (p. 485)

self-report A series of answers to a questionnaire that asks people to indicate the extent to which sets of statements or adjectives accurately describe their own behavior or mental state. (p. 347)

self-selection A problem that occurs when anything about a person determines whether he or she will be included in the experimental or control group. (p. 44)

self-serving bias People's tendency to take credit for their successes but downplay responsibility for their failures. (p. 369)

self-verification The tendency to seek evidence to confirm the self-concept. (p. 367)

semantic memory A network of associated facts and concepts that make up our general knowledge of the world. (p. 182)

sensation Simple stimulation of a sense organ. (p. 92)

sensorimotor stage A stage of development that begins at birth and lasts through infancy in which infants acquire information about the world by sensing it and moving around within it. (p. 313)

sensory adaptation Sensitivity to prolonged stimulation tends to decline over time as an organism adapts to current conditions. (p. 96)

sensory memory A type of storage that holds sensory information for a few seconds or less. (p. 170)

sensory neurons Neurons that receive information from the external world and convey this information to the brain via the spinal cord. (p. 58)

shaping Learning that results from the reinforcement of successive steps to a final desired behavior. (p. 216)

shared environment Those environmental factors that are experienced by all relevant members of a household (see *nonshared environment*). (p. 296)

short-term memory A type of storage that holds nonsensory information for more than a few seconds but less than a minute. (p. 171)

sick role A socially recognized set of rights and obligations linked with illness. (p. 482)

signal detection theory An observation that the response to a stimulus depends both on a person's sensitivity to the stimulus in the presence of noise and on a person's response criterion. (p. 95)

sleep apnea A disorder in which the person stops breathing for brief periods while asleep. (p. 145)

sleep paralysis The experience of waking up unable to move. (p. 146)

social cognition The processes by which people come to understand others. (p. 396)

social cognitive approach An approach that views personality in terms of how the person thinks about the situations encountered in daily life and behaves in response to them. (p. 361)

social exchange The hypothesis that people remain in relationships only as long as they perceive a favorable ratio of costs to benefits. (p. 387)

social influence The ability to control another person's behavior. (p. 389)

social phobia A disorder that involves an irrational fear of being publicly humiliated or embarrassed. (p. 413)

social psychology A subfield of psychology that studies the causes and consequences of interpersonal behavior. (p. 121)

social psychology The study of the causes and consequences of sociality. (p. 376)

social support The aid gained through interacting with others. (p. 479)

somatic nervous system A set of nerves that conveys information into and out of the central nervous system. (p. 66)

somatoform disorder A psychological disorder in which the patient displays physical symptoms not fully explained by a general medical condition. (p. 481)

somnambulism (sleepwalking) Occurs when the person arises and walks around while asleep. (p. 145)

source memory Recall of when, where, and how information was acquired. (p. 188)

specific phobia A disorder that involves an irrational fear of a particular object or situation that markedly interferes with an individual's ability to function. (p. 413)

spinal reflexes Simple pathways in the nervous system that rapidly generate muscle contractions. (p. 68)

spontaneous recovery The tendency of a learned behavior to recover from extinction after a rest period. (p. 204)

standard deviation A statistic that describes the average distance between the measurements in a frequency distribution and the mean of that distribution. (p. A-3)

state-dependent retrieval The tendency for information to be better recalled when the person is in the same state during encoding and retrieval. (p. 177)

stereotyping The process by which people draw inferences about others based on their knowledge of the categories to which others belong. (p. 396)

stimulants Substances that excite the central nervous system, heightening arousal and activity levels. (p. 154)

stimulus Sensory input from the environment. (p. 6)

storage The process of maintaining information in memory over time. (p. 166)

stress The physical and psychological response to internal or external stressors. (p. 466)

stressors Specific events or chronic pressures that place demands on a person or threaten the person's well-being. (p. 466)

structuralism The analysis of the basic elements that constitute the mind. (p. 6)

subcortical structures Areas of the forebrain housed under the cerebral cortex near the very center of the brain. (p. 71)

sublimation A defense mechanism that involves channeling unacceptable sexual or aggressive drives into socially acceptable and culturally enhancing activities. (p. 357)

subliminal perception A thought or behavior that is influenced by stimuli that a person cannot consciously report perceiving. (p. 140)

suggestibility The tendency to incorporate misleading information from external sources into personal recollections. (p. 190)

sunk-cost fallacy A framing effect in which people make decisions about a current situation based on what they have previously invested in the situation. (p. 283)

superego The mental system that reflects the internalization of cultural rules, mainly learned as parents exercise their authority. (p. 356)

surface structure How a sentence is worded. (p. 269)

sympathetic nervous system A set of nerves that prepares the body for action in threatening situations. (p. 67)

synapse The junction or region between the axon of one neuron and the dendrites or cell body of another. (p. 58)

syntactical rules A set of rules that indicate how words can be combined to form phrases and sentences. (p. 269)

systematic persuasion The process by which attitudes or beliefs are changed by appeals to reason. (p. 394)

taste buds The organ of taste transduction. (p. 124)

telegraphic speech Speech that is devoid of function morphemes and consists mostly of content words. (p. 272)

temperaments Characteristic patterns of emotional reactivity. (p. 322)

temporal code The mechanism by which the cochlea registers low frequencies via the firing rate of action potentials entering the auditory nerve. (p. 118)

temporal lobe A region of the cerebral cortex responsible for hearing and language. (p. 75)

teratogens Agents that damage the process of development, such as drugs and viruses. (p. 310)

terminal buttons Knoblike structures that branch out from an axon. (p. 63)

thalamus A subcortical structure that relays and filters information from the senses and transmits the information to the cerebral cortex. (p. 63)

Thematic Apperception Test (TAT) A projective personality test in which respondents reveal underlying motives, concerns, and the way they see the social

world through the stories they make up about ambiguous pictures of people. (p. 348)

theory A hypothetical explanation of a natural phenomenon. (p. 32)

theory of mind The idea that human behavior is guided by mental representations. (p. 317)

third-variable correlation The fact that two variables are correlated only because each is causally related to a third variable. (p. 41)

third-variable problem The fact that a causal relationship between two variables cannot be inferred from the naturally occurring correlation between them because of the ever-present possibility of third-variable correlation. (p. 42)

thought suppression The conscious avoidance of a thought. (p. 137)

timbre A listener's experience of sound quality or resonance. (p. 116)

token economy A form of behavior therapy in which clients are given "tokens" for desired behaviors, which they can later trade for rewards. (p. 442)

trait A relatively stable disposition to behave in a particular and consistent way. (p. 350)

transcranial magnetic stimulation (TMS) A treatment that involves placing a powerful pulsed magnet over a person's scalp, which alters neuronal activity in the brain. (p. 454)

transduction What takes place when many sensors in the body convert physical signals from the environment into encoded neural signals sent to the central nervous system. (p. 93)

transfer-appropriate processing The idea that memory is likely to transfer from one situation to another when the encoding contexts of the situations match. (p. 178)

transference An event that occurs in psychoanalysis when the analyst begins to assume a major significance in the client's life and the client reacts to the analyst based on unconscious childhood fantasies. (p. 440)

transience Forgetting what occurs with the passage of time. (p. 185)

two-factor theory A theory which asserts that emotions are inferences about the causes of physiological arousal. (p. 238)

two-factor theory of intelligence Spearman's theory suggesting that every task requires a combination of a general ability (which he called g) and skills that are specific to the task (which he called s). (p. 290)

Type A behavior pattern The tendency toward easily aroused hostility, impatience, a sense of time urgency, and competitive achievement strivings. (p. 472)

unconditioned response (UR) A reflexive reaction that is reliably produced by an unconditioned stimulus. (p. 200)

unconditioned stimulus (US) Something that reliably produces a naturally occurring reaction in an organism. (p. 200)

unconscious The part of the mind that operates outside of conscious awareness but influences conscious thoughts, feelings, and actions. (p. 10)

unconscious motivation A motivation of which one is not aware. (p. 261)

universality hypothesis The hypothesis that emotional expressions have the same meaning for everyone. (p. 244)

validity The extent to which a measurement and a property are conceptually related. (p. 35)

variable A property whose value can vary across individuals or over time. (p. 39)

variable interval (VI) schedule An operant conditioning principle in which behavior is reinforced based on an average time that has expired since the last reinforcement. (p. 214)

variable ratio (VR) schedule An operant conditioning principle in which the delivery of reinforcement is based on a particular average number of responses. (p. 215)

vestibular system The three fluid-filled semicircular canals and adjacent organs located next to the cochlea in each inner ear. (p. 122)

visual imagery encoding The process of storing new information by converting it into mental pictures. (p. 168)

visual-form agnosia The inability to recognize objects by sight. (p. 105)

Weber's law The just noticeable difference of a stimulus is a constant proportion despite variations in intensity. (p. 95)

working memory Active maintenance of information in short-term storage. (p. 172)

zygote A fertilized egg that contains chromosomes from both a sperm and an egg. (p. 309)

References

Aarts, H., Custers, R., & Marien, H. (2008). Preparing and motivating behavior outside of awareness. *Science, 319,* 1639.

Abbott, J. M., Klein, B., & Ciechomski, L. (2008). Best practices in online therapy. *Journal of Technology in Human Services, 26,* 360–375.

Abel, T., Alberini, C., Ghirardi, M., Huang, Y.-Y., Nguyen, P., & Kandel, E. R. (1995). Steps toward a molecular definition of memory consolidation. In D. L. Schacter (Ed.), *Memory distortion: How minds, brains and societies reconstruct the past* (pp. 298–328). Cambridge, MA: Harvard University Press.

Abelson, J., Curtis, G., Sagher, O., Albucher, R., Harrigan, M., Taylor, S., et al. (2009). Deep brain stimulation for refractory obsessive-compulsive disorder. *Biological Psychiatry, 57,* 510–516.

Abrams, M., & Reber, A. S. (1988). Implicit learning: Robustness in the face of psychiatric disorders. *Journal of Psycholinguistic Research, 17,* 425–439.

Abramson, L. Y., Seligman, M. E. P., & Teasdale, J. D. (1978). Learned helplessness in humans: Critique and reformulation. *Journal of Abnormal Psychology, 87,* 49–74.

Acevedo, B. P., & Aron, A. (2009). Does a long-term relationship kill romantic love? *Review of General Psychology, 13,* 59–65.

Acevedo-Garcia, D., McArdle, N., Osypuk, T. L., Lefkowitz, B., & Krimgold, B. K. (2007). *Children left behind: How metropolitan areas are failing America's children.* Boston: Harvard School of Public Health.

Acocella, J. (1999). *Creating hysteria: Women and multiple personality disorder.* San Francisco: Jossey-Bass.

Adams, H. E., Wright, L. W., Jr., & Lohr, B. A. (1996). Is homophobia associated with homosexual arousal? *Journal of Abnormal Psychology, 105,* 440–445.

Addis, D. R., Wong, A. T., & Schacter, D. L. (2007). Remembering the past and imagining the future: Common and distinct neural substrates during event construction and elaboration. *Neuropsychologia, 45,* 1363–1377.

Addis, D. R., Wong, A. T., & Schacter, D. L. (2008). Age-related changes in the episodic simulation of future events. *Psychological Science, 19,* 33–41.

Adelmann, P. K., & Zajonc, R. B. (1989). Facial efference and the experience of emotion. *Annual Review of Psychology, 40,* 249–280.

Adolphs, R., Russell, J. A., & Tranel, D. (1999). A role for the human amygdala in recognizing emotional arousal from unpleasant stimuli. *Psychological Science, 10,* 167–171.

Aggleton, J. (Ed.). (1992). *The amygdala: Neurobiological aspects of emotion, memory and mental dysfunction.* New York: Wiley-Liss.

Agin, D. (2007). *Junk science: An overdue indictment of government, industry, and faith groups that twist science for their own gain.* New York: Macmillan.

Aharon, I., Etcoff, N., Ariely, D., Chabris, C. F., O'Conner, E., & Breiter, H. C. (2001). Beautiful faces have variable reward value: fMRI and behavioral evidence. *Neuron, 32,* 537–551.

Ainsworth, M. D. S., Blehar, M. C., Waters, E., & Wall, S. (1978). *Patterns of attachment: A psychological study of the strange situation.* Hillsdale, NJ: Lawrence Erlbaum.

Albarracín, D., & Vargas, P. (2010). Attitudes and persuasion: From biology to social responses to persuasive intent. In S. T. Fiske, D. T. Gilbert, & G. Lindzey (Eds.), *The handbook of social psychology* (5th ed., Vol. 1, pp. 389–422). New York: Wiley.

Aleman, A., Sommer, I. E., & Kahn, R. S. (2007). Efficacy of slow repetitive transcranial magnetic stimulation in the treatment of resistant auditory hallucinations in schizophrenia: A meta-analysis. *Journal of Clinical Psychiatry, 68,* 416–421.

Allison, D. B., Fontaine, K. R., Manson, J. E., Stevens, J., & VanItallie, T. B. (1999). Annual deaths attributable to obesity in the United States. *Journal of the American Medical Association, 282,* 1530–1538.

Allport, G. W. (1937). *Personality: A psychological interpretation.* New York: Holt.

Allport, G. W. (1954). *The nature of prejudice.* Cambridge, MA: Addison-Wesley.

Allport, G. W., & Odbert, H. S. (1936). Trait-names: A psycholexical study. *Psychological Monographs, 47,* 592.

Alt, K. W., Jeunesse, C., Buitrago-Téllez, C. H., Wächter, R., Boës, E., & Pichler, S. L. (1997). Evidence for Stone Age cranial surgery. *Nature, 387,* 360.

Alvarez, L., & Eckholm, E. (2009, January 8). Pentagon: No Purple Hearts for PTSD. *The Boston Globe,* p. A4.

American Psychiatric Association. (2000). *Diagnostic and statistical manual of mental disorders* (*DSM-IV-TR*) (4th ed.). Washington, DC: American Psychiatric Press.

American Psychiatric Association. (2013). Diagnostic and Statistical Manual of Mental Disorders (DSM-5) (5th ed.) Washington, DC: American Psychiatric Publishing

American Psychological Association. (2002). *Ethical principles of psychologists and code of conduct.* Washington, DC: Author.

American Psychological Association. (2005). *Resolution in favor of empirically supported sex education and HIV prevention programs for adolescents.* Washington, DC: Author.

American Psychological Association. (2009). *Report of the American Psychological Association task force on appropriate therapeutic responses to sexual orientation.* Washington, DC: Author.

Andersen, S. M., & Berk, J. S. (1998). Transference in everyday experience: Implications of experimental research for relevant clinical phenomena. *Review of General Psychology, 2,* 81–120.

Anderson, C. A. (1989). Temperature and aggression: Ubiquitous effects of heat on occurrence of human violence. *Psychological Bulletin, 106,* 74–96.

Anderson, C. A., Berkowitz, L., Donnerstein, E., Huesmann, L. R., Johnson, J. D., Linz, D., et al. (2003). The influence of media violence on youth. *Psychological Science in the Public Interest, 4,* 81–110.

Anderson, C. A., & Bushman, B. J. (2001). Effects of violent video games on aggressive behavior, aggressive cognition, aggressive affect, physiological arousal, and prosocial behavior: A meta-analytic review of the scientific literature. *Psychological Science, 12*(5), 353–359.

Anderson, C. A., & Bushman, B. J. (2002). Human aggression. *Annual Review of Psychology, 53,* 27–51.

Anderson, C. A., Bushman, B. J., & Groom, R. W. (1997). Hot years and serious and deadly assault: Empirical tests of the heat hypothesis. *Journal of Personality and Social Psychology, 73,* 1213–1223.

Anderson, J. R., & Schooler, L. J. (1991). Reflections of the environment in memory. *Psychological Science, 2,* 396–408.

Anderson, J. R., & Schooler, L. J. (2000). The adaptive nature of memory. In E. Tulving & F. I. M. Craik (Eds.), *Handbook of memory* (pp. 557–570). New York: Oxford University Press.

Anderson, J. W., Johnstone, B. M., & Remley, D. T. (1999). Breastfeeding and cognitive development: A meta-analysis. *American Journal of Clinical Nutrition, 70,* 525–535.

Anderson, M. C. (2003). Rethinking interference theory: Executive control and the mechanisms of forgetting. *Journal of Memory and Language, 49,* 415–445.

Anderson, M. C., Bjork, R. A., & Bjork, E. L. (1994). Remembering can cause forgetting: Retrieval dynamics in long-term memory. *Journal of Experimental Psychology: Learning, Memory, & Cognition, 20,* 1063–1087.

Anderson, M. C., Ochsner, K. N., Kuhl, B., Cooper, J., Robertson, E., Gabrieli, S. W., et al. (2004). Neural systems underlying the suppression of unwanted memories. *Science, 303,* 232–235.

Anderson, R. C., Pichert, J. W., Goetz, E. T., Schallert, D. L., Stevens, K. V., & Trollip, S. R. (1976). Instantiation of general terms. *Journal of Verbal Learning and Verbal Behavior, 15,* 667–679.

Andrewes, D. (2001). *Neuropsychology: From theory to practice.* Hove, England: Psychology Press.

Antoni, M. H., Lehman, J. M., Klibourn, K. M., Boyers, A. E., Culver, J. L., Alferi, S. M., et al. (2001). Cognitive-behavioral stress management intervention decreases the prevalence of depression and enhances benefit finding among women under treatment for early-stage breast cancer. *Health Psychology, 20,* 20–32.

Antony, M. M., Roth, D., Swinson, R. P., Huta, V., & Devins, G. M. (1998). Illness intrusiveness in individuals with panic disorder, obsessive-compulsive disorder, or social phobia. *Journal of Nervous and Mental Disease, 186,* 311–315.

Arellano, D., Varona, J., & Perales, F. (2008). Generation and visualization of emotional states in virtual characters. *Computer Animation and Virtual Worlds, 19*(3–4), 259–270.

Ariyasu, H., Takaya, K., Tagami, T., Ogawa, Y., Hosoda, K., Akamizu, T., et al. (2001). Stomach is a major source of circulating ghrelin, and feeding state determines plasma ghrelin-like immunoreactivity levels in humans. *Journal of Clinical Endocrinology and Metabolism, 86,* 4753–4758.

Arlow, J. A. (2000). Psychoanalysis. In R. J. Corsini & D. Wedding (Eds.), *Current psychotherapies* (6th ed., pp. 16–53). Itasca, IL: Peacock.

Armstrong, D. M. (1980). *The nature of mind.* Ithaca, NY: Cornell University Press.

Arnold, M. B. (Ed.). (1960). *Emotion and personality: Psychological aspects* (Vol. 1). New York: Columbia University Press.

Aron, A., Fisher, H., Mashek, D., Strong, G., Li, H., & Brown, L. (2005). Reward, motivation, and emotion systems associated with early-stage intense romantic love. *Journal of Neurophysiology, 93,* 327–337.

Aronson, E. (1963). Effect of the severity of threat on the devaluation of forbidden behavior. *Journal of Abnormal and Social Psychology, 66,* 584–588.

Aronson, E. (1969). The theory of cognitive dissonance: A current perspective. In L. Berkowitz (Ed.), *Advances in experimental social psychology* (Vol. 4, pp. 1–34): Academic Press.

Aronson, E., & Worchel, P. (1966). Similarity versus liking as determinants of interpersonal attractiveness. *Psychonomic Science, 5,* 157–158.

Asch, S. E. (1951). Effects of group pressure on the modification and distortion of judgments. In H. Guetzkow (Ed.), *Groups, leadership, and men* (pp. 177–190). Pittsburgh: Carnegie Press.

Asch, S. E. (1955). Opinions and social pressure. *Scientific American, 193,* 31–35.

Asch, S. E. (1956). Studies of independence and conformity: 1. A minority of one against a unanimous majority. *Psychological Monographs: General and Applied, 70,* 1–70.

Aschoff, J. (1965). Circadian rhythms in man. *Science, 148,* 1427–1432.

Aserinsky, E., & Kleitman, N. (1953). Regularly occurring periods of eye motility, and concomitant phenomena, during sleep. *Science, 118,* 273–274.

Ashby, F. G., & Ell, S. W. (2001). The neurobiology of human category learning. *Trends in Cognitive Sciences, 5,* 204–210.

Ashcraft, M. H. (1998). *Fundamentals of cognition.* New York: Longman.

Astington, J. W., & Baird, J. (2005). *Why language matters for theory of mind.* Oxford, England: Oxford University Press.

Avery, D., Holtzheimer, P., III, Fawaz, W., Russo, J., Naumeier, J., Dunner, D., et al. (2009). A controlled study of repetitive transcranial magnetic stimulation in medication-resistant major depression. *Biological Psychiatry, 59,* 187–194.

Aviezer, H., Hassin, R. R., Ryan, J., Grady, C., Susskind, J., Anderson, A., et al. (2008). Angry, disgusted, or afraid? Studies on the malleability of emotion perception. *Psychological Science, 19,* 724–732.

Axelrod, R. (1984). *The evolution of cooperation.* New York: Basic Books.

Axelrod, R., & Hamilton, W. D. (1981). The evolution of cooperation. *Science, 211,* 1390–1396.

Ayduk, O., Shoda, Y., Cervone, D., & Downey, G. (2007). Delay of gratification in children: Contributions to social-personality psychology. In *Persons in context: Building a science of the individual* (pp. 97–109). New York: Guilford Press.

Azuma, H., & Kashiwagi, K. (1987). Descriptors for an intelligent person: A Japanese study. *Japanese Psychological Research, 29,* 17–26.

Baars, B. J. (1986). *The cognitive revolution in psychology.* New York: Guilford Press.

Back, M. D., Stropfer, J. M., Vazire, S., Gaddis, S., Schmukle, S. C., Egloff, B., & Gosling, S. (2010). Facebook profiles reflect actual personality not self-idealization. *Psychological Science, 21,* 372–374.

Backman, C. W., & Secord, P. F. (1959). The effect of perceived liking on interpersonal attraction. *Human Relations, 12,* 379–384.

Bäckman, L., Almkvist, O., Andersson, J., Nordberg, A., Winblad, B., Reineck, R., & Långström, B. (1997). Brain activation in young and older adults during implicit and explicit retrieval. *Journal of Cognitive Neuroscience, 9,* 378–391.

Bäckman, L., & Dixon, R. A. (1992). Psychological compensation: A theoretical framework. *Psychological Bulletin, 112,* 259–283.

Baddeley, A. D. (2001). Is working memory still working? *American Psychologist, 56,* 851–864.

Baddeley, A. D., & Hitch, G. J. (1974). Working memory. In S. Dornic (Ed.), *Attention and performance, 6,* 647–667. Hillsdale, NJ: Lawrence Erlbaum.

Baer, L., Rauch, S. L., Ballantine, H. T., Jr., Martuza, R., Cosgrove, R., Cassem, E., et al. (1995). Cingulotomy for intractable obsessive-compulsive disorder: Prospective long-term follow-up of 18 patients. *Archives of General Psychiatry, 52,* 384–392.

Bagby, R. M., Levitan, R. D., Kennedy, S. H., Levitt, A. J., & Joffe, R. T. (1999). Selective alteration of personality in response to noradrenergic and serotonergic antidepressant medication in depressed sample: Evidence of non-specificity. *Psychiatry Research, 86,* 211–216.

Bahrick, H. P. (1984). Semantic memory content in permastore: 50 years of memory for Spanish learned in school. *Journal of Experimental Psychology: General, 113,* 1–29.

Bahrick, H. P. (2000). Long-term maintenance of knowledge. In E. Tulving & F. I. M. Craik (Eds.), *The Oxford handbook of memory* (pp. 347–362). New York: Oxford University Press.

Bahrick, H. P., Hall, L. K., & Berger, S. A. (1996). Accuracy and distortion in memory for high school grades. *Psychological Science, 7,* 265–271.

Bailey, J. M., & Pillard, R. C. (1991). A genetic study of male sexual orientation. *Archives of General Psychiatry, 48,* 1089–1096.

Bailey, J. M., Pillard, R. C., Neale, M. C., & Agyes, Y. (1993). Heritable factors influence sexual orientation in women. *Archives of General Psychiatry, 50,* 217–223.

Bailey, R. (2002, March 6). Hooray for designer babies! *Reason.com.* Retrieved September 30, 2007, from http://www.reason.com/news/show/34776.html

Baillargeon, R., Spelke, E. S., & Wasserman, S. (1985). Object permanence in 5-month-old infants. *Cognition, 20,* 191–208.

Baker, T. B., Brandon, T. H., & Chassin, L. (2004). Motivational influences on cigarette smoking. *Annual Review of Psychology, 55,* 463–491.

Baker, T. B., McFall, R. M., & Shoham, V. (2009). Current status and future prospects of clinical psychology: Toward a scientifically principled approach to mental and behavioral health care. *Psychological Science in the Public Interest, 9,* 67–103.

Baldwin, M. W., Carrell, S. E., & Lopez, D. F. (1989). Priming relationship schemas: My advisor and the pope are watching me from the back of my mind. *Journal of Experimental Social Psychology, 26,* 435–454.

Baler, R. D., & Volkow, N. D. (2006). Drug addiction: The neurobiology of disrupted self-control. *Trends in Molecular Medicine, 12,* 559–566.

Baltes, P. B., & Reinert, G. (1969). Cohort effects in cognitive development of children as revealed by cross-sectional sequences. *Developmental Psychology, 1,* 169–177.

Banaji, M. R., & Heiphetz, L. (2010). Attitudes. In S. T. Fiske, D. T. Gilbert, & G. Lindzey (Eds.), *The handbook of social psychology* (5th ed., Vol. 1, pp. 348–388). New York: Wiley.

Bandura, A. (1977). *Social learning theory.* Englewood Cliffs, NJ: Prentice Hall.

Bandura, A. (1986). *Social foundations of thought and action: A social cognitive theory.* Englewood Cliffs, NJ: Prentice Hall.

Bandura, A. (1994). Social cognitive theory of mass communication. In J. Bryant & D. Zillmann (Eds.), *Media effects: Advances in theory and research* (pp. 61–90). Hillsdale, NJ: Lawrence Erlbaum.

Bandura, A., Ross, D., & Ross, S. (1961). Transmission of aggression through imitation of adult models. *Journal of Abnormal and Social Psychology, 63,* 575–582.

Bandura, A., Ross, D., & Ross, S. (1963). Vicarious reinforcement and imitative learning. *Journal of Abnormal and Social Psychology, 67,* 601–607.

Bard, P. (1934). On emotional experience after decortication with some remarks on theoretical views. *Psychological Review, 41,* 309–329.

Bargh, J. A., Gollwitzer, P. M., Lee-Chai, A., Barndollar, K., & Trötschel, R. (2001). The automated will: Nonconscious activation and pursuit of behavioral goals. *Journal of Personality and Social Psychology, 81,* 1014–1027.

Bargh, J. A., Gollwitzer, P. M., & Oettingen, G. (2010). Motivation. In S. T. Fiske, D. T. Gilbert, & G. Lindzey (Eds.), *The handbook of social psychology* (5th ed., Vol. 1, pp. 263–311). New York: Wiley.

Barkow, J. (1980). Prestige and self-esteem: A biosocial interpretation. In D. R. Omark, F. F. Stayer, & D. G. Freedman (Eds.), *Dominance relations* (pp. 319–322). New York: Garland.

Barlow, D. H., Gorman, J. M., Shear, M. K., & Woods, S. W. (2000). Cognitive-behavioral therapy, imipramine, or their combination for panic disorder: A randomized controlled trial. *Journal of the American Medical Association, 283*(19), 2529–2536.

Barnier, A. J., Levin, K., & Maher, A. (2004). Suppressing thoughts of past events: Are repressive copers good suppressors? *Cognition and Emotion, 18,* 457–477.

Baron-Cohen, S. (1991). Do people with autism understand what causes emotion? *Child Development, 62,* 385–395.

Baron-Cohen, S., Leslie, A., & Frith, U. (1985). Does the autistic child have a "theory of mind"? *Cognition, 21,* 37–46.

Bartlett, F. C. (1932). *Remembering: A study in experimental and social psychology.* Cambridge, England: Cambridge University Press.

Bartol, C. R., & Costello, N. (1976). Extraversion as a function of temporal duration of electric shock: An exploratory study. *Perceptual and Motor Skills, 42,* 1174.

Bartoshuk, L. M. (2000). Comparing sensory experiences across individuals: Recent psychophysical advances illuminate genetic variation in taste perception. *Chemical Senses, 25,* 447–460.

Bartoshuk, L. M., & Beauchamp, G. K. (1994). Chemical senses. *Annual Review of Psychology, 45,* 419–445.

Bates, E., & Goodman, J. C. (1997). On the inseparability of grammar and the lexicon: Evidence from acquisition, aphasia, and real-time processing. *Language and Cognitive Processes, 12,* 507–584.

Batson, C. D. (2002). Addressing the altruism question experimentally. In S. G. Post & L. G. Underwood (Eds.), *Altruism & altruistic love: Science, philosophy, & religion in dialogue* (pp. 89–105). London: Oxford University Press.

Baumeister, R. F., Bratslavsky, E., Muraven, M., & Tice, D. M. (1998). Ego depletion: Is the active self a limited resource? *Journal of Personality and Social Psychology, 74,* 1252–1265.

Baumeister, R. F., Cantanese, K. R., & Vohs, K. D. (2001). Is there a gender difference in strength of sex drive? Theoretical views, conceptual distinctions, and a review of relevant evidence. *Personality and Social Psychology Review, 5,* 242–273.

Baumeister, R. F., Heatherton, T. F., & Tice, D. M. (1995). *Losing control.* San Diego, CA: Academic Press.

Baumeister, R. F., & Leary, M. R. (1995). The need to belong: Desire for interpersonal attachments as a fundamental human motivation. *Psychological Bulletin, 117,* 497–529.

Baumeister, R. F., Smart, L., & Boden, J. M. (1996). Relation of threatened egotism to violence and aggression: The dark side of high self-esteem. *Psychological Review, 103,* 5–33.

Baumeister, R. F., Vohs, K. D., & Tice, D. M. (2007). The strength model of self-control. *Current Directions in Psychological Science, 16,* 351–355.

Baxter, L. R., Schwartz, J. M., Bergman, K. S., Szuba, M. P., Guze, B. H., Mazziotta, J. C., Alazraki, A., et al. (1992). Caudate glucose metabolic rate changes with both drug and behavior therapy for obsessive-compulsive disorder. *Archives of General Psychiatry, 49,* 681–689.

Bayley, P. J., Frascino, J. C., & Squire, L. R. (2005a). Robust habit learning in the absence of awareness and independent of the medial temporal lobe. *Nature, 436,* 550–553.

Bayley, P. J., Gold, J. J., Hopkins, R. O., & Squire, L. R. (2005b). The neuroanatomy of remote memory. *Neuron, 46,* 799–810.

Bechara, A., Damasio, A. R., Damasio, H., & Anderson, S. W. (1994). Insensitivity to future consequences following damage to human prefrontal cortex. *Cognition, 50,* 7–15.

Bechara, A., Damasio, H., Tranel, D., & Damasio, A. R. (1997). Deciding advantageously before knowing the advantageous strategy. *Science, 275,* 1293–1295.

Bechara, A., Dolan, S., Denburg, N., Hindes, A., & Anderson, S. W. (2001). Decision-making deficits, linked to a dysfunctional ventromedial prefrontal cortex, revealed in alcohol and stimulant abusers. *Neuropsychologia, 39,* 376–389.

Bechara, A., Tranel, D., & Damasio, H. (2000). Characterization of the decision-making deficit of patients with ventromedial prefrontal cortex lesions. *Brain, 123,* 2189–2202.

Beck, A. T., & Weishaar, M. (2000). Cognitive therapy. In R. J. Corsini & D. Wedding (Eds.), *Current psychotherapies* (6th ed., pp. 241–272). Itasca, IL: Peacock.

Beevers, C. G., & Meyer, B. (2008). I feel fine but the glass is still half empty: Thought suppression biases information processing despite recovery from a dysphoric mood state. *Cognitive Therapy and Research, 32,* 323–332.

Bekinschtein, T. A., Shalom, D. E., Forcato, C., Herrera, M., Coleman, M. R., Manes, F. F., & Sigman, M. (2009). Classical conditioning in the vegetative and minimally conscious state. *Nature Neuroscience, 12,* 1343–1350.

Bell, A. P., Weinberg, M. S., & Hammersmith, S. K. (1981). *Sexual preference: Its development in men and women.* Bloomington: Indiana University Press.

Bem, S. L. (1974). The measure of psychological androgyny. *Journal of Consulting and Clinical Psychology, 42,* 155–162.

Bennett, I. J., Romano, J. C., Howard, J. H., & Howard, D. V. (2008). Two forms of implicit learning in young adults with dyslexia. *Annals of the New York Academy of Sciences, 1145,* 184–198.

Benson, H. (Ed.). (1990). *The relaxation response.* New York: Harper Torch.

Bering, J. (2004). A critical review of the "enculturation hypothesis": The effects of human rearing on great ape social cognition. *Animal Cognition, 7,* 201–212.

Berkowitz, L. (1990). On the formation and regulation of anger and aggression: A cognitive-neoassociationistic analysis. *American Psychologist, 45,* 494–503.

Berridge, K. C. (2007). The debate over dopamine's role in reward: The case for incentive salience. *Psychopharmacology, 191,* 391–431.

Berscheid, E., Dion, K., Walster, E., & Walster, G. W. (1971). Physical attractiveness and dating choice: A test of the matching hypothesis. *Journal of Experimental Social Psychology, 7*(2), 173–189.

Berscheid, E., & Reiss, H. T. (1998). Interpersonal attraction and close relationships. In D. T. Gilbert, S. T. Fiske, & G. Lindzey (Eds.), *The handbook of social psychology* (4th ed., Vol. 2, pp. 193–281). New York: McGraw-Hill.

Bertelsen, B., Harvald, B., & Hauge, M. (1977). A Danish twin study of manic-depressive disorders. *British Journal of Psychiatry, 130,* 330–351.

Bertenthal, B. I., Rose, J. L., & Bai, D. L. (1997). Perception-action coupling in the development of visual control of posture. *Journal of Experimental Psychology: Human Perception & Performance, 23,* 1631–1643.

Berthoud, H.-R., & Morrison, C. (2008). The brain, appetite, and obesity. *Annual Review of Psychology, 59,* 55–92.

Best, J. B. (1992). *Cognitive psychology* (3rd ed.). New York: West Publishing.

Bettencourt, B., A., & Miller, N. (1996). Gender differences in aggression as a function of provocation: A meta-analysis. *Psychological Bulletin, 119,* 422–447.

Beutler, L. E. (2002). The dodo bird is extinct. *Clinical Psychology: Science and Practice, 9,* 30–34.

Bialystok, E. (1999). Cognitive complexity and attentional control in the bilingual mind. *Child Development, 70,* 636–644.

Bialystok, E. (2009). Bilingualism: The good, the bad, and the indifference. *Bilingualism: Language and Cognitive Processes, 12,* 3–11.

Bialystok, E., & Hakuta, K. (1994). *In other words: The science and psychology of second-language acquisition.* New York: Basic Books.

Billet, E., Richter, J., & Kennedy, J. (1998). Genetics of obsessive-compulsive disorder. In R. Swinson, M. Anthony, S. Rachman, & M. Richter (Eds.), *Obsessive-compulsive disorder: Theory, research, and treatment* (pp. 181–206). New York: Guilford Press.

Binet, A. (1909). *Les idées modernes sur les enfants.* Paris: Flammarion.

Binswanger, L. (1958). The existential analysis school of thought. In R. May (Ed.), *Existence: A new dimension in psychiatry and psychology.* New York: Basic Books.

Bjork, D. W. (1983). *The compromised scientist: William James in the development of American psychology.* New York: Columbia University Press.

Bjork, D. W. (1993). *B. F. Skinner: A life.* New York: Basic Books.

Bjork, R. A. (1975). Retrieval as a memory modifier: An interpretation of negative recency and related phenomena. In R. L. Solso (Ed.), *Information processing and cognition: The Loyola symposium* (pp. 123–144). Hillsdale, NJ: Lawrence Erlbaum.

Bjork, R. A., & Bjork, E. L. (1988). On the adaptive aspects of retrieval failure in autobiographical memory. In M. M. Gruneberg, P. E. Morris, & R. N. Sykes (Eds.), *Practical aspects of memory: Current research and issues* (pp. 283–288). Chichester, England: Wiley.

Blair, I. V. (2002). The malleability of automatic stereotypes and prejudice. *Personality and Social Psychology Review, 6,* 242–261.

Blair, J., Peschardt, K., & Mitchell, D. R. (2005). *Psychopath: Emotion and the brain.* Oxford, England: Blackwell.

Blascovich, J., & Tomaka, J. (1996). The biopsychosocial model of arousal regulation. In M. P. Zanna (Ed.), *Advances in experimental social psychology* (Vol. 28, pp. 1–51). San Diego, CA: Academic Press.

Blau, F. D., & Kahn, L. M. (2007). Changes in the labor supply behavior of married women: 1980–2000. *Journal of Labor Economics, 25*(3), 393–438.

Blazer, D. G., Hughes, D., & George, L. D. (1987). Stressful life events and the onset of a generalized anxiety syndrome. *American Journal of Psychiatry, 144,* 1178–1183.

Blazer, D. G., Hughes, D. J., George, L. K., Swartz, M., & Boyer, R. (1991). Generalized anxiety disorder. In L. N. Robins & D. A. Regier (Eds.), *Psychiatric disorders in America* (180–203). New York: Free Press.

Blesch, A., & Tuszynski, M. H. (2009). Spinal cord injury: Plasticity, regeneration and the challenge of translational drug development. *Trends in Neurosciences, 32,* 41–47.

Bliss, T. V. P. (1999). Young receptors make smart mice. *Nature, 401,* 25–27.

Bliss, T. V. P., & Lømo, W. T. (1973). Long-lasting potentiation of synaptic transmission in the dentate area of the anesthetized rabbit following stimulation of the perforant path. *Journal of Physiology, 232,* 331–356.

Bloch, C., Kaiser, A., Kuenzli, E., Zappatore, D., Haller, S., Franceschini, R., Luedi, G., Radue, E. W., & Nitsch, C. (2009). The age of second language acquisition determines the variability in activation elicited by narration in three languages in Broca's and Wernicke's area. *Neuropsychologia, 47,* 625–633.

Bloom, C. M., Venard, J., Harden, M., & Seetharaman, S. (2007). Non-contingent positive and negative reinforcement schedules of superstitious behaviors. *Behavioural Process, 75,* 8–13.

Bocanegra, B. R., & Zeelenberg, R. (2009). Emotion improves and impairs early vision. *Psychological Science, 20*(6), 707–713.

Boecker, H., Sprenger, T., Spilker, M. E., Henriksen, G., Koppenhoefer, M., Wagner, K. J., et al. (2008). The runner's high: Opioidergic mechanisms in the human brain. *Cerebral Cortex, 18,* 2523–2531.

Bohan, J. S. (1996). *Psychology and sexual orientation: Coming to terms.* New York: Routledge.

Boinski, S., Quatrone, R. P., & Swartz, H. (2000). Substrate and tool use by brown capuchins in Suriname: Ecological contexts and cognitive bases. *American Anthropologist, 102,* 741–761.

Boisvert, C. M., & Faust, D. (2002). Iatrogenic symptoms in psychotherapy: A theoretical exploration of the potential impact of labels, language, and belief systems. *American Journal of Psychotherapy, 56,* 244–259.

Bolton, G. E., & Ockenfels, A. (2000). ERC: A theory of equity, reciprocity, and competition. *American Economic Review, 90,* 166–193.

Boomsma, D., Busjahn, A., & Peltonen, L. (2002). Classical twin studies and beyond. *Nature Reviews Genetics, 3,* 872–882.

Bootzin, R. R., Manber, R., Perlis, M. L., Salvio, M. A., & Wyatt, J. K. (1993). Sleep disorders. In P. B. Sutker & H. E. Adams (Eds.), *Comprehensive handbook of psychopathology* (2nd ed.). New York: Plenum Press.

Borkenau, P., & Liebler, A. (1995). Observable attributes as manifestations and cues of personality and intelligence. *Journal of Personality, 63,* 1–25.

Born, R. T., & Bradley, D. C. (2005). Structure and function of visual area MT. *Annual Review of Neuroscience, 28,* 157–189.

Botwin, M. D., Buss, D. M., & Shackelford, T. K. (1997). Personality and mate preferences: Five factors in mate selection and marital satisfaction. *Journal of Personality, 65,* 107–136.

Bouchard, T. J., & McGue, M. (2003). Genetic and environmental influences on human psychological differences. *Journal of Neurobiology, 54,* 4–45.

Bourguignon, E. (1968). World distribution and patterns of possession states. In R. Prince (Ed.), *Trance and possession states* (pp. 3–34). Montreal, Canada: R. M. Burke Memorial Society.

Bouton, M. E. (1988). Context and ambiguity in the extinction of emotional learning: Implications for exposure therapy. *Behaviour Research and Therapy, 26,* 137–149.

Bowlby, J. (1969). *Attachment and loss: Vol. 1. Attachment.* New York: Basic Books.

Bowlby, J. (1973). *Attachment and loss: Vol. 2. Separation.* New York: Basic Books.

Bowlby, J. (1980). *Attachment and loss: Vol. 3. Loss: Sadness and depression.* New York: Basic Books.

Bozarth, M. A., & Wise, R. A. (1985). Toxicity associated with long-term intravenous heroin and cocaine self-administration in the rat. *Journal of the American Medical Association, 254,* 81–83.

Brackett, M. A., & Mayer, J. D. (2003). Convergent, discriminant, and incremental validity of competing measures of emotional intelligence. *Personality and Social Psychology Bulletin, 29,* 1147.

Brackett, M. A., Rivers, S. E., Shiffman, S., Lerner, N., & Salovey, P. (2006). Relating emotional abilities to social functioning: A comparison of self-report and performance measures of emotional intelligence. *Journal of Personality and Social Psychology, 91,* 780.

Brackett, M. A., Warner, R. M., & Bosco, J. (2005). Emotional intelligence and relationship quality among couples. *Personal Relationships, 12*(2), 197–212.

Bradford, D., Stroup, S., & Lieberman, J. (2002). Pharmacological treatments for schizophrenia. In P. E. Nathan & J. M. Gorman (Eds.), *A guide to treatments that work* (2nd ed., pp. 169–199). New York: Oxford University Press.

Bradmetz, J., & Schneider, R. (2004). The role of the counterfactually satisfied desire in the lag between false-belief and false-emotion attributions in children aged 4–7. *British Journal of Developmental Psychology, 22,* 185–196.

Braet, W., & Humphreys, G. W. (2009). The role of reentrant processes in feature binding: Evidence from neuropsychology and TMS on late onset illusory conjunctions. *Visual Cognition, 17,* 25–47.

Bramlett, M. D., & Mosher, W. D. (2002). *Cohabitation, marriage, divorce, and remarriage in the United States* (Vital and Health Statistics Series 23, No. 22). Hyattsville, MD: National Center for Health Statistics.

Brandt, K. R., Gardiner, J. M., Vargha-Khadem, F., Baddeley, A. D., & Mishkin, M. (2009). Impairment of recollection but not familiarity in a case of developmental amnesia. *Neurocase, 15,* 60–65.

Braun, A. R., Balkin, T. J., Wesensten, N. J., Gwadry, F., Carson, R. E., Varga, M., et al. (1998). Dissociated pattern of activity in visual cortices and their projections during rapid eye movement sleep. *Science, 279,* 91–95.

Breazeal, C. (2003). Emotion and sociable humanoid robots. *International Journal of Human-Computer Studies, 59,* 119–155.

Breazeal, C. (2009). Role of expressive behaviour for robots that learn from people. *Philosophical Transactions of the Royal Society B, 364,* 3527–3538.

Brédart, S., & Valentine, T. (1998). Descriptiveness and proper name retrieval. *Memory, 6,* 199–206.

Breggin, P. R. (2000). *Reclaiming our children.* Cambridge, MA: Perseus Books.

Breland, K., & Breland, M. (1961). The misbehavior of organisms. *American Psychologist, 16,* 681–684.

Brennan, P. A., & Zufall, F. (2006). Pheromonal communication in vertebrates. *Nature, 444,* 308–315.

Brenneis, C. B. (2000). Evaluating the evidence: Can we find authenticated recovered memory? *Journal of the American Psychoanalytic Association, 17,* 61–77.

Bretherton, I., & Munholland, K. A. (1999). Internal working models in attachment relationships: A construct revisited. In J. Cassidy & P. R. Shaver (Eds.), *Handbook of attachment: Theory, research and clinical applications* (pp. 89–114). New York: Guilford Press.

Brewer, M. B. (1979). In-group bias in the minimal intergroup situation: A cognitive-motivational analysis. *Psychological Bulletin, 86,* 307–324.

Broadbent, D. E. (1958). *Perception and communication.* London: Pergamon Press.

Broberg, D. J., & Bernstein, I. L. (1987). Candy as a scapegoat in the prevention of food aversions in children receiving chemotherapy. *Cancer, 60,* 2344–2347.

Brody, N. (2003). Construct validation of the Sternberg Triarchic Abilities Test: Comment and reanalysis. *Intelligence, 31*(4), 319–329.

Brooks, R., & Meltzoff, A. N. (2002). The importance of eyes: How infants interpret adult looking behavior. *Developmental Psychology, 38,* 958–966.

Brooks-Gunn, J., Graber, J. A., & Paikoff, R. L. (1994). Studying links between hormones and negative affect: Models and measures. *Journal of Research on Adolescence, 4,* 469–486.

Brown, A. S. (2004). *The déjà vu experience.* New York: Psychology Press.

Brown, B. B., Mory, M., & Kinney, D. (1994). Casting crowds in a relational perspective: Caricature, channel, and context. In G. A. R. Montemayor & T. Gullotta (Eds.), *Advances in adolescent development: Personal relationships during adolescence* (Vol. 5, pp. 123–167). Newbury Park, CA: Sage.

Brown, J. D., & McGill, K. L. (1989). The cost of good fortune: When positive life events produce negative health consequences. *Journal of Personality and Social Psychology, 57,* 1103–1110.

Brown, L. E., Wilson, E. T., & Gribble, P. L. (2009). Repetitive transcranial magnetic stimulation to the primary cortex interferes with motor learning by observing. *Journal of Cognitive Neuroscience, 21,* 1013–1022.

Brown, R., & Hanlon, C. (1970). Derivational complexity and order of acquisition in child speech. In J. R. Hayes (Ed.), *Cognition and the development of language* (pp. 11–53). New York: Wiley.

Brown, R., & Kulik, J. (1977). Flashbulb memories. *Cognition, 5,* 73–99.

Brown, R., & McNeill, D. (1966). The "tip-of-the-tongue" phenomenon. *Journal of Verbal Learning and Verbal Behavior, 5,* 325–337.

Brown, R. P., Osterman, L. L., & Barnes, C. D. (2009). School violence and the culture of honor. *Psychological Science, 20*(11), 1400–1405.

Brown, S. C., & Craik, F. I. M. (2000). Encoding and retrieval of information. In E. Tulving & F. I. M. Craik (Eds.), *The Oxford handbook of memory* (pp. 93–107). New York: Oxford University Press.

Brown, T. A., Campbell, L. A., Lehman, C. L., Grisham, J. R., & Mancill, R. B. (2001). Current and lifetime comorbidity of the *DSM-IV* anxiety and mood disorders in a large clinical sample. *Journal of Abnormal Psychology, 110,* 585–599.

Brownlee, S. (2002, March). Designer babies. *The Washington Monthly.*

Bruner, J. S. (1983). Education as social invention. *Journal of Social Issues, 39,* 129–141.

Brunet, A., Orr, S. P., Tremblay, J., Robertson, K., Nader, K., & Pitman, R. K. (2008). Effects of post-retrieval propranolol on psychophysiologic responding during subsequent script-driven traumatic imagery in posttraumatic stress disorder. *Journal of Psychiatric Research, 42,* 503–506.

Brunner, D. P., Dijk, D. J., Tobler, I., & Borbely, A. A. (1990). Effect of partial sleep deprivation on sleep stages and EEG power spectra. *Electroencephalography and Clinical Neurophysiology, 75,* 492–499.

Buchanan, C. M., Eccles, J. S., & Becker, J. B. (1992). Are adolescents the victims of raging hormones? Evidence for activational effects of hormones on moods and behavior at adolescence. *Psychological Bulletin, 111,* 62–107.

Buckner, R. L., Petersen, S. E., Ojemann, J. G., Miezin, F. M., Squire, L. R., & Raichle, M. E. (1995). Functional anatomical studies of explicit and implicit memory retrieval tasks. *The Journal of Neuroscience, 15,* 12–29.

Burdick, K. E., Lencz, T., Funke, B., Finn, C. T., Szeszko, P. R., Kane, J. M., et al. (2006). Genetic variation in dtnbp1 influences general cognitive ability. *Human Molecular Genetics, 15*(10), 1563–1568.

Bureau of Justice Statistics. (2008). *Prisoners in 2007* (No. NCJ224280 by H. C. West and W. J. Sabol). Washington, DC: U.S. Department of Justice.

Burger, J. M. (1999). The foot-in-the-door compliance procedure: A multiple-process analysis and review. *Personality and Social Psychology Review, 3,* 303–325.

Burger, J. M. (2009). Replicating Milgram: Would people still obey today? *American Psychologist, 64,* 1–11.

Burger, J. M., & Burns, L. (1988). The illusion of unique invulnerability and the use of effective contraception. *Personality and Social Psychology Bulletin, 14,* 264–270.

Burger, J. M., Sanchez, J., Imberi, J. E., & Grande, L. R. (2009). The norm of reciprocity as an internalized social norm: Returning favors even when no one finds out. *Social Influence, 4*(1), 11–17.

Burke, D., MacKay, D. G., Worthley, J. S., & Wade, E. (1991). On the tip of the tongue: What causes word failure in young and older adults? *Journal of Memory and Language, 30,* 237–246.

Burkham, D. T., Ready, D. D., Lee, V. E., & LoGerfo, L. F. (2004). Social-class differences in summer learning between kindergarten and first grade: Model specification and estimation. *Sociology of Education, 77,* 1–31.

Burnstein, E., Crandall, C., & Kitayama, S. (1994). Some neo-Darwinian decision rules for altruism: Weighing cues for inclusive fitness as a function of the biological importance of the decision. *Journal of Personality and Social Psychology, 67,* 773–789.

Burrelli, J. (2008). Thirty-three years of women in S&E faculty positions. *InfoBrief* (NSF 08-308). Arlington, VA: National Science Foundation.

Burris, C. T., & Branscombe, N. R. (2005). Distorted distance estimation induced by a self-relevant national boundary. *Journal of Experimental Social Psychology, 41,* 305–312.

Bushman, B. J., & Huesmann, L. R. (2010). Aggression. In S. T. Fiske, D. T. Gilbert, & G. Lindzey (Eds.), *The handbook of social psychology* (5th ed., Vol. 2). New York: Wiley.

Buss, D. M. (1985). Human mate selection. *American Scientist, 73,* 47–51.

Buss, D. M. (1989). Sex differences in human mate preferences: Evolutionary hypotheses tested in 37 cultures. *Behavioral and Brain Sciences, 12,* 1–49.

Buss, D. M. (1996). Social adaptation and five major factors of personality. In J. S. Wiggins (Ed.), *The five-factor model of personality: Theoretical perspectives* (pp. 180–208). New York: Guilford Press.

Buss, D. M. (1999). *Evolutionary psychology: The new science of the mind.* Boston: Allyn & Bacon.

Buss, D. M. (2000). *The dangerous passion: Why jealousy is as necessary as love and sex.* New York: Free Press.

Buss, D. M., Haselton, M. G., Shackelford, T. K., Bleske, A. L., & Wakefield, J. C. (1998). Adaptations, exaptations, and spandrels. *American Psychologist, 53,* 533–548.

Buss, D. M., & Schmitt, D. P. (1993). Sexual strategies theory: An evolutionary perspective on human mating. *Psychological Review, 100,* 204–232.

Butler, A. C., Chapman, J. E., Forman, E. M., & Beck, A. T. (2006). The empirical status of cognitive-behavioral therapy: A review of meta-analyses. *Clinical Psychology Review, 26,* 17–31.

Butler, M. A., Corboy, J. R., & Filley, C. M. (2009). How the conflict between American psychiatry and neurology delayed the appreciation of cognitive dysfunction in multiple sclerosis. *Neuropsychology Review, 19,* 399–410.

Byrne, D., Allgeier, A. R., Winslow, L., & Buckman, J. (1975). The situational facilitation of interpersonal attraction: A three-factor hypothesis. *Journal of Applied Social Psychology, 5,* 1–15.

Byrne, D., & Clore, G. L. (1970). A reinforcement model of evaluative responses. *Personality: An International Journal, 1,* 103–128.

Byrne, D., Ervin, C. R., & Lamberth, J. (1970). Continuity between the experimental study of attraction and real-life computer dating. *Journal of Personality and Social Psychology, 16,* 157–165.

Byrne, D., & Nelson, D. (1965). Attraction as a linear function of proportion of positive reinforcements. *Journal of Personality and Social Psychology, 1,* 659–663.

Cabeza, R. (2002). Hemispheric asymmetry reduction in older adults: The HAROLD model. *Psychology and Aging, 17,* 85–100.

Cabeza, R., Grady, C. L., Nyberg, L., McIntosh, A. R., Tulving, E., Kapur, S., et al. (1997). Age-related differences in neural activity during memory encoding and retrieval: A positron emission tomography study. *The Journal of Neuroscience, 17,* 391–400.

Cabeza, R., Rao, S., Wagner, A. D., Mayer, A., & Schacter, D. L. (2001). Can medial temporal lobe regions distinguish true from false? An event-related fMRI study of veridical and illusory recognition memory. *Proceedings of the National Academy of Sciences, USA, 98,* 4805–4810.

Cacioppo, J. T., & Patrick, B. (2008). *Loneliness: Human nature and the need for social connection.* New York: W. W. Norton & Company.

Cahill, L., Haier, R. J., Fallon, J., Alkire, M. T., Tang, C., Keator, D., et al. (1996). Amygdala activity at encoding correlated with long-term, free recall of emotional information. *Proceedings of the National Academy of Sciences, USA, 93,* 8016–8021.

Cahill, L., & McGaugh, J. L. (1998). Mechanisms of emotional arousal and lasting declarative memory. *Trends in Neurosciences, 21,* 294–299.

Calkins, M. W. (Ed.). (1930). *Mary Whiton Calkins* (Vol. 1). Worcester, MA: Clark University Press.

Callaghan, T., Rochat, P., Lillard, A., Claux, M. L., Odden, H., Itakura, S., et al. (2005). Synchrony in the onset of mental-state reasoning: Evidence from five cultures. *Psychological Science, 16,* 378–384.

Campbell, A. (1999). Staying alive: Evolution, culture, and women's intra-sexual aggression. *Behavioral & Brain Sciences, 22,* 203–252.

Campbell, C. M., Edward, R. R., & Fillingim, R. B. (2005). Ethnic differences in responses to multiple experimental pain stimuli. *Pain, 113,* 20–26.

Campbell, R., & Sais, E. (1995). Accelerated metalinguistic (phonological) awareness in bilingual children. *British Journal of Developmental Psychology, 13,* 61–68.

Canetto, S., & Lester, D. (1995). Gender and the primary prevention of suicide mortality. *Suicide and Life Threatening Behavior, 25,* 85–89.

Cannon, W. B. (1927). The James-Lange theory of emotion: A critical examination and alternate theory. *American Journal of Psychology, 39,* 106–124.

Cannon, W. B. (1942). "Voodoo" death. *American Anthropologist, 44,* 182–190.

Cantor, N. (1990). From thought to behavior: "Having" and "doing" in the study of personality and cognition. *American Psychologist, 45,* 735–750.

Caplan, A. L. (Ed.). (1992). *When medicine went mad: Bioethics and the Holocaust.* Totowa, NJ: Humana Press.

Carlson, C., & Hoyle, R. (1993). Efficacy of abbreviated progressive muscle relaxation training: A quantitative review of behavioral medicine research. *Journal of Consulting and Clinical Psychology, 61,* 1059–1067.

Carmichael Olson, H., Streissguth, A. P., Sampson, P. D., Barr, H. M., Bookstein, F. L., & Thiede, K. (1997). Association of prenatal alcohol exposure with behavioral and learning problems in early adolescence. *Journal of the American Academy of Child & Adolescent Psychiatry, 36*(9), 1187–1194.

Carolson, E. A. (1998). A prospective longitudinal study of attachment disorganization/disorientation. *Child Development, 69,* 1107–1128.

Carr, L., Iacoboni, M., Dubeau, M., Mazziotta, J. C., & Lenzi, G. L. (2003). Neural mechanisms of empathy in humans: A relay from neural systems for imitation to limbic areas. *Proceedings of the National Academy of Sciences, USA, 100,* 5497–5502.

Carroll, J. B. (1993). *Human cognitive abilities.* Cambridge, England: Cambridge University Press.

Carson, R. C., Butcher, J. N., & Mineka, S. (2000). *Abnormal psychology and modern life* (11th ed.). Boston: Allyn & Bacon.

Carstensen, L. L. (1992). Social and emotional patterns in adulthood: Support for socioemotional selectivity theory. *Psychology and Aging, 7,* 331–338.

Carstensen, L. L., & Turk-Charles, S. (1994). The salience of emotion across the adult life span. *Psychology and Aging, 9,* 259–264.

Carter, J. (1977). Drug abuse message to the Congress [Electronic version]. The American Presidency Project. Retrieved March 5, 2009, from http://www.presidency.ucsb.edu/ws/index.php?pid=7908

Carver, C. S. (2006). Approach, avoidance, and the self-regulation of affect and action. *Motivation and Emotion, 30,* 105–110.

Carver, C. S., Lehman, J. M., & Antoni, M. H. (2003). Dispositional pessimism predicts illness-related disruption of social and recreational activities among breast cancer patients. *Journal of Personality and Social Psychology, 84,* 813–821.

Carver, C. S., & White, T. L. (1994). Behavioral inhibition, behavioral activation, and affective responses to impending reward and punishment: The bis/bas scales. *Journal of Personality and Social Psychology, 67*(2), 319–333.

Caspi, A., & Herbener, E. S. (1990). Continuity and change: Assortative marriage and the consistency of personality in adulthood. *Journal of Personality and Social Psychology, 58,* 250–258.

Caspi, A., Lynam, D., Moffitt, T. E., & Silva, P. A. (1993). Unraveling girls' delinquency: Biological, dispositional, and contextual contributions to adolescent misbehavior. *Developmental Psychology, 29,* 19–30.

Caspi, A., & Moffitt, T. E. (1991). Individual differences are accentuated during periods of social change: The sample case of girls at puberty. *Journal of Personality and Social Psychology, 61,* 157–168.

Caspi, A., Roberts, B. W., & Shiner, R. L. (2005). Personality development: Stability and change. *Annual Review of Psychology, 56,* 453–484.

Cattell, R. B. (1950). *Personality: A systematic, theoretical, and factual study.* New York: McGraw-Hill.

Ceci, S. J. (1991). How much does schooling influence general intelligence and its cognitive components? A reassessment of the evidence. *Developmental Psychology, 27,* 703–722.

Ceci, S. J., DeSimone, M., & Johnson, S. (1992). Memory in context: A case study of "Bubbles P.," a gifted but uneven memorizer. In D. J. Herrmann, H. Weingartner, A. Searleman, & C. McEvoy (Eds.), *Memory improvement: Implications for memory theory* (pp. 169–186). New York: Springer-Verlag.

Ceci, S. J., & Williams, W. M. (1997). Schooling, intelligence, and income. *American Psychologist, 52,* 1051–1058.

Centers for Disease Control and Prevention (CDC). (2006). Epidemiology of HIV/AIDS—United States, 1981–2005. *Morbidity and Mortality Weekly Report, 55,* 589–592.

Centers for Disease Control Vietnam Experience Study (CDC). (1988). Health status of Vietnam veterans: I. Psychosocial characteristics. *Journal of the American Medical Association, 259*(18), 2701–2708.

Chaiken, S. (1980). Heuristic versus systematic information processing and the use of source versus message cues in persuasion. *Journal of Personality and Social Psychology, 39,* 752–766.

Chambless, D. L., Baker, M. J., Baucom, D. H., Beutler, L. E., Calhoun, K. S., Crits-Christoph, P., et al. (1998). Update on empirically validated therapies, II. *Clinical Psychologist, 51*(1), 3–14.

Chandler, J., & Schwarz, N. (2009). How extending your middle finger affects your perception of others: Learned movements influence concept accessibility. *Journal of Experimental Social Psychology, 45,* 123–128.

Chang, P. P., Ford, D. E., Meoni, L. A., Wang, N., & Klag, M. J. (2002). Anger in young men and subsequent premature cardiovascular disease. *Archives of Internal Medicine, 162,* 901–906.

Charles, S. T., Reynolds, C. A., & Gatz, M. (2001). Age-related differences and change in positive and negative affect over 23 years. *Journal of Personality and Social Psychology, 80,* 136–151.

Charlesworth, A., & Glantz, S. A. (2005). Smoking in the movies increases adolescent smoking: A review. *Pediatrics, 116,* 1516–1528.

Charness, N. (1981). Aging and skilled problem solving. *Journal of Experimental Psychology: General, 110,* 21–38.

Chartrand, T. L., & Bargh, J. A. (1999). The chameleon effect: The perception-behavior link and social interaction. *Journal of Personality and Social Psychology, 76,* 893–910.

Chartrand, T. L., & Kay, A. (2006). *Mystery moods and perplexing performance: Consequences of succeeding and failing at a nonconscious goal.* Unpublished manuscript.

Chebium, R. (2000). Kirk Bloodsworth, twice convicted of rape and murder, exonerated by DNA evidence. *CNN.com.* Retrieved June 20, 2000, from http://www.cnn.com/2000/LAW/06/20/bloodsworth.profile

Chen, E., Cohen, S., & Miller, G. E. (2010). How low socioeconomic status affects 2-year hormonal trajectories in children. *Psychological Science, 21*(1), 31–37.

Cheney, D. L., & Seyfarth, R. M. (1990). *How monkeys see the world.* Chicago: University of Chicago Press.

Cheng, D. T., Disterhoft, J. F., Power, J. M., Ellis, D. A., & Desmond, J. E. (2008). Neural substrates underlying human delay and trace eyeblink conditioning. *Proceedings of the National Academy of Sciences, USA, 105,* 8108–8113.

Cherlin, A. J. (Ed.). (1992). *Marriage, divorce, remarriage* (2nd ed.). Cambridge, MA: Harvard University Press.

Childress, C. A. (2000). Ethical issues in providing online psychotherapeutic interventions. *Journal of Medical Internet Research, 2*(1), e5.

Choi, I., Nisbett, R. E., & Norenzayan, A. (1999). Causal attribution across cultures: Variation and universality. *Psychological Bulletin, 125,* 47–63.

Chomsky, N. (1957). *Syntactic structures.* The Hague: Mouton.

Chomsky, N. (1959). A review of *Verbal Behavior* by B. F. Skinner. *Language, 35,* 26–58.

Chomsky, N. (1986). *Knowledge of language: Its nature, origin, and use.* New York: Praeger.

Christakis, N. A., & Fowler, J. H. (2007). The spread of obesity in a large social network over 32 years. *New England Journal of Medicine, 357*(4), 370–379.

Christianson, S.-Å., & Loftus, E. F. (1987). Memory for traumatic events. *Applied Cognitive Psychology, 1,* 225–239.

Chung, G. H., Flook, L., & Fuligni, A. J. (2009). Daily family conflict and emotional distress among adolescents from Latin American, Asian, and European backgrounds. *Developmental Psychology, 45,* 1406–1415.

Cialdini, R. B., & Trost, M. R. (1998). Social influence: Social norms, conformity, and compliance. In D. T. Gilbert, S. T. Fiske, & G. Lindzey (Eds.), *The handbook of social psychology* (4th ed., Vol. 2, pp. 151–192). New York: McGraw-Hill.

Cialdini, R. B., Trost, M. R., & Newsom, J. T. (1995). Preference for consistency: The development of a valid measure and the discovery of surprising behavioral implications. *Journal of Personality and Social Psychology, 69,* 318–328.

Cialdini, R. B., Vincent, J. E., Lewis, S. K., Catalan, J., Wheeler, D., & Darby, B. L. (1975). Reciprocal concessions procedure for inducing compliance: The door-in-the-face technique. *Journal of Personality and Social Psychology, 31,* 206–215.

Ciarrochi, J. V., Chan, A. Y., & Caputi, P. (2000). A critical evaluation of the emotional intelligence concept. *Personality & Individual Differences, 28,* 539.

Cicchetti, D., & Toth, S. L. (1998). Perspectives on research and practice in developmental psychopathology. In I. E. Sigel & K. A. Renninger (Eds.), *Handbook of child psychology: Vol. 4. Child psychology in practice* (5th ed., pp. 479–583). New York: Wiley.

Cieply, M. (2010, January 3). James Cameron responds to critics of smoking in *Avatar. New York Times.*

Clancy, S. A., McNally, R. J., Schacter, D. L., Lenzenweger, M. F., & Pitman, R. K. (2002). Memory distortion in people reporting abduction by aliens. *Journal of Abnormal Psychology, 111,* 455–461.

Clancy, S. A., Schacter, D. L., McNally, R. J., & Pitman, R. K. (2000). False recognition in women reporting recovered memories of sexual abuse. *Psychological Science, 11,* 26–31.

Clark, M. S., & Lemay, E. P. (2010). Close relationships. In S. T. Fiske, D. T. Gilbert, & G. Lindzey (Eds.), *The handbook of social psychology* (5th ed., Vol. 2). New York: Wiley.

Clark, R. D., & Hatfield, E. (1989). Gender differences in receptivity to sexual offers. *Journal of Psychology and Human Sexuality, 2,* 39–55.

Clark, R. E., & Squire, L. R. (1998). Classical conditioning and brain systems: The role of awareness. *Science, 280,* 77–81.

Cleckley, H. M. (1976). *The mask of sanity* (5th ed.). St. Louis: Mosby.

Coe, C. L., & Lubach, G. R. (2008). Fetal programming prenatal origins of health and illness. *Current Directions in Psychological Science, 17,* 36–41.

Cogan, R., Cogan, D., Waltz, W., & McCue, M. (1987). Effects of laughter and relaxation on discomfort thresholds. *Journal of Behavioral Medicine, 10,* 139–144.

Coghill, R. C., McHaffie, J. G., & Yen, Y. (2003). Neural correlates of individual differences in the subjective experience of pain. *Proceedings of the National Academy of Sciences, USA, 100,* 8538–8542.

Cohen, D., Nisbett, R. E., Bowdle, B. F., & Schwarz, N. (1996). Insult, aggression, and the southern culture of honor: An "experimental ethnography." *Journal of Personality and Social Psychology, 70,* 945–960.

Cohen, G. (1990). Why is it difficult to put names to faces? *British Journal of Psychology, 81,* 287–297.

Cohen, S. (1988). Psychosocial models of the role of social support in the etiology of physical disease. *Health Psychology, 7,* 269–297.

Cohen, S. (1999). Social status and susceptibility to respiratory infections. *New York Academy of Sciences, 896,* 246–253.

Cohen, S., Evans, G. W., Krantz, D. S., & Stokols, D. (1980). Physiological, motivational, and cognitive effects of aircraft noise on children. *American Psychologist, 35,* 231–243.

Cohen, S. J. (Ed.). (1979). *New directions in patient compliance.* Lexington, MA: Heath.

Coifman, K. G., Bonanno, G. A., Ray, R. D., & Gross, J. J. (2007). Does repressive coping promote resilience? Affective-autonomic response discrepancy during bereavement. *Journal of Personality and Social Psychology, 92,* 745–758.

Colcombe, S. J., Erickson, K. I., Scalf, P. E., Kim, J. S., Prakesh, R., McAuley, E., et al. (2006). Aerobic exercise training increases brain volume in aging humans. *Journals of Gerontology Series A: Biological Sciences and Medical Sciences, 61,* 1166–1170.

Colcombe, S. J., Kramer, A. F., Erickson, K. I., Scalf, P., McAuley, E., Cohen, N. J., et al. (2004). Cardiovascular fitness, cortical plasticity, and aging. *Proceedings of the National Academy of Sciences, USA, 101,* 3316–3321.

Cole, M. (1996). *Cultural psychology: A once and future discipline.* Cambridge, MA: Belknap Press of Harvard University Press.

Condon, J. W., & Crano, W. D. (1988). Inferred evaluation and the relation between attitude similarity and interpersonal attraction. *Journal of Personality and Social Psychology, 54,* 789–797.

Connors, E., Lundregan, T., Miller, N., & McEwen, T. (1997). *Convicted by juries, exonerated by science: Case studies in the use of DNA evidence to establish innocence after trial.* Collingdale, PA: Diane Publishing.

Conroy, D. E., Elliot, A. J., Thrash, T. M., Leary, M. R., & Hoyle, R. H. (2009). Achievement motivation. In *Handbook of individual differences in social behavior* (pp. 382–399). New York: Guilford Press.

Conwell, Y., Duberstein, P. R., Cox, C., Hermmann, J. H., Forbes, N. T., & Caine, E. D. (1996). Relationships of age and axis I diagnoses in victims of completed suicide: A psychological autopsy study. *American Journal of Psychiatry, 153,* 1001–1008.

Cook, E. P. (1985). *Psychological androgyny.* New York: Pergamon Press.

Cook, M., & Mineka, S. (1989). Observational conditioning of fear to fear-relevant versus fear-irrelevant stimuli in rhesus monkeys. *Journal of Abnormal Psychology, 98,* 448–459.

Coombs, R. H. (1991). Marital status and personal well-being: A literature review. *Family Relations, 40,* 97–102.

Coons, P. M. (1994). Confirmation of childhood abuse in child and adolescent cases of multiple personality disorder and dissociative disorder not otherwise specified. *Journal of Nervous and Mental Disease, 182,* 461–464.

Coontz, P. (2008). The responsible conduct of social research. In K. Yang & G. J. Miller (Eds.), *Handbook of research methods in public administration* (pp. 129–139). Boca Raton, FL: Taylor & Francis.

Cooper, H., Nye, B., Charlton, K., Lindsay, J., & Greathouse, S. (1996). The effects of summer vacation on achievement test scores: A narrative and meta-analytic review. *Review of Educational Research, 66*(3), 227–268.

Cooper, J., & Fazio, R. H. (1984). A new look at dissonance theory. In L. Berkowitz (Ed.), *Advances in experimental social psychology* (Vol. 17, pp. 229–266). New York: Academic Press.

Cooper, J. C., Hollon, N. G., Wimmer, G. E., & Knutson, B. (2009). Available alternative incentives modulate anticipatory nucleus accumbens activation. *Social Cognitive and Affective Neuroscience, 4,* 409–416.

Cooper, J. R., Bloom, F. E., & Roth, R. H. (2003). *Biochemical basis of neuropharmacology.* New York: Oxford University Press.

Cooper, M. L. (2006). Does drinking promote risky sexual behavior? A complex answer to a simple question. *Current Directions in Psychological Science, 15,* 19–23.

Cooper, W. H., & Withey, W. J. (2009). The strong situation hypothesis. *Personality and Social Psychology Review, 13,* 62–72.

Coren, S. (1997). *Sleep thieves.* New York: Free Press.

Corkin, S. (1984). Lasting consequences of bilateral medial temporal lobectomy: Clinical course and experimental findings in H. M. *Seminars in Neurology, 4,* 249–259.

Corkin, S. (2002). What's new with the amnesic patient HM? *Nature Reviews Neuroscience, 3,* 153–160.

Correll, J., Park, B., Judd, C. M., & Wittenbrink, B. (2002). The police officer's dilemma: Using ethnicity to disambiguate potentially threatening individuals. *Journal of Personality and Social Psychology, 83,* 1314–1329.

Correll, J., Park, B., Judd, C. M., Wittenbrink, B., Sadler, M. S., & Keesee, T. (2007). Across the thin blue line: Police officers and racial bias in the decision to shoot. *Journal of Personality and Social Psychology, 92,* 1006–1023.

Corti, E. (1931). *A history of smoking* (P. England, Trans.). London: Harrap.

Coryell, W., Endicott, J., Maser, J. D., Mueller, T., Lavori, P., & Keller, M. (1995). The likelihood of recurrence in bipolar affective disorder: The importance of episode recency. *Journal of Affective Disorders, 33,* 201–206.

Cottrell, C. A., Neuberg, S. L., & Li, N. P. (2007). What do people desire in others? A sociofunctional perspective on the importance of different valued characteristics. *Journal of Personality and Social Psychology, 92,* 208–231.

Couzin, J. (2008). Gene tests for psychiatric risk polarize researchers. *Science, 319,* 274–277.

Coyne, J. A. (2000, April 3). Of vice and men: Review of R. Tornhill and C. Palmer, *A natural history of rape. The New Republic,* pp. 27–34.

Craddock, N., & Jones, I. (1999). Genetics of bipolar disorder. *Journal of Medical Genetics, 36,* 585–594.

Craik, F. I. M., & Tulving, E. (1975). Depth of processing and the retention of words in episodic memory. *Journal of Experimental Psychology: General, 104,* 268–294.

Cramer, P. (2008). Seven pillars of defense mechanism theory. *Social and Personality Psychology Compass, 2*(5), 1963–1981.

Cramer, R. E., Schaefer, J. T., & Reid, S. (1996). Identifying the ideal mate: More evidence for male-female convergence. *Current Psychology, 15,* 157–166.

Craske, M. G. (1999). *Anxiety disorders: Psychological approaches to theory and treatment.* Boulder, CO: Westview Press.

Crick, N. R., & Grotpeter, J. K. (1995). Relational aggression, gender, and social-psychological adjustment. *Child Development, 66,* 710–722.

Crocker, J., & Wolfe, C. T. (2001). Contingencies of self-worth. *Psychological Review, 108*(3), 593–623.

Crombag, H. F. M., Wagenaar, W. A., & Van Koppen, P. J. (1996). Crashing memories and the problem of "source monitoring." *Applied Cognitive Psychology, 10,* 95–104.

Cross, E. S., Kraemer, D. J. M., Hamilton, A. F. de C., Kelley, W. M., & Grafton, S. T. (2009). Sensitivity of the action observation network to physical and observational learning. *Cerebral Cortex, 19,* 315–326.

Crowe, R. (1990). Panic disorder: Genetic considerations. *Journal of Psychiatric Researchers, 24,* 129–134.

Csikszentmihalyi, M. (1990). *Flow: The psychology of optimal experience.* New York: Harper & Row.

Csikszentmihalyi, M., & Larson, R. (1987). Validity and reliability of the experience-sampling method. *Journal of Nervous & Mental Disease, 175,* 526–536.

Cumming, S., Hay, P., Lee, T., & Sachdev, P. (1995). Neuropsychological outcome from psychosurgery for obsessive-compulsive disorder. *Australian and New Zealand Journal of Psychiatry, 29,* 293–298.

Curran, J. P., & Lippold, S. (1975). The effects of physical attraction and attitude similarity on attraction in dating dyads. *Journal of Personality, 43,* 528–539.

Curtiss, S. (1977). *Genie: A psycholinguistic study of a modern-day "wildchild."* New York: Academic Press.

Dabbs, J. M., Carr, T. S., Frady, R. L., & Riad, J. K. (1995). Testosterone, crime, and misbehavior among 692 male prison inmates. *Personality and Individual Differences, 18,* 627–633.

D'Agostino, P. R., & Fincher-Kiefer, R. (1992). Need for cognition and correspondence bias. *Social Cognition, 10,* 151–163.

Dahl, G., & Della Vigna, S. (2009). Does movie violence increase violent crime? *The Quarterly Journal of Economics, 124,* 677–734.

Dally, P. (1999). *The marriage of heaven and hell: Manic depression and the life of Virginia Woolf.* New York: St. Martin's Griffin.

Dalton, P. (2003). Olfaction. In H. Pashler & S. Yantis (Eds.), *Stevens' handbook of experimental psychology: Vol. 1. Sensation and perception* (3rd ed., pp. 691–746). New York: Wiley.

Daly, M., & Wilson, M. (1988). Evolutionary social psychology and family homicide. *Science, 242,* 519–524.

Damasio, A. R. (1989). Time-locked multiregional retroactivation: A systems-level proposal for the neural substrates of recall and recognition. *Cognition, 33,* 25–62.

Damasio, A. R. (1994). *Descartes' error: Emotion, reason, and the human brain.* New York: Putnam.

Damasio, A. R. (2005). *Descartes' error: Emotion, reason, and the human brain.* New York: Penguin.

Damasio, A. R., Grabowski, T. J., Bechara, A., Damasio, H., Ponto, L. L. B., Parvisi, J., et al. (2000). Subcortical and cortical brain activity during the feeling of self-generated emotions. *Nature Neuroscience, 3,* 1049–1056.

Damasio, H., Grabowski, T., Frank, R., Galaburda, A. M., & Damasio, A. R. (1994). The return of Phineas Gage: Clues about the brain from the skull of a famous patient. *Science, 264,* 1102–1105.

Damasio, H., Grabowski, T. J., Tranel, D., Hichwa, R. D., & Damasio, A. R. (1996). A neural basis for lexical retrieval. *Nature, 380,* 499–505.

Damsma, G., Pfaus, J. G., Wenkstern, D., Phillips, A. G., & Fibiger, H. C. (1992). Sexual behavior increases dopamine transmission in the nucleus accumbens and striatum of male rats: Comparison with novelty and locomotion. *Behavioral Neurosciences, 106,* 181–191.

Daniel, H. J., O'Brien, K. F., McCabe, R. B., & Quinter, V. E. (1985). Values in mate selection: A 1984 campus survey. *College Student Journal, 19,* 44–50.

Darley, J. M., & Berscheid, E. (1967). Increased liking caused by the anticipation of interpersonal contact. *Human Relations, 10,* 29–40.

Darley, J. M., & Latané, B. (1968). Bystander intervention in emergencies: Diffusion of responsibility. *Journal of Personality and Social Psychology, 8,* 377–383.

Dar-Nimrod, I., & Heine, S. J. (2006). Exposure to scientific theories affects women's math performance. *Science, 314,* 435.

Darwin, C. (1999). *On the origin of the species by means of natural selection.* New York: Bantam Classics. (Original work published 1859)

Darwin, C. (2007). *The expression of the emotions in man and animals.* New York: Bibliobazaar. (Original work published 1899)

Darwin, C. J., Turvey, M. T., & Crowder, R. G. (1972). An auditory analogue of the Sperling partial report procedure: Evidence for brief auditory storage. *Cognitive Psychology, 3,* 255–267.

Dauer, W., & Przedborski, S. (2003). Parkinson's disease: Mechanisms and models. *Neuron, 39,* 889–909.

Daum, I., Schugens, M. M., Ackermann, H., Lutzenberger, W., Dichgans, J., & Birbaumer, N. (1993). Classical conditioning after cerebellar lesions in humans. *Behavioral Neuroscience, 107,* 748–756.

Davidson, R. J. (2004). What does the prefrontal cortex "do" in affect: Perspectives on frontal EEG asymmetry research. *Biological Psychology, 67,* 219–233.

Davidson, R. J., Ekman, P., Saron, C., Senulis, J., & Friesen, W. V. (1990). Emotional expression and brain physiology I: Approach/withdrawal and cerebral asymmetry. *Journal of Personality and Social Psychology, 58,* 330–341.

Davidson, R. J., Pizzagalli, D., Nitschke, J. B., & Putnam, K. (2002). Depression: Perspectives from affective neuroscience. *Annual Review of Psychology, 53,* 545–574.

Davidson, R. J., Putnam, K. M., & Larson, C. L. (2000). Dysfunction in the neural circuitry of emotion regulation—a possible prelude to violence. *Science, 289,* 591–594.

Davies, G. (1988). Faces and places: Laboratory research on context and face recognition. In G. M. Davies & D. M. Thomson (Eds.), *Memory in context: Context in memory* (pp. 35–53). New York: Wiley.

Davila Ross, M., Menzler, S., & Zimmermann, E. (2008). Rapid facial mimicry in orangutan play. *Biology Letters, 4*(1), 27–30.

Dawes, R. M. (1994). *House of cards: Psychology and psychotherapy built on myth.* New York: Free Press.

Dawson, M., Soulieres, I., Gernsbacher, M. A., & Mottron, L. (2007). The level and nature of autistic intelligence. *Psychological Science, 18,* 657–662.

Dayan, P., & Huys, Q. J. M. (2009). Serotonin in affective control. *Annual Review of Neuroscience, 32,* 95–126.

de Araujo, I. E., Rolls, E. T., Velazco, M. I., Margot, C., & Cayeux, I. (2005). Cognitive modulation of olfactory processing. *Neuron, 46,* 671–679.

De Vries, M. H., Barth, A. C. R., Maiworm, S., Knecht, S., Zwitserlood, P., & Flöel, A. (in press). Electrical stimulation of Broca's area enhances implicit learning of an artificial grammar. *Journal of Cognitive Neuroscience.*

De Witte, P. (1996). The role of neurotransmitters in alcohol dependency. *Alcohol & Alcoholism, 31*(Suppl. 1), 13–16.

De Wolff, M., & van IJzendoorn, M. H. (1997). Sensitivity and attachment: A meta-analysis on parental antecedents of infant attachment. *Child Development, 68,* 571–591.

Deary, I. J. (2000). *Looking down on human intelligence: From psychometrics to the brain.* New York: Oxford University Press.

Deary, I. J., Batty, G. D., Pattie, A., & Gale, C. R. (2008). More intelligent, more dependable children live longer: A 55-year longitudinal study of a representative sample of the Scottish nation. *Psychological Science, 19,* 874.

Deary, I. J., Whiteman, M. C., Starr, J. M., Whalley, L. J., & Fox, H. C. (2004). The impact of childhood intelligence on later life: Following up the Scottish mental surveys of 1932 and 1947. *Journal of Personality and Social Psychology, 86,* 130–147.

DeCasper, A. J., & Spence, M. J. (1986). Prenatal maternal speech influences newborns' perception of speech sounds. *Infant Behavior and Development, 9,* 133–150.

Deci, E. L. (1971). Effects of externally mediated rewards on intrinsic motivation. *Journal of Personality and Social Psychology, 18,* 105–115.

Deci, E. L., Koestner, R., & Ryan, R. M. (1999). A meta-analytic review of experiments examining the effects of extrinsic rewards on intrinsic motivation. *Psychological Bulletin, 125,* 627–668.

Deese, J. (1959). On the prediction of occurrence of particular verbal intrusions in immediate recall. *Journal of Experimental Psychology, 58,* 17–22.

Delgado, M. R., Frank, R. H., & Phelps, E. A. (2005). Perceptions of moral character modulate the neural systems of reward during the trust game. *Nature Neuroscience, 8,* 1611–1618.

Delongis, A., Coyne, J. C., Dakof, G., Folkman, S., & Lazarus, R. S. (1982). Relationship of daily hassles, uplifts, and major life events to health status. *Health Psychology, 1,* 119–136.

Demb, J. B., Desmond, J. E., Wagner, A. D., Vaidya, C. J., Glover, G. H., & Gabrieli, J. D. E. (1995). Semantic encoding and retrieval in the left inferior prefrontal cortex: A functional MRI study of task difficulty and process specificity. *The Journal of Neuroscience, 15,* 5870–5878.

Dement, W. C. (1959, November 30). Dreams. *Time.*

Dement, W. C. (1978). *Some must watch while some must sleep.* New York: Norton.

Dement, W. C. (1999). *The promise of sleep.* New York: Delacorte Press.

Dennett, D. (1991). *Consciousness explained.* New York: Basic Books.

DePaulo, B. M., Lindsay, J. J., Malone, B. E., Muhlenbruck, L., Charlton, K., & Cooper, H. (2003). Cues to deception. *Psychological Bulletin, 129,* 74–118.

DePaulo, B. M., Stone, J. I., & Lassiter, G. D. (1985). Deceiving and detecting deceit. In B. R. Schlenker (Ed.), *The self and social life* (pp. 323–370). New York: McGraw-Hill.

Der, G., Batty, G. D., & Deary, I. J. (2009). The association between IQ in adolescence and a range of health outcomes at 40 in the 1979 U.S. national longitudinal study of youth. *Intelligence, 37*(6), 573–580.

DeRosnay, M., Pons, F., Harris, P. L., & Morrell, J. M. B. (2004). A lag between understanding false belief and emotion attribution in young children: Relationships with linguistic ability and mothers' mental-state language. *British Journal of Developmental Psychology, 24*(1), 197–218.

Des Jarlais, D. C., McKnight, C., Goldblatt, C., & Purchase, D. (2009). Doing harm reduction better: Syringe exchange in the United States. *Addiction, 104*(9), 1331–1446.

Deuenwald, M. (2003, June 12). Students find another staple of campus life: Stress. *New York Times.*

Deutsch, M. (1949). A theory of cooperation and competition. *Human Relations, 2,* 129–152.

DeVilliers, P. (2005). The role of language in theory-of-mind development: What deaf children tell us. In J. W. Astington & J. A. Baird (Eds.), *Why language matters for theory of mind* (pp. 266–297). Oxford, England: Oxford University Press.

DeYoung, C. G., & Gray, J. R. (2009). Personality neuroscience: Explaining individual differences in affect, behavior, and cognition. In P. J. Corr & G. Matthews (Eds.), *The Cambridge handbook of personality psychology* (pp. 323–346). New York: Cambridge University Press.

Diano, S., Farr, S. A., Benoit, S. C., McNay, E. C., da Silva, I., Horvath, B., et al. (2006). Ghrelin controls hippocampal spine synapse density and memory performance. *Nature Neuroscience, 9*(3), 381–388.

Dickens, W. T., & Flynn, J. R. (2001). Heritability estimates versus large environmental effects: The IQ paradox resolved. *Psychological Review, 108,* 346–369.

Diekelmann, S., Wilhelm, I., & Born, J. (2009). The whats and whens of sleep-dependent memory consolidation. *Sleep Medicine Reviews, 13,* 309–321.

Diener, E., Horwitz, J., & Emmons, R. A. (1985). Happiness of the very wealthy. *Social Indicators Research, 16,* 263–274.

Dijksterhuis, A. (2004). Think different: The merits of unconscious thought in preference development and decision making. *Journal of Personality and Social Psychology, 87,* 586–598.

Dijksterhuis, A., Aarts, H., & Smith, P. K. (2005). The power of the subliminal: On subliminal persuasion and other potential applications. In J. S. U. R. Hassin & J. A. Bargh (Eds.), *The new unconscious* (pp. 77–106). New York: Oxford University Press.

Dillbeck, M. C., & Orme-Johnson, D. W. (1987). Physiological differences between transcendental meditation and rest. *American Psychologist, 42,* 879–881.

Dimberg, U. (1982). Facial reactions to facial expressions. *Psychophysiology, 19,* 643–647.

Dion, K., Berscheid, E., & Walster, E. (1972). What is beautiful is good. *Journal of Personality and Social Psychology, 24,* 285–290.

DiTella, R., MacCulloch, R. J., & Oswald, A. J. (2003). The macroeconomics of happiness. *Review of Economics and Statistics, 85,* 809–827.

Dollard, J., Doob, L. W., Miller, N. E., Mowrer, O. H., & Sears, R. R. (1939). *Frustration and aggression.* Oxford, England: Yale University Press.

Domjan, M. (2005). Pavlovian conditioning: A functional perspective. *Annual Review of Psychology, 56,* 179–206.

Dornbusch, S. M., Hastorf, A. H., Richardson, S. A., Muzzy, R. E., & Vreeland, R. S. (1965). The perceiver and perceived: Their relative influence on categories of interpersonal perception. *Journal of Personality and Social Psychology, 1,* 434–440.

Dovidio, J. F., & Gaertner, S. L. (2010). Intergroup bias. In S. T. Fiske, D. T. Gilbert, & G. Lindzey (Eds.), *The handbook of social psychology* (5th ed., Vol. 2). New York: Wiley.

Downer, J. D. C. (1961). Changes in visual gnostic function and emotional behavior following unilateral temporal damage in the "split-brain" monkey. *Nature, 191,* 50–51.

Downing, P. E., Chan, A. W. Y., Peelen, M. V., Dodds, C. M., & Kanwisher, N. (2006). Domain specificity in visual cortex. *Cerebral Cortex, 16,* 1453–1461.

Dreifus, C. (2003, May 20). Living one disaster after another, and then sharing the experience. *New York Times,* p. D2.

Drigotas, S. M., & Rusbult, C. E. (1992). Should I stay or should I go? A dependence model of breakups. *Journal of Personality and Social Psychology, 62,* 62–87.

Druckman, D., & Bjork, R. A. (1994). *Learning, remembering, believing: Enhancing human performance.* Washington, DC: National Academy Press.

Duchaine, B. C., Yovel, G., Butterworth, E. J., & Nakayama, K. (2006). Prosopagnosia as an impairment to face-specific mechanisms: Elimination of the alternative hypotheses in a developmental case. *Cognitive Neuropsychology, 23,* 714–747.

Duckworth, A. L., & Seligman, M. E. P. (2005). Self-discipline outdoes IQ in predicting academic performance of adolescents. *Psychological Science, 16,* 939–944.

Dunbar, R. I. M., & Shultz, S. (2007). Evolution in the social brain. *Science, 317,* 1344–1347.

Dunlop, S. A. (2008). Activity-dependent plasticity: Implications for recovery after spinal cord injury. *Trends in Neurosciences, 31,* 410–418.

Dunphy, D. C. (1963). The social structure of urban adolescent peer groups. *Sociometry, 26,* 230–246.

Durkheim, E. (1951). *Suicide: A study in sociology* (G. Simpson, Trans.). New York: Free Press.

Dutton, D. G., & Aron, A. P. (1974). Some evidence for heightened sexual attraction under conditions of high anxiety. *Journal of Personality and Social Psychology, 30,* 510–517.

Duval, S., & Wicklund, R. A. (1972). *A theory of objective self-awareness.* New York: Academic Press.

Eacott, M. J., & Crawley, R. A. (1998). The offset of childhood amnesia: Memory for events that occurred before age 3. *Journal of Experimental Psychology: General, 127,* 22–33.

Eagly, A. H., Ashmore, R. D., Makhijani, M. G., & Longo, L. C. (1991). What is beautiful is good, but . . . : A meta-analytic review of research on the physical attractiveness stereotype. *Psychological Bulletin, 110,* 109–128.

Eagly, A. H., & Steffen, V. J. (1986). Gender and aggressive behavior: A meta-analytic review of the social psychological literature. *Psychological Bulletin, 100,* 309–330.

Eagly, A. H., & Wood, W. (1999). The origins of sex differences in human behavior: Evolved dispositions versus social roles. *American Psychologist, 54,* 408–423.

Eastwick, P. W., Finkel, E. J., Mochon, D., & Ariely, D. (2007). Selective versus unselective romantic desire: Not all reciprocity is created equal. *Psychological Science, 18,* 317–319.

Eaton, W. W., Kessler, R. C., Wittchen, H. U., & McGee, W. J. (1994). Panic and panic disorder in the United States. *American Journal of Psychiatry, 151,* 413–420.

Eaton, W. W., Shao, H., Nestadt, G., Lee, B. H., Bienvenu, O. J., & Zandi, P. (2008). Population-based study of first onset and chronicity of major depressive disorder. *Archives of General Psychiatry, 65,* 513–520.

Ebbinghaus, H. (1964). *Memory: A contribution to experimental psychology.* New York: Dover. (Original work published 1885)

Eddy, D. M. (1982). Probabilistic reasoning in clinical medicine: Problems and opportunities. In D. Kahneman, P. Slovic, & A. Tversky (Eds.), *Judgments under uncertainty: Heuristics and biases* (pp. 249–267). New York: Cambridge University Press.

Editorial. (2006, May 31). Bribing people to vote will not benefit system. *Yuma Sun.* Retrieved May 31, 2006, from http://www.yumasun.com/articles/people-21362-vote-voting.html

Edwards, W. (1955). The theory of decision making. *Psychological Bulletin, 51,* 201–214.

Efferson, C., Lalive, R., & Fehr, E. (2008). The coevolution of cultural groups and ingroup favoritism. *Science, 321,* 1844–1849.

Eich, J. E. (1995). Searching for mood dependent memory. *Psychological Science, 6,* 67–75.

Eichenbaum, H. (2008). *Learning & memory.* New York: Norton.

Eichenbaum, H., & Cohen, N. J. (2001). *From conditioning to conscious recollection: Memory systems of the brain.* New York: Oxford University Press.

Eimas, P. D., Siqueland, E. R., Jusczyk, P., & Vigorito, J. (1971). Speech perception in infants. *Science, 171,* 303–306.

Einstein, G. O., & McDaniel, M. A. (1990). Normal aging and prospective memory. *Journal of Experimental Psychology: Learning, Memory, and Cognition, 16,* 717–726.

Einstein, G. O., & McDaniel, M. A. (2005). Prospective memory: Multiple retrieval processes. *Current Directions in Psychological Science, 14,* 286–290.

Eisenberg, N., Fabes, R. A., Guthrie, I. K., & Reiser, M. (2000). Dispositional emotionality and regulation: Their role in predicting quality of social functioning. *Journal of Personality & Social Psychology, 78,* 136.

Eisenberger, N. I., Lieberman, M. D., & Williams, K. D. (2003). Does rejection hurt? An fMRI study of social exclusion. *Science, 302,* 290–292.

Eisenegger, C., Naef, M., Snozzi, R., Heinrichs, M., & Fehr, E. (2010). Prejudice and truth about the effect of testosterone on human bargaining behaviour. *Nature, 463,* 356–359.

Ekman, P. (1972). Universals and cultural differences in facial expressions of emotion. In J. K. Cole (Ed.), *Nebraska Symposium on Motivation, 1971* (pp. 207–283). Lincoln: University of Nebraska Press.

Ekman, P. (1992). *Telling lies.* New York: Norton.

Ekman, P. (2003). Darwin, deception, and facial expression. *Annals of the New York Academy of Sciences, 1000,* 205–221.

Ekman, P., & Friesen, W. V. (1968). Nonverbal behavior in psychotherapy research. In J. M. Shlien (Ed.), *Research in psychotherapy* (Vol. 3, pp. 179–216). Washington, DC: American Psychological Association.

Ekman, P., & Friesen, W. V. (1971). Constants across cultures in the face and emotion. *Journal of Personality and Social Psychology, 17,* 124–129.

Ekman, P., & Friesen, W. V. (1982). Felt, false, and miserable smiles. *Journal of Nonverbal Behavior, 6,* 238–252.

Ekman, P., Levenson, R. W., & Friesen, W. V. (1983). Autonomic nervous system activity distinguishes among emotions. *Science, 221,* 1208–1210.

Ekman, P., & O'Sullivan, M. (1991). Who can catch a liar? *American Psychologist, 46*(9), 913–920.

Ekman, P., O'Sullivan, M., & Frank, M. G. (1999). A few can catch a liar. *Psychological Science, 10,* 263–266.

Elder, G. H., & Conger, R. D. (2000). *Children of the land: Adversity and success in rural America.* Chicago: University of Chicago Press.

Eldridge, L. L., Knowlton, B. J., Furmanski, C. S., Bookheimer, S. Y., & Engel, S. A. (2000). Remembering episodes: A selective role for the hippocampus during retrieval. *Nature Neuroscience, 3,* 1149–1152.

Elfenbein, H. A., & Ambady, N. (2002). On the universality and cultural specificity of emotion recognition: A meta-analysis. *Psychological Bulletin, 128,* 203–235.

Elfenbein, H. A., Der Foo, M. D., White, J., & Tan, H. H. (2007). Reading your counterpart: The benefit of emotion recognition accuracy for effectiveness in negotiation. *Journal of Nonverbal Behavior, 31,* 205–223.

Ellenbogen, J. M., Payne, J. D., & Stickgold, R. (2006). The role of sleep in declarative memory consolidation: Passive, permissive, or none? *Current Opinion in Neurobiology, 16,* 716–722.

Elliott, R., Sahakian, B. J., Matthews, K., Bannerjea, A., Rimmer, J., & Robbins, T. W. (1997). Effects of methylphenidate on spatial working memory and planning in healthy young adults. *Psychopharmacology, 131,* 196–206.

Ellis, B. J., & Garber, J. (2000). Psychosocial antecedents of variation in girls' pubertal timing: Maternal depression, stepfather presence, and marital and family stress. *Child Development, 71,* 485–501.

Ellis, E. M. (1983). A review of empirical rape research: Victim reactions and response to treatment. *Clinical Psychology Review, 3,* 473–490.

Ellman, S. J., Spielman, A. J., Luck, D., Steiner, S. S., & Halperin, R. (1991). REM deprivation: A review. In S. J. Ellman & J. S. Antrobus (Eds.), *The mind in sleep: Psychology and psychophysiology* (2nd ed., pp. 329–376). New York: Wiley.

Ellsworth, P. C., & Scherer, K. R. (2003). Appraisal processes in emotion. In R. J. Davidson, K. R. Scherer, & H. H. Goldsmith (Eds.), *The handbook of affective science* (pp. 572–595). New York: Oxford University Press.

Emerson, R. C., Bergen, J. R., & Adelson, E. H. (1992). Directionally selective complex cells and the computation of motion energy in cat visual cortex. *Vision Research, 32,* 203–218.

Empson, J. A. (1984). Sleep and its disorders. In R. Stevens (Ed.), *Aspects of consciousness.* New York: Academic Press.

Epley, N., Savitsky, K., & Kachelski, R. A. (1999). What every skeptic should know about subliminal persuasion. *Skeptical Inquirer, 23,* 40–45, 58.

Epley, N., & Waytz, A. (2010). Mind perception. In S. T. Fiske, D. T. Gilbert, & G. Lindzey (Eds.), *The handbook of social psychology* (5th ed., Vol. 1, pp. 498–541). New York: Wiley.

Epstein, R. (2007). The myth of the teen brain. *Scientific American Mind, 18,* 27–31.

Etcoff, N. (1999). *Survival of the prettiest: The science of beauty.* New York: Doubleday.

Evans, G. W. (2004). The environment of childhood poverty. *American Psychologist, 59*(2), 77–92.

Everson, S. A., Lynch, J. W., Chesney, M. A., Kaplan, G. A., Goldberg, D. E., Shade, S. B., et al. (1997). Interaction of workplace demands and cardiovascular reactivity in progression of carotid atherosclerosis: Population based study. *British Medical Journal, 314,* 553–558.

Exner, J. E. (1993). *The Rorschach: A comprehensive system: Vol. 1. Basic foundations.* New York: Wiley.

Eysenck, H. J. (1957). The effects of psychotherapy: An evaluation. *Journal of Consulting Psychology, 16,* 319–324.

Eysenck, H. J. (1967). *The biological basis of personality.* Springfield, IL: Charles C. Thomas.

Fancher, R. E. (1979). *Pioneers of psychology.* New York: Norton.

Fantz, R. L. (1964). Visual experience in infants: Decreased attention to familiar patterns relative to novel ones. *Science, 164,* 668–670.

Farah, M. J., Illes, J., Cook-Deegan, R., Gardner, H., Kandel, E., King, P., et al. (2004). Neurocognitive enhancement: What can we do and what should we do? *Nature Reviews Neuroscience, 5,* 421–426.

Farooqi, I. S., Matarese, G., Lord, G. M., Keogh, J. M., Lawrence, E., Agwu, C., et al. (2002). Beneficial effects of leptin on obesity, T cell hyporesponsiveness, and neuroendocrine/metabolic dysfunction of human congenital leptin deficiency. *The Journal of Clinical Investigation, 110*(8), 1093–1103.

Farrar, M. J. (1990). Discourse and the acquisition of grammatical morphemes. *Journal of Child Language, 17,* 607–624.

Fazel, S., & Danesh, J. (2002). Serious mental disorder in 23,000 prisoners: A review of 62 surveys. *Lancet, 359,* 545–550.

Fechner, G. T. (1966). *Elements of psychophysics* (H. E. Alder, Trans.). New York: Holt, Rinehart and Winston. (Original work published 1860)

Feczer, D., & Bjorklund, P. (2009). Forever changed: Posttraumatic stress disorder in female military veterans, a case report. *Perspectives in Psychiatric Care, 45,* 278–291.

Fein, S., Hilton, J. L., & Miller, D. T. (1990). Suspicion of ulterior motivation and the correspondence bias. *Journal of Personality and Social Psychology, 58,* 753–764.

Feinberg, T. E. (2001). *Altered egos: How the brain creates the self.* New York: Oxford University Press.

Feingold, A. (1990). Gender differences in effects of physical attractiveness on romantic attraction: A comparison across five research paradigms. *Journal of Personality and Social Psychology, 59,* 981–993.

Feingold, A. (1992a). Gender differences in mate selection preferences: A test of the parental investment model. *Psychological Bulletin, 112,* 125–139.

Feingold, A. (1992b). Good-looking people are not what we think. *Psychological Bulletin, 111,* 304–341.

Feingold, A. (1994). Gender differences in personality: A meta-analysis. *Psychological Bulletin, 116,* 429–456.

Feldman, D. E. (2009). Synaptic mechanisms for plasticity in neocortex. *Annual Review of Neuroscience, 32,* 33–55.

Feldman, M. D. (2004). *Playing sick.* New York: Brunner-Routledge.

Ferster, C. B., & Skinner, B. F. (1957). *Schedules of reinforcement.* New York: Appleton-Century-Crofts.

Festinger, L. (1957). *A theory of cognitive dissonance.* Stanford, CA: Stanford University Press.

Festinger, L., Schachter, S., & Back, K. (1950). *Social pressures in informal groups: A study of human factors in housing.* Oxford, England: Harper & Row.

Fiedler, E. R., Oltmanns, T. F., & Turkheimer, E. (2004). Traits associated with personality disorders and adjustment to military life: Predictive validity of self and peer reports. *Military Medicine, 169,* 32–40.

Fields, G. (2009, May 14). White House czar calls for end to "War on Drugs." *The Wall Street Journal,* p. A3. Retrieved May 14, 2009, from http://online.wsj.com/article/SB124225891527617397.html

Finkel, E. J., & Eastwick, P. W. (2009). Arbitrary social norms influence sex differences in romantic selectivity. *Psychological Science, 20,* 1290–1295.

Finkelstein, E. A., Trogdon, J. G., Cohen, J. W., & Dietz, W. (2009). Annual medical spending attributable to obesity: Payer- and service-specific estimates. *Health Affairs, 28*(5), w822–w831.

Finkelstein, K. E. (1999, October 17). Yo-Yo Ma's lost Stradivarius is found after wild search. *New York Times*, p. 34.

Fiore, A. T., Taylor, L. S., Zhong, X., Mendelsohn, G. A., & Cheshire, C. (2010). Who's right and who writes: People, profiles, contacts, and replies in online dating. *Proceedings of Hawaii International Conferences on Systems Science, 43*.

Fiorentine, R. (1999). After drug treatment: Are 12-step programs effective in maintaining abstinence? *American Journal of Drug and Alcohol Abuse, 25*, 93–116.

Fiorillo, C. D., Newsome, W. T., & Schultz, W. (2008). The temporal precision of reward prediction in dopamine neurons. *Nature Neuroscience, 11*, 966–973.

Fisher, R. P., & Craik, F. I. M. (1977). The interaction between encoding and retrieval operations in cued recall. *Journal of Experimental Psychology: Human Learning and Perception, 3*, 153–171.

Fiske, S. T. (2009). *Social beings: A core motives approach to social psychology* (2nd ed.). New York: Wiley.

Fleeson, W. (2004). Moving personality beyond the person-situation debate: The challenge and opportunity of within-person variability. *Current Directions in Psychological Science, 13*, 83–87.

Fleming, R., Baum, A., Gisriel, M. M., & Gatchel, R. J. (1985). Mediating influences of social support on stress at Three Mile Island. In A. Monat & R. S. Lazarus (Eds.), *Stress and coping: An anthology* (2nd ed., pp. 95–106). New York: Columbia University Press.

Fletcher, P. C., Shallice, T., & Dolan, R. J. (1998). The functional roles of prefrontal cortex in episodic memory: I. Encoding. *Brain, 121*, 1239–1248.

Flynn, E. (2008). Investigating children as cultural magnets: Do young children transmit redundant information along diffusion chains? *Philosophical Transactions of the Royal Society of London Series B, 363*, 3541–3551.

Flynn, E., & Whiten, A. (2008). Cultural transmission of tool-use in young children: A diffusion chain study. *Social Development, 17*, 699–718.

Flynn, J. R. (1984). The mean IQ of Americans: Massive gains 1932 to 1978. *Psychological Bulletin, 95*, 29–51.

Flynn, J. R. (1987). Massive IQ gains in 14 nations: What IQ tests really measure. *Psychological Bulletin, 101*, 171–191.

Flynn, J. R. (2009). *What is intelligence? Beyond the Flynn Effect.* Cambridge, England: Cambridge University Press.

Foa, E. B., Dancu, C. V., Hembree, E. A., Jaycox, L. H., Meadows, E. A., & Street, G. P. (1999). A comparison of exposure therapy, stress inoculation training, and their combination for reducing posttraumatic stress disorder in female assault victims. *Journal of Consulting and Clinical Psychology, 67*, 194–200.

Fogassi, L., Ferrari, P. F., Gesierich, B., Rozzi, S., Chersi, F., & Rizzolatti, G. (2005). Parietal lobe: From action organization to intention understanding. *Science, 308*, 662–667.

Fombonne, E. (2009). Epidemiology of pervasive developmental disorders. *Pediatric Research, 65*, 5991–5998.

Forkstam, C., Hagoort, P., Fernández, G., Ingvar, M., & Petersson, K. M. (2006). Neural correlates of artificial syntactic structure classification. *NeuroImage, 32*, 956–967.

Fornazzari, L., Wilkinson, D. A., Kapur, B. M., & Carter, P. L. (1983). Cerebellar, cortical and functional impairment in toluene abusers. *Acta Neurologica Scandinavica, 67*, 319–329.

Foroni, F., & Semin, G. R. (2009). Language that puts you in touch with your bodily feelings: The multimodal responsiveness of affective expressions. *Psychological Science, 20*(8), 974–980.

Fournier, J. C., DeRubeis, R., Hollon, S. D., Dimidjian, S., Amsterdam, J. D., Shelton, R. C., et al. (2010). Antidepressant drug effects and depression severity. *Journal of the American Medical Association, 303*, 47–53.

Fox, M. J. (2009). *Always looking up.* New York: Hyperion.

Fox, R. E., DeLeon, P. H., Newman, R., Sammons, M. T., Dunivin, D. L., & Baker, D. C. (2009). Prescriptive authority and psychology: A status report. *American Psychologist, 64*, 257–268.

Fragaszy, D. M., Izar, P., Visalberghi, E., Ottoni, E. B., & de Oliveria, M. G. (2004). Wild capuchin monkeys (*Cebus libidinosus*) use anvils and stone pounding tools. *American Journal of Primatology, 64*, 359–366.

Frank, M. G., Ekman, P., & Friesen, W. V. (1993). Behavioral markers and recognizability of the smile of enjoyment. *Journal of Personality and Social Psychology, 64*, 83–93.

Frank, M. G., & Stennet, J. (2001). The forced-choice paradigm and the perception of facial expressions of emotion. *Journal of Personality and Social Psychology, 80*, 75–85.

Fredman, T., & Whiten, A. (2008). Observational learning from tool using models by human-reared and mother-reared capuchin monkeys (*Cebus apella*). *Animal Cognition, 11*, 295–309.

Fredrickson, B. L. (2000). Cultivating positive emotions to optimize health and well-being. *Prevention and Treatment, 3*.

Freedman, J. L., & Fraser, S. C. (1966). Compliance without pressure: The foot-in-the-door technique. *Journal of Personality and Social Psychology, 4*, 195–202.

Freeman, S., Walker, M. R., Borden, R., & Latané, B. (1975). Diffusion of responsibility and restaurant tipping: Cheaper by the bunch. *Personality and Social Psychology Bulletin, 1*, 584–587.

French, H. W. (1997, February 26). In the land of the small it isn't easy being tall. *New York Times*.

Freud, A. (1936). *The ego and the mechanisms of defense.* New York: International Universities Press.

Freud, S. (1965). *The interpretation of dreams* (J. Strachey, Trans.). New York: Avon. (Original work published 1900)

Freudenberger, H. J. (1974). Staff burnout. *Journal of Social Issues, 30*, 159–165.

Fried, P. A., & Watkinson, B. (2000). Visuoperceptual functioning differs in 9- to 12-year-olds prenatally exposed to cigarettes and marijuana. *Neurotoxicology and Teratology, 22*, 11–20.

Friedlander, L., & Desrocher, M. (2006). Neuroimaging studies of obsessive-compulsive disorder in adults and children. *Clinical Psychology Review, 26*, 32–49.

Friedman, J. M. (2003). A war on obesity, not the obese. *Science, 299*(5608), 856–858.

Friedman, J. M., & Halaas, J. L. (1998). Leptin and the regulation of body weight in mammals. *Nature, 395*(6704), 763–770.

Friedman, M., & Rosenman, R. H. (1974). *Type A behavior and your heart.* New York: Knopf.

Friedman, S. L., & Boyle, D. E. (2008). Attachment in U.S. children experiencing nonmaternal care in the early 1990s. *Attachment & Human Development, 10*(3), 225–261.

Friedman, W. J. (1993). Memory for the time of past events. *Psychological Bulletin, 113*, 44–66.

Friedman-Hill, S. R., Robertson, L. C., & Treisman, A. (1995). Parietal contributions to visual feature binding: Evidence from a patient with bilateral lesions. *Science, 269*, 853–855.

Friesen, W. V. (1972). *Cultural differences in facial expressions in a social situation: An experimental test of the concept of display rules.* Unpublished doctoral dissertation, University of California, San Francisco.

Frith, C. D., & Fletcher, P. (1995). Voices from nowhere. *Critical Quarterly, 37,* 71–83.

Frith, U. (2001). Mind blindness and the brain in autism. *Neuron, 32,* 969–979.

Frith, U. (2003). *Autism: Explaining the enigma.* Oxford, England: Blackwell.

Fryer, A. J., Mannuzza, S., Gallops, M. S., Martin, L. Y., Aaronson, C., Gorman, J. M., et al. (1990). Familial transmission of simple phobias and fears: A preliminary report. *Archives of General Psychiatry, 47,* 252–256.

Fukui, H., Murai, T., Fukuyama, H., Hayashi, T., & Hanakawa, T. (2005). Functional activity related to risk anticipation during performance of the Iowa gambling task. *Neuroimage, 24,* 253–259.

Funder, D. C. (2001). Personality. *Annual Review of Psychology, 52,* 197–221.

Furmark, T., Tillfors, M., Marteinsdottir, I., Fischer, H., Pissiota, A., Långström, B., et al. (2002). Common changes in cerebral blood flow in patients with social phobia treated with citalopram or cognitive-behavioral therapy. *Archives of General Psychiatry, 59*(5), 425–433.

Fuster, J. M. (2003). *Cortex and mind.* New York: Oxford University Press.

Gable, S. L., & Haidt, J. (2005). What (and why) is positive psychology? *Review of General Psychology, 9,* 102–110.

Gais, S., Albouy, G., Boly, M., Dang-Vu, T. T., Darsaud, A., Desseilles, M., et al. (2007). Sleep transforms the cerebral traces of declarative memories. *Proceedings of the National Academy of Sciences, USA, 104,* 18778–18783.

Gais, S., & Born, J. (2004). Low acetylcholine during slow-wave sleep is critical for declarative memory consolidation. *Proceedings of the National Academy of Sciences, USA, 101,* 2140–2144.

Galanter, E. (1962). Contemporary psychophysics. In R. Brown, E. Galanter, E. H. Hess, & G. Mandler (Eds.), *New directions in psychology* (pp. 87–156). New York: Holt, Rinehart and Winston.

Galati, D., Scherer, K. R., & Ricci-Bitt, P. E. (1997). Voluntary facial expression of emotion: Comparing congenitally blind with normally sighted encoders. *Journal of Personality and Social Psychology, 73,* 1363–1379.

Galef, B. (1998). Edward Thorndike: Revolutionary psychologist, ambiguous biologist. *American Psychologist, 53,* 1128–1134.

Gallistel, C. R. (2000). The replacement of general-purpose learning models with adaptively specialized learning modules. In M. S. Gazzaniga (Ed.), *The new cognitive neurosciences* (pp. 1179–1191). Cambridge, MA: The MIT Press.

Gallo, D. A. (2006). *Associative illusions of memory.* New York: Psychology Press.

Gallup, G. G. (1977). Self-recognition in primates: A comparative approach to the bidirectional properties of consciousness. *American Psychologist, 32,* 329–338.

Gallup, G. G. (1997). On the rise and fall of self-conception in primates. *Annals of the New York Academy of Sciences, 818,* 73–84.

Galton, F. (1869). *Hereditary genius: An inquiry into its laws and consequences.* London: Macmillan/Fontana.

Garb, H. N. (1998). *Studying the clinician: Judgment research and psychological assessment.* Washington, DC: American Psychological Association.

Garcia, J. (1981). Tilting at the windmills of academe. *American Psychologist, 36,* 149–158.

Garcia, J., & Koelling, R. A. (1966). Relation of cue to consequence in avoidance learning. *Psychonomic Science, 4,* 123–124.

Garofalo, R., Cameon, W., Wissow, L. S., Woods, E. R., & Goodman, E. (1999). Sexual orientation and risk of suicide. *Archives of Pediatrics and Adolescent Medicine, 513,* 487.

Garry, M., Manning, C., Loftus, E. F., & Sherman, S. J. (1996). Imagination inflation: Imagining a childhood event inflates confidence that it occurred. *Psychonomic Bulletin & Review, 3,* 208–214.

Gazzaniga, M. S. (Ed.). (2000). *The new cognitive neurosciences.* Cambridge, MA: The MIT Press.

Gazzaniga, M. S. (2006). Forty-five years of split brain research and still going strong. *Nature Reviews Neuroscience, 6,* 653–659.

Ge, X. J., Conger, R. D., & Elder, G. H. (1996). Coming of age too early: Pubertal influences on girls' vulnerability to psychological distress. *Child Development, 67,* 3386–3400.

Geen, R. G. (1984). Preferred stimulation levels in introverts and extraverts: Effects on arousal and performance. *Journal of Personality and Social Psychology, 46,* 1303–1312.

Gegenfurtner, K. R., & Kiper, D. C. (2003). Color vision. *Annual Review of Neuroscience, 26,* 181–206.

Geller, D. A., Hoog, S. L., Heiligenstein, J. H., Ricardi, R. K., Tamura, R., Kluszynski, S., Jacobson, J. G., et al. (2001). Fluoxetine treatment for obsessive-compulsive disorder in children and adolescents: A placebo-controlled clinical trial. *Journal of the American Academy of Child and Adolescent Psychiatry, 40,* 773–779.

George, D. (1981). *Sweet man: The real Duke Ellington.* New York: Putnam.

George, M. S., Lisanby, S. H., & Sackeim, H. A. (1999). Transcranial magnetic stimulation: Applications in neuropsychiatry. *Archives of General Psychiatry, 56,* 300–311.

Germain, V., Marchand, A., Bouchard, S., Drouin, M., & Guay, S. (2009). Effectiveness of cognitive behavioral therapy administered by videoconference for posttraumatic stress disorder. *Cognitive Behavior Therapy, 38,* 42–53.

Gershoff, E. T. (2002). Corporal punishment by parents and associated child behaviors and experiences: A meta-analytic and theoretical review. *Psychological Bulletin, 128,* 539–579.

Giedd, J. N., Blumenthal, J., Jeffries, N. O., Castellanos, F. X., Liu, H., Zijdenbos, A., et al. (1999). Brain development during childhood and adolescence: A longitudinal MRI study. *Nature Neuroscience, 2,* 861–863.

Gigerenzer, G. (1996). The psychology of good judgment: Frequency formats and simple algorithms. *Journal of Medical Decision Making, 16,* 273–280.

Gigerenzer, G., & Hoffrage, U. (1995). How to improve Bayesian reasoning without instruction: Frequency formats. *Psychological Review, 102,* 684–704.

Gilbert, D. T. (1991). How mental systems believe. *American Psychologist, 46,* 107–119.

Gilbert, D. T. (1998). Ordinary personology. In D. T. Gilbert, S. T. Fiske, & G. Lindzey (Eds.), *The handbook of social psychology* (4th ed., Vol. 2, pp. 89–150). New York: McGraw-Hill.

Gilbert, D. T. (2006). *Stumbling on happiness.* New York: Knopf.

Gilbert, D. T., Brown, R. P., Pinel, E. C., & Wilson, T. D. (2000). The illusion of external agency. *Journal of Personality and Social Psychology, 79,* 690–700.

Gilbert, D. T., Gill, M. J., & Wilson, T. D. (2002). The future is now: Temporal correction in affective forecasting. *Organizational Behavior and Human Decision Processes, 88,* 430–444.

Gilbert, D. T., & Malone, P. S. (1995). The correspondence bias. *Psychological Bulletin, 117,* 21–38.

Gilbert, D. T., & Wilson, T. D. (2009). Why the brain talks to itself: Sources of error in emotional prediction. *Philosophical Transactions of the Royal Society B: Biological Sciences, 364,* 1335–1341.

Gilbert, G. M. (1951). Stereotype persistence and change among college students. *Journal of Abnormal and Social Psychology, 46,* 245–254.

Gilbertson, M. W., Shenton, M. E., Ciszewski, A., Kasai, K., Lasko, N. B., Orr, S. P., et al. (2002). Smaller hippocampal volume predicts pathological vulnerability to psychological trauma. *Nature Neuroscience, 5,* 1242–1247.

Gillette, J., Gleitman, H., Gleitman, L., & Lederer, A. (1999). Human simulation of vocabulary learning. *Cognition, 73,* 135–176.

Ginzburg, K., Solomon, Z., & Bleich, A. (2002). Repressive coping style, acute stress disorder, and posttraumatic stress disorder after myocardial infarction. *Psychosomatic Medicine, 64,* 748–757.

Giovanello, K. S., Schnyer, D. M., & Verfaellie, M. (2004). A critical role for the anterior hippocampus in relational memory: Evidence from an fMRI study comparing associative and item recognition. *Hippocampus, 14,* 5–8.

Gladue, B. A. (1994). The biopsychology of sexual orientation. *Current Directions in Psychological Science, 3,* 150–154.

Glass, D. C., & Singer, J. E. (1972). *Urban stress.* New York: Academic Press.

Gleaves, D. H., Smith, S. M., Butler, L. D., & Spiegel, D. (2004). False and recovered memories in the laboratory and clinic: A review of experimental and clinical evidence. *Clinical Psychology: Science and Practice, 11,* 3–28.

Glenwick, D. S., Jason, L. A., & Elman, D. (1978). Physical attractiveness and social contact in the singles bar. *Journal of Social Psychology, 105,* 311–312.

Glynn, S. M. (1990). Token economy approaches for psychiatric patients: Progress and pitfalls over 25 years. *Behavior Modification, 14,* 383–407.

Gneezy, U., & Rustichini, A. (2000). A fine is a price. *Journal of Legal Studies, 29,* 1–17.

Gobert, A., Rivet, J. M., Cistarelli, L., Melon, C., & Millan, M. J. (1999). Buspirone modulates basal and fluoxetine-stimulated dialysate levels of dopamine, noradrenaline, and serotonin in the frontal cortex of freely moving rats: Activation of serotonin 1A receptors and blockade of alpha2-adrenergic receptors underlie its actions. *Neuroscience, 93,* 1251–1262.

Goddard, H. H. (1913). *The Kallikak family: A study in the heredity of feeble-mindedness.* New York: Macmillan.

Godden, D. R., & Baddeley, A. D. (1975). Context-dependent memory in two natural environments: On land and underwater. *British Journal of Psychology, 66,* 325–331.

Goehler, L. E., Gaykema, R. P. A., Hansen, M. K., Anderson, K., Maier, S. F., & Watkins, L. R. (2000). Vagal immune-to-brain communication: A visceral chemosensory pathway. *Autonomic Neuroscience: Basic and Clinical, 85,* 49–59.

Goetzman, E. S., Hughes, T., & Klinger, E. (1994). *Current concerns of college students in a midwestern sample.* Unpublished report, University of Minnesota, Morris.

Goff, L. M., & Roediger, H. L., III. (1998). Imagination inflation for action events—repeated imaginings lead to illusory recollections. *Memory & Cognition, 26,* 20–33.

Goldman, M. S., Brown, S. A., & Christiansen, B. A. (1987). Expectancy theory: Thinking about drinking. In H. T. Blane & K. E. Leonard (Eds.), *Psychological theories of drinking and alcoholism* (pp. 181–266). New York: Guilford Press.

Goldstein, R., & Herschkowitsch, A. (2008). *The wine trials.* Austin, TX: Fearless Critic Media.

Goldstein, S., Naglieri, J. A., & Ozonoff, S. (Eds.). (2008). *Assessment of autism spectrum disorders.* New York: Guilford Press.

Gomez, C., Argandota, E. D., Solier, R. G., Angulo, J. C., & Vazquez, M. (1995). Timing and competition in networks representing ambiguous figures. *Brain and Cognition, 29,* 103–114.

Gonzaga, G. C., Keltner, D., Londahl, E. A., & Smith, M. D. (2001). Love and the commitment problem in romantic relations and friendship. *Journal of Personality and Social Psychology, 81,* 247–262.

Goodale, M. A., & Milner, A. D. (1992). Separate visual pathways for perception and action. *Trends in Neurosciences, 15,* 20–25.

Goodale, M. A., & Milner, A. D. (2004). *Sight unseen.* Oxford, England: Oxford University Press.

Goodale, M. A., Milner, A. D., Jakobson, L. S., & Carey, D. P. (1991). A neurological dissociation between perceiving objects and grasping them. *Nature, 349,* 154–156.

Goodwin, F. K., & Ghaemi, S. N. (1998). Understanding manic-depressive illness. *Archives of General Psychiatry, 55,* 23–25.

Goodwin, P., McGill, B., & Chandra, A. (2009). *Who marries and when? Age at first marriage in the United States, 2002.* National Center for Health Statistics Data Brief 19.

Gootman, E. (2003, March 3). Separated at birth in Mexico, united at campuses on Long Island. *New York Times,* p. A25.

Gopie, N., & MacLeod, C. M. (2009). Destination memory: Stop me if I've told you this before. *Psychological Science, 20,* 1492–1499.

Gordon, P. (2004). Numerical cognition without words: Evidence from Amazonia. *Science, 306,* 496–499.

Gosling, S. D., Ko, S. J., Mannarelli, T., & Morris, M. E. (2002). A room with a cue: Personality judgments based on offices and bedrooms. *Journal of Personality and Social Psychology, 82,* 379–398.

Gottesman, I. I. (1991). *Schizophrenia genesis: The origins of madness.* New York: Freeman.

Gottesman, I. I., & Hanson, D. R. (2005). Human development: Biological and genetic processes. *Annual Review of Psychology, 56,* 263–286.

Gottfredson, L. S. (1997). Mainstream science on intelligence: An editorial with 52 signatories, history, and bibliography. *Intelligence, 24,* 13–23.

Gottfredson, L. S. (2003). Dissecting practical intelligence theory: Its claims and evidence. *Intelligence, 31*(4), 343–397.

Gottfredson, L. S., & Deary, I. J. (2004). Intelligence predicts health and longevity, but why? *Current Directions in Psychological Science, 13,* 1–4.

Gottfried, J. A. (2008). Perceptual and neural plasticity of odor quality coding in the human brain. *Chemosensory Perception, 1,* 127–135.

Gottman, J. M. (1994). *What predicts divorce? The relationship between marital processes and marital outcomes.* Hillsdale, NJ: Lawrence Erlbaum.

Gouldner, A. W. (1960). The norm of reciprocity. *American Sociological Review, 25,* 161–178.

Graf, P., & Schacter, D. L. (1985). Implicit and explicit memory for new associations in normal subjects and amnesic patients. *Journal of Experimental Psychology: Learning, Memory, and Cognition, 11,* 501–518.

Grant, A. M. (2008). Personal life coaching for coaches-in-training enhances goal attainment, insight, and learning. *Coaching, 1*(1), 54–70.

Grant, B. F., Hasin, D. S., Stinson, F. S., Dawson, D. A., Chou, S. P., & Ruan, W. J. (2004). Prevalence, correlates, and disability of personality disorders in the U.S.: Results from the National Epidemiologic Survey on Alcohol and Related Conditions. *Journal of Clinical Psychiatry, 65,* 948–958.

Grassian, S. (2006). Psychiatric effects of solitary confinement. *Journal of Law & Policy, 22,* 326–383.

Gray, H. M., Gray, K., & Wegner, D. M. (2007). Dimensions of mind perception. *Science, 315,* 619.

Gray, J. A. (1970). The psychophysiological basis of introversion-extraversion. *Behavior Research and Therapy, 8,* 249–266.

Gray, J. A. (1990). Brain systems that mediate both emotion and cognition. *Cognition and Emotion, 4,* 269–288.

Greeley, A. M. (1975). *The sociology of the paranormal: A reconnaissance.* Beverly Hills, CA: Sage.

Greely, H., Sahakian, B., Harris, J., Kessler, R. C., Gazzaniga, M., Campbell, P., et al. (2008). Towards responsible use of cognitive-enhancing drugs by the healthy. *Nature, 456*(7223), 702–705.

Green, D. A., & Swets, J. A. (1966). *Signal detection theory and psychophysics.* New York: Wiley.

Green, S. K., Buchanan, D. R., & Heuer, S. K. (1984). Winners, losers, and choosers: A field investigation of dating initiation. *Personality & Social Psychology Bulletin, 10,* 502–511.

Greenberg, J., Solomon, S., & Arndt, J. (2008). A basic but uniquely human motivation: Terror management. In J. Y. Shah & W. L. Gardner (Eds.), *Handbook of motivation science* (pp. 114–134). New York: Guilford Press.

Greenberg, P. E., Sisitsky, T., Kessler, R. C., Finkelstein, S. N., Berndt, E. R., Davidson, J. R. T., et al. (1999). The economic burden of anxiety disorders in the 1990s. *Journal of Clinical Psychiatry, 60,* 427–435.

Greene, J. D., Sommerville, R. B., Nystrom, L. E., Darley, J. M., & Cohen, J. D. (2001). An fMRI investigation of emotional engagement in moral judgment. *Science, 293,* 2105–2108.

Greenfield, P. M., Keller, H., Fuligni, A., & Maynard, A. (2003). Cultural pathways through universal development. *Annual Review of Psychology, 54,* 461–490.

Greenhouse, S. (2003, July 13). Going for the look, but risking discrimination. *New York Times.*

Greenwald, A. G., McGhee, D. E., & Schwartz, J. L. K. (1998). Measuring individual differences in implicit cognition: The implicit association test. *Journal of Personality and Social Psychology, 74,* 1464–1480.

Greenwald, A. G., & Nosek, B. A. (2001). Health of the Implicit Association Test at age 3. *Zeitschrift für Experimentelle Psychologie, 48,* 85–93.

Grigoriadis, S., & Robinson, G. E. (2007). Gender issues in depression. *Journal of Clinical Psychiatry, 19,* 247–255.

Gronlund, S. D., Carlson, C. A., Dailey, S. B., & Goodsell, C. A. (2009). Robustness of the sequential lineup advantage. *Journal of Experimental Psychology: Applied, 15*(2), 140–152.

Gropp, E., Shanabrough, M., Borok, E., Xu, A. W., Janoschek, R., Buch, T., et al. (2005). Agouti-related peptide-expressing neurons are mandatory for feeding. *Nature Neuroscience, 8,* 1289–1291.

Gross, J. J. (1998). Antecedent- and response-focused emotion regulation: Divergent consequences for experience, expression, and physiology. *Journal of Personality and Social Psychology, 74,* 224–237.

Gross, J. J., & Munoz, R. F. (1995). Emotion regulation and mental health. *Clinical Psychology: Science and Practice, 2,* 151–164.

Groves, B. (2004, August 2). Unwelcome awareness. *The San Diego Union-Tribune,* p. 24.

Guillery, R. W., & Sherman, S. M. (2002). Thalamic relay functions and their role in corticocortical communication: Generalizations from the visual system. *Neuron, 33,* 163–175.

Gustafsson, J.-E. (1984). A unifying model for the structure of intellectual abilities. *Intelligence, 8,* 179–203.

Guthrie, R. V. (2000). Kenneth Bancroft Clark (1914–). In A. E. Kazdin (Ed.), *Encyclopedia of Psychology* (Vol. 2, p. 91). Washington, DC: American Psychological Association.

Hackman, D. A., & Farah, M. J. (2008). Socioeconomic status and the developing brain. *Trends in Cognitive Sciences, 13,* 65–73.

Haggard, P., & Tsakiris, M. (2009). The experience of agency: Feelings, judgments, and responsibility. *Current Directions in Psychological Science, 18,* 242–246.

Haidt, J. (2001). The emotional dog and its rational tail: A social intuitionist approach to moral judgment. *Psychological Review, 108,* 814–834.

Haidt, J. (2006). *The happiness hypothesis: Finding modern truth in ancient wisdom.* New York: Basic Books.

Haidt, J. (2008). Morality. *Perspectives in Psychological Science, 3,* 65–72.

Haidt, J., & Keltner, D. (1999). Culture and facial expression: Open-ended methods find more expressions and a gradient of recognition. *Cognition and Emotion, 13,* 225–266.

Hakuta, K. (1986). *Cognitive development of bilingual children.* Center for Language Education and Research, University of California, Los Angeles.

Hakuta, K. (1999). The debate on bilingual education. *Journal of Developmental and Behavioral Pediatrics, 20,* 36–37.

Hallett, M., Cloninger, C. R., Fahn, S., & Jankovic, J. J. (Eds.). (2005). *The psychogenic movement disorders: Neurology and neuropsychiatry.* Philadelphia: Lippincott, Williams & Wilkins.

Halliday, R., Naylor, H., Brandeis, D., Callaway, E., Yano, L., & Herzig, K. (1994). The effect of D-amphetamine, clonidine, and yohimbine on human information processing. *Psychophysiology, 31,* 331–337.

Halpern, B. (2002). Taste. In H. Pashler & S. Yantis (Eds.), *Stevens' handbook of experimental psychology: Vol. 1. Sensation and perception* (3rd ed., pp. 653–690). New York: Wiley.

Halpern, D. F. (1997). Sex differences in intelligence: Implications for education. *American Psychologist, 52,* 1091–1102.

Halpern, D. F., Benbow, C. P., Geary, D. C., Gur, R. C., Hyde, J. S., & Gernsbacher, M. A. (2007). The science of sex differences in science and mathematics. *Psychological Science in the Public Interest, 8,* 1–51.

Hamermesh, D. S., & Biddle, J. E. (1994). Beauty and the labor market. *American Economic Review, 84,* 1174–1195.

Hamilton, W. D. (1964). The genetical evolution of social behaviour. *Journal of Theoretical Biology, 7,* 1–16.

Hamlin, J. K., Wynn, K., & Bloom, P. (2007). Social evaluation by preverbal infants. *Nature, 450*(7169), 557–559.

Hansen, E. S., Hasselbalch, S., Law, I., & Bolwig, T. G. (2002). The caudate nucleus in obsessive-compulsive disorder. Reduced metabolism following treatment with paroxetine: A PET study. *International Journal of Neuropsychopharmacology, 5,* 1–10.

Hansen, T., Olkkonen, M., Walter, S., & Gegenfurtner, K. R. (2006). Memory modulates color appearance. *Nature Neuroscience, 9,* 1367–1368.

Hanson, C. J., Stevens, L. C., & Coast, J. R. (2001). Exercise duration and mood state: How much is enough to feel better? *Health Psychology, 20,* 267–275.

Happé, F. G. E. (1995). The role of age and verbal ability in the theory-of-mind performance of subjects with autism. *Child Development, 66,* 843–855.

Happé, F. G. E., & Vital, P. (2009). What aspects of autism predispose to talent? *Philosophical Transactions of the Royal Society B: Biological Science, 364*, 1369–1375.

Hare, R. D. (1998). *Without conscience: The disturbing world of the psychopaths among us.* New York: Guilford Press.

Harlow, H. F. (1958). The nature of love. *American Psychologist, 13*, 573–685.

Harlow, H. F., & Harlow, M. L. (1965). The affectional systems. In A. M. Schrier, H. F. Harlow, & F. Stollnitz (Eds.), *Behavior of nonhuman primates* (Vol. 2). New York: Academic Press.

Harlow, J. M. (1848). Passage of an iron rod through the head. *Boston Medical and Surgical Journal, 39*, 389–393.

Harris, P. L., de Rosnay, M., & Pons, F. (2005). Language and children's understanding of mental states. *Current Directions in Psychological Science, 14*, 69–73.

Harris, P. L., Johnson, C. N., Hutton, D., Andrews, G., & Cooke, T. (1989). Young children's theory of mind and emotion. *Cognition and Emotion, 3*, 379–400.

Hart, B. L. (1988). Biological basis of the behavior of sick animals. *Neuroscience and Biobehavioral Reviews, 12*, 123–137.

Hart, B., & Risley, T. R. (1995). *Meaningful differences in the everyday experience of young American children.* Baltimore, MD: Brookes.

Hartshorne, H., & May, M. (1928). *Studies in deceit.* New York: Macmillan.

Haskell, E. (1869). *The trial of Ebenezer Haskell, in lunacy, and his acquittal before Judge Brewster, in November, 1868, together with a brief sketch of the mode of treatment of lunatics in different asylums in this country and in England: with illustrations, including a copy of Hogarth's celebrated painting of a scene in old Bedlam, in London, 1635.* Philadelphia, PA: Ebenezer Haskell.

Haslam, C., Wills, A. J., Haslam, S. A., Kay, J., Baron, R., & McNab, F. (2007). Does maintenance of colour categories rely on language? Evidence to the contrary from a case of semantic dementia. *Brain and Language, 103*, 251–263.

Hassabis, D., Kumaran, D., Vann, S. D., & Maguire, E. A. (2007). Patients with hippocampal amnesia cannot imagine new experiences. *Proceedings of the National Academy of Sciences, USA, 104*, 1726–1731.

Hasselmo, M. E. (2006). The role of acetylcholine in learning and memory. *Current Opinion in Neurobiology, 16*, 710–715.

Hassin, R. R., Bargh, J. A., & Zimerman, S. (2009). Automatic and flexible: The case of non-conscious goal pursuit. *Social Cognition, 27*, 20–36.

Hassmen, P., Koivula, N., & Uutela, A. (2000). Physical exercise and psychological well-being: A population study in Finland. *Preventive Medicine, 30*, 17–25.

Hasson, U., Hendler, T., Bashat, D. B., & Malach, R. (2001). Vase or face? A neural correlate of shape-selective grouping processes in the human brain. *Journal of Cognitive Neuroscience, 13*, 744–753.

Hatfield, E. (1988). Passionate and companionate love. In R. J. Sternberg & M. L. Barnes (Eds.), *The psychology of love* (pp. 191–217). New Haven, CT: Yale University Press.

Hatfield, E., & Rapson, R. L. (1992). Similarity and attraction in close relationships. *Communication Monographs, 59*, 209–212.

Hausser, M. (2000). The Hodgkin-Huxley theory of the action potential. *Nature Neuroscience, 3*, 1165.

Hawley, P. H. (2002). Social dominance and prosocial and coercive strategies of resource control in preschoolers. *International Journal of Behavioral Development, 26*, 167–176.

Haxby, J. V., Gobbini, M. I., Furey, M. L., Ishai, A., Schouten, J. L., & Pietrini, P. (2001). Distributed and overlapping representations of faces and objects in ventral temporal cortex. *Science, 293*, 2425–2430.

Hay, P., Sachdev, P., Cumming, S., Smith, J. S., Lee, T., Kitchener, P., et al. (1993). Treatment of obsessive-compulsive disorder by psychosurgery. *Acta Psychiatrica Scandinavica, 87*, 197–207.

Hayes, S. C., Strosahl, K., & Wilson, K. G. (1999). *Acceptance and commitment therapy: An experiential approach to behavior change.* New York: Guilford Press.

Health, United States. (2008). Hyattsville, MD: National Center for Health Statistics.

Heath, S. B. (1983). *Way with words: Language, life and work in communities and classrooms.* Cambridge, England: Cambridge University Press.

Heatherton, T. F., & Weinberger, J. L. (Eds.). (1994). *Can personality change?* Washington, DC: American Psychological Association.

Hebb, D. O. (1949). *The organization of behavior.* New York: Wiley.

Hebl, M. R., & Heatherton, T. F. (1997). The stigma of obesity in women: The difference is Black and White. *Personality and Social Psychology Bulletin, 24*, 417–426.

Hebl, M. R., & Mannix, L. M. (2003). The weight of obesity in evaluating others: A mere proximity effect. *Personality and Social Psychology Bulletin, 29*, 28–38.

Heerey, E. A., Keltner, D., & Capps, L. M. (2003). Making sense of self-conscious emotion: Linking theory of mind and emotion in children with autism. *Emotion, 3*, 394–400.

Heider, F., & Simmel, M. (1944). An experimental study of apparent behavior. *American Journal of Psychology, 57*, 243–259.

Heine, S. J. (2010). Cultural psychology. In S. T. Fiske, D. T. Gilbert, & G. Lindzey (Eds.), *The handbook of social psychology* (5th ed., Vol. 2). New York: Wiley.

Henderlong, J., & Lepper, M. R. (2002). The effects of praise on children's intrinsic motivation: A review and synthesis. *Psychological Bulletin, 128*, 774–795.

Henry, W. P., Strupp, H. H., Schacht, T. E., & Gaston, L. (1994). Psychodynamic approaches. In A. E. Bergin & S. L. Garfield (Eds.), *Handbook of psychotherapy and behavior change* (pp. 467–508). New York: Wiley.

Herman, C. P., Roth, D. A., & Polivy, J. (2003). Effects of the presence of others on food intake: A normative interpretation. *Psychological Bulletin, 129*, 873–886.

Herman-Giddens, M. E., Slora, E. J., Wasserman, R. C., Bourdony, C. J., Bhapkar, M. V., Koch, G. G., et al. (1997). Secondary sexual characteristics and menses in young girls seen in office practice: A study from the pediatric research in office settings network. *Pediatrics and Perinatal Epidemiology, 99*, 505–512.

Herrmann, D. J., Raybeck, D., & Gruneberg, M. (2002). *Improving memory and study skills: Advances in theory and practice.* Seattle: Hogrefe and Huber.

Herrnstein, R. J. (1977). The evolution of behaviorism. *American Psychologist, 32*, 593–603.

Hertwig, R., & Gigerenzer, G. (1999). The "conjunction fallacy" revisited: How intelligent inferences look like reasoning errors. *Journal of Behavioral Decision Making, 12*, 275–305.

Herz, R. S., & von Clef, J. (2001). The influence of verbal labeling on the perception of odors. *Perception, 30*, 381–391.

Hettema, J. M., Neale, M. C., & Kendler, K. S. (2001). A review and meta-analysis of the genetic epidemiology of anxiety disorders. *American Journal of Psychiatry, 158*, 1568–1578.

Heyes, C. M., & Foster, C. L. (2002). Motor learning by observation: Evidence from a serial reaction time task. *Quarterly Journal of Experimental Psychology (A), 55*, 593–607.

Heymsfield, S. B., Greenberg, A. S., Fujioka, K., Dixon, R. M., Kushner, R., Hunt, T., et al. (1999). Recombinant leptin for weight loss in obese and lean adults: A randomized, controlled, dose-escalation trial. *Journal of the American Medical Association, 282*(16), 1568–1575.

Higgins, E. T. (1987). Self-discrepancy theory: A theory relating self and affect. *Psychological Review, 94*, 319–340.

Higgs, S., Williamson, A. C., Rotshtein, P., & Humphreys, G. W. (2008). Sensory-specific satiety is intact in amnesics who eat multiple meals. *Psychological Science, 19*, 623–628.

Hilgard, E. R. (1965). *Hypnotic susceptibility.* New York: Harcourt, Brace and World.

Hillman, C. H., Erickson, K. I., & Kramer, A. F. (2008). Be smart, exercise your heart: Exercise effects on brain and cognition. *Nature Reviews Neuroscience, 9*, 58–65.

Hilts, P. (1995). *Memory's ghost: The strange tale of Mr. M and the nature of memory.* New York: Simon & Schuster.

Hirschfeld, D. R., Rosenbaum, J. F., Biederman, J., Bolduc, E. A., Faraone, S. V., Snidman, N., et al. (1992). Stable behavioral inhibition and its association with anxiety disorder. *Journal of the American Academy of Child and Adolescent Psychiatry, 31*, 103–111.

Hirschfeld, R. M. A. (1996). Panic disorder: Diagnosis, epidemiology, and clinical course. *Journal of Clinical Psychiatry, 57*, 3–8.

Hirst, W., Phelps, E. A., Buckner, R. L., Budson, A. E., Cuc, A., Gabrieli, J. D. E., et al. (2009). Long-term memory for the terrorist attack of September 11: Flashbulb memories, event memories, and the factors that influence their retention. *Journal of Experimental Psychology: General, 138*, 161–176.

Hishakawa, Y. (1976). Sleep paralysis. In C. Guilleminault, W. C. Dement, & P. Passouant (Eds.), *Narcolepsy: Advances in sleep research* (Vol. 3, pp. 97–124). New York: Spectrum.

Hobson, J. A. (1988). *The dreaming brain.* New York: Basic Books.

Hobson, J. A., & McCarley, R. W. (1977). The brain as a dream-state generator: An activation-synthesis hypothesis of the dream process. *American Journal of Psychiatry, 134*, 1335–1368.

Hockley, W. E. (2008). The effects of environmental context on recognition memory and claims of remembering. *Journal of Experimental Psychology: Learning, Memory, & Cognition, 34*, 1412–1429.

Hodgkin, A. L., & Huxley, A. F. (1939). Action potential recorded from inside a nerve fibre. *Nature, 144*, 710–712.

Hoek, H. W., & van Hoeken, D. (2003). Review of the prevalence and incidence of eating disorders. *International Journal of Eating Disorders, 34*, 383–396.

Hoffrage, U., & Gigerenzer, G. (1998). Using natural frequencies to improve diagnostic inferences. *Academic Medicine, 73*, 538–540.

Hogan, D. P., Sun, R., & Cornwell, G. T. (2000). Sexual and fertility behaviors of American females age 15–19 years: 1985, 1990 and 1995. *American Journal of Public Health, 90*, 1421–1425.

Holloway, G. (2001). *The complete dream book: What your dreams tell about you and your life.* Naperville, IL: Sourcebooks.

Holmbeck, G. N., & O'Donnell, K. (1991). Discrepancies between perceptions of decision making and behavioral autonomy. In R. L. Paikoff (Ed.), *New directions for child development: No. 51. Shared views in the family during adolescence.* San Francisco: Jossey-Bass.

Holmes, T. H., & Rahe, R. H. (1967). The social readjustment rating scale. *Journal of Psychosomatic Research, 11*, 213–318.

Hölzel, B. K., Carmody, J., Vangel, M., Congleton, C., Yerramsetti, S. M., Gard, T., & Lazar, S. W. (2011). Mindfulness practice leads to increases in regained gray matter density. *Psychiatry Research: Neuroimaging, 191*(1), 36–43.

Homans, G. C. (1961). *Social behavior.* New York: Harcourt, Brace and World.

Horn, J. L., & Cattell, R. B. (1966). Refinement and test of the theory of fluid and crystallized general intelligences. *Journal of Educational Psychology, 5*, 253–270.

Horner, V., Whiten, A., Flynn, E., & de Waal, F. B. M. (2006). Faithful replication of foraging techniques along cultural transmission chains by chimpanzees and children. *Proceedings of the National Academy of Sciences, USA, 103*, 13878–13883.

Horrey, W. J., & Wickens, C. D. (2006). Examining the impact of cell phone conversation on driving using meta-analytic techniques. *Human Factors, 48*, 196–205.

Horta, B. L., Victoria, C. G., Menezes, A. M., Halpern, R., & Barros, F. C. (1997). Low birthweight, preterm births and intrauterine growth retardation in relation to maternal smoking. *Pediatrics and Perinatal Epidemiology, 11*, 140–151.

Horwitz, A. V., & Wakefield, J. C. (2007). *The loss of sadness: How psychiatry transformed normal sorrow into depressive disorder.* New York: Oxford University Press.

Hosking, S. G., Young, K. L., & Regan, M. A. (2009). The effects of text messaging on young drivers. *Human Factors, 51*, 582–592.

House, J. S., Landis, K. R., & Umberson, D. (1988). Social relationships and health. *Science, 241*, 540–545.

Howard, I. P. (2002). Depth perception. In S. Yantis & H. Pashler (Eds.), *Stevens' handbook of experimental psychology: Vol. 1. Sensation and perception* (3rd ed., pp. 77–120). New York: Wiley.

Hubbard, E. M., & Ramachandran, V. S. (2003). Refining the experimental lever. *Journal of Consciousness Studies, 10*, 77–84.

Hubbard, E. M., & Ramachandran, V. S. (2005). Neurocognitive mechanisms of synesthesia. *Neuron, 48*, 509–520.

Hubel, D. H. (1988). *Eye, brain, and vision.* New York: Freeman.

Hubel, D. H., & Wiesel, T. N. (1962). Receptive fields, binocular interaction and functional architecture in the cat's visual cortex. *Journal of Physiology, 160*, 106–154.

Hubel, D. H., & Wiesel, T. N. (1998). Early exploration of the visual cortex. *Neuron, 20*, 401–412.

Huesmann, L. R., Moise-Titus, J., Podolski, C.-L., & Eron, L. D. (2003). Longitudinal relations between children's exposure to TV violence and their aggressive and violent behavior in young adulthood: 1977–1992. *Developmental Psychology, 39*, 201–221.

Humphreys, K., Winzelberg, A., & Klaw, E. (2000). Psychologists' ethical responsibilities in Internet-based groups: Issues, strategies, and a call for dialogue. *Professional Psychology: Research and Practice, 31*, 493–496.

Humphreys, N., & Dennett, D. C. (1989). Speaking for our selves. *Raritan: A Quarterly Review, 9*, 68–98.

Hunsley, J., & Di Giulio, G. (2002). Dodo bird, phoenix, or urban legend? The question of psychotherapy equivalence. *Scientific Review of Mental Health Practice, 1*, 13–24.

Huxley, A. (1932). *Brave new world.* London: Chatto and Windus.

Huxley, A. (1954). *The doors of perception.* New York: Harper & Row.

Hyde, J. S. (2005). The gender similarities hypothesis. *American Psychologist, 60*, 581–592.

Hyman, I. E., Jr., Boss, S. M., Wise, B. M., McKenzie, K. E., & Caggiano, J. M. (2010). Did you see the unicycling clown? Inattentional blindness while walking and talking on a cell phone. *Applied Cognitive Psychology, 24*(5), 597–607.

Hyman, I. E., Jr., & Pentland, J. (1996). The role of mental imagery in the creation of false childhood memories. *Journal of Memory and Language, 35,* 101–117.

Hypericum Depression Trial Study Group. (2002). Effect of *Hypericum perforatum* (St. John's wort) in major depressive disorder: A randomized controlled trial. *Journal of the American Medical Association, 287,* 1807–1814.

Iacoboni, M. (2009). Imitation, empathy, and mirror neurons. *Annual Review of Psychology, 60,* 653–670.

Iacoboni, M., & Dapretto, M. (2006). The mirror neuron system and the consequences of its dysfunction. *Nature Reviews Neuroscience, 7,* 942–951.

Iacoboni, M., Molnar-Szakacs, I., Gallese, V., Buccino, G., Mazziotta, J. C., & Rizzolatti, G. (2005). Grasping the intentions of others with one's own mirror neuron system. *PLoS Biology, 3,* 529–535.

Imbo, I., & LeFevre, J.-A. (2009). Cultural differences in complex addition: Efficient Chinese versus adaptive Belgians and Canadians. *Journal of Experimental Psychology: Learning, Memory, and Cognition, 35,* 1465–1476.

Inciardi, J. A. (2001). *The war on drugs III.* New York: Allyn & Bacon.

Ingvar, M., Ambros-Ingerson, J., Davis, M., Granger, R., Kessler, M., Rogers, G. A., et al. (1997). Enhancement by an ampakine of memory encoding in humans. *Experimental Neurology, 146,* 553–559.

Inui, A. (2001). Ghrelin: An orexigenic and somatotrophic signal from the stomach. *Nature Reviews Neuroscience, 2,* 551–560.

Irvine, J. T. (1978). Wolof magical thinking: Culture and conservation revisited. *Journal of Cross-Cultural Psychology, 9,* 300–310.

Isabelle, R. A. (1993). Origins of attachment: Maternal interactive behavior across the first year. *Child Development, 64,* 605–621.

Isacsson, G., & Rich, C. L. (1997). Depression and antidepressants, and suicide: Pharmacoepidemiological evidence for suicide prevention. In R. W. Maris, M. M. Silverman, & S. S. Canetton (Eds.), *Review of suicidology* (pp. 168–201). New York: Guilford Press.

Isen, A. M., & Patrick, R. (1983). The effect of positive feelings on risk-taking: When the chips are down. *Organizational Behavior and Human Performance, 31,* 194–202.

Ishii, K., Reyes, J. A., & Kitayama, S. (2003). Spontaneous attention to word content versus emotional tone. *Psychological Science, 14*(1), 39–46.

Ittelson, W. H. (1952). *The Ames demonstrations in perception.* Princeton, NJ: Princeton University Press.

Iverson, L. L. (2006). *Speed, ecstasy, Ritalin: The science of amphetamines.* New York: Oxford University Press.

Izard, C. E. (1971). *The face of emotion.* New York: Appleton-Century-Crofts.

Jablensky, A. (1997). The 100-year epidemiology of schizophrenia. *Schizophrenia Research, 28,* 111–125.

Jacobs, B. L. (1994). Serotonin, motor activity, and depression-related disorders. *American Scientist, 82,* 456–463.

James, W. (1890). *The principles of psychology.* Cambridge, MA: Harvard University Press.

Janicak, P. G., Dowd, S. M., Martis, B., Alam, D., Beedle, D., Krasuski, J., et al. (2002). Repetitive transcranial magnetic stimulation versus electroconvulsive therapy for major depression: Preliminary results of a randomized trial. *Biological Psychiatry, 51,* 659–667.

Jarvella, R. J. (1970). Effects of syntax on running memory span for connected discourse. *Psychonomic Science, 19,* 235–236.

Jarvella, R. J. (1971). Syntactic processing of connected speech. *Journal of Verbal Learning & Verbal Behavior, 10,* 409–416.

Jausovec, N., & Jausovec, K. (2005). Differences in induced gamma and upper alpha oscillations in the human brain related to verbal/performance and emotional intelligence. *International Journal of Psychophysiology, 56,* 223.

Jausovec, N., Jausovec, K., & Gerlic, I. (2001). Differences in event-related and induced electroencephalography patterns in the theta and alpha frequency bands related to human emotional intelligence. *Neuroscience Letters, 311,* 93.

Jaynes, J. (1976). *The origin of consciousness in the breakdown of the bicameral mind.* London: Allen Lane.

Jenkins, H. M., Barrera, F. J., Ireland, C., & Woodside, B. (1978). Signal-centered action patterns of dogs in appetitive classical conditioning. *Learning and Motivation, 9,* 272–296.

Jenkins, J. G., & Dallenbach, K. M. (1924). Obliviscence during sleep and waking. *American Journal of Psychology, 35,* 605–612.

John, O. P., Naumann, L. P., & Soto, C. J. (2008). Paradigm shift to the integrative Big-Five trait taxonomy: History, measurement, and conceptual issues. In O. P. John, R. W. Robins, & L. A. Pervin (Eds.), *Handbook of personality: Theory and research* (pp. 114–158). New York: Guilford Press.

John, O. P., & Srivastava, S. (1999). The Big Five trait taxonomy: History, measurement, and theoretical perspectives. In L. A. Pervin & O. P. John (Eds.), *Handbook of personality: Theory and research* (2nd ed., pp. 102–138). New York: Guilford Press.

Johnson, C. A., Xiao, L., Palmer, P., Sun, P., Wang, Q., Wei, Y. L., et al. (2008). Affective decision-making deficits, linked to dysfunctional ventromedial prefrontal cortex, revealed in 10th grade Chinese adolescent binge drinkers. *Neuropsychologia, 46,* 714–726.

Johnson, D. H. (1980). The relationship between spike rate and synchrony in responses of auditory-nerve fibers to single tones. *Journal of the Acoustical Society of America, 68,* 1115–1122.

Johnson, D. R., & Wu, J. (2002). An empirical test of crisis, social selection, and role explanations of the relationship between marital disruption and psychological distress: A pooled time-series analysis of four-wave panel data. *Journal of Marriage and the Family, 64,* 211–224.

Johnson, J. S., & Newport, E. L. (1989). Critical period effects in second language learning: The influence of maturational state on the acquisition of English as a second language. *Cognitive Psychology, 21,* 60–99.

Johnson, K. (2002). Neural basis of haptic perception. In H. Pashler & S. Yantis (Eds.), *Stevens' handbook of experimental psychology: Vol. 1. Sensation and perception* (3rd ed., pp. 537–583). New York: Wiley.

Johnson, M. K., Hashtroudi, S., & Lindsay, D. S. (1993). Source monitoring. *Psychological Bulletin, 114,* 3–28.

Johnson, R. (2005, February 12). A genius explains. *The Guardian.*

Johnson, S. L., Cuellar, A. K., & Miller, C. (2009). Unipolar and bipolar depression: A comparison of clinical phenomenology, biological vulnerability, and psychosocial predictors. In I. H. Gottlib & C. L. Hammen (Eds.), *Handbook of depression* (2nd ed., pp. 142–162). New York: Guilford Press.

Johnson, S. L., Cuellar, A. K., Ruggiero, C., Winnett-Perman, C., Goodnick, P., White, R., et al. (2008). Life events as predictors of mania and depression in bipolar 1 disorder. *Journal of Abnormal Psychology, 117,* 268–277.

Johnson, S. L., & Miller, I. (1997). Negative life events and time to recover from episodes of bipolar disorder. *Journal of Abnormal Psychology, 106,* 449–457.

Joiner, T. E., Jr. (2006). *Why people die by suicide*. Cambridge, MA: Harvard University Press.

Jonas, E., Graupmann, V., Kayser, D. N., Zanna, M., Traut-Mattausch, E., & Frey, D. (2009). Culture, self, and the emergence of reactance: Is there a "universal" freedom? *Journal of Experimental Social Psychology, 45,* 1068–1080.

Jones, B. C., Little, A. C., Penton-Voak, I. S., Tiddeman, B. P., Burt, D. M., & Perrett, D. I. (2001). Facial symmetry and judgements of apparent health: Support for a "good genes" explanation of the attractiveness-symmetry relationship. *Evolution and Human Behavior, 22,* 417–429.

Jones, E. E., & Harris, V. A. (1967). The attribution of attitudes. *Journal of Experimental Social Psychology, 3,* 1–24.

Jones, E. E., & Nisbett, R. E. (1972). The actor and the observer: Divergent perceptions of the causes of behavior. In E. E. Jones, D. E. Kanouse, H. H. Kelley, R. E. Nisbett, S. Valins, & B. Weiner (Eds.), *Attribution: Perceiving the causes of behavior* (pp. 79–94). Morristown, NJ: General Learning Press.

Jones, S. S. (2007). Imitation in infancy. *Psychological Science, 18*(7), 593–599.

Jonsson, H., & Hougaard, E. (2008). Group cognitive behavioural therapy for obsessive-compulsive disorder: A systematic review and meta-analysis. *Acta Psychiatrica Scandinavica, 117,* 1–9.

Joo, E., Greenwood, T. A., Schork, N., McKinney, R. A., Satdovnick, D., Remick, D. A., et al. (2009). Suggestive evidence for linkage of SDHD features in bipolar disorder to chromosome 10p14. *American Journal of Medical Genetics Part B: Neuropsychiatric Genetics, 153B,* 260–268.

Jordan, S. A., Cunningham, D. G., & Marles, R. J. (2010). Assessment of herbal medicinal products: Challenges and opportunities to increase the knowledge base for safety assessment. *Toxicology and Applied Pharmacology, 243,* 198–216.

Judd, L. L. (1997). The clinical course of unipolar major depressive disorders. *Archives of General Psychiatry, 54,* 989–991.

Jung-Beeman, M. (2005). Bilateral brain processes for comprehending natural language. *Trends in Cognitive Sciences, 9,* 512–518.

Kaas, J. H. (1991). Plasticity of sensory and motor maps in adult mammals. *Annual Review of Neuroscience, 14,* 137–167.

Kahneman, D., Krueger, A. B., Schkade, D. A., Schwarz, N., & Stone, A. A. (2004). A survey method for characterizing daily life experience: The day reconstruction method. *Science, 306,* 1776–1780.

Kahneman, D., & Tversky, A. (1973). On the psychology of prediction. *Psychological Review, 80,* 237–251.

Kahneman, D., & Tversky, A. (1979). Prospect theory: An analysis of decision under risk. *Econometrica, 47,* 263–291.

Kan, P. F., & Kohnert, K. (2008). Fast mapping by bilingual preschool children. *Journal of Child Language, 35,* 495–514.

Kandel, E. R. (2000). Nerve cells and behavior. In E. R. Kandel, G. H. Schwartz, & T. M. Jessell (Eds.), *Principles of neural science* (pp. 19–35). New York. McGraw-Hill.

Kandel, E. R. (2006). *In search of memory: The emergence of a new science of mind.* New York: Norton.

Kanner, A. D., Coyne, J. C., Schaefer, C., & Lazarus, R. S. (1981). Comparison of two modes of stress management: Daily hassles and uplifts versus major life events. *Journal of Behavioral Medicine, 4,* 1–39.

Kant, I. (1965). *Critique of pure reason* (N. K. Smith, Trans.). New York: St. Martin's Press. (Original work published 1781)

Kanwisher, N., McDermott, J., & Chun, M. M. (1997). The fusiform face area: A module in human extrastriate cortex specialized for face perception. *The Journal of Neuroscience, 17,* 4302–4311.

Kanwisher, N., & Yovel, G. (2006). The fusiform face area: A cortical region specialized for the perception of faces. *Philosophical Transactions of the Royal Society (B), 361,* 2109–2128.

Kapur, S., Craik, F. I. M., Tulving, E., Wilson, A. A., Houle, S., & Brown, G. M. (1994). Neuroanatomical correlates of encoding in episodic memory: Levels of processing effects. *Proceedings of the National Academy of Sciences, USA, 91,* 2008–2011.

Karlins, M., Coffman, T. L., & Walters, G. (1969). On the fading of social stereotypes: Studies in three generations of college students. *Journal of Personality and Social Psychology, 13,* 1–16.

Karney, B. R., & Bradbury, T. N. (1995). The longitudinal course of marital quality and stability: A review of theory, methods, and research. *Psychological Bulletin, 118,* 3–34.

Karno, M., & Golding, J. M. (1991). Obsessive-compulsive disorder. In L. N. Robins & D. A. Regier (Eds.), *Psychiatric disorders in America: The epidemiologic catchment area study.* New York: Free Press.

Karow, A., Pajonk, F. G., Reimer, J., Hirdes, F., Osterwald, C., Naber, D., et al. (2007). The dilemma of insight into illness in schizophrenia: Self- and expert-rated insight and quality of life. *European Archives of Psychiatry and Clinical Neuroscience, 258,* 152–159.

Karpicke, J. D., & Roediger, H. L., III (2008). The critical importance of retrieval for learning. *Science, 319,* 966–968.

Kassam, K. S., Gilbert, D. T., Swencionis, J. K., & Wilson, T. D. (2009). Misconceptions of memory: The Scooter Libby effect. *Psychological Science, 20,* 551–552.

Kasser, T., & Sharma, Y. S. (1999). Reproductive freedom, educational equality, and females' preference for resource-acquisition characteristics in mates. *Psychological Science, 10,* 374–377.

Katz, D., & Braly, K. (1933). Racial stereotypes of one hundred college students. *Journal of Abnormal and Social Psychology, 28,* 280–290.

Kaufman, A. S. (2001). WAIS-III IQs, Horn's theory, and generational changes from young adulthood to old age. *Intelligence, 29,* 131–167.

Kaufman, L. (2009, January 30). Utilities turn their customers green, with envy. *New York Times.*

Kawakami, K., Dovidio, J. F., Moll, J., Hermsen, S., & Russin, A. (2000). Just say no (to stereotyping): Effects of training in the negation of stereotypic associations on stereotype activation. *Journal of Personality and Social Psychology, 78,* 871–888.

Keefe, F. J., Abernathy, A. P., & Campbell, L. C. (2005). Psychological approaches to understanding and treating disease-related pain. *Annual Review of Psychology, 56,* 601–630.

Keefe, F. J., Lumley, M., Anderson, T., Lynch, T., & Carson, K. L. (2001). Pain and emotion: New research directions. *Journal of Clinical Psychology, 57,* 587–607.

Keisler, D. J. (1999). *Beyond the disease model of mental disorders.* New York: Praeger.

Kelley, H. H. (1983). Love and commitment. In H. H. Kelley, E. Berscheid, A. Christensen, & J. H. Harvey (Eds.), *Close relationships* (pp. 265–314). New York: W.H. Freeman and Company.

Kelly, C., & McCreadie, R. (2000). Cigarette smoking and schizophrenia. *Advances in Psychiatric Treatment, 6,* 327–331.

Kelly, G. (1955). *The psychology of personal constructs.* New York: Norton.

Keltner, D. (1995). Signs of appeasement: Evidence for the distinct displays of embarrassment, amusement, and shame. *Journal of Personality and Social Psychology, 68,* 441–454.

Keltner, D., & Buswell, B. N. (1996). Evidence for the distinctness of embarrassment, shame, and guilt: A study of recalled antecedents and facial expressions of emotion. *Cognition and Emotion, 10,* 155–171.

Keltner, D., & Haidt, J. (1999). Social functions of emotions at four levels of analysis. *Cognition and Emotion, 13,* 505–521.

Keltner, D., & Harker, L. A. (1998). The forms and functions of the nonverbal signal of shame. In P. Gilbert & B. Andrews (Eds.), *Shame: Interpersonal behavior, psychopathology, and culture* (pp. 78–98). New York: Oxford University Press.

Kendler, K. S., Myers, J., & Prescott, C. A. (2002). The etiology of phobias: An evaluation of the stress-diathesis model. *Archives of General Psychiatry, 59,* 242–248.

Kendler, K. S., Neale, M., Kessler, R. C., & Heath, A. (1992). Generalized anxiety disorder in women: A population-based twin study. *Archives of General Psychiatry, 49,* 267–272.

Kenrick, D. T., Sadalla, E. K., Groth, G., & Trost, M. R. (1990). Evolution, traits, and the stages of human courtship: Qualifying the parental investment model. *Journal of Personality, 58,* 97–116.

Kensinger, E. A., Clarke, R. J., & Corkin, S. (2003). What neural correlates underlie successful encoding and retrieval? A functional magnetic resonance imaging study using a divided attention paradigm. *The Journal of Neuroscience, 23,* 2407–2415.

Kensinger, E. A., & Schacter, D. L. (2005). Emotional content and reality monitoring ability: fMRI evidence for the influence of encoding processes. *Neuropsychologia, 43,* 1429–1443.

Kensinger, E. A., & Schacter, D. L. (2006). Amygdala activity is associated with the successful encoding of item, but not source, information for positive and negative stimuli. *The Journal of Neuroscience, 26,* 2564–2570.

Kessler, R. C., Berglund, P., Demler, M. A., Jin, R., Merikangas, K. R., & Walters, E. E. (2005). Lifetime prevalence and age-of-onset distributions of *DSM-IV* disorders in the National Comorbidity Survey replication. *Archives of General Psychiatry, 62,* 593–602.

Kessler, R. C., Chiu, W. T., Jin, R., Ruscio, A. M., Shear, K., & Walters, E. E. (2006). The epidemiology of panic attacks, panic disorder, and agoraphobia in the National Comorbidity Survey Replication. *Archives of General Psychiatry, 63,* 415–424.

Kessler, R. C., McGonagle, K. A., Zhao, S., Nelson, C. B., Hughes, M., Eshleman, S., et al. (1994). Lifetime and 12-month prevalence of *DSM-III-R* psychiatric disorders in the United States: Results from the National Comorbidity Study. *Archives of General Psychiatry, 51,* 8–19.

Kessler, R. C., Nelson, C. B., McGonagle, K. A., Liu, J., Swartz, M., & Blazer, D. (1996). Comorbidity of *DSM-III-R* major depressive disorder in the general population: Results from the U.S. national comorbidity survey. *British Journal of Psychiatry, 168,* 17–30.

Kessler, R. C., Sonnega, A., Bromet, E., Hughes, M., & Nelson, C. B. (1995). Posttraumatic stress disorder in the National Comorbidity Survey. *Archives of General Psychiatry, 52,* 1048–1060.

Kessler, R. C., Soukup, J., Davis, R. B., Foster, D. F., Wilkey, S. A., Van Rompay, M. I., et al. (2001). The use of complementary and alternative therapies to treat anxiety and depression in the United States. *American Journal of Psychiatry, 158,* 289–294.

Kiecolt-Glaser, J. K., Garner, W., Speicher, C., Penn, G., & Glaser, R. (1984). Psychosocial modifiers of immunocompetence in medical students. *Psychosomatic Medicine, 46,* 7–14.

Kiefer, H. M. (2004). Americans unruffled by animal testing. Retrieved August 8, 2009, from http://www.gallup.com/poll/11767/Americans-Unruffled-Animal-Testing.aspx

Kiefer, M., Schuch, S., Schenk, W., & Fiedler, K. (2007). Mood states modulate activity in semantic brain areas during emotional word encoding. *Cerebral Cortex, 17,* 1516–1530.

Kiehl, K. A., Smith, A. M., Hare, R. D., Mendrek, A., Forster, B. B., Brink, J., et al. (2001). Limbic abnormalities in affective processing by criminal psychopaths as revealed by functional magnetic resonance imaging. *Biological Psychiatry, 50,* 677–684.

Kihlstrom, J. F. (1985). Hypnosis. *Annual Review of Psychology, 36,* 385–418.

Kihlstrom, J. F. (1987). The cognitive unconscious. *Science, 237,* 1445–1452.

Kihlstrom, J. F. (2005). Dissociative disorders. *Annual Review of Clinical Psychology, 1,* 227–253.

Kihlstrom, J. F., Beer, J. S., & Klein, S. B. (2002). Self and identity as memory. In M. R. Leary & J. P. Tangney (Eds.), *Handbook of self and identity* (pp. 68–90). New York: Guilford Press.

Kim, G., Walden, T. A., & Knieps, L. J. (2010). Impact and characteristics of positive and fearful emotional messages during infant social referencing. *Infant Behavior and Development, 33,* 189–195.

Kim, K., & Smith, P. K. (1998). Childhood stress, behavioural symptoms and mother-daughter pubertal development. *Journal of Adolescence, 21,* 231–240.

Kim, U. K., Jorgenson, E., Coon, H., Leppert, M., Risch, N., & Drayna, D. (2003). Positional cloning of the human quantaitive trait locus underlying taste sensitivity to phenylthiocarbamide. *Science, 299,* 1221–1225.

King, C. A. (1997). Suicidal behavior in adolescence. In R. W. Maris, M. M. Silverman, & S. S. Canetton (Eds.), *Review of suicidology, 1997* (pp. 61–95). New York: Guilford Press.

Kinney, D. A. (1993). From nerds to normals—the recovery of identity among adolescents from middle school to high school. *Sociology of Education, 66,* 21–40.

Kirchner, W. H., & Towne, W. F. (1994). The sensory basis of the honeybee's dance language. *Scientific American, 270*(6), 74–80.

Kirsch, I., & Sapirstein, G. (1998). Listening to Prozac but hearing placebo: A meta-analysis of antidepressant medication. *Prevention and Treatment, 1,* Article 0002. Retrieved May 18, 2007, from www.journals.apa.org/pt/prevention/volume1/pre0010002a.html

Kirwan, C. B., Bayley, P. J., Galvan, V. V., & Squire, L. R. (2008). Detailed recollection of remote autobiographical memory after damage to the medial temporal lobe. *Proceedings of the National Academy of Sciences, USA, 105,* 2676–2680.

Klein, S. B. (2004). The cognitive neuroscience of knowing one's self. In M. Gazzaniga (Ed.), *The cognitive neurosciences* (3rd ed.). Cambridge, MA: The MIT Press.

Kleinman, A. M. (1986). *Social origins of distress and disease: Depression, neurasthenia and pain in modern China.* New Haven, CT: Yale University Press.

Kleinman, A. M. (1988). *Rethinking psychiatry: From cultural category to personal experience.* New York: Free Press.

Kleinschmidt, A., & Cohen, L. (2006). The neural bases of prosopagnosia and pure alexia: Recent insights from functional neuroimaging. *Current Opinion in Neurology, 19,* 386–391.

Klinger, E. (1975). Consequences of commitment to and disengagement from incentives. *Psychological Review, 82,* 1–25.

Klinger, E. (1977). *Meaning and void.* Minneapolis: University of Minnesota Press.

Kluft, R. P. (1991). Multiple personality disorder. In A. Tasman & S. M. Goldfinger (Eds.), *American Psychiatric Press review of psychiatry* (Vol. 10, pp. 161–188). Washington, DC: American Psychiatric Press.

Klüver, H. (1951). Functional differences between the occipital and temporal lobes with special reference to the interrelations of behavior and extracerebral mechanisms. In L. A. Jeffress (Ed.), *Cerebral mechanisms in behavior* (pp. 147–199). New York: Wiley.

Klüver, H., & Bucy, P. C. (1937). "Psychic blindness" and other symptoms following bilateral temporary lobectomy in rhesus monkeys. *American Journal of Physiology, 119,* 352–353.

Klüver, H., & Bucy, P. C. (1939). Preliminary analysis of functions of the temporal lobes in monkeys. *Archives of Neurology and Psychiatry, 42,* 979–1000.

Knowlton, B. J., Ramus, S. J., & Squire, L. R. (1992). Intact artificial grammar learning in amnesia: Dissociation of classification learning and explicit memory for specific instances. *Psychological Science, 3,* 173–179.

Knutson, B., Adams, C. M., Fong, G. W., & Hommer, D. (2001). Anticipation of increasing monetary reward selectively recruits nucleus accumbens. *The Journal of Neuroscience, 21,* 159.

Knutson, B., Wolkowitz, O. M., Cole, S. W., Chan, T., Moore, E. A., Johnson, R. C., et al. (1998). Selective alteration of personality and social behavior by serotonergic intervention. *American Journal of Psychiatry, 155,* 373–379.

Kobasa, S. (1979). Stressful life events, personality, and health: An inquiry into hardiness. *Journal of Personality and Social Psychology, 37,* 1–11.

Koenigs, M., Huey, E. D., Calamia, M., Raymont, V., Tranel, D., & Grafman, J. (2008). Distinct regions of prefrontal cortex mediate resistance and vulnerability to depression. *Journal of Neuroscience, 28,* 12341–12348.

Koffka, K. (1935). *Principles of Gestalt psychology.* New York: Harcourt, Brace and World.

Kohlberg, L. (1963). Development of children's orientation towards a moral order (Part I). Sequencing in the development of moral thought. *Vita Humana, 6,* 11–36.

Kohlberg, L. (1986). A current statement on some theoretical issues. In S. Modgil & C. Modgil (Eds.), *Lawrence Kohlberg.* Philadelphia: Falmer.

Kolb, B., & Whishaw, I. Q. (2003). *Fundamentals of human neuropsychology* (5th ed.). New York: Worth Publishers.

Kolotkin, R. L., Meter, K., & Williams, G. R. (2001). Quality of life and obesity. *Obesity Reviews, 2,* 219–229.

Komiya, N., Good, G. E., & Sherrod, N. B. (2000). Emotional openness as a predictor of college students' attitudes toward seeking psychological help. *Journal of Counseling Psychology, 47,* 138–143.

Komter, A. (2010). The evolutionary origins of human generosity. *International Sociology, 25*(3), 443–464.

Koss, M. P. (1990). The women's mental health research agenda: Violence against women. *American Psychologist, 45,* 374–380.

Kosslyn, S. M., Alpert, N. M., Thompson, W. L., Chabris, C. F., Rauch, S. L., & Anderson, A. K. (1993). Visual mental imagery activates topographically organized visual cortex: PET investigations. *Journal of Cognitive Neuroscience, 5,* 263–287.

Kosslyn, S. M., Pascual-Leone, A., Felician, O., Camposano, S., Keenan, J. P., Thompson, W. L., et al. (1999). The role of area 17 in visual imagery: Convergent evidence from PET and rTMS. *Science, 284,* 167–170.

Kramer, M. S., Aboud, F., Mironova, E., Vanilovich, I., Platt, R. W., Matush, L., et al. (2008). Breastfeeding and child cognitive development: New evidence from a large randomized trial. *Archives of General Psychiatry, 65,* 578–584.

Kramer, P. D. (1993). *Listening to Prozac.* New York: Viking.

Krantz, D. S., & McCeney, M. K. (2002). Effects of psychological and social factors on organic disease: A critical assessment of research on coronary heart disease. *Annual Review of Psychology, 53,* 341–369.

Kroeze, W. K., & Roth, B. L. (1998). The molecular biology of serotonin receptors: Therapeutic implications for the interface of mood and psychosis. *Biological Psychiatry, 44,* 1128–1142.

Kruk, M. R., Halasz, J., Meelis, W., & Haller, J. (2004). Fast positive feedback between the adrenocortical stress response and a brain mechanism involved in aggressive behavior. *Behavioral Neuroscience, 118,* 1062–1070.

Kubovy, M. (1981). Concurrent-pitch segregation and the theory of indispensable attributes. In M. Kubovy & J. R. Pomerantz (Eds.), *Perceptual organization* (pp. 55–96). Hillsdale, NJ: Lawrence Erlbaum.

Kuhl, B. A., Dudukovic, N. M., Kahn, I., & Wagner, A. D. (2007). Decreased demands on cognitive control reveal the neural processing benefits of forgetting. *Nature Neuroscience, 10,* 908–917.

Kunda, Z., & Oleson, K. C. (1997). When exceptions prove the rule: How extremity of deviance determines the impact of deviant examples on stereotypes. *Journal of Personality and Social Psychology, 72,* 965–979.

Kurtzman, T. L., Otsuka, K. N., & Wahl, R. A. (2001). Inhalant abuse by adolescents. *Journal of Adolescent Health, 28,* 170–180.

Kutchins, H., & Kirk, S. A. (1997). *Making us crazy: DSM: The psychiatric bible and the creation of mental disorders.* New York: Free Press.

Kvavilashvili, L., Mirani, J., Schlagman, S., Foley, K., & Kornbrot, D. E. (2009). Consistency of flashbulb memories of September 11 over long delays: Implications for consolidation and wrong time slice hypotheses. *Journal of Memory and Language, 61,* 556–572.

Kwan, V. S. Y., John, O. P., Robins, R. W., & Kuang, L. L. (2008). Conceptualizing and assessing self-enhancement bias: A componential approach. *Journal of Personality and Social Psychology, 94*(6), 1062–1077.

LaBar, K. S., & Phelps, E. A. (1998). Arousal-mediated memory consolidation: Role of the medial temporal lobe in humans. *Psychological Science, 9,* 490–493.

Lachman, R., Lachman, J. L., & Butterfield, E. C. (1979). *Cognitive psychology and information processing: An introduction.* Hillsdale, NJ: Lawrence Erlbaum.

Lackner, J. R., & DiZio, P. (2005). Vestibular, proprioceptive, and haptic contributions to spatial orientation. *Annual Review of Psychology, 56,* 115–147.

LaFraniere, S. (2007, July 4). In Mauritania, seeking to end an overfed ideal. *New York Times.*

Lai, Y., & Siegal, J. (1999). Muscle atonia in REM sleep. In B. Mallick & S. Inoue (Eds.), *Rapid eye movement sleep* (pp. 69–90). New Delhi, India: Narosa Publishing House.

Lake, J. (2009). Natural products used to treat depressed mood as monotherapies and adjuvants to antidepressants: A review of the evidence. *Psychiatric Times, 26,* 1–6.

Lalonde, J. K., Hudson, J. I., Gigante, R. A., & Pope, H. G., Jr. (2001). Canadian and American psychiatrists' attitudes toward dissociative disorders diagnoses. *Canadian Journal of Psychiatry, 46,* 407–412.

Langer, E. J., & Abelson, R. P. (1974). A patient by any other name . . . . Clinician group difference in labeling bias. *Journal of Consulting and Clinical Psychology, 42,* 4–9.

Langleben, D. D., Loughead, J. W., Bilker, W. B., Ruparel, K., Childress, A. R., Busch, S. I., et al. (2005). Telling truth from lie in individual subjects with fast event-related fMRI. *Human Brain Mapping, 26,* 262–272.

Langlois, J. H., Kalakanis, L., Rubenstein, A. J., Larson, A., Hallam, M., & Smoot, M. (2000). Maxims or myths of beauty? A meta-analytic and theoretical review. *Psychological Bulletin, 126,* 390–423.

Langlois, J. H., Ritter, J. M., Casey, R. J., & Sawin, D. B. (1995). Infant attractiveness predicts maternal behaviors and attitudes. *Developmental Psychology, 31,* 464–472.

Langlois, J. H., & Roggman, L. A. (1990). Attractive faces are only average. *Psychological Science, 1,* 115–121.

Langlois, J. H., Roggman, L. A., & Musselman, L. (1994). What is average and what is not average about attractive faces? *Psychological Science, 5,* 214–220.

Langston, J. W. (1995). *The case of the frozen addicts.* New York: Pantheon.

Lareau, A. (2003). *Unequal childhoods: Class, race, and family life.* Berkeley: University of California Press.

Larsen, S. F. (1992). Potential flashbulbs: Memories of ordinary news as baseline. In E. Winograd & U. Neisser (Eds.), *Affect and accuracy in recall: Studies of "flashbulb memories"* (pp. 32–64). New York: Cambridge University Press.

Larson, R., & Richards, M. H. (1991). Daily companionship in late childhood and early adolescence—changing developmental contexts. *Child Development, 62,* 284–300.

Lashley, K. S. (1960). In search of the engram. In F. A. Beach, D. O. Hebb, C. T. Morgan, & H. W. Nissen (Eds.), *The neuropsychology of Lashley.* New York: McGraw-Hill.

Laupa, M., & Turiel, E. (1986). Children's conceptions of adult and peer authority. *Child Development, 57,* 405–412.

Lavie, P. (2001). Sleep-wake as a biological rhythm. *Annual Review of Psychology, 52,* 277–303.

Lawrence, N. S., Jollant, F., O'Daly, O., Zelaya, F., & Phillips, M. L. (2009). Distinct roles of prefrontal cortical subregions in the Iowa Gambling Task. *Cerebral Cortex, 19,* 1134–1143.

Lawton, M. P., Kleban, M. H., Rajagopal, D., & Dean, J. (1992). The dimensions of affective experience in three age groups. *Psychology and Aging, 7,* 171–184.

Lazarus, R. S. (1984). On the primacy of cognition. *American Psychologist, 39,* 124–129.

Lazarus, R. S., & Folkman, S. (1984). *Stress, appraisal, and coping.* New York: Springer.

Leader, T., Mullen, B., & Abrams, D. (2007). Without mercy: The immediate impact of group size on lynch mob atrocity. *Personality and Social Psychology Bulletin, 33*(10), 1340–1352.

Leary, M. R. (1990). Responses to social exclusion: Social anxiety, jealousy, loneliness, depression, and low self-esteem. *Journal of Social and Clinical Psychology, 9,* 221–229.

Leary, M. R. (2010). Affiliation, acceptance, and belonging: The pursuit of interpersonal connection. In S. T. Fiske, D. T. Gilbert, & G. Lindzey (Eds.), *The handbook of social psychology* (5th ed., Vol. 2). New York: Wiley.

Leary, M. R., & Baumeister, R. F. (2000). The nature and function of self-esteem: Sociometer theory. In M. P. Zanna (Ed.), *Advances in experimental social psychology* (Vol. 32, pp. 1–62). San Diego: Academic Press.

Leary, M. R., Cox, C. B., Shah, J. Y., & Gardner, W. L. (2008). Belongingness motivation: A mainspring of social action. In *Handbook of motivation science* (pp. 27–40). New York: Guilford Press.

Lecky, P. (1945). *Self-consistency: A theory of personality.* New York: Island Press.

Lecrubier, Y., Clerc, G., Didi, R., & Kieser, M. (2002). Efficacy of St. John's wort extract WS 5570 in major depression: A double-blind, placebo-controlled trial. *American Journal of Psychiatry, 159,* 1361–1366.

Lederman, S. J., & Klatzky, R. L. (2009). Haptic perception: A tutorial. *Attention, Perception, & Psychophysics, 71,* 1439–1459.

LeDoux, J. E. (2002). *The synaptic self: How our brains become who we are.* New York: Viking.

LeDoux, J. E., Iwata, J., Cicchetti, P., & Reis, D. J. (1988). Different projections of the central amygdaloid nucleus mediate autonomic and behavioral correlates of conditioned fear. *Journal of Neuroscience, 8,* 2517–2529.

Lee, D. N., & Aronson, E. (1974). Visual proprioceptive control of standing in human infants. *Perception & Psychophysics, 15,* 529–532.

Lee, I., Hunsaker, M. R., & Kesner, R. P. (2005). The role of hippocampal subregions in detecting spatial novelty. *Behavioral Neuroscience, 119,* 145–153.

Lee, L., Loewenstein, G., Ariely, D., Hong, J., & Young, J. (2008). If I'm not hot, are you hot or not? Physical-attractiveness evaluations and dating preferences as a function of one's own attractiveness. *Psychological Science, 19,* 669–677.

Lefcourt, H. M. (1982). *Locus of control: Current trends in theory and research* (2nd ed.). Hillsdale, NJ: Lawrence Erlbaum.

Lefkowitz, E. S., & Zeldow, P. B. (2006). Masculinity and femininity predict optimal mental health: A belated test of the androgyny hypothesis. *Journal of Personality Assessment, 87,* 95–101.

Lempert, D. (2007). *Women's increasing wage penalties from being overweight and obese:* Washington, DC: U.S. Bureau of Labor Statistics.

Lentz, M. J., Landis, C. A., Rothermel, J., & Shaver, J. L. (1999). Effects of selective slow wave sleep disruption on musculoskeletal pain and fatigue in middle-aged women. *Journal of Rheumatology, 26,* 1586–1592.

Leon, D. A., Lawlor, D. A., Clark, H., Batty, G. D., & Macintyre, S. (2009). The association of childhood intelligence with mortality risk from adolescence to middle age: Findings from the Aberdeen children of the 1950s cohort study. *Intelligence, 37*(6), 520–528.

Lepage, M., Ghaffar, O., Nyberg, L., & Tulving, E. (2000). Prefrontal cortex and episodic memory retrieval mode. *Proceedings of the National Academy of Sciences, USA, 97,* 506–511.

Lepper, M. R., Greene, D., & Nisbett, R. E. (1973). Undermining children's intrinsic interest with extrinsic rewards: A test of the "overjustification" hypothesis. *Journal of Personality and Social Psychology, 28,* 129–137.

Lerman, D. (2006). Consumer politeness and complaining behavior. *Journal of Services Marketing, 20,* 92–100.

Levin, R., & Nielsen, T. (2009). Nightmares, bad dreams, and emotion dysregulation: A review and new neurocognitive model of dreaming. *Current Directions in Psychological Science, 18,* 84–88.

Levine, R. V., Norenzayan, A., & Philbrick, K. (2001). Cross-cultural differences in helping strangers. *Journal of Cross-Cultural Psychology, 32,* 543–560.

Lewin, K. (1951). Behavior and development as a function of the total situation. In K. Lewin, *Field theory in social science: Selected theoretical papers* (pp. 791–843). New York: Harper & Row.

Lewis, M., & Brooks-Gunn, J. (1979). *Social cognition and the acquisition of self.* New York: Plenum Press.

Li, F., & Tsien, J. Z. (2009). Memory and the NMDA receptors. *New England Journal of Medicine, 361,* 302–303.

Li, W., & Zinbarg, R. E. (2007). Anxiety sensitivity and panic attacks. *Behavior Modification, 31,* 145–161.

Libet, B. (1985). Unconscious cerebral initiative and the role of conscious will in voluntary action. *Behavioral and Brain Sciences, 8,* 529–566.

Lieberman, M. D., & Rosenthal, R. (2001). Why introverts can't always tell who likes them: Multitasking and nonverbal decoding. *Journal of Personality and Social Psychology, 80,* 294–310.

Lilienfeld, S. O., Lynn, S. J., & Lohr, J. M. (Eds.). (2003). *Science and pseudoscience in clinical psychology.* New York: Guilford Press.

Lindquist, K., & Barrett, L. F. (2008). Constructing emotion: The experience of fear as a conceptual act. *Psychological Science, 19,* 898–903.

Lindstrom, M. (2005). *Brand sense: How to build powerful brands through touch, taste, smell, sight and sound.* London: Kogan Page.

Little, B. R. (1983). Personal projects: A rationale and method for investigation. *Environment and Behavior, 15,* 273–309.

Liu, D., Wellman, H. M., Tardif, T., & Sabbagh, M. A. (2008). Theory of mind development in Chinese children: A meta-analysis of false-belief understanding across cultures and languages. *Developmental Psychology 44,* 523–531.

Livingstone, M., & Hubel, D. (1988). Segregation of form, color, movement, and depth: Anatomy, physiology, and perception. *Science, 240,* 740–749.

Loehlin, J. C. (1992). *Genes and environment in personality development.* Newbury Park, CA: Sage.

Loftus, E. F. (1993). The reality of repressed memories. *American Psychologist, 48,* 518–537.

Loftus, E. F. (2003). Make-believe memories. *American Psychologist, 58,* 867–873.

Loftus, E. F., & Ketchum, K. (1994). *The myth of repressed memory.* New York: St. Martin's Press.

Loftus, E. F., & Pickrell, J. E. (1995). The formation of false memories. *Psychiatric Annals, 25,* 720–725.

Lopes, P. N., Grewal, D., Kadis, J., Gall, M., & Salovey, P. (2006). Emotional intelligence and positive work outcomes. *Psichothema, 18,* 132.

Lorenz, K. (1952). *King Solomon's ring.* New York: Crowell.

Lozano, B. E., & Johnson, S. L. (2001). Can personality traits predict increases in manic and depressive symptoms? *Journal of Affective Disorders, 63,* 103–111.

Luborsky, L., Rosenthal, R., Diguer, L., Andrusyna, T. P., Berman, J. S., Levitt, J. T., et al. (2002). The dodo bird verdict is alive and well—mostly. *Clinical Psychology: Science and Practice, 9,* 2–12.

Luborsky, L., & Singer, B. (1975). Comparative studies of psychotherapies: Is it true that "everyone has won and all must have prizes"? *Archives of General Psychiatry, 32*(8), 995–1008.

Lucas, R. E., Clark, A. E., Georgellis, Y., & Diener, E. (2003). Reexamining adaptation and the set point model of happiness: Reactions to changes in marital status. *Journal of Personality and Social Psychology, 84,* 527–539.

Ludwig, A. M. (1966). Altered states of consciousness. *Archives of General Psychiatry, 15,* 225–234.

Lustman, P. J., Caudle, M. L., & Clouse, R. E. (2002). Case study: Nondysphoric depression in a man with type 2 diabetes. *Clinical Diabetes, 20,* 122–123.

Lykken, D. T. (1995). *The antisocial personalities.* Hillsdale, NJ: Lawrence Erlbaum.

Lykken, D. T., & Tellegen, A. (1996). Happiness is a stochastic phenomenon. *Psychological Science, 7,* 186–189.

Lynn, M., & Shurgot, B. A. (1984). Responses to lonely hearts advertisements: Effects of reported physical attractiveness, physique, and coloration. *Personality and Social Psychology Bulletin, 10,* 349–357.

Lynn, R. (2009). What has caused the Flynn effect? Secular increases in the development quotients of infants. *Intelligence, 37*(1), 16–24.

Lyubomirsky, S. (2008). *The how of happiness: A scientific approach to getting the life you want.* New York: Penguin.

Lyubomirsky, S., & Lepper, H. S. (1999). A measure of subjective happiness: Preliminary reliability and construct validation. *Social Indicators Research, 46,* 137–155.

MacDonald, S., Uesiliana, K., & Hayne, H. (2000). Cross-cultural and gender differences in childhood amnesia. *Memory, 8,* 365–376.

Mack, A. H., Franklin, J. E., Jr., & Frances, R. J. (2003). Substance use disorders. In R. E. Hales & S. C. Yudofsky (Eds.), *The American Psychiatric Publishing textbook of clinical psychiatry* (4th ed., pp. 309–377). Washington, DC: American Psychiatric Publishing.

MacLeod, M. D. (2002). Retrieval-induced forgetting in eyewitness memory: Forgetting as a consequence of remembering. *Applied Cognitive Psychology, 16,* 135–149.

MacLeod, M. D., & Saunders, J. (2008). Retrieval inhibition and memory distortion: Negative consequences of an adaptive process. *Current Directions in Psychological Science, 17,* 26–30.

Macmillan, M. (2000). *An odd kind of fame: Stories of Phineas Gage.* Cambridge, MA: The MIT Press.

Macmillan, N. A., & Creelman, C. D. (2005). *Detection theory.* Mahwah, NJ: Lawrence Erlbaum.

Maddi, S. R., Harvey, R. H., Khoshaba, D. M., Fazel, M., & Resurreccion, N. (2009). Hardiness training facilitates performance in college. *The Journal of Positive Psychology, 4,* 566–577.

Maddi, S. R., Kahn, S., & Maddi, K. L. (1998). The effectiveness of hardiness training. *Consulting Psychology Journal: Practice and Research, 50,* 78–86.

Maes, M. (1995). Evidence for an immune response in major depression: A review and hypothesis. *Progress in Neuro-Psychopharmacology and Biological Psychiatry, 19,* 11–38.

Magee, W. J., Eaton, W. W., Wittchen, H.-U., McGonagle, K. A., & Kessler, R. C. (1996). Agoraphobia, simple phobia, and social phobia in the National Comorbidity Survey. *Archives of General Psychiatry, 53,* 159–168.

Maguire, E. A., Woollett, K., & Spiers, H. J. (2006). London taxi drivers and bus drivers: A structural MRI and neuropsychological analysis. *Hippocampus, 16,* 1091–1101.

Mahon, B. Z., Anzellotti, S., Schwarzbach, J., Zampini, M., & Caramazza, A. (2009). Category-specific organization in the human brain does not require visual experience. *Neuron, 63,* 397–405.

Maier, S. F., & Watkins, L. R. (1998). Cytokines for psychologists: Implications of bidirectional immune-to-brain communication for understanding behavior, mood, and cognition. *Psychological Review, 105,* 83–107.

Maier, S. F., & Watkins, L. R. (2000). The immune system as a sensory system: Implications for psychology. *Current Directions in Psychological Science, 9,* 98–102.

Makin, J. E., Fried, P. A., & Watkinson, B. (1991). A comparison of active and passive smoking during pregnancy: Long-term effects. *Neurotoxicology and Teratology, 16,* 5–12.

Maldonado, J. R., & Butler, L. D. (1998). *Treatments for dissociative disorders.* New York: Oxford University Press.

Malina, R. M., Bouchard, C., & Beunen, G. (1988). Human growth: Selected aspects of current research on well-nourished children. *Annual Review of Anthropology, 17,* 187–219.

Mandle, C. L., Jacobs, S. C., Arcari, P. M., & Domar, A. D. (1996). The efficacy of relaxation response interventions with adult patients: A review of the literature. *Journal of Cardiovascular Nursing, 10,* 4–26.

Mandler, G. (1967). Organization and memory. In K. W. Spence & J. T. Spence (Eds.), *The psychology of learning and motivation* (Vol. 1, pp. 327–372). New York: Academic Press.

Mankiw, N. G., & Weinzierl, M. (2010). The optimal taxation of height: A case study of utilitarian income redistribution. *American Economic Journal: Economic Policy, 2,* 155–176.

Marangell, L. B., Silver, J. M., Goff, D. M., & Yudofsky, S. C. (2003). Psychopharmacology and electroconvulsive therapy. In R. E. Hales & S. C. Yudofsky (Eds.), *The American Psychiatric Publishing textbook of clinical psychiatry* (4th ed., pp. 1047–1149). Washington, DC: American Psychiatric Publishing.

Markus, H. (1977). Self-schemata and processing information about the self. *Journal of Personality and Social Psychology, 35,* 63–78.

Marlatt, G. A., & Rohsenow, D. (1980). Cognitive processes in alcohol use: Expectancy and the balanced placebo design. In N. K. Mello (Ed.), *Advances in substance abuse: Behavioral and biological research* (pp. 159–199). Greenwich, CT: JAI Press.

Martin, A. (2007). The representation of object concepts in the brain. *Annual Review of Psychology, 58,* 25–45.

Martin, A., & Caramazza, A. (2003). Neuropsychological and neuroimaging perspectives on conceptual knowledge: An introduction. *Cognitive Neuropsychology, 20,* 195–212.

Martin, A., & Chao, L. L. (2001). Semantic memory and the brain: Structure and processes. *Current Opinion in Neurobiology, 11,* 194–201.

Marucha, P. T., Kiecolt-Glaser, J. K., & Favagehi, M. (1998). Mucosal wound healing is impaired by examination stress. *Psychosomatic Medicine, 60,* 362–365.

Masand, P. S., & Gupta, S. (2002). Long-term side effects of newer-generation antidepressants: SSRIs, venlafaxine, nefazodone, bupropion, and mirtazipine. *Annals of Clinical Psychiatry, 14,* 175–182.

Maslach, C. (2003). Job burnout: New directions in research and intervention. *Current Directions in Psychological Science, 12,* 189–192.

Maslow, A. H. (1937). Dominance-feeling, behavior, and status. In R. J. Lowry (Ed.), *Dominance, self-esteem, self-actualization: Germinal papers by A. H. Maslow.* Monterey, CA: Brooks-Cole.

Maslow, A. H. (1954). *Motivation and personality.* New York: Harper & Row.

Maslow, A. H. (1970). *Motivation and personality* (2nd ed.). New York: Harper & Row.

Masserman, J. H. (1961). *Principles of dynamic psychiatry* (2nd ed.). Philadelphia: W. B. Saunders.

Mather, M., Canli, T., English, T., Whitfield, S., Wais, P., Ochsner, K., et al. (2004). Amygdala responses to emotionally valenced stimuli in older and younger adults. *Psychological Science, 15,* 259–263.

Mather, M., & Carstensen, L. L. (2003). Aging and attentional biases for emotional faces. *Psychological Science, 14,* 409–415.

Mather, M., & Carstensen, L. L. (2005). Aging and motivated cognition: The positivity effect in attention and memory. *Trends in Cognitive Sciences, 9*(10), 496–502.

Mathis, J. L. (1964). A sophisticated version of voodoo death. *Psychosomatic Medicine, 26,* 104–107.

Matsumoto, D., & Willingham, B. (2009). Spontaneous facial expressions of emotion of congenitally and noncongenitally blind individuals. *Journal of Personality and Social Psychology, 96,* 1–10.

Mattar, A. A. G., & Gribble, P. L. (2005). Motor learning by observing. *Neuron, 46,* 153–160.

Matthews, G., & Gilliland, K. (1999). The personality theories of H. J. Eysenck and J. A. Gray: A comparative review. *Personality and Individual Differences, 26,* 583–626.

Mattingly, J. B. (2009). Attention, automaticity, and awareness in synesthesia. *Annals of the New York Academy of Sciences, 1156,* 141–167.

May, R. (1983). *The discovery of being: Writings in existential psychology.* New York: Norton.

Mayberg, H., Lozano, A., Voon, V., McNeely, H., Seminowicz, D., Hamani, C., et al. (2005). Deep brain stimulation for treatment-resistant depresssion. *Neuron, 45,* 651–660.

Mayer, J. D., Caruso, D. R., & Salovey, P. (1999). Emotional intelligence meets traditional standards for an intelligence. *Intelligence, 27,* 267.

Mayer, J. D., Roberts, R. D., & Barsade, S. G. (2008). Human abilities: Emotional intelligence. *Annual Review of Psychology, 59,* 507–536.

McAdams, D. (1993). *The stories we live by: Personal myths and the making of the self.* New York: Morrow.

McCann, I. L., & Holmes, D. S. (1984). Influence of aerobic exercise on depression. *Journal of Personality and Social Psychology, 46,* 1142–1147.

McClelland, D. C., Atkinson, J. W., Clark, R. A., & Lowell, E. L. (1953). *The achievement motive.* New York: Appleton-Century-Crofts.

McClure, S. M., Li, J., Tomlin, D., Cypert, K. S., Montague, L. M., & Montague, P. R. (2004). Neural correlates of behavioral preference for culturally familiar drinks. *Neuron, 44,* 379–387.

McConkey, K. M., Barnier, A. J., & Sheehan, P. W. (1998). Hypnosis and pseudomemory: Understanding the findings and their implications. In S. J. Lynn & K. M. McConkey (Eds.), *Truth in memory* (pp. 227–259). New York: Guilford Press.

McCrae, R. R., & Costa, P. T. (1990). *Personality in adulthood.* New York: Guilford Press.

McCrae, R. R., & Costa, P. T. (1999). A five-factor theory of personality. In L. A. Pervin & O. P. John (Eds.), *Handbook of personality: Theory and research.* New York: Guilford Press.

McEvoy, S. P., Stevenson, M. R., McCartt, A. T., Woodward, M., Haworth, C., Palamara, P., et al. (2005). Role of mobile phones in motor vehicle crashes resulting in hospital attendance: A case-crossover study. *British Medical Journal, 331,* 428–430.

McFall, R. M., & Treat, T. A. (1999). Quantifying the information value of clinical assessments with signal detection theory. *Annual Review of Psychology, 50,* 215–241.

McFarlane, A. H., Norman, G. R., Streiner, D. L., Roy, R., & Scott, D. J. (1980). A longitudinal study of the influence of the psychosocial environment on health status: A preliminary report. *Journal of Health and Social Behavior, 21,* 124–133.

McGaugh, J. L. (2000). Memory: A century of consolidation. *Science, 287,* 248–251.

McGlinchey-Berroth, R., Carrillo, M. C., Gabrieli, J. D., Brawn, C. M., & Disterhoft, J. F. (1997). Impaired trace eyeblink conditioning in bilateral, medial-temporal lobe amnesia. *Behavioral Neuroscience, 111,* 873–882.

McGrath, J., Saha, S., Chant, D., & Welham, J. (2008). Schizophrenia: A concise overview of incidence, prevalence, and mortality. *Epidemiologic Reviews, 30,* 67–76.

McGue, M., & Bouchard, T. J. (1998). Genetic and environmental influences on human behavioral differences. *Annual Review of Neuroscience, 21,* 1–24.

McKetin, R., McLaren, J., Lubman, D. I., & Hides, L. (2006). The prevalence of psychotic symptoms among methamphetamine users. *Addiction, 101,* 1473–1478.

McKetin, R., Ward, P. B., Catts, S. V., Mattick, R. P., & Bell, J. R. (1999). Changes in auditory selective attention and event-related potentials following oral administration of D-amphetamine in humans. *Neuropsychopharmacology, 21,* 380–390.

McKinney, C. H., Antoni, M. H., Kumar, M., Tims, F. C., & McCabe, P. M. (1997). Effects of guided imagery and music (GIM) therapy on mood and cortisol in healthy adults. *Health Psychology, 16,* 390–400.

McLean, K. C. (2008). The emergence of narrative identity. *Social and Personality Psychology Compass, 2*(4), 1685–1702.

McNally, R. J. (2003). *Remembering trauma.* Cambridge, MA: Belknap Press of Harvard University Press.

McNally, R. J., & Steketee, G. S. (1985). Etiology and maintenance of severe animal phobias. *Behavioral Research and Therapy, 23,* 431–435.

McWilliams, N. (1994). *Psychoanalytic diagnosis: Understanding personality structure in the clinical process.* New York: Guilford Press.

McWilliams, P. (1993). *Ain't nobody's business if you do: The absurdity of consensual crimes in a free society.* Los Angeles: Prelude Press.

Mead, G. H. (1934). *Mind, self, and society.* Chicago: University of Chicago Press.

Mead, M. (1968). *Sex and temperament in three primitive societies.* New York: Dell. (Original work published 1935)

Mechelli, A., Crinion, J. T., Noppeney, U., O'Doherty, J., Ashburner, J., Frackowiak, R. S., et al. (2004). Neurolinguistics: Structural plasticity in the bilingual brain. *Nature, 431,* 757.

Mecklenburg, S. H., Bailey, P. J., & Larsen, M. R. (2008). The Illinois field study: A significant contribution to understanding real world witness identification issues. *Law and Human Behavior, 32,* 22–27.

Medin, D. L., & Schaffer, M. M. (1978). Context theory of classification learning. *Psychological Review, 85,* 207–238.

Medvec, V. H., Madey, S. F., & Gilovich, T. (1995). When less is more: Counterfactual thinking and satisfaction among Olympic medalists. *Journal of Personality and Social Psychology, 69,* 603–610.

Meeren, H. K. M., van Heijnsbergen, C. C. R. J., & de Gelder, B. (2005). Rapid perceptual integration of facial expression and emotional body language. *Proceedings of the National Academy of Sciences, USA, 102*(45), 16518–16523.

Mehl, M. R., Vazire, S., Ramirez-Esparza, N., Slatcher, R. B., & Pennebaker, J. W. (2009). Are women really more talkative than men? *Science, 317,* 82.

Mellon, R. C. (2009). Superstitious perception: Response-independent reinforcement and punishment as determinants of recurring eccentric interpretations. *Behaviour Research and Therapy, 47,* 868–875.

Meltzoff, A. N. (1995). Understanding the intentions of others: Reenactment of intended acts by 18-month-old children. *Developmental Psychology, 31,* 838–850.

Meltzoff, A. N., Kuhl, P. K., Movellan, J., & Sejnowski, T. J. (2009). Foundations for a new science of learning. *Science, 325,* 284–288.

Meltzoff, A. N., & Moore, M. K. (1977). Imitation of facial and manual gestures by human neonates. *Science, 198,* 75–78.

Melzack, R., & Wall, P. D. (1965). Pain mechanisms: A new theory. *Science, 150,* 971–979.

Mendle, J., Turkheimer, E., & Emery, R. E. (2007). Detrimental psychological outcomes associated with early pubertal timing in adolescent girls. *Developmental Review, 27,* 151–171.

Mennella, J. A., Johnson, A., & Beauchamp, G. K. (1995). Garlic ingestion by pregnant women alters the odor of amniotic fluid. *Chemical Senses, 20,* 207–209.

Mervis, C. B., & Bertrand, J. (1994). Acquisition of the "Novel Name" Nameless Category (N3C) principle. *Child Development, 65,* 1646–1662.

Messick, D. M., & Cook, K. S. (1983). *Equity theory: Psychological and sociological perspectives.* New York: Praeger.

Meston, C. M., & Buss, D. M. (2007). Why humans have sex. *Archives of Sexual Behavior, 36,* 477–507.

Mestre, J. M., Guil, R., Lopes, P. N., Salovey, P., & Gil-Olarte, P. (2006). Emotional intelligence and social and academic adaptation to school. *Psicothema, 18,* 112.

Metcalfe, J. (2009). Metacognitive judgments and control of study. *Current Directions in Psychological Science, 18,* 159–163.

Metcalfe, J., & Finn, B. (2008). Evidence that judgments of learning are causally related to study choice. *Psychonomic Bulletin & Review, 15,* 174–179.

Michelson, D., Pollack, M., Lydiard, R. D., Tamura, R., Tepner, R., & Tollefson, G. (1999). Continuing treatment of panic disorder after acute responses: Randomized, placebo-controlled trial with fluoxetine. The Fluoxitine Panic Disorder Study Group. *British Journal of Psychiatry, 174,* 213–218.

Michotte, A. (1963). *The perception of causality.* New York: Basic Books.

Miklowitz, D. J., Goldstein, M. J., Nuechterlein, K. H., Snyder, K. S., & Mintz, J. (1988). Family factors and the course of bipolar affective disorder. *Archives of General Psychiatry, 45,* 225–231.

Milgram, S. (1963). Behavioral study of obedience. *Journal of Abnormal and Social Psychology, 67,* 371–378.

Milgram, S., Bickman, L., & Berkowitz, O. (1969). Note on the drawing power of crowds of different size. *Journal of Personality and Social Psychology, 13,* 79–82.

Miller, D. T., & Prentice, D. A. (1996). The construction of social norms and standards. In E. T. Higgins & A. W. Kruglanski (Ed.), *Social psychology: Handbook of basic principles* (pp. 799–829). New York: Guilford Press.

Miller, D. T., & Ratner, R. K. (1998). The disparity between the actual and assumed power of self-interest. *Journal of Personality and Social Psychology, 74,* 53–62.

Miller, G. A. (1956). The magical number seven, plus or minus two: Some limits on our capacity for processing information. *Psychological Review, 63,* 81–96.

Miller, K. F., Smith, C. M., & Zhu, J. (1995). Preschool origins of cross-national differences in mathematical competence: The role of number-naming systems. *Psychological Science, 6,* 56–60.

Miller, N. E. (1960). Motivational effects of brain stimulation and drugs. *Federation Proceedings, 19,* 846–854.

Miller, T. W. (Ed.). (1996). *Theory and assessment of stressful life events.* Madison, CT: International Universities Press.

Milne, E., & Grafman, J. (2001). Ventromedial prefrontal cortex lesions in humans eliminate implicit gender stereotyping. *Journal of Neuroscience, 21,* 1–6.

Milner, A. D., & Goodale, M. A. (1995). *The visual brain in action.* Oxford, England: Oxford University Press.

Milner, B. (1962). Laterality effects in audition. In V. B. Mountcastle (Ed.), *Interhemispheric relations and cerebral dominance* (pp. 177–195). Baltimore: Johns Hopkins University Press.

Mingroni, M. A. (2007). Resolving the IQ paradox: Heterosis as a cause of the Flynn effect and other trends. *Psychological Review, 114,* 806–829.

Minsky, M. (1986). *The society of mind.* New York: Simon & Schuster.

Mischel, W. (1968). *Personality and assessment.* New York: Wiley.

Mischel, W. (2004). Toward an integrative science of the person. *Annual Review of Psychology, 55,* 1–22.

Mischel, W., Ayduk, O., Baumeister, R. F., & Vohs, K. D. (2004). Willpower in a cognitive-affective processing system: The dynamics of delay of gratification. In *Handbook of self-regulation: Research, theory, and applications* (pp. 99–129). New York: Guilford Press.

Mischel, W., & Shoda, Y. (1999). Integrating dispositions and processing dynamics within a unified theory of personality: The cognitive-affective personality system. In L. A. Pervin & O. P. John (Eds.), *Handbook of personality: Theory and research.* New York: Guilford Press.

Mischel, W., Shoda, Y., & Rodriguez, M. L. (1989). Delay of gratification in children. *Science, 244,* 933–938.

Mitchell, D. B. (2006). Nonconscious priming after 17 years. *Psychological Science, 17,* 925–929.

Mitchell, J. P. (2006). Mentalizing and Marr: An information processing approach to the study of social cognition. *Brain Research, 1079,* 66–75.

Mitchell, K. J., & Johnson, M. K. (2009). Source monitoring 15 years later: What have we learned from fMRI about the neural mechanisms of source memory? *Psychological Bulletin, 135,* 638–677.

Miura, I. T., Okamoto, Y., Kim, C. C., & Chang, C. M. (1994). Comparisons of children's cognitive representation of number: China, France, Japan, Korea, Sweden and the United States. *International Journal of Behavioral Development, 17,* 401–411.

Moffitt, T. E. (1993). Adolescence-limited and life-course-persistent antisocial behavior: A developmental taxonomy. *Psychological Review, 100,* 674–701.

Molden, D., Lee, A. Y., & Higgins, E. T. (2009). Motivations for promotion and prevention. In J. Shah & W. Gardner (Eds.), *Handbook of motivation science* (pp. 169–187). New York: Guilford Press.

Monroe, S. M., & Reid, M. W. (2009). Life stress and major depression. *Current Directions in Psychological Science, 18,* 68–72.

Montague, C. T., Farooqi, I. S., Whitehead, J. P., Soos, M. A., Rau, H., Wareham, N. J., et al. (1997). Congenital leptin deficiency is associated with severe early-onset obesity in humans. *Nature, 387*(6636), 903–908.

Mook, D. G. (1983). In defense of external invalidity. *American Psychologist, 38,* 379–387.

Moore, D. W. (2003). Public lukewarm on animal rights. Retrieved June 22, 2010, from http://www.gallup.com/poll/8461/publiclukewarm-animal-rights.aspx

Morewedge, C. K., & Norton, M. I. (2009). When dreaming is believing: The (motivated) interpretation of dreams. *Journal of Personality and Social Psychology, 96,* 249–264.

Morgan, H. (1990). Dostoevsky's epilepsy: A case report and comparison. *Surgical Neurology, 33,* 413–416.

Morgenstern, J., Labouvie, E., McCrady, B. S., Kahler, C. W., & Frey, R. M. (1997). Affiliation with Alcoholics Anonymous after treatment: A study of its therapeutic effects and mechanisms of action. *Journal of Consulting and Clinical Psychology, 65,* 768–777.

Morin, A. (2005). Levels of consciousness and self-awareness: A comparison of various neurocognitive views. *Consciousness & Cognition, 15,* 358–371.

Morris, C. D., Bransford, J. D., & Franks, J. J. (1977). Levels of processing versus transfer-appropriate processing. *Journal of Verbal Learning and Verbal Behavior, 16,* 519–533.

Morris, R. G., Anderson, E., Lynch, G. S., & Baudry, M. (1986). Selective impairment of learning and blockade of long-term potentiation by an N-methyl-D-aspartate receptor antagonist, AP5. *Nature, 319,* 774–776.

Morrow, D., Leirer, V., Altiteri, P., & Fitzsimmons, C. (1994). When expertise reduces age differences in performance. *Psychology and Aging, 9,* 134–148.

Moruzzi, G., & Magoun, H. W. (1949). Brain stem reticular formation and activation of the EEG. *Electroencephalography and Clinical Neurophysiology, 1,* 455–473.

Moscovitch, M. (1994). Memory and working-with-memory: Evaluation of a component process model and comparisons with other models. In D. L. Schacter & E. Tulving (Eds.), *Memory systems 1994* (pp. 269–310). Cambridge, MA: The MIT Press.

Moscovitch, M., Nadel, L., Winocur, G., Gilboa, A., & Rosenbaum, R. S. (2006). The cognitive neuroscience of remote episodic, semantic and spatial memory. *Current Opinion in Neurobiology, 16,* 179–190.

Moulin, C. J. A., Conway, M. A., Thompson, R. G., James, N., & Jones, R. W. (2005). Disordered memory awareness: Recollective confabulation in two cases of persistent déjà vecu. *Neuropsychologia, 43,* 1362–1378.

Moura, A. C. A. de, & Lee, P. C. (2004). Capuchin stone tool use in Caatinga dry forest. *Science, 306,* 1909.

Mueller, T. E., Gavin, L. E., & Kulkarni, A. (2008). The association between sex education and youth's engagement in sexual intercourse, age at first intercourse, and birth control use at first sex. *The Journal of Adolescent Health, 42*(1), 89–96.

Mueller, T. I., Leon, A. C., Keller, M. B., Solomon, D. A., Endicott, J., Coryell, W., et al. (1999). Recurrence after recovery from major depressive disorder during 15 years of observational follow-up. *American Journal of Psychiatry, 156,* 1000–1006.

Muenter, M. D., & Tyce, G. M. (1971). L-dopa therapy of Parkinson's disease: Plasma L-dopa concentration, therapeutic response, and side effects. *Mayo Clinic Proceedings, 46,* 231–239.

Mukherjee, S., Sackeim, H. A., & Schnur, D. B. (1994). Electroconvulsive therapy of acute manic episodes: A review of 50 years' experience. *American Journal of Psychiatry, 151,* 169–176.

Mullen, M. K. (1994). Earliest recollections of childhood: A demographic analysis. *Cognition, 52,* 55–79.

Multhaup, K. S., Johnson, M. D., & Tetirick, J. C. (2005). The wane of childhood amnesia for autobiographical and public event memories. *Memory, 13,* 161–173.

Murphy, N. A., Hall, J. A., & Colvin, C. R. (2003). Accurate intelligence assessments in social interactions: Mediators and gender effects. *Journal of Personality, 71,* 465–493.

Murray, H. A. (1943). *Thematic Apperception Test manual.* Cambridge, MA: Harvard University Press.

Murray, H. A., & Kluckhohn, C. (1953). Outline of a conception of personality. In C. Kluckhohn, H. A. Murray, & D. M. Schneider (Eds.),

Personality in nature, society, and culture (2nd ed., pp. 3–52). New York: Knopf.

Myers, D. G., & Diener, E. (1995). Who is happy? *Psychological Science, 6,* 10–19.

Nadasdy, A. (1995). Phonetics, phonology, and applied linguistics. *Annual Review of Applied Linguistics, 15,* 68–77.

Nader, K., & Hardt, O. (2009). A single standard for memory: The case of reconsolidation. *Nature Reviews Neuroscience, 10,* 224–234.

Nader, K., Shafe, G., & LeDoux, J. E. (2000). Fear memories require protein synthesis in the amygdala for reconsolidation after retrieval. *Nature, 406,* 722–726.

Nagasako, E. M., Oaklander, A. L., & Dworkin, R. H. (2003). Congenital insensitivity to pain: An update. *Pain, 101,* 213–219.

Nagell, K., Olguin, R. S., & Tomasello, M. (1993). Processes of social learning in the tool use of chimpanzees (*Pan troglodytes*) and human children (*Homo sapiens*). *Journal of Comparative Psychology, 107,* 174–186.

Nahemow, L., & Lawton, M. P. (1975). Similarity and propinquity in friendship formation. *Journal of Personality and Social Psychology, 32,* 205–213.

Nairne, J. S., & Pandeirada, J. N. S. (2008). Adaptive memory: Remembering with a Stone Age brain. *Current Directions in Psychological Science, 17,* 239–243.

Nairne, J. S., Thompson, S. R., & Pandeirada, J. N. S. (2007). Adaptive memory: Survival processing enhances retention. *Journal of Experimental Psychology: Learning, Memory, & Cognition, 33,* 263–273.

Nakazato, M., Murakami, N., Date, Y., Kojima, M., Matsuo, H., Kangawa, K., et al. (2001). A role for ghrelin in the central regulation of feeding. *Nature, 409,* 194–198.

Naqvi, N., Shiv, B., & Bechara, A. (2006). The role of emotion in decision making: A cognitive neuroscience perspective. *Current Directions in Psychological Science, 15,* 260–264.

Narrow, W. E., Rae, D. S., Robins, L. N., & Regier, D. A. (2002). Revised prevalence estimates of mental disorders in the United States: Using a clinical significance criterion to reconcile 2 surveys' estimates. *Archives of General Psychiatry, 59,* 115–123.

Nathan, P. E., & Gorman, J. M. (2007). *A guide to treatments that work* (3rd ed.). New York: Oxford University Press.

Nathanson, C., Paulhus, D. L., & Williams, K. M. (2006). Personality and misconduct correlates of body modification and other cultural deviance markers. *Journal of Research in Personality, 40,* 779–802.

National Center for Health Statistics. (2004). *Health, United States, 2004, with chartbook on trends in the health of Americans.* Hyattsville, MD: Author.

National Center for Health Statistics. (2008). *Health, United States.* Retrieved January 25, 2010, from http://www.cdc.gov/nchs/hus.htm

National Institute of Mental Health. (2003). *In harm's way* (NIH Publication No. 03-4594). Washington, DC: National Institutes of Health, U.S. Department of Health and Human Services.

National Research Council. (2003). *The polygraph and lie detection.* Washington, DC: National Academies Press.

National Science Board. (2008). *Science and engineering indicators 2008.* Two volumes. Arlington, VA: National Science Foundation (Vol. 1, NSB 08-01; Vol. 2, NSB 08-01A).

Naumann, L. P., Vazire, S., Rentfrow, P. J., & Gosling, S. D. (2009). Personality judgments based on physical appearance. *Personality & Social Psychology Bulletin, 35,* 1661–1671.

Neimeyer, R. A., & Mitchell, K. A. (1988). Similarity and attraction: A longitudinal study. *Journal of Social and Personal Relationships, 5,* 131–148.

Neisser, U. (Ed.). (1998). *The rising curve: Long-term gains in IQ and related measures.* Washington, DC: American Psychological Association.

Neisser, U., & Becklen, R. (1975). Selective looking: Attending to visually significant events. *Cognitive Psychology, 7,* 480–494.

Neisser, U., Boodoo, G., Bouchard, T. J., Jr., Boykin, A. W., Brody, N., Ceci, S. J., et al. (1996). Intelligence: Knowns and unknowns. *American Psychologist, 51,* 77–101.

Neisser, U., & Harsch, N. (1992). Phantom flashbulbs: False recollections of hearing the news about *Challenger*. In E. Winograd & U. Neisser (Eds.), *Affect and accuracy in recall: Studies of "flashbulb memories"* (pp. 9–31). Cambridge, England: Cambridge University Press.

Nemeth, C., & Chiles, C. (1988). Modelling courage: The role of dissent in fostering independence. *European Journal of Social Psychology, 18,* 275–280.

Netherlands Ministry of Justice. (1999). Fact sheet: Dutch drugs policy. Utrecht: Trimbos Institute, Netherlands Institute of Mental Health and Addiction.

Neugebauer, R., Hoek, H. W., & Susser, E. (1999). Prenatal exposure to wartime famine and development of antisocial personality in early adulthood. *Journal of the American Medical Association, 282,* 455–462.

Newberg, A., Alavi, A., Baime, M., Pourdehnad, M., Santanna, J., & d'Aquili, E. (2001). The measurement of regional cerebral blood flow during the complex cognitive task of meditation: A preliminary SPECT study. *Psychiatry Research: Neuroimaging, 106,* 113–122.

Newell, A., Shaw, J. C., & Simon, H. A. (1958). Elements of a theory of human problem solving. *Psychological Review, 65,* 151–166.

Newman, L. S., Baumeister, R. F., & Duff, K. J. (1995). A new look at defensive projection: Thought suppression, accessibility, and biased person perception. *Journal of Personality and Social Psychology, 72,* 980–1001.

Newman, M. G., & Stone, A. A. (1996). Does humor moderate the effects of experimentally induced stress? *Annals of Behavioral Medicine, 18,* 101–109.

Newsome, W. T., & Paré, E. B. (1988). A selective impairment of motion perception following lesions of the middle temporal visual area (MT). *Journal of Neuroscience, 8,* 2201–2211.

Niaura, R., Todaro, J. F., Stroud, L., Spiro, A., III, Ward, K. D., Weiss, S., et al. (2002). Hostility, the metabolic syndrome, and incident coronary heart disease. *Health Psychology, 21,* 588–593.

Nicoladis, E., & Genesee, F. (1997). Language development in preschool bilingual children. *Journal of Speech-Language Pathology & Audiology, 21,* 258–270.

Nikles, C. D., II, Brecht, D. L., Klinger, E., & Bursell, A. L. (1998). The effects of current concern- and nonconcern-related waking suggestions on nocturnal dream content. *Journal of Personality and Social Psychology, 75,* 242–255.

Nisbett, R. E. (2009). *Intelligence and how to get it.* New York: Norton.

Nisbett, R. E., Caputo, C., Legant, P., & Maracek, J. (1973). Behavior as seen by the actor and as seen by the observer. *Journal of Personality and Social Psychology, 27,* 154–164.

Nisbett, R. E., & Cohen, D. (1996). *Culture of honor: The psychology of violence in the South.* Boulder, CO: Westview Press.

Nishino, S., Mignot, E., & Dement, W. C. (1995). Sedative-hypnotics. In A. F. Schatzberg & C. B. Nemeroff (Eds.), *American*

Psychiatric Press textbook of psychopharmacology (pp. 405–416). Washington, DC: American Psychiatric Press.

Nissen, M. J., & Bullemer, P. (1987). Attentional requirements of learning: Evidence from performance measures. *Cognitive Psychology, 19,* 1–32.

Norcross, J. C., Hedges, M., & Castle, P. H. (2002). Psychologists conducting psychotherapy in 2001: A study of the Division 29 membership. *Psychotherapy: Theory/Research/Practice/Training, 39,* 97–102.

Norrholm, S. D., & Ressler, K. J. (2009). Genetics of anxiety and trauma-related disorders. *Neuroscience, 164,* 272–287.

North, R. J., & Swann, W. B., Jr. (2009). Self-verification 360°: Illuminating the light and dark sides. *Self and Identity, 8*(2–3), 131–146.

Nosanchuk, T. A., & Lightstone, J. (1974). Canned laughter and public and private conformity. *Journal of Personality and Social Psychology, 29,* 153–156.

Nowak, M. A. (2006). Five rules for the evolution of cooperation. *Science, 314,* 1560–1563.

Nunn, J. A., Gregory, L. J., & Brammer, M. (2002). Functional magnetic resonance imaging of synesthesia: Activation of V4/V8 by spoken words. *Nature Neuroscience, 5,* 371–375.

Nuttin, J. M. (1985). Narcissism beyond Gestalt and awareness: The name letter effect. *European Journal of Social Psychology, 15,* 353–361.

Nyborg, H., & Jensen, A. R. (2001). Occupation and income related to psychometric g. *Intelligence, 29,* 45–55.

Oakes, L. M., & Cohen, L. B. (1990). Infant perception of a causal event. *Cognitive Development, 5,* 193–207.

Ochsner, K. N. (2000). Are affective events richly recollected or simply familiar? The experience and process of recognizing feelings past. *Journal of Experimental Psychology: General, 129,* 242–261.

Ochsner, K. N., Bunge, S. A., Gross, J. J., & Gabrieli, J. D. E. (2002). Rethinking feelings: An fMRI study of the cognitive regulation of emotion. *Journal of Cognitive Neuroscience, 14,* 1215–1229.

Ochsner, K. N., Ray, R. R., Hughes, B., McRae, K., Cooper, J. C., Weber, J., et al. (2009). Bottom-up and top-down processes in emotion generation: Common and distinct neural mechanisms. *Psychological Science, 20,* 1322–1331.

Ofshe, R. J. (1992). Inadvertent hypnosis during interrogation: False confession due to dissociative state, misidentified multiple personality, and the satanic cult hypothesis. *International Journal of Clinical and Experimental Hypnosis, 40,* 125–126.

Ofshe, R., & Watters, E. (1994). *Making monsters: False memories, psychotherapy, and sexual hysteria.* New York: Scribner/Macmillan.

Öhman, A. (1996). Preferential preattentive processing of threat in anxiety: Preparedness and attentional biases. In R. M. Rapee (Ed.), *Current controversies in the anxiety disorders.* New York: Guilford Press.

Öhman, A., Dimberg, U., & Öst, L. G. (1985). Animal and social phobias: Biological constraints on learned fear responses. In S. Reiss & R. Bootzin (Eds.), *Theoretical issues in behavior therapy* (pp. 123–175). New York: Academic Press.

Okagaki, L., & Sternberg, R. J. (1993). Parental beliefs and children's school performance. *Child Development, 64,* 36–56.

Okuda, J., Fujii, T., Ohtake, H., Tsukiura, T., Tanji, K., Suzuki, K., Kawashima, R., Fukuda, H., Itoh, M., & Yamadori, A. (2003). Thinking of the future and the past: The roles of the frontal pole and the medial temporal lobes. *Neuroimage, 19,* 1369–1380.

Okulicz-Kozaryn, A. (2011). Europeans work to live and Americans live to work (who is happy to work more: Americans or Europeans?). *Journal of Happiness Studies, 12*(2), 225–243.

O'Laughlin, M. J., & Malle, B. F. (2002). How people explain actions performed by groups and individuals. *Journal of Personality and Social Psychology, 82,* 33–48.

Olausson, P. O., Haglund, B., Weitoft, G. R., & Cnattingius, S. (2001). Teenage child-bearing and long-term socioeconomic consequences: A case study in Sweden. *Family Planning Perspectives, 33,* 70–74.

Oldham, J. M., Skodol, A. E., & Bender, D. S. (2005). *The American Psychiatric Publishing textbook of personality disorders.* Washington, DC: American Psychiatric Publishing.

Olds, J. (1956, October). Pleasure center in the brain. *Scientific American, 195,* 105–116.

Olds, J., & Fobes, J. I. (1981). The central basis of motivation: Intracranial self-stimulation studies. *Annual Review of Psychology, 32,* 523–574.

Ollers, D. K., & Eilers, R. E. (1988). The role of audition in infant babbling. *Child Development, 59,* 441–449.

Olsson, A., & Phelps, E. A. (2007). Social learning of fear. *Nature Neuroscience, 10,* 1095–1102.

Oltmanns, T. F., Neale, J. M., & Davison, G. C. (1991). *Case studies in abnormal psychology* (3rd ed.). New York: Wiley.

Oltmanns, T. F., & Turkheimer, E. (2006). Perceptions of self and others regarding pathological personality traits. In R. Kreuger & J. Tackett (Eds.), *Personality and psychopathology* (pp. 71–111). New York: Guilford Press.

Olton, D. S., & Samuelson, R. J. (1976). Remembrance of places passed: Spatial memory in rats. *Journal of Experimental Psychology: Animal Behavior Processes, 2,* 97–116.

Ono, K. (1987). Superstitious behavior in humans. *Journal of the Experimental Analysis of Behavior, 47,* 261–271.

Ophir, E., Nass, C., & Wagner, A. D. (2009). Cognitive control in media multitaskers. *Proceedings of the National Academy of Sciences, USA, 106,* 15583–15587.

Oppenheimer, M. (2008, May 4). The queen of the new age. *New York Times.*

Orban, G. A., Van Essen, D., & Vanduffel, W. (2004). Comparative mapping of higher visual areas in monkeys and humans. *Trends in Cognitive Sciences, 8,* 315–324.

Orban, P., Lungu, O., & Doyon, J. (2008). Motor sequence learning and developmental dyslexia. *Annals of the New York Academy of Sciences, 1145,* 151–172.

O'Sullivan, L. F., & Allegeier, E. R. (1998). Feigning sexual desire: Consenting to unwanted sexual activity in heterosexual dating relationships. *Journal of Sex Research, 35,* 234–243.

Owens, W. A. (1966). Age and mental abilities: A second adult follow-up. *Journal of Educational Psychology, 57,* 311–325.

Oztekin, I., Curtis, C. E., & McElree, B. (2009). The medial temporal lobe and left inferior prefrontal cortex jointly support interference resolution in verbal working memory. *Journal of Cognitive Neuroscience, 21,* 1967–1979.

Pagnin, D., de Queiroz, V., Pini, S., & Cassano, G. B. (2008). Efficacy of ECT in depression: A meta-analytic review. *Focus, 6,* 155–162.

Paivio, A. (1971). *Imagery and verbal processes.* New York: Holt, Rinehart and Winston.

Paivio, A. (1986). *Mental representations: A dual coding approach.* New York: Oxford University Press.

Palmeri, T. J., Blake, R. B., Marois, R., Flanery, M. A., & Whetsell, W. O. (2002). The perceptual reality of synesthetic color. *Proceedings of the National Academy of Sciences, 99,* 4127–4131.

Parker, E. S., Cahill, L. S., & McGaugh, J. L. (2006). A case of unusual autobiographical remembering. *Neurocase, 12,* 35–49.

Parker, H. A., & McNally, R. J. (2008). Repressive coping, emotional adjustment, and cognition in people who have lost loved ones to suicide. *Suicide and Life-Threatening Behavior, 38,* 676–687.

Parkinson, B., & Totterdell, P. (1999). Classifying affect-regulation strategies. *Cognition and Emotion, 13,* 277–303.

Parrott, A. C. (2001). Human psychopharmacology of ecstasy (MDMA): A review of 15 years of empirical research. *Human Psychopharmacology, 16,* 557–577.

Parrott, A. C., Morinan, A., Moss, M., & Scholey, A. (2004). *Understanding drugs and behavior.* Chichester, England: Wiley.

Parsons, T. (1975). The sick role and the role of the physician reconsidered. *Milbank Memorial Fund Quarterly, Health and Society,* 53(3), 257–278.

Partinen, M. (1994). Epidemiology of sleep disorders. In M. H. Kryger, T. Roth, & W. C. Dement (Eds.), *Principles and practice of sleep medicine* (2nd ed.). Philadelphia: Saunders.

Pascoe, E. A., & Richman, L. S. (2009). Perceived discrimination and health: A meta-analytic review. *Psychological Bulletin, 135,* 531–554.

Pascual-Leone, A., Amedi, A., Fregni, F., & Merabet, L. B. (2005). The plastic human brain cortex. *Annual Review of Neuroscience, 28,* 377–401.

Patrick, C. J., Cuthbert, B. N., & Lang, P. J. (1994). Emotion in the criminal psychopath: Fear image processing. *Journal of Abnormal Psychology, 103,* 523–534.

Patterson, C. J. (1995). Lesbian mothers, gay fathers, and their children. In A. R. D'Augelli & C. J. Patterson (Eds.), *Lesbian, gay and bisexual identities across the lifespan: Psychological perspectives* (pp. 262–290). New York: Oxford University Press.

Paul, A. M. (2004). *The cult of personality testing.* New York: Free Press.

Pavlidis, I., Eberhardt, N. L., & Levine, J. A. (2002). Human behaviour: Seeing through the face of deception. *Nature, 415,* 35.

Pavlidou, E. V., Williams, J. M., & Kelly, L. M. (2009). Artificial grammar learning in primary school children with and without developmental dyslexia. *Annals of Dyslexia, 59,* 55–77.

Pavlov, I. P. (1923a). New researches on conditioned reflexes. *Science, 58,* 359–361.

Pavlov, I. P. (1923b, July 23). Pavloff. *Time, 1*(21), 20–21.

Pawlowski, B., Dunbar, R. I. M., & Lipowicz, A. (2000). Tall men have more reproductive success. *Nature, 362,* 156.

Pearce, J. M. (1987). A model of stimulus generalization for Pavlovian conditioning. *Psychological Review, 84,* 61–73.

Peck, J., & Shu, S. B. (2009). The effect of mere touch on perceived ownership. *Journal of Consumer Research, 36,* 434–447.

Pelham, B. W. (1985). Self-investment and self-esteem: Evidence for a Jamesian model of self-worth. *Journal of Personality and Social Psychology, 69,* 1141–1150.

Pelham, B. W., Carvallo, M., & Jones, J. T. (2005). Implicit egotism. *Current Directions in Psychological Science, 14,* 106–110.

Pelham, B. W., Mirenberg, M. C., & Jones, J. T. (2002). Why Susie sells seashells by the seashore: Implicit egotism and major life decisions. *Journal of Personality and Social Psychology, 82,* 469–487.

Penfield, W., & Rasmussen, T. (1950). *The cerebral cortex of man: A clinical study of localization of function.* New York: Macmillan.

Pennebaker, J. W., & Chung, C. K. (2007). Expressive writing, emotional upheavals, and health. In H. Friedman & R. Silver (Eds.), *Handbook of health psychology* (pp. 263–284). New York: Oxford University Press.

Pennebaker, J. W., Kiecolt-Glaser, J. K., & Glaser, R. (1988). Disclosure of traumas and immune function: Health implications for psychotherapy. *Journal of Consulting and Clinical Psychology, 56,* 239–245.

Pennebaker, J. W., & Sanders, D. Y. (1976). American graffiti: Effects of authority and reactance arousal. *Personality and Social Psychology Bulletin, 2,* 264–267.

Perkins, D. N., & Grotzer, T. A. (1997). Teaching intelligence. *American Psychologist, 52,* 1125–1133.

Perlmutter, J. S., & Mink, J. W. (2006). Deep brain stimulation. *Annual Review of Neuroscience, 29,* 229–257.

Perloff, L. S., & Fetzer, B. K. (1986). Self-other judgments and perceived vulnerability to victimization. *Journal of Personality and Social Psychology, 50,* 502–510.

Perrett, D. I., Burt, D. M., Penton-Voak, I. S., Lee, K. J., Rowland, D. A., & Edwards, R. (1999). Symmetry and human facial attractiveness. *Evolution and Human Behavior, 20,* 295–307.

Persons, J. B. (1986). The advantages of studying psychological phenomena rather than psychiatric diagnoses. *American Psychologist, 41,* 1252–1260.

Petersen, A. C. (1985). Pubertal development as a cause of disturbance—myths, realities, and unanswered questions. *Genetic Social and General Psychology Monographs, 111,* 205–232.

Petersen, A. C., & Grockett, L. (1985). Pubertal timing and grade effects on adjustment. *Journal of Youth and Adolescence, 14,* 191–206.

Peterson, C., & Siegal, M. (1999). Representing inner worlds: Theory of mind in autistic, deaf and normal hearing children. *Psychological Science, 10,* 126–129.

Peterson, L. R., & Peterson, M. J. (1959). Short-term retention of individual verbal items. *Journal of Experimental Psychology, 58,* 193–198.

Petersson, K. M., Forkstam, C., & Ingvar, M. (2004). Artificial syntactic violations activate Broca's region. *Cognitive Science, 28,* 383–407.

Petitto, L. A., & Marentette, P. F. (1991). Babbling in the manual mode: Evidence for the ontogeny of language. *Science, 251,* 1493–1496.

Petrie, K. P., Booth, R. J., & Pennebaker, J. W. (1998). The immunological effects of thought suppression. *Journal of Personality and Social Psychology, 75,* 1264–1272.

Petty, R. E., & Cacioppo, J. T. (1986). The elaboration likelihood model of persuasion. In L. Berkowitz (Ed.), *Advances in experimental social psychology* (Vol. 19, pp. 123–205). New York: Academic Press.

Petty, R. E., Cacioppo, J. T., & Goldman, R. (1981). Personal involvement as a determinant of argument-based persuasion. *Journal of Personality and Social Psychology, 41,* 847–855.

Petty, R. E., & Wegener, D. T. (1998). Attitude change: Multiple roles for persuasion variables. In D. T. Gilbert, S. T. Fiske, & G. Lindzey (Eds.), *The handbook of social psychology* (4th ed., Vol. 1, pp. 323–390). Boston: McGraw-Hill.

Pew Hispanic Center. (2009). Between two worlds: How young Latinos come of age in America. Retrieved April 22, 2010, from http://pewhispanic.org/reports/report.php?ReportID=117

Pew Research Center for People & the Press. (1997). *Motherhood today: A tougher job, less ably done.* Pew Research Center: Author.

Pew Research Center for People & the Press. (2006). Attitudes toward homosexuality in African countries. Pew Research Center: Author.

Pew Research Center for People & the Press. (2009a). Growing old in America: Expectations vs. reality. Retrieved May 3, 2010, from http://pewsocialtrends.org/pubs/736/getting-old-in-america

Pew Research Center for People & the Press. (2009b). Majority continues to support civil unions: Most still oppose same-sex marriage. Retrieved March 20, 2010, from http://people-press.org/report/553/same-sex-marriage

Phelan, J., Link, B., Stueve, A., & Pescosolido, B. (1997). *Public conceptions of mental illness in 1950 in 1996: Has sophistication increased? Has stigma declined?* Paper presented at the American Sociological Association, Toronto, Ontario.

Phelps, E. A. (2006). Emotion and cognition: Insights from studies of the human amygdala. *Annual Review of Psychology, 24,* 27–53.

Phelps, E. A., & LeDoux, J. L. (2005). Contributions of the amygdala to emotion processing: From animal models to human behavior. *Neuron, 48,* 175–187.

Phillips, F. (2002, January 24). Jump in cigarette sales tied to Sept. 11 attacks. *Boston Globe,* p. B1.

Piaget, J. (1954). *The child's conception of number.* New York: Norton.

Piaget, J. (1965). *The moral judgment of the child.* New York: Free Press. (Originally published 1932)

Piaget, J. (1977). The first year of life of the child. In H. E. Gruber & J. J. Voneche (Eds.), *The essential Piaget: An interpretative reference and guide* (pp. 198–214). New York: Basic Books. (Originally published 1927)

Pinel, J. P. J., Assanand, S., & Lehman, D. R. (2000). Hunger, eating, and ill health. *American Psychologist, 55,* 1105–1116.

Pines, A. M. (1993). Burnout: An existential perspective. In W. B. Schaufeli, C. Maslach, & T. Marek (Eds.), *Professional burnout: Recent developments in theory and research* (pp. 33–51). Washington, DC: Taylor & Francis.

Pines, A., M., & Aronson, E. (1988). *Career burnout: Causes and cures* (2nd ed.). New York: Free Press.

Pinker, S. (1994). *The language instinct.* New York: Morrow.

Pinker, S. (1997). Evolutionary psychology: An exchange. *New York Review of Books, 44,* 55–58.

Pinker, S. (2003). *The blank slate: The modern denial of human nature.* New York: Viking.

Pinker, S., & Bloom, P. (1990). Natural language and natural selection. *Behavioral & Brain Sciences, 13,* 707–784.

Piper, A., & Merskey, H. (2004). The persistence of folly: A critical examination of dissociative identity disorder. Part I. The excesses of an improbable concept. *Canadian Journal of Psychiatry, 49*(9), 592–600.

Planty, M., Hussar, W., Snyder, T., Provasnik, S., Kena, G., Dinkes, R., Kewal Ramani, A., & Kemp, J. (2008). *The condition of education 2008* (NCES 2008–031). National Center for Education Statistics, Institute of Education Sciences, U.S. Department of Education, Washington, DC.

Plassman, H., O'Doherty, J., Shiv, B., & Rangel, A. (2008). Marketing actions can modulate neural representations of experienced pleasantness. *Proceedings of the National Academy of Sciences, USA, 105,* 1050–1054.

Pleis, J. R., Lucas, J. W., & Ward, B. W. (2009). Summary of health statistics for U.S. adults: National health interview survey, 2008, *Vital Health Stat 10*(242). National Center for Health Statistics.

Plomin, R., DeFries, J. C., McClearn, G. E., & Rutter, M. (1997). *Behavioral genetics* (3rd ed.). New York: Freeman.

Plotnik, J. M., de Waal, F. B. M., & Reiss, D. (2006). Self-recognition in an Asian elephant. *Proceedings of the National Academy of Sciences, USA, 103,* 17053–17057.

Poliak, S., & Peles, E. (2003). The local differentiation of myelinated axons at nodes of Ranvier. *Nature Reviews Neuroscience, 4,* 968–980.

Poole, D. A., Lindsay, S. D., Memon, A., & Bull, R. (1995). Psychotherapy and the recovery of memories of childhood sexual abuse: U.S. and British practitioners' opinions, practices, and experiences. *Journal of Consulting and Clinical Psychology, 63,* 426–487.

Pope, A. W., & Bierman, K. L. (1999). Predicting adolescent peer problems and antisocial activities: The relative roles of aggression and dysregulation. *Developmental Psychology, 35,* 335–346.

Porter, S., & ten Brinke, L. (2008). Reading between the lies: Identifying concealed and falsified emotions in universal facial expressions. *Psychological Science, 19,* 508–514.

Portocarrero, J. S., Burright, R. G., & Donovick, P. J. (2007). Vocabulary and verbal fluency of bilingual and monolingual college students. *Archives of Clinical Neuropsychology, 22,* 415–422.

Posey, T. B., & Losch, M. E. (1983). Auditory hallucinations of hearing voices in 375 normal subjects. *Imagination, Cognition and Personality, 3,* 99–113.

Posner, M. I., & Raichle, M. E. (1994). *Images of mind.* New York: Freeman.

Post, R. M., Frye, M. A., Denicoff, G. S., Leverich, G. S., Dunn, R. T., Osuch, E. A., et al. (2008). Emerging trends in the treatment of rapid cycling bipolar disorder: A selected review. *Bipolar Disorders, 2,* 305–315.

Postman, L., & Underwood, B. J. (1973). Critical issues in interference theory. *Memory & Cognition, 1,* 19–40.

Postmes, T., & Spears, R. (1998). Deindividuation and anti-normative behavior: A meta-analysis. *Psychological Bulletin, 123,* 238–259.

Powers, M. B., & Emmelkamp, P. M. (2008). Virtual reality exposure therapy for anxiety disorders: A meta-analysis. *Journal of Anxiety Disorders, 22,* 561–569.

Prasada, S., & Pinker, S. (1993). Generalizations of regular and irregular morphology. *Language and Cognitive Processes, 8,* 1–56.

Pratkanis, A. R. (1992). The cargo-cult science of subliminal persuasion. *Skeptical Inquirer, 16,* 260–272.

Pressman, S. D., Cohen, S., Miller, G. E., Barkin, A., Rabin, B. S., & Treanor, J. J. (2005). Loneliness, social network size, and immune response to influenza vaccination in college freshmen. *Health Psychology, 24,* 297–306.

Price, J. L., & Davis, B. (2008). *The woman who can't forget: The extraordinary story of living with the most remarkable memory known to science.* New York: Free Press.

Prior, H., Schwartz, A., & Güntürkün, O. (2008). Mirror-induced behavior in the magpie (*Pica pica*): Evidence of self-recognition. *PLoS Biology, 6,* e202.

Prochaska, J. J., & Sallis, J. F. (2004). A randomized controlled trial of single versus multiple health behavior change: Promoting physical activity and nutrition among adolescents. *Health Psychology, 23,* 314–318.

Procopio, M., & Marriott, P. (2007). Intrauterine hormonal environment and risk of developing anorexia nervosa. *Archives of General Psychiatry, 64*(12), 1402–1407.

Pruitt, D. G. (1998). Social conflict. In D. T. Gilbert, S. T. Fiske, & G. Lindzey (Eds.), *The handbook of social psychology* (4th ed., Vol. 2, pp. 470–503). New York: McGraw-Hill.

Putnam, F. W., Guroff, J. J., Silberman, E. K., Barban, L., & Post, R. M. (1986). The clinical phenomenology of multiple personality disorder: Review of 100 recent cases. *Journal of Clinical Psychiatry, 47,* 285–293.

Pyers, J. E., & Senghas, A. (2009). Language promotes false-belief understanding: Evidence from learners of a new sign language. *Psychological Science, 20*(7), 805–812.

Quattrone, G. A. (1982). Behavioral consequences of attributional bias. *Social Cognition, 1,* 358–378.

Querleu, D., Lefebvre, C., Titran, M., Renard, X., Morillon, M., & Crepin, G. (1984). Réactivité de nouveau-né de moins de deux heures de vie á la voix maternelle. *Journal de Gynecologie Obstetrique et de Biologie de la Reproduction* [Reactivity of newborns less than 2 hours old to the mother's voice], *13,* 125–134.

Radford, E., & Radford, M. A. (1949). *Encyclopedia of superstitions.* New York: Philosophical Library.

Raichle, M. E., & Mintun, M. A. (2006). Brain work and brain imaging. *Annual Review of Neuroscience, 29,* 449–476.

Ramachandran, V. S., & Altschuler, E. L. (2009). The use of visual feedback, in particular mirror visual feedback, in restoring brain function. *Brain, 132,* 1693–1710.

Ramachandran, V. S., & Blakeslee, S. (1998). *Phantoms in the brain: Probing the mysteries of the human mind.* New York: Morrow.

Ramachandran, V. S., & Hubbard, E. M. (2003). Hearing colors, tasting shapes. *Scientific American, 288,* 52–59.

Ramachandran, V. S., Rodgers-Ramachandran, D., & Stewart, M. (1992). Perceptual correlates of massive cortical reorganization. *Science, 258,* 1159–1160.

Rapaport, D. (1946). *Diagnostic psychological testing: The theory, statistical evaluation, and diagnostic application of a battery of tests.* Chicago: Year Book Publishers.

Rappoport, J. L. (1990). Obsessive compulsive disorder and basal ganglia dysfunction. *Psychological Medicine, 20,* 465–469.

Rauschecker, J. P., & Scott, S. K. (2009). Maps and streams in the auditory cortex: Nonhuman primates illuminate human speech processing. *Nature Neuroscience, 12,* 718–724.

Raz, N. (2000). Aging of the brain and its impact on cognitive performance: Integration of structural and functional findings. In F. I. M. Craik & T. A. Salthouse (Eds.), *The handbook of aging and cognition* (pp. 1–90). Mahwah, NJ: Lawrence Erlbaum.

Read, K. E. (1965). *The high valley.* London: Allen and Unwin.

Reason, J., & Mycielska, K. (1982). *Absent-minded?: The psychology of mental lapses and everyday errors.* Englewood Cliffs: Prentice-Hall.

Reber, A. S. (1967). Implicit learning of artificial grammars. *Journal of Verbal Learning and Verbal Behavior, 6,* 855–863.

Reber, A. S. (1996). *Implicit learning and tacit knowledge: An essay on the cognitive unconscious.* New York: Oxford University Press.

Reber, P. J., Gitelman, D. R., Parrish, T. B., & Mesulam, M. M. (2003). Dissociating explicit and implicit category knowledge with fMRI. *Journal of Cognitive Neuroscience, 15,* 574–583.

Recanzone, G. H., & Sutter, M. L. (2008). The biological basis of audition. *Annual Review of Psychology, 59,* 119–142.

Rechsthaffen, A., Gilliland, M. A., Bergmann, B. M., & Winter, J. B. (1983). Physiological correlates of prolonged sleep deprivation in rats. *Science, 221,* 182–184.

Reed, C. L., Klatzky, R. L., & Halgren, E. (2005). What vs. where in touch: An fMRI study. *NeuroImage, 25,* 718–726.

Reed, D. R. (2008). Birth of a new breed of supertaster. *Chemical Senses, 33,* 489–491.

Reed, G. (1988). *The psychology of anomalous experience* (rev. ed.). Buffalo, NY: Prometheus Books.

Reeve, C. L., Heggestad, E. D., & Lievens, F. (2009). Modeling the impact of test anxiety and test familiarity on the criterion-related validity of cognitive ability tests. *Intelligence, 37*(1), 34–41.

Regan, P. C. (1998). What if you can't get what you want? Willingness to compromise ideal mate selection standards as a function of sex, mate value, and relationship context. *Personality and Social Psychology Bulletin, 24,* 1294–1303.

Regier, D. A., Narrow, W. E., Rae, D. S., Manderscheid, R. W., Locke, B. Z., & Goodwin, F. K. (1993). The de facto U.S. mental and addictive disorders service system: Epidemiologic Catchment Area prospective 1-year prevalence rates of disorders and services. *Archives of General Psychiatry, 41,* 934–941.

Reinarman, C., Cohen, P. D. A., & Kaal, H. L. (2004). The limited relevance of drug policy: Cannabis in Amsterdam and San Francisco. *American Journal of Public Health, 94,* 836–842.

Reis, H. T., & Aron, A. (2008). Love: What is it, why does it matter, and how does it operate? *Perspectives on Psychological Science, 3,* 80–86.

Reiss, D., & Marino, L. (2001). Mirror self-recognition in the bottlenose dolphin: A case of cognitive convergence. *Proceedings of the National Academy of Sciences, USA, 98,* 5937–5942.

Reissland, N. (1988). Neonatal imitation in the first hour of life: Observations in rural Nepal. *Developmental Psychology, 24,* 464–469.

Renner, M. J., & Mackin, R. (1998). A life stress instrument for classroom use. *Teaching of Psychology, 25,* 46–48.

Rensink, R. A. (2002). Change detection. *Annual Review of Psychology, 53,* 245–277.

Rensink, R. A., O'Regan, J. K., & Clark, J. J. (1997). To see or not to see: The need for attention to perceive changes in scenes. *Psychological Science, 8,* 368–373.

Rentfrow, P. J., & Gosling, S. D. (2003). The do re mi's of everyday life: The structure and personality correlates of music preferences. *Journal of Personality and Social Psychology, 84,* 1236–1256.

Rescorla, R. A. (1966). Predictability and number of pairings in Pavlovian fear conditioning. *Psychonomic Science, 4,* 383–384.

Rescorla, R. A. (1988). Classical conditioning: It's not what you think it is. *American Psychologist, 43,* 151–160.

Rescorla, R. A. (2006). Stimulus generalization of excitation and inhibition. *Quarterly Journal of Experimental Psychology, 59,* 53–67.

Rescorla, R. A., & Wagner, A. R. (1972). A theory of Pavlovian conditioning: Variations in effectiveness of reinforcement and nonreinforcement. In A. Black & W. F. Prokasky, Jr. (Eds.), *Classical conditioning II.* New York: Appleton-Century-Crofts.

Ressler, K. J., & Nemeroff, C. B. (1999). Role of norepinephrine in the pathophysiology and treatment of mood disorders. *Biological Psychiatry, 46,* 1219–1233.

Revkin, A. C., & Seelye, K. Q. (2003, June 19). Report by EPA leaves out data on climate change. *New York Times.*

Rhode, D. L. (2010). *The beauty bias: The injustice of appearance in life and law.* Oxford, England: Oxford University Press.

Richards, M., Black, S., Mishra, G., Gale, C. R., Deary, I. J., & Batty, D. G. (2009). IQ in childhood and the metabolic syndrome in middle age: Extended follow-up of the 1946 British birth cohort study. *Intelligence, 37*(6), 567–572.

Richards, M. H., Crowe, P. A., Larson, R., & Swarr, A. (1998). Developmental patterns and gender differences in the experience of peer companionship during adolescence. *Child Development, 69,* 154–163.

Rieber, R. W. (Ed.). (1980). *Wilhelm Wundt and the making of scientific psychology.* New York: Plenum Press.

Risman, J. E., Coyle, J. T., Green, R. W., Javitt, D. C., Benes, F. M., Heckers, S., et al. (2008). Circuit-based framework for understanding neurotransmitter and risk gene interactions in schizophrenia. *Trends in Neurosciences, 31,* 234–242.

Rizzolatti, G., & Craighero, L. (2004). The mirror-neuron system. *Annual Review of Neuroscience, 27,* 169–192.

Rizzolatti, G., Fabbri-Destro, M., & Cattaneo, L. (2009). Mirror neurons and their clinical relevance. *Nature Clinical Practice Neurology, 5,* 24–34.

Roberts, B. W., & Mroczek, D. (2008). Personality trait change in adulthood. *Current Directions in Psychological Science, 17,* 31–35.

Roberts, G. A. (1991). Delusional belief and meaning in life: A preferred reality? *British Journal of Psychiatry, 159,* 20–29.

Roberts, G. A., & McGrady, A. (1996). Racial and gender effects on the relaxation response: Implications for the development of hypertension. *Biofeedback and Self-Regulation, 21,* 51–62.

Robertson, L. C. (1999). What can spatial deficits teach us about feature binding and spatial maps? *Visual Cognition, 6,* 409–430.

Robertson, L. C. (2003). Binding, spatial attention and perceptual awareness. *Nature Reviews Neuroscience, 4,* 93–102.

Robins, L. N., Helzer, J. E., Hesselbrock, M., & Wish, E. (1980). Vietnam veterans three years after Vietnam. In L. Brill & C. Winick (Eds.), *The yearbook of substance use and abuse* (Vol. 11). New York: Human Sciences Press.

Robins, R. W., Fraley, R. C., & Krueger, R. F. (Eds.). (2007). *Handbook of research methods in personality psychology.* New York: Guilford Press.

Robinson, D. N. (1995). *An intellectual history of psychology.* Madison: University of Wisconsin Press.

Rochlen, A. B., Zack, J. S., & Speyer, C. (2004). Online therapy: Review of relevant definitions, debates, and current empirical support. *Journal of Clinical Psychology, 60,* 269–283.

Rodgers, A., Ezzati, M., Vander Hoorn, S., Lopez, A. D., Lin, B., Murray, C. J., et al. (2004). Distribution of major health risks: Findings from the Global Burden of Disease study. *PLoS Med, 1*(1), e27.

Roediger, H. L., III. (2000). Why retrieval is the key process to understanding human memory. In E. Tulving (Ed.), *Memory, consciousness, and the brain: The Tallinn conference* (pp. 52–75). Philadelphia: Psychology Press.

Roediger, H. L., III, & Karpicke, J. D. (2006). Test-enhanced learning: Taking memory tests improves long-term retention. *Psychological Science, 17,* 249–255.

Roediger, H. L., III, & McDermott, K. B. (1995). Creating false memories: Remembering words not presented in lists. *Journal of Experimental Psychology: Learning, Memory, and Cognition, 21,* 803–814.

Roediger, H. L., III, & McDermott, K. B. (2000). Tricks of memory. *Current Directions in Psychological Science, 9,* 123–127.

Roediger, H. L., III, Weldon, M. S., & Challis, B. H. (1989). Explaining dissociations between implicit and explicit measures of retention: A processing account. In H. L. I. Roediger & F. I. M. Craik (Eds.), *Varieties of memory and consciousness: Essays in honor of Endel Tulving* (pp. 3–41). Hillsdale, NJ: Lawrence Erlbaum.

Rosch, E. H. (1973). Natural categories. *Cognitive Psychology, 4,* 328–350.

Rosch, E. H. (1975). Cognitive representations of semantic categories. *Journal of Experimental Psychology: General, 104,* 192–233.

Rosch, E. H., & Mervis, C. B. (1975). Family resemblances: Studies in the internal structure of categories. *Cognitive Psychology, 7,* 573–605.

Rose, S. P. R. (2002). Smart drugs: Do they work? Are they ethical? Will they be legal? *Nature Reviews Neuroscience, 3,* 975–979.

Roseman, I. J. (1984). Cognitive determinants of emotion: A structural theory. *Review of Personality and Social Psychology, 5,* 11–36.

Roseman, I. J., & Smith, C. A. (2001). Appraisal theory: Overview, assumptions, varieties and controversies. In K. R. Scherer, A. Schorr, & T. Johnstone (Eds.), *Appraisal processes in emotion: Theory, methods, research* (pp. 3–19). New York: Oxford University Press.

Rosenberg, M. (1965). *Society and the adolescent self-image.* Princeton, NJ: Princeton University Press.

Rosenhan, D. (1973). On being sane in insane places. *Science, 179,* 250–258.

Rosenkranz, K., Williamon, A., & Rothwell, J. C. (2007). Motor-cortical excitability and synaptic plasticity is enhanced in professional musicians. *The Journal of Neuroscience, 27,* 5200–5206.

Rosenstein, M. J., Milazzo-Sayre, L. J., & Manderscheid, R. W. (1990). Characteristics of persons using specifically inpatient, outpatient, and partial care programs in 1986. In M. A. Sonnenschein (Ed.), *Mental health in the United States* (pp. 139–172). Washington, DC: U.S. Government Printing Office.

Rosenthal, R., & Fode, K. L. (1963). The effect of experimenter bias on the performance of the albino rat. *Behavioral Science, 8,* 183–189.

Ross, D. F., Ceci, S. J., Dunning, D., & Toglia, M. P. (1994). Unconscious transference and mistaken identity: When a witness misidentifies a familiar but innocent person. *Journal of Applied Psychology, 79,* 918–930.

Ross, L. (1977). The intuitive psychologist and his shortcomings: Distortions in the attribution process. *Advances in Experimental Social Psychology, 10,* 173–220.

Ross, L., Amabile, T. M., & Steinmetz, J. L. (1977). Social roles, social control, and biases in social-perception processes. *Journal of Personality and Social Psychology, 35,* 485–494.

Ross, L., & Nisbett, R. E. (1991). *The person and the situation.* New York: McGraw-Hill.

Rothbart, M. K., & Bates, J. E. (1998). Temperament. In N. Eisenberg (Ed.), *Handbook of child psychology: Vol. 3. Social, emotional and personality development* (5th ed., pp. 105–176). New York: Wiley.

Rothbaum, B. O., Hodges, L., Watson, B. A., Kessler, G. D., & Opdyke, D. (1996). Virtual reality exposure therapy in the treatment of fear of flying: A case report. *Behaviour Research and Therapy, 34,* 477–481.

Rothbaum, B. O., & Schwartz, A. C. (2002). Exposure therapy for posttraumatic stress disorder. *American Journal of Psychotherapy, 56,* 59–75.

Rotstein, A. H. (2006, November 11). Despite 2–1 defeat on Election Day, backer of $1 million voter lottery still likes the idea. *Associated Press.*

Rotter, J. B. (1966). Generalized expectancies for internal versus external locus of control of reinforcement. *Psychological Monographs: General and Applied, 80,* 1–28.

Rouw, R., & Scholte, H. S. (2007). Increased structural connectivity in grapheme-color synesthesia. *Nature Neuroscience, 10,* 792–797.

Rowa, K., Antony, M. M., Brar, S., Summerfeldt, L. J., & Swinson, R. P. (2000). Treatment histories of patients with three anxiety disorders. *Depression and Anxiety, 12,* 92–98.

Roy-Byrne, P. P., & Cowley, D. (1998). *Pharmacological treatment of panic, generalized anxiety, and phobic disorders.* New York: Oxford University Press.

Roy-Byrne, P. P., & Cowley, D. S. (2002). Pharmacological treatments for panic disorder, generalized anxiety disorder, specific phobia, and social anxiety disorder. In P. E. Nathan & J. M. Gorman (Eds.), *A guide to treatments that work* (2nd ed., pp. 337–365). New York: Oxford University Press.

Rozin, P. (1968). Are carbohydrate and protein intakes separately regulated? *Journal of Comparative and Physiological Psychology, 65,* 23–29.

Rozin, P., Bauer, R., & Catanese, D. (2003). Food and life, pleasure and worry, among American college students: Gender differences and regional similarities. *Journal of Personality and Social Psychology, 85,* 132–141.

Rozin, P., & Kalat, J. W. (1971). Specific hungers and poison avoidance as adaptive specializations of learning. *Psychological Review, 78,* 459–486.

Rubin, B. D., & Katz, L. C. (1999). Optical imaging of odorant representations in the mammalian olfactory bulb. *Neuron, 23,* 499–511.

Rubin, Z. (1973). *Liking and loving.* New York: Holt, Rinehart and Winston.

Rudman, L. A., Ashmore, R. D., & Gary, M. L. (2001). "Unlearning" automatic biases: The malleability of implicit prejudice and stereotypes. *Journal of Personality and Social Psychology, 81,* 856–868.

Rusbult, C. E. (1983). A longitudinal test of the investment model: The development (and deterioration) of satisfaction and commitment in heterosexual involvements. *Journal of Personality and Social Psychology, 45,* 101–117.

Rusbult, C. E., & Van Lange, P. A. M. (2003). Interdependence, interaction and relationships. *Annual Review of Psychology, 54,* 351–375.

Rusbult, C. E., Verette, J., Whitney, G. A., & Slovik, L. F. (1991). Accommodation processes in close relationships: Theory and preliminary empirical evidence. *Journal of Personality and Social Psychology, 60,* 53–78.

Rushton, J. P. (1995). Asian achievement, brain size, and evolution: Comment on A. H. Yee. *Educational Psychology Review, 7,* 373–380.

Rushton, J. P., & Templer, D. I. (2009). National differences in intelligence, crime, income, and skin color. *Intelligence, 37*(4), 341–346.

Russell, B. (1945). *A history of Western philosophy.* New York: Simon & Schuster.

Rutter, M., & Silberg, J. (2002). Gene–environment interplay in relation to emotional and behavioral disturbance. *Annual Review of Psychology, 53,* 463–490.

Ryan, R. M., & Deci, E. L. (2000). Self-determination theory and the facilitation of intrinsic motivation, social development, and well-being. *American Psychologist, 55,* 68–78.

Sachs, J. S. (1967). Recognition of semantic, syntactic, and lexical changes in sentences. *Psychonomic Bulletin & Review, 1,* 17–18.

Sackeim, H. A., & Devanand, D. P. (1991). Dissociative disorders. In M. Hersen & S. M. Turner (Eds.), *Adult psychopathology and diagnosis* (2nd ed., pp. 279–322). New York: Wiley.

Sacks, O. (1995). *An anthropologist on Mars.* New York: Knopf.

Sagiv, N., Heer, J., & Robertson, L. (2006). Does binding of synesthetic color to the evoking grapheme require attention? *Cortex, 42,* 232–242.

Sahakian, B., & Morein-Zamir, S. (2007). Professor's little helper. *Nature, 450*(7173), 1157–1159.

Salmon, D. P., & Bondi, M. W. (2009). Neuropsychological assessment of dementia. *Annual Review of Psychology, 60,* 257–282.

Salovey, P., & Grewal, D. (2005). The science of emotional intelligence. *Current Directions in Psychological Science, 14*(6), 281–285.

Salthouse, T. A. (1984). Effects of age and skill in typing. *Journal of Experimental Psychology: General, 113,* 345–371.

Salthouse, T. A. (1987). Age, experience, and compensation. In C. Schooler & K. W. Schaie (Eds.), *Cognitive functioning and social structure over the life course* (pp. 142–150). New York: Ablex.

Salthouse, T. A. (1996a). General and specific mediation of adult age differences in memory. *Journal of Gerontology: Series B: Psychological Sciences and Social Sciences, 51B,* P30–P42.

Salthouse, T. A. (1996b). The processing-speed theory of adult age differences in cognition. *Psychological Review, 103,* 403–428.

Salthouse, T. A. (2000). Pressing issues in cognitive aging. In D. Park & N. Schwartz (Eds.), *Cognitive aging: A primer.* Philadelphia: Psychology Press.

Salthouse, T. A. (2006). Mental exercise and mental aging. *Perspectives on Psychological Science, 1*(1), 68–87.

Sampson, R. J., & Laub, J. H. (1995). Understanding variability in lives through time: Contributions of life-course criminology. *Studies of Crime Prevention, 4,* 143–158.

Sandin, R. H., Enlund, G., Samuelsson, P., & Lenmarken, C. (2000). Awareness during anesthesia: A prospective case study. *Lancet, 355,* 707–711.

Sara, S. J. (2000). Retrieval and reconsolidation: Toward a neurobiology of remembering. *Learning and Memory, 7,* 73–84.

Sarris, V. (1989). Max Wertheimer on seen motion: Theory and evidence. *Psychological Research, 51,* 58–68.

Sarter, M. (2006). Preclinical research into cognition enhancers. *Trends in Pharmacological Sciences, 27,* 602–608.

Satcher, D. (2001). *The Surgeon General's call to action to promote sexual health and responsible sexual behavior.* Washington, DC: U.S. Government Printing Office.

Sato, S. (2001). Autonomy and relatedness in psychopathology and treatment: A cross-cultural formulation. *Genetic, Social, and General Psychology Monographs, 127,* 89–127.

Savage, C. R., Deckersbach, T., Heckers, S., Wagner, A. D., Schacter, D. L., Alpert, N. M., et al. (2001). Prefrontal regions supporting spontaneous and directed application of verbal learning strategies: Evidence from PET. *Brain, 124,* 219–231.

Saver, J. L., & Rabin, J. (1997). The neural substrates of religious experience. *Journal of Neuropsychiatry and Clinical Neurosciences, 9,* 498–510.

Savic, I., Berglund, H., & Lindstrom, P. (2005). Brain response to putative pheromones in homosexual men. *Proceedings of the National Academy of Sciences, USA, 102,* 7356–7361.

Savic, I., & Lindstrom, P. (2008). PET and MRI show differences in cerebral asymmetry and functional connectivity between homo- and heterosexual subjects. *Proceedings of the National Academy of Sciences, USA, 105*(27), 9403–9408.

Sawa, A., & Snyder, S. H. (2002). Schizophrenia: Diverse approaches to a complex disease. *Science, 295,* 692–695.

Sawyer, T. F. (2000). Francis Cecil Sumner: His views and influence on African American higher education. *History of Psychology, 3*(2), 122–141.

Scarborough, E., & Furumoto, L. (1987). *Untold lives: The first generation of American women psychologists.* New York: Columbia University Press.

Schachter, S. (1982). Recidivism and self-cure of smoking and obesity. *American Psychologist, 37,* 436–444.

Schachter, S., & Gross, L. P. (1968). Manipulated time and eating behavior. *Journal of Personality and Social Psychology, 10,* 98–106.

Schachter, S., & Singer, J. E. (1962). Cognitive, social, and psychological determinants of emotional state. *Physiological Review, 69,* 379–399.

Schacter, D. L. (1987). Implicit memory: History and current status. *Journal of Experimental Psychology: Learning, Memory, and Cognition, 13,* 501–518.

Schacter, D. L. (1996). *Searching for memory: The brain, the mind, and the past.* New York: Basic Books.

Schacter, D. L. (1999). The seven sins of memory: Insights from psychology and cognitive neuroscience. *American Psychologist, 54*(3), 182–203.

Schacter, D. L. (2001a). *Forgotten ideas, neglected pioneers: Richard Semon and the story of memory.* Philadelphia: Psychology Press.

Schacter, D. L. (2001b). *The seven sins of memory: How the mind forgets and remembers.* Boston: Houghton Mifflin.

Schacter, D. L., & Addis, D. R. (2007). The cognitive neuroscience of constructive memory: Remembering the past and imagining the future. *Philosophical Transactions of the Royal Society of London. Series B: Biological Sciences, 362,* 773–786.

Schacter, D. L., Addis, D. R., & Buckner, R. L. (2007). Remembering the past to imagine the future: The prospective brain. *Nature Reviews Neuroscience, 8,* 657–661.

Schacter, D. L., Addis, D. R., & Buckner, R. L. (2008). Episodic simulation of future events: Concepts, data, and applications. *Annals of the New York Academy of Sciences, 1124,* 39–60.

Schacter, D. L., Alpert, N. M., Savage, C. R., Rauch, S. L., & Albert, M. S. (1996a). Conscious recollection and the human hippocampal formation: Evidence from positron emission tomography. *Proceedings of the National Academy of Sciences, USA, 93,* 321–325.

Schacter, D. L., & Curran, T. (2000). Memory without remembering and remembering without memory: Implicit and false memories. In M. S. Gazzaniga (Ed.), *The new cognitive neurosciences* (2nd ed.). Cambridge, MA: The MIT Press.

Schacter, D. L., Dawes, R., Jacoby, L. L., Kahneman, D., Lempert, R., Roediger, H. L., & Rosenthal, R. (2008). Studying eyewitness investigations in the field. *Law and Human Behavior, 32,* 3–5.

Schacter, D. L., Dobbins, I. G., & Schnyer, D. M. (2004). Specificity of priming: A cognitive neuroscience perspective. *Nature Reviews Neuroscience, 5,* 853–862.

Schacter, D. L., Harbluk, J. L., & McLachlan, D. R. (1984). Retrieval without recollection: An experimental analysis of source amnesia. *Journal of Verbal Learning and Verbal Behavior, 23,* 593–611.

Schacter, D. L., Israel, L., & Racine, C. A. (1999). Suppressing false recognition in younger and older adults: The distinctiveness heuristic. *Journal of Memory and Language, 40,* 1–24.

Schacter, D. L., Reiman, E., Curran, T., Yun, L. S., Bandy, D., McDermott, K. B., et al. (1996b). Neuroanatomical correlates of veridical and illusory recognition memory: Evidence from positron emission tomography. *Neuron, 17,* 267–274.

Schacter, D. L., & Tulving, E. (1994). *Memory systems 1994.* Cambridge, MA: The MIT Press.

Schacter, D. L., Wagner, A. D., & Buckner, R. L. (2000). Memory systems of 1999. In E. Tulving & F. I. M. Craik (Eds.), *The Oxford handbook of memory.* New York: Oxford University Press.

Schaeffer, M. A., McKinnon, W., Baum, A., Reynolds, C. P., Rikli, P., & Davidson, L. M. (1985). Immune status as a function of chronic stress at Three-Mile Island [Abstract]. *Psychosomatic Medicine, 47,* 85.

Schafer, R. B., & Keith, P. M. (1980). Equity and depression among married couples. *Social Psychology Quarterly, 43,* 430–435.

Schaie, K. W. (1996). *Intellectual development in adulthood: The Seattle Longitudinal Study.* New York: Cambridge University Press.

Schaie, K. W. (2005). *Developmental influences on adult intelligence: The Seattle Longitudinal Study.* New York: Oxford University Press.

Schapira, A. H. V., Emre, M., Jenner, P., & Poewe, W. (2009). Levodopa in the treatment of Parkinson's disease. *European Journal of Neurology, 16,* 982–989.

Scheier, M. F., Matthews, K. A., Owens, J. F., Schulz, R., Bridges, M. W., Magovern, G. J., Sr., et al. (1999). Optimism and rehospitalization after coronary artery bypass graft surgery. *Archives of Internal Medicine, 159,* 829–835.

Scherer, K. R. (1999). Appraisal theory. In T. Dalgleish & M. Power (Eds.), *Handbook of cognition and emotion* (pp. 637–663). New York: Wiley.

Scherer, K. R. (2001). The nature and study of appraisal: A review of the issues. In K. R. Scherer, A. Schorr, & T. Johnstone (Eds.), *Appraisal processes in emotion: Theory, methods, research* (pp. 369–391). New York: Oxford University Press.

Schlegel, A., & Barry, H., III. (1991). *Adolescence: An anthropological inquiry.* New York: Free Press.

Schneier, F., Johnson, J., Hornig, C. D., Liebowitz, M. R., & Weissman, M. M. (1992). Social phobia: Comorbidity and morbidity in an epidemiologic sample. *Archives of General Psychiatry, 49,* 282–288.

Schnorr, J. A., & Atkinson, R. C. (1969). Repetition versus imagery instructions in the short- and long-term retention of paired associates. *Psychonomic Science, 15,* 183–184.

Schoenemann, P. T., Sheenan, M. J., & Glotzer, L. D. (2005). Prefrontal white matter volume is disproportionately larger in humans than in other primates. *Nature Neuroscience, 8,* 242–252.

Schooler, J. W., Bendiksen, M., & Ambadar, Z. (1997). Taking the middle line: Can we accommodate both fabricated and recovered memories of sexual abuse? In M. A. Conway (Ed.), *Recovered memories and false memories* (pp. 251–292). Oxford, England: Oxford University Press.

Schott, B. J., Henson, R. N., Richardson-Klavehn, A., Becker, C., Thoma, V., Heinze, H. J., & Duzel, E. (2005). Redefining implicit and explicit memory: The functional neuroanatomy of priming, remembering, and control of retrieval. *Proceedings of the National Academy of Sciences, USA, 102,* 1257–1262.

Schouwenburg, H. C. (1995). Academic procrastination: Theoretical notions, measurement, and research. In J. R. Ferrari, J. L. Johnson, & W. G. McCown (Eds.), *Procrastination and task avoidance: Theory, research, and treatment.* New York: Plenum Press.

Schreiner, C. E., Read, H. L., & Sutter, M. L. (2000). Modular organization of frequency integration in primary auditory cortex. *Annual Review of Neuroscience, 23,* 501–529.

Schreiner, C. E., & Winer, J. A. (2007). Auditory cortex mapmaking: Principles, projections, and plasticity. *Neuron, 56,* 356–365.

Schubert, T. W., & Koole, S. L. (2009). The embodied self: Making a fist enhances men's power-related self-conceptions. *Journal of Experimental Social Psychology, 45,* 828–834.

Schultz, D., Izard, C. E., & Bear, G. (2004). Children's emotion processing: Relations to emotionality and aggression. *Development and Psychopathology, 16*(2), 371–387.

Schultz, D. P., & Schultz, S. E. (1987). *A history of modern psychology* (4th ed.). San Diego: Harcourt Brace Jovanovich.

Schultz, W. (2006). Behavioral theories and the neurophysiology of reward. *Annual Review of Psychology, 57,* 87–115.

Schultz, W. (2007). Behavioral dopamine signals. *Trends in Neurosciences, 30,* 203–210.

Schwartz, B. L. (2002). *Tip-of-the-tongue states: Phenomenology, mechanisms, and lexical retrieval.* Mahwah, NJ: Lawrence Erlbaum.

Schwartz, C. E., Wright, C. I., Shin, L. M., Kagan, J., & Rauch, S. L. (2003). Inhibited and uninhibited infants "grown up": Adult amygdalar response to novelty. *Science, 300,* 1952–1953.

Schwartz, J. H., & Westbrook, G. L. (2000). The cytology of neurons. In E. R. Kandel, G. H. Schwartz, & T. M. Jessell (Eds.), *Principles of neural science* (pp. 67–104). New York: McGraw-Hill.

Schwartz, S., & Maquet, P. (2002). Sleep imaging and the neuropsychological assessment of dreams. *Trends in Cognitive Sciences, 6,* 23–30.

Schwartzman, A. E., Gold, D., & Andres, D. (1987). Stability of intelligence: A 40-year follow-up. *Canadian Journal of Psychology, 41,* 244–256.

Schwarz, N., & Clore, G. L. (1983). Mood, misattribution, and judgments of well-being: Informative and directive functions of affective states. *Journal of Personality and Social Psychology, 45,* 513–523.

Schwarz, N., Mannheim, Z., & Clore, G. L. (1988). How do I feel about it? The informative function of affective states. In K. Fiedler & J. Forgas (Eds.), *Affect cognition and social behavior: New evidence and integrative attempts* (pp. 44–62). Toronto: C. J. Hogrefe.

Scoville, W. B., & Milner, B. (1957). Loss of recent memory after bilateral hippocampal lesions. *Journal of Neurology, Neurosurgery, and Psychiatry, 20,* 11–21.

Scribner, S. (1984). Studying working intelligence. In B. Rogoff & J. Lave (Eds.), *Everyday cognition: Its development in social context* (pp. 9–40). Cambridge, MA: Harvard University Press.

Sedikides, C., & Gregg, A. P. (2008). Self-enhancement: Food for thought. *Perspectives on Psychological Science, 3*(2), 102–116.

Segall, M. H., Campbell, D. T., & Herskovits, M. J. (1963). Cultural differences in the perception of geometric illusions. *Science, 139,* 769–771.

Segall, M. H., Lonner, W. J., & Berry, J. W. (1998). Cross-cultural psychology as a scholarly discipline: On the flowering of culture in behavioral research. *American Psychologist, 53*(10), 1101–1110.

Segerstrom, S. C. (2005). Optimism and immunity: Do positive thoughts always lead to positive effects? *Brain, Behavior, and Immunity, 19,* 195–200.

Seligman, M. E. P. (1971). Phobias and preparedness. *Behavior Therapy, 2,* 307–320.

Seligman, M. E. P. (1995). The effectiveness of psychotherapy: The consumer reports study. *American Psychologist, 48,* 966–971.

Selye, H., & Fortier, C. (1950). Adaptive reaction to stress. *Psychosomatic Medicine, 12,* 149–157.

Semenza, C. (2009). The neuropsychology of proper names. *Mind & Language, 24,* 347–369.

Semenza, C., & Zettin, M. (1989). Evidence from aphasia from proper names as pure referring expressions. *Nature, 342,* 678–679.

Senghas, A., Kita, S., & Ozyurek, A. (2004). Children create core properties of language: Evidence from an emerging sign language in Nicaragua. *Science, 305,* 1782.

Senju, A., Southgate, V., White, S., & Frith, U. (2009). Mind-blind eyes: An absence of spontaneous theory of mind in Asperger syndrome. *Science, 325,* 883–885.

Serpell, R. (1974). Aspects of intelligence in a developing country. *African Social Research, 17,* 578–596.

Seymour, K., Clifford, C. W. G., Logothetis, N. K., & Bartels, A. (2010). Coding and binding of color and form in visual cortex. *Cerebral Cortex.* doi:10.1093/cercor/bhp265

Shah, J. Y., & Gardner, W. L. (Eds.). (2008). *Handbook of motivation science.* New York: Guilford Press.

Shallice, T., Fletcher, P., Frith, C. D., Grasby, P., Frackowiak, R. S. J., & Dolan, R. J. (1994). Brain regions associated with acquisition and retrieval of verbal episodic memory. *Nature, 368,* 633–635.

Shapiro, N. (2005, October 5–11). The day care scare. *Seattle Weekly.*

Shaw, J. S., Bjork, R. A., & Handal, A. (1995). Retrieval-induced forgetting in an eyewitness paradigm. *Psychonomic Bulletin & Review, 13,* 1023–1027.

Shedler, J. (2010). The efficacy of psychodynamic psychotherapy. *American Psychologist, 65,* 98–109.

Sheehan, P. (1979). Hypnosis and the process of imagination. In E. Fromm & R. S. Shor (Eds.), *Hypnosis: Developments in research and new perspectives.* Chicago: Aldine.

Sheingold, K., & Tenney, Y. J. (1982). Memory for a salient childhood event. In U. Neisser (Ed.), *Memory observed* (pp. 201–212). New York: Freeman.

Shenton, M. E., Dickey, C. C., Frumin, M., & McCarley, R. W. (2001). A review of MRI findings in schizophrenia. *Schizophrenia Research, 49,* 1–52.

Shepherd, G. M. (1988). *Neurobiology.* New York: Oxford University Press.

Sherrod, D. (1974). Crowding, perceived control, and behavioral aftereffects. *Journal of Applied Social Psychology, 4,* 171–186.

Sherry, D. F., & Schacter, D. L. (1987). The evolution of multiple memory systems. *Psychological Review, 94,* 439–454.

Shiffman, S., Gnys, M., Richards, T. J., Paty, J. A., & Hickcox, M. (1996). Temptations to smoke after quitting: A comparison of lapsers and maintainers. *Health Psychology, 15,* 455–461.

Shimamura, A. P., & Squire, L. R. (1987). A neuropsychological study of fact memory and source amnesia. *Journal of Experimental Psychology: Learning, Memory, and Cognition, 13,* 464–473.

Shinskey, J. L., & Munakata, Y. (2005). Familiarity breeds searching. *Psychological Science, 16*(8), 596–600.

Shiv, B., Loewenstein, G., Bechara, A., Damasio, H., & Damasio, A. R. (2005). Investment behavior and the negative side of emotion. *Psychological Science, 16,* 435–439.

Shomstein, S., & Yantis, S. (2004). Control of attention shifts between vision and audition in human cortex. *Journal of Neuroscience, 24,* 10702–10706.

Shore, C. (1986). Combinatorial play: Conceptual development and early multiword speech. *Developmental Psychology, 22,* 184–190.

Shweder, R. A., & Sullivan, M. A. (1993). Cultural psychology: Who needs it? *Annual Review of Psychology, 44,* 497–523.

Siegel, B. (1988, October 30). Can evil beget good? Nazi data: A dilemma for science. *Los Angeles Times.*

Siegel, S. (1984). Pavlovian conditioning and heroin overdose: Reports by overdose victims. *Bulletin of the Psychonomic Society, 22,* 428–430.

Siegel, S. (2005). Drug tolerance, drug addiction, and drug anticipation. *Current Directions in Psychological Science, 14,* 296–300.

Siegel, S., Baptista, M. A. S., Kim, J. A., McDonald, R. V., & Weise-Kelly, L. (2000). Pavlovian psychopharmacology: The associative basis of tolerance. *Experimental and Clinical Psychopharmacology, 8,* 276–293.

Silver, R. L., Boon, C., & Stones, M. H. (1983). Searching for meaning in misfortune: Making sense of incest. *Journal of Social Issues, 39,* 81–102.

Simon, L. (1998). *Genuine reality: A life of William James.* New York: Harcourt Brace.

Simons, D. J., & Levin, D. T. (1998). Failure to detect changes to people during a real-world interaction. *Psychonomic Bulletin & Review, 5,* 644–649.

Simons, D. J., & Rensink, R. A. (2005). Change blindness: Past, present, and future. *Trends in Cognitive Sciences, 9,* 16–20.

Singer, T., Seymour, B., O'Doherty, J., Kaube, H., Dolan, R. J., & Frith, C. D. (2004). Empathy for pain involves the affective but not sensory components of pain. *Science, 303,* 1157–1162.

Skinner, B. F. (1938). *The behavior of organisms: An experimental analysis.* New York: Appleton-Century-Crofts.

Skinner, B. F. (1948). "Superstition" in the pigeon. *Journal of Experimental Psychology, 38,* 168–172.

Skinner, B. F. (1953). *Science and human behavior.* New York: Macmillan.

Skinner, B. F. (1957). *Verbal behavior.* New York: Appleton-Century-Crofts.

Skinner, B. F. (1971). *Beyond freedom and dignity.* New York: Bantam Books.

Skinner, B. F. (1979). *The shaping of a behaviorist: Part two of an autobiography.* New York: Knopf.

Skinner, B. F. (1986). *Walden II.* Englewood Cliffs, NJ: Prentice Hall. (Original work published 1948)

Slater, A., Morison, V., & Somers, M. (1988). Orientation discrimination and cortical function in the human newborn. *Perception, 17,* 597–602.

Slotnick, S. D., & Schacter, D. L. (2004). A sensory signature that distinguished true from false memories. *Nature Neuroscience, 7,* 664–672.

Smetacek, V. (2002). Balance: Mind-grasping gravity. *Nature, 415,* 481.

Smetana, J. G. (1981). Preschool children's conceptions of moral and social rules. *Child Development, 52,* 1333–1336.

Smetana, J. G., & Braeges, J. L. (1990). The development of toddlers' moral and conventional judgments. *Merrill-Palmer Quarterly, 36,* 329–346.

Smith, A. R., Seid, M. A., Jimanez, L. C., & Wcislo, W. T. (2010). Socially induced brain development in a facultatively eusocial sweat bee *Megalopta genalis* (Halictidae). *Proceedings of the Royal Society B: Biological Sciences.*

Smith, E. E., & Jonides, J. (1997). Working memory: A view from neuroimaging. *Cognitive Psychology, 33,* 5–42.

Smith, M. L., Glass, G. V., & Miller, T. I. (1980). *The benefits of psychotherapy.* Baltimore: Johns Hopkins University Press.

Smith, N., & Tsimpli, I.-M. (1995). *The mind of a savant.* Oxford, England: Oxford University Press.

Snedeker, J., Geren, J., & Shafto, C. (2007). Starting over: International adoption as a natural experiment in language development. *Psychological Science, 18,* 79–87.

Snyder, C. R., & Lopez, S. J. (Eds.). (2009). *Oxford handbook of positive psychology* (2nd ed.). New York: Oxford University Press.

Solomon, S., Greenberg, J., & Pyszczynski, T. (1991). A terror management theory of social behavior: The psychological functions of self-esteem and cultural worldviews. In M. P. Zanna (Ed.), *Advances in experimental social psychology* (Vol. 24, pp. 93–159). New York: Academic Press.

Solomon, S., Greenberg, J., Pyszczynski, T., Greenberg, J., Koole, S. L., & Pyszczynski, T. (2004). The cultural animal: Twenty years of terror management theory and research. In *Handbook of experimental existential psychology* (pp. 13–34). New York: Guilford Press.

Somers, J. M., Goldner, E. M., Waraich, P., & Hsu, L. (2006). Prevalence and incidence studies of anxiety disorders: A systematic review of the literature. *Canadian Journal of Psychiatry, 51,* 100–113.

Sonnby-Borgstrom, M., Jonsson, P., & Svensson, O. (2003). Emotional empathy as related to mimicry reactions at different levels of information processing. *Journal of Nonverbal Behavior, 27,* 3–23.

Sperling, G. (1960). The information available in brief visual presentations. *Psychological Monographs, 74* (Whole No. 48).

Sperry, R. W. (1964). The great cerebral commissure. *Scientific American, 210,* 42–52.

Spitz, R. A. (1949). Motherless infants. *Child Development, 20,* 145–155.

Spitzer, R. L., Gibbon, M., Skodol, A. E., Williams, J. B. W., & First, M. B. (1994). *DSM-IV casebook: A learning companion to the Diagnostic & Statistical Manual of Mental Disorders* (4th ed.). Washington, DC: American Psychiatric Press.

Sprecher, S. (1999). "I love you more today than yesterday": Romantic partners' perceptions of changes in love and related affect over time. *Journal of Personality and Social Psychology, 76,* 46–53.

Squire, L. R. (1992). Memory and the hippocampus: A synthesis from findings with rats, monkeys, and humans. *Psychological Review, 99,* 195–231.

Squire, L. R. (2009). The legacy of patient HM for neuroscience. *Neuron, 61,* 6–9.

Squire, L. R., & Kandel, E. R. (1999). *Memory: From mind to molecules.* New York: Scientific American Library.

Squire, L. R., Knowlton, B., & Musen, G. (1993). The structure and organization of memory. *Annual Review of Psychology, 44,* 453–495.

Srivistava, S., John, O. P., Gosling, S. D., & Potter, J. (2003). Development of personality in early and middle adulthood: Set like plaster or persistent change? *Journal of Personality and Social Psychology, 84,* 1041–1053.

Staddon, J. E. R., & Simmelhag, V. L. (1971). The "superstition" experiment: A reexamination of its implications for the principles of adaptive behavior. *Psychological Review, 78,* 3–43.

Staw, B. M., & Hoang, H. (1995). Sunk costs in the NBA: Why draft order affects playing time and survival in professional basketball. *Administrative Science Quarterly, 40,* 474–494.

Steele, C. M., & Aronson, J. (1995). Stereotype threat and the intellectual test performance of African Americans. *Journal of Personality and Social Psychology, 69,* 797–811.

Steele, C. M., & Josephs, R. A. (1990). Alcohol myopia: Its prized and dangerous effects. *American Psychologist, 45,* 921–933.

Steele, H. (2008). Day care and attachment re-visited. *Attachment & Human Development, 10,* 223.

Stein, M., Federspiel, A., Koenig, T., Wirth, M., Lehmann, C., Wiest, R., Strik, W., Brandeis, D., & Dierks, T. (2009). Reduced frontal activation with increasing second language proficiency. *Neuropsychologia, 47,* 2712–2720.

Stein, M. B. (1998). Neurobiological perspectives on social phobia: From affiliation to zoology. *Biological Psychiatry, 44,* 1277–1285.

Stein, M. B., Chavira, D. A., & Jang, K. L. (2001). Bringing up bashful baby: Developmental pathways to social phobia. *Psychiatric Clinics of North America, 24,* 661–675.

Stein, M. B., Koverola, C., Hanna, C., Torchia, M. G., & McClarty, B. (1997). Hippocampal volume in women victimized by childhood sexual abuse. *Psychological Medicine, 27,* 951–959.

Stein, Z., Susser, M., Saenger, G., & Marolla, F. (1975). *Famine and development: The Dutch hunger winter of 1944–1945.* Oxford, England: Oxford University Press.

Steinbaum, E. A., & Miller, N. E. (1965). Obesity from eating elicited by daily stimulation of hypothalamus. *American Journal of Physiology, 208,* 1–5.

Steinberg, L. (1999). *Adolescence* (5th ed.). Boston: McGraw-Hill.

Steinberg, L., & Monahan, K. C. (2007). Age differences in resistance to peer influence. *Developmental Psychology, 43,* 1531–1543.

Steinberg, L., & Morris, A. S. (2001). Adolescent development. *Annual Review of Psychology, 52,* 83–110.

Steiner, F. (1986). Differentiating smiles. In E. Branniger-Huber & F. Steiner (Eds.), *FACS in psychotherapy research* (pp. 139–148). Zurich: Department of Clinical Psychology, Universität Zürich.

Steiner, J. E. (1973). The gustofacial response: Observation on normal and anencephalic newborn infants. In J. F. Bosma (Ed.), *Fourth symposium on oral sensation and perception: Development in the fetus and infant* (pp. 254–278). Bethesda, MD: U.S. Department of Heath, Education, and Welfare (DHEW 73-546).

Steiner, J. E. (1979). Human facial expressions in response to taste and smell stimulation. *Advances in Child Development and Behavior, 13,* 257–295.

Stellar, J. R., Kelley, A. E., & Corbett, D. (1983). Effects of peripheral and central dopamine blockade on lateral hypothalamic self-stimulation: Evidence for both reward and motor deficits. *Pharmacology, Biochemistry, and Behavior, 18,* 433–442.

Stellar, J. R., & Stellar, E. (1985). *The neurobiology of motivation and reward.* New York: Springer-Verlag.

Stelmack, R. M. (1990). Biological bases of extraversion: Psychophysiological evidence. *Journal of Personality, 58,* 293–311.

Stephens, R. S. (1999). Cannabis and hallucinogens. In B. S. McCrady & E. E. Epstein (Eds.), *Addictions: A comprehensive guidebook.* New York: Oxford University Press.

Sterelny, K., & Griffiths, P. E. (1999). *Sex and death: An introduction to philosophy of biology.* Chicago: University of Chicago Press.

Stern, J. A., Brown, M., Ulett, A., & Sletten, I. (1977). A comparison of hypnosis, acupuncture, morphine, Valium, aspirin, and placebo in the management of experimentally induced pain. In W. E. Edmonston (Ed.), *Conceptual and investigative approaches to hypnosis and hypnotic phenomena* (Vol. 296, pp. 175–193). New York: Annals of the New York Academy of Sciences.

Sternberg, R. J. (1986). A triangular theory of love. *Psychological Review, 93,* 119–135.

Stevens, G., & Gardner, S. (1982). *The women of psychology* (Vol. 1). Rochester: Schenkman Books.

Stevens, J. (1988). An activity approach to practical memory. In M. M. Gruneberg, P. E. Morris, & R. N. Sykes (Eds.), *Practical aspects of memory: Current research and issues* (Vol. 1, pp. 335–341). New York: Wiley.

Stevens, L. A. (1971). *Explorers of the brain.* New York: Knopf.

Stickgold, R., Hobson, J. A., Fosse, R., & Fosse, M. (2001). Sleep, learning, and dreams: Off-line memory reprocessing. *Science, 294,* 1052–1057.

Stone, A. A., Schwarts, J. E., Broderick, J. E., & Deaton, A. (2010). A snapshot of the age distribution of psychological well-being in the United States. *Proceedings of the National Academy of Sciences, USA, 107,* 9985–9990.

Stone, J., Perry, Z. W., & Darley, J. M. (1997). "White men can't jump": Evidence for the perceptual confirmation of racial stereotypes following a basketball game. *Basic and Applied Social Psychology, 19,* 291–306.

Stoodley, C. J., Ray, N., J., Jack, A., & Stein, J. F. (2008). Implicit learning in control, dyslexic, and garden-variety poor readers. *Annals of the New York Academy of Sciences, 1145,* 173–183.

Storms, M. D. (1973). Videotape and the attribution process: Reversing actors' and observers' points of view. *Journal of Personality and Social Psychology, 27,* 165–175.

Strack, F., Martin, L. L., & Stepper, S. (1988). Inhibiting and facilitating conditions of the human smile: A nonobtrusive test of the facial feedback hypothesis. *Journal of Personality and Social Psychology, 54,* 768–777.

Strahan, E. J., Spencer, S. J., & Zanna, M. P. (2002). Subliminal priming and persuasion: Striking while the iron is hot. *Journal of Experimental Social Psychology, 38,* 556–568.

Strayer, D. L., Drews, F. A., & Johnston, W. A. (2003). Cell phone induced failures of visual attention during simulated driving. *Journal of Experimental Psychology: Applied, 9,* 23–32.

Streissguth, A. P., Barr, H. M., Bookstein, F. L., Sampson, P. D., & Carmichael Olson, H. (1999). The long-term neurocognitive consequences of prenatal alcohol exposure: A 14-year study. *Psychological Science, 10,* 186–190.

Striano, T., & Reid, V. M. (2006). Social cognition in the first year. *Trends in Cognitive Sciences, 10*(10), 471–476.

Strickland, L. H. (1991). Russian and Soviet social psychology. *Canadian Psychology, 32,* 580–595.

Striegel-Moore, R. H., & Bulik, C. M. (2007). Risk factors for eating disorders. *American Psychologist, 62,* 181–198.

Strohmetz, D. B., Rind, B., Fisher, R., & Lynn, M. (2002). Sweetening the till: The use of candy to increase restaurant tipping. *Journal of Applied Social Psychology, 32,* 300–309.

Strueber, D., Lueck, M., & Roth, G. (2006). The violent brain. *Scientific American Mind, 17.*

Stuss, D. T., & Benson, D. F. (1986). *The frontal lobes.* New York: Raven Press.

Suarez-Morales, L., & Lopez, B. (2009). The impact of acculturative stress and daily hassles on pre-adolescent psychological adjustment: Examining anxiety symptoms. *Journal of Primary Prevention, 30,* 335–349.

Substance Abuse and Mental Health Services Administration. (2005). *Suicide warning signs.* Washington, DC: U.S. Department of Health and Human Services.

Suchman, A. L., Markakis, K., Beckman, H. B., & Frankel, R. (1997). A model of empathic communication in the medical interview. *Journal of the American Medical Association, 277,* 678–682.

Suddendorf, T., & Corballis, M. C. (2007). The evolution of foresight: What is mental time travel and is it unique to humans? *Behavioral and Brain Sciences, 30,* 299–313.

Suler, J. (2004). The online disinhibition effect. *Cyberpsychology and Behavior, 7,* 321–326.

Sulloway, F. J. (1992). *Freud, biologist of the mind.* Cambridge, MA: Harvard University Press.

Sundet, J. M., Eriksen, W., & Tambs, K. (2008). Intelligence correlations between brothers decrease with increasing age difference: Evidence for shared environmental effects in young adults. *Psychological Science, 19,* 843–847.

Susman, S., Dent, C., McAdams, L., Stacy, A., Burton, D., & Flay, B. (1994). Group self-identification and adolescent cigarette smoking: A 1-year prospective study. *Journal of Abnormal Psychology, 103,* 576–580.

Susser, E. B., Brown, A., & Matte, T. D. (1999). Prenatal factors and adult mental and physical health. *Canadian Journal of Psychiatry, 44*(4), 326–334.

Sussman, L. K., Robins, L. N., & Earls, F. (1987). Treatment-seeking for depression by Black and White Americans. *Social Science and Medicine, 24,* 187–196.

Suzuki, L. A., & Valencia, R. R. (1997). Race-ethnicity and measured intelligence: Educational implications. *American Psychologist, 52,* 1103–1114.

Swann, W. B., Jr. (1983). Self-verification: Bringing social reality into harmony with the self. In J. M. Suls & A. G. Greenwald (Ed.), *Psychological perspectives on the self* (Vol. 2, pp. 33–66). Hillsdale, NJ: Lawrence Erlbaum.

Swann, W. B., Jr. (in press). Self-verification theory. In A. W. Kruglanski, E. T. Higgins, & P. A. M. Lange (Eds.), *Handbook of theories of social psychology*. London: Sage.

Swann, W. B., Jr., & Rentfrow, P. J. (2001). Blirtatiousness: Cognitive, behavioral, and physiological consequences of rapid responding. *Journal of Personality and Social Psychology, 181*(6), 1160–1175.

Swann, W. B., Jr., Rentfrow, P. J., Guinn, J. S., Leary, M. R., & Tangney, J. P. (2003). Self-verification: The search for coherence. In *Handbook of self and identity* (pp. 367–383). New York: Guilford Press.

Swets, J. A., Dawes, R. M., & Monahan, J. (2000). Psychological science can improve diagnostic decisions. *Psychological Science in the Public Interest, 1,* 1–26.

Szasz, T. S. (1987). *Insanity.* New York: Wiley.

Szpunar, K. K., Watson, J. M., & McDermott, K. B. (2007). Neural substrates of envisioning the future. *Proceedings of the National Academy of Sciences, USA, 104,* 642–647.

Tajfel, H. (1970). Experiments in intergroup discrimination. *Scientific American, 223,* 96–102.

Tajfel, H., Billig, M. G., Bundy, R. P., & Flament, C. (1971). Social categorization and intergroup behaviour. *European Journal of Social Psychology, 1,* 149–178.

Takahashi, K. (1986). Examining the strange-situation procedure with Japanese mothers and 12-month-old infants. *Developmental Psychology, 22,* 265–270.

Tamis-LeMonda, C. S., Adolph, K. E., Lobo, S. A., Karasik, L. B., Ishak, S., & Dimitropoulou, K. A. (2008). When infants take mothers' advice: 18-month-olds integrate perceptual and social information to guide motor action. *Developmental Psychology, 44,* 734–746.

Tamminga, C. A., Nemeroff, C. B., Blakely, R. D., Brady, L., Carter, C. S., Davis, K. L., Dingledine, R., et al. (2002). Developing novel treatments for mood disorders: Accelerating discovery. *Biological Psychiatry, 52,* 589–609.

Tanaka, F., Cicourel, A., & Movellan, J. R. (2007). Socialization between toddlers and robots at an early childhood education center. *Proceedings of the National Academy of Sciences, USA, 104*(46), 17954–17958.

Tanaka, K. (1996). Inferotemporal cortex and object vision. *Annual Review of Neuroscience, 19,* 109–139.

Tang, T. Z., DeRubeis, R., Hollon, S. D., Amsterdam, J., Shelton, R., & Schalet, B. (2009). Personality change during depression treatment: A placebo-controlled trial. *Archives of General Psychiatry, 66,* 1322–1330.

Tang, Y.-P., Shimizu, E., Dube, G. R., Rampon, C., Kerchner, G. A., Zhuo, M., et al. (1999). Genetic enhancement of learning and memory in mice. *Nature, 401,* 63–69.

Tart, C. T. (Ed.). (1969). *Altered states of consciousness.* New York: Wiley.

Task Force on Promotion and Dissemination of Psychological Procedures. (1995). Training in and dissemination of empirically validated psychological treatments: Report and recommendations. *Clinical Psychologist, 48,* 3–23.

Taylor, D., & Lambert, W. (1990). *Language and culture in the lives of immigrants and refugees.* Austin, TX: Hogg Foundation for Mental Health.

Taylor, E. (2001). *William James on consciousness beyond the margin.* Princeton, NJ: Princeton University Press.

Taylor, S. E. (1986). *Health psychology.* New York: Random House.

Taylor, S. E. (1989). *Positive illusions.* New York: Basic Books.

Taylor, S. E. (2002). *The tending instinct: How nurturing is essential to who we are and how we live.* New York: Times Books.

Taylor, S. E., & Brown, J. D. (1988). Illusion and well-being: A social psychological perspective on mental health. *Psychological Bulletin, 103,* 193–210.

Taylor, S. E.,, & Fiske, S. T. (1975). Point-of-view and perceptions of causality. *Journal of Personality and Social Psychology, 32,* 439–445.

Teasdale, J. D., Segal, Z. V., & Williams, J. M. G. (2000). Prevention of relapse/recurrence in major depression by mindfulness-based cognitive therapy. *Journal of Consulting and Clinical Psychology, 68,* 615–623.

Tejada-Vera, B., & Sutton, P. D. (2009). Births, marriages, divorces, and deaths: Provisional data for 2008. *National Vital Statistics Reports, 57.*

Telch, M. J., Lucas, J. A., & Nelson, P. (1989). Non-clinical panic in college students: An investigation of prevalence and symptomology. *Journal of Abnormal Psychology, 98,* 300–306.

Tellegen, A., & Atkinson, G. (1974). Openness to absorbing and self-altering experiences ("absorption"), a trait related to hypnotic susceptibility. *Journal of Abnormal Psychology, 83,* 268–277.

Tellegen, A., Lykken, D. T., Bouchard, T. J., Wilcox, K., Segal, N., & Rich, A. (1988). Personality similarity in twins reared together and apart. *Journal of Personality and Social Psychology, 54,* 1031–1039.

Temerlin, M. K., & Trousdale, W. W. (1969). The social psychology of clinical diagnosis. *Psychotherapy: Theory, Research & Practice, 6,* 24–29.

Tempini, M. L., Price, C. J., Josephs, O., Vandenberghe, R., Cappa, S. F., Kapur, N., et al. (1998). The neural systems sustaining face and proper-name processing. *Brain, 121,* 2103–2118.

Terman, L. M. (1916). *The measurement of intelligence.* Boston: Houghton Mifflin.

Terman, M., Terman, J. S., Quitkin, F. M., McGrath, P. J., Stewart, J. W., & Rafferty, B. (1989). Light therapy for seasonal affective disorder. A review of efficacy. *Neuropsychopharmacology, 2,* 1–22.

Teyler, T. J., & DiScenna, P. (1986). The hippocampal memory indexing theory. *Behavioral Neuroscience, 100,* 147–154.

Thase, M. E., & Howland, R. H. (1995). Biological processes in depression: An updated review and integration. In E. E. Beckham & W. R. Leber (Eds.), *Handbook of depression* (2nd ed., pp. 213–279). New York: Guilford Press.

Thibaut, J. W., & Kelley, H. H. (1959). *The social psychology of groups.* New Brunswick, NJ: Transaction Publishers.

Thomaes, S., Bushman, B. J., Stegge, H., & Olthof, T. (2008). Trumping shame by blasts of noise: Narcissism, self-esteem, shame, and aggression in young adolescents. *Child Development, 79*(6), 1792–1801.

Thomas, A., & Chess, S. (1977). *Temperament and development.* New York: Brunner/Mazel.

Thompson, B., Coronado, G., Chen, L., Thompson, L. A., Halperin, A., Jaffe, R., et al. (2007). Prevalence and characteristics of smokers at 30 Pacific Northwest colleges and universities. *Nicotine & Tobacco Research, 9,* 429–438.

Thompson, P. M., Vidal, C., Giedd, J. N., Gochman, P., Blumenthal, J., Nicolson, R., et al. (2001). Accelerated gray matter loss in very early-onset schizophrenia. *Proceedings of the National Academy of Sciences, USA, 98,* 11650–11655.

Thompson, R. F. (2005). In search of memory traces. *Annual Review of Psychology, 56,* 1–23.

Thompson, S. C., Schlehofer, M. l. M., Shah, J. Y., & Gardner, W. L. (2008). The many sides of control motivation: Motives for high, low, and illusory control. In *Handbook of motivation science* (pp. 41–56). New York: Guilford Press.

Thorndike, E. L. (1898). Animal intelligence: An experimental study of associative processes in animals. *Psychological Review Monograph Supplements, 2,* 4–160.

Thornhill, R., & Gangestad, S. W. (1993). Human facial beauty: Averageness, symmetry, and parasite resistance. *Human Nature, 4,* 237–269.

Thurber, J. (1956). *Further fables of our time.* New York: Simon & Schuster.

Thurstone, L. L. (1938). *Primary mental abilities.* Chicago: University of Chicago Press.

Tice, D. M., & Baumeister, R. F. (1997). Longitudinal study of procrastination, performance, stress, and health: The costs and benefits of dawdling. *Psychological Science, 8*(6), 454–458.

Tickle, J. J., Sargent, J. D., Dalton, M. A., Beach, M. L., & Heatherton, T. F. (2001). Favourite movie stars, their tobacco use in contemporary movies, and its association with adolescent smoking. *Tobacco Control, 10,* 16–22.

Tienari, P., Wynne, L. C., Sorri, A., Lahti, I., Läksy, K., Moring, J., et al. (2004). Genotype–environment interaction in schizophrenia spectrum disorder: Long-term follow-up study of Finnish adoptees. *British Journal of Psychiatry, 184,* 216–222.

Time poll. (2005, January 17). Just how happy are we? *Time,* p. A4.

Tittle, P. (Ed.). (2004). *Should parents be licensed?: Debating the issues.* New York: Prometheus Books.

Tolman, E. C., & Honzik, C. H. (1930a). "Insight" in rats. *University of California Publications in Psychology, 4,* 215–232.

Tolman, E. C., & Honzik, C. H. (1930b). Introduction and removal of reward and maze performance in rats. *University of California Publications in Psychology, 4,* 257–275.

Tolman, E. C., Ritchie, B. F., & Kalish, D. (1946). Studies in spatial learning: I. Orientation and short cut. *Journal of Experimental Psychology, 36,* 13–24.

Tomasello, M., & Call, J. (2004). The role of humans in the cognitive development of apes revisited. *Animal Cognition, 7,* 213–215.

Tomasello, M., Davis-Dasilva, M., Camak, L., & Bard, K. (1987). Observational learning of tool use by young chimpanzees. *Human Evolution, 2,* 175–183.

Tomasello, M., Savage-Rumbaugh, S., & Kruger, A. C. (1993). Imitative learning of actions on objects by children, chimpanzees, and enculturated chimpanzees. *Child Development, 64,* 1688–1705.

Tomkins, S. S. (1981). The role of facial response in the experience of emotion. *Journal of Personality and Social Psychology, 40,* 351–357.

Tooby, J., & Cosmides, L. (2000). Mapping the evolved functional organization of mind and brain. In M. S. Gazzaniga (Ed.), *The cognitive neurosciences* (pp. 1185–1198). Cambridge, MA: The MIT Press.

Tootell, R. B. H., Reppas, J. B., Dale, A. M., Look, R. B., Sereno, M. I., Malach, R., et al. (1995). Visual-motion aftereffect in human cortical area MT revealed by functional magnetic resonance imaging. *Nature, 375,* 139–141.

Torgensen, S. (1983). Genetic factors in anxiety disorders. *Archives of General Psychiatry, 40,* 1085–1089.

Torgensen, S. (1986). Childhood and family characteristics in panic and generalized anxiety disorder. *American Journal of Psychiatry, 143,* 630–639.

Torrey, E. F., Bower, A. E., Taylor, E. H., & Gottesman, I. I. (1994). *Schizophrenia and manic-depressive disorder: The biological roots of mental illness as revealed by the landmark study of identical twins.* New York: Basic Books.

Treede, R. D., Kenshalo, D. R., Gracely, R. H., & Jones, A. K. (1999). The cortical representation of pain. *Pain, 79,* 105–111.

Treisman, A. (1998). Feature binding, attention and object perception. *Philosophical Transactions of the Royal Society (B), 353,* 1295–1306.

Treisman, A. (2006). How the deployment of attention determines what we see. *Visual Cognition, 14,* 411–443.

Treisman, A., & Gelade, G. (1980). A feature integration theory of attention. *Cognitive Psychology, 12,* 97–136.

Treisman, A., & Schmidt, H. (1982). Illusory conjunctions in the perception of objects. *Cognitive Psychology, 14,* 107–141.

Trimble, M. R. (2007). *The soul in the brain: The cerebral basis of language, art, and belief.* Baltimore, MD: Johns Hopkins University Press.

Trivers, R. L. (1971). The evolution of reciprocal altruism. *Quarterly Review of Biology, 46,* 35–57.

Trivers, R. L. (1972). Parental investment and sexual selection. In B. Campbell (Ed.), *Sexual selection and the descent of man, 1871–1971* (pp. 139–179). Chicago: Aldine.

Trull, T. J., & Durrett, C. A. (2005). Categorical and dimensional models of personality disorder. *Annual Review of Clinical Psychology, 1,* 355–380.

Tulving, E. (1972). Episodic and semantic memory. In E. Tulving & W. Donaldson (Eds.), *Organization of memory* (pp. 381–403). New York: Academic Press.

Tulving, E. (1983). *Elements of episodic memory.* Oxford, England: Clarendon Press.

Tulving, E. (1985). Memory and consciousness. *Canadian Psychologist, 25,* 1–12.

Tulving, E. (1998). Neurocognitive processes of human memory. In C. von Euler, I. Lundberg, & R. Llins (Eds.), *Basic mechanisms in cognition and language* (pp. 261–281). Amsterdam: Elsevier.

Tulving, E., Kapur, S., Craik, F. I. M., Moscovitch, M., & Houle, S. (1994). Hemispheric encoding/retrieval asymmetry in episodic memory: Positron emission tomography findings. *Proceedings of the National Academy of Sciences, USA, 91,* 2016–2020.

Tulving, E., & Schacter, D. L. (1990). Priming and human memory systems. *Science, 247,* 301–306.

Tulving, E., Schacter, D. L., & Stark, H. (1982). Priming effects in word-fragment completion are independent of recognition memory. *Journal of Experimental Psychology: Learning, Memory, and Cognition, 8,* 336–342.

Tulving, E., & Thomson, D. M. (1973). Encoding specificity and retrieval processes in episodic memory. *Psychological Review, 80,* 352–373.

Turiel, E. (2006). Thought, emotions, and social interactional processes in moral development. In M. Killen & J. G. Smetana (Eds.), *Handbook of moral development* (pp. 7–35). Mahwah, NJ: Lawrence Erlbaum.

Turkheimer, E. (2000). Three laws of behavior genetics and what they mean. *Current Directions in Psychological Science, 9,* 160–164.

Turner, D. C., Robbins, T. W., Clark, L., Aron, A. R., Dowson, J., & Sahakian, B. J. (2003). Cognitive enhancing effects of modafinil in healthy volunteers. *Psychopharmacology, 165,* 260–269.

Turner, D. C., & Sahakian, B. J. (2006). Neuroethics of cognitive enhancement. *BioSocieties, 1,* 113–123.

Turtle, J., Read, J. D., Lindsay, D. S., & Brimacombe, C. A. E. (2008). Toward a more informative psychological science of eyewitness evidence. *Applied Cognitive Psychology, 22,* 769–778.

Tversky, A., & Kahneman, D. (1973). Availability: A heuristic for judging frequency and probability. *Cognitive Psychology, 5,* 207–232.

Tversky, A., & Kahneman, D. (1974). Judgment under uncertainty: Heuristics and biases. *Science, 185,* 1124–1131.

Tversky, A., & Kahneman, D. (1981). The framing of decisions and the psychology of choice. *Science, 211,* 453–458.

Tversky, A., & Kahneman, D. (1983). Extensional versus intuitive reasoning: The conjunction fallacy in probability judgment. *Psychological Review, 90,* 293–315.

Tversky, A., & Kahneman, D. (1992). Advances in prospect theory: Cumulative representation of uncertainty. *Journal of Risk and Uncertainty, 5,* 297–323.

Twenge, J. M., Campbell, W. K., & Foster, C. A. (2003). Parenthood and marital satisfaction: A meta-analytic review. *Journal of Marriage and Family, 65,* 574–583.

Tyler, T. R. (1990). *Why people obey the law.* New Haven, CT: Yale University Press.

Umberson, D., Williams, K., Powers, D. A., Liu, H., & Needham, B. (2006). You make me sick: Marital quality and health over the life course. *Journal of Health and Social Behavior, 47,* 1–16.

Uncapher, M. R., & Rugg, M. D. (2008). Fractionation of the component processes underlying successful episodic encoding: A combined fMRI and divided-attention study. *Journal of Cognitive Neuroscience, 20,* 240–254.

Ungerleider, L. G., & Mishkin, M. (1982). Two cortical visual systems. In D. J. Ingle, M. A. Goodale, & R. J. W. Mansfield (Eds.), *Analysis of visual behavior* (pp. 549–586). Cambridge, MA: The MIT Press.

Ursano, R. J., & Silberman, E. K. (2003). Psychoanalysis, psychoanalytic psychotherapy, and supportive psychotherapy. In R. E. Hales & S. C. Yudofsky (Eds.), *The American Psychiatric Publishing textbook of clinical psychiatry* (4th ed., pp. 1177–1203). Washington, DC: American Psychiatric Publishing.

U.S. Department of Transportation. (2008). Traffic safety facts 2006: Alcohol-impaired driving [Electronic version]. Retrieved December 2, 2008, from http://www-nrd.nhtsa.dot.gov/Pubs/810801.PDF

Usher, J. A., & Neisser, U. (1993). Childhood amnesia and the beginnings of memory for four early life events. *Journal of Experimental Psychology: General, 122,* 155–165.

Valentine, T., Brennen, T., & Brédart, S. (1996). *The cognitive psychology of proper names: On the importance of being Ernest.* London: Routledge.

Vallacher, R. R., & Wegner, D. M. (1985). *A theory of action identification.* Hillsdale, NJ: Lawrence Erlbaum.

Vallacher, R. R., & Wegner, D. M. (1987). What do people think they're doing? Action identification and human behavior. *Psychological Review, 94,* 3–15.

van den Boon, D. C. (1994). The influence of temperament and mothering on attachment and exploration: An experimental manipulation of sensitive responsiveness among lower-class mothers with irritable infants. *Child Development, 65,* 1457–1477.

van den Boon, D. C. (1995). Do first year intervention effects endure? Follow-up during toddlerhood of a sample of Dutch irritable infants. *Child Development, 66,* 1798–1816.

Van Der Werf, Y. D., Van Der Helm, W., Schoonheim, M., Ridderikhoff, A., & Van Smeren, E. J. W. (2009). Learning by observation requires an early sleep window. *Proceedings of the National Academy of Sciences, USA, 106,* 18926–18930.

Van Essen, D. C., Anderson, C. H., & Felleman, D. J. (1992). Information processing in the primate visual system: An integrated systems perspective. *Science, 255,* 419–423.

van IJzendoorn, M. H. (1995). Adult attachment representations, parental responsiveness, and infant attachment: A meta-analysis on the predictive validity of the Adult Attachment Interview. *Psychological Bulletin, 117,* 387–403.

van IJzendoorn, M. H., & Kroonenberg, P. M. (1988). Cross-cultural patterns of attachment: A meta-analysis of the strange situation. *Child Development, 59,* 147–156.

van IJzendoorn, M. H., Juffer, F., & Klein Poelhuis, C. W. (2005). Adoption and cognitive development: A meta-analytic comparison of adopted and nonadopted children's IQ and school performance. *Psychological Bulletin, 131,* 301–316.

van Praag, H. (2009). Exercise and the brain: Something to chew on. *Trends in Neuroscience, 32,* 283–290.

van Stegeren, A. H., Everaerd, W., Cahill, L., McGaugh, J. L., & Gooren, L. J. G. (1998). Memory for emotional events: Differential effects of centrally versus peripherally acting blocking agents. *Psychopharmacology, 138,* 305–310.

Van Velzen, C. J. M., & Emmelkamp, P. M. G. (1996). The assessment of personality disorders: Implications for cognitive and behavior therapy. *Behaviour Research and Therapy, 34,* 655–668.

Vargha-Khadem, F., Gadian, D. G., Watkins, K. E., Connelly, A., Van Paesschen, W., & Mishkin, M. (1997). Differential effects of early hippocampal pathology on episodic and semantic memory. *Science, 277,* 376–380.

Vinter, A., & Perruchet, P. (2002). Implicit motor learning through observational training in adults and children. *Memory & Cognition, 30,* 256–261.

Vitkus, J. (1996). *Casebook in abnormal psychology* (3rd ed.). New York: McGraw-Hill.

Vitkus, J. (1999). *Casebook in abnormal psychology* (4th ed.). New York: McGraw-Hill.

Von Frisch, K. (1974). Decoding the language of the bee. *Science, 185,* 663–668.

Vygotsky, L. S. (1978). *Mind in society: The development of higher psychological processes.* Cambridge, MA: Harvard University Press.

Wadhwa, P. D., Sandman, C. A., & Garite, T. J. (2001). The neurobiology of stress in human pregnancy: Implications for prematurity and development of the fetal central nervous system. *Progress in Brain Research, 133,* 131–142.

Wagner, A. D., Schacter, D. L., Rotte, M., Koutstaal, W., Maril, A., Dale, A. M., et al. (1998). Remembering and forgetting of verbal experiences as predicted by brain activity. *Science, 281,* 1188–1190.

Wagner, G., & Morris, E. (1987). Superstitious behavior in children. *Psychological Record, 37,* 471–488.

Wahba, M. A., & Bridwell, L. G. (1976). Maslow reconsidered: A review of research on the need hierarchy theory. *Organizational Behavior & Human Performance, 15,* 212–240.

Waite, L. J. (1995). Does marriage matter? *Demography, 32,* 483–507.

Walden, T. A., & Ogan, T. A. (1988). The development of social referencing. *Child Development, 59,* 1230–1240.

Walker, C. (1977). Some variations in marital satisfaction. In R. C. J. Peel (Ed.), *Equalities and inequalities in family life* (pp. 127–139). London: Academic Press.

Walker, L. J. (1988). The development of moral reasoning. *Annals of Child Development, 55*, 677–691.

Walker, M. P., & Stickgold, R. (2006). Sleep, memory, and plasticity. *Annual Review of Psychology, 57*, 139–166.

Walster, E., Aronson, V., Abrahams, D., & Rottmann, L. (1966). Importance of physical attractiveness in dating behavior. *Journal of Personality and Social Psychology, 4*, 508–516.

Walster, E., Walster, G. W., & Berscheid, E. (1978). *Equity: Theory and research.* Boston: Allyn & Bacon.

Wang, L. H., McCarthy, G., Song, A. W., & LaBar, K. S. (2005). Amygdala activation to sad pictures during high-field (4 tesla) functional magnetic resonance imaging. *Emotion, 5*, 12–22.

Wansink, B., & Linder, L. R. (2003). Interactions between forms of fat consumption and restaurant bread consumption. *International Journal of Obesity, 27*, 866–868.

Wansink, B., Painter, J. E., & North, J. (2005). Bottomless bowls: Why visual cues of portion size may influence intake. *Obesity Research, 13*, 93–100.

Wansink, B., & Wansink, C. S. (2010). The largest last supper: Depictions of food portions and plate size increased over the millennium. *International Journal of Obesity, 34*, 943–944.

Ward, J., Parkin, A. J., Powell, G., Squires, E. J., Townshend, J., & Bradley, V. (1999). False recognition of unfamiliar people: "Seeing film stars everywhere." *Cognitive Neuropsychology, 16*, 293–315.

Warneken, F., & Tomasello, M. (2009). Varieties of altruism in children and chimpanzees. *Trends in Cognitive Sciences, 13*, 397–402.

Warnock, M. (2003). *Making babies: Is there a right to have children?* Oxford, England: Oxford University Press.

Warren, K. R., & Hewitt, B. G. (2009). Fetal alcohol spectrum disorders: When science, medicine, public policy, and laws collide. *Developmental Disabilities Research Reviews, 15*, 170–175.

Warrington, E. K., & McCarthy, R. A. (1983). Category specific access dysphasia. *Brain, 106*, 859–878.

Warrington, E. K., & Shallice, T. (1984). Category specific semantic impairments. *Brain, 107*, 829–854.

Watanabe, S., Sakamoto, J., & Wakita, M. (1995). Pigeons' discrimination of painting by Monet and Picasso. *Journal of the Experimental Analysis of Behavior, 63*, 165–174.

Watkins, L. R., & Maier, S. F. (2005). Immune regulation of central nervous system functions: From sickness responses to pathological pain. *Journal of Internal Medicine, 257*, 139–155.

Watson, D., & Pennebaker, J. W. (1989). Health complaints, stress, and distress: Exploring the central role of negative affectivity. *Psychological Review, 96*, 234–254.

Watson, J. B. (1913). Psychology as the behaviorist views it. *Psychological Review, 20*, 158–177.

Watson, J. B. (1924). *Behaviorism.* New York: People's Institute.

Watson, J. B., & Rayner, R. (1920). Conditioned emotional reactions. *Journal of Experimental Psychology, 3*, 1–14.

Watzlawick, P., Beavin, J., & Jackson, D. D. (1967). *Pragmatics of human communication: A study of interactional patterns, pathologies, and paradoxes.* New York: Norton.

Weber, R., & Crocker, J. (1983). Cognitive processes in the revision of stereotypic beliefs. *Journal of Personality and Social Psychology, 45*, 961–977.

Webster Marketon, J. I., & Glaser, R. (2008). Stress hormones and immune function. *Cellular Immunology, 252*, 16–26.

Wechsler, H., Davenport, A., Dowdall, G., Moeykens, B., & Castillo, S. (1994). Health and behavioral consequences of binge drinking in college: A national survey of students at 140 campuses. *Journal of the American Medical Association, 272*, 1672–1677.

Wegner, D. M. (1989). *White bears and other unwanted thoughts.* New York: Viking.

Wegner, D. M. (1994a). Ironic processes of mental control. *Psychological Review, 101*, 34–52.

Wegner, D. M. (1994b). *White bears and other unwanted thoughts: Suppression, obsession, and the psychology of mental control.* New York: Guilford Press.

Wegner, D. M. (1997). Why the mind wanders. In J. D. Cohen & J. W. Schooler (Eds.), *Scientific approaches to consciousness* (pp. 295–315). Mahwah, NJ: Lawrence Erlbaum.

Wegner, D. M. (2002). *The illusion of conscious will.* Cambridge, MA: The MIT Press.

Wegner, D. M. (2009). How to think, say, or do precisely the worst thing for any occasion. *Science, 325*, 48–51.

Wegner, D. M., Ansfield, M., & Pilloff, D. (1998). The putt and the pendulum: Ironic effects of the mental control of action. *Psychological Science, 9*, 196–199.

Wegner, D. M., Broome, A., & Blumberg, S. J. (1997). Ironic effects of trying to relax under stress. *Behavior Research and Therapy, 35*, 11–21.

Wegner, D. M., Erber, R. E., & Zanakos, S. (1993). Ironic processes in the mental control of mood and mood-related thought. *Journal of Personality and Social Psychology, 65*, 1093–1104.

Wegner, D. M., & Gilbert, D. T. (2000). Social psychology: The science of human experience. In H. Bless & J. Forgas (Eds.), *The message within: Subjective experience in social cognition and behavior* (pp. 1–9). Philadelphia: Psychology Press.

Wegner, D. M., Schneider, D. J., Carter, S. R., & White, T. L. (1987). Paradoxical effects of thought suppression. *Journal of Personality and Social Psychology, 53*, 5–13.

Wegner, D. M., Vallacher, R. R., Macomber, G., Wood, R., & Arps, K. (1984). The emergence of action. *Journal of Personality and Social Psychology, 46*, 269–279.

Wegner, D. M., & Wenzlaff, R. M. (1996). Mental control. In E. T. Higgins & A. Kruglanski (Eds.), *Social psychology: Handbook of basic mechanisms and processes* (pp. 466–492). New York: Guilford Press.

Wegner, D. M., Wenzlaff, R. M., & Kozak, M. (2004). Dream rebound: The return of suppressed thoughts in dreams. *Psychological Science, 15*, 232–236.

Wegner, D. M., & Zanakos, S. (1994). Chronic thought suppression. *Journal of Personality, 62*, 615–640.

Weinstock, S., Berman, S., & Cates, W., Jr. (2004). Sexually transmitted diseases among American youth: Incidence and prevalence estimates, 2000. *Perspectives on Sexual and Reproductive Health, 36*, 6–10.

Weisfeld, G. (1999). *Evolutionary principles of human adolescence.* New York: Basic Books.

Weiss, P. H., Zilles, K., & Fink, G. R. (2005). When visual perception causes feeling: Enhanced cross-modal processing in grapheme-color synesthesia. *NeuroImage, 28*, 859–868.

Weissman, M. M., Bland, R. C., Canino, G. J., Faravelli, C., Greenwald, S., Hwu, H. G., et al. (1997). The cross-national epidemiology of panic disorder. *Archives of General Psychiatry, 54*, 305–309.

Wells, G. L., Malpass, R. S., Lindsay, R. C. L., Fisher, R. P., Turtle, J. W., & Fulero, S. M. (2000). From the lab to the police station: A successful application of eyewitness research. *American Psychologist, 55*, 581–598.

Wells, G. L., Small, M., Penrod, S., Malpass, R. S., Fulero, S. M., & Brimacombe, C. A. E. (1998). Eyewitness identification procedures: Recommendations for lineups and photospreads. *Law and Human Behavior, 22,* 603–647.

Wenner, L. A. (2004). On the ethics of product placement in media entertainment. In M. L. Galacian (Ed.), *Handbook of product placement in the mass media* (pp. 101–132). Binghamton, NY: Haworth Press.

Wenzlaff, R. M. (2005). Seeking solace but finding despair: The persistence of intrusive thoughts in depression. In D. A. Clark (Ed.), *Intrusive thoughts in clinical disorders: Theory, research, and treatment* (pp. 54–85). New York: Guilford Press.

Wenzlaff, R. M., & Bates, D. E. (1998). Unmasking a cognitive vulnerability to depression: How lapses in mental control reveal depressive thinking. *Journal of Personality and Social Psychology, 75,* 1559–1571.

Wenzlaff, R. M., & Eisenberg, A. R. (2001). Mental control after dysphoria: Evidence of a suppressed, depressive bias. *Behavior Therapy, 32,* 27–45.

Wenzlaff, R. M., & Wegner, D. M. (2000). Thought suppression. In S. T. Fiske (Ed.), *Annual review of psychology* (Vol. 51, pp. 51–91). Palo Alto, CA: Annual Reviews.

Westrin, A., & Lam, R. W. (2007). Seasonal affective disorder: A clinical update. *Journal of Clinical Psychiatry, 19,* 239–246.

Wexler, K. (1999). Maturation and growth of grammar. In W. C. Ritchie & T. K. Bhatia (Eds.), *Handbook of child language acquisition* (pp. 55–110). San Diego: Academic Press.

Whalen, P. J., Rauch, S. L., Etcoff, N. L., McInerney, S. C., Lee, M. B., & Jenike, M. A. (1998). Masked presentations of emotional facial expressions modulate amygdala activity without explicit knowledge. *The Journal of Neuroscience, 18,* 411–418.

Whalley, L. J., & Deary, I. J. (2001). Longitudinal cohort study of childhood IQ and survival up to age 76. *British Medical Journal, 322,* 1–5.

Wheeler, M. A., Petersen, S. E., & Buckner, R. L. (2000). Memory's echo: Vivid recollection activates modality-specific cortex. *Proceedings of the National Academy of Sciences, USA, 97,* 11125–11129.

White, B. L., & Held, R. (1966). Plasticity of motor development in the human infant. In J. F. Rosenblith & W. Allinsmith (Eds.), *The cause of behavior* (pp. 60–70). Boston: Allyn & Bacon.

White, G. M., & Kirkpatrick, J. (Eds.). (1985). *Person, self, and experience: Exploring Pacific ethnopsychologies.* Berkeley: University of California Press.

Wicker, B., Keysers, C., Plailly, J., Royet, J.-P., Gallese, V., & Rizzolatti, G. (2003). Both of us disgusted in *my* insula: The common neural basis of seeing and feeling disgust. *Neuron, 40,* 655–664.

Wiggs, C. L., & Martin, A. (1998). Properties and mechanisms of perceptual priming. *Current Opinion in Neurobiology, 8,* 227–233.

Wilcoxon, H. C., Dragoin, W. B., & Kral, P. A. (1971). Illness-induced aversions in rats and quail: Relative salience of visual and gustatory cues. *Science, 171,* 826–828.

Wiley, J. L. (1999). Cannabis: Discrimination of "internal bliss"? *Pharmacology, Biochemistry, & Behavior, 64,* 257–260.

Wilkinson, L., Teo, J. T., Obeso, I., Rothwell, J. C., & Jahanshahi, M. (2010). The contribution of primary motor cortex is essential for probabilistic implicit sequence learning: Evidence from theta burst magnetic stimulation. *Journal of Cognitive Neuroscience, 22,* 427–436.

Williams, A. C. (2002). Facial expression of pain: An evolutionary account. *Behavioral and Brain Sciences, 25,* 439–488.

Williams, C. M., & Kirkham, T. C. (1999). Anandamide induces overeating: Mediation by central cannabinoid (CB1) receptors. *Psychopharmacology, 143,* 315–317.

Wilson, T. D. (2002). *Strangers to ourselves: Discovering the adaptive unconscious.* Cambridge, MA: Harvard University Press.

Wilson, T. D., Meyers, J., & Gilbert, D. T. (2003). "How happy was I, anyway?" A retrospective impact bias. *Social Cognition, 21,* 421–446.

Wimber, M., Rutschmann, R. N., Greenlee, M. W., & Bauml, K.-H. (2009). Retrieval from episodic memory: Neural mechanisms of interference resolution. *Journal of Cognitive Neuroscience, 21,* 538–549.

Wimmer, H., & Perner, J. (1983). Beliefs about beliefs: Representations and constraining function of wrong beliefs in young children's understanding of deception. *Cognition, 13,* 103–128.

Windham, G. C., Eaton, A., & Hopkins, B. (1999). Evidence for an association between environmental tobacco smoke exposure and birthweight: A meta-analysis and new data. *Pediatrics and Perinatal Epidemiology, 13,* 35–57.

Winterer, G., & Weinberger, D. R. (2004). Genes, dopamine and cortical signal-to-noise ratio in schizophrenia. *Trends in Neuroscience, 27,* 683–690.

Wise, R. A. (1989). Brain dopamine and reward. *Annual Review of Psychology, 40,* 191–225.

Wise, R. A. (2005). Forebrain substrates of reward and motivation. *Journal of Comparative Neurology, 493,* 115–121.

Wittchen, H., Knauper, B., & Kessler, R. C. (1994). Lifetime risk of depression. *British Journal of Psychiatry, 165,* 16–22.

Wittgenstein, L. (1999). *Philosophical investigations.* Upper Saddle River, NJ: Prentice Hall. (Original work published 1953)

Wixted, J. T., & Ebbesen, E. (1991). On the form of forgetting. *Psychological Science, 2,* 409–415.

Wolf, J. (2003, May 18). Through the looking glass. *The New York Times Magazine,* p. 120.

Wolpe, J. (1958). *Psychotherapy by reciprocal inhibition.* Stanford, CA: Stanford University Press.

Wood, J. M., & Bootzin, R. R. (1990). Prevalence of nightmares and their independence from anxiety. *Journal of Abnormal Psychology, 99,* 64–68.

Wood, J. M., Bootzin, R. R., Rosenhan, D., Nolen-Hoeksema, S., & Jourden, F. (1992). Effects of the 1989 San Francisco earthquake on frequency and content of nightmares. *Journal of Abnormal Psychology, 101,* 219–224.

Woods, E. R., Lin, Y. G., Middleman, A., Beckford, P., Chase, L., & DuRant, R. H. (1997). The associations of suicide attempts in adolescents. *Pediatrics, 99,* 791–796.

Woods, S. C., Seeley, R. J., Porte, D., Jr., & Schwartz, M. W. (1998). Signals that regulate food intake and energy homeostasis. *Science, 280,* 1378–1383.

Woods, S. M., Natterson, J., & Silverman, J. (1966). Medical students' disease: Hypochondriasis in medical education. *Journal of Medical Education, 41,* 785–790.

Woody, S. R., & Nosen, E. (2008). Psychological models of phobic disorders and panic. In M. M. Anthony & M. B. Stein (Eds.), *Oxford handbook of anxiety and related disorders* (pp. 209–224). New York: Oxford University Press.

Woody, S. R., & Sanderson, W. C. (1998). Manuals for empirically supported treatments: 1998 update. *Clinical Psychologist, 51,* 17–21.

Wrangham, R., & Peterson, D. (1997). *Demonic males: Apes and the origin of human violence.* New York: Mariner.

Wren, A. M., Seal, L. J., Cohen, M. A., Brynes, A. E., Frost, G. S., Murphy, K. G., et al. (2001). Ghrelin enhances appetite and increases food intake in humans. *Journal of Clinical Endocrinology and Metabolism, 86,* 5992–5995.

Wrenn, C. C., Turchi, J. N., Schlosser, S., Dreiling, J. L., Stephenson, D. A., & Crawley, J. N. (2006). Performance of galanin transgenic mice in the 5-choice serial reaction time attentional task. *Pharmacology Biochemistry and Behavior, 83,* 428–440.

Wulf, S. (1994, March 14). Err Jordan. *Sports Illustrated.*

Wundt, W. (1900–20). *Völkerpsychologie. Eine untersuchung der entwicklungsgesetze von sprache, mythos und sitte* [Völkerpsychologie: An examination of the developmental laws of language, myth, and custom]. Leipzig, Germany: Engelmann & Kroner.

Xiaohe, X., & Whyte, K. J. (1990). Love matches and arranged marriages: A Chinese replication. *Journal of Marriage and the Family, 52,* 709–722.

Yamaguchi, S. (1998). Basic properties of umami and its effects in humans. *Physiology and Behavior, 49,* 833–841.

Yang, S., & Sternberg, R. J. (1997). Conceptions of intelligence in ancient Chinese philosophy. *Journal of Theoretical and Philosophical Psychology, 17,* 101–119.

Yelsma, P., & Athappilly, K. (1988). Marital satisfaction and communication practices: Comparisons among Indian and American couples. *Journal of Comparative Family Studies, 19,* 37–53.

Yin, R. K. (1970). Face recognition by brain-injured patients: A dissociable ability. *Neuropsychologia, 8,* 395–402.

Young, A. S., Klap, R., Sherbourne, C. D., & Wells, K. B. (2001). The quality of care for depressive and anxiety disorders in the United States. *Archives of General Psychiatry, 58,* 55–61.

Yzerbyt, V., & Demoulin, S. (2010). Intergroup relations. In S. T. Fiske, D. T. Gilbert, & G. Lindzey (Eds.), *The handbook of social psychology* (5th ed., Vol. 2). New York: Wiley.

Zahn-Waxler, C., Radke-Yarrow, M., Wagner, E., & Chapman, M. (1992). Development of concern for others. *Developmental Psychology, 28,* 126–136.

Zajonc, R. B. (1989). Feeling the facial efference: Implications of the vascular theory of emotion. *Psychological Review, 96,* 395–416.

Zebrowitz, L. A., Hall, J. A., Murphy, N. A., & Rhodes, G. (2002). Looking smart and looking good: Facial cues to intelligence and their origins. *Personality and Social Psychology Bulletin, 28,* 238–249.

Zeki, S. (1993). *A vision of the brain.* London: Blackwell Scientific Publications.

Zeki, S. (2001). Localization and globalization in conscious vision. *Annual Review of Neuroscience, 24,* 57–86.

Zentall, T. R., Sutton, J. E., & Sherburne, L. M. (1996). True imitative learning in pigeons. *Psychological Science, 7,* 343–346.

Zihl, J., von Cramon, D., & Mai, N. (1983). Selective disturbance of movement vision after bilateral brain damage. *Brain, 106,* 313–340.

Zillmann, D., Katcher, A. H., & Milavsky, B. (1972). Excitation transfer from physical exercise to subsequent aggressive behavior. *Journal of Experimental Psychology, 8,* 247–259.

Zimprich, D., & Martin, M. (2002). Can longitudinal changes in processing speed explain longitudinal age changes in fluid intelligence? *Psychology and Aging, 17,* 690–695.

Zuckerman, M., DePaulo, B. M., & Rosenthal, R. (1981). Verbal and nonverbal communication of deception. In L. Berkowitz (Ed.), *Advances in experimental social psychology* (Vol. 14, pp. 1–59). New York: Academic Press.

Zuckerman, M., & Driver, R. E. (1985). Telling lies: Verbal and nonverbal correlates of deception. In W. Seigman & S. Feldstein (Eds.), *Multichannel integrations of nonverbal behavior* (pp. 129–147). Hillsdale, NJ: Lawrence Erlbaum.

Name Index

Subject Index

Note: Page numbers followed by f indicate figures; those followed by t indicate tables.